D0048767

COLLINS SHUBUN

ENGLISH JAPANESE DICTIONARY

コリンズ
秀　　文　英和辞典

COLLINS SHUBUN

ENGLISH JAPANESE DICTIONARY

コリンズ 英和辞典
秀　文

HarperCollins*Publishers*
Shubun International Co., Ltd.
ハーパーコリンズ／秀文インターナショナル

First published in this edition 1993

© HarperCollins Publishers &
Shubun International Co., Ltd. 1993

ISBN 0 00 433405-1

Original material by
CollinsBilingual

Japanese language edition
Richard C. Goris
Yukimi Okubo

editorial administration
Jill Campbell

---

*A catalogue record for this book is
available from the British Library*

Typeset by Tosho Printing Co., Ltd.

Printed in Great Britain by Clays Ltd., St Ives plc

CONTENTS

Authors' Foreword

Dictionary compilers have been labeled "harmless drudges", but we have found little drudgery in compiling the Collins-Shubun English-Japanese Dictionary. On the contrary, we have experienced great pleasure in rising to the challenge of producing a book that was not run-of-the-mill.

To begin with, we had several advantages. We had the dictionary framework provided in electronic form by Collins Dictionary Division. Then we had computers running powerful Japanese word processing software. Together these factors saved us from the drudgery (and writer's cramp) caused by writing thousands and thousands of manuscript pages by hand. They also eliminated the drudgery of correcting in proof the innumerable mistakes introduced by typesetters misinterpreting our handwriting.

The challenge of producing "a better mousetrap" also provided motivation that eliminated drudgery.

In order to keep the dictionary truly pocket-sized, we aimed at providing one translation for each word, or for each meaning of a word. Where several possible translations existed, we chose the one with the highest frequency of usage in modern Japanese. We also tried to give translations that were the cultural equivalent of the English. Thus, if the English word conveyed a sense of dignity, we used a dignified Japanese expression; if the English was a slangy word, we provided a slangy Japanese word or phrase. Where this was not possible, we have provided glosses to clarify the difference.

There were some exceptions. When the English word had several Japanese equivalents, each used with equal frequency, and generally interchangeable, we gave the two or three most frequent, separated by commas.

In this category fell words that could be expressed either by a Chinese compound (2 or more Chinese characters used as a single word) or by a purely Japanese word. There were also words that could be expressed by a Japanese translation or a "Japanized" foreign loan word of equal frequency. In this case we gave the Japanese translation first, followed by a comma and the loan word. Where the Japanese translation existed, but was outlandish and seldom used, we gave only the loan word. In such cases the loan word is generally listed as a headword in standard Japanese dictionaries.

Finally, we discussed every entry thoroughly before adopting it. Thus we feel we have met our goal of providing a small, portable, but extremely useful dictionary - useful to the language student and the native speaker alike.

Our efforts would have been futile without the support, aid, and counsel of the editorial staff of Collins Dictionaries and Shubun. Shubun's board of experts and editors included Kazuo Shibuya, Shiruki Furukawa, Ari Matsue, and Kazuko Namiki. On the other side of the ocean we had in particular the aid of Lorna Sinclair-Knight, Jeremy Butterfield, and the hard-working Jill Campbell, in addition to other anonymous advisors.

To all and sundry, a handshake and a deep bow of gratitude.

Richard C. Goris
Yukimi Okubo

著 者 前 書

辞書を書く人というと「ひたすらこつこつ働く，人畜無害な凡人」と見る向きもあるが，当の私達はコリンズ・秀文英和辞典を書くに際し，ことさら単調な仕事を余儀なくされたという感じは全く覚えなかった．平凡でない辞書を作ろうというチャレンジに答えることにむしろ大きな喜びを感じた．

第一に苦労を軽減する要素がいくつかあった．まずコリンズ社の辞書部門よりコービルドのデータベースから頻度によって抽出され，フォーマット化されたた語彙リストのフロッピーディスクが提供された．これを強力な日本語ワープロソフトでコンピュータ操作し，日本語訳等を入力した．こうして何千枚もの原稿を手書きする苦労（と書痙の危険）を避けられ，同時に植字段階で起こるエラーを校正で直す苦労も避けることができた．

第二に，「より優れたもの」を作るというチャレンジも作業の単調さを吹き飛ばす動機にもなった．

当書をポケット版の限度内に抑えるためには，原則として一見出し語に対して，あるいは見出し語の一意味に対して一つだけの訳語をつけることにした．複数の訳語が可能な場合，最も頻度の高いものを選んだ．また，英語の語彙に対して文化的に同じ含みの訳語を選ぶように努力した．例えば，英単語が格調の高い語であれば，格調の高い日本語訳をつけた．一方，俗語のような英語に対してはそれに相当する日本語の俗語をつけた．これが不可能な場合，補足説明をつけた．

いくつか例外がある．複数の日本語訳が可能で，頻度が同じぐらいで置き換えもきく場合，二つか三つを併記してコンマで分けた．こういう語には漢語的表現またはやまとことばに訳せる語が多かった．その他に純粋な日本語もしくは外来語で表せる語もあった．その場合，日本語と外来語を併記してコンマで分けた．しかし日本語訳がおかしかったり頻度が低かったりする場合，外来語だけを記載した．この様な外来語はたいがい国語辞典で見出し語として使われている．

熟考と討論を重ねて最後に訳語を選択した．こうして小型でポケット版であるにもかかわらず，language student，native speaker 双方に大いに役立つ画期的な辞典の作成に成功したと確信する．

コリンズ社辞典編集部門及び秀文インターナショナルの編集スタッフの支援と助言なしには私達の努力だけではこの辞書を作れなかったと思う．秀文側にあっては特に渋谷一夫，古川知己，松江亜里，並木和子，そして海の向こうにあっては Lorna Sinclair-Knight, Jeremy Butterfield, Jill Campbell, その他の皆さん方に深く感謝の意を表する．

R. C. ゴリス

大久保 雪美

PUBLISHER'S FOREWORD

As the 21st century approaches and the countries of the world become more internationalized, the importance of English as a world language is felt ever more keenly by society. This awareness spotlights certain problems concerning the bilingual dictionaries, particularly English-Japanese dictionaries, published in Japan.

To begin with, there is the habit of crowding into each entry, without rhyme or reason, all the possible translations of a headword that can be thought of, a habit that has persisted since the Meiji Era.

Secondly, in a great many cases, scientific data on the use of words and phrases is very scarce, making it extremely difficult to improve on the present situation.

Dictionary users are becoming increasingly dissatisfied with the growing volume of unsorted data that is being thrust at them. Things have reached a point where the dictionary makers appear to have lost touch with the needs of their users.

What the users really want is well-ordered data, that is, clear, uncluttered information on the meaning of the words of a language. They need fundamental information on actual usage of the words of a language, information on situation and context in which a word or phrase is used, information on what normally comes before or after various words and phrases. This in turn requires a wealth of background information about the actual state of a language. Fortunately, we have been able to join forces with HarperCollins Publishers of Britain, who have at their disposal the largest data bank in the world of the English language. This data bank furnished us with, among other things, information on word frequency, which guided the choice of headwords; and information on situation, context, variation in meaning etc, which is shown in parentheses (the "indicators") in each entry. The result has been the revolutionary dictionary that we present here, for use throughout the world, in preparation for the 21st century, a truly original publication.

Instead of being laboriously typeset from a hand-written manuscript, the dictionary was composed entirely on a computer in a form that permitted electronic typesetting machines to transform the data directly into the printed page. Throughout the project the authors maintained constant, real-time contact with the editorial staff of Collins Dictionary Division through electronic mail and other modern means.

All Japanese entries in the main text have their pronunciation indicated in romaji, so that anyone anywhere in the world can use this dictionary to study Japanese through the medium of English.

At the same time Japanese users of the dictionary, even if already proficient in English, can gain confidence in their use of the language by noting the information about usage given in the parenthetical "indicators" in each entry.

Shubun International, Ltd.

出版する立場から

21世紀の幕開けが近づく一方，さらに国際化が一層進展し世界語としての英語の重要性がますます高まっているのが昨今の社会情勢と言えましょう．このような背景を踏まえ，我が国の外国語特に英和辞典の将来を考えてみるといくつかの問題点がはっきりしてくる．

まず第一に明治以来の伝統に従って狭い紙面に未整理のままと言ってよい程の訳語という名称の語義の網羅振りが指摘できよう．

第二に多くの場合，言語使用に付いて科学的データに乏しく，思い切った革新の道を拓くことが極めて困難といった状況が指摘できましょう．

肥大化する情報量に辞典使用者もうんざりの感さえするのである．使用者が何を求めているのか図りかねているのが現状とも言える状況である．

辞典使用者は小気味よく整理された情報の提供，すなわち今や簡潔・明解な言語の意味を求めている．ある言語の意味とは，ある語（句）がどのような場面・文脈・前後関係の中で何を伝達しようとしているのか示すことであり，かつ最も基本的なことである，このためには当該言語使用の実態について豊富なデータが必要となる．幸いなことに今日世界最大規模のdata bank of the English languageを活用する英国ハーパーコリンズ社と提携，使用頻度及び語句の意味の使用範囲「indicators」のデータを駆使した21世紀を指向した世界で使える画期的な英和辞典の完成をここに見る運びと相成った次第である．これこそ独創の知的生産物財産とも言うべきかなである．

原稿執筆も従来のような組み上げられた順序ではなく項目単位と言うべき方式で完全にコンピュータ化完成され，原稿執筆終了即組版完了ともなった点は画期的な技術革新の成果でもあった．電子時代の申し子でもある電子メール等最新の記述によりコリンズ社辞典編集部門と執筆のデスクが結ばれ，リアルタイムに意志伝達が行われたのである．

このように完成された本辞典は，日本語全てにローマ字による発音表記を付し，世界の何処にあっても英語を媒介とし日本語の習得を可能ならしめる効果的な内容とした．

また特に我が国の英語既習者の社会人にとって意味使用範囲「indicators」の明示による活用は英語使用に自信を与える英語習得への開眼となると信ずる．

株式会社　秀文インターナショナル

INTRODUCTION

We are delighted you have decided to buy the Collins Shubun Pocket English-Japanese Dictionary and hope you will enjoy and benefit from using it at school, at home, on holiday or at work.

This introduction gives you a few tips on how to get the most out of your dictionary-not simply from its comprehensive wordlist but also from the information provided in each entry.

The Collins Shubun English-Japanese Dictionary begins by listing the abbreviations used in the text and follows with a guide to Japanese pronunciation and a chart of the two Japanese scripts "hiragana" and "katakana" together with the Roman letter transliteration used in this dictionary.

USING YOUR COLLINS SHUBUN POCKET DICTIONARY

A wealth of information is presented in the dictionary, using various typefaces, sizes of type, symbols, abbreviations and brackets. The conventions and symbols used are explained in the following sections.

Headwords

The words you look up in a dictionary -"headwords"- are listed alphabetically. They are printed in bold type for rapid identification. The headwords appearing at the top of each page indicate the first and last word dealt with on the page in question.

Information about the usage or form of certain headwords is given in brackets after the phonetic spelling. This usually appears in abbreviated form (e. g., *(fam)*, (COMM).

Common expressions in which the headword appears are shown in bold italic type (e. g., **account**... *of no account*).

When such expressions are preceded by a colon, it means that the headword is used mainly in that particular expression (e. g., **aback**... *adv*: *to be taken aback*).

Phonetic spellings

The phonetic spelling of each headword (indicating its pronunciation) is given in square brackets immediately after the headword (e. g., **able** [ei'bəl]). The phonetics show a standardized US English pronunciation in IPA (International Phonetic Alphabet) symbols. A list of these symbols is given on page (13).

Translations

Headword translations are given in ordinary type and, where more than one meaning or usage exists, these are separated by a semicolon. You will often find other words in brackets before the translations. These offer suggested contexts in which the headword might appear (e. g., **absentee** (from school, meeting etc) or provide synonyms (e. g. **able** (capable) or (skilled)). A white lozenge precedes a gloss giving information for the non-English native speaker.

"Keywords"

Special status is given to certain English words which are considered as "key" words in the language. They may, for example, occur very frequently or have several types of usage (e. g., **a**, **be**). A combination of lozenges and numbers helps you to distinguish different parts of speech and different meanings. Further helpful information is provided in brackets.

Grammatical Information

Parts of speech are given in abbreviated form in italics after the phonetic spellings of headwords (e. g., *vt*, *adv*, *conj*) and headwords with several parts of speech have a black lozenge before each new part of speech (e. g., **wash**).

使用上の注意

本辞典は英単語の意味を知りたい日本人だけでなく日本語を勉強している外国人も使えるよう，すべての訳語，補足説明などを日本文字とローマ字で併記した．ローマ字は原則としてヘボン式に従い，ローマ字：仮名対照表を (17)－(18) ページに示した．またローマ字には日本語のアクセントも加えた．右上がりのアクセント記号 (á) は声の上がりを，右下がりの記号 (à) は声の下がりを，記号のない場合は平坦に発音する事を示す．

見出し語は太字の立体活字で示した．つづりは米国の標準に従ったが，英国の標準がそれと異なる場合，アルファベット順にこれも示した．

> 例：**anaemia** [əniˈmiːə] *etc* (*BRIT*) = **anemia** *etc*

続いて発音を [ ] の中に国際音表文字で示した．発音記号表は (13) ページにある．アクセントは ['] の記号でアクセントのある音節の後に示した．

> 例：**able** [eiˈbəl]

品詞は斜字の略語で示した．例：**able** [eiˈbəl] *adj*

品詞に続いて訳語を日本語とローマ字で示した．原則として1つの意味に対して1つだけ最も頻度の高い訳語を採用した．

> 例：**blockade**... 封鎖 fúsa

頻度が同じぐらいで複数の訳語がある場合，これを示すと共にコンマ (,) で分けた．

> 例：**blood**... 血 chi，血液 ketsúèki

訳語の前に丸括弧 ( ) の中でその見出し語についての情報を記した．

立体の大文字はその語が使われる「分野」などを示す．

> 例：**blood**... (BIO) 血 chi，血液 ketsúèki

すなわち，**blood** は「生物学」という分野の語である．

立体の小文字はその他の情報を示す．

> 例：**bleat**... *vi* (goat, sheep) 鳴く nakú

すなわち，bleat という動詞はヤギやヒツジについて使う語である．

> 例：**aperture**... (hole) 穴 aná; (gap) すき間 sukíma; (PHOT) アパーチャ ápàcha

この例では類語を使って見出し語の意味をはっきりさせている．また，このように1つの見出し語に対して複数の意味がある場合，セミコロン (;) で分ける．

見出し語の成句はその都度改行して太字の斜字で示した．

> 例：**bearing**...
>   *to take a bearing*...
>   *to find one's bearings*...

成句は主語＋動詞形式のものでも文頭の大文字と文尾のピリオドをつけずにあくまでも
成句として扱った．ただし疑問を表す成句には？をつけた．

> 例：**anyone**...
>> *anyone could do it*
>> *can you see anyone?*

表示，標識，立て札などに使う成句は「**...**」で囲んだ．

> 例：**entry**...
>> 「*no entry*」...

改行なしで品詞などに続くコロン（**:**）＋ 太斜字の成句は見出し語などがその成句以外
には殆ど使われない事を示す．

> 例：**aback** [əbǽk'] *adv*: *to be taken aback* 仰天する gyóten suru

丸括弧の中で *also*: に続く立体太字の語句はその意味では同意語である事を示す．

> 例：**go about** *vi* (*also*: **go around**: rumor) 流れる nagárerù.

ここでは「噂が流れる」という意味では go about でも go around でも使える事を示して
いる．

特殊記号：

♦：最初に示した品詞と品詞が異なったものにつけた．

> 例：**abdicate**... *vt* (responsibility, right) 放棄する ...
>> ♦*vi* (monarch) 退位する ...

◇：補足説明を示す．

／：見出し語，成句の中で置き換えられる部分を示す．日本語訳やローマ字の中でこれ
を〔 〕で示した．

> 例：**abide**... *vt*: *I can't abide it/him* 私はそれ〔彼〕が大嫌いだ watáku-
>> shi wá soré〔karè〕ga dáikirai da

KEYWORD: このタイトルは頻度の高い重要な語で特に徹底的に取り扱った見出し語
（たとえば **be, can**）を示す．

発音記号表

[ɑ:] f*a*ther, h*o*t, kn*o*wledge

[æ] *a*t, h*a*ve, c*a*t

[ai] m*y*, b*uy*, l*i*ke

[au] h*ow*, m*ou*th

[e] m*e*n, s*ay*s, fr*ie*nd

[ei] s*ay*, t*a*ke, r*ai*n

[e:r] *air*, c*are*, wh*ere*

[ə] *a*bove, paym*e*nt, lab*e*l

[ə:r] g*ir*l, l*ear*n, b*ur*n, w*or*m

[i] s*i*t, wom*e*n, bus*y*

[i:] s*ee*, b*ea*n, cit*y*

[ou] n*o*, kn*ow*, b*oa*t

[ɔi] b*oy*, b*oi*l

[u] b*oo*k, c*oul*d, p*u*t

[u:] t*oo*l, s*ou*p, bl*ue*

[ɔ:] l*aw*, w*a*lk, st*o*ry

[ʌ] *u*p, c*u*t, ab*o*ve

[p] *p*ut, cu*p*

[b] *b*e, ta*b*

[d] *d*own, ha*d*

[t] *t*oo, ho*t*

[k] *c*ome, ba*ck*

[g] *g*o, ta*g*

[s] *s*ee, cup*s*, for*c*e

[z] ro*s*e, bu*zz*

[ʃ] *sh*e, *s*ugar

[ʒ] vi*s*ion, plea*s*ure

[tʃ] *ch*ur*ch*

[dʒ] *j*am, *g*em, *j*u*dg*e

[f] *f*arm, hal*f*, *ph*one

[v] *v*ery, e*v*e

[θ] *th*in, bo*th*

[ð] *th*is, o*th*er

[l] *l*itt*l*e, ba*ll*

[r] *r*at, b*r*ead

[m] *m*ove, co*m*e

[n] *n*o, ru*n*

[ŋ] si*ng*, ba*nk*

[h] *h*at, re*h*eat

[j] *y*es

[w] *w*ell, a*w*ay

Table of Abbreviations 略語表

adj	adjective	形容詞
abbr	abbreviation	略語
adv	adverb	副詞
ADMIN	administration	管理
AGR	agriculture	農業
ANAT	anatomy	解剖学
ARCHIT	architecture	建築
AUT	automobiles	自動車関係
aux vb	auxiliary verb	助動詞
AVIAT	aviation	航空
BIO	biology	生物学
BOT	botany	植物学
BRIT	British English	英国つづり／用法
CHEM	chemistry	化学
COMM	commerce, finance, banking	商業，金融関係
COMPUT	computing	コンピュータ関係
conj	conjunction	接続詞
cpd	compound	形容詞的名詞
CULIN	cookery	料理
def art	definite article	定冠詞
dimin	diminutive	指小辞
ECON	economics	経済学
ELEC	electricity, electronics	電気，電子工学
excl	exclamation, interjection	感嘆詞
fam(!)	colloquial usage (! particularly offensive)	口語（！特に悪質なもの）
fig	figurative use	比喩
fus	(phrasal verb) where the particle cannot be separated from the main verb	vt fusを見よ
gen	in most or all senses; generally	たいがいの意味では，一般に
GEO	geography, geology	地理学，地質学
GEOM	geometry	幾何学
indef art	indefinite article	不定冠詞

inf(!)	colloquial usage (! particularly offensive)	口語（！特に悪質なもの）
infin	infinitive	不定詞
inv	invariable	変化しない
irreg	irregular	不規則な
LING	grammar, linguistics	文法，語学
lit	literal use	文字通りの意味
MATH	mathematics	数学
MED	medical term, medicine	医学
METEOR	the weather, meteorology	気象関係
MIL	military matters	軍事
MUS	music	音楽
n	noun	名詞
NAUT	sailing, navigation	海事
num	numeral adjective or noun	数詞
obj	(grammatical) object	目的語
pej	pejorative	蔑称
PHOT	photography	写真
PHYSIOL	physiology	生理学
pl	plural	複数
POL	politics	政治
pp	past participle	過去分詞形
prep	preposition	前置詞
pron	pronoun	代名詞
PSYCH	psychology, psychiatry	精神医学
pt	past tense	過去形
RAIL	railroad, railway	鉄道
REL	religion	宗教
SCOL	schooling, schools and universities	学校教育
sing	singular	単数
subj	(grammatical) subject	主語
superl	superlative	最上級
TECH	technical term, technology	技術(用語)，テクノロジー
TEL	telecommunications	電信電話
TV	television	テレビ
TYP	typography, printing	印刷

US	American English	米国つづり／用法
vb	verb	動詞
vi	verb or phrasal verb used intransitively	自動詞
vt	verb or phrasal verb used transitively	他動詞
vt fus	phrasal verb where the particle cannot be separated from main verb	パーチクルを動詞から分けられない句動詞
ZOOL	zoology	動物学
®	registered trademark	登録商標

THE ROMANIZATION AND PRONUNCIATION OF JAPANESE

There are several systems for writing Japanese in Roman characters, but the most understandable and least confusing to the speaker of English is the Hepburn ("hebon" in Japanese) system. The following table illustrates this system, with its "hiragana" and "katakana" equivalents, as it has been adopted in this dictionary.

a	i	u	e	o		ā	ī	ū	ē	ō
あ	い	う	え	お		—	—	うう	—	おお/おう
ア	イ	ウ	エ	オ		アー	イー	ウー	エー	オー

ka	ki	ku	ke	ko		kya	—	kyu	—	kyo
か	き	く	け	こ		きゃ	—	きゅ	—	きょ
カ	キ	ク	ケ	コ		キャ	—	キュ	—	キョ

ga	gi	gu	ge	go		gya	—	gyu	—	gyo
が	ぎ	ぐ	げ	ご		ぎゃ	—	ぎゅ	—	ぎょ
ガ	ギ	グ	ゲ	ゴ		ギャ	—	ギュ	—	ギョ

sa	shi	su	se	so		sha	shi	shu	she	sho
さ	し	す	せ	そ		しゃ	し	しゅ	しぇ	しょ
サ	シ	ス	セ	ソ		シャ	シ	シュ	シェ	ショ

za	ji	zu	ze	zo		ja	ji	ju	je	jo
ざ	じ	ず	ぜ	ぞ		じゃ	じ	じゅ	じぇ	じょ
ザ	ジ	ズ	ゼ	ゾ		ジャ	ジ	ジュ	ジェ	ジョ

ta	chi	tsu	te	to		cha	chi	chu	che	cho
た	ち	つ	て	と		ちゃ	ち	ちゅ	ちぇ	ちょ
タ	チ	ツ	テ	ト		チャ	チ	チュ	チェ	チョ

da	ji	zu	de	do		ja	ji	ju	je	jo
だ	ぢ	づ	で	ど		ぢゃ	ぢ	ぢゅ	ぢぇ	ぢょ
ダ	ヂ	ヅ	デ	ド		ヂャ	ヂ	ヂュ	ヂェ	ヂョ

na	ni	nu	ne	no	nya	—	nyu	—	nyo
な	に	ぬ	ね	の	にゃ	—	にゅ	—	にょ
ナ	ニ	ヌ	ネ	ノ	ニャ	—	ニュ	—	ニョ

ha	hi	fu	he	ho	hya	—	hyu	—	hyo
は	ひ	ふ	へ	ほ	ひゃ	—	ひゅ	—	ひょ
ハ	ヒ	フ	ヘ	ホ	ヒャ	—	ヒュ	—	ヒョ

ba	bi	bu	be	bo	bya	—	byu	—	byo
ば	び	ぶ	べ	ぼ	びゃ	—	びゅ	—	びょ
バ	ビ	ブ	ベ	ボ	ビャ	—	ビュ	—	ビョ

pa	pi	pu	pe	po	pya	—	pyu	—	pyo
ぱ	ぴ	ぷ	ぺ	ぽ	ぴゃ	—	ぴゅ	—	ぴょ
パ	ピ	プ	ペ	ポ	ピャ	—	ピュ	—	ピョ

ma	mi	mu	me	mo	mya	—	myu	—	myo
ま	み	む	め	も	みゃ	—	みゅ	—	みょ
マ	ミ	ム	メ	モ	ミャ	—	ミュ	—	ミョ

ya	—	yu	—	yo
や	—	ゆ	—	よ
ヤ	—	ユ	—	ヨ

ra	ri	ru	re	ro	rya	—	ryu	—	ryo
ら	り	る	れ	ろ	りゃ	—	りゅ	—	りょ
ラ	リ	ル	レ	ロ	リャ	—	リュ	—	リョ

wa	—	—	—	wo	n
わ	—	—	—	を	ん
ワ	—	—	—	ヲ	ン

Consonants:

Pronounce the consonants as you would in English. Exceptions are "w" in the objective particle "wo", "r", "g", and "f". In "wo" the "w" is normally not pronounced, but is written to distinguish it easily from other words that are pronounced "o". (Japanese word-processing software also usually requires that you type "wo" to get を or ヲ.)

"R" is pronounced with a very slight trill. Do not pronounce it as in the English word "rich"; you probably will not be understood. If you trill it as in Italian or Spanish, you can be understood, but you will sound foreign. The best strategy is to listen and imitate. Lacking access to native speakers, try pronouncing "r" as you would "d", but with the tongue farther forward, touching the upper teeth instead of the palate.

"G" is perfectly understandable pronounced as in English "get", "go" etc, and many Japanese always pronounce it in this way. Cultured people, however, prefer a softer, slightly nasal pronunciation, which they call a "half-voiced" or "nasal-voiced" "k". It is similar to the "ng" in "sing", but coming at the beginning of a syllable.

"F" also is quite understandable when given its usual English fricative value, with the lower lip touching the upper teeth. The Japanese, however, normally pronounce it by simply narrowing the gap between the lower lip and the teeth, without actually touching the lip to the teeth. Thus some individuals pronounce it much closer to "h" than to the English "f".

"N" at the end of a syllable or word is syllabic, that is, it is a syllable in its own right, with full syllabic length, as in English "butt*on*". In this dictionary when syllabic "n" is followed by a vowel or "y", a hyphen is inserted to indicate the proper pronunciation: e. g., 勧誘 かんゆう kan-yū, as opposed to 加入 かにゅう kanyū.

Before "p", "b", or "m", "n" naturally becomes an "m" sound; but in this dictionary, in keeping with the practice of other romanized dictionaries, the Japanese ん is consistently transliterated as "n", not "m": e. g., 文法 ぶんぽう bunpō, not bumpō.

Double consonants are pronounced in Japanese, as in US English "cattail". In "katakana" and "hiragana" they are indicated by a lowercase っ or ッ before the consonant to be doubled, and in this dictionary are printed as double consonants: かっぱ "kappa", いった "itta". The one exception is the combination っち, which we express as "tch": マッチ, "matchi".

A few Japanese exclamations are written with a lowercase っ at the end, indicating an articulated "t" sound at the end. These we have romanized with a quarter-sized "t": しっ "shit" (equivalent to the English "ssh !").

The sounds [tiː] and [diː] do not exist in Japanese. They are usually expressed as

ティ and ディ, which we romanize as "ti" and "di". Other sounds in loan words without Japanese equivalents are generally corrupted to some similar sound, e. g., "v" to "b".

Vowels:

The 5 Japanese vowels are the fundamental Latin vowels: [ɑ:], [i:], [u:], [e], and [o]. "U" is pronounced without rounding the lips, keeping them relaxed. A rounded "u" is understandable, but sounds outlandishly foreign. Again, listen and imitate.

The vowels can be long or short. Long vowels are pronounced the same as short vowels, but for double their length, with no break. Pay strict attention to this, for vowel length is essential to both meaning and comprehension. Using a short vowel for a long one, or vice versa, can produce a word of entirely different meaning from the one intended. In this dictionary, long vowels are marked with a macron: ā, ī, ū, ē, ō.

The syllable "-su" at the end of a word, especially in the verbal ending "-masu" frequently drops the "u", so that only the "s" is heard. This occurs more often in the east than in the west of the country. There are no hard and fast rules, so the student needs to rely on his experience from listening to spoken Japanese.

Japanese accents:

Japanese words do not have a strong tonic accent as in most European languages. Instead they are inflected, with the voice rising or falling gently on certain syllables, and remaining flat on others. Using the correct "accent" or inflection is necessary for intelligibility of speech, and often serves to distinguish between words of similar spelling. For example, depending on the "accent", "momo" can mean either "peach" or "thigh"; "kaki" can be either "persimmon" or "oyster"; "atsui" can be "hot" or "thick".

The Japanese accent is difficult to depict graphically with any accuracy, for there are no standard conventions. Many dictionaries simply ignore the problem, leaving the foreign student to his own devices. Language classes for foreigners both in Japan and abroad frequently do not teach accents explicitly, but rely on imitation of pronunciation by a native Japanese model.

We felt that the foreign student needed something to aid the memory in trying to pronounce words already learned in the past, as well as a guide to pronunciation of words being looked up in the dictionary. We settled on the accute accent (á) to indicate a rising inflection, and the grave accent (à) to indicate a falling inflection. No mark at all means that the voice is held flat on that syllable.

The one exception in this dictionary is when two "i"s occur together, as in the word for "good" いい ii. In most cases like this, the first "i" requires a rising inflection (í), and the second a falling inflection (ì). However, with standard typefaces this produces an unesthetic effect (íì). Therefore, we have omitted the accent mark of the second "i" in such cases: a rising inflection on the first of a "double i" combination indicates also a falling inflection on the second letter: íi = í ì.

Doubtless the foreign student will be somewhat disconcerted to see such inflection marks on "n" in this dictionary. Remember that final "n" is always syllabic and may be pronounced by itself in Japanese. Thus, "n" can also have a rising or falling inflection, or be flat, as the case may be.

Accent differs markedly from region to region in Japan, particularly between the east and the west. The speech patterns of the Kanto region have generally been adopted as the standards for a "common" language, to be taught in the schools and used by television and radio announcers. Although the accents in this dictionary have followed the guidance of an expert in the field, we lay no claim to absolute accuracy. Our aim has been to guide the foreign student to a pronunciation that, if used, will be understandable in any part of the country, even when the listeners themselves follow a different standard of pronunciation.

English Irregular Verb Forms 不規則動詞表

arise 　arising	arose	arisen	持ち上る mochíagaru
awake 　awaking	awoke	awaked	目が覚める me ga samérù
be 　am, is, are 　being	was, were	been	である de árù
bear	bore	born(e)	支える sasáerù
beat	beat	beaten	殴る nagúrù
become 　becoming	became	become	なる nárù
begin 　beginning	began	begun	始める hajímeru
behold	beheld	beheld	見る mírù
bend	bent	bent	曲げる magéru
beseech	besought	besought	嘆願する tañgan suru
beset 　besetting	beset	beset	襲う osóu
bet 　betting	bet, betted	bet, betted	かける kakérù
bid 　bidding	bid, bade	bid, bidden	競りに加わる serí ni kuwawarù
bind	bound	bound	縛る shibárù
bite 　biting	bit	bitten	かむ kámù
bleed	bled	bled	出血する shukkétsu suru
blow	blew	blown	吹く fúkù
break	broke	broken	割る warú
breed	bred	bred	繁殖させる hañshoku saséru
bring	brought	brought	持って来る motté kurù
build	built	built	建てる tatérù
burn	burned, burnt	burned, burnt	燃やす moyásu
burst	burst	burst	破裂させる harétsu saséru
buy	bought	bought	買う kaú
can	could	(been able)	出来る dekírù

cast	cast	cast	投げる nagérù
catch	caught	caught	捕まえる tsukámaeru
choose	chose	chosen	選ぶ erábù
choosing			
cling	clung	clung	しがみつく shigámitsukù
come	came	come	来る kúrù
coming			
cost	cost	cost	の値段である no nedán de arù
creep	crept	crept	忍び足で歩く shinóbiàshi de arúkù
cut	cut	cut	切る kirù
cutting			
deal	dealt	dealt	配る kubárù
dig	dug	dug	掘る hórù
digging			
dive	dived	dived	飛込む tobíkomù
diving	*also US* dove		
do	did	done	する sùrú
does			
draw	drew	drawn	描く kákù
dream	dreamed, dreamt	dreamed, dreamt	夢を見る yumé wo mirù
drink	drank	drunk	飲む nómù
drive	drove	driven	運転する uñten suru
driving			
dwell	dwelt	dwelt	住む súmù
eat	ate	eaten	食べる tabérù
fall	fell	fallen	落ちる ochírù
feed	fed	fed	食べさせる tabésaserù
feel	felt	felt	感じる kañjirù
fight	fought	fought	戦う tatákaù
find	found	found	見付ける mitsúkeru
flee	fled	fled	逃げる nigérù
fling	flung	flung	投げる nagérù
fly	flew	flown	飛ぶ tobú
flies			
forbid	forbade	forbidden	禁ずる kiñzurù
forbidding			

forecast	forecast	forecast	予報する yohṓ suru
forego	forewent	foregone	なしで我慢する náshì de gámàn suru
foresee	foresaw	foreseen	予想する yosṓ suru
foretell	foretold	foretold	予言する yogén suru
forget forgetting	forgot	forgotten	忘れる wasúrerù
forgive forgiving	forgave	forgiven	許す yurúsù
forsake forsaking	forsook	forsaken	見捨てる misúterù
freeze freezing	froze	frozen	凍る kṓrù
get getting	got	got US gotten	手に入れる té ni irerù
give giving	gave	given	与える atáerù
go goes	went	gone	行く ikú
grind	ground	ground	ひく hikú
grow	grew	grown	成長する seíchō suru
hang	hung, hanged	hung, hanged	掛ける kakérù
have has ; having	had	had	持っている móttè iru
hear	heard	heard	聞く kikú
hide hiding	hid	hidden	隠す kakúsù
hit hitting	hit	hit	打つ utsú
hold	held	held	持つ mótsù
hurt	hurt	hurt	痛める itámerù
keep	kept	kept	保管する hokán suru
kneel	knelt, kneeled	knelt, kneeled	ひざまずく hizámazukù
know	knew	known	知っている shitté irù
lay	laid	laid	置く okú
lead	led	led	先導する seńdō suru
lean	leaned, leant	leaned, leant	傾く katámukù
leap	leaped, leapt	leaped, leapt	跳躍する chṓyaku suru

learn	learned, learnt	learned, learnt	学ぶ manábù
leave	left	left	去る sárù
leaving			
lend	lent	lent	貸す kásù
let	let	let	許す yurúsù
letting			
lie	lay	lain	横になる yokó ni narù
lying			
light	lighted, lit	lighted, lit	火を付ける hí wo tsukérù
lose	lost	lost	失う ushínaù
losing			
make	made	made	作る tsukúrù
making			
may	might	—	かも知れない ka mo shirenài
mean	meant	meant	意味する ímì suru
meet	met	met	会う áù
mistake	mistook	mistaken	間違える machígaerù
mistaking			
mow	mowed	mowed, mown	刈る karú
must	(had to)	(had to)	しなければならない shinákereba naranài
pay	paid	paid	払う haráù
put	put	put	置く okú
putting			
quit	quit, quitted	quit, quitted	やめる yamérù
quitting			
read	read	read	読む yómù
rid	rid	rid	取除く torínozokù
ridding			
ride	rode	ridden	乗る nórù
riding			
ring	rang	rung	鳴る narú
rise	rose	risen	上がる agárù
rising			
run	ran	run	走る hashírù
running			
saw	sawed	sawn	のこぎりで切る nokógirì de kírù
say	said	said	言う iú

see	saw	seen	見る mírù
seek	sought	sought	求める motómerù
sell	sold	sold	売る urú
send	sent	sent	送る okúrù
set	set	set	置く ókù
setting			
shake	shook	shaken	振る fúrù
shaking			
shall	should	—	しましょう shimashō
shear	sheared	sheared, shorn	毛を刈る kê wò karú
shed	shed	shed	落す otósù
shedding			
shine	shone	shone	照る térù
shining			
shoot	shot	shot	そ撃する sogéki suru
show	showed	shown	見せる misérù
shrink	shrank	shrunk	縮む chijímù
shut	shut	shut	閉める shimérù
shutting			
sing	sang	sung	歌う utáù
sink	sank	sunk	沈没する chiñbotsu suru
sit	sat	sat	座る suwárù
sitting			
slay	slew	slain	殺す korósù
sleep	slept	slept	眠る nemúrù
slide	slid	slid	滑る subérù
sliding			
sling	slung	slung	投げる nagérù
slit	slit	slit	切り開く kiríhirakù
slitting			
smell	smelled, smelt	smelled, smelt	匂う nióù
sneak	sneaked	sneaked	こっそり行く kossórì ikú
	also US snuck	*also US* snuck	
sow	sowed	sown, sowed	まく mákù
speak	spoke	spoken	話す hanásù
speed	sped, speeded	sped, speeded	スピードを出す supídò wo dásù
spell	spelled, spelt	spelled, spelt	つづりを言う tsuzúri wò iú
spend	spent	spent	過ごす sugósù

spill	spilled, spilt	spilled, spilt	こぼす kobósù
spin	spun	spun	紡ぐ tsumúgù
spinning			
spit	spat	spat	つばを吐く tsúbà wo hákù
spitting			
split	split	split	裂く sákù
splitting			
spoil	spoiled, spoilt	spoiled, spoilt	台無しにする daínashi ni surù
spread	spread	spread	広げる hirógerù
spring	sprang	sprung	跳ぶ tobú
stand	stood	stood	立つ tátsù
steal	stole	stolen	盗む nusúmù
stick	stuck	stuck	くっつく kuttsúkù
sting	stung	stung	刺す sásù
stink	stank	stunk	におう nióù
stride	strode	stridden	大またに歩く ốmàta ni arúkù
striding			
strike	struck	struck, stricken	打つ útsù
striking			
strive	strove	striven	努力する dóryòku suru
striving			
swear	swore	sworn	誓う chikáù
sweep	swept	swept	掃く hákù
swell	swelled	swelled, swollen	はれる harérù
swim	swam	swum	泳ぐ oyógù
swimming			
swing	swung	swung	振る furú
take	took	taken	とる tórù
taking			
teach	taught	taught	教える oshíerù
tear	tore	torn	破る yabúrù
tell	told	told	述べる nobérù
think	thought	thought	考える kañgaerù
throw	threw	thrown	投げる nagérù
thrust	thrust	thrust	強く押す tsúyòku osú
tread	trod	trodden	歩く arúkù
wake	waked, woke	waked, woken	起す okósù
waking			

waylay	waylaid	waylaid	待伏せする machíbuse suru
wear	wore	worn	着る kirú
weave weaving	wove, weaved	woven, weaved	織る orù
wed wedding	wedded, wed	wedded, wed	結婚する kekkón suru
weep	wept	wept	泣く naku
win winning	won	won	勝つ katsù
wind	wound	wound	巻く makú
withdraw	withdrew	withdrawn	取出す torídasu
withhold	withheld	withheld	拒む kobámù
withstand	withstood	withstood	耐える taérù
wring	wrung	wrung	絞る shibórù
write writing	wrote	written	書く kakù

A

A [ei] *n* (MUS: note) イ音 í-òn; (: key) イ調 íchò

KEYWORD

---

a [ei, ə] (*before vowel or silent h:* **an**) *indef art* **1** 1つの hitótsu no, ある árù ◇通常日本語では表現しない tsújō nihongo de wa hyōgen shínái

a book/girl/mirror 本〔少女, 鏡〕hòn 〔shójo, kagámi〕

an apple りんご ríngo

she's a doctor 彼女は医者です kánojo wa ishá desu

2 (*instead of the number "one"*) 1つの hitótsu no

a loaf and 2 pints of milk, please パン1本とミルク2パイント下さい pan íppoñto mírùku nipáìnto kudasái

a year ago 1年前 ichinen máè

a hundred/thousand etc pounds 100〔1000〕ポンド hyaku〔sen〕póñdò

3 (*in expressing ratios, prices etc*) 1つ当り... hitótsu átàri...

3 a day/week 1日〔1週間〕当り3つ ichinichi〔isshūkan〕átàri mittsú

10 km an hour 時速10キロメーター jísòku jukkirométa

£5 a person 1人当たり5ポンド hitori átàri gopóñdò

30p a kilo 1キロ30ペンス ichíkìro sanjuppéñsù

AA [eiei'] *n abbr* (= *Alcoholics Anonymous*) アルコール依存症自主治療協会 arúkōru izoñshō jishúchiryō kyōkai; (*BRIT*: = *Automobile Association*) 英国自動車連盟 eíkoku jidōsha reñmei

AAA [trip'əlei] *n abbr* (= *American Automobile Association*) 米国自動車連盟 beíkoku jidōsha reñmei

aback [əbæk'] *adv*: *to be taken aback* 仰天する gyóten suru

abandon [əbæn'dən] *vt* (person) 見捨てる misúterù; (car) 乗捨てる norísuterù;

(give up: search, idea, research) やめる yaméru

◆*n* (wild behavior): *with abandon* 羽目を外して hamé wò hazúshite

abashed [əbæʃt'] *adj* (person) 恥ずかしがっている hazúkashigatté irú

abate [əbeit'] *vi* (lessen: storm, terror, anger) 治まる osámarù

abattoir [æbətwɑːr'] (*BRIT*) *n* と殺場 tosátsujō

abbey [æb'iː] *n* 修道院 shúdòin

abbot [æb'ət] *n* 修道院長 shúdòinchò

abbreviate [əbriː'viːeit] *vt* (essay, word) 短縮する tañshuku suru

abbreviation [əbriːviːei'ʃən] *n* (short form) 短縮形 tañshukukei

abdicate [æb'dikeit] *vt* (responsibility, right) 放棄する hóki suru

◆*vi* (monarch) 退位する táì-i suru

abdication [æbdikei'ʃən] *n* (of responsibility, right) 放棄 hóki; (by monarch) 退位 táì-i

abdomen [æb'dəmən] *n* 腹部 fukúbù

abduct [æbdʌkt'] *vt* ら致する ráchì suru

aberration [æbərei'ʃən] *n* (unusual behavior, event etc) 異状 ijō

abet [əbet'] *vt see* **aid**

abeyance [əbei'əns] *n*: *in abeyance* (law) 無視されて múshì sarete; (matter) 保留されて horyú sarete

abhor [æbhɔːr'] *vt* (cruelty, violence etc) ひどく嫌う hídòkù kiráu

abide [əbaid'] *vt*: *I can't abide it/him* 私はそれ〔彼〕が大嫌いだ watákushi wà soré〔karè〕gà dáìkirai da

abide by *vt fus* (law, decision) ...に従う ...ni shitágaù

ability [əbil'itiː] *n* (capacity) 能力 nóryoku; (talent, skill) 才能 saínō

abject [æb'dʒekt] *adj* (poverty) 極度の kyókùdo no; (apology) 卑屈な hikútsu na

ablaze [əbleiz'] *adj* (building etc) 炎上している eñjō shite iru

able [ei'bəl] *adj* (capable) 出来る dekíru;

(skilled) 有能な yū́nō na

to be able to do something ...をする事が出来る ...wo suru koto gà dékirù

able-bodied [ei'bɔlbɑːdʲiːd] *adj* (person) がん健な gáñken na

ably [ei'bliː] *adv* (skilfully, well) 上手に jōzú ni

abnormal [æbnɔːr'məl] *adj* (behavior, child, situation) 異常な ijṓ na

aboard [əbɔːrd'] *adv* (NAUT, AVIAT) ...に乗って ...ni nottē
◆*prep* (NAUT, AVIAT) ...に乗って ...ni nottē

abode [əboud'] *n* (LAW): *of no fixed abode* 住所不定の jū́shofutèi no

abolish [əbɑːl'iʃ] *vt* 廃止する haíshi suru

abolition [æbəliʃ'ən] *n* 廃止 haíshi

abominable [əbɑːm'inəbəl] *adj* (conditions) ひどい hídoì; (behavior) 忌わしい imáwashiì

aborigine [æbəridʒ'əniː] *n* 原住民 geñjū́mìn

abort [əbɔːrt'] *vt* (MED: fetus) 流産する ryū́zan suru; (plan, activity) 中止する chū́shi suru

abortion [əbɔːr'ʃən] *n* (MED) 妊娠中絶 niñshinchūzètsu

to have an abortion 妊娠を中絶する niñshin wò chū́zetsu suru

abortive [əbɔːr'tiv] *adj* (attempt, action) 不成功の fuséikō no

abound [əbaund'] *vi* (exist in large numbers) ...が多い ...ga ōí

to abound in/with (possess in large numbers) ...に富む ...ni tómù

KEYWORD

about [əbaut'] *adv* 1 (approximately) 約 yákù, 大よそ ōyoso, ...ぐらい ...gúrài

about a hundred/thousand etc dollars 約100(1000)ドル yákù hyakú(sen) dòru

it takes about 10 hours 10時間ぐらいかかります jūjikan gúrài kakarimásù

at about 2 o'clock 2時頃 niji górò

I've just about finished 終わったところです hóbò owatta tokoro desù

2 (referring to place) あちこちに achíko-

chì ni

to leave things lying about 物をあちこちに散らかしたままにする monō wo achíkochì ni chirakashita mamá ni sùrú

to run/walk etc about あちこち走り回る〔歩き回る〕achíkochì hashirimawárù〔arukimawárù〕

3: *to be about to do something* ...するところである ...suru tokoro dè árù

he was about to cry/leave/wash the dishes/go to bed 彼は泣き出す〔帰る、皿を洗う、寝る〕ところだった kárè wa nakidasu(kaeru, sara wo arau, neru) tokoro dattà

◆*prep* 1 (relating to) ...について ...ni tsúìte, ...に関して ...ni kànshite

a book about London ロンドンについての本 róndòn ni tsúìte no hon

what is it about? それは何についてですか sore wa nán ni tsúìte desu ká

we talked about it 私たちはそれについて話し合った watakushitachì a sore ni tsúìte hanashiáttà

what/how about having some coffee? コーヒーでも飲みましょうか kōhī de mò nomimashṓ kà

2 (referring to place) ...のあちこちに ...no achíkochì ni

to walk about the town 町をあちこち歩き回る machí wo achíkochì arukimawárù

her clothes were scattered about the room 部屋のあちこちに彼女の服が散らかっていた heya no achíkochì ni kánojo no fukú gà chirakatte itá

about-face [əbaut'feis] *n* (MIL) 回れ右 mawáremigì; (*fig*): *to do an about-face* 一変する ippén suru

about-turn [əbaut'təːrn] *n* = about-face

above [əbʌv'] *adv* (higher up, overhead) 上の方に ué no hṓ ni; (greater, more) 以上に ijṓ ni
◆*prep* (higher than) ...より上に ...yórì ué ni; (greater than, more than: in number, amount etc) ...以上 ...ijṓ; (: in rank etc) 上である ué de arù

mentioned above 上記の jṓki no

above all まず第一に mázu daî-ichi ni

aboveboard [əbʌv'bourd] *adj* 公明正大な kṓmeiseidai na

abrasive [əbrei'siv] *adj* (substance) 研磨の kênma no; (person, manner) とげとげしい togétogeshii

abreast [əbrest'] *adv* (people, vehicles) 横に並んで yokó ni narande

to keep abreast of (fig: news etc) ...についていく ...ni tsúite ikú

abridge [əbridʒ'] *vt* (novel, play) 短縮する tañshuku suru

abroad [əbrɔːd'] *adv* 海外に káigai ni

abrupt [əbrʌpt'] *adj* (sudden: action, ending etc) 突然の totsúzen no; (curt: person, behavior) ぶっきらぼうな bukkírabṓ na

abruptly [əbrʌpt'li:] *adv* (leave, end) 突然 totsúzen; (speak) ぶっきらぼうに bukkírabṓ ni

abscess [æb'ses] *n* のうよう nṓyō

abscond [æbskɑːnd'] *vi* (thief): *to abscond with* ...を持ち逃げする ...wo mochínige suru; (prisoner): *to abscond (from)* (...から) 逃亡する (...kara) tṓbō suru

absence [æb'səns] *n* (of person: from home etc) 不在 fuzái; (: from school, meeting etc) 欠席 kesséki; (: from work) 欠勤 kekkín; (of thing) 無い事 naî kotó

absent [æb'sənt] *adj* (person: from home etc) 不在の fuzái no; (: from school, meeting etc) 欠席の kesséki no; (: from work) 欠勤の kekkín no; (thing) 無い naî

absentee [æbsənti:'] *n* (from school, meeting etc) 欠席者 kessékishà; (from work) 欠勤者 kekkíñsha

absent-minded [æb'səntmain'did] *adj* 忘れっぽい wasúreppoì

absolute [æb'səlu:t] *adj* (complete) 全くの mattáku no; (monarch, rule, power) 専制的な señseiteki na; (principle, rule etc) 絶対的な zettáiteki na

absolutely [æbsəlu:t'li:] *adv* (totally) 全く mattáku; (certainly) その通り sonṓ tṓri

absolution [æbsəlu:'ʃən] *n* (REL) 罪の許

absolve [æbzɑːlv'] *vt*: *to absolve someone (from blame, responsibility, sin)* ...の (...を) 許す ...no (...wò) yurúsù

absorb [æbsɔːrb'] *vt* 吸収する kyúshū suru; (assimilate: group, business) 併合する heígō suru

to be absorbed in a book 本に夢中になっている hoñ ni muchū ni nattè irú

absorbent cotton [æbsɔːr'bənt-] (*US*) *n* 脱脂綿 dasshímèn

absorbing [æbsɔːr'biŋ] *adj* 夢中にさせる muchū ni saserù

absorption [æbsɔːrp'ʃən] *n* 吸収 kyúshū; (assimilation: of group, business etc) 併合 heígō; (interest) 夢中になる事 muchū ni narù kotó

abstain [æbstein'] *vi*: *to abstain (from)* (eating, drinking) 控える hikáerù; (voting) 棄権する kikén suru

abstemious [æbsti:'mi:əs] *adj* (person) 節制する sesséi suru

abstention [æbsten'ʃən] *n* (refusal to vote) 棄権 kikén

abstinence [æb'stənəns] *n* 禁欲 kiń-yoku

abstract [æb'strækt] *adj* (idea, quality) 抽象的な chúshōteki na; (ART) 抽象派の chúshōha no; (LING): *abstract noun* 抽象名詞 chúshōmeishi

abstruse [æbstru:s'] *adj* 分かりにくい wakárinikuì

absurd [æbsəːrd'] *adj* ばかげた bakágetà

abundance [əbʌn'dəns] *n* 豊富さ hṓfusa

abundant [əbʌn'dənt] *adj* 豊富な hṓfuku na

abuse [*n* əbjuːs' *vb* əbjuːz'] *n* (insults) ののしり nonóshiri; (ill-treatment) 虐待 gyakútai; (misuse: of power, drugs etc) 乱用 rañ-yō

♦*vt* (insult) ののしる nonóshirù; (ill-treat) 虐待する gyakútai suru; (misuse) 乱用する rañ-yō suru

abusive [əbjuː'siv] *adj* (person) 口の悪い kuchí no waruì; (language) 侮辱的な bujókuteki na

abysmal [əbiz'məl] *adj* (performance, failure) 最低の saítei no; (ignorance etc)

ひどい hidói

abyss [əbis'] *n* 深えん shín-en

AC [ei'si:] *abbr* = **alternating current**

academic [ækədem'ik] *adj* (person) イン
テリの ínteri no; (year, system, books,
freedom etc) 教育関係の kyóikukaṅkei
no; (pej: issue) 理論的な rirónteki na
♦*n* 学者 gakúsha

academy [əkæd'əmi:] *n* (learned body)
アカデミー akádèmī; (school) 学院 gakú-
in
　　academy of music 音楽学院 oṅgaku
gakúin

accelerate [æksel'əreit] *vt* (process) 早
める hayámerù
♦*vi* (AUT) 加速する kasóku suru

acceleration [ækselərei'ʃən] *n* (AUT) 加
速 kasóku

accelerator [æksel'əreitər] *n* アクセル
ákùseru

accent [æk'sent] *n* (pronunciation) な ま
り namári; (written mark) アクセント符
号 akúsento fugǒ; (fig: emphasis, stress)
強調 kyóchō, アクセント akùsento

accept [æksept'] *vt* (gift, invitation) 受取
る ukétoru; (fact, situation, risk) 認める
mitómeru; (responsibility, blame) 負 う
oú

acceptable [æksep'təbəl] *adj* (offer, gift)
受入れられる uké-irerarerù; (risk etc) 許
容できる kyoyǒ dekirù

acceptance [æksep'təns] *n* (of gift, offer
etc) 受取る事 ukétoru koto; (of risk etc)
許容 kyoyǒ; (of responsibility etc) 負 う
事 oú koto

access [æk'ses] *n* (to building, room) 入
る事 háiru kotǒ; (to information, papers)
利用する権利 riyǒ suru keṅri
　　to have access to (child etc) ...への面会
権のある ...e no meṅkaikeṅ ga árù

accessible [ækses'əbəl] *adj* (place) 行 き
やすい ikíyasuì; (person) 面会しやすい
meṅkai shiyasuì; (available: knowledge,
art etc) 利用しやすい riyǒ shiyasuì

accessory [ækses'ə:ri:] *n* (dress, COMM,
TECH, AUT) アクセサリー ákùsesarī;
(LAW): *accessory to* ...の共 犯 者 ...no
kyóhaṅsha

accident [æk'sidənt] *n* (chance event) 偶
然 gúzen; (mishap, disaster) 事故 jíkð
　　by accident (unintentionally) うっかり
ukkárì; (by chance) 偶然に gúzen ni

accidental [æksiden'təl] *adj* (death) 事
故による jíkð ni yorú; (damage) 偶発的
な gúhatsuteki na

accidentally [æksiden'təli:] *adv* (b y
accident) 偶然に gúzen ni

accident-prone [æk'sidəntproun'] *adj*
事故に会いがちな jíkð ni aigachi na

acclaim [əkleim'] *n* 賞賛 shósan
♦*vt: to be acclaimed for one's
achievements* 功績で有名である kóseki
dè yúmei de arù

acclimate [əklai'mit] *(US) vt* = **acclimatize**

acclimatize [əklai'mətaiz] *vt: t o
become acclimatized (to)* (...に) 慣
れる (...ni) narérù

accolade [ækəleid'] *n* (fig) 賞賛 shósan

accommodate [əkɑm'ədeit] *vt* (subj:
person) 泊める toméru; (: car, hotel etc)
収容できる shúyō dekirù; (oblige, help)
...に親切にして上げる ...ni shíṅsetsu ni
shite agérù

accommodating [əkɑm'ədeitiŋ] *adj* 親
切な shíṅsetsu na

accommodation [əkɑ:mədei'ʃən] *n* 宿
設備 shukúhakusetsùbi

accommodations [əkɑ:mədei'ʃənz] *(US)
npl* 宿泊設備 shukúhakusetsùbi

accompaniment [əkʌm'pənimənt] *n* 伴
奏 bańsō

accompany [əkʌm'pəni:] *vt* (escort, go
along with) ...に付きそう ...ni tsukísoù;
(MUS) ...の伴奏をする ...no bańsō wò suru

accomplice [əkɑ:m'plis] *n* 共犯者 kyóhaṅsha

accomplish [əkɑ:m'pliʃ] *vt* (finish: task)
成遂げる nashítogerù; (achieve: goal) 達
成する tasséi suru

accomplished [əkɑ:m'pliʃt] *adj* (person)
熟練の jukúren no; (performance) 優れた
sugúretà

accomplishment [əkɑ:m'pliʃmənt] *n*
(completion, bringing about) 遂行 suíkō;

(skill: *gen pl*) 才能 saínō

accord [əkɔ:rd'] *n* (treaty) 協定 kyótei
♦*vt* 与える atáeru
of his own accord 自発的に jihátsuteki ni

accordance [əkɔ:r'dəns] *n*: *in accordance with* (someone's wishes, the law etc) ...に従って ...ni shitágatte

according [əkɔ:r'diŋ]: *according to* *prep* (person, account) ...によると ...ni yorú to

accordingly [əkɔ:r'diŋli:] *adv* (appropriately) それに応じて soré nī ōjite; (as a result) それで soré de

accordion [əkɔ:r'di:ən] *n* アコーデオン ákōdeon

accost [əkɔ:st'] *vt* ...に近寄って話し掛ける ...ni chikáyottè hanáshikakerù

account [əkaunt'] *n* (COMM: bill) 勘定書 kañjōgaki; (: monthly account) 計算書 keísansho; (in bank) 口座 kōza; (report) 報告 hōkoku
of no account 構わない kamáwanài
on account つけで tsuké de
on no account 何があっても... (すべき) でない naní ga atte mo ...(subeki) de naì
on account of ...のために ...no tamé ni
to take into account, take account of ...を考慮に入れる ...wò kōryò ni iréru

accountable [əkaun'təbəl] *adj*: *accountable (to)* (...に) 申開きする義務がある (...ni) mōshihiraki suru gimù ga árù

accountancy [əkaun'tənsi:] *n* 会計士の職 kaíkeìshi no shokú

accountant [əkaun'tənt] *n* 会計士 kaíkeìshi

account for *vt fus* (explain) 説明する setsúmei suru; (represent) ... (の割合) を占める ...(no waríai) wò shimérù

account number *n* (at bank etc) 口座番号 kōzabañgō

accounts [əkaunts'] *npl* (COMM) 勘定 kañjō

accredited [əkred'itid] *adj* (agent etc) 資格のある shikáku no arù

accrued interest [əkru:d'-] *n* 累積利息 ruísekirisòku

accumulate [əkju:m'jəleit] *vt* 貯める taméru
♦*vi* 貯まる tamáru

accuracy [æk'jə:rəsi:] *n* 正確さ seíkakusa

accurate [æk'jə:rit] *adj* 正確な seíkaku na

accurately [æk'jə:ritli:] *adv* (count, shoot, answer) 正確に seíkaku ni

accusation [ækju:zei'ʃən] *n* 非難 hínàn

accuse [əkju:z'] *vt*: *to accuse someone (of something)* (crime, incompetence) (...だと) ...を責める (...dá tò) ...wo semérù

accused [əkju:zd'] *n* (L A W): *the accused* 容疑者 yōgishà

accustom [əkʌs'təm] *vt* 慣れさせる naréraseru

accustomed [əkʌs'təmd] *adj* (usual): *accustomed to* ...に慣れている ...ni narétè irú

ace [eis] *n* (CARDS, TENNIS) エースèsu

ache [eik] *n* 痛み itámi
♦*vi* (be painful) 痛む itámù, ...が痛い ...ga itáì
my head aches 頭が痛い atáma gà itáì

achieve [ətʃi:v'] *vt* (aim) 成遂げる nashítogerù; (result) 上げる agéru; (victory, success) 獲得する kakútoku suru

achievement [ətʃi:v'mənt] *n* (completion) 完成 kañsei; (success, feat) 業績 gyóseki

acid [æs'id] *adj* (CHEM: soil etc) 酸性の sañsei no; (taste) 酸っぱい suppáI
♦*n* (CHEM) 酸 sáñ; (*inf*: LSD) LSD erúesudì

acid rain *n* 酸性雨 sañseiù

acknowledge [æknɑ:l'idʒ] *vt* (letter, parcel: *also*: **acknowledge receipt of**) 受け取った事を知らせる ukétotta koto wò shiráserù; (fact, situation, person) 認める mitómeru

acknowledgement [æknɑ:l'idʒmənt] *n* (of letter, parcel) 受領通知 juryótsūchi

acne [æk'ni:] *n* にきび níkîbi

acorn [ei'kɔ:rn] *n* ドングリ dóñguri

acoustic [əkuːs'tik] adj (related to hearing) 聴覚の chōkaku no; (guitar etc) アコースティックの akōsutikku no

acoustics [əkuːs'tiks] n (science) 音響学 oñkyōgaku
♦npl (of hall, room) 音響効果 oñkyōkōka

acquaint [əkweint'] vt: *to acquaint someone with something* (inform) ...に ...を知らせる ...ni ...wo shiráseru
to be acquainted with (person) ...と面識がある ...to meñshiki ga arù

acquaintance [əkwein'təns] n (person) 知合い shiríai; (with person, subject) 知識 chíshìki

acquiesce [ækwiːes'] vi: *to acquiesce (to)* (...) を承諾する (...wò) shōdaku suru

acquire [əkwai'əːr] vt (obtain, buy) 手に入れる te ni iréru; (learn, develop: interest, skill) 取得する shutóku suru

acquisition [ækwiziʃ'ən] n (obtaining etc) 入手 nyúshu; (development etc) 獲得 kakútoku; (thing acquired) 取得物 shutókubùtsu

acquit [əkwit'] vt (free) 無罪とする múzài to suru
to acquit oneself well 見事な働きをする mígòto na határaki wo suru

acquittal [əkwit'əl] n 無罪判決 muzái hañketsu

acre [ei'kəːr] n エーカー ēka

acrid [æk'rid] adj (smell, taste, smoke) 刺激的な shigékiteki na

acrimonious [ækrəmou'niːəs] adj (remark, argument) 辛らつな shiñratsu na

acrobat [æk'rəbæt] n アクロバット akúrobattò

acrobatic [ækrəbæt'ik] adj (person, movement, display) アクロバット的な akúrobattòteki na

acronym [æk'rənim] n 頭字語 tōjigo

across [əkrɔːs'] prep (from one side to the other of) ...を渡って ...wo watátte; (on the other side of) ...の向こう側に ...no mukōgawa ni; (crosswise over) ...と交差して ...to kōsa shíte
♦adv (direction) 向こう側へ mukōgawa e; (measurement) 直径が...で chokkéi ga

...de
to run/swim across 走って〔泳いで〕渡る hashítte〔oyóide〕wataru
across from ...の向かいに ...no mukái ni

acrylic [əkril'ik] adj アクリルの ákùriru no
♦n アクリル ákùriru

act [ækt] n (action) 行為 kōi; (of play) 幕 makú; (in a show etc) 出し物 dashímòno; (LAW) 法 hō
♦vi (do something, take action) 行動する kódō suru; (behave) 振舞う furúmaù; (have effect: drug, chemical) 作用する sáyò suru; (THEATER) 出演する shutsúen suru; (pretend) ...の振りをする ...no furí wò suru
♦vt (part) ...に扮する ...ni fuñ surù
in the act of ...しているさなかに ...shité iru sanàka ni
to act as ...として勤める ...toshite tsutómerù

acting [æk'tiŋ] adj (manager, director etc) 代理の daíri no
♦n (activity) 演技 éñgi; (profession) 演劇 eñgeki

action [æk'ʃən] n (deed) 行為 kōi; (motion) 動き ugókí; (MIL) 戦闘 señtō; (LAW) 訴訟 soshō
out of action (person) 活動不能で katsúdōfunò de; (thing) 作動不能で sadōfunò de
to take action 行動を起す kódō wò okósù

action replay n (TV) 即時ビデオ再生 sokúji bideo saísei

activate [æk'təveit] vt (mechanism) 作動させる sadōsaserù

active [æk'tiv] adj (person, life) 活動的な katsúdōteki na
active volcano 活火山 kakkázàn

actively [æk'tivli] adv (participate) 積極的に sekkyókuteki ni; (discourage) 強く tsúyòku; (dislike) 非常に hijō ni

activist [æk'tivist] n 活動家 katsúdōka

activity [æktiv'əti:] n (being active) 活動 katsúdo; (action) 動き ugóki; (pastime, pursuit) 娯楽 goráku

actor [æk'təːr] n 俳優 haíyū

actress [æk'tris] *n* 女優 joyū̀

actual [æk'tʃuːəl] *adj* 実際の jissái no

actually [æk'tʃuːəliː] *adv* (really) 本当に hoñtō ni; (in fact) 実は jitsú wa

acumen [əkjuː'mən] *n* 判断力 hañdañryoku

acupuncture [æk'jupʌŋktʃəːr] *n* 針 hárì

acute [əkjuːt'] *adj* (illness) 急性の kyūsei no; (anxiety, pain) 激しい hagéshiî; (mind, person) 抜け目の無い nukéme no nai; (MATH): **acute angle** 鋭角 eíkaku; (LING): **acute accent** 鋭アクセント eíakùsento

ad [æd] *n abbr* = **advertisement**

A.D. [eidiː'] *adv abbr* (= *Anno Domini*) 西暦...年 seíreki ...neñ

adamant [æd'əmənt] *adj* (person) 譲らない yuzúranai

Adam's apple [æd'əms-] *n* のど仏 nodó-botòke

adapt [ədæpt'] *vt* (alter, change) 適応させる tekíō saserù
   ♦*vi*: **to adapt (to)** (に) 適応する (...ni) tekíō suru

adaptable [ədæp'təbəl] *adj* (device, person) 適応性のある tekíōsei no arù

adapter [ədæp'təːr] *n* (ELEC) アダプター adáputà

adaptor [ədæp'təːr] *n* = **adapter**

add [æd] *vt* (to a collection etc) 加える kuwáeru; (comment etc) 付加える tsukékuwaerù; (figures: *also*: **add up**) 合計する gōkei suru
   ♦*vi*: **to add to** (increase) ...を増す ...wo masú

adder [æd'əːr] *n* ヨーロッパクサリヘビ yōroppà kusárihebì

addict [æd'ikt] *n* (to drugs etc) 中毒者 chūdokushà; (enthusiast) マニア máñia

addicted [ədik'tid] *adj*: **to be addicted to** (drink etc) ...中毒にかかっている ...chūdoku ni kakáttè irú; (*fig*: football etc) ...マニアである ...máñia de arù

addiction [ədik'ʃən] *n* (to drugs etc) 中毒 chūdoku

addictive [ədik'tiv] *adj* (drug) 習慣性のある shūkansei no arù; (activity) 癖になる kusé ni narù

addition [ədiʃ'ən] *n* (adding up) 足し算 tashízàn; (thing added) 加えられた物 kuwáeraretà monò
   in addition なお náò
   in addition to ...の外に ...no hoká ni

additional [ədiʃ'ənəl] *adj* 追加の tsuíka no

additive [æd'ətiv] *n* 添加物 teñkabùtsu

address [ədres'] *n* (postal address) 住所 jūsho; (speech) 演説 eñzetsu
   ♦*vt* (letter, parcel) ...に宛名を書く ...ni aténa wo kákù; (speak to: person) ...に話し掛ける ...ni hanáshikakerù; (: audience) ...に演説する ...ni eñzetsu suru; (problem): **to address (oneself to) a problem** 問題に取組む moñdai ni torikumù

adept [ədept'] *adj*: **adept at** ...が上手な ...ga jōzu na

adequate [æd'əkwit] *adj* (enough: amount) 十分な jūbuñ na; (satisfactory: performance, response) 満足な máñzoku na

adhere [ædhiːr'] *vi*: **to adhere to** (stick to) ...にくっつく ...ni kuttsúkù; (*fig*: abide by: rule, decision, treaty etc) ...を守る ...wo mamórù; (: hold to: opinion, belief etc) ...を固守する ...wo kóshù suru

adhesive [ædhiː'siv] *n* 粘着材 neñchakuzài

adhesive tape *n* (*US*: MED) ばん創こう bañsōkō; (*BRIT*) 粘着テープ neñchaku tēpu

ad hoc [æd hɑːk'] *adj* (decision, committee) 特別な tokúbetsu na

adjacent [ədʒei'sənt] *adj*: **adjacent to** ...の隣の ...no tonári no

adjective [ædʒ'iktiv] *n* 形容詞 keíyòshi

adjoining [ədʒɔi'niŋ] *adj* (room etc) 隣の tonári no

adjourn [ədʒəːrn'] *vt* (trial) 休廷にする kyūtei ni suru; (meeting, discussion) 休会にする kyūkai ni suru
   ♦*vi* (trial) 休廷する kyūtei suru; (meeting) 休止する kyūshi suru

adjudicate [ədʒuː'dikeit] *vt* (contest) ...の審査員を勤める ...no shiñsa-ìn wo tsutómerù

adjust [ədʒʌst'] *vt* (change: approach etc) 調整する chōsei suru; (rearrange: clothing, machine etc) 調節する chōsetsu suru

♦*vi*: **to adjust (to)** 適応する tekíō suru

adjustable [ədʒʌst'əbəl] *adj* 調節できる chōsetsu dekirù

adjustment [ədʒʌst'mənt] *n* (PSYCH) 適応 tekíō; (to machine) 調節 chōsetsu; (of prices, wages) 調整 chōsei

ad-lib [ædlib'] *vi* アドリブで話す adóribu dè hanásù

ad lib [ædlib'] *adv* (speak) アドリブで a-dóribu de

administer [ædmin'istə:r] *vt* (country) 統治する tōchi suru; (department) 管理する kánri suru; (MED: drug) 投与する tōyo suru

   to administer justice 裁く sabákù

administration [ædministrei'ʃən] *n* (management) 管理 kánri; (government) 政権 seíken

administrative [ædmin'istreitiv] *adj* (work, error etc) 管理的な kaíriteki na

administrator [ædmin'istreitə:r] *n* 管理者 kaírishà

admiral [æd'mə:rəl] *n* 海軍大将 kaígun taíshō

Admiralty [æd'mə:rəlti:] (*BRIT*) *n*: **the Admiralty** (*also*: **Admiralty Board**) 海軍省 kaígunshō

admiration [ædmərei'ʃən] *n* 感心 kaíshin

admire [ædmai'ə:r] *vt* (respect) ...に感心する ...ni kańshin suru; (appreciate) 観賞する kańshō suru

admirer [ædmai'ə:rə:r] *n* (suitor) 男女達 otókotomodachi; (fan) ファン fáń

admission [ædmiʃ'ən] *n* (admittance) 入場 nyūjō; (entry fee) 入場料 nyūjōryō; (confession) 自白 jiháku

admit [ædmit'] *vt* (confess) 自白する jiháku suru; (permit to enter) 入場させる nyūjō saserù; (to club, organization) 入会させる nyūkai saserù; (to hospital) 入院させる nyūin saserù; (accept: defeat, responsibility etc) 認める mitómeru

admittance [ædmit'əns] *n* 入場 nyūjō

admittedly [ædmit'idli:] *adv* 確かに...であるが táshìka ni ... de árù ga

admit to *vt fus* (murder etc) ...を自白する ...wo jiháku suru

admonish [ædmɑ:n'iʃ] *vt* (rebuke) たしなめる tashínamerù; (LAW) 忠告する chūkoku suru

ad nauseam [æd nɔː'zi:əm] *adv* (repeat, talk) いやという程 iyá to iú hodô

ado [ədu:'] *n*: *without (any) more ado* さっさと sássà to

adolescence [ædəles'əns] *n* 10代 jūdai

adolescent [ædəles'ənt] *adj* 10代の jūdai no

♦*n* ティーンエージャー tínèjā

adopt [ədɑːpt'] *vt* (child) 養子にする yōshi ni suru; (policy, attitude) とる torù; (accent) まねる manéru

adopted [ədɑːp'tid] *adj* (child) 養子の yōshi no

adoption [ədɑːp'ʃən] *n* (of child) 養子縁組 yōshìengumi; (of policy etc) 採択 saítaku

adoptive [ədɑːp'tiv] *adj*: *adoptive father/mother* 養父(母) yōfu(bo)
   adoptive country 第2の祖国 dāî ni no sókòku

adore [ədɔːr'] *vt* (person) 崇拝する sūhai suru

adorn [ədɔːrn'] *vt* (decorate) 飾る kazáru

adrenalin [ədren'əlin] *n* アドレナリン a-dórenarìn

Adriatic [eidri:æt'ik] *n*: *the Adriatic (Sea)* アドリア海 adóriakài

adrift [ədrift'] *adv* (NAUT: loose) 漂流して hyōryū shite

adult [ədʌlt'] *n* (person) 大人 otóna; (animal, insect) 成体 seítai

♦*adj* (grown-up: person) 大人の otóna no; (: animal etc) 成体の seítai no; (for adults: literature, education) 成人向きの seíjinmuki no

adultery [ədʌl'tə:ri:] *n* かん通 kańtsū

advance [ædvæns'] *n* (movement, progress) 進歩 shíñpo; (money) 前借り maégari

♦*adj* (booking, notice, warning) 事前の jizén no

♦vt (money) 前貸する maégashi suru
♦vi (move forward) 前進する zeńshin suru; (make progress) 進歩する shińpo suru

to make advances (to someone) (gen) (...に) 言い寄る (...ni) iíyorù

in advance (book, prepare etc) 前もって maémottè

advanced [ædvænst'] adj (SCOL: studies) 高等の kótō no; (country) 先進の seńshin no; (child) ませた máseta

advancement [ædvæns'mənt] n (improvement) 進歩 shínpo; (in job, rank) 昇進 shóshin

advantage [ædvæn'tidʒ] n (supremacy) 有利な立場 yúri na táchiba; (benefit) 利点 ríten; (TENNIS) アドバンテージ adóbańtēji

to take advantage of (person) ...に付け込む ...ni tsukékomù; (opportunity) 利用する riyṓ suru

advantageous [ædvəntei'dʒəs] adj: **advantageous (to)** (...に) 有利な (...ni) yúri na

advent [æd'vent] n (appearance: of innovation) 出現 shutsúgen; (REL): **Advent** 待降節 taíkōsetsù

adventure [ædven't∫ər] n 冒険 bóken

adventurous [ædven't∫ərəs] adj (bold, outgoing) 大胆な daítan na

adverb [æd'vərb] n 副詞 fukúshi

adversary [æd'vərse:ri:] n (opponent, also MIL) 敵 tekí

adverse [ædvə:rs'] adj (effect, weather, publicity etc) 悪い warúi

adversity [ædvə:r'siti:] n 逆境 gyakkyṓ

advert [æd'və:rt] (BRIT) n abbr = **advertisement**

advertise [æd'və:rtaiz] vi (COMM: in newspaper, on television etc) 広告する kókoku suru
♦vt (product, event, job) ...を広告する ...wo kókoku suru

to advertise for (staff, accommodation etc) ...を求める広告を出す ...wo motómerù kókoku wo dasu

advertisement [ædvə:rtaiz'mənt] n 広告 kókoku

advertiser [æd'və:rtaizə:r] n (in newspaper, on television etc) 広告主 kókoku-nùshi

advertising [æd'və:rtaiziŋ] n (advertisements) 広告 kókoku; (industry) 広告業界 kókokugyōkai

advice [ædvais'] n (counsel) 忠告 chúkoku; (notification) 知らせ shiráse

a piece of advice 一つの忠告 hítotsu no chúkoku

to take legal advice 弁護士に相談する beńgoshì ni sṓdan suru

advisable [ædvai'zəbəl] adj 望ましい no-zómashiì

advise [ædvaiz'] vt (give advice to: person, company etc) ...に忠告する ...ni chúkoku suru; (inform): **to advise someone of something** ...に ...を知らせる ...ni ...wo shiráserù

to advise against something/doing something ... (するの) を避けた方がいいと忠告する ... (surú no) wo sakéta hṓ gà íi to chúkoku suru

advisedly [ædvai'zidli:] adv (deliberately) 意図的に itóteki ni

adviser [ædvai'zə:r] n (counsellor, consultant: to private person) 相談相手 sódan aitè; (: to company etc) 顧問 kómon

advisor [ædvai'zə:r] n = **adviser**

advisory [ædvai'zə:ri:] adj (role, capacity, body) 顧問の kómòn no

advocate [æd'vəkit] vt (support, recommend) 主張する shuchṓ suru
♦n (LAW: barrister) 弁護士 beńgoshì; (supporter): **advocate of** ...の主張者 ...no shuchṓsha

Aegean [idʒi:'ən] n: **the Aegean (Sea)** エーゲ海 ḗgekài

aerial [e:r'i:əl] n アンテナ añtena
♦adj (attack, photograph) 航空の kókū no

aerobics [e:rou'biks] n エアロビクス eárobikùsu

aerodynamic [e:roudainæm'ik] adj 空力的な kúrikiteki na

aeroplane [e:r'əplein] (BRIT) n 飛行機 híkōki

aerosol [e:r'əso:l] n スプレー缶 supúrē

kan

aerospace industry [ɛːrˈəspeis-] *n* 宇宙
開発業界 uchŭkaɪ̄hatsugyōkai

aesthetic [esθetˈik] *adj* 美的な bitḗki na

afar [əfɑːrˈ] *adv*: **from afar** 遠くから tồku karà

affable [æfˈəbəl] *adj* (person) 愛想の良い aīsồ no yoɪ̄; (behavior) 感じの良い kaɲji no yoɪ̄

affair [əferˈ] *n* (matter, business, question) 問題 moɲdai; (romance: *also*: **love affair**) 浮気 uwáki

affect [əfektˈ] *vt* (influence, concern: person, object) …に影響を与える …ni eɪ̄kyō wò atáerù; (subj: disease: afflict) 冒す okásù; (move deeply) 感動させる kaɲdō saserù

affected [əfekˈtid] *adj* (behavior, person) 気取った kidốtta

affection [əfekˈʃən] *n* (fondness) 愛情 aɪ̄jō

affectionate [əfekˈʃənit] *adj* (person, kiss) 愛情深い aɪ̄jōbukaɪ̄; (animal) 人なつこい hitồnatsukoɪ̄

affiliated [əfilˈiːeitid] *adj* (company, body) 関連の kaɲren no

affinity [əfinˈəti] *n* (bond, rapport): **to have an affinity with/for** …に魅力を感じる …ni miryốku wò kaɲjiru; (resemblance): **to have an affinity with** … …に似ている …ni nité iru

affirmative [əfəːrˈmətiv] *adj* (answer, nod etc) 肯定の kốtei no

affix [əfiksˈ] *vt* (stamp) はる harú

afflict [əfliktˈ] *vt* (subj: pain, sorrow, misfortune) 苦しめる kurúshimerù

affluence [æfˈluːəns] *n* 裕福さ yū́fukusà

affluent [æfˈluːənt] *adj* (wealthy: family, background, surroundings) 裕福な yū́fuku na

the affluent society 豊かな社会 yútaka na shákaɪ̄

afford [əfɔːrdˈ] *vt* (have enough money for) 買う余裕がある kaú yoyū ga arù; (permit oneself: time, risk etc) する余裕がある surú yoyū ga arù; (provide) 与える atáeru

affront [əfrʌntˈ] *n* (insult) 侮辱 bujóku

Afghanistan [æfgænˈistæn] *n* アフガニスタン afúganisùtan

afield [əfiːldˈ] *adv*: **far afield** 遠く tốku

afloat [əfloutˈ] *adv* (floating) 浮んで ukáñde

afoot [əfutˈ] *adv*: **there is something afoot** 何か怪しい事が起っている náñka ayáshii koto gà okốttè irú

afraid [əfreidˈ] *adj* (frightened) 怖がっている kowágattè irú

to be afraid of (person, thing) …を怖がる …wo kowágarù

to be afraid to …をするのを怖がる …wo suru no wồ kowágarù

I am afraid that (apology) 申訳ないが … mốshiwakenai ga

I am afraid so/not 残念ですがその通りです〔違います〕zaññeñ desu ga sonồ tồri desu〔chigáimasù〕

afresh [əfreʃˈ] *adv* (begin, start) 新たに árāta ni

Africa [æfˈrikə] *n* アフリカ afúrika

African [æfˈrikən] *adj* アフリカの afúrika no

♦*n* アフリカ人 afúrikajìn

aft [æft] *adv* (to be) 後方に kốhō ni; (to go) 後方へ kốhō e

after [æfˈtər] *prep* (of time) …の後に …no átồ ni; (of place) …の後ろに …no ushíro ni; (of order) …の次に …no tsugí ni

♦*adv* 後に átồ ni

♦*conj* …してから …shité kara

what/who are you after? 何〔だれ〕を捜していますか nánì〔dárè〕wo sagáshitè imásu ka

after he left 彼が帰ってから kárè ga kaétte kara

after having done …してから …shité kara

to name someone after someone …に因んで…に名を付ける …ni chínàñde …ni na wo tsukérù

it's twenty after eight (*US*) 8時20分だ hachíji nijippùn da

to ask after someone …の事を尋ねる …no kotồ wồ tazúnerù

after all (in spite of everything) どうせ

dőse; (in spite of contrary expectations etc) 予想を裏切って yosố wò urágittè

after you! お先にどうぞ o-sáki ni dốzo

after-effects [ǽf'tə:rifekts] *npl* (of illness, radiation, drink etc) 結果 kekká

aftermath [ǽf'tə:rmæθ] *n* (period after) ...直後の期間 ...chókùgo no kikáñ; (aftereffects) 結果 kekká

afternoon [æftə:rnu:n'] *n* 午後 gógò

afters [ǽf'tə:rz] (*BRIT*:*inf*) *n* (dessert) デザート dézàto

after-sales service [ǽf'tə:rseilz-](*BRIT*) *n* (for car, washing machine etc) アフターサービス afútāsābisu

after-shave (lotion) [ǽf'tə:rʃeiv-] *n* アフターシェーブローション afútāshēburōshon

afterthought [ǽf'tə:rθɔ:t] *n*: *as an afterthought* 後の思い付きで átò no omóitsuki de

afterwards [ǽf'tə:rwə:rdz] (*US also*: **afterward**) *adv* その後 sonó àtò

again [əgen'] *adv* (once more) もう1度 mố ichido, 再び futátabi

not ... again もう...ない mố ... nai

to do something again ...をもう1度する ...wo mố ichido surù

again and again 何度も nǎndo mo

against [əgenst'] *prep* (leaning on, touching) ...にもたれ掛って ...ni motárekakattè; (in opposition to, at odds with) ...に反対して ...ni hañtai shite; (compared to) ...に較べて ...ni kurábete

age [eid3] *n* (of person, object) 年齢 nefirei; (period in history) 時代 jidái

◆*vi* (person) 年を取る toshí wo torù

◆*vt* (subj: hairstyle, dress, make-up etc) ...を実際の年以上に見せる ...wo jissái no toshi ijồ ni misérù

20 years of age 年齢二十 nefirei hatàchi

to come of age 成人する sefjin suru

it's been ages since ...は久し振りだ ...wa hisáshiburi da

aged[1] [ei'd3d] *adj*: *aged 10* 10才の jússai no

aged[2] [ei'd3id] *npl*: *the aged* 老人 rốjin

◇総称 sốshō

age group *n* 年齢層 nefireìsō

age limit *n* 年齢制限 nefireiseìgen

agency [ei'd3ənsi:] *n* (COMM) 代理店 daírìten; (government body) ...局 ...kyokú, ...庁 ...chố

agenda [ədʒen'də] *n* (of meeting) 議題 gidái

agent [ei'd3ənt] *n* (representative: COMM, literary, theatrical etc) 代理人 daírinin, エージェント ềjento; (spy) スパイ supáì; (CHEM, *fig*) 試薬 shiyáku

aggravate [æg'rəveit] *vt* (exacerbate: situation) 悪化させる akká saserù; (annoy: person) 怒らせる okóraserù

aggregate [æg'rəgit] *n* (total) 合計 gốkei

aggression [əgreʃ'ən] *n* (aggressive behavior) 攻撃 kốgeki

aggressive [əgres'iv] *adj* (belligerent, assertive) 攻撃的な kốgekiteki na

aggrieved [əgri:vd'] *adj* 不満を抱いた fumán wò idáìtà

aghast [əgæst'] *adj* あっけにとられた akké ni toráretà

agile [ædʒ'əl] *adj* (physically, mentally) 身軽な migáru na; (mentally) 機敏な kibín na

agitate [ædʒ'əteit] *vt* (person) 動揺させる dốyò saserù

◆*vi*: *to agitate for/against* ...の運動〔反対運動〕をする ...no uñdō (hañtaiundồ) wò suru

agitator [ædʒ'iteitə:r] *n* 扇動者 sefidốsha

AGM [eid3i:em'] *n abbr* = **annual general meeting**

agnostic [ægnɑ:s'tik] *n* 不可知論者 fukáchironsha

ago [əgou'] *adv*: *2 days ago* 2日前 futsúkamaè

not long ago 少し前に súkòshi máè ni

how long ago? どのぐらい前に? donó gurǎi máè ni?

agog [əgɑ:g'] *adj* (excited, eager) わくわくしている wákùwaku shitế irù

agonizing [æg'ənaiziŋ] *adj* 苦しい kurúshiî

agony [æg'əni:] *n* (pain) 苦もん kumốn

to be in agony 苦しむ kurúshimù

agree [əgriː'] *vt* (price, date) 合意して決める gói shité kiméru

♦*vi* (have same opinion) ...と意見が合う ...to íkèn ga áù; (correspond) ...と一致する ...to itchí suru; (consent) 承諾する shôdaku suru

to agree with someone (subj: person) ...と同意する ...to dôi suru; (: food) ...に合う ...ni áù

to agree (with) (statements etc) (...に)同意する (...ni) dôi suru; (LING) (...と)一致する (...to) itchí suru

to agree to something/to do something ...に〔することに〕同意する ...ni 〔surú koto ni〕dôi suru

to agree that (admit) ...だと認める ...dá tò mitómeru

agreeable [əgriː'əbəl] *adj* (sensation, person: pleasant) 気持の良い kimóchi no yoì; (willing) 承知する shôchi suru

agreed [əgriːd'] *adj* (time, place, price) 同意で決めた dôi de kimétà

agreement [əgriː'mənt] *n* (concurrence, consent) 同意 dôi; (arrangement, contract) 契約 keíyaku

in agreement 同意して dôi shite

agricultural [ægrəkʌl'tʃəːrəl] *adj* (land, implement, show) 農業の nôgyō no

agriculture [æg'rəkʌltʃəːr] *n* 農業 nôgyō

aground [əgraund'] *adv*: *to run aground* (NAUT) ざ折する zasétsu suru

ahead [əhed'] *adv* (in front: of place, time) 前に máè ni; (into the future) 先さき sakí

ahead of (in progress) ...より進んで ...yórì susúnde; (in ranking) ...の上に ...no ué ni; (in advance of: person, time, place) ...の前に ...no máè ni

ahead of time 早目に hayáme ni

go right/straight ahead (direction) 真っ直ぐに行って下さい mássùgu ni itté kudasai; (permission) どうぞ, どうぞ dôzo, dôzo

aid [eid] *n* (assistance: to person, country) 援助 êñjo; (device) ...を助けるもの

...wo tasúkerù monó

♦*vt* (help: person, country) 援助する êñjo suru

in aid of (BRIT) ...のために ...no támè ni

to aid and abet (LAW) ほう助する hôjo suru ¶ *see also* **hearing**

aide [eid] *n* (person, *also* MIL) 側近 sokkín

AIDS [eidz] *n abbr* (= *acquired immunodeficiency syndrome*) エイズ êìzu

ailing [ei'liŋ] *adj* (person) 病気の byôki no

ailment [eil'mənt] *n* 病気 byôki

aim [eim] *vt*: *to aim (at)* (gun, missile, camera, remark) (...に)向ける (...ni) mukérù

♦*vi* (*also*: *take aim*) ねらう neráu

♦*n* (objective) 目的 mokúteki; (in shooting: skill) ねらい nerái

to aim at (with weapon; *also* objective) ねらう neráu

to aim a punch at げんこつで...を殴うとする geñkotsu de ...wò nágùro to suru

to aim to do ...するつもりである ...surú tsumóri de arù

aimless [eim'lis] *adj* (person, activity) 当てのない até no naì

ain't [eint] (*inf*) = **am not; aren't; isn't**

air [eːr] *n* (atmosphere) 空気 kûki; (tune) メロディー méròdī; (appearance) 態度 táìdo

♦*vt* (room) ...の空気を入れ替える ...no kûki wo irékaerù; (clothes) 干す hósù; (grievances, ideas) 打明ける uchíakeru

♦*cpd* (currents etc) 空気の kûki no; (attack) 空からの sorá kara no

to throw something into the air (ball etc) ...を投上げる ...wo nagéageru

by air (travel) 飛行機で híkòki de

on the air (RADIO, TV: programme, station) 放送中 hôsōchū

airbed [eːr'bed] (BRIT) *n* 空気布団 kûki-butòn

airborne [eːr'bɔːrn] *adj* (airplane) 飛行中の hikôchū no

air-conditioned [eːr'kəndiʃənd] *adj* 空

調付きの kúchōtsuki no

air conditioning [-kəndiʃ'əniŋ] n 空調 kúchō

aircraft [ɛːr'kræft] n inv 航空機 kókūki

aircraft carrier n 空母 kūbo

airfield [ɛːr'fiːld] n 飛行場 hikójō

Air Force n 空軍 kúgun

air freshener [-freʃ'ənəːr] n 消臭剤 shōshūzai

airgun [ɛːr'gʌn] n 空気銃 kúkijū

air hostess (BRIT) n スチュワーデス suchúwàdesu

air letter (BRIT) n エアログラム eárogurāmu

airlift [ɛːr'lift] n エアリフト eárifùto

airline [ɛːr'lain] n エアライン eáraìn

airliner [ɛːr'lainəːr] n 旅客機 ryokákukì

airmail [ɛːr'meil] n: **by airmail** 航空便で kōkūbin de

airplane [ɛːr'plein] (US) n 飛行機 hǐkōki

airport [ɛːr'pɔːrt] n 空港 kúkō

air raid n 空襲 kúshū

airsick [ɛːr'sik] adj: **to be airsick** 飛行機に酔う hǐkōki ni yóù

airspace [ɛːr'speis] n 領空 ryókū

air terminal n 空港ターミナルビル kúkōtāminarubìru

airtight [ɛːr'tait] adj 気密の kimítsu no

air-traffic controller [ɛːr'træfik-] n 管制官 kańseìkan

airy [ɛːr'iː] adj (room, building) 風通しの良い kazétoshi no yoì; (casual: manner) 軽薄な keíhaku na

aisle [ail] n 通路 tsúro

ajar [ədʒɑːr'] adj (door) 少し開いている sukóshi aite irù

akin [əkin'] adj: **akin to** (similar) ...の様な ...no yō na

alacrity [əlæk'riti:] n 敏速さ bińsokusa

alarm [əlɑːrm'] n (anxiety) 心配 shińpai; (in shop, bank) 警報 keíhō
  ♦vt (person) 心配させる shińpai saserù

alarm call n (in hotel etc) モーニングコール móningukòru

alarm clock n 目覚し時計 mezámashidokèi

alas [əlæs'] excl 残念ながら zańnennagàra

Albania [ælbei'niːə] n アルバニア arúbania

albeit [ɔːlbiː'it] conj (although) ...ではあるが ...de wa árù ga

album [æl'bəm] n (gen, also: LP) アルバム arúbamu

alcohol [æl'kəhɔːl] n アルコール arúkōru

alcoholic [ælkəhɔː'lik] adj アルコールの入った arúkōru no haìtta
  ♦n アルコール中毒者 arúkōru chúdokùsha

alcoholism [æl'kəhɔːlizəm] n アルコール中毒 arúkōru chúdoku

alcove [æl'kouv] n アルコーブ arúkobù

ale [eil] n (drink) エール êru

alert [ələːrt'] adj 注意している chúi shité irù
  ♦n (alarm) 警報 keíhō
  ♦vt (guard, police etc) ...に知らせる ...ni shiráserù
  to be on the alert (also MIL) 警戒している keíkai shite irù

algebra [æl'dʒəbrə] n 代数 daísū

Algeria [ældʒiː'riːə] n アルジェリア arújeria

algorithm [æl'gəriðəm] n アルゴリズム arúgorizùmu

alias [ei'liːəs] adv 別名は betsúmei wa
  ♦n (of criminal, writer etc) 偽名 giméi

alibi [æl'əbai] n (LAW: also gen) アリバイ aríbai

alien [eil'jən] n (foreigner) 外国人 gaíkokujìn; (extraterrestrial) 宇宙人 uchūjin
  ♦adj: **alien (to)** (...) の性に合わない (...no) shō ni awánaì

alienate [eil'jəneit] vt (person) ...と仲たがいする ...to nakátagaì suru

alight [əlait'] adj (burning) 燃えている moéte iru; (eyes, expression) 輝いている kagáyaìte irú
  ♦vi (bird) とまる tomáru; (passenger) 降りる orírù

align [əlain'] vt (objects) 並べる naráberu

alike [əlaik'] adj 似ている nité iru
  ♦adv (similarly) 同様に dóyō ni;

(equally) ...共に ...tomo ni
to look alike 似ている nitē iru

alimony [ǽləmouni:] n (payment) 離婚手当 rikónteàte

alive [əláiv'] adj (living) 生きている íkìte irú; (lively: person) 活発な kappátsu na; (place) 活気に満ちた kakkí ni michíta

alkali [ǽl'kəlài] n アルカリ arúkari

KEYWORD

all [ɔ:l] adj 皆の mi(n)ná no, 全ての subète nó, 全部の zènbu nó, ...中...jū
all day/night 1日〔1晩〕中 ichinichi(hitoban)jū
all men are equal 全ての人間は平等である subète nó nínGen wa byōdō de árù
all five came 5人とも来ました gonín tomo kimáshìta
all the books/food 本〔食べ物〕は全部 hòn〔tabémono〕wa zènbu
all the time いつも ítsumo
he lived here all his life 彼は一生ここで暮らしました kàre wa isshō koko de kuráshimashìta

◆pron 1 皆 miná, 全て subète, 全部 zènbu
I ate it all, I ate all of it それを全部食べました soré wo zènbu tabémashìta
all of us/the boys went 私たち〔少年たち〕は皆行きました watákushitàchi 〔shōnèntachi〕wa miná íkimashìta
we all sat down 私たちは皆腰掛けました watákushitàchi wa miná koshíkakemashìta
is that all? それで全部ですか soré de zènbu desu ká; (in shop) 外にはよろしいでしょうか hoká ni wà yoróshiì deshō ká
2 (in phrases): **above all** 何よりも nánì yori mo
after all 何しろ nánì shiro
at all: not at all (in answer to question) 少しも...ない sùkóshì mo ...nài; (in answer to thanks) どういたしまして dō itáshimashìtē
I'm not at all tired 少しも疲れていません sùkóshi mo tsùkárete ìmasen
anything at all will do 何でもいいで

す nán de mo iì desú
all in all 全般的に見て zénpanteki ni mítè

◆adv 全く máttaku
all alone 1人だけで hítorí dake dè
it's not as hard as all that 言われている程難しくありません iwárete iru hodo mùzúkashiku arímasèn
all the more なお更... nàósara...
all the better 更にいい sàra ni iì
all but (regarding people) ...を除いて皆 ...wo nózoite miná; (regarding things) ...を除いて全て ...wo nózoite sùbete
I had all but finished もう少しで終るところだった mō sukoshì de owáru tokoro dáttà
the score is 2 all カウントはツーオールです kaúnto wa tsūórù désù

---

allay [əléi'] vt (fears) 和らげる yawáragerù

all clear n (after attack etc) 警報解除信号 keíhōkaijoshiǹgō; (fig: permission) 許可 kyóka

allegation [æləgei'∫ən] n (of misconduct, impropriety) 主張 shuchō

allege [əledʒ'] vt (claim) 主張する shuchō suru

allegedly [əledʒ'idli:] adv 主張によると shuchō ni yoru to

allegiance [əli:'dʒəns] n (loyalty, support) 忠誠 chūsei

allegory [æl'əgɔ:ri:] n (painting, story) 比ゆ híyù

allergic [ələr'dʒik] adj (reaction, rash) アレルギーの arérùgī no
allergic to (foods etc) ...に対してアレルギー体質である ...ni taíshite arérugítaishìtsu de aru; (fig: work etc) ...が大嫌いである ...ga daíkirai de aru

allergy [æl'ərdʒi:] n (MED) アレルギー arérùgī

alleviate [əli:'vi:eit] vt (pain, difficulty) 軽減する keígen suru

alley [æl'i:] n (street) 横丁 yokóchō

alliance [əlai'əns] n (of states, people) 連合 reńgō

allied [əlaid'] adj (POL, MIL: forces) 連

合の refgō no

alligator [ǽl'əgeitə:r] n (ZOOL) アリゲーター arígēta

all-in [ɔ:l'in] (BRIT) adj (also adv: price, cost, charge) 込みの〔で〕kómì no 〔de〕

all-in wrestling (BRIT) n プロレスリング puróresùringu

all-night [ɔ:l'nait] adj (cafe, cinema, party) オールナイトの ốrunaìto no

allocate [ǽl'əkeit] vt (earmark: time, money, tasks, rooms etc) 割当てる waríaterù

allot [əlɑt'] vt: **to allot (to)** (time, money etc) 割当てる waríaterù

allotment [əlɑt'mənt] n (share) 配分 haíbun; (BRIT: garden) 貸家庭菜園 kashíkateisaèn

all-out [ɔ:l'aut'] adj (effort, dedication etc) 徹底的な tettéiteki na
all out adv 徹底的に tettéiteki ni

allow [əlau'] vt (permit, tolerate: practice, behavior, goal) 許す yurúsù; (sum, time estimate) 見積る mitsúmorù; (claim) 認める mitómeru; (concede): **to allow that** ...だと認める ...da to mitómerù

to allow someone to do ...に...をするのを許す ...ni ...wò suru no wò yúrusù

he is allowed to ... 彼は...してよいとなっている kárè wa ...shité yoì to natte irù

allowance [əlau'əns] n (money given to someone: gen) 支給金 shikyúkin; (: welfare payment) 福祉手当 fukúshiteàte; (: pocket money) 小遣い kózùkai; (tax allowance) 控除 kòjo

to make allowances for (person, thing) 考慮する kōryo suru

allow for vt fus (shrinkage, inflation etc) ...を考慮する ...wo kōryo suru

alloy [ǽl'ɔi] n (mix) 合金 gókin

all right adv (well: get on) うまく úmàku; (correctly: function, do) しかるべく shikárubekù; (as answer: in agreement) いいですよ íi desu yo

I feel all right 大丈夫です daíjōbu desu

all-rounder [ɔ:l'raun'də:r] (BRIT) n 多才の人 tasái no hito

all-time [ɔ:l'taim] adj (record) 史上最...の shijōsai... no

allude [əlu:d'] vi: **to allude to** 暗に言及する án ni geñkyū suru

alluring [əlu:'riŋ] adj (person, prospect) 魅力的な miryóteki na

allusion [əlu:'ʒən] n (reference) さりげない言及 sarígenaì geñkyū

ally [ǽl'ai] n (friend, also POL, MIL) 味方 mikáta
♦vt: **to ally oneself with** ...に味方する ...ni mikáta suru

almighty [ɔ:lmai'ti:] adj (omnipotent) 全能の zeñnō no; (tremendous: row etc) ものすごい monòsugoí

almond [ɑ:'mənd] n (fruit) アーモンド ā̀mondo

almost [ɔ:l'moust] adv (practically) ほとんど hotôndo; (with verb): **I almost fell** 私は転ぶところだった watákushi wà koróbu tokoro dattà

alms [ɑ:mz] npl 施し hodókoshi

aloft [əlɔ:ft'] adv (hold, carry) 高く tákàku

alone [əloun'] adj (by oneself, unaccompanied) 一人きりの hitórikiri no
♦adv (unaided) 単独で tañdoku de
to leave someone alone ...をほうっておく ...wo hôtte oku
to leave something alone ...をいじらない ...wo íjiranai
let alone ... ...は言うまでもなく ...wa iú made mo naku

along [əlɔ:ŋ'] prep (way, route, street, wall etc) ...に沿って ...ni sôtte
♦adv: **is he coming along with us?** 彼も付いて来るのですか kárè mo tsúite kurú no desu ká
he was limping along 彼はびっこを引いて歩いていた kárè wa bíkkò wo hiite árùite itá
along with (together with) ...と一緒に ...to isshó ni
all along (all the time) ずっと zuttô

alongside [əlɔ:ŋ'said'] prep (come, be: vehicle, ship) ...の横に ...no yokô ni
♦adv (see prep) ...の横に ...no yokô ni

aloof [əlu:f'] adj よそよそしい yosóyososhiî

◆*adv*: *to stand aloof* 知らぬ顔をする shiránu kao wò suru

aloud [əlaud'] *adv* (read, speak) 声を出して kôê wo dáshîte

alphabet [æl'fəbet] *n* アルファベット a-rúfabettô

alphabetical [ælfəbet'ikəl] *adj* アルファベットの arúfabettô no

alpine [æl'pain] *adj* (sports, meadow, plant) 山の yamá no

Alps [ælps] *npl*: *the Alps* アルプス山脈 arúpusu saǹmyaku

already [ɔ:lred'i:] *adv* もう mô, 既に súdèni

alright [ɔ:lrait'] (*BRIT*) *adv* = **all right**

Alsatian [ælsei'ʃən] *n* (*BRIT*: dog) シェパード犬 shepádoken

also [ɔ:l'sou] *adv* (too) も mo; (moreover) なお nâô

altar [ɔ:l'tə:r] *n* (REL) 祭壇 saídan

alter [ɔ:l'tə:r] *vt* (change) 変える kaéru
◆*vi* (change) 変る kawáru

alteration [ɔ:ltərei'ʃən] *n* (to plans) 変更 heǹkō; (to clothes) 寸法直し suǹpōnaôshi; (to building) 改修 kaíshū

alternate [*adj* ɔ:l'tə:rnit *vb* ɔ:l'tə:rneit] *adj* (actions, events, processes) 交互の kôgo no; (*US*: alternative: plans) 代りの kawári no
◆*vi*: *to alternate (with)* (...と) 交替する (...to) kôtai suru
on alternate days 1日置きに ichínichi oki ni

alternating current [ɔ:l'tə:rneitiŋ-] *n* 交流 kôryū

alternative [ɔ:ltə:r'nətiv] *adj* (plan, policy) 代りの kawári no
◆*n* (choice: other possibility) 選択 seǹtaku

alternative comedy 新コメディー shíǹkomèdî ◇近年若手コメディアンの間ではやっている反体制の落語、喜劇などを指す kíǹnen wakátekomedîan no aída dè hayátte iru haǹtaisei no rakúgo, kígèki nado wo sásù

alternative medicine 代替医学 daítaiigàku ◇はり, 指圧など, 西洋医学以外の

治療法を指す hárî, shiátsu nadò, seíyōigàku ígài no chiryôhō wo sasù

alternatively [ɔ:ltə:r'nətivli:] *adv*: *alternatively one could ...* 一方...する事もできる íppô ...surú koto mo dekirù

alternator [ɔ:l'tə:rneitə:r] *n* (AUT) 交流発電機 kôryūhatsudeǹki

although [ɔ:lðou'] *conj* (despite the fact that) ...にもかかわらず ...ni mo kakáwaràzu

altitude [æl'tətu:d] *n* (of place) 海抜 kaíbatsu; (of plane) 高度 kôdo

alto [æl'tou] *n* (female) アルト árùto; (male) コントラテノール koǹtoratenôru

altogether [ɔ:ltəgeð'ə:r] *adv* (completely) 全く mattáku; (on the whole, in all) 合計は gôkei wa

altruistic [æltru:is'tik] *adj* (motive, behavior) 愛他的な aítateki na

aluminium [ælu:min'i:əm] (*BRIT*) = **aluminum**

aluminum [əlu:'mənəm] *n* アルミニウム arúminiùmu, アルミ arúmi

always [ɔ:l'weiz] *adv* (at all times) いつも ítsumo; (forever) いつまでも ítsu made mò; (if all else fails) いざとなれば ízà to nárèba

am [æm] *vb see* **be**

a.m. [ei'em'] *adv abbr* (= *ante meridiem*) 午前 gózen

amalgamate [əmæl'gəmeit] *vi* (organizations, companies) 合併する gappéi suru
◆*vt* (see vi) 合併させる gappéi saseru

amass [əmæs'] *vt* (fortune, information, objects) 貯め込む tamékomù

amateur [æm'ətʃə:r] *n* (non-professional) 素人 shíroùto, アマチュア amáchua

amateurish [æmətʃu:'riʃ] *adj* (work, efforts) 素人っぽい shirótoppoi

amaze [əmeiz'] *vt* 仰天させる gyóten saseru
to be amazed (at) (...に) びっくり仰天する (...ni) bíkkùrigyôten suru

amazement [əmeiz'mənt] *n* 仰天 gyôten

amazing [əmei'ziŋ] *adj* (surprising) 驚くべき odórokubekî; (fantastic) 素晴らし

い subárashiì

Amazon [æm'əzɑːn] n (GEO: river) アマゾン川 amázoṅgawa

ambassador [æmbæs'ədər] n (diplomat) 大使 táìshi

amber [æm'bər] n (substance) こはく koháku

at amber (BRIT: AUT: of traffic light) 黄色になって kíìro ni nattè

ambiguity [æmbəgjuː'itiː] n (lack of clarity: in thoughts, word, phrase etc) あいまいさ aímaisa

ambiguous [æmbig'juːəs] adj (word, phrase, reply) あいまいな aímai na

ambition [æmbiʃ'ən] n (desire, thing desired) 野心 yáshìn

ambitious [æmbiʃ'əs] adj (person, plan) 野心的な yashínteki na

ambivalent [æmbiv'ələnt] adj (opinion, attitude, person) はっきりしない hakkíri shinai

amble [æm'bəl] vi (gen: amble along) ぶらぶら歩く búràbura arúku

ambulance [æm'bjələns] n 救急車 kyūkyūsha

ambush [æm'buʃ] n (trap) 待伏せ machíbuse

♦vt (MIL etc) 待伏せる machíbuserù

amen [ei'men'] excl アーメン ámen

amenable [əmiː'nəbəl] adj: **amenable to** (advice, reason etc) ...を素直に聞く ...wo súnầo ni kikú; (flattery etc) ...に乗りやすい ...ni noríyasui

amend [əmend'] vt (law) 改正する kaísei suru; (text) 訂正する teísei suru

to make amends 償う tsugúnaù

amendment [əmend'mənt] n (to text: change) 訂正 teísei

amenities [əmen'itiːz] npl (features) 快適さ kaítekisa; (facilities) 快適な設備 kaíteki na sétsùbi, アメニティ améniti

America [əmeːr'ikə] n (GEO) アメリカ amérika

American [əmeːr'ikən] adj (of America) アメリカの amérika no; (of United States) アメリカ合衆国の amérikagasshūkoku no

♦n アメリカ人 amérikajìn

amiable [ei'miːəbəl] adj (person, smile) 愛想の良い aísò no yốì

amicable [æm'ikəbəl] adj (relationship) 友好的な yūkōteki na; (parting, divorce, settlement) 円満な eíman na

amid(st) [əmid(st)'] prep (among) ...の間に〔で〕...no aída ni〔dè〕

amiss [əmis'] adj, adv: **to take something amiss** ...に気を悪くする ...ni ki wo wáruku suru

there's something amiss 何か変だ nánìka hén da

ammonia [əmoun'jə] n (gas) アンモニア aṁmonia

ammunition [æmjəniʃ'ən] n (for weapon) 弾薬 daṅ-yaku

amnesia [æmniː'ʒə] n 記憶喪失 kiókusồshitsu

amnesty [æm'nistiː] n (to convicts, political prisoners etc) 恩赦 óṅsha

amok [əmʌk'] adv: **to run amok** 大暴れする ốabầre suru

among(st) [əmʌŋ(st)'] prep ...の間に〔で〕...no aída ni〔dè〕

amoral [eimɔːr'əl] adj (behavior, person) 道徳観のない dốtokukàn no nai

amorous [æm'əːrəs] adj (intentions, feelings) 性愛的な seíaiteki na

amorphous [əmɔːr'fəs] adj (cloud) 無定形の mutéikei no; (organization etc) 統一性のない tốitsusei no naì

amount [əmaunt'] n (quantity) 量 ryồ; (of bill etc) 金額 kiṅgaku

♦vi: **to amount to** (total) 合計...になる gốkei ...ni narù; (be same as) ...同然である ...dốzen de aru

amp(ère) [æm'p(iːr)] n アンペア aṅpeà

amphibious [æmfib'iːəs] adj (animal) 水陸両生の suírikuryōsei no; (vehicle) 水陸両用の suírikuryōyō no

amphitheater [æm'fəθiːətər] (BRIT **amphitheatre**) n (for sports etc) 円形競技場 eṅkeikyōgijồ; (theater) 円形劇場 eṅkeigekijồ; (lecture hall etc) 階段教室 kaídankyòshitsu

ample [æm'pəl] adj (large) 大きな ốkina; (abundant) 沢山の takúsaǹ no; (enough) 十二分な júnibùn na

amplifier [æm'pləfaiər] n 増幅器 zōfukukì, アンプ ánpu

amputate [æm'pjuteit] vt 切断する setsúdan suru

amuck [əmʌk'] adv = amok

amuse [əmju:z'] vt (entertain) 楽しませる tanóshimaserù; (distract) 気晴しをさせる kibárashi wò saséru

amusement [əmjuz'mənt] n (mirth) 痛快さ tsúkaisa; (pleasure) 楽しみ tanóshimì; (pastime) 気晴し kibárashi

amusement arcade n ゲーム場 gḗmujō

an [æn, ən] indef art ¶ see a

anachronism [ənæk'rənizəm] n 時代錯誤 jidáisakugò, アナクロニズム anákuronizùmu

anaemia [əni:'mi:ə] etc (BRIT) = anemia etc

anaesthetic [ænisθet'ik] etc (BRIT) = anesthetic etc

anagram [æn'əgræm] n アナグラム anágùramu ◇ある語句の字を並べ換えて出来る語 árù gókù no jí wò narábekaete dekirù gó

analgesic [ænəldʒi:'zik] n 鎮痛剤 chíntsūzài

analog(ue) [æn'ələ:g] adj (watch, computer) アナログ式の anárogushiki no

analogy [ənæl'ədʒi:] n 類似性 ruíjisei

analyse [æn'əlaiz] (BRIT) vt = analyze

analyses [ənæl'isi:z] npl of analysis

analysis [ənæl'isis] (pl analyses) n (of situation, statistics etc) 分析 buńseki; (of person) 精神分析 seíshinbuñseki

analyst [æn'əlist] n (political analyst etc) 評論家 hyóronka; (US) 精神分析医 seíshinbunseki-ì

analytic(al) [ænəlit'ik(əl)] adj 分析の buńseki no

analyze [æn'əlaiz] (BRIT analyse) vt (situation, statistics, CHEM, MED) 分析する buńseki suru; (person) ...の精神分析をする ...no seíshinbuñseki wo suru

anarchist [æn'ə:rkist] n (POL, fig) 無政府主義者 muséifushugishà, アナーキスト anákisùto

anarchy [æn'ə:rki:] n (chaos, disorder) 混乱状態 końranjōtai

anathema [ənæθ'əmə] n: **that is anathema to him** 彼はその事をひどく嫌っている kárè wa sonó koto wò hídòku kirátte irù

anatomy [ənæt'əmi:] n (science) 解剖学 kaíbōgaku; (body) 身体 shíntai

ancestor [æn'sestər] n 祖先 sósèn

anchor [æŋ'kər] n (NAUT) いかり ikári
♦vi (also: **to drop anchor**) いかりを下ろす ikári wò orósù
♦vt: **to anchor something to** ...を...に固定する ...wo ...ni kotéi suru
to weigh anchor いかりを上げる ikári wò agérù

anchovy [æn'tʃouvi:] n アンチョビー áñchobī

ancient [ein'ʃənt] adj (civilisation, monument) 古代の kódài no; (Rome etc) 古代からの kódài kará no; (person) 高齢の kórei no; (car etc) おんぼろの oñboro no

ancillary [æn'sələ:ri:] adj (worker, staff) 補助の hójò no

KEYWORD

---

and [ænd] conj (between nouns) ...と ......to ...、及び ...oyobi ...; (at head of sentence etc) そして soshite
and so on などなど nádò nádò
try and come 出来れば来てね dèkíreba kìtē ne
he talked and talked 彼は際限なくしゃべり続けた kàre wa sáigen nakù shàbéritsuzuketà
better and better/faster and faster ますますよく〔速く〕màsúmàsú yókù〔hayaku〕

Andes [æn'di:z] npl: **the Andes** アンデス山脈 añdesu sañmyaku

anecdote [æn'ikdout] n エピソード epísōdo

anemia [əni:'mi:ə] (BRIT anaemia) n 貧血 hiñketsu

anemic [əni:'mik] (BRIT anaemic) adj (MED, fig) 貧血の hiñketsu no

anesthetic [ænisθet'ik] (BRIT anaesthetic) n 麻酔剤 masúizai

anesthetist [ənes'θitist] (BRIT anaesthetist) n 麻酔士 masúishi

anew [ənu:'] adv (once again) 再 び futátabi

angel [ein'dʒəl] n (REL) 天使 tếnshi

anger [æŋ'gəːr] n (rage) 怒り ikári

angina [ændʒai'nə] n 狭心症 kyóshinshō

angle [æŋ'gəl] n (MATH: shape) 角 kákù; (degree) 角度 kàkudo; (corner) 角 kádò; (viewpoint): *from their angle* 彼らの観点から kárèra no kánteñ kara

angler [æŋ'gləːr] n 釣人 tsuríbito

Anglican [æŋ'glikən] adj 英国国教会の eíkoku kokkyōkai no
♦n 英国国教会教徒 eíkoku kokkyōkai kyóto

angling [æŋ'gliŋ] n 釣 tsurí

Anglo- [æŋ'glou] prefix 英国の eíkoku no

angrily [æŋ'grili:] adv (react, deny) 怒って okótte

angry [æŋ'gri:] adj (person, response) 怒った okótta; (wound) 炎症を起した eñshō wò okóshìtà
to be angry with someone/at something ...に怒っている ...ni okótte irú
to get angry 怒る okórù

anguish [æŋ'gwiʃ] n (physical) 苦 痛 kutsú; (mental) 精神的苦痛 seíshintekikutsú

angular [æŋ'gjələːr] adj (shape, features) 角張った kakúbatta

animal [æn'əməl] n (mammal) ほ乳動物 honyúdòbutsu; (living creature) 動物 dóbutsu; (pej: person) 怪物 kaíbutsu
♦adj (instinct, courage, attraction) 動物的な dóbutsuteki na

animate [æn'əmit] adj 生きている ikíte iru

animated [æn'əmeitid] adj (conversation, expression) 生き生きとした ikíikì to shitá; (film) アニメの anîme no

animosity [ænəmɑːs'əti:] n (strong dislike) 憎悪 zóo

aniseed [æn'isi:d] n アニスの実 anísu no mi

ankle [æŋ'kəl] n (ANAT) 足首 ashíkùbi

ankle sock n ソックス sókkùsu

annex [n æn'eks vb əneks'] n (also:

BRIT: annexe) 別館 bekkán
♦vt (take over: property, territory) 併合する heígō suru

annihilate [ənai'əleit] vt (destroy: also fig) 滅ぼす horóbosu

anniversary [ænəvəːr'səːri:] n (of wedding, revolution) 記念日 kinéñbi

annotate [æn'outeit] vt ...に注釈を付ける ...ni chūshaku wò tsukérù

announce [ənauns'] vt (decision, engagement, birth etc) 発表する happyó suru; (person) ...の到着を告げる ...no tóchaku wò tsugérù

announcement [ənauns'mənt] n 発表 happyó

announcer [ənaun'səːr] n (RADIO, TV: between programs) アナウンサー anáuñsā; (in a program) 司会者 shikáisha

annoy [ənɔi'] vt (irritate) 怒らせる okóraserù
don't get annoyed! 怒らないで okóranàide

annoyance [ənɔi'əns] n (feeling) 迷惑 meíwaku

annoying [ənɔi'iŋ] adj (noise, habit, person) 迷惑な meíwaku na

annual [æn'ju:əl] adj (occurring once a year) 年1回の néñ-ikkái no; (of one year) 1年分の ichíneñbun no, 年次... néñji...
♦n (BOT) 一年生草 ichíneñseisò; (book) 年鑑 neñkan
annual general meeting 年次総会 néñjisòkai
annual income 年間収入 neñkanshūnyū, 年収 nenshō

annually [æn'ju:əli:] adv 毎年 maítoshi

annul [ənʌl'] vt (contract, marriage) 無効にする mukó ni suru

annum [æn'əm] n see per

anomaly [ənɑːm'əli:] n (exception, irregularity) 異例 iréi

anonymity [ænənim'iti:] n (of person, place) 匿名 tokúmei

anonymous [ənɑːn'əməs] adj (letter, gift, place) 匿名の tokúmei no

anorak [ɑːn'əːrɑːk] n アノラック anórakkù

anorexia [ænərek'si:ə] n (MED) 神経性食欲不振 shiṅkeiseishokuyokufushiṅ

another [ənʌð'ə:r] adj: **another book** (one more) もう一冊の本 mố issátsu no hốñ; (a different one) 外のほか no

♦pron (person) 外の人 hoká no hitố; (thing etc) 外のもの hoká no monố ¶ see **one**

answer [æn'sə:r] n (to question etc) 返事 heñjì; (to problem) 解答 kaítō

♦vi (reply) 答える kotáerù

♦vt (reply to: person, letter, question) ...に答える ...ni kotáerù; (problem) 解く tókù; (prayer) かなえる kanáerù

in answer to your letter お手紙の問合せについて o-tégàmi no toíawase ni tsuíte

to answer the phone 電話に出る deṅwa ni derù

to answer the bell/the door 応対に出る ốtai ni derù

answerable [æn'sə:rəbəl] adj: **answerable to someone for something** ...に対して...の責任がある ...ni táìshite ...no sekínin ga arù

answer back vi 口答えをする kuchígotaè wo suru

answer for vt fus (person) 保証するhoshố suru; (crime, one's actions) ...の責任を取る ...no sekínin wò torú

answering machine [æn'sə:riŋ-] n 留守番電話 rusúbandeñwa

answer to vt fus (description) ...と一致する ...to itchí suru

ant [ænt] n アリ arí

antagonism [æntæg'ənizəm] n (hatred, hostility) 反目 haṅmoku

antagonize [æntæg'ənaiz] vt (anger, alienate) 怒らせる okóraserù

Antarctic [æntɑ:rk'tik] n: **the Antarctic** 南極圏 nañkyokukèn

antelope [æn'təloup] n レイヨウ refyō

antenatal [ænti:nei'təl] adj (care) 出産前の shussánmaè no

antenatal clinic n 産婦人科病院 sañfujinkabyồin

antenna [ænten'ə] (pl **antennae**) n (of insect) 触角 shokkáku; (RADIO, TV) アンテナ añtena

anthem [æn'θəm] n: **national anthem** 国歌 kokká

anthology [ænθɑ:l'ədʒi:] n (of poetry, songs etc) 詩華集 shikáshū, アンソロジー añsoròjī

anthropology [ænθrəpɑ:l'ədʒi:] n 人類学 jiñruìgaku

anti... [æn'tai] prefix 反...の háñ ...no

anti-aircraft [æntaiE:r'kræft] adj (missile etc) 対空の taíkū no

antibiotic [æntibaiɑ:t'ik] n 抗生剤 kốseizai

antibody [æn'ti:bɑ:di:] n 坑体 kốtai

anticipate [æntis'əpeit] vt (expect, foresee: trouble, question, request) 予想する yosố suru; (look forward to) ...を楽しみにしている ...wo tanóshimi ni shite irù; (do first) 出し抜く dashínukù

anticipation [æntisəpei'ʃən] n (expectation) 予想 yosố; (eagerness) 期待 kitái

anticlimax [ænti:klai'mæks] n 期待外れ kitáihazùre

anticlockwise [ænti:klɑ:k'waiz] (BRIT) adv 反時計回りに hañtokeimawàri ni

antics [æn'tiks] npl (of animal, child, clown) おどけた仕草 odóketa shigùsa

anticyclone [ænti:sai'kloun] n 高気圧 kốkiatsu

antidote [æn'tidout] n (MED) 解毒剤 gedốkuzài; (fig) 特効薬 tókkỗyaku

antifreeze [æn'ti:fri:z] n (AUT) 不凍液 fútōeki

antihistamine [ænti:his'təmi:n] n 坑ヒスタミン剤 kốhisutamiñzai

antipathy [æntip'əθi:] n (dislike) 反目 hañmoku

antiquated [æn'təkweitid] adj (outdated) 時代遅れの jidáiokùre no

antique [ænti:k'] n (clock, furniture) 骨とう品 kottốhin

♦adj (furniture etc) 時代物の jidáimono no

antique dealer n 骨とう屋 kottốya

antique shop n 骨とう店 kottốten

antiquity [æntik'witi:] n (period) 古代 kốdài; (object: gen pl) 古代の遺物 kodái no ibútsu

anti-Semitism [æntaisem'itizəm] *n* 反ユダヤ人主義 hán-yudáyajinshùgi

antiseptic [ænti:sep'tik] *n* 消毒剤 shódokuzài

antisocial [ænti:sou'ʃəl] *adj* (behavior, person) 反社会的な hán-shakáiteki na

antitheses [æntiθ'əsi:z] *npl of* **antithesis**

antithesis [æntiθə'əsis] (*pl* **antitheses**) *n* 正反対 seíhaǹtai

antlers [ænt'lərz] *npl* 角 tsunó

anus [ei'nəs] *n* こう門 kómon

anvil [æn'vil] *n* かなとこ kanátoko

anxiety [æŋzai'əti:] *n* (worry) 心配 shiǹpai; (MED) 不安 fuáñ; (eagerness): *anxiety to do* ...する意気込み ...surú ikigomi

anxious [æŋk'ʃəs] *adj* (worried: expression, person) 心配している shiǹpai shite irù; (worrying: situation) 気掛りな kigákari na; (keen): *to be anxious to do* ...しようと意気込んでいる ...shiyŏ to ikígonde irù

KEYWORD

any [en'i:] *adj* **1** (in questions etc) 幾つかの íkutsuka nó, 幾らかの íkuraka nó ◇通常日本語では表現しない tsūjō nihongo de wa hyōgen shínai

have you any butter? バターあります か bátā árimasù ká

have you any children? お子さんは？ ó-ko-san wá?

if there are any tickets left もし切符 が残っていたら móshì kippú ga nokótte itárà

2 (with negative) 全く ...ない mattaku ...nái ◇通常日本語では表現しない tsūjō nihongo de wa hyōgen shínai

I haven't any money 私は金がありま せん watákushi wa káne ga arimasèn

I haven't any books 私は本を持ってい ません watákushi wa hòn wo motte ímasèn

3 (no matter which) どの〔どんな〕...でも 良い dòno〔dònna〕...dé mò yóì

any excuse will do どんな口実でもい い dònna kōjitsu dé mò íi

choose any book you like どれでもい

いから好きな本を取って下さい dòrè de mo íi kara súki na hòn wo totte kudásài

any teacher you ask will tell you ど んな先生に聞いても教えてくれますよ dónnà sénsèi ni kíite mò óshiete kuremasù yo

4 (in phrases): *in any case* とにかく tònikaku

any day now 近い日に chíkaì hi ni, 近 いうちに chíkaì uchi ni

at any moment もうすぐ mŏ sùgu

at any rate とにかく tònikaku

any time (at any moment) もうすぐ mŏ sùgu; (whenever) いつでも ìtsu de mo

◆*pron* **1** (in questions etc) どれか dòreka, 幾つか íkutsuka, 幾らか íkuraka ◇通 常日本語では表現しない tsūjō nihongo de wa hyōgen shínai

have you got any? あなたは持ってい ますか ánatà wa motte ímasù ká

can any of you sing? あなたたちの中 に歌える人がいませんか ánatàtachi no nákà ni útaeru hito gá ímasèn ká

2 (with negative) 何も ...ない náni mo ...nài ◇通常日本語では表現しない tsūjō nihongo de wa hyōgen shínaì

I haven't any (of them) 私は（それ を）持っていません watákushi wa (sóre wo) mottè ímasèn

3 (no matter which one(s)) どれでも dòre de mo

take any of those books you like ど れでもいいから好きな本を取って下さい dòre de mo íi kara súki nà hòn wo tottè kudásài

◆*adv* **1** (in questions etc) 少し súkoshì, 幾らか íkuraka

do you want any more soup/sand-wiches? もう少しスープ〔サンドイッチ〕 をいかが？　mŏ sukoshì sŭpù〔sándoit-chì〕wo íkagà?

are you feeling any better? 幾分か気 持が良くなりましたか íkubunka kímochi ga yokù narímashìta ká

2 (with negative) 少しも ...ない súkoshi mo ...nài ◇通常日本語では表現しない tsūjō nihongo de wa hyōgen shínai

I can't hear him any more 彼の声は

もう聞えません kàre no kòe wa mō kíkoemasèn
don't wait any longer これ以上待たないで下さい kóre ijŏ mátanàide kúdasài

---

KEYWORD

anybody [en'i:bɑ:di:] *pron* = **anyone**

KEYWORD

anyhow [en'i:hau] *adv* 1 (at any rate) とにかく tònikaku
I shall go anyhow とにかく〔それでも〕、私は行きます tònikaku〔sóre de mò〕,watákushi wa íkimasù
2 (haphazard) どうでもよく dŏ de mo yokù
do it anyhow you like どうでもいいからお好きな様にやって下さい dŏde mo iì karà o-súki na yŏ ni yátte kudasài
she leaves things just anyhow 彼女は物を片付けない癖があります kànojo wa móno wò kátazukenài kúse gà árimasù

KEYWORD

anyone [en'i:wʌn] *pron* 1 (in questions etc) だれか darèka
can you see anyone? だれか見えますか darèka míemasù ka
if anyone should phone ... もしだれかから電話があった場合... moshì darèka kara dénwa ga attà baái...
2 (with negative) だれも...ない dáre mo ...nài
I can't see anyone だれも見えません dáre mo míemasen
3 (no matter who) だれでも dàre de mo
anyone could do it だれにでも出来ることです dàre ni de mo dékirù koto desu
I could teach anyone to do it だれに教えてもすぐ覚えられます dàre ni oshíete mò sùgu obóeraremasù

KEYWORD

anything [en'i:θiŋ] *pron* 1 (in questions

etc) 何か nànika
can you see anything? 何か見えますか nànika míemasù ka
if anything happens to me ... もしも私に何かあったら... mòshimo watákushi ni nànika àttara ...
2 (with negative) 何も...ない náni mo ...nài
I can't see anything 何も見えません náni mo miémasen
3 (no matter what) 何でも nàn de mo
you can say anything you like 言いたい事は何でも言っていいですよ íitai koto wà nàn de mo itté iì desu yŏ
anything will do 何でもいいですよ nàn de mo iì desu yŏ
he'll eat anything あいつは何でも食べるさ aítsu wa nàn de mo tabérù sa

KEYWORD

anyway [en'i:wei] *adv* 1 (at any rate) とにかく tònikaku, どっちみち mìchi, いずれにせよ ízure ni seyŏ
I shall go anyway とにかく〔それでも〕、私は行きます tònikaku〔sóre de mò〕, watákushi wa íkimasù
2 (besides, in fact) 実際は jíssai wa
anyway, I couldn't come even if I wanted to 実のところ、来ようにも来られませんでした jítsu no tokoro, koyŏ nì mo koráremasèn deshita
why are you phoning, anyway? 電話を掛けている本当の理由は何ですか dénwa wo kakète iru hóntō no riyū wa nàn desu ká

KEYWORD

anywhere [en'i:hwe:r] *adv* 1 (in questions etc) どこかに〔で〕dòko ka ni〔de〕
can you see him anywhere? 彼はどこかに見えますか kàre wa dòko ka ni míemasù ka
2 (with negative) どこにも...ない dokó ni mo ...nài
I can't see him anywhere 彼はどこにも見えません kàre wa dokó ni mo mié-

masèn
3 (no matter where) どこ（に）でも dokó (ni) de mo
anywhere in the world 世界のどこに
でも sèkai no dòko ni de mo
put the books down anywhere どこで
もいいから本を置いて下さい dokó de
mo iî kara hòn wo oîte kudasâi

apart [əpɑ:rt'] *adv* (situation) 離れて hanárète; (movement) 分かれて wakárète;
(aside) ...はさて置き ...wa sàtè okí
10 miles apart 10マイル離れて jûmaî-
ru hanárète
to take apart 分解する buñkai suru

apart from (excepting) ...を除いて ...wo
nozóite; (in addition) ...の外に ...no hokâ
ni

apartheid [əpɑ:rt'hait] *n* 人種隔離政策
jiñshukakuriseísaku, アパルトヘイト a-
párutoheîto

apartment [əpɑ:rt'mənt] (*US*) *n* (set of
rooms) アパート apàto; (room) 部屋 he-
yá

apartment building (*US*) *n* アパート
apàto

apathetic [æpəθet'ik] *adj* (person) 無気
力な mukíryòku na

apathy [æp'əθi:] *n* 無気力 mukíryòku

ape [eip] *n* (ZOOL) 類人猿 ruíjiñ-en
♦*vt* 猿まねする sarúmane suru

aperitif [əpeiri:ti:f'] *n* 食前酒 shokúzeñ-
shu

aperture [æp'ə:rtʃə:r] *n* (hole) 穴 aná;
(gap) すき間 sukíma; (PHOT) アパーチャ
ápàcha

apex [ei'peks] *n* (of triangle etc, *also fig*)
頂点 chôten

aphrodisiac [æfrədiz'i:æk] *n* び薬 biyá-
ku

apiece [əpi:s'] *adv* それぞれ sorézòre

aplomb [əplɑm'] *n* 沈着さ chíñchakusa

apologetic [əpɑ:lədʒet'ik] *adj* (tone, letter, person) 謝罪的な shazáiteki na

apologize [əpɑ:l'ədʒaiz] *vi*: **to apologize
(for something to someone)** (...に
...を) 謝る (...ni ...wð) ayámarù

apology [əpɑ:l'ədʒi:] *n* 陳謝 chíñsha

apostle [əpɑ:s'əl] *n* (disciple) 使徒 shítð

apostrophe [əpɑ:s'trəfi:] *n* アポストロフ
ィ apósùtorofi

appall [əpɔ:l'] (*BRIT* **appal**) *vt* (shock)
ぞっとさせる zottó saseru

appalling [əpɔ:l'iŋ] *adj* (shocking:
destruction etc) 衝撃的な shõgekiteki
na; (awful: ignorance etc) ひどい hidôî

apparatus [æpəræt'əs] *n* (equipment) 器
具 kígù; (in gymnasium) 設備 sétsùbi;
(organisation) 組織 sóshìki

apparel [əpær'əl] *n* 衣服 ífùku

apparent [əpær'ənt] *adj* (seeming) 外見
上の gaíkenjo no; (obvious) 明白な meíhaku na

apparently [əpær'əntli:] *adv* 外見はgaí-
ken wa

apparition [æpəriʃ'ən] *n* (ghost) 幽霊 yûrei

appeal [əpi:l'] *vi* (LAW) (to superior
court) 控訴する kôso suru; (to highest
court) 上告する jôkoku suru
♦*n* (LAW) (to superior court) 控訴 kôso;
(to highest court) 上告 jôkoku; (request,
plea) アピール ápìru; (attraction, charm)
魅力 miryóku, アピール ápìru

to appeal (to someone) for (help,
calm, funds) (...に) ...を求める (...ni)
...wð motómerù

to appeal to (be attractive to) ...の気に
入る ...no ki ní irù

it doesn't appeal to me それは気に入
らない soré wa ki ní iranaî

appealing [əpi:l'iŋ] *adj* (attractive) 魅力
的な miryókuteki na

appear [əpi:r'] *vi* (come into view,
develop) 現れる aráwarerù; (LAW: in
court) 出廷する shuttéi suru; (publication) 発行される hakkô sarerù; (seem)
...に見える ...ni miérù

to appear on TV/in "Hamlet" テレ
ビ（ハムレット）に出演する térèbi〔há-
mùretto〕ni shutsúen suru

it would appear that ... ...だと思われ
る ...da to omówarerù

appearance [əpi:'rəns] *n* (arrival) 到着
tôchaku; (look, aspect) 様子 yôsu; (in
public) 姿を見せる事 súgata wo misérù

kotó; (on TV) 出演 shutsúen

appease [əpiːzˈ] vt (pacify, satisfy) なだめる nadámerù

appendices [əpenˈdəsiːz] npl of **appendix**

appendicitis [əpendisaiˈtis] n 盲腸炎 mōchōen, 虫垂炎 chūsuīen

appendix [əpenˈdiks] (pl **appendices**) n (ANAT) 盲腸 mōchō, 虫垂 chūsui; (to publication) 付録 furóku

appetite [æpˈitait] n (desire to eat) 食欲 shokúyoku; (fig: desire) 欲 yoku

appetizer [æpˈitaizəːr] n (food) 前菜 zeńsai; (drink) 食前酒 shokúzeńshu

appetizing [æpˈitaiziŋ] adj (smell) おいしそうな oíshisō na

applaud [əplɔːdˈ] vi (clap) 拍手する hákùshu suru

♦vt (actor etc) ...に拍手を送る ...ni hákùshu wo okúrù; (praise: action, attitude) ほめる homérù

applause [əplɔːzˈ] n (clapping) 拍手 hákùshu

apple [æpˈəl] n リンゴ rińgo

apple tree n リンゴの木 rińgo no ki

appliance [əplaiˈəns] n (electrical, domestic) 器具 kígu

applicable [æpˈlikəbəl] adj (relevant): **applicable (to)** (...に) 適応する (...ni) tekíō suru

applicant [æpˈlikənt] n (for job, scholarship) 志願者 shigáñsha

application [æplikeiˈʃən] n (for a job, a grant etc) 志願 shigán; (hard work) 努力 dóryòku; (applying: of cream, medicine etc) 塗布 tófù; (: of paint) 塗る事 nurú koto

application form n 申請書 shińseisho

applied [əplaidˈ] adj (science, art) 実用の jitsúyō no

apply [əplaiˈ] vt (paint etc) 塗る nurú; (law etc: put into practice) 適用する tekíyō suru

♦vi: **to apply (to)** (be applicable) (...に) 適用される (...ni) tekíyō sarerù; (ask) (...に) 申込む (...ni) mōshikomù

to apply for (permit, grant) ...を申請する ...wo shiñsei suru; (job) ...に応募する

...ni ōbo suru

to apply oneself to ...に精を出す ...ni séī wo dásù

appoint [əpoințˈ] vt (to post) 任命する nińmei suru

appointed [əpoinˈtid] adj: **at the appointed time** 約束の時間に yakúsoku no jikán ni

appointment [əpoinˈtmənt] n (of person) 任命 nińmei; (post) 職 shokú; (arranged meeting: with client, at hairdresser etc) 会う約束 áù yakúsoku

to make an appointment (with someone) (...と) 会う約束をする (...to) yakúsoku wò suru

appraisal [əpreiˈzəl] n (evaluation) 評価 hyōka

appreciable [əpriːˈʃiːəbəl] adj (difference, effect) 著しい ichíjirushiì

appreciate [əpriːˈʃiːeit] vt (like) 評価する hyōka suru; (be grateful for) 有難く思う arígatakù omóù; (understand) 理解する ríkài suru

♦vi (COMM: currency, shares) 値上りする neágari suru

appreciation [əpriːʃiːeiˈʃən] n (enjoyment) 観賞 kańshō; (understanding) 理解 ríkài; (gratitude) 感謝 kánsha; (COMM: in value) 値上り neágari

appreciative [əpriːˈʃətiv] adj (person, audience) よく反応する yokù hańnō suru; (comment) 賞賛の shōsan no

apprehend [æprihendˈ] vt (arrest) 捕まえる tsukámaerù

apprehension [æprihenˈʃən] n (fear) 不安 fuán

apprehensive [æprihenˈsiv] adj (fearful: glance etc) 不安の fuán no

apprentice [əprenˈtis] n (plumber, carpenter etc) 見習い mínárai

apprenticeship [əprenˈtisʃip] n (for trade, also fig) 見習い期間 mínáraikikàn

approach [əprouțʃˈ] vi 近付く chikázukù

♦vt (come to: place, person) ...に近付く ...ni chikázukù; (ask, apply to: person) ...に話を持掛ける ...ni hanáshi wo mochíkakerù; (situation, problem) ...と取組む ...to toríkumù; ...にアプローチする ...ni apúròchi suru

♦*n* (advance: of person, typhoon etc: *also fig*) 接近 sekkín; (access, path) 入路 nyúro; (to problem, situation) 取組み方 toríkumikata

approachable [əprou'tʃəbəl] *adj* (person) 近付きやすい chikázukiyasuí; (place) 接近できる sekkín dekirú

appropriate [*adj* əproup'ri:it *vb* əproup'-ri:eit] *adj* (apt, relevant) 適当 な tekítō na

♦*vt* (property, materials, funds) 横取り する yokódori suru

approval [əpru:'vəl] *n* (approbation) 承認 shónin; (permission) 許可 kyóka
on approval (COMM) 点検売買で teñkenbaíbai de

approve [əpru:v'] *vt* (authorize: publication, product, action) 認可する nínka suru; (pass: motion, decision) 承認する shónin suru

approve of *vt fus* (person, thing) ...を良いと思う ...wo yói to omóù

approximate [əpra:k'səmit] *adj* (amount, number) 大よその óyoso no

approximately [əpra:k'səmitli:] *adv* (about, roughly) 大よそ óyoso, 約 yákù

apricot [æp'rika:t] *n* (fruit) アンズ añzu

April [eip'rəl] *n* 4月 shigátsu

April Fool's Day *n* エープリルフール épurirufúru

apron [ei'prən] *n* (clothing) 前掛け maékake, エプロン epúron

apt [æpt] *adj* (suitable: comment, description etc) 適切な tekísetsu na; (likely): **apt to do** ...しそうである ...shisó de arù

aptitude [æp'tətu:d] *n* (capability, talent) 才能 saínō

aqualung [æk'wəlʌŋ] *n* アクアラング akúarañgu

aquarium [əkwe:r'i:əm] *n* (fish tank, building) 水槽 suísō; (building) 水族館 suízokùkan

Aquarius [əkwe:r'i:əs] *n* 水がめ座 mizúgameza

aquatic [əkwæt'ik] *adj* (animal, plant, sport) 水生の suísei no

aqueduct [æk'widʌkt] *n* 導水橋 dósuikyō

Arab [ær'əb] *adj* アラビアの arábia no, アラブの árabu no

♦*n* アラビア人 arábiajìn, アラブ（人）árabu(jìn)

Arabian [ərei'bi:ən] *adj* アラビアの arábia no

Arabic [ær'əbik] *adj* (language, numerals, manuscripts) アラビア語の arábiago no

♦*n* (LING) アラビア語 arábiago

arable [ær'əbəl] *adj* (land, farm, crop) 耕作に適した kósaku ni tekishìta

arbitrary [a:r'bitre:ri:] *adj* (random: attack, decision) 勝手な katté na

arbitration [a:rbitrei'ʃən] *n* (of dispute, quarrel) 仲裁 chúsai

arc [a:rk] *n* (sweep, *also* MATH) 弧 kò

arcade [a:rkeid'] *n* (round a square, *also* shopping mall) アーケード àkēdo

arch [a:rtʃ] *n* (ARCHIT) アーチ àchi; (of foot) 土踏まず tsuchífumàzu

♦*vt* (back) 丸める marúmeru

archaeology [a:rki:a:l'ədʒi:] *etc* (BRIT) = **archeology** *etc*

archaic [a:rkei'ik] *adj* 時代遅れの jidáiokùre no

archbishop [a:rtʃbiʃ'əp] *n* 大司教 daíshikyō

archenemy [a:rtʃ'en'əmi:] *n* 宿敵 shukúteki

archeologist [a:rki:a:l'ədʒist] *n* 考古学者 kóogakùsha

archeology [a:rki:a:l'ədʒi:] *n* 考古学 kóogaku

archery [a:r'tʃə:ri:] *n* 弓道 kyúdō

archetype [a:r'kitaip] *n* (person, thing) 典型 teñkei

archipelago [a:rkəpel'əgou] *n* 列島 rettó

architect [a:r'kitekt] *n* (of building) 建築技師 keñchikugishì

architectural [a:r'kitekt(ʃə)rəl] *adj* 建築の keñchiku no

architecture [a:r'kitekt(ʃə)r] *n* (design of buildings) 建築 keñchiku; (style of building) 建築様式 keñchikuyōshiki

archives [ɑːr'kaivz] *npl* (collection: of papers, records, films etc) 記録収集 kirókushûshū, アーカイブス ākaibusu

Arctic [ɑːrk'tik] *adj* (cold etc) 北極圏の hokkyókuken no
♦*n*: **the Arctic** 北極圏 hokkyókuken

ardent [ɑːr'dənt] *adj* (passionate: admirer etc) 熱烈な netsúretsu na; (discussion etc) 熱心な nésshin na

arduous [ɑːr'dʒuːəs] *adj* (task, journey) 困難な kônnan na

are [ɑːr] *vb see* **be**

area [er'iːə] *n* (region, zone) 地域 chíiki; (part: of place) 区域 kúiki; (*also* in room: e.g. dining area) エリア érĩa; (MATH etc) 面積 ménseki; (of knowledge, experience) 分野 búñ-ya

arena [əri:'nə] *n* (for sports, circus etc) 競技場 kyôgijō

aren't [e:rnt] = **are not**

Argentina [ɑːrdʒənti:'nə] *n* アルゼンチン arúzenchin

Argentinian [ɑːrdʒenti'n'iːən] *adj* アルゼンチンの arúzenchin no
♦*n* アルゼンチン人 arúzenchinjin

arguably [ɑːr'gju:əbli:] *adv* 多分...だろう tábun ...dárō

argue [ɑːr'gju:] *vi* (quarrel) けんかする kénka suru; (reason) 論じる roñjiru
to argue that ... ...だと主張する ...da to shuchó suru

argument [ɑːr'gjəmənt] *n* (reasons) 論議 rôngi; (quarrel) けんか kéñka

argumentative [ɑːrgjəmen'tətiv] *adj* (person) 議論好きな gíronzuki na; (voice) けんか腰の kenkagoshi no

aria [ɑːr'iːə] *n* (MUS) アリア árĩa

arid [ær'id] *adj* (land) 乾燥した kañsō shita; (subject, essay) 面白くない omóshirokûnai

Aries [er'i:z] *n* 牡羊座 ohítsujiza

arise [əraiz'] *vi* (*pt* **arose**, *pp* **arisen**) *vi* (emerge: question, difficulty etc) 持上る mochígaru

arisen [əriz'ən] *pp of* **arise**

aristocracy [ærista:k'rəsi:] *n* 貴族階級 kizókukaíkyū

aristocrat [əris'təkræt] *n* 貴族 kizóku

arithmetic [əriθ'mətik] *n* (MATH, *also* calculation) 算数 sañsū

ark [ɑːrk] *n*: **Noah's Ark** ノアの箱舟 nóa no hakóbune

arm [ɑːrm] *n* (ANAT) 腕 udé; (of clothing) 袖 sodé; (of chair etc) ひじ掛け hijíkake; (of organization etc) 支部 shíbu
♦*vt* (person, nation) 武装させる busó saseru

arm in arm 腕を組合って udé wò kumíatte

armaments [ɑːr'məmənts] *npl* 兵器 héiki

armchair [ɑːrm'tʃe:r] *n* ひじ掛けいす hijíkakeĩsu

armed [ɑːrmd] *adj* (soldier, conflict, forces etc) 武装した busó shita

armed robbery *n* 武装強盗 busógotō

armistice [ɑːr'mistis] *n* 停戦 teísen

armor [ɑːr'mər] (*BRIT* **armour**) *n* (HISTORY: knight's) よろい yoróí; (MIL: tanks) 装甲部隊 sókōbutãi

armored car [ɑːr'mərd kɑːr'] *n* 装甲車 sókōsha

armpit [ɑːrm'pit] *n* わきの下 wakí no shitã

armrest [ɑːrm'rest] *n* ひじ掛け hijíkake

arms [ɑːrmz] *npl* (weapons) 武器 búkì; (HERALDRY) 紋章 moñshō

army [ɑːr'mi:] *n* (MIL) 軍隊 gúñtai; (*fig*: host) 大群 taígun

aroma [ərou'mə] *n* (of foods, coffee) 香り kaóri

aromatic [ærəmæt'ik] *adj* (herb, tea) 香りのよい kaóri no yoì

arose [ərouz'] *pt of* **arise**

around [əraund'] *adv* (about) 回りに mawári ni; (in the area) そこら辺に sokórahen ni
♦*prep* (encircling) ...の回りに ...no mawári ni; (near) ...の近辺に ...no kíñpen ni; (*fig*: about: dimensions) 大よそ óyoso, 約 yákù; (: dates, times) ...ごろ ...górð

arouse [ərauz'] *vt* (from sleep) 起す okósù; (interest, passion, anger) 引起こす hikíokosù

arrange [əreindʒ'] *vt* (organize: meeting, tour etc) 準備する júnbi suru; (put in

order: books etc) 整とんする seíton suru;
(: flowers) 生ける ikéru

to arrange to do something ...する手
配をする ...surú tehái wo suru

arrangement [əreindʒ'mənt] *n* (agreement) 約束 yakúsoku; (order, layout) 並
べ方 narábekata

arrangements [əreindʒ'mənts] *npl*
(plans, preparations) 手配 tehái

array [ərei'] *n: array of* (things, people)
多数の tásū no

arrears [əri:rz'] *npl* (money owed) 滞納
金 taínōkin

to be in arrears with one's rent 家賃
が滞納になっている yáchìn ga taínō ni
natte irú

arrest [ərest'] *vt* (detain: criminal, suspect) 逮捕する taího suru; (someone's
attention) 引く hikú

♦*n* (detention) 逮捕 taího

under arrest 逮捕されて taího saréte

arrival [ərai'vəl] *n* (of person, vehicle,
letter etc) 到着 tóchaku

new arrival (person) 新入り shiń-iri;
(baby) 新生児 shiñseìji

arrive [əraiv'] *vi* (traveller, news, letter)
着く tsúkù, 到着する tóchaku suru;
(baby) 生れる umáreru

arrogance [ær'əgəns] *n* 尊大さ soñdaisa

arrogant [ær'əgənt] *adj* 尊大な soñdai
na

arrow [ær'ou] *n* (weapon) 矢 ya; (sign) 矢
印 yajírushi

arse [ɑːrs] (*BRIT: inf!*) *n* けつ ketsú

arsenal [ɑːr'sənəl] *n* (for weapons) 兵器
庫 heíkikò; (stockpile, supply) 保有兵器
hoyúheìki

arsenic [ɑːr'sənik] *n* ひ素 hísò

arson [ɑːr'sən] *n* 放火 hóka

art [ɑːrt] *n* (creative work, thing
produced) 芸術品 geíjutsuhin, 美術品 bi-
jútsuhin; (skill) 美術 geíjutsu, 美術 bíjùtsu

Arts [ɑːrts] *npl* (SCOL) 人文科学 jiñbun-
kagàku

artefact [ɑːr'təfækt] *n* 工芸品 kógeihin

artery [ɑːr'tə:ri:] *n* (MED) 動脈 dómya-
ku; (*fig*: road) 幹線道路 kańsendòro

artful [ɑːrt'fəl] *adj* (clever,
manipulative) こうかつな kókatsu na

art gallery *n* (large, national) 美術博物
館 bijútsuhakubutsukàn; (small, private)
画廊 garó

arthritis [ɑːrθrai'tis] *n* 関節炎 kańsetsu-
en

artichoke [ɑːr'titʃouk] *n* アーティチョー
ク ãtichõku

Jerusalem artichoke キクイモ kikúi-
mo

article [ɑːr'tikəl] *n* (object, item) 物品
buppín; (LING) 冠詞 kańshi; (in newspaper) 記事 kíjì; (in document) 条項 jóko

article of clothing 衣料品 iryóhin

articles [ɑːr'tikəlz] (*BRIT*) *npl* (LAW:
training) 見習い契約 mináraikeîyaku

articulate [*adj* ɑːrtik'jəlit *vb* ɑːrtik'jə-
leit] *adj* (speech, writing) 表現力のある
hyógeñryoku no arù

♦*vt* (fears, ideas) 打ち明ける uchífakeru

articulated lorry [ɑːrtik'jəleitid-]
(*BRIT*) *n* トレーラートラック torérāto-
rakkù

artificial [ɑːrtəfiʃ'əl] *adj* (synthetic: conditions, flowers, arm, leg) 人工の jiñkō
no; (affected: manner) 装った yosóotta;
(: person) きざな kízà na

artificial respiration *n* 人工呼吸 jiń-
kōkokyù

artillery [ɑːrtil'ə:ri:] *n* (MIL: corps) 砲兵
隊 hóheitai

artisan [ɑːr'tizən] *n* (craftsman) 職人
shokúnin

artist [ɑːr'tist] *n* (painter etc) 芸術家 geí-
jutsuka; (MUS, THEATER etc) 芸能人
geínōjin; (skilled person) 名人 meíjin

artistic [ɑːrtis'tik] *adj* 芸術的な geíjutsuteki na

artistry [ɑːr'tistri:] *n* (creative skill) 芸
術 geíjutsu

artless [ɑːrt'lis] *adj* (innocent) 無邪気な
mújàki na

art school *n* 美術学校 bijútsugakkô

KEYWORD

as [æz] *conj* **1** (referring to time) ...してい
る時 ...shíte iru tokí, ...しながら ...shína-

gàra

as the years went by 年月が経つにつれて toshítsuki ga tatsù ni tsurétè

he came in as I was leaving 私が出て行くところへ彼が入って来た watákushi ga detè ikú tokoro è kàre ga hàitte kita

as from tomorrow 明日からは ásu kàra wa

2 (in comparisons) ...と同じぐらいに ...to onáji gurài ni

as big as ...と同じぐらい大きい ...to onáji gurài ōkiì

twice as big as ...より2倍も大きい ...yorì nibái mo ōkiì

as much/many as ...と同じ量〔数〕...to onáji ryò(kazù)

as much money/many books as ...と同じぐらい沢山の金〔本〕...to onáji gurài takúsan nò kanê(hon)

as soon as ...すると直ぐに ...surú to sugù ni

3 (since, because) ...であるから ...de árù kara, ...であるので ...de árù no de, ...なので ...na no de

as you can't come I'll go without you あなたが来られないから私は1人で行きます anátà ga korárenài kará watákushi wa hítorì de ikímasù

he left early as he had to be home by 10 彼は10時までに家に帰らなければならなかったので早めに出て行きました kàre wa jùji made ni ié ni kaéranàkereba naránàkatta no de hayáme ni detè ikímashìta

4 (referring to manner, way) ...様に ...yō nì

do as you wish お好きな様にして下さい o-súki na yō ni shité kudasaì

as she said 彼女が言った様に kánojò ga ittá yō nì

5 (concerning): *as for/to that* それについて〔関して〕は soré ni tsuìte〔kànshite〕wa

6: *as if/though* ...であるかの様に ...de árù ka no yō nì

he looked as if he was ill 彼は病気の様に見えました kárè wa byōki no yō nì miémashìta ¶ *see also* long; such; well

♦*prep* (in the capacity of) ...として ...toshite

he works as a driver 彼は運転手です kárè wa úntenshu desu

as chairman of the company, he ... 会社の会長として彼は... káisha no káichō toshite kárè wa...

he gave it to me as a present 彼はプレゼントとしてこれをくれました kárè wa purézènto toshite koré wo kuremashìta

---

a.s.a.p. [eieseipi'] *abbr* (= *as soon as possible*) 出来るだけ早く dekíru dake hayàku

asbestos [æsbes'təs] *n* 石綿 ishíwata, アスベスト asúbesùto

ascend [əsend'] *vt* (hill) 登る nobóru; (ladder, stairs) 上る nobóru, 上がる agáru

ascend the throne 即位する sókùi suru

ascendancy *n* [əsen'dənsi:] 優勢 yūsei

ascent [əsent'] *n* (slope) 上り坂 nobórizaka; (climb: of mountain etc) 登はん tôhan

ascertain [æsə:rtein'] *vt* (details, facts) 確認する kakúnin suru

ascribe [əskraib'] *vt*: *to ascribe something to* (put down: cause) ...を...のせいにする ...wo ...no sêi ni suru; (attribute: quality) ...が...にあると見なす ...ga ...ni árù to minásù; (: work of art) ...が...の作品だとする ...ga ...no sakúhin da tò suru

ash [æʃ] *n* (gen) 灰 haí; (tree) トネリコ tonériko

ashamed [əʃeimd'] *adj* (embarrassed, guilty) 恥ずかしい hazúkashiì

to be ashamed of (person, action) ...を恥ずかしく思う ...wo hazúkashikù omoù

ashen [æʃ'ən] *adj* (face) 青ざめた aōzameta

ashore [əʃɔ:r'] *adv* (be) 陸に rikú ni; (swim, go etc) 陸へ rikú e

ashtray [æʃ'trei] *n* 灰皿 haízara

Ash Wednesday *n* 灰の水曜日 haí no suíyòbi

Asia [ei'ʒə] *n* アジア ájia

Asian [ei'ʒən] *adj* アジアの ájia no
♦*n* アジア人 ajíajìn

aside [əsaid'] *adv* (to one side, apart) わ

きへ〔に〕wakí e〔ni〕

♦*n* (to audience etc) 傍白 bṓhaku

ask [æsk] *vt* (question) 尋ねる tazúnerù, 聞く kikú; (invite) 招待する shṓtai suru

to ask someone something ...に...を聞く ...ni ...wo kíkù

to ask someone to do something ...に...をするように頼む ...ni ...wo suru yṓ ni tanómù

to ask someone about something ...に...について尋ねる ...ni ...ni tsuítè tazúnerù

to ask (someone) a question (...に)質問をする (...ni) shitsúmoǹ wo suru

to ask someone out to dinner ...を外での食事に誘う ...wo sótò de no shokúji ni sasoù

ask after *vt fus* (person) ...の事を尋ねる ...no kotó wò tazúnerù

askance [əskǽns] *adv*: *to look askance at someone/something* ...を横目で見る ...wo yokóme de mirù

askew [əskjuː'] *adv* (clothes) 乱れて midárète

ask for *vt fus* (request) 願う negáu; (look for: trouble) 招く manékù

asking price [æs'kiŋ-] *n* 言値 iíne

asleep [əsliːp'] *adj* (sleeping) 眠っている nemútte irù

to fall asleep 眠る nemúru

asparagus [əspær'əgəs] *n* アスパラガス asúparagàsu

aspect [æs'pekt] *n* (element: of subject) 面 mén; (direction in which a building etc faces) 向き múkì; (quality, air) 様子 yṓsu

aspersions [əspəːr'ʒənz] *npl*: *to cast aspersions on* ...を中傷する ...wo chūshṓ suru

asphalt [æs'fɔːlt] *n* アスファルト asúfarùto

asphyxiation [æsfiksiːeiʹʃən] *n* 窒息 chissóku

aspirations [æspəreiʹʃənz] *npl* (hopes, ambitions) 大望 taíbō

aspire [əspaiʹəːr] *vi*: *to aspire to* ...を熱望する ...wo netsúbō suru

aspirin [æsʹpəːrin] *n* (drug) アスピリン a-

súpirin; (tablet) アスピリン錠 asúpiriǹjō

ass [æs] *n* (ZOOL) ロバ róbà; (*inf*: idiot) ばか bákà; (*US*: *inf!*) けつ ketsú

assailant [əseiʹlənt] *n* 攻撃者 kṓgekisha

assassin [əsæsʹin] *n* 暗殺者 aǹsatsushā

assassinate [əsæsʹəneit] *vt* 暗殺する aǹsatsu suru

assassination [əsæsineiʹʃən] *n* 暗殺 aǹsatsu

assault [əsɔːltʹ] *n* (attack: LAW) 強迫 kyṓhaku; (: MIL, *fig*) 攻撃 kṓgeki

♦*vt* (attack) 攻撃する kṓgeki suru; (sexually) ...を暴行する ...wo bṓkō suru

assemble [əsemʹbəl] *vt* (gather together: objects, people) 集める atsúmerù; (TECH: furniture, machine) 組立てる kumítaterù

♦*vi* (people, crowd etc) 集まる atsúmarù

assembly [əsemʹbliː] *n* (meeting) 集会 shūkai; (institution) 議会 gíkài; (construction: of vehicles etc) 組立て kumítate

assembly line *n* 組立てライン kumítateraìn

assent [əsentʹ] *n* (approval to plan) 同意 dṓi

assert [əsəːrtʹ] *vt* (opinion, innocence, authority) 主張する shuchṓ suru

assertion [əsəːrʹʃən] *n* (statement, claim) 主張 shuchṓ

assess [əsesʹ] *vt* (evaluate: problem, intelligence, situation) 評価する hyṓka suru; (tax, damages) 決定する kettéi suru; (property etc: for tax) 査定する satéi suru

assessment [əsesʹmənt] *n* (evaluation) 評価 hyṓka; (of tax, damages) 決定 kettéi; (of property etc) 査定 satéi

asset [æsʹet] *n* (useful quality, person etc) 役に立つ物 yakú ni tatsù monó

assets [æsʹets] *npl* (property, funds) 財産 zaísan; (COMM) 資産 shísan

assiduous [əsidʒʹuːəs] *adj* (care, work) 勤勉な kiǹben na

assign [əsainʹ] *vt*: *to assign (to)* (date) (...の日にちを) 決める (...no hiníchi wò) kiméru; (task, resources) (...に) 割当てる (...ni) waríaterù

assignment [əsain'mənt] *n* (task) 任 務 nínmu; (SCOL) 宿題 shukúdai

assimilate [əsim'əleit] *vt* (learn: ideas etc) 身に付ける mi ni tsukérù; (absorb: immigrants) 吸収する kyúshū suru

assist [əsist'] *vt* (person: physically, financially, with information etc) 援助する éñjo suru

assistance [əsis'təns] *n* (help: with advice, money etc) 援助 éñjo

assistant [əsis'tənt] *n* (helper) 助 手 jo-shú, アシスタント ashísutanto; (BRIT: also: **shop assistant**) 店員 teñ-in

associate [adj, *n* əsou'ʃi:it *vb* əsou'ʃi:eit]
♦adj: **associate member** 準会員 juñkaìin
♦*n* (at work) 仲間 nakáma
♦*vt* (mentally) 結び付ける musúbitsukerù
♦*vi*: **to associate with someone** ...と交際する ...to kōsai suru
associate professor 助教授 jókyòju

association [əsousi:ei'ʃən] *n* (group) 会 kaî; (involvement, link) 関係 kañkei; (PSYCH) 連想 reñsō

assorted [əsɔːr'tid] *adj* (various, mixed) 色々な iróiro na

assortment [əsɔːrt'mənt] *n* (*gen*) ...の 色々 ...no iróiro; (of things in a box etc) 詰合せ tsuméawase

assume [əsuːm'] *vt* (suppose) 仮定する katéi suru; (responsibilities etc) 引受ける hikíukerù; (appearance, attitude) 装う yosóoù

assumed name [əsuːmd'-] *n* 偽名 giméi

assumption [əsʌmp'ʃən] *n* (supposition) 仮定 katéi; (of power etc) 引受ける事 hikíukerù kotó

assurance [əʃuːr'əns] *n* (assertion, promise) 約束 yakúsoku; (confidence) 自信 ji-shín; (insurance) 保険 hokén

assure [əʃuːr'] *vt* (reassure) 安心させる añshin saseru; (guarantee: happiness, success etc) 保証する hoshō suru

asterisk [æs'tərisk] *n* 星 印 hoshíjirùshi, アステリスク asúterisùku

asteroid [æs'tərɔid] *n* 小 惑 星 shōwakù-sei

asthma [æz'mə] *n* ぜん息 zeñsoku

astonish [əstɑːn'iʃ] *vt* 仰天させる gyōten saserù

astonishment [əstɑːn'iʃmənt] *n* 仰 天 gyōten

astound [əstaund'] *vt* びっくり仰天させ る bikkúrì gyōten saserù

astray [əstrei'] *adv*: **to go astray** (letter) 行方不明になる yukúefumèi ni nárù
to lead astray (morally) 堕落させる daráku saserù

astride [əstraid'] *prep* ...をまたいで ...wo matáide

astrologer [əstrɑːl'ədʒər] *n* 星 占 い 師 hoshíuranaìshi

astrology [əstrɑːl'ədʒi:] *n* 占星術 señseíjutsu

astronaut [æs'trənɔːt] *n* 宇 宙 飛 行 士 u-chū́hìkòshi

astronomer [əstrɑːn'əmər] *n* 天文学者 teñmongakùsha

astronomical [æstrənɑːm'ikəl] *adj* (science, telescope) 天文学の teñmoñgaku no; (fig: odds, price) 天文学的な teñmongakuteki na

astronomy [əstrɑːn'əmi:] *n* 天文学 teñmoñgaku

astute [əstuːt'] *adj* (operator, decision) 抜け目のない nukéme no naì

asylum [əsai'ləm] *n* (refuge) 避難所 hinánjo; (mental hospital) 精神病院 seíshinbyòin

---

KEYWORD

---

at [æt] *prep* **1** (referring to position, direction) ...に〔で〕... ni〔de〕, ...の 方 へ ...no hṓ è
at the top 一番上に〔で〕ichíban ue nì〔de〕
at home/school 家〔学校〕に〔で〕ié〔gákkō〕nì〔dè〕
at the baker's パン屋に〔で〕pàn-ya ní〔de〕
to look at something ...の方に目を向ける ...no hṓ ni mè wo mukéru, ...を見る ...wo míru
to throw something at someone ...目掛けて...を投げる ...megákète ...wo nagérù

2 (referring to time) ...に ...ni
at 4 o'clock 4時に yójì ni
at night 夜 (に) yórù (ni)
at Christmas クリスマスに kurísumàsu ni
at times 時々 tokídoki
3 (referring to rates, speed etc) ...で〔に〕 ...de〔ni〕
at £1 a kilo 1キロ1ポンドで ichíkìro ichípondo de
two at a time 1度に2つ ichído nì futátsu
at 50 km/h 時速50キロメーターで jisóku gòjúkkiromētā de
4 (referring to manner) ...で〔に〕 ...de〔ni〕
at a stroke 一撃で ichígeki de
at peace 平和に heíwa ni
5 (referring to activity) ...して ...shíte
to be at work 仕事している shígoto shite iru
to play at cowboys カウボーイごっこをして遊ぶ kaúbōigokkō wo shité asobu
to be good at something ...するのがうまい ...surú nò ga umáì
6 (referring to cause) ...に〔で〕 ni〔de〕
shocked/surprised/annoyed at something ...にショックを感じて〔驚いて，怒って〕...ni shókkù wo kánjite(odóroìte, okóttè)
I went at his suggestion 彼の勧めで私は行きました kárè no susúme de wàtákushi wa ìkímashìta

ate [eit] *pt of* **eat**
atheist [ei'θi:ist] *n* 無神論者 mushínroňsha
Athens [æθ'ənz] *n* アテネ átène
athlete [æθ'li:t] *n* 運動家 uňdōka, スポーツマン supótsumàn
athletic [æθlet'ik] *adj* (tradition, excellence etc) 運動の uňdō no, スポーツのsúpōtsu no; (sporty: person) スポーツ好きの supótsuzuki no; (muscular: build) たくましい takúmashiì
athletics [æθlet'iks] *n* 運動競技 uňdōkyōgì
Atlantic [ætlæn'tik] *adj* (coast, waves etc) 太平洋の taíheìyō no

◆*n: the Atlantic (Ocean)* 太平洋 taiheìyō
atlas [æt'ləs] *n* 地図帳 chizúchō, アトラス atórasu
atmosphere [æt'məsfi:r] *n* (of planet) 大気 taíki; (of place) 雰囲気 fuň-ikì
atom [æt'əm] *n* (PHYSICS) 原子 geňshi
atomic [ətɑ:m'ik] *adj* 原子の geňshi no
atom(ic) bomb *n* 原子爆弾 geňshibakùdan
atomizer [æt'əmaizə:r] *n* 噴霧器 fuňmukì
atone [ətoun'] *vi: to atone for* (sin, mistake) 償う tsugúnaù
atrocious [ətrou'ʃəs] *adj* (very bad) ひどい hidóì
atrocity [ətrɑ:s'iti:] *n* (act of cruelty) 残虐行為 zaňgyakukòi
attach [ətætʃ'] *vt* (fasten, join) 付ける tsukérù; (document, letter) とじる tojírù; (importance etc) 置く okú
to be attached to someone/something (like) ...に愛着がある ...ni aíchaku ga arù
attaché [ætæʃei'] *n* 大使館員 taíshikaň-in
attaché case *n* アタッシェケース atásshekēsu
attachment [ətætʃ'mənt] *n* (tool) 付属品 fuzókuhin; (love): *attachment (to someone)* (...への) 愛着 (...é no) aíchaku
attack [ətæk'] *vt* (MIL) 攻撃する kógeki suru; (subj: criminal: assault) 襲う osóu; (idea: criticize) 非難する hínàn suru; (task etc: tackle) ...に取掛る ...ni toríkakarù
◆*n* (assault: MIL) 攻撃 kógeki; (on someone's life) 襲撃 shúgekì; (fig: criticism) 非難 hínàn; (of illness) 発作 hossá
heart attack 心臓発作 shiňzōhossà
attacker [ətæk'ə:r] *n* 攻撃者 kógekìsha
attain [ətein'] *vt* (also: **attain to**: results, rank) 達する tassúru; (: happiness) 手に入れる te ni irérù; (: knowledge) 得る érù
attainments [ətein'mənts] *npl* (achievements) 業績 gyóseki
attempt [ətempt'] *n* (try) 試み kokóromi
◆*vt* (try) 試みる kokóromirù

attempted [ətemp'tid] *adj* (murder, burglary, suicide) …未遂 mísùi

attend [ətend'] *vt* (school, church) …に通う …ni kayóu; (lectures) …に出席する …ni shusséki suru; (patient) 看護する kángo suru

attendance [əten'dəns] *n* (presence) 出席 shusséki; (people present) 出席率 shussékirìtsu

attendant [əten'dənt] *n* (helper) 付添い tsukísoi; (in garage etc) 係 kákàri
◆*adj* (dangers, risks) 付き物の tsukímòno no

attend to *vt fus* (needs etc) …の世話をする …no sewá wò suru; (affairs etc) …を片付ける …wo katázukerù; (patient) …を看護する …wo kángo suru; (customer) …の用を聞く …no yô wo kikú

attention [əten'ʃən] *n* (concentration, care) 注意 chùi
◆*excl* (MIL) 気を付け ki wo tsuké
for the attention of … (ADMIN) …気付け …kitsúke

attentive [əten'tiv] *adj* (intent: audience etc) 熱心に聞く nésshìn ni kikú; (polite: host) 気配り十分の kikúbàrijúbùn no

attest [ətest'] *vi*: *to attest to* (demonstrate) …を立証する …wo risshô suru; (LAW: confirm) …を確認する …wo kakúnin suru

attic [æt'ik] *n* 屋根裏部屋 yanéurabeya

attitude [æt'ətu:d] *n* (mental view) 態度 táìdo; (posture) 姿勢 shiséi

attorney [ətə:r'ni:] *n* (lawyer) 弁護士 beńgoshì

Attorney General *n* 法務長官 hômuchôkan

attract [ətrækt'] *vt* (draw) 引付ける hikítsukerù; (someone's interest, attention) 引く hikú

attraction [ətræk'ʃən] *n* (charm, appeal) 魅力 miryóku; (*gen pl*: amusements) 呼び物 yobímono, アトラクション atórakùshon; (PHYSICS) 引力 fìhryoku; (*fig*: towards someone, something) 引かれる事 hikáreru koto

attractive [ətræk'tiv] *adj* (man, woman) 美ぼうの bibô no; (interesting: price, idea, offer) 魅力的な miryôkuteki na

attribute [*n* æt'rəbju:t *vb* ətrib'ju:t] *n* 属性 zokúsei
◆*vt: to attribute something to* (cause) …を…のせいにする …wo …no seí ni surù; (poem, painting) …が…の作とする …ga …no sakú to surù; (quality) …に…がある と考える …ni …ga arú to kañgaerù

attrition [ətriʃ'ən] *n*: *war of attrition* 消耗戦 shômôsen

aubergine [ou'bə:rʒi:n] *n* (BRIT) (vegetable) なす nasù; (color) なす紺 nasúkon

auburn [ɔ:'bə:rn] *adj* (hair) くり色 kurírò

auction [ɔ:k'ʃən] *n* (also: sale by auction) 競り serî
◆*vt* 競りに掛ける serî ni kakérù

auctioneer [ɔ:kʃəni:r'] *n* 競売人 kyôbainìn

audacity [ɔ:dæs'iti:] *n* (boldness, daring) 大胆さ daítansa; (*pej*: impudence) ずうずうしさ zûzûshisà

audible [ɔ:d'əbəl] *adj* 聞える kikóeru

audience [ɔ:d'i:əns] *n* (at event) 観客 kañkyaku; (RADIO) 聴取者 chôshushà; (TV) 視聴者 shíchôsha; (public) 世間 sekén; (interview: with queen etc) 謁見 ekkén

audio-typist [ɔ:d'i:outai'pist] *n* (BRIT) 書取りタイピスト kakítori taipisùto ◇口述の録音テープを聞いてタイプを打つ人 kôjutsu nò rokúon tēpù wo kiíte taipù wo utsu hitô

audio-visual [ɔ:d'i:ouvi:ʒ'u:əl] *adj* (materials, equipment) 視聴覚の shíchôkaku no

audio-visual aid *n* 視聴覚教材 shíchôkakukyôzai

audit [ɔ:d'it] *vt* (COMM: accounts) 監査する kañsa suru

audition [ɔ:diʃ'ən] *n* (CINEMA, THEATER etc) オーディション ôdishòn

auditor [ɔ:'dətə:r] *n* (accountant) 監査役 kañsayaku

auditorium [ɔ:ditɔ:r'i:əm] *n* (building) 講堂 kôdô; (audience area) 観客席 kañkyakusèki

augment [ɔ:gment'] vt (income etc) 増やす fuyásù

augur [ɔ:'gə:r] vi: **it augurs well** いい兆しだ íi kizáshi da

August [ɔ:g'əst] n 8月 hachígatsu

aunt [ænt] n 伯(叔)母 obá

auntie [æn'ti:] n dimin of **aunt**

aunty [æn'ti:] n = **auntie**

au pair [ɔ: pe:r'] n (also: **au pair girl**) オペア（ガール）opéa(gàru)

aura [ɔ:r'ə] n (fig: air, appearance) 雰囲気 fuń-ikì

auspices [ɔ:s'pisiz] npl: **under the auspices of** ...の後援で ...no kōen de

auspicious [ɔ:spij'əs] adj (opening, start, occasion) 前途有望な zéntoyûbō na

austere [ɔ:sti:r'] adj (room, decoration) 質素な shíssò na; (person, lifestyle, manner) 厳格な geñkaku na

austerity [ɔ:ster'iti:] n (simplicity) 質素さ shissòsa; (ECON: hardship) 苦労 kúrò

Australia [ɔ:streil'jə] n オーストラリア ōsutorarīa

Australian [ɔ:streil'jən] adj オーストラリアの ōsutorarīa no
♦n オーストラリア人 ōsutorariajín

Austria [ɔ:s'tri:ə] n オーストリア ōsutorīa

Austrian [ɔ:s'tri:ən] adj オーストリアの ōsutorīa no
♦n オーストリア人 ōsutoriajín

authentic [ɔ:θen'tik] adj (painting, document, account) 本物の hoñmono no

author [ɔ:'θə:r] n (of text) 著者 chóshà; (profession) 作家 sakká; (creator: of plan, character etc) 発案者 hatsúañsha

authoritarian [əθɔ:rite:r'i:ən] adj (attitudes, conduct) 独裁的な dokúsaiteki na

authoritative [əθɔ:r'iteitiv] adj (person, manner) 権威ありげな kéñ-i aríge na; (source) 信頼できる shiñrai dekirù

authority [əθɔ:r'iti:] n (power) 権限 keñgeñ; (expert) 権威 kéñ-i; (government body) 当局 tókyoku; (official permission) 許可 kyókà
   the authorities 当局 tòkyoku

authorize [ɔ:'θə:raiz] vt (publication etc)

autistic [ɔ:tis'tik] adj 自閉症の jihéishō no

auto [ɔ:'tou] (US) n (car) 自動車 jídòsha, カーkā

autobiography [ɔ:təbaiɑ:g'rəfi:] n 自叙伝 jijódèn

autocratic [ɔ:təkræt'ik] adj (government, ruler) 独裁的な dokúsaiteki na

autograph [ɔ:'təgræf] n サイン sáiñ
♦vt (photo etc) ...にサインする ...ni sáiñ suru

automata [ɔ:tɑ:m'ətə] npl of **automaton**

automated [ɔ:'təmeitid] adj (factory, process) 自動化した jidōka shita

automatic [ɔ:təmæt'ik] adj (process, machine) 自動の jidō no; (reaction) 自動的な jidōteki na
♦n (gun) 自動ピストル jidōpìsutòru, オートマチック ōtomachikkù; (BRIT: washing machine) 自動洗濯機 jidōsentakùki; (car) オートマチック車 ōtomachikkushà

automatically [ɔ:təmæt'ikli:] adv (also fig) 自動的に jidōteki ni

automation [ɔ:təmei'ʃən] n (of factory process, office) 自動化 jidōka, オートメーション ōtomēshon

automaton [ɔ:tɑ:m'ətɑ:n] (pl **automata**) n (robot) ロボット robótto

automobile [ɔ:təməbi:l'] (US) n 自動車 jídòsha

autonomous [ɔ:tɑ:n'əməs] adj (region, area) 自治の jíchì no; (organization, person) 独立の dokúritsu no

autonomy [ɔ:tɑ:n'əmi:] n (of organization, person, country) 独立 dokúritsu

autopsy [ɔ:'tɑ:psi:] n (post-mortem) 司法解剖 shihōkaìbō, 検死解剖 keñshikaìbō

autumn [ɔ:'təm] n (season) 秋 ákì
   in autumn 秋に ákì ni

auxiliary [ɔ:gzil'jə:ri:] adj (assistant) 補助の hójò no; (back-up) 予備の yóbì no
♦n 助手 joshú

avail [əveil'] vt: **to avail oneself of** (offer, opportunity, service) ...を利用する ...wo riyō suru
♦n: **to no avail** 無駄に mudá ni

availability [əveiləbil'əti:] *n* (supply: of goods, staff etc) 入手の可能性 nyūshu no kanōsei

available [əvei'ləbəl] *adj* (obtainable: article etc) 手に入る te ni haírù; (service, time etc) 利用できる riyō dekiru; (person: unoccupied) 手が空いている te ga aíte iru; (: unattached) 相手がいない aíte gà ínái

avalanche [æv'əlæntʃ] *n* (of snow) 雪崩 nadáre; (*fig*: of people, mail, events) 殺到 sattō

avant-garde [ævɑːntgɑːrd'] *adj* 前衛の zeñ-ei no, アバンギャルドの abáñgyarùdo no

avarice [æv'ə:ris] *n* どん欲 dóñ-yoku

Ave. [æv] *abbr* = **avenue**

avenge [əvendʒ'] *vt* (person, death etc) ...の復しゅうをする ...no fukúshū wò suru

avenue [æv'ənuː] *n* (street) 通り tōri; (drive) 並木通り namíkidòri; (means, solution) 方法 hōhō

average [æv'ə:ridʒ] *n* (mean, norm) 平均 heíkin
♦*adj* (mean) 平均の heíkin no; (ordinary) 並な namí no
♦*vt* (reach an average of: in speed, output, score) 平均 ...で ...する heíkin ...de ...surú
on average 平均で heíkin de

average out *vi*: *to average out at* 平均が...になる heíkin ga ...ni nárù

averse [əvə:rs'] *adj*: *to be averse to something/doing* ...(...するの)が嫌いである ...(...surú nò) ga kirái de arù

aversion [əvə:r'ʒən] *n* (to people, work etc) 嫌悪 kéñ-o

avert [əvə:rt'] *vt* (prevent: accident, war) 予防する yobō suru; (ward off: blow) 受け止める ukétomerù; (turn away: one's eyes) そらす sorásù

aviary [ei'vi:e:ri:] *n* 鳥用大型ケージ torí-yō ōgata kèji

aviation [eivi:ei'ʃən] *n* 航空 kōkū

avid [æv'id] *adj* (supporter, viewer) 熱心な nésshiñ na

avocado [ævəkɑːd'ou] *n* (*BRIT*: also:

avocado pear) アボカド abókado

avoid [əvɔid'] *vt* (person, obstacle, danger) 避ける sakérù

avuncular [əvʌŋ'kjələ:r] *adj* (expression, tone, person) 伯(叔)父の様に優しい ojí no yō ni yasáshiì

await [əweit'] *vt* 待つ mátsù

awake [əweik'] *adj* (from sleep) 目が覚めている me ga sámète irú
♦*vb* (*pt* **awoke**, *pp* **awoken** *or* **awaked**)
♦*vt* 起す okósù
♦*vi* 目が覚める me ga samérù
to be awake 目が覚めている me ga samète irù

awakening [əwei'kəniŋ] *n* (*also fig*: of emotion) 目覚め mezáme

award [əwɔːrd'] *n* (prize) 賞 shō; (LAW: damages) 賠償 baíshō
♦*vt* (prize) 与える atáeru; (LAW: damages) 命ずる meízuru

aware [əwe:r'] *adj*: *aware (of)* (conscious) (...に) 気が付いている (...ni) ki gá tsuíte irù; (informed) (...を) 知っている (...wo) shitté iru
to become aware of/that (become conscious of) ...に(...という事に)気が付く ...ni(...to iú koto ni)ki gá tsukù; (learn) ...を(...という事を)知る ...wo(...to iú koto wò)shírù

awareness [əwe:r'nis] *n* (consciousness) 気が付いている事 ki gá tsuíte irú koto; (knowing) 知っている事 shitté iru koto

awash [əwɑːʃ'] *adj* (with water) 水浸しの mizúbitashi no; (*fig*: *awash with* ...だらけの ...daráke no

away [əwei'] *adv* (movement) 離れて hanárète; (position) 離れた所に hanárèta tokóro ni; (not present) 留守で rúsù de; (in time) ...先で ...sáki de; (far away) 遠くに tóku ni
two kilometers away 2キロメートル離れて nikíromètoru hanarete
two hours away by car 車で2時間走った所に kurúma de nijíkaǹ hashítta tokoro ni
the holiday was two weeks away 休暇は2週間先だった kyūka wa nishūkan saki dattá

he's away for a week 彼は1週間の予定で留守です kárè wa isshúkan no yotei de rusù desu

to take away (remove) 片付ける katázukerù; (subtract) 引く hikú

to work/pedal etc away 一生懸命に働く〔ペダルを踏む〕etc isshókenmei ni határaku〔pedáru wò fumù〕etc

to fade away (color) さめる sameru; (enthusiasm) 冷める samérù; (light, sound) 消えてなくなる kiéte nakunarù

away game n (SPORT) ロードゲーム ródogēmu

awe [ɔː] n (respect) い敬 ikéi

awe-inspiring [ɔːˈinspaiəriŋ] adj (overwhelming: person, thing) い敬の念を抱かせる ikéi no neǹ wo idákaserù

awesome [ɔːˈsəm] adj = **awe-inspiring**

awful [ɔːˈfəl] adj (frightful: weather, smell) いやな iyá na; (dreadful: shock) ひどい hidóì; (number, quantity): **an awful lot (of)** いやに沢山の iyá ni takusaǹ no

awfully [ɔːˈfəliː] adv (very) ひどく hídóku

awhile [əwaiˈl] adv しばらく shibáraku

awkward [ɔːkˈwəːrd] adj (clumsy: person, movement) ぎこちない gikóchinaì; (difficult: shape) 扱いにくい atsúkainikuì; (embarrassing: problem, situation) 厄介な yákkai na

awning [ɔːˈniŋ] n 日よけ hiyóke

awoke [əwouk] pt of **awake**

awoken [əwouˈkən] pp of **awake**

awry [əraiˈ] adv: **to be awry** (order, clothes, hair) 乱れている midárète irú

to go awry (outcome, plan) 失敗する shippái suru

axe [æks] (US: also: **ax**) n 斧 ónò
◆vt (project etc) 廃止する haíshi suru

axes[1] [ækˈsiz] npl of **ax(e)**

axes[2] [ækˈsiz] npl of **axis**

axis [ækˈsis] (pl **axes**) n (of earth, on graph) 軸 jikú

axle [ækˈsəl] n (AUT) 車軸 shajíku

aye [ai] excl (yes) はい haì

azalea [əzeilˈjə] n ツツジ tsutsújì

B

B [biː] n (MUS: note) ロ音 ro-óǹ; (: key) ロ調 róchō

B.A. [biːeiˈ] abbr = **Bachelor of Arts**

babble [bæbˈəl] vi (person, voices) ぺちゃくちゃしゃべる péchakucha shabérù; (brook) さらさら流れる sáràsara nagárerù

baby [beiˈbiː] n (infant) 赤ん坊 ákánbō, 赤ちゃん akáchan; (US: inf: darling) あなた anátà, ベビー bébì

baby carriage (US) n 乳母車 ubágurùma

baby-sit [beiˈbiːsit] vi 子守をする komórì wo suru, ベビーシッターをする bebíshittà wo suru

baby-sitter [beiˈbiːsitər] n 子守役 komóriyaku, ベビーシッター bebíshittà

bachelor [bætʃˈələːr] n 独身の男 dokúshin no otóko

Bachelor of Arts/Science (person) 文〔理〕学士 buń(ri)gakùshi; (qualification) 文〔理〕学号 buń(ri)gakùshigō

back [bæk] n (of person, animal) 背中 senáka; (of hand) 甲 kṑ; (of house, page, book) 裏 urá; (of car, train) 後ろ ushíro, 後部 kōbu; (of chair) 背もたれ semótàre; (of crowd, audience) 後ろの方 ushíro no hṑ; (SOCCER) バック bákkù
◆vt (candidate: also: **back up**) 支援する shién suru; (horse: at races) …に かける …ni kakérù; (car) バックさせる bákkù saséru
◆vi (also: **back up**: person) 後ずさりする atózusari suru; (: : car etc) バックする bákkù suru
◆cpd (payment, rent) 滞納の taínō no; (AUT: seat, wheels) 後部の kōbu no
◆adv (not forward) 後ろへ〔に〕ushíro e〔ni〕; (returned): **he's back** 彼は帰って来た kárè wa kaétte kità; (return): **throw the ball back** ボールを投げ返して下さい bốru wò nagékaeshite kudasaì; (again): **he called back** 彼は電話を掛け直してきた kárè wa deńwa wò kakénao-

shite kita

he ran back 彼は駆け戻った kárè wa kakémodottà

can I have it back? それを返してくれませんか soré wò kaéshite kuremaseñ ka

backbencher [bæk'bentʃər] (*BRIT*) *n* 平議員 hirágìin

backbone [bæk'boun] *n* (ANAT) 背骨 sebóne; (*fig*: main strength) 主力 shúryòku; (: courage) 勇気 yùki

backcloth [bæk'klɔːθ] (*BRIT*) *n* = **backdrop**

backdate [bækdeit'] *vt* (document, pay raise etc) ...にさかのぼって有効にする ...ni sakánobottè yūkō ni suru

back down *vi* 譲る yuzúru

backdrop [bæk'drɑːp] *n* 背景幕 haíkeìmaku

backfire [bæk'faiər] *vi* (AUT) バックファイアする bakkúfaìa suru; (plans) 裏目に出る uráme ni derù

background [bæk'graund] *n* (of picture, events: also COMPUT) 背景 haíkei, バック bákkù; (basic knowledge) 予備知識 yobíchishìki; (experience) 経歴 keíreki

family background 家庭環境 kateikankyō

backhand [bæk'hænd] *n* (TENNIS: also: **backhand stroke**) バックハンド bakkúhañdo

backhanded [bæk'hændid] *adj* (*fig*: compliment) 当てこすりの atékosuri no

backhander [bæk'hændər] (*BRIT*) *n* (bribe) 賄ろ waíro

backing [bæk'iŋ] *n* (*fig*) 支援 shíen

backlash [bæk'læʃ] *n* (*fig*) 反動 haňdō

backlog [bæk'lɔːg] *n*: **backlog of work** たまった仕事 tamátta shigoto

back number *n* (of magazine etc) バックナンバー bakkúnañbā

back out *vi* (of promise) 手を引く te wo hikú

backpack [bæk'pæk] *n* リュックサック ryukkúsakkù

back pay *n* 未払いの給料 mihárài nó kyūryò

backside [bæk'said] (*inf*) *n* おしり o-shí-

ri

backstage [bæk'steidʒ'] *adv* (THEATER) 楽屋に〔で〕 gakúya ni〔de〕

backstroke [bæk'strouk] *n* 背泳ぎ seóyògi

back up *vt* (support: person, theory etc) 支援する shíen suru; (COMPUT) バックアップコピーを作る bakkúappukopì wo tsukúrù

backup [bæk'ʌp] *adj* (train, plane) 予備の yóbi no; (COMPUT) バックアップ用の bakkúappu yō no

♦*n* (support) 支援 shíen; (*also*: **backup file**) バックアップファイル bakkúappu faìru

backward [bæk'wərd] *adj* (movement) 後ろへの ushíro e no; (person, country) 遅れた okúreta

backwards [bæk'wərdz] *adv* (move, go) 後ろに〔へ〕 ushíro ni〔e〕; (read a list) 逆に gyakú nì; (fall) 仰向けに aōmuke ni; (walk) 後ろ向きに ushíromuki ni

backwater [bæk'wɔːtər] *n* (*fig*) 後進地 kōshìnchi

backyard [bæk'jɑːrd] *n* (of house) 裏庭 urániwa

bacon [bei'kən] *n* ベーコン bèkon

bacteria [bækti'riːə] *npl* 細菌 saíkin

bad [bæd] *adj* (gen) 悪い warúî; (mistake, accident, injury) 大きな ōkina; (meat, food) 悪くなった wárùku nattá

his bad leg 彼の悪い方の脚 kárè no warúî hō nò ashí

to go bad (food) 悪くなる warúku narù

bade [bæd] *pt of* **bid**

badge [bædʒ] *n* (of school etc) 記章 kishṑ; (of policeman) バッジ bájjî

badger [bædʒ'ər] *n* アナグマ anáguma

badly [bæd'liː] *adv* (work, dress etc) 下手に hetá ni; (reflect, think) 悪く wárùku

badly wounded 重傷を負った jūshṑ wò ottá

he needs it badly 彼にはそれがとても必要だ kárè ni wa soré gà totémo hitsuyṑ da

to be badly off (for money) 生活が苦しい seíkatsu ga kurushiî

badminton [bæd'mintən] *n* バドミント

ン badómiǹton

bad-tempered [bǽd'tem'pə:rd] *adj* (person: by nature) 怒りっぽい okórippoì; (: on one occasion) 機嫌が悪い kigén gà warúî

baffle [bæf'əl] *vt* (puzzle) 困惑させる koń-waku saserù

bag [bæg] *n* (of paper, plastic) 袋 fukúro; (handbag) ハンドバッグ hańdobaggù; (satchel, case) かばん kabán

bags of (*inf*: lots of) 沢山の takúsan no

baggage [bæg'idʒ] *n* (luggage) 手荷物 te-nímòtsu

baggy [bæg'i:] *adj* だぶだぶの dabúdabu no

bagpipes [bæg'paips] *npl* バグパイプ ba-gúpaìpu

Bahamas [bəhɑːm'əz] *npl*: *the Bahamas* バハマ諸島 bahámashotò

bail [beil] *n* (LAW: payment) 保釈金 ho-shákukin; (: release) 保釈 hosháku

♦*vt* (prisoner: *gen*: grant bail to) 保釈する hosháku suru; (boat: *also*: **bail out**) ...から水をかい出す ...kará mizú wò kaídasù

on bail (prisoner) 保釈中 (の) hoshákuchů (no)

bailiff [bei'lif] *n* (LAW: *US*) 廷吏 teîri; (: *BRIT*) 執行吏 shíkkòri

bail out *vt* (prisoner) 保釈させる hoshá-ku saseru ¶ *see also* **bale**

bait [beit] *n* (for fish, animal) えさ esá; (for criminal etc) おとり otóri

♦*vt* (hook, trap) ...にえさをつける ...ni esá wò tsukérù; (person: tease) からかう karákaù

bake [beik] *vt* (CULIN: cake, potatoes) オーブンで焼く ǒbun de yakú; (TECH: clay etc) 焼く yakú

♦*vi* (cook) オーブンに入っている ǒbun ni háîtte iru

baked beans [beikt-] *npl* ベークトビーンズ bêkutobìnzu

baker [bei'kə:r] *n* パン屋 pán-ya

bakery [bei'kə:ri:] *n* (building) パン屋 pán-ya

baking [bei'kiŋ] *n* (act) オーブンで焼く事 ǒbun de yakú koto; (batch) オーブン

で焼いたもの ǒbun de yaíta mono

baking powder *n* ふくらし粉 fukúra-shikò, ベーキングパウダー bêkingupaù-dā

balance [bæl'əns] *n* (equilibrium) 均衡 kińkò, バランス baránsu; (COMM: sum) 残高 zańdaka; (remainder) 残り nokóri; (scales) 天びん teńbin

♦*vt* (budget) ...の収入と支出を合せる ...no shúnyū tò shishútsu wò awáserù; (account) ...の決算をする ...no kessán wò suru; (make equal) 釣合を取る tsuríai wo torù

balance of trade 貿易収支 bốekishùshi

balance of payments 国際収支 kokú-saishùshi

balanced [bæl'ənst] *adj* (report) バランスの良い baránsu no yoì; (personality) 安定した ańtei shita

a balanced diet 均衡食 kińkò shòku

balance sheet *n* 貸借対照表 taíshakuta-ishôhyồ, バランスシート baránsu shîto

balcony [bæl'kəni:] *n* バルコニー barúkonì; (in theater) 天井さじき teńjōsajìki

bald [bɔːld] *adj* (head) はげた hágèta; (tire) 坊主になった bồzu ni nattá

bale [beil] *n* (of paper, cotton, hay) こり korí

baleful [beil'fəl] *adj* (glance) 邪悪な jaá-ku na

bale out *vi* (of a plane) パラシュートで脱出する paráshùto de dasshútsù suru

ball [bɔːl] *n* (SPORT) 球 tamá, ボール bồ-ru; (of wool, string) 玉 tamá; (dance) 舞踏会 bútòkai

to play ball (co-operate) 協力する kyố-ryoku suru

ballad [bæl'əd] *n* (poem, song) バラード bárādo

ballast [bæl'əst] *n* (on ship, balloon) バラスト barásùto

ball bearings *npl* ボールベアリング bồ-rubeàringu

ballerina [bæləri:'nə] *n* バレリーナ barérìna

ballet [bælei'] *n* (art) バレエ bárèe; (an artistic work) バレエ曲 baréekyokù

ballet dancer *n* バレエダンサー baréedańsā

ballistics [bəlis'tiks] n 弾道学 dańdōgaku

balloon [bəlu:n'] n (child's) 風船 fūsen; (hot air balloon) 熱気球 netsúkikyū

ballot [bæl'ət] n (vote) 投票 tōhyō

ballot paper n 投票用紙 tōhyōyōshi

ballpoint (pen) [bɔ:l'pɔint] n ボールペン bōrupen

ballroom [bɔ:l'ru:m] n 舞踏の間 butō no ma

balm [bɑm] n バルサム bárùsamu

Baltic [bɔ:l'tik] n: **the Baltic (Sea)** バルト海 barútokài

balustrade [bæl'əstreid] n (on balcony, staircase) 手すり tesúri

bamboo [bæmbu:'] n (plant) 竹 take; (material) 竹材 takézai

ban [bæn] n (prohibition) 禁止 kińshi
♦vt (prohibit) 禁止する kińshi suru

banal [bənæl'] adj (remark, idea, situation) 陳腐な chíńpu na

banana [bənæn'ə] n バナナ bánàna

band [bænd] n (group) 一団 ichídan; (MUS: jazz, rock, military etc) バンド bańdo; (strip of cloth etc) バンド bańdo; (stripe) 帯状の物 obíjō no mono

bandage [bæn'didʒ] n 包帯 hōtai
♦vt ...に包帯を巻く ...ni hōtai wò makú

bandaid [bænd'eid'] ® (US) n バンドエイド bańdoeìdo ◇ばん創こうの一種 bańsōkō no isshù

bandit [bæn'dit] n 盗賊 tōzoku

band together vi 団結する danketsu suru

bandwagon [bænd'wægən] n: **to jump on the bandwagon** (fig) 便乗する bińjō suru

bandy [bæn'di:] vt (jokes, insults, ideas) やり取りする yarítòri surù

bandy-legged [bæn'di:legid] adj がにまたの ganímata no

bang [bæŋ] n (of door) ばたんという音 bátàn to iú oto; (of gun, exhaust) ぱんという音 páñ to iú otò; (blow) 打撃 dagéki
♦excl ぱんぱん páñpan
♦vt (door) ばたんと閉める batán to shimerù; (one's head etc) ぶつける butsúke-

ru
♦vi (door) ばたんと閉まる batán to shimárù; (fireworks) ぱんぱんと爆発する báñban to bakúhatsu suru

bangle [bæŋ'gəl] n (bracelet) 腕飾り udékazari

bangs [bæŋz] (US) npl (fringe) 切下げ前髪 kirísagemaegamì

banish [bæn'iʃ] vt (exile: person) 追放する tsuíhō suru

banister [bæn'istə:r(z)] n(pl) (on stairway) 手すり tesúri

bank [bæŋk] n (COMM: building, institution: also of blood etc) 銀行 gińkō, バンク báňku; (of river, lake) 岸 kishí; (of earth) 土手 doté
♦vi (AVIAT) 傾く katámukù
data bank データバンク détabañku

bank account n 銀行口座 gińkōkòza

bank card n ギャランティーカード gyarántikàdo ◇小切手を使う時に示すカード.カードのサインと小切手のサインが照合される kogítte wo tsukáù tokí nì shimésu kàdo. kàdo no saín to kogítte no saín ga shōgō sarerù

banker [bæŋk'ə:r] n 銀行家 gińkōka

banker's card (BRIT) n = **bank card**

Bank Holiday (BRIT) n 銀行定休日 gińkōteikyūbi

banking [bæŋk'iŋ] n 銀行業 gińkōgyò

banknote [bæŋk'nout] n 紙幣 shíhèi

bank on vt fus ...を頼りにする ...wo táyòri ni suru

bank rate n 公定歩合 kōteibuài

bankrupt [bæŋk'rʌpt] adj (person, organization) 倒産した tōsan shita
to go bankrupt 倒産する tōsan suru
to be bankrupt 返済能力がない heñsaino̅ryoku ga naí

bankruptcy [bæŋk'rʌptsi:] n (COMM) 倒産 tōsan

bank statement n 勘定照合表 kańjōshōgōhyō

banner [bæn'ə:r] n (for decoration, advertising) 横断幕 ōdañmaku; (in demonstration) 手持ち横断幕 temóchi ōdañmaku

banns [bænz] npl: **the banns** 結婚予告

kekkón-yokóku

banquet [bæŋ'kwit] *n* 宴会 eńkai

baptism [bæp'tizəm] *n* (REL) 洗礼 seńrei

baptize [bæptaiz'] *vt* ...に洗礼を施す ...ni seńrei wò hodókosù

bar [bɑːr] *n* (place: for drinking) バー bā; (counter) カウンター kaúntā; (rod: of metal etc) 棒 bố; (slab: of soap) 1個 ikkó; (*fig*: obstacle) 障害 shốgai; (prohibition) 禁止 kińshi; (MUS) 小節 shốsetsu

♦*vt* (road) ...を通るのを禁止する ...ga ...surú no wò kíńshi suru; (person) ...が ...するのを禁止する ...ga ...surú no wò kińshi suru; (activity) 禁止する kińshi suru

a bar of chocolate 板チョコ itachoko

the Bar (LAW: profession) 弁護士 beńgoshi ◊総称 sốshō

bar none 例外なく reigai nakù

barbaric [bɑːrbær'ik] *adj* (uncivilized, cruel) 野蛮な yabán na

barbarous [bɑːr'bərəs] *adj* (uncivilized, cruel) 野蛮な yabán na

barbecue [bɑːr'bəkjuː] *n* (grill) バーベキューこん炉 bấbekyūkòńro; (meal, party) バーベキューパーティ bấbekyūpàti

barbed wire [bɑːrbd'-] *n* 有刺鉄線 yúshitessèn, バラ線 barásen

barber [bɑːr'bər] *n* 理髪師 rihátsushì, 床屋 tokóya

bar code *n* (on goods) バーコード bãkōdo

bare [beːr] *adj* (naked: body) 裸の hadáka no; (: tree) 葉の落ちた ha no óchìta; (countryside) 木のない ki no nái; (minimum: necessities) ほんの hońno

♦*vt* (one's body, teeth) むき出しにする mukídashi ni suru

bareback [beːr'bæk] *adv* くらなしで kuránashì de

barefaced [beːr'feist] *adj* (lie, cheek) 厚かましい atsúkamashìi

barefoot [beːr'fut] *adj* 裸足の hadáshi no

♦*adv* 裸足で hadáshi de

barely [beːr'liː] *adv* (scarcely) 辛うじて kárōjite

bargain [bɑːr'gin] *n* (deal, agreement) 取引 toríhìki; (good buy) 掘出し物 horída-

shimono, バーゲン bãgen

♦*vi* (negotiate): *to bargain (with someone)* (...と) 交渉する (...to) kốshō suru; (haggle) 駆引きする kakéhìki suru

into the bargain おまけに o-máke ni

bargain for *vt fus*: *he got more than he bargained for* 彼はそんな結果を予想していなかった kárè wa sofina kekká wò yosố shite inakattà

barge [bɑːrdʒ] *n* (boat) はしけ hashíke

barge in *vi* (enter) いきなり入り込む ikínari hairikomù; (interrupt) 割込む waríkomù

bark [bɑːrk] *n* (of tree) 皮 kawá; (of dog) ほえ声 hoégoe

♦*vi* (dog) ほえる hoérù

barley [bɑːr'liː] *n* 大麦 ốmugi

barley sugar *n* 氷砂糖 kốrizatò

barmaid [bɑːr'meid] *n* 女性バーテン joséibāten

barman [bɑːr'mən] (*pl* **barmen**) *n* バーテン bāten

barn [bɑːrn] *n* 納屋 náyà

barometer [bərɑːm'itəːr] *n* (for weather) 気圧計 kiátsukei

baron [bær'ən] *n* (nobleman) 男爵 dańshaku; (of press, industry) 大立て者 ốdatemòno

baroness [bær'ənis] *n* 男爵夫人 dańshakufujìn

barracks [bær'əks] *npl* (MIL) 兵舎 héisha

barrage [bərɑːʒ'] *n* (MIL) 弾幕 dańmaku; (dam) ダム dámù; (*fig*: of criticism, questions etc) 連発 reńpatsu

barrel [bær'əl] *n* (of wine, beer) たる tarú; (of oil) バレル bárèru; (of gun) 銃身 júshin

barren [bær'ən] *adj* (land) 不毛の fumố no

barricade [bær'əkeid] *n* バリケード barírkèdo

♦*vt* (road, entrance) バリケードでふさぐ barírkèdo de fuságu

to barricade oneself (in) (...に) ろう城する (...ni) rốjō suru

barrier [bær'iːr] *n* (at frontier, entrance) 関門 kańmon; (*fig*: to progress, communication etc) 障害 shōgai

barring [bɑːrʾiŋ] *prep* ...を除いて ...wo nozóite

barrister [bærʾistəːr] (*BRIT*) *n* 法廷弁護士 hôteibengoshì

barrow [bærʾou] *n* (wheelbarrow) 一輪車 ichírìnsha

bars [bɑːrz] *npl* (on window etc: grille) 格子 kōshi

behind bars (prisoner) 刑務所に〔で〕 keímushò ni〔de〕

bartender [bɑːrʾtendəːr] (*US*) *n* バーテン báten

barter [bɑːrʾtəːr] *vt*: **to barter something for something** ...を...と交換する ...wo ...to kōkan suru

base [beis] *n* (foot: of post, tree) 根元 nemóto; (foundation: of food) 主成分 shuséibun; (: of make-up) ファウンデーション faúndèshon; (center: for military, research) 基地 kichí; (: for individual, organization) 本拠地 honkyochi
♦*vt*: **to base something on** (opinion, belief) ...が...に基づく ...ga ...ni motózuku
♦*adj* (mind, thoughts) 卑しい iyáshiì

baseball [beisʾbɔːl] *n* 野球 yakyū, ベースボール bésubòru

basement [beisʾmənt] *n* 地下室 chikáshìtsu

bases[1] [beisʾiz] *npl of* **base**

bases[2] [beisʾiːz] *npl of* **basis**

bash [bæʃ] (*inf*) *vt* (beat) ぶん殴る buńnagurù

bashful [bæʃʾfəl] *adj* 内気な uchíki na

basic [beiʾsik] *adj* (fundamental: principles, problem, essentials) 基本的な kihónteki na; (starting: wage) 基本の kihón no; (elementary: knowledge) 初歩的な shohôteki na; (primitive: facilities) 最小限の saíshōgen no

basically [beiʾsikliː] *adv* (fundamentally) 根本的に końponteki ni; (in fact, put simply) はっきり言って hakkírì itté

basics [beiʾsiks] *npl*: **the basics** 基本 kihón

basil [bæzʾəl] *n* メボウキ mébòki, バジル bájìru

basin [beiʾsin] *n* (vessel) たらい taráì;

(*also*: **wash basin**) 洗面台 seńmendai; (GEO: of river, lake) 流域 ryūiki

basis [beiʾsis] (*pl* **bases**) *n* (starting point, foundation) 基礎 kisó
on a part-time/trial basis パートタイム〔見習い〕で pátotaìmù(minarai)de

bask [bæsk] *vi*: **to bask in the sun** 日光浴をする nikkōyoku wo suru, 日なたぼっこをする hinátabokkò wo suru

basket [bæsʾkit] *n* (container) かご kagó, バスケット basúkettò

basketball [bæsʾkitbɔːl] *n* バスケットボール basúkettobòru

bass [beis] *n* (part, instrument) バス básù; (singer) バス歌手 basúkashù

bassoon [bæsuːnʾ] *n* (MUS) バスーン básùn

bastard [bæsʾtərd] *n* (offspring) 私生児 shiséìji; (*inf!*) くそ野郎 kusóyarō

bastion [bæsʾtʃən] *n* (of privilege, wealth etc) とりで toríde

bat [bæt] *n* (ZOOL) コウモリ kômori; (for ball games) バット báttò; (*BRIT*: for table tennis) ラケット rakéttò
♦*vt*: **he didn't bat an eyelid** 彼は瞬き1つしなかった kárè wa mabátàki hitotsu shinákàtta

batch [bætʃ] *n* (of bread) 1かま分 hitókamabùn; (of letters, papers) 1山 hitóyàma

bated [beiʾtid] *adj*: **with bated breath** 息を殺して íkì wo koróshite

bath [bæθ] *n* (bathtub) 風呂 fúrò, 湯船 yúbùne; (act of bathing) 入浴 nyūyoku
♦*vt* (baby, patient) 風呂に入れる fúrò ni iréru
to have a bath 風呂に入る fúrò ni haíru
¶ *see also* **baths**

bathe [beið] *vi* (swim) 泳ぐ oyógù, 遊泳する yūei suru; (*US*: have a bath) 風呂に入る fúrò ni haíru
♦*vt* (wound) 洗う aráu

bather [beiʾðəːr] *n* 遊泳〔水泳〕する人 yūei(suíei) suru hito

bathing [beiʾðiŋ] *n* (taking a bath) 入浴 nyūyoku; (swimming) 遊泳 yūei, 水泳 suíei

bathing cap *n* 水泳帽 suíeibō

bathing suit (*BRIT* **bathing costume**)

n 水着 mizúgi

bathrobe [bæθ'roub] *n* バスローブ basúrōbu

bathroom [bæθ'ruːm] *n* トイレ tôīre; (without toilet) 浴室 yokúshitsu

baths [bæðz] (BRIT) *npl* (*also*: **swimming baths**) 水泳プール suíeipūru

bath towel *n* バスタオル basútaðru

baton [bætɑːn'] *n* (MUS) 指揮棒 shikíbō; (ATHLETICS) バトン batón; (policeman's) 警棒 keíbō

battalion [bətæl'jən] *n* 大隊 daítai

batter [bæt'əːr] *vt* (child, wife) ...に暴力を振るう ...ni bōryoku wo furûú; (subj: wind, rain) ...に強く当たる ...ni tsúyòku atáru

♦*n* (CULIN) 生地 kíjì

battered [bæt'əːrd] *adj* (hat, pan) 使い古した tsukáifurushìta

battery [bæt'əːri] *n* (of flashlight etc) 乾電池 kańdeñchi; (AUT) バッテリー battérī

battle [bæt'əl] *n* (MIL, *fig*) 戦い tatákai
♦*vi* 戦う tatákau

battlefield [bæt'əlfiːld] *n* 戦場 seńjō

battleship [bæt'əlʃip] *n* 戦艦 seńkan

bawdy [bɔː'diː] *adj* (joke, song) わいせつな waísetsu na

bawl [bɔːl] *vi* (shout: adult) どなる donárù; (wail: child) 泣きわめく nakíwamekù

bay [bei] *n* (GEO) 湾 wáñ
to hold someone at bay ...を寄付けない ...wo yosétsukenaí

bay leaf *n* ゲッケイジュの葉 gekkéīju no ha, ローリエ rōrie, ベイリーフ beírīfu

bayonet [bei'ənet] *n* 銃剣 júken

bay window *n* 張出し窓 harídashimadò

bazaar [bəzɑːr'] *n* (market) 市場 íchìba; (fete) バザー bazā

B. & B. [biː' ænd biː'] *n abbr* = **bed and breakfast**

BBC [biːbiːsiː'] *n abbr* (= *British Broadcasting Company*) 英国放送協会 eíkoku hōsō kyōkai

B.C. [biːsiː'] *adv abbr* (= *before Christ*) 紀元前 kigéñzen

---

be [biː] (*pt* **was, were**, *pp* **been**) *aux vb* **1** (with present participle: forming continuous tenses) ...している ...shíte iru

what are you doing? 何をしていますか nâni wo shité imasù ká

it is raining 雨が降っています ámè ga fúttè imásù

they're coming tomorrow 彼らは明日来る事になっています kárèra wa asú kurù koto ni náttè imásù

I've been waiting for you for hours 何時間もあなたを待っていますよ nánjikàn mo anátà wo máttè imásù yo

2 (with *pp*: forming passives) ...される ...saréru

to be killed 殺される korósareru

the box had been opened 箱は開けられていた hakó wa àkérarete ita

the thief was nowhere to be seen 泥棒はどこにも見当らなかった doróbō wa dòkó ni mo mìátaranakàtta

3 (in tag questions) ...ね ...né, ...でしょう ...deshő

it was fun, wasn't it? 楽しかったね tanóshikàtta né

he's good-looking, isn't he? 彼は男前だね kárè wa otókomae da ne

she's back again, is she? 彼女はまた来たのか kánojò wa matá kita nò ká

4 (+ **to** + *infinitive*) ...すべきである ...subékì de aru

the house is to be sold 家は売る事になっている ié wà urú koto nì náttè iru

you're to be congratulated for all your work 立派な仕事を完成しておめでとう rippá na shigoto wo kansei shite ōmédetō

he's not to open it 彼はそれを開けてはならない kárè wa soré wo akete wà naránaî

♦*vb* + *complement* **1** (*gen*) ...である ...de árù

I'm English 私はイングランド人です watákushi wa íngurandojìn desu

I'm tired/hot/cold 私は疲れた（暑い，寒い）watákushi wa tsùkárèta〔atsûî, samúi]

he's a doctor 彼は医者です kárè wa ishá desù

2 and 2 are 4 2足す2は4 ní tasù ní wà yóñ

she's tall/pretty 彼女は背が高い〔きれいです〕 kánojò wa sé gà takái〔kírèi desu〕

be careful/quiet/good! 注意〔静かに，行儀よく〕して下さい chúi〔shízùka ni, gyógì yokù〕shité kudasài

2 (of health): *how are you?* お元気ですか o-génkì desu ká

he's very ill 彼は重病です kárè wa jū́byō desù

I'm better now もう元気になりました mó génkì ni narímashìta

3 (of age) ...才です ...sài desu

how old are you? 何才ですか nánsai desu ka, (お) 幾つですか (ó)ikùtsu desu ka

I'm sixteen (years old) 16才です jūrokusài desu

4 (cost): *how much was the meal?* 食事はいくらでしたか shokúji wa ikùra deshìta ká

that'll be $5.75, please 5ドル75セント頂きます gódòru nanájūgosèntò itádakimasù

♦*vi* **1** (exist, occur etc) 存在する sónzai suru

the best singer that ever was 史上最高の歌手 shijó saikò no kashù

is there a God? 神は存在するか kámì wa sónzai suru kà

be that as it may それはそれとして soré wa sore toshite

so be it それでよい soré de yoì

2 (referring to place) ...にある〔いる〕...ni árù〔ìrú〕

I won't be here tomorrow 明日ここに来ません asú wà kokó ni kìmàseñ

Edinburgh is in Scotland エジンバラはスコットランドにある ejínbàra wa sukóttorandò ni árù

it's on the table それはテーブルにあります soré wa tēburu ni árímasù

we've been here for ages 私たちはずっと前からここにいます watákushitàchi wa zuttó maè kara kokó ni ìmásù

3 (referring to movement) 行って来る itté kurù

where have you been? どこへ行っていましたか dókò e itté imashìta ká

I've been to the post office/to China 郵便局〔中国〕へ行って来ました yūbìn-kyoku〔chūgòku〕e itté kimashìta

I've been in the garden 庭にいました niwá ni imashìta

♦*impers vb* **1** (referring to time): *it's 5 o'clock* 5時です gójì desu

it's the 28th of April 4月28日です shigátsu nijūhachìnichi dèsu

2 (referring to distance): *it's 10 km to the village* 村まで10キロメーターです murá màde jukkíromētà desu

3 (referring to the weather): *it's too hot* 暑過ぎる atsúsugirù

it's too cold 寒過ぎる samúsugirù

it's windy today 今日は風が強い kyó wà kazé ga tsuyoì

4 (emphatic): *it's only me/the postman* ご心配なく，私〔郵便屋さん〕です go-shínpai nakù, watákushi〔yūbin-ya-san〕desù

it was Maria who paid the bill 勘定を払ったのはマリアでした kánjō wò haráttà no wa márià deshita

beach [biːtʃ] *n* 浜 hamá

♦*vt* (boat) 浜に引上げる hamá ni hikíagerù

beacon [biːˈkən] *n* (lighthouse) 燈台 tódai; (marker) 信号 shíñgō

bead [biːd] *n* (glass, plastic etc) ビーズ bízu; (of sweat) 玉 tamá

beak [biːk] *n* (of bird) くちばし kuchíbashi

beaker [biːˈkəːr] *n* (cup) コップ koppú, グラス gúràsu

beam [biːm] *n* (ARCHIT) はり harí; (of light) 光線 kósen

♦*vi* (smile) ほほえむ hohóemù

bean [biːn] *n* マメ mamé

runner bean サヤインゲン sayáiñgen

broad bean ソラマメ sorámàme

coffee bean コーヒーマメ kóhīmàme

beansprouts [biːnˈsprauts] *npl* マメモヤシ mamémoyàshi

bear [beːr] *n* (ZOOL) クマ kumá
♦*vb* (*pt* **bore**, *pp* **borne**)
♦*vt* (carry, support: weight) 支える sasáerù; (: responsibility) 負う oú; (: cost) 払う haráù; (tolerate: examination, scrutiny, person) ...に耐える ...ni taérù; (produce: children) 産む umú
♦*vi*: *to bear right/left* (AUT) 右〔左〕に曲る mígì〔hidári〕ni magárù

to bear fruit ...に実がなる ...ni mi ga narú

beard [biːrd] *n* ひげ higé

bearded [biːrˈdid] *adj* ひげのある higé no arù

bearer [beːrˈəːr] *n* (of letter, news) 運ぶ人 hakóbu hito; (of cheque) 持参人 jisánnin; (of title) 持っている人 móttè irú hito

bearing [beːrˈiŋ] *n* (air) 態度 táĭdo; (connection) 関係 kañkei

to take a bearing 方角を確かめる hôgaku wò tashíkamerù

to find one's bearings 自分の位置を確かめる jibún no ichi wò tashíkamerù

bearings [beːrˈiŋz] *npl* (*also*: **ball bearings**) ボールベアリング bôrubeàringu

bear out *vt* (person) ...の言う事を保証する ...no iu koto wo hoshô suru; (suspicions etc) ...の事実を証明する ...no jijítsu wo shômei suru

bear up *vi* (person) しっかりする shikkárí surú

beast [biːst] *n* (animal) 野獣 yajū́; (*inf*: person) いやなやつ iyá na yatsù

beastly [biːstˈliː] *adj* (awful: weather, child, trick etc) ひどい hídoì

beat [biːt] *n* (of heart) 鼓動 kodô; (MUS) 拍子 hyôshi, ビート bîto; (of policeman) 巡回区域 juñkaikuìki
♦*vb* (*pt* **beat**, *pp* **beaten**)
♦*vt* (strike: wife, child) 殴る nagúrù; (eggs, cream) 泡立てる awádaterù, ホイップする hoíppù suru; (defeat: opponent) ...に勝つ ...ni kátsù; (: record) 破る yabúrù
♦*vi* (heart) 鼓動する kodô suru; (rain) た

たき付ける様に降る tatákitsukeru yô ni fúrù; (wind) たたき付ける様に吹く tatákitsukeru yô ni fúkù; (drum) 鳴る narú

off the beaten track へんぴな所に héñpi na tokóro ni

to beat it (*inf*) ずらかる zurákarù

beating [biːˈtiŋ] *n* (punishment with whip etc) むち打ち muchíuchi; (violence) 殴ける abの暴行 nagurukeru no bôkō

beat off *vt* (attack, attacker) 撃退する gekítai surù

beat up *vt* (person) 打ちのめす uchínomesù; (mixture) かく拌する kakúhan suru; (eggs, cream) 泡立てる awádaterù, ホイップする hoíppù suru

beautiful [bjuːˈtəfəl] *adj* (woman, place) 美しい utsúkushiì; (day, weather) 素晴しい subárashiì

beautifully [bjuːˈtəfəliː] *adv* (play music, sing, drive etc) 見事に mígòto ni

beauty [bjuːˈtiː] *n* (quality) 美しさ utsúkushìsa; (beautiful woman) 美女 bíjò, 美人 bíjìn; (*fig*: attraction) 魅力 miryóku

beauty salon *n* 美容院 bíyòin

beauty spot *n* (*BRIT*: TOURISM) 景勝地 keíshōchī

beaver [biːˈvəːr] *n* (ZOOL) ビーバー bîbā

became [bikeim] *pt of* **become**

because [bikɔːzˈ] *conj* ...だから ...dá kàra, ...であるので ...de árù nodé

because of ...のため ...no tamé, ...のせいで ...no seí de

beck [bek] *n*: *to be at the beck and call of* ...の言いなりになっている ...no iínari ni nattè irú

beckon [bekˈən] *vt* (*also*: **beckon to**: person) ...に来いと合図する ...ni kôĭ to áĭzu suru

become [bikʌmˈ] (*pt* **became**, *pp* **become**) *vi* ...になる ...ni nárù

to become fat 太る futôrù

to become thin やせる yasérù

becoming [bikʌmˈiŋ] *adj* (behavior) ふさわしい fusáwashì; (clothes) 似合う niáù

bed [bed] *n* (piece of furniture) ベッド béddò; (of coal, clay) 層 sô; (bottom: of river, sea) 底 sokó; (of flowers) 花壇 kádàn *to go to bed* 寝る nerú

bed and breakfast *n* (place) 民宿 miń-shuku; (terms) 朝食付き宿泊 chóshoku-tsuki shukúhaku

bedclothes [bed'klouz] *npl* シーツと毛布 shítsu to mófu

bedding [bed'iŋ] *n* 寝具 shíŋgu

bedlam [bed'ləm] *n* 大騒ぎ ősawági

bedraggled [bidræg'əld] *adj* (person, clothes, hair) びしょ濡れの bishónure no

bedridden [bed'ridən] *adj* 寝たきりの ne-tákiri no

bedroom [bed'ru:m] *n* 寝室 shińshitsu

bedside [bed'said] *n*: *at someone's bedside* …の枕元に …no makúramòto ni

bedsit(ter) [bed'sit(ə:r)] (*BRIT*) *n* 寝室兼居間 shińshitsu keń imá

bedspread [bed'spred] *n* ベッドカバー beddókabà

bedtime [bed'taim] *n* 寝る時刻 nerú jíkòku

bee [bi:] *n* ミツバチ mitsúbachi

beech [bi:tʃ] *n* (tree) ブナ búna; (wood) ブナ材 bunázai

beef [bi:f] *n* 牛肉 gyúniku

roast beef ローストビーフ rősutobìfu

beefburger [bi:f'bə:rgə:r] *n* ハンバーガー hańbāgà

Beefeater [bi:f'i:tə:r] *n* ロンドン塔の守衛 rońdontō no shuéi

beehive [bi:'haiv] *n* ミツバチの巣箱 mi-tsúbachi no súbàko

beeline [bi:'lain] *n*: *to make a beeline for* まっしぐらに…に向かう masshígùra ni …ni mukáu

been [bin] *pp of* be

beer [bi:r] *n* ビール bíru

beet [bi:t] *n* (vegetable) サトウダイコン satódaikòn, ビート bíto; (*US: also:* red beet) ビーツ bítsu

beetle [bi:t'əl] *n* 甲虫 kóchū

beetroot [bi:t'ru:t] (*BRIT*) *n* ビーツ bítsu

before [bifɔ:r'] *prep* (of time, space) …の前に〔で〕 …no máè ni〔de〕

♦*conj* …する前に …surú maè ni

♦*adv* (time, space) 前に máè ni

before going 行く前に ikú maè ni

before she goes 彼女が行く前に kánojo ga ikú maè ni

the week before (week past) 1週間前 isshúkan maè

I've never seen it before これまで私はそれを見た事はない koré madè watákushi wa soré wò mitá koto wà nái

beforehand [bifɔ:r'hænd] *adv* あらかじめ arákajime, 前もって maémottè

beg [beg] *vi* (as beggar) こじきをする ko-jíki wò suru

♦*vt* (*also:* beg for: food, money) こい求める koímotomerù; (: forgiveness, mercy etc) 願う negáù

to beg someone to do something …に…してくれと頼む …ni …shité kurè to ta-nómù ¶ *see also* pardon

began [bigæn'] *pt of* begin

beggar [beg'ə:r] *n* こじき kojíki

begin [bigin'] (*pt* began, *pp* begun) *vt* 始める hajímeru

♦*vi* 始まる hajímaru

to begin doing/to do something …し始める …shihajímeru

beginner [bigin'ə:r] *n* 初心者 shoshíñsha

beginning [bigin'iŋ] *n* 始め hajíme

begun [bigʌn'] *pp of* begin

behalf [bihæf'] *n*: *on behalf of* (as representative of) …を代表して …wo daíhyō shité; (for benefit of) …のために …no ta-mé ni

on my/his behalf 私〔彼〕のために wa-tákukushi〔kárè〕nò tamé ni

behave [biheiv'] *vi* (person) 振舞う furú-maù; (well: *also:* behave oneself) 行儀良くする győgi yokù suru

behavior [biheiv'jə:r] (*BRIT* behaviour) *n* 行動 kődō

behead [bihed'] *vt* …の首を切る …no kubí wò kírù

beheld [biheld'] *pt, pp of* behold

behind [bihaind'] *prep* (position: at the back of) …の後ろに〔で〕 …no ushíro ni〔de〕; (supporting) …を支援して …wo shi-én shite; (lower in rank, etc) …に劣って …ni otótte

♦*adv* (at/towards the back) 後ろに〔の方へ〕 ushíro ni〔no hő è〕; (leave, stay) 後に

átō ni

♦*n* (buttocks) しり shirí

to be behind (schedule) 遅れている okúrete irù

behind the scenes (*fig*) 非公式に hikóshiki ni

behold [bihould'] (*pt, pp* **beheld**) *vt* 見る mírù

beige [beiʒ] *adj* ベージュ bḗju

Beijing [bei'dʒiŋ'] *n* 北京 pékìn

being [bi:'iŋ] *n* (creature) 生き物 ikímonò; (existence) 存在 sońzai

Beirut [beiru:t'] *n* ベイルート beírūto

belated [bilei'tid] *adj* (thanks, welcome) 遅ればせの okúrebase no

belch [beltʃ] *vi* げっぷをする geppú wò suru

♦*vt* (*gen*: belch out: smoke etc) 噴出する fuńshutsu suru

belfry [bel'fri:] *n* 鐘楼 shṓrō

Belgian [bel'dʒən] *adj* ベルギーの berúgì no

♦*n* ベルギー人 berúgìjìn

Belgium [bel'dʒəm] *n* ベルギー berúgì

belie [bilai'] *vt* (contradict) 隠す kakúsù; (disprove) 反証する hańshō suru

belief [bili:f'] *n* (opinion) 信念 shíñnen; (trust, faith) 信仰 shíñkō

believe [bili:v'] *vt* 信じる shiñjirù

♦*vi* 信じる shiñjirù

to believe in (God, ghosts) ...の存在を信じる ...no soñzai wò shiñjirù; (method) ...が良いと考える ...ga yóì to kańgaerù

believer [bili:v'ə:r] *n* (in idea, activity) ...が良いと考える人 ...ga yóì to kańgaeru hito; (REL) 信者 shiñja

belittle [bilit'əl] *vt* 軽視する keíshi suru

bell [bel] *n* (of church) 鐘 kanḗ; (small) 鈴 suzú; (on door, *also* electric) 呼び鈴 yobírin, ベル bérù

belligerent [bəlidʒ'ə:rənt] *adj* (person, attitude) けんか腰の keńkagoshi no

bellow [bel'ou] *vi* (bull) 大声で鳴く ṓgoè de nakú; (person) どなる donárù

bellows [bel'ouz] *npl* (for fire) ふいご fuígo

belly [bel'i:] *n* (ANAT: of person, animal) 腹 hará

belong [biloːŋ'] *vi*: *to belong to* (person) ...の物である ...no monó de arù; (club etc) ...に所属している ...ni shozóku shite irù; (group) ...の会員である ...no kaíìn de arù

this book belongs here この本はここにしまうことになっている konó hoǹ wa kokó ni shimaù kotó ni nattè irú

belongings [biloːŋ'iŋz] *npl* 持物 mochímòno

beloved [bilʌv'id] *adj* (person) 最愛の saíai no; (place) 大好きな dɑísuki na; (thing) 愛用の aíyō no

below [bilou'] *prep* (beneath) ...の下に〔で〕 ...no shitá ni〔de〕; (less than: level, rate) ...より低く ...yórì hikúkù

♦*adv* (beneath) 下に shitá ni

see below (in letter etc) 下記参照 kakísañshō

belt [belt] *n* (of leather etc: *also* TECH) ベルト berúto; (*also*: **belt of land**) 地帯 chítài

♦*vt* (thrash) 殴る nagúrù

beltway [belt'wei] (*US*) *n* (AUT: ring road) 環状道路 kañjōdōro

bemused [bimju:zd'] *adj* (person, expression) ぼう然とした bṓzen to shitá

bench [bentʃ] *n* (seat) ベンチ beńchi; (work bench) 作業台 sagyṓdai; (*BRIT*: POL) 議員席 giíñseki

the Bench (LAW: judges) 裁判官 saíbañkan◇総称 sṓshō

bend [bend] (*pt, pp* **bent**) *vt* (leg, arm, pipe) 曲げる magéru

♦*vi* (person) かがむ kagámu

♦*n* (*BRIT*: in road) カーブ kầbu; (in pipe, river) 曲った所 magátta tokoro

bend down *vi* 身をかがめる mi wo kagámeru

bend over *vi* 身をかがめる mi wo kagámeru

beneath [bini:θ'] *prep* (position) ...の下に〔で〕 ...no shitá ni〔de〕; (unworthy of) ...のこけんに関わる ...no kokéñ ni kakawarù

♦*adv* 下に shitá ni

benefactor [ben'əfæktə:r] *n* (to person, institution) 恩人 oñjin

beneficial [benəfiʃ'əl] *adj* (effect, influ-

ence) 有益な yū́eki na
beneficial (to) (...に) 有益な (...ni) yū́eki na
benefit [ben'əfit] n (advantage) 利益 ríèki; (money) 手当て tēate
♦vt ...の利益になる ...no ríèki ni narū
♦vi: **he'll benefit from it** それは彼のためになるだろう soré wà kárè no tamé ni narū darō
Benelux [ben'əlʌks] n ベネルクス benérukùsu
benevolent [bənev'ələnt] adj (person) 温和な oñwa na; (organization) 慈善の jizén no
benign [binain'] adj (person, smile) 優しい yasáshii; (MED) 良性の ryṓsei no
bent [bent] pt, pp of **bend**
♦n 才能 saínō
♦adj (inf: corrupt) 不正な fuséi na
to be bent on doing ...しようと心掛けている ...shíyŏ to kokórogakete irù
bequest [bikwest'] n (to person, charity) 遺贈 izṓ
bereaved [biri:vd'] n: **the bereaved** 喪中の人々 mochū no hitóbìto
beret [bərei'] n ベレー帽 bérèbō
Berlin [bə:rlin'] n ベルリン berúrin
berm [bə:rm] (US) n (AUT) 路肩 rokáta
Bermuda [bə:rmju:d'ə] n バーミューダ bámyùda
berry [be:r'i:] n ベリー berī ◇総称 sṓshō
berserk [bə:rsə:rk'] adj: **to go berserk** (madman, crowd) 暴れ出す abáredasù
berth [bə:rθ] n (on ship or train) 寝台 shíñdai; (for ship) バース bāsu
♦vi (ship) 接岸する setsúgan suru
beseech [bisi:tʃ] (pt, pp **besought**) vt (person, God) ...に嘆願する ...ni tañgan suru
beset [biset'] (pt, pp **beset**) vt (subj: fears, doubts, difficulties) 襲う osóu
beside [bisaid'] prep (next to) ...の横に〔で〕...no yokó ni〔de〕
to be beside oneself (with anger) 逆上している gyakújṑ shite irù
that's beside the point それは問題外です soré wà moñdaigài desu
besides [bisaidz'] adv (in addition) それ

に soré ni, その上 sonó ue; (in any case) とに角 toníkaku
♦prep (in addition to, as well as) ...の外に ...no hoká ni
besiege [bisi:dʒ'] vt (town) 包囲攻撃する hōikōgeki suru; (fig: subj: journalists, fans) ...に押寄せる ...ni oshíyoserù
besought [bisɔ:t'] pt, pp of **beseech**
best [best] adj (quality, suitability, extent) 最も良い mottomò yoì
♦adv 最も良く mottómò yókù
the best part of (quantity) ...の大部分 ...no daíbubun
at best 良くても yókùte mo
to make the best of something ...を出来るだけ我慢する ...wo dekíru dake gamàn suru
to do one's best 最善を尽す saízen wo tsukúsù, ベストを尽くす bésùto wo tsukúsù
to the best of my knowledge 私の知っている限りでは watákushi no shittè irú kagiri de wa
to the best of my ability 私に出来る限り watákushi ni dekírù kagíri
best man n 新郎付添い役 shiñrōtsukisoiyàku
bestow [bistou'] vt (honor, title): **to bestow something on someone** ...に...を授ける ...ni ...wo sazúkerù
bestseller [best'selə:r] n (book) ベストセラー besútoserà
bet [bet] n (wager) かけ kaké
♦vb (pt, pp **bet** or **betted**)
♦vt (wager): **to bet someone something** ...と...をかける ...to ...wo kakérù
♦vi (wager) かける kakérù
to bet money on something ...に金をかける ...ni kané wò kakérù
betray [bitrei'] vt (friends, country, trust, confidence) 裏切る urágirù
betrayal [bitrei'əl] n (action) 裏切り urágiri
better [bet'ə:r] adj (quality, skill, sensation) より良い yorí yoì; (health) 良くなった yókù nattá
♦adv より良く yorí yókù
♦vt (score) ...より高い得点をする ...yorí

takaî tokúten wo suru; (record) 破る ya-búrù

♦*n*: *to get the better of* ...に勝つ ...ni kátsù

you had better do it あなたはそうした方が良い anátà wa sô shita hô ga yóî

he thought better of it 彼は考え直した kárè wa kañgaenaoshita

to get better (MED) 良くなる yókù naru, 回復する kaífuku suru

better off *adj* (wealthier) ...より金がある ...yórì kané ga arù; (more comfortable etc) ...の方が良い ...no hô ga yoî

betting [bet'iŋ] *n* (gambling, odds) かけ事 kakégòto, ギャンブル gyáñburu

betting shop (*BRIT*) *n* 私営馬券売り場 shiéibaken-urìba

between [bitwi:n'] *prep* (all senses) ...の間に〔で〕...no aída ni〔de〕

♦*adv* 間に aída ni

beverage [bev'ə:ridʒ] *n* 飲物 nomímòno, 飲料 íñryò

beware [biwe:r'] *vi*: *to beware (of)* (dog, fire) (...を)用心する (...wo) yójin suru

「*beware of the dog*」猛犬注意 môkenchûi

bewildered [biwil'də:rd] *adj* (stunned, confused) 当惑した tôwaku shita

bewitching [biwitʃ'iŋ] *adj* (smile, person) うっとりさせる uttórì saséru

beyond [bi:ɑːnd'] *prep* (in space) ...より先に〔で〕...yórì sakí ni〔de〕; (past: understanding) ...を越えて ...wo koête; (after: date) ...以降を ...íkô ni; (above) ...以上に ...íjô ni

♦*adv* (in space, time) 先に sakí ni

beyond doubt 疑いもなく utágai mo nakù

beyond repair 修理不可能で shûri fukánô de

bias [bai'əs] *n* (prejudice) 偏見 heñken

bias(s)ed [bai'əst] *adj* (jury) 偏見を持った heñken wo mottá; (judgement, reporting) 偏見に基づいた heñken ni motózuìta

bib [bib] *n* (child's) よだれ掛け yodárekàke

Bible [bai'bəl] *n* (REL) 聖書 séîsho, バイブル báîburu

biblical [bib'likəl] *adj* 聖書の séîsho no

bibliography [bibli:ɑːg'rəfi:] *n* (in text) 文献目録 buñkenmokùroku

bicarbonate of soda [baiəkɑːr'bənit-] *n* 重炭酸ソーダ jûtansaňsòda, 重曹 jûsô

bicker [bik'əːr] *vi* (squabble) 口論する kôron suru

bicycle [bai'sikəl] *n* 自転車 jiteñsha

bid [bid] *n* (at auction) 付値 tsukéně; (in tender) 入札 nyûsatsu; (attempt) 試みkokóromi

♦*vb* (*pt* **bade** *or* **bid**, *pp* **bidden** *or* **bid**)

♦*vi* (at auction) 競りに加わる serí ni kuwawarù

♦*vt* (offer) ...と値を付ける ...to né wò tsukérù

to bid someone good day (hello) ...に今日はと言う ...ni konnichi wa to iu; (farewell) ...にさようならと言う ...ni sayónara to iu

bidder [bid'əːr] *n*: *the highest bidder* 最高入札者 saíkônyûsatsùsha

bidding [bid'iŋ] *n* (at auction) 競り serí

bide [baid] *vt*: *to bide one's time* (for opportunity) 時期を待つ jíkì wo mátsù

bidet [bi:dei'] *n* ビデ bídè

bifocals [baifou'kəlz] *npl* 二重焦点眼鏡 nijûshôtenmegàne

big [big] *adj* (gen) 大きい ôkiî, 大きな ô-kina

big brother 兄 áni, 兄さん níisan

big sister 姉 anê, 姉さん nêsan

bigamy [big'əmi:] *n* 重婚 jûkon

big dipper [-dip'əːr] (*BRIT*) *n* (at fair) ジェットコースター jettôkôsutâ

bigheaded [big'hedid] *adj* うぬぼれたu-núboreta

bigot [big'ət] *n* (on race, religion) 偏狭な人 heñkyô na hito

bigoted [big'ətid] *adj* (on race, religion) 偏狭な heñkyô na

bigotry [big'ətri:] *n* 偏狭さ heñkyôsà

big top *n* (at circus) 大テント ôteňto

bike [baik] *n* (bicycle) 自転車 jiteñsha

bikini [biki:'ni:] *n* ビキニ bíkìni

bilateral [bailæt'əːrəl] *adj* (agreement)

双務的な sṓmuteki na

bile [bail] n (BIO) 胆汁 tañjū

bilingual [bailiŋ'gwəl] adj (dictionary) 二か国語の nikákokugo no; (secretary) 二か国語を話せる nikákokugo wò hanáserù

bill [bil] n (account) 勘定書 kañjōgaki; (invoice) 請求書 seíkyūsho; (POL) 法案 hōan; (US: banknote) 紙幣 shíhèi; (of bird) くちばし kuchíbashi; (THEATER: of show: on the bill) 番組 bañgumi

「*post no bills*」張紙厳禁 harígamigenkin

to fit/fill the bill (fig) 丁度いい chṓdo iì

billboard [bil'bɔːrd] n 広告板 kṓkokuban

billet [bil'it] n (MIL) 軍人宿舎 guñjinshukūsha

billfold [bil'fould] (US) n 財布 saífu

billiards [bil'jəːrdz] n ビリヤード biríyàdo

billion [bil'jən] n (BRIT) 兆 chṓ; (US) 10億 jūoku

bin [bin] n (BRIT: for rubbish) ごみ入れ gomíire; (container) 貯蔵箱 chózōbako, 瓶 bíñ

binary [bai'nəːriː] adj (MATH) 二進法の nishínhō no

bind [baind] (pt, pp **bound**) vt (tie, tie together) 縛る shibárù; (constrain) 束縛する sokúbaku suru; (book) 製本する seíhon suru

♦n (inf: nuisance) いやな事 iyá na koto

binding [bain'diŋ] adj (contract) 拘束力のある kōsokuryòku no aru

binge [bindʒ] (inf) n: *to go on a binge* (drink a lot) 酒浸りになる sakébitari ni narù

bingo [biŋ'gou] n ビンゴ bíñgo

binoculars [bənɑːk'jələːrz] npl 双眼鏡 sṓgankyō

biochemistry [baioukem'istriː] n 生化学 seíkagàku

biography [baiɑːg'rəfiː] n 伝記 deñki

biological [baiəlɑːdʒ'ikəl] adj (science, warfare) 生物学の seíbutsugàku no; (washing powder) 酵素洗剤 kōsoseñzai

biology [baiɑːl'ədʒiː] n 生物学 seíbutsu-

gàku

birch [bəːrtʃ] n (tree) カバノキ kabá no ki; (wood) カバ材 kabázài

bird [bəːrd] n (ZOOL) 鳥 torí; (BRIT: inf: girl) 女の子 ofína no ko

bird's-eye view [bəːrdzai-] n (aerial view) 全景 zeñkei; (overview) 概観 gaíkan

bird-watcher [bəːrd'wɑːtʃəːr] n バードウォッチャー bádowotchà

bird-watching [bəːrd'wɑːtʃiŋ] n バードウォッチング bádowotchìngu

Biro [bai'rou] ® n ボールペン bṓrupen

birth [bəːrθ] n (of baby, animal, also fig) 誕生 tañjō

to give birth to (BIO: subj: woman, animal) ...を生む ...wo umú

birth certificate n 出生証明書 shusshṓ〔shussei〕shṓmeisho

birth control n (policy) 産児制限 sañjiseígen; (methods) 避妊 hinín

birthday [bəːrθ'dei] n 誕生日 tañjòbi

♦cpd (cake, card, present etc) 誕生日の tañjōbi no ¶ see also **happy**

birthplace [bəːrθ'pleis] n (country, town etc) 出生地 shusshṓchi〔shusséichi〕, 生地 umárekokyò; (house etc) 生家 seíka

birth rate n 出生率 shusshṓritsu〔shusséiritsu〕

Biscay [bis'kei] n: *the Bay of Biscay* ビスケー湾 bisúkèwan

biscuit [bis'kit] (BRIT) n ビスケット bisúkettò

bisect [baisekt'] vt (angle etc) 二等分する nitṓbun suru

bishop [biʃ'əp] n (REL: Catholic etc) 司教 shíkyò; (: Protestant) 監督 kañtoku; (: Greek Orthodox) 主教 shúkyò; (CHESS) ビショップ bíshoppu

bit [bit] pt of **bite**

♦n (piece) 欠けら kakéra; (COMPUT) ビット bíttò; (of horse) はみ hámì

a bit of 少しの sukóshì no, ちょっとの chottṓ no

a bit mad ちょっと頭がおかしい chóttô atáma ga okáshìì

a bit dangerous ちょっと危ない chóttô abúnaì

bit by bit 少しずつ sukóshi zutsù

bitch [bitʃ] *n* (dog) 雌犬 mesúinu; (*inf!*: woman) あま ámà

bite [bait] (*pt* **bit**, *pp* **bitten**) *vt* (subj: person) かむ kámù; (: dog etc) …にかみ付く …ni kamítsuku; (: insect etc) 刺す sásù
♦*vi* (dog etc) かみ付く kamítsuku; (insect etc) 刺す sásù
♦*n* (insect bite) 虫刺され mushísasàre; (mouthful) 一口 hitókùchi

to bite one's nails つめをかむ tsumé wo kamù

let's have a bite (to eat) (*inf*) 何か食べよう nàni ka tabéyò

bitten [bit'ən] *pp* of **bite**

bitter [bit'əːr] *adj* (person) 恨みを持った urámi wò mottá; (taste, experience, disappointment) 苦い nigáì; (wind) 冷たい tsumétaì; (struggle) 激しい hagéshiì; (criticism) 辛らつな shínratsu na
♦*n* (*BRIT*: beer) ビター bitá ◇ホップの利いた苦いビール hoppù no kíìta nigáì bīru

bitterness [bit'əːrnis] *n* (anger) 恨み urámi; (bitter taste) 苦み nigámi

bizarre [bizɑːr'] *adj* (conversation, contraption) 奇妙な kímyò na

blab [blæb] (*inf*) *vi* (to the press) しゃべる shabérù

black [blæk] *adj* (color) 黒い kuróì; (person) 黒人の kokújin no; (tea, coffee) ブラックの burákkù no
♦*n* (color) 黒 kúrò; (person): *Black* 黒人 kokújin
♦*vt* (*BRIT*: INDUSTRY) ボイコットする boíkottò suru

black humor ブラックユーモア burákkuyùmoa

to give someone a black eye …を殴って目にあざを作る …wo nagútte me ni azá wo tsukúrù

black and blue (bruised) あざだらけの azá daràke no

to be in the black (in credit) 黒字である kuróji de arù

blackberry [blæk'beːriː] *n* ブラックベリー burákkuberì ◇キイチゴの一種 kiíchigo no isshù

blackbird [blæk'bəːrd] *n* (European bird) クロウタドリ kuróutadòri

blackboard [blæk'bɔːrd] *n* 黒板 kokúban

black coffee *n* ブラックコーヒー burákku kòhī

blackcurrant [blækʌr'ənt] *n* クロスグリ kurósugùri

blacken [blæk'ən] *vt* (*fig*: name, reputation) 汚す kegásù

black ice (*BRIT*) *n* (on road) 凍結路面 tóketsuromèn

blackleg [blæk'leg] (*BRIT*) *n* (INDUSTRY) スト破り sutóyabùri

blacklist [blæk'list] *n* ブラックリスト burákkurisùto

blackmail [blæk'meil] *n* ゆすり yusúri
♦*vt* ゆする yusúru

black market *n* やみ市 yamíchi

blackout [blæk'aut] *n* (MIL) 灯火管制 tókakañsei; (power cut) 停電 teíden; (TV, RADIO) 放送中止 hósōchūshi; (faint) 一時的の意識喪失 ichíjitekiishìkisōshitsu, ブラックアウト burákkuaùto

Black Sea *n*: *the Black Sea* 黒海 kókkài

black sheep *n* (*fig*) 持て余し者 motéamashimòno

blacksmith [blæk'smiθ] *n* 鍛冶屋 kajíya

black spot *n* (*BRIT*: AUT) 事故多発地点 jikótahàtsuchitèn; (: for unemployment etc) …が深刻になっている地域 …ga shíñkoku ni nattè irú chìki

bladder [blæd'əːr] *n* (ANAT) ぼうこう bókò

blade [bleid] *n* (of knife, sword) 刃 hà; (of propeller) 羽根 hanè

a blade of grass 草の葉 kusá no ha

blame [bleim] *n* (for error, crime) 責任 sekínin
♦*vt*: *to blame someone for something* …を…のせいにする …wo …no seí ni suru
to be to blame 責任が…にある sekínin ga …ni arù

blameless [bleim'lis] *adj* (person) 潔白な keppáku na

bland [blænd] *adj* (taste, food) 味気ない ajíke naì

blank [blæŋk] *adj* (paper etc) 空白の kúhaku no; (look) ぼう然とした bŏzen to shitá

♦*n* (of memory) 空白 kŭhaku; (on form) 空所 kŭsho; (*also*: **blank cartridge**) 空包 kŭhō

a blank sheet of paper 白紙 hakúshi

blank check *n* 金額未記入の小切手 kíngakumiki-nyū no kogíttè

blanket [blæŋ'kit] *n* (of cloth) 毛布 mŏfu; (of snow, fog etc) 一面の… ichímen no …

blare [ble:r] *vi* (brass band, horns, radio) 鳴り響く naríhibikù

blasé [blɑːzei'] *adj* (reaction, tone) 無関心な mukánshin na

blasphemy [blæs'fəmi:] *n* (REL) 冒とく bŏtoku

blast [blæst] *n* (of wind) 突風 toppŭ; (of explosive) 爆発 bakúhatsu

♦*vt* (blow up) 爆破する bakúha suru

blast-off [blæst'ɔːf] *n* (SPACE) 発射 hasshá

blatant [blei'tənt] *adj* (discrimination, bias) 露骨な rokótsu na

blaze [bleiz] *n* (fire) 火事 kájì; (*fig*: of color, glory) きらめき kirámeki; (: publicity) 大騒ぎ ŏsawàgi

♦*vi* (fire) 燃え盛る moésakerù; (guns) 続け様に発砲する tsuzúkezama ni happŏ suru; (*fig*: eyes) 怒りで燃える ikári de moérù

♦*vt*: *to blaze a trail* (*fig*) 先べんを付ける señben wo tsúkerù

blazer [blei'zəːr] *n* (of school, team etc) ブレザー burézà

bleach [bliːtʃ] *n* (*also*: **household bleach**) 漂白剤 hyŏhakuzài

♦*vt* (fabric) 漂白する hyŏhaku suru

bleached [bliːtʃt] *adj* (hair) 漂白した hyŏhaku shitá

bleachers [bliːtʃəːrz] (*US*) *npl* (SPORT) 外野席 gaíyasèki

bleak [bliːk] *adj* (countryside) もの寂しい monósabishiì; (weather) 悪い warúì; (prospect, situation) 暗い kurái; (smile) 悲しそうな kanáshisò na

bleary-eyed [bliː'riːaid] *adj* 目がしょぼしょぼしている me ga shobòshobo shité

bleat [bliːt] *vi* (goat, sheep) 鳴く nakú

bled [bled] *pt, pp of* **bleed**

bleed [bliːd] (*pt, pp* **bled**) *vi* (MED) 出血する shukkétsu suru

my nose is bleeding 鼻血が出ている hanáji ga dete irù

bleeper [bliː'pəːr] *n* (device) ポケットベル pokétto berù

blemish [blem'iʃ] *n* (on skin) 染み shimí; (on fruit) 傷 kizú; (on reputation) 汚点 otén

blend [blend] *n* (of tea, whisky) 混合 koñgō, ブレンド buréndo

♦*vt* 混ぜ合せる mazéawaserù, 混合する koñgō suru

♦*vi* (colors etc: *also*: **blend in**) 溶け込む tokékomù

bless [bles] (*pt, pp* **blessed** *or* **blest**) *vt* (REL) 祝福する shukúfuku suru

bless you! (after sneeze) お大事に o-dáiji ni

blessing [bles'iŋ] *n* (approval) 承認 shŏnin; (godsend) 恵み megúmi; (REL) 祝福 shukúfuku

blew [bluː] *pt of* **blow**

blight [blait] *vt* (hopes, life etc) 駄目にする damé ni suru

blimey [blai'miː] (*BRIT*: *inf*) *excl* おやおや oyá

blind [blaind] *adj* (MED) 盲目の mŏmoku no; (*pej*) めくらの mekúra no; (euphemistically) 目の不自由な me no fujíyù na; (*fig*): *blind (to)* (…を) 見る目がない (…wo) mirù mé ga naì

♦*n* (for window) ブラインド buráindo; (: *also*: **Venetian blind**) ベネシアンブラインド benéshian buraìndo

♦*vt* (MED) 失明させる shitsúmei sasérù; (dazzle) …の目をくらます …no me wo kurámasù; (deceive) だます damásù

the blind (blind people) 盲人 mŏjiñ ◇総称 sŏshō

blind alley *n* (*fig*) 行き詰り yukízumari

blind corner (*BRIT*) *n* 見通しの悪い曲り角 mitŏshi no waruì magárikadò

blindfold [blaind'fould] *n* 目隠し mekákùshi

♦*adj* 目隠しをした mekákùshi wo shitá

♦*adv* 目隠しをして mekákùshi wo shitế

♦*vt* 目隠しする mekákùshi suru

blindly [blaind'li:] *adv* (without seeing) よく見ないで yốkù mináide; (without thinking) めくら滅法に mekúramepp̀o ni

blindness [blaind'nis] *n* (MED) 盲目 mốmoku; (euphemistically) 目の障害 me no shốgai

blind spot *n* (AUT) 死角 shikáku; (*fig*: weak spot) 盲点 mốten

blink [blink] *vi* (person, animal) 瞬く mabátakù; (light) 点滅する teńmetsu suru

blinkers [blink'ə:rz] *npl* 馬の目隠し umá no mekákùshi

bliss [blis] *n* (complete happiness) 至福 shifúku

blister [blis'tə:r] *n* (on skin) 水膨れ mizúbukùre; (in paint, rubber) 気胞 kihố

♦*vi* (paint) 気胞ができる kihố ga dekirù

blithely [blaið'li:] *adv* (proceed, assume) 軽率に keísotsu ni

blitz [blits] *n* (MIL) 空襲 kữshū

blizzard [bliz'ə:rd] *n* 吹雪 fubúki, ブリザード burízàdo

bloated [blou'tid] *adj* (face, stomach: swollen) はれた haréta; (person: full) たらふく食べた taráfùku tabèta

blob [blɑːb] *n* (of glue, paint) 滴 shizúku; (something indistinct) はっきり見えないもの hakkírì miénai monó

bloc [blɑːk] *n* (POL) 連合 refigō, ブロック burókkù

block [blɑːk] *n* (of buildings) 街区 gaíku, ブロック burókkù; (of stone, wood) ブロック burókkù; (in pipes) 障害物 shốgaibutsu

♦*vt* (entrance, road) 塞ぐ fuságu; (progress) 邪魔する jamá suru

block of flats (*BRIT*) マンション mańshon

mental block 精神的ブロック seíshinteki burokkù

blockade [blɑːkeid'] *n* 封鎖 fấsa

blockage [blɑːk'idʒ] *n* 閉そく heísoku

blockbuster [blɑːk'bʌstə:r] *n* (film, book) センセーション seńsêshon

block letters *npl* 活字体 katsújitai

bloke [blouk] (*BRIT*: *inf*) *n* 男 otóko, 野郎 yárồ

blond(e) [blɑːnd] *adj* (hair) 金髪の kíñpatsu no, ブロンドの buróndo no

♦*n* (woman) 金髪の女性 kíñpatsu no joséi, ブロンド buróndo

blood [blʌd] *n* (BIO) 血 chi, 血液 ketsúeki

blood donor *n* 献血者 keńketsùsha

blood group *n* 血液型 ketsúekigata

bloodhound [blʌd'haund] *n* ブラッドハウンド buráddohaùndo

blood poisoning [-poi'zəniŋ] *n* 敗血症 haíketsushô

blood pressure *n* 血圧 ketsúatsu

bloodshed [blʌd'ʃed] *n* 流血 ryúketsu

bloodshot [blʌd'ʃɑːt] *adj* (eyes) 充血した júketsu shitá

bloodstream [blʌd'striːm] *n* 血流 ketsúryū

blood test *n* 血液検査 ketsúekikeñsa

bloodthirsty [blʌd'θə:rsti:] *adj* (tyrant, regime) 血に飢えた chi ni úeta

blood vessel *n* 血管 kekkán

bloody [blʌd'i:] *adj* (battle) 血みどろの chímìdoro no; (nose) 鼻血を出した hanáji wo dashìta; (*BRIT*: *inf!*): *this bloody ...* くそったれ... kusóttarè...

bloody strong/good (*inf!*) すごく強い〔良い〕sugókù tsuyóī〔yoì〕

bloody-minded [blʌd'i:main'did] (*BRIT*: *inf*) *adj* 意地悪な ijíwàru na

bloom [bluːm] *n* (BOT: flower) 花 haná

♦*vi* (tree) ...の花が咲く ... no hana ga sakú; (flower) 咲く sakú

blossom [blɑːs'əm] *n* (BOT) 花 haná

♦*vi* (BOT) 花が咲く haná ga sakú; (*fig*): *to blossom into* 成長して...になる seíchōshite ...ni narù

blot [blɑːt] *n* (on text) 染み shimí; (*fig*: on name etc) 傷 kizú

♦*vt* (with ink etc) 汚す yogósu

blotchy [blɑːtʃ'i:] *adj* (complexion) 染みだらけの shimídaràke no

blot out *vt* (view) 見えなくする miénàku suru; (memory) 消す kesú

blotting paper [blɑːt'iŋ-] *n* 吸取り紙 suítorigàmi

blow [blou] n (punch etc: *also fig*) 打撃 dagéki; (with sword) 一撃 ichígeki

♦vb (pt **blew**, pp **blown**)

♦vi (wind) 吹く fúkù; (person) 息を吹掛ける íkì wo fukíkakerù

♦vt (subj: wind) 吹飛ばす fukítobasù; (instrument, whistle) 吹く fúkù; (fuse) 飛ばす tobásu

to blow one's nose 鼻をかむ haná wo kamú

blow away vt 吹飛ばす fukítobasù

blow down vt (tree) 吹倒す fukítaosù

blow-dry [blou'drai] n (hairstyle) ブロー仕上げ burôshiàge

blowlamp [blou'læmp] (*BRIT*) n = **blowtorch**

blow off vt (hat etc) 吹飛ばす fukítobasù

blow out vi (fire, flame) 吹消す fukíkesù

blow-out [blou'aut] n (of tire) パンク páñku

blow over vi (storm) 静まる shizúmarù; (crisis) 収まる osámarù

blowtorch [blou'tɔːrtʃ] n ブローランプ burôrañpu, トーチランプ tôchirañpu

blow up vi (storm) 起きる okírù; (crisis) 起る okórù

♦vt (bridge: destroy) 爆破する bakúha suru; (tire: inflate) 膨らます fukúramasu; (PHOT: enlarge) 引延ばす hikínobasù

blue [bluː] adj (color) 青い aóì, ブルーの burû no; (depressed) 憂うつな yúutsu na

blue film ポルノ映画 porúnoeìga

blue joke わいせつなジョーク waísetsu na jôku

out of the blue (*fig*) 青天のへきれきの様に seíten no hekíreki no yô ni

bluebell [bluː'bel] n ツルボ tsurúbò

bluebottle [bluː'baːtəl] n (insect) アオバエ aóbae

blueprint [bluː'print] n (*fig*): *a blueprint (for)* (...の) 計画 (...no) keíkaku, (...の) 青写真 (...no) aójashìn

blues [bluːz] n: *the blues* (MUS) ブルース búrùsu

bluff [blʌf] vi (pretend, threaten) はったりを掛ける hattári wo kakérù

♦n (pretense) はったり hattári

to call someone's bluff ...に挑戦する ...ni chôsen suru

blunder [blʌn'dəːr] n (political) へまhémà

♦vi (bungle something) へまをする hémà wo suru

blunt [blʌnt] adj (pencil) 先が太い sakí ga futóì; (knife) 切れない kirénaì; (person, talk) 率直な sotchóku na

blur [bləːr] n (shape) かすんで見える物 kasúnde miérù monó

♦vt (vision) くらます kurámasu; (distinction) ぼかす bokásu

blurb [bləːrb] n (for book, concert etc) 宣伝文句 señdenmoñku

blurt out [bləːrt-] vt 出し抜けに言い出す dashínuke ni iídasù

blush [blʌʃ] vi (with shame, embarrassment) 赤面する sekímen suru

♦n 赤面 sekímen

blustering [blʌs'təːriŋ] adj (person) 威張り散らす ibárichirasù

blustery [blʌs'təːriː] adj (weather) 風の強い kazé no tsuyóì

boar [bɔːr] n イノシシ inóshishì

board [bɔːrd] n (cardboard) ボール紙 bôrugami; (wooden) 板 ítà; (on wall: notice board) 掲示板 keíjiban; (for chess etc) ...盤 ...bañ; (committee) 委員会 iíñkai; (in firm) 役員会 yakúiñkai; (NAUT, AVIAT): *on board* ...に乗って ...ni notte

♦vt (ship, train) ...に乗る ...ni norú

full/half board (*BRIT*) 3食〔2食〕付き sañshoku〔nishóku〕tsukí

board and lodging 賄い付き下宿 makánaitsuki geshúku

to go by the board (*fig*) 捨てられる sutérareru

boarder [bɔːr'dəːr] n (SCOL) 寄宿生 kishúkusèi

boarding card [bɔːr'diŋ-] n = **boarding pass**

boarding house n 下宿屋 geshúkuya

boarding pass n (AVIAT, NAUT) 搭乗券 tôjōken

boarding school n 全寮制学校 zeñryō-

seigakkō

board room n 役員会議室 yakúinkaigi-shìtsu

board up vt (door, window) ...に板を張る ...ni ítà wo harú

boast [boust] vi: *to boast (about/of)* (...を) 自慢する (...wo) jimán suru

boat [bout] n (small) ボート bōto; (ship) 船 fúnè

boater [bou'tə:r] n (hat) かんかん帽 kańkanbò

boatswain [bou'sən] n 甲板長 kōhaǹchō, ボースン bōsun

bob [ba:b] vi (boat, cork on water: also: **bob up and down**) 波に揺れる namí ni yuréru

bobby [ba:b'i:] (BRIT: inf) n (policeman) 警官 keíkan

bobsleigh [ba:b'slei] n ボブスレー bobù-surē

bob up vi (appear) 現れる aráwarerù

bode [boud] vi: *to bode well/ill (for)* (...にとって) 良い〔悪い〕前兆である (...ni tottè) yoi(warúi)zeńchō de arù

bodily [ba:d'əli:] adj (needs, functions) 身体の shíntai no
♦adv (lift, carry) 体ごと karádagoto

body [ba:d'i:] n (ANAT: gen) 体 karáda, 身体 shíntai; (corpse) 死体 shitái; (object) 物体 buttái; (main part) 本体 hôntai; (of car) 車体 shatái, ボディー bódì; (fig: group) 団体 dańtai; (: organization) 組織 sóshìki; (quantity: of facts) 量 ryó; (of wine) こく kokú

body-building [ba:d'i:bil'diŋ] n ボディービル bodíbiru

bodyguard [ba:d'i:ga:rd] n (of statesman, celebrity) 護衛 goéi, ボディーガード bodígàdo

bodywork [ba:d'i:wə:rk] n (AUT) 車体 shatái

bog [ba:g] n (GEO) 沼沢地 shṓtakùchì
♦vt: *to get bogged down* (fig) 泥沼にはまり込む dorónuma ni hamárikomù

boggle [ba:g'əl] vi: *the mind boggles* 理解できない ríkài dekínai

bogus [bou'gəs] adj (claim, workman etc) 偽の nisé no

boil [boil] vt (water) 沸かす wakásu; (eggs, potatoes etc) ゆでる yudérù
♦vi (liquid) 沸く wakú; (fig: with anger) かんかんに怒る kańkan ni okórù; (: with heat) うだるような暑さになる udárù yō na atsùsa ni narú
♦n (MED) 出来物 dekímonò
to come to a (US)/the (BRIT) boil 沸き始める wakíhajimerù

boil down to vt fus (fig) 要するに...である yō surú ni ...de arù

boiled egg [boild-] n ゆで卵 yudétamà-go

boiled potatoes npl ゆでジャガイモ yu-déjagàimo

boiler [boi'lə:r] n (device) ボイラー bôirā

boiler suit (BRIT) n つなぎの作業着 tsunági no sagyōgi

boiling point [boi'liŋ-] n (of liquid) 沸騰点 fúttōten

boil over vi (kettle, milk) 吹こぼれる fu-kíkoborerù

boisterous [bois'tə:rəs] adj (noisy, excitable: person, crowd) 騒々しい sōzōshìì

bold [bould] adj (brave) 大胆な daítan na; (pej: cheeky) ずうずうしい zūzūshìì; (pattern) 際立った kiwádattà; (line) 太い futôì; (color) 派手な hadé na

Bolivia [bouliv'i:ə] n ボリビア boríbìa

bollard [ba:l'ə:rd] (BRIT) n (AUT) 標識柱 hyṓshikichū ◇安全地帯などを示す ańzenchítai nadò wo shimésù

bolster [boul'stə:r] n (pillow) 長まくら nagámakùra

bolster up vt (case) 支持する shíjì suru

bolt [boult] n (lock) ラッチ rátchì; (with nut) ボルト borúto
♦adv: *bolt upright* 背筋を伸ばして sesúji wo nobàshite
♦vt (door) ...のラッチを掛ける ...no ratchì wo kakérù; (also: **bolt together**) ボルトで止める borúto de tomérù; (food) 丸のみする marúnomi suru
♦vi (run away: horse) 逃出す nigédasu

bomb [ba:m] n (device) 爆弾 bakúdan
♦vt 爆撃する bakúgeki suru

bombard [ba:m'ba:rd] vt (MIL: with big guns etc) 砲撃する hốgeki suru; (: from planes) 爆撃する bakúgeki suru; (*fig*: with questions) ...に浴びせる ...ni abíseru

bombardment [bɑːmbɑːrdˈmənt] *n*: **bombardment from guns** 砲撃 hṓgeki **bombardment from planes** 爆撃 bakúgeki

bombastic [bɑːmbæsˈtik] *adj* (person, language) もったい振った mottáibuttà

bomb disposal *n*: **bomb disposal unit** 爆弾処理班 bakúdanshorihàn

bomber [bɑːmˈəːr] *n* (AVIAT) 爆撃機 bakúgekikì

bombshell [bɑːmˈʃel] *n* (*fig*: revelation) 爆弾 bakúdan

bona fide [bouˈnəfaidˈ] *adj* (traveler etc) 本物の hofímono no

bond [bɑːnd] *n* (of affection, *also gen*: link) きずな kizúna; (binding promise) 約束 yakúsoku; (FINANCE) 証券 shŏken; (COMM): **in bond** (of goods) 保税倉庫で hozéisòko de

bondage [bɑːnˈdidʒ] *n* (slavery) 奴隷の身分 doréi no mìbun

bone [boun] *n* (ANAT, *gen*) 骨 honé
♦*vt* (meat, fish) 骨を抜く honé wò nukú

bone idle *adj* ぐうたらの gútara no

bonfire [bɑːnˈfaiəːr] *n* たき火 takíbi

bonnet [bɑːnˈit] *n* (hat: *also BRIT*: of car) ボンネット bofínettò

bonus [bouˈnəs] *n* (payment) ボーナス bŏnasu; (*fig*: additional benefit) おまけ o-máke

bony [bouˈniː] *adj* (MED: tissue) 骨のほね no; (arm, face) 骨振った honébattà; (meat, fish) 骨の多い honé no ŏi

boo [buː] *excl* (to surprise someone) わっ wá; (to show dislike) ぶー bū
♦*vt* 野次る yajírù

booby trap [buːˈbiː-] *n* (MIL) 仕掛爆弾 shikákebakùdan

book [buk] *n* (novel etc) 本 hófí; (of stamps, tickets) 1つづり hitótsuzùri
♦*vt* (ticket, seat, room) 予約する yoyáku suru; (subj: traffic warden, policeman) ...に違反切符を書く ...ni ihánkippù wo kakú; (: referee) ...に勧告を与える ...ni kañkoku wò atáeru

bookcase [bukˈkeis] *n* 本棚 hófídana

booking office [bukˈiŋ-] (*BRIT*) *n* (RAIL, THEATER) 切符売り場 kippú urìba

book-keeping [bukkiːˈpiŋ] *n* 簿記 bókì

booklet [bukˈlit] *n* 小冊子 shŏsasshì, パンフレット páfífurettó

bookmaker [bukˈmeikəːr] *n* 馬券屋 bakén-ya

books [buks] *npl* (COMM: accounts) 帳簿 chŏbo

bookseller [bukˈseləːr] *n* 本屋 hófí-ya

bookshop [bukˈʃɑːp] *n* = **bookstore**

bookstore [bukˈstɔːr] *n* 本屋 hófí-ya, 書店 shotén

boom [buːm] *n* (noise) とどろき todóroki; (in prices, population etc) ブーム bŭmu
♦*vi* (guns, thunder) とどろく todórokù; (voice) とどろく様で言う todórokù yŏ na koè de iú; (business) 繁盛する hafíjō suru

boomerang [buːˈməːræŋ] *n* ブーメラン bŭmeran

boon [buːn] *n* (blessing, benefit) 有難い物 arígataì monó

boost [buːst] *n* (to confidence, sales etc) 増す事 masú kotó
♦*vt* (confidence, sales etc) 増す masú; (economy) 促進する sokúshin suru

booster [buːsˈtəːr] *n* (MED) ブースター bŭsutā

boot [buːt] *n* (knee-length) 長靴 nagágutsu, ブーツ bŭtsu; (*also*: **hiking/climbing boots**) 登山靴 tozáfígutsu; (*also*: **soccer boots**) サッカーシューズ sakkáshùzu; (*BRIT*: of car) トランク torâfíku
♦*vt* (COMPUT) 起動する kidŏ suru
... to boot (in addition) おまけに o-máke ni

booth [buːθ] *n* (at fair) 屋台 yátài; (telephone booth, voting booth) ボックス bokkùsu

booty [buːˈtiː] *n* 戦利品 señrihin

booze [buːz] (*inf*) *n* 酒 sakê

border [bɔːrˈdəːr] *n* (of a country) 国境 kokkyŏ; (*also*: **flower border**) ボーダー花壇 bŏdakadàn; (band, edge: on cloth etc) へり herí
♦*vt* (road; subject: trees etc) ...に沿って

立っている ...ni sottě tattě irú; (another country: *also*: **border on**) ...に隣接する ...ni rińsetsu suru

borderline [bɔːr'dəːrlain] *n* (*fig*): **on the borderline** 際どいところで kiwádoì tokóro de, ボーダーラインすれすれで bŏdāraìn surésure de

borderline case *n* 決めにくいケース kiménikuì kêsu

border on *vt fus* (*fig*: insanity, brutality) ...に近い ...ni chikáì

Borders [bɔːr'dəːrz] *n*: **the Borders** ボーダーズ州 bŏdāzùshū ◊イングランドに隣接するスコットランド南部の1州 ińgurando ni rińsetsu surú sukóttòrando nańbu no isshū

bore [bɔːr] *pt of* **bear**
◆*vt* (hole) ...に穴を開ける ...ni aná wo akéru; (oil well, tunnel) 掘る hórù; (person) 退屈させる taíkutsu saséru
◆*n* (person) 詰まらない話で退屈させる人 tsumáranaì hanáshi de taíkutsu saséru hitó; (of gun) 口径 kŏkei
to be bored 退屈する taíkutsu suru

boredom [bɔːr'dəm] *n* (condition) 退屈 taíkutsu; (boring quality) 詰まらなさ tsumáranasà

boring [bɔːr'iŋ] *adj* (tedious, unimaginative) 退屈な taíkutsu na

born [bɔːrn] *adj*: **to be born** 生れる umáreru
I was born in 1960 私は1960年に生れました watákushi wa sénkyúhyàkurokújūnen ni umáremashìta

borne [bɔːrn] *pp of* **bear**

borough [bʌr'ə] *n* (POL) 区 ku

borrow [bɑːr'ou] *vt*: **to borrow something** (from someone) ...を借りる ...wo karíru

bosom [buz'əm] *n* (ANAT) 胸 muné

bosom friend *n* 親友 shiń-yū

boss [bɔːs] *n* (employer) 雇い主 yatóìnushi; (supervisor, superior) 上司 jŏshi, 親方 oyákata, ボス bósù
◆*vt* (*also*: **boss around**, **boss about**) こき使う kokítsukaù

bossy [bɔːs'iː] *adj* (overbearing) 威張り散らす ibárichirasù

bosun [bou'sən] *n* (NAUT) = **boatswain**

botany [bɑːt'əniː] *n* 植物学 shokúbutsugàku

botch [bɑːtʃ] *vt* (bungle: *also*: **botch up**) 不手際で...をしくじる futégìwa de ...wo shikújirù

both [bouθ] *adj* 両方の ryóhŏ no
◆*pron* (things, people) 両方 ryóhŏ
◆*adv*: **both A and B** AもBも A mo B mo
both of us went, we both went 私たち2人共行きました watákushitàchi futáritomo ikímashìta

bother [bɑːð'əːr] *vt* (worry) 心配させる shińpai saséru; (disturb) ...に迷惑を掛ける ...ni meíwaku wo kakéru
◆*vi* (*also*: **bother oneself**) ...に気付かう ...ni kizúkaù
◆*n* (trouble) 迷惑 meíwaku; (nuisance) いやな事 iyá na kotó
to bother doing わざわざ...する wázàwaza ...surú

bottle [bɑːt'əl] *n* (container: for milk, wine, perfume etc) 瓶 bíñ; (of wine, whiskey etc) ボトル botóru; (amount contained) 瓶一杯 bíñ ippaí; (baby's) 乳瓶 hō-nyūbin
◆*vt* (beer, wine) 瓶に詰める bíñ ni tsumérù

bottleneck [bɑːt'əlnek] *n* (AUT: *also fig*: of supply) ネック nékkù

bottle-opener [bɑːt'əloupənəːr] *n* 栓抜き seńnukì

bottle up *vt* (emotion) 抑える osáerù

bottom [bɑːt'əm] *n* (of container, sea etc) 底 sokó; (buttocks) しり shirí; (of page, list) 一番下の所 ichíban shitá no tokóro; (of class) びり bíri
◆*adj* (lower: part) 下の方の shitá no hŏ no; (last: rung, position) 一番下の ichíban shitá no

bottomless [bɑːt'əmlis] *adj* (funds, store) 際限のない saígeñ no naì

bough [bau] *n* 枝 edá

bought [bɔːt] *pt, pp of* **buy**

boulder [boul'dəːr] *n* 大きな丸石 ŏkinà marúishi

bounce [bauns] *vi* (ball) 跳ね返る hané-

kaèru; (check) 不渡りになる fuwátàri ni
narù
♦vt (ball) 跳ねさせる hanésaserù
♦n (rebound) 跳ね返る事 hanékaèru kotó

bouncer [baun'sə:r] (inf) n (at dance,
club) 用心棒 yójìnbō

bound [baund] pt, pp of **bind**
♦n (leap) 一飛び hitótòbi; (gen pl: limit)
限界 geńkai
♦vi (leap) 跳ぶ tobù
♦vt (border) ...の境界になる ...no kyókai
ni narù
♦adj: **bound by** (law, regulation) ...に拘
束されている ...ni kósoku saréte irù
to be bound to do something (obliged)
やむを得ず...しなければならない yamú
wo ezù ...shinákereba naranaì; (likely)
必ず...するだろう kanárazu ...surú darò
bound for (NAUT, AUT, RAIL) ...行き
の ...yukí no
out of bounds (fig: place) 立入禁止で
tachíirikinshi de

boundary [baun'də:ri:] n (border, limit)
境界 kyókai

boundless [baund'lis] adj (energy etc) 果
てし無い hatéshinaì

bouquet [bu:kei'] n (of flowers) 花束 ha-
nátàba, ブーケ bùke

bourgeois [bur'ʒwa:] adj ブルジョア根性
の burújoakoñjō no

bout [baut] n (of malaria etc) 発作 hossá;
(of activity) 発作的にする事 hossáteki ni
suru kotó; (BOXING etc) 試合 shiái

boutique [bu:ti:k'] n ブティック butíkku

bow[1] [bou] n (knot) チョウ結び chómusù-
bi; (weapon, MUS) 弓 yumí

bow[2] [bau] n (of the head) 会釈 éshàku;
(of the head and body) お辞儀 ojígi;
(NAUT: also: **bows**) 船首 séñshu, へ先
hesáki
♦vi (with head) 会釈する éshàku suru;
(with head and body) お辞儀する ojígi
suru; (yield): **to bow to/before** (reason,
pressure) ...に屈服する ...ni kuppúku suru

bowels [bau'əlz] npl (ANAT) 腸 chó; (of
the earth etc) 深い所 fukáì tokóro

bowl [boul] n (container) 鉢 hachí, ボー
ル bóru; (contents) ボール一杯 bóru ippá-
i; (ball) 木球 mokkyū, ボール bóru
♦vi (CRICKET) 投球する tókyū suru

bow-legged [bou'legid] adj がにまたの
ganímata no

bowler [bou'lə:r] n (CRICKET) 投手 tó-
shu, ボウラー bóra; (BRIT: also: **bowler
hat**) 山高帽 yamátakabō

bowling [bou'liŋ] n (game) ボーリング
bóringu

bowling alley n (building) ボーリング
場 bóringujō; (track) レーン rèn

bowling green n ローンボーリング場
róñbōringujō

bowls [boulz] n (game) ローンボーリング
róñbōringu

bow tie n チョウネクタイ chónekùtai

box [ba:ks] n (gen) 箱 hakó; (also: **cardboard box**) 段ボール箱 dañbōrubàko;
(THEATER) ボックス bókkùsu
♦vt (put in a box) 箱に詰める hakó ni
tsumérù
♦vi (SPORT) ボクシングする bókùshingu suru

boxer [ba:k'sə:r] n (person) ボクシング選
手 bokúshing señshu, ボクサー bókùsā

boxing [ba:k'siŋ] n (SPORT) ボクシング
bókùshingu

Boxing Day (BRIT) n ボクシングデー
bokúshingudě

boxing gloves npl ボクシンググローブ
bokúshingugurōbu

boxing ring n リング riñgu

box office n 切符売り場 kippú uríba

boxroom [ba:ks'ru:m] (BRIT) n 納戸 nañ-
do

boy [bɔi] n (young) 少年 shóneñ, 男の子 o-
tóko no kò; (older) 青年 seíneñ; (son) 息
子 musúko

boycott [bɔi'ka:t] n ボイコット boíkottò
♦vt (person, product, place etc) ボイコッ
トする boíkottò suru

boyfriend [bɔi'frend] n 男友達 otókoto-
mòdachi, ボーイフレンド bóifureñdo

boyish [bɔi'iʃ] adj (man) 若々しい waká-
wakashiì; (looks, smile, woman) 少年の
様な shóneñ no yō na

B.R. [bi:a:r'] n abbr = **British Rail**

bra [brɑ:] n ブラジャー burájã

brace [breis] n (on teeth) 固定器 koteîki, ブレース burêsu; (tool) 曲り柄ドリル magáriedorĭru
♦vt (knees, shoulders) ...に力を入れる ...ni chikára wo iréru
to brace oneself (for weight) 構えて待つ kamáete matsù; (for shock) 心を静めて待つ kokóro wo shizúmete matsu

bracelet [breis'lit] n 腕輪 udéwa, ブレスレット burésùretto

braces [brei'siz] (BRIT) npl ズボンつり zubóñtsuri, サスペンダー sasúpeñdà

bracing [brei'siŋ] adj (air, breeze) さわやかな sawáyàka na

bracken [bræk'ən] n ワラビ warábi

bracket [bræk'it] n (TECH) 腕 金 udégane; (group) グループ gúrŭpu; (range) 層 sō; (also: **brace bracket**) 中括弧 chúkakkò, ブレース búrèsu; (also: **round bracket**) 小括弧 shókakkò, 丸括弧 marúkakkò, パーレン páren; (also: **square bracket**) かぎ括弧 kagíkakkò
♦vt (word, phrase) ...に括弧を付ける ...ni kakkò wo tsúkerù

brag [bræg] vi 自慢する jimán suru

braid [breid] n (trimming) モール mōru; (of hair) お下げ o-ságe

Braille [breil] n 点字 teñji

brain [brein] n (ANAT) 脳 nō; (fig) 頭脳 zúnò

brainchild [brein'tʃaild] n (project) 発案 hatsúan; (invention) 発明 hatsúmei

brains [breinz] npl (CULIN) 脳みそ nômisò; (intelligence) 頭脳 zúnò

brainwash [brein'wɑ:ʃ] vt 洗脳する señnō suru

brainwave [brein'weiv] n 脳波 nòha

brainy [brei'ni:] adj (child) 頭の良い atáma no yoÍ

braise [breiz] vt (CULIN) いためてから煮込む itámète kará nikómù

brake [breik] n (AUT) 制動装置 seídōsòchi, ブレーキ burèki; (fig) 歯止め hadóme
♦vi ブレーキを掛ける burèki wo kakérù

brake fluid n ブレーキ液 burékièki

brake light n ブレーキライト burêkiraìto

bramble [bræm'bəl] n (bush) イバラ ibára

bran [bræn] n ふすま fusúma

branch [bræntʃ] n (of tree) 枝 edá; (COMM) 支店 shitén

branch out vi (fig): ***to branch out into*** ...に手を広げる ...ni te wo hirógeru

brand [brænd] n (trademark: also: **brand name**) 銘柄 meígara, ブランド burándo; (fig: type) 種類 shúrùi
♦vt (cattle) 焼印 yakíin

brandish [bræn'diʃ] vt (weapon) 振り回す furímawasù

brand-new [brænd'nu:'] adj 真新しい maátarashiÍ

brandy [bræn'di:] n ブランデー burándē

brash [bræʃ] adj (forward, cheeky) ずうずうしい zúzushiÍ

brass [bræs] n (metal) 真ちゅう shiñchū
the brass (MUS) 金管楽器 kiñkangàkki

brass band n 吹奏楽団 suísōgakùdan, ブラスバンド burásubañdo

brassiere [brəzi:r'] n ブラジャー burájã

brat [bræt] (pej) n (child) がき gakí

bravado [brəvɑ:'dou] n 空威張り karáibàri

brave [breiv] adj (attempt, smile, action) 勇敢な yūkan na
♦vt (face up to) ...に立ち向う ...ni tachímukaù

bravery [brei'vəri:] n 勇気 yūki

bravo [brɑ:'vou] excl ブラボー burabò

brawl [brɔ:l] n (in pub, street) けんか keñka

brawny [brɔ:'ni:] adj (arms etc) たくましい takúmashiÍ

bray [brei] vi (donkey) 鳴く nakú

brazen [brei'zən] adj (woman) ずうずうしい zúzushiÍ; (lie, accusation) 厚かましい atsúkamashiÍ
♦vt: ***to brazen it out*** 最後までしらばくれる saígo madé shirábakurerù

brazier [brei'ʒə:r] n (on building site etc) 野外用簡易暖炉 yagáiyō kañ-i dañro

Brazil [brəzil'] n ブラジル burájiru

Brazilian [brəzil'i:ən] adj ブラジルの burájiru no

♦*n* ブラジル人 burájirujìn

breach [briːtʃ] *vt* (defence, wall) 突破する toppá suru

♦*n* (gap) 突破口 toppákò; (breaking):
breach of contract 契約不履行 keíyakufurikò

breach of the peace 治安妨害 chiánbògai

bread [bred] *n* (food) パン pán

bread and butter *n* バターを塗ったパン bátà wo nuttá pán; (*fig*: source of income) 金づる kanézuru

breadbox [bred'bɑːks] (*BRIT* **breadbin**) *n* パン入れ pań-ìre

breadcrumbs [bred'krʌmz] *npl* (*gen*) パンくず pańkuzù; (CULIN) パン粉 pańko

breadline [bred'lain] *n*: *on the breadline* 貧しい mazúshiì

breadth [bredθ] *n* (of cloth etc) 幅 habá; (*fig*: of knowledge, subject) 広さ híròsa

breadwinner [bred'winəːr] *n* (in family) 稼ぎ手 kaségìte

break [breik] (*pt* **broke**, *pp* **broken**) *vt* (cup, glass) 割る warú; (stick, leg, arm) 折る orù; (machine etc) 壊す kowású; (promise, law, record) 破る yabúrù; (journey) 中断する chúdan suru

♦*vi* (crockery) 割れる waréru; (stick, arm, leg) 折れる orérù; (machine etc) 壊れる kowárerù; (storm) 起る okórù; (weather) 変る kawáru; (story, news) 報道される hódò saréru; (dawn): *dawn breaks* 夜が明ける yo ga akéru

♦*n* (gap) 途切れた所 togírèta tokóro; (fracture: *gen*) 破損 hasón; (: of limb) 骨折 kossétsu; (pause for rest) 休憩 kyúkei; (at school) 休み時間 yasúmijikàn; (chance) チャンス cháñsu

to break the news to someone ...に知らせる ...ni shiráseru

to break even (COMM) 収支がとんとんになる shúshi ga tofiton ni narù

to break free/loose (person, animal) 逃出す nigédasu

to break open (door etc) ...を壊して開ける ...wo kowáshite akéru

breakage [brei'kidʒ] *n* (act of breaking)

壊す事 kowású kotó; (object broken) 損傷 sofishō

break down *vt* (figures, data) 分析する bufiseki suru

♦*vi* (machine, car) 故障する koshō suru; (person) 取乱す torímidasù; (talks) 物別れになる monówakàre ni narù

breakdown [breik'daun] *n* (AUT) 故障 koshō; (in communications) 中断 chúdan; (of marriage) 破たん hatán; (MED: *also*: **nervous breakdown**) 神経衰弱 shifikeisuìjaku; (of statistics) 分析 bufiseki

breakdown van (*BRIT*) *n* レッカー車 rékkàsha

breaker [brei'kəːr] *n* (wave) 白波 shiránami

breakfast [brek'fəst] *n* 朝ご飯 asá gohàn, 朝食 chōshoku

break in *vt* (horse etc) 慣らす narásù

♦*vi* (burglar) 押入る oshíirù; (interrupt) 割込む waríkomù

break-in [breik'in] *n* 押入り oshíiri

breaking and entering [breik'iŋ ænd en'təːriŋ] *n* (LAW) 不法侵入 fuhō-shiñ-nyū

break into *vt fus* (house) ...に押入る ...ni oshíirù

break off *vi* (branch) 折れる orérù; (speaker) 話を中断する hanáshi wo chúdan suru

break out *vi* (begin: war) ぼっ発する boppátsu suru; (: fight) 始まる hajímaru; (escape: prisoner) 脱出する dasshútsu suru

to break out in spots/a rash にきび〔湿しん〕になる níkibi[shisshín] ni narù

breakthrough [breik'θruː] *n* (*fig*: in technology etc) 躍進 yakúshin

break up *vi* (ship) 分解する buñkai suru; (crowd, meeting) 解散する kaísan suru; (marriage) 離婚に終る rikón ni owáru; (SCOL) 終る owáru

♦*vt* (rocks, biscuit etc) 割る warú; (fight etc) やめさせる yamésaseru

breakwater [breik'wɔːtəːr] *n* 防波堤 bóhatei

breast [brest] *n* (of woman) 乳房 chíbùsa; (chest) 胸 muné; (of meat) 胸肉 munénīkù

breast-feed [brest'fi:d] (*pt*, *pp* **breast-fed**) *vt* ...に母乳を飲ませる ...ni bonyū wo nomáserù

♦*vi* 子供に母乳を飲ませる kodómo ni bonyū wo nomáserù

breaststroke [brest'strouk] *n* 平泳ぎ hiráoyògi

breath [breθ] *n* 息 íkì

out of breath 息を切らせて íkì wo kirásete

Breathalyser [breθ'əlaizə:r] ® *n* 酒気検査器 shukíkensakì

breathe [bri:ð] *vt* 呼吸する kokyū suru

♦*vi* 呼吸する kokyū suru

breathe in *vt* 吸込む suíkomù

♦*vi* 息を吸込む íkì wo suíkomù

breathe out *vt* 吐出す hakídasu

♦*vi* 息を吐く íkì wo hakù

breather [bri:'ðə:r] *n* (break) 休憩 kyūkei

breathing [bri:'ðiŋ] *n* 呼吸 kokyū

breathless [breθ'lis] *adj* (from exertion) 息を切らせている íkì wo kirásète irú; (MED) 呼吸困難の kokyūkonnan no

breathtaking [breθ'teikiŋ] *adj* (speed) 息が止る様な íkì ga tomáru yō na; (view) 息を飲むような íkì wo nomù yō na

bred [bred] *pt*, *pp* of **breed**

breed [bri:d] (*pt*, *pp* **bred**) *vt* (animals) 繁殖させる hańshoku saséru; (plants) 栽培する saíbai suru

♦*vi* (ZOOL) 繁殖する hańshoku suru

♦*n* (ZOOL) 品種 hińshu; (type, class) 種類 shúrùi

breeding [bri:'diŋ] *n* (upbringing) 育ち sodáchi

breeze [bri:z] *n* そよ風 soyókàze

breezy [bri:'zi:] *adj* (manner, tone) 快活な kaíkatsu na; (weather) 風の多い kazé no ōi

brevity [brev'iti:] *n* (shortness, conciseness) 簡潔さ kańketsusa

brew [bru:] *vt* (tea) 入れる iréru; (beer) 醸造する jōzō suru

♦*vi* (storm) 起ろうとしている okórō to shité irù; (fig: trouble, a crisis) 迫ってい

る semátte irù

brewery [bru:'ə:ri:] *n* 醸造所 jōzōshò

bribe [braib] *n* 賄ろ waíro

♦*vt* (person, witness) 買収する baíshū suru

bribery [brai'bə:ri:] *n* (with money, favors) 贈賄 zōwai

bric-a-brac [brik'əbræk] *n* 置物類 okímonòrùi

brick [brik] *n* (for building) れんが réñga

bricklayer [brik'leiə:r] *n* れんが職人 reñgashokùnin

bridal [braid'əl] *adj* (gown) 花嫁の hanáyòme no; (suite) 新婚者の shińkoñsha no

bride [braid] *n* 花嫁 hanáyòme, 新婦 shiñpu

bridegroom [braid'gru:m] *n* 花婿 hanámùko, 新郎 shíñrō

bridesmaid [braidz'meid] *n* 新婦付き添いの女性 shíñputsukísoi no joséi

bridge [bridʒ] *n* (TECH, ARCHIT) 橋 hashî; (NAUT) 船橋 seńkyō, ブリッジ burijjî; (CARDS, DENTISTRY) ブリッジ burîjjì

♦*vt* (*fig*: gap, gulf) 乗越える noríkoerù

bridge of the nose 鼻柱 hanábashira

bridle [braid'əl] *n* くつわ kutsúwa

bridle path *n* 乗馬用の道 jōbayō no michí

brief [bri:f] *adj* (period of time, description, speech) 短い mijíkaì

♦*n* (LAW) 事件摘要書 jikéntekiyōsho; (*gen*: task) 任務 niñmu

♦*vt* (inform) ...に指示を与える ...ni shijî wo atáeru

briefcase [bri:f'keis] *n* かばん kabán, ブリーフケース burīfukèsu

briefing [bri:'fiŋ] *n* (*gen*, PRESS) 説明 setsúmei

briefly [bri:f'li:] *adv* (smile, glance) ちらっと chiráttò; (explain, say) 短く mijíkakù

briefs [bri:fs] *npl* (for men) パンツ pańtsu, ブリーフ burīfu; (for women) パンティー pañtī, ショーツ shōtsu

brigade [brigeid'] *n* (MIL) 旅団 ryodán

brigadier [brigədi'ə:r] *n* (MIL) 准将 juñshō

bright [brait] *adj* (*gen*) 明るい akárui; (person, idea: clever) 利口な rikṓ na; (person: lively) 明朗な meírō na

brighten [brait'ən] (*also*: **brighten up**) *vt* (room) 明るくする akáruku suru; (event) 楽しくする tanóshìkù suru
♦*vi* 明るくなる akáruku narù

brilliance [bril'jəns] *n* (of light) 明るさ akárusa; (of talent, skill) 素晴らしさ subárashisà

brilliant [bril'jənt] *adj* (person, idea) 天才的な teñsaiteki na; (smile, career) 輝かしい kagáyakashìi; (sunshine, light) 輝く kagáyakù; (*BRIT*: *inf*: holiday etc) 素晴らしい subárashìi

brim [brim] *n* (of cup etc) 縁 fuchí; (of hat) つば tsubá

brine [brain] *n* (CULIN) 塩水 shiómizu

bring [briŋ] (*pt*, *pp* **brought**) *vt* (thing) 持って来る motté kurù; (person) 連れて来る tsuréte kurù; (*fig*: satisfaction) もたらす motárasù; (trouble) 起す okósù

bring about *vt* (cause) 起こす okósù

bring back *vt* (restore: hanging etc) 復帰させる fukkí saséru; (return: thing/person) 持って〔連れて〕帰る motté(tsuréte)kaèrù

bring down *vt* (government) 倒す taósù; (MIL: plane) 撃墜する gekítsui suru; (price) 下げる sagérù

bring forward *vt* (meeting) 繰り上げる kuríagerù; (proposal) 提案する teían suru

bring off *vt* (task, plan) ...に成功する ...ni seíkō suru

bring out *vt* (gun) 取出す torídasu; (meaning) 明らかにする akíraka ni suru; (publish, produce: book) 出版する shuppán suru; (: album) 発表する happyṓ suru

bring round *vt* (unconscious person) 正気付かせる shṓkizukaserù

bring up *vt* (carry up) 上に持って来る〔行く〕ué ni motté kurù(ikú); (educate: person) 育てる sodáterù; (question, subject) 持出す mochídasù; (vomit: food) 吐く hakú

brink [briŋk] *n* (of disaster, war etc) 瀬戸際 setógiwa

brisk [brisk] *adj* (tone, person) きびきびした kíbìkibi shitá; (pace) 早い hayáî; (trade) 盛んな sakán na

bristle [bris'əl] *n* (animal hair, hair of beard) 剛毛 gōmō; (of brush) 毛 ke
♦*vi* (in anger) 怒る okórù

Britain [brit'ən] *n* (*also*: **Great Britain**) 英国 eíkoku, イギリス igírisu ◇イングランド, スコットランド, ウェールズを含む iñgurañdo, sukóttorañdo, uéruzu wo fukúmù

British [brit'iʃ] *adj* 英国の eíkoku no, イギリスの igírisu no
♦*npl*: **the British** 英国人 eíkokujìn, イギリス人 igírisujìn

British Isles *npl*: **the British Isles** イギリス諸島 igírisushotṓ

British Rail *n* 英国国有鉄道 eíkoku kokúyū tetsùdō

Briton [brit'ən] *n* 英国人 eíkokujìn, イギリス人 igírisujìn

brittle [brit'əl] *adj* (fragile: glass etc) 割れやすい waréyasuî; (: bones etc) もろい morṓî

broach [broutʃ] *vt* (subject) 持出す mochídasu

broad [brɔːd] *adj* (street, shoulders, smile, range) 広い hiróî; (general: outlines, distinction etc) 大まかな ṓmakà na; (accent) 強い tsuyóî
in broad daylight 真っ昼間に mappíruma ni

broadcast [brɔːd'kæst] *n* (TV, RADIO) 放送 hṓsō
♦*vb* (*pt*, *pp* **broadcast**)
♦*vt* (TV, RADIO) 放送する hṓsō suru; (TV) 放映する hóei suru
♦*vi* (TV, RADIO) 放送する hṓsō suru

broaden [brɔːd'ən] *vt* (scope, appeal) 広くする híròku suru, 広げる hirógeru
♦*vi* (river) 広くなる híròku narú, 広がる hirógaru
to broaden one's mind 心を広くする kokóro wo hiróku suru

broadly [brɔːd'li:] *adv* (in general terms) 大まかに ṓmakà ni

broad-minded [brɔːd'main'did] *adj* 心の広い kokóro no hiróî

broccoli [brɑ:k'əli:] n (BOT, CULIN) ブロッコリー burókkòrī

brochure [brouʃur'] n (booklet) 小冊子 shōsasshî, パンフレット pánfuretto

broil [brɔil] vt (CULIN) じか火で焼く jikábi de yakú

broke [brouk] pt of **break**
♦adj (inf: person, company) 無一文になった muíchimon ni nattá

broken [brou'kən] pp of **break**
♦adj (window, cup etc) 割れた waréta; (machine: also: **broken down**) 壊れた kowáretà
a broken leg 脚の骨折 ashí no kossetsú
in broken English/Japanese 片言の英語〔日本語〕で katákoto no eígo(nihóngo)de

broken-hearted [brou'kənhɑːr'tid] adj 悲嘆に暮れた hitán ni kuréta

broker [brou'kər] n (COMM: in shares) 証券ブローカー shōken burôkā; (: insurance broker) 保険代理人 hokén dairinin

brolly [brɑːl'i:] (BRIT: inf) n 傘 kása

bronchitis [brɑːŋkai'tis] n 気管支炎 kikánshièn

bronze [brɑːnz] n (metal) 青銅 seídō, ブロンズ burônzu; (sculpture) 銅像 dôzō

brooch [broutʃ] n ブローチ burôchi

brood [bruːd] n (of birds) 一腹のひな hitôhàra no hiná
♦vi (person) くよくよする kuyôkuyo suru

brook [bruk] n 小川 ogáwa

broom [bruːm] n (for cleaning) ほうき hôki; (BOT) エニシダ eníshòda

broomstick [bruːm'stik] n ほうきの柄 hôki no e

Bros. abbr (= brothers) 兄弟 kyôdai

broth [brɔːθ] n (CULIN) スープ sûpu

brothel [brɑːθ'əl] n 売春宿 baíshun-yadò

brother [brʌð'əːr] n (also: **older brother**) 兄 anî, 兄さん nîisan; (also: **younger brother**) 弟 otôtô; (REL) 修道士 shûdōshi

brother-in-law [brʌð'əːrinlɔː] (pl **brothers-in-law**) n (older) 義理の兄 girî no anî; (younger) 義理の弟 girî no otôtô

brought [brɔːt] pt, pp of **bring**

brow [brau] n (forehead) 額 hitái; (rare: gen: eyebrow) まゆ mayù; (of hill) 頂上 chôjō

brown [braun] adj (color) 褐色の kasshôku no, 茶色の chaíro no; (tanned) 日焼けした hiyáke shitá
♦n (color) 褐色 kasshóku, 茶色 chaíro
♦vt (CULIN) ...に焼き目を付ける ...ni yakíme wo tsukérù

brown bread n 黒パン kurópan

brownie [brau'ni:] n (Brownie guide) ブラウニー burâûnī◇ガールスカウトの幼年団員 gárusukaùto no yônendan-in; (US: cake) チョコレートクッキーの一種 chokórētokukkî no isshù

brown paper n クラフト紙 kuráfutoshî

brown sugar n 赤砂糖 akásatô

browse [brauz] vi (through book) 拾い読みする hirôiyomi suru; (in shop) 商品を見て回る shôhin wo mitè mawáru

bruise [bruːz] n (on face etc) 打撲傷 dabôkushō, あざ azá
♦vt (person) ...に打撲傷を与える ...ni dabôkushō wo atáeru

brunch [brʌntʃ] n ブランチ burânchi

brunette [bruːnet'] n (woman) ブルネット burúnettò

brunt [brʌnt] n: *to bear the brunt of* (attack, criticism) ...の矢面に立つ ...no yaômòte ni tatsù

brush [brʌʃ] n (for cleaning, shaving etc) ブラシ burâshi; (for painting etc) 刷毛 haké; (artist's) 筆 fudé, 絵筆 efúde; (quarrel) 小競り合い kozerîai
♦vt (sweep etc) ...にブラシを掛ける ...ni búrashi wo kakérù; (clean: teeth etc) 磨く migáku; (groom) ブラシでとかす búrashi de tokásù; also: **brush against**: person, object) ...に触れる ...ni furéru

brush aside vt (emotion, criticism) 無視する mushî suru

brush up vt (subject, language) 復習する fukúshū suru

brushwood [brʌʃ'wud] n (sticks) しば shibá

brusque [brʌsk] adj (person, manner) 無愛想な buáîso na; (apology) ぶっきらぼうな bukkírabô na

Brussels [brʌs'əlz] n ブリュッセル buryússèru

Brussels sprout n メキャベツ mekyábètsu

brutal [bru:t'əl] adj (person, actions) 残忍な zañnin na; (honesty, frankness) 厳しい程の kibíshiì hodó no

brutality [bru:tæl'iti:] n 残忍さ zañninsa

brute [bru:t] n (person) 人でなし hitódenashi, けだもの kedámono; (animal) 獣 kemóno

♦adj: **by brute force** 暴力で bóryoku de

B.Sc. [bi:essi:'] abbr = **Bachelor of Science**

bubble [bʌb'əl] n (in liquid, soap) 泡 awá; (of soap etc) シャボン玉 shabóndama

♦vi (liquid) 沸く wakú; (: sparkle) 泡立つ awádatsù

bubble bath n 泡風呂 awáburo

bubble gum n 風船ガム fūsengamù

buck [bʌk] n (rabbit) 雄ウサギ osúusàgi; (deer) 雄ジカ ojíka; (US: inf: dollar) ドル dorù

♦vi (horse) 乗手を振り落そうとする noríte wo furíotosò to surù

to pass the buck (to someone) (...に) 責任をなすり付ける (...ni) sekínin wo nasúritsukerù

bucket [bʌk'it] n (pail) バケツ bakétsu; (contents) バケツ一杯 bakétsu ippái

buckle [bʌk'əl] n (on shoe, belt) バックル bakkúru

♦vt (shoe, belt) ...のバックルを締める ...no bakkúru wo shimérù

♦vi (wheel) ゆがむ yugámu; (bridge, support) 崩れる kuzúrerù

buck up vi (cheer up) 元気を出す géñki wo dasù

bud [bʌd] n (of tree, plant, flower) 芽 me

♦vi 芽を出す me wo dasù

Buddhism [bu:'dizəm] n (REL) 仏教 bukkyō

budding [bʌd'iŋ] adj (actor, entrepreneur) 有望な yūbō na

buddy [bʌd'i:] (US) n (friend) 相棒 aíbo

budge [bʌdʒ] vt (object) ちょっと動かす chóttò ugókasù; (fig: person) 譲歩させる

jóho saséru

♦vi (object, person) ちょっと動く chóttò ugókù; (fig: person) 譲歩する jóho suru

budgerigar [bʌdʒ'ə:ri:gɑ:r] n セキセイインコ sekíseiiñko

budget [bʌdʒ'it] n (person's, government's) 予算 yosán, 予算案 yosán-an

♦vi: **to budget for something** ...を予算案に入れる ...wo yosáñ-an ni iréru

I'm on a tight budget 台所が苦しい daídokoro ga kúrushiì

budgie [bʌdʒ'i:] n = **budgerigar**

buff [bʌf] adj (color: envelope) 薄茶色 usúchairo

♦n (inf: enthusiast) マニア mánia

buffalo [bʌf'əlou] (pl **buffalo** or **buffaloes**) n (BRIT) スイギュウ suígyū; (US: bison) バイソン báison

buffer [bʌf'ə:r] n (COMPUT) バッファ báffà; (RAIL) 緩衝機 kañshòki

buffet[1] [bufei'] (BRIT) n (in station) ビュッフェ byúffè; (food) 立食 risshóku

buffet[2] [bʌf'it] vt (subj: wind, sea) もみ揺さぶる momíyusaburù

buffet car (BRIT) n (RAIL) ビュッフェ車 byufféshà

bug [bʌg] n (esp US: insect) 虫 mushí; (COMPUT: of program) バグ bágù; (fig: germ) 風邪 kazé; (hidden microphone) 盗聴器 tóchòki

♦vt (inf: annoy) 怒らせる okóraserù; (room, telephone etc) ...に盗聴器を付ける ...ni tóchòki wo tsukérù

buggy [bʌg'i:] n (baby buggy) 乳母車 ubágurùma

bugle [bju:'gəl] n (MUS) らっぱ rappá

build [bild] n (of person) 体格 taíkaku

♦vb (pt, pp **built**)

♦vt (house etc) 建てる tatérù, 建築する keñchiku suru; (machine, cage etc) 作る tsukúrù

builder [bil'də:r] n (contractor) 建築業者 keñchikugyòsha

building [bil'diŋ] n (industry, construction) 建築業 keñchikugyò; (structure) 建物 tatémonò, ビル birù

building society (BRIT) n 住宅金融組合 jūtakukin-yūkumìai

build up vt (forces, production) 増やす fuyásù; (morale) 高める takámerù; (stocks) 蓄積する chikúseki suru

built [bilt] pt, pp of **build**
♦adj: **built-in** (oven, wardrobes etc) 作り付けの tsukúritsuke no

built-up area [bilt'ʌp-] n 市街化区域 shigáikakuìki

bulb [bʌlb] n (BOT) 球根 kyúkon; (ELEC) 電球 deñkyū

Bulgaria [bʌlge:r'i:ə] n ブルガリア burúgaria

Bulgarian [bʌlge:r'i:ən] adj ブルガリアの burúgaria no
♦n ブルガリア人 burúgariajìn

bulge [bʌldʒ] n (bump) 膨らみ fukúrami
♦vi (pocket, file, cheeks etc) 膨らむ fukúramu

bulk [bʌlk] n (mass: of thing) 巨大な姿 kyodái na sugàta; (: of person) 巨体 kyotái
in bulk (COMM) 大口で ŏguchi de
the bulk of (most of) ...の大半 ...no taíhan

bulky [bʌl'ki:] adj (parcel) かさばった kasábattà; (equipment) 大きくて扱いにくい ŏkikute atsúkainikuì

bull [bul] n (ZOOL) 雄牛 oúshi; (male elephant/whale) 雄 osú

bulldog [bul'dɔ:g] n ブルドッグ burúdoggù

bulldozer [bul'douzə:r] n ブルドーザー burúdōzà

bullet [bul'it] n 弾丸 dañgan

bulletin [bul'itən] n (TV etc: news update) 速報 sokúhō; (journal) 会報 kaíhō, 紀要 kiyŏ

bulletproof [bul'itpru:f] adj (glass, vest, car) 防弾の bŏdan no

bullfight [bul'fait] n 闘牛 tŏgyū

bullfighter [bul'faitə:r] n 闘牛士 tŏgyūshi

bullfighting [bul'faitiŋ] n 闘牛 tŏgyū

bullhorn [bul'hɔ:rn] n (US) n ハンドマイク hañdomaìku

bullion [bul'jən] n (gold, silver) 地金 jigáne

bullock [bul'ək] n 去勢した雄牛 kyoséi

shitá oúshi

bullring [bul'riŋ] n 闘牛場 tŏgyūjō

bull's-eye [bulz'ai] n (on a target) 的の中心 matŏ no chūshin

bully [bul'i:] n 弱い者いじめ yowáimonoijìme
♦vt いじめる ijímeru

bum [bʌm] (inf) n (backside) しり shirí; (esp US: tramp) ルンペン ruñpen; (: good-for-nothing) ろくでなし rokúdenashi

bumblebee [bʌm'bəlbi:] n クマンバチ kumáñbachi

bump [bʌmp] n (in car: minor accident) 衝突 shŏtotsu; (jolt) 衝撃 shŏgeki; (swelling: on head) こぶ kobú; (on road) 段差 dañsa
♦vt (strike) ...にぶつかる ...ni butsúkaru

bumper [bʌm'pə:r] n (AUT) バンパー bañpā
♦adj: **bumper crop/harvest** 豊作 hŏsaku

bumper cars npl (in amusement park) バンパーカー bañpākā

bump into vt fus (strike: obstacle) ...にぶつかる ...ni butsúkaru; (inf: meet: person) ...に出くわす ...ni dekúwasu

bumptious [bʌmp'ʃəs] adj (person) うぬぼれた unúboreta

bumpy [bʌm'pi:] adj (road) 凸凹な dekóboko na

bun [bʌn] n (CULIN) ロールパン rŏrupan, パン bán; (of hair) まげ magé, シニヨン shíníyon

bunch [bʌntʃ] n (of flowers, keys) 束 tábà; (of bananas) 房 fusá; (of people) グループ gúrupu

bunches [bʌntʃ'iz] npl (in hair) 左右のポニーテール sáyù no poníteru

bundle [bʌn'dəl] n (parcel: of clothes, samples etc) 包み tsutsúmi; (of sticks, papers) 束 tabá
♦vt (also: **bundle up**) 厚着させる atsúgi sasèru; (put): **to bundle something/someone into** ...にほうり[押]込む ...ni hŏri[oshí]komu

bungalow [bʌŋ'gəlou] n バンガロー bañgarō

bungle [bʌŋ'gəl] vt (job, assassination) ...にしくじる ...ni shikújirù

bunion [bʌn'jən] n (MED) けん膜りゅう kefimakuryū, バニオン bánion

bunk [bʌŋk] n (bed) 作り付けベッド tsukúritsukebeddò

bunk beds npl 二段ベッド nidánbeddò

bunker [bʌŋ'kə:r] n (also: **coal bunker**) 石炭庫 sekítaǹko; (MIL) えんぺいごう eñpeìgō; (GOLF) バンカー bañkā

bunny [bʌn'i:] n (also: **bunny rabbit**) ウサちゃん usáchan

bunting [bʌn'tiŋ] n (flags) 飾り小旗 kazárikobàta

buoy [bu:'i:] n (NAUT) ブイ buì

buoyant [bɔi'ənt] adj (ship) 浮力のある fúryòku no arù; (economy, market) 活気のある kakkí no arù; (fig: person, nature) 朗らかな hogáràka na

buoy up vt (fig) 元気づける geñkizukerù

burden [bə:r'dən] n (responsibility, worry) 負担 fután; (load) 荷物 nímòtsu
♦vt (trouble): **to burden someone with** (oppress) ...を打明けて...に心配を掛ける ...wo uchíakete ...ni shiñpai wo kakérù

bureau [bjur'ou] (pl **bureaus** or **bureaus**) n (BRIT: writing desk) 書き物机 kakímonozukùe ◇ふたが書く面になる机を指す futá ga kakù meň ni narù tsukúe wo sasù; (US: chest of drawers) 整理だんす seíridànsu; (office: government, travel, information) 局 kyókù, 課 ka

bureaucracy [bjura:k'rəsi:] n (POL, COMM) 官僚制 kañryōsei

bureaucrat [bjur'əkræt] n (administrator) 官僚 kañryō; (pej: pen-pusher) 小役人 koyákùnin

bureaux [bjur'ouz] npl of **bureau**

burglar [bə:r'glə:r] n 押込み強盗 oshíkomigòtō

burglar alarm n 盗難警報機 tōnankeihòki

burglary [bə:r'glə:ri:] n (crime) 住居侵入罪 jūkyoshiñnyūzai

burial [be:r'i:əl] n 埋葬 maísō

burly [bə:r'li:] adj (figure, workman etc) ごつい gotsúī

Burma [bə:rm'ə] n ビルマ bírùma

burn [bə:rn] (pt, pp **burned** or **burnt**) vt (papers, fuel etc) 燃やす moyásu; (toast, food etc) 焦がす kogású; (house etc: arson) ...に放火する ...ni hōka suru
♦vi (house, wood etc) 燃える moéru; (cakes etc) 焦げる kogérù; (sting) ひりひりする hírìhiri suru
♦n やけど yakédo

burn down vt 全焼させる zeńshō saséru

burner [bə:r'nə:r] n (on cooker, heater) 火口 hígùchi, バーナー bầnā

burning [bə:r'niŋ] adj (house etc) 燃えている moéte irù; (sand) 焼ける様に熱い yakéru yỗ ni atsuì; (desert) しゃく熱の shakúnetsu no; (ambition) 熱烈な netsúretsu na

burnt [bə:rnt] pt, pp of **burn**

burrow [bə:r'ou] n (of rabbit etc) 巣穴 suána
♦vi (dig) 掘る hórù; (rummage) あさる asáru

bursary [bə:r'sə:ri:] (BRIT) n (SCOL) 奨学金 shōgakukin

burst [bə:rst] (pt, pp **burst**) vt (bag, balloon, pipe etc) 破裂させる harétsu saséru; (subj: river: banks etc) 決壊させる kekkái saséru
♦vi (pipe, tire) 破裂する harétsu suru
♦n (also: **burst pipe**) 破裂した水道管 harétsu shita suídōkan

a burst of energy/speed/enthusiasm 突発的なエネルギー〔スピード, 熱心さ〕toppátsuteki na enérugī〔supído, nesshíñsa〕

a burst of gunfire 連射 reñsha

to burst into flames 急に燃え出す kyū ni moédasu

to burst into tears 急に泣き出す kyū ni nakídasù

to burst out laughing 急に笑い出す kyū ni waráidasù

to be bursting with (subj: room, container) はち切れんばかりに...で一杯になっている hachíkireñbakari ni ...de ippái ni natté irù; (: person: emotion) ...で胸が一杯になっている ...de muné ga ippái ni natté irù

burst into vt fus (room etc) ...に飛込む

...ni tobíkomù

bury [ber'ri:] vt (gen) 埋める uméru; (at funeral) 埋葬する maísō suru

bus [bʌs] n (vehicle) バス básù

bush [buʃ] n (in garden) 低木 teíboku; (scrubland) 未開地 mikáìchi, ブッシュ bússhù

    to beat about the bush 遠回しに言う tōmawàshi ni iú

bushy [buʃ'i:] adj (tail, hair, eyebrows) ふさふさした fúsàfusa shitá

busily [biz'ili:] adv (actively) 忙しく isógashikù

business [biz'nis] n (matter, question) 問題 moñdai; (trading) 商売 shōbai; (firm) 会社 kaísha; (occupation) 仕事 shigóto

    to be away on business 出張して留守である shutchō shite rusù de arù

    it's my business to ...するのは私の務めです ...surú no wa watákushi no tsutóme desù

    it's none of my business 私の知った事じゃない watákushi no shittá kotó ja naì

    he means business 彼は本気らしい karè wa hoñki rashìì

businesslike [biz'nislaik] adj てきぱきした tekípaki shitá

businessman [biz'nismæn] (pl **businessmen**) n 実業家 jitsúgyōka

business trip n 出張 shutchō

businesswoman [biz'niswumən] (pl **businesswomen**) n 女性実業家 joséijitsugyōka

busker [bʌs'kə:r] (BRIT) n 大道芸人 daídōgeìnin

bus-stop [bʌs'stɑ:p] n バス停留所 básùteíryùjo

bust [bʌst] n (ANAT) 乳房 chíbùsa, 胸 munè; (measurement) バスト básùto; (sculpture) 胸像 kyōzō

    ♦adj (inf: broken) 壊れた kowárèta

    to go bust (company etc) つぶれる tsubúreru

bustle [bʌs'əl] n (activity) 雑踏 zattō

    ♦vi (person) 忙しく飛回る isógashikù tobímawarù

bustling [bʌs'liŋ] adj (town, place) にぎ

やかな nígiyàka na

busy [biz'i:] adj (person) 忙しい isógashiì; (shop, street) にぎやかな nígiyàka na; (TEL: line) 話し中の hanáshichū no

    ♦vt: *to busy oneself with* 忙しそうに...する isógashisō ni ...suru

busybody [biz'i:bɑːdi:] n でしゃばり屋 deshábariya

busy signal (US) n (TEL) 話中音 wáchùon

<hr>
KEYWORD
<hr>

but [bʌt] conj 1 (yet) ...であるが ...de árù ga, ...であるけれども ...de árù keredomo, しかし shikáshì

    he's not very bright, but he's hard-working 彼はあまり頭は良くないが, よく働きます kárè wa amári àtama wà yókùnaì ga, yókù határakimasù

    I'm tired but Paul isn't 私は疲れていますが, ポールは疲れていません watákushi wa tsukárète imasu ga, pốrù wa tsukárète imásèn

    the trip was enjoyable but tiring 旅行は楽しかったけれども, 疲れました ryokō wa tánòshikàtta keredomo, tsukáremashìta

2 (however) ...であるが ...de árù ga, ...であるけれども ...de árù keredomo, しかし shikáshì

    I'd love to come, but I'm busy 行きたいが, 今忙しいんです ikítaì ga, ímà isógashiìn desu

    she wanted to go, but first she had to finish her homework 彼女は行きたかったけれども, 先に宿題を済ます必要がありました kánojò wa ikítakàtta keredomo, sakí ni shùkúdai wo sùmásù hitsúyō ga àrímashìta

    I'm sorry, but I don't agree 済みませんが, 私は同意できません sumímasèn ga, watákushi wa dối dekimasèn

3 (showing disagreement, surprise etc) しかし shikáshì

    but that's far too expensive! しかしそれは高過ぎますよ shikáshì sorè wa tàkásugimasù yo

    but that's fantastic! しかし素晴らし

いじゃありませんか shikáshì subárashiî ja arímasèn ka

♦*prep* (apart from, except) ...を除いて ...wo nozóite, ...以外に ...ígài ni

he was nothing but trouble 彼は厄介な問題ばかり起していました kárè wa yákkài na móndai bakàri okóshìte imáshìta

we've had nothing but trouble 厄介な問題ばかり起っています yákkài na móndai bakàri okóttè imásù

no one but him can do it 彼を除けば出来る人はいません kárè wo nozókebà dekírù hito wa imásèn

who but a lunatic would do such a thing? 気違いを除けばそんな事をする人はいないでしょう kichígaì wo nozókebà sónna koto wò suru hito wà ináî deshô

but for you あなたがいなかったら anátà ga inákàttara

but for your help あなたが助けてくれなかったら anátà ga tasúketè kurénakàttara

I'll do anything but that それ以外なら何でもします sorè igài nara nán de mo shimasù

♦*adv* (just, only) ただ tádà, ...だけ ...dàkè, ...しか...ない ...shika ...náî

she's but a child 彼女はほんの子供です kánojò wa hôn no kòdómo desù

had I but known 私がそれを知ってさえいたら watákushi ga sòrè wo shitte saè itárà

I can but try やってみるしかありません yátte mirù shika arímasèn

all but finished もう少しで出来上りです mô sukoshì de dekíagari desù

butcher [butʃ'ə:r] *n* (tradesman) 肉屋 nikúyà

♦*vt* (cattle etc for meat) と殺する tosátsu suru; (prisoners etc) 虐殺する gyakúsatsu suru

butcher's (shop) [butʃ'ə:rz-] *n* 精肉店 seínikutèn, 肉屋 nikúyà

butler [bʌt'lə:r] *n* 執事 shítsùji

butt [bʌt] *n* (large barrel) たる tarú; (of pistol) 握り nigíri; (of rifle) 床尾 shōbí; (of cigarette) 吸い殻 suígara; (*fig*: target: of teasing, criticism etc) 的 matô

♦*vt* (subj: goat, person) 頭で突く atáma de tsukù

butter [bʌt'ə:r] *n* (CULIN) バター bátà

♦*vt* (bread) ...にバターを塗る ...ni bátà wo nurú

buttercup [bʌt'ə:rkʌp] *n* キンポウゲ kínpòge

butterfly [bʌt'ə:rflai] *n* (insect) チョウチョウ chôchō; (SWIMMING: *also*: **butterfly stroke**) バタフライ bátàfurai

butt in *vi* (interrupt) ...に割込む ...ni waríkomù

buttocks [bʌt'əks] *npl* (ANAT) しり shirí

button [bʌt'ən] *n* (on clothes) ボタン botán; (on machine) 押しボタン oshíbotàn; (*US*: badge) バッジ bájjì

♦*vt* (*also*: **button up**) ...のボタンをはめる ...no botán wo haméru

♦*vi* ボタンで止まる botán de tomáru

buttress [bʌt'tris] *n* (ARCHIT) 控え壁 hikáekàbe

buxom [bʌk'səm] *adj* (woman) 胸の豊かな muné no yutàka na

buy [bai] (*pt, pp* **bought**) *vt* 買う kaú

♦*n* (purchase) 買物 kaímono

to buy someone something/something for someone ...に...を買って上げる ...ni ...wo katté agéru

to buy something from someone ...から...を買う ...kará ...wo kaú

to buy someone a drink ...に酒をおごる ...ni saké wo ogóru

buyer [bai'ə:r] *n* (purchaser) 買手 kaíte; (COMM) 仕入係 shíregakàri, バイヤー báíyā

buzz [bʌz] *n* (noise: of insect) ぶんぶんという音 bunbun to iú otò; (: of machine etc) うなり unári; (*inf*: phone call): *to give someone a buzz* ...に電話を掛ける ...ni deñwa wo kakérù

♦*vi* (insect) ぶんぶん羽音を立てる buñbun haòto wo taterù; (saw) うなる unárù

buzzer [bʌz'ə:r] *n* (ELEC) ブザー búzà

buzz word (*inf*) *n* 流行語 ryúkōgo

KEYWORD

by [bai] *prep* **1** (referring to cause, agent) ...に（よって）...ni (yotte)

killed by lightning 雷に打たれて死んだ kamínari ni útárète shínda

surrounded by a fence 塀に囲まれた heí ni kakomareta

a painting by Picasso ピカソの絵画 pikásò no káîga

it's by Shakespeare シェイクスピアの作品です sheíkusupìa no sakúhin desù

2 (referring to method, manner, means) ...で...de

by bus/car/train バス〔車，列車〕で básù(kurúma, rèssha)de

to pay by check 小切手で払う kogíttè de haráù

by moonlight/candlelight 月明かり〔ろうそくの灯〕で tsukíakàri(rósoku no akari)de

by saving hard, he ... 一生懸命に金を貯めて彼は... isshókènmei ni kanê wo tamete karê wa...

3 (via, through) ...を通って...wo tóttè, ...経由で...kêîyu de

we came by Dover ドーバー経由で来ました dóbākeìyu de kimáshìta

he came in by the back door 彼は裏口から入りました kárè wa uráguchi kara hairimashìta

4 (close to) ...のそばに〔で〕...no sôba ni〔de〕, ...の近くに〔で〕...no chikákù ni〔de〕

the house by the river 川のそばにある家 kawá no sôba ni árù ié

a holiday by the sea 海辺の休暇 umíbe no kyúka

she sat by his bed 彼女は彼のベッドのそばに座っていました kánojò wa kárè no béddò no sôba ni suwátte imashìta

5 (past) ...を通り過ぎて...wo tórisugìte

she rushed by me 彼女は足早に私の前を通り過ぎた kánojò wa ashíbaya ni watákushi no maè wo tórisugìta

I go by the post office every day 私は毎日郵便局の前を通ります watákushi wa maìnichi yúbìnkyoku no maê wo

tórimasù

6 (not later than) ...までに...mádè ni

by 4 o'clock 4時までに yójì made ni

by this time tomorrow 明日のこの時間までに myónichì no konô jikan madè ni

by the time I got here it was too late 私がここに着いたころにはもう手遅れでした watákushi ga kókò ni tsuíta koro ni wá mô teôkùre deshìta

7 (during): *by daylight* 日中に nitchû ni

8 (amount) ...単位で...tàn-i de

by the kilo/meter キロ〔メーター〕単位で kíró(méta)tàn-i de

paid by the hour 時給をもらって jikyú wo moratte

one by one (people) 1人ずつ hitórizutsù; (animals) 1匹ずつ ippíkizutsù; (things) 1つずつ hitótsuzutsù

little by little 少しずつ sukóshizutsù

9 (MATH, measure): *to divide by 3* 3で割る sán de waru

to multiply by 3 3を掛ける sán wo kakerù

a room 3 meters by 4 3メーター掛ける4メーターの部屋 sánmēta kakérù yónmētā no heyá

it's broader by a meter 1メーターも広くなっている ichímēta mó hiròku náttè iru

10 (according to) ...に従って...nì shitágatte

to play by the rules ルールを守る rûrù wo mamórù

it's all right by me 私は構いませんよ watákushi wa kàmáimasèn yó

11: *(all) by oneself* *etc* 一人だけで hitórì daké dè

he did it (all) by himself 彼は彼1人だけの力でやりました kárè wa kárè hitórì dake nò chikára dè yarímashìta

he was standing (all) by himself in the corner 彼は1人ぼっちで隅に立っていました kárè wa hitóribotchì de súmì ni táttè imáshìta

12: *by the way* ところで tokóro dè

by the way, did you know Claire was back? ところでね，クレアが帰って来たのをご存知？ tokóro dè ne, kùrea

ga káètte kita no wo go-zònjî?
this wasn't my idea by the way しか
しね, これを提案したのは私じゃないか
らね shikáshì nê, koré wo teian shita nò
wa watákushi ja nài kara nê

♦*adv* 1 *see* **go**; **pass** *etc*
2: *by and by* やがて yagáte
*by and by they came to a fork in the
road* やがて道路はY字路になりました
yagáte dòro ha waîjirò ni narímashìta
they'll come back by and by そのう
ち帰って来ますよ sonô uchi kaètte kimásù yo
by and large (on the whole) 大体におい
て dáitai ni òîte, 往々にして ōō ni shite
*by and large I would agree with
you* 大体あなたと同じ意見です dáitai a-
natà to onáji ikèn desu
*Britain has a poor image abroad, by
and large* 海外における英国のイメージ
は往々にして悪い kâîgai ni okêru êîko-
ku no îmèjì wa ōō ni shite wârûî

---

bye(-bye) [bai'(bai')] *n excl* じゃあねじゃ
ね, バイバイ bâîbai
by(e)-law [bai'lɔ:] *n* 条例 jôrei
by-election [bai'ilekʃən] (*BRIT*) *n* 補欠
選挙 hokétsuseñkyo
bygone [bai'gɔ:n] *adj* (age, days) 昔の
mukáshi no
♦*n*: *let bygones be bygones* 済んだ事を
水に流す súuda kotô wo mizú ni nagásù
bypass [bai'pæs] *n* (*AUT*) バイパス baî-
pasu; (*MED*: operation) 冠状動脈バイパ
ス kañjōdōmyakubaîpasu
♦*vt* (town) ...にバイパスを設ける ...ni ba-
îpasu wo môkerù
by-product [bai'prɑ:dəkt] *n* (of industrial process) 副産物 fukúsañbutsu; (of
situation) 二次的結果 nijîtekikèkka
bystander [bai'stændər] *n* (at accident,
crime) 居合せた通行人 iáwasèta tsúkō-
nin
byte [bait] *n* (*COMPUT*) バイト bâîto
byword [bai'wə:rd] *n*: *to be a byword
for* ...の代名詞である ...no daímeìshi de
arû
by-your-leave [baiju:rli:v'] *n*: *without*

---

so much as a by-your-leave 自分勝手
に jibúnkattè ni

C

C [si:] *n* (*MUS*: note) ハ音 há-òn; (: key) ハ
調 háchō
C. [si:] *abbr* = **centigrade**
C.A. [si:ei'] *abbr* = **chartered accountant**
cab [kæb] *n* (taxi) タクシー tákùshī; (of
truck, tractor etc) 運転台 uñtendai
cabaret [kæbərei'] *n* (nightclub) キャバ
レー kyábàrē; (floor show) フロアショー
furóashò
cabbage [kæb'idʒ] *n* キャベツ kyábètsu
cabin [kæb'in] *n* (on ship) キャビン kyá-
bìn; (on plane) 操縦室 sōjùshìtsu; (house)
小屋 koyá
cabin cruiser *n* 大型モーターボート ṑ-
gata mótābòto, クルーザー kúrūzà ◇居
室，炊事場などのある物を指す kyóshì-
tsu, suîjiba nádò no árù monó wo sásù
cabinet [kæb'ənit] *n* (piece of furniture)
戸棚 todána, キャビネット kyábìnettò;
(*also*: **display cabinet**) ガラス戸棚 garásu tódàna; (*POL*) 内閣 nâîkaku
cable [kei'bəl] *n* (strong rope) 綱 tsuná;
(*ELEC*, *TEL*, *TV*) ケーブル kêburu
♦*vt* (message, money) 電信で送る deñshin de okúru
cable-car [kei'bəlkɑ:r] *n* ケーブルカー
kêburukà
cable television *n* 有線テレビ yúsente-
rèbi
cache [kæʃ] *n*: *a cache of drugs* 隠匿さ
れた麻薬 iñtoku saretà mayáku
a weapons cache 隠匿武器 iñtokubùki
cackle [kæk'əl] *vi* (person, witch) 薄気味
悪い声で笑う usúkimiwaruî kôè de wa-
râù; (hen) こhere と鳴く kokoko to nákù
cacti [kæk'tai] *npl of* **cactus**
cactus [kæk'təs] (*pl* **cacti**) *n* サボテン
sabóten
caddie [kæd'i:] *n* (*GOLF*) キャディー
kyádì
caddy [kæd'i:] *n* = **caddie**

cadet [kədet'] n (MIL) 士官候補生 shikán-kōhosèi; (POLICE) 警察学校の生徒 keísatsugakkō no sēíto

cadge [kædʒ] (inf) vt (lift, cigarette etc) ねだる nedáru

Caesarean [size:r'i:ən] (BRIT) = **Cesarean**

café [kæfei'] n (snack bar) 喫茶店 kíssàten

cafeteria [kæfiti:'ri:ə] n (in school, factory, station) 食堂 shokúdō

caffein(e) [kæ'fi:n] n カフェイン kaféīn

cage [keidʒ] n (of animal) おり orí, ケージ kēji; (also: **bird cage**) 鳥かご toríkago, ケージ kēji; (of lift) ケージ kēji

cagey [kei'dʒi:] (inf) adj 用心深い yōjinbukaì

cagoule [kəgu:l'] (BRIT) n カグール kágūru ◇薄手の雨ガッパ usúde no amágappa

Cairo [kai'rou] n カイロ kâîro

cajole [kədʒoul'] vt 丸め込む marúmekomù

cake [keik] n (CULIN: large) デコレーションケーキ dekórēshonkèki; (: small) 洋菓子 yōgashì
  a cake of soap 石けん1個 sekkén íkkò

caked [keikt] adj: *caked with* (blood, mud etc) ...の塊で覆われた ...no katámari de ōwareta

calamity [kəlæm'iti:] n (disaster) 災難 saínaǹ

calcium [kæl'si:əm] n (in teeth, bones etc) カルシウム karúshiùmu

calculate [kæl'kjəleit] vt (work out: cost, distance, numbers etc) 計算する keísan suru; (: effect, risk, impact etc) 予測する yosóku suru

calculating [kæl'kjəleitiǹg] adj (scheming) ずる賢い zurúgashikoì

calculation [kælkjəlei'ʃən] n (MATH) 計算 keísan; (estimate) 予測 yosóku

calculator [kæl'kjəleitə:r] n 電卓 deñtaku

calculus [kæl'kjələs] n (MATH) 微積分学 bisékibungàku

calendar [kæl'əndə:r] n (of year) カレンダー káreñdā; (timetable, schedule) 予定表 yotéihyō

calendar month/year n 暦月〔年〕 rekígetsu〔nen〕

calf [kæf] (pl **calves**) n (of cow) 子ウシ koúshi; (of elephant, seal etc) ...の子 ...no ko; (also: **calfskin**) 子牛革 koúshigàwa, カーフスキン káfusukiǹ; (ANAT) ふくらはぎ fukúrahàgi

caliber [kæl'əbə:r] (BRIT **calibre**) n (of person) 能力 nōryoku; (of skill) 程度 téido; (of gun) 口径 kōkéi

call [kɔ:l] vt (christen, name) 名付ける nazúkerù; (label) ...を...と呼ぶ ...wo...to yobú; (TEL) ...に電話を掛ける ...ni deñwa wo kakérù; (summon: doctor etc) 呼ぶ yobú; (: witness etc) 召喚する shōkan suru; (arrange: meeting) 召集する shōshū suru

♦vi (shout) 大声で言う ōgoè de iú; (telephone) 電話を掛ける deñwa wo kakérù; (visit: also: **call in**, **call round**) 立寄る tachíyoru

♦n (shout) 呼声 yobígoè; (TEL) 電話 deñwa; (of bird) 鳴声 nakígoè
  : *to be called* ...と呼ばれる ...to yobárerù, ...という ...to íù
  on call (nurse, doctor etc) 待機して taíki shité

call back vi (return) また寄る matá yorú; (TEL) 電話を掛け直す deñwa wo kakénaosù

callbox [kɔ:l'bɑ:ks] (BRIT) n 電話ボックス deñwabokkùsu

caller [kɔ:l'ə:r] n (visitor) 訪問客 hōmoñkyaku; (TEL) 電話を掛けてくる人 deñwa wo kakète kurù hitò

call for vt fus (demand) 要求する yōkyū suru; (fetch) 迎えに行く mukáe ni ikú

call girl n (prostitute) コールガール kōrugāru

call-in [kɔ:l'in] (US) n (phone-in) ◇視聴者が電話で参加する番組 shíchōsha ga deñwa de sañka suru bañgumi

calling [kɔ:l'iǹg] n (occupation) 職業 shokùgyō; (also: **religious calling**) 神のお召し kámì no o-méshi

calling card (US) n 名刺 meíshi

call off vt (cancel) 中止する chūshi suru

call on vt fus (visit) 訪ねる tazúnerù, 訪問する hṓmon suru; (appeal to) ...に...を求める ...ni ...wo motómerù

callous [kæl'əs] adj (heartless) 冷淡な reítañ na

call out vt (name etc) 大声でいう ṓgoè de iù; (summon for help etc) 呼び出す yobídasu
♦vi (shout) 大声で言う ṓgoè de iú

call up vt (MIL) 召集する shṓshū suru; (TEL) ...に電話をかける ...ni deñwa wo kakérù

calm [kɑːm] adj (unworried) 落着いている ochítsuite irú; (peaceful) 静かな shízùka na; (weather, sea) 穏やかな odáyàka na
♦n (quiet, peacefulness) 静けさ shizúkesà
♦vt (person, child) 落着かせる ochítsukasèru; (fears, grief etc) 鎮める shizúmerù

calm down vi (person) 落着く ochítsukù
♦vt (person) 落着かせる ochítsukasèru

Calor gas [kæl'ɔːr-]® n ◇携帯用燃料ガスボンベの商品名 keítaiyō neñryō gasuboñbe no shṓhìñmei

calorie [kæl'əːriː] n カロリー káròrī

calves [kævz] npl of **calf**

camber [kæm'bəːr] n (of road) 真ん中が高くなっている事 mañnaka ga takakù nattè irú kotó

Cambodia [kæmbou'diːə] n カンボジア kañbojìa

came [keim] pt of **come**

camel [kæm'əl] n (ZOOL) ラクダ rakúda

cameo [kæm'iːou] n (jewellery) カメオ kámèo

camera [kæm'əːrə] n (PHOT) 写真機 shashíñki, カメラ kámèra; (CINEMA) 映画カメラ eíga kámèra; (also: **TV camera**) テレビカメラ terébi kamèra
in camera (LAW) 非公開で híkòkai de

cameraman [kæm'əːrəmæn] (pl **cameramen**) n (CINEMA, TV) カメラマン kaméràmàn

camouflage [kæm'əflɑːʒ] n (MIL) カムフラージュ kamúfuràju; (ZOOL) 隠ぺいの擬態 iñpeitekigitài
♦vt (conceal: also MIL) 隠す kakúsù

camp [kæmp] n (encampment) キャンプ場 kyañpujō; (MIL: barracks) 基地 kichí; (for prisoners) 収容所 shúyòjo; (faction) 陣営 jiñ-ei
♦vi (in tent) キャンプする kyañpu suru
♦adj (effeminate) 女々しい meméshiî

campaign [kæmpein'] n (MIL) 作戦 sakúsen; (POL etc) 運動 uñdō, キャンペーン kyañpèn
♦vi (objectors, pressure group etc) 運動をする uñdō wo suru

camp bed (BRIT) n 折畳みベッド orítatami beddò

camper [kæm'pəːr] n (person) キャンパー kyañpā; (vehicle) キャンピングカー kyañpingukā

camping [kæm'piŋ] n 野営 yaéi, キャンピング kyañpiñgu
to go camping キャンピングに行く kyañpiñgu ni iku

campsite [kæmp'sait] n キャンプ場 kyañpujō

campus [kæm'pəs] n (SCOL) キャンパス kyáñpasu

can¹ [kæn] n (container: for foods, drinks, oil etc) 缶 kâñ
♦vt (foods) 缶詰にする kañzume ni suru

KEYWORD

can² [kæn] (negative **cannot**, **can't** conditional and pt **could**) aux vb **1** (be able to) 出来る dekírù

you can do it if you try 努力すればできますよ dóryòku surébà dekímasù yo

I'll help you all I can できるだけ力になりましょう dekíru dake chîkára nì narímashṓ

she couldn't sleep that night その晩彼女は眠れませんでした sònó ban kanòjo wa nemúremasèn deshita

I can't go on any longer 私はもうこれ以上やっていけません watákushi wa mṓ koré ijō yatté ikemasèn

I can't see you あなたの姿が見えません anátà no súgàta ga miémasèn

can you hear me? 私の声が聞こえますか watákushi no koè ga kikóemasù ká

I can see you tomorrow, if you're

free 明日でよかったらお会いできますよ asú dè yókàttara o-ái dekimasù yó

2 (know how to) ...の仕方が分かる ...no shikáta ga wakarù, ...ができる ...ga dekírù

I can swim/play tennis/drive 私は水泳〔テニス，運転〕ができます watákushi wa suíei(ténisù, únten)ga dèkimasu ká

can you speak French? あなたはフランス語ができますか anátà wa furánsugo ga dèkimasù ká

3 (may) ...してもいいですか ...shìté mò íi desu ká

can I use your phone? 電話をお借りしてもいいですか dénwa wo ò-kári shite mò íi desu ká

could I have a word with you? ちょっと話しがあるんですが chóttò hanáshi gà árùn desu gá

you can smoke if you like タバコを吸いたければ遠慮なくどうぞ tabáko wo suitakèreba énryo nakù dózò

can I help you with that? 手を貸しましょうか té wò kashímashò ka

4 (expressing disbelief, puzzlement): *it can't be true!* うそでしょう úsò deshó

what CAN he want? あいつは何をねらっているだろうね àitsu wa nánì wo neráttè iru dàrò né

5 (expressing possibility, suggestion, etc) ...かも知れない ...ka mò shirenai

he could be in the library 彼は図書室にいるかも知れません kárè wa toshóshìtsu ni irú ka mo shiremasen

she could have been delayed 彼女は何かの原因で出発が遅れたかも知れません kánòjo wa nánìka no gén-in de shùppátsu ga òkureta kà mo shirémasèn

Canada [kæn'ədə] *n* カナダ kánàda

Canadian [kənei'di:ən] *adj* カナダの kánàda no
♦*n* カナダ人 kanádajìn

canal [kənæl'] *n* (for ships, barges, irrigation) 運河 úñga; (ANAT) 管 káñ

canary [kəner'i:] *n* カナリヤ kanáriya

cancel [kæn'səl] *vt* (meeting) 中止する chúshi suru; (appointment, reservation,

contract, order) 取消す toríkesu, キャンセルする kyáñseru suru; (cross out: words, figures) 線を引いて消す séñ wo hiíte kesú

the flight was canceled その便は欠航になった sonó bìñ wa kekkó ni nattá

the train was canceled その列車は運休になった sonó resshà wa uñkyú ni nattá

cancellation [kænsəlei'ʃən] *n* (of meeting) 中止 chúshi; (of appointment, reservation, contract, order) 取消し toríkeshi, キャンセル kyáñseru; (of flight) 欠航 kekkó; (of train) 運休 uñkyú

cancer [kæn'sɔːr] *n* (MED) がん gáñ
Cancer (ASTROLOGY) かに座 kaníza

candid [kæn'did] *adj* (expression, comment) 率直な sotchóku na

candidate [kæn'dideit] *n* (for job) 候補者 kóhoshà; (in exam) 受験者 jukéñsha; (POL) 立候補者 rikkóhoshà

candle [kæn'dəl] *n* ろうそく rósokù

candlelight [kæn'dəllait] *n*: *by candlelight* ろうそくの明りで rósokù no akári de

candlestick [kæn'dəlstik] *n* (*also*: **candle holder**: plain) ろうそく立て rósokutàte; (: bigger, ornate) しょく台 shokúdai

candor [kæn'dəːr] (*BRIT* **candour**) *n* (frankness) 率直さ sotchókusà

candy [kæn'diː] *n* (*also*: **sugar-candy**) 氷砂糖 kórizatò; (*US*: sweet) あめ amé

candy-floss [kæn'diːflɔːs] (*BRIT*) *n* 綿あめ watá-àme, 綿菓子 watágashì

cane [kein] *n* (BOT) 茎 kukí ◊竹などの様に中が空洞になっている植物を指す takénadò no yò ni nakà ga kúdò ni natté irú shokúbùtsu wo sasù; (for furniture) 藤 tò; (stick) 棒 bó; (for walking) 杖 tsúè, ステッキ sutékkì
♦*vt* (*BRIT*: SCOL) むち打つ muchíutsù

canine [kei'nain] *adj* イヌの inú no

canister [kæn'istəːr] *n* (container: for tea, sugar etc) 容器 yóki ◊茶筒の様な物を指す chazútsu no yò na monó wo sasù; (pressurized container) スプレー缶 supúrēkàñ; (of gas, chemicals etc) ボンベ bóñbe

cannabis [kænˈəbis] *n* マリファナ marífàna

canned [kænd] *adj* (fruit, vegetables etc) 缶詰の kañzume no

cannibal [kænˈəbəl] *n* (person) 人食い人間 hitókui niñgen; (animal) 共食いする動物 tomógui suru dóbutsu

cannon [kænˈən] (*pl* **cannon** *or* **cannons**) *n* (artillery piece) 大砲 taíhō

cannot [kænˈɑːt] = **can not**

canny [kænˈiː] *adj* (quick-witted) 抜け目ない nukémenaì

canoe [kənuːˈ] *n* (boat) カヌー kánù

canon [kænˈən] *n* (clergyman) 司教座聖堂参事会員 shikyőzaseídō sañjikàiin; (rule, principle) 規準 kijún

canonize [kænˈənaiz] *vt* (REL) 聖人の列に加える seíjin no retsù ni kuwáerù

can opener *n* 缶切 kañkiri

canopy [kænˈəpiː] *n* (above bed, throne etc) 天がい teñgai

can't [kænt] = **can not**

cantankerous [kæntæŋˈkəːrəs] *adj* (fault-finding, complaining) つむじ曲りの tsumújimagàri no

canteen [kæntiːnˈ] *n* (in workplace, school etc) 食堂 shokúdō; (*also*: **mobile canteen**) 移動食堂 időshokudò; (*BRIT*: of cutlery) 収納箱 shūnōbàko ◊ナイフ, フォークなどを仕舞う箱 naífu, főku nadð wo shimáu hakð

canter [kænˈtəːr] *vi* (horse) キャンターで走る kyañta de hashirù

canvas [kænˈvəs] *n* (fabric) キャンバス kyáñbasu; (painting) 油絵 abúraè; (NAUT) 帆 hð ◊総称 sóshō

canvass [kænˈvəs] *vi* (POL): **to canvass for** ...のために選挙運動をする ...no tamè ni señkyoundō wo suru
◆*vt* (investigate: opinions, views) 調査する chōsa surù

canyon [kænˈjən] *n* 峡谷 kyőkoku

cap [kæp] *n* (hat) 帽子 bőshi ◊主につばのある物を指す ốmð ni tsubá no arù monő wo sásù; (of pen) キャップ kyáppù; (of bottle) ふた futá; (contraceptive) ペッサリー péssàrī; (for toy gun) 紙雷管 kamíraìkan

◆*vt* (outdo) しのぐ shinőgù

capability [keipəbilˈəti:] *n* (competence) 能力 nőryoku

capable [keiˈpəbəl] *adj* (person, object): **capable of doing** ...ができる ...ga dekírù; (able: person) 有能な yūnō na

capacity [kəpæsˈiti:] *n* (of container, ship etc) 容積 yőseki; (of stadium etc) 収容力 shūyōryòku; (capability) 能力 nőryoku; (position, role) 資格 shikáku; (of factory) 生産能力 seísannōryòku

cape [keip] *n* (GEO) 岬 misáki; (short cloak) ケープ kếpu

caper [keiˈpəːr] *n* (CULIN: *gen*: capers) ケーパー kếpā; (prank) いたずら itázura

capital [kæpˈitəl] *n* (*also*: **capital city**) 首都 shútð; (money) 資本金 shihőñkin; (*also*: **capital letter**) 大文字 őmoji

capital gains tax *n* 資本利得税 shihőnritokuzèi

capitalism [kæpˈitəlizəm] *n* 資本主義 shihőnshùgi

capitalist [kæpˈitəlist] *adj* 資本主義の shihőnshùgi no
◆*n* 資本主義者 shihőnshugishà

capitalize [kæpˈitəlaiz]: **capitalize on** *vt fus* (situation, fears etc) 利用する riyố suru

capital punishment 死刑 shikéi

capitulate [kəpitʃˈuleit] *vi* (give in) 降参する kősan suru

capricious [kəpriʃˈəs] *adj* (fickle: person) 気まぐれの kimágure no

Capricorn [kæpˈrikɔːrn] *n* (ASTROLOGY) やぎ座 yagíza

capsize [kæpˈsaiz] *vt* (boat, ship) 転覆させる teñpuku saséru
◆*vi* (boat, ship) 転覆する teñpuku suru

capsule [kæpˈsəl] *n* (MED) カプセル kápùseru; (spacecraft) 宇宙カプセル uchűkapùseru

captain [kæpˈtin] *n* (of ship) 船長 señchō; (of plane) 機長 kichő; (of team) 主将 shushő; (in army) 大尉 tâî-i; (in navy) 大佐 taísa; (*US*: in air force) 大尉 tâî-i; (*BRIT*: SCOL) 主席の生徒 shuséki no seíto

caption [kæpˈʃən] *n* (to picture) 説明文

setsúmeìbun

captivate [kǽp'təveit] *vt* (fascinate) 魅了する miryŏ suru

captive [kǽp'tiv] *adj* (person) とりこの toríko no; (animal) 飼育下の shiíkukà no
♦*n* (person) とりこ toríko; (animal) 飼育下の動物 shiíkukà no dŏbutsu

captivity [kæptív'əti:] *n* 監禁状態 kańkinjŏtai

capture [kǽp'tʃər] *vt* (animal, person) 捕まえる tsukámaerù; (town, country) 占領する seńryŏ suru; (attention) 捕える toráerù; (COMPUT) 収納する shúnō suru
♦*n* (seizure: of animal) 捕獲 hokáku; (: of person: by police) 逮捕 táìho; (: of town, country: by enemy) 占領 seńryŏ; (COMPUT) 収納 shúnō

car [kɑːr] *n* (AUT) 自動車 jídŏsha, 車 kurúma; (: *US*: carriage) 客車 kyakúsha; (RAIL: dining car, buffet car) 特殊車両 tokúshusharyò

carafe [kəræf'] *n* 水差し mizúsashì

caramel [kær'əməl] *n* (CULIN: sweet) キャラメル kyarámeru; (: burnt sugar) カラメル karámeru

carat [kær'ət] *n* (of diamond, gold) カラット karáttò

caravan [kær'əvæn] *n* (*BRIT*: vehicle) キャンピングカー kyañpingukầ; (in desert) 隊商 taíshō, キャラバン kyáràban

caravan site (*BRIT*) *n* オートキャンプ場 ŏtokyanpujō

carbohydrate [kɑːrbouhai'dreit] *n* (CHEM, food) 炭水化物 tańsuikabùtsu

carbon [kɑːr'bən] *n* 炭素 táñso

carbon copy *n* カーボンコピー kẩboñ kopì

carbon dioxide [-daiɑːk'said] *n* 二酸化炭素 nisánkatañso

carbon monoxide [-mənɑːk'said] *n* 一酸化炭素 issánkatañso

carbon paper *n* カーボン紙 kǎboñshi

carburetor [kɑːr'bəreitəːr] (*BRIT* **carburettor**) *n* (AUT) キャブレター kyábùretā

carcass [kɑːr'kəs] *n* (of animal) 死体 shitái

card [kɑːrd] *n* (cardboard) ボール紙 bŏrugami; (greetings card, index card etc) カード kẩdo; (playing card) トランプのカード toráñpu no kẩdo; (visiting card) 名刺 meíshi

cardboard [kɑːrd'bɔːrd] *n* ボール紙 bŏrugami

card game *n* トランプゲーム toráñpugẽmu

cardiac [kɑːr'diːæk] *adj* (arrest, failure) 心臓の shiñzō no

cardigan [kɑːr'digən] *n* カーディガン kẩdigàn

cardinal [kɑːr'dənəl] *adj* (chief: principle) 重要な júyō na
♦*n* (REL) 枢機けい sǘkikèi
of cardinal importance 極めて重要で kiwámète júyō de

cardinal number 基数 kisǘ

card index *n* カード式索引 kẩdoshiki sakúin

care [keːr] *n* (attention) 注意 chǘi; (worry) 心配 shiñpai; (charge) 管理 kánri
♦*vi*: *to care about* (person, animal) ...を気に掛ける ...wo ki ni kakérù, ...を愛する ...wo aí surù; (thing, idea etc) ...に関心を持つ ...ni kañshin wo motsù
care of (on mail) ...方 ...gatá
in someone's care ...の管理に任せ(られ)て ...no kanri ni makáse(rarè)tè
to take care (to do) ...をする様心掛ける ...wo suru yŏ kokórogakerù
to take care of (patient, child etc) ...の世話をする ...no sewá wo suru; (problem, situation) ...の始末を付ける ...no shimátsu wo tsukerù
I don't care 私は構いません watákushi wa kamáimasèn
I couldn't care less 私はちっとも気にしない watákushi wa chittô mò ki ni shinaì

career [kəriːr'] *n* (job, profession) 職業 shokùgyō; (life: in school, work etc) キャリア kyaría
♦*vi* (*also*: **career along**: car, horse) 猛スピードで走る mŏsupìdo de hashirù

career woman (*pl* **career women**) *n* キャリアウーマン kyaríaùman

care for vt fus (look after) ...の世話をする...no sewá wo suru; (like) ...が好きである...ga sukí de arù, ...を愛している...wo aí shité irú

carefree [ke:r'fri:] adj (person, attitude) 気苦労のない kigurǒ no naì

careful [ke:r'fəl] adj (cautious) 注意深い chǔibukaì; (thorough) 徹底的な tettéiteki na

(be) careful! 気を付けてね ki wo tsukéte ne

carefully [ke:r'fəli:] adv (cautiously) 注意深く chǔibukakù; (methodically) 念入りに nefi-iri ni

careless [ke:r'lis] adj (negligent) 不注意な fuchǔi na; (heedless) 軽率な keísotsu na

carelessness [ke:r'lisnis] n (negligence) 不注意 fuchǔi; (lack of concern) 無とん着 mutoñchaku

caress [kəres'] n (stroke) 愛ぶ aíbu
♦vt (person, animal) 愛ぶする aíbu suru

caretaker [ke:r'teikə:r] n (of flats etc) 管理人 kaírinin

car-ferry [ka:r'fe:ri:] n カーフェリー kǎferī

cargo [ka:r'gou] n (pl **cargoes**) (of ship, plane) 積荷 tsumíni, 貨物 kámotsu

car hire (BRIT) n レンタカーサービス reńtakǎ sābisu

Caribbean [kæræbi:'ən] n: **the Caribbean (Sea)** カリブ海 karíbukaì

caricature [kær'əkətʃə:r] n (drawing) 風刺漫画 fǔshimaǹga, カリカチュア karíkachùa; (description) 風刺文 fǔshibùn; (exaggerated account) 真実のわい曲 shiñjitsu no waikyoku

caring [ke:r'iŋ] adj (person, society, behavior) 愛情深い aíjōbukaì; (organization) 健康管理の keñkōkaǹri no

carnage [ka:r'nidʒ] n (MIL) 虐殺 gyakúsatsu

carnal [ka:r'nəl] adj (desires, feelings) 肉体的な nikútaiteki na

carnation [ka:rnei'ʃən] n カーネーション kǎnēshon

carnival [ka:r'nəvəl] n (festival) 謝肉祭 shaníkusài, カーニバル kǎnibaru; (US: funfair) カーニバル kǎnibàru

carnivorous [ka:rniv'ə:rəs] adj (animal, plant) 肉食の nikúshoku no

carol [kær'əl] n: **(Christmas) carol** クリスマスキャロル kurísumasu kyaròru

carp [ka:rp] n (fish) コイ koì

car park (BRIT) n 駐車場 chǔshajō

carp at vt fus (criticize) とがめ立てする togámedate suru

carpenter [ka:r'pəntə:r] n 大工 daìku

carpentry [ka:r'pəntri:] n 大工仕事 daíkushigòto

carpet [ka:r'pit] n (in room etc) じゅうたん jūtan, カーペット kǎpettð; (fig: of pine needles, snow etc) じゅうたんの様な... jūtan no yǒ na...
♦vt (room, stairs etc) ...にじゅうたんを敷く ...ni jūtan wo shikú

carpet slippers npl スリッパ súrippa

carpet sweeper [-swi:'pə:r] n じゅうたん掃除機 jūtan sōjikì

carriage [kær'idʒ] n (BRIT: RAIL) 客車 kyakúsha; (also: **horse-drawn carriage**) 馬車 bashá; (of goods) 運搬 uńpan; (transport costs) 運送料 uńsōryō

carriage return n (on typewriter etc) 復帰キー fukkí kì

carriageway [kær'idʒwei] (BRIT) n (part of road) 車線 shaseǹ ◇自動車道の上りまたは下り半分を指す jidōshadō no nobóri mata wá kudári haǹbuǹ wo sasù

carrier [kær'i:ə:r] n (transporter, transport company) 運送会社 uńsōgaìsha; (MED) 保菌者 hókiǹsha, キャリア kyárìa

carrier bag (BRIT) n 買い物袋 kaímonobukùro, ショッピングバッグ shoppíngubaggù

carrot [kær'ət] n (BOT, CULIN) ニンジン niǹjin

carry [kær'i:] vt (take) 携帯する keítai suru; (transport) 運ぶ hakóbu; (involve: responsibilities etc) 伴う tomónaù; (MED: disease, virus) 保有する hoyǔ suru
♦vi (sound) 通る tǒru

to get carried away (fig: by enthusiasm, idea) 夢中になる muchǔ ni narù

carrycot [kær'i:ka:t] (BRIT) n 携帯ベビ

ーベッド keítai bebíbèddò

carry on *vi* (continue) 続ける tsuzúkeru
♦*vt* (continue) 続ける tsuzúkeru
carry-on [kær'i:a:n] (*inf*) *n* (fuss) 大騒ぎ
ōsawági
carry out *vt* (orders) 実行する jikkṓ suru; (investigation) 行う okónau
cart [ka:rt] *n* (for grain, silage, hay etc)
荷車 nígùruma; (*also*: **horsedrawn cart**)
馬車 basha; (*also*: **handcart**) 手押し車 te-
ōshigurùma
♦*vt* (*inf*: people) 否応なしに連れて行く
iyáō nashi ni tsuréte ikú; (objects) 引きず
る hikízuru
cartilage [ka:r'təlidʒ] *n* (ANAT) 軟骨
nańkotsu
carton [ka:r'tən] *n* (large box) ボール箱
bṓrubako; (container: for yogurt, milk
etc) 容器 yṓki; (of cigarettes) カートン
kāton
cartoon [ka:rtu:n'] *n* (drawing) 漫画 mañga; (*BRIT*: comic strip) 漫画 mañga ◇四
こま漫画などを指す yońkoma manga
nadò wo sasù; (CINEMA) アニメ映画 a-
níme-eìga
cartridge [ka:r'tridʒ] *n* (for gun) 弾薬筒
dań-yakutō, 実弾 jitsúdan; (of record-
player) カートリッジ kátorijjì; (of pen)
インクカートリッジ íñku kátorijjì
carve [ka:rv] *vt* (meat) 切り分ける kiríwakerù, スライスする suráisu surù; (wood,
stone) 彫刻する chṓkoku suru; (initials,
design) 刻む kizámu
carve up *vt* (land, property) 切り分ける kiríwakerù
carving [ka:r'viŋ] *n* (object made from
wood, stone etc) 彫刻 chṓkoku; (in wood
etc: design) 彫り物 horímonð; (: art) 彫刻
chṓkoku
carving knife *n* カービングナイフ ká-
bingunaìfu
car wash *n* 洗車場 seńshajō, カーウォッ
シュ kắuosshù
cascade [kæskeid'] *n* (waterfall) 小さい
滝 chíísaì takí
♦*vi* (water) 滝になって流れ落ちる takí
ni natté nagáreochirù; (hair, people,
things) 滝の様に落ちる takí no yṓ ni o-

chirù
case [keis] *n* (situation, instance) 場合
baái; (MED) 症例 shōrei; (LAW) 事件 jíkèn; (container: for spectacles etc) ケー
ス kḕsu; (box: of whisky etc) 箱 hakó, ケ
ース kḕsu; (*BRIT*: *also*: **suitcase**) スーツ
ケース sûtsukḕsu
in case (of) (fire, emergency) ...の場合
に ...no baái ni
in any case とにかく toníkaku
just in case 万一に備えて mán-ichi ni
sonáete
cash [kæʃ] *n* (money) 現金 geńkin
♦*vt* (check etc) 換金する kańkin suru
to pay (in) cash 現金で払う geńkin de
haraù
cash on delivery 着払い chakúbarài
cash-book [kæʃ'buk] *n* 出納簿 suítōbo
cash card (*BRIT*) *n* (for cash dispenser)
キャッシュカード kyasshúkàdo
cash desk (*BRIT*) *n* 勘定カウンター kań-
jōkauńtà
cash dispenser *n* 現金自動支払い機 geńkin jidōshiharaìki, カード機 kắdokì
cashew [kæʃ'u:] *n* (*also*: **cashew nut**) カ
シューナッツ kashúnattsù
cash flow *n* 資金繰り shikínguri
cashier [kæʃi'ə:r] *n* (in bank) 出納係 suítōgakàri; (in shop, restaurant) レジ係 re-
jígakàri
cashmere [kæʒ'mi:r] *n* (wool, jersey) カ
シミア kashímia
cash register *n* レジスター réjìsutā
casing [kei'siŋ] *n* (covering) 被覆 hífùku
casino [kəsi:'nou] *n* カジノ kájìno
cask [kæsk] *n* (of wine, beer) たる tarú
casket [kæs'kit] *n* (for jewelery) 宝石箱
hōsekibakò; (*US*: coffin) 棺 kán
casserole [kæs'əroul] *n* (of lamb,
chicken etc) キャセロール kyaséròru;
(pot, container) キャセロールなべ kyasé-
rōrunabè
cassette [kəset'] *n* (tape) カセットテープ
kasétto tḕpu
cassette player *n* カセットプレーヤー
kasétto purḕyà
cassette recorder *n* カセットレコーダ
ー kasétto rekṓdà

cast [kæst] (*pt, pp* **cast**) *vt* (throw: light, shadow) 映す utsúsù; (: object, net) 投げる nagérù; (: fishing-line) キャストする kyásùto surù; (: aspersions, doubts) 投拐ける nagékakerù; (glance, eyes) 向ける mukérù; (THEATER) ...に ...の役を振当てる ...ni ...no yakú wo furísaterù; (make: statue) 鋳込む ikómù

♦*n* (THEATER) キャスト kyásùto; (*also*: **plaster cast**) ギプス gípùsu

to cast a spell on (subject: witch etc) ...に魔法を掛ける ...ni mahô wò kakérù

to cast one's vote 投票する tōhyō suru

castaway [kæs'təwei] *n* 難破した人 nañpa shita hitó

caste [kæst] *n* (social class) カースト kâsùto; (*also*: **caste system**) 階級制 kaíkyūsei, カースト制 kâsutosei

caster [kæs'tə:r] *n* (wheel) キャスター kyásutā

caster sugar (*BRIT*) *n* 粉砂糖 konázatō

casting vote [kæs'tiŋ-] (*BRIT*) *n* 決定票 kettéihyō, キャスティングボート kyásutingubōto

cast iron [kæs'ai'ə:rn] *n* 鋳鉄 chûtetsu

castle [kæs'əl] *n* (building) 城 shirô; (CHESS) 城将 jôshō

cast off *vi* (NAUT) 綱を解く tsuná wo tokù; (KNITTING) 編み終える amíoerù

cast on *vi* (KNITTING) 編み始める amíhajimerù

castor [kæs'tə:r] (*BRIT*) *n* = **caster**

castor oil *n* ひまし油 himáshiyu

castrate [kæs'treit] *vt* (bull, man) 去勢する kyoséi suru

casual [kæʒ'u:əl] *adj* (by chance) 偶然の gúzen no; (irregular: work etc) 臨時の riñji no; (unconcerned) さりげない sarígenaì; (informal: clothes) 普段用の fudányō no

casually [kæʒ'u:əli:] *adv* (in a relaxed way) さりげなく sarígenakù; (dress) 普段着で fudángi de

casualty [kæʒ'u:əlti:] *n* (of war, accident: someone injured) 負傷者 fushôsha; (: someone killed) 死者 shishá; (of situation, event: victim) 犠牲者 giséisha;

(MED: *also*: **casualty department**) 救急病棟 kyúkyūbyōtō

cat [kæt] *n* (pet) ネコ nekð; (wild animal) ネコ科の動物 nekóka no dôbutsu

catalogue [kæt'ələːg] (*US also*: **catalog**) *n* (COMM: for mail order) カタログ katárogu; (of exhibition, library) 目録 mokúroku

♦*vt* (books, collection, events) ...の目録を作る ...no mokúroku wo tsukurù

catalyst [kæt'əlist] *n* (CHEM, *fig*) 触媒 shokúbai

catapult [kæt'əpʌlt] (*BRIT*) *n* (slingshot) ぱちんこ pachínko

cataract [kæt'ərækt] *n* (MED) 白内障 hakúnaìshō

catarrh [kətɑːr'] *n* カタル kátàru

catastrophe [kətæs'trəfiː] *n* (disaster) 災害 saígai

catastrophic [kætəstrɑːf'ik] *adj* (disastrous) 破局的な hakyókuteki na

catch [kætʃ] (*pt, pp* **caught**) *vt* (animal) 捕る tôrù, 捕まえる tsukámaeru; (fish: with net) 捕る tôrù; (: with line) 釣る tsurú; (ball) 捕る tôrù; (bus, train etc) ...に乗る ...ni norù; (arrest: thief etc) 逮捕する taího suru; (surprise: person) びっくりさせる bikkúri saséru; (attract: attention) 引く hikú; (hear: comment, whisper etc) 聞く kikú; (MED: illness) ...に掛る ...ni kakarù; (person: *also*: **catch up with/to**) ...に追い付く ...ni oítsukù

♦*vi* (fire) 付く tsukù; (become trapped: in branches, door etc) 引っ掛る hikkákarù

♦*n* (of fish etc) 獲物 emóno; (of ball) 捕球 hokyû; (hidden problem) 落し穴 otóshiana; (of lock) 留金 tomégane; (game) キャッチボール kyátchibōru

to catch one's breath (rest) 息をつく íkì wo tsukù, 一休みする hitoyàsumi surù

to catch fire 燃え出す moédasù

to catch sight of 見付ける mitsúkeru

catching [kætʃ'iŋ] *adj* (infectious) 移る utsurù

catchment area [kætʃ'mənt-] (*BRIT*) *n* (of school) 学区 gákkù; (of hospital) 通院

圏 tsúiǹken

catch on vi (understand) 分かる waka-rù; (grow popular) 流行する ryúkō suru

catch phrase n キャッチフレーズ kyá-tchífurèzu

catch up vi (fig: with person, on work) 追付く oítsukù
♦vt (person) ...に追い付く ...ni oítsukù

catchy [kætʃ'i:] adj (tune) 覚え易い obóe-yasuì

catechism [kæt'əkizəm] n (REL) 公教要理 kókyōyōri

categoric(al) [kætəgɔ:r'ik(əl)] adj (certain, absolute) 絶対的な zettáiteki na

category [kæt'əgɔ:ri:] n (set, class) 範ちゅう haňchū

cater [kei'tər] vi: **to cater for** (BRIT: person, group) ...向きである ...mukí de arù; (needs) ...を満たす ...wo mitasù; (COMM: weddings etc) ...の料理を仕出しする ...no ryōri wo shidáshi suru

caterer [kei'tərər] n 仕出し屋 shidáshi-ya

catering [kei'təriŋ] n (trade, business) 仕出し shidáshi

caterpillar [kæt'ərpilər] n (with hair) 毛虫 kemúshi; (without hair) 芋虫 imo-mùshi

caterpillar track n キャタピラ kyatá-pirà

cathedral [kəθi:'drəl] n 大聖堂 daíseidō

catholic [kæθ'əlik] adj (tastes, interests) 広い hiroì

Catholic [kæθ'əlik] adj (REL) カトリック教の katórikkukyō no
♦n (REL) カトリック教徒 katórikku-kyòto

cat's-eye [kæts'ai'] (BRIT) n (AUT) 反射りょう haňshabyō ◊夜間の目印として道路の中央またはわきに埋込むガラスなどの反射器 yakán no mejírushi toshitè dōro no chūō mata wa wakí ni umékomù garásu nadò no haňshakì

cattle [kæt'əl] npl ウシ ushí ◊総称 sōshō

catty [kæt'i:] adj (comment, woman) 意地悪な ijíwarù na

caucus [kɔ:'kəs] n (POL: group) 実力者会議 jitsúryokusha kaìgi; (: US) 党部会 tô-

bukái

caught [kɔ:t] pt, pp of **catch**

cauliflower [kɔ:'ləflauər] n カリフラワー karífurawà

cause [kɔ:z] n (of outcome, effect) 原因 geñ-in; (reason) 理由 riyū; (aim, principle: also POL) 目的 mokúteki
♦vt (produce, lead to: outcome, effect) 引起こす hikíokosù

caustic [kɔ:s'tik] adj (CHEM) 腐食性の fushókusei no; (fig: remark) 辛らつな shiňratsu na

caution [kɔ:'ʃən] n (prudence) 慎重さ shiňchōsa; (warning) 警告 keíkoku, 注意 chūi
♦vt (warn: also POLICE) 警告する keíkoku suru

cautious [kɔ:'ʃəs] adj (careful, wary) 注意深い chūibukaì

cautiously [kɔ:'ʃəsli:] adv 注意深く chūibukakù

cavalier [kævəliər'] adj (attitude, fashion) 威張り腐った ibárikusattà

cavalry [kæv'əlri:] n (MIL: mechanized) 装甲部隊 sōkōbutài; (: mounted) 騎兵隊 kihéitai

cave [keiv] n (in cliff, hill) 洞穴 horá-ana

cave in vi (roof etc) 陥没する kaňbotsu suru, 崩れる kuzúrerù

caveman [keiv'mən] (pl **cavemen**) n 穴居人 kékkyòjin

cavern [kæv'ə:rn] n どうくつ dōkutsu

caviar(e) [kæv'i:ɑ:r] n キャビア kyàbia

cavity [kæv'iti:] n (in wall) 空どう kūdō; (ANAT) 腔 kō; (in tooth) 虫歯の穴 mu-shíba no aná

cavort [kəvɔ:rt'] vi (romp) はしゃぎ回る hashágimawarù

CB [si:bi:'] n abbr (= Citizens' Band (Radio)) 市民バンド shimínbaňdo, シチズンバンド shichízunbaňdo

CBI [si:bi:ai'] n abbr (= Confederation of British Industry) 英国産業連盟 eíkokusaňgyōreňmei

cc [si:si:'] abbr (= cubic centimeter(s)) 立方センチメートル rippósenchimètoru, cc shíshì; = **carbon copy**

cease [si:s] vt (end, stop) 終える oéru
♦vi (end, stop) 終る owáru, 止る tomáru

ceasefire [si:s'faiǝr'] n (MIL) 停戦 teſsen

ceaseless [si:s'lis] adj (chatter, traffic) 絶間ない taēma naī

cedar [si:'dǝr] n (tree) ヒマラヤスギ himárayasugī; (wood) シーダー材 shídāzāi

cede [si:d] vt (land, rights etc) 譲る yuzúru

ceiling [si:'liŋ] n (in room) 天井 teñjō; (upper limit: on wages, prices etc) 天井 teñjō, 上限 jṓgen

celebrate [sel'ǝbreit] vt (gen) 祝う iwáu; (REL: mass) 挙げる agéru
♦vi お祝いする o-íwai suru

celebrated [sel'ǝbreitid] adj (author, hero) 有名な yū́mei na

celebration [selǝbrei'ʃǝn] n (party, festival) お祝い o-íwai

celebrity [sǝleb'riti:] n (famous person) 有名人 yū́meijin

celery [sel'ǝ:ri:] n セロリ séròri

celestial [sǝles'tʃǝl] adj (heavenly) 天上的な teñjōteki na

celibacy [sel'ǝbǝsi:] n 禁欲生活 kiñ-yoku seīkatsu

cell [sel] n (in prison: gen) 監房 kañbō; (: solitary) 独房 dokúbō; (in monastery) 個室 koshítsu; (BIO, also of revolutionaries) 細胞 saíbō; (ELEC) 電池 déñchi

cellar [sel'ǝr] n (basement) 地下室 chikáshitsu; (also: wine cellar) ワイン貯蔵室 waín chozṓshitsu

cello [tʃel'ou] n (MUS) チェロ chéro

cellophane [sel'ǝfein] n セロハン séròhan

cellular [sel'jǝlǝr] adj (BIO: structure, tissue) 細胞の saíbō no; (fabrics) 保温効果の高い hoónkōka no takaī, 防寒の bṓkan no

cellulose [sel'jǝlous] n (tissue) 繊維素 señ-isò

Celt [selt, kelt] n ケルト人 kerútòjin

Celtic [sel'tik, kel'tik] adj ケルト人の kerútòjin no; (language etc) ケルトの kérùto no

cement [siment'] n (powder) セメント seménto; (concrete) コンクリート koñkurī́to

cement mixer n セメントミキサー seménto mikisà

cemetery [sem'ite:ri:] n 墓地 bóchì

cenotaph [sen'ǝtæf] n (monument) 戦没者記念碑 señbotsusha kineñhi

censor [sen'sǝr] n (POL, CINEMA etc) 検閲官 keñ-etsùkan
♦vt (book, play, news etc) 検閲する keñ-etsu suru

censorship [sen'sǝ:rʃip] n (of book, play, news etc) 検閲 keñ-etsu

censure [sen'ʃǝr] vt (reprove) とがめる togámerù

census [sen'sǝs] n (of population) 国勢調査 kokúzeichōsa

cent [sent] n (US: also: one-cent coin) 1 セント玉 isséntodamá ¶ see also per

centenary [sen'tǝne:ri:] n (of birth etc) 100周年 hyakúshūnen

center [sen'tǝr] (BRIT centre) n (of circle, room, line) 中心 chūshin; (of town) 中心部 chūshinbu, 繁華街 hañkagài; (of attention, interest) 的 matō; (heart: of action, belief etc) 核心 kakúshin; (building: health center, community center) センター séntā; (POL) 中道 chū́dō
♦vt (weight) ...の中心に置く ...no chūshin ni okú; (sights) ...にぴったり合わせる ...ni pittari awaseru; (SOCCER: ball) グランド中央へ飛ばす gurándo chū́ō e tobásu; (TYP: on page) 中央に合わせる chū́ō ni awáseru

center forward n (SPORT) センターフォワード señtāfowàdo

center half n (SPORT) センターハーフ señtāhāfu

centigrade [sen'tigreid] adj 摂氏 sesshī́

centimeter [sen'tǝmi:tǝr] (BRIT **centimetre**) n センチメートル señchimḕtoru

centipede [sen'tǝpi:d] n ムカデ mukáde

central [sen'trǝl] adj (in the center) 中心点の chūshiñten no; (near the center) 中心の chūshin no; (committee, government) 中央の chū́ō no; (idea, figure) 中心の chūshin no

Central America n 中米 chū́bei

central heating n セントラルヒーティング señtoraruhī́tiñgu

centralize [sen'trəlaiz] *vt* (decision-making, authority) 中央に集中させる chūō ni shūchū saséru

central reservation (*BRIT*) *n* (AUT: of road) 中央分離帯 chūōbunritai

centre [sen'tə:r] (*etc BRIT*) = **center** *etc*

century [sen'tʃə:ri:] *n* 世紀 séìki
20th century 20世紀 nijússeìki

ceramic [sərəm'ik] *adj* (art, tiles) セラミックの serámikku no

ceramics [sərəm'iks] *npl* (objects) 焼物 yakímono

cereal [si:r'i:əl] *n* (plant, crop) 穀物 kókùmotsu; (food) シリアル shiríarù

cerebral [se:r'əbrəl] *adj* (MED: of the brain) 脳の nō no; (intellectual) 知的な chitéki na

ceremony [se:r'əmouni:] *n* (event) 式 shikí; (ritual) 儀式 gíshìki; (behavior) 形式 kéíshiki
to stand on ceremony 礼儀にこだわる reígi ni kodáwarù

certain [sə:r'tən] *adj* (sure: person) 確信している kakúshin shité irú; (: fact) 確実な kakújitsu na; (person): *a certain Mr Smith* スミスと呼ばれる男 sumísù to yobareru otóko; (particular): *certain days/places* ある日〔場所〕árù hi 〔bashó〕; (some): *a certain coldness/pleasure* ある程度の冷たさ〔喜び〕árù teido no tsumétasa 〔yorókobi〕
for certain 確実に kakújitsu ni

certainly [sə:r'tənli:] *adv* (undoubtedly) 間違いなく machígai nakù; (of course) もちろん mochíròn

certainty [sə:r'tənti:] *n* (assurance) 確実性 kakújitsusei; (inevitability) 必然性 hitsúzensei

certificate [sərtif'əkit] *n* (of birth, marriage etc) 証明書 shōmeisho; (diploma) 資格証明書 shikákushōmeisho

certified mail [sə:r'təfaid-] (*US*) *n* 配達証明付き書留郵便 haítatsushōmei tsukí kakítome yūbin

certified public accountant (*US*) *n* 公認会計士 kōnin kaikèishi

certify [sə:r'təfai] *vt* (fact) 証明する shō-

mei suru; (award a diploma to) ...に資格を与える ...ni shikáku wo atáeru; (declare insane) 精神異常と認定する seíshinijō to niñtei suru

cervical [sə:r'vikəl] *adj* (smear, cancer) 子宮けい部の shikyúkeibu no

cervix [sə:r'viks] *n* (ANAT) 子宮けい部 shikyúkeibu

Cesarean [size:r'i:ən] (*BRIT* **Caesarean**) *adj*: *Cesarean (section)* 帝王切開 teíōsekkài

cesspit [ses'pit] *n* (sewage tank) 汚水だめ osúidame

cf. *abbr* = **compare**

ch. *abbr* = **chapter**

chafe [tʃeif] *vt* (rub: skin) 擦る súrù

chagrin [ʃəgrin'] *n* (annoyance) 悔しさ kuyáshisa; (disappointment) 落胆 rakútan

chain [tʃein] *n* (for anchor, prisoner, dog etc) 鎖 kusári; (on bicycle) チェーン chēn; (jewelery) 首飾り kubíkazàri; (of shops, hotels) チェーン chēn; (of events, ideas) 連鎖 reñsa
◆*vt* (*also:* **chain up**: prisoner, dog) 鎖につなぐ kusári ni tsunágu
an island chain/a chain of islands 列島 rettō
a mountain chain/a chain of mountains 山脈 sañmyaku

chain reaction *n* 連鎖反応 reñsahaǹnō

chain-smoke [tʃein'smouk] *vi* 立続けにタバコを吸う tatétsuzuke ni tabáko wo suú

chain store *n* チェーンストア chéñsutoà

chair [tʃe:r] *n* (seat) いす isú; (armchair) 安楽いす añrakuisú; (of university) 講座 kōza; (of meeting) 座長 zachō; (of committee) 委員長 iíñchō
◆*vt* (meeting) 座長を務める zachō wo tsutómerù

chairlift [tʃe:r'lift] *n* リフト rífùto

chairman [tʃe:r'mən] (*pl* **chairmen**) *n* (of committee) 委員長 iíñchō; (*BRIT*: of company) 社長 shachō

chalet [ʃælei'] *n* 山小屋 yamágoya

chalice [tʃæl'is] *n* (REL) 聖さん杯 seísañhai

chalk [tʃɔ:k] n (GEO) 白亜 hákùa; (for writing) 白墨 hakuboku, チョーク chōku

challenge [tʃǽl'indʒ] n (of new job, unknown, new venture etc) 挑戦 chṓsen; (to authority, received ideas etc) 反抗 hańkō; (dare) 挑戦 chṓsen

♦vt (SPORT) ...に試合を申込む ...ni shiái wo mṓshikomù; (rival, competitor) 挑戦 する chṓsen suru; (authority, right, idea etc) ...に反抗する ...ni hańkō suru

to challenge someone to do something ...に...をやれるものならやってみろ と挑戦する ...ni ...wo yaréru monó nara yatté miro to chṓsen suru

challenging [tʃǽl'indʒiŋ] adj (career, task) やりがいを感じさせる yarígai wo kańji saséru; (tone, look etc) 挑発的な chṓhatsuteki na

chamber [tʃeim'bə:r] n (room) 部屋 heyá; (POL: house) 院 íñ; (BRIT: LAW: gen pl) 弁護士事務所 beńgoshi jimushḯtsu; (: of judge) 判事室 hańjishḯtsu

chamber of commerce 商工会議所 shṓkōkaigisho

chambermaid [tʃeim'bə:rmeid] n (in hotel) メード mḗdo

chamber music n 室内音楽 shitsúnai oñgaku

chamois [ʃæm'i:] n (ZOOL) シャモア shamòa; (cloth) セーム革 sḗmugawa

champagne [ʃæmpein'] n シャンペン shańpeñ

champion [tʃæm'pi:ən] n (of league, contest, fight) 優勝者 yúshōsha, チャンピオ ン chańpion; (of cause, principle, person) 擁護者 yògosha

championship [tʃæm'pi:ənʃip] n (contest) 選手権決定戦 seńshukèn kettéisen; (title) 選手権 seńshuken

chance [tʃæns] n (likelihood, possibility) 可能性 kańōsei; (opportunity) 機会 kikái, チャンス cháñsu; (risk) 危険 kikén, か け kaké

♦vt (risk): *to chance it* 危険を冒す kikén wo okasù, 冒険をする bṓken wo suru

♦adj 偶然の gūzen no

to take a chance 危険を冒す kikén wo okasù, 冒険をする bṓken wo suru

by chance 偶然に gūzen ni

chancellor [tʃæn'səlɚ] n (head of government) 首相 shushṓ

Chancellor of the Exchequer (BRIT) n 大蔵大臣 ōkuradaìjin

chandelier [ʃændəli'ə:r] n シャンデリア shańderìa

change [tʃeindʒ] vt (alter, transform) 変 える kaéru; (wheel, bulb etc) 取替える toríkaeru; (clothes) 着替える kigáeru; (job, address) 変える kaéru; (baby, diaper) 替える kaéru; (exchange: money) 両 替する ryṓgae suru

♦vi (alter) 変る kawáru; (change one's clothes) 着替える kigáeru; (change trains, buses) 乗換える noríkaeru; (traffic lights) 変る kawáru; (be transformed): *to change into* ...に変る ...ni kawáru, ...になる ...ni narù

♦n (alteration) 変化 héñka; (difference) 違い chigái; (also: **change of clothes**) 着 替え kigáe; (of government, climate, job) 変る事 kawáru kotó; (coins) 小銭 kozéni; (money returned) お釣 o-tsúri

to change one's mind 気が変る ki gá kawarù

for a change たまには tamá ni wa

changeable [tʃein'dʒəbəl] adj 変りやすい kawáriyasuì

change machine n 両替機 ryṓgaeki

changeover [tʃeindʒ'ouvə:r] n (to new system) 切替え kiríkae

changing [tʃein'dʒiŋ] adj (world, nature) 変る kawáru

changing room (BRIT) n 更衣室 kōishìtsu

channel [tʃæn'əl] n (TV) チャンネル chánneru; (in sea, river etc) 水路 suíro; (groove) 溝 mizó; (fig: means) 手続 tetsuzùki, ルート rūto

♦vt (money, resources) 流す nagásù

the (English) Channel イギリス海峡 igírisu kaíkyō

the Channel Islands チャネル諸島 chanéru shotō

chant [tʃænt] n (of crowd, fans etc) 掛声 kakégoè; (REL: song) 詠唱歌 eíshōka

♦vt (word, name, slogan) 唱える tonáerù

chaos [kei'ɑ:s] n (disorder) 混乱 koñran

chaotic [keiɑ'tik] adj (mess, jumble) 混乱した koñran shitá

chap [tʃæp] (BRIT: inf) n (man) やつ yátsu

chapel [tʃæp'əl] n (in church) 礼拝堂 reíhaidō; (in hospital, prison, school etc) チャペル chápèru; (BRIT: non-conformist chapel) 教会堂 kyōkaidō

chaperone [tʃæp'əroun] n (for woman) 付添い tsukísoi, シャペロン shapéroñ

♦vt (woman, child) ...に付添う ...ni tsukísoù

chaplain [tʃæp'lin] n (REL, MIL, SCOL) 付属牧師 fuzókubokùshi

chapped [tʃæpt] adj (skin, lips) あかぎれした akágire shitá

chapter [tʃæp'tər] n (of book) 章 shō; (of life, history) 時期 jíkì

char [tʃɑ:r] vt (burn) 黒焦げにする kurókoge ni suru

♦n (BRIT) = **charwoman**

character [kær'iktər] n (nature) 性質 seíshitsu; (moral strength) 気骨 kikótsu; (personality) 人格 jiñkaku; (in novel, film) 人物 jíñbutsu; (letter) 文字 mójì

characteristic [kæriktəris'tik] adj (typical) 特徴的な tokúchōteki na

♦n (trait, feature) 特徴 tokúchō

characterize [kær'iktəraiz] vt (typify) ...の特徴である ...no tokúchō de arú; (describe the character of) ...の特徴を描写する ...no tokúchō wo byōsha suru

charade [ʃəreid'] n (sham, pretence) 装いyosóoi

charcoal [tʃɑ:r'koul] n (fuel) 炭 sumí, 木炭 mokútañ; (for drawing) 木炭 mokútañ

charge [tʃɑ:rdʒ] n (fee) 料金 ryōkin; (LAW: accusation) 容疑 yōgi; (responsibility) 責任 sekínin

♦vt (for goods, services) ...の料金を取る ...no ryōkin wo torú; (LAW: accuse): **to charge someone (with)** 起訴する kisó suru; (battery) 充電する jūden suru; (MIL: enemy) ...に突撃する ...ni totsúgeki suru

♦vi (animal) 掛って来る〔行く〕kakáttè

kurù〔ikú〕; (MIL) 突撃する totsúgeki suru

to take charge of (child) ...の面倒を見る ...no meñdō wo mirù; (company) ...の指揮を取る ...no shíki wo torú

to be in charge of (person, machine) ...の責任を持っている ...no sekínin wo motté irù; (business) ...の責任者である ...no sekíninshà de arù

how much do you charge? 料金はいくらですか ryōkin wa ikùra desù ka

to charge an expense (up) to someone's account ...の勘定に付ける ...no kañjō ni tsukerù

charge card n (for particular shop or organization) クレジットカード kuréjittokàdo ◊特定の店でしか使えない物を指す tokútei nò mise de shika tsukáenai monò wo sásù

charges [tʃɑr'dʒiz] npl (bank charges, telephone charges etc) 料金 ryōkin

to reverse the charges (TEL) 先方払いにする señpōbarài ni surù

charisma [kəriz'mə] n カリスマ性 karísumasei

charitable [tʃær'itəbəl] adj (organization) 慈善の jízen no

charity [tʃær'iti:] n (organization) 慈善事業 jizéñjigyō; (kindness) 親切さ shíñsetsusa; (generosity) 寛大さ kañdaisa; (money, gifts) 施し hodókoshi

charlady [tʃɑr'leidi:] (BRIT) n = **charwoman**

charlatan [ʃɑr'lətən] n 偽者 nisémono

charm [tʃɑrm] n (attractiveness) 魅力 miryóku; (to bring good luck) お守 o-mámori; (on bracelet etc) 飾り kazári

♦vt (please, delight) うっとりさせる uttórì saséru

charming [tʃɑr'miŋ] adj (person, place) 魅力的な miryókuteki na

chart [tʃɑrt] n (graph) グラフ gúràfu; (diagram) 図 zu; (map) 海図 kâizu

♦vt (course) 地図に書く chízù ni kakú; (progress) 図に書く zù ni kakú

charter [tʃɑr'tər] vt (plane, ship etc) チャーターする chátā surù

♦n (document, constitution) 憲章 keñ

shō; (of university, company) 免許 mênkyo

chartered accountant [tʃɑːrˈtəːrd-] (*BRIT*) *n* 公認会計士 kōnin kaikeîshi

charter flight *n* チャーターフライト châtāfuraîto

charts [tʃɑːrts] *npl* (hit parade): *the charts* ヒットチャート hittóchāto

charwoman [tʃɑːrˈwumən] (*pl* **charwomen**) *n* 掃除婦 sōjifu

chase [tʃeis] *vt* (pursue) 追掛ける oîkakerù; (*also*: **chase away**) 追払う oîharaù

♦*n* (pursuit) 追跡 tsuîseki

chasm [kæzˈəm] *n* (GEO) 深い割れ目 fúkài warême

chassis [ʃæsˈiː] *n* (AUT) シャシ shashî

chastity [tʃæsˈtitiː] *n* (REL) 純潔 juñketsu

chat [tʃæt] *vi* (*also*: **have a chat**) おしゃべりする o-shábeři surù

♦*n* (conversation) おしゃべり o-shábeřî

chat show (*BRIT*) *n* トーク番組 tōku baňgumi

chatter [tʃætˈəːr] *vi* (person) しゃべりまくる shabérimakurù; (animal) きゃっきゃっと鳴く kyákkyattò nakú; (teeth) がちがち鳴る gachígachi narú

♦*n* (of people) しゃべり声 shabérigoè; (of birds) さえずり saézuri; (of animals) きゃっきゃっという鳴き声 kyákkyattò iú nakígoè

chatterbox [tʃætˈəːrbɑːks] (*inf*) *n* おしゃべり好き o-shábeřizuki

chatty [tʃætˈiː] *adj* (style, letter) 親しみやすい shitáshimiyasuì; (person) おしゃべりな o-shábeřî na

chauffeur [ʃouˈfəːr] *n* お抱え運転手 okákae-unteñshu

chauvinist [ʃouˈvənist] *n* (male chauvinist) 男性優越主義者 dañseiyūetsushugishà; (nationalist) 熱狂的愛国主義者 nekkyōtekiaikokushugishà

cheap [tʃiːp] *adj* (inexpensive) 安い yasuî; (poor quality) 安っぽい yasúppoì; (behavior, joke) 下劣な gerétsu na

♦*adv*: *to buy/sell something cheap* 安く買う（売る）yasúkù kaú〔urú〕

cheaper [tʃiːˈpəːr] *adj* (less expensive) もっと安い móttò yasuî

cheaply [tʃiːpˈliː] *adv* (inexpensively) 安く yasuku

cheat [tʃiːt] *vi* (in exam) カンニングする kañningu suru; (at cards) いかさまをする ikásama wo suru

♦*vt*: *to cheat someone (out of something)* ...から ...をだまし取る ...kara ...wo damáshitorù

♦*n* (person) いかさま師 ikásamashî

check [tʃek] *vt* (examine: bill, progress) 調べる shiráberù; (verify: facts) 確認する kakúnin suru; (halt: enemy, disease) 食止める kuîtomerù; (restrain: impulse, person) 抑える osáerù

♦*n* (inspection) 検査 kêñsa; (curb) 抑制 yokúsei; (*US*: bill) 勘定書 kañjōgaki; (BANKING) 小切手 kogittè; (pattern: *gen pl*) 市松模様 ichímatsumoyò

♦*adj* (pattern, cloth) 市松模様の ichímatsumoyò no

checkbook [tʃekˈbuk] (*US*) *n* 小切手帳 kogittechō

checkerboard [tʃekˈəːrbɔːrd] *n* チェッカ一盤 chekkában

checkered [tʃekˈəːrd] (*BRIT* **chequered**) *adj* (*fig*: career, history) 起伏の多い kifúku no ôi

checkers [tʃekˈəːrz] (*US*) *npl* (game) チェッカー chékkā

check in *vi* (at hotel, airport) チェックインする chekkûin surù

♦*vt* (luggage) 預ける azúkerù

check-in (desk) [tʃekˈin-] *n* フロント furônto

checking account [tʃekˈiŋ-] (*US*) *n* (current account) 当座預金 tōzayokìn

checkmate [tʃekˈmeit] *n* (CHESS) 王手 ôte

check out *vi* (of hotel) チェックアウトする chekkúaùto surù

checkout [tʃekˈaut] *n* (in shop) 勘定カウンター kañjō kauñtā

checkpoint [tʃekˈpɔint] *n* (on border) 検問所 keñmonjo

checkroom [tʃekˈruːm] (*US*) *n* (left-luggage office) 手荷物一時預り所 tenímòtsu ichíjìazúkarijo

check up vi: *to check up on something/someone* ...を調べておく ...wo shirábetè okù

checkup [tʃek'ʌp] n (MED) 健康診断 keñkōshindan

cheek [tʃiːk] n (ANAT) ほお hő; (impudence) ずうずうしさ zúzūshisà; (nerve) 度胸 dokyō

cheekbone [tʃiːk'boun] n ほお骨 hőbone

cheeky [tʃiː'kiː] adj (impudent) ずうずうしい zúzūshiì

cheep [tʃiːp] vi (bird) ぴよぴよ鳴く piyópiyo nakù

cheer [tʃiːr] vt (team, speaker) 声援する seíen suru; (gladden) 喜ばす yorókobasù
♦vi (shout) 声援する seíen suru
♦n (shout) 声援 seíen

cheerful [tʃiːr'fəl] adj (wave, smile, person) 朗らかな hogaràka na

cheerio [tʃiːr'iːou] (BRIT) excl じゃあね já ne

cheers [tʃiːrz] npl (of crowd etc) 声援 seíen, かっさい kassái
cheers! (toast) 乾杯 kañpai

cheer up vi (person) 元気を出す geñki wo dasù
♦vt (person) 元気づける geñkizukerù

cheese [tʃiːz] n チーズ chízu

cheeseboard [tʃiːz'bourd] n チーズボード chízubōdo ◇チーズを盛り合せる板または皿 chízu wo moríawaserù ità mata wa sará

cheetah [tʃiː'tə] n チーター chítā

chef [ʃef] n (in restaurant, hotel) コック kókkù

chemical [kem'ikəl] adj (fertilizer, warfare) 化学の kágàku no
♦n 化学薬品 kagákuyakùhin

chemist [kem'ist] n (BRIT: pharmacist) 薬剤師 yakúzaìshi; (scientist) 化学者 kagákùsha

chemistry [kem'istriː] n 化学 kágàku

chemist's (shop) [kem'ists-] (BRIT) n 薬局 yakkyóku

cheque [tʃek] (BRIT: BANKING) n = check

chequebook [tʃek'buk] (BRIT) n = checkbook

cheque card (BRIT) n (to guarantee cheque) 小切手カード kogítte kàdo

chequered [tʃek'əːrd] (BRIT) adj = checkered

cherish [tʃeːr'iʃ] vt (person) 大事にする daíji ni suru; (memory, dream) 心に抱く kokórò ni idakù

cherry [tʃeːr'iː] n (fruit) サクランボウ sakúranbō; (also: cherry tree) サクラ sakúra

chess [tʃes] n チェス chésù

chessboard [tʃes'bourd] n チェス盤 chésuban

chest [tʃest] n (ANAT) 胸 muné; (box) ひつ hitsú
chest of drawers 整理だんす seíridañsu

chestnut [tʃes'nʌt] n クリ kurí; (also: chestnut tree) クリの木 kurí no ki

chew [tʃuː] vt (food) かむ kamù

chewing gum [tʃuː'iŋ-] n チューインガム chúingamù

chic [ʃiːk] adj (dress, hat etc) スマートな súmāto na; (person, place) 粋な ikí na

chick [tʃik] n (bird) ひな hínà; (inf: girl) べっぴん beppín

chicken [tʃik'ən] n (bird) ニワトリ niwátori; (meat) 鶏肉 keíniku; (inf: coward) 弱虫 yowamùshi

chicken out (inf) vi おじ気付いて...から手を引く ojíkezuìte ...kara te wo hikú

chickenpox [tʃik'ənpɑks] n 水ぼうそう mizúbōsō

chicory [tʃik'əːriː] n チコリ chíkòri

chief [tʃiːf] n (of tribe) しゅう長 shúchō; (of organization, department) ...長 ...chō
♦adj (principal) 主な ómò na

chief executive n 社長 shachō

chiefly [tʃiːf'liː] adv (principally) 主に ómò ni

chiffon [ʃifɑn'] n (fabric) シフォン shífòn

chilblain [tʃil'blein] n 霜焼け shimóyake

child [tʃaild] (pl **children**) n 子供 kodómo
do you have any children? お子さんは? o-kó-san wa?

childbirth [tʃaild'bəːrθ] n お産 osán

childhood [tʃaild'hud] n 子供時分 kodómojìbun

childish [tʃail'diʃ] *adj* (games, attitude, person) 子供っぽい kodómoppoì

childlike [tʃaild'laik] *adj* 無邪気な mújàki na

child minder (*BRIT*) *n* 保母 hóbò

children [tʃil'drən] *npl of* **child**

Chile [tʃil'i:] *n* チリ chírì

Chilean [tʃil'eiən] *adj* チリの chírì no
♦*n* チリ人 chírìjin

chill [tʃil] *n* (coldness: in air, water etc) 冷え hié; (MED: illness) 風邪 kazé
♦*vt* (cool: food, drinks) 冷す hiyasù; (person: make cold): **to be chilled** 体が冷える karáda ga hierù

chilli [tʃil'i:] *n* チリ chirì

chilly [tʃil'i:] *adj* (weather) 肌寒い hadásamuì; (person) 寒気がする samúke ga suru; (response, look) 冷たい tsumétai

chime [tʃaim] *n* (of bell, clock) チャイム cháìmu
♦*vi* チャイムが鳴る chaìmu ga narú

chimney [tʃim'ni:] *n* (of house, factory) 煙突 eńtotsu

chimney sweep *n* 煙突掃除夫 eńtotsu sōjifù

chimpanzee [tʃimpænzi:'] *n* チンパンジー chińpañjī

chin [tʃin] *n* あご agó

China [tʃai'nə] *n* 中国 chūgoku

china [tʃai'nə] *n* (clay) 陶土 tòdo; (crockery) 瀬戸物 setómono

Chinese [tʃaini:z'] *adj* 中国の chūgoku no; (LING) 中国語の chūgokugo no
♦*n inv* (person) 中国人 chūgokujin; (LING) 中国語 chūgokugo

chink [tʃiŋk] *n* (crack: in door, wall etc) 透き間 sukíma; (clink: of bottles etc) かちん kachín

chip [tʃip] *n* (*BRIT: gen pl*: CULIN) フライドポテト furáidopotèto; (*US: also:* **potato chip**) ポテトチップス potétochippusu; (of wood, glass, stone) 欠けら kakéra; (COMPUT) チップ chippù
♦*vt*: **to be chipped** (cup, plate) 縁が欠けている fuchí ga kakéte irú

chip in (*inf*) *vi* (contribute) 寄付する kífù surù; (interrupt) 口を挟む kuchí wo

hasamù

chiropodist [kirɑ:p'ədist] (*BRIT*) *n* 足治療師 ashí chiryòshi

chirp [tʃə:rp] *vi* (bird) ちゅうちゅう鳴く chūchū nakú

chisel [tʃiz'əl] *n* (for wood) のみ nómì; (for stone) たがね tagáne

chit [tʃit] *n* (note) メモ mémò; (receipt) 領収書 ryōshūsho

chitchat [tʃit'tʃæt] *n* 世間話 sekénbanàshi

chivalrous [ʃiv'əlrəs] *adj* 親切な shínsetsu na

chivalry [ʃiv'əlri:] *n* (behavior) 親切さ shińsetsusa; (medieval system) 騎士道 kishídò

chives [tʃaivz] *npl* (herb) チャイブ cháìbu

chlorine [klɔ:r'i:n] *n* (CHEM) 塩素 éñso

chock-a-block [tʃɑ:k'əblɑ:k'] *adj* 一杯で íppài de

chock-full [tʃɑ:k'ful'] *adj* = **chock-a-block**

chocolate [tʃɔ:k'əlit] *n* (bar, sweet, cake) チョコレート chokórèto; (drink) ココア kókòa

choice [tʃɔis] *n* (selection) 選んだ物 eráñda monò; (option) 選択 señtaku; (preference) 好み konómi
♦*adj* (fine: cut of meat, fruit etc) 一級の ikkyū no

choir [kwai'ə:r] *n* (of singers) 聖歌隊 seíkatai; (area of church) 聖歌隊席 seíkataisèki

choirboy [kwaiə:r'bɔi] *n* 少年聖歌隊員 shóñen seikataiin

choke [tʃouk] *vi* (on food, drink etc) ...がのどに詰る ...ga nodò ni tsumarù; (with smoke, dust, anger etc) むせる muséru
♦*vt* (strangle) ...ののどを締める ...no nodò wo shimerù; (block): **to be choked (with)** (...で)詰っている (...de) tsumattè irú
♦*n* (AUT) チョーク chôku

cholera [kɑ:l'ə:rə] *n* コレラ kórèra

cholesterol [kəles'tərɔ:l] *n* (fat) コレステロール korésuterôru

choose [tʃu:z] (*pt* chose, *pp* chosen) *vt* 選

ぶ erábù
to choose to do ...をする事に決める
...wo suru kotō ni kiméru
choosy [tʃuːˈziː] *adj* (difficult to please)
えり好みする erígonomi suru
chop [tʃɑp] *vt* (wood) 割る warú;
(CULIN: *also*: **chop up**: vegetables, fruit,
meat) 刻む kizámu
♦*n* (CULIN) チョップ chóppù, チャップ
cháppu
chopper [tʃɑˈpəːr] *n* (helicopter) ヘリコ
プター heríkopùtā
choppy [tʃɑˈpiː] *adj* (sea) しけの shiké no
chops [tʃɑps] *npl* (jaws) あご agó
chopsticks [tʃɑˈpˈstiks] *npl* はし háshì
choral [kɔːrˈəl] *adj* (MUS) 合唱の gasshō
no
chord [kɔːrd] *n* (MUS) 和音 wáòn
chore [tʃɔːr] *n* (domestic task) 家事 kájì;
(routine task) 毎日の雑用 máìnichi no
zatsúyo
choreographer [kɔːriːɑˈgˈrəfəːr] *n* 振付
師 furítsukeshì
chortle [tʃɔːrˈtəl] *vi* 楽しそうに笑う tanó-
shisō ni waraù
chorus [kɔːrˈəs] *n* (MUS: group) 合唱隊
gasshōtai, コーラス kōrasu; (: song) 合唱
gasshō; (: refrain) リフレーン rifúrēn; (of
musical play) コーラス kōrasu
chose [tʃouz] *pt of* **choose**
chosen [tʃouˈzən] *pp of* **choose**
Christ [kraist] *n* キリスト kirísuto
christen [krisˈən] *vt* (REL: baby) ...に洗
礼を施す ...ni sénrei wo hodókosù; (nickname) ...を...と呼ぶ ...wo ...to yobú
Christian [krisˈtʃən] *adj* キリスト教の
kirísutokyō no
♦*n* キリスト教徒 kirísutokyòto
Christianity [kristʃiːænˈitiː] *n* キリスト
教 kirísutokyō
Christian name *n* ファーストネーム fá-
sutonèmu
Christmas [krisˈməs] *n* (REL: festival)
クリスマス kurísumàsu; (period) クリスマ
スの季節 kurísumàsu no kisetsù
Merry Christmas! メリークリスマス！
merī́ kurisumàsu!
Christmas card *n* クリスマスカード

kurísumasu kàdo
Christmas Day *n* クリスマス kurísumàsu
Christmas Eve *n* クリスマスイブ kurísumasu ibù
Christmas tree *n* クリスマスツリー kurísumasu tsurī́
chrome [kroum] *n* クロームめっき kurō-
mumekkì
chromium [krouˈmiːəm] *n* = **chrome**
chromosome [krouˈməsoum] *n* 染色体
seńshokutai
chronic [krɑnˈik] *adj* (continual: ill-
health, illness etc) 慢性の mańsei no;
(: drunkenness etc) 常習的な jōshūteki
na; (severe: shortage, lack etc) ひどい
hídòi
chronicle [krɑnˈikəl] *n* (of events) 記録
kiróku ◇年代順または日付順の記録を指
す neńdaijuñ mata wa hizúkejuñ no
kiróku wo sasù
chronological [krɑnələˈdʒˈikəl] *adj*
(order) 日付順の hizúkejuñ no
chrysanthemum [krisænˈθəməm] *n* キ
ク kikú
chubby [tʃʌbˈiː] *adj* (cheeks, child) ぽっち
ゃりした potchárì shitá
chuck [tʃʌk] (*inf*) *vt* (throw: stone, ball
etc) 投げる nagerù; (*BRIT*: *also*: **chuck
up**) やめる yaméru
chuckle [tʃʌkˈəl] *vi* くすくす笑う kúsùkusu waraù
chuck out *vt* (person) 追い出す oídasù;
(rubbish etc) 捨てる sutéru
chug [tʃʌg] *vi* (machine, car engine etc)
ぽっぽっと音を立てる póppòtto otó wo
taterù; (car, boat: *also*: **chug along**) ぽっ
ぽっと音を立てて行く poppòtto otó wo
tatète ikú
chum [tʃʌm] *n* (friend) 友達 tomódachi
chunk [tʃʌŋk] *n* (of stone, meat) 塊 katámari
church [tʃəːrtʃ] *n* (building) 教会 kyókai;
(denomination) 教派 kyōha, ...教 ...kyō
churchyard [tʃəːrtʃˈjɑːrd] *n* 教会墓地
kyókaibochì
churlish [tʃəːrˈliʃ] *adj* (silence, behavior)
無礼な burèi na

churn [tʃəːrn] *n* (for butter) かく乳器 kakúnyǔki; (BRIT: also: **milk churn**) 大型ミルク缶 ōgata mirukukan

churn out *vt* (mass-produce: objects, books etc) 大量に作る taíryō ni tsukurù

chute [ʃuːt] *n* (also: **rubbish chute**) ごみ捨て場 gomísuteba; (for coal, parcels etc) シュート shūto

chutney [tʃʌtniː] *n* チャツネ chátsune

CIA [siːaiei'] (US) *n abbr* (= *Central Intelligence Agency*) 中央情報局 chūōjōhōkyoku

CID [siːaidi'] (BRIT) *n abbr* (= *Criminal Investigation Department*) 刑事部 keíjibù

cider [sai'dəːr] *n* リンゴ酒 ríngoshù

cigar [sigɑːr'] *n* 葉巻 hamáki

cigarette [sigəret'] *n* (紙巻) タバコ (kamímaki) tābako

cigarette case *n* シガレットケース shigárettokèsu

cigarette end *n* 吸殻 suígara

Cinderella [sindərel'ə] *n* シンデレラ shíndererà

cinders [sin'dəːrz] *npl* (of fire) 燃え殻 moégara

cine-camera [sin'iːkæməːrə] (BRIT) *n* 映画カメラ eíga kamèra

cine-film [sin'iːfilm] (BRIT) *n* 映画用フィルム eígayò fírùmu

cinema [sin'əmə] *n* (THEATER) 映画館 eígakàn; (film-making) 映画界 eígakài

cinnamon [sin'əmən] *n* (CULIN) ニッケイ nikkéi, シナモン shinámoñ

cipher [sai'fəːr] *n* (code) 暗号 añgō

circle [səːr'kəl] *n* (shape) 円 eñ; (of friends) 仲間 nakáma; (in cinema, theater) 二階席 nikáisekì

♦*vi* (bird, plane) 旋回する señkai suru

♦*vt* (move round) 回る mawáru; (surround) 囲む kakómu

circuit [səːr'kit] *n* (ELEC) 回路 kaíro; (tour) 1周 isshū; (track) サーキット sā̀kitto; (lap) 1周 isshū, ラップ ráppù

circuitous [səːrkjuːˈitəs] *adj* (route, journey) 遠回りの tōmawàri no

circular [səːr'kjəlàːr] *adj* (plate, pond etc) 丸い marúi

♦*n* (letter) 回状 kaíjō

circulate [səːr'kjəleit] *vi* (traffic) 流れる nagárerù; (blood) 循環する juñkan suru; (news, rumour, report) 出回る demáwaru; (person: at party etc) 動き回る ugókimawarù

♦*vt* (report) 回す mawásu

circulation [səːrkjəlei'ʃən] *n* (of report, book etc) 回される事 mawásareru kotó; (of traffic) 流れ nagáre; (of air, water, also MED: of blood) 循環 juñkan; (of newspaper) 発行部数 hakkóbusù

circumcise [səːr'kəmsaiz] *vt* (MED) ...の包皮を切除する ...no hōhi wo setsùjo surù; (REL) ...に割礼を行う ...ni katsúrei wo okónau

circumference [səːrkʌmˈfəːrəns] *n* (edge) 周囲 shūi; (distance) 周囲の長さ shūi no nagàsa

circumflex [səːr'kəmfleks] *n* (also: **circumflex accent**) 曲折アクセント kyokúsetsu akùsento

circumspect [səːr'kəmspekt] *adj* (cautious, careful) 慎重な shíñchō na

circumstances [səːr'kəmstænsiz] *npl* (of accident, death) 状況 jōkyō; (conditions, state of affairs) 状態 jōtai; (also: **financial circumstances**) 経済状態 keízaijōtai

circumvent [səːrkəmvent'] *vt* (regulation) ...に触れない様にする ...ni furénai yō ni surù; (difficulty) 回避する káîhi surù

circus [səːr'kəs] *n* (show) サーカス sā̀kasu; (performers) サーカス団 sā̀kasudaǹ

CIS [siːaies'] *n abbr* = **Commonwealth of Independent States**

cistern [sis'təːrn] *n* (water tank) 貯水タンク chosúitaǹku; (of toilet) 水槽 suísō

cite [sait] *vt* (quote: example, author etc) 引用する in-yō suru; (LAW) 召喚する shōkan suru

citizen [sit'əzən] *n* (gen) 住民 jūmin; (of a country) 国民 kokúmin, 市民 shímìn; (of a city) 市民 shímìn; (of other political divisions) ...民 ...mín

citizenship [sit'əzənʃip] *n* (of a country) 市民権 shimíñken

citrus fruit [sit'rəs fru:t] n カンキツ類 kańkitsuruì

city [sit'i:] n 都市 toshì
 the City (FINANCE) シティー shitî ◇ロンドンの金融業の中心地 rondon no kiń'yūgyō no chūshińchi

civic [siv'ik] adj (leader, duties, pride) 公民の kŏmin no; (authorities) 自治体の ji-chítai no

civic centre (BRIT) n 自治体中心部 ji-chítaichūshinbu

civil [siv'əl] adj (gen) 市民の shímin no, 公民の kŏmin no; (authorities) 行政の gyŏsei no; (polite) 礼儀正しい reígitadashiì

civil defense n 民間防衛 mińkanbōei

civil disobedience n 市民的不服従 shi-mínтekifufukujù

civil engineer n 土木技師 dobŏkugishì

civilian [sivil'jən] adj (attitudes, casu-alties, life) 民間の mińkan no
 ♦ n 民間人 mińkanjin

civilization [sivəlazei'ʃən] n (a society) 文明社会 buńmeishakài; (social organi-zation) 文化 buńka

civilized [siv'əlaizd] adj (society) 文明的な buńmeiteki na; (person) 洗練された seńren saréta

civil law n 民法 mínpō

civil rights npl 公民権 kŏminken

civil servant n 公務員 kŏmuìn

Civil Service n 文官職 buńkanshokù

civil war n 内乱 naíran

clad [klæd] adj: **clad (in)** ...を着た ...wo kitá

claim [kleim] vt (expenses) 請求する sei-kyū suru; (inheritance) 要求する yōkyū suru; (rights) 主張する shuchō suru; (assert): **to claim that/to be** ...であると主張する ...de arù to shuchō suru
 ♦ vi (for insurance) 請求する seikyū suru
 ♦ n (assertion) 主張 shuchō; (for pension, wage rise, compensation) 請求 seíkyū; (to inheritance, land) 権利 kênri
 to claim responsibility (for) (...の) 犯行声明を出す (...no) hańkōseimeì wo dasù
 to claim credit (for) (...が) 自分の業績

であると主張する (...ga) jibún no gyŏseki de arù to shuchŏ suru

claimant [klei'mənt] n (ADMIN) 要求者 yŏkyūshà; (LAW) 原告 geńkoku

clairvoyant [kle:rvɔi'ənt] n (psychic) 霊媒 reíbai

clam [klæm] n (ZOOL, CULIN) ハマグリ hamagùri ◇英語では食用二枚貝の総称として使われる eígo de wa shokúyōnimaì-gai no sŏshō toshité tsukáwarerù

clamber [klæm'bə:r] vi (aboard vehicle) 乗る norú; (up hill etc) 登る nobŏru ◇手足を使って物に乗ったり登ったりするという含みがある teàshi wo tsukátte mo-nŏ ni nottári nobŏttari suru to iú fukúmi ga arù

clammy [klæm'i:] adj (hands, face etc) 冷たくてべとべとしている tsumétakùte betŏbeto shité irù

clamor [klæm'ə:r] (BRIT clamour) vi: **to clamor for** (change, war etc) ...をやかましく要求する ...wo yakámashikù yŏ-kyū suru

clamp [klæmp] n (device) 留め金 tomḗga-ne, クランプ kurańpu
 ♦ vt (two things together) クランプで留める kurańpu de toméru; (put: one thing on another) 締付ける shimétsukerù

clamp down on vt fus (violence, specu-lation etc) 取り締る toríshimarù

clan [klæn] n (family) 一族 ichízoku

clandestine [klændes'tin] adj (activity, broadcast) 秘密の himítsu no

clang [klæŋ] vi (bell, metal object) かんと鳴る kań to narú

clap [klæp] vi (audience, spectators) 拍手する hákushu surù

clapping [klæp'iŋ] n (applause) 拍手 há-kùshu

claret [klær'it] n クラレット kuráret-tò ◇ボルドー産の赤ワイン bŏrudōsań no aká waiñ

clarify [klær'əfai] vt (argument, point) はっきりさせる hakkíri saséru

clarinet [klærənet'] n (MUS: instru-ment) クラリネット kurárinettò

clarity [klær'iti:] n (of explanation, thought) 明りょうさ meíryōsa

clash [klæʃ] n (of opponents) 衝突 shōtotsu; (of beliefs, ideas, views) 衝突 shōtotsu; 対立 tairitsu; (of colors) 不調和 fuchōwa; (of styles) つり合わない事 tsuríawanai kotò; (of two events, appointments) かち合い kachíai; (noise) ぶつかる音 butsúkaru otó

♦vi (fight: rival gangs etc) 衝突する shōtotsu suru; (disagree: political opponents, personalities) 角突合いをする tsunótsukiaì wo surù; (beliefs, ideas, views) 相容れない aírénai; (colors, styles) 合わない awánai; (two events, appointments) かち合う kachíaù; (make noise: weapons, cymbals etc) 音を立てて ぶつかり合う otó wo tatéte butsúkariaù

clasp [klæsp] n (hold: with hands) 握る事 nigíru kotó, 握り nigíri; (: with arms) 抱締めること dakíshimerù kotò, 抱擁 hōyō; (of necklace, bag) 留金 tomégane, クラスプ kurásupù

♦vt (hold) 握る nigíru; (embrace) 抱締める dakíshimerù

class [klæs] n (SCOL: pupils) 学級 gakkyū, クラス kurásu; (: lesson) 授業 jugyō; (of society) 階級 kaíkyū; (type, group) 種類 shurùi

♦vt (categorize) 分類する buńrui suru

classic [klǽsik] adj (example, illustration) 典型的な teńkeiteki na; (film, work etc) 傑作の kessáku no; (style, dress) 古典的な kotenteki na

♦n (film, novel etc) 傑作 kessáku

classical [klǽsikəl] adj (traditional) 伝統的な deńtōteki na; (MUS) クラシックの kuráshikkù no; (Greek, Roman) 古代の kōdai no

classification [klæsəfəkei'ʃən] n (process) 分類する事 buńrui suru kotò; (category, system) 分類 buńrui

classified [klǽs'əfaid] adj (information) 秘密の himítsu no

classified advertisement n 分類広告 buńruikōkoku

classify [klǽs'əfai] vt (books, fossils etc) 分類する buńrui suru

classmate [klǽs'meit] n 同級生 dṓkyūsei, クラスメート kurásumḕto

classroom [klǽs'ruːm] n 教室 kyṓshitsu

clatter [klǽt'əːr] n (of dishes, pots etc) がちゃがちゃ gáchàgacha; (of hooves) かたかた kátàkata

♦vi (dishes, pots etc) がちゃがちゃいう gachàgacha iú; (hooves) かたかた鳴る kátàkata narú

clause [klɔːz] n (LAW) 条項 jōkō; (LING) 文節 buńsetsu

claustrophobia [klɔːstrəfou'biːə] n (PSYCH) 閉所恐怖症 heíshokyōfushō

claw [klɔː] n (of animal, bird) つめ tsumé; (of lobster) はさみ hasámi

claw at vt fus (curtains, door etc) 引っかく hikkáku

clay [klei] n 粘土 neńdo

clean [kliːn] adj (person, animal) きれい好きな kiréizuki na; (place, surface, clothes etc) 清潔な seíketsu na; (fight) 反則のない hańsoku no naì; (record, reputation) 無傷の múkizu no; (joke, story) 下品でない gehín de naì; (MED: fracture) 単純な tańjun na

♦vt (car, hands, face etc) 洗う aráu; (room, house) 掃除する sōji suru

clean-cut [kliːn'kʌt] adj (person) 品の良い hiń no yoí

cleaner [kliː'nəːr] n (person) 掃除係 sōjigakàri; (substance) 洗剤 seńzai

cleaner's [kliː'nəːrz] n (also: dry cleaner's) クリーニング店 kuríningùten

cleaning [kliː'niŋ] n (of room, house) 掃除 sōji

cleanliness [klen'liːnis] n 清潔 seíketsu

clean out vt (cupboard, drawer) 中身を出してきれいにする nakámi wo dashíte kiréi ni suru

cleanse [klenz] vt (purify) 清める kiyómerù; (face, cut) 洗う aráu

cleanser [klen'zəːr] n (for face) 洗顔料 seńganryō

clean-shaven [kliːn'ʃei'vən] adj ひげのない higé no naì

cleansing department [klen'ziŋ-] (BRIT) n 清掃局 seísōkyoku

clean up vt (mess) 片付ける katázukerù; (child) 身ぎれいにする migírei ni surù

clear [kliː'əːr] adj (easy to understand:

report, argument) 分かりやすい wakáriyasuǐ; (easy to see, hear) はっきりした hakkírǐ shitá; (obvious: choice, commitment) 明らかな akíraka na; (glass, plastic) 透明な tōmei na; (water, eyes) 澄んだ súnda; (road, way, floor etc) 障害のない shōgai no naǐ; (conscience) やましい所のない yamashiǐ tokóro no naǐ; (skin) 健康そうな keñkōsō na; (sky) 晴れたharèta

♦vt (space, room) 開ける akéru; (LAW: suspect) 容疑を晴す yōgi wo harasù; (fence, wall) 飛越える tobíkoerù; (check) 払う haraù

♦vi (weather, sky) 晴れる harerù; (fog, smoke) 消える kierù

♦adv: **clear of** (trouble) …を避けて …wo sakète; (ground) …から離れて …kara hanárete

to clear the table 食卓を片付ける shokútaku wo katázukerù

clearance [kli:ʹrəns] n (removal: of trees, slums) 取り払う事 toríharaù kotó; (permission) 許可 kyókà

clear-cut [kli:ʹərkʌtʹ] adj (decision, issue) 明白な meñhaku na

clearing [kli:ʹriŋ] n (in woods) 開けた所 hiráketà tokóro

clearing bank (BRIT) n 手形交換組合銀行 tegátakōkankumiaigiñkō ◊ロンドンの中央手形交換所を通じて他の銀行との取引を行う銀行 róñdon no chūō tegata kōkañjo wo tsūjitè tá no giñkō to no toríhiki wò okónaù giñkō

clearly [kli:ʹrli:] adv (distinctly, coherently) はっきりと hakkírǐ to; (evidently) 明らかに akíraka ni

clear up vt (room, mess) 片付ける katázukerù; (mystery, problem) 解決する kaíketsu suru

clearway [kli:ʹrwei] (BRIT) n 駐停車禁止道路 chūteíshakinshidōro

cleaver [kli:ʹvəʹr] n 骨割包丁 honéwaribōchō ◊なたに似た物で，肉のブロックをたたき切ったり骨を割ったりするのに使う natá ni nitá monó de，nikú no burokkù wo tatákikittarǐ honé wo wattárǐ surù no ni tsukaù

clef [klef] n (MUS) 音部記号 oñbukigō

cleft [kleft] n (in rock) 割れ目 warème

clemency [klemʹənsi:] n 恩情 óñjo

clench [klentʃ] vt (fist) 握り締める nigírishimerù; (teeth) 食いしばる kuíshibarù

clergy [klə:rʹdʒi:] n 聖職者 seíshoku-sha ◊総称 sōshō

clergyman [klə:rʹdʒi:mən] (pl **clergymen**) n (Protestant) 牧師 bōkùshi; (Catholic) 神父 shíñpu

clerical [kleʹrʹikəl] adj (worker, job) 事務の jímù no; (REL) 聖職者の seíshokù-sha no

clerk [klə:rk] n (BRIT: office worker) 事務員 jimúìn; (US: sales person) 店員 teñ-in

clever [klevʹəːr] adj (intelligent) 利口なrikō na; (deft, crafty) こうかつな kōkatsu na; (device, arrangement) 良く工夫した yókù kufú shitá

cliché [kli:ʃeiʹ] n 決り文句 kimárimoñku

click [klik] vt (tongue) 鳴らす narásu; (heels) 打鳴らす uchínarasu

♦vi (device, switch etc) かちっと鳴る kachíttò narú

client [klaiʹənt] n (of bank, company) 客 kyakú; (of lawyer) 依頼人 iráinìn

cliff [klif] n (GEO) 断崖 dañgai

climate [klaiʹmit] n (weather) 気候 kikō; (of opinion etc) 雰囲気 fuñ-ikì

climax [klaiʹmæks] n (of battle, career) 頂点 chōten; (of film, book) クライマックス kuráimakkùsu; (sexual) オルガズム orúgazumù

climb [klaim] vi (sun, plant) 上がる agáru; (plant) はい上がる haíagarù; (plane) 上昇する jōshō suru; (prices, shares) 上昇する jōshō suru; (move with effort): **to climb over a wall** 塀を乗り越える heí wo noríkoerù

♦vt (stairs, ladder) 上がる agáru, 登るnobóru; (hill) 登る nobóru; (tree) …に登る …ni nobóru

♦n (of hill, cliff etc) 登る事 nobóru kotó; (of prices etc) 上昇 jōshō

to climb into a car 車に乗り込む kurúma ni noríkomù

climb-down [klaimʹdaun] n (retraction)

撤回 tekkái

climber [klai'mə:r] n (mountaineer) 登山者 tozánsha; (plant) つる性植物 tsurúseishokubùtsu

climbing [klai'miŋ] n (mountaineering) 山登り yamánobòri, 登山 tózàn

clinch [klintʃ] vt (deal) まとめる matómeru; (argument) ...に決着を付ける ...ni ketcháku wo tsukerù

cling [kliŋ] (pt, pp **clung**) vi: **to cling to** (mother, support) ...にしがみつく ...ni shigámitsukù; (idea, belief) 固執する koshū suru; (subj: clothes, dress) ...にぴったりくっつく ...ni pittàri kuttsùku

clinic [klin'ik] n (MED: center) 診療所 shíñryòjo

clinical [klin'ikəl] adj (MED: tests) 臨床の ríñshò no; (: teaching) 臨床の ríñshò no; (fig: thinking, attitude) 冷淡な reítañ na; (: building, room) 潤いのない uróoi no naì

clink [kliŋk] vi (glasses, cutlery) ちんと鳴る chíñ to narú

clip [klip] n (also: **paper clip**) クリップ kuríppù; (also: **hair clip**) 髪留 kamídome; (TV, CINEMA) 断片 dañpen

♦vt (fasten) 留める toméru; (cut) はさみで切る hasámi de kiru

clippers [klip'ə:rz] npl (for gardening) せん ばさみ señteibasàmi; (also: **nail clippers**) つめ切り tsumékiri

clipping [klip'iŋ] n (from newspaper) 切抜き kirínuki

clique [kli:k] n 徒党 totó

cloak [klouk] n (cape) マント máñto

♦vt (fig: in mist, secrecy) 隠す kakúsù

cloakroom [klouk'ru:m] n (for coats etc) クローク kuróku; (BRIT: WC) お手洗 o-téarài

clock [klɑk] n 時計 tokéi

clock in vi (for work) 出勤する shukkín suru

clock off vi (from work) 退社する taísha suru

clock on vi = **clock in**

clock out vi = **clock off**

clockwise [klɑk'waiz] adv 時計回りに tokéimawàri ni

clockwork [klɑk'wə:rk] n 時計仕掛 tokéijikàke

♦adj (model, toy) 時計仕掛の tokéijikàke no

clog [klɑg] n (leather) 木底の靴 kizóko no kutsú; (also: **wooden clog**) 木靴 kígùtsu

♦vt (drain, nose) ふさぐ fuságu

♦vi (also: **clog up**: sink) 詰る tsumáru

cloister [klɔis'tə:r] n 回廊 kaírō

clone [kloun] n (of animal, plant) クローン kúrōn

close[1] [klous] adj (near) 近くの chikákù no; (friend) 親しい shitáshiì; (relative) 近縁の kiñ-en no; (contact) 密な mítsù na; (link, ties) 密接な missétsu na; (examination, watch) 注意深い chúibukaì; (contest) 互角な gokáku no; (weather) 重苦しい omókurushiì

♦adv (near) 近くに chikákù ni

close to ...の近くに ...no chikákù ni

close at hand, close by adj 近くの chikákù no

♦adv 近くに chikákù ni

to have a close shave (fig) 間一髪で助かる kañ-ippátsu de tasúkaru

close[2] [klouz] vt (shut: door, window) しめる shimérù; (finalize: sale) 取決める toríkimerù; (end: case, speech) 終える oéru

♦vi (shop etc) 閉店する heíten suru; (door, lid) 閉る shimàru; (end) 終る owáru

closed [klouzd] adj (door, window, shop etc) 閉まった shimátte irú

close down vi (factory) 廃業する haígyō suru; (magazine) 廃刊する haíkan suru

closed shop n (fig) クローズドショップ kuróuzudo shoppù ◇特定の労働組合員だけしか雇わない事業所 tokútei no ródōkumiaìñ dake shika yatówanaì jigyósho

close-knit [klous'nit'] adj (family, community) 堅く結ばれた katáku musúbareta

closely [klous'li:] adv (examine, watch) 注意深く chúibukakù; (connected) 密接に missétsu ni; (related) 近縁になって kiñ-en ni natté; (resemble) そっくり sokkúrì

closet [klɑ:z'it] n (cupboard) たんす tańsu

close-up [klous'ʌp] n (PHOT) クローズアップ kurôzuappù

closure [klou'ʒər] n (of factory) 閉鎖 heísa; (of magazine) 廃刊 haíkan

clot [klɑ:t] n (gen: blood clot) 血の塊 chi no katámari; (inf: idiot) ばか bákà
♦vi (blood) 固まる katámaru, 凝固する gyôko suru

cloth [klɔ:θ] n (material) 布 nunó; (rag) ふきん fukíñ

clothe [klouð] vt (dress) …に服を着せる …ni fukú wo kiséru

clothes [klouz] npl 服 fukú

clothes brush n 洋服ブラシ yôfukuburàshi

clothes line n 物干綱 monóhoshizùna

clothes pin (BRIT **clothes peg**) n 洗濯ばさみ señtakubasàmi

clothing [klou'ðiŋ] n = **clothes**

cloud [klaud] n (in sky) 雲 kúmð
a cloud of smoke/dust もうもうとした煙〔ほこり〕mômō to shita kemúri〔hokori〕

cloudburst [klaud'bə:rst] n 集中豪雨 shúchūgòu

cloudy [klau'di:] adj (sky) 曇った kumottà; (liquid) 濁った nigottà

clout [klaut] vt (hit, strike) 殴る nagurù

clove [klouv] n (spice) チョウジ chôji, クローブ kurôbu
clove of garlic ニンニクの一粒 niñniku no hitótsubu

clover [klou'vər] n クローバー kurôbà

clown [klaun] n (in circus) ピエロ pîero
♦vi (also: **clown about, clown around**) おどける odôkeru

cloying [klɔi'iŋ] adj (taste, smell) むかつかせる mukátsukaseru

club [klʌb] n (society, place) クラブ kúràbu; (weapon) こん棒 koñbō; (also: **golf club**) クラブ kúràbu
♦vt (hit) 殴る nagurù
♦vi: to club together (BRIT: for gift, card) 金を出し合う kané wo dashiaù

club car (US) n (RAIL) ラウンジカー raúnjikà ◇休憩用客車 kyúkeiyō kyakùsha

clubhouse [klʌb'haus] n (of sports club) クラブハウス kurábuhaùsu ◇スポーツクラブのメンバーが集まる部屋, 建物など supôtsukuràbu no meñba ga atsúmarù heyá, tatèmono nadð

clubs [klʌbz] npl (CARDS) クラブ kúràbu

cluck [klʌk] vi (hen) こっこっと鳴く kőkkðtto nakú

clue [klu:] n (pointer, lead) 手掛かり tégàkari; (in crossword) かぎ kagí
I haven't a clue さっぱり分らない sáppàri wakáranaì

clump [klʌmp] n (gen) 塊 katámari; (of buildings etc) 一連 ichíren
a clump of trees 木立 kódàchi

clumsy [klʌm'zi:] adj (person, movement) 不器用な búkiyò na; (object) 扱いにくい atsúkainikuì; (effort, attempt) 下手な hetá na

clung [klʌŋ] pt, pp of **cling**

cluster [klʌs'tə:r] n (of people, stars, flowers etc) 塊 katámari
♦vi 固まる katámaru, 群がる murágaru

clutch [klʌtʃ] n (grip, grasp) つかむ事 tsukamù kotó; (AUT) クラッチ kurátchi
♦vt (purse, hand, stick) しっかり持つ shíkkàri motsù

clutter [klʌt'əːr] vt (room, table) 散らかす chirákasu

cm abbr = **centimeter**

CND [si:endi:'] n abbr (= Camgaign for Nuclear Disarmament) 核廃絶運動 kakúhaizetsu uñdō

Co. abbr = **county; company**

c/o abbr = **care of**

coach [koutʃ] n (bus) バス básù; (also: **horse-drawn coach**) 馬車 báshà; (of train) 客車 kyakúsha; (SPORT: trainer) コーチ kôchi; (tutor) 個人教師 kojíñkyòshi
♦vt (sportsman/woman) コーチする kôchi suru; (student) …に個人指導をする …ni kojíñshidò wo surù

coach trip n バス旅行 basúryokò

coagulate [kouæg'jəleit] vi (blood, paint etc) 凝固する gyôko surú

coal [koul] n (substance) 石炭 sekítañ,

(also: **lump of coal**) 石炭1個 sekítaǹ ik-kò

coal face n 石炭切り場 sekítankiríba

coalfield [koul'fiːld] n 炭田 taǹden

coalition [kouəliʃ'ən] n (POL: also: **coalition government**) 連合政権 reǹgōseikeǹ; (of pressure groups etc) 連盟 reǹmei

coalman [koul'mən] (pl **coalmen**) n 石炭屋 sekítanya

coal merchant n = **coalman**

coalmine [koul'main] n 炭坑 taǹkō

coarse [kɔːrs] adj (texture: rough) 荒い arái; (person: vulgar) 下品な gehìn na

coast [koust] n 海岸 kaígan
♦vi (car, bicycle etc) 惰力走行する daryókusōkō suru

coastal [kous'təl] adj (cities, waters) 海岸沿いの kaíganzòi no

coastguard [koust'gɑːrd] n (officer) 沿岸警備隊員 eǹgankeibitàiin; (service) 沿岸警備隊 eǹgankeibitài

coastline [koust'lain] n 海岸線 kaígansen

coat [kout] n (overcoat) コート kòto; (of animal) 毛 ke; (of paint) 塗り nurí
♦vt: **coated with** ...で覆われた ...de ōwaréta

coat hanger n ハンガー háǹgā

coating [kou'tiŋ] n (of dust, mud etc) 覆う物 ōù monó; (of chocolate, plastic etc) 被覆 hifúku

coat of arms n 紋 móǹ

coax [kouks] vt (person: persuade) 説得する settóku suru

cob [kɑːb] n see **corn**

cobbler [kɑːb'ləːr] n (maker/repairer of shoes) 靴屋 kutsúyà

cobbles [kɑːb'əlz] npl 敷石 shikíishi

cobblestones [kɑːb'əlstounz] npl = **cobbles**

cobweb [kɑːb'web] n クモの巣 kúmò no su

cocaine [koukein'] n コカイン kókàin

cock [kɑːk] n (rooster) おん鳥 oǹdori; (male bird) 鳥の雄 torí no osú
♦vt (gun) ...の撃鉄を起す ...no gekítetsu wo okosù

cockerel [kɑːk'əːrəl] n 雄のひな鳥 osú no hinàdori

cock-eyed [kɑːk'aid] adj (fig: idea, method) ばかな báka na

cockle [kɑːk'əl] n ホタテガイ hotátègai

cockney [kɑːk'niː] n コックニー kókkùnī ◇ロンドンのEast End地区生れの人 roǹdon no Eàst End chikú umáre no hitó

cockpit [kɑːk'pit] n (in aircraft) 操縦室 sōjūshitsu, コックピット kokkúpittò; (in racing car) 運転席 uǹteǹseki, コックピット kokkúpittò

cockroach [kɑːk'routʃ] n ゴキブリ gokíburi

cocktail [kɑːk'teil] n (drink) カクテル kákùteru; (mixture: fruit cocktail, prawn cocktail etc) ...カクテル ...kakùteru

cocktail cabinet n ホームバー hōmubā

cocktail party n カクテルパーティ kakúterupàti

cocoa [kou'kou] n (powder, drink) ココア kókòa

coconut [kou'kənʌt] n (fruit) ヤシの実 yáshì no mi; (flesh) ココナッツ kokónattsu

cocoon [kəkuːn'] n (of butterfly) 繭 máyù

cod [kɑːd] n タラ tárà

C.O.D. [siːoudiː'] abbr (= cash or also (US) collect on delivery) 着払い chakúbarài

code [koud] n (of practice, behavior) 規定 kitéi; (cipher) 暗号 aǹgō; (dialling code, post code) 番号 baǹgō

cod-liver oil [kɑːd'livəːr-] n 肝油 kaǹ-yu

coercion [kouəːr'ʃən] n (pressure) 強制 kyōsei

coffee [kɔːf'iː] n (drink, powder) コーヒー kōhī; (cup of coffee) コーヒー一杯 kōhī ippái

coffee bar (BRIT) n 喫茶店 kíssàten

coffee bean n コーヒー豆 kōhìmamè

coffee break n コーヒーブレーク kōhībureˋku

coffeepot [kɔːf'iːpɑːt] n コーヒーポット kōhīpottò

coffee table n コーヒーテーブル kōhītĕburu

coffin [kɔːf'in] n ひつぎ hitsúgi

cog [kɑːg] n (TECH: wheel) 歯車 hágùruma; (: tooth) 歯車の歯 hágùruma no há

cogent [kou'dʒənt] adj (argument etc) 説得力ある settókuryòku arù

cognac [koun'jæk] n コ ニ ャ ッ ク kónyàkku

coherent [kouhi:'rənt] adj (answer, theory, speech) 筋の通った sujî no tôtta; (person) 筋の通った事を言う sujî no tôtta kotô no iú

cohesion [kouhi:'ʒən] n (political, ideological etc) 団結 daǹketsu

coil [kɔil] n (of rope, wire) 一巻 hitòmaki; (ELEC) コイル kôîru; (contraceptive) 避妊リング hiníǹrìngu

♦vt (rope) 巻く makú

coin [kɔin] n (money) 硬貨 kôka, コイン kôîn

♦vt (word, slogan) 造る tsukúru

coinage [kɔi'nidʒ] n 貨幣制度 kahéiseìdo

coin-box [kɔin'bɑːks] (BRIT) n コイン電話 koíndeǹwa ◇公衆電話でカードだけしか使えない物に対比して言う kôshúdeǹwa de kâdo dakê shiká tsukáenai monó ni taíhi shité iú

coincide [kouinsaid'] vi (events) 同時に起る dôji ni okôru; (ideas, views) 一致する itchí suru

coincidence [kouin'sidəns] n 偶然の一致 gûzen no itchí

Coke [kouk] ® n (drink) コカコーラ kokákòra

coke [kouk] n (coal) コークス kôkusu

colander [kɑːl'əndər] n 水切り mizúkiri ◇ボール型で穴の比較的大きい物を指す bórugata de aná no hikákuteki ôkií monô wo sasú

cold [kould] adj (water, food) 冷たい tsumétai; (weather, room) 寒い samúî; (person, attitude: unemotional) 冷たい tsumétai, 冷淡な reítaǹ na

♦n (weather) 寒さ samùsa; (MED) 風邪 kazé

it's cold 寒い samui

to be cold (person, object) 冷たい tsumétai

to catch (a) cold 風邪を引く kazé wo hikú

in cold blood (kill etc) 冷酷に reíkoku ni

coldly [kould'li:] adv (speak, behave) 冷たく tsumétaku, 冷淡に reítaǹ ni

cold-shoulder [kould'ouldər] vt 冷たくあしらう tsumétaku ashíraù

cold sore n 口角炎 kôkakuèn

coleslaw [koul'slɔ:] n コールスロー kôrusurò

colic [kɑːl'ik] n (MED) 腹痛 fukútsû

collaborate [kəlæb'əreit] vi (on book, research) 協同する kyôdō suru; (with enemy) 協力する kyôryoku suru

collaboration [kəlæbərei'ʃən] n 協力 kyôryoku

collage [kəlɑːʒ'] n コラージュ kôràju

collapse [kəlæps'] vi (building, system, resistance) 崩れる kuzúrerù, 崩壊する hôkai suru; (government) 倒れる taôrerù; (MED: person) 倒れる taôrerù; (table) 壊れる kowárerù, つぶれる tsubúrerù; (company) つぶれる tsubúrerù, 破産する hasán suru

♦n (of building, system, government, resistance) 崩壊 hôkai; (MED: of person) 倒れる事 taôreru kotô; (of table) 壊れる〔つぶれる〕事 kowáreru〔tsubureru〕kotô; (of company) 破産 hasán

collapsible [kəlæps'əbəl] adj (seat, bed, bicycle) 折畳みの orítatami no

collar [kɑːl'ər] n (of coat, shirt) 襟 erí, カラー kárà; (of dog, cat) 首輪 kubíwa, カラー karà

collarbone [kɑːl'ə:rboun] n (ANAT) 鎖骨 sakótsu

collateral [kəlæt'ə:rəl] n (COMM) 担保 táǹpo

colleague [kɑːl'i:g] n 同僚 dôryō

collect [kəlekt'] vt (gather: wood, litter etc) 集める atsúmerù; (as a hobby) 収集する shûshū suru; (BRIT: call and pick up: person) 迎えに行く mukáe ni ikú; (: object) 取りに行く torî ni ikú; (for charity, debts, taxes etc) 集金する shûkin suru; (mail) 取集する shushû suru

♦*vi* (crowd) 集る atsúmarù
to call collect (US: TEL) コレクトコールする korékutokòru suru

collection [kəlek'ʃən] *n* (of art, stamps etc) コレクション kórekushon; (of poems, stories etc) ...集 ...shū; (from place, person) 受取る事 ukétoru kotò; (for charity) 募金 bokín; (of mail) 取集 shushū

collective [kəlek'tiv] *adj* (farm, decision) 共同の kyōdō no

collector [kəlek'tə:r] *n* (of art, stamps etc) 収集家 shūshūka; (of taxes etc) 集金人 shūkíñnin

college [ka:l'idʒ] *n* (SCOL: of university) 学寮 gakúryō; (: of agriculture, technology) 大学 daígaku

collide [kəlaid'] *vi* (cars, people) ぶつかる butsúkaru, 衝突する shōtotsu suru

collie [ka:l'i:] *n* コリー犬 koríken

colliery [ka:l'jə:ri:] (BRIT) *n* 炭坑 tañkō

collision [kəliʒ'ən] *n* (of vehicles) 衝突 shōtotsu

colloquial [kəlou'kwi:əl] *adj* (LING: informal) 口語の kṓgo no

collusion [kəlu:'ʒən] *n* (collaboration) 結託 kettáku

colon [kou'lən] *n* (punctuation mark) コロン kórðn; (ANAT) 大腸 dáìchō

colonel [kə:r'nəl] *n* 大佐 taísa

colonial [kəlou'ni:əl] *adj* 植民地の shokúmiñchi no

colonize [ka:l'ənaiz] *vt* (country, territory) 植民地にする shokúmiñchi ni surù

colony [ka:l'əni:] *n* (subject territory) 植民地 shokúmiñchi; (of people) ...人街 ...jiñgai; (of animals) 個体群 kotáigùn

color [kʌl'ə:r] (BRIT **colour**) *n* (gen) 色 iro

♦*vt* (paint) ...に色を塗る ...ni iró wo nurú; (dye) 染める soméru; (fig: account) ...に色を付ける ...ni iró wo tsukerù; (judgment) ゆがめる yugámerù

♦*vi* (blush) 赤面する sekímen suru
in color 天然色で teñneñshoku de, カラーで kárā de

color bar *n* 人種差別 jiñshusabètsu ◇有色人種、特に黒人に対する差別を指す yūshokujiñshu, tokù ni kokújin ni taí suru sabètsu wo sasú

color-blind [kʌl'ə:rblaind'] *adj* 色盲の shikímō no

colored [kʌl'ə:rd] *adj* (person) 有色の yúshoku no; (illustration etc) カラーの kárā no

color film *n* カラーフィルム karáfirùmu

colorful [kʌl'ə:rfəl] *adj* (cloth) 色鮮やかな iró azàyaka na; (account, story) 華やかな hanáyaka na; (personality) 華々しい hanábanashiì

color in *vt* (drawing) ...に色を塗る ...ni iró wo nurú

coloring [kʌl'ə:riŋ] *n* (complexion) 肌の色合い hadà no iróai; (also: food coloring) 着色料 chakúshokùryō

colors [kʌl'ə:rz] *npl* (of party, club etc) 色 iró

color scheme *n* 配色計画 haíshokukeìkaku

color television *n* カラーテレビ karáterèbi

colossal [kəla:s'əl] *adj* 巨大な kyodái na

colour [kʌl'ə:r] *etc* (BRIT) *n* = **color** *etc*

colt [koult] *n* 子ウマ koúma

column [ka:l'əm] *n* (ARCHIT) 円柱 eñchū; (of smoke) 柱 hashíra; (of people) 縦隊 jūtai; (gossip column, sports column) コラム kóràmu

columnist [ka:l'əmist] *n* コラムニスト korámunisùto

coma [kou'mə] *n* (MED) こん睡状態 koñsuijōtai

comb [koum] *n* くし kushí
♦*vt* (hair) くしでとかす kushí de tokasù; (fig: area) 捜索する sōsaku suru

combat [*n* ka:m'bæt *vb* kəmbæt'] *n* (MIL: fighting) 戦闘 señtō; (fight, battle) 戦い tatákai
♦*vt* (oppose) 反抗する hañkō suru

combination [ka:mbənei'ʃən] *n* (mixture) 組合せ kumíawase; (for lock, safe etc) 組合せ番号 kumíawasebañgō

combine [*vb* kəmbain' *n* ka:m'bain] *vt*:
to combine something with something ...を...と組合せる ...wo ...to kumía-

waserù; (qualities) 兼備える kanésonaerù; (two activities) 兼任する keńnin suru
♦*vi* (people, groups) 合併する gappéi suru
♦*n* (ECON) 連合 reńgō

combine (harvester) [kɑːm'bain(hɑːr'vestəːr)] *n* コンバイン końbaìn

combustion [kəmbʌs'tʃən] *n* (act, process) 燃焼 neńshō

KEYWORD

come [kʌm] (*pt* **came**, *pp* **come**) *vi* **1**
(movement towards) 来る kúrù

come here! ここにおいでkokó ni oide

I've only come for an hour 1時間しかいられません ichíjikàn shika iráremasèn

come with me ついて来て下さい tsúite kite kudasai

are you coming to my party? 私のパーティに来てくれますね watákushi no pāti ni kité kùrémasu né

to come running 走って来る hashíttè kúrù

2 (arrive) 着く tsúkù, 到着する tóchaku suru, 来る kúrù

he's just come from Aberdeen 彼はアバーディーンから来たばかりです kárè wa abádìn kara kitá bakàri desu

he's come here to work 彼はここには働きに来ました kárè wa kokó ni wà határaki ni kimashìta

they came to a river 彼らは川に着きました kárèra wa kawá nì tsukímashìta

to come home 家に戻って来る ié nì modótte kuru

3 (reach): *to come to* ...に届く ...ni todókù, ...になる ...ni nárù

the bill came to £40 勘定は計40ポンドだった kánjò wa kéi yónjuppòndo datta

her hair came to her waist 彼女の髪の毛は腰まで届いていた kánojò no kamí no kè wa koshí madè todóìte ita

to come to power 政権を握る seíken wo nigiru

to come to a decision 結論に達する ketsúron ni tassuru

4 (occur): *an idea came to me* いい考え

が浮かびました íi kángaè ga ukábimashìta

5 (be, become) なる nárù

to come loose/undone etc 外れる hazúreru

I've come to like him 彼が好きになりました kárè ga sukí nì narímashìta

---

come about *vi* 起る okórù

come across *vt fus* (person, thing) ...に出会う ...ni deáù

come away *vi* (leave) 帰る káeru, 出て来る détè kure; (become detached) 外れる hazúreru

come back *vi* (return) 帰って来る káette kuru

comeback [kʌm'bæk] *n* (of film star etc) 返り咲き kaérizaki, カムバック kamúbakkù

come by *vt fus* (acquire) 手に入れる té nì iréru

comedian [kəmi:'di:ən] *n* (THEATER, TV) コメディアン kómèdian

comedienne [kəmi:di:en'] *n* 女性コメディアン joséi komèdian

come down *vi* (price) 下がる sagárù; (tree) 倒れる taórerù; (building) 崩れ落ちる kuzúreochirù

comedy [kɑːm'idi:] *n* (play, film) 喜劇 kígèki, コメディー kómèdī; (humor) 喜劇性 kigékisei, ユーモア yúmoa

come forward *vi* (volunteer) 進んで...する susúnde ...sùrù

come from *vt fus* (place, source etc) ...から来る ...kara kúrù

come in *vi* (visitor) 入る háìru; (on deal etc) 加わる kuwáwarù; (be involved) 関係する kánkei suru

come in for *vt fus* (criticism etc) 受ける ukérù

come into *vt fus* (money) 相続する sózoku suru; (be involved) ...に関係する ...ni kánkei suru

to come into fashion 流行する ryúkō suru

come off *vi* (button) 外れる hazúreru; (attempt) 成功する seíkō suru

come on *vi* (pupil, work, project) 進歩す

る shínpo suru; (lights, electricity) つく tsùkú

come on! さあさあ sāsā

come out vi (fact) 発覚する hakkáku suru; (book) 出版される shúppan sareru; (stain) 取れる torérù, 落ちる ochírù; (sun) 出る dérù

come round vi (after faint, operation) 正気に返る shóki ni kaèrù, 目が覚める mé gà samérù, 気が付く ki ga tsukù

comet [kɑːm'it] n すい星 suísei

come to vi (regain consciousness) 正気に戻る shóki ni modorù, 目が覚める mé gà samérù

come up vi (sun) 出る dérù; (problem) 起る okórù, 出る dérù; (event) 起る okórù; (in conversation) 出る dérù

come up against vt fus (resistance, difficulties) ぶつかる butsúkaru

come upon vt fus (find) 見付ける mitsúkeru

comeuppance [kʌmʌp'əns] n: **to get one's comeuppance** 当然の罰を受ける tôzen no batsù wo ukerù

come up with vt fus (idea) 持出す mochídasù; (money) 出す dásù

comfort [kʌm'fəːrt] n (well-being: physical, material) 安楽 ánraku; (relief) 慰め nagúsame

♦vt (console) 慰める nagúsamerù

comfortable [kʌm'fəːrtəbəl] adj (person: physically) 楽な rákù na; (: financially) 暮しに困らない kuráshi ni kománaì; (furniture) 座り心地の良い suwárigokochi no yoî; (room) 居心地のよい igókochi nò yoî; (patient) 苦痛のない kutsû no naî; (easy: walk, climb etc) 楽な rákù na

comfortably [kʌm'fəːrtəbliː] adv (sit, live etc) 楽に rákù ni

comforts [kʌm'fəːrts] npl (of home etc) 生活を楽にするもの seíkatsu wo rakú ni suru monò

comfort station (US) n お手洗 o-teàrài

comic [kɑːm'ik] adj (also: **comical**) こっけいな kokkéi na

♦n (comedian) コメディアン kómèdian; (BRIT: magazine) 漫画(雑誌) maň-

ga(zasshī)

comic strip n 連続漫画 reňzokumaňga

coming [kʌm'iŋ] n (arrival) 到着 tôchaku

♦adj (event, attraction) 次の tsugî no, これからの koré kara no

coming(s) and going(s) n(pl) 行き来 yukíki, 往来 ôrai

comma [kɑːm'ə] n コンマ kóňma

command [kəmænd'] n (order) 命令 meírei; (control, charge) 指揮 shikî; (MIL: authority) 司令部 shíreìbu; (mastery: of subject) マスターしていること masútà shité irù kotô

♦vt (give orders to): **to command someone to do something** ...に...をする様に命令する ...ni ...wo suru yô ni meírei suru; (troops) ...の司令官である ...no shiréìkan de arù

commandeer [kɑːməndiːr'] vt (requisition) 徴発する chôhatsu suru; (fig) 勝手に取って使う katté ni totté tsukáù

commander [kəmæn'dəːr] n (MIL) 司令官 shíreìkan

commandment [kəmænd'mənt] n (REL) 戒律 kaíritsu

commando [kəmæn'dou] n (group) コマンド部隊 kómándobùtai; (soldier) コマンド隊員 kómándotaìin

commemorate [kəmem'əːreit] vt (with statue, monument, celebration, holiday) 記念する kinén suru

commence [kəmens'] vt (begin, start) 始める hajímeru

♦vi 始まる hajímaru

commend [kəmend'] vt (praise) ほめる homérù; (recommend) ゆだねる yudánerù

commensurate [kəmen'səːrit] adj: **commensurate with** ...に相応した ...ni sôô shitá

comment [kɑːm'ent] n (remark: written or spoken) コメント koménto

♦vi: **to comment (on)** (...について) コメントする (...ni tsuìté) koménto surù

no comment ノーコメント nôkomento

commentary [kɑːm'anteːriː] n (TV, RADIO) 実況放送 jikkyôhōsō; (book, article) 注解 chúkai

commentator [kɑ:m'ənteitə:r] n (TV, RADIO) 解説者 kaísetsùsha

commerce [kɑ:m'ə:rs] n 商業 shôgyō

commercial [kəmə:r'ʃəl] adj (organization, activity) 商業 の shôgyō no; (success, failure) 商業上の shôgyōjō no
♦n (TV, RADIO: advertisement) コマーシャル kômāsharu, CM shîemu

commercialized [kəmə:r'ʃəlaizd] (pej) adj (place, event etc) 営利本意の efrihoñi no

commercial radio/television n 民間ラジオ〔テレビ〕放送 miñkan rajio〔terebi〕hôsō, 民放 miñpō

commiserate [kəmiz'əreit] vi: to commiserate with ...をいたわる ...wo itáwarù

commission [kəmiʃ'ən] n (order for work: esp of artist) 依頼 iráì; (COMM) 歩合 buái, コミッション kômîsshon; (committee) 委員会 iíñkai
♦vt (work of art) 依頼する iráì suru
out of commission (not working) 故障して koshô shité

commissionaire [kəmiʃənɛ:r'] (BRIT) n ドアマン dôaman

commissioner [kəmiʃ'ənə:r] n (POLICE) 長官 chôkan

commit [kəmit'] vt (crime, murder etc) 犯す okásu; (money, resources) 充当する jútō suru; (to someone's care) 任せる makáserù
to commit oneself (to do) (...する事を) 約束する (...surú kotó wo) yakúsoku suru
to commit suicide 自殺する jisátsu suru

commitment [kəmit'mənt] n (to ideology, system) 献身 keńshin; (obligation) 責任 sekínin; (undertaking) 約束 yakúsoku

committee [kəmit'i:] n (of organization, club etc) 委員会 iíñkai

commodity [kəmɑ:d'iti:] n (saleable item) 商品 shôhin

common [kɑ:m'ən] adj (shared by all: knowledge, property, good) 共同の kyô-

dō no; (usual, ordinary: event, object, experience etc) 普通の futsū no; (vulgar: person, manners) 下品な gehíñ na
♦n (area) 共有地 kyôyũchi
in common 共通で kyôtsū de

commoner [kɑ:m'ənə:r] n 庶民 shomín

common law n コモン・ロー komón rō ◇成文化されてない慣習に基づく英米の一般法を指す seíbunka saréte naì kañshū ni motózukù eíbei no ippánhō wo sasù

commonly [kɑ:m'ənli:] adv (usually) 通常 tsújō

Common Market n ヨーロッパ共同市場 yôroppa kyôdōshijō

commonplace [kɑ:m'ənpleis] adj 平凡な heíbon na

common room n (SCOL) 談話室 dañwashítsu

Commons [kɑ:m'ənz] (BRIT) npl: the Commons 下院 ká-ìn

common sense n 常識 jôshiki, コモンセンス komónseñsu

Commonwealth [kɑ:m'ənwelθ] n (British Commonwealth): the Commonwealth イギリス連邦 igírisureñpō
the Commonwealth of Independent States 独立国家共同体 dokúritsu kòkka kyôdōtai

commotion [kəmou'ʃən] n (uproar) 騒ぎ sáwàgi

communal [kəmju:'nəl] adj (shared) 共同の kyôdō no

commune [n kɑ:m'ju:n vb kəmju:n'] n (group) コミューン komyũn
♦vi: to commune with (nature, God) ...に親しむ ...ni shitáshimù

communicate [kəmju:'nikeit] vt (idea, decision, feeling) 伝える tsutáerù
♦vi: to communicate (with) ...と通信する ...to tsúshin suru

communication [kəmju:nikei'ʃən] n (process) 通信 tsúshin; (letter, call) 連絡 refraku

communication cord (BRIT) n (on train) 非常通報装置 hijôtsūhōsōchi

communion [kəmju:n'jən] n (also: Holy Communion) 聖体拝領 seítaihaìryō

communiqué [kəmjuːnikeiˈ] n (POL, PRESS) コミュニケ kómyùnike

communism [kɑːmˈjənizəm] n 共産主義 kyōsanshùgi

communist [kɑːmˈjənist] adj 共産主義の kyōsanshùgi no
♦n 共産主義者 kyōsanshugishà

community [kəmjuːˈniːtiː] n (group of people) 共同体 kyōdòtai; (within larger group) 社会 shákài

community center n 公民館 kōmìnkan

community chest (US) n 共同募金 kyōdòbòkin

community home (BRIT) n 養育施設 yōikushisètsu

commutation ticket [kɑːmjəteiˈʃən-] (US) n 定期券 teíkìkèn

commute [kəmjuːtˈ] vi (to work) 通う kayóu
♦vt (LAW: sentence) 減刑する geñkei suru

commuter [kəmjuːtˈəːr] n 通勤者 tsūkìñsha

compact [kɑːmˈpækt] adj (taking up little space) 小型の kogáta no
♦n (also: **powder compact**) コンパクト kóñpakuto

compact disk n コンパクトディスク kóñpakuto disùko

companion [kəmpænˈjən] n 相手 aíte

companionship [kəmpænˈjənʃip] n つきあい tsukíai

company [kʌmˈpəniː] n (COMM) 会社 kaísha; (THEATER) 劇団 gekídan; (companionship) 付合い tsukíai
to keep someone company ...の相手になる ...no aíte ni narù

company secretary (BRIT) n 総務部長 sōmubùchō

comparable [kɑːmˈpəːrəbəl] adj (size, style, extent) 匹敵する hittéki suru

comparative [kəmpærˈətiv] adj (peace, stranger, safety) 比較的 hikákuteki; (study) 比較の hikáku no

comparatively [kəmpærˈətivliː] adv (relatively) 比較的に hikákuteki ni

compare [kəmpeːrˈ] vt: **to compare someone/something with/to** (set side

by side) ...を...と比較する ...wo ...to hikáku suru; (liken) ...を...に例える ...wo ...ni tatóerù
♦vi: **to compare (with)** (...に) 匹敵する (...ni) hittéki suru

comparison [kəmpærˈisən] n (setting side by side) 比較 hikáku; (likening) 例えたとえ tatóe
in comparison (with) ...と比較して ...to hikáku shitè

compartment [kəmpɑːrtˈmənt] n (RAIL) 客室 kyakúshitsu, コンパートメント kóñpātomènto; (section: of wallet, fridge etc) 区画 kukáku

compass [kʌmˈpəs] n (instrument: NAUT, GEO) 羅針盤 rashínban, コンパス kóñpasu

compasses [kʌmˈpəsiz] npl (MATH) コンパス koñpasu

compassion [kəmpæʃˈən] n (pity, sympathy) 同情 dōjō

compassionate [kəmpæʃˈənit] adj (person, look) 情け深い nasákebukaì

compatible [kəmpætˈəbəl] adj (people) 気が合う ki ga aù; (ideas etc) 両立できる ryōritsu dekírù; (COMPUT) 互換性のある gokáñsei no arù

compel [kəmpelˈ] vt (force) 強制する kyōsei suru

compelling [kəmpelˈiŋ] adj (fig: argument, reason) 止むに止まれぬ yamú ni yamárenù

compensate [kɑːmˈpənseit] vt (employee, victim) ...に補償する ...ni hoshō suru
♦vi: **to compensate for** (loss, disappointment, change etc) ...を埋め合せる ...wo uméawaserù

compensation [kɑːmpənseiˈʃən] n (to employee, victim) 補償 hoshō; (for loss, disappointment, change etc) 埋め合せ uméawase

compère [kɑːmˈpeːr] (BRIT) n (TV, RADIO) 司会者 shíkàisha

compete [kəmpiːtˈ] vi (companies, rivals): **to compete (with)** (...と) 競り合う (...to) serîaù; (in contest, game) 参加する sañka suru

competence [kɑːmˈpitəns] n (of worker

etc) 能力 nṓryoku

competent [kɑ:m'pitənt] *adj* 有能 な yū́-
nō na

competition [kɑ:mpitiʃ'ən] *n* (between
firms, rivals) 競争 kyṓsō; (contest) コン
クール koñkū́ru; (ECON) ライバル商品
raíbaru shṓhin

competitive [kəmpet'ətiv] *adj* (industry,
society) 競争の激しい kyṓsō no hagéshiî;
(person) 競争心の強い kyṓsōshin no tsuyóî; (price, product) 競争できる kyṓsō
dekírù

competitive sports 競技 kyṓgi

competitor [kəmpet'itəːr] *n* (rival) 競争
相手 kyṓsōaìte; (participant) 参加者 sañkashà

compile [kəmpail'] *vt* (book, film,
report) 編集する heñshū́ suru

complacency [kəmplei'sənsi:] *n* (smug-
ness) 自己満足 jikṓmañzoku

complacent [kəmplei'sənt] *adj* (smug)
自己満足にふける jikṓmañzoku ni fukḗ-
rù

complain [kəmplein'] *vi* (grumble) 不平
不満を言う fuhéifùman wo iú; (protest:
to authorities, shop etc) 訴える uttáerù

to complain of (pain) ...を訴える ...wo
uttáerù

complaint [kəmpleint'] *n* (objection) 訴
え uttáe; (criticism) 非難 hínàn; (MED:
illness) 病気 byṓki

complement [*n* kɑ:m'pləmənt *vb* kɑ:m'-
pləmənt] *n* (supplement) 補う物 ogínaù
monó; (esp ship's crew) 人員 jiń-in

♦*vt* (enhance) 引立たせる hikítataserù

complementary [kɑ:mpləmən'tə:ri:] *adj*
(mutually supportive) 補足し合う hosó-
ku shiaù

complete [kəmpli:t'] *adj* (total, whole)
完全な kañzen na; (finished: building,
task) 完成した kañsei shitá

♦*vt* (finish: building, task) 完成する kañsei suru; (: set, group etc) そろえる soróerù; (fill in: a form) ...に記入する ...ni
kinyū́ suru

completely [kəmpli:t'li:] *adv* (totally) 全
く mattáku, 完全に kañzen ni

completion [kəmpli:'ʃən] *n* (of building)

完成 kañsei; (of contract) 履行 rikṓ

complex [*adj* kəmpleks' *n* kɑ:m'pleks]
adj (structure, problem, decision) 複雑な
fukúzatsu na

♦*n* (group: of buildings) 団地 dañchi;
(PSYCH) コンプレックス koñpurekkùsu

complexion [kəmplek'ʃən] *n* (of face) 顔
の肌 kaó no hadà

complexity [kəmplek'siti:] *n* (of problem, law) 複雑さ fukúzatsusa

compliance [kəmplai'əns] *n* (submission) 服従 fukújù; (agreement) 同意 dṓi

in compliance with ...に従って ...ni shitágatte

complicate [kɑ:m'pləkit] *vt* (matters,
situation) 複雑にする fukúzatsu ni suru

complicated [kɑ:m'pləkeitid] *adj* (explanation, system) 複雑な fukúzatsu na

complication [kɑ:mpləkei'ʃən] *n* (problem) 問題 moñdai; (MED) 合併症 gappéi-
shō

complicity [kəmplis'əti:] *n* (in crime) 共
犯 kyṓhan

compliment [*n* kɑ:m'pləmənt *vb* kɑ:m'-
pləmənt] *n* (expression of admiration)
ほめ言葉 homékotòba

♦*vt* (express admiration for) ほめる homérù

to pay someone a compliment ...をほ
める ...wo homéru

complimentary [kɑ:mpləmən'tə:ri:] *adj*
(remark) 賛辞の sañji no; (ticket, copy
of book etc) 無料の muryṓ no

compliments [kɑ:m'pləmənts] *npl*
(regards) 挨拶 aísatsu

comply [kəmplai'] *vi*: *to comply with*
(law, ruling) ...に従う ...ni shitágaù

component [kəmpou'nənt] *adj* (parts,
elements) 構成している kṓsei shité irù

♦*n* (part) 部分 búbùn

compose [kəmpouz'] *vt* (form): *to be
composed of* ...から出来ている ...kará
dekíte irù; (write: music, poem, letter)
書く kákù

to compose oneself 心を落着かせる kokórò wo ochítsukaserù

composed [kəmpouzd'] *adj* (calm) 落着
いている ochítsuite irù

composer [kəmpou'zə:r] n (MUS) 作曲家 sakkyōkuka

composition [ka:mpəzíʃ'ən] n (of substance, group etc) 構成 kōsei; (essay) 作文 sakúbun; (MUS) 作曲 sakkyōku

compost [ka:m'poust] n たい肥 taíhi

composure [kəmpou'ʒə:r] n (of person) 落着き ochítsuki

compound [ka:m'paund] n (CHEM) 化合物 kágōbutsu; (enclosure) 囲い地 kakóichi; (LING) 複合語 fukúgōgo
♦adj (fracture) 複雑な fukúzatsu na
compound interest 複利 fúkūri

comprehend [ka:mprihend'] vt (understand) 理解する rikái suru

comprehension [ka:mprihen'ʃən] n (understanding) 理解 ríkài

comprehensive [ka:mprihen'siv] adj (description, review, list) 包括的な hōkatsuteki na; (INSURANCE) 総合的な sōgōteki na

comprehensive (school) (*BRIT*) n 総合中等学校 sōgōchūtōgakkō ◇あらゆる能力の子供に適した課程のある中等学校 aráyurù nōryoku no kodómo ni tekí shita katéi no arù chūtōgakkō

compress [vb ka:mpres' n ka:m'pres] vt (air, cotton, paper etc) 圧縮する asshúku suru; (text, information) 要約する yōyaku suru
♦n (MED) 湿布 shippú

comprise [kəmpraiz'] vt (also: *be comprised of*) ...からなる ...kará narù; (constitute) 構成する kōsei suru

compromise [ka:m'prəmaiz] n 妥協 dakyō
♦vt (beliefs, principles) 傷つける kizú tsukerù
♦vi (make concessions) 妥協する dakyō suru

compulsion [kəmpʌl'ʃən] n (desire, impulse) 強迫観念 kyōhakukaǹnen; (force) 強制 kyōsei

compulsive [kəmpʌl'siv] adj (liar, gambler etc) 病的な byōteki na; (viewing, reading) 止められない yamérarenài

compulsory [kəmpʌl'sə:ri:] adj (attendance, retirement) 強制的な kyōseiteki

computer [kəmpju:'tə:r] n コンピュータ końpyūta

computerize [kəmpju:'təraiz] vt (system, filing, accounts etc) コンピュータ化する końpyūtaka suru; (information) コンピュータに覚えさせる końpyūta ni oboesaserù

computer programmer n プログラマー puróguramā

computer programming n プログラミング puróguramiǹgu

computer science n コンピュータ科学 końpyūta kagàku

computing [kəmpju:'tiŋ] n (activity, science) コンピュータ利用 końpyūta riyō

comrade [ka:m'ræd] n (POL, MIL) 同志 dōshi; (friend) 友人 yūjin

comradeship [ka:m'rædʃip] n 友情 yūjō

con [ka:n] vt (deceive) だます damásù; (cheat) ぺてんに掛ける petén ni kakérù
♦n (trick) いかさま ikásama

concave [ka:nkeiv'] adj 凹面の ōmen no

conceal [kənsi:l'] vt (hide: weapon, entrance) 隠す kakúsù; (keep back: information) 秘密にする himítsu ni surù

concede [kənsi:d'] vt (admit: error, point, defeat) 認める mitómeru

conceit [kənsi:t'] n (arrogance) うぬぼれ unúbore

conceited [kənsi:'tid] adj (vain) うぬぼれた unúboreta

conceivable [kənsi:v'əbəl] adj (reason, possibility) 考えられる kańgaerarerù

conceive [kənsi:v'] vt (child) はらむ harámù; (plan, policy) 考え出す kańgaedasù
♦vi (BIO) 妊娠する nińshin suru

concentrate [ka:n'səntreit] vi (on problem, activity etc) 専念する seńnen suru; (in one area, space) 集中する shūchū suru
♦vt (energies, attention) 集中させる shūchū saséru

concentration [ka:nsəntrei'ʃən] n (on problem, activity) 専念 seńnen; (in one area, space) 集中 shūchū; (attention) 注意 chūi; (CHEM) 濃縮 nōshuku

concentration camp n 強制収容所 kyóseishūyòjo

concept [ka:n'sept] n (idea, principle) 概念 gáinen

conception [kənsep'ʃən] n (idea) 概念 gáinen; (of child) 妊娠 nińshin

concern [kənsə:rn'] n (affair) 責任 sekínin; (anxiety, worry) 心配 shińpai; (COMM: firm) 企業 kígyō
♦vt (worry) 心配させる shińpai saséru; (involve, relate to) ...に関係がある ...ni kańkē ga arù
to be concerned (about) (person, situation etc) (...について) 心配する (...ni tsuité) shińpai suru

concerning [kənsə:r'niŋ] prep (regarding) ...について ...ni tsuíte

concert [ka:n'sə:rt] n (MUS) 演奏会 eńsōkai, コンサート końsàto

concerted [kənsə:r'tid] adj (effort etc) 共同の kyódō no

concert hall n コンサートホール końsātohòru

concertina [ka:nsə:rti:'nə] n (MUS: instrument) コンサーティーナ końsātīna ◇六角形の小型アコーディオン rokkákkèi no kogáta akòdion

concerto [kəntʃe:r'tou] n 協奏曲 kyósōkyoku, コンチェルト kóncheruto

concession [kənseʃ'ən] n (compromise) 譲歩 jòho; (COMM: right) 特権 tokkén
tax concession 減税 geńzei

conciliatory [kənsil'i:ətɔ:ri:] adj (gesture, tone) 懐柔的な kaíjūteki na

concise [kənsais'] adj (description, text) 簡潔な kańketsu na

conclude [kənklu:d'] vt (finish: speech, chapter) 終える oéru; (treaty) 締結する teíketsu suru; (deal etc) まとめる matómeru; (decide) (...だと) 結論する (...da to) ketsúron suru

conclusion [kənklu:'ʒən] n (of speech, chapter) 終り owári; (of treaty) 締結 teíketsu; (of deal etc) まとめる事 matómeru kotó; (decision) 結論 ketsúron

conclusive [kənklu:'siv] adj (evidence, defeat) 決定的な kettéiteki na

concoct [kənka:kt'] vt (excuse) でっち上げる detchíagerù; (plot) 企てる kuwádaterù; (meal, sauce) 工夫して作る kufú shité tsukúrù

concoction [kənka:k'ʃən] n (mixture) 調合物 chógòbutsu

concourse [ka:n'kɔ:rs] n (hall) 中央ホール chūōhòru, コンコース końkòsu

concrete [ka:n'kri:t] n コンクリート końkurīto
♦adj (block, floor) コンクリートの końkurīto no; (proposal, idea) 具体的な gutáiteki na

concur [kənkə:r'] vi 同意する dói suru

concurrently [kənkə:r'əntli:] adv (happen, run) 同時に dóji ni

concussion [kənkʌʃ'ən] n (MED) 脳震とう nóshiñtō

condemn [kəndem'] vt (denounce: action, report etc) 非難する hínàn suru; (sentence: prisoner) ...に...刑を宣告する ...ni...keí wo señkoku suru; (declare unsafe: building) 使用に耐えない物と決定する shiyō ni taénai monó to kettéi suru

condemnation [ka:ndemnei'ʃən] n (criticism) 非難 hínàn

condensation [ka:ndensei'ʃən] n (on walls, windows) 結露 kétsuro

condense [kəndens'] vi (vapor) 液化する ekíka suru
♦vt (report, book) 要約する yóyaku suru

condensed milk [kəndenst'-] n 練乳 reńnyū

condescending [ka:ndisen'diŋ] adj (reply, attitude) 恩着せがましい ońkisegamashìi

condition [kəndiʃ'ən] n (state: gen) 状態 jótai; (MED: of illness) 病状 byójō; (requirement) 条件 jóken; (MED: illness) 病気 byóki
♦vt (person) 慣れさせる narésaserù
on condition that ...という条件で ...to iú jóken de

conditional [kəndiʃ'ənəl] adj 条件付きの jókentsuki no

conditioner [kəndiʃ'ənə:r] n (also: hair conditioner) ヘアコンディショナー heákondishònā; (for fabrics) 柔軟剤 jūnańzai

conditions [kəndiʃ'ənz] *npl* (circumstances) 状況 jōkyō

condolences [kəndou'lənsiz] *npl* お悔み o-kúyami

condom [kɑːn'dəm] *n* コンドーム koǹdōmu, スキン sukín

condominium [kɑːndəmin'iːəm] (*US*) *n* 分譲マンション buǹjōmaǹshon

condone [kəndoun'] *vt* (misbehavior, crime) 容認する yōnin suru

conducive [kənduː'siv] *adj*: **conducive to** (rest, study) ...を助ける ...wo tasúkerù

conduct [*n* kɑːn'dʌkt *vb* kəndʌkt'] *n* (of person) 振舞 furúmai
♦*vt* (survey, research etc) 行う okónaù; (orchestra, choir etc) 指揮する shikí suru; (heat, electricity) 伝導する deńdō suru
to conduct oneself (behave) 振舞う furúmaù

conducted tour [kəndʌk'tid-] *n* ガイド付き見物 gaídotsuki keńbutsu

conductor [kəndʌk'təːr] *n* (of orchestra) 指揮者 shikíshà; (*BRIT*: on bus, *US*: on train) 車掌 shashō; (ELEC) 伝導体 deńdōtai

conductress [kəndʌk'tris] *n* (on bus) 女性車掌 joséishashò, バスガール basúgāru

cone [koun] *n* (shape) 円すい形 eńsuikei; (on road) カラーコーン karákōn, セーフティコーン sēfutikòn; (BOT) 松かさ matsúkasà; (ice cream cornet) コーン kôn

confectioner [kənfek'ʃənəːr] *n* (person) 菓子職人 kashíshokunìn

confectioner's (shop) [kənfek'ʃənəːrz-] *n* (sweet shop) 菓子屋 kashíyà

confectionery [kənfek'ʃəneːriː] *n* (sweets, candies) 菓子類 kashírui

confederation [kənfedərei'ʃən] *n* (POL, COMM) 連合 reńgō

confer [kənfəːr'] *vt*: **to confer something (on someone)** (honor, degree, advantage) (...に) ...を与える (...ni) ...wo atáerù
♦*vi* (panel, team) 協議する kyōgi suru

conference [kɑːn'fəːrəns] *n* (meeting) 会議 kaígi

confess [kənfes'] *vt* (sin, guilt, crime) 白状する hákùjō suru; (weakness, ignorance) 認める mitómeru
♦*vi* (admit) 認める mitómeru

confession [kənfeʃ'ən] *n* (admission) 白状 hákùjō; (REL) ざんげ zâǹge

confetti [kənfet'iː] *n* コンフェティ kôǹfeti ◇紙吹雪き用に細かく切った色紙 kamífubuki yô ni komákaku kittá irôgami

confide [kənfaid'] *vi*: **to confide in** ...に打明ける ...ni uchíakerù

confidence [kɑːn'fidəns] *n* (faith) 信用 shiń-yō; (*also*: **self-confidence**) 自信 jishín; (secret) 秘密 himítsu
in confidence (speak, write) 内緒で naísho de

confidence trick *n* いかさま ikásama

confident [kɑːn'fidənt] *adj* (self-assured) 自信のある jishín no arù; (positive) 確信している kakúshin shité irù

confidential [kɑːnfiden'ʃəl] *adj* (report, information) 秘密の himítsu no; (tone) 親しげな shitáshige na

confine [kənfain'] *vt* (limit) 限定する geńtei suru; (shut up) 閉じ込める tojíkomerù

confined [kənfaind'] *adj* (space) 限られた kagírareta

confinement [kənfain'mənt] *n* (imprisonment) 監禁 kańkin

confines [kɑːn'fainz] *npl* (of area) 境 sakái

confirm [kənfəːrm'] *vt* (belief, statement) 裏付ける urázukerù; (appointment, date) 確認する kakúnin suru

confirmation [kɑːnfəːrmei'ʃən] *n* (of belief, statement) 裏付け urázuke; (of appointment, date) 確認 kakúnin; (REL) 堅信礼 keńshiǹrei

confirmed [kənfəːrmd'] *adj* (bachelor, teetotaller) 常習的な jōshūteki na

confiscate [kɑːn'fiskeit] *vt* (impound, seize) 没収する bosshū suru

conflict [*n* kɑːn'flikt *vb* kənflikt'] *n* (disagreement) 論争 roǹsō; (difference: of interests, loyalties etc) 対立 taíritsu; (fighting) 戦闘 seńtō
♦*vi* (opinions) 対立する taíritsu suru; (research etc) 矛盾する mujún suru

conflicting [kənflik'tiŋ] *adj* (reports) 矛盾する mujún suru; (interests etc) 対立する taíritsu suru

conform [kənfɔːrm'] *vi* (comply) 従う shitágaù
to conform to (law, wish, ideal) ...に従う ...ni shitágaù

confound [kənfaund'] *vt* (confuse) 当惑させる tówaku saséru

confront [kənfrʌnt'] *vt* (problems, task) ...と取組む ...to toríkumù; (enemy, danger) ...に立向かう ...ni tachímukaù

confrontation [kɑːnfrəntei'ʃən] *n* (dispute, conflict) 衝突 shótotsu

confuse [kənfjuːz'] *vt* (perplex: person) 当惑させる tówaku saséru; (mix up: two things, people etc) 混同する kofídō suru; (complicate: situation, plans) 混乱させる koñran saséru

confused [kənfjuːzd'] *adj* (bewildered) 当惑した tówaku shitá; (disordered) 混乱した koñran shitá

confusing [kənfjuː'ziŋ] *adj* (plot, instructions) 分かりにくい wakárinikuí

confusion [kənfjuː'ʒən] *n* (perplexity) 当惑 tówaku; (mix-up) 混同 kofídō; (disorder) 混乱 koñran

congeal [kəndʒiːl'] *vi* (blood, sauce) 凝結する gyóketsu suru

congenial [kəndʒiːn'jəl] *adj* (person) 気の合った ki no attá; (atmosphere etc) 楽しい tanóshiì

congenital [kəndʒen'itəl] *adj* (MED: defect, illness) 先天性の señtensei no

congested [kəndʒes'tid] *adj* (MED: with blood) うっ血した ukkétsu shitá; (: with mucus: nose) 詰まった tsumátta; (road) 渋滞した jútai shitá; (area) 人口密集の jiñkōmisshû no

congestion [kəndʒes'tʃən] *n* (MED: with blood) うっ血 ukkétsu; (: with mucus) 鼻詰まり hanázumàri; (of road) 渋滞 jútai; (of area) 人口密集 jiñkōmisshû

conglomerate [kənglɑːm'ər:it] *n* (COMM) 複合企業 fukúgōkigyð, コングロマリット koñguromaríttò

conglomeration [kənglɑːmərei'ʃən] *n* (group, gathering) 寄せ集め yoséatsume

congratulate [kəngrætʃ'uleit] *vt* (parents, bridegroom etc) ...にお祝いを言う ...ni o-íwai wo iú

congratulations [kəngrætʃulei'ʃənz] *npl* 祝詞 shukúji
congratulations! おめでとうございます omédetō gozáimasù

congregate [kɑːŋ'grəgeit] *vi* (people) 集まる atsúmarù; (animals) 群がる murágarù

congregation [kɑːŋgrəgei'ʃən] *n* (of a church) 会衆 kaíshū

congress [kɑːŋ'gris] *n* (conference) 大会 taíkai; (US): **Congress** 議会 gikài

congressman [kɑːŋ'grismən] (*US*: *pl* **congressmen**) *n* 下院議員 ka-íngiìn

conical [kɑːn'ikəl] *adj* (shape) 円すい形の eñsuikei no

conifer [kou'nifəːr] *n* 針葉樹 shiñ-yōju

conjecture [kəndʒek'tʃəːr] *n* (speculation) 憶測 okúsoku

conjugal [kɑːn'dʒəgəl] *adj* 夫婦間の fúfùkàn no

conjugate [kɑːn'dʒəgeit] *vt* (LING) ...の活用形を挙げる ...no katsúyōkei wo agérù

conjunction [kəndʒʌŋk'ʃən] *n* (LING) 接続詞 setsúzokushì

conjunctivitis [kəndʒʌŋktəvai'tis] *n* (MED) 結膜炎 ketsúmakuèn

conjure [kɑːn'dʒəːr] *vi* (magician) 奇術をする kijútsu wo suru

conjurer [kɑːn'dʒəːr:r] *n* (magician) 奇術師 kijútsushì, マジシャン majíshan

conjure up *vt* (ghost, spirit) 呼出す yobídasù; (memories) 思い起す omóiokosù

conk out [kɑːŋk-] (*inf*) *vi* (machine, engine) 故障する koshó suru

con man [kɑːn'mən] (*pl* **con men**) *n* ぺてん師 petéňshi

connect [kənekt'] *vt* (join, *also* TEL) つなぐ tsunágu; (ELEC) 接続する setsúzoku suru; (*fig*: associate) 関係付ける kañkeizùkeru

♦*vi*: **to connect with** (train, plane etc) ...に連絡する ...ni reñraku suru
to be connected with (associated) 関係付ける kañkeizùkeru

connection [kənekˈʃən] n (joint, link) つなぎ tsunági; (ELEC, TEL) 接続 setsúzoku; (train, plane etc) 連絡 refraku; (fig: association) 関係 kaňkei

connive [kənaivˈ] vi: **to connive at** (misbehavior) ...を容認する ...wo yőnin suru

connoisseur [kɑːnisəːrˈ] n (of food, wine, art etc) 通 tsū

connotation [kɑːnəteiˈʃən] n (implication) 含み fukúmi

conquer [kɑːŋˈkəːr] vt (MIL: country, enemy) 征服する seífuku suru; (fear, feelings) 克服する kokúfuku suru

conqueror [kɑːŋˈkəːrəːr] n (MIL) 征服者 seífukushà

conquest [kɑːnˈkwest] n (MIL) 征服 seífuku; (prize) 勝ち得た物 kachíeta monó; (mastery: of space etc) 征服 seífuku

cons [kɑːnz] npl see **convenience; pro**

conscience [kɑːnˈʃəns] n (sense of right and wrong) 良心 ryōshin

conscientious [kɑːnʃiːenˈʃəs] adj (worker) 良心的な ryōshinteki na

conscious [kɑːnˈʃəs] adj (aware): **conscious (of)** (...に) 気が付いている (...ni) ki ga tsuíte irú; (deliberate) 意識的な ishíkiteki na; (awake) 目が覚めている me ga saméte irú

consciousness [kɑːnˈʃəsnis] n (awareness, mentality: also MED) 意識 ishíki

conscript [kɑːnˈskript] n (MIL) 徴集兵 chōshūhei

conscription [kɑːnskripˈʃən] n (MIL) 徴兵 chōhei

consecrate [kɑːnˈsəkreit] vt (building, place) 奉献する hōken suru

consecutive [kɑːnsekˈjətiv] adj (days, wins) 連続の refzoku no

consensus [kɑːnsenˈsəs] n 合意 gōi

consent [kɑːnsentˈ] n (permission) 許可 kyóka
♦vi: **to consent to** ...に同意する ...ni dői suru

consequence [kɑːnˈsəkwens] n (result) 結果 kekká; (significance) 重要さ jűyōsa

consequently [kɑːnˈsəkwentliː] adv (as a result, so) 従って shitágàtte

conservation [kɑːnsəːrveiˈʃən] n (of the environment) 保護 hogð, 保全 hozén; (of energy) 節約 setsúyaku; (of paintings, books) 保全 hozén

conservative [kənsəːrˈvətiv] adj (traditional, conventional: person, attitudes) 保守的な hoshúteki na; (cautious: estimate etc) 控え目の hikáeme no; (BRIT: POL): **Conservative** 保守党の hoshútō no
♦n (BRIT: POL): **Conservative** 保守党員 hoshútðin

conservatory [kənsəːrˈvətɔːriː] n (greenhouse) 温室 oñshitsu; (MUS) 音楽学校 oñgaku gakkō

conserve [vb kənsəːrvˈ n kɑːnˈsəːrv] vt (preserve) 保護する hőgð suru; (supplies, energy) 節約する setsúyaku suru
♦n (jam) ジャム jámu

consider [kənsidˈəːr] vt (believe) ...だと思う ...da to omőù; (study) 熟考する jukkō suru; (take into account) 考慮に入れる kőryo ni irérù
to consider doing something ...しようかと考える ...shiyő ka to kángaerù

considerable [kənsidˈəːrəbəl] adj (amount, expense, difference etc) かなりの kanári no

considerably [kənsidˈəːrəbliː] adv (improve, deteriorate) かなり kanári

considerate [kənsidˈəːrit] adj (person) 思いやりのある omóiyari no arù

consideration [kənsidəreiˈʃən] n (deliberation) 熟考 jukkő; (factor) 考慮すべき点 kőryo subeki tén; (thoughtfulness) 思いやり omóiyarì

considering [kənsidˈəːriŋ] prep (bearing in mind) ...を考慮すると ...wo kőryo surù to

consign [kənsainˈ] vt (something unwanted): **to consign to** (place) ...にしまっておく ...ni shimátte okù; (person): **to consign to** (someone's care etc) ...に委ねる ...ni yudánerù; (poverty etc) ...に追込む ...ni oíkomù

consignment [kənsainˈmənt] n (COMM) 輸送貨物 yusőkamòtsu

consist [kənsistˈ] vi: **to consist of** (comprise) ...から成る ...kará narù

consistency [kənsis'tənsi:] *n* (of actions, policies etc) 一貫性 ikkánsei; (of yoghurt, cream etc) 固さ katása

consistent [kənsis'tənt] *adj* (person) 変らない kawáranaì; (argument, idea) 一貫性のある ikkánsei no arù

consolation [kɑːnsəlei'ʃən] *n* (comfort) 慰め nagúsame

console [*vb* kənsoul' *n* kɑːn'soul] *vt* (comfort) 慰める nagúsamerù
♦*n* (panel) コンソール konsôru

consolidate [kənsɑːl'ideit] *vt* (position, power) 強化する kyóka suru

consommé [kɑːnsəmei'] *n* (CULIN) コンソメ konsome

consonant [kɑːn'sənənt] *n* (LING) 子音 shíìn

consortium [kənsɔːr'ʃiːəm] *n* (COMM) 協会 kyókai

conspicuous [kənspik'juːəs] *adj* (noticeable: person, feature) 目立つ medátsu

conspiracy [kənspir'əsiː] *n* (plot) 陰謀 iñbō

conspire [kənspai'əːr] *vi* (criminals, revolutionaries etc) 共謀する kyóbō suru; (events) 相重なる aíkasanarù

constable [kɑːn'stəbəl] (*BRIT*) *n* 巡査 juñsa
chief constable (*BRIT*) 警察本部長 keísatsu hoñbuchō

constabulary [kənstæb'jələːriː] (*BRIT*) *n* 警察 keísatsu ◇一地区の警察隊を指す ichíchiku no keísatsutai wo sasù

constant [kɑːn'stənt] *adj* (continuous: criticism, pain) 絶えない taénài; (fixed: temperature, level) 一定の ittéi no

constantly [kɑːn'stəntliː] *adv* (continually) 絶間なく taémanàku

constellation [kɑːnstəlei'ʃən] *n* (ASTRONOMY) 星座 seíza

consternation [kɑːnstəːrnei'ʃən] *n* (dismay) ろうばい rōbai

constipated [kɑːn'stəpeitid] *adj* (MED) 便秘している beñpi shité irù

constipation [kɑːnstəpei'ʃən] *n* (MED) 便秘 beñpi

constituency [kənstitʃ'uːənsiː] *n* (POL: area) 選挙区 señkyokù; (: electors) 選挙民 señkyomìn

constituent [kənstitʃ'uːənt] *n* (POL) 有権者 yūkeñsha; (component) 部分 búbùn

constitute [kɑːn'stituːt] *vt* (represent: challenge, emergency) ...である ...de arù; (make up: whole) 構成する kósei suru

constitution [kɑːnstituː'ʃən] *n* (of country) 憲法 kéñpō; (of club etc) 会則 kaísoku; (health) 体質 taíshitsu; (make-up: of committee etc) 構成 kósei

constitutional [kɑːnstituː'ʃənəl] *adj* (government, reform etc) 憲法の kéñpō no

constraint [kənstreint'] *n* (restriction) 制限 seígen; (compulsion) 強制 kyósei

construct [kɑːn'strʌkt] *vt* (building) 建てる tatérù; (bridge, road etc) 建設する keñsetsu suru; (machine) 作る tsukúrù

construction [kənstrʌk'ʃən] *n* (of building etc) 建築 keñchiku; (of bridge, road etc) 建設 keñsetsu; (of machine) 製作 seísaku; (structure) 構造物 kózōbutsu

constructive [kənstrʌk'tiv] *adj* (remark, criticism) 建設的な keñsetsuteki na

construe [kənstruː'] *vt* (statement, event) 解釈する kaíshaku suru

consul [kɑːn'səl] *n* 領事 ryóji

consulate [kɑːn'səlit] *n* 領事館 ryójikan

consult [kənsʌlt'] *vt* (doctor, lawyer, friend) ...に相談する ...ni sódan suru; (reference book) 調べる shirábèru

consultant [kənsʌl'tənt] *n* (MED) 顧問医 komón-i; (other specialist) 顧問 kómòn, コンサルタント koñsarùtanto

consultation [kɑːnsəltei'ʃən] *n* (MED) 診察 shiñsatsu; (discussion) 協議 kyógi

consulting room [kənsʌl'tiŋ-] (*BRIT*) *n* 診察室 shiñsatsushitsu

consume [kənsuːm'] *vt* (food) 食べる tabérù; (drink) 飲む nómù; (fuel, energy, time etc) 消費する shóhi suru

consumer [kənsuː'məːr] *n* (COMM) 消費者 shóhishà

consumer goods *npl* 消費財 shóhizài

consumerism [kənsuː'məːrizəm] *n* 消費者運動 shóhishaundō

consumer society n 消費社会 shōhishakāi

consummate [kɑːnˈsəmeit] vt (ambition etc) 全うする mattō suru

  to consummate a marriage 床入りする tokó-iri suru

consumption [kənsʌmpʃ(ə)n] n (of food) 食べる事 tabérù kotó; (of drink) 飲む事 nōmù kotó; (of fuel, energy, time etc) 消費 shōhi; (amount consumed) 消費量 shōhiryō; (buying) 消費 shōhi

cont. abbr (= continued) 続く tsuzúku

contact [kɑːnˈtækt] n (communication) 連絡 reńraku; (touch) 接触 sesshóku; (person) 連絡相手 refirakuaìte

  ♦vt (by phone, letter) …に連絡する …ni reńraku suru

contact lenses npl コンタクトレンズ końtakutoreńzu

contagious [kənteiˈdʒəs] adj (MED: disease) 伝染性の deńsensei no; (fig: laughter, enthusiasm) 移りやすい utsúriyasuī

contain [kənteiˈn] vt (hold: objects) …に…が入っている …ni …ga haítte irù; (have: component, ingredient etc) …に…が含まれている …ni …ga fukúmarète irù; (subj: piece of writing, report etc) …に…が書いてある …ni …ga kaíte arù; (curb: growth, spread, feeling) 抑える osáerù

  to contain oneself 自制する jiséi suru

container [kənteiˈnəːr] n (box, jar etc) 入れ物 irémono; (COMM: for shipping etc) コンテナー kóñtenā

contaminate [kəntæməˈneit] vt (water, food, soil etc) 汚染する oséñ suru

contamination [kəntæməneiˈʃ(ə)n] n (of water, food, soil etc) 汚染 oséñ

cont'd abbr (= continued) 続く tsuzuku

contemplate [kɑːnˈtəmpleit] vt (idea, subject, course of action) じっくり考える jikkúrì kańgaerù; (person, painting etc) 眺める nagámerù

contemporary [kəntemˈpəreːriː] adj (present-day) 現代の geñdai no; (belonging to same time) 同時代の dōjidai no

  ♦n (person) 同時代の人 dōjidai no hitó

contempt [kəntempt'] n (scorn) 軽べつ keíbetsu

contempt of court (LAW) 法廷侮辱罪 hōteibujokuzāi

contemptible [kəntempˈtəbəl] adj (conduct) 卑劣な hirétsu na

contemptuous [kəntempˈtʃʊəs] adj (attitude) 軽べつ的な keíbetsuteki na

contend [kəntend'] vt (assert): **to contend that** …だと主張する …da to shuchō suru

  ♦vi (struggle): **to contend with** (problem, difficulty) …と戦う …to tatákaù; (compete): **to contend for** (power etc) …を争う …wo arásoù

contender [kəntendˈəːr] n (in competition) 競争者 kyōsōshà; (POL) 候補者 kōhoshà; (SPORT) 選手 séñshu

content [adj, vb kəntent' n kɑːntent'] adj (happy and satisfied) 満足して mañzoku shité

  ♦vt (satisfy) 満足させる mañzoku saséru

  ♦n (of speech, novel) 内容 naíyō; (fat content, moisture content etc) 含有量 gañ-yūryō

contented [kəntenˈtid] adj (happy and satisfied) 満足して mañzoku shité

contention [kəntenˈʃ(ə)n] n (assertion) 主張 shuchō; (disagreement, argument) 論争 rofisō

contentment [kəntentˈmənt] n (happiness, satisfaction) 満足 mañzoku

contents [kɑːnˈtents] npl (of bottle, packet) 中身 nakámî; (of book) 内容 naíyō

  (table of) contents 目次 mokúji

contest [n kɑːnˈtest vb kəntest'] n (competition) コンテスト kóñtesuto, コンクール kóñkūru; (struggle: for control, power etc) 争い arásoì

  ♦vt (election, competition) …で競う …de kisóù; (statement, decision: also LAW) …に対して異義を申立てる …ni taíshite igí wo mōshítaterù

contestant [kəntesˈtənt] n (in quiz, competition) 参加者 sańkashà; (in fight) 競争者 kyōsōshà

context [kɑːnˈtekst] n (circumstances: of events, ideas etc) 背景 haíkei; (of word, phrase) 文脈 buńmyaku

continent [kɑːnʹtənənt] n (land mass) 大陸 taíriku

the **Continent** (*BRIT*) ヨーロッパ大陸 yŏroppa tairíku

continental [kɑːntənenʹtəl] *adj* 大陸の taírĭku no

continental quilt (*BRIT*) n 掛布団 kakébuton

contingency [kəntinʹdʒənsiː] n 有事 yŭji

contingent [kəntinʹdʒənt] n (group of people: *also* MIL) 一団 ichídan

continual [kəntinʹjuːəl] *adj* (movement, process, rain etc) 絶間ない taémanài

continually [kəntinʹjuːəliː] *adv* 絶間なく taémanàku

continuation [kəntinjuːeiʹʃən] n 継続 keízoku

continue [kəntinʹjuː] *vi* 続く tsuzúkù
♦*vt* 続ける tsuzúkerù

continuity [kɑːntənuːʹitiː] n (in policy, management etc) 連続性 reńzokusei; (TV, CINEMA) 撮影台本 satsúeidaìhon, コンテ kóǹte

continuous [kəntinʹjuːəs] *adj* (process, growth etc) 絶間ない taémanài; (line) 途切れのない togíre no naì; (LING) 進行形の shiñkōkei no

continuous stationery n 連続用紙 reńzokuyòshi

contort [kəntɔːrtʹ] *vt* (body) ねじる nejírù; (face) しかめる shikámerù

contortion [kəntɔːrʹʃən] n (of body) ねじれ nejíre; (of face) こわばり kowábari

contour [kɑːnʹtuːr] n (on map: *also*: **contour line**) 等高線 tókōsen; (shape, outline: *gen pl*) 輪郭 riñkaku

contraband [kɑːnʹtrəbænd] n 密輸品 mitsúyuhìn

contraception [kɑːntrəsepʹʃən] n 避妊 hinín

contraceptive [kɑːntrəsepʹtiv] *adj* (method, technique) 避妊の hinín no
♦n (device) 避妊用具 hinín yŏgu; (pill etc) 避妊薬 hínín-yaku

contract [n kɑːnʹtrækt vb kəntræktʹ] n (LAW, COMM) 契約 keíyaku
♦*vi* (become smaller) 収縮する shŭshuku suru; (COMM): **to contract to do**

something ...をする契約をする ...wo suru keíyaku wo suru
♦*vt* (illness) ...に掛かる ...ni kakárù

contraction [kəntrækʹʃən] n (of metal, muscle) 収縮 shŭshuku; (of word, phrase) 短縮形 tañshukukei

contractor [kɑːnʹtræktər] n (COMM) 請負人 ukéoinìn

contradict [kɑːntrədiktʹ] *vt* (person) ...の言う事を否定する ...no iú kotŏ wo hitéi suru; (statement etc) 否定する hitéi suru

contradiction [kɑːntrədikʹʃən] n (inconsistency) 矛盾 mujún

contradictory [kɑːntrədikʹtəːriː] *adj* (ideas, statements) 矛盾する mujún suru

contraption [kəntræpʹʃən] (*pej*) n (device, machine) 珍妙な機械 chiñmyō na kikáī

contrary[1] [kɑːnʹtreːriː] *adj* (opposite, different) 反対の hañtai no
♦n (opposite) 反対 hañtai

on the **contrary** それどころか sorédokoro ka

unless you hear to the contrary そうではないと聞かされない限り só de wa nài to kikásarenài kagíri

contrary[2] [kəntreːrʹiː] *adj* (perverse) つむじ曲りな tsumújimagàri na、へそ曲りな hesómagari na

contrast [n kɑːnʹtræst vb kəntræstʹ] n (difference) 相違 sŏi、コントラスト koñtorasùto
♦*vt* (techniques, texts etc) 対照する taíshō suru

in contrast to ...と違って ...to chigátte

contrasting [kəntræsʹtiŋ] *adj* (colors, attitudes) 対照的な taíshōteki na

contravene [kɑːntrəviːnʹ] *vt* (law) ...に違反する ...ni ihán suru

contribute [kəntribʹjuːt] *vi* (give) 寄付する kifú suru
♦*vt*: **to contribute an article to** (commissioned) ...に記事を寄稿する ...ni kíjĭ wo kikŏ suru; (unsolicited) ...に記事を投稿する ...ni kíjĭ wo tŏkō suru; **to contribute $10** 10ドルを寄付する jŭdòru wo kifú suru

to contribute to (charity) ...に寄付する ...ni kifú suru; (newspaper: commissioned) ...に寄稿する ...ni kikō suru; (unsolicited) ...に投稿する ...ni tōkō suru; (discussion) 意見を言う ikén wo iú; (problem etc) ...を悪くする ...wo warúkù surú

contribution [kɑːntrəbjuː'ʃən] *n* (donation) 寄付 kifu; (*BRIT*: for social security) 掛金 kakékin; (to debate, campaign) 貢献 kōken; (to journal: commissioned) 寄稿 kikō; (: unsolicited) 投稿 tōkō

contributor [kəntrib'jətər] *n* (to appeal) 寄付者 kifúshà; (to newspaper) 投稿者〔寄稿者〕tōkōshà〔kikōshà〕

contrive [kəntraiv'] *vi*: *to contrive to do* 努力して...に成功する doryòku shite ...ni seīkō suru

control [kəntroul'] *vt* (country, organization) 支配する shihái suru; (machinery, process) 制御する seígyo suru; (wages, prices) 規制する kiséi suru; (temper) 自制する jiséi suru; (disease) 抑制する yokúsei suru

◆*n* (of country, organization) 支配 shihái; (of oneself, emotions) 自制心 jiséishin

to be in control of (situation) ...を掌握している ...wo shōaku shité irù; (car etc) ...を思いのままに動かしている ...wo omói no mamá ni ugókashite irù

under control (crowd) 指示に従って shijì ni shitágatte; (situation) 収拾が付いて shūshū ga tsuíte; (dog) 言う事を聞いて iú kotó wo kiíte

out of control (crowd) 制止が利かなくなって seíshi ga kikánakù natté; (situation) 手に負えなくなって te ni oénakù natté; (dog) 言う事を聞かなくなって iú kotó wo kikánakù natté

control panel *n* 制御盤 seígyoban

control room *n* 制御室 seígyoshìtsu

controls [kəntroulz'] *npl* (of vehicle) ハンドル hándoru ◊ブレーキ，クラッチなど全ての運転制御装置を含む burèki, kurátchì nadò subéte no uńtenseigyosòchi wo fukúmù; (on radio, television etc) コントロール盤 końtorōruban ◊全てのス

イッチ，調節用つまみ，ボタンなどを含む subete no suítchì, chōsetsu yō tsumami, botán nadò wo fukúmù; (governmental) 規制 kiséi

control tower *n* (AVIAT) 管制塔 kańseitō

controversial [kɑːntrəvəːr'ʃəl] *adj* (topic, person) 論争の的になっている rońsō no matō ni natté irù

controversy [kɑːn'trəvəːrsiː] *n* 論争 rońsō

conurbation [kɑːnəːrbei'ʃən] *n* 大都市圏 daítoshikèn

convalesce [kɑːnvəles'] *vi* (MED) 回復する kaífuku suru

convalescence [kɑːnvəles'əns] *n* (MED) 回復期 kaífukukì

convector [kənvek'təːr] *n* (heater) 対流式暖房器 taíryūshikidanbōkì, コンベクター końbekūtā

convene [kənviːn'] *vt* (meeting, conference) 召集する shōshū suru

◆*vi* (parliament, inquiry) 開会する kaíkai suru

convenience [kənviːn'jəns] *n* (easiness: of using something, doing something) 便利 bénri; (suitability: of date, meeting, house etc) 好都合 kōtsugō; (advantage, help) 便宜 béñgi

at your convenience ご都合の良い時に go-tsúgō no yoì tokí ni

all modern conveniences, (*BRIT*) *all mod cons* 近代設備完備 kińdaisetsubikañbi ◊不動産の広告などに使われる語句 fudōsan no kōkoku nadò ni tsukáwarerù gokù

convenient [kənviːn'jənt] *adj* (handy) 便利な bénri na; (suitable) 都合の良い tsugō no yoì

convent [kɑːn'vent] *n* (REL) 女子修道院 joshíshūdòin

convention [kənven'ʃən] *n* (custom) 慣例 kańrei; (conference) 大会 taíkai; (agreement) 協定 kyōtei

conventional [kənven'ʃənəl] *adj* (person) 型にはまった katá ni hamátta; (method) 伝統的な deńtōteki na

converge [kənvəːrdʒ'] *vi* (roads) 合流す

g góryū suru; (people): **to converge on** (place, person) ...に集まる ...ni atsúmarù

conversant [kənvəːrʹsənt] *adj*: **to be conversant with** (problem, requirements) ...に通じている ...ni tsújite irù

conversation [kɑːnvəːrseiʹʃ(ə)n] *n* (talk) 会話 kaíwa

conversational [kɑːnvəːrseiʹʃənəl] *adj* (tone, language, skills) 会話的な kaíwateki na

converse [*n* kɑːnʹvəːrs *vb* kənvəːrsʹ] *n* (of statement) 逆 gyakú

♦*vi* (talk): **to converse (with someone)** (...と) 話をする (...to) hanáshi wo suru

conversely [kənvəːrsʹliː] *adv* 逆に gyakú ni

conversion [kənvəːrʹʒən] *n* (of weights, substances etc) 変換 heñkan; (REL) 改宗 kaíshū

convert [*vb* kənvəːrtʹ *n* kɑːnʹvəːrt] *vt* (change): **to convert something into/ to** ...を...に変換する ...wo ...ni heñkan suru; (person: REL) 改宗させる kaíshū saséru; (: POL) 党籍を変えさせる tóseki wo kaésaserù

♦*n* (REL) 改宗者 kaíshūsha; (POL) 党籍を変える人 tóseki wo kaéru hitó

convertible [kənvəːrʹtəbəl] *n* (AUT) コンバーチブル koñbāchibùru ◊畳み込み式屋根を持つ乗用車 tatámikomishiki yané wo motsù jóyōsha

convex [kɑːnveksʹ] *adj* 凸面の totsúmen no

convey [kənveiʹ] *vt* (information, idea, thanks) 伝える tsutáerù; (cargo, traveler) 運ぶ hakóbu

conveyor belt [kənveiʹəːr-] *n* ベルトコンベヤー berútokonbeyà

convict [*vb* kənviktʹ *n* kɑːnʹvikt] *vt* (of a crime) ...に有罪の判決を下す ...ni yúzai no hañketsu wo kudásù

♦*n* (person) 囚人 shūjin

conviction [kənvikʹʃən] *n* (belief) 信念 shíñnen; (certainty) 確信 kakúshin; (LAW) 有罪判決 yūzaihañketsu

convince [kənvinsʹ] *vt* (assure) 分からせる wakáraserù; (persuade) 納得させる

nattóku saséru

convinced [kənvinstʹ] *adj*: **convinced of/that** ...を〔だと〕確信している ...wo 〔dáto〕kakúshin shité irù

convincing [kənvinʹsiŋ] *adj* (case, argument) 納得のいく nattóku no ikú

convoluted [kɑːnʹvəluːtid] *adj* (statement, argument) 入込った komíttta

convoy [kɑːnʹvɔi] *n* (of trucks) 護衛付き輸送車隊 goéitsuki yusóshatai; (of ships) 護衛付き輸送船団 goéitsukiyusóseñdan

convulse [kənvʌlsʹ] *vt*: **to be convulsed with laughter** 笑いこける waráikokerù

to be convulsed with pain もだえる modáerù

convulsion [kənvʌlʹʃən] *n* (MED) けいれん keíren

coo [kuː] *vi* (dove, pigeon) くーくー鳴く kūkū nakú; (person) 優しい声で言う yasáshii koè de iú

cook [kuk] *vt* (food, meal) 料理する ryóri suru

♦*vi* (person) 料理する ryóri suru; (meat, pie etc) 焼ける yakéru

♦*n* 料理人 ryórinìn, コック kokkù

cookbook [kukʹbuk] *n* 料理の本 ryóri no hoñ

cooker [kukʹəːr] *n* (stove) レンジ réñji

cookery [kukʹəːriː] *n* 料理する事 ryóri suru kotó

cookery book (*BRIT*) *n* = **cookbook**

cookie [kukʹiː] (*US*) *n* ビスケット bisúkettò, クッキー kúkkì

cooking [kukʹiŋ] *n* (activity) 料理すること ryóri suru kotó; (food) 料理 ryóri

cool [kuːl] *adj* (temperature, clothes) 涼しい suzúshiì; (drink) 冷たい tsumétai; (person: calm) 落着いている ochítsuite irù; (: unfriendly) そっけない sokkénaì

♦*vt* (make colder: tea) 冷ます samásù; (: room) 冷やす hiyásù

♦*vi* (become colder: water) 冷たくなる tsumétaku narù; (: air) 涼しくなる suzúshiku narù

coolness [kuːlʹnis] *n* (of temperature, clothing) 涼しさ suzúshisà; (of drink) 冷たさ tsumétasà; (calm) 落着き ochítsuki;

(unfriendliness) そっけなさ sokkénasà

coop [ku:p] *n* (*also*: **rabbit coop**) ウサギ 小屋 uságigoya; (*also*: **hen coop**) ニワト リ小屋 niwátorigoya

♦*vt*: **to coop up** (*fig*: imprison) 閉込める tojíkomerù

cooperate [kouɑːp'əreit] *vi* (collaborate) 協同する kyódō suru; (assist) 協力する kyóryoku suru

cooperation [kouɑːpərei'ʃən] *n* (collaboration) 協同 kyódō; (assistance) 協力 kyóryoku

cooperative [kouɑːp'rətiv] *adj* (farm, business) 協同組合の kyódōkùmiai no; (person) 協力的な kyóryokuteki na

♦*n* (factory, business) 協同組合 kyódō-kùmiai

coordinate [*vb* kouɔːr'dəneit *n* kouɔːr'-dənit] *vt* (activity, attack) 指揮する shi-kí suru; (movements) 調整する chósei su-ru

♦*n* (MATH) 座標 zahyó

coordinates [kouɔːr'dənits] *npl* (clothes) コーディネートされた服 kódi-nèto saréta fukú

coordination [kouɔːrdənei'ʃən] *n* (of services) 指揮 shikí; (of one's move-ments) 調整 chósei

co-ownership [kouou'nə:rʃip] *n* 協同所 有 kyódōshoyū

cop [kɑːp] (*inf*) *n* (policeman/woman) 警官 keíkan

cope [koup] *vi*: **to cope with** (problem, situation etc) …に対応する …ni taíō suru

copious [kou'pi:əs] *adj* (helpings) たっぷ りの táppùri no

copious amounts of 多量の taryó no

copper [kɑːp'ə:r] *n* (metal) 銅 dó; (*inf*: policeman/woman) 警官 keíkan

coppers [kɑːp'ə:rz] *npl* (small change, coins) 小銭 kozéni

coppice [kɑːp'is] *n* 木立 kodáchi

copse [kɑːps] *n* = **coppice**

copulate [kɑːp'jəleit] *vi* (people) 性交す る seíkō suru; (animals) 交尾する kóbi suru

copy [kɑːp'iː] *n* (duplicate) 複写 fukúsha, コピー kópì; (of book) 1冊 issátsu; (of record) 1枚 ichímaì; (of newspaper) 1部 ichíbù

♦*vt* (person, idea etc) まねる manérù; (something written) 複写する fukúsha suru, コピーする kópì suru

copyright [kɑːp'iːrait] *n* 著作権 chosá-kukèn

coral [kɔːr'əl] *n* (substance) さんご saǹgo

coral reef *n* さんご礁 saǹgoshō

cord [kɔːrd] *n* (string) ひも himó; (ELEC) コード kódo; (fabric) コールテン kóruten

cordial [kɔːr'dʒəl] *adj* (person, welcome) 暖かい atátakaì; (relationship) 親密な shiǹmitsu na

♦*n* (BRIT: drink) フルーツシロップ fu-rútsu shiròppu

cordon [kɔːr'dən] *n* (MIL, POLICE) 非常 線 hijōsen

cordon off *vt* 非常線を張って…への立入 りを禁止する hijōsen wo hatté …e no tachíiri wo kiñshi suru

corduroy [kɔːr'dərɔi] *n* コールテン kóru-ten

core [kɔːr] *n* (of fruit) しん shiǹ; (of orga-nization, system, building) 中心部 chú-shiñbu; (heart? of matter) 核心 kakúshin

♦*vt* (an apple, pear etc) …のしんをくりぬ く …no shiǹ wo kurínukù

coriander [kɔːriːænˈdəːr] *n* (spice) コリ アンダー koríañdā

cork [kɔːrk] *n* (stopper) 栓 séǹ; (bark) コ ルク kóruku

corkscrew [kɔːrk'skruː] *n* 栓抜き seńnu-ki

corn [kɔːrn] *n* (US: maize) トウモロコシ tómoròkoshi; (BRIT: cereal crop) 穀物 kokúmòtsu; (on foot) 魚の目 uó no me

corn on the cob 軸付きトウモロコシ ji-kútsuki tómoròkoshi

cornea [kɔːr'niːə] *n* (of eye) 角膜 kakú-maku

corned beef [kɔːrnd-] *n* コーンビーフ kóǹbīfu

corner [kɔːr'nə:r] *n* (outside) 角 kádò; (inside) 隅 súmì; (in road) 角 kádò; (SOC-CER) コーナーキック kónākikkù; (BOX-ING) コーナー kóǹā

♦*vt* (trap) 追詰める oítsumerù, 袋のネズ

ミにする fukúro no nezumi ni suru;
(COMM: market) 独占する dokúsen suru

♦*vi* (in car) コーナリングする kōnaringu
surù

cornerstone [kɔːr'nəːrstoun] *n* (*fig*) 土台
dodái

cornet [kɔːrnet'] *n* (MUS) コルネット
korúnettò; (*BRIT*: of ice-cream) アイス
クリームコーン aísukurīmukòn

cornflakes [kɔːrn'fleiks] *npl* コーンフレ
ーク kōnfurēku

cornflour [kɔːrn'flauəːr] (*BRIT*) *n* =
cornstarch

cornstarch [kɔːrn'stɑːrtʃ] (*US*) *n* コーン
スターチ kōnsutāchi

Cornwall [kɔːrn'wɔːl] *n* コーンウォール
kōn-uōru

corny [kɔːr'niː] (*inf*) *adj* (joke) さえない
saénài

corollary [kɔːr'əleːriː] *n* (of fact, idea) 当
然の結果 tōzen no kekkà

coronary [kɔːr'əneːriː] *n* (*also*: **coronary
thrombosis**) 肝動脈血栓症 kańdōmyaku-
kesséñshō

coronation [kɔːrənei'ʃən] *n* たい冠式 taíkañshiki

coroner [kɔːr'ənəːr] *n* (LAW) 検死官 keñ-
shikàn

coronet [kɔːr'ənit] *n* コロネット korő-
nettò ◇貴族などがかぶる小さな冠 kiző-
ku nadò ga kabúrù chíisana kañmuri

corporal [kɔːr'pəːrəl] *n* (MIL) ご長 gō-
chō

♦*adj*: **corporal punishment** 体罰 taíba-
tsu

corporate [kɔːr'pəːrit] *adj* (action,
effort, ownership) 共同の kyōdō no;
(finance, image) 企業の kigyō no

corporation [kɔːrpərei'ʃən] *n* (COMM)
企業 kigyō; (of town) 行政部 gyōseibù

corps [kɔːr *pl* kɔːrz] (*pl* **corps**) *n* (MIL)
兵団 heídan; (of diplomats, journalists)
...団 ...dàn

corpse [kɔːrps] *n* 遺体 itái

corpuscle [kɔːr'pəsəl] *n* (BIO) 血球 kek-
kyū

corral [kəræl'] *n* (for cattle, horses) 囲い

kakói

correct [kərekt'] *adj* (right) 正しい tadá-
shiî; (proper) 礼儀正しい reígitadashiî

♦*vt* (mistake, fault) 直す naősù; (exam)
採点する saíten suru

correction [kərek'ʃən] *n* (act of correcting) 直す事 naősù kotð; (instance) 直し
naőshi

correlation [kɔːrəlei'ʃən] *n* (link) 相互関
係 sögokañkei

correspond [kɔːrəspɑːnd'] *vi* (write): **to
correspond (with)** (...と) 手紙のやり
取りをする (...to) tegámi no yarítòri
wo surù; (be equivalent): **to correspond
(to)** (...に) 相当する (...ni) sōtō suru;
(be in accordance): **to correspond
(with)** (...と) 一致する (...to) itchí
suru

correspondence [kɔːrəspɑːn'dəns] *n*
(letters) 手紙 tegámi; (communication
by letters) 文通 buńtsū; (relationship) 一
致 itchí

correspondence course *n* (SCOL) 通
信講座 tsūshinkōza

correspondent [kɔːrəspɑːn'dənt] *n*
(journalist) 特派員 tokúhaìn

corridor [kɔːr'idəːr] *n* (in house, building
etc) 廊下 rōka; (in train) 通路 tsūro

corroborate [kərɑːb'əreit] *vt* (facts,
story) 裏付ける urázukerù

corrode [kəroud'] *vt* (metal) 浸食する
shiñshoku suru

♦*vi* (metal) 腐食する fushőku suru

corrosion [kərou'ʒən] *n* 腐食 fushőku

corrugated [kɔːr'əgeitid] *adj* (roof,
cardboard) 波型の namígata no

corrugated iron *n* なまこ板 namákoi-
tà

corrupt [kərʌpt'] *adj* (person) 腐敗した
fuhái shitá; (COMPUT: data) 化けた ba-
kétà, 壊れた kowáretà

♦*vt* (person) 買収する baíshū suru;
(COMPUT: data) 化けさせる bakésase-
rù

corruption [kərʌp'ʃən] *n* (of person) 汚
職 oshőku; (COMPUT: of data) 化ける事
bakérù kotð

corset [kɔːr'sit] *n* (undergarment: *also*

MED) コルセット kórùsetto

Corsica [kɔːr'sikə] *n* コルシカ島 korúshikatō

cosh [kɑːʃ] (*BRIT*) *n* (cudgel) こん棒 koñbō

cosmetic [kɑːzmet'ik] *n* (beauty product) 化粧品 keshōhin
♦*adj* (*fig*: measure, improvement) 表面的な hyōmenteki na

cosmic [kɑːz'mik] *adj* 宇宙の uchū no

cosmonaut [kɑːz'mənɔːt] *n* 宇宙飛行士 uchūhikōshi

cosmopolitan [kɑːzməpɑːl'itən] *adj* (place, person) 国際的な kokúsaiteki na

cosmos [kɑːz'məs] *n* 宇宙 uchū

cosset [kɑːs'it] *vt* (person) 甘やかす amáyakasù

cost [kɔːst] *n* (price) 値段 nedán; (expenditure) 費用 híyō
♦*vt* (*pt*, *pp* cost) (be priced at) ...の値段である ...no nedán de arù; (find out cost of: project, purchase etc: *pt*, *pp* costed) ...の費用を見積る ...no hiyō wo mitsúmorù

how much does it cost? いくらですか ikùra desu ká

to cost someone time/effort ...に時間〔労力〕を要する ...ni jikán 〔rōryoku〕 wo yō surù

it cost him his life そのために彼は命をなくした sono tamé ni kárè wa íñochi wo nákù shitá

at all costs 何があっても nanî ga atté mò

co-star [kou'stɑːr] *n* (TV, CINEMA) 共演者 kyōeñsha

cost-effective [kɔːstifek'tiv] *adj* 費用効果比の高い hiyōkōkahi no takáî

costly [kɔːst'liː] *adj* (high-priced) 値段の高い nedán no takáî; (involving much expenditure) 費用の掛かる hiyō no kakárù

cost-of-living [kɔːstəvliv'iŋ] *adj* (allowance, index) 生計費の seíkeìhi no

cost price (*BRIT*) *n* 原価 géñka

costs [kɔːsts] *npl* (overheads) 経費 kéìhi; (LAW) 訴訟費用 soshōhìyō

costume [kɑːs'tuːm] *n* (outfit, style of dress) 衣装 íshō; (*BRIT*: also: **swimming costume**) 水着 mizúgi

costume jewelery *n* 模造宝石類 mozōhōsekìruì

cosy [kou'ziː] (*BRIT*) *adj* = **cozy**

cot [kɑːt] *n* (*BRIT*: child's) ベビーベッド bebíbeddò; (*US*: campbed) キャンプベッド kyañpubeddò

cottage [kɑːt'idʒ] *n* (house) 小さな家 chíisa na ie, コッテージ kottēji

cottage cheese *n* カッテージチーズ kattēji chīzù

cotton [kɑːt'ən] *n* (fabric) 木綿 momén, コットン kőttòn; (*BRIT*: thread) 縫い糸 nuí-itò

cotton batting [-bæt'iŋ] *n* (*US*) 脱脂綿 dasshímèn

cotton candy (*US*) *n* (candy floss) 綿菓子 watágashì, 綿あめ watá-àme

cotton on to (*inf*) *vt fus* ...に気が付く ...ni kî ga tsúkù

cotton wool (*BRIT*) *n* = **cotton batting**

couch [kautʃ] *n* (sofa) ソファー sófà; (doctor's) 診察台 shiñsatsudai

couchette [kuːʃet'] *n* (on train, boat) 寝台 shiñdai ◇昼間壁に畳み掛けるか普通の座席に使う物を指す hiruma kabé ni tatámikakerù ka futsú no zaséki ni tsukáù monó wo sasù

cough [kɔːf] *vi* (person) せきをする sekí wo surù
♦*n* (noise) せき sekí; (illness) せきの多い病気 sekí no ōi byōki

cough drop *n* せき止めドロップ sekídome doróppu

could [kud] *pt of* **can**

couldn't [kud'ənt] = **could not**

council [kaun'səl] *n* (committee, board) 評議会 hyōgikài
city/town council 市〔町〕議会 shi〔chō〕gíkài

council estate (*BRIT*) *n* 公営住宅団地 kōeijūtakudañchi

council house (*BRIT*) *n* 公営住宅 kōeijūtaku

councillor [kaun'sələːr] *n* 議員 gíin

counsel [kaun'səl] *n* (advice) 助言 jogén;

(lawyer) 弁護人 beńgonin

♦vt (advise) ...に助言する ...ni jogén suru

counsel(l)or [kaun'sələr] n (advisor) カウンセラー kaúnserä; (US: lawyer) 弁護人 beńgonin

count [kaunt] vt (add up: numbers, money, things, people) 数える kazóerù; (include) 入れる iréru, 含む fukúmù

♦vi (enumerate) 数える kazóerù; (be considered) ...と見なされる ...to minasareru; (be valid) 効果をもつ kõka wo mótsù

♦n (of things, people, votes) 数 kazú; (level: of pollen, alcohol etc) 値 atái, 数値 súchi; (nobleman) 伯爵 hakúshaku

countdown [kaunt'daun] n (to launch) 秒読み byõyomi

countenance [kaun'tənəns] n (face) 顔 kaő

♦vt (tolerate) 容認する yőnin suru

counter [kaun'tər] n (in shop, café, bank etc) カウンター kaúntä; (in game) こま komá

♦vt (oppose) ...に対抗する ...ni taikõ suru

♦adv: **counter to** ...に反して ...ni hań shite

counteract [kauntərækt'] vt (effect, tendency) 打消す uchíkesu

counter-espionage [kauntə:res'pi:ə-nɑ:ʒ] n 対抗的スパイ活動 taíkōteki supáikatsudõ

counterfeit [kaun'tə:rfit] n (forgery) 偽物 nisémono

♦vt (forge) 偽造する gizõ suru

♦adj (coin) 偽物の nisémono no

counterfoil [kaun'tə:rfoil] n (of check, money order) 控え hikáe

countermand [kauntə:rmænd'] vt (order) 取消す toríkesu

counterpart [kaun'tə:rpɑ:rt] n: **counterpart of** (person) ...に相当する人 ...ni sõtō suru hitõ; (thing) ...に相当するもの ...ni sõtō suru mono

counterproductive [kauntə:rprədʌk'-tiv] adj (measure, policy etc) 逆効果的な gyakúkōkateki na

countersign [kaun'tə:rsain] vt (document) ...に副署する ...ni fukúsho surù

countess [kaun'tis] n 伯爵夫人 hakúsha-kufùjin

countless [kaunt'lis] adj (innumerable) 無数の músū no

count on vt fus (expect) ...の積りでいる ...no tsumőri de irù; (depend on) ...を頼りにする ...wo táyðri ni suru

country [kʌn'tri:] n (state, nation) 国 kuní; (native land) 母国 bőkðku; (rural area) 田舎 ináka; (region) 地域 chíiki

country dancing (BRIT) n 英国郷土舞踏 eíkokukyōdðbuyõ

country house n 田舎の大邸宅 ináka no daíteitàku

countryman [kʌn'tri:mən] (pl countrymen) n (compatriot) 同国人 dőkokujìn; (country dweller) 田舎者 ináகamòno

countryside [kʌn'tri:said] n 田舎 ináka

county [kaun'ti:] n (POL, ADMIN) 郡 gún

coup [ku:] (pl coups) n (MIL, POL: also: **coup d'état**) クーデター kúdetà; (achievement) 大成功 daíseikõ

coupé [ku:pei'] n (AUT) クーペ kúpe

couple [kʌp'əl] n (also: **married couple**) 夫婦 fûfu; (cohabiting etc) カップル káppùru; (of things) 一対 ittsúi

a couple of (two people) 2人の futári no; (two things) 2つの futátsu no; (a few people) 数人の súnin no; (a few things) 幾つかの ikùtsuka no

coupon [ku:'pɑ:n] n (voucher) クーポン券 kúpoňken; (detachable form) クーポン kúpon

courage [kə:r'idʒ] n (bravery) 勇気 yúki

courageous [kərei'dʒəs] adj (person, attempt) 勇敢な yúkan na

courgette [kurʒet'] (BRIT) n ズッキーニ zúkkìni

courier [kə:r'i:ər] n (messenger) メッセンジャー méssènjā; (for tourists) 添乗員 teñjóin

course [kɔ:rs] n (SCOL) 課程 katéi; (process: of life, events, time etc) 過程 katéi; (of treatment) クール kûru; (direction: of argument, action) 方針 hőshin; (of ship) 針路 shíñro; (part of meal) 一品 ippín, コース kõsu; (for golf) コース kõsu *the course of a river* 川筋 kawásuji

of course (naturally) もちろん mochíron, 当然 tōzen; (certainly) いいとも íi to mo

court [kɔːrt] *n* (royal) 宮殿 kyúden; (LAW) 法廷 hōtei; (for tennis, badminton etc) コート kōto

♦*vt* (woman) 妻にしようとして…と交際 する tsumá ni shiyō to shité …to kōsai suru

to take someone to court (LAW) …を 相手取って訴訟を起す …wo aítedottè so-shō wo okósù

courteous [kɔːrˈtiːəs] *adj* (person, conduct) 丁寧な teínei na

courtesan [kɔːrˈtizən] *n* 宮廷しょう婦 kyūteishōfu

courtesy [kəːrˈtisiː] *n* (politeness) 礼儀正 しさ reígitadashìsa

(by) courtesy of (thanks to) …のお陰で …no okáge de

court-house [kɔːrtˈhaus] (*US*) *n* 裁判所 saíbansho

courtier [kɔːrˈtiːər] *n* 廷臣 teíshin

court-martial [kɔːrtˈmɑːrˈʃəl] (*pl* **courts-martial**) *vt* (MIL) 軍法会議 guńpōkaìgi

courtroom [kɔːrtˈruːm] *n* 法廷 hōtei

courtyard [kɔːrtˈjɑːrd] *n* (of castle, house) 中庭 nakániwa

cousin [kʌzˈin] *n* (relative) 親せき shínseki

first cousin いとこ itókò

second cousin はとこ hatókò, またいとこ mata-itoko

cove [kouv] *n* (bay) 入江 iríe

covenant [kʌvˈənənt] *n* (promise) 契約 keíyaku

cover [kʌvˈər] *vt* (hide: face, surface, ground): *to cover (with)* …で覆う …de ōù; (hide: feelings, mistake): *to cover (with)* …で隠す …de kakúsù; (shield: book, table etc): *to cover (with)* …に (…を) 掛ける …ni (…wo) kakérù; (with lid): *to cover (with)* …にふたをする …ni futá wo suru; (travel: distance) 行く ikú; (protect: *also* INSURANCE) カバーする kábā suru; (discuss: topic, subject: *also* PRESS) 取上げる toríagerù; (include) 含

む fukúmù

♦*n* (for furniture) 覆い ōi; (lid) ふた futá; (on bed) 上掛 uwágake; (of book, magazine) 表紙 hyōshi; (shelter: for hiding) 隠 れ場所 kakúrebasho; (: from rain) 雨宿 りの場所 amáyadòri no bashō; (INSURANCE) 保険 hokén; (of spy) 架空の身分 kakū no míbùn

to take cover (shelter: from rain) 雨宿 りをする amáyadòri wo suru; (: from gunfire etc) 隠れる kakúrerù

under cover (indoors) 屋根の下で〔に〕 yané no shitá de 〔ni〕

under cover of darkness やみに紛れ て yamí ni magíretè

under separate cover (COMM) 別便で betsúbin de

coverage [kʌvˈəːridʒ] *n* (TV, PRESS) 報 道 hōdō

cover charge *n* (in restaurant) サービ ス料 sābisuryō

covering [kʌvˈəːriŋ] *n* (layer) 覆い ōi; (of snow, dust etc) 覆う物 ōu monò

covering letter (*US also*: **cover letter**) *n* 添状 soéjō

cover note (*BRIT*) *n* (INSURANCE) 仮保険証 karíhokeñshò

covert [kouvˈəːrt] *adj* (glance, threat) 隠 れた kakúretà

cover up *vi*: *to cover up for someone* …をかばう …wo kabáù

cover-up [kʌvˈəːrʌp] *n* もみ消し momíkeshi

covet [kʌvˈit] *vt* (desire) 欲しがる hoshígarù

cow [kau] *n* (animal) 雌ウシ meúshi; (*infl*: woman) あま amã

♦*vt* (oppress): *to be cowed* おびえる obíerù

coward [kauˈəːrd] *n* おく病者 okúbyōmono

cowardice [kauˈəːrdis] *n* おく病 okúbyō

cowardly [kauˈəːrdliː] *adj* おく病な okúbyō na

cowboy [kauˈbɔi] *n* (in US) カウボーイ kaúbōi

cower [kauˈəːr] *vi* に縮する ishúku suru

coxswain [kɑːkˈsin] *n* (ROWING: abbr:

cox) コックス kókkùsu

coy [kɔi] *adj* (demure, shy) はにかんでみ
せる haníkañde misérù

coyote [kaiout'i:] *n* コヨーテ kóyòte

cozy [kou'zi:] (*BRIT* **cosy**) *adj* (room,
house) こじんまりした kojíñmarî shita;
(person) 心地よい kokóchi yoì

CPA [si:pi:ei'] (*US*) *abbr* = **certified
public accountant**

crab [kræb] *n* カニ kaní

crab apple *n* ヒメリンゴ himérìñgo

crack [kræk] *n* (noise: of gun) パン páñ;
(: of thunder) ばりばり bárìbari; (: of
twig) ぽっきり pokkíri; (: of whip) バン
bañ; (gap) 割れ目 waréme; (in bone, dish,
glass, wall) ひび hibí

♦*vt* (whip, twig) 鳴らす narásù; (bone,
dish, glass, wall) ひびを入れる hibí wo
irérù; (nut) 割る warú; (solve: problem)
解決する kaíketsu suru; (: code) 解く tókù; (joke) 飛ばす tobásu

♦*adj* (expert) 優秀な yūshù na

crack down on *vt fus* (crime, expenditure etc) 取り締る toríshimarù

cracker [kræk'əːr] *n* (biscuit, Christmas
cracker) クラッカー kurákkà

crackle [kræk'əl] *vi* (fire) ぱちぱちと音
を立てる páchìpachi to otó wo tatérù;
(twig) ぽきぽきと音を立てる pókìpoki to
otó wo tatérù

crack up *vi* (PSYCH) 頭がおかしくなる
atáma ga okáshìku nárù

cradle [krei'dəl] *n* (baby's) 揺りかご yurí-
kago

craft [kræft] *n* (skill) 芸術 geíjutsu;
(trade) 職業 shokúgyò; (boat: *pl inv*) 船
fúnè; (plane: *pl inv*) 飛行機 hikóki

craftsman [kræfts'mən] (*pl* **craftsmen**)
n (artisan) 職人 shokúnin

craftsmanship [kræfts'mənʃip] *n* (quality) 芸術 geíjutsu

crafty [kræf'ti:] *adj* (sneaky) 腹黒い haráguroì, こうかつな kókatsu na

crag [kræg] *n* 険しい岩山 kewáshiĩ iwá-
yama

cram [kræm] *vt* (fill): **to cram something with** ...を ...で一杯にする ...wo
...de ippái ni surù; (put): **to cram some-**

thing into ...を...に詰込む ...wo ...ni tsumékomù

♦*vi*: **to cram for exams** 一夜漬の試験
勉強をする ichíyazuke no shikénbenkyò
wo suru

cramp [kræmp] *n* (MED) けいれん keíren

cramped [kræmpt] *adj* (accommodation) 窮屈な kyúkutsu na

crampon [kræm'pɑːn] *n* (CLIMBING)
アイゼン áizen

cranberry [kræn'beːri:] *n* (berry) コケモ
モ kokémòmo, クランベリー kuránberī

crane [krein] *n* (machine) クレーン kúrèn;
(bird) ツル tsurú

crank [kræŋk] *n* (person) 変人 heñjiñ;
(handle) クランク kuráñku

crankshaft [kræŋk'ʃæft] *n* (AUT) クラ
ンクシャフト kuráñkushafùto

cranny [kræn'iː] *n see* **nook**

crash [kræʃ] *n* (noise) 大音響 daíonkyò ◇
物が落ちる、ぶつかるなどの大きな音を
指す monó ga ochírù, butsúkarù nádò
no ōkina otó wo sásù; (of car, train etc)
衝突 shótotsu; (of plane) 墜落 tsuíraku;
(COMM: of stock-market) 暴落 bóraku;
(COMM: of business etc) 倒産 tósan

♦*vt* (car etc) 衝突させる shótotsu saséru;
(plane) 墜落させる tsuíraku saséru

♦*vi* (car) 衝突する shótotsu suru; (plane)
墜落する tsuíraku suru; (COMM: market) 暴落する bóraku suru; (COMM:
firm) 倒産する tósan suru

crash course *n* 速成コース sokúseikòsu

crash helmet *n* ヘルメット herúmettò

crash landing *n* (AVIAT) 不時着陸 fujíchakùriku

crass [kræs] *adj* (behavior, comment,
person) 露骨な rokótsu na

crate [kreit] *n* (box) 箱 hakó; (for bottles) ケース kēsu

crater [krei'təːr] *n* (of volcano) 噴火口
fuñkakò; (on moon etc) クレーター kuré-
tā

bomb crater 爆弾孔 bakúdankò

cravat [krəvæt'] *n* アスコットタイ asú-
kottaì

crave [kreiv] *vt, vi*: **to crave for** ...を強
く欲しがる ...wo tsuyókù hoshígarù

crawl [krɔːl] *vi* (person) 四つんばいには
う yotsúnbai ni háù; (insect) はう háù;
(vehicle) のろのろと進む nórònoro ni susúmù
♦*n* (SWIMMING) クロール kúròru

crayfish [krei'fiʃ] *n inv* (freshwater) ザ
リガニ zaríganì; (saltwater) エビガニ e-
bígani

crayon [krei'ɑːn] *n* クレヨン kuréyòn

craze [kreiz] *n* (fashion) 大流行 dáiryūkō

crazy [krei'ziː] *adj* (insane) 正気でない
shōki de náì; (*inf*: keen): **crazy about**
someone/something ...が大好きである
...ga daísuki de arù

crazy paving (*BRIT*) *n* 不ぞろい舗装
fuzóroi hosō ◇不ぞろいの敷石からなる
舗装 fuzóroi no shikíìshi kara narù hosō

creak [kriːk] *vi* (floorboard, door etc) き
しむ kishímù

cream [kriːm] *n* (of milk) (生)クリーム
(namá)kúrìmu; (*also*: **artificial cream**)
人造クリーム jinzōkurìmu; (cosmetic) 化
粧クリーム keshōkurìmu; (élite) 名士た
ち meíshi tachì
♦*adj* (color) クリーム色の kúrìmuírò no

cream cake *n* クリームケーキ kurímu-
kèki

cream cheese *n* クリームチーズ kurí-
muchìzu

creamy [kriː'miː] *adj* (color) クリーム色
のkurímuirò no; (taste) 生クリームたっ
ぷりの namákurìmu táppùri no

crease [kriːs] *n* (fold) 折り目 oríme; (wrinkle) しわ shiwá; (in trousers) 折目 oríme
♦*vt* (wrinkle) しわくちゃにする shiwákucha ni suru
♦*vi* (wrinkle up) しわくちゃになる shi-
wakucha ni naru

create [kriːeit'] *vt* (cause to happen,
exist) 引き起こす hikíokosù; (produce,
design) 作る tsukúrù

creation [kriːei'ʃən] *n* (causing to happen, exist) 引き起こす事 hikíokosu kotó;
(production, design) 作る事 tsukúrù kotó; (REL) 天地創造 teńchisōzō

creative [kriːei'tiv] *adj* (artistic) 芸術的
な geíjutsuteki na; (inventive) 創造性の
ある sōzōsei no árù

creator [kriːei'tər] *n* (maker, inventor)
作る人 tsukúrù hitó

creature [kriː'tʃər] *n* (living animal) 動
物 dōbutsu; (person) 人 hitó

crèche [kreʃ] *n* 託児所 takújisho

credence [kriː'dəns] *n*: **to lend cre-**
dence to (prove) ...を信じさせる ...wo
shińji saséru
to give credence to (prove) ...を信じさ
せる ...wo shińji saséru; (believe) 信じる
shińjirù

credentials [kriden'ʃəlz] *npl* (refer-
ences) 資格 shikáku; (identity papers) 身
分証明証 mibúnshōmeishō

credibility [kredəbil'əti:] *n* (of person,
fact) 信頼性 shińraisei

credible [kred'əbəl] *adj* (believable) 信じ
られる shińjirarerù; (trustworthy) 信用
できる shiń-yō dekírù

credit [kred'it] *n* (COMM: loan) 信用 shiń-
yō; (recognition) 名誉 meíyo
♦*vt* (COMM) ...の入金にする ...no nyúkin
ni suru; (believe: *also*: **give credit to**) 信
じる shińjirù
to be in credit (person, bank account)
黒字になっている kuróji ni natté irù
to credit someone with (*fig*) ...に...の美
徳があると思う ...ni...no bitóku ga arù to
omóù

credit card *n* クレジットカード kuréjittokàdo

creditor [kred'itər] *n* (COMM) 債権者
saíkeñsha

credits [kred'its] *npl* (CINEMA) クレジ
ット kuréjitto

creed [kriːd] *n* (REL) 信条 shińjō

creek [kriːk] *n* (*US*: stream) 小川 ogáwa;
(*BRIT*: inlet) 入江 iríe

creep [kriːp] (*pt*, *pp* **crept**) *vi* (person,
animal) 忍び足で歩く shinóbiàshi de arú-
kù

creeper [kriː'pər] *n* (plant) つる tsurú

creepy [kriː'piː] *adj* (frightening: story,
experience) 薄気味悪い usúkimiwaruî

cremate [kriː'meit] *vt* (corpse) 火葬にす
る kasō ni surù

cremation [krimei'ʃən] *n* 火葬 kasō

crematoria [kriː'mətɔːr'iːə] *npl of* **cre-**

matorium

crematorium [kri:mətɔːr'i:əm] (*pl* **crematoria**) *n* 火葬場 kasōba

crêpe [kreip] *n* (fabric) クレープ kúrēpu; (rubber) クレープゴム kurḗpugomù ◇靴底に使う表面がしわ状のゴム kutsúzoko ni tsukáù hyṓmen ga shiwájō no gṓmù

crêpe bandage (*BRIT*) *n* 伸縮性包帯 shifshukuseihōtai

crept [krept] *pt, pp of* **creep**

crescent [kres'ənt] *n* (shape) 三日月形 mikázukigata; (street) ...通り ...dōri ◇特にカーブになっている通りの名前に使う tókù ni kâbu ni natté irú tòri no namáe ni tsukáù

cress [kres] *n* (BOT, CULIN) クレソン kurésoṅ

crest [krest] *n* (of hill) 頂上 chōjō; (of bird) とさか tosáka; (coat of arms) 紋章 mōṅ

crestfallen [krest'fɔːlən] *adj* しょんぼりした shofiborí shitá

Crete [krit] *n* クレタ kurétà

crevice [krev'is] *n* (gap, crack) 割れ目 waréme

crew [kru:] *n* (NAUT) 乗組員 noríkumìn; (AVIAT) 乗員 jōin; (TV, CINEMA) カメラ班 kaméràhan ◇3つの意味とも総称として使う mittsú no imí to mo sōshō toshité tsukáù

crew-cut [kru:'kʌt] *n* 角刈り kakúgari

crew-neck [kru:'nek] *n* (of jersey) 丸首 marúkubi

crib [krib] *n* (cot) ベビーベッド bebíbeddò
◆*vt* (*inf*: copy: during exam etc) カンニングする kańningu suru; (: from writings etc of others) 盗用する tóyō suru

crick [krik] *n*: **to have a crick in one's neck** 首が痛い kubí ga itáî

cricket [krik'it] *n* (game) クリケット kuríkettò; (insect) コオロギ kōrogi

crime [kraim] *n* (no pl: illegal activities) 犯罪 hańzai; (illegal action) 犯罪 (行為) hańzai(kôi); (*fig*) 罪 tsumî

criminal [krim'ənəl] *n* 犯罪者 hańzaîsha
◆*adj* (illegal) 違法の ihō no; (morally wrong) 罪悪の zaîaku no

crimson [krim'zən] *adj* 紅色の beníiro no

cringe [krindʒ] *vi* (in fear, embarrassment) 縮こまる chijîkomarù

crinkle [kriŋ'kəl] *vt* (crease, fold) しわくちゃにする shiwákucha ni suru

cripple [krip'əl] *n* (MED) 身障者 shifishṓsha
◆*vt* (person) 不具にする fúgu ni suru

crises [krai'si:z] *npl of* **crisis**

crisis [krai'sis] (*pl* **crises**) *n* 危機 kikî

crisp [krisp] *adj* (vegetables) ぱりぱりした párîpari shitá; (bacon) かりかりした kárîkari shitá; (weather) からっとした karáttò shitá; (manner, tone, reply) 無愛想な buáîsō na

crisps [krisps] (*BRIT*) *npl* ポテトチップ potétochippù

criss-cross [kris'krɔːs] *adj* (pattern, design) 十字模様の jūjimoyō no

criteria [kraiti:'ri:ə] *npl of* **criterion**

criterion [kraiti:r'i:ən] (*pl* **criteria**) *n* (standard) 規準 kijûn

critic [krit'ik] *n* (of system, policy etc) 反対者 hańtaîsha; (reviewer) 評論家 hyṓronka

critical [krit'ikəl] *adj* (time, situation) 重大な jūdai na; (opinion, analysis) 批評的な hihyṓteki na; (person: fault-finding) 粗捜し好きな arásagashizùki na; (illness) 危険な kikén na

critically [krit'ikli:] *adv* (speak, look etc) 批判的に hihánteki ni
critically ill 重症で jōshō de

criticism [krit'isizəm] *n* (disapproval, complaint) 非難 hínàn; (of book, play etc) 批評 hihyṓ

criticize [krit'əsaiz] *vt* (find fault with) 非難する hínàn suru

croak [krouk] *vi* (frog) げろげろ鳴く gérògero nakú; (bird etc) かーかー鳴く kâkā nakú; (person) がらがら声で言う garágaragaroe de iu

crochet [krouʃei'] *n* かぎ針編み kagíbariami

crockery [krɑk'əːri:] *n* (dishes) 皿類 saráruî

crocodile [krɑk'ədail] *n* ワニ wánî

crocus [krou'kəs] n クロッカス kurôk-kāsu

croft [krɔːft] (*BRIT*) n (small farm) 小農場 shônōjō

crony [krou'niː] (*inf: pej*) n 仲間 nakáma

crook [kruk] n (criminal) 悪党 akútō; (*also*: **shepherd's crook**) 羊飼のつえ hitsújikai no tsúe ◇片端の曲った物を指す katáhashi no magátta monó wo sásù

crooked [kruk'id] adj (bent, twisted) 曲った magátta; (dishonest) 不正の fuséi no

crop [krɑːp] n (of fruit, cereals, vegetables) 作物 sakúmòtsu; (harvest) 収穫 shûkaku; (riding crop) むち múchi ◇乗馬用の物を指す jôbayō no monó wo sásù
♦vt (hair) 刈込む karíkomù

crop up vi (problem, topic) 持ち上る mochíagarù

croquet [kroukei'] n クロッケー kurôkkē ◇複雑なゲートボールに似た球技 fukúzatsu na gétobòru ni nitá kyûgi

croquette [krouket'] n (CULIN) コロッケ kóròkke

cross [krɔːs] n (shape) 十字 jûji; (REL) 十字架 jûjika; (mark) ばつ(印) bátsù(jírùshi); (hybrid) 合の子 aínoko
♦vt (street, room etc) 横断する ôdan suru; (arms, legs) 組む kúmù; (animal, plant) 交雑する kôzatsu suru
♦vt (angry) 不機嫌な fukígen na
to cross a check 線引小切手にする señbiki kogítte ni suru

crossbar [krɔːs'bɑːr] n (SPORT) ゴールの横棒 gôru no yokóbō

cross country (*race*) n クロスカントリーレース kurósukantorīrèsu

cross-examine [krɔːs'igzæm'in] vt (LAW) 反対尋問する hañtaijiñmon suru

cross-eyed [krɔːs'aid] adj 寄り目の yoríme no

crossfire [krɔːs'faiəːr] n 十字射撃 jûjishagèki

crossing [krɔːs'iŋ] n (sea passage) 船旅 funátabi; (*also*: **pedestrian crossing**) 横断歩道 ôdanhodō

crossing guard (*US*) n 交通指導員 kôtsūshidòin ◇交通事故を防ぐために横断歩道に立って学童などの横断を助ける係員 kôtsūshidōin wo fuségu tamé ni ôdanhodō ni tattě gakúdō nádò no ôdan wo tasúkerù kakáriìn

cross out vt (delete) 線を引いて消す señ wo híite kesú

cross over vi (move across) 横断する ôdan suru

cross-purposes [krɔːs'pəːr'pəsiz] npl: *to be at cross-purposes* 話が食違っている hanáshi ga kuíchigatte irù

cross-reference [krɔːs'ref'əːrəns] n 相互参照 sôgosañshò

crossroads [krɔːs'roudz] n 交差点 kôsatèn

cross section n (of an object) 断面 dañmeñ; (sketch) 断面図 dañmeñzu
cross section of the population 国民を代表する人々 kokumin wo daíhyō suru hítòbìto

crosswalk [krɔːs'wɔːk] (*US*) n 横断歩道 ôdanhodō

crosswind [krɔːs'wind] n 横風 yokókaze

crossword [krɔːs'wəːrd] n クロスワードパズル kurósuwādopazùru

crotch [krɑːtʃ] n (ANAT, of garment) また matá

crotchet [krɑːtʃ'it] n (MUS) 四分音符 shibúoñpu

crotchety [krɑːtʃ'əti:] adj (person) 気難しい kimúzukashiì

crouch [krautʃ] vi (person, animal) うずくまる uzúkumarù

croupier [kruː'pi:əːr] n (in casino) とばく台の元締 tobákudai no motójime, ディーラー dīrā

crow [krou] n (bird) カラス káràsu; (of cock) 鳴き声 nakígoè
♦vi (cock) 鳴く nakú

crowbar [krou'bɑːr] n バール bằru

crowd [kraud] n: *crowd of people* 群衆 guñshū
♦vt (fill: room, stadium etc) ...にぎっしり入る ...ni gisshírì haírù
♦vi (gather): *to crowd round* ...の回りに群がる ...no mawári ni murágarù; (cram): *to crowd in* ...の中へ詰めかける ...no nákà e tsumékakerù

a crowd of fans 大勢のファン ōzei nò fáñ

crowded [krau'did] *adj* (full) 込み入った komſitta; (densely populated) 人口密度の高い jiñkōmitsùdo no takái

crown [kraun] *n* (gen) 冠 kañmuri; (of monarch) 王冠 ōkan; (monarchy): *the Crown* 国王 kokúō; (of head, hill) てっぺん tēppéñ; (of tooth) 歯冠 shikáñ
♦*vt* (monarch) 王位に就かせる ōi ni tsukáserù; (fig: career, evening) ...に有終の美を飾る ...ni yūshū no bí wo kazárù

crown jewels *npl* 王位の象徴 ōi no shôchō ◇王冠、しゃくなど国家的儀式で王または女王が王位の象徴として用いる物を指す ōkan, shákù nádò kokkáteki gishíki de ō matá wa jóō ga ōi no shôchō toshité mochíirù monó wo sásù

crown prince *n* 皇太子 kōtaìshi

crow's feet *npl* 目じりの小じわ mējíri no kojíwa, カラスの足跡 káràsu no ashíatò

crucial [kru:'ʃəl] *adj* (decision, vote) 重大な jūdai na

crucifix [kru:'səfiks] *n* (REL) 十字架像 jūjikazō

crucifixion [kru:'səfik'ʃən] *n* (REL) キリストのはりつけ kirísuto no harítsuke

crude [kru:d] *adj* (materials) 原...géñ...; (fig: basic) 原始的な geñshiteki na; (: vulgar) 露骨な rokótsu na

crude (oil) *n* 原油 geñ-yu

cruel [kru:'əl] *adj* (person, action) 残酷な zañkoku na; (situation) 悲惨な hisán na

cruelty [kru:'əlti:] *n* (of person, action) 残酷さ zañkokusa; (of situation) 悲惨さ hisánsa

cruise [kru:z] *n* (on ship) 船旅 funátabi
♦*vi* (ship) 巡航する juñkō suru; (car) 楽に走行する rákù ni sōkō suru

cruiser [kru:'zə:r] *n* (motorboat) 大型モーターボート ōgata mótābòto, クルーザー kurūzà; (warship) 巡洋艦 juñ-yōkan

crumb [krʌm] *n* (of bread, cake) くず kúzù

crumble [krʌm'bəl] *vt* (bread, biscuit etc) 崩す kuzúsù
♦*vi* 崩れる kuzúrerù

crumbly [krʌm'bli:] *adj* (bread, biscuits etc) 崩れやすい kuzúreyasùi, ぼろぼろした pórðporo shitá

crumpet [krʌm'pit] *n* クランペット kuránpettò ◇マフィンの一種 mafíñ no isshù

crumple [krʌm'pəl] *vt* (paper, clothes) しわくちゃにする shiwákucha ni suru

crunch [krʌntʃ] *vt* (food etc) かみ砕く kamíkudakù; (underfoot) 踏み砕く fumíkudakù
♦*n* (fig: moment of truth) いざという時 izá no iú tokí

crunchy [krʌn'tʃi:] *adj* (food) ぱりぱりした parípari shitá

crusade [kru:seid'] *n* (campaign) 運動uñdō

crush [krʌʃ] *n* (crowd) 人込み hitógomi; (love): *to have a crush on someone* ...にのぼせる ...ni noboseru; (drink): *lemon crush* レモンスカッシュ remónsukasshù
♦*vt* (press, squeeze) 押しつぶす oshítsubusù; (crumple: paper, clothes) しわくちゃにする shiwákucha ni suru; (defeat: army, opposition) 圧倒する attô suru; (devastate: hopes) 台無しにする daínashi ni suru; (: person) 落胆させる rakútan saséru

crust [krʌst] *n* (of bread, pastry) 皮 kawá; (of snow, ice) アイスバーン aísubàn; (of the earth) 地殻 chikáku

crutch [krʌtʃ] *n* (support, stick) 松葉づえ matsúbazùe

crux [krʌks] *n* (of problem, matter) 核心 kakúshin

cry [krai] *vi* (weep) 泣く nakú; (shout: *also*: **cry out**) 叫ぶ sakébù
♦*n* (shriek) 悲鳴 himéi; (shout) 叫び声 sakébigoè; (of bird, animal) 鳴き声 nakígoè

cry off *vi* (change one's mind, cancel) 手を引く te wo hikú

crypt [kript] *n* 地下室 chikáshitsu ◇特に納骨堂などに使われる教会の地下室を指す tókù ni nôkotsudō nadò ni tsukáwarerù kyōkai no chikáshitsu wo sásù

cryptic [krip'tik] *adj* (remark, clue) なぞめいた nazómeità

crystal [kris'təl] n (mineral) 結晶 kesshō; (in jewelry) 水晶 suíshō; (glass) クリスタル kurísùtaru

crystal-clear [kris'təlkli'ə:r] adj (transparent) よく澄んだ yókù súnda; (fig: easy to understand) 明白な meíhaku na

crystallize [kris'təlaiz] vt (opinion, thoughts) まとめる matómerù
♦vi (sugar etc) 結晶する kesshō suru

cub [kʌb] n (of lion, wolf etc) ...の子 ...no ko; (also: **cub scout**) カブスカウト kábùsukaùto

Cuba [kju:'bə] n キューバ kyūba

Cuban [kju:'bən] adj キューバの kyūba no
♦n キューバ人 kyūbajìn

cubbyhole [kʌb'i:houl] n 小さな納戸 chiísa na naǹdo

cube [kju:b] n (shape) 立方体 rippótai; (MATH: of number) ...の3乗 ...no saǹjō
♦vt (MATH) 三乗する saǹjō suru

cube root n (MATH) 立方根 ríppòkon

cubic [kju:'bik] adj (volume) 立方の rippó no

cubic capacity n 体積 taíseki

cubicle [kju:'bikəl] n (at pool) 更衣室 kōishìtsu ◇小さい個室について言う chiísaí koshìtsu ni tsuíte iú; (in hospital) カーテンで仕切った1病床分のスペース kâten de shikítta ichíbyōshōbùn no supḕsu

cuckoo [ku'ku:] n カッコウ kákkō

cuckoo clock n はと時計 hatódokèi

cucumber [kju:'kʌmbə:r] n キューリ kyūri

cuddle [kʌd'əl] vt (baby, person) 抱締める dakíshimerù
♦vi (lovers) 抱合う dakíaù

cue [kju:] n (snooker cue) キュー kyū; (THEATER etc) 合図 aízu, キュー kyū

cuff [kʌf] n (of sleeve) カフス káfùsu; (US: of trousers) 折返し oríkaeshi; (blow) 平手打ち hiráteuchi
off the cuff (impromptu) 即座に〔の〕sókùza ni [no]

cufflinks [kʌf'liŋks] npl カフスボタン kafúsubotàn

cuisine [kwizi:n'] n (of country, region) 料理 ryòri

cul-de-sac [kʌl'dəsæk'] n (road) 行き止まり yukídomari

culinary [kju:'ləne:ri:] adj 料理の ryōri no

cull [kʌl] vt (story, idea) えり抜く erínukù
♦n (of animals) 間引き mabíki

culminate [kʌl'məneit] vi: **to culminate in** (gen) 遂に...となる tsuí ni ...to narù; (unpleasant outcome) 挙句の果てに...となってしまう agéku no hatè ni ...to nattè shimáù

culmination [kʌlmənei'ʃən] n (of career, process etc) 頂点 chōten

culottes [kju:lots'] npl キュロット kyúròtto

culpable [kʌl'pəbəl] adj (blameworthy) とがむべき togámùbeki

culprit [kʌl'prit] n (of crime) 犯人 haǹnin

cult [kʌlt] n (REL: worship) 崇拝 sūhai; (: sect, group) 宗派 shūha; (fashion) 流行 ryūkō

cultivate [kʌl'təveit] vt (land) 耕す tagáyasù; (crop) 栽培する saíbai suru; (person) 近付きになろうとする chikázuki ni nárð to suru

cultivation [kʌltəvei'ʃən] n (AGR) 耕作 kōsaku

cultural [kʌl'tʃə:rəl] adj (traditions etc) 文化文明の buńkabuńmei no; (activities etc) 芸術の geíjutsu no

culture [kʌl'tʃə:r] n (of a country, civilization) 文明 buńmei, 文化 buńka; (the arts) 芸術 geíjutsu; (BIO) 培養 baíyō

cultured [kʌl'tʃə:rd] adj (individual) 教養のある kyóyō no arù

cumbersome [kʌm'bə:rsəm] adj (object) 扱いにくい atsúkainikui ◇かさ張る物、重い物、大きくて不格好な物などについて言う kasábarù monó, omói monó, ókikùte bukákkō na monó nadò ni tsuíte iú; (process) 面倒な meńdō na

cumulative [kju:m'jələtiv] adj (effect, result) 累積する ruíseki suru

cunning [kʌn'iŋ] n (craftiness) こうかつさ kōkatsusa
♦adj (crafty) こうかつな kōkatsu na

cup [kʌp] n (for drinking) カップ káppù;

(as prize) 賞杯 shṓhai, カップ káppù; (of bra) カップ káppù

cupboard [kʌb'ə:rd] n 戸棚 todána

Cupid [kju:'pid] n キューピッド kyū́piddo

cup-tie [kʌp'tai] (BRIT) n (SOCCER) トーナメント tṓnamento

curate [kju:'rit] n 助任牧師 jonínbokùshi

curator [kjurei'tə:r] n (of museum, gallery) キューレーター kyū́rḕtā ◇学芸員の管理職に相当する人を指す gakúgeìin no kańrishòku ni sṓtō suru hitó wo sásù

curb [kə:rb] vt (powers, expenditure) 制限する seígen suru; (person) 抑える osáerù

◆n (restraint) 抑制 yokúsei; (US: kerb) 縁石 fuchíishi

curdle [kə:r'dəl] vi (milk) 凝結する gyṓketsu suru

cure [kju:r] vt (illness, patient) 治す naósù; (CULIN) 保存食にする hozónshoku ni suru

◆n (MED) 治療法 chiryṓhō; (solution) 解決 kaíketsu

curfew [kə:r'fju:] n (MIL, POL) 夜間外出禁止令 yakán gaíshutsu kińshirei

curio [kju:'ri:ou] n 骨とう品 kottṓhin

curiosity [kju:ri:ɑ:s'əti:] n (of person) 好奇心 kṓkishìn; (object) 珍しい物 mezúrashiì monó

curious [kju:'ri:əs] adj (person: interested) 好奇心がある kṓkishìn ga arù; (: nosy) せん索好きな señsakuzùki na; (thing: strange, unusual) 変った kawátta

curl [kə:rl] n (of hair) カール kắru

◆vt (hair) カールする kắru suru

◆vi (hair) カールになっている kắru ni natté irù

curler [kə:r'lə:r] n (for hair) カーラー kā́rā

curl up vi (person, animal) 縮こまる chijíkomarù

curly [kə:r'li:] adj 巻毛の makíge no

currant [kə:r'ənt] n (dried fruit) レーズン rēzun ◇小型の種無しブドウから作った物を指す kogáta no tanénashibudō kara tsukúttá monó wo sásù; (bush, fruit: blackcurrant, redcurrant) スグリ súgùri

currency [kə:r'ənsi:] n (system) 通貨 tsū́ka; (money) 貨幣 káhèi

to gain currency (fig) 通用する様になる tsúyō suru yṓ ni nárù

current [kə:r'ənt] n (of air, water) 流れ nagáre; (ELEC) 電流 dénryū

◆adj (present) 現在の geńzai no; (accepted) 通用している tsúyō shité irù

current account (BRIT) n 当座預金 tṓzayokìn

current affairs npl 時事 jiji

currently [kə:r'əntli:] adv 現在は geńzai wa

curricula [kərik'jələ] npl of **curriculum**

curriculum [kərik'jələm] (pl **curriculums** or **curricula**) n (SCOL) 指導要領 shidṓyōryō

curriculum vitae [-vi:'tai] n 履歴書 rirékisho

curry [kə:r'i:] n (dish) カレー karḗ

◆vt: *to curry favor with* ...にへつらう ...ni hetsurau

curry powder n カレー粉 karḗko

curse [kə:rs] vi (swear) 悪態をつく akútai wo tsukù

◆vt (swear at) ののしる nonóshirù; (bemoan) のろう norou

◆n (spell) 呪い norói; (swearword) 悪態 akútai; (problem, scourge) 災の元 wazáwai no motó

cursor [kə:r'sə:r] n (COMPUT) カーソル kā́soru

cursory [kə:r'sə:ri:] adj (glance, examination) 何気ない nanígenài

curt [kə:rt] adj (reply, tone) 無愛想な buáisō na

curtail [kə:rteil'] vt (freedom, rights) 制限する seígen suru; (visit etc) 短くする mijíkakù suru; (expenses etc) 減らす herásu

curtain [kə:r'tən] n (at window) カーテン kā́ten; (THEATER) 幕 makú

curts(e)y [kə:rt'si:] vi (woman, girl) ひざを曲げて御辞儀をする hizá wo magéte ojígi wo suru

curve [kə:rv] n (bend: in line etc) 曲線 kyokúsen; (: in road) カーブ kā́bu

cushion [kuʃʼən] n (on sofa, chair) クッション kusshòn, 座布団 zabútòn; (also: **air cushion**) エアクッション eákusshòn ◇ホバークラフトなどを支える空気の事 hobâkurafùto nádò wo sasáeru kúki no kotò

♦vt (collision, fall) …の衝撃を和らげる …no shốgeki wo yawáragerù; (shock, effect) 和らげる yawáragerù

custard [kʌsʼtəːrd] n カスタード kasútàdo

custodian [kʌstouʼdiːən] n (of building, collection) 管理人 kańrinìn

custody [kʌsʼtədiː] n (LAW: of child) 親権 shińken

to take into custody (suspect) 逮捕する taího suru

custom [kʌsʼtəm] n (tradition) 伝統 deńtō; (convention) 慣習 kańshū; (habit) 習慣 shūkan; (COMM) ひいき hiíki

customary [kʌsʼtəmeːriː] adj (behavior, method, time) いつもの itsùmo no, 相変らずの aíkawarazu no

customer [kʌsʼtəmər] n (of shop, business etc) 客 kyakú

customized [kʌsʼtəmaizd] adj (car etc) 改造した kaízō shitá

custom-made [kʌsʼtəmmeidʼ] adj (shirt, car etc) あつらえの atsúraè no, オーダーメードの ốdāmèdo no

customs [kʌsʼtəmz] npl (at border, airport etc) 税関 zeíkan

customs duty n 関税 kańzei

customs officer n 税関吏 zeíkanri

cut [kʌt] (pt, pp **cut**) vt (bread, meat, hand etc) 切る kírù; (shorten: grass, hair) 刈る karú; (: text, program) 短くする mijíkakù suru; (reduce: prices, spending, supply) 減らす herásù

♦vi (knife, scissors) 切れる kirérù

♦n (in skin) 切り傷 kiríkìzu; (in salary) 減給 geńkyū; (in spending etc) 削減 sakúgen; (of meat) ブロック burókkù; (of garment) カット káttò

to cut a tooth 歯が生える há ga haérù

cutback [kʌtʼbæk] n 削減 sakúgen

cut down vt (tree) 切り倒す kirítaosù;

(consumption) 減らす herásu

cute [kjuːt] adj (US: pretty) かわいい kawáìi; (sweet) 陳腐なる chíńpu na

cuticle [kjuːʼtikəl] n (of nail) 甘皮 amákawa

cutlery [kʌtʼləːriː] n ナイフとフォークとスプーン naîfu to fôku to súpùn ◇総称 sốshō

cutlet [kʌtʼlit] n (piece of meat) カツ(レツ) katsú(retsu); (vegetable cutlet, nut cutlet) コロッケ kórokke

cut off vt (limb) 切断する setsúdan suru; (piece) 切る kírù, 切り分ける kiríwakerù; (person, village) 孤立させる korítsu saséru; (supply) 遮断する shadán suru; (TEL) 切る kírù

cut out vt (shape, article from newspaper) 切抜く kirínukù; (stop: an activity etc) やめる yaméru; (remove) 切除する setsùjo suru

cutout [kʌtʼaut] n (switch) 非常遮断装置 hijōshadansōchi, 安全器 añzeñki; (shape) 切抜き kirínuki

cut-rate [kʌtʼreit] (BRIT **cut-price**) adj 安売りの yasúuri no

cutthroat [kʌtʼθrout] n (murderer) 人殺し hitógoroshi

♦adj (business, competition) 殺人的な satsújinteki na

cutting [kʌtʼiŋ] adj (remark) 辛らつな shifratsu na

♦n (from newspaper) 切抜き kirínuki; (from plant) 穂木 hogí, さし穂 sashího

cut up vt (paper, meat) 刻む kizámu

CV [siːviːʼ] n abbr = **curriculum vitae**

cwt abbr = **hundredweight(s)**

cyanide [saiʼənaid] n 青酸化物 seísankabùtsu

cyclamen [sikʼləmən] n シクラメン shikúramèn

cycle [saiʼkəl] n (bicycle) 自転車 jitéñsha; (series: of events, seasons etc) 周期 shūki; (: TECH) サイクル saîkuru; (: of songs etc) 一連 ichíren

♦vi (on bicycle) 自転車で行く jitéñsha de ikú

cycling [saikʼliŋ] n サイクリング saîkuringu

cyclist [saik'list] n サイクリスト saíkurisuto

cyclone [saik'loun] n (storm) サイクロン saíkuron

cygnet [sig'nit] n (young) 若いハクチョウ wakáî hakúchō

cylinder [sil'ində:r] n (shape) 円柱 eñchū; (of gas) ボンベ bôñbe; (in engine, machine etc) 気筒 kitô, シリンダー shírîñdā

cylinder-head gasket [sil'ində:rhed-] n (AUT) シリンダーヘッドのパッキング shirîñdāheddô no pakkîñgu

cymbals [sim'bəlz] npl (MUS) シンバル shîñbaru

cynic [sin'ik] n 皮肉屋 hiníkuya, シニック shînîkku

cynical [sin'ikəl] adj (attitude, view) 皮肉な hiníku na, シニカルな shínikaru na

cynicism [sin'əsizəm] n シニカルな態度 shínîkaru na taído

cypress [sai'pris] n (tree) イトスギ itósùgi

Cypriot [sip'ri:ət] adj キプロスの kípùrosu no
♦n キプロス人 kipúrosujin

Cyprus [sai'prəs] n キプロス kípùrosu

cyst [sist] n (MED) のうしゅ nôshu

cystitis [sistai'tis] n (MED) ぼうこう炎 bôkōen

czar [za:r] n = **tsar**

Czech [tʃek] adj チェコスロバキアの chékòsurôbakìa no
♦n (person) チェコスロバキア人 chékòsurôbakìajìn; (language) チェコスロバキア語 chékòsurôbakiago

Czechoslovak [tʃekəslou'væk] adj, n = **Czechoslovakian**

Czechoslovakia [tʃekəsləva:ki'ə] n チェコスロバキア chékòsurôbakìa

Czechoslovakian [tʃekəsləva:ki:ən] adj チェコスロバキアの chékòsurôbakìa no
♦n (person) チェコスロバキア人 chékòsurôbakìajìn

D

D [di:] n (MUS: note) ニ音 nîòn; (: key) ニ調 níchò

dab [dæb] vt (eyes, wound) 軽くふく karúku fukú; (paint, cream) 軽く塗る karúku nurú

dabble [dæb'əl] vi: to dabble in (politics, antiques etc) 趣味でやる shúmì de yarú

dad [dæd] (inf) n 父ちゃん tôchàn

daddy [dæd'i:] (inf) n = **dad**

daffodil [dæf'ədil] n ラッパ水仙 suísen

daft [dæft] adj (silly) ばかな bákà ná

dagger [dæg'ə:r] n 短刀 tántō

daily [dei'li:] adj (dose, wages, routine etc) 毎日の maínichi no
♦n (also: daily paper) 日刊新聞 nikkanshínbun
♦adv (pay, see) 毎日 maínichi

dainty [dein'ti:] adj (petite) 繊細な sénsai na

dairy [de:r'i:] n (BRIT: shop) 牛乳店 gyúnyūten; (on farm) 牛乳 小屋 gyúnyūgoya ◇酪農場で牛乳を置いたり加工したりする小屋 rakúnōjō dè gyúnyū wò oítarí kakô shitarî suru koyá

dairy farm n 酪農場 rakúnōjō

dairy products npl 乳製品 nyúseihin

dairy store (US) n 牛乳店 gyúnyūten

dais [dei'is] n 演壇 éndan

daisy [dei'zi:] n デイジー deíjī

daisy wheel n (on printer) デイジーホイール deíjìhoírù

dale [deil] n (valley) 谷 taní

dam [dæm] n (on river) ダム dámù
♦vt (river, stream) ...にダムを造る ...ni dámù wo tsukúrù

damage [dæm'idʒ] n (harm: also fig) 害 gaì; (dents etc) 損傷 soñshō
♦vt (harm: reputation etc) 傷付ける kizutsukérù; (spoil, break: toy, machine etc) 壊す kowásù

damages [dæm'idʒiz] npl (LAW) 損害賠償 sóngaibaîshō

damn [dæm] vt (curse at) ...に悪態を浴びせる ...ni akútai wo àbíseru; (condemn) 非難する hínàn suru
♦n (inf): I don't give a damn おれの知った事じゃない oré no shìttá koto ja nâî

♦adj (inf: also: **damned**) くそったれの kusóttare no, 畜生の chikúshō no
damn (it)! 畜生 chikúshō

damning [dæm'iŋ] adj (evidence) 動かぬ ugókanù

damp [dæmp] adj (building, wall) 湿っぽい shiméppoì; (cloth) 湿った shimétta
♦n (in air, in walls) 湿り気 shimérike
♦vt (also: **dampen**: cloth, rag) 湿らす shimérasu; (: enthusiasm etc) ...に水を差す ...ni mizú wo sasù

damson [dæm'zən] n (fruit) ダムソンス モモ damúsonsumòmo

dance [dæns] n (movements, MUS, dancing) 踊り odóri, ダンス dànsu; (social event) 舞踏会 butṓkai, ダンスパーティ dánsupàti
♦vi (person) 踊る odóru

dance hall n ダンスホール dánsuhòru

dancer [dæn'sə:r] n (for pleasure) 踊る人 odóru hito; (professional) ダンサー dànsā

dancing [dæn'siŋ] n (skill, performance) 踊り odóri, ダンス dànsu

dandelion [dæn'dəlaiən] n タンポポ tànpopo

dandruff [dæn'drəf] n ふけ fukē

Dane [dein] n デンマーク人 dénmākujìn

danger [dein'dʒə:r] n (hazard, risk) 危険 kikén; (possibility): **there is a danger of ...** ...の危険がある ...no kikén ga arù
「**danger!**」 (on sign) 危険 kikén
in danger 危険にさらされて kikén ni sàrásareté
to be in danger of (risk, be close to) ...される危険がある ...saréru kikén ga arù

dangerous [dein'dʒə:rəs] adj 危険な kikén na

dangle [dæŋ'gəl] vt (keys, toy) ぶら下げる burásageru; (arms, legs) ぶらぶらさせる buràbura saséru
♦vi (earrings, keys) ぶら下がる burásagaru

Danish [dei'niʃ] adj デンマークの dénmāku no; (LING) デンマーク語の dénmāku-go no
♦n (LING) デンマーク語 dénmākugo

dapper [dæp'ə:r] adj (man, appearance) きびきびした kíbìkibì shitá

dare [de:r] vt: **to dare someone to do** 出来るものならしてみろと...にけし掛ける dekírù monó nàrá shité mirò to ...ni keshíkakerù
♦vi: to dare (to) do something 敢えて ...する áète ...surú
I dare say (I suppose) 多分 tábùn

daredevil [de:r'devəl] n 無謀な人 mubṓ na hito

daring [de:r'iŋ] adj (escape, person, dress, film, raid, speech) 大胆な daítàn na
♦n 大胆さ daítànsa

dark [dɑːrk] adj (room, night) 暗い kurái; (hair) 黒っぽい kuróppoì; (complexion) 浅黒い aságuroì; (color: blue, green etc) 濃い kôì
♦n: in the dark やみの中で〔に〕yamí no nakà de〔ni〕
to be in the dark about (fig) ...について何も知らない ...ni tsúite naní mo shírá-nai
after dark 暗くなってから kuráku nattè kará

darken [dɑːr'kən] vt (color) 濃くする kôkù suru
♦vi (sky, room) 暗くなる kuráku narù

dark glasses npl サングラス sánguràsu

darkness [dɑːrk'nis] n (of room, night) 暗やみ kuráyami

darkroom [dɑːrk'ruːm] n (PHOT) 暗室 ánshitsu

darling [dɑːr'liŋ] adj (child, spouse) 愛する aí surù
♦n (dear) あなた anátà; (favorite) ひいきの人 híiki no hitò

darn [dɑːrn] vt (sock, jersey) 繕う tsukúroù

dart [dɑːrt] n (in game) 投げ矢 nagéya, ダート dàto; (in sewing) ダーツ dātsu
♦vi 素早く走る subáyakù hashírù
to dart away/along 素早く走っていく subáyakù hashíttè ikú

dartboard [dɑːrt'bɔːrd] n ダーツの的 dàtsu no matô

darts [dɑːrts] n (game) ダーツ dàtsu

dash [dæʃ] n (small quantity) 少々 shô-shō; (sign) ダッシュ dásshù
♦vt (throw) 投付ける nagétsukerù; (hopes) くじく kujíkù
♦vi 素早く行く subáyakù ikú

dash away vi 走って行く hashíttè ikú

dashboard [dæʃ'bɔːrd] n (AUT) ダッシュボード dasshúbōdò

dashing [dæʃ'iŋ] adj さっそうとした sàssô to shita

dash off vi = dash away

data [dei'tə] npl (ADMIN, COMPUT) 情報 jôhō, データ dèta

database [dei'təbeis] n データベース dêtabèsu

data processing n 情報処理 jôhōshorì

date [deit] n (day) 日にち hiníchi; (with boy/girlfriend) デート dèto; (fruit) ナツメヤシの実 natsúmeyashî no mí
♦vt (event) ...の年代を決める ...no néndai wo kìmérù; (letter) ...に日付を書く ...ni hizúke wo kakù; (person) ...とデートをする ...to dèto wo suru
date of birth 生年月日 seínengàppi
to date (until now) 今まで imá madè

dated [dei'tid] adj (expression, style) 時代遅れの jidáiokùre no

daub [dɔːb] vt (mud, paint) 塗付ける nurítsukerù

daughter [dɔː'təːr] n 娘 musúme

daughter-in-law [dɔː'təːrinlɔː] (pl **daughters-in-law**) n 嫁 yomé

daunting [dɔːn'tiŋ] adj (task, prospect) しりごみさせる様な shirígomi saséru yô na, ひるませる様な hirúmaserù yô na

dawdle [dɔːd'əl] vi (go slow) ぐずぐずする gúzùguzu suru

dawn [dɔːn] n (of day) 夜明け yoáke; (of period, situation) 始まり hajímari
♦vi (day) 夜が明ける yó gà akérù; (fig): **it dawned on him that ...** 彼は...だと気が付いた kárè wa ...da tò ki gá tsuìta

day [dei] n (period) 日 hi, 1日 ichínichi; (daylight) 昼間 hirúma; (heyday) 全盛期 zenséîki
the day before 前の日 maé no hi, 前日 zénjitsu
the day after 翌日 yokújitsu

the day after tomorrow 明後日 asáttè
the day before yesterday 一昨日 otótoi
the following day 次の日 tsugí nò hi, 翌日 yokújitsu
by day 昼間に hirúma nì

daybreak [dei'breik] n 明け方 akégata, 夜明け yoáke

daydream [dei'driːm] vi 空想にふける kūsō ni fukérù

daylight [dei'lait] n (sunlight) 日光 níkkō; (daytime) 昼間 hirúma, 日中 nítchū

day return (BRIT) n (ticket) 往復券 ófukukèn

daytime [dei'taim] n 昼間 hirúma

day-to-day [deitu:dei'] adj (life, organization) 日常の nichíjō no

daze [deiz] vt (stun) ぼう然とさせる bôzen to sàséru
♦n: **in a daze** (confused, upset) ぼう然として bôzen to shite

dazzle [dæz'əl] vt (bewitch) 感嘆させる kántan sàséru; (blind) ...の目をくらます ...no mê wò kurámasu

DC [di:si:'] abbr (= direct current) 直流 chokúryū

D-day [di:'dei] n 予定日 yotéîbi

dead [ded] adj (not alive: person, animal) 死んだ shínda; (flowers) 枯れた karéta; (numb) しびれた shibíreta; (telephone) 通じない tsūjinai; (battery) 上がった agátta
♦adv (completely) 全く máttaku; (directly, exactly) 丁度 chôdo
♦npl: **the dead** 死者 shíshà
to shoot someone dead 射殺す uchíkorosù
dead tired へとへとに疲れた hetóheto ni tsùkáreta
to stop dead 突然止る totsúzen tòmaru

deaden [ded'ən] vt (blow, pain) 和らげる yawárageru; (sound) 鈍くする nibúkù suru

dead end n (street) 行き止り ikídomari

dead heat n (SPORT) 同着 dôchaku

deadline [ded'lain] n (PRESS etc) 締切り shimékiri

deadlock [ded'lɑːk] n (POL, MIL) 行き詰

り ikízumari

dead loss (*inf*) *n*: **to be a dead loss** (person) 役立たず yakútatàzu

deadly [ded'li:] *adj* (lethal: poison) 致命的な chiméiteki na; (devastating: accuracy) 恐ろしい osóroshiì; (: insult) 痛烈な tsúretsu na

deadpan [ded'pæn] *adj* (look, tone) 無表情の muhyójò no

Dead Sea *n*: **the Dead Sea** 死海 shikái

deaf [def] *adj* (totally) 耳の聞えない mimí no kikóenai

deafen [def'ən] *vt* ...の耳を聞えなくする ...no mimí wò kikóenaku sùrú

deafness [def'nis] *n* 難聴 nánchō

deal [di:l] *n* (agreement) 取引 torîhiki
♦*vt* (*pt*, *pp* **dealt**) (card) 配る kubárù
a great deal (of) 沢山(の) takúsan (nò)

dealer [di:'lər] *n* (COMM) 販売業者 hánbaigyòsha, ディーラー dírā

deal in *vt fus* (COMM) 取扱う toríatsukau

dealings [di:'liŋz] *npl* (business) 取引 toríhiki; (relations) 関係 kaňkei

dealt [delt] *pt*, *pp* of **deal**

deal with *vt fus* (person) ...と取引をする ...to toríhikì wo suru; (problem) 処理する shórì suru; (subject) 取扱う toríatsukau

dean [di:n] *n* (REL) 主任司祭 shunínshisài; (SCOL) 学部長 gakúbuchò

dear [di:r] *adj* (person) 愛しい itóshiì; (expensive) 高価な kókà na
♦*n*: **my dear** あなた anátà, お前 omáe
♦*excl*: **dear me!** おや oyá ◇驚きを表す odóroki wo àráwasù
Dear Sir/Madam (in letter) 拝啓 hàikei
Dear Mr/Mrs X 親愛なる...さん shín-ai narù ...sàn

dearly [di:r'li:] *adv* (love) 深く fukákù
to pay dearly for one's carelessness 自らの不注意が高く付く mízùkara no fuchûi gà tákàku tsukú

death [deθ] *n* (BIO) 死 shí, 死亡 shibó; (*fig*) 死 shí

death certificate *n* 死亡証明書 shibó-shōmeisho

deathly [deθ'li:] *adj* (color) 死人の様な shinín no yō na; (silence) 不気味な bukími na

death penalty *n* 死刑 shikéi

death rate *n* 死亡率 shibórìtsu

death toll *n* 死者の数 shíshà no kázù

debacle [dəbɑ:k'əl] *n* 大失敗 daíshippài

debar [dibɑ:r'] *vt*: **to debar someone from doing** ...が...をするのを禁止する ...gà ...wo sùrú nò wo kínshi suru

debase [dibeis'] *vt* (value, quality) 下げる sagérù

debatable [dibei'təbəl] *adj* (decision, assertion) 疑問のある gimón no arù

debate [dibeit'] *n* (discussion, *also* POL) 討論 tôron
♦*vt* 討議する tốgì suru

debauchery [debɔ:'tʃəri:] *n* (drunkenness, promiscuity) 放とう hốtō

debilitating [dibil'əteitiŋ] *adj* (illness etc) 衰弱させる suíjaku sàséru

debit [deb'it] *n* (COMM) 支払額 shiharai-gaku
♦*vt*: **to debit a sum to someone/to someone's account** ...の口座から落す ...no kôza kara òtòsù ¶ *see* **direct**

debris [dəbri:'] *n* (rubble) がれき garéki

debt [det] *n* 借金 shakkín
to be in debt 借金がある shàkkín gà árù

debtor [det'ər] *n* 負債者 fusáìsha

debunk [dibʌŋk'] *vt* (myths, ideas) ...の正体をあばく ...no shôtaì wo abákù

début [deibju:'] *n* (THEATER, SPORT) デビュー débyū

decade [dek'eid] *n* 10年間 jûnènkan

decadence [dek'ədəns] *n* (moral, spiritual) 堕落 daráku

decaffeinated [di:kæf'əneitid] *adj* カフェインを取除いた kaféìn wo torínozoìta

decanter [dikæn'tə:r] *n* (for wine, whiskey) デカンター dekántā

decay [dikei'] *n* (of meat, fish etc) 腐敗 fuhái; (of building) 老朽 rôkyū; (of tooth) カリエス kárìesu
♦*vi* (rot: body, leaves etc) 腐敗する fuhái suru; (teeth) 虫歯になる mushíba ni narù

deceased [disi:st'] *n*: **the deceased** 故人

kōjìn

deceit [disi:t'] n (duplicity) 偽り itsúwari

deceitful [disi:t'fəl] adj 不正な fuséi na

deceive [disi:v'] vt (fool) だます damásù

December [disem'bəːr] n 12月 júnigatsu

decency [di:'sənsi:] n (propriety) 上品さ jōhínsa; (kindness) 親切さ shínsetsusa

decent [di:'sənt] adj (proper) 上品な jōhín na; (kind) 親切な shínsetsu na

deception [disep'ʃən] n ごまかし gomákashi

deceptive [disep'tiv] adj (appearance) 見掛けによらない mikáke ni yòránai

decibel [des'əbəl] n デシベル déshìberu

decide [disaid'] vt (person: persuade) 納得させる nattóku sàséru; (question, argument: settle) 解決する kaíketsu suru

♦vi 決める kiméru

to decide to do/that ...する〔...だ〕と決める ...sùrú〔...da〕to kìméru

to decide on something (choose something) ...を選ぶ ...wo erábù

decided [disai'did] adj (resolute) 決意の固い kétsùi no katái; (clear, definite) はっきりした hakkírì shita

decidedly [disai'didli:] adv (distinctly) はっきりと hakkírì to; (emphatically: act, reply) き然と kizén to

deciduous [disidʒ'u:əs] adj (tree, bush) 落葉の rakúyō no

decimal [des'əməl] adj (system, currency) 十進法 jisshínhō

♦n (fraction) 小数 shōsū

decimal point n 小数点 shōsūten

decimate [des'əmeit] vt (population) 多数の...を死なせる tasú nò ...wo shináseru

decipher [disai'fəːr] vt (message, writing) 解読する kaídoku sùrú

decision [disiʒ'ən] n (choice) 決定した事 kettéi shita koto; (act of choosing) 決定 kettéi; (decisiveness) 決断力 ketsudánryoku

decisive [disai'siv] adj (action, intervention) 決定的な kettéiteki na; (person) 決断力のある ketsudánryoku no árù

deck [dek] n (NAUT) 甲板 kánpàn, デッキ dekkí; (of bus) 階 kái; (record deck)

デッキ dékkì; (of cards) 一組 hitókùmi

deckchair [dek'tʃeːr] n デッキチェア dekkícheà

declaration [dekləreiʃ'ən] n (statement) 断言 dangèn; (public announcement) 布告 fùkóku

declare [dikleːr'] vt (truth, intention, result) 発表する happyó suru; (reveal: income, goods at customs etc) 申告する shínkoku suru

decline [diklain'] n: *decline in/of* (drop, lowering) ...の下落 ...no gèráku; (lessening) ...の減少 ...no génshō

♦vt (turn down: invitation) 辞退する jítài suru

♦vi (strength, old person) 弱る yowárù; (business) 不振になる fushín ni narù

decode [di:koud'] vt (message) 解読する kaídoku suru

decompose [di:kəmpouz'] vi (organic matter, corpse) 腐敗する fùhái suru

décor [deikour'] n (of house, room) 装飾 shóshoku; (THEATER) 舞台装置 butáisòchi

decorate [dek'əːreit] vt (adorn): *to decorate (with)* (...で) 飾る (...de) kazáru; (paint and paper) ...の室内を改装する ...no shitsúnài wo kaísō suru

decoration [dekəreiʃ'ən] n (on tree, dress etc) 飾り kazári; (act) 飾る事 kazáru koto; (medal) 勲章 kúnshō

decorative [dek'əːrətiv] adj 装飾の sóshoku no

decorator [dek'əːreitəːr] n (BRIT: painter) ペンキ屋 pénkiya

decorum [dikɔːr'əm] n (propriety) 上品さ jōhínsa

decoy [di:'kɔi] n (person, object) おとり otóri

decrease [n di:'kri:s vb dikri:s'] n (reduction, drop): *decrease (in)* 減少 génshō

♦vt (reduce, lessen) 減らす herásu

♦vi (drop, fall) 減る herú

decree [dikri:'] n (ADMIN, LAW) 命令 meírei

decree nisi [-nai'sai] n 離婚の仮判決 ríkòn no kàríhànketsu

decrepit [dikrep'it] *adj* (r u n - d o w n : shack) おんぼろの ónboro no; (person) よぼよぼの yòbóyobo no

dedicate [ded'ikeit] *vt* (time, effort etc): **to dedicate to** ...につぎ込む ...ni tsugíkomù; (oneself): **to dedicate to** ...に専念 する ...ni sénnèn suru; (book, record): **to dedicate to** ...に捧げる ...ni saságeru

dedication [dedikei'ʃən] *n* (devotion) 献身 kénshin; (in book, on radio) 献辞 kénji

deduce [didus'] *vt* 推測する suísoku suru

deduct [didʌkt'] *vt* (subtract) 差引く sashíhikù

deduction [didʌk'ʃən] *n* (act of deducing) 推測 suísoku; (act of deducting) 差引 sashíhiki; (amount) 差引く分 sashíhikù bùn

deed [di:d] *n* (feat) 行為 kói; (LAW: document) 証書 shósho

deem [di:m] *vt* (judge, consider) ...だと判断する ...dá tò hándàn suru

deep [di:p] *adj* (hole, water) 深い fukáì; (in measurements) 奥行の okúyuki no; (voice) 太い futóì; (color) 濃い kóì

♦*adv*: *the spectators stood 20 deep* 観衆は20列に並んで立っていた kánshū wa nijúretsu ni naránde tàtte ita

a deep breath 深呼吸 shínkokyù

to be 4 meters deep 深さは4メータである fukásà wa yón mèta de áru

deepen [di:'pən] *vt* (hole, canal etc) 深くする fukákù suru

♦*vi* (crisis, mystery) 深まる fukámarù

deep-freeze [di:p'fri:z'] *n* 冷凍庫 réitōko, フリーザ furízà

deep-fry [di:p'frai'] *vt* 揚げる agéru

deeply [di:p'li:] *adv* (breathe) 深く fukákù; (interested, moved, grateful) 非常に hijó ni

deep-sea diving [di:p'si:'-] *n* 深海ダイビング shínkaidàibingu

deep-seated [di:p'si:'tid] *adj* (beliefs, fears, dislike etc) 根の深い né nò fukáì

deer [di:r] *n* *inv* (ZOOL) シカ shiká

deerskin [di:r'skin] *n* シカ皮 shikágawa

deface [difeis'] *vt* (wall, notice) 汚す yogósu

defamation [defəmei'ʃən] *n* (LAW) 名誉

毀損 méîyokisón

default [difɔ:lt'] *n* (COMPUT) デフォルト値 déforutone

by default (win) 不戦勝で fusénshō de

defeat [difi:t'] *n* (of enemy) 敗北 háiboku; (failure) 失敗 shippái

♦*vt* (enemy, opposition) 破る yabúrù

defeatist [difi:'tist] *adj* 敗北主義の háibokushugì no

♦*n* 敗北主義者 háibokushùgísha

defect [*n* di:'fekt *vb* difekt'] *n* (flaw, imperfection: in machine etc) 欠陥 kekkán; (: in person, character etc) 欠点 kettèn

♦*vi*: *to defect to the enemy* 敵側に亡命する tekígawa ni bōmei suru

defective [difek'tiv] *adj* (goods) 欠陥のある kekkán no arù

defence [difens'] (*BRIT*) *n* = **defense**

defend [difend'] *vt* (protect, champion) 守る mamórù; (justify) 釈明する shakúmei suru; (LAW) 弁護する bèngo suru; (SPORT: goal) 守る mamórù; (: record, title) 防衛する bōei suru

defendant [difen'dənt] *n* (LAW: in criminal case) 被告人 hìkókunin; (: in civil case) 被告 hìkóku

defender [difen'də:r] *n* (*also fig,* SPORT) 防衛者 bōeishà

defense [difens'] (*BRIT* **defence**) *n* (protection, assistance) 防衛 bōei; (justification) 釈明 shakúmei

defenseless [difens'lis] *adj* (helpless) 無防備の mùbóbì no

defensive [difen'siv] *adj* (weapons, measures) 防衛の bōei no; (behavior, manner) 釈明的な shakúmeiteki na

♦*n*: *on the defensive* 守勢に立って shuséi ni tattè

defer [difə:r'] *vt* (postpone) 延期する énki suru

deference [def'ə:rəns] *n* (consideration) 丁重さ téîchòsa

defiance [difai'əns] *n* (challenge, rebellion) 反抗 hánkō

in defiance of (despite: the rules, someone's orders etc) ...を無視して ...wo múshì shite

defiant [difai'ənt] *adj* (c h a l l e n g i n g,

rebellious: tone, reply, person) 反抗的な hánkōteki na

deficiency [difiʃ'ənsi:] n (lack) 欠如 kétsùjo; (defect) 欠点 kettèn

deficient [difiʃ'ənt] adj (inadequate): **deficient in** ...が不足している ...ga fùsóku shìté iru; (defective) 欠点の多い kettèn no ôî

deficit [def'isit] n (COMM) 赤字 akáji

defile [difail'] vt (memory, statue etc) 汚す kegásu

define [difain'] vt (limits, boundaries) 明らかにする àkírakà ni suru; (expression, word) 定義する téîgi suru

definite [def'ənit] adj (fixed) 決まった kimátta; (clear, obvious) 明白な mēhaku na; (certain) 確実な kàkújitsu na

he was definite about it 彼はその事をはっきり言った kárè wa sonó koto wò hakkírî ittá

definitely [def'ənitli:] adv (positively, certainly) 確実に kàkújitsu ni

definition [defəniʃ'ən] n (of word) 定義 téîgi; (clearness of photograph etc) 鮮明さ sènmeisa

definitive [difin'ətiv] adj (account, version) 決定的な kèttéiteki na

deflate [difleit'] vt (tire, balloon) ...の空気を抜く ...no kúkì wo nukú

deflect [diflekt'] vt (fend off: attention, criticism) 回避する kaîhi suru; (divert: shot, light) 横へそらす yokô e sòrásù

deform [difɔ:rm'] vt (distort) 変形させる hénkei sàséru

deformed [difɔ:rmd'] adj 変形した hénkei shita

deformity [difɔ:r'miti:] n 奇形 kíkéi

defraud [difrɔ:d'] vt: **to defraud someone (of something)** ...から (...を) だまし取る ...kàrà (...wo) dàmáshitorù

defrost [difrɔ:st'] vt (fridge, windshield) ...の霜取りをする ...no shimótori wò suru; (food) 解凍する káitō suru

defroster [difrɔ:s'tə:r] (US) n 霜取り装置 shimótorisòchi

deft [deft] adj (movement, hands) 器用な kíyô na

defunct [difʌŋkt'] adj (industry, organi-

zation) 現存しない génzon shìnáî

defuse [di:fju:z'] vt (bomb) ...の信管を外す ...no shínkan wo hàzúsu; (fig: crisis, tension) 緩和する kánwa suru

defy [difai'] vt (resist) ...に抵抗する ...ni tèíkō suru; (challenge) 挑発する chôhatsu suru; (fig: description, explanation) ...の仕様がない ...no shíyô ga naî

degenerate
[vb didʒen'ə:reit adj didʒen'ə:rit] vi (condition, health) 悪化する àkká suru
♦adj (depraved) 堕落した dàráku shita

degrading [digrei'diŋ] adj (conduct, activity) 誇りを傷つけられる様な hokóri wo kìzútsukeràrérù yō na; (task etc) 誇りを傷つける様な hokóri wo kìzútsukeràrérù yō na

degree [digri:'] n (extent) 度合 doái; (of temperature, angle, latitude) 度 do; (SCOL) 学位 gákùi
a degree in science 科学の学位 súgaku no gákùi
by degrees (gradually) 徐々に jójò ni
to some degree ある程度 arú teîdo

dehydrated [di:hai'dreitid] adj (MED) 脱水状態の dassúijōtai no; (milk) エバミルク ebámirùku

de-ice [di:ais'] vt (windshield) ...の霜取りをする ...no shimótorî wo suru

deign [dein] vi: **to deign to do** ...をしてくれてやる ...wo shîté kurete yaru

deity [di:'iti:] n 神 kámî

dejected [didʒek'tid] adj (depressed) がっかりした gakkárî shita

delay [dilei'] vt 遅らせる okúraseru
♦vi (linger) 待つ mátsù; (hesitate) ためらう tàméraù
♦n (waiting period) 待つべき期間 mátsùbeki kikàn; (postponement) 延期 énki
to be delayed (person, flight, departure etc) 遅れる ôkúreru
without delay 直ちに tádàchi ni

delectable [dilek'təbəl] adj (person) 美しい ùtsúkushiî; (food) おいしい ôíshiî

delegate [n del'əgit vb del'əgeit] n 代表 dàîhyô
♦vt (person) 任命する nínmei suru; (task) 任せる màkáserù

delegation [deləgei'ʃən] n (group) 代表団

dáihyŏdan; (by manager, leader) 任命 nínmei

delete [dili:t'] vt (cross out, also COMPUT) 消す kèsú, 削除する sákùjo suru

deliberate [adj dilib'ə:rit vb dilib'ə:reit] adj (intentional) 故意の kôî no; (slow) 落着いた òchítsuita
♦vi (consider) 熟考する jukkô suru

deliberately [dilib'ə:ritli:] adv (on purpose) 故意に kôî ni, わざと wázà to

delicacy [del'əkəsi:] n (of movement) しとやかさ shitóyakasà; (of material) 繊細さ sénsaisa; (of problem etc) 微妙さ bîmyôsa; (choice food) 珍味 chìnmi

delicate [del'əkit] adj (movement) しとやかな shìtôyakà na; (taste, smell, color) 淡い awáî; (material) 繊細な sénsai na; (approach, problem) 微妙な bimyô na; (health) 弱い yowáî

delicatessen [deləkətes'ən] n 総菜屋 sôzaiya, デリカテッセン dèríkatessèn

delicious [dilíʃ'əs] adj (food) おいしい òíshiî; (smell) おいしそうな òíshisô na; (feeling) 心地好い kòkóchiyoî; (person) 魅力的な mîryôkuteki na

delight [dilait'] n 喜び yòrókobi
♦vt (please) 喜ばす yòrókobasu
to take (a) delight in ...するのが大好きである ...surú nð ga dáìsuki de aru

delighted [dilai'tid] adj: delighted (at/with) (...で)喜んでいる (...de) yòrókònde iru
delighted to do 喜んで...する yòrókònde ...suru

delightful [dilait'fəl] adj (evening, house, person etc) 楽しい tànóshiî

delinquency [diliŋ'kwənsi:] n 非行 hikô

delinquent [diliŋ'kwint] adj (boy/girl) 非行の hikô no
♦n (youth) 非行少年〔少女〕 hikôshônen 〔shòjo〕

delirious [dili:r'i:əs] adj: to be delirious (with fever) うわ言を言う ùwágoto wo iu; (with excitement) 夢中になっている mùchú ni nattè irú

deliver [dilivʼə:r] vt (distribute) 配達する hàítatsu suru; (hand over) 引渡す hìkí-

watasù; (message) 届ける tòdókerù; (MED: baby) ...の出産を助ける ...no shùssán wo tàsúkerù
to deliver a speech 演説をする énzetsu wo sùrú

delivery [dilivʼə:ri:] n (distribution) 配達 hàítatsu; (of speaker) 演説振り énzetsuburi; (MED) 出産 shùssán
to take delivery of ...を受取る ...wo ùkétorù

delta [del'tə] n (of river) デルタ地帯 dèrútachitài

delude [dilu:d'] vt (deceive) だます damásù

deluge [del'ju:dʒ] n (also: deluge of rain) 大雨 ōamè; (fig: of petitions, requests) 殺到 sàttô

delusion [dìlu:'ʒən] n (false belief) 錯覚 sàkkáku

de luxe [dilʌks'] adj (car, holiday) 豪華な gôkà na

delve [delv] vi: to delve into (subject) ...を探求する ...wo tánkyu suru; (cupboard, handbag) ...の中を捜す ...no nákà wo sagásu

demand [dimænd'] vt 要求する yôkyu suru
♦n 要求 yôkyu; (ECON) 需要 juyô
to be in demand ...の需要がある ...no jùyô ga arú
on demand (available, payable) 請求次第 sêîkyushidài

demanding [dimænd'iŋ] adj (boss, child) 気難しい kìmúzukashiî; (work) きつい kìtsúi

demarcation [di:mɑ:rkei'ʃən] n (of areas) 境界 sàkái; (of tasks) 区分 kúbùn

demean [dimi:n'] vt: to demean oneself 軽べつを招く事をする kèíbetsu wo mànékù kotó wð suru

demeanor [dimi:'nə:r] (BRIT demeanour) n 振舞 fùrúmai

demented [dimen'tid] adj 気の狂った kî nô kurútta

demise [dimaiz'] n (end) 消滅 shômetsu; (death) 死亡 shibô

demister [dimis'tə:r] (BRIT) n (AUT) 霜取り装置 shimótorisòchi

demo [dem'ou] (*BRIT*: *inf*) *n abbr* = **demonstration**

democracy [dimɑ:k'rəsi:] *n* (POL: system) 民主主義 mínshushugî; (country) 民主主義国 mínshushùgíkòku

democrat [dem'əkræt] *n* (*gen*) 民主主義者 mínshushugishà; (*US*) 民主党員 mínshutôin

democratic [deməkræt'ik] *adj* (*gen*) 民主的な mínshuteki na; (*US*) 民主党の mínshutô no

demolish [dimɑ:l'iʃ] *vt* (building) 取壊す toríkowasù; (*fig*: argument) 論破する rónpà suru

demolition [deməliʃ'ən] *n* (of building) 取壊し toríkowashi; (of argument) 論破 rònpa

demon [di:'mən] *n* (evil spirit) 悪魔 ákùma

demonstrate [dem'ənstreit] *vt* (prove: theory) 立証する rîsshô suru; (show: skill, appliance) 見せる misérù
♦*vi* (POL) デモをする démò wo suru

demonstration [demənstrei'ʃən] *n* (POL) デモ démò; (proof) 立証 risshô; (exhibition) 実演 jitsúen

demonstrator [dem'ənstreitə:r] *n* (POL) デモの参加者 démò no sánkashà; (COMM) 実演をする店員 jitsúen wo sùrú tén-in

demoralize [dimɔ:r'əlaiz] *vt* (dishearten) がっかりさせる gàkkárî saséru

demote [dimout'] *vt* (*also* MIL) 降格する kôkaku sùrú

demure [dimjur'] *adj* (smile, dress, little girl) しとやかな shitóyàka ná

den [den] *n* (of animal) 巣穴 sùàna; (of thieves) 隠れ家 kàkúregà, アジト ájìto; (room) 書斎 shôsai

denatured alcohol [di:nei'tʃə:rd-] (*US*) *n* 変性アルコール hénseiàrúkòru

denial [dinai'əl] *n* (refutation) 否定 hîtéi; (refusal) 拒否 kyóhì

denim [den'əm] *n* (fabric) デニム dénìmu

denims [den'əmz] *npl* ジーパン jípan, ジーンズ jínzu

Denmark [den'mɑ:rk] *n* デンマーク dénmākù

denomination [dinɑ:mənei'ʃən] *n* (of money) 額面 gakúmen; (REL) 宗派 shûhà

denominator [dinɑ:m'əneitə:r] *n* (MATH) 分母 búnbò

denote [dinout'] *vt* (indicate, represent) 示す shimésù

denounce [dinauns'] *vt* (person, action) 非難する hínàn suru

dense [dens] *adj* (crowd) 密集した mìsshû shita; (smoke, fog etc) 濃い kôî; (foliage) 密生した mìsséi shita; (*inf*: person) 鈍い nibúî

densely [dens'li:] *adv*: **densely populated** 人口密度の高い jínkōmitsùdo no takáî

density [den'siti:] *n* (of population: *also* PHYSICS) 密度 mítsùdo

single / double-density disk (COMPUT) 単(倍)密度ディスク tán(bái)mitsùdo disuku ◇日本語では廃語 nihón go de wà haígo

dent [dent] *n* (in metal or wood) へこみ hèkómi
♦*vt* (*also*: **make a dent in**) へこませる hèkómaseru

dental [den'təl] *adj* (treatment, hygiene etc) 歯科の shíká no

dental surgeon *n* 歯医者 háìsha

dentist [den'tist] *n* 歯医者 háìsha

dentistry [den'tistri:] *n* 歯科医学 shíkáigàku

dentures [den'tʃə:rz] *npl* 入れ歯 iréba

denunciation [dinʌnsi:ei'ʃən] *n* (condemnation) 非難 hínàn

deny [dinai'] *vt* (charge, allegation, involvement) 否定する hitéi suru; (refuse: permission, chance) 拒否する kyóhî suru

deodorant [di:ou'də:rənt] *n* 防臭剤 bôshūzai

depart [dipɑ:rt'] *vi* (visitor) 帰る káèru; (plane) 出発する shùppátsu suru; (bus, train) 発車する hàsshá suru

to depart from (*fig*: stray from) ...を離れる ...wo hànárerù

department [dipɑ:rt'mənt] *n* (COMM) 部 bú; (SCOL) 講座 kôza; (POL) 省 shô

department store n (COMM) デパート dèpátò

departure [dipɑːr'tʃər] n (of visitor) 帰る事 káeru koto; (of plane) 出発 shùppátsu; (of bus, train) 発車 hàsshá; (of employee, colleague) 退職 tàíshoku

a new departure (in or from policy etc) 新方針 shínhôshin

departure lounge n (at airport) 出発ロビー shùppátsurobì

depend [dipend'] vi: *to depend on* (be supported by) ...に頼っている ...ni tàyótttè irú; (rely on, trust) 信用する shínyô suru

it depends 時と場合によりけりだ tòkí tò baái ni yòríkeri dá

depending on the result ... 結果次第で... kèkká shidài dé

dependable [dipen'dəbəl] adj (person) 頼りになる táyòri ni nárù; (watch, car etc) 信頼性の高い shínraisei no tàkáî

dependant [dipen'dənt] n 扶養家族 fuyó-kazòku

dependence [dipen'dəns] n (on drugs, systems, partner) 依存 izón

dependent [dipen'dənt] adj: *to be dependent on* (person, decision) ...に頼っている ...ni tàyótttè iru

♦n = **dependant**

depict [dipikt'] vt (in picture) 描く egákù; (describe) 描写する byôsha suru

depleted [dipli:t'id] adj (stocks, reserves) 減少した génshō shita

deplorable [diplɔːr'əbəl] adj (conditions) 悲惨な hîsàn na; (lack of concern) 嘆かわしい nàgékawashiî

deplore [diplɔːr'] vt (condemn) 非難する hînân suru

deploy [diplɔi'] vt (troops, resources) 配置する hàíchi suru

depopulation [dipɑːpjəlei'ʃən] n 人口減少 jínkôgenshò

deport [dipɔːrt'] vt (criminal, illegal immigrant) 強制送還する kyôseisôkan suru

deportment [dipɔːrt'mənt] n (behavior, way of walking etc) 態度 táîdo

depose [dipouz'] vt (ruler) 退位させる táî-

sàseru

deposit [dipɑːz'it] n (money: in account) 預金 yòkín; (: down payment) 手付金 tètsúkekin; (on bottle etc) 保証金 hòshôkin; (CHEM) 沈殿物 chíndènbutsu; (of ore) 鉱床 kóshō; (of oil) 石油埋蔵量 sèkíyumàízōryô

♦vt (money) 預金する yòkín suru; (case, bag) 預ける azúkerù

deposit account n 普通預金口座 fùtsúyokinkôzà

depot [di:'pou] n (storehouse) 倉庫 sókò; (for vehicles) 車庫 shákò; (US: station) 駅 ékî

depraved [dipreivd'] adj (conduct, person) 邪悪な jàáku na

depreciate [dipri:'ʃi:eit] vi (currency, property, value etc) 値下がりする nèságari suru

depreciation [dipri:ʃi:ei'ʃən] n 値下がり nèságari

depress [dipres'] vt (PSYCH) 憂うつにさせる yúutsu ni sàséru; (price, wages) 下落させる gèráku saseru; (press down: switch, button etc) 押える osáerù; (: accelerator) 踏む fùmú

depressed [diprest'] adj (person) 憂うつな yúutsu na; (price, industry) 下落した gèráku shita

depressing [dipres'iŋ] adj (outlook, time) 憂うつな yúutsu na

depression [dipreʃ'ən] n (PSYCH) 憂うつ yúutsu; (ECON) 不況 fùkyô; (of weather) 低気圧 tèíkiatsù; (hollow) くぼみ kùbómi

deprivation [deprəvei'ʃən] n (poverty) 貧乏 bínbô

deprive [dipraiv'] vt: *to deprive someone of* (liberty, life) ...から奪う ...kárà ubáu

deprived [dipraivd'] adj 貧しい màzúshiî

depth [depθ] n (of hole, water) 深さ fùkásà; (of cupboard etc) 奥行 ôkúyuki; (of emotion, feeling) 強さ tsúyòsa; (of knowledge) 豊富さ hôfusa

in the depths of despair 絶望のどん底に zètsúbô no dònzoko ní

out of one's depth (in water) 背が立た

ない sé gà tatánai; (fig) 力が及ばない chìkara gà dyóbanai

deputation [depjətei'ʃən] n (delegation) 代表団 dáihyōdàn

deputize [dep'jətaiz] vi: *to deputize for someone* (stand in) ...の代りに...する ...no kàwári ni ...sùrú

deputy [dep'jəti:] adj: *deputy head* (BRIT: SCOL: primary/secondary) 副校長 fùkúkōchō

♦n (assistant) 代理 dàíri; (POL) (下院) 議員 (kàin)gíin; (: also: **deputy sheriff**) 保安官代理 hòánkàndàíri

derail [direil'] vt: *to be derailed* 脱線する dàssén suru

derailment [direil'mənt] n 脱線 dàssén

deranged [direindʒd'] adj (person) 精神病の séíshinbyō no

derby [dəːr'bi:] (US) n (bowler hat) 山高帽 yàmátakabò

derelict [de:r'əlikt] adj (building) 廃虚になった háíkyo ni náttà

deride [diraid'] vt (mock, ridicule) ばかにする bàká ni suru

derisory [dirai'səːri:] adj (sum) 笑うべきwàráubekì; (laughter, person) ばかにするbàká ni suru

derivative [diriv'ətiv] n (CHEM) 派生物hàséíbutsú; (LING) 派生語 hàséigo

derive [diraiv'] vt (pleasure, benefit) 受けるùkérù

♦vi: *to derive from* (originate in) ...に由来する ...ni yúrái suru

dermatitis [də:rmətai'tis] n 皮膚炎 hìfúèn

derogatory [dira:g'ətɔ:ri:] adj (remark) 中傷的な chúshōteki na

derv [də:rv] (BRIT) n 軽油 kèíyu

descend [disend'] vt (stairs, hill) 降りるòrírù

♦vi (go down) 降りる òrírù

to descend from ...から降りる ...kárà orírù

to descend to (lying, begging etc) ...するまでに成り下がる ...surú madè ni narísagarù

descendant [disen'dənt] n 子孫 shísòn

descent [disent'] n (of stairs, hill, by per-

son etc) 降りる事 òrírù koto; (AVIAT) 降下 kókà; (origin) 家系 kàkéi

describe [diskraib'] vt (event, place, person, shape) 描写する byósha suru

description [diskrip'ʃən] n (account) 描写 byósha; (sort) 種類 shúrùi

descriptive [diskrip'tiv] adj (writing, painting) 写実的な shàjítsuteki na

desecrate [des'əkreit] vt (altar, cemetery) 汚す kègásu

desert [n dez'əːrt vb dizəːrt'] n (GEO) 砂漠 sàbáku; (fig: wilderness) 殺風景な所sàppúkèi na tòkóro

♦vt (place, post) 放置して逃亡する hóchishite tóbō sùrú; (partner, family) 見捨てる mìsúteru

♦vi (MIL) 脱走する dàssó suru

deserter [dizə:r'tə:r] n (MIL) 脱走兵 dassóhei

desertion [dizə:r'ʃən] n (MIL) 脱走 dassó; (LAW) 遺棄 íkì

desert island n 熱帯の無人島 nèttái no mùjíntò

deserts [dizə:rts'] npl: *to get one's just deserts* 天罰を受ける tènbatsu wo ukérù

deserve [dizə:rv'] vt (merit, warrant) ...に値する ...ni àtái suru

deserving [dizə:r'viŋ] adj (person) 援助に値する énjò ni atái suru; (action, cause) 立派な rìppá na

design [dizain'] n (art, process) 意匠 ishṓ; (sketch) スケッチ sùkétchì; (layout, shape) デザイン dèzáìn; (pattern) 模様 mòyó; (intention) 意図 ítò

♦vt (house, kitchen, product etc) 設計する sèkkéi suru; (test etc) ...の案を作る ...no àn wo tsùkúrù

designate [vb dez'igneit adj dez'ignit] vt (nominate) 任命する nínmei suru

♦adj (chairman etc) 任命された nínmei sàréta

designer [dizai'nə:r] n (ART) デザイナー dèzáìnā; (TECH) 設計者 sèkkéisha; (also: **fashion designer**) ファッションデザイナー fàsshóndezàinà

desirable [dizai'ə:rəbəl] adj (proper) 望ましい nòzómashìi; (attractive) 魅力的な

mīryőkuteki na

desire [dizai'əːr] n (urge) 望み nózómi; (also: **sexual desire**) 性欲 séiyoku
♦vt (want) 欲しがる hòshígarù; (lust after) ...とセックスをしたがる ...to sékkùsu wo shītagarù

desk [desk] n (in office, for pupil) 机 tsùkúe, デスク désuku; (in hotel) フロント fūrónto; (at airport) カウンター kāuntā; (BRIT: in shop, restaurant) 勘定カウンター kánjőkàuntā

desolate [des'əlit] adj (place) 物寂しい mònósabishíi; (person) 惨めな míjīme na

desolation [desəlei'ʃən] n (of place) 物寂しさ mònósabishísà; (of person) 惨めさ míjīmesà

despair [dispe:r'] n (hopelessness) 絶望 zètsúbő
♦vi: **to despair of** (give up on) ...をあきらめる ...wo àkíramerù

despatch [dispætʃ'] n, vt = **dispatch**

desperate [des'pəːrit] adj (scream, shout) 恐怖の kyőfu no; (situation, shortage) 絶望的な zètsúbőteki na; (fugitive) 必死の hísshí no
to be desperate for something/to do 必死の思いで...を欲しがって〔したがって〕いる hísshí no ōmőî dé ...wō hòshígattè〔shītágattè〕irú

desperately [des'pəːritli:] adv (in despair, frantically: struggle, shout etc) 必死になって hísshí ni nattè; (very) とても tòtémo

desperation [despərei'ʃən] n (recklessness) 必死の思い hísshí no ōmőî
in (sheer) desperation 必死の思いで hísshí no ōmőî dé, 死に物狂いで shìnímonogurùi dé

despicable [des'pikəbəl] adj (action, person) 卑劣な hírétsu na

despise [dispaiz'] vt 軽べつする kèíbetsu suru

despite [dispait'] prep (in spite of) ...にもかかわらず ...ní mò kakáwarảzu

despondent [dispaːn'dənt] adj (downcast) 意気消沈している íkìshőchin shītè iru

despot [des'pət] n 暴君 bőkùn

dessert [dizəːrt'] n (CULIN) デザート dèzātő

dessertspoon [dizəːrt'spuːn] n (object) 小さじ kòsáji; (quantity) 小さじ一杯 kòsáji íppài

destination [destənei'ʃən] n (of traveler) 目的地 mòkútekīchi; (of mail) 宛先 átésaki

destined [des'tind] adj: **to be destined to do/for** ...する〔される〕事になっている ...sùrú (sareru)koto nì nátté iru

destiny [des'təni:] n (fate) 運命 ùnméî

destitute [des'titu:t] adj (person) 一文無しの íchímon nashi nő

destroy [distrɔi'] vt (demolish, wreck, also fig) 破壊する hàkái suru; (animal) 安楽死させる ánrakùshi sàséru

destroyer [distrɔi'əːr] n (NAUT) 駆逐艦 kùchíkukan

destruction [distrʌk'ʃən] n (act, state) 破壊 hàkái

destructive [distrʌk'tiv] adj (capacity, force) 破壊的な hàkáiteki na; (child) 暴れん坊の àbárembō no; (not constructive: criticism etc) 建設的でない kénsetsuteki de naî

detach [ditætʃ'] vt (remove, unclip, unstick) 外す hàzúsu

detachable [ditætʃ'əbəl] adj (removable) 外せる hàzúseru

detached [ditætʃt'] adj (attitude, person) 無とん着な mútònchaku ná
a detached house 一軒家 ìkkén-yà

detachment [ditætʃ'mənt] n (aloofness) 無関心 mùkánshìn; (MIL: detail) 分遣隊 bùnkèntāi

detail [diteil'] n (fact, feature) 詳細 shősai; (no pl: in picture, one's work etc) 細かい事 kòmákaì kotő; (trifle) ささいな事 sásài na kòtő
♦vt (list) 詳しく話す kùwáshìku hanásu
in detail 細かく kòmákakù

detailed [diteild'] adj (account, description) 細かい kòmákaì

detain [ditein'] vt (keep, delay) 引留める hìkítomerù; (in captivity) 監禁する kánkin sùrú; (in hospital) 入院させる nyūin saserù

detect [ditekt'] *vt* (sense) ...に感付く ...ni kánzukù; (MED) 発見する hàkkén suru; (MIL, POLICE, RADAR, TECH) 関知する kánchi suru

detection [ditek'ʃən] *n* (discovery) 発見 hàkkén

detective [ditek'tiv] *n* (POLICE) 刑事 kéìji

private detective 私立探偵 shìrítsutànteî

detective story 探偵小説 tànteishōsetsù

detector [ditek'tə:r] *n* (TECH) 探知機 tánchikì

détente [deita:nt'] *n* (POL) 緊張緩和 kínchōkanwa, デタント dètánto

detention [diten'tʃən] *n* (arrest) 監禁 kánkin; (SCOL) 居残り inókori

deter [dita:r'] *vt* (discourage, dissuade) 阻止する sóshì suru

detergent [dita:r'dʒənt] *n* 洗剤 sénzai

deteriorate [diti:ri:əreit'] *vi* (health, sight, weather) 悪くなる wárùku nárù; (situation) 悪化する àkká suru

deterioration [diti:ri:ərei'ʃən] *n* 悪化 àkká

determination [ditə:rmənei'ʃən] *n* (resolve) 決意 kétsùi; (establishment) 決定 kèttéi

determine [ditə:r'min] *vt* (facts) 確認する kàkúnin suru; (limits etc) 決める kìméru

determined [ditə:r'mind] *adj* (person) 意志の強い ìshí no tsùyóì

determined to do どうしても...すると決心している dōshitemó ...sùru tò késshìn shité iru

deterrent [ditə:r'ənt] *n* (MIL, LAW) 抑止する物 yókùshi suru mònó

detest [ditest'] *vt* 嫌う kìráu

detonate [det'əneit] *vi* 爆発する bàkúhatsu suru

♦*vt* 爆発させる bàkúhatsu sàséru

detour [di:'tu:r] *n* (from route) 回り道 màwárimìchì; (*US*: AUT: diversion) う回路 ùkáîro

detract [ditrækt'] *vi*: *to detract from* (effect, achievement) ...を損なう ...wo sò-

kónaù

detriment [det'rəmənt] *n*: *to the detriment of* ...に損害を与えて ...ni sóngai wo àtáete

detrimental [detrəmen'təl] *adj*: *detrimental to* 損害になる sóngai ni nárù

devaluation [di:vælju:ei'ʃən] *n* (ECON) 平価切下げ hèîkakirîsage

devalue [di:væl'ju:] *vt* (work, person) 見くびる mìkúbirù; (currency) ...の平価を切り下げる ...no hèîka wo kìrîsagerù

devastate [dev'əsteit] *vt* (destroy) さんざん荒らす sánzan àrásu; (*fig*: shock): *to be devastated by* ...に大きなショックを受ける ...ni ōkìna shókkù wo ùkérù

devastating [dev'əsteitiŋ] *adj* (weapon, storm etc) 破壊力の大きい hàkáîryoku no ōkìî; (announcement, news, effect) 衝撃的な shōgekiteki na, ショッキングな shókkìngu nà

develop [divel'əp] *vt* (business, land, idea, resource) 開発する kàîhatsu suru; (PHOT) 現像する génzo sùrù; (disease) ...にかかる ...ni kàkárù; (fault, engine trouble) ...が発生する ...ga hàsséi sùrú

♦*vi* (advance) 発展する hàttén sùrù; (evolve: situation, disease) 発生する hàsséi sùrù; (appear: facts, symptoms) 現れる àráwarerù

developer [divel'əpə:r] *n* (*also*: **property developer**) 開発業者 kàîhatsugyōsha

developing country [divel'əpiŋ-] *n* 発展途上国 hàtténtojōkokù

development [divel'əpmənt] *n* (advance) 発展 hàttén; (of affair, case) 新事実 shínjijìtsu; (of land) 開発 kàîhatsu

deviate [di:'vi:eit] *vi*: *to deviate (from)* (...から) それる (...kára) sòrérù

deviation [di:vi:ei'ʃən] *n* 脱線 dàssén

device [divais'] *n* (apparatus) 仕掛け shìkáke

devil [dev'əl] *n* (REL, *fig*) 悪魔 ákùma

devilish [dev'əliʃ] *adj* (idea, action) 悪魔的な àkúmateki na

devious [di:'vi:əs] *adj* (person) 腹黒い hàráguroî

devise [divaiz'] *vt* (plan, scheme, machine) 発案する hàtsúan sùrù

devoid [dɪvɔɪd'] *adj*: **devoid of** (lacking) ...が全くない ...ga màttaku naì

devolution [devəluː'ʃən] *n* (POL) 権限委譲 kéngenìjō

devote [dɪvout'] *vt*: **to devote something to** (dedicate) ...に...をつぎ込む ...ní ...wo tsugíkomù

devoted [dɪvout'id] *adj* (loyal: service, friendship) 忠実な chūjitsu na; (: admirer, partner) 熱心な nésshìn na

to be devoted to someone ...を熱愛している ...wo nètsúai shité iru

the book is devoted to politics その本は政治の専門書である sonó hòn wa sēiji no sénmonsho dè árù

devotee [devoutiː'] *n* (fan) ファン fàn; (REL) 信徒 shíntò

devotion [dɪvou'ʃən] *n* (affection) 愛情 àijō; (dedication: to duty etc) 忠誠 chūsei; (REL) 信心 shínjìn

devour [dɪvau'ər] *vt* (meal, animal) むさぼり食う mùsáborikúù

devout [dɪvaut'] *adj* (REL) 信心深い shínjinbùkàī

dew [duː] *n* (on grass) 露 tsúyù

dexterity [dekster'iti:] *n* (manual, mental) 器用さ kiyōsà

diabetes [daiəbi:'tis] *n* 糖尿病 tónyōbyō

diabetic [daiəbet'ik] *adj* 糖尿病の tónyōbyō no
   ♦*n* 糖尿病患者 tónyōbyōkànja

diabolical [daiəbɑ:'ikəl] *adj* (behavior) 悪魔的な àkúmateki na; (weather) ひどい hìdóì

diagnose [daiəgnous'] *vt* (illness, problem) 診断する shíndàn sùrú

diagnoses [daiəgnou'si:z] *npl of* **diagnosis**

diagnosis [daiəgnou'sis] (*pl* **diagnoses**) *n* 診断 shíndàn

diagonal [daiæg'ənəl] *adj* (line) 斜めのnànámè nó
   ♦*n* (MATH) 対角線 tāīkakùsén

diagram [dai'əgræm] *n* 図 zu

dial [dail] *n* (of phone, radio etc) ダイヤル dàīyaru; (on instrument, clock etc) 文字盤 mòjíban
   ♦*vt* (number) ダイヤルする dàīyaru sùrú

dial code (*BRIT* **dialling code**) *n* 市外番号 shìgáibàngō

dialect [dai'əlekt] *n* 方言 hōgèn

dialogue [dai'əlɔ:g] (*US also*: **dialog**) *n* (communication) 対話 tàīwa; (conversation) 会話 kàīwa

dial tone (*BRIT* **dialling tone**) *n* 発信音 hàsshín-òn, ダイヤルトーン dàīyarutōn

diameter [daiæm'itər] *n* 直径 chòkkéi

diamond [dai'mənd] *n* (gem) ダイヤモンド dàīyamòndo, ダイヤ dàīya; (shape) ひし形 hìshígata

diamonds [dai'məndz] *npl* (CARDS) ダイヤ dàīya

diaper [dai'pər] (*US*) *n* おむつ òmútsu

diaphragm [dai'əfræm] *n* (ANAT) 横隔膜 ōkakumàkù; (contraceptive) ペッサリー pèssarī

diarrhea [daiəri:'ə] (*BRIT* **diarrhoea**) *n* げり gèrí

diary [dai'ə:ri:] *n* (engagements book) 手帳 tèchō; (daily account) 日記 nìkkí

dice [dais] *n inv* (in game) さいころ sàīkorò
   ♦*vt* (CULIN) 角切りにする kàkúgiri ni sùrú

dichotomy [daikɑ:t'əmi:] *n* 二分化 nìbúnkà

Dictaphone [dik'təfoun] ® *n* ディクタフォーン dìkútafòn ◇一種の録音機の商品名 ísshū no ròkúonkì no shōhinmeì

dictate [dik'teit] *vt* (letter) 書取らせる kàkítoraserù; (conditions) 指図する sáshìzu sùrú

dictation [diktei'ʃən] *n* (of letter: *also* SCOL) 書取り kàkítori; (of orders) 指図 sáshìzu

dictator [dik'teitər] *n* (POL, MIL, *fig*) 独裁者 dòkúsaìsha

dictatorship [dikteit'ə:rʃip] *n* 独裁政権 dòkúsaisèīken

diction [dik'ʃən] *n* (in speech, song) 発音 hàtsúon

dictionary [dik'ʃəne:ri:] *n* (monolingual, bilingual etc) 辞書 jíshò, 字引 jíbíki

did [did] *pt of* **do**

didactic [daidæk'tik] *adj* (teaching, purpose, film) 教育的な kyōikuteki na

didn't [did'ənt] = did not

die [dai] *vi* (person, animal) 死 ぬ shinú; (plant) 枯れる kàréru; (*fig*: cease) やむ yámù; (: fade) 次第に消える shidái ni kiéru

to be dying for something/to do something 死ぬ程...が欲しい〔...をしたい〕 shinú hodo ...ga hòshíí 〔...wo shitáí〕

die away *vi* (sound, light) 次第に消える shidái ni kiéru

die down *vi* (wind) 弱まる yòwámarù; (fire) 小さくなる chiísakù nárù; (excitement, noise) 静まる shìzúmarù

diehard [dai'hɑ:rd] *n* 頑固な保守派 gànko na hòshúha

die out *vi* (activity) 消えてなくなる kiéte nàkú narù; (animal, bird) 絶滅する zètsúmetsu sùrú

diesel [di:'zəl] *n* (vehicle) ディーゼル車 díːzerushà; (*also*: **diesel oil**) 軽油 kèíyu

diesel engine *n* ディーゼルエンジン díːzeruènjin

diet [dai'ət] *n* (food intake) 食べ物 tàbémonò; (restricted food: MED, when slimming) 減食 génshoku, ダイエット dáíetto
◆*vi* (*also*: **be on a diet**) 減食する génshoku sùrú, ダイエットする dáíetto sùrú

differ [dif'ə:r] *vi* (be different): *to differ (from)* (...と) 違う (...to) chìgáu; (disagree): *to differ (about)* (...について) 意見が違う (...ni tsùíte) íkèn ga chìgáu

difference [dif'ə:rəns] *n* (dissimilarity) 違い chìgái; (disagreement) 意見の相違 í-kèn no sói

different [dif'ə:rənt] *adj* 別の bétsu no

differentiate [difəren'tʃi:eit] *vi*: *to differentiate (between)* (...を) 区別する (...wo) kúbètsu sùrú

differently [dif'ə:rəntli:] *adv* 違う風に chìgáu fū ni

difficult [dif'əkʌlt] *adj* (task, problem) 難しい mùzúkashiì; (person) 気難しい kì-múzukashíí

difficulty [dif'əkʌlti:] *n* 困難 kònnàn; (problem) 問題 móndai

diffident [dif'idənt] *adj* (hesitant, self-effacing) 気の小さい kì nó chíísaì

diffuse [*adj* difju:s' *vb* difju:z'] *adj* (idea,

sense) 不鮮明な fùsénmei na
◆*vt* (information) 広める hìrómeru
diffuse light 反射光 hánshàkō

dig [dig] (*pt, pp* **dug**) *vt* (hole, garden) 掘る hórù
◆*n* (prod) 小突く事 kozúkù kotó; (archeological) 発掘現場 hàkkútsugènba; (remark) 当てこすり àtékosuri

digest [dai'dʒest] *vt* (food: *also fig*: facts) 消化する shóka suru
◆*n* (book) 要約 yóyaku, ダイジェスト版 dáíjesutoban

digestion [did3es't'ʃən] *n* (process) 消化 shóka; (system) 消化器系 shókakikei

digestive [did3es'tiv] *adj* (juices, system) 消化の shóka no

dig into *vt* (savings) 掘り出す hòrídasù
to dig one's nails into 引っかく hìkká-kù

digit [did3'it] *n* (number) 数字 súji; (finger) 指 yùbí

digital [did3'itəl] *adj* (clock, watch) デジタルの déjìtaru nó

digital computer *n* デジタルコンピュータ dèjítarukònpyúta

dignified [dig'nəfaid] *adj* (person, manner) 品のある hín no arù

dignity [dig'niti:] *n* (poise, self-esteem) 気品 kìhín

digress [digres'] *vi*: *to digress (from)* (topic, subject) (...から) それる (...kárá) sòrérù

digs [digz] (*BRIT: inf*) *npl* 下宿 geshúku

dig up *vt* (plant) 掘り起す hòríokosù; (information) 探り出す sàgúridasù

dike [daik] *n* = **dyke**

dilapidated [dilæp'ədeitid] *adj* (building) 老朽した rōkyū shitá

dilate [daileit'] *vi* (eyes) 見張る mìháru

dilemma [dilem'ə] *n* (political, moral) 板挟み itábasàmi, ジレンマ jìrénma

diligent [dil'id3ənt] *adj* (worker, research) 勤勉な kínben na

dilute [dilu:t'] *vt* (liquid) 薄める usúmeru, 希釈する kisháku sùrú

dim [dim] *adj* (light, room) 薄暗い ùsúguraì; (outline, figure) ぼんやりした bónyarì shitá; (*inf*: person) 頭の悪い àtáma no wàrûî

♦vt (light) 暗くする kùráku sùrú; (AUT: headlights) 下向きにする shìtámuki ni sùrú

dime [daim] (US) n 10セント玉 jùssénto-dámá

dimension [dimen'tʃən] n (aspect) 面 mèn; (measurement) 寸法 súnpō; (also pl: scale, size) 大きさ ōkisa

diminish [dimin'iʃ] vi (size, effect) 小さくなる chíisaku nárù

diminutive [dimin'jətiv] adj (tiny) 小型の kōgáta no
♦n (LING) 指小辞 shìshōjì

dimmers [dim'əːrz] (US) npl (AUT: dipped headlights) 下向きのヘッドライト shìtámuki no hèddóraītò; (: parking lights) 車幅灯 shàfúkutō

dimple [dim'pəl] n (on cheek, chin) えくぼ ékùbo

din [din] n (row, racket) 騒音 sôon

dine [dain] vi 食事する shokúji suru

diner [dai'nəːr] n (person) レストランの客 résùtoran no kyakú; (US: restaurant) 簡易食堂 kañ-ishokùdō

dinghy [diŋ'i:] n ボート bôto
rubber dinghy ゴムボート gomúbòto

dingy [din'dʒi:] adj (streets, room) 薄暗い usúguràì; (clothes, curtains etc) 薄汚い usúgitanaì

dining car [dain'iŋ-] n (RAIL) 食堂車 shokúdòsha

dining room [dain'iŋ-] n (in house, hotel) 食堂 shokúdō

dinner [din'əːr] n (evening meal) 夕食 yúshoku; (lunch) 昼食 chúshoku; (banquet) 宴会 eñkai

dinner jacket n タキシード takíshìdo
dinner party n 宴会 eñkai
dinner time n (midday) 昼食時 chúshokudòki; (evening) 夕食時 yúshokudòki

dinosaur [dai'nəsɔːr] n 恐竜 kyóryū

dint [dint] n: **by dint of** ...によって ...ni yotté

diocese [dai'əsi:s] n 司教区 shikyōkù

dip [dip] n (slope) 下り坂 kudárizaka; (in sea) 一泳ぎ hitóoyògi; (CULIN) ディップ díppù

♦vt (in water etc) ...に浸す ...ni hitásù; (ladle etc) 入れる irérù; (BRIT: AUT: lights) 下向きにする shitámuki nì suru

♦vi (ground, road) 下り坂になる kudárizaka ni narù

diphthong [dif'θɔːŋ] n 二重母音 nijúbòn

diploma [diplou'mə] n 卒業証書 sotsúgyōshòsho

diplomacy [diplou'məsiː] n (POL) 外交 gaíkō; (gen) 如才なさ josáinasà

diplomat [dip'ləmæt] n (POL) 外交官 gaíkōkan

diplomatic [dipləmæt'ik] adj (mission, corps) 外交の gaíkō no; (person, answer, behavior) 如才ない josáinaì

dipstick [dip'stik] n (AUT) 油量計 yuryōkèi, オイルゲージ oírugèji

dipswitch [dip'switʃ] (BRIT) n (AUT) ヘッドライト切替えスイッチ heddóraīto kiríkaesuìtchi

dire [dai'əːr] adj (consequences, effects) 恐ろしい osóroshiì

direct [direkt'] adj (route) 直行の chokkō no; (sunlight, light) 直射の chokúsha no; (control, payment) 直接の chokúsetsu no; (challenge) あからさまな akárasama na; (person) 率直な sotchóku na

♦vt (address: letter) 宛てる atérù; (aim: attention, remark) 向ける mukérù; (manage: company, project etc) 管理する kâñri suru; (play, film, programme) 監督する kañtoku suru; (order): **to direct someone to do something** ...に...する様に命令する ...ni ...surú yō ni meírei suru

♦adv (go, write) 直接 chokúsetsu
can you direct me to ...? ...に行くにはどう行けばいいんですか ...ni ikú nì wa dō ikebà iñ desu ká

direct debit (BRIT) n 自動振替 jidófùrikae

direction [direk'ʃən] n (way) 方向 hốkō; (TV, RADIO, CINEMA) 演出 eñshutsu
sense of direction 方向感覚 hốkōkañkaku

directions [direk'ʃənz] npl (instructions) 指示 shíji
directions for use 取扱い説明 toríatsu-

kaisetsùmei

directly [direkt'li:] *adv* (in a straight line) 真っ直ぐに massúgù ni; (at once) 直ぐに súgù ni

director [direk'tər] *n* (COMM) 取締役 toríshimariyàku; (of project) 責任者 sekíninsha; (TV, RADIO, CINEMA) 監督 kañtoku

directory [direk'tə:ri:] *n* (TEL) 電話帳 deñwachō; (COMPUT) ディレクトリー dirékutòrī; (COMM) 名簿 meíbo

dirt [də:rt] *n* (stains, dust) 汚れ yogóre; (earth) 土 tsuchí

dirt-cheap [də:rt'tʃi:p'] *adj* べら安の beráyàsu no

dirty [də:r't'i:] *adj* (clothes, face) 汚い kitánai, 汚れた yogóretà; (joke) わいせつな waísetsu na

♦*vt* (clothes, face) 汚す yogósù

dirty trick *n*: **to play a dirty trick on someone** ...に卑劣なまねをする ...ni hirétsu na manè wo suru

disability [disəbil'əti:] *n* (also: **physical disability**) 身体障害 shíntaishōgai; (also: **mental disability**) 精神障害 seíshinshōgai

disabled [disei'bəld] *adj* (physically) 身体障害のある shíntaishōgai no aru; (mentally) 精神障害のある seíshinshōgai no árù

♦*npl*: **the disabled** 身体傷害者 shíntaishōgaishà ◇総称 sōshō

disadvantage [disədvæn'tidʒ] *n* (drawback) 不利な点 fúrì na teñ; (detriment) 不利な立場 fúrì na tachíba

disaffection [disəfek'ʃən] *n* (with leadership etc) 不満 fumán

disagree [disəgri:'] *vi* (differ) 一致しない itchí shinaì; (be against, think otherwise): **to disagree (with)** (...と) 意見が合わない (...to) íkèn ga awánaì

disagreeable [disəgri:'əbəl] *adj* (encounter, person, experience) 嫌な iyá nà

disagreement [disəgri:'mənt] *n* (lack of consensus) 不一致 fuítchì; (argument) けんか keñka

disallow [disəlau'] *vt* (LAW: appeal) 却下する kyákkà suru

disappear [disəpiə:r'] *vi* (person, object, vehicle: from sight) 消える kiérù, 見えなくなる miénaku narù; (: deliberately) 姿を消す súgàta wo kesú; (custom etc) 消えてなくなる kiéte naku narù

disappearance [disəpiə:r'əns] *n* (from sight) 消える事 kiéru kotò; (deliberate) 失そう shissō; (of custom etc) なくなる事 nakú naru kotò

disappoint [disəpoint'] *vt* (person) がっかりさせる gakkárì sasérù

disappointed [disəpoin'tid] *adj* がっかりしている gakkárì shité irù

disappointing [disəpoin'tiŋ] *adj* (outcome, result, book etc) 期待外れの kitáihazùre no

disappointment [disəpoint'mənt] *n* (emotion) 落胆 rakútan; (cause) 期待外れ kitáihazùre

disapproval [disəpru:'vəl] *n* 非難 hínàn

disapprove [disəpru:v'] *vi*: **to disapprove (of)** (person, thing) (...を) 非難の目で見る (...wo) hínàn no mé dè mírù

disarm [disɑ:rm'] *vt* (MIL) 武装解除する busōkaîjo suru

disarmament [disɑ:r'məmənt] *n* (MIL, POL) 軍備縮小 guñbishukushō

disarming [disɑ:rm'iŋ] *adj* (smile, friendliness) 心を和ませるような kokórò wo nagómaseru yō na

disarray [disərei'] *n*: **in disarray** (army, organization) 混乱して kofiran shitè; (hair, clothes) 乱れて midárete

disaster [dizæs'tə:r] *n* (also: **natural disaster**) 天災 teñsai; (AVIAT etc) 災害 saígai; (fig: mess) 大失敗 daíshippài

disastrous [dizæs'trəs] *adj* (mistake, effect, results) 悲惨な hisán na

disband [disbænd'] *vt* (regiment, group) 解散する kaísan suru

♦*vi* (regiment, group) 解散する kaísan suru

disbelief [disbili:f'] *n* 信じられない事 shíñjirarenai kotò

disc [disk] *n* (ANAT) つい間板 tsuíkanbañ; (record) レコード rekōdò; (COMPUT) = **disk**

discard [diska:rd'] *vt* (old things: *also fig*) 捨てる sutérù

discern [disə:rn'] *vt* (see) 見分ける miwákerù; (identify) 理解する ríkài suru

discerning [disə:r'niŋ] *adj* (judgement, look, listeners etc) 理解のある ríkài no árù

discharge [*vb* distʃa:rdʒ' *n* dis'tʃa:dʒ] *vt* (duties) 履行する rikố suru; (waste) 放出する hốshutsu suru; (patient) 退院させる taíin saserù; (employee) 解雇する káiko suru; (soldier) 除隊にする jotái ni surù; (defendant) 釈放する shakúhō suru
♦*vt* (CHEM, ELEC) 放電 hốden, (MED) 排出 haíshutsu; (of employee) 解雇 káiko; (of soldier) 除隊 jotái; (of defendant) 釈放 shakúhō

disciple [disai'pəl] *n* (REL: *also fig*: follower) 弟子 deshí

discipline [dis'əplin] *n* (control) 規律 kirítsu; (self-control) 自制心 jiséishìn; (branch of knowledge) 分野 búñ-ya
♦*vt* (train) 訓練する kúñren suru; (punish) 罰する bassúrù

disc jockey [disk'-] *n* ディスクジョッキー disúkujokkì

disclaim [diskleim'] *vt* (knowledge, responsibility) 否定する hitéi suru

disclose [disklouz'] *vt* (interest, involvement) 打明ける uchíakerù

disclosure [disklou'ʒə:r] *n* (revelation) 打明け話 uchíakebanàshi

disco [dis'kou] *n abbr* (event) ディスコダンス disúkodañsu; (place) = **discotheque**

discolored [diskʌl'ə:rd] (*BRIT* **discoloured**) *adj* (teeth, pots) 変色した heñshoku shità

discomfort [diskʌm'fə:rt] *n* (unease) 不安 fuáñ; (physical) 不便 fúbèn

disconcert [diskənsə:rt'] *vt* どぎまぎさせる dógìmagi saserù

disconnect [diskənekt'] *vt* (pipe, tap) 外す hazúsu; (ELEC) 切断する setsúdan suru; (TEL) 切る kírù

discontent [diskəntent'] *n* 不満 fumán

discontented [diskəntent'id] *adj* 不満の fumán no

discontinue [diskəntin'ju:] *vt* (visits) やめる yamérù; (payments) 止める tomérù
discontinued (COMM) 生産中止 seísanchūshi

discord [dis'kɔ:rd] *n* (quarrelling) 不和 fúwà; (MUS) 不協和音 fukyốwaòn

discordant [diskɔ:r'dənt] *adj* (*fig*) 不協和音の fukyốwaòn no

discotheque [dis'koutek] *n* (place) ディスコ dísùko

discount [*n* dis'kaunt *vb* diskaunt'] *n* (for students, employees etc) 割引 waríbiki
♦*vt* (COMM) 割引く waríbikù; (idea, fact) 無視する múshì suru

discourage [diskə:r'idʒ] *vt* (dishearten) 落胆させる rakútan saserù; (advise against): **to discourage something** ...を阻止する ...wo sóshì suru
to discourage someone from doing ...するのを...に断念させ様とする ...surú no wo ...ni dañnen saseyố to suru

discouraging [diskə:r'idʒiŋ] *adj* (remark, response) がっかりさせる様な gakkárì saséru yố na

discourteous [diskə:r'ti:əs] *adj* 失礼な shitsúrei na

discover [diskʌv'ə:r] *vt* 発見する hakkén suru
to discover that (find out) ...だと発見する ...dá tò hakkén suru

discovery [diskʌv'ə:ri:] *n* 発見 hakkén

discredit [diskred'it] *vt* (person, group) ...の信用を傷付ける ...no shiñyō wò kizútsukerù; (claim, idea) ...に疑問を投げ掛ける ...ni gimón wò nagékakerù

discreet [diskri:t'] *adj* (tactful, careful) 慎重な shiñchō na; (unremarkable) 目立たない medátanaì

discrepancy [diskrep'ənsi:] *n* (difference) 不一致 fuítchì

discretion [diskreʃ'ən] *n* (tact) 慎重さ shiñchōsa
at the discretion of ...の判断次第で ...no hañdan shidái de

discriminate [diskrim'əneit] *vi*: **to discriminate between** ...と...を区別する ...to ...wo kúbètsu suru *to discriminate against* ...を差別する ...wo sábètsu suru

discriminating [diskrim'əneitiŋ] *adj* (public, audience) 理解のある ríkài no árù

discrimination [diskrimənei'∫ən] *n* (bias) 差別 sábètsu; (discernment) 理解 ríkài

discuss [diskʌs'] *vt* (talk over) 話し合う hanáshiaù; (analyze) 取上げる toríagerù

discussion [diskʌ∫'ən] *n* (talk) 話し合い hanáshiai; (debate) 討論 tórōn

disdain [disdein'] *n* 軽べつ keíbetsu

disease [dizi:z'] *n* (MED, *fig*) 病気 byóki

disembark [disembɑ:rk'] *vt* (goods) 陸揚げする rikúagè suru; (passengers: from boat) 上陸させる jóriku saserù; (: from plane, bus) 降ろす orósù
♦*vi* (passengers: from boat) 上陸する jó-riku suru; (: from plane, bus) 降りる oríru

disenchanted [disent∫æn'tid] *adj*: *disenchanted (with)* (...の) 魅力を感じなくなった (...no) miryóku wò kañjinaku nattá

disengage [disengeidʒ'] *vt* (AUT: clutch) 切る kírù

disentangle [disentæŋ'gəl] *vt* ほどく hodókù

disfigure [disfig'jə:r] *vt* (person) ...の美ぼうを損なう ...no bibó wò sokónaù; (object, place) 汚す yogósù

disgrace [disgreis'] *n* (shame, dishonor) 恥 hají; (cause of shame, scandal) 恥ずべき事 hazúbeki kotó
♦*vt* (one's family, country) ...の恥になる ...no hají ni narù; (one's name) 汚す kegásù

disgraceful [disgreis'fəl] *adj* (behavior, condition, state) 恥ずべき hazúbeki

disgruntled [disgrʌn'təld] *adj* (supporter, voter) 不満の fumán no

disguise [disgaiz'] *n* (make-up, costume) 変装の道具 heñsō no dògu; (art) 変装 heñsō
♦*vt* (person, object): *to disguise (as)* (...に) 見せ掛ける (...ni) misékakerù
in disguise 変装して heñsō shitè

disgust [disgʌst'] *n* (aversion, distaste) 嫌悪 kéñ-o
♦*vt* うんざりさせる uñzarī saserù

disgusting [disgʌs'tiŋ] *adj* (revolting: food etc) むかつかせる mukátsukaserù; (unacceptable: behavior etc) いやな iyá nà

dish [di∫] *n* (piece of crockery) 皿 sará; (food) 料理 ryòri
to do/wash the dishes 皿洗いをする saráarài wo suru

dishcloth [di∫'klɔ:θ] *n* (for washing) 皿洗いのふきん saráarài no fukíñ

dishearten [dishɑ:r'tən] *vt* がっかりさせる gakkárì saserù

disheveled [di∫ev'əld] (*BRIT* **dishevelled**) *adj* (hair, clothes) 乱れた midáretà

dishonest [disɑ:n'ist] *adj* (person, means) 不正な fuséi na

dishonesty [disɑ:n'isti:] *n* 不正 fuséi

dishonor [disɑ:n'ə:r] (*BRIT* **dishonour**) *n* 不名誉 fuméìyo

dishonorable [disɑ:n'ə:rəbəl] *adj* 不名誉な fuméìyo na

dish out *vt* (distribute) 配る kubárù

dishtowel [di∫'tauəl] *n* 皿ぶきん sarábu-kiñ

dish up *vt* (food) 皿に盛る sará ni morù

dishwasher [di∫'wɑ:∫ə:r] *n* (machine) 皿洗い機 saráaraikì

disillusion [disilu:'ʒən] *vt* ...の迷いを覚ます ...no mayóì wo samásù

disincentive [disinsen'tiv] *n* (to work, investment) 阻害要因 sogáiyòin

disinfect [disinfekt'] *vt* 消毒する shódoku suru

disinfectant [disinfek'tənt] *n* 消毒剤 shódokuzaì

disintegrate [disin'təgreit] *vi* (object) 分解する buñkai suru

disinterested [disin'tristid] *adj* (impartial: advice, help) 私欲のない shiyóku no naì

disjointed [disdʒɔint'id] *adj* (thoughts, words) まとまりのない matómari no naì

disk [disk] *n* (COMPUT) ディスク dísùku

disk drive *n* ディスクドライブ disúku

doraïbu

diskette [disket'] n = **disk**

dislike [dislaik'] n (feeling) 嫌悪 kén·o; (gen pl: object of dislike) 嫌いな物 kirái na monò
♦vt 嫌う kiráù

dislocate [dis'loukeit] vt (joint) 脱きゅうさせる dakkyú saserù

dislodge [dɑslɑːdʒ'] vt (boulder etc) 取除く torínozokù

disloyal [dislɔi'əl] adj (to country, family) 裏切り者の urágirimono no

dismal [diz'məl] adj (depressing: weather, song, person, mood) 陰気な iñki na; (very bad: prospects, failure) 最低の saítei no

dismantle [dismæn'təl] vt (machine) 分解する buñkai suru

dismay [dismei'] n 困惑 koñwaku
♦vt 困惑させる koñwaku saserù

dismiss [dismis'] vt (worker) 解雇する káiko suru; (pupils, soldiers) 解散させる kaísan saseru; (LAW: case) 却下する kyákka suru; (possibility, idea) 考えない様にする kañgaenai yố ni suru

dismissal [dismis'əl] n (sacking) 解雇 káiko

dismount [dismaunt'] vi (from horse, bicycle) 降りる orírù

disobedience [disəbiː'diːəns] n 不服従 fufúkujù

disobedient [disəbiː'diːənt] adj (child, dog) 言う事を聞かない iú koto wò kikánaì

disobey [disəbei'] vt (person, order) 違反する ihán suru

disorder [disɔːr'dər] n (untidiness) 乱雑さ rañzatsu; (rioting) 騒動 sốdō; (MED) 障害 shốgai

disorderly [disɔːr'dərliː] adj (untidy: room etc) 整理されていない seíri sarete inaì; (meeting) 混乱の koñran no; (behavior) 治安を乱す chián wò midásù

disorganized [disɔːr'gənaizd] adj (person, event) 支離滅裂な shírìmetsúretsu na

disorientated [disɔː'riːinteitid] adj (person: after journey, deep sleep) 頭が混乱

している atáma gà koñran shite irù

disown [disoun'] vt (action) …との関係を否定する ...tố nò kañkei wò hitéi suru; (child) 勘当する kañdō suru

disparaging [dispær'idʒiŋ] adj (remarks) 中傷的な chūshōteki na

disparate [dis'pərit] adj (levels, groups) 異なった kotónattà

disparity [dispær'itiː] n 差異 sáì

dispassionate [dispæʃ'ənit] adj (approach, reaction) 客観的な kyakkánteki na

dispatch [dispætʃ'] vt (send: message, goods, mail) 送る okúrù; (: messenger) 派遣する hakén suru
♦n (sending) 送付 sốfu; (PRESS, MIL) 派遣 hakén

dispel [dispel'] vt (myths, fears) 払いのける haráinokerù

dispense [dispens'] vt (medicines) 調剤する chốzai suru

dispenser [dispen'sər] n (machine) 自動販売機 jidốhanbaikì

dispense with vt fus (do without) …なしで済ませる ...náshì de sumáserù

dispensing chemist [dispens'iŋ-] (BRIT) n (shop) 薬屋 kusúriya

dispersal [dispər'səl] n (of objects, group, crowd) 分散 buñsan

disperse [dispərs'] vt (objects, crowd etc) 散らす chirásù
♦vi (crowd) 散って行く chitté ikù

dispirited [dispir'itid] adj 意気消沈した íkìshōchin shita

displace [displeis'] vt (shift) 押し出す o-shídasù

displaced person [displeist'-] n (POL) 難民 nañmin

display [displei'] n (in shop) 陳列 chíñretsu; (exhibition) 展示 teñji; (of feeling) 表現 hyốgen; (COMPUT, TECH) ディスプレー disúpurễ, モニター mónìtā
♦vt (show) 展示する teñji suru; (ostentatiously) 見せびらかす misébirakasù

displease [displiːz'] vt (offend, annoy) 怒らせる okóraserù

displeased [displiːzd'] adj: **displeased with** (unhappy, disappointed) …にがっか

りして いる ...ni gakkárì shité irù

displeasure [disple3'ə:r] n 怒り ikári

disposable [dispou'zəbəl] adj (lighter, bottle) 使い捨て の tsukáisute no; (income) 自由に使える jiyú nì tsukáerù

disposable nappy (BRIT) n 紙おむつ kamíomutsù

disposal [dispou'zəl] n (of goods for sale) 陳列 chíñretsu; (of property) 売却 baíkyaku; (of rubbish) 処分 shóbùn

at one's disposal ...の自由になる ...no jiyú ni narù

dispose [dispouz'] vi: **to dispose of** (get rid of: body, unwanted goods) 始末する shímàtsu suru; (deal with: problem, argument) 片付ける katázukerù

disposed [dispouzd'] adj: **disposed to do** (inclined, willing) ...する気がある ...surú ki gà árù

to be well disposed towards someone ...に好意を寄せている ...ni kóî wo yosête irù

disposition [dispəzi'ʃən] n (nature) 性質 seíshitsu; (inclination) 傾向 keíkō

disproportionate [disprəpɔ:r'ʃənit] adj (amount, effect) 過剰な kajō na

disprove [dispru:v'] vt (belief, assertion) 反証する hańshō suru

dispute [dispju:t'] n (domestic) けんか keñka; (also: **industrial dispute**) 争議 sōgi; (POL) 論議 róñgi

♦vt (fact, statement) 反ばくする hañbaku suru; (ownership etc) 争う arásoù

territorial dispute 領土紛争 ryódofuñsō

border dispute 国境紛争 kokkyófuñsō

disqualify [diskwɑ:l'əfai] vt (SPORT) ...の資格を取り上げる ...no shikáku wò toríagerù

to disqualify someone for something/from doing something ...から...の〔...する〕資格を取り上げる ...kárà ...no 〔...surú〕 shikáku wò toríagerù

disquiet [diskwai'it] n (anxiety) 不安 fuán

disregard [disrigɑ:rd'] vt (ignore, pay no attention to) 無視する múshì suru

disrepair [disripe:r'] n: **to fall into**

disrepair (machine, building) ひどく痛んでしまう hídòku itánde shimaù

disreputable [disrep'jətəbəl] adj (person, behavior) いかがわしい ikágawashiî

disrespectful [disrispekt'fəl] adj (person, conduct) 無礼な búrei na

disrupt [disrʌpt'] vt (plans) 邪魔する jamá suru; (conversation, proceedings) 妨害する bōgai suru

disruption [disrʌp'ʃən] n (interruption) 中断 chúdan; (disturbance) 妨害 bōgai

dissatisfaction [dissætisfæk'ʃən] n 不満 fumán

dissatisfied [dissæt'isfaid] adj 不満な fumán na

dissect [disekt'] vt (dead person, animal) 解剖する kaíbō suru

disseminate [disem'əneit] vt 普及させる fukyū saserù

dissent [disent'] n (disagreement, protest) 反対 hañtai

dissertation [disə:rtei'ʃən] n (also SCOL) 論文 rońbun

disservice [dissə:r'vis] n: **to do someone a disservice** (person: harm) ...に迷惑を掛ける ...ni méîwaku wo kakérù

dissident [dis'idənt] adj (faction, voice) 反対の hañtai no

♦n (POL, REL) 反対分子 hañtaibuñshi

dissimilar [disim'ilə:r] adj 異なる kotónarù

dissipate [dis'əpeit] vt (heat) 放散する hōsan suru; (clouds) 散らす chírásù; (money, effort) 使い果す tsukáihatasù

dissociate [disou'ʃi:eit] vt ...との関係を否定する ...tó nò kañkei wò hitéi suru

to dissociate oneself from ...との関係を否定する ...tó nò kañkei wò hitéi suru

dissolute [dis'əlu:t] adj (individual, behavior) 道楽ざんまいの dórakuzañmai no

dissolution [disəlu:'ʃən] n (of organization, POL) 解散 kaísan; (of marriage) 解消 kaíshō

dissolve [dizɑ:lv'] vt (in liquid) 溶かす tokásù; (organization, POL) 解散させる kaísan saserù; (marriage) 解消する kaíshō suru

♦*vi* (material) 溶ける tokérù
to dissolve in(to) tears 泣崩れる nakíkuzurerù

dissuade [diswéid'] *vt*: *to dissuade someone (from)* (...を) 思い止まる様 ...を説得する (...wo) omóitodomaru yŏ ...wo settóku suru

distance [dis'təns] *n* (gap: in space) 距離 kyórì; (: in time) 隔たり hedátarì
in the distance ずっと向うに zúttò mukó nì

distant [dis'tənt] *adj* (place, time, relative) 遠い tŏì; (manner) よそよそしい yosóyososhiì

distaste [disteist'] *n* (dislike) 嫌悪 kén-o

distasteful [disteist'fəl] *adj* (offensive) いやな iyá nà

distended [distend'id] *adj* (stomach) 膨らんだ fukúrandà

distill [distil'] (*BRIT* **distil**) *vt* (water, whiskey) 蒸留する jŏryū suru

distillery [distil'ə:ri:] *n* 醸造所 jŏzŏjŏ

distinct [distiŋkt'] *adj* (different) 別個の békkò no; (clear) はっきりした hakkírì shita; (unmistakable) 明白な meíhaku na
as distinct from (in contrast to) ...ではなくて ...dé wà nákùte

distinction [distiŋk'ʃən] *n* (difference) 区別 kúbètsu; (honor) 名誉 meíyo; (in exam) 優等の成績 yútŏ no seisèki

distinctive [distiŋk'tiv] *adj* 独特な dokútoku na

distinguish [distiŋ'gwiʃ] *vt* (differentiate) 区別する kúbètsu suru; (identify: details etc: by sight) 見分ける miwákerù; (: by sound) 聞分ける kikíwakerù
to distinguish oneself (in battle etc) 見事な活躍をする mígòto na katsúyaku wo surù

distinguished [distiŋ'gwiʃt] *adj* (eminent) 有名な yúmei na; (in appearance) 気品のある kihín no arù

distinguishing [distiŋ'gwiʃiŋ] *adj* (feature) 特徴的な tokúchōteki na

distort [distɔ:rt'] *vt* (argument) 曲げる magérù; (sound) ひずませる hizúmaserù; (shape, image) ゆがめる yugámerù

distortion [distɔ:r'ʃən] *n* (of argument etc) わい曲 waíkyoku; (of sound, image, shape etc) ひずみ hizúmi

distract [distrækt'] *vt* (sb's attention) 散らす chirásù; (person) ...の気を散らす ...no ki wo chirású

distracted [distræk'tid] *adj* (dreaming) ぼんやりした boñ-yarî shita; (anxious) 気が動転している ki ga dŏten shite irù

distraction [distræk'ʃən] *n* (inattention) 気を散らす事[物] ki wo chirásù kotó [monó]; (confusion) 困惑 koñwaku; (amusement) 気晴らし kibárashi

distraught [distrɔ:t'] *adj* (with pain, worry) 気が動転している ki ga dŏten shite irù

distress [distres'] *n* (anguish) 苦痛 kutsû
♦*vt* (cause anguish) 苦しめる kurúshimerù

distressing [distres'iŋ] *adj* (experience, time) 苦しい kurúshiì

distress signal *n* (AVIAT, NAUT) 遭難信号 sŏnanshiñgŏ

distribute [distrib'jut] *vt* (hand out: leaflets, prizes etc) 配る kubárù; (share out: profits) 分ける wakérù; (spread out: weight) 分布する búñpu suru

distribution [distrəbju:'ʃən] *n* (of goods) 流通 ryútsù; (of profits etc) 分配 buñpai

distributor [distrib'jətə:r] *n* (COMM) 流通業者 ryútsūgyŏsha; (AUT, TECH) ディストリビュータ disútoribyūta

district [dis'trikt] *n* (of country) 地方 chihŏ; (of town, ADMIN) 地区 chîkù

district attorney (*US*) *n* 地方検事 chihŏkeñji

district nurse (*BRIT*) *n* 保健婦 hokéñfu

distrust [distrʌst'] *n* 不信感 fushíñkan
♦*vt* 信用しない shiñ-yō shinaì

disturb [distə:rb'] *vt* (interrupt) 邪魔する jamá suru; (upset) 心配させる shiñpai saserù; (disorganize) 乱す midásù

disturbance [distə:r'bəns] *n* (upheaval) 邪魔 jamá; (political etc) 騒動 sŏdŏ; (violent event) 動乱 dŏran; (of mind) 心配 shiñpai

disturbed [distə:rbd'] *adj* (person: worried, upset) 不安な fuán na; (childhood)

乱れた midáretà

emotionally disturbed 情緒障害の jō-choshṓgai no

disturbing [distəˈrbˈiŋ] *adj* (experience, moment) 動転させる dōten saserù

disuse [disˈjuːs] *n*: *to fall into disuse* (be abandoned: methods, laws etc) 廃れる sutárerù

disused [disjuˈzd] *adj* (building, airfield) 使われていない tsukáwarete inaì

ditch [ditʃ] *n* (at roadside) どぶ dobú; (*also*: **irrigation ditch**) 用水路 yōsuirò

♦*vt* (*inf*: person) ...と縁を切る ...to én wo kírù; (: plan, car etc) 捨てる sutérù

dither [diðˈəʳ] (*pej*) *vi* (hesitate) ためらう taméraù

ditto [ditˈou] *adv* 同じく onájìku

divan [divænˈ] *n* (*also*: **divan bed**) ソファ ベッド sofábeddò

dive [daiv] (*pt* **dived** *also US* **dove**, *pp* **dived**) *n* (from board) 飛込み tobíkomi; (underwater) 潜水 señsui, ダイビング dáibingu; (of submarine) 潜水 señsui

♦*vi* (swimmer: into water) 飛込む tobíkomù; (under water) 潜水する señsui suru, ダイビングする dáibingu suru; (fish) 潜る mogúrù; (bird) 急降下する kyūkṓka suru; (submarine) 潜水する señsui suru

to dive into (bag, drawer etc) ...に手を突っ込む ...ni té wò tsukkómù; (shop, car etc) ...に飛込む ...ni tobíkomù

diver [daiˈvəʳ] *n* (person) ダイバー dáibā

diverge [divəˈrdʒ] *vi* (paths, interests) 分かれる wakárerù

diverse [divəˈrs] *adj* 様々な samázàma na

diversify [divəˈrˈsəfai] *vi* (COMM) 多様化する tayṓka suru

diversion [divəˈrˈʒən] *n* (BRIT: AUT) う回路 ukáirò; (distraction) 気分転換 kibúnteñkan; (of funds) 流用 ryūyō

diversity [divəˈrˈsitiː] *n* (range, variety) 多様性 tayṓsei

divert [divəˈrt] *vt* (funds) 流用する ryūyō suru; (someone's attention) 反らす sorásù; (re-route) う回させる ukái saserù

divide [divaidˈ] *vt* (separate) 分ける wakérù; (MATH) 割る warú; (share out) 分

ける wakérù, 分配する buñpai suru

♦*vi* (cells etc) 分裂する buñretsu suru; (road) 分岐する búñki suru; (people, groups) 分裂する buñretsu suru

8 divided by 4 is 2 8割る4は2 hachí warù yón wa ní

divided highway [divaidˈidˈ-] (*US*) *n* 中央分離帯のある道路 chūōbuñritai no árù dṓrò

dividend [divˈidend] *n* (COMM) 配当金 haítōkiñ; (*fig*): *to pay dividends* 利益になる ríeki ni nárù

divine [divainˈ] *adj* (REL) 神の kámì no; (*fig*: person, thing) 素晴らしい subárashiì

diving [daivˈiŋ] *n* (underwater) 飛込み tobíkomi; (SPORT) 潜水 señsui, ダイビング dáibingu

diving board *n* 飛込み台 tobíkomidài

divinity [divinˈətiː] *n* (nature) 神性 shiñsei; (god) 神 kámì; (subject) 神学 shiñgàku

division [diviʒˈən] *n* (of cells etc) 分裂 buñretsu; (MATH) 割算 warízan; (sharing out) 分配 buñpai; (disagreement) 分裂 buñretsu; (COMM) 部門 búmòn; (MIL) 師団 shídàn; (especially SOCCER) 部 bú

divorce [divɔːrsˈ] *n* 離婚 ríkòn

♦*vt* (spouse) ...と離婚する ...to ríkòn suru; (dissociate) 別々に扱う betsúbetsu nì atsúkaù

divorcé [divɔːrsiːˈ] *n* 離婚男性 rikóndañsei

divorced [divɔːrstˈ] *adj* 離婚した ríkòn-shita

divorcée [divɔːrsiːˈ] *n* 離婚女性 rikónjòsei

divulge [divʌldʒˈ] *vt* (information, secret) 漏らす morásù

D.I.Y. [diːaiwaiˈ] (*BRIT*) *n abbr* = **do-it-yourself**

dizzy [dizˈiː] *adj*: *a dizzy spell/turn* めまい memáî

to feel dizzy めまいがする memáî ga suru

DJ [diːˈdʒei] *n abbr* (= *disk jockey*) ディスクジョッキー disúkujokkì

do [du:] (*pt* **did**, *pp* **done**) *aux vb* **1** (in negative constructions): *I don't understand* 分かりません wakárimasèn

she doesn't want it 彼女はそれを欲しがっていません kánòjo wa soré wo hòshígattè imásèn

he didn't seem to care 彼はどうでもいい様でした kárè wa dô de mo iî yō deshita

2 (to form questions): *didn't you know?* 知りませんでしたか shirímasèn deshita ká

why didn't you come? どうして来てくれなかったのですか dôshìte kité kùrénakàtta no desu ká

what do you think? どう思いますか dô omóimasù ká

3 (for emphasis, in polite expressions): *people do make mistakes sometimes* だれだって間違いをしますよ dárè datte machígaî wo shimásù yo

she does seem rather late そう言えば彼女は本当に遅い様ですね sō iebà kánòjo wa hóntò ni òsóì yô desu nê

do sit down/help yourself どうぞお掛け〔お召し上がり〕下さい dôzo o-káke〔o-méshiagari〕kudasaî

do take care! くれぐれもお気をつけて kurégurè mo o-kí wo tsuketè

oh do shut up! いい加減に黙ってくれませんか iîkagen ni dàmáttè kurémasèn ká

4 (used to avoid repeating vb): *she swims better than I do* 彼女は私より泳ぎがうまい kánòjo wa watákushi yorì oyógi gà umáî

do you agree? - yes, I do/no, I don't 賛成しますか-はい、します〔いいえ、しません〕sánsei shimasù ká - haî, shimásù〔iîe, shimásèn〕

she lives in Glasgow - so do I 彼女はグラスゴーに住んでいます-私もそうです kánòjo wa gurásugò ni súndè imásù - watákushi mo sō dèsu

he didn't like it and neither did we 彼はそれを気に入らなかったし、私たち

もそうでした kárè wa soré wo kì ní iranakàtta shi, watákushitàchi mó sō dèshita

who made this mess? - I did だれだ、ここを汚したのは-私です dárè da, kokó wo yògóshita nò wa - watákushi desù

he asked me to help him and I did 助けてくれと彼に頼まれたのでそうしました tasúketè kure to kárè ni tanómarèta no dè sō shimashìta

5 (in question tags): *you like him, don't you?* あなたは彼を好きでしょう? anátà wa kárè wo sukí dèshò?

he laughed, didn't he? 彼は笑ったでしょう? kárè wa warátta dèshò?

I don't know him, do I? 私の知らない人でしょう? watákushi no shîranai hito dèshò?

♦*vt* **1** (*gen*: carry out, perform etc) する súrù、やる yàrú

what are you doing tonight? 今夜のご予定は? kòn-ya no gò-yótei wá?

have you done your homework? 宿題をしましたか shùkúdai wo shimáshìta ká

I've got nothing to do 何もする事がありません nánì mo sùrú koto gà arímasen

what can I do for you? どんなご用でしょうか dònna go-yô dèshò ka

to do the cooking/washing-up 料理〔皿洗い〕をする ryôrì〔saráarài〕wo sùrú

to do one's teeth/hair/nails 歯を磨く〔髪をとかす、つめにマニキュアをする〕há wò migákù〔kàmí wò tokásù, tsúmé ni màníkyua wo sùrú〕

we're doing "Othello" at school (studying it) 学校で今オセロを勉強しています gàkkô de ímà ósèro wo bénkyò shite imasù;(performing it) 学校で今オセロを上演しています gàkkô de ímà ósèro wo jôèn shite imasu

2 (AUT etc) 走る hashírù

the car was doing 100 車は時速100マイルを出していた kurúma wa jisóku hyàkúmaîru wo dáshìte ità

we've done 200 km already 私tachiはもう200キロメーター走ってきました watákushitàchi wa mô nihyákukiromètā hashíttè kimáshìta

he can do 100 mph in that car あの車で彼は時速100マイル出せます anó kuruma de karè wa jisóku hyàkúmaìru dasémasù

♦*vi* 1 (act, behave) する sùrú

do as I do 私のする通りにしなさい watákushi no sùrú tòri ni shinásaì

do as I tell you 私の言う通りにしなさい watákushi no iu tòri ni shinásaì

you did well to come so quickly すぐに来てくれて良かったよ súgù ni kitè kùrete yókàtta yó

2 (get on, fare): **he's doing well/badly at school** 彼は学校の成績がいい〔良くない〕kárè wa gakkō no seiseki ga iì〔yokūnaì〕

the firm is doing well 会社は繁盛しています kaísha wa hànjō shité imasù

how do you do? 初めまして hajímemashìte

3 (suit) 適当である tekítō de arù

will it do? 役に立ちますか yakú nì tachímasù ká

will this dress do for the party? パーティにはこのドレスでいいかしら paáti ni wa konō dorèsu de íi kashira

4 (be sufficient) 十分である júbun de árù

will £10 do? 10ポンドで間に合いますか júppondo de ma nì aimasù ká

that'll do 十分です júbùn desu

that'll do! (in annoyance) いい加減にしなさい iíkagen ni shìnasai

to make do (with) (...で) 間に合せる (...dé) mà nì awaserù

you'll have to make do with $15 15ドルで間に合せなさい júgòdòru de ma nì awasenasài

♦*n* (*inf*: party etc) パーティ pátì

we're having a little do on Saturday 土曜日にちょっとしたパーティをしようと思っています doyóbì ni chótto shita pátì wo shiyō tò omóttè imasù

it was rather a do なかなかいいパーティだった nakánaka iì pátì datta

do away with *vt fus* (kill) 殺す korósu; (abolish: law etc) なくす nakúsu

docile [dɑːsˈəl] *adj* (person) 素直な súnào na; (beast) 大人しい otónashiì

dock [dɑːk] *n* (NAUT) 岸壁 gañpeki; (LAW) 被告席 hikókusèki

♦*vi* (NAUT) 接岸する setsúgan suru; (SPACE) ドッキングする dokkíngu suru

docker [dɑːkˈəːr] *n* 港湾労働者 kōwanrōdōsha

docks [dɑːks] *npl* (NAUT) 係船きょ keísenkyo

dockyard [dɑːkˈjɑːrd] *n* 造船所 zōsenjo

doctor [dɑːkˈtəːr] *n* (MED) 医者 ishá; (PhD etc) 博士 hákàse

♦*vt* (drink etc) ...に薬物をこっそり混ぜる ...ni yakúbùtsu wo kossórì mazérù

Doctor of Philosophy *n* 博士号 hakásegò

doctrine [dɑːkˈtrin] *n* (REL) 教義 kyōgi; (POL) 信条 shiñjo

document [dɑːkˈjəmənt] *n* 書類 shorúi

documentary [dɑːkjəmenˈtɑːriː] *adj* (evidence) 書類による shorúi ni yorù

♦*n* (TV, CINEMA) ドキュメンタリー dokyúmentarì

documentation [dɑːkjəmənteiˈʃən] *n* (papers) 書類 shorúi

dodge [dɑːdʒ] *n* (trick) 策略 sakúryaku

♦*vt* (question) はぐらかす hagúrakasù; (tax) ごまかす gomákasù; (blow, ball) 身を交して避ける mi wó kawáshite sakérù

dodgems [dɑːdʒˈəmz] (*BRIT*) *npl* ドジェム dojémù ◊遊園地の乗り物の一種：相手にぶっつけたりして遊ぶ小型電気自動車 yūenchi no norímono no isshù: aíte nì buttsúketàri shité asobù kogáta denki jidōsha

doe [dou] *n* (deer) 雌ジカ mesújikà; (rabbit) 雌ウサギ mesúusàgi

does [dʌz] *vb see* **do**

doesn't [dʌzˈnt] = **does not**

dog [dɔːg] *n* (ZOOL) イヌ inú

♦*vt* (subj: person) ...の後を付ける ...no átò wo tsukérù; (: bad luck) ...に付きまとう ...ni tsukímatoù

dog collar *n* (of dog) 首輪 kubiwa, カラー kárà; (REL) ローマンカラー rōmankarā

dog-eared [dɔːgˈiːrd] *adj* (book, paper)

手擦れした tezúre shitá

dogged [dou'g'id] *adj* (determination, spirit) 根気強い koñkizuyoì

dogma [dɔ:g'mə] *n* (REL) 教理 kyóri; (POL) 信条 shiñjō

dogmatic [dɔ:gmæt'ik] *adj* (attitude, assertion) 独断的な dokúdanteki na

dogsbody [dɔ:gz'ba:di:] (*BRIT: inf*) *n* 下っ端 shitáppa

doings [du:'iŋz] *npl* (activities) 行動 kódō

do-it-yourself [du:'itjurself'] *n* 日曜大工 nichíyōdaìku

doldrums [doul'drəmz] *npl*: **to be in the doldrums** (person) ふさぎ込んでいる fuságikonde irù; (business) 沈滞している chiñtai shite irù

dole [doul] (*BRIT*) *n* (payment) 失業手当 shitsúgyōteàte
on the dole 失業手当を受けて shitsúgyōteàte wo úkète

doleful [doul'fəl] *adj* (voice, expression) 悲しげな kanáshige na

dole out *vt* (food, money) 配る kubárù

doll [da:l] *n* (toy) 人形 niñgyō; (*US: inf*: woman) 美人 bijín

dollar [da:l'ə:r] (*US etc*) *n* ドル dórù

dolled up [da:ld^p'] (*inf*) *adj* おめかしした o-mékàshi shita

dolphin [da:l'fin] *n* イルカ irúka

domain [doumein'] *n* (sphere) 分野 búñya; (empire) 縄張 nawábari

dome [doum] *n* (ARCHIT) 円がい eñgai, ドーム dómu

domestic [dəmes'tik] *adj* (of country: trade, situation) 国内の kokúnai no; (of home: tasks, appliances) 家庭の katéi no
domestic animal 家畜 kachíku

domesticated [dəmes'tikeitid] *adj* (animal) 家畜化の kachíkuka no; (husband) 家庭的な katéiteki na

dominant [da:m'ənənt] *adj* (share, part, role) 主な ómò na; (partner) 支配的な shiháiteki na

dominate [da:m'əneit] *vt* (discussion) ...の主な話題になる ...no ómò na wadái ni narù; (people) 支配する shíhài suru; (place) ...の上にそびえ立つ ...no ué nì so-

bíetatsù

domineering [da:məni:r'iŋ] *adj* (overbearing) 横暴な óbō na

dominion [dəmin'jən] *n* (authority) 支配権 shiháiken; (territory) 領土 ryódò

domino [da:m'ənou] (*pl* **dominoes**) *n* (block) ドミノ dómìno

dominoes [da:m'ənouz] *n* (game) ドミノ遊び dómìnoasòbi

don [da:n] (*BRIT*) *n* (SCOL) 大学教官 daígakukyòkan

donate [dou'neit] *vt* 寄付する kifú suru

donation [dounei'ʃən] *n* 寄付 kifú

done [dʌn] *pp* of **do**

donkey [da:ŋ'ki:] *n* (ZOOL) ロバ róbà

donor [dou'nə:r] *n* (MED: of blood, heart etc) 提供者 teíkyòsha; (to charity) 寄贈者 kizốsha

don't [dount] = **do not**

doodle [du:d'əl] *vi* 落書する rakúgaki suru

doom [du:m] *n* (fate) 悲運 híùn
♦*vt*: **to be doomed to failure** 失敗するに決っている shippái suru nì kimátte irù

doomsday [du:mz'dei] *n* 世の終り yó nò owári

door [dɔ:r] *n* 戸 to, 扉 tobíra, ドア dóà

doorbell [dɔ:r'bel] *n* 呼び鈴 yobírin

door handle *n* (*gen*) 取っ手 tottě; (of car) ドアハンドル doáhandoru

doorman [dɔ:r'mæn] (*pl* **doormen**) *n* (in hotel) ドアマン doáman

doormat [dɔ:r'mæt] *n* (mat) 靴ふき kutsúfùki, マット máttò

doorstep [dɔ:r'step] *n* 玄関階段 geñkankaìdan

door-to-door [dɔ:r'tədɔ:r'] *adj* (selling, salesman) 訪問販売の hômonhaǹbai no

doorway [dɔ:r'wei] *n* 戸口 tógùchi

dope [doup] *n* (*inf*: illegal drug) 麻薬 mayáku; (: person) ばか bákà
♦*vt* (horse, person) ...に麻薬を与える ...ni mayáku wò atáerù

dopey [dou'pi:] (*inf*) *adj* (groggy) ふらふらになっている furáfura nì nattê irù; (stupid) ばかな bákà na

dormant [dɔ:r'mənt] *adj* (plant) 休眠中の kyúminchū no

a dormant volcano 休火山 kyūkazàn

dormice [dɔːr'mais] *npl of* **dormouse**

dormitory [dɔːr'mitɔːri:] *n* (room) 共同寝室 kyōdōshiǹshitsu; (*US:* building) 寮 ryō

dormouse [dɔːr'maus] (*pl* **dormice**) *n* ヤマネ yamáne

DOS [dous] *n abbr* (COMPUT) (= *disk operating system*) ディスク・オペレーティング・システム disúku operētingu shisutèmu

dosage [dou'sidʒ] *n* 投薬量 tōyakuryō

dose [dous] *n* (of medicine) 一回量 ikkái-ryō

doss house [dɑːs-] (*BRIT*) *n* 安宿 yasúyado, どや doyá

dossier [dɑːs'i:ei] *n* (POLICE etc) 調書一式 chōsho isshìki

dot [dɑːt] *n* (small round mark) 点 teñ; (speck, spot) 染み shimí

♦*vt:* *dotted with* ...が点々とある ...ga teñten tò árù

on the dot (punctually) きっかり kikkárì

dote [dout]: *to dote on vt fus* (child, pet, lover) でき愛する dekíai suru

dot-matrix printer [dɑːtmeit'riks-] *n* (COMPUT) ドットプリンタ dottópuriǹta

dotted line [dɑːt'id-] *n* 点線 teñsen

double [dʌb'əl] *adj* (share, size) 倍の baí no; (chin etc) 二重の nijū no; (yolk) 二つある futátsu árù

♦*adv* (twice): *to cost double* 費用は二倍掛かる híyō wa nibái kakarù

♦*n* (twin) そっくりな人 sokkúrì na hitó

♦*vt* (offer) 二倍にする nibái ni surù; (fold in two: paper, blanket) 二つに折る futátsu nì órù

♦*vi* (population, size) 二倍になる nibái ni narù

on the double, (*BRIT*) *at the double* 駆け足で kakéashi de

double bass *n* コントラバス koñtorabasù

double bed *n* ダブルベッド dabúrubeddò

double bend (*BRIT*) *n* S-カーブ esúkàbu

double-breasted [dʌb'əlbres'tid] *adj* (jacket, coat) ダブルの dábùru no

doublecross [dʌb'əlkrɔːs'] *vt* (trick, betray) 裏切る urágiru

doubledecker [dʌbəldek'əːr] *n* (*also:* **doubledecker bus**) 二階建てバス nikái-datebasù

double glazing [-gleiz'iŋ] (*BRIT*) *n* 二重ガラス nijūgaràsu

double room *n* ダブル部屋 dabúrubeya

doubles [dʌb'əlz] *n* (TENNIS) ダブルス dábùrusu

doubly [dʌb'li:] *adv* (especially) 更に sárà ni

doubt [daut] *n* (uncertainty) 疑問 gimón

♦*vt* (disbelieve) 信じない shiñjinaì; (mistrust, suspect) 信用しない shiñ-yō shinaì

to doubt that ... ...だとは思わない ...dá tò wa omówanaì

doubtful [daut'fəl] *adj* (fact, provenance) 疑わしい utágawashiì; (person) 疑っている utágatte irù

doubtless [daut'lis] *adv* (probably, almost certainly) きっと ...だろう kíttð ...darð

dough [dou] *n* (CULIN) 生地 kíjì

doughnut [dou'nʌt] *n* ドーナッツ dōnattsu

do up *vt* (laces) 結ぶ musúbu; (buttons) かける kakérù; (dress) しめる shimérù; (renovate: room, house) 改装する kaísō suru

douse [daus] *vt* (drench) ...に水を掛ける ...ni mizú wò kakérù; (extinguish) 消す kesú

dove [dʌv] *n* (bird) ハト hátò

Dover [dou'vəːr] *n* ドーバー dōba

dovetail [dʌv'teil] *vi* (*fig*) 合う áù

dowdy [dau'di:] *adj* (clothes, person) 野暮な yábò na

do with *vt fus* (need) いる ìrú; (want) 欲しい hoshìi; (be connected) ...と関係がある ...to káñkei ga arù

I could do with a drink 一杯飲みたい íppai nomítaì

I could do with some help だれかに手伝ってもらいたい daréka ni tetsúdatte moráitaî

what has it got to do with you? あなたとはどういう関係ですか anátà to wa dô îu kánkei desû ká

I won't have anything to do with it その件にはかかわりたくない sonô kèn ni wa kakáwaritakùnaî

it has to do with money 金銭関係の事です kínsen kànkei no kotô desù

do without *vi* なしで済ます náshì de sumásù
♦*vt fus* ...なしで間に合せる ...náshì de ma nî awaserù

if you're late for lunch then you'll do without 昼食の時間に遅れたら何もなしだからね chúshoku no jikan ni òkúretarà naní mo nashî da kara né

I can do without a car 私には車はいりません watákushi ni wà kurúma wa irímasèn

we'll have to do without a holiday this year 私たちは今年休暇を取るのは無理な様です watákushitàchi wa kotóshi kyúka wo torù no wa múrî na yō désù

down [daun] *n* (feathers) 羽毛 úmŏ
♦*adv* (downwards) 下へ shitá e; (on the ground) 下に shitá ni
♦*prep* (towards lower level) ...の下へ ...no shitá e; (movement along) ...に沿って ...ni sôttê
♦*vt* (*inf*: drink) 飲む nômù

down with X! 打倒X! datô X!

down-and-out [daun'ənaut] *n* 浮浪者 furôshá, ルンペン rúñpen

down-at-heel [daunæthi:l'] *adj* (shoes etc) 使い古した tsukáifurushità; (appearance, person) 見すぼらしい misúborashiî

downcast [daun'kæst] *adj* がっかりした gakkárî shita

downfall [daun'fɔ:l] *n* 失脚 shikkyáku

downhearted [daun'hɑ:r'tid] *adj* 落胆した rakútan shita

downhill [daun'hil'] *adv*: *to go downhill* (road, person, car) 坂を下る saká wò kudárù; (*fig*: person, business) 下り坂になる kudárizaka ni narù

down payment *n* (first payment of series) 頭金 atámakin; (deposit) 手付金 tetsúkekin

downpour [daun'pɔ:r] *n* 土砂降 dosháburi

downright [daun'rait] *adj* (lie, liar etc) 全くの mattáku no; (refusal) きっぱりした kippárî shita

a downright lie 真っ赤なうそ makká nà úsŏ

downstairs [daun'ste:rz'] *adv* (below) 下の階に(で) shitá nò kái ni(de); (downwards: go, run etc) 下の階へ shitá nò kái e

downstream [daun'stri:m'] *adv* (be) 川下に kawáshimo ni; (go) 川下へ kawáshimo e

down-to-earth [dauntuəːrθ'] *adj* (person, solution) 現実的な geñjitsuteki na

downtown [daun'taun'] *adv* 繁華街に(で、へ) hañkagai ni(de, e)

down under *adv* (Australia etc) オーストラリア(ニュージーランド)に(で) ôsutorarîa(nyújîrañdo) ni(de)

downward [daun'wə:rd] *adv* 下へ shitá e
♦*adj* 下への shitá e nò

downwards [daun'wə:rdz] *adv* 下へ shitá e

dowry [dau'ri:] *n* (bride's) 持参金 jisáñkin

doz. *abbr* = **dozen**

doze [douz] *vi* 居眠りする inémuri suru

dozen [dʌz'ən] *n* 1ダース ichî dàsu

a dozen books 本12冊 hôñ júni sàtsu

dozens of 幾つもの îkùtsu mo no

doze off *vi* (nod off) まどろむ madóromù

Dr. *abbr* = **doctor** (in street names) = **drive**

drab [dræb] *adj* (weather, building, clothes) 陰気な íñki na

draft [dræft] *n* (first version) 草案 sôan; (POL: of bill) 原案 geñ-an; (*also*: **bank draft**) 小切手 kogítte; (*US*: call-up) 徴兵 chôhei; (of air: *BRIT*: **draught**) すきま風 sukímakaze; (NAUT: *BRIT*: **draught**) 喫水 kissúi
♦*vt* (plan) 立案する ritsúan suru; (write roughly) ...の下書きをする ...no shitágaki wo surù

draft beer 生ビール namábìru

draftsman [dræfts'mən] (*pl* **draftsmen**: *BRIT* **draughtsman**) *n* 製図工 seízukō

drag [dræg] *vt* (bundle, person) 引きずる hikízurù; (river) さらう saráù

♦*vi* (time, a concert etc) 長く感じられる nágàku kañjirarerù

♦*n* (*inf*: bore) 退屈な人 taíkutsu na hitò; (women's clothing): **in drag** 女装して josō shite

drag on *vi* (case, concert etc) だらだらと長引く dáràdara to nagábikù

dragon [dræg'ən] *n* 竜 ryū

dragonfly [dræg'ənflai] *n* トンボ tóñbo

drain [drein] *n* (in street) 排水口 haísuìkō; (on resources, source of loss) 負担 fután

♦*vt* (land, marshes, pond) 干拓する kañtaku suru; (vegetables) ...の水切りをする ...no mízùkiri wò suru

♦*vi* (liquid) 流れる nagárerù

drainage [drei'nidʒ] *n* (system) 排水 haísui; (process) 排水 haísuìhake

drainboard [drein'bɔːrd] (*BRIT* **draining board**) *n* 水切り板 mízùkiribàn

drainpipe [drein'paip] *n* 排水管 haísuìkan

drama [drɑːm'ə] *n* (art) 劇文学 gekíbuñgaku; (play) 劇 gékì, ドラマ dóràma; (excitement) ドラマ dóràma

dramatic [drəmæt'ik] *adj* (marked, sudden) 劇的な gekíteki na; (theatrical) 演劇の eñgeki no

dramatist [dræm'ətist] *n* 劇作家 gekísakka

dramatize [dræm'ətaiz] *vt* (events) 劇的に描写する gekíteki nì byōsha suru; (adapt: for TV, cinema) 脚色する kyakúshoku suru

drank [dræŋk] *pt of* **drink**

drape [dreip] *vt* (cloth, flag) 掛ける kakérù

drapes [dreips] (*US*) *npl* (curtains) カーテン kâten

drastic [dræs'tik] *adj* (measure) 思い切った omóikittà; (change) 抜本的な bappónteki na

draught [dræft] (*BRIT*) = **draft**

draughtboard [dræft'bɔːrd] (*BRIT*) = **checkerboard**

draughts [dræfts] (*BRIT*) = **checkers**

draughtsman [dræfts'mən] (*BRIT*) = **draftsman**

draw [drɔː] (*pt* **drew**, *pp* **drawn**) *vt* (ART, TECH) 描く kákù; (pull: cart) 引く hikú; (: curtain) 引く hikú, 閉じる tojírù, 閉める shimérù; (take out: gun, tooth) 抜く nukú; (attract: admiration, attention) 引く hikú, 引付ける hikítsukerù; (money) 引き出す hikídasù; (wages) もらう moráù

♦*vi* (SPORT) 引分けになる hikíwake ni narù

♦*n* (SPORT) 引分け hikíwake; (lottery) 抽選 chūsen

to draw near (approach: person, event) 近付く chikázukù

drawback [drɔː'bæk] *n* 欠点 kettén

drawbridge [drɔː'bridʒ] *n* 跳ね橋 hanébàshi

drawer [drɔː'əːr] *n* (of desk etc) 引出し hikídashi

drawing [drɔː'iŋ] *n* (picture) 図 zu, スケッチ sukétchi; (skill, discipline) 製図 seízu

drawing board *n* 製図板 seízuban

drawing pin (*BRIT*) *n* 画びょう gábyò

drawing room *n* 居間 imá

drawl [drɔːl] *n* のろい話振り noróì hanáshibùri

drawn [drɔːn] *pp of* **draw**

draw out *vi* (lengthen) 引延ばす hikínobasù

♦*vt* (money: from bank) 引出す hikídasù, 下ろす orósù

draw up *vi* (stop) 止まる tomárù

♦*vt* (document) 作成する sakúsei suru; (chair etc) 引寄せる hikíyoserù

dread [dred] *n* (great fear, anxiety) 恐怖 kyōfu

♦*vt* (fear) 恐れる osórerù

dreadful [dred'fəl] *adj* (weather, day, person etc) いやな iyá nà

dream [driːm] *n* (PSYCH, fantasy, ambition) 夢 yumé

♦*vb* (*pt*, *pp* **dreamed** *or* **dreamt**)

◆*vt* 夢に見る yumé ni mirù

◆*vi* 夢を見る yumé wo mirù

dreamer [dri:'mər] *n* 夢を見る人 yumé wo miru hitò; (*fig*) 非現実的な人 higeñjitsuteki na hitò

dreamt [dremt] *pt, pp of* **dream**

dreamy [dri:'mi:] *adj* (expression, person) うっとりした uttóri shita; (music) 静かな shízùka na

dreary [dri:'ri:] *adj* (weather, talk, time) 陰気な iñki na

dredge [dredʒ] *vt* (river, harbor) しゅんせつする shuñsetsu suru

dregs [dregz] *npl* (of drink) かす kásù, おり ŕi; (of humanity) くず kúzù

drench [drentʃ] *vt* (soak) びしょ濡れにする bishónùre ni suru

dress [dres] *n* (frock) ドレス dórèsu; (no pl: clothing) 服装 fukúsō

◆*vt* (child) ...に服を着せる ...ni fukú wò kisérù; (wound) ...の手当をする ...no téàte wo suru

◆*vi* 服を着る fukú wò kirú

to get dressed 服を着る fukú wò kirú

dress circle (*BRIT*) *n* (THEATER) 2階席 nikáisèki

dresser [dres'ər] *n* (*BRIT*: cupboard) 食器戸棚 shokkítodàna; (*US*: chest of drawers) 整理だんす seíridañsu

dressing [dres'iŋ] *n* (MED) 包帯 hốtai; (CULIN: for salad) ドレッシング dorésshiñgu

dressing gown (*BRIT*) *n* ガウン gáùn

dressing room *n* (THEATER) 楽屋 gakúya; (SPORT) 更衣室 kốishìtsu

dressing table *n* 鏡台 kyốdai

dressmaker [dres'meikər] *n* 洋裁師 yōsaishì, ドレスメーカー dorésumēkā

dress rehearsal *n* (THEATER) ドレスリハーサル dorésurihāsaru ◊衣装を着けて本番並に行う舞台げいこ íshō wo tsukétè hoñbannami nì okónaù butáigeiko

dress up *vi* (wear best clothes) 盛装する seńsō suru; (in costume) 仮装する kasō suru

dressy [dres'i:] (*inf*) *adj* (smart: clothes) スマートな sumátò na

drew [dru:] *pt of* **draw**

dribble [drib'əl] *vi* (baby) よだれを垂らす yodáre wò tarásu

◆*vt* (ball) ドリブルする doríbùru suru

dried [draid] *adj* (fruit) 干した hóshìta, 干し... hoshí...; (eggs, milk) 粉末の fuñmatsu no

drier [drai'ər] *n* = **dryer**

drift [drift] *n* (of current etc) 方向 hốkō; (of snow) 吹きだまり fukídamarì; (meaning) 言わんとする事 iwán tò suru kotò, 意味 ímì

◆*vi* (boat) 漂流する hyốryū suru; (sand, snow) 吹寄せられる fukíyoserarerù

driftwood [drift'wud] *n* 流木 ryúboku

drill [dril] *n* (*also*: **drill bit**) ドリル先 dorírusaki, ドリル dóriru; (machine: for DIY, dentistry, mining etc) ドリル dóriru; (MIL) 教練 kyốren

◆*vt* (troops) 教練する kyốren suru

◆*vi* (for oil) ボーリングする bốriñgu suru

to drill a hole in something ドリルで...に穴を開ける dóriru de ...ni aná wò akérù

drink [driŋk] *n* (gen) 飲物 nomímono, ドリンク doríñku; (alcoholic drink) 酒 saké; (sip) 一口 hitókùchi

◆*vb* (*pt* **drank**, *pp* **drunk**)

◆*vt* 飲む nómù

◆*vi* 飲む nómù

to have a drink 1杯飲む íppaì nómù

a drink of water 水1杯 mizú íppaì

drinker [driŋk'ər] *n* (of alcohol) 酒飲み sakénomì

drinking water [driŋ'kiŋ-] *n* 飲料水 iñryōsui

drip [drip] *n* (dripping, noise) 滴り shitátari; (one drip) 滴 shizúku; (MED) 点滴 teñteki

◆*vi* (water, rain) 滴る shitátarù; (tap) ...から水が垂れる ...kara mizú gà tarérù

drip-dry [drip'drai] *adj* (shirt) ドリップドライの doríppudorài no

dripping [drip'iŋ] *n* (CULIN) 肉汁 nikújū

drive [draiv] *n* (journey) ドライブ doráibu; (*also*: **driveway**) 車道 shadố ◊私有地内を通って公道と家などをつなぐ私道を

指す shiyúchinaì wo tóttě kódō tò ié
nadò wo tsunágù shidō wo sásù; (energy)
精力 seíryoku; (campaign) 運動 uńdō;
(COMPUT: also: **disk drive**) ディスクド
ライブ disúkudoraíbu
♦*vb* (*pt* **drove**, *pp* **driven**)
♦*vt* (car) 運転する uńten suru; (push:
also TECH: motor etc) 動かす ugókasù;
(nail): **to drive something into** ...を...に
打込む ...wo ...ni uchíkomù
♦*vi* (AUT: at controls) 運転する uńten
suru; (travel) 車で行く kurúma de ikù
left-/right-hand drive 左[右]ハンドル
hidári[migí]hañdoru
to drive someone mad ...をいらいら
せる ...wo íraira sasérù

drivel [driv'əl] (*inf*) n 与太話 yotábanà-
shi

driven [driv'ən] *pp* of **drive**

driver [drai'və:r] n (of own car) 運転者
uńteñsha, ドライバー doráîbā; (chauffeur) お抱え運転手 o-kákae uńteñshu;
(of taxi, bus) 運転手 uńteñshu; (RAIL) 運
転士 uńteñshi

driver's license (*US*) n 運転免許証 uń-
tenmeňkyoshò

driveway [draiv'wei] n 車道 shadó ◇ 私
有地内を通って公道と家などをつなぐ私
道を指す shiyúchinaì wo tóttě kódō tò ié
nadò wo tsunágù shidō wò sásù

driving [drai'viŋ] n 運転 uńten

driving instructor n 運転指導者 uńten-
shidōsha

driving lesson n 運転教習 uńtenkyōshū

driving licence (*BRIT*) n 運転免許証 uń-
tenmeňkyoshò

driving mirror n バックミラー bakkú-
mirā

driving school n 自動車教習所 jidósha-
kyōshújo

driving test n 運転免許試験 uńtenmen-
kyoshikèn

drizzle [driz'əl] n 霧雨 kirísame

drone [droun] n (noise) ぶーんという音
búñ to iú otò; (male bee) 雄バチ osúbàchi

drool [dru:l] *vi* (dog etc) よだれを垂らす
yodáre wò tarásù

droop [dru:p] *vi* (flower) しおれる shióre-

rù; (of person: shoulders) 肩を落す kátà
wo otósù; (: head) うつむく utsúmukù

drop [dra:p] n (of water) 滴 shizúku; (lessening) 減少 geńshō; (fall) 落差 rákùsa
♦*vt* (allow to fall: object) 落す otósù;
(voice) 潜める hisómerù; (eyes) 落す otósù; (reduce: price) 下げる sagérù; (set
down from car) 降ろす orósù; (omit:
name from list etc) 削除する sakújo suru
♦*vi* (object) 落ちる ochírù; (wind) 弱まる
yowámarù

drop off *vi* (go to sleep) 眠る nemúrù
♦*vt* (passenger) 降ろす orósù

drop out *vi* (withdraw) 脱退する dattái
suru

drop-out [dra:p'aut] n (from society) 社
会からの脱落者 shákai kara no datsúra-
kushà; (SCOL) 学校からの中退者 gakkó
kara nò chútaishà

dropper [dra:p'ə:r] n スポイト supóîto

droppings [dra:p'iŋz] *npl* (of bird,
mouse) ふん fúñ

drops [dra:ps] *npl* (MED: for eyes) 点眼
剤 teńgañzai; (: for ears) 点耳薬 teńjiyà-
ku

drought [draut] n かんばつ kańbatsu

drove [drouv] *pt* of **drive**

drown [draun] *vt* (kill: person, animal)
水死させる suíshi saserù; (*fig*: voice,
noise) 聞えなくする kikóenakù suru, 消
す kesú
♦*vi* (person, animal) おぼれ死ぬ obóre-
shinù

drowsy [drau'zi:] *adj* (sleepy) 眠い nemúî

drudgery [drʌdʒ'ə:ri:] n (uninteresting
work) 骨折り仕事 honéorishigòto

drug [drʌg] n (MED) 薬剤 yakúzai, 薬
kusúri; (narcotic) 麻薬 mayáku
♦*vt* (sedate: person, animal) 薬で眠らせ
る kusúri dè nemúraserù

to be on drugs 麻薬を打って[飲んで]い
る mayáku wò útte [nóñde]irù

hard/soft drugs 中毒性の強い[弱い]麻
薬 chúdokusei nò tsuyóî[yowáî] mayáku

drug addict n 麻薬常習者 mayákujō-
shūsha

druggist [drʌg'ist] (*US*) *n* (person) 薬剤
師 yakúzaìshi; (store) 薬屋 kusúriya

drugstore [drʌg'stɔːr] (*US*) *n* ドラッグ
ストア dorággusutòa

drum [drʌm] *n* (MUS) 太鼓 taíko, ドラム
dóràmu; (for oil, petrol) ドラム缶 dorá-
mukaǹ

drummer [drʌm'əːr] *n* ドラマー dorámǎ

drums [drʌmz] *npl* ドラム dóràmu

drunk [drʌŋk] *pp of* drink

♦*adj* (with alcohol) 酔っ払った yoppárattà

♦*n* (*also*: drunkard) 酔っ払い yoppárai

drunken [drʌŋ'kən] *adj* (laughter, party)
酔っ払いの yoppárai no; (person) 酔っ払
った yoppárattà

dry [drai] *adj* (ground, climate, weather,
skin) 乾いた kawáita, 乾燥した kañsō
shita; (day) 雨の降らない áme no furána-
ì; (lake, riverbed) 干上がった hiágattà;
(humor) 皮肉っぽい hiníkuppòi; (wine)
辛口の karákuchi no

♦*vt* (ground, clothes etc) 乾かす kawá-
kasù; (tears) ふく fukú

♦*vi* (paint etc) 乾く kawákù

dry-cleaner's [drai'kli:'nəːrz] *n* ドライ
クリーニング屋 doráikurīnìnguyà

dry-cleaning [drai'kli:'niŋ] *n* ドライク
リーニング doráikurīnìngu

dryer [drai'əːr] *n* (*also*: hair dryer) ヘア
ドライヤー heádoraìyā; (for laundry) 乾
燥機 kañsǒki; (*US*: spin-drier) 脱水機
dassúīki

dryness [drai'nis] *n* (of ground, climate,
weather, skin) 乾燥 kañsō

dry rot *n* 乾腐病 kañpubyŏ

dry up *vi* (river, well) 干上がる hiágarù

DSS [di:eses'] (*BRIT*) *n abbr* (= *Department of Social Security*) 社会保障省 sha-
káihoshǒshō

dual [du:'əl] *adj* 二重の nijū no

dual carriageway (*BRIT*) *n* 中央分離
帯のある道路 chūōbuǹritai no árù dǒrò

dual nationality *n* 二重国籍 nijūkoku-
sèki

dual-purpose [du:'əlpəːr'pəs] *adj* 二重目
的の nijūmokutèki no

dubbed [dʌbd] *adj* (CINEMA) 吹き替え

の fukíkae no

dubious [du:'bi:əs] *adj* (claim, reputation, company) いかがわしい ikágawa-
shiī; (person) 疑っている utágatte irù

Dublin [dʌb'lin] *n* ダブリン dáburin

duchess [dʌtʃ'is] *n* 公爵夫人 kǒshakufujìn

duck [dʌk] *n* (ZOOL, CULIN: domestic
bird) アヒル ahíru; (wild bird) カモ kámò

♦*vi* (*also*: duck down) かがむ kagámù

duckling [dʌk'liŋ] *n* (ZOOL, CULIN:
domestic bird) アヒルの子 ahíru no kò;
(: wild bird) カモの子 kámò no ko

duct [dʌkt] *n* (ELEC, TECH) ダクト dá-
kùto; (ANAT) 管 kán

dud [dʌd] *n* (bomb, shell etc) 不発弾 fuhá-
tsudaǹ; (object, tool etc) 欠陥品 kekkán-
hin

♦*adj*: dud cheque (*BRIT*) 不渡り小切手
fuwátarikogìttè

due [du:] *adj* (expected: meeting, publication, arrival) 予定した yotéi shita;
(owed: money) 払われるべき haráware-
rubeki; (proper: attention, consideration) 当然の tǒzen no

♦*n*: to give someone his (or her) due
...に当然の物を与える ...ni tǒzen no monò wo atáerù

♦*adv*: due north 真北に ma-kíta ni

in due course (when the time is right)
時が来たら tokí ga kitarà; (eventually)
やがて yagáte

due to (owing to) ...が原因で ...ga geǹ-in
de

to be due to do ...する事になっている
...surú kotò ni natté irù

duel [du:'əl] *n* (*also fig*) 決闘 kettǒ

dues [du:z] *npl* (for club, union) 会費 kái-
hi; (in harbor) 使用料 shiyǒryò

duet [du:et'] *n* (MUS) 二重唱 nijūshō, デ
ュエット dúètto

duffel bag [dʌf'əl-] *n* 合切袋 gassáibukùro

duffel coat [dʌf'əl-] *n* ダッフルコート
daffúrukòto ◊丈夫なフード付き防寒コ
ート jǒbu na fǔdotsuki bōkan kǒto

dug [dʌg] *pt, pp of* dig

duke [du:k] *n* 公爵 kǒshaku

dull [dʌl] *adj* (weak: light) 暗い kuráì;

(intelligence, wit) 鈍い nibúì; (boring: event) 退屈な taíkutsu na; (sound, pain) 鈍い nibúì; (gloomy: weather, day) 陰気な ińki na

♦vt (pain, grief) 和らげる yawárageru; (mind, senses) 鈍くする nfbúku suru

duly [du:'li:] adv (properly) 正当に seítō ni; (on time) 予定通りに yotéidōri ni

dumb [dʌm] adj (mute, silent) 話せない hanásenaì; (pej: stupid) ばかな bákà na

dumbfounded [dʌmfaund'id] adj あ然とした azén tò shita

dummy [dʌm'i:] n (tailor's model) 人台 jińdai; (TECH, COMM: mock-up) 模型 mokéi; (BRIT: for baby) おしゃぶり o-shábùri

♦adj (bullet) 模擬の mógì no; (firm) ダミーの dámì no

dump [dʌmp] n (also: **rubbish dump**) ごみ捨て場 gomísuteba; (inf: place) いやな場所 iyá na bashò

♦vt (put down) 落す otósù; (get rid of) 捨てる sutérù; (COMPUT: data) 打ち出す uchídasù, ダンプする dáǹpu suru

dumpling [dʌmp'liŋ] n (CULIN: with meat etc) 団子 dańgo

dumpy [dʌmp'i:] adj (person) ずんぐりした zuńgurì shita

dunce [dʌns] n (SCOL) 劣等生 rettósei

dune [du:n] n (in desert, on beach) 砂丘 sakyū

dung [dʌŋ] n (AGR, ZOOL) ふん fúǹ

dungarees [dʌŋgəri:z'] npl オーバーオール ōbāòru

dungeon [dʌn'dʒən] n 地下ろう chikárō

duo [du:'ou] n (gen, MUS) ペア péà

dupe [du:p] n (victim) かも kámò

♦vt (trick) だます damásù

duplex [du:p'leks] (US) n (house) 2世帯用住宅 nisétaiyōjūtaku; (apartment) 複層式アパート fukúsōushikiapàto

duplicate [n du:'plikit vb du:'plikeit] n (of document, key etc) 複製 fukúsei

♦vt (copy) 複製する fukúsei suru; (photocopy) ...のコピーを取る ...no kópì wo torù; (repeat) 再現する saígen suru

in duplicate 2部で nfbù de

duplicity [du:plis'əti:] n (deceit) いかさま ikásama

durable [du:r'əbəl] adj (goods, materials) 丈夫な jōbu na

duration [durei'ʃən] n (of process, event) 継続期間 keízokukikaǹ

duress [dures'] n: **under duress** (moral, physical) 強迫 kyóhaku

during [du:r'iŋ] prep ...の間に ...no aída ni

dusk [dʌsk] n 夕暮 yūgure

dust [dʌst] n ほこり hokóri

♦vt (furniture) ...のほこりを拭く ...no hokóri wò fukú; (cake etc): **to dust with** ...に...を振掛ける ...ni ...wo furíkakerù

dustbin [dʌst'bin] (BRIT) n ごみ箱 gomíbàko

duster [dʌs'tə:r] n (cloth) 雑きん zókin

dustman [dʌst'mæn] (pl **dustmen**) n ごみ収集人 gomíshūshūnin

dusty [dʌs'ti:] adj (road) ほこりっぽい hokórippoì; (furniture) ほこりだらけの hokóridaràke no

Dutch [dʌtʃ] adj オランダの oráńda no; (LING) オランダ語の orándagò no

♦n (LING) オランダ語 orándagò

♦npl: **the Dutch** オランダ人 orándajìn

to go Dutch (inf) 割勘にする waríkan ni surù

Dutchman/woman [dʌtʃ'mən/wumən] (pl **Dutchmen/Dutchwomen**) n オランダ人男性〔女性〕orándajin dańsei 〔joséì〕

dutiful [du:'tifəl] adj (son, daughter) 従順な jújun na

duty [du:'ti:] n (responsibility) 義務 gfmù; (tax) 税金 zeíkin

on/off duty (policeman, nurse) 当番〔非番〕で tóban〔hibán〕de

duty-free [du:'ti:fri:] adj (drink, cigarettes) 免税の meńzei no

duvet [du:'vei] (BRIT) n 掛布団 kakébutòn

dwarf [dwɔ:rf] (pl **dwarves**) n (person) 小人 kobíto; (animal, plant) わい小種 waíshōshù

♦vt 小さく見せる chíisaku misérù

dwarves [dwɔ:rvz] npl of **dwarf**

dwell [dwel] (pt, pp **dwelt**) vi (reside,

stay) 住む súmù

dwelling [dwel'iŋ] n (house) 住居 júkyò

dwell on vt fus (brood on) 長々と考える nagánaga tò kañgaerù

dwelt [dwelt] pt, pp of **dwell**

dwindle [dwin'dəl] vi (interest, attendance) 減る herù

dye [dai] n (for hair, cloth) 染料 señryò
♦vt 染める somérù

dying [dai'iŋ] adj (person, animal) 死に掛けている shiñkakatte irù

dyke [daik] (BRIT) n (wall) 堤防 teíbō

dynamic [dainæm'ik] adj (leader, force) 力強い chikárazuyoì

dynamite [dai'nəmait] n ダイナマイト daínamaìto

dynamo [dai'nəmou] n (ELEC) 発電機 hatsúdeñki, ダイナモ daínamo

dynasty [dai'nəsti:] n (family, period) 王朝 ốchō

dyslexia [dislek'si:ə] n 読書障害 dokúshoshōgai

E

E [i:] n (MUS: note) ホ音 hó-oñ; (: key) ホ調 hóchō

each [i:tʃ] adj (thing, person, idea etc) それぞれの soréezòre no
♦pron (each one) それぞれ soréezòre
each other 互いを(に) tagái wò (nì)
they hate each other 彼らは互いに憎み合っている kárèra wa tagái nì nikúmiatte irù
they have 2 books each 彼らはそれぞれ2冊の本を持っている kárèra wa soréezòre nísàtsu no hóñ wo motté irù

eager [i:'gə:r] adj (keen) 熱心な nesshíñ na
to be eager to do something 一生懸命に...をしたがっている isshókeñmei ni ... wo shitágatte irú
to be eager for とても...をほしがっている totémo ...wo hoshígatte irú

eagle [i:'gəl] n ワシ washí

ear [i:r] n (ANAT) 耳 mimí; (of corn) 穂 hố

earache [i:r'eik] n 耳の痛み mimí nò itámi

eardrum [i:r'drʌm] n 鼓膜 komáku

earl [ə:rl] (BRIT) n 伯爵 hakúshaku

earlier [ə:r'li:ə:r] adj (date, time, edition etc) 前の máè no
♦adv (leave, go etc) もっと早く móttó háyàku

early [ə:r'li:] adv (in day, month etc) 早く háyàku; (ahead of time) 早めに hayáme ni
♦adj (near the beginning: work, hours) 早朝の sốchō no; (Christians, settlers) 初期の shókì no; (sooner than expected: departure) 早めの hayáme no; (quick: reply) 早期の sốki no
an early death 早死に hayájinì
to have an early night 早めに寝る hayáme nì nérù
in the early/early in the spring 春先に harúsaki ni
in the early/early in the 19th century 19世紀の初めに júkyūseīki no hajíme ni

early retirement n 早めの引退 hayáme nő iñtai

earmark [i:r'ma:rk] vt: *to earmark (for)* (...に) 当てる (...ni) atérù

earn [ə:rn] vt (salary etc) 稼ぐ kaségù; (COMM: interest) 生む umú; (praise) 受ける ukérù

earnest [ə:r'nist] adj (wish, desire) 心からの kokórò kara no; (person, manner) 真剣な shiñken na
in earnest 真剣に shiñken ni

earnings [ə:r'niŋz] npl (personal) 収入 shứnyū; (of company etc) 収益 shốeki

earphones [i:r'founz] npl イヤホーン i-yáhòn

earring [i:r'riŋ] n イヤリング íyàringu

earshot [i:r'ʃɑːt] n: *within earshot* 聞える範囲に kikóerù hán-i ni

earth [ə:rθ] n (planet) 地球 chikyū; (land surface) 地面 jímèn; (soil) 土 tsuchí; (BRIT: ELEC) アース ãsu
♦vt (BRIT: ELEC) アースに落す āsu ni otósù

earthenware [ə:r'θənwe:r] n 土器 dốki

earthquake [ərθ'kweik] n 地震 jishín

earthy [ər'θi:] adj (fig: humor: vulgar) 下品な gehín na

ease [i:z] n (easiness) 容易さ yṓisà; (comfort) 楽 rakú
♦vt (lessen: problem, pain) 和らげる yawáragerù; (: tension) 緩和する kańwa suru

to ease something in/out ゆっくりと ...を入れる〔出す〕yukkúrì to ...wo irérù〔dásù〕

at ease! (MIL) 休め! yasúmè!

easel [i:'zəl] n 画架 gákà, イーゼル ízèru

ease off vi (lessen: wind) 弱まる yowámarù; (: rain) 小降りになる kobúri ni narù; (slow down) スピードを落とす supídò wo otósù

ease up vi = **ease off**

easily [i:'zili:] adv (with ease) 容易に yṓi ni; (in comfort) 楽に rakú ni

east [i:st] n (direction) 東 higáshi; (of country, town) 東部 tṓbù
♦adj (region) 東の higáshi no; (wind) 東からの higáshi karà no
♦adv 東に〔へ〕higáshi ni〔e〕

the East (Orient) 東洋 tṓyō; (POL) 東欧 tṓō, 東ヨーロッパ higáshi yōroppa

Easter [i:s'tər] n 復活祭 fukkátsusài, イースター ísutā

Easter egg n イースターエッグ ísutaeggù◇復活祭の飾り、プレゼントなどに使う色や模様を塗ったゆで卵 fukkátsusài no kazári, purézènto nádò ni tsukáu irò ya moyṓ wo nuttá yudétamàgo

easterly [i:s'tə:rli:] adj (to the east: direction, point) 東への higáshi e nò; (from the east: wind) 東からの higáshi karà no

eastern [i:s'tə:rn] adj (GEO) 東の higáshi no; (oriental) 東洋の tṓyō no; (communist) 東欧の tṓō no, 東ヨーロッパの higáshi yōroppa no

East Germany n 東ドイツ higáshi dóìtsu

eastward(s) [i:st'wə:rd(z)] adv 東へ higáshi e

easy [i:'zi:] adj (simple) 簡単な kańtan na; (relaxed) 寛いだ kutsúroìda; (comfortable) 楽な rakú na; (victim) だまされやすい damásareyasuì; (prey) 捕まりやすい tsukámariyasuì
♦adv: *to take it/things easy* (go slowly) 気楽にやる kiráku ni yarù; (not worry) 心配しない shiñpai shinaì; (rest) 休む yasúmù

easy chair n 安楽いす ańrakuisù

easy-going [i:'zi:gou'iŋ] adj 穏やかな odáyàka na

eat [i:t] (pt ate, pp eaten) vt (breakfast, lunch, food etc) 食べる tabérù
♦vi 食べる tabérù

eat away vt fus = **eat into**

eat into vt fus (metal) 腐食する fushóku suru; (savings) ...に食込む ...ni kuíkomù

eau de Cologne [ou' də kəloun'] n オーデコロン ódekoròn

eaves [i:vz] npl (of house) 軒 nokí

eavesdrop [i:vz'drɑːp] vi: *to eavesdrop (on)* (person, conversation) (...を) 盗み聞きする (...wo) nusúmigiki suru

ebb [eb] n (of sea, tide) 引く事 hikú kotó
♦vi (tide, sea) 引く hikú; (fig: also: **ebb away**: strength, feeling) 段々なくなる dańdan nakúnaru

ebony [eb'əni:] n (wood) 黒たん kokútan

EC [i:'si:'] n abbr (= European Community) 欧州共同体 ṓshūkyōdōtai

eccentric [iksen'trik] adj (choice, views) 風変りな fúgawarì na
♦n (person) 変り者 kawárimono

ecclesiastical [ikli:zi:æs'tikəl] adj 教会の kyṓkai no

echo [ek'ou] (pl echoes) n (of noise) こだま kodáma, 反響 hańkyō
♦vt (repeat) 繰返す kuríkaesù
♦vi (sound) 反響する hańkyō suru; (place) ...で鳴り響く ...de naríhibikù

echoes [ek'ouz] npl of **echo**

éclair [ikler'] n (cake) エクレア ekúrea

eclipse [iklips'] n (also: **eclipse of the sun**) 日食 nisshóku; (also: **eclipse of the moon**) 月食 gesshóku

ecology [ikɑːl'ədʒi:] n (environment) 環境 kańkyō, エコロジー ekórojì; (SCOL) 生態学 seítaigàku

economic [i:kənɑːm'ik] adj (system, history) 経済の keízai no; (BRIT: profitable: business etc) もうかる mókarù

economical [i:kənə:m'ikəl] *adj* (system, car, machine) 経済的な keízaiteki na; (person) 倹約な keñ-yaku na

economics [i:kənə:m'iks] *n* (SCOL) 経済学 keízaigàku
♦*npl* (of project, situation) 経済問題 keízaimoñdai

economist [ikɑ:n'əmist] *n* 経済学者 keízaigakùsha

economize [ikɑ:n'əmaiz] *vi* (make savings) 節約する setsúyaku suru

economy [ikɑ:n'əmi:] *n* (of country) 経済 keízai; (financial prudence) 節約 setsúyaku

economy class *n* (AVIAT) エコノミークラス ekónomìkuràsu

economy size *n* (COMM) お買い得サイズ o-káidoku saìzu

ecstasy [ek'stəsi:] *n* (rapture) 狂喜 kyó-ki, エクスタシー ekúsutashì

ecstatic [ekstæt'ik] *adj* (welcome, reaction) 熱烈な netsúretsu na; (person) 無我夢中になった múgàmuchú ni nattà

ecumenical [ekju:men'ikəl] *adj* 超宗派の chóshùha no

eczema [ek'səmə] *n* (MED) 湿しん shisshín

edge [edʒ] *n* (border: of lake, table, chair etc) 縁 fuchí; (of knife etc) 刃 há
♦*vt* (trim) 縁取りする fuchídori suru
on edge (*fig*) = **edgy**
to edge away from じりじり...から離れる jírìjiri ...kara hanárerù

edgeways [edʒ'weiz] *adv*: *he couldn't get a word in edgeways* 何一つ発言出来なかった nanihitótsu hatsúgen dekinakattà

edgy [edʒ'i:] *adj* (nervous, agitated) いらいらした fràira shita

edible [ed'əbəl] *adj* (mushroom, plant) 食用の shokúyō no

edict [i:'dikt] *n* (order) 政令 seírei

edifice [ed'əfis] *n* (building, structure) 大建造物 daíkenzōbùtsu

Edinburgh [ed'ənbə:rə] *n* エジンバラ ejínbara

edit [ed'it] *vt* (text, report) 校正する kósei suru; (book, film, newspaper etc) 編集する heñshū suru

edition [idiʃ'ən] *n* (of book) 版 háñ; (of newspaper, magazine) 号 gó; (TV, RADIO) 回 kaí

editor [ed'itə:r] *n* (of newspaper) 編集局長 heñshūkyokuchó, デスク désùku; (of magazine) 編集長 heñshūchò; (of column: foreign/political editor) 編集主任 heñshūshuniñ; (of book) 編集者 heñshūsha

editorial [editɔ:r'i:əl] *adj* (staff, policy, control) 編集の heñshū no
♦*n* (of newspaper) 社説 shasétsu

educate [edʒ'u:keit] *vt* (teach) 教育する kyóiku suru; (instruct) ...に教える ...ni oshíerù

education [edʒu:kei'ʃən] *n* (schooling, teaching) 教育 kyóiku; (knowledge, culture) 教養 kyóyō

educational [edʒu:kei'ʃənəl] *adj* (institution, policy etc) 教育の kyóiku no; (experience, toy) 教育的な kyóikuteki na

EEC [i:i:si:'] *n abbr* (= *European Economic Community*) 欧州経済共同体 ó-shūkeizaikyōdótai

eel [i:l] *n* ウナギ unági

eerie [i:'ri:] *adj* (strange, mysterious) 不気味な bukími na

effect [ifekt'] *n* (result, consequence) 結果 kekká; (impression: of speech, picture etc) 効果 kóka
♦*vt* (repairs) 行う okónau; (savings etc) ...に成功する ...ni seíkō suru
to take effect (law) 実施される jisshí sarerù; (drug) 効き始める kikíhajimerù
in effect 要するに yó surù ni

effective [ifek'tiv] *adj* (successful) 効果的な kókateki na; (actual: leader, command) 実際の jissái no

effectively [ifek'tivli:] *adv* (successfully) 効果的に kókateki ni; (in reality) 実際には jissái ni wa

effectiveness [ifek'tivnis] *n* (success) 有効性 yúkōsei

effeminate [ifem'ənit] *adj* (boy, man) 女々しい memēshiì

effervescent [efə:rves'ənt] *adj* (drink) 炭酸ガス入りの tańsangasuirı̂ no

efficacy [ef'ikəsi:] *n* (effectiveness) 有効性 yūkōsei

efficiency [ifif'ənsi:] *n* (of person, organization) 能率 nôritsu; (of machine) 効率 kôritsu

efficient [ifif'ənt] *adj* (person, organization) 能率的な nôritsuteki na; (machine) 効率の良い kôritsu no yoî

effigy [ef'idʒi:] *n* (image) 像 zō

effort [ef'ə:rt] *n* (endeavor) 努力 dôryòku; (determined attempt) 試み kokóromì, 企て kuwádate; (physical/mental exertion) 苦労 kúrò

effortless [ef'ə:rtlis] *adj* (achievement) 楽な rakú nà; (style) ごく自然な gôkù shizén na

effrontery [ifrʌn'tə:ri:] *n* (cheek, nerve) ずうずうしさ zûzūshisà

effusive [ifju:'siv] *adj* (handshake, welcome) 熱烈な netsúretsu na

e.g. [i:dʒi:'] *adv abbr* (= *exempli gratia*) 例えば tatóèba

egg [eg] *n* 卵 tamágò
hard-boiled/soft-boiled egg 堅ゆで〔半熟〕卵 katáyude〔hańjuku〕tamágo

eggcup [eg'kʌp] *n* エッグカップ eggúkappù

egg on *vt* (in fight etc) そそのかす sosónokasù

eggplant [eg'plænt] *(esp US)* *n* (aubergine) ナス násù

eggshell [eg'ʃel] *n* 卵の殻 tamágò no karấ

ego [i:'gou] *n* (self-esteem) 自尊心 jisóñshin

egotism [i:'gətizəm] *n* 利己主義 rikóshugì

egotist [i:'gətist] *n* 利己主義者 rikóshugishà, エゴイスト egôisùto

Egypt [i:'dʒipt] *n* エジプト ejíputo

Egyptian [idʒip'ʃən] *adj* エジプトの ejíputo no
♦*n* エジプト人 ejíputojìn

eiderdown [ai'də:rdaun] *n* (quilt) 羽布団 hanébutòn

eight [eit] *num* 八（の）hachí(no), 八つ

（の）yattsú no

eighteen [ei'ti:n'] *num* 十八（の）júhachi (no)

eighth [eitθ] *num* 第八の dáìhachi no

eighty [ei'ti:] *num* 八十（の）hachíjū(no)

Eire [e:r'ə] *n* アイルランド aíruratdo

either [i:'ðə:r] *adj* (one or other) どちらかの dôchìraka no; (both, each) 両方の ryôhò no
♦*pron*: **either (of them)** どちらも...ない dôchìra mo ...nai
♦*adv* ...も...ない ...mo ...nâî
♦*conj*: **either yes or no** はいかいいえかhâî ka iíè kâ
on either side 両側に ryôgawa ni
I don't like either どちらも好きじゃない dôchìra mo sukí ja naî
no, I don't either いいえ, 私もしないiíè, watákushi mò shinâî

eject [idʒekt'] *vt* (object) 放出する hôshutsu suru; (tenant) 立ちのかせる tachínokaserù; (gatecrasher etc) 追出す oídasù

eke [i:k]: **to eke out** *vt* (make last) 間に合せる ma ní awaserù

elaborate [*n* ilæb'ə:rit *vb* ilæb'ə:reit] *adj* (complex: network, plan, ritual) 複雑な fukúzatsu na
♦*vt* (expand) 拡張する kakúchō suru; (refine) 洗練する seńren suru
♦*vi*: **to elaborate (on)** (idea, plan etc) (...を) 詳しく説明する (...wo) kuwáshikù setsúmei suru

elapse [ilæps'] *vi* (time) 過ぎる sugírù

elastic [ilæs'tik] *n* (material) ゴムひも gomúhimo
♦*adj* (stretchy) 弾力性のある dańryokusei no arù; (adaptable) 融通の利く yúzū no kikù

elastic band *(BRIT)* *n* 輪ゴム wagómu

elated [ilei'tid] *adj*: **to be elated** 大喜びになっている ôyoròkobi ni natté irù

elation [ilei'ʃən] *n* (happiness, excitement) 大喜び ôyoròkobi

elbow [el'bou] *n* (ANAT: *also* of sleeve) ひじ hijî

elder [el'də:r] *adj* (brother, sister etc) 年上の toshíue no

◆*n* (tree) ニワトコ niwátoko; (older person: *gen pl*) 年上の人々 toshíue no hitóbìto

elderly [el'də:rli:] *adj* (old) 年寄の toshíyorì no

◆*npl: the elderly* 老人 rójin

eldest [el'dist] *adj* 最年長の saínenchō no

◆*n* 最年長の人 saínenchō no hitó

the eldest child/son/daughter 長子〔長男, 長女〕chōshì〔chōnàn, chōjò〕

elect [ilekt'] *vt* (government, representative, spokesman etc) 選出する senshutsu suru

◆*adj: the president elect* 次期大統領 jíkìdaítōryò ◇当選したものの、まだ就任していない人について言う tōsen shita mono no, mádà shúnin shite inaì hitó nì tsúìte iú

to elect to do (choose) …する事にする …surú kotó ni suru

election [ilek'ʃən] *n* (voting) 選挙 sénkyo; (installation) 当選 tōsen

electioneering [ilekʃəni:'riŋ] *n* (campaigning) 選挙運動 senkyoundō

elector [ilek'tə:r] *n* (voter) 有権者 yúkensha

electoral [ilek'tə:rəl] *adj* (register, roll) 有権者の yúkensha no

electorate [ilek'tə:rit] *n* (of constituency, country) 有権者 yúkensha ◇総称 sóshō

electric [ilek'trik] *adj* (machine, current, power) 電気の dénki no

electrical [ilek'trikəl] *adj* (appliance, system, energy) 電気の dénki no

electric blanket *n* 電気毛布 denkimófu

electric chair (*US*) *n* 電気いす denkíìsu

electric fire *n* 電気ヒーター denkihītā

electrician [ilektriʃ'ən] *n* 電気屋 denkíyà

electricity [ilektris'əti:] *n* 電気 dénki

electrify [ilek'trəfai] *vt* (fence) 帯電させる taíden saserù; (rail network) 電化する denka suru; (audience) ぎょっとさせる gyóttò saserù

electrocute [ilek'trəkju:t] *vt* 感電死させる kandenshi saserù

electrode [ilek'troud] *n* 電極 denkyoku

electron [ilek'tra:n] *n* (PHYSICS) 電子 denshi

electronic [ilektra:n'ik] *adj* (device, equipment) 電子の dénshi no

electronic mail *n* 電子郵便 denshiyúbin

electronics [ilektra:n'iks] *n* (industry, technology) 電子工学 denshikōgaku

elegance [el'əgəns] *n* (of person, building) 優雅さ yúgàsa, エレガンス érègansu; (of idea, plan) 見事さ migótosà

elegant [el'əgənt] *adj* (person, building) 優雅な yúgà na; (idea, plan) 洗練された senren saretà

element [el'əmənt] *n* (part: of whole, job, process) 要素 yōso; (CHEM) 元素 genso; (of heater, kettle etc) ヒーター素子 hītāsoshi

elementary [elimen'tə:ri:] *adj* (basic) 基本的な kihónteki na; (primitive) 原始的な genshiteki na; (school, education) 初等の shotō no

elephant [el'əfənt] *n* ゾウ zō

elevation [eləvei'ʃən] *n* (raising, promotion) 向上 kójō; (height) 海抜 káìbatsu

elevator [el'əveitə:r] *n* (*US*: lift) エレベーター erébētā

eleven [ilev'ən] *num* 十一 (の) júichi no

elevenses [ilev'ənziz] (*BRIT*) *npl* (coffeebreak) 午前のおやつ gózen no o-yátsu

eleventh [ilev'ənθ] *num* 第十一の dáìjúichi no

elf [elf] (*pl* **elves**) *n* 小妖精 shóyōsei

elicit [ilis'it] *vt: to elicit (from)* (information, response, reaction) (…から)…を引出す (…karà) …wò hikídasù

eligible [el'idʒəbəl] *adj* (qualified, suitable) 資格のある shikáku no arù; (man, woman) 好ましい結婚相手である konómashiì kekkón aìte de árù

to be eligible for something (qualified, suitable) …する資格がある …suru shikáku ga arù

eliminate [əlim'əneit] *vt* (eradicate: poverty, smoking) 無くす nakúsù; (candidate, team, contestant) 除外する jogái suru

elimination [əlimənei'ʃən] *n* (eradication) 根絶 koňzetsu; (of candidate, team etc) 除外 jogái

élite [ilí:t'] *n* エリート eríto

elm [elm] *n* (tree) ニレ nire; (wood) ニレ材 nirézai

elocution [eləkju:'ʃən] *n* 話術 wájutsu

elongated [ilɔ:ŋ'geitid] *adj* (body, shadow) 細長い hosónagaí

elope [iloup'] *vi* 駆落ちする kakéochi suru

elopement [iloup'mənt] *n* 駆落ち kakéochi

eloquence [el'əkwəns] *n* (of person, description, speech) 雄弁 yúben

eloquent [el'əkwənt] *adj* (person, description, speech) 雄弁な yúben na

else [els] *adv* (other) 外に hoká nì
  something else 外の物 hoká no monò
  somewhere else 外の場所 hoká no bashò
  everywhere else 外はどこも hoká wà dókò mo
  where else? 外にどこ? hoká nì dókò?
  there was little else to do 外にする事はなかった hoká nì suru kotò wa nákàtta
  nobody else spoke 外にだれもしゃべらなかった hoká nì daré mò shabéranakattà

elsewhere [els'we:r] *adv* (be) 外の所に hoká no tokorò ni; (go) 外の所へ hoká no tokorò e

elucidate [ilu:'sideit] *vt* (argument, point) 解明する kaímei suru

elude [ilu:d'] *vt* (subj: fact, idea: not realized) 気付かれない kizúkarenaì; (: : not remembered) 思い出せない omóidasenaì; (: : not understood) 理解されない ríkai sarénaì; (captor) ...から逃げる ...kara nigérù; (capture) 免れる manúgarerù

elusive [ilu:'siv] *adj* (person, animal) 見付けにくい mitsúkenikuì; (quality) 分かりにくい wakárinikuì

elves [elvz] *npl of* elf

emaciated [imei'ʃi:eitid] *adj* (person, animal) 衰弱した suíjaku shita

emanate [em'əneit] *vi*: *to emanate from* (idea, feeling) ...から放たれる ...kara hanatárerù; (sound) ...から聞える ...kara kikóerù; (light) ...から放射される ...kara hósha sarerù

emancipate [imæn'səpeit] *vt* (poor, slave, women) 解放する kaíhō suru

emancipation [imænsəpei'ʃən] *n* (of poor, slaves, women) 解放 kaíhō

embankment [embæŋk'mənt] *n* (of road, railway) 土手 doté; (of river) 堤防 teíbō

embargo [embɑ:r'gou] (*pl* **embargoes**) *n* (POL, COMM) 通商停止 tsúshōteíshi

embark [embɑ:rk'] *vi* (NAUT): *to embark (on)* (...に) 乗船する (...ni) jósen suru
  ♦*vt* (passengers, cargo) 乗せる nosérù
  to embark on (journey) ...に出発する ...ni shuppátsu surù; (task, course of action) ...に乗出す ...ni norídasù

embarkation [embɑ:rkei'ʃən] *n* (of people) 乗船 jósen; (of cargo) 船積み funázumi

embarrass [embær'əs] *vt* (emotionally) 恥をかかせる hají wò kakáserù; (politician, government) 困らせる komáraserù

embarrassed [embær'əst] *adj* (laugh, silence) 極り悪そうな kimáriwarusó na

embarrassing [embær'əsiŋ] *adj* (statement, situation, moment) 恥ずかしい hazúkashiì

embarrassment [embær'əsmənt] *n* (shame) 恥 hají; (embarrassing problem) 厄介な問題 yákkài na moñdai

embassy [em'bəsi:] *n* (diplomats) 使節団 shisétsudàn; (building) 大使館 taíshikàn

embedded [embed'id] *adj* (object) 埋め込まれた umékomaretà

embellish [embel'iʃ] *vt* (place, dress) 飾る kazáru; (account) 潤色する juñshoku suru

embers [em'bə:rz] *npl*: *the embers (of the fire)* 残り火 nokóribì

embezzle [embez'əl] *vt* (LAW) 横領する óryō suru

embezzlement [embez'əlmənt] *n* 横領 óryō

embitter [embit'ə:r] *vt* (fig: sour) 世の中を憎ませる yo nó nàka wo nikúmaserù

emblem [em'bləm] *n* (design) 標章 hyṓshō, マーク māku; (symbol) 象徴 shṓchō

embody [əmbɑ:d'i:] *vt* (idea, principle) 現す aráwasù; (features: include, contain) 含む fukúmù

embossed [embɔ:st'] *adj* (design, word) 浮き出しの ukídashi no

embrace [embreis'] *vt* (hug) 抱く dakú; (include) 含む fukúmù
♦*vi* (hug) 抱合う dakíaù
♦*n* (hug) 抱擁 hṓyō

embroider [embrɔi'də:r] *vt* (cloth) 刺しゅうする shishū́ suru

embroidery [embrɔi'də:ri:] *n* 刺しゅう shishū́

embryo [em'bri:ou] *n* (BIO) はい haí

emerald [em'ə:rəld] *n* エメラルド emérarùdo

emerge [imə:rdʒ'] *vi*: **to emerge (from)** (...から) 出て来る (...kara) déte kuru; (fact: from discussion etc) (...で) 明らかになる (...de) akíràka ni nárù; (new idea, industry, society) 現れる aráwarerù
to emerge from sleep 目が覚める mé gà samérù
to emerge from prison 釈放される shakúhō sarerù

emergency [imə:r'dʒənsi:] *n* (crisis) 非常時 hijṓjì
in an emergency 緊急の場合 kíñkyu no baàí
state of emergency 緊急事態 kíñkyūjitài

emergency cord (*US*) *n* 非常の際に引くコード hijṓ no saí ni hikú kòdo

emergency exit *n* 非常口 hijṓgùchi

emergency landing *n* (AVIAT) 不時着陸 fujíchakùriku

emergency services *npl* (fire, police, ambulance) 非常時のサービス機関 hijṓjì no sábisukikàn

emergent [imə:r'dʒənt] *adj* (nation) 最近独立した saíkin dokùritsu shità; (group) 最近創立された saíkin sṓritsu saretà

emery board [em'ə:ri:-] *n* つめやすり tsuméyasùri ◊ボール紙製の物を指す bṓrugamisei no monò wo sásù

emigrant [em'əgrənt] *n* (from native country) 移住者 ijū́shà

emigrate [em'əgreit] *vi* (from native country) 移住する ijū́ suru

emigration [eməgrei'ʃən] *n* 移住 ijū́

eminent [em'ənənt] *adj* (scientist, writer) 著名な choméi na

emission [imiʃ'ən] *n* (of gas) 放出 hṓshutsu; (of radiation) 放射 hōsha

emit [imit'] *vt* (smoke, smell, sound) 出す dásù; (light, heat) 放射する hṓsha suru

emotion [imou'ʃən] *n* 感情 kañjō

emotional [imou'ʃənəl] *adj* (needs, exhaustion, person, issue etc) 感情的な kañjōteki na; (scene etc) 感動的な kañdōteki na

emotive [imou'tiv] *adj* (subject, language) 感情に訴える kañjō nì uttáerù

emperor [em'pə:rə:r] *n* (gen) 皇帝 kṓtei; (of Japan) 天皇 teñnō

emphases [em'fəsi:z] *npl of* **emphasis**

emphasis [em'fəsis] (*pl* **emphases**) *n* (importance) 重点 jū́ten; (stress) 強調 kyṓchō

emphasize [em'fəsaiz] *vt* (word, point) 強調する kyṓchō suru; (feature) 浮彫にする ukfbori ni surù

emphatic [əmfæt'ik] *adj* (statement, denial, manner, person) 断固とした dáñko to shita

emphatically [əmfæt'ikli:] *adv* (forcefully) 断固として dáñko to shité; (certainly) 絶対に zéttái ni

empire [em'paiə:r] *n* (*also fig*) 帝国 teíkoku

empirical [empir'ikəl] *adj* (knowledge, study) 経験的な keíkenteki na

employ [emplɔi'] *vt* (workforce, person) 雇う yatóù; (tool, weapon) 使用する shiyṓ suru

employee [emplɔi'i:] *n* 雇用人 koyṓnìn

employer [emplɔi'ə:r] *n* 雇い主 yatóinùshi

employment [emplɔi'mənt] *n* (work) 就職 shū́shoku

employment agency *n* 就職あっ旋会社 shū́shokuassengaìsha

empower [empau'ə:r] *vt*: **to empower**

someone to do something (LAW, ADMIN) ...に...する権限を与える ...ni ...suru keñgen wò atáerù

empress [em'pris] *n* (woman emperor) 女帝 jotéi; (wife of emperor) 皇后 kōgō

emptiness [emp'ti:nis] *n* (of area, region etc) 何もない事 nanî mo naî kotó; (of life etc) むなしさ munáshìsa

empty [emp'ti:] *adj* (container) 空の kará no, 空っぽの karáppò no; (place, street) だれもいない darê mó inaî; (house, room, space) 空きの akî no
♦*vt* 空にする kará ni suru
♦*vi* (house, container) 空になる kará nì nárù; (liquid) 注ぐ sosógù

an empty threat こけおどし kokéodòshi

an empty promise 空約束 karáyakùsoku

empty-handed [empti:hæn'did] *adj* 手ぶらの tebúra no

emulate [em'jəleit] *vt* (hero, idol) まねる manérù

emulsion [imʌl'ʃən] *n* (liquid) 乳剤 nyúzai; (*also:* **emulsion paint**) 水溶ペンキ suíyōpeñki

enable [enei'bəl] *vt*: *to enable someone to do* (permit, allow) ...が...する事を許可する ...ga ...surú kotò wo kyőkà suru; (make possible) ...が...する事を可能にする ...ga ...surú kotò wo kanő ni surù

enact [enækt'] *vt* (law) 制定する seítei suru; (play, role) 上演する jően suru

enamel [enæm'əl] *n* (for decoration) エナメル enámerù; (*also:* **enamel paint**) エナメルペイント enámerupeìnto; (of tooth) エナメル質 enámerushìtsu

enamored [enæm'ə:rd] *adj*: *to be enamored of* (person, pastime, idea, belief) ...に惚れる ...ni horérù

encased [enkeist'] *adj*: *encased in* (plaster, shell) ...に覆われた ...ni őwareta

enchant [entʃænt'] *vt* (delight) 魅了する miryő suru

enchanted [entʃæn'tid] *adj* (castle, island) 魔法の mahő no

enchanting [entʃæn'tiŋ] *adj* (appearance, behavior, person) 魅力的な miryő-

encircle [ensə:r'kəl] *vt* (place, prisoner) 囲む kakómù

encl. *abbr* (= enclosed) 同封の dőfū no

enclave [en'kleiv] *n* 飛び地 tobíchi

enclose [enklouz'] *vt* (land, space) 囲む kakómù; (object) 閉じ込める tojíkomerù; (letter etc): *to enclose (with)* (...に) 同封する (...ni) dőfū suru

please find enclosed ...を同封します ...wo dőfū shimasù

enclosure [enklou'ʒə:r] *n* (area of land) 囲い kakói

encompass [enkʌm'pəs] *vt* (include: subject, measure) 含む fukúmù

encore [ɑːŋ'kɔːr] *excl* アンコール añkőru
♦*n* (THEATER) アンコール añkőru

encounter [enkaun'tə:r] *n* (with person etc) 出会い deái; (with problem etc) 直面 chokúmen
♦*vt* (person) ...に出会う ...ni deâù; (new experience, problem) 直面する chokúmen suru

encourage [enkə:r'idʒ] *vt* (person): *to encourage someone (to do something)* (...する事を) ...に勧める (...surú kotò wo) ...ni susúmerù; (activity, attitude) 激励する gekírei suru; (growth, industry) 刺激する shigéki suru

encouragement [enkə:r'idʒmənt] *n* (to do something) 勧め susúme; (of activity, attitude) 激励 gekírei; (of growth, industry) 刺激 shigéki

encroach [enkroutʃ'] *vi*: *to encroach (up)on* (rights) ...を侵す ...wo okásù; (property) ...に侵入する ...ni shíñnyū suru; (time) ...の邪魔をする ...no jamá wo surù

encrusted [enkrʌs'tid] *adj*: *encrusted with* (gems) ...をちりばめられた ...wo chiríbameraretà; (snow, dirt) ...に覆われた ...ni őwareta

encumber [enkʌm'bə:r] *vt*: *to be encumbered with* (suitcase, baggage etc) ...が邪魔になっている ...ga jamá nì natté irù; (debts) ...を背負っている ...wo seőtte irù

encyclop(a)edia [ensaikləpi:'di:ə] *n* 百

...になってしまう ...ni natté shimaù

end [end] *n* (of period, event, book etc) 終り owári; (of table, street, line, rope) 端 hashí; (of town) 外れ hazúre; (of pointed object) 先 sakí; (aim) 目的 mokúteki

♦*vt* (finish) 終える oérù; (stop: activity, protest etc)

JPNや止める yamérù

♦*vi* (situation, activity, period etc) 終る owárù

in the end 仕舞いには shimái ni wà

on end (object) 縦になって táte ni natté

to stand on end (hair) よだつ yodátsù

for hours on end ぶっ続けで何時間も buttsúzuke dè nañjikàn mo

endanger [endein'dʒər] *vt* (lives, prospects) 危険にさらす kikén nì sarásù

endearing [endiːr'iŋ] *adj* (personality, conduct) 愛敬のある aíkyo no arù

endeavor [endev'əːr] (*BRIT* **endeavour**) *n* (attempt) 試み kokóromi; (effort) 努力 dóryoku

♦*vi: to endeavor to do* (attempt) ...しようとする ...shiyó tò surù; (strive) ...しようと努力する ...shiyó tò dóryokù suru

endemic [endem'ik] *adj* (poverty, disease) 地方特有の chihótokuyū no

ending [en'diŋ] *n* (of book, film, play etc) 結末 ketsúmatsu; (LING) 語尾 góbì

endive [en'daiv] *n* (curly) エンダイブ eñdaìbu; (smooth: chicory) チコリ chikórì

endless [end'lis] *adj* (argument, search) 果てし無い hatéshinaì; (forest, beach) 延々と続く eñ-en tò tsuzúkù

endorse [endɔːrs'] *vt* (check) ...に裏書きする ...ni urágaki suru; (approve: proposal, plan, candidate) 推薦する suísen suru

endorsement [endɔːrs'mənt] *n* (approval) 推薦 suísen; (*BRIT*: on driving licence) 違反記録 ihánkiròku

endow [endau'] *vt* (provide with money) ...に金を寄付する ...ni kané wò kifú suru

to be endowed with (talent, quality) ...の持主である ...no mochínùshi de árù

end up *vi: to end up in* (place) ...に行ってしまう ...ni itté shimaù; (condition)

endurance [enduːr'əns] *n* (stamina) 耐久力 taíkyūryòku; (patience) 忍耐強さ niñtaizuÿòsa

endure [enduːr'] *vt* (bear: pain, suffering) 耐える taérù

♦*vi* (last: friendship, love etc) 長続きする nagátsuzùki suru

an enduring work of art 不朽の名作 fukyū no meísaku

enemy [en'əmiː] *adj* (forces, strategy) 敵の tekí no

♦*n* 敵 tekí

energetic [enəːrdʒet'ik] *adj* (person, activity) 精力的な seíryokuteki na

energy [en'əːrdʒiː] *n* (strength, drive) 精力 seíryoku; (power: nuclear energy etc) エネルギー enérùgī

enforce [enfɔːrs'] *vt* (LAW) 実施する jisshí suru

engage [engeidʒ'] *vt* (attention, interest) 引く hikú; (employ: consultant, lawyer) 雇う yatóù; (AUT: clutch) つなぐ tsunágù

♦*vi* (TECH) 掛る kakárù

to engage in (commerce, study, research etc) ...に従事する ...ni jūji suru

to engage someone in conversation ...に話し掛ける ...ni hanáshikakerù

engaged [engeidʒd'] *adj* (betrothed) 婚約している koñ-yaku shite irù; (*BRIT*: busy, in use) 使用中 shiyóchū

to get engaged 婚約する koñ-yaku suru

engaged tone (*BRIT*) *n* (TEL) 話し中の信号音 hanáshichū no shiñgðon

engagement [engeidʒ'mənt] *n* (appointment) 約束 yakúsoku; (booking: for musician, comedian etc) 仕事 shigóto; (to marry) 婚約 koñ-yaku

engagement ring *n* 婚約指輪 koñ-yaku yubíwa, エンゲージリング eñgējiriñgu

engaging [engei'dʒiŋ] *adj* (personality, trait) 愛敬のある aíkyo no arù

engender [endʒen'dəːr] *vt* (feeling, sense) 生む umú

engine [en'dʒən] *n* (AUT) エンジン éñjin; (RAIL) 機関車 kikáñsha

engine driver n (RAIL) 運転手 uñteñshu

engineer [endʒəniːr'] n (designer) 技師 gíshì; (BRIT: for repairs) 修理工 shúrikō; (US: RAIL) 運転手 uñteñshu; (on ship) 機関士 kikáñshi

engineering [endʒəniːr'iŋ] n (science) 工学 kōgaku; (design, construction: of roads, bridges) 建設 keñsetsu; (: of cars, ships, machines) 製造 seízō

England [iŋ'glənd] n イングランド íñgurando

English [iŋ'gliʃ] adj イングランドの íñgurando no; (LING) 英語の eígo no
♦n (LING) 英語 eígo
♦npl: **the English** イングランド人 iñgurandojíñ ◇総称 sōshō

English Channel n: **the English Channel** イギリス海峡 igírisukaíkyō

Englishman/woman [iŋ'gliʃmən/wumən] (pl **Englishmen/women**) n イングランド人男性〔女性〕 íñgurandojin dañsei〔jōsei〕

engraving [engrei'viŋ] n (picture, print) 版画 hañga

engrossed [engroust'] adj: **engrossed in** (book, program) ...に夢中になった ...ni muchū ni nattá

engulf [engʌlf'] vt (subj: fire) 巻込む makíkomù; (water) 飲込む nomíkomù; (: panic, fear) 襲う osóù

enhance [enhæns'] vt (enjoyment, reputation) 高める takámerù; (beauty) 増す masú

enigma [enig'mə] n (mystery) なぞ nazó

enigmatic [enigmæt'ik] adj (smile) なぞめいた nazómeìta; (person) 得体の知れない etái no shirenaí

enjoy [endʒɔi'] vt (like) ...が好きである ...ga sukí de arù; (take pleasure in) 楽しむ tanóshimù; (have benefit of: health, fortune, success) ...に恵まれる ...ni megúmarerù
to enjoy oneself 楽しむ tanóshimù

enjoyable [endʒɔi'əbəl] adj (pleasant) 楽しい tanóshiì

enjoyment [endʒɔi'mənt] n (feeling of pleasure) 楽しさ tanóshìsa; (activity) 楽

しみ tanóshimì]

enlarge [enlɑːrdʒ'] vt (size, scope) 拡大する kakúdai suru; (PHOT) 引伸ばす hikínobasù
♦vi: **to enlarge on** (subject) 詳しく話す kuwáshikù hanásù

enlargement [enlɑːrdʒ'mənt] n (PHOT) 引伸ばし hikínobashi

enlighten [enlait'ən] vt (inform) ...に教える ...ni oshíerù

enlightened [enlait'ənd] adj (person, policy, system) 聡明な sōmei na

enlightenment [enlait'ənmənt] n: **the Enlightenment** (HISTORY) 啓もう運動 keímōuñdō

enlist [enlist'] vt (soldier) 入隊させる nyútai saserù; (person) ...の助けを借りる ...no tasúke wò karírù; (support, help) 頼む tanómù
♦vi: **to enlist in** (army, navy etc) ...に入隊する ...ni nyútai suru

enmity [en'miti:] n (hostility) 恨み urámi

enormity [inɔːr'miti:] n (of problem, danger) 物すごさ monósugòsa

enormous [inɔːr'məs] adj (size, amount) 巨大な kyodái na; (delight, pleasure, success etc) 大きな ōkìna

enough [inʌf'] adj (time, books, people etc) 十分な júbuñ na
♦pron 十分 júbuñ
♦adv: **big enough** 十分に大きい júbuñ ni ōkìì
he has not worked enough 彼の努力が足りない kárè no dóryòku ga tarínaì
have you got enough? 足りましたか tarímashìta ká
enough to eat 食べ物が足りる tabémonò ga tarírù
enough! もういい! mō iì!
that's enough, thanks もう沢山です. 有難う. mō takusañ desu. arígàtō.
I've had enough of him 彼にはもううんざりだ kárè ni wa mō uñzari dá
... which, funnily/oddly enough ... おかしいけれども、それは... okáshii kerèdomo, soré wa ...

enquire [enkwai'əːr] vt, vi = **inquire**

enrage [enreidʒ'] vt (anger, madden) 激

怒させる gékìdo saseru

enrich [enritʃ'] vt (morally, spiritually) 豊かにする yútàka ni suru; (financially) 金持にする kanémochi ni surù

enroll [enroul'] (BRIT: **enrol**) vt (at school, university) 入学させる nyûgaku saserù; (on course) 登録する tôroku suru; (in club etc) 入会させる nyúkai saserù

♦vi (at school, university) 入学する nyûgaku suru; (on course) 参加手続きをする sañkatetsuzùki wo suru; (in club etc) 入会する nyúkai suru

enrollment [enroul'mənt] (BRIT: **enrolment**) n (registration) 登録 tôroku

en route [ɑːn ruːt'] adv (on the way) 途中で tochû dè

ensue [ensuː'] vi (follow) ...の結果として起る ...no kekká toshitè okórù

ensure [enʃuːr'] vt (result, safety) 確実にする kakújitsu ni surù

entail [enteil'] vt (involve) 要する yô suru

entangled [entæŋ'gəld] adj: **to become entangled (in)** (in net, rope etc) ...に絡まる ...ni karámarù

enter [en'tər] vt (room, club) ...に入る ...ni hâīru; (race, competition) ...に参加する ...ni sañka suru, ...に出場する ...ni shutsújō suru; (someone for a competition) ...に...の参加を申込む ...ni ...no sañka wò mốshikomù; (write down) 記入する kinyû suru; (COMPUT: data) 入力する nyúryòku suru

♦vi (come or go in) 入る hâīru

enter for vt fus (race, competition, examination) ...に参加を申込む ...ni sañka wò mốshikomù

enter into vt fus (discussion, correspondence, negotiations) 始める hajímerù; (agreement) 結ぶ musúbù

enterprise [en'tərpraiz] n (company, business) 企業 kigyố; (undertaking) 企画 kikáku; (initiative) 進取の気 shíñshu no ki

free enterprise 自由企業 jiyúkigyố

private enterprise (private company) 民間企業 miñkankigyố, 私企業 shikígyố

enterprising [en'tərpraiziŋ] adj (adventurous) 進取の気に富んだ shíñshu no ki ni tôñda

entertain [entəːrtein'] vt (amuse) 楽しませる tanóshimaserù; (invite: guest) 接待する séttai suru; (idea, plan) 考える kañgaerù

entertainer [entəːrtein'əːr] n (TV etc) 芸能人 geínojìn

entertaining [entəːrtei'niŋ] adj 面白い omóshiroì

entertainment [entəːrtein'mənt] n (amusement) 娯楽 goráku; (show) 余興 yokyố

enthralled [enθrɔːld'] adj (engrossed, captivated) 魅せられた misératetà

enthusiasm [enθuː'ziːæzəm] n (eagerness) 熱心さ nesshíñsa

enthusiast [enθuː'ziːæst] n (fan) マニア mánìa

enthusiastic [enθuːziːæs'tik] adj (excited, eager) 熱心な nesshíñ na

to be enthusiastic about ...に夢中になっている ...ni muchú nì natté irù

entice [entais'] vt (lure, tempt) 誘惑する yúwaku suru

entire [entai'əːr] adj (whole) 全体の zeñtai no

entirely [entaiəːr'liː] adv (completely) 全く mattákù

entirety [entai'əːrtiː] n: **in its entirety** 全体に zeñtai ni

entitle [entait'əl] vt: **to entitle someone to something** ...に...に対する権利を与える ...ni ...ni taísùru keñri wò atáerù

entitled [entait'əld] adj (book, film etc) ...という題の ...to iú daì no

to be entitled to do (be allowed) ...する権利がある ...suru kéñri ga árù

entity [en'titiː] n 物 monó

entourage [ɑːntuːrɑːʒ'] n (of celebrity, politician) 取巻き連 torímakireñ

entrails [en'treilz] npl (ANAT, ZOOL) 内臓 naízō

entrance [n en'trəns vb entræns'] n (way in) 入口 irígùchi; (arrival) 登場 tôjō

♦vt (enchant) 魅惑する miwáku suru

to gain entrance to (university, profession etc) ...に入る ...ni hâiru

entrance examination n 入学試験 nyúgakushikeñ, 入試 nyúshi

entrance fee n 入場料 nyújōryò

entrance ramp (US) n (AUT) 入口ランプ iríguchiraňpu

entrant [en'trənt] n (in race, competition etc) 参加者 sañkashà; (BRIT: in exam) 受験者 jukéñsha

entreat [entri:t'] vt (implore) 嘆願する tañgan suru

entrenched [entrentʃt'] adj (position, power) 固められた katámeraretà; (ideas) 定着した teíchakushità

entrepreneur [ɑːntrəprənəːr'] n (COMM) 企業家 kigyóka

entrust [entrʌst'] vt: **to entrust something to someone** ...を...に預ける ...wo ...ni azúkerù

entry [en'tri:] n (way in) 入口 iríguchi; (in competition) 参加者 sañkashà; (in register, account book) 記入 kinyú; (in reference book) 記事 kíji; (arrival) 登場 tójò; (to country) 入国 nyúkoku

「**no entry**」 (to room etc) 立入禁止 tachíirikiñshi; (AUT) 進入禁止 shiñnyūkiñshi

entry form n (for club etc) 入会申込書 nyúkaimōshikomishò; (for competition etc) 参加申込書 sañkamōshikomishò

entry phone n 玄関のインターホン géñkan no iñtàhon

enumerate [inuː'məreit] vt (list) 列挙する rékkyò suru

enunciate [inʌn'siːeit] vt (word) はっきりと発音する hakkírì to hatsúon suru; (principle, plan etc) 明確に説明する meíkaku nì setsúmei suru

envelop [envel'əp] vt (cover, enclose) 覆い包む őitsutsumù

envelope [en'vəloup] n 封筒 fútō

envious [en'viːəs] adj (person, look) うらやましい uráyamashiî

environment [envai'rənmənt] n (surroundings) 環境 kañkyō; (natural world): **the environment** 環境 kañkyō

environmental [envairənmen'təl] adj 環境の kañkyō no

envisage [enviz'idʒ] vt (foresee) 予想す

る yosō suru

envoy [en'vɔi] n (diplomat) 特使 tőkùshi

envy [en'vi:] n (jealousy) せん望 señbō
♦vt うらやましく思う uráyamashìku omóù

   to envy someone something ...の...をうらやましく思う ...no ...wo uráyamashìku omóù

enzyme [en'zaim] n (BIO, MED) 酵素 kőso

ephemeral [ifem'əːrəl] adj (fashion, fame) つかの間の tsuká no mà no

epic [ep'ik] n (poem) 叙事詩 jojíshì; (book, film) 大作 taisaku
♦adj (journey) 歴史的な rekíshiteki na

epidemic [epidem'ik] n (of disease) 流行病 ryúkōbyō

epilepsy [ep'əlepsi:] n (MED) てんかん teñkan

epileptic [epəlep'tik] adj てんかんの teñkan no
♦n てんかん患者 teñkankañja

episode [ep'isoud] n (period, event) 事件 jíkèn; (TV, RADIO: installment) 1回 ikkái

epistle [ipis'əl] n (letter: also REL) 書簡 shokán

epitaph [ep'itæf] n 墓碑銘 bohímei

epithet [ep'əθet] n 形容語句 keíyōgokù

epitome [ipit'əmi:] n (model, archetype) 典型 teñkei

epitomize [ipit'əmaiz] vt (characterize, typify) ...の典型である ...no teñkei dè árù

epoch [ep'ək] n (age, era) 時代 jidái

equable [ek'wəbəl] adj (climate) 安定した añteishità; (temper, reply) 落着いた ochítsuità

equal [i:'kwəl] adj (size, number, amount) 等しい hitóshiî; (intensity, quality) 同様な dőyō na; (treatment, rights, opportunities) 平等な byódō na
♦n (peer) 同輩 dőhai
♦vt (number) イコール ikőrù; (quality) ...と同様である ...to dőyō dè árù

   to be equal to (task) ...を十分出来る ...wo júbuñ dekírù

equality [ikwɑːl'iti:] n 平等 byódō

equalize [iː'kwəlaiz] vi (SPORT) 同点で

する dóten ni surù

equally [i:'kwəli:] *adv* (share, divide etc) 平等に byódō ni; (good, brilliant, bad etc) 同様な dóyō ni

equanimity [i:kwənim'iti:] *n* (calm) 平静さ heíseisà

equate [ikweit'] *vt*: *to equate something with* ...を...と同等視する ...wo ...to dótōshì suru

equation [ikwei'ʒən] *n* (MATH) 方程式 hóteishiki

equator [ikwei'tə:r] *n* 赤道 sekídō

equestrian [ikwes'tri:ən] *adj* 乗馬の jó-bà no

equilibrium [i:kwəlib'ri:əm] *n* (balance) 均衡 kíñkō; (composure) 平静さ heíseisà

equinox [i:'kwənɑ:ks] *n*: *spring/ autumn equinox* 春(秋)分の日 shuñ (shū)bun no hì

equip [ikwip'] *vt* (person, army, car etc) ...に...を装備させる ...ni ...wo sóbi saserù; (room) ...に...を備え付ける ...ni ...wo sonáetsukerù

to be well equipped 装備が十分である sóbi gà júbuñ de árù

to be equipped with ...を装備している ...wo sóbi shite irù

equipment [ikwip'mənt] *n* (tools, machinery) 設備 sétsùbi

equitable [ek'witəbəl] *adj* (settlement, agreement) 公正な kōsei na

equities [ek'witi:z] (*BRIT*) *npl* (COMM) 普通株 futsúkàbu

equivalent [ikwiv'ələnt] *adj*: *equivalent (to)* (...に)相当する (...ni) sótō suru
♦*n* (equal) 相当の物 sótō no monò

equivocal [ikwiv'əkəl] *adj* (ambiguous) あいまいな aímai na; (open to suspicion) いかがわしい ikágawashiì

era [i:'rə] *n* (age, period) 時代 jídai

eradicate [iræd'ikeit] *vt* (disease, problem) 根絶する koñzetsu suru

erase [ireis'] *vt* (tape, writing) 消す kesú

eraser [irei'sə:r] *n* (for pencil etc) 消しゴム keshígomu; (*US*: for blackboard etc) 黒板消し kokúbañkeshi

erect [irekt'] *adj* (posture) 直立の chokúritsu no; (tail, ears) ぴんと立てた píñ tò

tatétà
♦*vt* (build) 建てる tatérù; (assemble) 組立てる kumítaterù

erection [irek'ʃən] *n* (of building) 建築 keñchiku; (of statue) 建立 koñryū; (of tent) 張る事 harú kotò; (of machinery etc) 組立て kumítate; (PHYSIOL) ぼっ起 bokkí

ermine [ə:r'min] *n* (fur) アーミン ámiñ

erode [iroud'] *vt* (soil, rock) 侵食する shiñshoku suru; (metal) 腐食する fushóku suru; (confidence, power) 揺るがす yurúgasù

erosion [irou'ʒən] *n* (of soil, rock) 侵食 shiñshoku; (of metal) 腐食 fushóku; (of confidence, power) 揺るがされる事 yurúgasarerù kotò

erotic [irɑ:t'ik] *adj* (activities) 性的な seíteki na; (dreams, books, films) 扇情的な señjōteki na, エロチックな eróchikkù na

eroticism [irɑ:t'isizəm] *n* 好色 kóshoku, エロチシズム eróchishizùmu

err [ə:r] *vi* (formal: make a mistake) 過ちを犯す ayámachi wð okásù

errand [e:r'ənd] *n* お使い o-tsúkai

erratic [iræt'ik] *adj* (behavior) 突飛な toppí na; (attempts, noise) 不規則な fukísoku na

erroneous [irou'ni:əs] *adj* (belief, opinion) 間違った machígattà

error [e:r'ə:r] *n* (mistake) 間違い machígaì, エラー érà

erudite [e:r'judait] *adj* (person) 博学な hakúgaku na

erupt [irʌpt'] *vi* (volcano) 噴火する fuñka suru; (war, crisis) ぼっ発する boppátsu suru

eruption [irʌp'ʃən] *n* (of volcano) 噴火 fuñka; (of fighting) ぼっ発 boppátsu

escalate [es'kəleit] *vi* (conflict, crisis) 拡大する kakúdai suru, エスカレートする esúkarèto suru

escalator [es'kəleitə:r] *n* エスカレータ ー esúkarètā

escapade [es'kəpeid] *n* (adventure) 冒険 bóken

escape [eskeip'] *n* (from prison) 脱走 dassó; (from person) 逃げる事 nigéru kotò; (of gas) 漏れる事 moréru kotò

♦vi (get away) 逃げる nigérù; (from jail) 脱走する dassō suru; (leak) 漏れる morérù

♦vt (consequences, responsibility etc) 回避する kaíhi suru; (elude): *his name escapes me* 彼の名前を思い出せない kárè no namáe wò omóidasenaì

to escape from (place) ...から脱出する ...kara dasshútsu suru; (person) ...から逃げる ...kara nigérù

escapism [eskeiˈpizəm] n 現実逃避 geñjitsutōhi

escort [n esˈkɔːrt vb eskɔːrt'] n (MIL, POLICE) 護衛 goéi; (companion) 同伴者 dōhañsha

♦vt (person) ...に同伴する ...ni dōhan suru

Eskimo [esˈkəmou] n エスキモー人 esúkimōjìn

esoteric [esəteːrˈik] adj 難解な nañkai na

especially [espeʃˈəliː] adv (above all, particularly) 特に tókù ni

espionage [esˈpiːɑːnɑːʒ] n (POL, MIL, COMM) スパイ行為 supáikòi

esplanade [espləneidˈ'] n (by sea) 海岸の遊歩道 kaígan nò yúhodō

espouse [espauzˈ] vt (policy) 採用する saíyō suru; (idea) 信奉する shiñpō suru

Esq. n abbr = **Esquire**

Esquire [esˈkwaiər] n: *J. Brown, Esquire* J.ブラウン様 jē buráun samá

essay [esˈei] n (SCOL) 小論文 shōroñbun; (LITERATURE) 随筆 zuíhitsu, エッセーéssè

essence [esˈəns] n (soul, spirit) 本質 hoñshitsu; (CULIN) エキス ékìsu, エッセンス éssènsu

essential [əsenˈtʃəl] adj (necessary, vital) 不可欠な fukáketsu na; (basic) 根本的な koñponteki na

♦n (necessity) 不可欠な事柄 fukáketsu nà kotógarà

essentially [əsenˈtʃəliː] adv (basically) 根本的に koñponteki ni

establish [əstæbˈliʃ] vt (organization, firm) 創立する sōritsu suru; (facts,

proof) 確認する kakúnin suru; (relations, contact) 樹立する jurítsu suru; (reputation) 作り上げる tsukúriagerù

established [əstæbˈliʃt] adj (business) 定評のある teíhyō no arù; (custom, practice) 定着した teíchaku shitā

establishment [əstæbˈliʃmənt] n (of organization etc) 創立 sōritsu; (of facts etc) 確認 kakúnin; (of relations etc) 樹立 jurítsu; (of reputation) 作り上げる事 tsukúriageru kotō; (shop etc) 店 mìsé; (business, firm) 会社 kaísha; (institution) 施設 shísètsu

the Establishment 体制 taísei

estate [əsteitˈ] n (land) 屋敷 yashíki, (BRIT: also: **housing estate**) 住宅団地 jūtakudañchi; (LAW) 財産 zaísan

estate agent (BRIT) n 不動産屋 fudōsan'ya

estate car (BRIT) n ステーションワゴン sutḗshonwagòn

esteem [əstiːmˈ] n: *to hold someone in high esteem* (admire, respect) ...を尊敬する ...wo soñkei suru

esthetic [esθetˈik] (US) adj = **aesthetic**

estimate [n esˈtəmit vb esˈtəmeit] n (calculation) 概算 gaísan; (assessment) 推定 suítei; (COMM: builder's etc) 見積 mitsúmori

♦vt (reckon, calculate) 推定する suítei suru

estimation [estəmeiˈʃən] n (opinion) 意見 íkèn; (calculation) 推定 suítei

estranged [estreindʒdˈ'] adj (from spouse) ...と別居している ...to bekkyō shite irù; (from family, friends) ...と仲たがいしている ...to nakátagai shite irù

estuary [esˈtʃuːeːriː] n 河口 kakō

etc abbr (= *et cetera*) など nádò

etching [etʃˈiŋ] n 版画 hañga, エッチング etchíngu

eternal [itəːrˈnəl] adj (everlasting, unceasing) 永遠の efen no; (unchanging: truth, value) 不変的な fuhénteki na

eternity [itəːrˈnitiː] n (REL) 永遠 efen

ether [iːˈθəːr] n (CHEM) エーテル ḗteru

ethical [eθˈikəl] adj (question, problem) 道徳的な dōtokuteki na

ethics [eθ'iks] n (science) 倫理学 riñrigáku

♦npl (morality) 道徳 dṓtoku

Ethiopia [i:θi:ou'pi:ə] n エチオピア echíopīa

ethnic [eθ'nik] adj (population, music, culture etc) 民族の miñzoku no

ethos [i:'θɑ:s] n 気風 kifū

etiquette [et'əkit] n (manners, conduct) 礼儀作法 reígisahō, エチケット échiketto

eucalyptus [ju:kəlip'təs] n (tree) ユーカリ yūkari

euphemism [ju:'fəmizəm] n えん曲表現 eñkyokuhyṓgen

euphoria [ju:fɔ:r'i:ə] n (elation) 幸福感 kōfukukañ

Eurocheque [ju:'rout∫ek] n ユーロチェック yūrochekkù ◊ヨーロッパ諸国で通用する小切手 yōroppa shokõku de tsũyō surù kogíttè

Europe [ju:'rəp] n 欧州 ṓshū, ヨーロッパ yṓroppà

European [ju:rəpi:'ən] adj 欧州の ṓshū no, ヨーロッパの yṓroppà no

♦ヨーロッパ人 yṓroppàjin

euthanasia [ju:θənei'ʒə] n 安楽死 añrakushī

evacuate [ivæk'ju:eit] vt (people) 避難させる hínan sasérù; (place) ...から避難させる ...kara hínan sasérù

evacuation [ivækju:ei'∫ən] n 避難 hínan

evade [iveid'] vt (tax, duty) 脱税する datsúzei suru; (question) 言逃れる iínogarerù; (responsibility) 回避する kálhi suru; (person) 避ける sakérù

evaluate [ivæl'ju:eit] vt (importance, achievement, situation etc) 評価する hyṓka suru

evaporate [ivæp'ə:reit] vi (liquid) 蒸発する jōhatsu suru; (feeling, attitude) 消えてなくなる kiéte nakunarù

evaporated milk [ivæp'əreitid-] n エバミルク ebámirùku

evasion [ivei'ʒən] n (of responsibility, situation etc) 回避 kálhi

tax evasion 脱税 datsúzei

evasive [ivei'siv] adj (reply, action) 回避

的な kaíhiteki na

eve [i:v] n: on the eve of ...の前夜に ...no zéñ-ya ni

even [i:'vən] adj (level) 平らな taíra na; (smooth) 滑らかな naméràka na; (equal) 五分五分の gobúgobu no

♦adv (showing surprise) ...さえ ...sáe; (introducing a comparison) 更に sárà ni

an even number 偶数 gū̃sū

even if 例え...だとしても tatóe ...dá tò shité mò

even though 例え...だとしても tatóe ...dá tò shité mò

even more なおさら naósara

even so それにしても soré ni shite mò

not even ...さえも...ない ...sáe mo ...náî

even he was there 彼さえもいた kárè sáè mo itá

even on Sundays 日曜日にも nichíyòbi ni mo

to get even with someone ...に復しゅうする ...ni fukúshū suru

evening [i:v'niŋ] n (early) 夕方 yūgata; (late) 夜 yórù; (whole period, event) ...の夕べ ...no yū̃be

in the evening 夕方に yūgata ni

evening class n 夜間学級 yakángakkyū

evening dress n (no pl: formal clothes) 夜会服 yakáifùku; (woman's) イブニングドレス ibúningu dorèsu

even out vi (ground) 平らになる taíra ni narù; (prices etc) 安定する añtei suru

event [ivent'] n (occurrence) 事件 jíkèn; (SPORT) イベント ibéñto

in the event of ...の場合 ...no baái

eventful [ivent'fəl] adj (day) 忙しい isógashī; (life, game) 波乱の多い háràn no ōî

eventual [iven't∫u:əl] adj (outcome, goal) ゆくゆくの yukúyuku no

eventuality [iven't∫u:æl'iti:] n (possibility) 可能性 kanṓsei

eventually [iven't∫u:əli:] adv (finally) 結局 kekkyóku; (in time) やがて yagáte

ever [ev'ə:r] adv (always) 常に tsúnè ni; (at any time) ...いつ ítsù ka; (in question): why ever not? どうしてまたしないのか dṓshite matá shinaì no ká *the best ever* 絶対に一番良い物 zettái nǐ ichíban yoǐ monó

have you ever seen it? それを見た事がありますか soré wǒ mǐta kotó gǎ arímasǔ ká

better than ever なお一層良くなった náô issô yokǔ náttá

ever since adv それ以来 soré iraî
♦*conj* ...して以来 ...shité iraî

evergreen [ev'ə:rgri:n] *n* (tree, bush) 常緑樹 jôryokujû

everlasting [evə:rlæs'tiŋ] *adj* (love, life etc) 永遠の eíen no

---

KEYWORD

every [ev'ri:] *adj* 1 (each) すべての subète no, 皆の mǐna nǒ

every one of them (persons) 彼らは〔を〕皆 karéra wa 〔wo〕mǐná; (objects) それらは〔を〕皆 sorérá wa〔wo〕mǐná

I interviewed every applicant 私は応募者全員に面接しました watákushi wa ôbosha zén-in ni ménsetsu shimashǐta

every shop in the town was closed 町中の店が閉っていました machíjū no mise gǎ shimátte imáshǐta

2 (all possible) 可能な限りすべての kanô na kagîri súbète no

I gave you every assistance 私は可能な限りあなたを助けました watákushi wa kanô na kagîri anátá wo tasúkemashǐta

I have every confidence in him 私は完全に彼を信用しています watákushi wa kánzen ni karě wo shín-yôshite imasǔ

we wish you every success ご成功を祈ります go-seíkô wo inórimasǔ

he's every bit as clever as his brother 才能に関しては彼は彼の兄に少しも引けを取りません saínô ni kàn shite wa karě wa karě no ánǐ ni sukóshi mo hike wo tòrímasèn

3 (showing recurrence) 毎... maî...

every day/week 毎日〔週〕maînichi〔shû〕

every Sunday 毎日曜日 máinichiyôbì

every other car (had been broken

into) 車は2台に1台ドアが壊されていた kurúma wa nidái ni ichídài doa ga kowásarète ita

she visits me every other/third day 彼女は1日〔2日〕置きに面会に来てくれます kánojo wa ichínichi(futsúka)oki nǐ ménkai ni kite kùrémasǔ

every now and then 時々 tokídoki

---

everybody [ev'ri:bɑ:di:] *pron* (gen) だれも dáre mo; (form of address) 皆さん mǐnásàn

everyday [ev'ri:dei] *adj* (daily) 毎日の maînichi no; (usual, common) 平凡な heíbon na

everyone [ev'ri:wʌn] *pron* = **everybody**

everything [ev'ri:θiŋ] *pron* 何もかも nǎnǐ mo ká mǒ

everywhere [ev'ri:hwe:r] *adv* (all over) いたる所に itárù tokoro ni; (wherever) どこにでも dókò ni de mo

evict [ivikt'] *vt* (squatter, tenant) 立ちのかせる tachínokaserù

eviction [ivik'ʃən] *n* (from house, land) 立ちのかせる事 tachínokaseru kotǒ

evidence [ev'idəns] *n* (proof) 証拠 shôko; (of witness) 証言 shôgen; (sign, indication) 印 shirúshi

to give evidence 証言する shôgen suru

evident [ev'idənt] *adj* (obvious) 明らかな akíràka na

evidently [ev'idəntli:] *adv* (obviously) 明らかに akíràka ni; (apparently) ...らしい ...rashiî

evil [i:'vəl] *adj* (person, system, influence) 悪い warúî
♦*n* (wickedness, sin) 罪悪 zaíaku; (unpleasant situation or activity) 悪 ákù

evocative [ivɑ:k'ətiv] *adj* (description, music) 想像を刺激する sôzô wǒ shigéki suru

evoke [ivouk'] *vt* (feeling, memory, response) 呼び起す yobíokosù

evolution [evəlu:'ʃən] *n* (BIO: process) 進化 shínka; (also: **theory of evolution**) 進化論 shínkaròn; (development) 発展 hattén

evolve [ivɑ:lv'] *vt* (scheme, style) 練上げ

る neríagerù

♦vi (animal, plant etc) 進化する shíñka suru; (plan, idea, style etc) 展開する teñkai suru

ewe [ju:] n 雌ヒツジ mesúhitsùji

ex- [eks] prefix 元... mótò...

exacerbate [igzæs'ə:rbeit] vt (crisis, problem) 悪化させる akká saserù

exact [igzækt'] adj (correct: time, amount, word etc) 正確な seíkaku na; (person, worker) は帳面な kichōmen na

♦vt: **to exact something (from)** (obedience, payment etc) (...に) ...を強要する (...ni) ...wo kyóyò suru

exacting [igzæk'tiŋ] adj (task, conditions) 難しい muzúkashiì; (person, master etc) 厳しい kibíshiì

exactly [igzækt'li:] adv (precisely) 正確に seíkaku ni, 丁度 chōdo; (indicating emphasis) 正にmásà ni; (indicating agreement) その通り sonó tòri

exaggerate [igzædʒ'əreit] vt (difference, situation, story etc) 大げさに言う ōgesa nì iú

♦vi 大げさな事を言う ōgesa na kotò wo iú

exaggeration [igzædʒərei'ʃən] n 大げさ ōgesa

exalted [igzɔ:l'tid] adj (prominent) 著名な choméi na

exam [igzæm'] n abbr (SCOL) = **examination**

examination [igzæmənei'ʃən] n (of object, accounts etc) 検査 kéñsa; (of idea, plan etc) 検討 keñtō; (SCOL) 試験 shikéñ; (MED) 診察 shiñsatsu

examine [igzæm'in] vt (inspect: object, idea, plan, accounts etc) 調べる shiráberù; (SCOL: candidate) 試験する shikéñ suru; (MED: patient) 診察する shiñsatsu suru

examiner [igzæm'inə:r] n (SCOL) 試験官 shikéñkan

example [igzæm'pəl] n (typical illustration) 例 reí; (model: of good behavior etc) 手本 tehóñ

for example 例えば tatóèba

exasperate [igzæs'pəreit] vt (annoy,

frustrate) 怒らせる okóraserù

exasperating [igzæs'pəreitiŋ] adj いらいらさせる fráira saserù

exasperation [igzæspərei'ʃən] n いらだち irádachi

excavate [eks'kəveit] vt (site) 発掘する hakkútsu suru

excavation [eks'kəvei'ʃən] n (act) 発掘 hakkútsu; (site) 発掘現場 hakkútsugeñba

exceed [iksi:d'] vt (number, amount, budget) 越える koérù; (speed limit etc) 越す kosú; (powers, hopes) 上回る uwámawarù

exceedingly [iksi:'diŋli:] adv (enormously) 極めて kiwámète

excel [iksel'] vi: **to excel (in/at)** (sports, business etc) (...に) 優れる (...ni) sugúrerù

excellence [ek'sələns] n 優れる事 sugúreru kotò

Excellency [ek'seləns:] n: **His Excellency** 閣下 kákkà

excellent [ek'sələnt] adj (idea, work etc) 優秀な yúshū na

except [iksept'] prep (apart from: also: **except for**, **excepting**) ...を除いて ...nozóite

♦vt: **to except someone (from)** (attack, criticism etc) (...から) ...を除く (...kara) ...wo nozókù

except if/when ...する場合を除いて ...suru baái wò nozóite

except that がしくし... ga shikáshì...

exception [iksep'ʃən] n (special case) 例外 reígai

to take exception to ...が気に食わない ...ga ki ní kuwanaì

exceptional [iksep'ʃənəl] adj (person, talent) 優れた sugúretà; (circumstances) 例外的な reígaiteki na

excerpt [ek'sə:rpt] n (from text, film) 抜粋 bassúi

excess [ek'ses] n (surfeit) 過剰 kajő

excess baggage n 超過手荷物 chōkatenimőtsu

excesses [ekses'iz] npl (of cruelty, stupidity etc) 極端な行為 kyokútan na kṍi

excess fare (BRIT) n (RAIL) 乗越し運賃 noríkoshi uńchin

excessive [ikses'iv] adj (amount, extent) 過剰の kajō no

exchange [ikstʃeindʒ'] n (of presents, prisoners etc) 交換 kṓkan; (conversation) 口論 kṓron; (also: **telephone exchange**) 電話局 deṅwakyòku

♦vt: **to exchange (for)** (goods etc) (...と) 交換する (...to) kṓkan suru

exchange rate n 為替相場 kawásesòba

Exchequer [eks'tʃekər] (BRIT) n: **the Exchequer** 大蔵省 ōkurashṓ

excise [ek'saiz] n (tax) 消費税 shṓhizèi

excite [iksait'] vt (stimulate) 興奮させる kṓfun saserù; (arouse) 性的に刺激する seíteki nì shigéki suru

to get excited 興奮する kṓfun suru

excitement [iksait'mənt] n (agitation) 興奮 kṓfun; (exhilaration) 喜び yorókobì

exciting [iksai'tiŋ] adj (time, event, place) 興奮の kṓfun no, エキサイティングな ekísaitiñgu na

exclaim [ikskleim'] vi (cry out) 叫ぶ sakébù

exclamation [eksklɑmei'ʃən] n (cry) 叫び sakébi

exclamation mark n 感嘆符 kaítañfu

exclude [iksklu:d'] vt (fact, possibility, person) 除外する jogái suru

exclusion [iksklu:'ʒən] n 除外 jogái

exclusive [iksklu:'siv] adj (club, district) 高級な kōkyū na; (use, story, interview) 独占の dokúsen no

exclusive of tax 税別の zeíbetsu no

exclusively [iksklu:'sivli:] adv (only, entirely) 独占的に dokúsenteki ni

excommunicate [ekskəmju:'nəkeit] vt (REL) 破門する hamón suru

excrement [eks'krəmənt] n ふん fúñ

excruciating [ikskru:'ʃi:eitiŋ] adj (pain, agony, embarrassment etc) 極度の kyókùdo no, 耐えがたい taégataì; (noise) 耳をつんざくような mimí wò tsuñzaku yō na

excursion [ikskər'ʒən] n (tourist excursion, shopping excursion) ツアー tsúà

excuse [n ekskju:s' vb eksku:z'] n (justification) 言訳 iíwake

♦vt (justify: personal fault, mistake) ...の言訳をする ...no iíwake wo suru; (forgive: someone else's mistake) 許す yurúsù

to excuse someone from doing something ...する義務を ...に免除する ...suru gímù wo ...ni méñjo suru

excuse me! (attracting attention) 済みません(が) sumímaseñ (ga)...; (as apology) 済みません sumímaseñ

if you will excuse me ... ちょっと失礼します chóttò shitsúrei shimasù

ex-directory [eksdirek'tə:ri:] (BRIT) adj 電話帳に載っていない deñwachō ni notté inaì

execute [ek'səkju:t] vt (person) 死刑にする shikéi ni surù; (plan, order) 実行する jikkṓ suru; (maneuver, movement) する surú

execution [eksəkju:'ʃən] n (of person) 死刑 shikéi; (of plan, order, maneuver etc) 実行 jikkṓ

executioner [eksəkju:'ʃənər] n 死刑執行人 shikéishikkōnìn

executive [igzek'jətiv] n (person: of company) 重役 jūyaku; (committee: of organization, political party etc) 執行委員会 shikkṓiñkai

♦adj (board, role) 幹部の káñbu no

executor [igzek'jətər] n (LAW) 執行人 shikkṓnìn

exemplary [igzem'plə:ri:] adj (conduct) 模範的な mohánteki na; (punishment) 見せしめの misésime no

exemplify [igzem'pləfai] vt (typify) ...の典型である ...no teñkei dè árù; (illustrate) ...の例を挙げる ...no reí wò agérù

exempt [igzempt'] adj: **exempt from** (duty, obligation) ...を免除された ...wo méñjo sarétà

♦vt: **to exempt someone from** (duty, obligation) ...の...を免除する ...no ...wo méñjo suru

exemption [igzemp'ʃən] n 免除 méñjo

exercise [ek'sərsaiz] n (no pl: keep-fit) 運動 uñdō; (energetic movement) 体操 taísō; (SCOL) 練習問題 reñshūmoñdai;

(MUS) 練習曲 reñshúkyoku; (MIL) 軍事演習 guñjieñshū; (of authority etc) 行使 kóshì

♦vt (right) 行使する kóshì suru; (dog) ...に運動をさせる ...ni uñdō wò saserù; (mind) 働かせる határakaserù

♦vi (also: **to take exercise**) 運動する uñdō suru

to exercise patience 我慢する gámàn suru

exercise book n (SCOL) ノート nòto

exert [igzə:rt'] vt (influence) 及ぼす oyóbosù; (authority) 行使する kóshi suru

to exert oneself 努力する dóryòku suru

exertion [igzə:r'ʃən] n 努力 dóryòku

exhale [eksheil'] vt (air, smoke) 吐き出す hakídasù

♦vi (breathe out) 息を吐く íkì wo hákù

exhaust [igzɔːst'] n (AUT: also: **exhaust pipe**) 排気管 haíkikàn; (: fumes) 排気ガス haíkigasù

♦vt (person) へとへとに疲れさせる hetóhetò ni tsukáresaserù; (money, resources etc) 使い果す tsukáihatasù; (topic) ...について語り尽す ...ni tsúìte katáritsukusù

exhausted [igzɔːs'tid] adj (person) へとへとに疲れた hetóhetò ni tsukáretà

exhaustion [igzɔːs'tʃən] n (tiredness) 極度の疲労 kyókùdo no hiró

nervous exhaustion 神経衰弱 shiñkeisuijàku

exhaustive [igzɔːs'tiv] adj (search, study) 徹底的な tettéiteki na

exhibit [igzib'it] n (ART) 展示品 teñjihìn; (LAW) 証拠品 shôkohìn

♦vt (quality, ability, emotion) 見せる misérù; (paintings) 展示する tenji suru

exhibition [eksəbiʃ'ən] n (of paintings etc) 展示会 teñjikai; (of ill-temper etc) 極端な態度 kyokútañ na tàìdo; (of talent etc) 素晴らしい例 subárashiì reí

exhibitionist [eksəbiʃ'ənist] n (show-off) 気取り屋 kidóriya

exhilarating [igzil'əreitiŋ] adj (experience, news) 喜ばしい yorókobashiì

exhort [igzɔːrt'] vt 訓戒する kuñkai suru

exile [eg'zail] n (condition, state) 亡命 bômei; (person) 亡命者 bômeìsha

♦vt 追放する tsuíhō suru

exist [igzist'] vi (be present) 存在する soñzai suru; (live) 生活する seíkatsu suru

existence [igzis'təns] n (reality) 存在 soñzai; (life) 生活 seíkatsu

existing [igzis'tiŋ] adj (present) 現存の geñzon no, geñson no

exit [eg'zit] n (from room, building, motorway etc) 出口 déguchi; (departure) 出ていく事 détè ikú kotò

♦vi (THEATER) 退場する taíjō suru; (COMPUT) プログラムを終了する puró-guràmu wo shúryō suru

exit ramp (US) n (AUT) 出口ランプ degúchirañpu

exodus [ek'sədəs] n 大脱出 daídasshùtsu

exonerate [igzɑːn'əreit] vt: **to exonerate someone from something** (blame, guilt etc) ...について ...の容疑を晴らす ...ni tsúìte ...no yôgi wò harásù

exorbitant [igzɔːr'bətənt] adj (prices, rents) 法外な hôgai na

exorcize [ek'sɔːrsaiz] vt (spirit) 追い払う oíharaù; (person, place) ...から悪魔を追い払う ...kara ákùma wo oíharaù

exotic [igzɑːt'ik] adj (food, place) 異国的な ikókuteki na, エキゾチックな ekízochikkù na

expand [ikspænd'] vt (business etc) 拡張する kakúchō suru; (staff, numbers etc) 増やす fuyásù

♦vi (population etc) 増える fuérù; (business etc) 大きくなる ōkíku nárù; (gas, metal) 膨張する bôchō suru

expanse [ikspæns'] n (of sea, sky etc) 広がり hirógarì

expansion [ikspæn'tʃən] n (of business, population, economy etc) 増大 zôdai

expatriate [ekspei'tri:it] n 国外在住者 kokúgai zaíjùsha

expect [ikspekt'] vt (anticipate) 予想する yosō suru; (await) 待つ mátsù; (require) 要求する yókyū suru; (suppose) ...だと思う ...dá tò omóu

♦vi: **to be expecting** (be pregnant) 妊娠している niñshin shite irù

expectancy [ikspɛk'tənsi:] n (anticipation) 期待 kitái
life expectancy 寿命 jumyō

expectant mother [ikspɛk'tənt-] n 妊婦 nínpu

expectation [ɛkspɛktei'ʃən] n (hope, belief) 期待 kitái

expedience [ikspi:'di:əns] n (convenience) 便宜 béñgi, 都合 tsugō

expediency [ikspi:'di:ənsi:] n = **expedience**

expedient [ikspi:'di:ənt] adj (useful, convenient) 都合の良い tsugō no yoì
♦n (measure) 便法 benpō

expedition [ɛkspədiʃ'ən] n (for exploration) 探検旅行 tañkenryokō; (for shopping etc) ツアー tsúā

expel [ikspel'] vt (person: from school) 退学させる taīgaku saserù; (: from organization, place) 追出す oídasù; (gas, liquid) 排出する haīshutsu suru

expend [ikspend'] vt (money, time, energy) 費やす tsuíyasù

expendable [ikspen'dəbəl] adj (person, thing) 消耗品な shṓmōhinteki na

expenditure [ikspen'ditʃər] n (of money, energy, time) 消費 shṓhi

expense [ikspens'] n (cost) 費用 híyō; (expenditure) 出費 shuppí
at the expense of ...を犠牲にして ...wo giséi ni shitè

expense account n 交際費 kōsaíhi

expenses [ikspen'siz] npl (traveling expenses, hotel expenses etc) 経費 keíhi

expensive [ikspen'siv] adj (article) 高価な kōka na; (mistake, tastes) 高く付く tákkaku tsukú

experience [ikspi:r'i:əns] n 経験 keíken
♦vt (situation, feeling etc) 経験する keíken suru

experienced [ikspi:r'i:ənst] adj (in job) 熟練した jukúren shitá

experiment [ikspe:r'əmənt] n (trial: also SCIENCE) 実験 jikkén
♦vi: *to experiment (with/on)* (...を使って) 実験する (...wo tsukáttè) jikkén suru

experimental [ikspe:rəmen'təl] adj 実験

的な jikkénteki na

expert [ek'spə:rt] adj (opinion, help) 専門家の señmonka no; (driver etc) 熟練した jukúren shitá
♦n (specialist) 専門家 señmonka, エキスパート ekísupāto

expertise [ɛkspə:rti:z'] n (know-how) 技術 gíjùtsu, ノーハウ nṓhaù

expire [ikspai'ə:r] vi (passport, licence etc) 切れる kirérù

expiry [ikspaiə:r'i:] n (of passport, lease etc) 満期 máñki

explain [iksplein'] vt 説明する setsúmei suru

explanation [ɛksplənei'ʃən] n 説明 setsúmei

explanatory [iksplæn'ətɔ:ri:] adj (statement, comment) 説明の setsúmei no

explicit [iksplis'it] adj (clear) 明白な meíhaku na; (frank) 隠し立てしない kakúshidate shinaí

explode [iksploud'] vi (bomb) 爆発する bakúhatsu suru; (population) 爆発的に増える bakúhatsuteki nì fuérù; (person: with rage etc) 激怒する gékìdo suru

exploit [n eks'plɔit vb iksplɔit'] n (deed, feat) 手柄 tegára
♦vt (workers) 搾取する sákùshu suru; (person, idea) 私利私欲に利用する shírìshíyòku ni riyō suru; (opportunity, resources) 利用する riyō suru

exploitation [ɛksplɔitei'ʃən] n (of workers) 搾取 sákùshu; (of person, idea, resources, opportunity etc) 利用 riyō

exploration [ɛksplərei'ʃən] n (of place, space) 探検 tañken; (with hands etc) 探る事 sagúru kotò; (of idea, suggestion) 検討 keñtō

exploratory [iksplɔ:r'ətɔ:ri:] adj (expedition) 探検の tañken no; (talks, operation) 予備的な yobíteki na

explore [iksplɔ:r'] vt (place, space) 探検する tañken suru; (with hands etc) 探る sagúrù; (idea, suggestion) 検討する keñtō suru

explorer [iksplɔ:r'ə:r] n (of place, country etc) 探検家 tañkenka

explosion [iksplou'ʒən] n (of bomb) 爆発

bakúhatsu; (increase: of population etc) 爆発的増加 bakúhatsutekizōka; (outburst: of rage, laughter etc) 激怒 gékìdo

explosive [iksplou'siv] *adj* (device, effect) 爆発の bakúhatsu no; (situation, temper) 爆発的な bakúhatsuteki na
♦*n* (substance) 爆薬 bakúyaku; (device) 爆弾 bakúdaǹ

exponent [ekspou'nent] *n* (of idea, theory) 擁護者 yōgoshà; (of skill, activity) 達人 tatsújin

export [*vb* ekspo:rt' *n* eks'po:rt] *vt* (goods) 輸出する yushútsu suru
♦*n* (process) 輸出 yushútsu; (product) 輸出品 yushútsuhiǹ
♦*cpd* (duty, permit) 輸出... yushútsu...

exporter [ekspo:r'tə:r] *n* 輸出業者 yushútsugyōsha

expose [ikspouz'] *vt* (reveal: object) むき出しにする mukídashi ni surù; (unmask: person) ...の悪事を暴く ...no ákùji wo abákù

exposed [ikspouzd'] *adj* (house, place etc) 雨風にさらされた ámèkaze ni sarásaretà

exposure [ikspou'ʒə:r] *n* (to heat, cold, radiation) さらされる事 sarásareru kotò; (publicity) 報道 hōdō; (of person) 暴露 bákùro; (PHOT) 露出 roshútsu
to die from exposure (MED) 低体温症で死ぬ teítaíoǹshō de shinú

exposure meter *n* (PHOT) 露出計 roshútsukei

expound [ikspaund'] *vt* (theory, opinion) 説明する setsúmei suru

express [ikspres'] *adj* (clear: command, intention etc) 明白な meíhaku na; (*BRIT*: letter etc) 速達の sokútatsu no
♦*n* (train, bus, coach) 急行 kyūkō
♦*vt* (idea, view) 言表す iíarawasù; (emotion, quantity) 表現する hyōgen suru

expression [ikspreʃ'ən] *n* (word, phrase) 言方 iíkata; (of idea, emotion) 表現 hyōgen; (on face) 表情 hyōjō; (of actor, singer etc: feeling) 表現力 hyōgeǹryoku

expressive [ikspres'iv] *adj* (glance) 意味ありげな ímìarige na; (ability) 表現の hyōgen no

expressly [ikspres'li:] *adv* (clearly, intentionally) はっきりと hakkírì to

expressway [ikspres'wei] (*US*) *n* (urban motorway) 高速道路 kōsokudòro

expulsion [ikspʌl'ʃən] *n* (SCOL) 退学処分 taígakushobùn; (from organization etc) 追放 tsuíhō; (of gas, liquid etc) 排出 haíshutsu

expurgate [eks'pə:rgeit] *vt* (text, recording) 検閲する keñ-etsu suru

exquisite [ekskwiz'it] *adj* (perfect: face, lace, workmanship, taste) 見事な mígòto na

extend [ikstend'] *vt* (visit) 延ばす nobásù; (street) 延長する eñchō suru; (building) 増築する zōchiku suru; (arm, hand) 伸ばす nobásù
♦*vi* (land) 広がる hirógarù; (road) 延びる nobírù; (period) 続く tsuzúkù
to extend an offer of help 援助を申出る éñjo wo mōshiderù
to extend an invitation to ...を招待する ...wo shōtai suru

extension [iksten'tʃən] *n* (of building) 増築 zōchiku; (of time) 延長 eñchō; (of campaign, rights) 拡大 kakúdai; (ELEC) 延長コード eñchōkòdo; (TEL: in private house, office) 内線 naísen

extensive [iksten'siv] *adj* (area) 広い hirōí; (effect, damage) 甚大な jiñdai na; (coverage, discussion) 広範囲の kōhaǹ-i no

extensively [iksten'sivli:] *adv*: *he's traveled extensively* 彼は広く旅行している kárè wa híròku ryokō shite irù

extent [ikstent'] *n* (size: of area, land etc) 広さ híròsa; (: of problem etc) 大きさ ōkìsa
to some extent ある程度 árù teído
to the extent of ...までも ...máde mo
to such an extent that ...という程...to iú hodò
to what extent? どのぐらい? donó guraí?

extenuating [iksten'ju:eitiŋ] *adj*: *extenuating circumstances* 酌量すべき情状 shakúryō subèki jōjō

exterior [iksti:r'i:ə:r] *adj* (external) 外部 の gáibu no
♦*n* (outside) 外部 gáibu; (appearance) 外 見 gaíken

exterminate [ikstə:r'məneit] *vt* (animals) 撲滅する bokúmetsu suru; (people) 根絶する koṅzetsu suru

external [ikstə:r'nəl] *adj* (walls etc) 外部 の gáibu no; (examiner, auditor) 部外の búgai no

external evidence 外的証拠 gaítekishō-ko

「*for external use*」 外用薬 gaíyōyaku

extinct [ikstiŋkt'] *adj* (animal, plant) 絶 滅した zetsúmetsu shitá

an extinct volcano 死火山 shikázàn

extinction [ikstiŋk'ʃən] *n* (of species) 絶 滅 zetsúmetsu

extinguish [ikstiŋ'gwiʃ] *vt* (fire, light) 消 す kesú

extinguisher [ikstiŋ'gwiʃə:r] *n* 消 火 器 shōkaкì

extort [iksto:rt'] *vt* (money) ゆすり取る yusúritorù; (confession) 強要する kyōyō suru

extortion [iksto:r'ʃən] *n* (of money etc) ゆすり yusúri; (confession) 強要 kyōyō

extortionate [iksto:r'ʃənit] *adj* (price, demands) 法外な hōgai na

extra [eks'trə] *adj* (thing, person, amount) 余分の yobún no
♦*adv* (in addition) 特別に tokúbetsu ni
♦*n* (luxury) 特別の物 tokúbetsu no monð, 余分の物 yobún no monð; (surcharge) 追加料金 tsuíkaryōkin; (CINEMA, THEATER) エキストラ ekísutòra

extra-... [eks'trə] *prefix* 特別に ... tokúbetsu ni ...

extract [*vt* ikstrækt' *n* eks'trækt] *vt* (take out: object) 取出す torídasù; (: tooth) 抜く nukú, 抜歯する basshí suru; (mineral: from ground) 採掘する saíkutsu suru, 抽出する chūshutsu suru; (money) 強要して取る kyōyō shité tórù; (promise) 無理強いする muríjii suru
♦*n* (of novel, recording) 抜粋 bassúi; (malt extract, vanilla extract etc) エキ ス ékìsu, エッセンス éssènsu

extracurricular [ekstrəkərik'jələ:r] *adj* (activities) 課外の kagái no

extradite [eks'trədait] *vt* (from country) 引渡す hikíwatasù; (to country) ...の引渡 しを受ける ...no hikíwatashi wò ukérù

extradition [ekstrədiʃ'ən] *n* 外国への犯 人引渡し gaíkoku e nð háñnin hikíwata-shi

extramarital [ekstrəmær'itəl] *adj* (affair, relationship) 婚外の koñgai no, 不倫の furín no

extramural [ekstrəmju:r'əl] *adj* (lectures, activities) 学外の gakúgai no

extraordinary [ikstro:r'dəne:ri:] *adj* (person) 抜きん出た nukíndetà; (conduct, situation) 異常な ijō na; (meeting) 臨時の riñji no

extravagance [ikstræv'əgəns] *n* (no pl: spending) 浪費 rōhi; (example of spending) ぜいたく zeítaku

extravagant [ikstræv'əgənt] *adj* (lavish: person) 気前の良い kimáe no yoì; (: gift) ぜいたくな zeítaku na; (wasteful: person) 金遣いの荒い kanézukai no arai; (: machine) 不経済な fukéizai na

extreme [ikstri:m'] *adj* (cold, poverty etc) 非常な hijō na; (opinions, methods etc) 極端な kyokútan na; (point, edge) 末 端の mattán no
♦*n* (of behavior) 極端 kyokútan

extremely [ikstri:m'li:] *adv* 非 常 に hijō ni

extremity [ikstrem'iti:] *n* (edge, end) 端 hashí; (of situation) 極限 kyokúgen

extricate [ek'strikeit] *vt*: *to extricate someone/something (from)* (trap, situation) (...から)...を救い出す (...kara) ...wo sukúidasù

extrovert [ek'strouvə:rt] *n* 外向的な人 gaíkōteki na hitð

exuberant [igzu:'bə:rənt] *adj* (person etc) 元気一杯の geñkiippài no; (imagination etc) 豊かな yútàka na

exude [igzu:d'] *vt* (liquid) にじみ出させる nijímidasaserù; (smell) 放つ hanátsu
to exude confidence 自信満々である jishín mañman dè árù
to exude enthusiasm 意気込む ikígo-

mù

exult [igzʌlt'] *vi* (rejoice) 喜び勇む yoró-kobiisamù

eye [ai] *n* (ANAT) 目 mé

♦*vt* (look at, watch) 見詰める mitsúmerù
the eye of a needle 針の目 hárĩ no mé
to keep an eye on ...を見張る ...wo mihárù

eyeball [ai'bɔ:l] *n* 眼球 gañkyū

eyebath [ai'bæθ] *n* 洗眼カップ señgan-kappù

eyebrow [ai'brau] *n* 眉毛 máyùge

eyebrow pencil *n* アイブローペンシル aíburōpeñshiru

eyedrops [ai'drɑ:ps] *npl* 点眼薬 teñgaň-yaku

eyelash [ai'læʃ] *n* まつげ mátsùge

eyelid [ai'lid] *n* まぶた mábùta

eyeliner [ai'lainə:r] *n* アイライナー aíraĩ-nā

eye-opener [ai'oupənə:r] *n* (revelation) 驚くべき新事実 odórokubèki shiñjijĩtsu

eyeshadow [ai'ʃædou] *n* アイシャドー aí-shadŏ

eyesight [ai'sait] *n* 視力 shíryòku

eyesore [ai'sɔ:r] *n* (building) 目障り me-záwàri

eye witness *n* (to crime, accident) 目撃者 mokúgekishà

F

F [ef] *n* (MUS: note) ヘ音 hé-òn; (: key) ヘ調 héchŏ

F. *abbr* (= *Fahrenheit*) 華氏 káshĩ

fable [fei'bəl] *n* (story) ぐう話 gū́wa

fabric [fæb'rik] *n* (cloth) 生地 kíjĩ

fabrication [fæbrikei'ʃən] *n* (lie) うそ ú-sò; (making) 製造 sefzō

fabulous [fæb'jələs] *adj* (*inf*: super) 素晴らしい subárashiĩ; (extraordinary) 途方もない tohŏ mo nài; (mythical) 伝説的な deñsetsuteki na

facade [fəsɑːd'] *n* (of building) 正面 shŏ-men; (*fig*: pretence) 見せ掛け misékake

face [feis] *n* (ANAT) 顔 kaŏ; (expression) 表情 hyŏjō; (of clock) 文字盤 mojĩ-

ban; (of cliff) 面 mêñ; (of building) 正面 shŏmen

♦*vt* (particular direction) ...に向かう ...ni mukáù; (facts, unpleasant situation) 直視する chókushi suru

face down (person) 下向きになって shi-tmuki ni nattè; (card) 伏せてあって fu-sête attè

to lose face 面目を失う meñboku wo ushínaù

to make/pull a face 顔をしかめる kaŏ wo shikámerù

in the face of (difficulties etc) ...にめげず ...ni megézù

on the face of it (superficially) 表面は hyŏmen wa

face to face (with person, problem) 面と向かって meñ to mukattè

face cloth (*BRIT*) *n* フェースタオル fé-sutaòru

face cream *n* フェースクリーム fésuku-rĩmu

face lift *n* (of person) 顔のしわ取り手術 kaŏ no shiwátori shujùtsu; (of building etc) 改造 kaízō

face powder *n* フェースパウダー fésu-paùdā

face-saving [feis'seiviŋ] *adj* (compromise, gesture) 面子を立てる méñtsu wo tatérù

facet [fæs'it] *n* (of question, personality) 側面 sokúmen; (of gem) 切子面 kirĩko-mèn

facetious [fəsi:'ʃəs] *adj* (comment, remark) ふざけた fuzáketà

face up to *vt fus* (obligations, difficulty) ...に立ち向かう ...ni tachímukaù

face value *n* (of coin, stamp) 額面 gakú-men

to take something at face value (*fig*) そのまま信用する sonŏ mama shiñ-yŏ suru

facial [fei'ʃəl] *adj* (hair, expression) 顔の kaŏ no

facile [fæs'əl] *adj* (comment, reaction) 軽々しい karúgarushiĩ

facilitate [fəsil'əteit] *vt* 助ける tasúkerù

facilities [fəsil'əti:z] *npl* (buildings,

equipment) 設備 setsúbi

credit facilities 分割払い取扱い buñkatsubarài toríatsukai

facing [feiˈsiŋ] *prep* (opposite) ...の向い側の ...no mukáigawa no

facsimile [fækˈsimˈəliː] *n* (exact replica) 複製 fukúsei; (*also*: **facsimile machine**) ファックス fákkùsu; (transmitted document) ファックス fákkùsu

fact [fækt] *n* (true piece of information) 事実 jijítsu; (truth) 真実 shíñjitsu

in fact 事実は jijítsu wa

faction [fækˈʃən] *n* (group: *also* REL, POL) 派 há

factor [fækˈtər] *n* (of problem, decision etc) 要素 yóso

factory [fækˈtəˌriː] *n* (building) 工場 kốjō

factual [fækˈtʃuˌəl] *adj* (analysis, information) 事実の jijítsu no

faculty [fækˈəltiː] *n* (sense, ability) 能力 nōryoku; (of university) 学部 gakúbu; (*US*: teaching staff) 教職員 kyōshokuin ◇総称 sōshō

fad [fæd] *n* (craze) 一時的流行 ichíjitekiryūkō

fade [feid] *vi* (color) あせる asérù; (light, sound) 次第に消える shidái ni kiérù; (flower) しぼむ shibómù; (hope, memory, smile) 消える kiérù

fag [fæg] (*BRIT*: *inf*) *n* (cigarette) もく mokú

fail [feil] *vt* (exam) 落第する rakúdai surù; (candidate) 落第させる rakúdai saserù; (subj: leader) ...の期待を裏切る ...no kitái wo urágirù; (: courage, memory) なくなる nakúnarù

◆*vi* (candidate, attempt etc) 失敗する shippái suru; (brakes) 故障する koshố suru; (eyesight, health) 衰える otóroerù; (light) 暗くなる kuráku narù

to fail to do something (be unable) ...する事が出来ない ...surú koto gà dekínài; (neglect) ...する事を怠る ...surú koto wŏ okótarù

without fail 必ず kanárazu

failing [feiˈliŋ] *n* (weakness) 欠点 kettéñ

◆*prep* ...がなければ ...ga nakéreba

failure [feilˈjəːr] *n* (lack of success) 失敗 shippái; (person) 駄目人間 daméniǹgen; (mechanical etc) 故障 koshố

faint [feint] *adj* かすかな kásùka na

◆*n* (MED) 気絶 kizétsu

◆*vi* (MED) 気絶する kizétsu suru

to feel faint 目まいがする memái ga suru

fair [feːr] *adj* (reasonable, right) 公平な kōhei na; (quite large) かなりな kánàri na; (quite good) 悪くない warúkunài; (skin) 白い shirối; (hair) 金色の kiñ-iro no; (weather) 晴れの haré no

◆*adv* (play) 正々堂々と seíseidōdō to

◆*n* (*also*: **trade fair**) トレードフェアー torédofeà; (*BRIT*: funfair) 移動遊園地 idṓyūeñchi

fairly [feːrˈliː] *adv* (justly) 公平に kṓhei ni; (quite) かなり kánàri

fairness [feːrˈnis] *n* (justice, impartiality) 公平さ kṓheisa

fair play *n* 公平さ kṓheisa

fairy [feːrˈiː] *n* (sprite) 妖精 yṓsei

fairy tale *n* おとぎ話 otógibanàshi

faith [feiθ] *n* (trust) 信用 shiñ-yō; (religion) 宗教 shū́kyō; (religious belief) 信仰 shíñkō

faithful [feiθˈfəl] *adj* 忠実な chū́jitsu na

faithfully [feiθˈfəliː] *adv* 忠実に chū́jitsu ni

yours faithfully (*BRIT*: in letters) 敬具 kéîgu

fake [feik] *n* (painting etc) 偽物 nisémono; (person) ぺてん師 peténshi

◆*adj* (phoney) いんちきの íñchiki no

◆*vt* (painting etc) 偽造する gizṓ suru; (illness, emotion) ...だと見せ掛ける ...da to mísekakerù

falcon [fælˈkən] *n* ハヤブサ hayábusa

fall [fɔːl] *n* (of person, object: from height) 転落 teñraku; (of person, horse: from standing position) 転倒 teñtō; (of price, temperature, dollar) 下がる事 sagáru kotŏ; (of government, leader, country) 倒れる事 taṓreru kotŏ; (*US*: autumn) 秋 ákì

◆*vi* (*pt* **fell**, *pp* **fallen**) (person, object: from height) 落ちる ochírù; (person, horse: from standing position) 転ぶ korōbù; (snow, rain) 降る fúrù; (price, temperature, dollar) 下がる sagárù; (government, leader, country) 倒れる taórerù; (night, darkness) (...に) なる (...ni) nárù

snowfall 降雪 kṓsetsu

rainfall 降雨 kṓu

the fall of darkness 暗くなる事 kuráku naru kotò

the fall of night 夜になる事 yórù ni náru kotò

to fall flat (on one's face) うつぶせに 倒れる utsúbuse ni taórerù; (plan) 失敗す る shippái suru; (joke) 受けない ukénaì

fallacy [fæl'əsiː] n (misconception) 誤信 goshín

fall back vt fus (retreat) 後ずさりする atōzusàri suru; (MIL) 後退する kṓtaisuru

fall back on vt fus (remedy etc) ...に頼 る ...ni tayórù

fall behind vi 遅れる okúrerù

fall down vi (person) 転ぶ korōbù; (building) 崩壊する hṓkai suru

fallen [fɔːl'ən] pp of fall

fall for vt fus (trick) ...にだまされる ...ni damásarerù; (person) ...にほれる ...ni horérù

fallible [fæl'əbəl] adj (person, memory) 間違いをしがちな machígaì wo shigáchi na

fall in vi (roof) 落込む ochíkomù; (MIL) 整列する seíretsu suru

fall off vi (person, object) 落ちる ochírù; (takings, attendance) 減る herú

fall out vi (hair, teeth) 抜ける nukérù; (friends etc) けんかする keńka suru

fallout [fɔːl'aut] n (radiation) 放射性落下 物 hṓshaseìràkkabutsu, 死の灰 shí nò hai

fallout shelter n 放射性落下物待避所 hṓshaseìràkkabutsu taíhijò

fallow [fæl'ou] adj (land, field) 休閑中の kyúkaǹchū no

falls [fɔːlz] npl (waterfall) 滝 takí

fall through vi (plan, project) 失敗に終 る shippái ni owarù

false [fɔːls] adj (untrue: statement, accusation) うその usó no; (wrong: impression, imprisonment) 間違った machígattà; (insincere: person, smile) 不誠実な fuséijitsu na

false alarm n 誤った警報 ayámattà keíhō

false pretenses npl: **under false pretenses** うその申立てで usó nò mṓshitate de

false teeth npl 入れ歯 iréba

falter [fɔːl'təːr] vi (engine) 止りそうにな る tomárisō ni nárù; (person: hesitate) た めらう tamérauù; (: stagger) よろめく yorómekù

fame [feim] n 名声 meísei

familiar [fəmil'jəːr] adj (well-known: face, voice) おなじみの onájimi no; (intimate: behavior, tone) 親しい shitáshiì
　to be familiar with (subject) よく知っ ている yókù shitté iru

familiarize [fəmil'jəraiz] vt: **to familiarize oneself with** ...になじむ ...ni najímù

family [fæm'li:] n (relations) 家族 kázòku; (children) 子供 kodómo ◇総称 sṓshō

family business n 家族経営の商売 kazókukeìei no shōbai

family doctor n 町医者 machí-ìsha

famine [fæm'in] n 飢饉 kígà

famished [fæm'iʃt] adj (hungry) 腹がペ こぺこの haráがペkopeko no

famous [fei'məs] adj 有名な yūmei na

famously [fei'məsli:] adv (get on) 素晴ら しく subárashikù

fan [fæn] n (person) ファン fáñ; (folding) 扇子 séñsu; (ELEC) 扇風機 señpūki
　♦vt (face, person) あおぐ aṓgù; (fire, quarrel) あおる aōrù

fanatic [fənæt'ik] n (extremist) 熱狂者 nekkyṓshà; (enthusiast) マニア mánìa

fan belt n (AUT) ファンベルト faǹberùto

fanciful [fæn'sifəl] adj (notion, idea) 非 現実的な hígeǹjitsuteki na; (design, name) 凝った kóttà

fancy [fæn'si:] n (whim) 気まぐれ kimágurè; (imagination) 想像 sōzō; (fantasy) 夢 yumé
　♦adj (clothes, hat, food) 凝った kóttà;

(hotel etc) 高級の kốkyū no
♦vt (feel like, want) 欲しいなと思う hoshíi na to omoú; (imagine) 想像する sốzō suru; (think) ...だと思う ...da to omoú
to take a fancy to ...を気に入る ...wo kí ni irú
he fancies her (inf) 彼は彼女が好きだ kárè wa kanójò ga sukí dà
fancy dress n 仮装の衣装 kasố no ishō
fancy-dress ball n 仮装舞踏会 kasóbutōkai
fanfare [fæn'fe:r] n ファンファーレ fanfāre
fang [fæŋ] n (tooth) きば kibá
fan out vi 扇形に広がる ốgigata nì hirógarù
fantastic [fæntæs'tik] adj (enormous) 途方もない tohốmonầi; (strange, incredible) 信じられない shiñjirarenầi; (wonderful) 素晴らしい subá rashiî
fantasy [fæn'təsi:] n (dream) 夢 yumé; (unreality, imagination) 空想 kū́sō
far [fɑːr] adj (distant) 遠い tối
♦adv (a long way) 遠く tốku; (much) はるかに hárùka ni
far away/off 遠く tốku
far better ...の方がはるかにいい ...no hố ga hárùka ni ii
far from 決して...でない kesshíte ...de nầi ◇強い否定を表す tsuyói hitéi wo aráwasù
by far はるかに hárùka ni
go as far as the farm 農場まで行って下さい nốjō madè ittè kudasaí
as far as I know 私の知る限り watákushi nò shirú kagirî
how far? (distance) どれぐらいの距離 doré gurai no kyòri; (referring to activity, situation) どれ程 doré hodò
faraway [fɑːr'əwei] adj (place) 遠くの tốku no; (look) 夢見る様な yumémiru yố na; (thought) 現実離れの geñjitsubanare no
farce [fɑːrs] n (THEATER) 笑劇 shốgeki, ファース fā́sù; (fig) 茶番劇 chabáñgeki
farcical [fɑːr'sikəl] adj (situation) ばかげた bakágèta

fare [fe:r] n (on trains, buses) 料金 ryốkin; (also: **taxi fare**) タクシー代 takúshīdai; (food) 食べ物 tabémono
half/full fare 半〔全〕額 hañ〔zeñ〕gaku
Far East n: **the Far East** 極東 kyokútō
farewell [fe:r'wel'] excl さようなら sayốnarà
♦n 別れ wakáre
farm [fɑːrm] n 農場 nốjō
♦vt (land) 耕す tagáyasù
farmer [fɑːr'mə:r] n 農場主 nốjōshù
farmhand [fɑːrm'hænd] n 作男 sakúotòko
farmhouse [fɑːrm'haus] n 農家 nốka
farming [fɑːr'miŋ] n (agriculture) 農業 nốgyō; (of crops) 耕作 kốsaku; (of animals) 飼育 shiíku
farmland [fɑːrm'lænd] n 農地 nốchi
farm worker n = **farmhand**
farmyard [fɑːrm'jɑːrd] n 農家の庭 nốka no niwà
far-reaching [fɑːr'ri:'tʃiŋ] adj (reform, effect) 広範囲の kốhaǹ-i no
fart [fɑːrt] (inf!) vi おならをする onára wo surú
farther [fɑːr'ðə:r] compar of **far**
farthest [fɑːr'ðist] superl of **far**
fascinate [fæs'əneit] vt (intrigue, interest) うっとりさせる uttóri saserù
fascinating [fæs'əneitiŋ] adj (story, person) 魅惑的な miwákuteki na
fascination [fæsənei'tʃən] n 魅惑 miwáku
fascism [fæʃ'izəm] n (POL) ファシズム fashízùmu
fashion [fæʃ'ən] n (trend: in clothes, thought, custom etc) 流行 ryū́kō, ファッション fásshòn; (also: **fashion industry**) ファッション業界 fasshòn gyōkai; (manner) やり方 yaríkata
♦vt (make) 作る tsukúrù
in fashion 流行して ryū́kō shite
out of fashion 廃れて sutárete
fashionable [fæʃ'ənəbəl] adj (clothes, club, subject) 流行の ryū́kō no
fashion show n ファッションショー fasshòn shố

fast [fæst] *adj* (runner, car, progress) 速い hayáî; (clock): *to be fast* 進んでいる susúnde irù; (dye, color) あせない asénài
♦*adv* (run, act, think) 速く hayákù; (stuck, held) 固く katáku
♦*n* (REL etc) 断食 dañjiki
♦*vi* (REL etc) 断食する dañjiki suru
fast asleep ぐっすり眠っている gussúrî nemútte irù

fasten [fæsʼən] *vt* (tie, join) 縛る shibárù; (buttons, belt etc) 締める shimérù
♦*vi* 締まる shimárù

fastener [fæsʼənər] *n* (button, clasp, pin etc) ファスナー fásūnā

fastening [fæsʼəniŋ] *n* = **fastener**

fast food *n* (hamburger etc) ファーストフード fásutofūdo

fastidious [fæstidʼiːəs] *adj* (fussy) やかましい yakámashiî

fat [fæt] *adj* (person, animal) 太った futóttà; (book, profit) 厚い atsúi; (wallet) 金がたんまり入った kané gà tañmarî haîttà; (profit) 大きな ōkina
♦*n* (on person, animal: *also* CHEM) 脂肪 shibō; (on meat) 脂身 abúramî; (for cooking) ラード rādo

fatal [feitʼəl] *adj* (mistake) 重大な júdai na; (injury, illness) 致命的な chiméiteki na

fatalistic [feitəlisʼtik] *adj* (person, attitude) 宿命論的な shukúmeironteki na

fatality [feitælʼiti:] *n* (road death etc) 死亡事故 shibōjikò

fatally [feitʼəli:] *adv* (mistaken) 重大に júdai ni; (injured etc) 致命的に chiméiteki ni

fate [feit] *n* (destiny) 運命 ûnmei; (of person) 安否 âñpi

fateful [feitʼfəl] *adj* (moment, decision) 決定的な kettéiteki na

father [fɑːʼðər] *n* 父 chichî, 父親 chichîoya, お父さん o-tósàn

father-in-law [fɑːʼðəːrinlɔː] *n* しゅうと shûto

fatherly [fɑːʼðəːrliː] *adj* (advice, help) 父親の様な chichîoya no yō na

fathom [fæðʼəm] *n* (NAUT) 尋 hírò ◊水深の単位, 約1.83メーター suîshin no táñ-i,

yáku 1.83métâ
♦*vt* (understand: mystery, reason) 理解する rikái suru

fatigue [fətiːgʼ] *n* (tiredness) 疲労 hirō
metal fatigue 金属疲労 kiñzokuhirō

fatten [fætʼən] *vt* (animal) 太らせる futóraserù
♦*vi* 太る futórù

fatty [fætʼiː] *adj* (food) 脂肪の多い shibō no ōi
♦*n* (*inf*: person) でぶ débù

fatuous [fætʃʼuːəs] *adj* (idea, remark) ばかな bákà na

faucet [fɔːʼsit] (*US*) *n* (tap) 蛇口 jagúchi

fault [fɔːlt] *n* (blame) 責任 sekínin; (defect: in person) 欠点 kettén; (: in machine) 欠陥 kekkán; (GEO: crack) 断層 dañsō; (TENNIS) フォールト fórùto
♦*vt* (criticize) 非難する hínan suru
it's my fault 私が悪かった watákushi gà warúkattà
to find fault with ...を非難する ...wo hínan suru
at fault ...のせいで ...no seî de

faulty [fɔːlʼtiː] *adj* (machine) 欠陥のある kekkán no arù

fauna [fɔːʼnə] *n* 動物相 dôbutsusō

faux pas [fou pɑː] *n inv* 非礼 hiréi

favor [feiʼvər] (*BRIT* **favour**) *n* (approval) 賛成 sañsei; (help) 助け tasúke
♦*vt* (prefer: solution etc) ...の方に賛成する ...no hô nî sañsei surù; (: pupil etc) ひいきする hiîki suru; (assist: team, horse) ...に味方する ...ni mikáta suru
to do someone a favor ...の頼みを聞く ...no táñomi wo kîkù
to find favor with ...の気に入る ...no kî ni irù
in favor of ...に賛成して ...ni sañsei shite

favorable [feiʼvərəbəl] *adj* (*gen*) 有利な yūri na; (reaction) 好意的な kôiteki na; (impression) 良い yôî; (comparison) 賞賛的な shôsanteki na; (conditions) 好適な kôteki na

favorite [feiʼvəːrit] *adj* (child, author etc) 一番好きな ichíban suki na
♦*n* (of teacher, parent) お気に入り o-kî-

niiri; (in race) 本命 honmei

favoritism [fei'vərritizəm] n えこひいき ekóhiĭki

favour [fei'vər] etc = **favor** etc

fawn [fɔːn] n (young deer) 子ジカ kojíka
♦adj (also: **fawn-colored**) 薄茶色 usúcha-iro
♦vi: **to fawn (up)on** ...にへつらう ...ni hetsúraù

fax [fæks] n (machine, document) ファックス fákkùsu
♦vt (transmit document) ファックスで送る fákkùsu de okúrù

FBI [efbiːai'] (US) n abbr (= Federal Bureau of Investigation) 連邦捜査局 reńpōsōsakyòku

fear [fiːr] n (being scared) 恐怖 kyófu; (worry) 心配 shińpai
♦vt (be scared of) 恐れる osóreru; (be worried about) 心配する shińpai suru
for fear of (in case) ...を恐れて ...wo osóretè

fearful [fiːr'fəl] adj (person) 怖がっている kowágatte irù; (risk, noise) 恐ろしい osóroshiǐ

fearless [fiːr'lis] adj (unafraid) 勇敢な yúkan na

feasible [fiː'zəbəl] adj (proposal, idea) 可能な kanó na

feast [fiːst] n (banquet) 宴会 eńkai; (delicious meal) ごちそう gochísò; (REL: also: **feast day**) 祝日 shukújitsu
♦vi (take part in a feast) ごちそうを食べる gochísò wò tabérù

feat [fiːt] n (of daring, skill) 目覚しい行為 mezámashiì kòi

feather [feð'əːr] n (of bird) 羽根 hané

feature [fiː'tʃəːr] n (characteristic) 特徴 tokúchò; (of landscape) 目立つ点 medátsu tèn; (PRESS) 特別記事 tokúbetsukijì; (TV) 特別番組 tokúbetsu bangumi
♦vt (subj: film) 主役とする shuyáku to surù
♦vi: **to feature in** (situation, film etc) ...で主演する ...de shuén suru

feature film n 長編映画 chóhen eiga

features [fiː'tʃəːrz] npl (of face) 顔立ち kaódachi

February [feb'jəweːriː] n 2月 nigátsu

fed [fed] pt, pp of **feed**

federal [fed'əːrəl] adj (system, powers) 連邦の reńpō no

federation [fedərei'ʃən] n (association) 連盟 reńmei

fed up [fed ʌp'] adj: **to be fed up** うんざりしている ufizari shite iru

fee [fiː] n (payment) 料金 ryókin; (of doctor, lawyer) 報酬 hóshū; (for examination, registration) 手数料 tesúryō
school fees 授業料 jugyóryō

feeble [fiː'bəl] adj (weak) 弱い yowáì; (ineffectual: attempt, joke) 効果的でない kókateki dè náì

feed [fiːd] n (of baby) ベビーフード bebífūdo; (of animal) えさ esá; (on printer) 給紙装置 kyúshisòchi
♦vt (pt, pp **fed**) (person) ...に食べさせる ...ni tabésaserù; (baby) ...に授乳する ...ni junyú suru; (horse etc) ...にえさをやる ...ni esá wò yárù; (machine) ...に供給する ...ni kyókyū suru; (data, information): **to feed into** ...に入力する ...ni nyúryoku suru

feedback [fiːd'bæk] n (response) フィードバック fídobàkku

feeding bottle [fiː'diŋ-] (BRIT) n ほ乳瓶 honyúbìn

feed on vt fus (gen) ...を食べる ...wo tabérù, ...を常食とする ...wo jóshoku to surù; (fig) ...にはぐくまれる ...ni hagúkumarerù

feel [fiːl] n (sensation, touch) 感触 kańshoku; (impression) 印象 ińshó
♦vt (pt, pp **felt**) (touch) ...に触る ...ni sawárù; (experience: desire, anger) 覚える obóerù; (: cold, pain) 感じる kańjirù; (think, believe) ...だと思う ...da to omóù
to feel hungry おなかがすく onáka gà sukú
to feel cold 寒がる samúgarù
to feel lonely 寂しがる sabíshigarù
to feel better 気分がよくなる kíbùn ga yóku narù
I don't feel well 気分が悪い kíbùn ga warúì
it feels soft 柔らかい感じだ yawárakai

kañji da
  to feel like (want) ...が欲しい ...ga hoshíi

feel about/around vi ...を手探りで捜す ...wo teságuri de sagásù

feeler [fiːˈləːr] n (of insect) 触角 shokkáku
  to put out a feeler/feelers (fig) 打診する dashín suru

feeling [fiːˈliŋ] n (emotion) 感情 kañjố; (physical sensation) 感触 kañshoku; (impression) 印象 iñshō

feet [fiːt] npl of **foot**

feign [fein] vt (injury, interest) 見せ掛ける misékakerù

feline [fiːˈlain] adj (cat-like) ネコの様な nékò no yố na

fell [fel] pt of **fall**
  ♦vt (tree) 倒す taósù

fellow [felˈou] n (man) 男 otóko; (comrade) 仲間 nakáma; (of learned society) 会員 kaíin

fellow citizen n 同郷の市民 dốkyō nò shímìn

fellow countryman (pl **countrymen**) n 同国人 dốkokujìn

fellow men npl 外の人間 hoká no niñgen

fellowship [felˈouʃip] n (comradeship) 友情 yűjố; (society) 会 káì; (SCOL) 大学特別研究員 daígaku tokubetsu kenkyűin

felony [felˈəni:] n 重罪 jūzai

felt [felt] pt, pp of **feel**
  ♦n (fabric) フェルト férùto

felt-tip pen [felt'tip-] n サインペン saínpen

female [fiːˈmeil] n (ZOOL) 雌 mesű; (pej: woman) 女 oñna
  ♦adj (BIO) 雌の mesű no; (sex, character, child) 女の oñna no, 女性の joséi no; (vote etc) 女性たちの joséitachi no

feminine [femˈənin] adj (clothes, behavior) 女性らしい joséi rashíi; (LING) 女性の joséi no

feminist [femˈənist] n 男女同権論者 dañjodōkenroñsha, フェミニスト fémínisùto

fence [fens] n (barrier) 塀 heí
  ♦vt (also: **fence in**: land) 塀で囲む heí de kakómù

fencing [fenˈsiŋ] n (SPORT) フェンシングをする féñshingu wo suru

fencing [fenˈsiŋ] n (SPORT) フェンシング féñshingu

fend [fend] vi: **to fend for oneself** 自力でやっていく jíriki dè yatté ikù

fender [fenˈdəːr] n (of fireplace) 火格子 higóshi; (on boat) 防げん物 bốgenbùtsu; (US: of car) フェンダー feñdà

fend off vt (attack etc) 受流す ukénagasù

ferment [vb fəːrment' n fəːr'ment] vi (beer, dough etc) 発酵する hakkố suru
  ♦n (fig: unrest) 動乱 dốran

fern [fəːrn] n シダ shídà

ferocious [fərou'ʃəs] adj (animal, behavior) どう猛な dốmō na; (competition) 激しい hagéshìi

ferocity [fəra:s'iti:] n (of animal, behavior) どう猛さ dốmōsa; (of competition) 激しさ hagéshìsà

ferret [feːr'it] n フェレット férètto

ferret out vt (information) 捜し出す sagáshidasù

ferry [feːr'i:] n (also: **ferry boat**) フェリー férì, フェリーボート feríbòto
  ♦vt (transport: by sea, air, road) 輸送する yusố suru

fertile [fəːr'təl] adj (land, soil) 肥よくな hiyốku na; (imagination) 豊かな yútàka na; (woman) 妊娠可能な niñshinkanō na

fertility [fəːrtil'əti:] n (of land) 肥よくさ hiyốkusa; (of imagination) 独創性 dokúsōsei; (of woman) 繁殖力 hañshokuryòku

fertilize [fəːr'təlaiz] vt (land) ...に肥料をやる ...ni hiryố wò yárù; (BIO) 受精させる juséi saserù

fertilizer [fəːr'təlaizəːr] n (for plants, land) 肥料 hiryố

fervent [fəːr'vənt] adj (admirer, belief) 熱心な nesshín na

fervor [fəːr'vəːr] n 熱心さ nesshíñsa

fester [fesˈtəːr] vi (wound) 化のうする kanố suru

festival [fesˈtəvəl] n (REL) 祝日 shukújitsu; (ART, MUS) フェスティバル fésùtibaru

festive [fes'tiv] *adj* (mood, atmosphere) お祭気分の o-mátsurikibùn no
the festive season (BRIT: Christmas) クリスマスの季節 kurísumasu no kisétsù

festivities [festiv'iti:z] *npl* (celebrations) お祝い o-íwai

festoon [festu:n'] *vt*: *to festoon with* ...で飾る ...de kazárù

fetch [fetʃ] *vt* (bring) 持って来る motté kurù; (sell for) ...の値で売れる ...no ne de urérù

fetching [fetʃ'iŋ] *adj* (woman, dress) 魅惑的な miwákuteki na

fête [feit] *n* (at church, school) バザー bazá

fetish [fet'iʃ] *n* (obsession) 強迫観念 kyóhakukañnen

fetus [fi:'təs] (BRIT **foetus**) *n* (BIO) 胎児 táiji

feud [fju:d] *n* (quarrel) 争い arásoì

feudal [fju:d'əl] *adj* (system, society) 封建的な hókenteki na

fever [fi:'vəːr] *n* (MED) 熱 netsú

feverish [fi:'vəːriʃ] *adj* (MED) 熱がある netsú ga arù; (emotion) 激しい hagéshiì; (activity) 慌ただしい awátadashiì

few [fju:] *adj* (not many) 少数の shósū no; (some): *a few* 幾つかの íkùtsuka no
♦*pron* (not many) 少数 shósū; (some): *a few* 幾つかの íkùtsuka

fewer [fju:'əːr] *adj compar of* **few**

fewest [fju:'ist] *adj superl of* **few**

fiancé [fi:ɑːnsei'] *n* 婚約者 koñ-yakushà, フィアンセ fiáñse ◊男性 dañsei

fiancée [fi:ɑːnsei'] *n* 婚約者 koñ-yakushà, フィアンセ fiáñse ◊女性 joséi

fiasco [fi:æs'kou] *n* (disaster) 失敗 shippái

fib [fib] *n* (lie) うそ úsò

fiber [fai'bəːr] (BRIT **fibre**) *n* (thread, roughage) 繊維 séñ-i; (cloth) 生地 kíji; (ANAT: tissue) 神経繊維 shiñkeiseñ-i

fiber-glass [fai'bəːrglæs] *n* ファイバーグラス faíbàguràsu

fickle [fik'əl] *adj* (person) 移り気な utsúrigi na; (weather) 変りやすい kawáriyasuì

fiction [fik'ʃən] *n* (LITERATURE) フィクション fíkùshon; (invention) 作り事 tsukúrigoto; (lie) うそ úsò

fictional [fik'ʃənəl] *adj* (character, event) 架空の kakú no

fictitious [fiktiʃ'əs] *adj* (false, invented) 架空の kakú no

fiddle [fid'əl] *n* (MUS) バイオリン baíorin; (inf: fraud, swindle) 詐欺 ságì
♦*vt* (BRIT: accounts) ごまかす gomákasù

fiddle with *vt fus* (glasses etc) いじくる ijíkurù

fidelity [fidel'iti:] *n* (faithfulness) 忠誠 chūsei

fidget [fidʒ'it] *vi* (nervously) そわそわする sówàsowa suru; (in boredom) もぞもぞする mózòmozo suru

field [fi:ld] *n* (on farm) 畑 hatáke; (SPORT: ground) グランド guráñdo; (fig: subject, area of interest) 分野 búñya; (range: of vision) 視野 shíyà; (: of magnet: also ELEC) 磁界 jíkài

field marshal *n* (MIL) 元帥 geñsui

fieldwork [fi:ld'wəːrk] *n* (research) 現地調査 geñchichòsa, 実地調査 jitchíchòsa, フィールドワーク fírudowàku

fiend [fi:nd] *n* (monster) 怪物 kaíbutsu

fiendish [fi:n'diʃ] *adj* (person, problem) 怪物の様な kaíbutsu no yò na; (problem) ものすごく難しい monósugokù muzúkashiì

fierce [fi:rs] *adj* (animal, person) どう猛な dómō na; (fighting) 激しい hagéshiì; (loyalty) 揺るぎない yurúginaì; (wind) 猛烈な mōretsu na; (heat) うだる様な udáru yò na

fiery [fai'əːri:] *adj* (burning) 燃え盛る moésakarù; (temperament) 激しい hagéshiì

fifteen [fif'ti:n'] *num* 十五 (の) jūgo (no)

fifth [fifθ] *num* 第五 (の) dáigo (no)

fifty [fif'ti:] *num* 五十 (の) gojū (no)

fifty-fifty [fif'ti:fif'ti:] *adj* (deal, split) 五分五分の gobúgobu no
♦*adv* 五分五分に gobúgobu ni

fig [fig] *n* (fruit) イチジク ichíjìku

fight [fait] *n* 戦い tatákai
♦*vb* (*pt, pp* **fought**)
♦*vt* (person, enemy, cancer etc: *also* MIL) …と戦う …to tatákaù; (election) …に出馬する …ni shutsúba suru; (emotion) 抑える osáerù
♦*vi* (people: *also* MIL) 戦う tatákaù

fighter [fai'tə:r] *n* (combatant) 戦う人 tatákaù hitó, (plane) 戦闘機 seńtōkì

fighting [fai'tiŋ] *n* (battle) 戦い tatákai; (brawl) けんか keńka

figment [fig'mənt] *n*: *a figment of the imagination* 気のせい kí nò séì

figurative [fig'jə:rətiv] *adj* (expression, style) 比ゆ的な hiyúteki na

figure [fig'jə:r] *n* (DRAWING, GEOM) 図 zu; (number, statistic etc) 数字 sújì; (body, shape, outline) 形 katáchi; (person, personality) 人 hitó
♦*vt* (think: esp US) (…だと) 思う (…da to) omóù
♦*vi* (appear) 見える miérù

figurehead [fig'jə:rhed] *n* (NAUT) 船首像 seńshuzò; (*pej*: leader) 名ばかりのリーダー na bákarì no rīdā

figure of speech *n* 比ゆ híyú

figure out *vt* (work out) 理解する rikái suru

filament [fil'əmənt] *n* (ELEC) フィラメント fírament

filch [filtʃ] (*inf*) *vt* (steal) くすねる kusúnerù

file [fail] *n* (dossier) 資料 shiryố; (folder) 書類ばさみ shorúibàsami; (COMPUT) ファイル fáìru; (row) 列 rétsù; (tool) やすり yasúrì
♦*vt* (papers) 保管する hokán suru; (LAW: claim) 提出する teíshutsu suru; (wood, metal, fingernails) …にやすりを掛ける …ni yasúrì wo kakérù

file in/out *vi* 1列で入る〔出る〕ichíretsu dè haírù〔dérù〕

filing cabinet [fai'liŋ-] *n* ファイルキャビネット fáìru kyabínètto

fill [fil] *vt* (container, space): *to fill (with)* (…で) 一杯にする (…de) ippái ni surù; (vacancy) 補充する hojū suru; (need) 満たす mitásù

♦*n*: *to eat one's fill* たらふく食べる taráfuku taberù

fillet [filei'] *n* (of meat, fish) ヒレ hiré

fillet steak *n* ヒレステーキ hirésutèki

fill in *vt* (hole) うめる umérù; (time) つぶす tsubúsù; (form) …に書入れる …ni kakíirerù

filling [fil'iŋ] *n* (for tooth) 充てん jūten; (CULIN) 中身 nakami

filling station *n* (AUT) ガソリンスタンド gasórinsutaǹdo

fill up *vt* (container, space) 一杯にする ippái ni surù
♦*vi* (AUT) 満タンにする mańtan ni surù

film [film] *n* (CINEMA, TV) 映画 eíga; (PHOT) フィルム fírùmu; (of powder, liquid etc) 膜 makú
♦*vt* (scene) 撮影する satsúei suru
♦*vi* 撮影する satsúei suru

film star *n* 映画スター eígasutà

film strip *n* (slide) フィルムスライド firúmusuraìdo

filter [fil'tə:r] *n* (device) ろ過装置 rokásōchi, フィルター fírùtā; (PHOT) フィルター fírùtā
♦*vt* (liquid) ろ過する rokā suru

filter lane (*BRIT*) *n* (AUT) 右〔左〕折車線 u〔sa〕sétsu shasèn

filter-tipped [fil'tə:rtipt] *adj* フィルター付きの fírùtatsuki no

filth [filθ] *n* (dirt) 汚物 obútsu

filthy [fil'θi:] *adj* (object, person) 不潔な fukétsu na; (language) みだらな mídàra na

fin [fin] *n* (of fish) ひれ hiré

final [fai'nəl] *adj* (last) 最後の saígo no; (ultimate) 究極の kyúkyoku no; (definitive: answer, decision) 最終的な saíshūteki na
♦*n* (SPORT) 決勝戦 kesshốsen

finale [finæl'i:] *n* フィナーレ fínàre

finalist [fai'nəlist] *n* (SPORT) 決勝戦出場選手 kesshōsen shutsujō seńshu

finalize [fai'nəlaiz] *vt* (arrangements, plans) 最終的に決定する saíshūteki nì kettéi surù

finally [fai'nəli:] *adv* (eventually) ようやく yốyaku; (lastly) 最後に saígo ni

finals [fai'nəlz] *npl* (SCOL) 卒業試験 so-tsúgyōshikèn

finance [*n* fai'næns *vb* finæns'] *n* (money, backing) 融資 yúshi; (money management) 財政 zaísei

♦*vt* (back, fund) 融資する yúshi suru

finances [finæn'siz] *npl* (personal finances) 財政 zaísei

financial [finæn'tʃəl] *adj* (difficulties, year, venture) 経済的な keízaiteki na

financial year *n* 会計年度 kaíkeinèndo

financier [finænsi:r'] *n* (backer, funder) 出資者 shusshísha

find [faind] (*pt, pp* **found**) *vt* (person, object, answer) 見付ける mitsúkeru; (discover) 発見する hakkén suru; (think) …だと思う …da to omóu

♦*n* (discovery) 発見 hakkén

to find someone guilty (LAW) …に有罪判決を下す …ni yūzaihañketsu wo kudásù

findings [fain'diŋz] *npl* (LAW, of report) 調査の結果 chōsa no kekkà

find out *vt* (fact, truth) 知る shírù; (person) …の悪事を知る …no ákùji wo shírù

to find out about (subject) 調べる shiráberù; (by chance) 知る shírù

fine [fain] *adj* (excellent: quality, performance etc) 見事な mígòto na; (thin: hair, thread) 細い hosóì; (not coarse: sand, powder etc) 細かい komákaì; (subtle: detail, adjustment etc) 細かい komákaì

♦*adv* (well) うまく úmàku

♦*n* (LAW) 罰金 bakkín

♦*vt* (LAW) …に罰金を払わせる …ni bakkín wò haráwaserù

to be fine (person) 元気である géñki de árù; (weather) 良い天気である yóì téñki de árù

fine arts *npl* 美術 bíjùtsu

finery [fai'nə:ri:] *n* (dress) 晴着 harégi; (jewelery) 取って置きの装身具 tottéoki nò sōshiñgu

finesse [fines'] *n* 手腕 shúwàn

finger [fiŋ'gə:r] *n* (ANAT) 指 yubí

♦*vt* (touch) …に指で触る …ni yubí dè sawárù

little/index finger 小〔人差し〕指 ko-

(hitósashi)yúbi

fingernail [fiŋ'gə:rneil] *n* つめ tsumé

fingerprint [fiŋ'gə:rprint] *n* (mark) 指紋 shimón

fingertip [fiŋ'gə:rtip] *n* 指先 yubísaki

finicky [fin'iki:] *adj* (fussy) 気難しい kimúzukashiì

finish [fin'iʃ] *n* (end) 終り owárì; (SPORT) ゴール gōru; (polish etc) 仕上り shiágari

♦*vt* (work, eating, book etc) 終える oérù

♦*vi* (person, course, event) 終る owárù

to finish doing something …し終える …shi óerù

to finish third (in race etc) 3着になる sañchaku ni naru

finishing line [fin'iʃiŋ-] *n* ゴールライン gōruraìn

finishing school [fin'iʃiŋ-] *n* 花嫁学校 hanáyomegàkkō

finish off *vt* (complete) 仕上げる shiágerù; (kill) 止めを刺す todóme wo sasù

finish up *vt* (food, drink) 平らげる taíragerù

♦*vi* (end up) 最後に…に行ってしまう saígo ni …ni itté shimaù

finite [fai'nait] *adj* (time, space) 一定の ittéi no; (verb) 定形の teíkei no

Finland [fin'lənd] *n* フィンランド fíñrando

Finn [fin] *n* フィンランド人 fíñrandojìn

Finnish [fin'iʃ] *adj* フィンランドの fíñrando no; (LING) フィンランド語の fíñrandogo no

♦*n* (LING) フィンランド語 fíñrandogo

fiord [fjourd] = **fjord**

fir [fə:r] *n* モミ mómì

fire [fai'ə:r] *n* (flames) 火 hí; (in hearth) たき火 takíbi; (accidental) 火事 kají; (gas fire, electric fire) ヒーター hītā

♦*vt* (shoot: gun etc) うつ útsù; (: arrow) 射る írù; (stimulate: imagination, enthusiasm) 刺激する shigéki suru; (*inf*: dismiss: employee) 首にする kubí ni surù

♦*vi* (shoot) 発砲する happō suru

on fire 燃えて moéte

fire alarm *n* 火災警報装置 kasáikeihōsōchi

firearm [faiə:r'ɑ:rm] *n* 銃砲 jūhō ◇特に

ピストルを指す tőkù ni pisútoru wò sásù

fire brigade n 消防隊 shőbōtai

fire department (*US*) n = **fire brigade**

fire engine n 消防自動車 shőbōjidōsha

fire escape n 非常階段 hijőkaĭdan

fire extinguisher n 消化器 shőkakì

fireman [faiəːrˈmən] (*pl* **firemen**) n 消防士 shőbōshi

fireplace [faiəːrˈpleis] n 暖炉 dánro

fireside [faiəːrˈsaid] n 暖炉のそば dánro no sőbà

fire station n 消防署 shőbōsho

firewood [faiəːrˈwud] n まき makí

fireworks [faiəːrˈwəːrks] *npl* 花火 hánàbi

firing squad [faiəːrˈiŋ-] n 銃殺隊 jűsatsutai

firm [fəːrm] *adj* (mattress, ground) 固い katái; (grasp, push, tug) 強い tsuyőì; (decision) 断固とした dánko to shita; (faith) 固い katái; (measures) 強固な kyőko na; (look, voice) しっかりした shikkárì shita

♦n (company) 会社 kaísha

firmly [fəːrmˈliː] *adv* (grasp, pull, tug) 強く tsuyőku; (decide) 断固として dánko to shite; (look, speak) しっかりと shikkárì to

first [fəːrst] *adj* (before all others) 第一の dáìchi no, 最初の saísho no

♦adv (before all others) 一番に ichíban ni, 一番最初に ichíban saísho ni; (when listing reasons etc) 第一に dáìchi ni

♦n (person: in race) 1着 itcháku; (AUT) ローギヤ rőgiya; (BRIT SCOL: degree) 1級優等卒業学位 íkkyū yūtō sotsugyō gakùi ◇英国では優等卒業学位は成績の高い順に1級、2級、3級に分けられる eíkoku de wà yūtō sotsugyō gakùi wa seísèki no takái jùn ni ikkyû, nikyû, sankyû ni wakérarerù

at first 最初は saísho wa

first of all まず第一に mázu dáìchi ni

first aid n 応急手当 őkyūteate

first-aid kit n 救急箱 kyūkyûbako

first-class [fəːrstˈklæs] *adj* (excellent: mind, worker) 優れた sugúretà; (car-

riage, ticket, post) 1等の ittő no

first-hand [fəːrstˈhænd] *adj* (account, story) 直接の chokúsetsu no

first lady (*US*) n 大統領夫人 daítōryō-fujìn

firstly [fəːrstˈliː] *adv* 第一に daíichi ni

first name n 名 na, ファーストネーム fásutonēmu

first-rate [fəːrstˈreit] *adj* (player, actor etc) 優れた sugúretà

fiscal [fisˈkəl] *adj* (year) 会計の kaíkei no; (policies) 財政の zaísei no

fish [fiʃ] n *inv* 魚 sakána

♦vt (river, area) ...で釣をする ...de tsurí wo surù

♦vi (commercially) 漁をする ryő wo surù; (as sport, hobby) 釣をする tsurí wo surù

to go fishing 釣に行く tsurí ni ikù

fisherman [fiʃˈəːrmən] (*pl* **fishermen**) n 漁師 ryőshi

fish farm n 養魚場 yőgyojō

fish fingers (*BRIT*) *npl* = **fish sticks**

fishing boat [fiʃˈiŋ-] n 漁船 gyosén

fishing line n 釣糸 tsuríìto

fishing rod n 釣ざお tsurízao

fishmonger's (**shop**) [fiʃˈmʌŋgəːrz-] n 魚屋 sakánaya

fish sticks (*US*) *npl* フィッシュスティック fisshûsutikkù ◇細長く切った魚にパン粉をまぶして揚げた物 hosónagaku kittá sakána ni pánko wo mabúshite agéta monò

fishy [fiʃˈiː] (*inf*) *adj* (tale, story) 怪しい ayáshiì

fission [fiʃˈən] n 分裂 buñretsu

fissure [fiʃˈəːr] n 亀裂 kirétsu

fist [fist] n こぶし kőbùshi, げんこつ geñkotsu

fit [fit] *adj* (suitable) 適当な tekítō na; (healthy) 健康な keñkō na

♦vt (subj: clothes, shoes) ...にぴったり合う ...ni pittárì au; (put in) ...に入れる ...ni irérù; (attach, equip) ...に取付ける ...ni torítsukeru; (suit) ...に合う ...ni áù

♦vi (clothes) ぴったり合う pittárì áù; (parts) 合う áù; (in space, gap) ぴったりはいる pittárì haírù

♦n (MED) 発作 hossá; (of coughing, giggles) 発作的に...する事 hossáteki ni ...suru kotó

fit to (ready) ...出来る状態にある ...dekirù jōtai ni arù

fit for (suitable for) ...に適当である ...ni tekítō de arù

a fit of anger かんしゃく kańshaku

this dress is a good fit このドレスはぴったり体に合う konó dorèsu wa pittárì karáda ni aù

by fits and starts 動いたり止ったりして ugóitarì tomáttarì shité

fitful [fit'fəl] *adj* (sleep) 途切れ途切れの togíretogìre no

fit in *vi* (person) 溶込む tokékomù

fitment [fit'mənt] *n* (in room, cabin) 取付け家具 torítsukekagù ◇つり戸棚など壁などに固定した家具を指す tsurítodàna nadò kabé nadò ni kotéi shita kagù wo sásù

fitness [fit'nis] *n* (MED) 健康 keñkō

fitted carpet [fit'id-] *n* 敷込みじゅうたん shikíkomijùtan

fitted kitchen [fit'id-] *n* システムキッチン shisútemu kitchiñ

fitter [fit'əːr] *n* (of machinery, equipment) 整備工 seíbikō

fitting [fit'iŋ] *adj* (compliment, thanks) 適切な tekísetsu na

♦n (of dress) 試着 shicháku; (of piece of equipment) 取付け torítsuke

fitting room *n* (in shop) 試着室 shichákushìtsu

fittings [fit'iŋz] *npl* (in building) 設備 sétsubi

five [faiv] *num* 五（の）gó (no)、五つ（の）itsútsù (no)

fiver [fai'vəːr] *n* (*inf*: *BRIT*: 5 pounds) 5ポンド札 gópondo satsù; (*US*: 5 dollars) 5ドル札 gódoru satsù

fix [fiks] *vt* (attach) 取付ける torítsukerù; (sort out, arrange) 手配する tehái suru; (mend) 直す naósu; (prepare: meal, drink) 作る tsukúrù

♦n: *to be in a fix* 困っている komátte irù

fixation [fiksei'ʃən] *n* 固着 kocháku

fixed [fikst] *adj* (price, amount etc) 一定の ittéi no

a fixed idea 固定観念 kotéikaññen

a fixed smile 作り笑い tsukúriwarài

fixture [fiks'tʃəːr] *n* (bath, sink, cupboard etc) 設備 sétsubi; (SPORT) 試合の予定 shiái no yotèi

fix up *vt* (meeting) 手配する tehái surù

to fix someone up with something ...のために...を手に入れる ...no tamé ni ...wo té ni irerù

fizzle out [fiz'əl-] *vi* (event) しりすぼみに終ってしまう shirísùbomi ni owátte shimàu; (interest) 次第に消えてしまう shidái ni kiète shimáù

fizzy [fiz'i:] *adj* (drink) 炭酸入りの tañsan-iri no

fjord [fjourd] *n* フィヨルド fíyòrudo

flabbergasted [flæb'əːrgæstid] *adj* (dumbfounded, surprised) あっけにとられた akké ni toraretà

flabby [flæb'i:] *adj* (fat) 締まりのない shimárì no nái

flag [flæg] *n* (of country, organization) 旗 hatá; (for signalling) 手旗 tebáta; (*also*: flagstone) 敷石 shikíishi

♦vi (person, spirits) 弱る yowárù

to flag someone down (taxi, car etc) 手を振って...を止める té wo futtè ...wo tomérù

flagpole [flæg'poul] *n* 旗ざお hatázao

flagrant [fleig'rənt] *adj* (violation, injustice) 甚だしい hanáhadashiî

flagship [flæg'ʃip] *n* (of fleet) 旗艦 kikáñ; (*fig*) 看板施設 kañbanshisètsu

flair [fleːr] *n* (talent) 才能 saínō; (style) 粋なセンス ikí na señsu

flak [flæk] *n* (MIL) 対空砲火 taíkūhòka; (*inf*: criticism) 非難 hínàn

flake [fleik] *n* (of rust, paint) はげ落ちた欠けら hagéochità kakéra; (of snow, soap powder) 一片 ippéñ

♦vi (*also*: flake off): paint, enamel) はげ落ちる hagéochirù

flamboyant [flæmbɔi'ənt] *adj* (dress, design) けばけばしい kebákebashiì; (person) 派手な hadé na

flame [fleim] *n* (of fire) 炎 honó-ò

flamingo [fləmiŋ'gou] n フラミンゴ fu-rámiṅgo

flammable [flæm'əbəl] adj (gas, fabric) 燃えやすい moéyasuî

flan [flæn] (BRIT) n フラン fúràn ◊菓子の一種 kashí no isshù

flank [flæŋk] n (of animal) わき腹 wakí-bàra; (of army) 側面 sokúmèn
♦vt ...のわきにある〔いる〕...no wakí ni arù (iru)

flannel [flæn'əl] n (fabric) フランネル furánneru; (BRIT: also: **face flannel**) フェースタオル fêsutaðru

flannels [flæn'əlz] npl フランネルズボン furánneruzubòn

flap [flæp] n (of pocket, envelope, jacket) ふた futá
♦vt (arms, wings) ばたばたさせる bátà-bata saserù
♦vi (sail, flag) はためく hátamekù; (inf: also: **be in a flap**) 興奮している kốfun shite irù

flare [fle:r] n (signal) 発煙筒 hatsúentò; (in skirt etc) フレア furéa

flare up vi (fire) 燃え上る moéagarù; (fig: person) 怒る okórù; (: fighting) ぼっ発する boppátsu suru

flash [flæʃ] n (of light) 閃光 seńkō; (also: **news flash**) ニュースフラッシュ nyûsu-furasshù; (PHOT) フラッシュ furásshù
♦vt (light, headlights) 点滅させる teńmetsu saserù; (send: news, message) 速報する sokúhō suru; (: look, smile) 見せる misérù
♦vi (lightning, light) 光る hikárù; (light on ambulance etc) 点滅する teńmetsu suru

in a flash 一瞬にして isshún nĩ shite
to flash by/past (person) 走って通り過ぎる hashíttè tốrisugirù

flashback [flæʃ'bæk] n (CINEMA) フラッシュバック furásshubakkù

flashbulb [flæʃ'bʌlb] n フラッシュバルブ furásshubarùbu

flashcube [flæʃ'kju:b] n フラッシュキューブ furásshukyùbu

flashlight [flæʃ'lait] n 懐中電灯 kaíchū-deñtō

flashy [flæʃ'i:] (pej) adj 派手な hadé na

flask [flæsk] n (bottle) 瓶 bíñ; (also: **vacuum flask**) 魔法瓶 máhòbin, ポット pôt-tò

flat [flæt] adj (ground, surface) 平な taírana; (tire) パンクした páñku shita; (battery) 上がった agáttà; (beer) 気が抜けた ki gá nùketa; (refusal, denial) きっぱりした kippárî shita; (MUS: note) フラットの furáttò no; (: voice) そっけない sokkénai; (rate, fee) 均一の kiñ-itsu no
♦n (BRIT: apartment) アパート ápàto; (AUT) パンク páñku; (MUS) フラット furáttò

to work flat out 力一杯働く chikára ippài hataraku

flatly [flæt'li:] adv (refuse, deny) きっぱりと kippárî to

flatten [flæt'ən] vt (also: **flatten out**) 平にする taíra ni surù; (building, city) 取壊す toríkowasù

flatter [flæt'ə:r] vt (praise, compliment) ...にお世辞を言う ...ni oséji wò iú

flattering [flæt'ə:riŋ] adj (comment) うれしい uréshiî; (dress) よく似合う yókù niáû

flattery [flæt'ə:ri:] n お世辞 oséji

flaunt [flɔːnt] vt (wealth, possessions) 見せびらかす misébirakasù

flavor [flei'və:r] (BRIT **flavour**) n (of food, drink) 味 ajî; (of ice-cream etc) 種類 shúrui
♦vt ...に味を付ける ...ni ajî wo tsukerù
strawberry-flavored イチゴ味の ichí-goajî no

flavoring [flei'və:riŋ] n 調味料 chốmi-ryô

flaw [flɔː] n (in argument, policy) 不備な点 fúbî na teñ; (in character) 欠点 kettén; (in cloth, glass) 傷 kízû

flawless [flɔː'lis] adj 完璧な kañpeki na

flax [flæks] n 亜麻 amá

flaxen [flæk'sən] adj (hair) ブロンドの buróñdo no

flea [fliː] n (human, animal) ノミ nomí

fleck [flek] n (mark) 細かいはん点 ko-mákaî hañten

fled [fled] pt, pp of **flee**

flee [fli:] (*pt, pp* **fled**) *vt* (danger, famine, country) 逃れる nogárerù, ...から逃げる ...kara nigérù

♦*vi* (refugees, escapees) 逃げる nigérù

fleece [fli:s] *n* (sheep's wool) 羊毛一頭分 yōmōitòbùn; (sheep's coat) ヒツジの毛 hitsúji no kè

♦*vt* (*inf*: cheat) ...から大金をだまし取る ...kara taíkin wò dámashitorù

fleet [fli:t] *n* (of ships: for war) 艦隊 kañtai; (: for fishing etc) 船団 señdan; (of trucks, cars) 車両団 sharyōdan

fleeting [fli:'tiŋ] *adj* (glimpse) ちらっと 見える chiráttò míerù; (visit) 短い míjìkaì; (happiness) つかの間の tsuká no mà no

Flemish [flem'iʃ] *adj* フランダースの furándàsu no; (LING) フランダース語の furándàsugo no

♦*n* (LING) フランダース語 furándàsugo

flesh [fleʃ] *n* (ANAT) 肉 nikú; (skin) 肌 hadá; (of fruit) 果肉 kaníku

flesh wound *n* 軽傷 keíshō

flew [flu:] *pt of* **fly**

flex [fleks] *n* (of appliance) コード kōdo

♦*vt* (leg, muscles) 曲げたり伸したりする magétarì nobáshitarì suru

flexibility [fleksəbil'əti:] *n* (of material) しなやかさ shináyakasà; (of response, policy) 柔軟性 jūnañsei

flexible [flek'səbəl] *adj* (material) 曲げ やすい magéyasuì; (response, policy) 柔 軟な jūnan na

flick [flik] *n* (of hand, whip etc) 一振り hitófùri

♦*vt* (with finger, hand) はじき飛ばす hajíkitobasù; (towel, whip) ぴしっと振る pishíttò furù; (switch: on) 入れる iréru; (: off) 切る kírù

flicker [flik'ə:r] *vi* (light) ちらちらする chíràchira suru; (flame) ゆらゆらする yúràyura suru; (eyelids) まばたく mabátakù

flick through *vt fus* (book) ぱらぱらと ...のページをめくる páràpara to ...no pèji wo mekúrù

flier [flai'ə:r] *n* (pilot) パイロット paírottò

flight [flait] *n* (action: of birds, plane) 飛 行 hikō; (AVIAT: journey) 飛行機旅行 hikōkiryokō; (escape) 逃避 tōhi; (*also*: **flight of steps/stairs**) 階段 kaídan

flight attendant (*US*) *n* 乗客係 jōkyakugakàri

flight deck *n* (AVIAT) 操縦室 sōjūshìtsu; (NAUT) 空母の飛行甲板 kūbo no hikōkañpan

flimsy [flim'zi:] *adj* (shoes) こわれやすい kowáreyasuì; (clothes) 薄い usúi; (building) もろい moróì; (excuse) 見え透いた miésuità

flinch [flintʃ] *vi* (in pain, shock) 身震いす る mibúrùi suru

to flinch from (crime, unpleasant duty) ...するのをしり込みする ...surú no wò shirígomi surù

fling [fliŋ] (*pt, pp* **flung**) *vt* (throw) 投げ る nagérù

flint [flint] *n* (stone) 火打石 hiúchiishì; (in lighter) 石 ishí

flip [flip] *vt* (switch) はじく hajíkù; (coin) トスする tósù suru

flippant [flip'ənt] *adj* (attitude, answer) 軽率な keísotsu na

flipper [flip'ə:r] *n* (of seal etc) ひれ足 hiréashì; (for swimming) フリッパー furíppā

flirt [flə:rt] *vi* (with person) いちゃつく ichátsuku

♦*n* 浮気者 uwákimono

flit [flit] *vi* (birds, insects) ひょいと飛ぶ hyoí tò tobú

float [flout] *n* (for swimming, fishing) 浮 き ukí; (vehicle in parade) 山車 dashí; (money) つり用の小銭 tsuríyō nò kozéni

♦*vi* 浮く ukú

flock [flɑ:k] *n* 群れ muré; (REL) 会衆 kaíshū

♦*vi*: **to flock to** (place, event) ぞくぞく 集まる zókùzoku atsúmarù

flog [flɑ:g] *vt* (whip) むち打つ múchìutsu

flood [flʌd] *n* (of water) 洪水 kōzui; (of letters, imports etc) 大量 taíryō

♦*vt* (subj: water) 水浸しにする mizúbitàshi ni suru; (: people) ...に殺到する ...ni sattō suru

♦*vi* (place) 水浸しになる mizúbitàshi ni nárù; (people): **to flood into** ...に殺到する ...ni sattő suru

flooding [flʌd'iŋ] *n* 洪水 kőzui

floodlight [flʌd'lait] *n* 照明灯 shőmeitő

floor [flɔːr] *n* (of room) 床 yuká; (storey) 階 kái; (of sea, valley) 底 sőkő

♦*vt* (subj: blow) 打ちのめす uchínomesù; (: question) 仰天させる győten saserù

ground floor 1階 ikkái

first floor (*US*) 1階 ikkai (*BRIT*) 2階 nikái

floorboard [flɔːr'bɔːrd] *n* 床板 yuká-ita

floor show *n* フロアショー furőashő

flop [flɑːp] *n* (failure) 失敗 shippái

♦*vi* (fail) 失敗する shippái suru; (fall: into chair, onto floor etc) どたっと座り込む dotáttò suwárikomù

floppy [flɑːp'i:] *adj* ふにゃふにゃした fúnyàfunya shita

floppy (disk) *n* (COMPUT) フロッピー（ディスク）furóppī(disùku)

flora [flɔːr'ə] *n* 植物相 shokúbutsuső

floral [flɔːr'əl] *adj* (dress, wallpaper) 花柄の hanágara no

florid [flɔːr'id] *adj* (style) ごてごてした gőtègote shitá; (complexion) 赤らんだ akáraǹda

florist [flɔːr'ist] *n* 花屋 hanáyà

florist's (shop) *n* 花屋 hanáyà

flounce [flauns] *n* (frill) 縁飾り fuchíkazarì

flounce out *vi* 怒って飛び出す okőttè tobídasù

flounder [flaun'dəːr] *vi* (swimmer) もがく mogákù; (*fig*: speaker) まごつく magótsukù; (economy) 停滞する teítai suru

♦*n* (ZOOL) ヒラメ hiráme

flour [flau'əːr] *n* (*gen*) 粉 koná; (*also*: **wheat flour**) 小麦粉 komúgiko

flourish [flɔːr'iʃ] *vi* (business) 繁栄する haň-ei suru; (plant) 生い茂る oíshigerù

♦*n* (bold gesture): **with a flourish** 大げさな身振りで őgesa na mibùri de

flourishing [flɔːr'iʃiŋ] *adj* (company) 繁栄する haň-ei suru; (trade) 盛んな sakán na

flout [flaut] *vt* (law, rules) 犯す okásù

flow [flou] *n* 流れ nagáre

♦*vi* 流れる nagárerù

flow chart *n* 流れ図 nagárezù, フローチャート furőchāto

flower [flau'əːr] *n* 花 haná

♦*vi* (plant, tree) 咲く sakú

flower bed *n* 花壇 kádàn

flowerpot [flau'əːrpɑːt] *n* 植木鉢 uékibàchi

flowery [flau'ə:ri:] *adj* (perfume) 花の様な haná no yő na; (pattern) 花柄の hanágara no; (speech) 華々しい győgyőshiì

flown [floun] *pp* of **fly**

flu [fluː] *n* (MED) 流感 ryúkan

fluctuate [flʌk'tʃuːeit] *vi* (price, rate, temperature) 変動する heńdő suru

fluctuation [flʌktʃuːei'ʃən] *n*: **fluctuation (in)** (...の) 変動 (...no) heńdő

fluent [fluː'ənt] *adj* (linguist) 語学たん能な gogákutaňnő na; (speech, writing etc) 滑らかな naméràka na

he speaks fluent French, he's fluent in French 彼はフランス語が堪能だ kárè wa furánsugo gà tańnő da

fluently [fluː'əntli:] *adv* (speak, read, write) 流ちょうに ryúchő ni

fluff [flʌf] *n* (on jacket, carpet) 毛羽 kebá; (fur: of kitten etc) 綿毛 watáge

fluffy [flʌf'i:] *adj* (jacket, toy etc) ふわふわした fúwàfuwa shitá

fluid [fluː'id] *adj* (movement) しなやかな shináyàka na; (situation, arrangement) 流動的な ryúdőteki na

♦*n* (liquid) 液 ékì

fluke [fluːk] (*inf*) *n* まぐれ magúrè

flung [flʌŋ] *pt*, *pp* of **fling**

fluorescent [fluːəres'ənt] *adj* (dial, paint, light etc) 蛍光の keíkő no

fluoride [fluː'əːraid] *n* フッ化物 fukkábùtsu

flurry [flɔːr'i:] *n*: **a snow flurry** にわか雪 niwákayùki

flurry of activity 慌ただしい動き awátadashiǐ ugőki

flush [flʌʃ] *n* (on face) ほてり hotéri; (*fig*: of youth, beauty etc) 輝かしさ kagáyakashisà

♦*vt* (drains, pipe) 水を流して洗う mizú

wǒ nagáshite araù
♦*vi* (become red) 赤くなる akáku narù
♦*adj*: **flush with** (level) ...と同じ高さの
...to onáji takasà no
to flush the toilet トイレの水を流す
tôíre no mizú wo nagasù

flushed [flʌʃt] *adj* 赤らめた akáramètá

flush out *vt* (game, birds) 茂みから追出
す shigémi kàra oídasù

flustered [flʌs'tə:rd] *adj* (nervous, confused) まごついた magótsuità

flute [flu:t] *n* フルート fúrùto

flutter [flʌt'ə:r] *n* (of wings) 羽ばたき habátaki; (of panic, excitement, nerves) うろたえ urôtae
♦*vi* (bird) 羽ばたきする habátaki suru

flux [flʌks] *n*: **in a state of flux** 流動的
状態で ryúdòtekijòtai de

fly [flai] *n* (insect) ハエ haé; (on trousers: also: **flies**) ズボンの前 zubóñ no máè
♦*vb* (*pt* **flew**, *pp* **flown**)
♦*vt* (plane) 操縦する sǒjū suru; (passengers, cargo) 空輸する kǘyū suru; (distances) 飛ぶ tobú
♦*vi* (bird, insect, plane) 飛ぶ tobú; (passengers) 飛行機で行く hikóki de ikú; (escape) 逃げる nigérù; (flag) 掲げられる kakágerarerù

fly away *vi* (bird, insect) 飛んで行く tofíde ikú

flying [flai'iŋ] *n* (activity) 飛行機旅行 hikókiryokò; (action) 飛行 hikǒ
♦*adj*: **a flying visit** ほんの短い訪問 hofíno mijíkaì hǒmon
with flying colors 大成功で daíseikō de

flying saucer *n* 空飛ぶ円盤 sórà tobú efíban

flying start *n*: **to get off to a flying start** 好調な滑りだしをする kǒchō na suberídàshi wo suru

fly off *vi* = **fly away**

flyover [flai'ouvə:r] (*BRIT*) *n* (overpass) 陸橋 rikkyǒ

flysheet [flai'ʃi:t] *n* (for tent) 入口の垂れ
布 iríguchi nò tarénuno

foal [foul] *n* 子ウマ koúma

foam [foum] *n* (of surf, water, beer) 泡

awá; (*also*: **foam rubber**) フォームラバー fǒmurabà
♦*vi* (liquid) 泡立つ awádàtsu
to foam at the mouth (person, animal)
泡をふく awá wo fukù

fob [fɑ:b] *vt*: **to fob someone off** ...をだ
ます ...wo damásù

focal point *n* (of room, activity etc) 中心 chúshin

focus [fou'kəs] (*pl* **focuses**) *n* (PHOT) 焦
点 shǒten; (of attention, storm etc) 中心 chúshin
♦*vt* (field glasses etc) ...の焦点を合せる
...no shǒten wò awáserù
♦*vi*: **to focus (on)** (with camera)
(...に) カメラを合せる (...ni) kámèra wò awáserù; (person) (...に) 注意を向ける
(...ni) chúi wo mukérù
in/out of focus 焦点が合っている〔いない〕shǒten ga attè irú [ináí]

fodder [fɑ:d'ə:r] *n* (food) 飼葉 kaíba

foe [fou] *n* (rival, enemy) 敵 tekí

foetus [fi:'təs] (*BRIT*) = **fetus**

fog [fɔ:g] *n* 霧 kirí

foggy [fɔ:g'i:] *adj*: **it's foggy** 霧が出てい
る kirí ga detè irú

fog light (*BRIT* **fog lamp**) *n* (AUT) フ
ォッグライト fǒggùraito

foil [fɔil] *vt* (attack, plan) くじく kujíkù
♦*n* (metal foil, kitchen foil) ホイル hóì-ru; (complement) 引立てる物 hikítaterù monò; (FENCING) フルーレ furúrè

fold [fould] *n* (bend, crease) 折り目 oríme;
(of skin etc) しわ shiwá; (in cloth, curtain etc) ひだ hidá; (AGR) ヒツジの囲い
hitsúji nò kakói; (*fig*) 仲間 nakáma
♦*vt* (clothes, paper) 畳む tatámu; (arms)
組む kúmù

folder [foul'də:r] *n* (for papers) 書類挟み
shorúibasàmi

folding [foul'diŋ] *adj* (chair, bed) 折畳み
式の orítatamishiki no

fold up *vi* (map, bed, table) 折畳める orí-tatamerù; (business) つぶれる tsubúrerù
♦*vt* (map, clothes etc) 畳む tatámu

foliage [fou'li:idʒ] *n* (leaves) 葉 ha ◇総称 sǒshō

folk [fouk] *npl* (people) 人々 hitobíto

◆*adj* (art, music) 民族の mínzoku no

folks (parents) 両親 ryóshin

folklore [fouk'lɔ:r] *n* 民間伝承 mińkandeńshō

folk song *n* 民謡 miń-yō

follow [fɑ:l'ou] *vt* (person) ...について行く ...ni tsúite ikú; (suspect) 尾行する bikó suru; (event) ...に注目する ...ni chūmoku suru; (story) 注意して聞く chūí shite kikú; (leader, example, advice, instructions) ...に従う ...ni shitágaù; (route, path) たどる tadórù

◆*vi* (person, period of time) 後に来る〔いく〕átò ni kúru〔ikú〕; (result) ...という結果になる ...to iú kekká ni nárù

to follow suit (*fig*) (...と) 同じ事をする (...to) onáji kotò wo suru

follower [fɑ:l'ouər] *n* (of person) 支持者 shijíshà; (of belief) 信奉者 shińpōsha

following [fɑ:l'ouiŋ] *adj* 次の tsugí no

◆*n* (of party, religion, group etc) 支持者 shijíshà ◇総称 sōshō

follow up *vt* (letter, offer) ...に答える ...ni kotáerù; (case) 追及する tsuíkyū suru

folly [fɑ:l'i:] *n* (foolishness) ばかな事 báka na kotó

fond [fɑ:nd] *adj* (memory) 楽しい tanóshiì; (smile, look) 愛情に満ちた aíjō ni michíta; (hopes, dreams) 愚かな óròka na

to be fond of ...が好きである ...ga sukí de arù

fondle [fɑ:n'dəl] *vt* 愛ぶする aíbu suru

font [fɑ:nt] *n* (in church) 洗礼盤 seńreiban; (TYP) フォント fóñto

food [fu:d] *n* 食べ物 tabémonò

food mixer *n* ミキサー míkīsā

food poisoning [-pɔi'zəniŋ] *n* 食中毒 shokúchūdoku

food processor [-prɑ:s'esə:r] *n* ミキサー míkīsā ◇食べ物を混ぜたりひいたりおろしたりするための家庭電気製品 tabemono wo mazetari hiitari oroshitari suru tame no katei denki seihin

foodstuffs [fu:d'stʌfs] *npl* 食料 shokúryō

fool [fu:l] *n* (idiot) ばか bákà; (CULIN)

フール fúru ◇果物入りムースの一種 kudámono-iri mūsu no ísshū

◆*vt* (deceive) だます damásù

◆*vi* (*also*: **fool around**: be silly) ふざける fuzákerù

foolhardy [fu:l'hɑːrdi:] *adj* (conduct) 無謀な mubó na

foolish [fu:l'iʃ] *adj* (stupid) ばかな bákà na; (rash) 無茶な muchá na

foolproof [fu:l'pru:f] *adj* (plan etc) 絶対確実な zettáikakùjitsu na

foot [fut] (*pl* **feet**) *n* (of person, animal) 足 ashí; (of bed, cliff) ふもと fumóto; (measure) フィート fíto

◆*vt* (bill) 支払う shiháraù

on foot 徒歩で tóhò de

footage [fut'idʒ] *n* (CINEMA) 場面 bámèn

football [fut'bɔ:l] *n* (ball: round) サッカーボール sakkábòru; (: oval) フットボール futtóbòru; (sport: *BRIT*) サッカー sakká; (: *US*) フットボール futtóbòru

football player *n* (*BRIT*: *also*: **footballer**) サッカー選手 sakká seńshu; (*US*) フットボール選手 futtóbōru seńshu

footbrake [fut'breik] *n* 足ブレーキ ashíburèki

footbridge [fut'bridʒ] *n* 橋 hashí ◇歩行者しか渡れない狭い物を指す hokóshà shika watárenài semái monó wo sasù

foothills [fut'hilz] *npl* 山ろくの丘陵地帯 sańroku nò kyūryōchìtai

foothold [fut'hould] *n* 足場 ashíba

footing [fut'iŋ] *n* (*fig*: position) 立場 tachíba

to lose one's footing 足を踏み外す ashí wo fumíhazusù

footlights [fut'laits] *npl* (THEATER) フットライト futtóraìto

footman [fut'mən] (*pl* **footmen**) *n* (servant) 下男 genán

footnote [fut'nout] *n* 脚注 kyakúchū

footpath [fut'pæθ] *n* 遊歩道 yūhodò

footprint [fut'print] *n* (of person, animal) 足跡 ashíato

footstep [fut'step] *n* (sound) 足音 ashíoto; (footprint) 足跡 ashíato

footwear [fut'weə:r] *n* (shoes, sandals

etc) 履物 hakímono

KEYWORD

for [fɔːr] *prep* **1** (indicating destination, intention) ...行きの ...yuki no, ...に向かって ...ni mùkátte, ...のために〔の〕 ...notaméní[no]
the train for London ロンドン行きの電車 róndonyuki no densha
he left for Rome 彼はローマへ出発しました kárè wa rốmà e shúppatsu shimashìta
he went for the paper 彼は新聞を取りに行きました kárè wa shínbun wo torí ni ikímashìta
is this for me? これは私に? korè wa wàtákushi nî?
there's a letter for you あなた宛の手紙が来ています ànáta ate no tegami ga kìté ìmasu
it's time for lunch 昼食の時間です chûshoku no jikan desù
2 (indicating purpose) ...のために〔の〕 ...no tamé nì[no]
what's it for? それは何のためですか soré wa nàn no tamé dèsu ká
give it to me - what for? それをよこせ-何で? soré wo yòkósè - nàndé?
clothes for children 子供服 kodómofùku
to pray for peace 平和を祈る héiwa wo inorù
3 (on behalf of, representing) ...の代理として ...no dàfrí toshite
the MP for Hove ホーブ選出の議員 hōbùsénshutsu no gìn
he works for the government/a local firm 彼は政府〔地元の会社〕に雇われています kárè wa sêfu(jimóto no kaisha)ni yatówarète imásù
I'll ask him for you あなたに代って私が彼に聞きましょう ànáta ni kawátte wàtákushi ga karè ni kikímashò
G for George GはジョージのG G wà jóji no G
4 (because of) ...の理由で ...no riyú de, ...のために ...no tamé nì
for this reason このため kònó tame

for fear of being criticized 批判を恐れて hìhán wo òsórète
the town is famous for its canals 町は運河で有名です machí wà úngà de yūmei desù
5 (with regard to) ...にしては ...ni shité wà
it's cold for July 7月にしては寒い shichígatsu nì shité wà samúì
he's mature for his age 彼はませている kárè wa másète iru
a gift for languages 語学の才能 gógàku no saínô
for everyone who voted yes, 50 voted no 賛成1に対して反対50だった sánsei ìchí nì tâî shite hántaihyò gojú dàtta
6 (in exchange for) ...と交換して ...to kôkan shite
I sold it for $5 5ドルでそれを売りました gốdòru de sorê wo ùrímashìta
to pay $2.50 for a ticket 切符を2ドル50セントで買う kìppú wo nídòru gojússeñto de kaú
7 (in favor of) ...に賛成して ...ni sánsei shite
are you for or against us? あなたは我々に賛成なのか反対なのかはっきり言いなさい ànátà wa waréware ni sánsei na nò ka hántai na nò ka hakkírì íinasaî
I'm all for it 私は無条件で賛成です watákushi wa mùjôkèn de sánsei desù
vote for X Xに投票する ékkùsu ni tôhyò suru
8 (referring to distance): *there are roadworks for 5 km* 5キロもの区間が工事中です gốkìro mo no kúkàn ga kôjichū desù
we walked for miles 何マイルも歩きました nánmaìru mo arúkimashìta
9 (referring to time) ...の間 ...no aída
he was away for 2 years 彼は2年間家を離れていました kárè wa nínêñkan iê wò hanárete imashìta
she will be away for a month 彼女は1か月間出掛ける事になっています kánojo wa ikkágetsukàn dekákeru kotô ni natté imasu

it hasn't rained for 3 weeks 雨は3週間も降っていません ámè wa sañshūkan mo futté imaseñ

I have known her for years 何年も前から彼女とは知り合いです náñnen mo máè kara kánòjo to wa shiríai desù

can you do it for tomorrow? 明日までに出来ますか asú madè ni dekímasù ká

10 (with infinitive clause): *it is not for me to decide* 私が決める事ではありません watákushi gà kiméru kotò de wa arímaseñ

it would be best for you to leave あなたは帰った方がいい anátà wa káètta hō ga íi

there is still time for you to do it あなたはまだまだをする時間があります anátà wa mádàmada soré wò suru jikañ ga arímasù

for this to be possible ... これが可能になるのには... koré gà kanō ni narù no ni wa...

11 (in spite of) ...にもかかわらず ...ní mò kakáwarazù

for all his complaints, he is very fond of her 彼は色々と文句を言うが, 結局彼女を愛しています kárè wa iróiro tò móñku wo iú gà, kekkyóku kanòjo wo âi shite imásù

for all he said he would write, in the end he didn't 手紙を書くと言っていましたけれども, 結局書いてくれませんでした tegámi wò kákù kákù to ittè imashità keredomo, kekkyóku kaitè kurémasen deshìta

♦*conj* (since, as: rather formal) なぜならば...だから názènaraba ...dá kàra

she was very angry, for he was late again 彼女はかんかんになっていました, というのは彼はまたも遅刻したからです kánòjo wa kañkañ ni natté imashìta, to iú no wà kárè wa matá mò chikóku shita kara desù

---

forage [fɔːrˈidʒ] *vi* (search: for food, interesting objects etc) ...をあさる ...wo asárù

foray [fɔːrˈei] *n* (raid) 侵略 shiñryaku

forbad(e) [fərbædˈ] *pt of* **forbid**

forbid [fərbidˈ] (*pt* **forbad(e)**, *pp* **forbidden**) *vt* (sale, marriage, event etc) 禁ずる kiñzurù

to forbid someone to do something ...を...するのを禁ずる ...ni ...surú no wò kiñzurù

forbidden [fərbidˈən] *pp of* **forbid**

forbidding [fərbidˈiŋ] *adj* (look, prospect) 怖い kowái

force [fɔːrs] *n* (violence) 暴力 bṓryoku; (PHYSICS, *also* strength) 力 chikára

♦*vt* (compel) 強制する kyṓsei suru; (push) 強く押す tsúyòku osú; (break open: lock, door) こじ開ける kojíakerù

in force (in large numbers) 大勢で ōzei de; (LAW) 有効で yūkō de

to force oneself to do 無理して...する múrì shite ...suru

forced [fɔːrst] *adj* (labor) 強制的な kyṓseiteki na; (smile) 作りの tsukúri no

forced landing (AVIAT) 不時着 fujíchaku

force-feed [fɔːrsˈfiːd] *vt* (animal, prisoner) ...に強制給餌をする ...ni kyṓseikyūji wo suru

forceful [fɔːrsˈfəl] *adj* (person) 力強い chikárazuyoì; (attack) 強烈な kyṓretsu na; (point) 説得力のある settókuryoku no arù

forceps [fɔːrˈsəps] *npl* ピンセット piñsettò

forces [fɔːrsˈiz] (BRIT) *npl*: *the Forces* (MIL) 軍隊 guñtai

forcibly [fɔːrsˈəbliː] *adv* (remove) 力ずくで chikárazukù de; (express) 力強く chikárazuyokù

ford [fɔːrd] *n* (in river) 浅瀬 asáse ◇船を使わないで川を渡れる場所を指す fúnè wo tsukáwanaìde kawá wò watáreru bashò wo sásù

fore [fɔːr] *n*: *to come to the fore* 前面に出て来る zeñmen ni dete kurù

forearm [fɔːrˈɑːrm] *n* 前腕 maéude

foreboding [fɔːrboudˈiŋ] *n* (of disaster) 不吉な予感 fukítsu na yokañ

forecast [fɔːrˈkæst] *n* (of profits, prices,

weather) 予報 yohō

♦vt (pt, pp **forecast**) (predict) 予報する yohō suru

forecourt [fɔːrˈkɔːrt] n (of garage) 前庭 maéniwa

forefathers [fɔːrˈfɑːðərz] npl (ancestors) 先祖 señzo

forefinger [fɔːrˈfiŋgəːr] n 人差指 hitósashiyúbi

forefront [fɔːrˈfrʌnt] n: **in the forefront of** (industry, movement) ...の最前線で ...no saízeñsen de

forego [fɔːrˈgou] (pt **forewent** pp **foregone**) vt (give up) やめる yamérù; (go without) ...なしで我慢する ...náshì de gáman suru

foregone [fɔːrˈgɔːn] adj: **it's a foregone conclusion** 結果は決まっている kekká wa kimattē irú

foreground [fɔːrˈgraund] n (of painting) 前景 zeñkei

forehead [fɔːrˈhed] n 額 hitái

foreign [fɔːrˈin] adj (country) 外国の gaíkoku no; (trade) 対外の taígai no; (object, matter) 異質の ishítsu no

foreigner [fɔːrˈənəːr] n 外国人 gaíkokujìn

foreign exchange n 外国為替 gaíkokukawàse; (currency) 外貨 gaíka

Foreign Office (BRIT) n 外務省 gaímushō

Foreign Secretary (BRIT) n 外務大臣 gaímudaìjin

foreleg [fɔːrˈleg] n (of animal) 前足 maéashi

foreman [fɔːrˈmən] (pl **foremen**) n (in factory, on building site etc)現場監督 geñbakañtoku

foremost [fɔːrˈmoust] adj (most important) 最も大事な mottómò dáijì na

♦adv: **first and foremost** 先ず第一に mázù dáìchi ni

forensic [fərenˈsik] adj (medicine, test) 法医学的な hōigàkuteki na

forerunner [fɔːrˈrʌnəːr] n 先駆者 señkushà

foresee [fɔːrsiːˈ] (pt **foresaw** pp **foreseen**) vt (problem, development) 予想す

る yosō suru

foreseeable [fɔːrsiːˈəbəl] adj (problem, development) 予想出来る yosō dekirù

foreshadow [fɔːrʃædˈou] vt (event) ...の前兆となる ...no zeńchō to narù

foresight [fɔːrˈsait] n 先見の明 señken nò meí

forest [fɔːrˈist] n 森 mórì

forestall [fɔːrstɔːlˈ] vt (person) 出し抜く dashínuku; (discussion) 防ぐ fuségù

forestry [fɔːrˈistriː] n 林業 riñgyō

foretaste [fɔːrˈteist] n 前兆 zeñchō

foretell [fɔːrtelˈ] (pt, pp **foretold**) vt (predict) 予言する yogén suru

forever [fərevˈəːr] adv (for good) 永遠に eíen ni; (continually) いつも ítsùmo

forewent [fɔːrwentˈ] pt of **forego**

foreword [fɔːrˈwəːrd] n (in book) 前書 maégaki

forfeit [fɔːrˈfit] vt (lose: right, friendship etc) 失う ushínaù

forgave [fərgeivˈ] pt of **forgive**

forge [fɔːrdʒ] n (smithy) 鍛冶屋 kajíyà

♦vt (signature, money) 偽造する gizō suru; (wrought iron) 鍛えて作る kitáetè tsukúrù

forge ahead vi (country, person) 前進する zeńshin suru

forger [fɔːrˈdʒəːr] n 偽造者 gizōshà

forgery [fɔːrˈdʒəːriː] n (crime) 偽造 gizō; (object) 偽物 nisémono

forget [fərgetˈ] (pt **forgot**, pp **forgotten**) vt (fact, face, skill, appointment) 忘れる wasúrerù; (leave behind: object) 置忘れる okíwasurerù; (put out of mind: quarrel, person) 考えない事にする kañgaeñai kotō ni surù

♦vi (fail to remember) 忘れる wasúrerù

forgetful [fərgetˈfəl] adj (person) 忘れっぽい wasúreppòi

forget-me-not [fərgetˈmiːnɑːt] n ワスレナグサ wasúrenagùsa

forgive [fərgivˈ] (pt **forgave**, pp **forgiven**) vt (pardon) 許す yurúsù

to forgive someone for something (excuse) ...の...を許す ...no ...wo yurúsù

forgiveness [fərgivˈnis] n 許し yurúshi

forgo [fɔːrgouˈ] vt = **forego**

forgot [fərˈgɑːt] *pt of* **forget**

forgotten [fərˈgɑːtˈən] *pp of* **forget**

fork [fɔːrk] *n* (for eating) フォーク fôku; (for gardening) ホーク hôku; (in road, river, railway) 分岐点 buńkiteń
♦*vi* (road) 分岐する buńki suru

fork-lift truck [fɔːrkˈlift-] *n* フォークリフト fôkurifùto

fork out (*inf*) *vt* (pay) 払う haráù

forlorn [fɔːrlɔːrn'] *adj* (person, place) わびしい wabíshiì; (attempt) 絶望的な zetsúbōteki na; (hope) 空しい munáshiì

form [fɔːrm] *n* (type) 種類 shúrùi; (shape) 形 katáchi; (SCOL) 学年 gakúnen; (questionnaire) 用紙 yôshi
♦*vt* (make: shape, queue, object, habit) 作る tsukúrù; (make up: organization, group) 構成する kôsei suru; (idea) まとめる matómerù

in top form 調子が最高で chôshi gà saíkō de

formal [fɔːrˈməl] *adj* (offer, statement, occasion) 正式な seíshiki na; (person, behavior) 堅苦しい katágurushiì; (clothes) 正装の seísō no; (garden) 伝統的な deńtōteki na ◇極めて幾何学的な配置の庭園について言う kiwámete kikágakuteki na haíchi nò teien ni tsuitè iú; (education) 正規の seíki no

formalities [fɔːrmælˈitiːz] *npl* (procedures) 手続き tetsúzùki

formality [fɔːrmælˈiti:] *n* (procedure) 形式 keíshiki

formally [fɔːrˈməli:] *adv* (make offer etc) 正式に seíshiki ni; (act) 堅苦しく katágurushikù; (dress): *to dress formally* 正装する seísō suru

format [fɔːrˈmæt] *n* (form, style) 形式 keíshiki
♦*vt* (COMPUT: disk) 初期化する shókìka suru, フォーマットする fômatto suru

formation [fɔːrmeiˈʃən] *n* (creation: of organization, business) 創立 sôritsu; (: of theory) 考案 kôan; (pattern) 編隊 heńtai; (of rocks, clouds) 構造 kôzō

formative [fɔːrˈmətiv] *adj* (years, influence) 形成的な keíseiteki na

former [fɔːrˈmər] *adj* (one-time) かつて

の kátsùte no; (earlier) 前の mâe no

the former ... the latter ... 前者... 後者... zeńshà... kôshà...

formerly [fɔːrˈmərli:] *adv* (previously) 前は mâe wa

formidable [fɔːrˈmidəbəl] *adj* (task, opponent) 手ごわい tegówaì

formula [fɔːrˈmjələ] (*pl* **formulae** *or* **formulas**) *n* (MATH, CHEM) 公式 kôshiki; (plan) 方式 hôshiki

formulate [fɔːrˈmjəleit] *vt* (plan, strategy) 練る nérù; (opinion) 表現する hyôgen suru

forsake [fɔːrseikˈ] (*pt* **forsook**, *pp* **forsaken**) *vt* (abandon: person) 見捨てる misúterù; (: belief) 捨てる sutérù

forsook [fɔːrsukˈ] *pt of* **forsake**

fort [fɔːrt] *n* とりで toríde

forte [fɔːrˈtei] *n* (strength) 得意 tokúì

forth [fɔːrθ] *adv* (out) 外へ sótò e

back and forth 行ったり来たりして ittárì kitárì shité

and so forth など nádò

forthcoming [fɔːrθˈkʌmˈiŋ] *adj* (event) 今度の końdo no; (help, evidence) 手に入る té ni hairù; (person) 率直な sotchôku na

forthright [fɔːrθˈrait] *adj* (condemnation, opposition) はっきりとした hakkírì to shitá

forthwith [fɔːrθwiθˈ] *adv* 直ちに tádàchi ni

fortify [fɔːrˈtəfai] *vt* (city) ...の防備を固める ...no bôbi wo katámerù; (person) 力付ける chikárazukerù

fortitude [fɔːrˈtətuːd] *n* 堅忍 keńnin

fortnight [fɔːrtˈnait] *n* (two weeks) 2週間 nishûkan

fortnightly [fɔːrtˈnaitliː] *adj* (payment, visit, magazine) 2週間置きの nishûkan-oki no
♦*adv* (pay, meet, appear) 2週間置きに nishûkan-oki ni

fortress [fɔːrˈtris] *n* 要塞 yôsai

fortuitous [fɔːrtuːˈitəs] *adj* (discovery, result) 偶然の gûzen no

fortunate [fɔːrˈtʃənit] *adj* (person) 運のいい úń no íì; (event) 幸運な kôun na *it is fortunate that ...* 幸いに... saíwai ni ...

fortunately [fɔːr'tʃənitli:] *adv* (happily, luckily) 幸いに saíwai ni

fortune [fɔːr'tʃən] *n* (luck) 運 úñ; (wealth) 財産 zaísan

fortune-teller [fɔːr'tʃəntelər] *n* 易者 e-kísha

forty [fɔːr'ti:] *num* 40 (の) yóñjū (no)

forum [fɔːr'əm] *n* フォーラム fôramu

forward [fɔːr'wərd] *adj* (in position) 前方の zeñpō no; (in movement) 前方への zeñpō e no; (in time) 将来のための shôrai nò tame no; (not shy) 出過ぎた desúgità
♦*n* (SPORT) フォワード fowádo
♦*vt* (letter, parcel, goods) 転送する teñsō suru; (career, plans) 前進させる zeñshin saserù

to move forward (progress) 進歩する shíñpo suru

forward(s) [fɔːr'wərd(z)] *adv* 前へ mâe e

fossil [fɑs'əl] *n* 化石 kaséki

foster [fɔːs'tər] *vt* (child) 里親として育てる satóoya toshitè sodáterù; (idea, activity) 助成する joséi suru

foster child *n* 里子 satógo

fought [fɔːt] *pt, pp of* **fight**

foul [faul] *adj* (state, taste, smell, weather) 悪い warúì; (language) 汚い kitánaì; (temper) ひどい hidôi
♦*n* (SPORT) 反則 hañsoku, ファウル fáùru
♦*vt* (dirty) 汚す yogósù

foul play *n* (LAW) 殺人 satsújin

found [faund] *pt, pp of* **find**
♦*vt* (establish: business, theater) 設立する setsúritsu suru

foundation [faundei'ʃən] *n* (act) 設立 setsúritsu; (base) 土台 dodái; (organization) 財団 zaídan; (*also*: **foundation cream**) ファンデーション fañdêshon

foundations [faundei'ʃənz] *npl* (of building) 土台 dodái

founder [faun'dər] *n* (of firm, college) 設立者 setsúritsushà
♦*vi* (ship) 沈没する chíñbotsu suru

foundry [faun'dri:] *n* 鋳造工場 chūzōkō-jò

fountain [faun'tin] *n* 噴水 fuñsui

fountain pen *n* 万年筆 mañneñhitsu

four [fɔːr] *num* 4 (の) yóñ (no), 四つ (の) yotsu (no)

on all fours 四つんばいになって yotsúñbai ni nattè

four-poster [fɔːr'pous'tər] *n* (*also*: **four-poster bed**) 天がい付きベット teñgaitsukibetto

foursome [fɔːr'səm] *n* 4人組 yoníñgumi

fourteen [fɔːr'ti:n'] *num* 14 (の) jûyon (no)

fourth [fɔːrθ] *num* 第4(の) daíyon (no)

fowl [faul] *n* 家きん kakín

fox [fɑːks] *n* キツネ kitsúne
♦*vt* (baffle) 困らす komárasu

foyer [fɔi'ər] *n* (of hotel, theater) ロビー rôbì

fraction [fræk'ʃən] *n* (portion) 一部 ichíbù; (MATH) 分数 buñsū

fracture [fræk'tʃər] *n* (of bone) 骨折 kossétsu
♦*vt* (bone) 折る órù

fragile [frædʒ'əl] *adj* (breakable) 壊れやすい kowáreyasuì

fragment [fræg'mənt] *n* (small piece) 破片 hahéñ

fragrance [freig'rəns] *n* (scent) 香り kaóri

fragrant [freig'rənt] *adj* 香り高い kaóritakaì

frail [freil] *adj* (person, invalid) か弱い kayówaì; (structure) 壊れやすい kowáreyasuì

frame [freim] *n* (of building, structure) 骨組 honégumi; (of human, animal) 体格 taíkaku; (of door, window) 枠 wakú; (of picture) 額縁 gakúbuchi; (of spectacles: *also*: **frames**) フレーム fúrēmu
♦*vt* (picture) 額縁に入れる gakúbuchi ni irerù

frame of mind *n* 気分 kibúñ

framework [freim'wərk] *n* (structure) 骨組 honégumi

France [fræns] *n* フランス furánsu

franchise [fræn'tʃaiz] *n* (POL) 参政権 sañseikèn; (COMM) フランチャイズ furánchaĭzu

frank [fræŋk] *adj* (discussion, look) 率直
な sotchóku na, フランクな furáňku na
♦*vt* (letter) ...に...料金別納の判を押す ...ni
ryōkinbetsunō no háň wo osú

frankly [fræŋk'li:] *adv* (honestly) 正直に
shōjikí ni; (candidly) 率直に sotchóku ni

frankness [fræŋk'nis] *n* (honesty) 正直
さ shōjikisà; (candidness) 率直さ sotchóku-
kusa

frantic [fræn'tik] *adj* (distraught) 狂乱
した kyōran shita; (hectic) てんてこ舞い
の teñtekomài no

fraternal [frətəːr'nəl] *adj* (greetings,
relations) 兄弟の様な kyōdai no yō na

fraternity [frətəːr'niti:] *n* (feeling) 友愛
yūjō; (group of people) 仲間 nakáma

fraternize [fræt'əːrnaiz] *vi* 付き合う
tsukíaù

fraud [frɔːd] *n* (crime) 詐欺 sagí; (person)
ぺてん師 peténshi

fraudulent [frɔː'dʒələnt] *adj* (scheme,
claim) 不正な fuséi na

fraught [frɔːt] *adj*: **fraught with** (danger, problems) ...をはらんだ ...wo haráñ-
da

fray [frei] *n* (battle, fight) 戦い tatákai
♦*vi* (cloth, rope) 擦切れる suríkirerù;
(rope end) ほつれる hotsúrerù
tempers were frayed 皆短気になって
いた miná táňki ni nátte itá

freak [friːk] *n* (person: in attitude,
behavior) 変人 heñjin; (: in appearance)
奇形 kikéi
♦*adj* (event, accident) まぐれの mágure
no

freckle [frek'əl] *n* そばかす sobákasù

free [friː] *adj* (person, press, movement)
自由な jíyū na; (not occupied: time) 暇な
hímà na; (: seat) 空いている aíte irù;
(costing nothing: meal, pen etc) 無料の
muryō no
♦*vt* (prisoner etc) 解放する kaíhō suru;
(jammed object) 動ける様にする ugóke-
ru yō ni suru
free (of charge) 無料で muryō de
for free = **free of charge**

freedom [friː'dəm] *n* (liberty) 自由 jíyū

free-for-all [friː'fəːrɔːl'] *n* 乱闘 rañtō

free gift *n* 景品 keíhin

freehold [friː'hould] *n* (of property) 自由
保有権 jiyúhoyùken

free kick *n* (SPORT) フリーキック furí-
kikkù

freelance [friː'læns] *adj* (journalist, photographer, work) フリーランサーの furí-
rañsā no

freely [friː'liː] *adv* (without restriction,
limits) 自由に jíyū ni; (liberally) 気ままに
kimáma ni

Freemason [friː'meisən] *n* フリーメーソ
ン furímèson

Freepost [friː'poust] (® *BRIT*) *n* (postal
service) 料金受取人払い ryōkin uketori-
ninbarài

free-range [friː'reindʒ] *adj* 放し飼いの
hanáshigài no ◇特にニワトリやその卵に
ついて言う tōkù ni niwátori yà sonó
tamagò ni tsúīte iú

free trade *n* 自由貿易 jiyúbōeki

freeway [friː'wei] (*US*) *n* 高速道路 kōsokudōro

free will *n* 自由意志 jiyúishì
of one's own free will 自発的に jihátsuteki ni

freeze [friːz] (*pt* **froze**, *pp* **frozen**) *vi*
(weather) 氷点下になる hyōteňka ni ná-
rù; (liquid, pipe) 凍る kōrù; (person: with
cold) 冷える hiérù; (: stop moving) 立ち
すくむ tachísukumù
♦*vt* (water, lake) 凍らせる kōraserù;
(food) 冷凍にする reítō ni surù; (prices,
salaries) 凍結する tōketsu suru
♦*n* (weather) 氷点下の天気 hyōteňka no
téňki; (on arms, wages) 凍結 tōketsu

freeze-dried [friːz'draid'] *adj* 凍結乾燥
の tōketsukañsō no

freezer [friː'zəːr] *n* フリーザー furízā

freezing [friː'zin] *adj* (wind, weather,
water) 凍る様な kōru yō na
3 degrees below freezing 氷点下3度
hyōteňka sáňdo

freezing point *n* 氷点 hyōten

freight [freit] *n* (goods) 貨物 kámotsu;
(money charged) 運送料 uñsōryō

freight train (*US*) *n* (goods train) 貨物

列車 kamótsuresshà

French [frentʃ] *adj* フランス の furánsu no; (LING) フランス語の furánsugo no

♦*n* (LING) フランス語 furánsugo

♦*npl*: **the French** (people) フランス人 furánsujìn

French bean *n* サヤインゲン sayá-ingen

French fried potatoes *npl* フレンチフライ（ポテト）furénchifurài(pótèto)

French fries [-fraiz] (*US*) *npl* = **French fried potatoes**

Frenchman/woman [fren'tʃmən /wumən] (*pl* **Frenchmen/women**) *n* フランス人男性〔女性〕furánsujìn dañsei (jòsei)

French window *n* フランス窓 furánsu madò

frenetic [frənet'ik] *adj* (activity, behavior) 熱狂的な nekkyóteki na

frenzy [fren'zi:] *n* (of violence) 逆上 gyakújō; (of joy, excitement) 狂乱 kyóran

frequency [fri:'kwənsi:] *n* (of event) 頻度 híndo; (RADIO) 周波数 shúhasù

frequent [*adj* fri:'kwint *vb* frikwent'] *adj* (intervals, visitors) 頻繁な hiñpan na

♦*vt* (pub, restaurant) ...によく行く ...ni yóku ikú

frequently [fri:'kwintli:] *adv* (often) しばしば shíbàshiba

fresco [fres'kou] *n* フレスコ画 furésukoga

fresh [freʃ] *adj* (food, vegetables, bread, air etc) 新鮮な shiñsen na; (memories, footprint) 最近の saíkin no; (instructions) 新たな árata na; (paint) 塗立ての nurítate no; (new: approach, start) 新しい atárashiì; (cheeky: person) 生意気な namáìki na

freshen [freʃ'ən] *vi* (wind) 強くなる tsuyóku narù; (air) 涼しくなる suzúshiku narù

freshen up *vi* (person) 化粧直しをする keshónaòshi wo suru

fresher [freʃ'ə:r] (*BRIT*: *inf*) *n* = **freshman**

freshly [freʃ'li:] *adv* (made, cooked, painted) ...されたばかりで ...saréta bakàri de

freshman [freʃ'mən] (*pl* **freshmen**) *n* (*US*: SCOL) 1年生 ichínensei ◇大学生や高校生について言う daígakùsei ya kókōsei ni tsuitè iú

freshness [freʃ'nis] *n* 新鮮さ shiñsensà

freshwater [freʃ'wɔ:tər] *adj* (lake, fish) 淡水の tañsui no

fret [fret] *vi* (worry) 心配する shiñpai suru

friar [frai'ə:r] *n* (REL) 修道士 shúdōshì

friction [frik'ʃən] *n* (resistance, rubbing) 摩擦 masátsu; (between people) 不仲 fúnàka

Friday [frai'dei] *n* 金曜日 kiñ-yòbi

fridge [fridʒ] (*BRIT*) *n* 冷蔵庫 reízòko

fried [fraid] *adj* (steak, eggs, fish etc) 焼いた yaíta; (chopped onions etc) いためた itámetà; (in deep fat) 揚げた agéta, フライした furái shita

friend [frend] *n* 友達 tomódachi

friendly [frend'li:] *adj* (person, smile) 愛想のいい aísō nò íi; (government) 友好的な yúkōteki na; (place, restaurant) 居心地の良い igókochi no yoï; (game, match) 親善の shiñzen no

friendship [frend'ʃip] *n* 友情 yújō

frieze [fri:z] *n* フリーズ fúrìzu ◇壁の一番高い所に付ける細長い飾り、彫刻などを指す kabé no ichíban takáì tokórò ni tsukérù hosónagaì kazárì, chókoku nadò wo sásù

frigate [frig'it] *n* フリゲート艦 furígètokan

fright [frait] *n* (terror) 恐怖 kyófu; (scare) 驚き odóroki
  to take fright 驚く odórokù

frighten [frait'ən] *vt* 驚かす odórokasù

frightened [frait'ənd] *adj* (afraid) 怖がった kowágattà; (worried, nervous) 不安に駆られた fúan ni karáreta

frightening [frait'niŋ] *adj* (experience, prospect) 恐ろしい osóroshiì

frightful [frait'fəl] *adj* (dreadful) 恐ろしい osóroshiì

frightfully [frait'fəli:] *adv* 恐ろしく osóroshikù

frigid [fridʒ'id] *adj* (woman) 不感症の fukánshō no

frill [fril] n (of dress, shirt) フリル fúriru

fringe [frindʒ] n (BRIT: of hair) 前髪 maégami; (decoration: on shawl, lampshade etc) 縁飾り fuchíkazàri; (edge: of forest etc) へり herí

fringe benefits npl 付加給付 fukákyùfu

frisk [frisk] vt (suspect) ボディーチェックする bodíchekkù suru

frisky [fris'ki:] adj (animal, youngster) はつらつとした hatsúratsu to shità

fritter [frit'ə:r] n (CULIN) フリッター furíttā

fritter away vt (time, money) 浪費する rōhi suru

frivolous [friv'ələs] adj (conduct, person) 軽率な keísotsu na; (object, activity) 下らない kudáranaì

frizzy [friz'i:] adj (hair) 縮れた chijíretà

fro [frou] see to

frock [frɑːk] n (dress) ドレス dórèsu

frog [frɔːg] n カエル kaérù

frogman [frɔːg'mæn] (pl **frogmen**) n ダイバー dáìbā

frolic [frɑːl'ik] vi (animals, children) 遊び回る asóbimawarù

KEYWORD

from [frʌm] prep 1 (indicating starting place) ...から ...kárà

where do you come from?, where are you from? (asking place of birth) ご出身はどちらですか go-shússhìn wa dóchìra désù ka

from London to Glasgow ロンドンからグラスゴーへ rôndon kara gurásugò e

to escape from something/someone ...から逃げる ...kárà nigérù

2 (indicating origin etc) ...から ...kárà

a letter/telephone call from my sister 妹からの手紙〔電話〕imôto karà no tegámi〔deñwa〕

tell him from me that ... 私からの伝言で彼に...と言って下さい watákushi karà no deñgon dè kárè ni ...to itté kudasaì

a quotation from Dickens ディケンズからの引用 díkènzu kara no iñyō

3 (indicating time) ...から ...kárà

from one o'clock to/until/till two 1時から2時まで ichíji karà níji madè

from January (on) 1月から（先）ichígatsu karà (sakí)

4 (indicating distance) ...から ...kárà

the hotel is 1 km from the beach ホテルは浜辺から1キロ離れています hôtèru wa hamabé karà ichíkiro hanaréte imásù

we're still a long way from home まだまだ家まで遠い mádàmada ié madè tôi

5 (indicating price, number etc) ...から ...kárà, ...ないし... ...náishi ...

prices range from $10 to $50 値段は10ドルないし50ドルです nedán wa júdòru náishi gojúdòru désù

there were from 20 to 30 people there 20ないし30人いました níjū náishi sañjúnìn imáshìta

the interest rate was increased from 9% to 10% 公定歩合は9パーセントから10パーセントに引き上げられましたkôteibùai wa kyúpāseñto kara juppáseñto ni hikíageraremashìta

6 (indicating difference) ...と ...tò

he can't tell red from green 彼は赤と緑の区別ができません kárè wa ákà to mídòri no kúbètsu ga dekímasèn

to be different from someone/something ...と違っている ...tò chigátte irù

7 (because of, on the basis of) ...から ...kárà, ...によって ...ni yotté

from what he says 彼の言う事によると kárè no iú kotò ni yorú tò

from what I understand 私が理解したところでは watákushi gà ríkài shita tokôro de wà

to act from conviction 確信に基づいて行動する kakúshin ni motozuìte kôdō suru

weak from hunger 飢えでぐったりになって ué dè guttárì ni nátté

---

front [frʌnt] n (of house, dress) 前面 zeñ-

meǹ; (of coach, train, car) 最前部 saízeǹbu; (promenade: *also*: **sea front**) 海岸沿いの遊歩道 kaígaǹzoi no yúhodō; (MIL) 戦線 seǹseń; (METEOROLOGY) 前線 zeǹseń; (*fig*: appearances) 外見 gaíkeń
♦*adj* (*gen*) 前の máè no, 一番前の ichíbanmaè no; (gate) 正面の shómeǹ no

in front (of) (...の) 前に (...no) máè ni
front tooth 前歯 máèba

frontage [frʌn'tidʒ] *n* (of building) 正面 shómeń

frontal [frʌn'təl] *adj* 真っ向からの makkő kara no

front door *n* 正面玄関 shómengeǹkan

frontier [frʌntiːr'] *n* (between countries) 国境 kokkyő

front page *n* (of newspaper) 第一面 daíichimen

front room (*BRIT*) *n* 居間 imá

front-wheel drive [frʌnt'wiː-l-] *n* (AUT) 前輪駆動 zeńrinkùdō

frost [frɔːst] *n* (weather) 霜が降りる事 shimó ga orírù koto; (*also*: **hoarfrost**) 霜 shímő

frostbite [frɔːst'bait] *n* 霜焼け shimóyake

frosted [frɔːs'tid] *adj* (glass) 曇の kumóri no

frosty [frɔːs'tiː] *adj* (weather, night) 寒い samúi ◇気温が氷点下であるが雪が降っていない状態について言う kíon ga hyőtenka de arù ga yukí ga futte inái jōtai ni tsuíte iú; (welcome, look) 冷たい tsumétaì

froth [frɔːθ] *n* (on liquid) 泡 awá

frown [fraun] *vi* 顔をしかめる káò wo shikámerù

froze [frouz] *pt of* **freeze**

frozen [frou'zən] *pp of* **freeze**

frugal [fruː'gəl] *adj* (person) 倹約的な keń-yakuteki na; (meal) つましい tsumáshiì

fruit [fruːt] *n inv* (AGR, BOT) 果物 kudámono; (*fig*: results) 成果 seíkà

fruiterer [fruː'tə:rə:r] (*BRIT*) *n* 果物屋 kudámonoyà

fruiterer's (shop) [fruː'tə:rə:rz-] (*BRIT*) *n* 果物屋 kudámonoyà

fruitful [fruːt'fəl] *adj* (meeting, discussion) 有益な yúeki na

fruition [fruːiʃ'ən] *n*: *to come to fruition* 実る minórù

fruit juice *n* 果汁 kajû, フルーツジュース furútsujùsu

fruit machine (*BRIT*) *n* スロットマシン suróttomashiǹ

fruit salad *n* フルーツサラダ furútsusaràda

frustrate [frʌs'treit] *vt* (upset) ...に 欲求不満を起させる ...ni yokkyűfumàn wo okósaserù; (block) ざ折させる zasétsu saserù

frustration [frʌstrei'ʃən] *n* (irritation) 欲求不満 yokkyűfumàn; (disappointment) がっかり gakkárì

fry [frai] (*pt*, *pp* **fried**) *vt* (CULIN: steak, eggs etc) 焼く yákù; (: chopped onions etc) いためる itámerù; (: in deep fat) 揚げる agérù ¶ *see also* **small fry**

frying pan [frai'iŋ-] *n* フライパン furáipan

ft. *abbr* = **foot**; **feet**

fuddy-duddy [fʌd'iː:dʌdiː] (*pej*) *n* 古臭い人 furúkusaì hitő

fudge [fʌdʒ] *n* (CULIN) ファッジ fájjì

fuel [fjuː'əl] *n* 燃料 neńryō

fuel oil *n* 重油 jűyu

fuel tank *n* 燃料タンク neńryōtaǹku

fugitive [fjuː'dʒətiv] *n* (runaway, escapee) 逃亡者 tőbősha

fulfil [fulfil'] *vt* (function) 果す hatásù; (condition) 満たす mitásù; (request, wish, desire) かなえる kanáerù; (order) 実行する jikkő suru

fulfilment [fulfil'mənt] *n* (satisfaction) 満足 máňzoku; (of promise, desire) 実現 jitsúgeň

full [ful] *adj* (container, cup, car, cinema) 一杯の ippái no; (maximum: use, volume) 最大級の saídaìgen no; (complete: details, information) 全ての súbete no; (price) 割引なしの waríbikinashì no; (skirt) ゆったりした yuttárì shitá
♦*adv*: *to know full well that* ...という事を重々承知している ...to iú kotò wo jújū shőchi shite irù

I'm full (up) 満腹だ manpuku da

a full two hours 2時間も nijíkàn mo

at full speed 全速力で zeńsokuryòku de

in full (reproduce, quote, pay) 完全に kańzen ni

full employment *n* 100パーセントの就業率 hyakú pāseǹto no shúgyōrìtsu

full-length [ful'leŋkθ'] *adj* (film, novel etc) 長編の chóhen no; (coat) 長い nágài; (portrait) 全身の zeńshin no

full moon *n* 満月 máǹgetsu

full-scale [ful'skeil'] *adj* (attack, war) 全面的な zeńmenteki na; (model) 実物大の jitsúbutsudai no

full stop *n* 終止符 shúshifù, ピリオド pírìodo

full-time [ful'taim] *adj* (work, study) 全時間制の zeńjikánsei no
◆*adv* 全時間で zeńjikàn de

fully [ful'i:] *adv* (completely) 完全に kańzen ni; (at least): *fully as big as* 少なくとも...と同じぐらいの大きさの sukúnàkutomo ...to onaji gurai no ōkisa no

fully-fledged [ful'i:fledʒd'] *adj* (teacher, barrister) 一人前の ichíninmaè no

fulsome [ful'səm] (*pej*) *adj* (praise, compliments) 大げさな ōgesa na

fumble [fʌm'bəl] *vi*: *to fumble with* (key, catch) ...でもたもたする ...de mótàmota suru

fume [fju:m] *vi* (rage) かんかんに怒る kánkan ni okórù

fumes (of fire, fuel, car) ガス gásu

fun [fʌn] *n* (amusement) 楽しみ tanóshimi

to have fun 楽しむ tanóshimù

for fun 冗談として jódan toshite

to make fun of (ridicule, mock) ばかにする báka ni suru

function [fʌŋk'ʃən] *n* (role) 役割 yakúwari, 機能 kínō; (product) ...による物 ...ni yórù monó; (social occasion) 行事 gyōji
◆*vi* (operate) 作動する sadō suru

functional [fʌŋk'ʃənəl] *adj* (operational) 作動できる sadō dekirù; (practical) 機能的な kínōteki na

fund [fʌnd] *n* (of money) 基金 kikíñ;

(source, store) 貯蓄 chochíku

fundamental [fʌndəmen'təl] *adj* (principle, change, mistake) 基本的な kihónteki na

fundamentalist [fʌndəmen'təlist] *n* 原理主義者 geńrishugìsha

funds [fʌndz] *npl* (money) 資金 shikíñ

funeral [fju:'nərəl] *n* 葬式 sōshiki

funeral parlor *n* 葬儀屋 sōgiya

funeral service *n* 葬式 sōshiki

funfair [fʌn'fe:r] (*BRIT*) *n* 移動遊園地 idōyūeǹchi

fungi [fʌn'dʒai] *npl of* **fungus**

fungus [fʌŋ'gəs] (*pl* **fungi**) *n* (plant) キノコ kínòko; (mold) かび kabí

funnel [fʌn'əl] *n* (for pouring) じょうご jōgo; (of ship) 煙突 eńtotsu

funny [fʌn'i:] *adj* (amusing) こっけいな kokkéi na; (strange) 変な heń na

fur [fə:r] *n* (on animal) 毛 ke; (animal skin for clothing etc) 毛皮 kegáwa; (*BRIT*: in kettle etc) 湯あか yuáka

fur coat *n* 毛皮コート kegáwakòto

furious [fjur'i:əs] *adj* 猛烈な mōretsu na

furlong [fə:r'lɔːŋ] *n* (HORSE-RACING) ハロン háròn ◇距離の単位で, 約201メーター kyórì no tañ-i de, yakú 201 mēta

furlough [fə:r'lou] *n* (MIL: leave) 休暇 kyúka

furnace [fə:r'nis] *n* (in foundry) 炉 ro; (in power plant) ボイラー bóīrā

furnish [fə:r'niʃ] *vt* (room, building) ...に家具調度を備える ...ni kagúchòdo wo sonáerù; (supply) ...に供給する ...ni kyōkyū suru

furnishings [fə:r'niʃiŋz] *npl* 家具と設備 kágù to sétsùbi

furniture [fə:r'nitʃə:r] *n* 家具 kágù

piece of furniture 家具一点 kágù itteń

furrow [fə:r'ou] *n* (in field) 溝 mizó; (in skin) しわ shiwá

furry [fə:r'i:] *adj* 毛で覆われた ke de ōwaretà

further [fə:r'ðə:r] *adj* (additional) その上の sonó ue no, 追加の tsuíka no
◆*adv* (farther) もっと遠くへ móttò tóku ni; (more) それ以上 soré ijò; (moreover) 更に sárà ni, なお náò

♦*vt* (career, project) 促進する sokúshin suru

further education (*BRIT*) *n* 成人教育 seíjin kyōiku

furthermore [fəːrˈðəːrmɔːr] *adv* (moreover) 更に sárà ni, なお nao

furthest [fəːrˈðist] *superl* of **far**

furtive [fəːrˈtiv] *adj* (glance, movement) こっそりとする kossórì to surù

fury [fjuːrˈiː] *n* (anger, rage) 憤慨 fuńgai

fuse [fjuːz] *n* (ELEC: in plug, circuit) ヒューズ hyūzu; (for bomb etc) 導火線 dókasèn

♦*vt* (metal) 融合させる yū́gō saserù; (*fig*: ideas, systems) 混合する końgō suru

♦*vi* (metal: also *fig*) 融合する yū́gō suru

to fuse the lights (*BRIT*: ELEC) ヒューズを飛ばす hyūzu wo tobásu

fuse box *n* (ELEC) ヒューズ箱 hyū́zubàko

fuselage [fjuːˈsəlɑːʒ] *n* (AVIAT) 胴体 dótai

fusion [fjuːˈʒən] *n* (of ideas, qualities) 混合 końgō; (*also*: **nuclear fusion**) 核融合 kakúyūgō

fuss [fʌs] *n* (anxiety, excitement) 大騒ぎ ósawàgi; (complaining, trouble) 不平 fuhéi

to make a fuss 大騒ぎをする ósawàgi wo suru

to make a fuss of someone ...をちやほやする ...wo chíyàhoya suru

fussy [fʌsˈiː] *adj* (person) 小うるさい koúrusaì; (clothes, room etc) 凝った kóttà

futile [fjuːˈtəl] *adj* (attempt, comment, existence) 無駄な mudá na

future [fjuːˈtʃəːr] *adj* (date, generations) 未来の mírai no; (president, spouse) 将来の shórai no

♦*n* (time to come) 未来 mírài; (prospects) 将来 shórai; (LING) 未来形 mirái-kei

in future 将来に shórai ni

fuze [fjuːz] (*US*) = **fuse**

fuzzy [fʌzˈiː] *adj* (PHOT) ぼやけた boyáketa; (hair) 縮れた chijíretà

G

G [dʒiː] *n* (MUS: note) ト音 to-óñ; (: key) ト調 tóchō

g. *abbr* = **gram(s)**

gabble [gæbˈəl] *vi* ぺちゃくちゃしゃべる péchàkucha shábèru

gable [geiˈbəl] *n* (of building) 切妻 kirízùma

gadget [gædʒˈit] *n* 装置 sóchi

Gaelic [geiˈlik] *adj* ゲール語の gérugo no

♦*n* (LING) ゲール語 gérugo

gaffe [gæf] *n* (in words) 失言 shitsúgen; (in actions) 失態 shittai

gag [gæg] *n* (on mouth) 猿ぐつわ sarúgutsùwa; (joke) ギャグ gyágù

♦*vt* (prisoner) ...に猿ぐつわをはめる ...ni sarúgutsùwa wo hamérù

gaiety [geiˈətiː] *n* お祭り騒ぎ o-mátsuri sawàgi

gaily [geiˈliː] *adv* (talk, dance, laugh) 楽しそうに tanóshisò ni; (colored) 華やかに hanáyàka ni

gain [gein] *n* (increase) 増加 zōka; (improvement) 進歩 shíñpo; (profit) 利益 ríeki

♦*vt* (speed, weight, confidence) 増す masú

♦*vi* (benefit): *to gain from something* ...から利益を得る ...kara ríeki wo érù; (clock, watch) 進む susúmù

to gain on someone ...に迫る ...ni semárù

to gain 3lbs (in weight) (体重が) 3ポンド増える (taíjū ga) sańpoñdo fuérù

gait [geit] *n* 歩調 hochō

gal. *abbr* = **gallon**

gala [geiˈlə] *n* (festival) 祝祭 shukúsai

galaxy [gælˈəksiː] *n* (SPACE) 星雲 seíun

gale [geil] *n* (wind) 強風 kyófū

gallant [gælˈənt] *adj* (brave) 勇敢な yū́kan na; (polite) 紳士的な shiñshiteki na

gallantry [gælˈəntriː] *n* (bravery) 勇気 yū́ki; (politeness) 礼儀正しさ reígitadashìsa

gall bladder [gɔːl-] *n* 胆のう tańnō

gallery [gǽlə:ri:] n (also: **art gallery**: public) 美術博物館 bijútsu hakubutsukáñ; (: private) 画廊 garō; (in hall, church, theater) 二階席 nikáiseki

galley [gǽli:] n (ship's kitchen) 調理室 chōrishítsu

gallon [gǽlən] n (= 8 pints; BRIT = 4.5 l; US = 3.8 l) ガロン gároñ

gallop [gǽləp] n ギャロップ gyároppu
♦vi (horse) ギャロップで走る gyároppu de hashírù

gallows [gǽlouz] n 絞首台 kōshudai

gallstone [gɔ́:lstoun] n (MED) 胆石 tañseki

galore [gəlɔ́:r] adv どっさり dossárì

galvanize [gǽlvənaiz] vt (audience) ぎょっとさせる gyóttò sasérù; (support) 求める motómerù

gambit [gǽmbit] n (fig): **(opening) gambit** 皮切り kawákiri

gamble [gǽmbəl] n (risk) かけ kaké
♦vt (money) かける kakérù
♦vi (take a risk) 冒険をする bōken wo surù; (bet) ばくちをする bakúchi wo surù, ギャンブルをする gyáñburu wo suru
to gamble on something (horses, race, success etc) ...にかける ...ni kakérù

gambler [gǽmblə:r] n (punter) ばくち打ち bakúchiuchi

gambling [gǽmbliŋ] n (betting) ばくち bakúchi, ギャンブル gyáñburu

game [geim] n (activity, sport) 遊び asóbi; (match) 試合 shiái; (part of match: esp TENNIS: also: **board game**) ゲーム gēmu; (strategy, scheme) 策略 sakúryaku; (HUNTING) 猟鳥獣 ryōchōjū; (CULIN) 猟鳥獣の肉 ryōchōjū no nikú
♦adj (willing): **game (for)** (...をする) 気がある (...wo surù) kí ga arù
big game 大型猟獣 ōgaturyōjū

gamekeeper [geim'ki:pə:r] n 猟番 ryōban

gammon [gǽmən] n (bacon) ベーコン bēkon; (ham) スモークハム sumókuhamù

gamut [gǽmət] n (range) 範囲 háñ-i

gang [gǽŋ] n (of criminals, hooligans) 一味 ichímì; (of friends, colleagues) 仲間 nakama; (of workmen) 班 háñ

gangrene [gǽŋgri:n] n (MED) えそ ésò

gangster [gǽŋstə:r] n (criminal) 暴力団員 bōryokudañ-in, ギャング gyáñgu

gang up vi: **to gang up on someone** 寄ってたかって...をやっつける yotté takatte ...wo yattsukerù

gangway [gǽŋwei] n (from ship) タラップ taráppu; (BRIT: in cinema, bus, plane etc) 通路 tsūro

gaol [dʒeil] (BRIT) n, vt = **jail**

gap [gǽp] n (space) すき間 sukíma, ギャップ gyappu; (: in time) 空白 kúhaku; (difference): **gap (between)** (...の)断絶 (...no) dañzetsu

gape [geip] vi (person) ぽかんと口を開けて見詰める pokáñ to kuchí wo aketè mitsúmerù; (shirt, hole) 大きく開いている ōkiku aíte irù

gaping [gei'piŋ] adj (shirt, hole) 大きく開いた ōkiku aítà

garage [gərɑ:ʒ'] n (of private house) 車庫 shákò; (for car repairs) 自動車修理工場 jidóshashūrikōjō

garbage [gɑ:r'bidʒ] n (US: rubbish) ごみ gomí; (inf: nonsense) でたらめ detárame

garbage can (US) n ごみ容器 gomíyōki

garbled [gɑ:r'bəld] adj (account, message) 間違った machígattà

garden [gɑ:r'dən] n (private) 庭 niwá

gardener [gɑ:rd'nə:r] n 庭師 niwáshi

gardening [gɑ:r'dəniŋ] n 園芸 éñgei

gardens [gɑ:r'dənz] npl (public park) 公園 kōen

gargle [gɑ:r'gəl] vi うがいする ugái suru

garish [ge:r'iʃ] adj けばけばしい kebákebashī

garland [gɑ:r'lənd] n (also: **garland of flowers**) 花輪 hanáwa

garlic [gɑ:r'lik] n (BOT, CULIN) ニンニク nifíniku

garment [gɑ:r'mənt] n (dress) 衣服 ífuku

garnish [gɑ:r'niʃ] vt (food) 飾る kazárù

garrison [gær'isən] n (MIL) 守備隊 shubítai

garrulous [gær'ələs] adj (talkative) 口数の多い kuchíkazu no ōi

garter [gɑ:r'tə:r] n (for sock etc) 靴下止め

め kutsúshitadome, ガーター gǎtā; (US: suspender) ガーターベルト gátāberùto

gas [gæs] n (CHEM) 気体 kítài; (fuel) ガス gásù; (US: gasoline) ガソリン gasórin
♦vt (kill) ガスで殺す gásù de korósù

gas cooker (BRIT) n ガスレンジ gasúreñji

gas cylinder n ガスボンベ gasúboñbe

gas fire (BRIT) n ガスストーブ gasúsutōbu

gash [gæʃ] n (wound) 切り傷 kiríkìzu; (tear) 裂け目 sakéme
♦vt (wound) 傷を負わせる kizú wò owáserù

gasket [gæs'kit] n (AUT) ガスケット gasúkettò

gas mask n ガスマスク gasúmasùku

gas meter n ガスメーター gasúmētā

gasoline [gæsəli:n'] (US) n ガソリン gasórin

gasp [gæsp] n (breath) 息切れ ikígire; (of shock, horror) はっとする事 háttò suru kotó
♦vi (pant) あえぐ aégù

gasp out vt (say) あえぎながら言う aéginagàra iú

gas station (US) n ガソリンスタンド gasórinsutañdo

gassy [gæs'i:] adj (beer etc) 炭酸ガスの入った tañsangasù no haítta

gastric [gæs'trik] adj 胃の í no

gastroenteritis [gæstrouentərai'tis] n 胃腸炎 ichōen

gate [geit] n (of garden, field, grounds) 門 móñ; (at airport) ゲート gēto

gatecrash [geit'kræʃ] (BRIT) vt ...に押し掛ける ...ni oshíkakerù

gateway [geit'wei] n (entrance: also fig) 入口 iríguchi

gather [gæð'ə:r] vt (flowers, fruit) 摘む tsúmù; (pick up) 拾う hiróù; (assemble, collect: objects, information) 集める atsúmerù; (understand) 推測する suísoku suru; (SEWING) ...にギャザーを寄せる ...ni gyázā wo yosérù
♦vi (assemble) 集まる atsúmerù
to gather speed スピードを上げる supído wo agerù

gathering [gæð'ə:riŋ] n 集まり atsúmarì

gauche [gouʃ] adj (adolescent, youth) ぎごちない gigóchinài

gaudy [gɔ:d'i:] adj 派手な hadé na

gauge [geidʒ] n (instrument) 計器 keíki
♦vt (amount, quantity) 計る hakárù; (fig: feelings, character etc) 判断する hañdan suru

gaunt [gɔ:nt] adj (haggard) やせこけた yasékoketà; (bare, stark) 荒涼とした kōryō to shita

gauntlet [gɔ:nt'lit] n (glove) 長手袋 nagátebukùro; (fig): **to run the gauntlet** 方々からやられる hōbō kara yarárerù
to throw down the gauntlet 挑戦する chōsen suru

gauze [gɔ:z] n (fabric: also MED) ガーゼ gāze

gave [geiv] pt of **give**

gay [gei] adj (homosexual) 同性愛の dōseìai no, ホモの hómò no; (cheerful) 陽気な yōki na; (color, music, dress etc) 華やかな hanáyàka na

gaze [geiz] n (look, stare) 視線 shisén
♦vi: **to gaze at something** ...をじっと見る ...wo jíttò mírù

gazelle [gəzel'] n ガゼル gázèru

gazetteer [gæziti:r'] n (index) 地名辞典 chiméijitèn

gazumping [gəzʌm'piŋ] (BRIT) n (of house buyer) 詐欺 ságì

GB [dʒi:bi:'] abbr = **Great Britain**

GCE [dʒi:si:i:'] (BRIT) n abbr (= General Certificate of Education) 普通教育証書 futsúkyōikushōsho ◇16才の時に受けるOレベルと大学入学前に受けるAレベルの2種類がある jūrokusài no tokí nì ukérù O rébèru to daígaku nyūgakumáè ni ukérù A rébèru no nishúrui ga arù

GCSE [dʒi:si:esi:'] (BRIT) n abbr (= General Certificate of Secondary Education) ◇1988年からGCEのOレベルはGCSEに置換えられた señkyūhyakuhachijūhachi nèn ni GCE no O rébèru wa GCSE ni okíkaeraretà

gear [gi:r] n (equipment) 道具 dōgu; (TECH) 歯車 hagúrùma; (AUT) ギヤ gí-

yà

♦*vt* (*fig*: adapt): *to gear something to* ...に...を適応させる ...ni ...wo tekíō sase-rù

high (*US*) *or top* (*BRIT*) / *low gear* ハイ〔ロー〕ギヤ haí〔rò〕giyà

in gear ギヤを入れて gíyà wo iréte

gear box *n* ギヤボックス giyábokkùsu

gear shift (*BRIT* **gear lever**) *n* シフトレバー shífùtorebā

geese [gi:s] *npl of* **goose**

gel [dʒel] *n* (for hair) ジェル jérù; (CHEM) ゲル gérù

gelatin(e) [dʒel'ətin] *n* (CULIN) ゼラチン zeráchìn

gelignite [dʒel'ignait] *n* (explosive) ゼリグナイト zerígunaìto

gem [dʒem] *n* (stone) 宝石 hőseki

Gemini [dʒem'ənai] *n* (ASTROLOGY) 双子座 futágoza

gender [dʒen'də:r] *n* (sex: *also* LING) 性 seí

gene [dʒi:n] *n* (BIO) 遺伝子 idénshi

general [dʒen'ə:rəl] *n* (MIL) 大将 taíshō

♦*adj* (overall, non-specific, miscellaneous) 一般の ippán no, 一般的な ippánteki na; (widespread: movement, interest) 全面的な zeńmenteki na

in general 一般に ippán ni

general delivery (*US*) *n* (poste restante) 局留 kyokúdome

general election *n* 総選挙 sōseñkyo

generalization [dʒenə:rəlʌzei'ʃən] *n* 一般化 ippáñka

generally [dʒen'ə:rəli:] *adv* (in general) 一般に ippán ni; (usually) 普通は futsū wa

general practitioner *n* 一般開業医 ippán kaigyői

generate [dʒen'ə:reit] *vt* (power, energy) 発生させる hasséi saserù; (jobs, profits) 生み出す umídasù

to generate electricity 発電する hatsúden suru

generation [dʒenərei'ʃən] *n* (period of time) 世代 sedái; (of people, family) 同じ世代の人々 onáji sedài no hitobito; (of heat, steam, gas etc) 発生 hasséi; (of electricity) 発電 hatsúden

generator [dʒen'ə:reitə:r] *n* (ELEC) 発電機 hatsúdeñki

generosity [dʒenərɑːs'əti:] *n* 寛大さ kańdaisa

generous [dʒen'ə:rəs] *adj* (person, measure, remuneration etc) 寛大な kańdai na

genetics [dʒənet'iks] *n* (science) 遺伝学 idéngàku

Geneva [dʒəni:'və] *n* ジュネーブ júnèbu

genial [dʒi:'ni:əl] *adj* (host, smile) 愛想の良い aíso no yoì

genitals [dʒen'itəlz] *npl* (ANAT) 性器 seíki

genius [dʒi:n'jəs] *n* (ability, skill, person) 天才 teńsai

genocide [dʒen'əsaid] *n* 民族虐殺 mińzokugyakusàtsu, ジェノサイド jénòsaido

gent [dʒent] *n* *abbr* = **gentleman**

genteel [dʒenti:l'] *adj* (person, family) 家柄の良い iégara no yoì

gentle [dʒen'təl] *adj* (person) 優しい yasáshiì; (animal) 大人しい otónashiì; (movement, shake) 穏やかな odáyàka na, 静かな shizúkà na; (slope, curve) 緩やかな yurúyàka na

a gentle breeze そよ風 soyókàze

gentleman [dʒen'təlmən] (*pl* **gentlemen**) *n* (man) 男の方 otóko no katà; (referring to social position: *also* well-mannered man) 紳士 shíñshì, ジェントルマン jéñtoruman

gentleness [dʒen'təlnis] *n* (of person) 優しさ yasáshisà; (of animal) 大人しさ otónashisà; (of movement, breeze, shake) 穏やかさ odáyàkasa, 静かさ shizúkàsa; (of slope, curve) 緩やかさ yurúyàkasa

gently [dʒen'tli:] *adv* (subj: person) 優しく yasáshikù; (: animal) 大人しく otónashikù; (: breeze etc) 静かに shizúkàni (: slope, curve) 緩やかに yurúyàka ni

gentry [dʒen'tri:] *n* 紳士階級 shińshikaìkyū

gents [dʒents] (*BRIT*) *n* (men's toilet) 男性トイレ dańseitoirè

genuine [dʒen'ju:in] *adj* (real) 本物の hońmonò no; (person) 誠実な seíjitsu na

geographic(al) [dʒiːəgrӕfˈik(əl)] *adj* 地理の chírî no

geography [dʒiːɑːgˈrəfiː] *n* (of town, country etc: *also* SCOL) 地理 chírî

geological [dʒiːələːdʒˈikəl] *adj* 地質学の chishítsugáku no

geologist [dʒiːɑːlˈədʒist] *n* 地質学者 chishítsugakushá

geology [dʒiːɑːlˈədʒiː] *n* (of area, rock etc) 地質 chíshitsu; (SCOL) 地質学 chishítsugáku

geometric(al) [dʒiːəmetˈrik(əl)] *adj* (problem, design) 幾何学的な kikágakuteki na

geometry [dʒiːɑːmˈətriː] *n* (MATH) 幾何学 kikágaku

geranium [dʒəreiˈniːəm] *n* ゼラニウム zeránîumu

geriatric [dʒeːriːӕtˈrik] *adj* (of old people) 老人の rôjin no

germ [dʒəːrm] *n* ばい菌 baíkin

German [dʒəːrˈmən] *adj* (of Germany) ドイツの doítsu no; (LING) ドイツ語の doítsugo no
♦*n* ドイツ人 doítsujin; (LING) ドイツ語 doítsugo

German measles *n* (rubella) 風しん fúshin

Germany [dʒəːrˈməniː] *n* ドイツ doítsu

germination [dʒəːrməneiˈʃən] *n* (of seed) 発芽 hatsúga

gesticulate [dʒestikˈjəleit] *vi* (with arms, hands) 手振りをする tébùri wo suru

gesture [dʒesˈtʃəːr] *n* (movement) 手振り tébùri, ジェスチャー jésùchā; (symbol, token) ジェスチャー jésùchā

KEYWORD

get [get] (*pt, pp* **got**, (US) *pp* **gotten**) *vi* 1 (become, be) ...になる ...ni nárù

to get old (thing) 古くなる fúrùku naru; (person) 年を取る toshí wò toru

to get cold 寒くなる sámùku naru

to get annoyed/bored/tired 怒る〔退屈する, 疲れる〕okórù〔taíkutsu surù, tsukárerù〕

to get drunk 酔っ払う yopparau

to get dirty 汚れる yogórerù

to get killed 殺される korósarerù

to get married 結婚する kekkón surù

when do I get paid? 金はいつ払ってくれますか kané wà ítsu harátte kuremasù ká

it's getting late 遅くなってきました osóku nattè kimáshìta

2 (go): *to get to/from* ...へ〔から〕行く ...ê〔kará〕iku

to get home 家に帰る iê ni kaerù

how did you get here? あなたはどうやってここへ来ましたか anátà wa dô yattè kokô è kimáshìta ká

3 (begin): *to get to know someone* ...と親しくなる ...tò shitáshikù naru

I'm getting to like him 彼を好きになってきました kárè wo sukí ni nattè kimáshìta

let's get going/started さあ，行きましょう sâ, ikímashô

♦*modal aux vb: you've got to do it* あなたはどうしてもそれをしなければなりません anátà wa dôshite mò soré wò shinákereba narimaseñ

I've got to tell the police 警察に知らせなければなりません keísatsu nì shirásenakereba narimaseñ

♦*vt* 1: *to get something done* (do) ...を済ます ...wò sumásù; (have done) ...をしてもらう ...wò shité moraù

to get the washing/dishes done 洗濯〔皿洗い〕を済ます señtaku〔saráarài〕wò sumásù

to get one's hair cut 散髪してもらう sañpatsu shite moraù

to get the car going/to go 車のエンジンをかける kurúma no eñjin wo kakérù

to get someone to do something ...に...をさせる ...nî ...wò sasérù

to get something ready ...を用意する ...wò yôî suru

to get someone ready ...に用意をさせる ...nì yôî wo sasérù

to get someone drunk/into trouble ...を酔っ払わせる〔困らせる〕...wò yoppárawaserù〔komáraserù〕

2 (obtain: money) 手に入れる té ni irerù;

(: permission, results) 得る érù; (find: job, flat) 見付ける mitsúkerù; (fetch: person, doctor) 呼んで来る yóñde kuru; (: object) 持って来る mottè kurù

to get something for someone ...のために...を持って来る ...no tamé nì ...wò mottè kurù

he got a job in London 彼はロンドンに仕事を見付けました kárè wa róñdon ni shigóto wò mitsúkemashìta

get me Mr Jones, please (TEL) ジョーンズさんをお願いしたいんですが jóñzu san wo o-négai shitaiñ dèsu ga

I think you should get the doctor 医者を呼んだ方がいいと思います ishá wò yoñda hō ga íì to omóimasù

can I get you a drink? 何か飲みませんか nánìka nomímaseñ ka

3 (receive: present, letter) 受ける ukérù; (acquire: reputation, prize) 得る érù, 獲得する kakútoku suru

what did you get for your birthday? お誕生日に何をもらいましたか o-táñjòbi ni nánì wo móraimashìta ká

he got a prize for French 彼はフランス語の成績で賞をもらいました kárè wa furáñsugò no seíseki dè shō wò móraimashìta

how much did you get for the painting? 絵画はいくらで売れましたか káìga wa íkùra de urémashìta ká

4 (catch) つかむ tsukámù; (hit: target etc) ...に当る ...ni atárù

to get someone by the arm/throat ...の腕〔のど〕をつかむ ...no udé〔nódò〕wò tsukámù

get him! やつを捕まえろ yátsù wo tsukámaerò

the bullet got him in the leg 弾丸は彼の脚に当った dañgan wà kárè no ashí ni atattà

5 (take, move) 連れて〔持って〕いく tsuréte〔mottè〕ikù, 移動する idő suru

to get something to someone ...に...を持って行く ...ní ...wò mottè ikù

do you think we'll get it through the door? それは戸口から入ると思いますか soré wà tóguchi kara haírù to omó-

imasù ká

I'll get you there somehow 何とかしてあなたを連れて行きます náñ to ka shite anátà wo tsuréte ikimasù

we must get him to (US the) hospital どうしても彼を病院に連れて行かなくちゃ dőshìte mo kárè wo byőiñ ni tsuréte ikanakùcha

6 (catch, take: plane, bus etc) 乗る norú

where do I get the train - Birmingham? 電車はどこで乗ればいいんですか -バーミンガムですか deñsha wà dőkò de noréba iin desù ká - bámìñgamu desu ká

7 (understand) 理解する ríkài suru; (hear) 聞き取る kikítorù

I've got it 分かった wakáttà

I don't get your meaning あなたが言おうとしている事が分かりません anátà ga iő to shite iru kotő ga wakárimaseñ

I'm sorry, I didn't get your name 済みませんが，お名前を聞き取れませんでした sumímaseñ ga, o-námae wò kikítoremasen deshìta

8 (have, possess): ***to have got*** 持つ mótsù

how many have you got? いくつ持っていますか íkùtsu mottè imasù ká

get about vi 動き回る ugőkimawarù; (news) 広まる hirőmarù

get along vi (agree) 仲良くする nákàyoku suru; (depart) 帰る káerù; (manage) = **get by**

get at vt fus (attack, criticize) 批判する hihán suru; (reach) ...に手が届く ...ni té gà todőkù

get away vi (leave) 帰る káèru; (escape) 逃げる nigérù

get away with vt fus ...をうまくやりおおせる ...wò úmàku yaríōseru

get back vi (return) 帰る káèru

◆vt 返す káèsu

get by vi (pass) 通る tőrù; (manage) やって行く yatté ikù

get down vi 降りる orírù

◆vt fus 降りる orírù

◆vt 降ろす orősù; (depress: person) がっかりさせる gakkárì saseru

get down to vt fus (work) ...に取り掛る ...ni toríkakarù

get in vi 入る haírù; (train) 乗る norú; (arrive home) 帰って来る kaétte kurù

get into vt fus ...に入る ...ni haírù; (vehicle) ...に乗る ...ni norú; (clothes) 着る kirú

to get into bed ベッドに入る béddò ni haírù

to get into a rage かんかんに怒る kánkan ni okórù

get off vi (from train etc) 降りる orírù; (depart: person, car) 出発する shuppátsu suru; (escape punishment etc) 逃れる nogárerù

♦vt (remove: clothes) 脱ぐ núgù; (: stain) 消す kesú, 落す otósù; (send off) 送る okúrù

♦vt fus (train, bus) 降りる orírù

get on vi (at exam etc): *how are you getting on?* 万事うまく行っていますか bánji úmàku itté imasù ká; (agree): *to get on (with)* (...と) 気が合う (...tò) ki gá aù

♦vt fus ...に乗る ...ni norú

get out vi 出る dérù; (of vehicle) 降りる orírù

♦vt 取り出す torídasù

get out of vt fus ...から出る ...kara dérù; (vehicle) ...から降りる ...kara orírù; (bed) ...から起きる ...kara okírù; (duty etc) 避ける sakérù, 逃れる nogárerù

get over vt fus (illness) ...が直る ...ga naórù

get round vt fus (problem, difficulty) 避ける sakérù; (law, rule) ...に触れないようにする ...ni furénai yồ ni suru; (fig: person) 言いくるめる ifkurumerù

get through vi (TEL) 電話が通じる deńwa gà tsújiru

get through to vt fus (TEL) ...に電話が通じる ...ni deńwa gà tsújiru

get together vi (people) 集まる atsúmarù

♦vt 集める atsúmerù

get up vi (rise) 起きる okírù

♦vt fus 起す okósù

get up to vt fus (reach) ...に着く ...ni

tsukú; (BRIT: prank etc) 仕出かす shidékasù

geyser [gai'zɔːr] n (GEO) 間欠温泉 kańketsu oñsen; (BRIT: water heater) 湯沸かし器 yuwákashikì

Ghana [gɑːnə] n ガーナ gầna

ghastly [gæst'liː] adj (horrible: person, behavior, situation) いやな íyà na, ひどい hídòi; (: building, appearance) 薄気味悪い usúkimiwaruì; (pale: complexion) 青白い aójiroì

gherkin [gɔːr'kin] n キュウリのピクルス kyűri no píkùrusu

ghetto [get'ou] n (ethnic area) ゲットー géttồ

ghost [goust] n (spirit) 幽霊 yûrei, お化け o-báke

giant [dʒai'ənt] n (in myths, children's stories) 巨人 kyojín, ジャイアント jáiāanto; (fig: large company) 大企業 daíkigyō

♦adj (enormous) 巨大な kyodái na

gibberish [dʒib'əːriʃ] n (nonsense) でたらめ detárame

gibe [dʒaib] n = **jibe**

giblets [dʒib'lits] npl 鳥の内臓 torí nò naízō

Gibraltar [dʒibrɔːl'tɔːr] n ジブラルタル jíbùrarutaru

giddy [gid'iː] adj (dizzy) めまいがする memái ga suru

gift [gift] n (present) 贈り物 okúrimonò, プレゼント purézènto, ギフト gífùto; (ability) 才能 saínō

gifted [gif'tid] adj (actor, sportsman, child) 才能ある saínō arù

gift token n ギフト券 gifútokèn

gift voucher n = **gift token**

gigantic [dʒaigæn'tik] adj 巨大な kyodái na

giggle [gig'əl] vi くすくす笑う kusúkùsu waráù

gill [dʒil] n (= 0.25 pints; BRIT = 0.15 l; US = 0.12 l) ギル gírù

gills [gilz] npl (of fish) えら erá

gilt [gilt] adj (frame, jewelery) 金めっきした kińmekkì shita

♦n 金めっき kińmekkì

gilt-edged [gilt'edʒd] adj (stocks, secu-

rities) 優良な yūryō na

gimmick [gim'ik] n (sales, electoral) 仕
掛け shikáke

gin [dʒin] n ジン jíń

ginger [dʒin'dʒəːr] n (spice) ショウガ
shōga

ginger ale n ジンジャーエール jíńjaèru

ginger beer n ジンジャービール jíńjābī-
ru

gingerbread [dʒin'dʒəːrbred] n (cake)
ジンジャーブレッドケーキ jíńjābureddo-
kḕki; (biscuit) ジンジャーブレッドクッキ
ー jíńjābureddokukkī

gingerly [dʒin'dʒəːrli:] adv (tentatively)
慎重に shińchō ni

gipsy [dʒip'si:] n = **gypsy**

giraffe [dʒəræf'] n キリン kírín

girder [gəːr'dəːr] n 鉄骨 tekkótsu

girdle [gəːr'dəl] n (corset) ガードル gā́do-
ru

girl [gəːrl] n (child) 女の子 ońna nò ko, 少
女 shōjo; (young unmarried woman) 若い
女性 wakáī jòséi, ガール gā́ru; (daughter) 娘 musúme

an English girl 若いイングランド人女
性 wakáī íńgurandojìn jòséi

girlfriend [gəːrl'frend] n (of girl) 女友達
ońna tomodàchi; (of boy) ガールフレン
ド gā́rufurendo

girlish [gəːr'liʃ] adj 少女の様な shōjo nó
yō na

giro [dʒai'rou] n (also: **bank giro**) 銀行振
替為替 gíńkōfurikaekawàse; (also: **post
office giro**) 郵便振替為替 yūbinfurikae-
kawàse; (BRIT: welfare check) 生活保
護の小切手 seíkatsuhogò no kogíttè

girth [gəːrθ] n (circumference) 周囲 shū́i;
(of horse) 腹帯 haráobi

gist [dʒist] n (of speech, program) 骨子
kósshī

KEYWORD

---

give [giv] (pt **gave**, pp **given**) vt **1** (hand
over): **to give someone something,
give something to someone** ...に...を与
える ...ní ...wò atáerù, ...に...を渡す ...ní
...wò watásu

I gave David the book, I gave the

book to David 私は本をデービッドに渡
しました watákushi wà hóñ wò débìddo
ni watáshimashīta

give him your key あなたのかぎを彼に
渡しなさい anátà no kagí wò kárè ni
watáshinasaì

he gave her a present 彼は彼女にプレ
ゼントをあげた kárè wa kánòjo ni puré-
zeñto wo agétà

give it to him, give him it それを彼に
渡しなさい soré wò kárè ni watáshi
nasaì

I'll give you £5 for it それを5ポンド
で私に売ってくれませんか soré wò go-
póñdo de watákushi nì utté kuremaseñ
ká

2 (used with noun to replace a verb): **to
give a sigh** ため息をつく taméiki wo
tsuku

to give a cry/shout 叫ぶ sakébù

to give a push 押す osú

to give a groan うめく umékù

to give a shrug 肩をすくめる kátà wo
sukúmerù

to give a speech/a lecture 演説〔講演〕
をする eñzetsu〔kōen〕wo surù

to give three cheers 万歳三唱をする
bañzaisañshō wo suru

3 (tell, deliver: news, advice, message
etc) 伝える tsutáerù, 言う iú, 与える atáerù

**did you give him the message/the
news?** 彼にメッセージ〔ニュース〕を伝え
ましたか kárè ni méssèji〔nyúsù〕wo tsu-
táemashīta ká

let me give you some advice ちょっと
忠告をあげよう chóttò chū́koku wo age-
yō

**he gave me his new address over the
phone** 彼は電話で新しい住所を教えてく
れました kárè wa deńwa dè atárashii
jūsho wo oshíete kuremashīta

to give the right/wrong answer 正し
い〔間違った〕答を言う tadáshii〔machí-
gatta〕kotàe wo iú

4 (supply, provide: opportunity, surprise,
job etc) 与える atáerù, 提供する teíkyo
suru; (bestow: title) 授与する júyò suru;

(: honor, right) 与える atáerù

I gave him the chance to deny it それを否定するチャンスを彼に与えました soré wo hitéi suru chansu wo kárè ni atáemashìta

the sun gives warmth and light 太陽は熱と光を我々に与えてくれる taíyo wa netsú tò hikári wò waréware nì atáete kurerù

what gives you the right to do that? 何の権利でそんな事をするのか nán no keńri de sońna kotò wo suru nò ka

that's given me an idea あれでいい事を思い付いたんですが aré de ii kotò wo omóitsuitan desù ga

5 (dedicate: time) 当てる atérù; (: one's life) 捧げる saságerù; (: attention) 払う haráù

you'll need to give me more time もっと時間を下さい móttò jikán wo kudasaì

she gave it all her attention 彼女はそれに専念した kánòjo wa soré nì seńnen shìta

6 (organize): *to give a party/dinner etc* パーティ〔晩さん会〕を開催する pátì 〔bańsańkai〕wo kaísai suru

♦vi 1 (also: **give way**: break, collapse) 崩れる kuzúrerù

his legs gave beneath him 彼は突然立てなくなった kárè wa totsúzen taténaku nattà

the roof/floor gave as I stepped on it 私が踏んだとたん屋根〔床〕が抜け落ちた watákushi ga funda totań yánè〔yuká〕ga nukéochìtà

2 (stretch: fabric) 伸びる nobírù

give away *vt* (money) 人にやる hitó nì yarú; (opportunity) 失う ushínaù; (secret, information) 漏らす morásù; (bride) 新郎に渡す shińrò ni watásu

give back *vt* 返す káèsu

give in *vi* (yield) 降参する kósan suru

♦vt (essay etc) 提出する teíshutsu suru

give off *vt* (heat) 放つ hanátsù; (smoke) 出す dásù

give out *vt* (distribute: prizes, books,

drinks etc) 配る kubárù; (make known: news etc) 知らせる shiráserù

give up *vi* (surrender) 降参する kósan suru

♦vt (renounce: job, habit) やめる yamérù; (boyfriend) ...との交際をやめる ...to no kósai wo yamérù; (abandon: idea, hope) 捨てる sutérù

to give up smoking タバコをやめる tabáko wo yamérù

to give oneself up 自首する jishú suru

give way *vi* (yield) 譲る yuzúru; (break, collapse: floor, ladder etc) 崩れる kuzúrerù, 壊れる kowárerù; (: rope) 切れる kirérù; (*BRIT*: AUT) 道を譲る michí wò yuzúru

glacier [gleí'ʒər] *n* 氷河 hyóga

glad [glæd] *adj* (happy, pleased) うれしい uréshiì

gladly [glæd'li:] *adv* (willingly) 喜んで yorókoǹde

glamorous [glæm'ə:rəs] *adj* 魅惑的な miwákuteki na

glamour [glæm'ə:r] *n* 魅惑 miwáku

glance [glæns] *n* (look) ちらっと見る事 chiráttò mírù koto

♦vi: *to glance at* ...をちらっと見る ...wo chiráttò mírù

glance off *vt fus* ...に当って跳ね返る ...ni attáte hanékaerù

glancing [glæn'siǹ] *adj* (blow) かすめる kasúmerù

gland [glænd] *n* せん sén

glare [gler] *n* (of anger) にらみ nirámi; (of light) まぶしさ mabúshisà; (of publicity) 脚光 kyakkó

♦vi (light) まぶしく光る mabúshikù hikárù

to glare at (glower) ...をにらみ付ける ...wo nirámitsukerù

glaring [gler'iǹ] *adj* (mistake) 明白な meíhaku na

glass [glæs] *n* (substance) ガラス garásu; (container) コップ koppù, グラス gúràsu; (contents) コップ一杯 koppú ippài

glasses [glæs'iz] *npl* 眼鏡 mégàne

glasshouse [glæs'haus] *n* 温室 ońshitsu

glassware [glæs'we:r] *n* グラス類 gurásurui

glassy [glæs'i:] *adj* (eyes) うつろな utsúro na

glaze [gleiz] *vt* (door, window) ...にガラスをはめる ...ni garásu wò hamérù; (pottery) ...にうわぐすりを掛ける ...ni uwágusùri wo kakérù

♦*n* (on pottery) うわぐすり uwágusùri

glazed [gleizd] *adj* (eyes) うつろなutsúro na; (pottery, tiles) うわぐすりを掛けた uwágusùri wo kakéta

glazier [glei'ʒəːr] *n* ガラス屋 garásuyà

gleam [gli:m] *vi* (shine: light, eyes, polished surface) 光る hikárù

glean [gli:n] *vt* (information) かき集める kakíatsumerù

glee [gli:] *n* (joy) 喜び yorókobi

glen [glen] *n* 谷間 taníaì

glib [glib] *adj* (person) 口達者な kuchídasshà na; (promise, response) 上辺だけの uwábe dake no

glide [glaid] *vi* (snake, dancer, boat etc) 滑る様に動く subéru yồ ni ugókù; (AVIAT, birds) 滑空する kakkū́ suru

glider [glai'dəːr] *n* (AVIAT) グライダー guráidà

gliding [glai'diŋ] *n* (AVIAT) 滑空 kakkū́

glimmer [glim'əːr] *n*: *a glimmer of light* かすかな光 kásùka na hikári
a glimmer of interest かすかな表情 kásùka na hyójồ
a glimmer of hope かすかな希望 kásùka na kibố

glimpse [glimps] *n* (of person, place, object) ...がちらっと見える事 ...ga chiráttò míerù koto

♦*vt* ...がちらっと見える ...ga chiráttò míerù

glint [glint] *vi* (flash: light, eyes, shiny surface) ぴかっと光る pikáttò hikárù

glisten [glis'ən] *vi* (with sweat, rain etc) ぎらぎらする gíràgira suru

glitter [glit'əːr] *vi* (sparkle: light, eyes, shiny surface) 輝く kagáyakù

gloat [glout] *vi*: *to gloat (over)* (exult) ...にほくそえむ ...ni hokúsoemu

global [glou'bəl] *adj* (worldwide) 世界的な sekáiteki na

globe [gloub] *n* (world) 地球 chikyū́; (model) 地球儀 chikyū́gì; (shape) 球 kyū́

gloom [glu:m] *n* (dark) 暗やみ kuráyami; (sadness) 失望 shitsúbò

gloomy [glu:'mi:] *adj* (dark) 薄暗い usúguraì; (sad) 失望した shitsúbō shita

glorious [glɔːr'i:əs] *adj* (sunshine, flowers, weather) 素晴らしい subárashiì; (victory, future) 栄光の eíkō no

glory [glɔːr'i:] *n* (prestige) 栄光 eíkō; (splendor) 華々しさ hanábanashisà

gloss [glɔːs] *n* (shine) つや tsuyá; (also: **gloss paint**) つや出しペイント tsuyádashipeìnto

glossary [glɑːs'əːri:] *n* 用語集 yógoshū́

gloss over *vt fus* (error) 言繕う iístukuroù; (problem) 言いくるめる iíkurumerù

glossy [glɑːs'i:] *adj* (hair) つやつやした tsuyátsùya shita; (photograph) つや出しの tsuyádashi no; (magazine) アート紙の átoshì no

glove [glʌv] *n* (gen) 手袋 tebúkùro; (in baseball) グローブ gúròbu, グラブ gúràbu

glove compartment *n* (AUT) グローブボックス gurốbubokkùsu

glow [glou] *vi* (embers) 赤く燃える akákù moérù; (stars) 光る hikárù; (face, eyes) 輝く kagáyakù

glower [glau'əːr] *vi*: *to glower at* ...をにらみ付ける ...wo nirámitsukerù

glucose [glu:'kous] *n* ブドウ糖 budótō, グルコース gurúkōsu

glue [glu:] *n* (adhesive) 接着剤 setchákuzài

♦*vt* 接着する setchákù suru

glum [glʌm] *adj* (miserable) ふさぎ込んだ fuságikoñda

glut [glʌt] *n* (of oil, goods etc) 生産過剰 seísankajō

glutton [glʌt'ən] *n* 大食らい ồgurai
a glutton for work 仕事の鬼 shigóto nò oní

gluttony [glʌt'əni:] *n* 暴食 bốshoku

glycerin(e) [glis'əːrin] *n* グリセリン guríserìn

gnarled [nɑːrld] *adj* (tree, hand) 節くれだった fushíkuredattà

gnat [næt] n ブヨ búyò
gnaw [nɔː] vt (bone) かじる kajírù
gnome [noum] n 地の小鬼 chi no koóni

KEYWORD
---

go [gou] (pt **went**, pp **gone**) vi **1** (travel, move) 行く ikú

she went into the kitchen 彼女は台所に行った kánòjo wa daídokoro ni ittá

shall we go by car or train? 車で行きましょうか、それとも電車で行きましょうか kurúma dè ikímashò ka, sorétomò dénsha dè ikímashò ka

a car went by 車が通り過ぎた kurúma gà tòri sugitá

to go round the back 裏へ回る urá e mawàru

to go by the shop 店の前を通る misé no maè wo tòrù

he has gone to Aberdeen 彼はアバーディーンへ行きました kárè wa abádìn e ikímashìta

2 (depart) 出発する shuppátsu suru、たつ tátsù、帰る káèru、行ってしまう itté shimaù

"I must go," she said「帰ります」と彼女は言った "kaérimasù" to kánòjo wa ittá

our plane went at 6 pm 我々の飛行機は夕方6時に出発しました waréware no hikòki wa yùgata rokujì ni shuppátsu shimashìta

they came at 8 and went at 9 彼らは8時に来て9時に帰った kárèra wa hachíji ni kitè kújì ni kaérimashìta

3 (attend) 通う kayóu

she went to university in Aberdeen 彼女はアバーディーンの大学に通った kánòjo wa abádìn no daígaku ni kayótta

she goes to her dancing class on Tuesdays 彼女がダンス教室に通うのは火曜日です kánòjo ga dañsukyòshitsu ni kayóu no wa kayòbì desu

he goes to the local church 彼は地元の教会に通っています kárè wa jimóto no kyòkai ni kayótte imasù

4 (take part in an activity) ...に行く ...ni ikú、...する ...surù

to go for a walk 散歩に行く sañpo ni ikù、散歩する sanpo suru

to go dancing ダンスに行く dáñsu ni iku

5 (work) 作動する sadò suru

the clock stopped going 時計が止りました tokéi gà tomárimashìta

is your watch going? あなたの時計は動いていますか anátà no tokéi wà ugóite imasù ká

the bell went just then 丁度その時ベルが鳴りました chòdo sono tokì bérù ga narímashìta

the tape recorder was still going テープレコーダーはまだ回っていました tèpurekòdà wa mádà mawátte imashìta

6 (become) ...になる ...ni nárù

to go pale 青白くなる aòjiroku narù

to go moldy かびる kabíru

7 (be sold): **to go for $10** 10ドルで売れる jùdoru de urérù

8 (fit, suit) 合う áù

to go with ...に合う ...ni áù

that tie doesn't go with that shirt そのネクタイはシャツと合いません sonó nekùtai wa shátsù to aímaseñ

9 (be about to, intend to): **he's going to do it** 彼は今それをやる所です kárè wa ìmà sorè wò yarú tokorò desu

we're going to leave in an hour 1時間したら出発します ichíjikan shitarà shuppátsu shimasù

are you going to come? あなたも一緒に来ますか anátà mo isshó nì kimásù ká

10 (time) 経つ tátsù

time went very slowly/quickly 時間が経つのがとても遅く〔早く〕感じられました jikán ga tatsù no ga totémò osòku 〔hàyaku〕 kanjiraremashèn

11 (event, activity) 行く ikú

how did it go? うまく行きましたか úmàku ìkimashìta ká

12 (be given) 与えられる atáerarerù

the job is to go to someone else そのポストは他の人のところへいきました sonó posùto wa hoká no hito no tokorò e ikímashìta

13 (break etc: glass etc) 割れる warérù;

(: stick, leg, pencil etc) 折れる orérù;
(: thread, rope, chain etc) 切れる kirérù

the fuse went ヒューズが切れた〔飛んだ〕hyúzù ga kiréta (tónda)

the leg of the chair went いすの脚が折れた isú no ashí ga óreta

14 (be placed) ...という事になっている ...ni shimáu kotó ni nátte irù

where does this cup go? このカップはどこにしまうのですか konó kappù wa dókò ni shimáu no desu ká

the milk goes in the fridge ミルクは冷蔵庫にしまう事になっています mírùku wa reízòko ni shimáu kotó ni nátte imasù

♦*n* (*pl* **goes**) **1** (try): *to have a go (at)* (...を) やってみる (...wo) yatté mirù

2 (turn) 番 bán

whose go is it? だれの番ですか dárè no bán desu ká

3 (move): *to be on the go* 忙しくする isógashiku surù

go about *vi* (*also:* **go around**: rumor) 流れる nagárerù
♦*vt fus*: *how do I go about this?* どういう風にやればいいんですか dó iu fū́ ni yareba íin desu ká

goad [goud] *vt* 刺激する shigéki suru

go ahead *vi* (make progress) 進歩する shíñpo suru; (get going) 取り掛かる toríkakarù

go-ahead [gou'əhed] *adj* (person, firm) 進取の気に富んだ shíñshu no ki ni tóñda
♦*n* (for project) 許可 kyókà, ゴーサイン gōsaìn

goal [goul] *n* (SPORT) ゴール gōrù; (aim) 目標 mokúhyò

goalkeeper [goul'ki:pə:r] *n* ゴールキーパー gōrukīpā

go along *vi* ついて行く tsuíte ikú
♦*vt fus* ...を行く ...wò ikú
to go along with (agree with: plan, idea, policy) ...に賛成する ...ni sañsei surù

goalpost [goul'poust] *n* ゴールポスト gōruposùto

goat [gout] *n* ヤギ yágì

go away *vi* (leave) どこかへ行く dókò ka e ikú

go back *vi* (return) 帰る káèru; (go again) また行く matá ikú

go back on *vt fus* (promise) 破る yabúrù

gobble [gɑ:b'əl] *vt* (*also:* **gobble down**, **gobble up**) むさぼり食う musáborikuù

go-between [gou'bitwi:n] *n* 仲介者 chúkaishà

go by *vi* (years, time) 経つ tátsù
♦*vt fus* (book, rule) ...に従う ...ni shitágaù

God [gɑ:d] *n* (REL) 神 kámì

god [gɑ:d] *n* (MYTHOLOGY, *fig*) 神 kámì

godchild [gɑ:d'tʃaild] *n* 名付け子 nazúkegò

goddaughter [gɑ:d'dɔ:tə:r] *n* 名付け娘 nazúkemusùme

goddess [gɑ:d'is] *n* (MYTHOLOGY, REL, *fig*) 女神 mégàmi

godfather [gɑ:d'fɑ:ðə:r] *n* 名付け親 nazúkeòya, 代父 daífù, 教父 kyófù

godforsaken [gɑ:d'fə:rsei'kən] *adj* (place, spot) 荒れ果てた aréhatetà

godmother [gɑ:d'mʌðə:r] *n* 名付け親 nazúkeòya, 代母 daíbò, 教母 kyóbò

go down *vi* (descend) 降りる orírù; (ship) 沈む shizúmu, 沈没する chiñbotsu suru; (sun) 沈む shizúmu
♦*vt fus* (stairs, ladder) ...を降りる ...wo orírù

godsend [gɑ:d'send] *n* (blessing) 天の恵み teñ nò megúmî

godson [gɑ:d'sʌn] *n* 名付け息子 nazúkemusùko゚

go for *vt fus* (fetch) 取りに行く tórì ni ikú; (like) 気に入る ki ní irù; (attack) ...に襲い掛る ...ni osóikakarù

goggles [gɑ:g'əlz] *npl* (for skiing, motorcycling) ゴーグル gōguru

go in *vi* (enter) 入る háìru

go in for *vt fus* (competition) ...に参加する ...ni sañka suru; (like) ...が好きである ...ga sukí de arù, ...を気に入る ...wò ki ní irù

going [gou'iŋ] *n* (conditions) 状況 jókyò

♦*adj: the going rate* 相場 sóba

go into *vt fus* (enter) ...に入る ...ni háiru; (investigate) 調べる shiráberù; (embark on) ...に従事する ...ni jújì suru

gold [gould] *n* (metal) 金 kíñ

♦*adj* (jewelery, watch, tooth etc) 金の kíñ no

gold reserves 金の正貨準備 kíñ no séìka juñbi

golden [goul'dən] *adj* (made of gold) 金 の kíñ no; (gold in color) 金色の kiñ-iro no

goldfish [gould'fiʃ] *n* 金魚 kíñgyo

goldmine [gould'main] *n* 金山 kíñzan; (fig) ドル箱 dorúbako

gold-plated [gouldplei'tid] *adj* 金めっき の kíñmekkì no

goldsmith [gould'smiθ] *n* 金細工師 kiñzaikushì

golf [gɑːlf] *n* ゴルフ górùfu

golf ball *n* (for game) ゴルフボール gorúfubòru; (on typewriter) 電動タイプライターのボール deñdōtaipuraìta no bòru

golf club *n* (organization, stick) ゴルフクラブ gorúfukuràbu

golf course *n* ゴルフコース gorúfukòsu

golfer [gɑːl'fəːr] *n* ゴルファー górùfā

gondola [gɑːn'dələ] *n* (boat) ゴンドラ góñdora

gone [gɔːn] *pp of* **go**

gong [gɔːŋ] *n* どら dorá, ゴング góñgu

good [gud] *adj* (pleasant, satisfactory etc) 良い yóì; (high quality) 高級な kőkyū na; (tasty) おいしい oíshiì; (kind) 親切な shińsetsu na; (well-behaved: child) 行儀の良い győgi no yoì; (morally correct) 正当な seítō na

♦*n* (virtue, morality) 善 zéñ; (benefit) 利益 ríèki

good! よろしい! yoróshiì!

to be good at ...が上手である ...ga jőzu dè árù

to be good for (useful) ...に使える ...ni tsukáerù

it's good for you あなたのためにいい anáta no tamè ni íi

would you be good enough to ...? 済みませんが...して下さいませんか sumímaseñ ga ...shite kudásaimaseñ ká

a good deal (of) 沢山（の）takúsan (no)

a good many 沢山の takúsaǹ no

to make good (damage, loss) 弁償する beñshō suru

it's no good complaining 不平を言ってもしようがない fuhéi wo ittè mo shiyő ga nái

for good (forever) 永久に eíkyū ni

good morning! お早うございます o-háyō gozaimasù

good afternoon! 今日は koñnichi wa

good evening! 今晩は koñban wa

good night! お休みなさい o-yásumi nasaì

goodbye [gudbai'] *excl* さようなら sayőnarà

to say goodbye 別れる wakárerù

Good Friday *n* (REL) 聖金曜日 seíkinyòbi

good-looking [gud'luk'iŋ] *adj* (woman) 美人の bijín no; (man) ハンサムな háñsamu na

good-natured [gud'nei'tʃəːrd] *adj* (person, pet) 気立ての良い kidáte no yoì

goodness [gud'nis] *n* (of person) 優しさ yasáshisà

for goodness sake! 後生だから goshő da kara

goodness gracious! あらまあ! ará má

goods [gudz] *npl* (COMM) 商品 shőhin

goods train (*BRIT*) *n* 貨物列車 kamótsuresshà

goodwill [gud'wil'] *n* (of person) 善意 zéñ-i

go off *vi* (leave) どこかへ行く dókò ka é ikù; (food) 悪くなる warúku naru; (bomb) 爆発する bakúhatsu suru; (gun) 暴発する bőhatsu suru; (event): *to go off well* うまくいく úmàku iku

♦*vt fus* (person, place, food etc) 嫌いになる kirái ni narù

go on *vi* (continue) 続く tsuzúku; (happen) 起る okórù

to go on doing something ...をし続ける ...wò shitsuzúkerù

goose [guːs] (*pl* **geese**) *n* ガチョウ gachő

gooseberry [guːs'beːri:] *n* (tree, fruit) ス

グリ súguri

to play gooseberry (BRIT) アベックの
邪魔をする abékkù no jamá wo surù

gooseflesh [guːsˈfleʃ] n 鳥肌 toríhada

goose pimples npl = **gooseflesh**

go out vi (leave: room, building) 出る dérù; (for entertainment) **are you going
out tonight?** 今夜どこかへ出掛けます
か kôn-ya dókòka e dekákemasù ká;
(couple): **they went out for 3 years** 彼
らは3年交際した kárèra wa sañnen kō-
sai shita; (fire, light) 消える kiérù

go over vi (ship) 転覆する teñpuku surù
♦vt fus (check) 調べる shiráberù

gore [gɔːr] vt (subj: bull, buffalo) 角で刺
す tsunó dè sásù
♦n (blood) 血のり chinóri

gorge [gɔːrdʒ] n (valley) 峡谷 kyôkoku
♦vt: **to gorge oneself (on)** (...を) た
らふく食う (...wo) taráfuku kúù

gorgeous [gɔːrˈdʒəs] adj (necklace, dress
etc) 豪華な gôka na; (weather) 素晴らし
い subárashiì; (person) 美しい utsúkushiì

gorilla [gərílˈə] n ゴリラ górìra

gorse [gɔːrs] n ハリエニシダ haríenishì-
da

gory [gɔːˈriː] adj (details, situation) 血み
どろの chimídoro no

go-slow [gouˈslouˈ] (BRIT) n 遵法闘争
juñpōtōsō

gospel [gɑːsˈpəl] n (REL) 福音 fukúìn

gossip [gɑːsˈəp] n (rumors) うわさ話 u-
wásabanashi, ゴシップ goshíppù; (chat)
雑談 zatsúdan; (person) おしゃべり o-
sháberi, ゴシップ屋 goshíppùya
♦vi (chat) 雑談する zatsúdan suru

got [gɑːt] pt, pp of **get**

go through vt fus (town etc) ...を通る
...wò tôrù; (search through: files, papers)
...を一つ一つ調べる ...wò hitótsu hitotsù
shiráberù; (examine: list, book, story) 調
べる shiráberù

gotten [gɑːtˈən] (US) pp of **get**

go up vi (ascend) 登る nobóru; (price,
level) 上がる agáru

gout [gaut] n 痛風 tsúfū

govern [gʌvˈərn] vt (country) 統治する
tôchi suru; (event, conduct) 支配する shi-

hái suru

governess [gʌvˈəːrnis] n (children's) 女
性家庭教師 joséikateikyōshi

government [gʌvˈəːrnmənt] n (act of
governing) 政治 seíji; (governing body)
政府 seífu; (BRIT: ministers) 内閣 naí-
kaku

governor [gʌvˈəːrnəːr] n (of state) 知事
chíjì; (of colony) 総督 sôtoku; (of bank,
school, hospital) 理事 ríjì; (BRIT: of
prison) 所長 shochô

go without vt fus (food, treats) ...無し
で済ます ...náshì de sumásù

gown [gaun] n (dress: also of teacher) ガ
ウン gâun; (BRIT: of judge) 法服 hôfuku

GP [dʒiːpiːˈ] n abbr = **general practitioner**

grab [græb] vt (seize) つかむ tsukámù
♦vi: **to grab at** ...をつかもうとする
...wo tsukámô to suru

grace [greis] n (REL) 恩恵 oñkei;
(gracefulness) しとやかさ shitóyakasà
♦vt (honor) ...に栄誉を与える ...ni êîyo
wo atáerù; (adorn) 飾る kazárù

5 days' grace 5日間の猶予 itsúkakañ
no yúyo

graceful [greisˈfəl] adj (animal, athlete)
しなやかな shináyàka na; (style, shape)
優雅な yúga na

gracious [greiˈʃəs] adj (person) 親切な
shiñsetsu na

grade [greid] n (COMM: quality) 品質 hiñshitsu; (in hierarchy) 階級 kaíkyū;
(SCOL: mark) 成績 seíseki; (US: school
class) 学年 gakùnen
♦vt (rank, class) 格付けする kakúzuke
suru; (exam papers etc) 採点する saíten
suru

grade crossing (US) n 踏切 fumíkiri

grade school (US) n 小学校 shôgakkô

gradient [greiˈdiːənt] n (of road, slope)
こう配 kôbai

gradual [grædʒˈuːəl] adj (change, evolution) 少しずつの sukóshizutsù no

gradually [grædʒˈuːəliː] adv 徐々に jójò
ni

graduate [n grædʒˈuːit vb grædʒˈuːeit]
n (also: **university graduate**) 大学の卒

業生 daígaku nò sotsúgyòsei; (*US: also:*
high school graduate) 高校の卒業生 kô-
kō nò sotsúgyòsei
♦*vi* 卒業する sotsúgyō suru

graduation [grædʒuːei'ʃən] *n* (*also:*
graduation ceremony) 卒業式 sotsúgyò-
shiki

graffiti [grəfiː'tiː] *npl* 落書 rakúgaki

graft [græft] *n* (AGR) 接木 tsugíki;
(MED) 移植 ishóku; (*BRIT: inf:* hard
work) 苦労 kúrò; (bribery) 汚職 oshóku
♦*vt* (AGR) 接木する tsugíki suru; (MED)
移植する ishóku suru

grain [grein] *n* (of rice, wheat, sand,
salt) 粒 tsúbù; (no pl: cereals) 穀物 kokúmòtsu; (of wood) 木目 mokúme

gram [græm] *n* グラム gúràmu

grammar [græm'əːr] *n* (LING) 文法 buñpō; (book) 文法書 buñpósho

grammar school (*BRIT*) *n* 公立高等学
校 kôritsukōtōgakkô ◇大学進学教育を
する公立高校 daígakushingakukyōiku
wo suru kôritsukōkô; (*US*) 小学校 shôgakkô

grammatical [grəmæt'ikəl] *adj* (LING)
文法の buñpō no

gramme [græm] *n* = **gram**

gramophone [græm'əfoun] *n* 蓄音機
chikúoñki

grand [grænd] *adj* (splendid, impressive)
壮大な sôdai na; (*inf:* wonderful) 素晴ら
しい subárashiì; (*also* humorous: gesture
etc) 大げさな ôgesa na

grandchildren [græn'tʃil'drən] *npl* 孫
mágò

granddad [græn'dæd] *n* (*inf*) おじいち
ゃん ojíichan

granddaughter [græn'dɔːtəːr] *n* 孫娘
magómusùme

grandeur [græn'dʒəːr] *n* (of scenery etc)
壮大さ sôdaisa

grandfather [græn'fɑːðəːr] *n* 祖父 sófù

grandiose [græn'diːous] *adj* (scheme,
building) 壮大な sôdai na; (*pej*) 大げさな
ôgesa na

grandma [græm'ə] *n* (*inf*) おばあちゃん
obáàchan

grandmother [græm'mʌðəːr] *n* 祖母 sô-

bò

grandpa [græm'pə] *n* (*inf*) = **granddad**

grandparents [græm'peːrənts] *npl* 祖父
母 sófùbo

grand piano *n* グランドピアノ gurán-
dopiàno

grandson [græm'sʌn] *n* 孫息子 magómu-
sùko

grandstand [græm'stænd] *n* (SPORT)
観覧席 kañrañseki, スタンド sutáñdo

granite [græm'it] *n* 御影石 mikágeìshi

granny [græm'iː] *n* (*inf*) おばあちゃん o-
báàchan

grant [grænt] *vt* (money) 与える atáèru;
(request etc) かなえる kanáèru; (visa) 交
付する kôfu suru; (admit) 認める mitómerù
♦*n* (SCOL) 助成金 joséikin; (ADMIN:
subsidy) 交付金 kôfukin

*to take someone/something for
granted* ...を軽く見る ...wo karúkù mírù

granulated sugar [græn'jəleitid-] *n* グ
ラニュー糖 gurányùtō

granule [græn'juːl] *n* (of coffee, salt) 粒
tsúbù

grape [greip] *n* ブドウ budô

grapefruit [greip'fruːt] (*pl* **grapefruit**
or **grapefruits**) *n* グレープフルーツ gu-
rêpufurùtsu

graph [græf] *n* (diagram) グラフ gúràfu

graphic [græf'ik] *adj* (account, description) 写実的な shajítsuteki na; (art,
design) グラフィックの guráfikkù no

graphics [græf'iks] *n* (art, process) グラ
フィックス guráfikkùsu
♦*npl* (drawings) グラフィックス guráfikkùsu

grapple [græp'əl] *vi: to grapple with
someone* ...ともみ合う ...to momíaù
to grapple with something (problem
etc) ...と取組む ...to toríkumù

grasp [græsp] *vt* (hold, seize) 握る nigírù;
(understand) 理解する rikái suru
♦*n* (grip) 握り nigírì; (understanding) 理
解 rikái

grasping [græs'piŋ] *adj* (money-
grabbing) 欲深い yokúfukaì

grass [græs] *n* (BOT) 草 kusá; (lawn) 芝生 shibáfu

grasshopper [græs'hɑːpər] *n* バッタ battá

grass-roots [græs'ruːts] *adj* (level, opinion) 一般人の ippánjìn no

grate [greit] *n* (for fire) 火格子 higóshi
♦*vi* (metal, chalk): **to grate (on)** (...にすれて) きしる (...ni suréte) kishírù
♦*vt* (CULIN) すりおろす suríorosù

grateful [greit'fəl] *adj* (thanks) 感謝の kánsha no; (person) 有難く思っている arígatakù omótte irù

grater [grei'tər] *n* (CULIN) 卸し金 oróshigàne

gratifying [græt'əfaiiŋ] *adj* (pleasing, satisfying) 満足な máñzoku na

grating [grei'tiŋ] *n* (iron bars) 鉄格子 tetsúgōshi
♦*adj* (noise) きしる kishírù

gratitude [græt'ətuːd] *n* 感謝 kánsha

gratuity [grətuː'itiː] *n* (tip) 心付け kokórozùke, チップ chíppù

grave [greiv] *n* (tomb) 墓 haká
♦*adj* (decision, mistake) 重大な júdai na; (expression, person) 重々しい omómoshiì

gravel [græv'əl] *n* 砂利 jarí

gravestone [greiv'stoun] *n* 墓石 hakáishi

graveyard [greiv'jɑːrd] *n* 墓場 hakába, 墓地 bóchi

gravity [græv'itiː] *n* (PHYSICS) 引力 iñryoku; (seriousness) 重大さ júdaisa

gravy [grei'viː] *n* (juice of meat) 肉汁 nikújū; (sauce) グレービーソース gurébīsòsu

gray [grei] *adj* = **grey**

graze [greiz] *vi* (animal) 草を食う kusá wo kuù
♦*vt* (touch lightly) かすめる kasúmerù; (scrape) こする kosúrù
♦*n* (MED) かすり傷 kasúrikìzu

grease [griːs] *n* (lubricant) グリース gurísù; (fat) 脂肪 shibó
♦*vt* ...にグリースを差す ...ni gurísù wo sásù

greaseproof paper [griːs'pruːf-] (*BRIT*)

n パラフィン紙 paráfiñshi

greasy [griː'siː] *adj* (food) 脂っこい abúrakkoỉ; (tools) 油で汚れた abúra de yogóretà; (skin, hair) 脂ぎった abúragittà

great [greit] *adj* (large: area, amount) 大きい ōkii; (intense: heat, pain) 強い tsuyóỉ; (important, famous: city, man) 有名な yūmei na; (*inf*: terrific) 素晴らしい subárashiî

Great Britain *n* 英国 eíkoku, イギリス igírisu

great-grandfather [greit'græn'fɑːðər] *n* そう祖父 sósofù

great-grandmother [greit'græn'mʌðəːr] *n* そう祖母 sósobò

greatly [greit'liː] *adv* とても totémo

greatness [greit'nis] *n* (importance) 偉大さ idáisa

Greece [griːs] *n* ギリシア gírìshia

greed [griːd] *n* (*also*: **greediness**) どん欲 dóñ-yoku

greedy [griː'diː] *adj* どん欲な dóñ-yoku na

Greek [griːk] *adj* ギリシアの gírìshia no; (LING) ギリシア語の giríshiago no
♦*n* (person) ギリシア人 giríshiajìn; (LING) ギリシア語 giríshiago

green [griːn] *adj* (color) 緑（色）の mídòri(iro) no; (inexperienced) 未熟な mijúku na; (POL) 環境保護の kañkyōhogò no
♦*n* (color) 緑（色）mídòri(iro); (stretch of grass) 芝生 shibáfu; (on golf course) グリーン guríñ

green belt *n* (round town) 緑地帯 ryokúchitài, グリーンベルト guríñberùto

green card *n* (*BRIT*: AUT) グリーンカード guríñkàdo ◇海外自動車保険証 kaígai jidōsha hokeñshō; (*US*: ADMIN) グリーンカード guríñkàdo ◇外国人入国就労許可書 gaíkokujìn nyūkoku shūrō kyokàsho

greenery [griː'nəːriː] *n* 緑 mídòri ◇主に人為的に植えた樹木などを指す ómò ni jiñ-iteki ni ueta júmòku nádà wo sásù

greengrocer [griːn'grousəːr] (*BRIT*) *n* 八百屋 yaóya

greenhouse [griːn'haus] *n* 温室 oñshitsu

greenish [griː'niʃ] *adj* 緑がかった midórigakattā

Greenland [gri:n'lənd] *n* グリーンランド gurīnrañdo

greens [gri:nz] *npl* (vegetables) 葉物 hamóno, 葉菜 yōsai

greet [gri:t] *vt* (welcome: person) ...にあいさつする ...ni áĭsatsu suru, 歓迎する kañgei suru; (receive: news) 受けとめる ukétomerù

greeting [gri:'tiŋ] *n* (welcome) あいさつ áĭsatsu, 歓迎 kañgei

greeting(s) card *n* グリーティングカード gurītingukādo

gregarious [grige:'ri:əs] *adj* (person) 社交的な shakōteki na

grenade [grineid'] *n* (*also*: **hand grenade**) 手りゅう弾 teryūdan, shuryūdan

grew [gru:] *pt of* **grow**

grey [grei] *adj* (color) 灰色 haíiro; (dismal) 暗い kuráĭ

grey-haired [grei'he:rd] *adj* 白髪頭の shirágaatāma no, 白髪の hakúhatsu no

greyhound [grei'haund] *n* グレーハウンド gurēhaùndo

grid [grid] *n* (pattern) 碁盤の目 góbàn no me; (ELEC: network) 送電網 sōdenmō

grief [gri:f] *n* (distress, sorrow) 悲しみ kanáshimi

grievance [gri:'vəns] *n* (complaint) 苦情 kujō

grieve [gri:v] *vi* (feel sad) 悲しむ kanáshimù

♦*vt* (cause sadness or distress to) 悲しませる kanáshimaserù

to grieve for (dead spouse etc) ...を嘆く ...wo nagékù

grievous [gri:'vəs] *adj*: **grievous bodily harm** (LAW) 重傷 jūshō

grill [gril] *n* (on cooker) グリル gúrìru; (grilled food: *also*: **mixed grill**) グリル料理 guríruryòri

♦*vt* (BRIT: food) グリルで焼く gúrìru de yákù; (*inf*: question) 尋問する jiñmon suru

grille [gril] *n* (screen: on window, counter etc) 鉄格子 tetsúgōshi; (AUT) ラジエーターグリル rajíētàgùriru

grim [grim] *adj* (unpleasant: situation)

厳しい kibíshiĭ; (unattractive: place) 陰気な íñki na; (serious, stern) 険しい kewáshiĭ

grimace [grim'əs] *n* (ugly expression) しかめっ面 shikámettsura

♦*vi* しかめっ面をする shikámetsura wo surú

grime [graim] *n* (dirt) あか aká

grin [grin] *n* (smile) にやにや笑い níyàni-yawarai

♦*vi* にやにやと笑う níyàniya to waráù

grind [graind] (*pt, pp* **ground**) *vt* (crush) もみつぶす momítsubusù; (coffee, pepper etc: *also US*: meat) 挽く hikú; (make sharp: knife) 研ぐ tógù

♦*n* (work) 骨折れ仕事 honéoreshigòto

grip [grip] *n* (hold) 握り nigíri; (control, grasp) 支配 shihái; (of tire, shoe) グリップ guríppù; (handle) 取っ手 tottè; (holdall) 旅行かばん ryokōkabàn

♦*vt* (object) つかむ tsukámù, 握る nigírù; (audience, attention) 引付ける hikítsukerù

to come to grips with (problem, difficulty) ...と取組む ...to toríkumù

gripping [grip'iŋ] *adj* (story, film) 引付ける hikítsukerù

grisly [griz'li:] *adj* (death, murder) ひどい hidóĭ

gristle [gris'əl] *n* (on meat) 軟骨 náñkotsu

grit [grit] *n* (sand, stone) 砂利 jarí; (determination, courage) 根性 koñjō

♦*vt* (road) ...に砂利を敷く ...ni jarí wo shíkù

to grit one's teeth 歯を食いしばる há wo kuíshibarù

groan [groun] *n* (of person) うめき声 umékigoè

♦*vi* うめく umékù

grocer [grou'sə:r] *n* 食料品商 shokúryō-hiñshō

groceries [grou'sə:ri:z] *npl* (provisions) 食料品 shokúryōhin

grocer's (shop) [grou'sə:rz-] *n* 食料品店 shokúryōhiñten

groggy [grɑ:g'i:] *adj* ふらふらする fúráfura suru, グロッキーの gurókkī no

groin [grɔin] n そけい部 sokéibu

groom [gru:m] n (for horse) 馬丁 batéi; (also: **bridegroom**) 花婿 hanámukò

♦vt (horse) ...の手入れをする ...no teíre wò suru; (fig): **to groom someone for** (job) 仕込む shikómù

well-groomed (person) 身だしなみのいい midáshìnami no íi

groove [gru:v] n 溝 mizó

grope [group] vi (fumble): **to grope for** 手探りで探す teságuri de sagásù

gross [grous] adj (flagrant: neglect, injustice) 甚だしい hanáhadashiì; (vulgar: behavior, building) 下品な géhìn na; (COMM: income, weight) 全体の zeítai no

grossly [grous'li:] adv (greatly) 甚だしく hanáhadashikù

grotesque [groutesk'] adj (exaggerated, ugly) 醜悪な shūaku na, グロテスクな gurótesùku na

grotto [grɑ:t'ou] n (cave) 小さな洞穴 chíisana horáana

grotty [grɑ:t'i:] (BRIT inf) adj (dreadful) ひどい hídòi

ground [graund] pt, pp of **grind**

♦n (earth, soil) 土 tsuchí; (land) 地面 jímèn; (SPORT) グランド gurándo; (US: also: **ground wire**) アース線 ásùsen; (reason: gen pl) 根拠 koñkyo

♦vt (plane) 飛べない様にする tobénai yō ni suru; (US: ELEC) ...のアースを取付ける ...no ásu wò torítsukerù

on the ground 地面に〔で〕jímèn ni 〔de〕

to the ground 地面へ jímèn e

to gain/lose ground 前進〔後退〕する zeńshin〔kōtai〕surù

ground cloth (US) n = **groundsheet**

grounding [graun'diŋ] n (in education) 基礎 kisó

groundless [graund'lis] adj (fears, suspicions) 根拠のない koñkyo no nài

grounds [graundz] npl (of coffee etc) かす kásù; (gardens etc) 敷地 shikíchi

groundsheet [graund'ʃi:t] n グラウンドシート gurául doshîto

ground staff n (AVIAT) 整備員 seíbiìn

◇総称 sốshō

ground swell n (of opinion) 盛り上がり moríagarì

groundwork [graund'wə:rk] n (preparation) 準備 júnbi

group [gru:p] n (of people) 集団 shúdan, グループ gúrùpu; (of trees etc) 一群れ hitómùre; (of cars etc) 一団 ichídan; (also: **pop group**) グループ gúrùpu; (COMM) グループ gúrùpu

♦vt (also: **group together**: people, things etc) 一緒にする íssho ni suru, グループにする gúrùpu ni suru

♦vi (also: **group together**) 群がる murágarù, グループになる gúrùpu ni nárù

grouse [graus] n inv (bird) ライチョウ ráìchō

♦vi (complain) 不平を言う fuhéi wò iú

grove [grouv] n 木立 kodáchì

grovel [grʌv'əl] vi (fig): **to grovel (before)** (boss etc) (...に) ぺこぺこする (...ni) pékòpeko suru

grow [grou] (pt **grew**, pp **grown**) vi (plant, tree) 生える haérù; (person, animal) 成長する seíchō suru; (increase) 増える fuérù; (become) なる nárù; (develop): **to grow (out of/from)** (...から) 発生する (...kara) hasséi suru

♦vt (roses, vegetables) 栽培する saíbai suru; (beard) 生やす hayásù

grower [grou'ə:r] n (BOT, AGR) 栽培者 saíbaishà

growing [grou'iŋ] adj (fear, awareness, number) 増大する zṓdai suru

growl [graul] vi (dog, person) うなる unárù

grown [groun] pp of **grow**

grown-up [groun'ʌp'] n (adult) 大人 otóna

growth [grouθ] n (development, increase: of economy, industry) 成長 seíchō; (what has grown: of weeds, beard etc) 生えた物 haéta monò; (growing: of child, animal etc) 発育 hatsúiku; (MED) しゅよう shuyṓ

grow up vi (child) 育つ sodátsù

grub [grʌb] n (larva) 幼虫 yṓchū; (inf: food) 飯 meshí

grubby [grʌb'i:] *adj* (dirty) 汚い kitánaì

grudge [grʌdʒ] *n* (grievance) 恨み urámì

♦*vt*: **to grudge someone something** (be unwilling to give) ...に...を出し惜しみする ...ni ...wo dashíoshimi suru; (envy) ...の...をねたむ ...no ...wo netámù

to bear someone a grudge ...に恨みがある ...ni urámi ga arù

gruelling [gru:'əliŋ] *adj* (trip, journey, encounter) きつい kitsúi

gruesome [gru:'səm] *adj* (tale, scene) むごたらしい mugótarashiì

gruff [grʌf] *adj* (voice, manner) ぶっきらぼうな bukkírabò na

grumble [grʌm'bəl] *vi* (complain) 不平を言う fuhéi wò iú

grumpy [grʌm'pi:] *adj* (bad-tempered) 機嫌が悪い kigén ga warúì

grunt [grʌnt] *vi* (pig) ぶーぶー言う būbū iú; (person) うなる unáru

G-string [dʒi:'striŋ] *n* (garment) バタフライ bátáfurai

guarantee [gærənti:'] *n* (assurance) 保証 hoshố; (COMM: warranty) 保証書 hoshốshò

♦*vt* 保証する hoshố suru

guard [gɑːrd] *n* (one person) 警備員 keíbìn, ガードマン gádoman; (squad) 護衛隊 goéitai; (BRIT: RAIL) 車掌 shashố; (on machine) 安全カバー añzenkabā; (also: **fireguard**) 安全格子 añzenkồshi

♦*vt* (protect: place, person, secret etc):

to guard (against) (...から) 守る (...kara) mamórù; (prisoner) 見張る mihárù

to be on one's guard 警戒する keíkai suru

guard against *vt fus* (prevent: disease, damage etc) 防ぐ fuségù

guarded [gɑːr'did] *adj* (statement, reply) 慎重な shiñchồ na

guardian [gɑːr'di:ən] *n* (LAW: of minor) 保護者 hógòsha; (defender) 監視人 kañshinìn

guard's van (BRIT) *n* (RAIL) 乗務員車 jốmuinsha

guerrilla [gəril'ə] *n* ゲリラ gérìra

guess [ges] *vt, vi* (estimate: number, dis-

tance etc) 推定する suítei suru; (correct answer) 当ててみる atétè mírù; (US: think) ...だと思う ...da to omóù

♦*n* (attempt at correct answer) 推定 suítei

to take/have a guess 推定する suítei suru, 当ててみる atétè mírù

guesswork [ges'wərk] *n* (speculation) 当て推量 atézuiryồ

guest [gest] *n* (visitor) 客 kyákù; (in hotel) 泊り客 tomárikyàku

guest-house [gest'haus] *n* 民宿 mínshuku

guest room *n* 客間 kyakúma

guffaw [gʌfɔ:'] *vi* ばか笑い bakáwarai

guidance [gaid'əns] *n* (advice) 指導 shidố

guide [gaid] *n* (person: museum guide, tour guide, mountain guide) 案内人 añnáinìn, ガイド gáido; (book) ガイドブック gaídobukkù; (BRIT: also: **girl guide**) ガールスカウト gárusukaùto

♦*vt* (round city, museum etc) 案内する añnái suru; (lead) 導く michíbikù; (direct) ...に道を教える ...ni michí wò oshíerù

guidebook [gaid'buk] *n* ガイドブック gaídobukkù

guide dog *n* 盲導犬 mốdōkèn

guidelines [gaid'lainz] *npl* (advice) 指針 shishín, ガイドライン gaídorain

guild [gild] *n* (association) 組合 kumíaì, 協会 kyốkai

guile [gail] *n* (cunning) 悪意 akúì

guillotine [gil'əti:n] *n* (for execution) 断頭台 dañtốdai, ギロチン giróchin; (for paper) 裁断機 saídañki

guilt [gilt] *n* (remorse) 罪の意識 tsumí nò ishíki; (culpability) 有罪 yúzai

guilty [gil'ti:] *adj* (person) 有罪の yúzai no; (expression) 後ろめたそうな ushírometasồ na; (secret) やましい yamáshiì

guinea [gin'i:] *n* (BRIT) (old money) ギニー gínì

guinea pig *n* (animal) モルモット morúmottò; (fig: person) 実験台 jikkéñdai

guise [gaiz] *n*: **in/under the guise of** ...の装いで ...no yosóoì de

guitar [gita:r'] n ギター gítā

gulf [gʌlf] n (GEO) 湾 wáñ; (abyss: *also fig*: difference) 隔たり hedátarì

gull [gʌl] n カモメ kamóme

gullet [gʌl'it] n 食道 shokúdō

gullible [gʌl'əbəl] *adj* (naive, trusting) だまされやすい damásareyàsui

gully [gʌl'i:] n (ravine) 峡谷 kyōkoku

gulp [gʌlp] vi (swallow) 息を飲込む íkì wo nomíkomù

♦vt (*also*: **gulp down**: drink) がぶがぶ飲込む gábùgabu nomíkomù; (: food) 急いで食べる isóìde tabérù

gum [gʌm] n (ANAT) 歯茎 hágùki; (glue) アラビア糊 arábia nòri; (sweet: *also*: **gumdrop**) ガムドロップ gamúdoroppù; (*also*: **chewing-gum**) チューインガム chūingugàmu, ガム gámù

♦vt (stick): **to gum (together)** 張り合わせる haríawaserù

gumboots [gʌm'bu:ts] (*BRIT*) *npl* ゴム靴 gomúgùtsu

gumption [gʌmp'ʃən] n (sense, wit) 度胸 dokyō

gun [gʌn] n (small: revolver, pistol) けん銃 keñjū, ピストル písùtoru, ガン gáñ; (medium-sized: rifle) 銃 jū, ライフル raífùru; (: *also*: **airgun**) 空気銃 kūkijū; (large: cannon) 大砲 taíhō

gunboat [gʌn'bout] n 砲艦 hōkan

gunfire [gʌn'faiə:r] n 銃撃 jūgeki

gunman [gʌn'mən] (*pl* **gunmen**) n (criminal) ガンマン gáñman

gunpoint [gʌn'pɔint] n: **at gunpoint** (pointing a gun) ピストルを突付けて písùtoru wo tsukítsuketè; (threatened with a gun) ピストルを突付けられて písùtoru wo tsukítsukerarète

gunpowder [gʌn'paudə:r] n 火薬 kayákù

gunshot [gʌn'ʃɑ:t] n (act) 発砲 happō; (sound) 銃声 jūsei

gurgle [gə:r'gəl] vi (baby) のどを鳴らす nodó wò narásù; (water) ごぼごぼ流れる góbògobo nagárerù

guru [gu:'ru:] n (REL: *also fig*) 教師 kyōshi

gush [gʌʃ] vi (blood, tears, oil) どっと流れ出る dóttò nagárederù; (person) 大げさに言う ōgesa ni iu

gusset [gʌs'it] n (SEWING) まち máchì

gust [gʌst] n (*also*: **gust of wind**) 突風 toppū; (of smoke) 渦巻 uzúmàki

gusto [gʌs'tou] n (enthusiasm) 楽しみ tanóshimì

gut [gʌt] n (ANAT: intestine) 腸 chō

guts [gʌts] *npl* (ANAT: of person, animal) 内臓 naízō; (*inf*: courage) 勇気 yūki, ガッツ gáttsù

gutter [gʌt'ə:r] n (in street) どぶ dobu; (of roof) 雨どい amádòi

guttural [gʌt'ə:rəl] *adj* (accent, sound) のどに絡まった様な nódò ni karámatta yồ na

guy [gai] n (*inf*: man) 野郎 yarō, やつ yátsù; (*also*: **guyrope**) 支線 shisén; (figure) ガイフォークスの人形 gaífồkusu no niñgyō

guzzle [gʌz'əl] vt (drink) がぶがぶ飲む gábùgabu nómù; (food) がつがつ食う gátsùgatsu kúù

gym [dʒim] n (building, room: *also*: **gymnasium**) 体育館 taíikukàn; (activity: *also*: **gymnastics**) 体操 taísō

gymnast [dʒim'næst] n 体操選手 taísōseñshu

gymnastics [dʒimnæs'tiks] n 体操 taísō

gym shoes *npl* 運動靴 uñdōgùtsu, スニーカー súnīkā

gym slip (*BRIT*) n (tunic) スモックスモック ♦そで無しの上っ張りでかつて女子学童の制服として使われた物 sodénashi no uwápparì de katsútè joshí gakudō no seífuku toshite tsukáwaretà monó

gynecologist [gainəkɑ:l'ədʒist] (*BRIT* **gynaecologist**) n 婦人科医 fujíñka-i

gypsy [dʒip'si:] n ジプシー jípùshī

gyrate [dʒai'reit] vi (revolve) 回転する kaíten suru

H

haberdashery [hæb'ə:rdæʃə:ri:] n (*US*) 紳士服店 shiñshifukutèn; (*BRIT*) 小間物店 komámonotèn

habit [hǽb'it] *n* (custom, practice) 習慣 shúkan; (addiction) 中毒 chúdoku; (REL: costume) 修道服 shúdōfùku

habitable [hǽb'itəbəl] *adj* 住める suméru

habitat [hǽb'itæt] *n* 生息地 seísokuchì

habitual [həbitʃ'u:əl] *adj* (action) 習慣的な shúkanteki na; (drinker, liar) 常習的な jōshūteki na

hack [hæk] *vt* (cut, slice) ぶった切る buttágirù
◆*n* (*pej*: writer) 三文文士 safimonbuñshi

hacker [hæk'ə:r] *n* (COMPUT) コンピュータ破り cofipyūtayaburì, ハッカー hákkā

hackneyed [hæk'ni:d] *adj* 陳腐な chífipu na

had [hæd] *pt*, *pp* of **have**

haddock [hæd'ək] (*pl* **haddock** *or* **haddocks**) *n* タラ tárà

hadn't [hæd'ənt] = **had not**

haemorrhage [hem'ə:ridʒ] (*BRIT*) *n* = **hemorrhage**

haemorrhoids [hem'ə:rɔidz] (*BRIT*) *npl* = **hemorrhoids**

haggard [hæg'ə:rd] *adj* (face, look) やつれた yatsúretà

haggle [hæg'əl] *vi* (bargain) 値切る negírù

Hague [heig] *n*: **The Hague** ハーグ hǎgù

hail [heil] *n* (frozen rain) ひょう hyǒ; (of objects, criticism etc) 降り注ぐ物 furísosogù monó
◆*vt* (call: person) 呼ぶ yobú; (flag down: taxi) 呼び止める yobítomerù; (acclaim: person, event etc) ほめる homérù
◆*vi* (weather) ひょうが降る hyǒ ga fúrù

hailstone [heil'stoun] *n* ひょうの粒 hyǒ no tsubú

hair [he:r] *n* (of animal: *also* gen) 毛 ke; (of person's head) 髪の毛 kamí no kè
to do one's hair 髪をとかす kamí wò tokásu

hairbrush [he:r'brʌʃ] *n* ヘアブラシ heáburashì

haircut [he:r'kʌt] *n* (action) 散髪 safipatsu; (style) 髪型 kamígata, ヘアスタイル heásutaìru

hairdo [he:r'du:] *n* 髪型 kamígata, ヘアスタイル heásutaìru

hairdresser [he:r'dresə:r] *n* 美容師 biyóshì

hairdresser's [he:r'dresə:rz] *n* (shop) 美容院 biyóìn

hair dryer *n* ヘアドライヤー heádoraìyā

hairgrip [he:r'grip] *n* 髪止め kamídome

hairnet [he:r'net] *n* ヘアネット heánettò

hairpin [he:r'pin] *n* ヘアピン heápìn

hairpin curve (*BRIT* **hairpin bend**) *n* ヘアピンカーブ heápinkābu

hair-raising [he:r'reiziŋ] *adj* (experience, tale) ぞっとする様な zóttò suru yō na

hair remover [-rimu:'və:r] *n* (cream) 脱毛クリーム datsúmōkurīmù

hair spray *n* ヘアスプレー heásupurè

hairstyle [he:r'stail] *n* 髪型 kamígata, ヘアスタイル heásutaìru

hairy [he:r'i:] *adj* (person, animal) 毛深い kebúkaì; (inf: situation) 恐ろしい osóroshiì

hake [heik] (*pl inv or* **hakes**) *n* タラ tárà

half [hæf] (*pl* **halves**) *n* (of amount, object) 半分 hafibuñ; (of beer etc) 半パイント hafipaìnto; (RAIL, bus) 半額 hafigaku
◆*adj* (bottle, fare, pay etc) 半分の hafibuñ no
◆*adv* (empty, closed, open, asleep) 半ば nakábà

two and a half 2と2分の1 nf tò nibún no ichi

two and a half years/kilos/hours 2年〔キロ，時間〕半 niñeñ〔kíro, jíkan〕hàn

half a dozen 半ダース hafidàsu

half a pound 半ポンド hafipoñdo

to cut something in half ...を半分に切る ...wo hafibuñ ni kírù

half-baked [hæf'beikt'] *adj* (idea, scheme) ばかげた bakágetà

half-caste [hæf'kæst] *n* 混血児 koñketsujì, ハーフ hǎfu

half-hearted [hæf'hɑ:r'tid] *adj* (attempt) いい加減な iíkagen na

half-hour [hæf'au'ə:r] *n* 半時間 hañjikàn

half-mast [hæf'mæst']: *a flag at half-mast* 半旗 háñki

halfpenny [hei'pəni:] (*BRIT*) *n* 半ペニー hañpenì

half-price [hæf'prais'] *adj* 半額の hañgaku no
♦*adv* 半額で hañgaku de

half term (*BRIT*) *n* (SCOL) 中間休暇 chúkankyūka

half-time [hæf'taim'] *n* (SPORT) ハーフタイム háfutaimù

halfway [hæf'wei'] *adv* (between two points in place, time) 中途で chúto de

halibut [hæl'əbət] *n inv* オヒョウ ohyő

hall [hɔ:l] *n* (entrance way) 玄関ホール geñkanhòru; (for concerts, meetings etc) 講堂 kődō, ホール hőru

hall of residence (*BRIT*) *n* 学生寮 gakúseiryö

hallmark [hɔ:l'mɑ:rk] *n* (on metal) 太鼓判 taíkoban; (of writer, artist etc) 特徴 tokúchò

hallo [hələu'] *excl* = **hello**

Hallowe'en [hæləwi:n'] *n* ハロウイーン harőuìn

hallucination [həlu:sənei'[ən] *n* 幻覚 geñkaku

hallway [hɔ:l'wei] *n* (entrance hall) 玄関ホール geñkanhòru

halo [hei'lou] *n* (of saint) 後光 gokő

halt [hɔ:lt] *n* (stop) 止る事 tomáru kotò
♦*vt* (progress, activity, growth etc) 止める tomérù
♦*vi* (stop) 止る tomárù

halve [hæv] *vt* (reduce) 半分に減らす hañbuñ ni herásù; (divide) 半分に切る hañbuñ ni kírù

halves [hævz] *pl of* **half**

ham [hæm] *n* (meat) ハム hámù

hamburger [hæm'bə:rgə:r] *n* ハンバーガー hañbágà

hamlet [hæm'lit] *n* (village) 小さな村 chíisana murá

hammer [hæm'ə:r] *n* (tool) 金づち kanázuchì, とんかち toñkàchi
♦*vt* (nail) たたく tatákù
♦*vi* (on door, table etc) たたく tatákù

to hammer an idea into someone ...に ある考え方をたたき込む ...ni árù kañgaekata wo tátakikomù

to hammer a message across ある考え を繰返し強調する aru kañgaè wo kuríkaeshì kyőchō suru

hammock [hæm'ək] *n* (on ship, in garden) ハンモック hañmokkù

hamper [hæm'pə:r] *vt* (person, movement, effort) 邪魔する jamá suru
♦*n* (basket) ふた付きバスケット futátsukibasukettò

hamster [hæm'stə:r] *n* ハムスター hámùsutā

hand [hænd] *n* (ANAT) 手 té; (of clock) 針 hárì; (handwriting) 筆跡 hisséki; (worker) 使用人 shíyònin; (of cards) 持札 mochífùda
♦*vt* (pass, give) 渡す watásù

to give/lend someone a hand ...の手伝 いをする ...no tetsúdaì wo suru

at hand 手元に temóto nì

in hand (time) 空いていて aíte itè; (job, situation) 当面の tőmen no

on hand (person, services etc) 利用でき る ríyō dekirù

to hand (information etc) 手元に temóto nì

on the one hand ..., on the other hand ... 一方では...他方では... ippő de wa ..., táhō de wa ...

handbag [hænd'bæg] *n* ハンドバッグ hañdobaggù

handbook [hænd'buk] *n* (manual) ハンドブック hañdobukkù

handbrake [hænd'breik] *n* (AUT) サイドブレーキ saídoburèki

handcuffs [hænd'kʌfs] *npl* (POLICE) 手錠 tejő

handful [hænd'ful] *n* (of soil, stones) 一握り hitónigirì

a handful of people 数人 súnin

handicap [hæn'di:kæp] *n* (disability) 障害 shőgai; (disadvantage) 不利 fúrì; (SPORT) ハンデ háñde
♦*vt* (hamper) 不利にする fúrì ni suru

mentally/physically handicapped 精神的〔身体〕障害のある seíshinteki〔shíñtai) shōgai no árù

handicraft [hǽn'di:kræft] n (activity) 手芸 shúgèi; (object) 手芸品 shugéihìn

hand in vt (essay, work) 提出する teíshutsu suru

handiwork [hǽn'di:wə:rk] n やった事 yattá kotò

handkerchief [hǽŋ'kə:rtʃif] n ハンカチ hańkachi

handle [hǽn'dəl] n (of door, window, drawer etc) 取っ手 totté; (of cup, knife, brush etc) 柄 e; (for winding) ハンドル hańdòru

♦vt (touch: object, ornament etc) いじる ijírù; (deal with: problem, responsibility etc) 処理する shórì suru; (treat: people) 扱う atsúkaù

「*handle with care*」取扱い注意 toríatsukai chùi

to fly off the handle 怒る okórù

handlebar(s) [hǽn'dəlbɑːr(z)] n(pl) ハンドル hańdòru

hand luggage n 手荷物 teńmótsu

handmade [hǽnd'meid'] adj (clothes, jewellery, pottery etc) 手作りの tezúkùri no

hand out vt (object, information) 配る kubárù; (punishment) 与える atáerù

handout [hǽnd'aut] n (money, clothing, food) 施し物 hodókoshimono; (publicity leaflet) パンフレット pánfuretto; (summary: of lecture) 講演の要約 kōen nò yōyaku

hand over vt (thing) 引渡す hikíwatasù; (responsibility) 譲る yuzúrù

handrail [hǽnd'reil] n (on stair, ledge) 手すり tesúri

handshake [hǽnd'ʃeik] n 握手 ákùshu

handsome [hǽn'səm] adj (man) 男前の otókomaè no, ハンサムな háńsamu na; (woman) きりっとした kiríttò shita; (building) 立派な rippá na; (fig: profit, return) 相当な sōtō na

handwriting [hǽnd'raitiŋ] n (style) 筆跡 hisséki

handy [hǽn'di:] adj (useful) 便利な bénrì na; (skilful) 手先の器用な tesáki nò kíyō na; (close at hand) 手元にある temóto nì

árù

handyman [hǽn'di:mæn] (pl **handymen**) n (at home) 手先の器用な人 tesáki nò kíyō na hitò; (in hotel etc) 用務員 yōmuin

hang [hæŋ] (pt, pp **hung**) vt (painting, coat etc) 掛ける kakérù; (criminal: pt, pp hanged) 絞首刑にする kōshukei ni surù

♦vi (painting, coat, drapery etc) 掛っている kakátte irù; (hair etc) 垂れ下がる tarésagarù

to get the hang of something (inf) ...のこつが分かる ...no kótsù ga wakárù

hang about vi (loiter) ぶらつく burátsukù

hangar [hǽŋ'ə:r] n (AVIAT) 格納庫 kakúnōko

hang around vi = hang about

hanger [hǽŋ'ə:r] n (for clothes) 洋服掛け yōfukukàke, ハンガー háńgā

hanger-on [hǽŋ'ə:rɑːn'] n (parasite) 取巻き torímaki

hang-gliding [hǽŋ'glaidiŋ] n (SPORT) ハンググライダー hańguguraídā

hang on vi (wait) 待つ mátsù

hangover [hǽŋ'ouvə:r] n (after drinking) 二日酔い futsúkayoì

hang up vi (TEL) 電話を切る deńwa wò kírù

♦vt (coat, painting etc) 掛ける kakérù

hang-up [hǽŋ'ʌp] n (inhibition) ノイローゼ noírōze

hanker [hǽŋ'kə:r] vi: *to hanker after* (desire, long for) 渇望する katsúbō suru

hankie [hǽŋ'ki:] n abbr = **handkerchief**

hanky [hǽŋ'ki:] n abbr = **handkerchief**

haphazard [hǽp'hǽz'ɑːrd] adj (system, arrangement) いい加減な iíkagen na

happen [hǽp'ən] vi (event etc: occur) 起る okórù; (chance): *to happen to do something* 偶然に...する gūzen ni ...surù

as it happens 実は jitsú wà

happening [hǽp'əniŋ] n (incident) 出来事 dekígòto

happily [hǽp'ili:] adv (luckily) 幸い saíwai; (cheerfully) 楽しそうに tanóshisò ni

happiness [hæp'i:nis] *n* (contentment) 幸せ shiáwase

happy [hæp'i:] *adj* (pleased) うれしい uréshiî; (cheerful) 楽しい tanóshiî

  to be happy (with) (content) (...に) 満足する (...ni) mañzoku suru

  to be happy to do (willing) 喜んで...する yorókoñde ...surù

  happy birthday! 誕生日おめでとう! tañjôbi ómédetô!

happy-go-lucky [hæp'i:goulʌk'i:] *adj* (person) のんきな nôñki na

harangue [həræŋ'] *vt* (audience, class) ...に向かって熱弁を振るう ...ni mukátte netsúben wò furúû

harass [həræs'] *vt* (annoy, pester) ...にいやがらせをする ...ni iyágarase wo surù

harassment [həræs'mənt] *n* (hounding) 嫌がらせ iyágarase

harbor [hɑːr'bəːr] (*BRIT* **harbour**) *n* (NAUT) 港 mináto

  ♦*vt* (hope, fear etc) 心に抱く kokóro ni idákù; (criminal, fugitive) かくまう kakúmaù

hard [hɑːrd] *adj* (surface, object) 堅い katái; (question, problem) 難しい muzúkashiî; (work) 骨の折れる honé no orérù; (life) 苦しい kurúshiî; (person) 非情な hijô na; (facts, evidence) 確実な kakújitsu na

  ♦*adv* (work, think, try) 一生懸命に isshôkeñmei ni

  to look hard at ...を見詰める ...wo mitsúmerù

  no hard feelings! 悪く思わないから warúkù omówanài kará

  to be hard of hearing 耳が遠い mimí ga tôi

  to be hard done by 不当な扱いを受けた futô na atsukài wo ukétá

hardback [hɑːrd'bæk] *n* (book) ハードカバー hâdokabà

hard cash *n* 現金 geñkin

hard disk *n* (COMPUT) ハードディスク hâdodisùku

harden [hɑːr'dən] *vt* (wax, glue, steel) 固める katámerù; (attitude, person) かたくなにする katákùna ni suru

  ♦*vi* (wax, glue, steel) 固まる katámarù; (attitude, person) かたくなになる katákùna ni nárù

hard-headed [hɑːrd'hed'id] *adj* (businessman) 現実的な geñjitsuteki na

hard labor *n* (punishment) 懲役 chôeki

hardly [hɑːrd'li:] *adv* (scarcely) ほとんど...ない hotóñdo ...nâî; (no sooner) ...するや否や ...surú ya inà ya

  hardly ever ほとんど...しない hotóñdo ...shinâî

hardship [hɑːrd'ʃip] *n* (difficulty) 困難 kofinañ

hard up (*inf*) *adj* (broke) 金がない kané ga naî, 懐が寂しい futókoro ga sabishiî

hardware [hɑːrd'weːr] *n* (ironmongery) 金物 kanámono; (COMPUT) ハードウエア hâdouèà; (MIL) 兵器 hêíki

hardware shop *n* 金物屋 kanámonoya

hard-wearing [hɑːrd'weːr'iŋ] *adj* (clothes, shoes) 丈夫な jôbu na

hard-working [hɑːrd'wəːr'kiŋ] *adj* (employee, student) 勤勉な kiñben na

hardy [hɑːr'di:] *adj* (plants, animals, people) 丈夫な jôbu na

hare [heːr] *n* ノウサギ noúsàgi

hare-brained [her'breind] *adj* (scheme, idea) バカげた bakágetà

harem [her'əm] *n* (of wives) ハーレム hâremu

harm [hɑːrm] *n* (injury) 害 gâî; (damage) 損害 soñgai, ダメージ damêji

  ♦*vt* (person) ...に危害を加える ...ni kígài wo kuwáerù; (thing) 損傷する soñshô suru

  out of harm's way 安全な場所に añzen na bashò ni

harmful [hɑːrm'fəl] *adj* (effect, toxin, influence etc) 有害な yûgai na

harmless [hɑːrm'lis] *adj* (animal, person) 無害な mugái na; (joke, pleasure, activity) たわいのない tawai no nai

harmonica [hɑːrmɑːn'ikə] *n* ハーモニカ hâmonika

harmonious [hɑːrmou'ni:əs] *adj* (discussion, relationship) 友好的な yúkôteki na; (layout, pattern) 調和の取れた chôwa no tóretà; (sound, tune) 調子の良い chôshi no yoï

harmonize [haːrˈmənaiz] vi (MUS) ハーモニーを付ける hāmonī wo tsukérù; (colors, ideas): **to harmonize (with)** (...と)調和する (...to) chōwa suru

harmony [haːrˈməniː] n (accord) 調和 chōwa; (MUS) ハーモニー hāmonī

harness [haːrˈnis] n (for horse) 馬具 bágù; (for child, dog) 胴輪 dōwa, ハーネス hānesù; (safety harness) 安全ハーネス añzenhānesu
♦vt (resources, energy etc) 利用する riyō suru; (horse) ...に馬具をつける ...ni bágù wo tsukérù; (dog) ...にハーネスを付ける ...ni hānesù wo tsukérù

harp [haːrp] n (MUS) たて琴 tatégòto, ハープ hāpu
♦vi: **to harp on about** (pej) ...の事をくどくどと話し続ける ...no kotó wò kúdòkudo to hanáshitsuzukerù

harpoon [haːrpuːn] n もり mórì

harrowing [hærˈouiŋ] adj (experience, film) 戦りつの señritsu no

harsh [haːrʃ] adj (sound) 耳障りな mimízawàri na; (light) どぎつい dogítsui; (judge, criticism) 酷な kakóku na; (life, winter) 厳しい kibíshiì

harvest [haːrˈvist] n (harvest time) 収穫期 shūkakukì; (of barley, fruit etc) 収穫 shūkaku
♦vt (barley, fruit etc) 収穫する shūkaku suru

has [hæz] vb see **have**

hash [hæʃ] n (CULIN) ハッシュ hásshù; (fig: mess) めちゃめちゃな有様 mechámecha na arisama

hashish [hæʃˈiːʃ] n ハシシ háshìshi

hasn't [hæzˈənt] = **has not**

hassle [hæsˈəl] (inf) n (bother) 面倒 mendō

haste [heist] n (hurry) 急ぎ isógi

hasten [heiˈsən] vt (decision, downfall) 早める hayámerù
♦vi (hurry): **to hasten to do something** 急いで...する isóide ...surù

hastily [heisˈtiliː] adv (hurriedly) 慌ただしく awátadashikù; (rashly) 軽はずみに karúhazùmi ni

hasty [heisˈtiː] adj (hurried) 慌ただしい awátadashiì; (rash) 軽はずみの karúhazùmi no

hat [hæt] n (headgear) 帽子 bōshi

hatch [hætʃ] n (NAUT: also: **hatchway**) 倉口 sōkō, ハッチ hátchì; (also: **service hatch**) サービス口 sābisugùchi, ハッチ hátchì
♦vi (bird) 卵からかえる tamágò kara kaérù; (egg) かえる kaérù, ふ化する fuká suru

hatchback [hætʃˈbæk] n (AUT) ハッチバック hatchíbakkù

hatchet [hætʃˈit] n (axe) おの ónò

hate [heit] vt (wish ill to: person) 憎む nikúmù; (dislike strongly: person, thing, situation) 嫌う kiráu
♦n (illwill) 増悪 zōo; (strong dislike) 嫌悪 kén'o

hateful [heitˈfəl] adj ひどい hidóî

hatred [heiˈtrid] n (illwill) 増悪 zōo; (strong dislike) 嫌悪 kén'o

haughty [hɔːˈtiː] adj (air, attitude) 尊大な soñdai na

haul [hɔːl] vt (pull) 引っ張る hippáru
♦n (of stolen goods etc) 獲物 emóno; (also: **a haul of fish**) 漁獲 gyokáku

haulage [hɔːˈlidʒ] n (business, costs) 運送 uñsō

hauler [hɔːˈləːr] (BRIT **haulier**) n 運送屋 uñsōya

haunch [hɔːntʃ] n (ANAT) 腰 koshí; (of meat) 腰肉 koshíniku

haunt [hɔːnt] vt (subj: ghost) (place) ...に出る ...ni dérù; (person) ...に付きまとう ...ni tsukimatou; (: problem, memory etc) 悩ます nayámasù
♦n (of crooks, childhood etc) 行き付けの場所 ikítsuke nò bashó
haunted house お化け屋敷 obákeyashìki

KEYWORD

---

have [hæv] (pt, pp **had**) aux vb 1 (gen)
to have arrived/gone/eaten/slept 着いた〔行った, 食べた, 眠った〕tsuíta〔ittá, tábèta, nemúttá〕
he has been kind/promoted 彼は親切

だった〔昇格した〕kárè wa shíñsetsu dáttà〔shōkaku shita〕

has he told you? 彼はあなたにそれを話しましたか kárè wa anátà ni soré wò hanáshimashìta ká

having finished/when he had finished, he left 仕事が済むと彼は帰った shigòto ga sumù to kárè wa kâètta

2 (in tag questions): **you've done it, haven't you?** あなたはその仕事をやったんでしょう anátà wa sonó shigòto wo yattáñ deshō

he hasn't done it, has he? 彼は仕事をやらなかったんでしょう kárè wa shigòto wò yaránakattàn deshō

3 (in short answers and questions): **you've made a mistake - no I haven't!** - **I have** あなたは間違いをしました-違いますよ〔そうですね〕anátà wa machígai wo shimáshìta - chigáimasù yó〔sō desu né〕

we haven't paid - yes we have! 私たちはまだ金を払っていません-払いましたよ watákushitàchi wa mádà kané wo haráttè imaseñ - haráimashìta yó

I've been there before, have you? 私は前にあそこへ行った事がありますが、あなたは? watákushi wà máè ni asóko è ittá kotò ga arímasù ga, anátà wà?

♦**modal aux vb** (be obliged): **to have (got) to do something** ...をしなければならない ...wò shinákereba naranài

she has (got) to do it 彼女はどうしてもそれをしなければなりません kánòjo wa dôshitè mo soré wò shinákereba narimaseñ

I have (got) to finish this work 私はこの仕事を済まさなければなりません watákushi wà konó shigòto wo sumásanakereba narimaseñ

you haven't to tell her 彼女に言わなくてもいい〔言ってはならない〕kánòjo ni iwánakute mò íi〔itté wa naránaì〕

I haven't got/I don't have to wear glasses 私は眼鏡を掛けなくてもいいwatákushi wà mégàne wò kakénakute mò íi

this has to be a mistake これは何かの

間違いに違いない koré wa nánìka no machígaì ni chigái naì

♦**vt 1** (possess) 持っている móttè iru, ...がある ...gá arù

he has (got) blue eyes/dark hair 彼は目が青い〔髪が黒い〕kárè wa mé gà aóì〔kamí gà kuróì〕

do you have/have you got a car/phone? あなたは車〔電話〕を持っていますか anátà wa kurúma〔deñwa〕wò móttè imasu ká

I have (got) an idea いい考えがあります íi kañgae ga arímasù

have you any more money? もっとお金がありませんか móttò o-káne gà arímaseñ ká

2 (take: food) 食べる tabérù; (: drink) 飲む nómù

to have breakfast/lunch/dinner 朝食〔昼食, 夕食〕を食べる chōshoku〔chúshoku, yūshoku〕wò tabérù

to have a drink 何かを飲む nánìka wo nómù

to have a cigarette タバコを吸う tabáko wo suù

3 (receive, obtain etc) 受ける ukérù, 手に入れる té ni irerù

may I have your address? ご住所を教えて頂けますか go-jūsho wò oshíete itadakemasù ká

you can have it for $5 5ドルでそれを譲ります gódòru de soré wò yuzúrimasù

I must have it by tomorrow どうしても明日までにそれをもらいたいのですdôshite mò ashíta made nì soré wò morăitai no desù

to have a baby 子供を産む kodómo wo umù

4 (maintain, allow) 主張する shuchō suru, 許す yurúsù

he will have it that he is right 彼は自分が正しいと主張している kárè wa jibún gà tadáshiì to shuchō shite irù

I won't have it/this nonsense! それ〔こんなばかげた事〕は許せません soré〔koñna bakageta kotò〕wà yurúsemaseñ

we can't have that そんな事は許せません soñna kotò wa yurúsemaseñ

5: *to have something done* ...をさせる ...wò sasérù, ...をしてもらう ...wò shité mòraù

to have one's hair cut 散髪をしてもらう sañpatsu wò shité moraù

to have a house built 家を建てる ié wò tatérù

to have someone do something ...に ...をさせる ...ní ...wò sasérù

he soon had them all laughing/working まもなく彼は皆を笑わせて〔働かせて〕いた ma mó nàku kárè wa miná wò waráwasete〔határakasete〕ità

6 (experience, suffer) 経験する keíken suru

to have a cold 風邪を引いている kazé wò hiíte irù

to have (the) flu 感冒にかかっている kañbō nì kakátte irù

she had her bag stolen/her arm broken 彼女はハンドバッグを盗まれた〔腕を折った〕 kánòjo wa hañdobaggù wò nusúmaretà〔udé wo ottà〕

to have an operation 手術を受ける shújùtsu wo ukérù

7 (+ noun: take, hold etc) ...する ... suru

to have a swim/walk/bath/rest 泳ぐ〔散歩する, 風呂に入る, ひと休みする〕oyógù〔sañpo suru, fúrò ni háìru, hitóyàsumi suru〕

let's have a look 見てみましょう mítè mimashō

to have a meeting/party 会議〔パーティ〕を開く kàígi〔pâti〕wo hirákù

let me have a try 私に試させて下さい watákushi nì tamésasete kudasaí

8 (*inf*: dupe) だます damásù

he's been had 彼はだまされた kárè wa damásaretà

---

haven [heí'vən] *n* (harbor) 港 minàto; (safe place) 避難所 hinâñjo

haven't [hæv'ənt] = **have not**

have out *vt*: *to have it out with someone* (settle a problem etc) ...と決着をつける ...tò ketcháku wò tsukérù

haversack [hæv'ə:rsæk] *n* (of hiker, soldier) リュックサック ryukkúsakkù

---

havoc [hæv'ək] *n* (chaos) 混乱 koñran

Hawaii [həwaí'jiː] *n* ハワイ háwài

hawk [hɔːk] *n* タカ takå

hay [heí] *n* 干草 hoshíkusa

hay fever *n* 花粉症 kafúñshō

haystack [heí'stæk] *n* 干草の山 hoshíkusa no yama

haywire [heí'waiə:re] (*inf*) *adj*: *to go haywire* (machine etc) 故障する koshó suru; (plans etc) とんざする tôñza suru

hazard [hæz'ə:rd] *n* (danger) 危険 kikén
♦*vt* (risk: guess, bet etc) やってみる yatté mirù

hazardous [hæz'ə:rdəs] *adj* (dangerous) 危険な kikén na

hazard (warning) lights *npl* (AUT) 非常点滅灯 hijóteñmetsutō

haze [heíz] *n* (of heat, smoke, dust) かすみ kasúmi

hazelnut [heí'zəlnʌt] *n* ヘーゼルナッツ hézerunattsù

hazy [heí'ziː] *adj* (sky, view) かすんだ kasúnda; (idea, memory) ぼんやりとした boñ-yarí to shita

he [hiː] *pron* 彼は〔が〕kárè wa〔ga〕
he who ... ...する人は ...surú hitò wa

head [hed] *n* (ANAT, mind) 頭 atáma; (of table) 上席 jōseki; (of queue) 先頭 señtō; (of company, organization) 最高責任者 saíkōsekiniñsha; (of school) 校長 kǒchō
♦*vt* (list, queue) ...の先頭にある〔いる〕...no señtō ni arù〔irù〕; (group, company) 取仕切る toríshikirù

heads (or tails) 表か（裏か）omóte kà (urá kà)

head first (fall) 真っ逆様に massákàsama ni; (rush) 向こう見ずに mukó mìzu ni

head over heels (in love) ぞっこん zokkóñ

to head a ball ボールをヘディングで飛ばす bòru wo hedíñgu de tobásu

headache [hed'eik] *n* 頭痛 zutsū

headdress [hed'dres] (*BRIT*) *n* (of bride) ヘッドドレス heddódoresù

head for *vt fus* (place) ...に向かう ...ni mukáù; (disaster) ...を招く ...wo manékù

heading [hed'iŋ] *n* (of chapter, article)

表題 hyódai, タイトル táîtoru

headlamp [hed'læmp] (*BRIT*) *n* = **headlight**

headland [hed'lænd] *n* 岬 misáki

headlight [hed'lait] *n* ヘッドライト heddóraîto

headline [hed'lain] *n* (PRESS, TV) 見出し midáshi

headlong [hed'lɔːŋ] *adv* (fall) 真っ逆様に massákàsama ni; (rush) 向こう見ずに mukó mîzu ni

headmaster [hed'mæs'təːr] *n* 校長 kốchō ◊男性の場合 dańsei nò baái

headmistress [hed'mis'tris] *n* 校長 kốchō ◊女性の場合 joséi nò baái

head office *n* (of company etc) 本社 hóńsha

head-on [hed'ɑːn'] *adj* (collision, confrontation) 正面の shốmen no

headphones [hed'founz] *npl* ヘッドホン heddóhòn

headquarters [hed'kwɔːrtəːrz] *npl* (of company, organization) 本部 hóńbu; (MIL) 司令部 shiréîbu

headrest [hed'rest] *n* (AUT) ヘッドレスト heddôrèsuto

headroom [hed'ruːm] *n* (in car) 天井の高さ teńjō no tákàsa; (under bridge) 通行可能な高さ tsúkōkanô na takàsa

headscarf [hed'skɑːrf] *n* スカーフ sukáfù

headstrong [hed'strɔːŋ] *adj* (determined) 強情な gốjō na

head waiter *n* (in restaurant) 給仕頭 kyúĵigashira

headway [hed'wei] *n*: **to make headway** 進歩する shíñpo suru

headwind [hed'wind] *n* 向かい風 mukáikaze

heady [hed'iː] *adj* (experience, time) 陶酔の tốsui no; (drink, atmosphere) 酔わせる yowáserù

heal [hiːl] *vt* (injury, patient) 治す naósù
♦*vi* (injury, damage) 治る naórù

health [helθ] *n* (condition: *also* MED) 健康状態 keńkōjōtai; (good health) 健康 keńkō

health food *n* 健康食品 keńkōshokùhin

Health Service (*BRIT*) *n*: **the Health Service** 公共衛生機構 kốkyōeiseikikò

healthy [hel'θiː] *adj* (person, appetite etc) 健康な keńkõ na; (air, walk) 健康に良い keńkõ ni yoî; (economy) 健全な keńzen na; (profit etc) 大いなる ối naru

heap [hiːp] *n* (pile: of clothes, papers, sand etc) 山 yamá
♦*vt* (stones, sand etc): **to heap (up)** 積み上げる tsumíagerù

to heap something with (plate) ...に...を山盛りする ...ni...wo yamámori suru; (sink, table etc) ...に...を山積みする ...ni...wo yamázumi suru

to heap something on (food) ...を...に山盛りする ...wo ...ni yamámori suru; (books etc) ...を...に山積みする ...wo ...ni yamázumi suru

heaps of (*inf*: time, money, work etc) 一杯の ippái no

hear [hiːr] (*pt*, *pp* **heard**) *vt* (sound, voice etc) ...を聞く ...wo kikú, ...が聞こえる ...ga kikóeru; (news, information) ...を聞く ...wo kikú, ...で聞いて知る ...de kíîte shirú; (LAW: case) 審理する shińri suru

to hear about (event, person) ...の事を聞く ...no kotô wo kikú

to hear from someone ...から連絡を受ける ...kara refraku wò ukérù

heard [həːrd] *pt*, *pp of* **hear**

hearing [hiː'riŋ] *n* (sense) 聴覚 chốkaku; (of facts, witnesses etc) 聴聞会 chốmoñkai

hearing aid *n* 補聴器 hochốki

hearsay [hiːr'sei] *n* (rumor) うわさ uwása

hearse [həːrs] *n* 霊きゅう車 reíkyùsha

heart [hɑːrt] *n* (ANAT) 心臓 shiñzõ; (*fig*: emotions, character) 心 kokórò; (of problem) 核心 kakúshin; (of city) 中心部 chúshiňbu; (of lettuce) しん shíñ; (shape) ハート形 hátogata

to lose heart (courage) 落胆する rakútan suru

to take heart (courage) 勇気を出す yúki wò dásù

at heart (basically) 根は... né wà ...

by heart (learn, know) 暗記で ańki de

heart attack n (MED) 心臓発作 shínzō-hossā

heartbeat [hɑːrtˈbiːt] n 心拍 shiñpaku

heartbreaking [hɑːrtˈbreikiŋ] adj (news, story) 悲痛な hitsū na

heartbroken [hɑːrtˈbroukən] adj: **to be heartbroken** 悲嘆に暮れている hitán ni kurete irú

heartburn [hɑːrtˈbəːrn] n (indigestion) 胸焼け muñyake

heart failure n (MED) 心不全 shiñfūzen

heartfelt [hɑːrtˈfelt] adj (prayer, wish) 心からの kokórō kara no

hearth [hɑːrθ] n (fireplace) 炉床 roshō

heartland [hɑːrtˈlænd] n (of country, region) 中心地 chūshiñchi

heartless [hɑːrtˈlis] adj (person, attitude) 非情な hijō na

hearts [hɑːrts] npl (CARDS) ハート hāto

hearty [hɑːrtiː] adj (person) 明朗な mefrō na; (laugh) 大きな ōkina; (appetite) お盛んな ōsei na; (welcome) 熱烈な netsúretsu na; (dislike) 絶対的な zettáiteki na; (support) 心からの kokórō kara no

heat [hiːt] n (warmth) 暑さ átsùsa; (temperature) 温度 óñdo; (excitement) 熱気 nekkí; (SPORT: also: **qualifying heat**) 予選 yosén

♦vt (water) 沸かす wákasù; (food) ...に火を通す ...ni hǐ wǒ tōsu; (room, house) 暖める atátamerù

heated [hiːˈtid] adj (pool) 温水の oñsui no; (room etc) 暖房した dañbō shita; (argument) 激しい hageshíì

heater [hiːˈtəːr] n ヒーター hǐtā

heath [hiːθ] n (BRIT) 荒野 aréno

heathen [hiːˈðən] n (REL) 異教徒 ikyótò

heather [heðˈəːr] n エリカ erīka, ヒース hǐsù

heating [hiːˈtiŋ] n (system, equipment) 暖房 dáñbō

heatstroke [hiːtˈstrouk] n (MED) 熱射病 nesshábyō

heat up vi (water, room) 暖まる atátamarù

♦vt (food, water, room) 暖める atátamerù

heatwave [hiːtˈweiv] n 熱波 néppà

heave [hiːv] vt (pull) 強く引く tsúyðku hikú; (push) 強く押す tsúyðku osú; (lift) ぐいと持上げる gǔi to mochíagerù

♦vi (vomit) 吐く hákù; (feel sick) むかつく mukátsukù

♦n (of chest) あえぎ aḗgi; (of stomach) むかつき mukátsuki

to heave a sigh ため息をつく tamḗikḯ wo tsukú

his chest was heaving 彼はあえいでいた kárè wa aéide itá

heaven [hevˈən] n (REL: also fig) 天国 téñgoku

heavenly [hevˈənliː] adj (REL) 天からの téñ kara no; (fig: day, place) 素晴らしい subárashiì

heavily [hevˈiliː] adv (land, fall) どしんと dóshìn to; (drink, smoke) 大量に taíryō ni; (sleep) ぐっすりと gussúrḯ to; (sigh) 深く fukákù; (depend, rely) すっかり sukkárḯ

heavy [hevˈiː] adj (person, load, responsibility) 重い omói; (clothes) 厚い atsúi; (rain, snow) 激しい hageshíì; (of person: build, frame) がっしりした gasshírḯ shita; (blow) 強い tsúyðì; (breathing) 荒い aráì; (sleep) 深い fukáì; (schedule, week) 過密な kamítsu na; (work) きつい kitsúi; (weather) 蒸し暑い mushíatsuì; (food, meal) もたれる motárerù

a heavy drinker 飲兵衛 nóñbē

a heavy smoker ヘビースモーカー hebísumōkā

heavy goods vehicle (BRIT) n 大型トラック ōgatatorákku

heavyweight [hevˈiːweit] n (SPORT) ヘビー級選手 hebíkyūseñshu

Hebrew [hiːˈbruː] adj (REL) ヘブライの hebúrai no; (LING) ヘブライ語の hebúraigo no

♦n (LING) ヘブライ語 hebúraigo

Hebrides [hebˈridiːz] npl: **the Hebrides** ヘブリディーズ諸島 hebúridīzushotō

heckle [hekˈəl] vt (speaker, performer) 野次る yajírù

hectic [hekˈtik] adj (event, week) やたらに忙しい yatára ni isogashíì

he'd [hiːd] = **he would; he had**

hedge [hedʒ] n (in garden, on roadside)

生け垣 ikégàki
◆vi (stall) あいまいな態度を取る aímai
nà táìdo wo tórù

to hedge one's bets (*fig*) 失敗に備える
shippái nì sonáerù

hedgehog [hedʒ'hɑ:g] n ハリネズミ harí-
nezùmi

heed [hi:d] vt (*also*: **take heed of**: advice,
warning) 聞き入れる kikíirerù

heedless [hi:d'lis] adj: **heedless (of)**
(...を) 無視して (...wo) múshì shité

heel [hi:l] n (of foot, shoe) かかと kákáto
◆vt: *to heel shoes* 靴のかかとを修理す
る kutsú nò kakáto wò shúri suru

hefty [hef'ti:] adj (person) がっしりした
gasshírì shita; (parcel etc) 大きくて重い
ōkikute omói; (profit) 相当な sótō na

heifer [hef'ə:r] n 若い雌ウシ wakái mèú-
shi ◇まだ子を生んだ事のない物を指す
mádà ko wo ùnda kotò no náì monó wo
sásù

height [hait] n (of tree, building, mountain) 高さ takása; (of person) 身長 shíñchō; (of plane) 高度 kōdo; (high ground)
高地 kōchi; (*fig*: of powers) 絶頂期 zet-
chōkī; (: of season) 真っ最中 massáìchū;
(: of luxury, stupidity) 極み kiwámi

heighten [hait'ən] vt (fears, uncertainty)
高める takámerù

heir [e:r] n (to throne) 継承者 keíshōshà;
(to fortune) 相続人 sōzokuniñ

heiress [e:r'is] n 大遺産の相続人 daíisan
no sōzokuniñ ◇女性について言う joséi ni
tsuité iù

heirloom [e:r'lu:m] n 家宝 kahō

held [held] pt, pp of **hold**

helicopter [hel'əkɑ:ptə:r] n (AVIAT) ヘ
リコプター heríkoputā

heliport [hel'əpɔ:rt] n (AVIAT) ヘリポ
ート herípòto

helium [hi:'li:əm] n ヘリウム heríūmu

he'll [hi:l] = **he will**, **he shall**

hell [hel] n (life, situation: *also* REL) 地
獄 jigóku

hell! (*inf*) 畜生！ chikúshò!, くそ！ kusó!

hellish [hel'iʃ] (*inf*) adj (traffic, weather,
life etc) 地獄の様な jigóku no yō na

hello [helou'] excl (as greeting) や あ yā,
今日は koñnichi wa; (to attract attention) おい ôí; (on telephone) もしもし
móshìmoshi; (expressing surprise) お や
oyá

helm [helm] n (NAUT: stick) かじ棒 ka-
jíbō, チラー chirā; (: wheel) だ輪 daríñ

helmet [hel'mit] n (*gen*) ヘルメット herúmettò

help [help] n (assistance, aid) 助け tasúke, 手伝い tétsùdau; (charwoman) お手伝
いさん o-tétsùdaisan
◆vt (person) 助ける tasúkerù, 手伝う tétsùdau; (situation) ...に役に立つ ...ni yakú ni tatsù

help! 助けてくれ！ tasúketè kuré!

help yourself (to) (...を) 自由に取っ
て下さい (...wo) jiyú ni tottè kudásai

he can't help it 彼はそうせざるを得な
い kárè wa sō sezarù wo énài

helper [hel'pə:r] n (assistant) 助手 joshú,
アシスタント ashísùtanto

helpful [hel'fəl] adj (person, advice,
suggestion etc) 役に立つ yakú ni tatsù

helping [hel'piŋ] n (of food) 一盛り hitó-
mòri

a second helping お代り o-káwarì

helpless [help'lis] adj (incapable) 何もで
きない naní mo dekínài; (defenceless) 無
防備の mubóbi no

hem [hem] n (of skirt, dress) すそ susó
◆vt (skirt, dress etc) ...のすそ縫いをする
...no susónui wo suru

hem in vt 取囲む toríkakomù

hemisphere [hem'isfi:r] n 半球 hañkyū

hemorrhage [hem'ə:ridʒ] (*BRIT* **haemorrhage**) n 出血 shukkétsu

hemorrhoids [hem'ə:rɔidz] (*BRIT*
haemorrhoids) npl じ ji

hen [hen] n (female chicken) メンドリ
meñdori; (female bird) 雌の鳥 mesú no
torí

hence [hens] adv (therefore) 従って shitágattè

2 years hence 今から2年先 ímà kara
nínen sakì

henceforth [hens'fɔ:rθ] adv (from now
on) 今後 kóñgo; (from that time on) その

後 sonō go

henchman [hentʃ'mən] (*pej: pl* **henchmen**) *n* (of gangster, tyrant) 手下 teshíta, 子分 kóbùn

henpecked [hen'pekt] *adj* (husband) 妻のしりに敷かれた tsúmà no shirí ni shikaretà

hepatitis [hepətai'tis] *n* (MED) 肝炎 kâñen

her [hər] *pron* (direct) 彼女を kánojo wo; (indirect) 彼女に kánòjo ni
♦*adj* 彼女の kánòj no ¶ *see also* **me; my**

herald [her'əld] *n* (forerunner) 兆し kizáshi
♦*vt* (event, action) 予告する yokóku suru

heraldry [her'əldri:] *n* (study) 紋章学 mofishōgàku; (coat of arms) 紋章 mofishō ◊総称 sóshō

herb [əːrb] *n* (*gen*) ハーブ hābu; (BOT, MED) 薬草 yakúsō; (CULIN) 香草 kôsō

herd [həːrd] *n* (of cattle, goats, zebra etc) 群れ muré

here [hiːr] *adv* (this place): *she left here yesterday* 彼女は昨日ここを出ました kanójo wa kínō kokó wò demáshità; (beside me): *I have it here* ここに持っています kokó ni mottè imásù; (at this point): *here he stopped reading ...* その時彼は読むのをやめて... sonó tokì kárè wa yómù no wo yaméte ...
here! (I'm present) はい！ hâî!; (take this) はいどうぞ hâî dôzo
here is/are はい、...です hâî, ...désù
here she is! 彼女はここにいました！ kanójo wa kokó ni imáshità!

hereafter [hiːræf'təːr] *adv* (in the future) 今後 kôñgo

hereby [hiːrbai'] *adv* (in letter) これをもって koré wo mottè

hereditary [həred'iteːri:] *adj* (disease) 先天的な señtenteki na; (title) 世襲の seshū no

heredity [həred'iti:] *n* (BIO) 遺伝 idéñ

heresy [herˈisi:] *n* (opposing belief: *also* REL) 異端 itán

heretic [herˈitik] *n* 異端者 itáñsha

heritage [herˈitidʒ] *n* (of country, nation) 遺産 isán

hermetically [hərmet'ikli:] *adv*: *hermetically sealed* 密閉した mippéi shita

hermit [hərˈmit] *n* 隠とん者 iñtoñsha

hernia [hərˈniːə] *n* (MED) 脱腸 datchō

hero [hiːˈrou] (*pl* **heroes**) *n* (in book, film) 主人公 shujíñkō, ヒーロー hīrō ◊男性を指す dansei wo sasu; (of battle, struggle) 英雄 eíyū; (idol) アイドル âîdoru

heroic [hiroui'k] *adj* (struggle, sacrifice, person) 英雄的な eíyūteki na

heroin [herˈouin] *n* ヘロイン herôîn

heroine [herˈouin] *n* (in book, film) 女主人公 ofnashujiñkō, ヒロイン hírōn; (of battle, struggle) 英雄的女性 eíyūtekijosei; (idol) アイドル âîdoru

heroism [herˈouizəm] *n* (bravery, courage) 勇敢さ yūkansa

heron [herˈən] *n* アオサギ aósagi

herring [herˈiŋ] *n* (fish) ニシン níshìn

hers [həːrz] *pron* 彼女の物 kanójo no mono ¶ *see also* **mine**

herself [hərˈself] *pron* 彼女自身 kanójojishìn ¶ *see also* **oneself**

he's [hiːz] = **he is; he has**

hesitant [hezˈətənt] *adj* (smile, reaction) ためらいがちな taméraigachi na

hesitate [hezˈəteit] *vi* (pause) ためらう taméraù; (be unwilling) 後込みする shirígomì suru

hesitation [hezəteiˈʃən] *n* (pause) ためらい tamérai; (unwillingness) 後込み shirígomì

heterosexual [hetəːrəsek'ʃuːəl] *adj* (person, relationship) 異性愛の iséiai no

hew [hjuː] *vt* (stone, wood) 刻む kizámu

hexagonal [heksæg'ənəl] *adj* (shape, object) 六角形の rokkákukèi no

heyday [hei'dei] *n*: *the heyday of* ...の全盛時代 ...no zeñseijidài

HGV [eitʃgiːviː'] (*BRIT*) *n abbr* = **heavy goods vehicle**

hi [hai] *excl* (as greeting) やあ yá, 今日は kóñnichi wa; (to attract attention) おい ôî

hiatus [haieiˈtəs] *n* (gap: in manuscript etc) 脱落個所 datsúrakukashò; (pause)

中断 chúdan

hibernate [hai'bə:rneit] *vi* (animal) 冬眠
する tốmin suru

hiccough [hik'ʌp] *vi* しゃっくりする
shákkùri suru

hiccoughs [hik'ʌps] *npl* しゃっくり
shákkùri

hiccup [hik'ʌp] *vi* = **hiccough**

hiccups [hik'ʌps] *npl* = **hiccoughs**

hid [hid] *pt of* **hide**

hidden [hid'ən] *pp of* **hide**

hide [haid] *n* (skin) 皮 kawá
◆*vb* (*pt* **hid**, *pp* **hidden**)
◆*vt* (person, object, feeling, information)
隠す kakúsù; (obscure: sun, view) 覆い隠
す ốikakusù
◆*vi*: **to hide (from someone)** (...に見
つからない様に) 隠れる (...ni mitsúkara-
nai yố ni) kakúrerù

hide-and-seek [haid'ənsiːk'] *n* (game)
隠れん坊 kakúreñbō

hideaway [haid'əwei] *n* (retreat) 隠れ家
kakúregà

hideous [hid'i:əs] *adj* (painting, face) 醜
い miníkuî

hiding [hai'diŋ] *n* (beating) むち打ち muchíuchi
to be in hiding (concealed) 隠れている
kakúrete irù

hierarchy [hai'ə:rɑːrki:] *n* (system of
ranks) 階 級 制 kaíkyūsei; (people in
power) 幹部 káñbu ◇総称 sōshō

hi-fi [hai'fai'] *n* ステレオ sutéreo
◆*adj* (equipment, system) ステレオ sutéreo no

high [hai] *adj* (*gen*) 高い takáî; (speed) 速
い hayáî; (wind) 強い tsuyóî; (quality) 上
等な jốtō na; (principles) 崇高な súkō na
◆*adv* (climb, aim etc) 高く tákàku
it is 20 m high その高さは20メーター
です sonó takàsa wa nijū mētā desu
high in the air 空高く sóràtakaku

highbrow [hai'brau] *adj* (intellectual) 知
的な chitéki na

highchair [hai'tʃe:r] *n* (for baby) ベビー
チェア bebíchèa

higher education [hai'ə:r-] *n* 高等教育
kốtōkyoîku

high-handed [hai'hæn'did] *adj* (decision, rejection) 横暴な ốbō na

high-heeled [hai'hi:ld] *adj* (shoe) ハイヒ
ールの haíhīru no

high jump *n* (SPORT) 走り高飛び ha-
shíritakàtobi

highlands [hai'ləndz] *npl*: **the Highlands** スコットランド高地地方 sukốtto-
rañdo kốchichihồ

highlight [hai'lait] *n* (*fig*: of event) 山場
yamába, ハイライト haíraîto; (of news
etc) 要点 yốten, ハイライト haíraîto; (in
hair) 光る部分 hikárù búbùn, ハイライト
haíraîto
◆*vt* (problem, need) ...に焦点を合せる
...ni shốten wò awáserù

highly [hai'li:] *adv* (critical, confidential)
非常に hijố ni; (a lot): **to speak highly
of** ...をほめる ...wo homérù
to think highly of ...を高く評価する
...wo tákàku hyốka suru
highly paid 高給取りの kốkyūtòri no

highly strung (*BRIT*) *adj* = **high-
strung**

highness [hai'nis] *n*: **Her (*or* His)
Highness** 陛下 heîka

high-pitched [hai'pitʃt'] *adj* (voice,
tone, whine) 調子の高い chốshi no tákaî

high-rise block [hai'raiz'-] *n* 摩天楼
matéñrō

high school *n* (*US*: for 14-18 year-olds)
高等学校 kốtōgakkố, ハイスクール haí-
sūkuru; (*BRIT*: for 11-18 year-olds) 総合
中等学校 sốgōchūtōgakkố

high season (*BRIT*) *n* 最盛期 saiseiki,
シーズン shízun

high street (*BRIT*) *n* 本通り hoñdòri

high-strung [hai'strʌŋ'] (*US*) *adj* 神経
質な shiñkeishitsu na

highway [hai'wei] *n* 幹線道路 kańsendồ-
ro, ハイウエー haíuè

Highway Code (*BRIT*) *n* 道路交通法
dốrokōtsūhồ

hijack [hai'dʒæk] *vt* (plane, bus) 乗っ取
る nottốrù, ハイジャックする haíjakkù
suru

hijacker [hai'dʒækə:r] *n* 乗っ取り犯 not-
tốrihañ

hike [haik] *vi* (go walking) ハイキングする haíkingu suru
♦*n* (walk) ハイキング haíkingu

hiker [hai'kər] *n* ハイカー haíkā

hilarious [hiler'i:əs] *adj* (account, adventure) こっけいな kokkéi na

hill [hil] *n* (small) 丘 okấ; (fairly high) 山 yamấ; (slope) 坂 sakấ

hillside [hil'said] *n* 丘の斜面 okấ no shamẽn

hilly [hil'i:] *adj* 丘の多い okấ no ői
a hilly area 丘陵地帯 kyűryōchitái

hilt [hilt] *n* (of sword, knife) 柄 e
to the hilt (*fig*: support) とことんまで tokóton made

him [him] *pron* (direct) 彼を kárẽ wo; (indirect) 彼に kárẽ ni ¶ *see also* **me**

himself [himself'] *pron* 彼自身 kárẽjishin ¶ *see also* **oneself**

hind [haind] *adj* (legs, quarters) 後ろの ushíro no

hinder [hin'dər] *vt* (progress, movement) 妨げる samátageru

hindrance [hin'drəns] *n* 邪魔 jamá

hindsight [haind'sait] *n*: *with hindsight* 後になってみると áto ni nátte míru to

Hindu [hin'du:] *adj* ヒンズーの hińzū no

hinge [hindʒ] *n* (on door) ちょうつがい chőtsugái
♦*vi* (*fig*): *to hinge on* ...による ...ni yórú

hint [hint] *n* (suggestion) 暗示 añji, ヒント hínto; (advice) 勧め susúme, 提言 teígen; (sign, glimmer) 兆し kizáshi
♦*vt*: *to hint that* (suggest) ...だとほのめかす ...da to honómekasù
♦*vi*: *to hint at* (suggest) ほのめかす honómekasù

hip [hip] *n* (ANAT) 腰 koshí, ヒップ híppù

hippopotamus [hipəpα:t'əməs] (*pl* **hippopotamuses** *or* **hippopotami**) *n* カバ kábà

hire [haiə:r] *vt* (*BRIT*: car, equipment, hall) 賃借りする chiñgari suru; (worker) 雇う yatóù
♦*n* (*BRIT*: of car, hall etc) 賃借り chiñgari

for hire (taxi, boat) 賃貸し用の chiñgashiyő no

hire purchase (*BRIT*) *n* 分割払い購入 buñkatsubaraikőnyú

his [hiz] *pron* 彼の物 kárẽ no monő
♦*adj* 彼の kárẽ no ¶ *see also* **my; mine**

hiss [his] *vi* (snake, gas, roasting meat) しゅーっと言う shűtto iű; (person, audience) しーっと野次る shíttò yajírù

historian [histɔ:r'i:ən] *n* 歴史学者 rekíshigakushá

historic(al) [histɔ:r'ik(əl)] *adj* (event, person) 歴史上の rekíshijő no, 歴史的な rekíshiteki na; (novel, film) 歴史に基づく rekíshi ni motőzukù

history [his'tə:ri:] *n* (of town, country, person: *also* SCOL) 歴史 rekíshi

hit [hit] (*pt*, *pp* **hit**) *vt* (strike: person, thing) 打つ utsű, たたく tatáku; (reach: target) ...に当る ...ni atárù; (collide with: car) ...にぶつかる ...ni butsúkarù; (affect: person, services, event etc) ...に打撃を与える ...ni dagéki wò atáerù
♦*n* (knock) 打撃 dagéki; (success: play, film, song) 大当り őatári, ヒット híttő
to hit it off with someone ...と意気投合する ...to íkîtőgő suru

hit-and-run driver [hit'ənrʌn'-] *n* ひき逃げ運転者 hikínige unteñsha

hitch [hitʃ] *vt* (fasten) つなぐ tsunágù; (*also*: **hitch up**: trousers, skirt) 引上げる hikíagerù
♦*n* (difficulty) 問題 mońdai
to hitch a lift ヒッチハイクをする hitchíhaìku wo suru

hitch-hike [hitʃ'haik] *vi* ヒッチハイクをする hitchíhaìku wo suru

hitch-hiker [hitʃ'haikə:r] *n* ヒッチハイクをする人 hitchíhaìku wo suru hitő

hi-tech [hai'tek'] *adj* ハイテクの haíteku no
♦*n* ハイテク haíteku

hitherto [hið'ə:rtu:] *adv* (until now) 今まで imá madè

hive [haiv] *n* (of bees) ミツバチの巣箱 mitsúbachi no súbàko

hive off (*inf*) *vt* (company) ...の一部を切放す ...no ichíbu wo kiríhanasù

HMS [eitʃemes'] *abbr* (= *Her/His Majesty's Ship*) 軍艦...号 gunkaṅ ...gô ◇英国海軍の軍艦の名前の前に付ける eŕkoku-kaigùn no gunkaṅ no namáê no mâê ni tsukérù

hoard [hɔːrd] *n* (of food etc) 買いだめ kaŕdame; (of money, treasure) 蓄え takúwaè

♦*vt* (food etc) 買いだめする kaŕdamesuru

hoarding [hɔːr'diŋ] (*BRIT*) *n* (for posters) 掲示板 keŕjiban

hoarfrost [hɔːr'frɔːst] *n* (on ground) 霜 shimó

hoarse [hɔːrs] *adj* (voice) しわがれた shiwágaretà

hoax [houks] *n* (trick) いんちき ińchiki, いかさま ikásama

hob [hɑːb] *n* (of cooker, stove) レンジの上部 reńji no jôbu

hobble [hɑːb'əl] *vi* (limp) びっこを引く bîkkò wo hikú

hobby [hɑːb'iː] *n* (pastime) 趣味 shúmì

hobby-horse [hɑːb'iːhɔːrs] *n* (*fig*: favorite topic) 十八番の話題 oháko nò wadái

hobo [hou'bou] (*US*) *n* (tramp) ルンペン ruńpen

hockey [hɑːk'iː] *n* (game) ホッケー hôkkè

hoe [hou] *n* (tool) くわ kuwá, ホー hồ

hog [hɔːg] *n* (pig) ブタ butá ◇去勢した雄ブタを指す kyoséi shita osubùta wo sasu

♦*vt* (*fig*: road, telephone etc) 独り占めにする hitórijime nì suru

to go the whole hog とことんまでやる tokótoṅ made yarú

hoist [hɔist] *n* (apparatus) 起重機 kijúkì, クレーン kuréṅ

♦*vt* (heavy object) 引上げる hikíagerù; (flag) 掲げる kakágerù; (sail) 張る harú

hold [hould] (*pt*, *pp* **held**) *vt* (bag, umbrella, someone's hand etc) 持つ mótsù; (contain: subj: room, box etc) ...に ...が入っている ...ni ...ga hâîtte iru; (have: power, qualification, opinion) を持っている ...wo móttè iru, ...がある ...ga árù; (meeting) 開く hirákù; (detain: prisoner,

hostage) 監禁する kańkin suru; (consider): *to hold someone responsible/liable etc* ...の責任と見なす ...no sekínin tô mínàsù; (keep in certain position): *to hold one's head up* 頭を上げる atáma wò agérù

♦*vt* (withstand pressure) 持ちこたえる mochíkotaeru; (be valid) 当てはまる atéhamarù

♦*n* (grasp) 握り nigíri; (of ship) 船倉 seńsō; (of plane) 貨物室 kamótsushìtsu; (control): *to have a hold over* ...の急所を握っている ...no kyúsho wò nigítte irù

to hold a conversation with ...と話し合う ...to hanáshiaù

hold the line! (*TEL*) 少々お待ち下さい shôshō o-máchì kudasai

hold on! ちょっと待って chótto mâttè

to hold one's own (*fig*) 引けを取らない hiké wò toránaì, 負けない makénaì

to catch/get (a) hold of ...に捕まる ...ni tsukámarù

holdall [hould'ɔːl] (*BRIT*) *n* 合切袋 gassáibukùro

hold back *vt* (person, thing) 制止する seíshi suru; (thing, emotion) 押さえる osáerù; (secret, information) 隠す kakúsù

hold down *vt* (person) 押さえつける o-sáetsukerù; (job) ...についている ...ni tsúìte iru

holder [houl'dər] *n* (container) 入れ物 irémono, ケース kêsu, ホールダー hôrudầ; (of ticket, record, title) 保持者 hojísha; (of office) 在職者 zaíshokusha

holding [houl'diŋ] *n* (share) 持株 mochíkabu; (small farm) 小作農地 kosákunôchi

hold off *vt* (enemy) ...に持ちこたえる ...ni mochíkotaerù

hold on *vi* (hang on) 捕まる tsukámarù; (wait) 待つ mátsù

hold on to *vt fus* (for support) ...に捕まる ...ni tsukámarù; (keep) 預かる azúkarù

hold out *vt* (hand) 差伸べる sashínoberù; (hope, prospect) 持たせる motáserù

♦*vi* (resist) 抵抗する teŕkō suru

hold up *vt* (raise) 上げる agérù; (support) 支える sasáerù; (delay) 遅らせる o-kúraserù; (rob: person, bank) 武器を突付けて...から金を奪う búkì wo tsukítsuketè ...kara kané wò ubáù

hold-up [hould'ʌp] n (robbery) 強盗 gṓtō; (delay) 遅れ okúre; (BRIT: in traffic) 渋滞 jūtai

hole [houl] n 穴 aná
♦vt (ship, building etc) ...に穴を開ける ...ni aná wò akérù

holiday [ha:l'idei] n (BRIT: vacation) 休暇 kyúka; (day off) 休暇の日 kyúka no hi; (public holiday) 祝日 shukújitsu
on holiday 休暇中 kyúkachū

holiday camp (BRIT) n (also: **holiday centre**) 休暇村 kyúkamùra

holiday-maker [ha:l'ideimeikə:r] (BRIT) n 行楽客 kṓrakukyàku

holiday resort n 行楽地 kṓrakuchì, リゾート rizṓtò

holiness [hou'li:nis] n (of shrine, person) 神聖さ shifseisa

Holland [ha:l'ənd] n オランダ oráñda

hollow [ha:l'ou] adj (container) 空っぽの karáppo no; (log, tree) うろのある uró no arù; (cheeks, eyes) くぼんだ kubóñda; (laugh) わざとらしい wazátorashiì; (claim) 根拠のない kofíkyo no naì; (sound) うつろな utsúro na
♦n (in ground) くぼみ kubómi
♦vt: **to hollow out** (excavate) がらんどうにする garándò ni surù

holly [ha:l'i:] n (tree, leaves) ヒイラギ híìragi

holocaust [ha:l'əkɔ:st] n 大虐殺 daígyakùsatsu

hologram [hou'ləgræm] n ホログラム horógurầmu

holster [houl'stə:r] n (for pistol) ホルスター horúsutầ

holy [hou'li:] adj (picture, place, person) 神聖な shiñsei na
holy water 聖水 seísui

homage [ha:m'idʒ] n (honor, respect) 敬意 kéìi
to pay homage to (hero, idol) ...に敬意を表する ...ni kéìi wo aráwasù

home [houm] n (house) 家 ié, 住い sumáì;

(area, country) 故郷 kokyṓ; (institution) 収容施設 shúyōshisètsu
♦cpd (domestic) 家庭の katéi no; (ECON, POL) 国内の kokúnai no; (SPORT: team, game) 地元の jimóto no
♦adv (go, come, travel etc) 家に ié ni
at home (in house) 家に〔で〕ié ni 〔de〕; (in country) 本国に〔で〕hóñgoku ni 〔de〕; (in situation) ...に通じて ...ni tsújite
make yourself at home どうぞお楽にdṓzo o-ráku ni
to drive something home (nail etc) ...を打込む ...wo uchíkomù; (fig: point etc) ...を強調する ...wo kyṓchō suru

home address n 自宅の住所 jitáku no jūsho

home computer n パーソナルコンピュータ pāsonarukonpyūta, パソコン pasṓkon

homeland [houm'lænd] n 母国 bókòku

homeless [houm'lis] adj (family, refugee) 家のない ié no naì

homely [houm'li:] adj (simple, plain) 素朴な sobóku na; (US: not attractive: person) 不器量な bukíryō na

home-made [houm'meid'] adj (bread, bomb) 手製の teséi no, 自家製の jikásei no

Home Office (BRIT) n 内務省 naímushō

homeopathy [houmi:a:p'əθi:] (BRIT **homoeopathy**) n (MED) ホメオパシー homéopashī

home rule n (POL) 自治権 jichíkèn

Home Secretary (BRIT) n 内務大臣 naímudaìjin

homesick [houm'sik] adj ホームシックの hṓmushikkù no

hometown [houmtaun'] n 故郷 kokyṓ

homeward [houm'wə:rd] adj (journey) 家に帰る ié ni kaerù

homework [houm'wə:rk] n (SCOL) 宿題 shukúdai

homicide [ha:m'isaid] (US) n 殺人 satsújin

homoeopathy [houmi:a:p'əθi:] (BRIT) n = **homeopathy**

homogeneous [houmədʒi:'ni:əs] adj

(group, class) 均質の kínshitsu no

homosexual [houməsek'ʃuːəl] *adj* (person, relationship: *gen*) 同性愛の dóseiai no; (man) ホモの hómò no; (woman) レズの rézù no
♦*n* (man) 同性愛者 dóseiaishà, ホモ hómò; (woman) 同姓愛者 dóseiaishà, レズ rézù

honest [ɑ:n'ist] *adj* (truthful, trustworthy) 正直な shójiki na; (sincere) 率直な sotchóku na

honestly [ɑ:n'istli:] *adv* (truthfully) 正直に shójiki ni; (sincerely, frankly) 率直に sotchóku ni

honesty [ɑ:n'isti:] *n* (truthfulness) 正直 shójiki; (sincerity, frankness) 率直さ sotchókusa

honey [hʌn'i:] *n* (food) はちみつ hachímitsu

honeycomb [hʌn'i:koum] *n* (of bees) ミツバチの巣 mitsúbàchi no su

honeymoon [hʌn'i:muːn] *n* (holiday, trip) 新婚旅行 shiñkonryokò, ハネムーン hanémùn

honeysuckle [hʌn'i:sʌkəl] *n* (BOT) スイカズラ suíkazùra

honk [hɑːŋk] *vi* (AUT: horn) 鳴らす narásu

honorary [ɑ:n'əːreːri:] *adj* (unpaid: job, secretary) 無給の mukyú no; (title, degree) 名誉の meíyo no

honor [ɑ:n'əːr] (*BRIT* **honour**) *vt* (hero, author) ほめたたえる hométataerù; (commitment, promise) 守る mamórù
♦*n* (pride, self-respect) 名誉 meíyo; (tribute, distinction) 光栄 kóei

honorable [ɑ:n'əːrəbəl] *adj* (person, action, defeat) 名誉ある meíyo aru

honors degree [ɑ:n'əːrz-] *n* (SCOL) 専門学士号 señmongakushigò

hood [hud] *n* (of coat, cooker etc) フードfúdo; (*US*: AUT: engine cover) ボンネット boñnettò; (*BRIT*: AUT: folding roof) 折畳み式トップ orítatamishiki toppù

hoodlum [huːd'ləm] *n* (thug) ごろつき gorótsuki, 暴力団員 bóryokudan-ìn

hoodwink [hud'wiŋk] *vt* (con, fool) だます damásu

hoof [huf] (*pl* **hooves**) *n* ひづめ hizúme

hook [huk] *n* (for coats, curtains etc) かぎ kagí, フック fúkkù; (on dress) ホック hókkù; (*also*: **fishing hook**) 釣針 tsuríbàri
♦*vt* (fasten) 留める tomérù; (fish) 釣る tsurú

hooligan [huː'ligən] *n* ちんぴら chíñpira

hoop [huːp] *n* (ring) 輪 wá

hooray [həreí'] *excl* = **hurrah, hurray**

hoot [huːt] *vi* (AUT: horn) クラクションを鳴らす kurákùshon wo narásù; (siren) 鳴る narú; (owl) ほーほーと鳴く hóhò to nakú

hooter [huː'təːr] *n* (*BRIT*: AUT) クラクション kurákùshon, ホーン hòn; (NAUT, factory) 警報機 keíhòkì

hoover [huː'vəːr] ⓇⓇ(*BRIT*) *n* (vacuum cleaner) (真空) 掃除機 (shiñkū)sòjikì
♦*vt* (carpet) ...に掃除機を掛ける ...ni sójikì wo kakérù

hooves [huvz] *npl of* **hoof**

hop [hɑːp] *vi* (on one foot) 片足で跳ぶ katáashi de tobù; (bird) ぴょんぴょん跳ぶ pyóñpyon tobú

hope [houp] *vt*: *to hope that/to do* ...だと〔する事を〕望む ...da to〔surú kotò wo〕nozómù
♦*vi* 希望する kibó suru
♦*n* (desire) 望み nozómi; (expectation) 期待 kitái; (aspiration) 希望 kibó

I hope so/not そうだ〔でない〕といいがsó dà〔de naí〕to íi ga

hopeful [houp'fəl] *adj* (person) 楽観的な rakkánteki na; (situation) 見込みのある mikómi no arù

hopefully [houp'fəli:] *adv* (expectantly) 期待して kitái shite; (one hopes) うまくいけば úmàku ikébà

hopeless [houp'lis] *adj* (grief, situation, future) 絶望的な zetsúbōteki na; (person: useless) 無能な munóna

hops [hɑːps] *npl* (BOT) ホップ hóppù

horde [hɔːrd] *n* (of critics, people) 大群 taígun

horizon [həraí'zən] *n* (skyline) 水平線 suíheìsen

horizontal [hɔːrizɑːn'təl] *adj* 水平の suíhei no

hormone [hɔːrˈmoun] n (BIO) ホルモン hórùmon

horn [hɔːrn] n (of animal) 角 tsunó; (material) 角質 kakúshitsu; (MUS: also: **French horn**) ホルン hórùn; (AUT) クラクション kurákùshon, ホーン hòn

hornet [hɔːrˈnit] n (insect) スズメバチ suzúmebàchi

horny [hɔːrˈniː] (inf) adj (aroused) セックスをしたがっている sékkùsu wo shitágatte irù

horoscope [hɔːrˈəskoup] n (ASTROL-OGY) 星占い hoshíuranai

horrendous [hɔːrenˈdəs] adj (crime) 恐ろしい osóroshiî; (error) ショッキングな shókkìngu na

horrible [hɔːrˈəbəl] adj (unpleasant: color, food, mess) ひどい hidóî; (terrifying: scream, dream) 恐ろしい osóroshiî

horrid [hɔːrˈid] adj (person, place, thing) いやな iyá na

horrify [hɔːrˈəfai] vt (appall) ぞっとさせる zóttò sasérù

horror [hɔːrˈəːr] n (alarm) 恐怖 kyófù; (abhorrence) 憎悪 zòo; (of battle, war-fare) むごたらしさ mugótarashisà

horror film n ホラー映画 horáeìga

hors d'oeuvre [ɔːr dəːrvˈ] n (CULIN: gen) 前菜 zeñsai; (: Western food) オードブル ódobùru

horse [hɔːrs] n 馬 umá

horseback [hɔːrsˈbæk]: **on horseback** adj 乗馬の jōba no
♦adv 馬に乗って umá ni nottè

horse chestnut n (tree) トチノキ tochí no kì; (nut) とちの実 tochí no mì

horseman/woman [hɔːrsˈmən/wumən] (pl **horsemen/women**) n (rider) 馬の乗り手 umá nò noríte

horsepower [hɔːrsˈpauəːr] n (of engine, car etc) 馬力 barírki

horse-racing [hɔːrsˈreisiŋ] n (SPORT) 競馬 keíba

horseradish [hɔːrsˈrædiʃ] n (BOT, CULIN) ワサビダイコン wasábidaìkon, セイヨウワサビ seíyowasàbi

horseshoe [hɔːrsˈʃuː] n てい鉄 teítetsu

horticulture [hɔːrˈtəkʌltʃəːr] n 園芸 eñgei

hose [houz] n ホース hòsu

hosiery [houˈʒəːriː] n (in shop) 靴下類 kutsúshitarùi

hospice [hɑːsˈpis] n (for the dying) ホスピス hósupisu

hospitable [hɑːspitˈəbəl] adj (person) 持て成しの良い moténashi no yoî; (behav-ior) 手厚い teátsuî

hospital [hɑːsˈpitəl] n 病院 byóin

hospitality [hɑːspətælˈitiː] n (of host, welcome) 親切な持て成し shiñsetsu nà moténashì

host [houst] n (at party, dinner etc) 主人 shújìn, ホスト hósùto; (TV, RADIO) 司会者 shikáishà; (REL) 御聖体 go-séitai; (large number): **a host of** 多数の tasú no

hostage [hɑːsˈtidʒ] n (prisoner) 人質 hitó-jichi

hostel [hɑːsˈtəl] n (for homeless etc) 収容所 shúyòjo; (also: **youth hostel**) ユースホステル yúsuhosùteru

hostess [housˈtis] n (at party, dinner etc) 女主人 ofnashujìn, ホステス hósùtesu; (BRIT: air hostess) スチュワーデス su-chúwàdesu; (TV, RADIO) (女性) 司会者 (josei)shikáishà

hostile [hɑːsˈtəl] adj (person, attitude: aggressive) 敵対する tekítai suru, 敵意のある tékì no árù; (: unwelcoming): **hostile to** ...に対して排他的な ...ni táìshite haítateki na; (conditions, environ-ment) か酷な kakóku na

hostilities [hɑːstilˈətiːz] npl (fighting) 戦闘 señtō

hostility [hɑːstilˈətiː] n (antagonism) 敵対 tekítai, 敵意 tékì-i; (lack of welcome) 排他的態度 haítatekitaìdo; (of condi-tions, environment) か酷な kakókusa

hot [hɑːt] adj (moderately hot) 暖かい a-tátakaî; (very hot) 熱い atsúi; (weather, room etc) 暑い atsúi; (spicy: food) 辛い karáî; (fierce: temper, contest, argu-ment etc) 激しい hageshiî

it is hot (weather) 暑い atsúi; (object) 熱い atsúi

I am hot (person) 私は暑い watákushi wà atsúî

he is hot 彼は暑がっている kárè wa atsúgatte irù

hotbed [hɑːt'bed] *n* (*fig*) 温床 onshō

hot dog *n* (snack) ホットドッグ hottódoggù

hotel [houtel'] *n* ホテル hótèru

hotelier [ɔːteljei'] *n* (owner) ホテルの経営者 hótèru no keíeîsha; (manager) ホテルの支配人 hótèru no shihâînin

hotheaded [hɑːt'hedid] *adj* (impetuous) 気の早い kí no hayaî

hothouse [hɑːt'haus] *n* (BOT) 温室 onshitsu

hot line *n* (POL) ホットライン hottóraîn

hotly [hɑːt'liː] *adv* (speak, contest, deny) 激しく hagéshikù

hotplate [hɑːt'pleit] *n* (on cooker) ホットプレート hottópurèto

hot-water bottle [hɑːtwɔːtˈəːr-] *n* 湯たんぽ yutánpo

hound [haund] *vt* (harass, persecute) 迫害する hakúgai suru

♦*n* (dog) 猟犬 ryṓken, ハウンド haúndo

hour [au'əːr] *n* (sixty minutes) 1時間 ichí jikan; (time) 時間 jíkan

hourly [auəːr'liː] *adj* (service, rate) 1時間当りの ichí jikan atàri no

house [*n* haus *vb* hauz] *n* (home) 家 ié, うち uchí; (family) 家族 kazóku; (company) 会社 kaísha; (POL) 議院 gíin; (THEATER) 客席 kyakúseki; (dynasty) ...家 ...ké

♦*vt* (person) ...に住宅を与える ...ni jútaku wò atáerù; (collection) 収容する shúyō suru

on the house (*fig*) サービスで sābisu de

house arrest *n* (POL, MIL) 軟禁 nañkin

houseboat [haus'bout] *n* 屋形船 yakátabunè, ハウスボート haúsubòto ◇住宅用の船を指す jútakuyṓ no funè wo sásù

housebound [haus'baund] *adj* (invalid) 家から出られない ié kara derárenaî

housebreaking [haus'breikiŋ] *n* 家宅侵入 kátakushiñnyū

housecoat [haus'kout] *n* 部屋着 heyági

household [haus'hould] *n* (inhabitants)

家族 kazóku; (home) 家 ié

housekeeper [haus'kiːpəːr] *n* (servant) 家政婦 kaséifu

housekeeping [haus'kiːpiŋ] *n* (work) 家事 kájì; (money) 家計費 kakéihi

house-warming party [haus'wɔːrmiŋ-] *n* 新居祝いのパーティ shinkyo-iwaî no pàti

housewife [haus'waif] (*pl* **housewives**) *n* 主婦 shúfu

housework [haus'wəːrk] *n* (chores) 家事 kájì

housing [hau'ziŋ] *n* (houses) 住宅 jútaku; (provision) 住宅供給 jútakukyōkyū

housing development *n* 住宅団地 jútakudañchi

housing estate (*BRIT*) *n* 住宅団地 jútakudañchi

hovel [hʌv'əl] *n* (shack) あばら屋 abáraya

hover [hʌv'əːr] *vi* (bird, insect) 空中に止まる kúchū ni tomarù

hovercraft [hʌv'əːrkræft] *n* (vehicle) ホバークラフト hobákurafùto

KEYWORD

how [hau] *adv* **1** (in what way) どう dṓ, どの様に donó yō ni, どうやって dṓ yattè

how did you do it? どうやってそれができたんですか dṓ yattè soré gà dekítan desù ká

I know how you did it あなたがどの様にしてそれができたか私には分かっています anátā ga donó yō ni shite soré gà dekíta kà watákushi ni wà wakátte imasù

to know how to do something ...の仕方を知っている ...no shikáta wò shitté irù

how is school? 学校はどうですか gakkṓ wa dō desu ká

how was the film? 映画はどうでしたか eíga wa dō deshita ká

how are you? お元気ですか o-génki desu ká

2 (to what degree) どのくらい donó kurai

how much milk? どのくらいのミルク

donố kurai nố míruku

how many people? 何人の人々 nánnin no hitóbito

how much does it cost? 値段はいくらですか nedán wà íkùra desu ká

how long have you been here? いつからここにいますか ítsu kara kokó nì imásù ká

how old are you? お幾つですか o-íkùtsu desu ká

how tall is he? 彼の身長はどれくらいですか kárè no shifíchō wà dorè gùrai desu ká

how lovely/awful! なんて美しい〔ひどい〕 nánte utsúkushiì〔hidôí〕

howl [haul] *vi* (animal) 遠ぼえする tốboe suru; (baby, person) 大声で泣く ốgoè de nakú; (wind) うなる unárù

H.P. [eitʃpiː'] *abbr* = **hire purchase**

h.p. *abbr* = **horsepower**

HQ [eitʃkjuː'] *abbr* = **headquarters**

hub [hʌb] *n* (of wheel) ハブ hábù; (*fig*: centre) 中心 chūshin

hubbub [hʌb'ʌb] *n* (din, commotion) どよめき doyốmeki

hubcap [hʌb'kæp] *n* (AUT) ホイールキャップ hoírukyappù

huddle [hʌd'əl] *vi*: **to huddle together** (for heat, comfort) 体を寄せ合う karáda wò yoséaù

hue [hjuː] *n* (color) 色 iró; (shade of color) 色合い iróaì

hue and cry *n* (outcry) 騒ぎ sáwàgi

huff [hʌf] *n*: **in a huff** (offended) 怒って okóttè

hug [hʌg] *vt* (person, thing) 抱締める dakíshimerù

huge [hjuːdʒ] *adj* (enormous) ばくだいな bakúdai na

hulk [hʌlk] *n* (ship) 廃船 haísen; (person) 図体ばかり大きい人 zūtai bakari ốkiì hitó, うどの大木 udo no taiboku; (building etc) ばかでかい物 bakádekai monô

hull [hʌl] *n* (of ship) 船体 sefítai, ハル hárù

hullo [həluə'] *excl* = **hello**

hum [hʌm] *vt* (tune, song) ハミングで歌

う hamingu de utau

♦*vi* (person) ハミングする hámìngu suru; (machine) ぶーんと鳴る bûn to narú; (insect) ぶんぶんいう búnbun iu

human [hjuː'mən] *adj* (existence, body) 人の hitô no, 人間の ninîgen no; (weakness, emotion) 人間的な ninígenteki na

♦*n* (person) 人 hitô, 人間 nifígen

humane [hjuːmein'] *adj* (treatment, slaughter) 苦痛を与えない kutsū́ wò atáenai

humanitarian [hjuːmæniteːr'iːən] *adj* (aid, principles) 人道的な jifídōteki na

humanity [hjuːmæn'itiː] *n* (mankind) 人類 jífrui, 人間 nifígen; (human nature) 人間性 nifígensei; (humaneness, kindness) 思いやり omôiyari

humble [hʌm'bəl] *adj* (modest) 謙虚な kéñkyo na; (lowly: background) 身分の低い mífbun no hikúì

♦*vt* (humiliate, crush) ...の高慢な鼻を折る ...no kôman na haná wò órù

humbug [hʌm'bʌg] *n* (of statement, writing) でたらめ detárame; (*BRIT*: sweet) はっかあめ hakká-ame

humdrum [hʌm'drʌm] *adj* (dull, boring) 退屈な tafíkutsu na

humid [hjuː'mid] *adj* (atmosphere, climate) 湿度の高い shitsúdò no takáì

humidity [hjuːmid'ətiː] *n* 湿度 shitsúdò

humiliate [hjuːmil'iːeit] *vt* (rival, enemy) ...の高慢な鼻を折る ...no kôman na haná wò órù

humiliation [hjuːmiliːei'ʃən] *n* (embarrassment) 恥 hají; (situation, experience) 恥辱 chijóku

humility [hjuːmil'ətiː] *n* (modesty) 謙そん keñson

humor [hjuː'məːr] (*BRIT* **humour**) *n* (comedy, mood) ユーモア yūmoa

♦*vt* (child, person) ...の機嫌を取る ...no kigén wo tôrù

humorous [hjuː'məːrəs] *adj* (remark, book) おどけた odôketa; (person) ユーモアのある yūmoa no árù

hump [hʌmp] *n* (in ground) 小山 koyáma; (of camel: *also* deformity) こぶ kobú

humpbacked [hʌmp'bækt] *adj*: **hump-**

backed bridge 反り橋 soríhàshi

hunch [hʌntʃ] *n* (premonition) 直感 chokkán

hunchback [hʌntʃ'bæk] *n* せむしの人 semúshi nò hitò ◇べっ称 besshô

hunched [hʌntʃt] *adj* (bent, stooped: shoulders) 曲げた magéta; (: person) 肩を落とした kátà wo otóshità

hundred [hʌn'drid] *num* 百 (の) hyakú (no); (before *n*): *a/one hundred books* 100冊の本 hyakúsatsu nò hôñ: *a/one hundred people* 100人の人 hyakúnin nò hitò: *a/one hundred dollars* 100ドル hyakú doru

hundreds of 何百もの nañbyaku mo no

hundredweight [hʌn'dridweit] *n* (*US* = 45.3 kg, 100 lb; *BRIT* = 50.8 kg, 112 lb)

hung [hʌŋ] *pt, pp of* **hang**

Hungarian [hʌŋɡeːr'iːən] *adj* ハンガリーの hañgarī no; (LING) ハンガリー語の hañgarīgo no
♦*n* (person) ハンガリー人 hañgarījìn; (LING) ハンガリー語 hañgarīgo

Hungary [hʌŋ'ɡəːriː] *n* ハンガリー hañgarī

hunger [hʌŋ'ɡəːr] *n* (lack of food) 空腹 kúfuku; (starvation) 飢餓 kígà
♦*vi*: *to hunger for* (desire) ...に飢える ...ni uérù

hunger strike *n* ハンガーストライキ hañgāsutoraìki, ハンスト hañsuto

hungry [hʌŋ'griː] *adj* (person, animal) 空腹な kúfuku na; (keen, avid): *hungry for* ...に飢えた ...ni uétà

to be hungry おなかがすいた onáka ga suità

hunk [hʌŋk] *n* (of bread etc) 塊 katámari

hunt [hʌnt] *vt* (for food: subj: animal) 捜し求める sagáshimotomerù, あさる asárù; (SPORT) 狩る kárù, ...の狩りをする ...no kárì wo suru; (criminal, fugitive) 捜す sagásu, 捜索する sôsaku suru
♦*vi* (search): *to hunt (for)* (...を) 捜す (...wo) sagásu; (SPORT) (...の) 狩りをする (...no) kárì wo suru
♦*n* (for food: *also* SPORT) 狩り kárì; (search) 捜す事 sagásu kotò; (for crimi-

nal) 捜索 sôsaku

hunter [hʌn'təːr] *n* (sportsman) ハンター háñtā

hunting [hʌn'tiŋ] *n* (for food: *also* SPORT) 狩り kárì

hurdle [həːr'dəl] *n* (difficulty) 障害 shôgai; (SPORT) ハードル hâdoru

hurl [həːrl] *vt* (object) 投げる nagérù; (insult, abuse) 浴びせ掛ける abísekakerù

hurrah [həːrɑː'] *n* (as cheer) 歓声 kañsei

hurray [həːrei'] *n* = **hurrah**

hurricane [həːr'əkein] *n* (storm) ハリケーン haríkēn

hurried [həːr'iːd] *adj* (hasty, rushed) 大急ぎの ôisôgi no

hurriedly [həːr'iːdliː] *adv* 大急ぎで ôisôgi de

hurry [həːr'iː] *n* (haste, rush) 急ぎ isógi
♦*vi* (*also:* **hurry up**) hasten, rush) 急ぐ isógù
♦*vt* (*also:* **hurry up**: person) 急がせる isógaserù; (: work) 急いでする isóide suru

to be in a hurry 急いでいる isóide irù

hurt [həːrt] (*pt, pp* **hurt**) *vt* (cause pain to) 痛める itámerù; (injure, *fig*) 傷付ける kizútsukerù
♦*vi* (be painful) 痛む itámù

it hurts! 痛い! itâi!

hurtful [həːrt'fəl] *adj* (remark) 傷付ける様な kizútsukeru yô na

hurtle [həːr'təl] *vi*: *to hurtle past* (train, car) 猛スピードで通り過ぎる môsupîdo de tôrisugirù

to hurtle down (fall) 落ちる ochírù

husband [hʌz'bənd] *n* 夫 ottô

hush [hʌʃ] *n* (silence) 沈黙 chiñmoku; (stillness) 静けさ shizúkesà
♦*vt* (silence) 黙らせる damáraserù

hush! 静かに shízùka ni

hush up *vt* (scandal etc) もみ消す momíkesù

husk [hʌsk] *n* (of wheat, rice) 殻 kará; (of maize) 皮 kawá

husky [hʌs'kiː] *adj* (voice) しわがれた shiwágaretà, ハスキーな hásùkī na
♦*n* (dog) ハスキー hásùkī

hustle [hʌs'əl] *vt* (hurry) 急がせる isógaserù

♦n: *hustle and bustle* 雑踏 zattô

hut [hʌt] *n* (house) 小屋 koyá; (shed) 物置 monô-oki

hutch [hʌtʃ] *n* (*also*: **rabbit hutch**) ウサギ小屋 uságigoya

hyacinth [hai'əsinθ] *n* ヒヤシンス hiyáshiñsu

hybrid [hai'brid] *n* (plant, animal) 交雑種 kôzatsushù, ハイブリッド haíburiddò; (mixture) 混成物 koñseibùtsu

hydrant [hai'drənt] *n* (*also*: **fire hydrant**) 消火栓 shôkasen

hydraulic [haidrɔː'lik] *adj* (pressure, system) 油圧の yuátsu no

hydroelectric [haidrouilek'trik] *adj* (energy, complex) 水力発電の suíryokuhatsûden no

hydrofoil [hai'drəfoil] *n* (boat) 水中翼船 suíchūyokùsen

hydrogen [hai'drədʒən] *n* (CHEM) 水素 sûiso

hyena [haii'nə] *n* ハイエナ haíena

hygiene [hai'dʒiːn] *n* (cleanliness) 衛生 eísei

hygienic [haidʒiːen'ik] *adj* 衛生的な eíseiteki na

hymn [him] *n* 賛美歌 sañbika

hype [haip] *n* (*inf*) 誇大広告 uríkomi-kôjò

hypermarket [hai'pəːrmɑːrkit] *n* (*BRIT*) *n* 大型スーパー ôgatasûpā

hyphen [hai'fən] *n* (dash) ハイフン háifun

hypnosis [hipnou'sis] *n* 催眠 saímin

hypnotic [hipnɑːt'ik] *adj* (trance) 催眠術の saímiñjutsu no; (rhythms) 催眠的な saímiñteki na

hypnotism [hip'nətizəm] *n* 催眠術 saímiñjutsu

hypnotist [hip'nətist] *n* (person) 催眠術師 saíminjutsushì

hypnotize [hip'nətaiz] *vt* (MED etc) ...に催眠術を掛ける ...ni saímiñjutsu wo kakérù; (*fig*: mesmerise) 魅惑する miwáku suru

hypochondriac [haipəkɑːn'driːæk] *n* 心気症患者 shiñkishōkaǹja

hypocrisy [hipɑːk'rəsiː] *n* (falseness, in-sincerity) 偽善 gizén

hypocrite [hip'əkrit] *n* (phoney) 偽善者 gizéñsha

hypocritical [hipəkrit'ikəl] *adj* (person) 偽善の gizén no; (behavior) 偽善者的な gizéñshateki na

hypothermia [haipəθəːr'miːə] *n* (MED) 低体温症 teítaioñshō

hypothesis [haipɑː'θəsis] (*pl* **hypotheses**) *n* (theory) 仮説 kasétsu

hypothetic(al) [haipəθet'ik(əl)] *adj* (question, situation) 仮定の katéi no

hysteria [histi'riːə] *n* (panic: *also* MED) ヒステリー hisúterī

hysterical [histeːr'ikəl] *adj* (person, rage) ヒステリックな hisúterikkù na; (situation: funny) 笑いが止らない様な warái gà tomáranai yô na

hysterical laughter ばか笑い bakáwa-ràì

hysterics [histeːr'iks] *npl* (anger, panic) ヒステリー hisúterī; (laughter) 大笑い ô-warài

I

I [ai] *pron* 私は〔が〕watákushi wa 〔ga〕

ice [ais] *n* (frozen water) 氷 kôri; (*also*: **ice cream**) アイスクリーム aísukurîmu

♦*vt* (cake) ...にアイシングを掛ける ...ni áishingu wo kakérù

♦*vi* (*also*: **ice over**, **ice up**: road, window etc) 氷に覆われる kôri nì ôwarerù

iceberg [ais'bəːrg] *n* 氷山 hyôzan

icebox [ais'bɑːks] *n* (*US*: fridge) 冷蔵庫 reízōko; (*BRIT*: compartment) 冷凍室 reítōshitsu; (insulated box) クーラー kûrā

ice cream *n* アイスクリーム aísukurîmu

ice cube *n* 角氷 kakúgôri

iced [aist] *adj* (cake) アイシングを掛けた áishingu wo kákèta; (beer) 冷した hiyáshita

iced tea アイスティー aísutî

ice hockey *n* (SPORT) アイスホッケー aísuhokkê

Iceland [ais'lənd] *n* アイスランド aísurañdo

ice lolly [-lɑ:'li:] (*BRIT*) *n* アイスキャンディー aísukyaṅdī

ice rink *n* スケートリンク sukḗtoriṅku

ice-skating [ais'skeitiŋ] *n* アイススケート aísusukḗto

icicle [ai'sikəl] *n* (on gutter, ledge etc) つらら tsurára

icing [ai'siŋ] *n* (CULIN) 砂糖衣 satógoròmo, アイシング aíshiṅgu

icing sugar (*BRIT*) *n* 粉砂糖 konázatò

icon [ai'kɑ:n] *n* (REL) 聖像画 seízòga, イコン íkòn

icy [ai'si:] *adj* (air, water, temperature) 冷たい tsumétai; (road) 氷に覆われた kṓri ni ówareta

I'd [aid] = I would; I had

idea [aidi:'ə] *n* (scheme, notion) 考え kaṅgaè; (opinion) 意見 íkèn; (objective) つもり tsumóri

ideal [aidi:'əl] *n* (principle) 理想 risṓ; (epitome) 模範 mohán
♦*adj* (perfect) 理想的な risṓteki na

idealist [aidi:'əlist] *n* 理想主義者 risṓshugishà

identical [aiden'tikəl] *adj* 同一の dṓitsu no

identification [aidentəfəkei'ʃən] *n* (process) 識別 shikíbetsu; (of person, dead body) 身元の確認 mimóto nò kakúnin
(means of) identification 身分証明書 mibúnshōmeìsho

identify [aiden'təfai] *vt* (recognize) 見分ける miwákerù; (distinguish) 識別する shikíbetsu suru; (associate): *to identify someone/something (with)* ...を (...と) 関連付ける ...wo (...to) kaṅrenzukerù

Identikit [aiden'təkit] ® *n*: *Identikit (picture)* モンタージュ写真 moṅtáju-shashìn

identity [aiden'titi:] *n* (of person, suspect etc) 身元 mimóto, 正体 shṓtai; (of group, culture, nation etc) 特性 tokúsei

identity card *n* 身分証明書 mibúnshōmeìsho

ideology [aidi:ɑ:l'ədʒi:] *n* (beliefs) 思想 shisṓ, イデオロギー idéorògī

idiom [id'i:əm] *n* (style) 作風 sakúfū; (phrase) 熟語 jukúgo, イディオム ídìomu

idiomatic [idi:əmæt'ik] *adj* 熟語的な jukúgoteki na

idiosyncrasy [idi:əsiŋ'krəsi:] *n* (foible) 特異性 tokúisei

idiot [id'i:ət] *n* (fool) ばか bákà

idiotic [idi:ɑ:t'ik] *adj* (stupid) ばかな bá-kà na

idle [ai'dəl] *adj* (inactive) 暇な himá na; (lazy) 怠惰な taída na; (unemployed) 失業中の shitsúgyōchū no; (machinery) 動いていない ugóite inaì; (factory) 休業中の kyúgyōchū no; (question, conversation) 無意味な muími na; (pleasure) むなしい munáshiì
♦*vi* (machine, engine) 空回りする kára-mawàri suru, アイドリングする aídoriṅgu suru

idle away *vt*: *to idle away the time* のらくらする nórakura suru

idol [ai'dəl] *n* (hero) アイドル aídoru; (REL) 偶像 gūzō

idolize [ai'dəlaiz] *vt* ...に心酔する ...ni shiṅsui suru

idyllic [aidil'ik] *adj* のどかな nódòka na

i.e. [aii:'] *abbr* (= *id est*: *that is*) 即ち sunáwàchi

| KEYWORD |

if [if] *conj* 1 (conditional use: given that, providing that etc) (もし)...すれば〔するならば〕(móshi)...surébà〔surú narābà〕

I'll go if you come with me あなたが一緒に来れば，私は行ってもいいです a-nátà ga isshó ni kuréba watákushi wà itté mò íi desu

I'd be pleased if you could do it あなたがそれをやって下されば私は助かりますが anátà ga soré wò yatté kudasare-ba watákushi wà tasúkarimasù ga

if anyone comes in だれかが入って来れば dáreka ga háitte kuréba

if necessary 必要であれば hitsúyō de aréba

if I were you 私があなただったら wa-tákushi gà anátà dáttàra

2 (whenever) ...の時 ...no tókì

if we are in Scotland, we always go to see her スコットランドにいる時私たちは必ず彼女に会いに行きます sukóttorañdo ni irú tokì watákushitàchi wa kanárazù kánòjo ni aì nì ikímasù

3 (although): *(even) if* たとえ...でも tatóè ...dé mò

I am determined to finish it, (even) if it takes all week たとえ今週いっぱいかかっても私はこの仕事を片付けたいtatóè koñshū ippài kakátte mò watákushi wà konó shigoto wò katázuketaì

I like it, (even) if you don't あなたがいやでも、私はこれが好きです anátà ga iyá de mò, watákushi wà koré gà sukí desù

4 (whether) ...かどうか ...ka dò ka

I don't know if he is here 彼がここにいるかどうか私には分かりません kárè ga kokó nì irú ka dòka watákushi ni wà wakárimaseñ

ask him if he can come 来られるかどうか彼に聞いて下さい koráreru ka dò ka kárè ni kíìte kudasaì

5: *if so/not* そうであれば〔なければ〕só de arèba〔nakerèba〕

if only ...であったらなあ ...de áttara ná

if only I could 私にそれができたらなあ watákushi nì soré gà dékìtara ná

¶ *see also* **as**

---

igloo [ig'lu:] *n* イグルー ígùrū

ignite [ignait'] *vt* (set fire to) ...に火をつける ...ni hí wò tsukérù
♦*vi* 燃え出す moédasù

ignition [igníʃʼən] *n* (AUT: process) 点火 teñka; (: mechanism) 点火装置 teñkasòchi

to switch on/off the ignition エンジンスイッチを入れる〔切る〕 eñjinsuìtchi wo irérù〔kírù〕

ignition key *n* (AUT) カーキー kákì

ignorance [ig'nəːrəns] *n* (lack of knowledge) 無知 múchì

ignorant [ig'nəːrənt] *adj* (uninformed, unaware) 無学な múgàku na, 無知な múchì na

to be ignorant of (subject, events) ...を知らない ...wo shìránaì

ignore [ignɔːr'] *vt* (person, advice, event, fact) 無視する mushí suru

I'll [ail] = **I will; I shall**

ill [il] *adj* (sick) 病気の byóki no; (harmful: effects) 害 gaì; (trouble) warúì
♦*n* (evil) 悪 ákù; (trouble) 凶兆 kyóchō
♦*adv*: *to speak ill of someone* ...の悪口を言う ...no warúgùchi wo iú

to think ill (of someone) (...を）悪く思う (...wo) warúkù omóù

to be taken ill 病気になる byóki ni narù, 倒れる taórerù

ill-advised [il'ædvaizd'] *adj* (decision) 軽率な keísotsu na; (person) 無分別な mufúñbetsu na

ill-at-ease [il'əti:z'] *adj* (awkward, uncomfortable) 落着かない ochítsukanaì

illegal [ili:'gəl] *adj* (not legal: activity, organization, immigrant etc) 不法の fuhṓ no

illegible [iledʒ'əbəl] *adj* (writing) 読めない yoménaì

illegitimate [ilidʒit'əmit] *adj*: *an illegitimate child* 私生児 shiséiji

ill-fated [il'fei'tid] *adj* (doomed) 不運な fúùn na

ill feeling *n* (animosity, bitterness) 恨み urámi

illicit [ilis'it] *adj* (unlawful: sale, association, substance) 不法の fuhṓ no

illiterate [ilit'əːrit] *adj* (person) 文盲の mofúmō no; (letter) 無学な múgàku na

ill-mannered [il'mæn'əːrd] *adj* (rude: child etc) 行儀の悪い gyṓgi no warùi

illness [il'nis] *n* 病気 byóki

illogical [ilɑːdʒ'ikəl] *adj* (fear, reaction, argument) 不合理な fugṓri na

ill-treat [il'tri:t] *vt* (child, pet, prisoner) 虐待する gyakútai suru

illuminate [ilu:'məneit] *vt* (light up: room, street) 明るくする akárukù suru; (decorate with lights: building, monument etc) ライトアップする raítoappù suru; (shine light on) 照らす terásù

illumination [ilu:mənei'ʃən] *n* (lighting) 照明 shṓmei

illuminations [ilu:mənei'ʃənz] *npl* (decorative lights) 電飾 denshoku, イルミネーション irumineshon

illusion [ilu:'ʒən] *n* (false idea, belief) 錯覚 sakkáku; (trick) いんちき inchiki, トリック toríkkù

illusory [ilu:'sə:ri:] *adj* (hopes, prospects) 錯覚の sakkáku no

illustrate [il'əstreit] *vt* (point) 例を挙げて説明する rei wò agétè setsúmei suru; (book) ...に挿絵を入れる ...ni sashíè wo irérù; (talk) ...にスライド (など) を使う ...ni suráìdo (nádò) wo tsukáù

illustration [iləstrei'ʃən] *n* (act of illustrating) 図解 zukái; (example) 例 reí; (in book) 挿絵 sashíè

illustrious [ilʌs'tri:əs] *adj* (career) 輝かしい kagáyakashiî; (predecessor) 著名な chomèi na

ill will *n* (hostility) 恨み urámi

I'm [aim] = **I am**

image [im'idʒ] *n* (picture) 像 zó; (public face) イメージ íměji; (reflection) 姿 sugáta

imagery [im'idʒri:] *n* (in writing, painting etc) 比ゆ híyù

imaginary [imædʒ'əne:ri:] *adj* (being, danger) 想像上の sózòjō no

imagination [imædʒənei'ʃən] *n* (part of the mind) 想像 sózò; (inventiveness) 想像力 sózòryoku

imaginative [imædʒ'ənətiv] *adj* (person) 想像力に富んだ sózòryoku ni toñdà; (solution) 奇抜な kibátsu na

imagine [imædʒ'in] *vt* (visualise) 想像する sózò suru; (dream) ...だと錯覚する ...da to sakkáku suru; (suppose) ...だと思う ...da to omóù

imbalance [imbæl'əns] *n* (inequality) 不均等 fukíñtō, アンバランス añbaransu

imbecile [im'bəsil] *n* (idiot) ばか bákà

imbue [imbju:'] *vt*: **to imbue someone/ something with** ...に ...を吹き込む ...ni ...wo fukíkomù

imitate [im'əteit] *vt* (copy) まねる manérù; (mimic) ...の物まねをする ...no monómane wò suru

imitation [imətei'ʃən] *n* (act of copying)

まね mané; (act of mimicking) 物まね monómane; (copy) 偽物 nisémono

immaculate [imæk'jəlit] *adj* (room) 汚れ一つない yogóre hitotsù náî; (appearance) 清潔な seíketsu na; (piece of work) 完璧な kañpeki na; (REL) 原罪のない geñzai nò náî

immaterial [iməti:'ri:əl] *adj* (unimportant) どうでもいい dó dè mo íi

immature [imətu:r'] *adj* (fruit, cheese) 熟していない jukú shite inài; (organism) 未成熟の miséijuku no; (person) 未熟な mijúku na

immediate [imi:'di:it] *adj* (reaction, answer) 即時の sokúji no; (pressing: need) 緊迫した kiñpaku shita; (nearest: neighborhood, family) 最も近い mottómò chikáî

immediately [imi:'di:itli:] *adv* (at once) 直ぐに súgù ni, 直ちに tádàchi ni; (directly) 真っ直ぐに massúgù ni
immediately next to ...の直ぐ隣に ...no súgù tonárì ni

immense [imens'] *adj* (huge: size) 巨大な kyodái na; (: progress, importance) 大変な taíheñ na

immerse [imə:rs'] *vt* (submerge) 浸す hitásù
to be immersed in (*fig*: work, study etc) ...に熱中している ...ni netchú shite irú
to be immersed in thought 考え込んでいる kañgaekoñde irú

immersion heater [imə:r'ʒən-] (*BRIT*) *n* 投込式湯沸かし器 tónyūshiki yuwakashikí

immigrant [im'əgrənt] *n* 移民 imín

immigration [iməgrei'ʃən] *n* (process) 移住 ijú; (control: at airport etc) 入国管理局 nyúkoku kañrikyoku

imminent [im'ənənt] *adj* (arrival, departure) 差迫った sashísematta

immobile [imou'bəl] *adj* (motionless) 動かない ugókanaî

immobilize [imou'bəlaiz] *vt* (person, machine) 動けなくする ugókenakù suru

immoral [imɔ:r'əl] *adj* (person, behavior, idea etc) 不道徳な fudótoku na

immorality [iməræl'iti:] *n* 不道徳 fudő-toku

immortal [imɔ:r'təl] *adj* (living for ever: god) 永遠に生きる efen ni ikfrù; (unforgettable: poetry, fame) 不滅の fumétsu no

immortalize [imɔ:r'təlaiz] *vt* (hero, event) ...に不朽の名声を与える ...ni fukyú no meísei wo atáerù

immune [imju:n'] *adj*: **immune (to)** (disease) (...に) 免疫がある (...ni) meñ-eki ga arù; (flattery) (...が) ...に通じない (...ga) ...ni tsújinai; (criticism, attack) ...に (...の) しようがない ...ni (...no) shíyō ga nai

immunity [imju:'niti:] *n* (to disease etc) 免疫 meñ-eki; (from prosecution, taxation etc) 免除 méñjo

diplomatic immunity 外交特権 gaíko-utokkèn

immunize [im'jənaiz] *vt* (MED: *gen*) ...に免疫性を与える ...ni meñ-ekisei wð atáerù; (with injection) ...に予防注射をする ...ni yobóchùsha wo suru

imp [imp] *n* (small devil) 小鬼 ko-óni; (child) いたずらっ子 itázurakkð

impact [im'pækt] *n* (of bullet, crash) 衝撃 shőgeki, インパクト íñpakuto; (of law, measure) 影響 efkyō

impair [impe:r'] *vt* (vision, judgement) 損なう sokónaù

impale [impeil'] *vt* くし刺にする kushízashi ni suru

impart [impɑ:rt'] *vt* (make known: information) 与える atáerù; (bestow: flavor) 添える soérù

impartial [impɑr'ʃəl] *adj* (judge, observer) 公平な kőhei na

impassable [impæs'əbəl] *adj* (river) 渡れない watárenaì; (road, route etc) 通行不可能な tsúkōfukanð na

impasse [im'pæs] *n* (in war, negotiations) 行き詰り ikízumari

impassive [impæs'iv] *adj* (face, expression) 無表情な muhyőjō na

impatience [impei'ʃəns] *n* (annoyance due to waiting) じれったさ jiréttasà; (irritation) 短気 táñki; (eagerness) 意欲 í-yòku

impatient [impei'ʃənt] *adj* (annoyed by waiting) じれったい jiréttaì; (irritable) 短気な táñki na; (eager, in a hurry): **impatient to ...** ...に従っている ...shitágatte irù

to get/grow impatient もどかしがる modőkashigarù

impeccable [impek'əbəl] *adj* (perfect: manners, dress) 申分のない mőshibùn no náì

impede [impi:d'] *vt* (progress, development etc) 妨げる samátagerù

impediment [impe'dəmənt] *n* (to growth, movement) 障害 shőgai; (*also*: **speech impediment**) 言語障害 geñgoshő-gai

impending [impen'diŋ] *adj* (arrival, catastrophe) 差迫る sashísemarù

impenetrable [impen'itrəbəl] *adj* (wall, jungle) 通れない tőrenaì; (*fig*: law, text) 難解な nañkai na

imperative [impe:r'ətiv] *adj* (need) 緊急の kiñkyū no; (tone) 命令的な meíreiteki na

♦*n* (LING) 命令形 meíreikei

imperceptible [impə:rsep'təbəl] *adj* (change, movement) 気付かれない kizúkarenaì

imperfect [impə:r'fikt] *adj* (goods, system etc) 不完全な fukánzen na

♦*n* (LING: *also*: **imperfect tense**) 過去進行形 kakőshinkōkei

imperfection [impə:rfek'ʃən] *n* (failing, blemish) 欠点 kettéñ

imperial [impi:r'i:əl] *adj* (history, power) 帝国の teíkoku no; (*BRIT*: measure) ヤードポンド法の yádopondohő no

imperialism [impi:r'i:əlizəm] *n* 帝国主義 teíkokushùgi

impersonal [impə:r'sənəl] *adj* (place, organization) 人間味のない niñgeñmi no náì

impersonate [impə:r'səneit] *vt* (another person, police officer etc) ...の名をかたる ...no ná wð katárù, ...に成り済ます ...ni narísumasù; (THEATER) ...にふんする ...ni fuñ surù

impertinent [impər'tənənt] adj (pupil, question) 生意気な namáiki na

impervious [impəːr'viːəs] adj (fig): **impervious to** (criticism etc) ...に影響されない ...ni eíkyō sarenái

impetuous [impet∫'uːəs] adj (impulsive) 無鉄砲な mutéppō na

impetus [im'pitəs] n (momentum: of flight, runner) 惰性 daséi; (fig: driving force) 原動力 geńdōryoku

impinge [impindʒ']: **to impinge on** vt fus (person) ...の行動を制限する ...no kốdō wò seígen suru; (rights) 侵害する shíñgai suru

implacable [implæk'əbəl] adj (hatred, anger etc) なだめがたい nadámegàtai; (opposition) 執念深い shúnenbùkai

implement [n im'pləmənt vb im'pləment] n (tool: for farming, gardening, cooking etc) 道具 dōgu
♦vt (plan, regulation) 実行する jikkố suru

implicate [im'plikeit] vt (in crime, error) ...のかかわり合いを立証する ...no kakáwariaì wo risshó suru

implication [implikei'∫ən] n (inference) 含み fukúmi; (involvement) 係り合い kakáwariai

implicit [implis'it] adj (inferred: threat, meaning etc) 暗黙の añmoku no; (unquestioning: belief, trust) 盲目的な mố-mokuteki na

implore [imploːr'] vt (beg) ...に嘆願する ...ni tañgan suru

imply [implai'] vt (hint) ...の意味を含む ...no ímì wo fukúmù; (mean) ...を意味する ...wo ímì suru

impolite [impəlait'] adj (rude, offensive) 失礼な shitsúrei na

import [vb impoːrt' n im'poːrt] vt (goods etc) 輸入する yunyú suru
♦n (COMM: article) 輸入品 yunyúhin; (: importation) 輸入 yunyú

importance [impoːr'təns] n (significance) 重大さ júdaisa; (of person) 有力 yúryoku

important [impoːr'tənt] adj (significant: decision, difference etc) 重要な júyō na, 重大な júdai na; (influential: person) 偉い eráì
it's not important 大した事じゃない taíshita kotò ja náì

importer [impoːr'təːr] n (COMM) 輸入業者 yunyúgyōsha

impose [impouz'] vt (sanctions, restrictions, discipline etc) 負わせる owáserù
♦vi: **to impose on someone** ...に付込む ...ni tsukékomù, ...に迷惑を掛ける ...ni méìwaku wo kakérù

imposing [impou'ziŋ] adj (building, person, manner) 貫ろくある kañroku arù

imposition [impəzi∫'ən] n (of tax etc) 賦課 fukấ
to be an imposition on (person) ...に付込む ...ni tsukékomù, ...に迷惑を掛ける ...ni méìwaku wo kakérù

impossible [impɑːs'əbəl] adj (task, demand etc) 不可能な fukánō na; (situation) 厄介な yakkáì na; (person) どうしようもない dố shiyõ mo naí

impostor [impɑːs'təːr] n 偽者 nisémono

impotence [im'pətəns] n (lack of power) 無力 múryòku; (MED) 性交不能 seíkōfunō, インポテンツ iñpotentsu

impotent [im'pətənt] adj (powerless) 無力な múryòku na; (MED) 性交不能の seíkōfunō no

impound [impaund'] vt (belongings, passports) 没収する bosshū suru

impoverished [impɑːv'əːri∫t] adj (country, person etc) 貧しくなった mazúshiku nattá

impracticable [impræk'tikəbəl] adj (idea, solution) 実行不可能な jikkốfukanō na

impractical [impræk'tikəl] adj (plan) 実用的でない jitsúyōteki de naî; (person) 不器用な bukíyō na

imprecise [imprisais'] adj (inexact) 不正確な fuséikaku na

impregnable [impreg'nəbəl] adj (castle, fortress) 難攻不落の nañkōfuràku no

impregnate [impreg'neit] vt (saturate) ...に染込ませる ...ni shimíkomaserù

impresario [imprəsɑː'riːou] n (THEA-

TER) 興業師 kṓgyōshī

impress [impres'] vt (person) ...に印象を与える ...ni ińshō wò atáerù; (mark) ...に押付ける ...ni oshítsukerù

to impress something on someone ...に...を強く言い聞かす ...ni ...wo tsuyókù iíkikasù

impression [impreʃ'ən] n (of place, situation, person) 印象 ińshō; (of stamp, seal) 判 hán, 刻印 kokúiň; (idea) 思い込み omóikomi; (effect) 効果 kṓka; (mark) 跡 átò; (imitation) 物まね monómane

to be under the impression that ...だと思い込んでいる ...da to omóikoňde irú

impressionable [impreʃ'ənəbəl] adj (child, person) 感じやすい kaňjiyasui

impressionist [impreʃ'ənist] n (entertainer) 物真似芸人 monómanegeìnin; (ART): *Impressionist* 印象派画家 ińshōhagaka

impressive [impres'iv] adj (reputation, collection) 印象的な ińshōteki na

imprint [im'print] n (outline: of hand etc) 跡 ato; (PUBLISHING) 奥付 okúzuke

imprison [impriz'ən] vt (criminal) 拘置する kṓchi suru, 刑務所に入れる keímushò ni irérù

imprisonment [impriz'ənmənt] n 拘置 kṓchi

improbable [impra:b'əbəl] adj (unlikely: outcome) ありそうもない arísō mò náì; (: explanation, story) 本当らしくない hońtōrashikù náì

impromptu [impra:mp'tu:] adj (celebration, party) 即席の sokúseki no

improper [impra:p'ə:r] adj (unsuitable: conduct, procedure) 不適切な futékisetsu na; (dishonest: activities) 不正な fuséi na

improve [impru:v'] vt (make better: character, housing, result) 改善する kaízen suru

♦vi (get better: weather, pupil, patient, health etc) 良くなる yókù naru

improvement [impru:v'mənt] n (making better) 改善 kaízen; (getting better) 良くなる事 yókù naru kotó: *improve-*

ment (in) (making better) (...を) 改善する事 (...wo) kaízen surù kotó; (getting better) (...が) 良くなる事 (...ga) yókù naru kotó

improvise [im'prəvaiz] vt (meal, bed etc) 有り合せの物で作る aríawase no mono dè tsukúrù

♦vi (THEATER, MUS) 即興的にしゃべる〔演奏する〕sokkyṓteki nì shabérù〔eńsō suru〕、アドリブする adóribu suru

imprudent [impru:d'ənt] adj (unwise) 賢明でない keńmei de naì

impudent [im'pjədənt] adj (child, comment, remark) 生意気な namáiki na

impulse [im'pʌls] n (urge: gen) 衝動 shṓdō; (: to do wrong) 出来心 dekígokòro; (ELEC) 衝撃 shṓgeki, インパルス íňparusu

to act on impulse 衝動的に行動する shṓdōteki ni kōdṓ suru

impulsive [impʌl'siv] adj (purchase, gesture, person) 衝動的な shṓdōteki na

impunity [impju:'niti:] n: *with impunity* 罰せられずに bassérarezù ni

impure [impju:r'] adj (adulterated) 不純な fujún na; (sinful) みだらな mídàra na

impurity [impju:r'iti:] n (foreign substance) 不純物 fujúňbutsu

KEYWORD
---

in [in] prep 1 (indicating place, position) ...に〔で〕... nì〔dè〕

in the house/garden 家〔庭〕に〔で〕ié〔niwá〕nì〔dè〕

in the box/fridge/drawer 箱〔冷蔵庫、引き出し〕に〔で〕hakó〔reízōko, hikídashi〕nì〔dè〕

I have it in my hand 手に持っています tè nì mòttě imasu

to spend a day in town/the country 町〔田舎〕で1日を過ごす machí〔ínáka〕dè ichínichi wò sugósù

in school 学校に〔で〕gakkṓ nì〔dè〕

in here/there ここ〔あそこ〕に〔で〕kokó〔asóko〕nì〔dè〕

2 (with place names: of town, region, country) ...に〔で〕... nì〔dè〕

in London ロンドンに〔で〕róňdon ni

〔de〕

in England/Japan/Canada/the United States 英国〔日本, カナダ, アメリカ〕に〔で〕eíkoku〔nippón, kánàda, amérĩka〕nì〔dè〕

in Burgundy バーガンディーに〔で〕bágañdī ni〔dè〕

3 (indicating time: during) ...に ...nĩ

in spring/summer 春〔夏〕に hárù〔natsú〕ni

in 1998 1998年に señkyùhyakukyújùhachi néñ ni

in May 5月に gógatsu ni

I'll see you in July 7月に会いましょう shichígatsu ni aímashō

in the afternoon 午後に gógò ni

at 4 o'clock in the afternoon 午後4時に gógò yójî ni

4 (indicating time: in the space of) ...で ...dè

I did it in 3 hours/days 3時間〔3日〕でやりました sañjikàn〔mikkà〕de yarímashìta

I'll see you in 2 weeks/in 2 weeks' time 2週間したらまた会いましょう nishūkàn shitara matá aímashō

5 (indicating manner etc) ...で ...dè

in a loud/soft voice 大きな〔小さな〕声で ōkìna〔chíisana〕kóè de

in pencil/ink 鉛筆〔インク〕で eñpitsu〔íñku〕dè

in English/French 英語〔フランス語〕で eígo〔furánsugo〕dè

the boy in the blue shirt 青いシャツの少年 aóì shátsu no shōnen

6 (indicating circumstances): **in the sun** 直射日光に当って chokúshanikkô ni atáttè, 日なたに hinátà ni

in the rain 雨の中 ámè no nákà

in the shade 日陰で hikáge de

a change in policy 政策の変更 seísaku nò heñkō

a rise in prices 物価の上昇 búkkà no jōshō

7 (indicating mood, state): **in tears** 泣いて naíte

in anger 怒って okóttè

in despair 失望して shitsúbō shitè

in good condition 無事に bují nĩ

to live in luxury ぜいたくに暮す zeítaku ni kuràsu

8 (with ratios, numbers): **1 in 10 households has a second car, 1 household in 10 has a second car** 10世帯中1世帯は車を2台持っている jussétaichū issétai wà kurúma wò nídai mótte irù

6 months in the year 1年の内6か月 ichínen no uchî rokkágetsu

they lined up in twos 彼らは2人ずつ並んだ kárèra wa futárizùtsu naráñda

9 (referring to people, works): **the disease is common in children** この病気は子供によく見られる konó byōki wa kodómo nĩ yókù mirárerù

in (the works of) Dickens ディケンズの作品の中に díkènzu no sakúhin no nakà ni

she has it in her to succeed 彼女には成功する素質がある kánòjo ni wa seíkō suru soshìtsu ga árù

they have a good leader in him 彼らにとって彼は素晴らしいリーダーです kárèra ni tóttè kárè wa subárashiì rídā desu

10 (indicating profession etc): **to be in teaching** 教員である kyōín de árù

to be in publishing 出版関係の仕事をしている shuppánkañkei no shigóto wò shité irù

to be in the army 軍人である guñjìn de árù

11 (after superlative): **the best pupil in the class** クラスで最優秀の生徒 kúrasu de saíyūshū no seíto

the biggest/smallest in Europe ヨーロッパ中で最も大きな〔小さな〕物 yōroppajū de mottómò ōkìna〔chíisana〕monó

12 (with present participle): **in saying this** こう言って kō ittè

in doing things the way she did, she alienated everyone 彼女のやり方は皆の反感を買った kánòjo no yaríkata wà miná nò hañkan wo kattà

♦**adv**: **to be in** (person: at home) 在宅である zaítaku de arù; (: at work) 出社して

いる shusshá shite irù; (train, plane) 到着
している tōchaku shite irù; (ship) 入港し
ている nyūkō shite irù; (in fashion) 流行
している ryūkō shite irù

he'll be in later today 2-3時間したら
出社すると思います nisánjikàn shitárà
shusshá suru tò omóimasù

miniskirts are in again this year 今
年ミニスカートが再び流行しています
kotóshi minísukàto ga futátabi ryūkō
shite imasù

to ask someone in ...を家に上がらせる
...wò ié nì agáraserù

to run/limp etc in 走って〔びっこを引
いて〕入って来る hashíttè〔bíkkò wo híi-
tè〕háitte kuru

♦*n: the ins and outs* (of proposal,
situation etc) 詳細 shōsai

*he explained all the ins and outs of
the deal to me* 彼は私に取引の詳細を
説明してくれました kárè wa watákushi
nì toríhiki no shōsai wo setsúmei shite
kuremashìta

in. *abbr* = **inch**

inability [inəbil'əti:] *n* (incapacity): *inability (to do)* (...する事が) できない
事 (...surú kotò ga) dekínaì kotó

inaccessible [inækses'əbəl] *adj* (place)
入りにくい haírinikùi, 近付きにくい chi-
kázukinikùi; (*fig:* text, music) 難解な nań-
kai na

inaccurate [inæk'jə:rit] *adj* (account,
answer, person) 不正確な fuséikaku na

inactivity [inæktiv'iti:] *n* (idleness) 活動
しない事 katsúdōshinai kotó

inadequate [inæd'əkwit] *adj* (income,
amount, reply) 不十分な fujūbùn na;
(person) 無能な munō na

inadvertently [inədvə:r'təntli:] *adv* (unintentionally) うっかり ukkárì

inadvisable [inədvai'zəbəl] *adj* 得策でな
い tokúsaku de naì

inane [inein'] *adj* (smile, remark) 愚かな
óròka na

inanimate [inæn'əmit] *adj* 生命のない
seímei no naì

inappropriate [inəprou'pri:it] *adj* (un-

suitable) 不適切な futékisetsu na; (improper: word, expression) 非難すべき hi-
nánsubeki

inarticulate [inɑ:rtik'jəlit] *adj* (person)
口下手な kuchíbeta na; (speech) 分かり
にくい wakárinikuì

inasmuch as [inəzmʌtʃ'-] *adv* (in that)
...という点で ...to iú teñ de; (insofar as)
できる限り dekíru kagiri

inaudible [inɔ:'dəbəl] *adj* (voice, aside)
聞取れない kikítorenaí

inaugural [inɔ:'gjə:rəl] *adj* (speech) 就 任
の shūnin no; (meeting) 発会の hakkái
no

inaugurate [inɔ:'gjə:reit] *vt* (president,
official) ...の就任式を行う ...no shúniñshiki wo okonau; (system, measure) 始
める hajímeru; (organization) 発足させ
る hossóku saserù

inauguration [inɔ:gjərei'ʃən] *n* (of president, official) 就任式 shúniñshiki; (of
system, measure) 開始 kaíshi; (of organization) 発足 hossóku

in-between [in'bitwi:n'] *adj* (intermediate) 中間的な chūkanteki na

inborn [in'bɔ:rn] *adj* (quality) 生れ付きの
umáretsuki no

inbred [in'bred] *adj* (quality) 生まれつき
の umaretsuki no; (family) 近親交配の
kiñshinkōhai no

Inc. *abbr* = **incorporated**

incalculable [inkæl'kjələbəl] *adj* (effect,
loss) 途方もない tohō mo naì

incapable [inkei'pəbəl] *adj* (helpless) 無
能な munō na; (unable to): *to be incapable of something/doing something* ...が〔する事が〕できない ...ga〔surú
kotò ga〕dekínaì

incapacitate [inkəpæs'əteit] *vt* 不 具 に
する fúgù ni suru

incapacity [inkəpæs'iti:] *n* (weakness)
弱さ yówàsa; (inability) 不能 funō

incarcerate [inkɑ:r'sə:rit] *vt* 拘置する
kōchi suru, 刑務所に入れる keímushò ni
irérù

incarnation [inkɑ:rnei'ʃən] *n* (of beauty)
化身 késhìn; (of evil) 権化 góñge; (REL)
神が人間の姿を取る事 kámì ga niñgen

no sugatā wo tōrù kotó

incendiary [insen'di:e:ri:] *adj* (device) 放火の hōka no

an incendiary bomb 焼い弾 shōidàn

incense [*n* in'sens *vb* insens'] *n* (perfume: *also* REL) 香 kō

♦*vt* (anger) 怒らせる okóraserù

incentive [insen'tiv] *n* (inducement) 動機 dōki, 刺激 shigéki

incessant [inses'ənt] *adj* (bickering, criticism) 引っ切り無しの hikkíri nashí no

incessantly [inses'əntli:] *adv* 引っ切り無しに hikkíri nashí ni

incest [in'sest] *n* 近親相かん kińshinsòkan

inch [intʃ] *n* (measurement) インチ ińchi

to be within an inch of doing 危うく...するところである ayáuku ...surú tokóro de árù

he didn't give an inch (*fig*: back down, yield) 一寸も譲ろうとしなかった issún mo yuzúrō to shinákatta

inch forward *vi* 一寸刻みに進む issúñkizami ni susúmù

incidence [in'sidəns] *n* (of crime, disease) 発生率 hasséiritsu

incident [in'sidənt] *n* (event) 事件 jíkèn

incidental [insiden'təl] *adj* (additional, supplemental) 付随的な fuzúiteki na

incidental to ...に対して二次的な ...ni táishite nijíteki na

incidentally [insiden'təli:] *adv* (by the way) ところで tokóro dè

incinerator [insin'ə:reitə:r] *n* (for waste, refuse) 焼却炉 shōkyakurò

incipient [insip'i:ənt] *adj* (baldness, madness) 初期の shókì no

incision [insiʒ'ən] *n* (cut: *also* MED) 切開 sékkài

incisive [insai'siv] *adj* (comment, criticism) 痛烈な tsūretsu na

incite [insait'] *vt* (rioters, violence) 扇動する seńdō suru; (hatred) あおりたてる aóritatèru

inclination [inklənei'ʃən] *n* (tendency) 傾向 keíkō; (disposition, desire) 望み nozōmi

incline [in'klain] *n* (slope) 坂 saká

♦*vt* (bend: head) 下げる sagérù

♦*vi* (surface) 傾斜する keísha suru

to be inclined to (tend) ...する傾向がある ...suru keíkō ga arù

include [inklu:d'] *vt* (incorporate: in plan, team etc) 入れる irérù; (: in price) 含む fukúmù

including [inklu:d'iŋ] *prep* ...を含めて ...wo fukúmète

inclusion [inklu:'ʒən] *n* (incorporation: in plan etc) 入れる事 irérù kotó; (: in price) 含む事 fukúmù kotó

inclusive [inklu:'siv] *adj* (price, terms) 含んでいる fukúñde iru

inclusive of ...を含めて ...wo fukúmète

incognito [inkɑ:gni:'tou] *adv* (travel) 御忍びで o-shínobi de

incoherent [inkouhi:'rənt] *adj* (argument, speech, person) 分かりにくい wakárinikuī

income [in'kʌm] *n* 収入 shūnyu

income tax *n* 所得税 shotókuzèi

incoming [in'kʌmiŋ] *adj* (flight, passenger) 到着の tōchaku no; (call, mail) 着信の chakúshin no; (government, official) 新任の shińnin no; (wave) 寄せて来る yoséte kurù

the incoming tide 上げ潮 agéshio

incomparable [inkɑ:m'pə:rəbəl] *adj* (genius, efficiency etc) 類のない ruī no naī

incompatible [inkəmpæt'əbəl] *adj* (lifestyles, systems, aims) 相容れない aíìrenai

incompetence [inkɑ:m'pitəns] *n* 無能 munố

incompetent [inkɑ:m'pitənt] *adj* (person) 無能な munố na; (job) 下手な hetá na

incomplete [inkəmpli:t'] *adj* (unfinished: book, painting etc) 未完成の mikáñsei no; (partial: success, achievement) 部分的な bubúnteki na

incomprehensible [inkɑ:mprihen'səbəl] *adj* (conduct) 不可解な fukákai na; (language) 分からない wakáranai

inconceivable [inkənsi:'vəbəl] *adj* (unthinkable) 考えられない kańgaerarenaī

incongruous [inkɑːŋ'gruːəs] *adj* (strange: situation, figure) 変った kawátta; (inappropriate: remark, act) 不適当な futékitō na

inconsiderate [inkənsid'əːrit] *adj* (person, action) 心ない kokóronaī

inconsistency [inkənsis'tənsiː] *n* (of behavior, person etc) 一貫しない事 ikkán shinai koto; (in work) むら murá; (in statement, action) 矛盾 mujún

inconsistent [inkənsis'tənt] *adj* (behavior, person) 変りやすい kawáriyasuī; (work) むらの多い murá no ōi; (statement, action) 矛盾した mujún shita
  inconsistent with (beliefs, values) ...と矛盾する ...to mujún suru

inconspicuous [inkənspik'juːəs] *adj* (person, color, building etc) 目立たない medátanaī

incontinent [inkɑːn'tənənt] *adj* (MED) 失禁の shikkín no

inconvenience [inkənviːn'jəns] *n* (problem) 問題 mondai; (trouble) 迷惑 meíwaku
  ♦*vt* ...に迷惑を掛ける ...ni meíwaku wò kakérù

inconvenient [inkənviːn'jənt] *adj* (time, place, house) 不便な fubén na; (visitor, incident etc) 厄介な yakkái na

incorporate [inkɔːr'pəːrit] *vt* (make part of) 取入れる torírerù; (contain) 含む fukúmù

incorporated company [inkɔːr'pəːreitid-] (*US*) *n* (*abbr* **Inc.**) 会社 kaísha

incorrect [inkərekt'] *adj* (information, answer, attitude etc) 間違った machígattā

incorrigible [inkɔːr'idʒəbəl] *adj* (liar, crook) 救い様のない sukúiyō no naī

incorruptible [inkərʌp'təbəl] *adj* (not open to bribes) 買収のできない baíshū no dekínaī

increase [*n* in'kriːs *vb* inkriːs'] *n* (rise): *increase (in/of)* (...の) 増加 (...no) zṓka
  ♦*vi* (: price, level, productivity etc) 増す masú
  ♦*vt* (make greater: price, knowledge etc) 増す masú

increasing [inkriːs'iŋ] *adj* (number, use) 増加する zṓka suru

increasingly [inkriːs'iŋliː] *adv* (more intensely, more often) ますます masúmàsu

incredible [inkred'əbəl] *adj* (unbelievable) 信じられない shiñjirarenaī; (enormous) ばく大な bakúdai na

incredulous [inkred'ʒələs] *adj* (tone, expression) 半信半疑の hañshiñhangi no

increment [in'krəmənt] *n* (in salary) 定期昇給 teíkishōkyū

incriminate [inkrim'əneit] *vt* (LAW) ...の罪を立証する ...no tsúmì wo risshṓ suru

incubation [inkjəbei'ʃən] *n* (of eggs) ふ卵 furán; (of illness) 潜伏期間 señpukukikàn

incubator [in'kjəbeitəːr] *n* (for babies) 保育器 hoíkukì

incumbent [inkʌm'bənt] *n* (official: POL, REL) 現役 gén-eki
  ♦*adj*: *it is incumbent on him to ...* ...するのが彼の義務である ...surú no gà kárè no gímù de arù

incur [inkəːr'] *vt* (expenses) ...が掛る ...ga kakárù; (loss) 受ける ukérù; (debt) こしらえる koshíraerù; (disapproval, anger) 被る kṓmurù

incurable [inkjuːr'əbəl] *adj* (disease) 不治の fújì no

incursion [inkəːr'ʒən] *n* (MIL: invasion) 侵入 shiñnyū

indebted [indet'id] *adj*: *to be indebted to someone* (grateful) ...に感謝している ...ni kánsha shité irù

indecent [indiː'sənt] *adj* (film, book) みだらな mídàra na

indecent assault (*BRIT*) *n* 強制わいせつ罪 kyṓsei waisetsuzaì

indecent exposure *n* 公然わいせつ罪 kṓzen waisetsuzaì

indecisive [indisai'siv] *adj* (person) 決断力のない ketsúdanryoku no naī

indeed [indiːd'] *adv* (certainly) 確かに táshìka ni, 本当に hoñtṓ ni; (in fact) 実は jitsú wà; (furthermore) なお náò *yes indeed!* 確かにそうだ! táshǐka ni sō dà!

indefinite [indef'ənit] *adj* (answer, view) 不明確な fuméikaku na; (period, number) 不定の futéi no

indefinitely [indef'ənitli:] *adv* (continue, wait) いつまでも ítsub made mo

indelible [indel'əbəl] *adj* (mark, stain, ink) 消せない kesénaì

indelible pen 油性フェルトペン yuséi ferútopen

indemnity [indem'niti:] *n* (insurance) 賠償保険 baíshōhokèn; (compensation) 賠償 baíshō

independence [indipen'dəns] *n* (of country, person etc) 独立 dokúritsu; (of thinking etc) 自主性 jishúsei

independent [indipen'dənt] *adj* (country, business etc) 独立した dokúritsu shita; (person, thought) 自主的な jishúteki na; (school) 私立の shíritsu no; (broadcasting company) 民間の mińkan no; (inquiry) 独自の dokúji to

indestructible [indistrʌk'təbəl] *adj* 破壊できない hakái dekinaì

indeterminate [inditəːr'mənit] *adj* (number, nature) 不明の fuméi to

index [in'deks] (*pl* **indexes**) *n* (in book) 索引 sakúin, インデックス ińdekkùsu; (in library etc) 蔵書目録 zōshomokùroku; (*pl*: **indices**: ratio) 率 rítsù, 指数 shísù; (: sign) 印 shirúshi

index card *n* インデックスカード ińdekkusukàdo

indexed [in'dekst] (*BRIT* **index-linked**) *adj* (income, payment) スライド制のsuráidosei no

index finger *n* 人差指 hitósashiyùbi

India [in'di:ə] *n* インド ińdo

Indian [in'di:ən] *adj* インドの ińdo no
Red Indian アメリカインディアン amérika indian

Indian Ocean *n*: *the Indian Ocean* インド洋 ińdoyō

indicate [in'dikeit] *vt* (show) 示す shimésù; (point to) 指す sásù; (mention) 示唆する shisá suru

indication [indikei'ʃən] *n* (sign) しるし shirúshi

indicative [indik'ətiv] *adj*: *indicative of* …のしるしである …no shirúshi de aru
♦*n* (LING) 直接法 chokúsetsuhō

indicator [in'dikeitəːr] *n* (marker, signal) しるし shirúshi; (AUT) 方向指示器 hōkōshijìki, ウインカー uíńkā

indices [in'disi:z] *npl of* **index**

indictment [indait'mənt] *n* (denunciation) 避難 hínàn; (charge) 起訴 kisó

indifference [indif'əːrəns] *n* (lack of interest) 無関心 mukánshin

indifferent [indif'əːrənt] *adj* (uninterested: attitude) 無関心な mukánshin na; (mediocre: quality) 平凡な heíbon na

indigenous [indidʒ'ənəs] *adj* (wildlife) 固有の koyū no
the indigenous population 原住民 geńjūmin

indigestion [indidʒes'tʃən] *n* 消化不良 shōkafuryō

indignant [indig'nənt] *adj*: *to be indignant at something/with someone* (angry) …に怒っている …ni okótte irù

indignation [indignei'ʃən] *n* (outrage, resentment) 立腹 rippúku

indignity [indig'niti:] *n* (humiliation) 侮辱 bujóku

indigo [in'dəgou] *n* (color) あい aí

indirect [indirekt'] *adj* (way, route) 遠回しの tómawashì no; (answer, effect) 間接的な kańsetsuteki na

indirectly [indirekt'li:] *adv* (responsible) 間接的に kańsetsuteki ni

indiscreet [indiskri:t'] *adj* (person, behavior, comment) 軽率な keísotsu na

indiscriminate [indiskrim'ənit] *adj* (bombing) 無差別の musábetsu no; (taste) はっきりしない hakkíří shinái

indispensable [indispen'səbəl] *adj* (tool, worker) 掛替えのない kakégae no naì

indisposed [indispouzd'] *adj* (unwell) 体調の悪い taíchō no warúì

indisputable [indispju:'təbəl] *adj* (undeniable) 否めない inárenaì

indistinct [indistiŋkt'] *adj* (image, memory) ぼんやりした boń-yarì shita; (noise) かすかな kásùka na

individual [indəvidʒ'u:əl] *n* (person: different from all others) 個人 kójìn; (: with *adj*) 人 人 hitó, 人物 jinbutsu

◆*adj* (personal) 個人個人 の kojínkòjin no; (single) それぞれの sorézòre no; (particular: characteristic) 独特な dokútoku na

individualist [indəvidʒ'u:əlist] *n* 個人主義者 kojínshugishà

individually [indəvidʒ'u:əli:] *adv* (singly: persons) 一人一人で hitórihitòri de; (: things) 一つ一つで hitótsuhitòtsu de

indivisible [indəviz'əbəl] *adj* (matter, power) 分割できない bunkatsu dekinài

indoctrinate [indɑːk'trəneit] *vt* ...に ...を教え込む ...ni ...wo oshíekomù, 洗脳する sefnō suru

indoctrination [indɑːktrənei'ʃən] *n* 教え込む事 oshíekomù kotó, 洗脳 sefnō

indolent [in'dələnt] *adj* (lazy) 怠惰な táída na

Indonesia [indəni:'ʒə] *n* インドネシア ifdoneshìa

indoor [in'dɔːr] *adj* 屋内の okúnai no

indoors [indɔːrz'] *adv* (inside) 屋内でo-kúnai de

induce [indus'] *vt* (bring about) 引起こす hikíokosù; (persuade) 説得する settóku suru; (MED: birth) 誘発する yūhatsu suru

inducement [indus'mənt] *n* (incentive) 動機 dōki, 刺激 shigéki; (*pej*: bribe) 賄ろ wáîro

indulge [indʌldʒ'] *vt* (desire, whim) 満たす mitásù; (person, child) 気ままにさせる kimáma ni saserù

◆*vi*: **to indulge in** (vice, hobby) ...にふける ...ni fukérù

indulgence [indʌl'dʒəns] *n* (pleasure) 楽しみ tanóshimi; (leniency) 寛大さ kafdaisa

indulgent [indʌl'dʒənt] *adj* (parent, smile) 甘やかす amáyakasù

industrial [indʌs'tri:əl] *adj* 産業の sañgyō no, 工業の kógyō no

industrial action (*BRIT*) *n* 争議行為 sōgikòi

industrial estate (*BRIT*) *n* = **industrial park**

industrialist [indʌs'tri:əlist] *n* 実業家 ji-tsúgyōka

industrialize [indʌs'tri:əlaiz] *vt* (country, society) 工業化する kógyōka suru

industrial park (*US*) *n* 工業団地 kógyōdañchi

industrious [indʌs'tri:əs] *adj* (student, worker) 勤勉な kiñben na

industry [in'dəstri:] *n* (manufacturing) 産業 sañgyō, 工業 kógyō; (oil industry, textile industry etc) ...業界 ...gyōkai; (diligence) 勤勉さ kiñbensa

inebriated [inib'ri:eitid] *adj* (drunk) 酔っ払った yoppáratta

inedible [ined'əbəl] *adj* (disgusting) 食べられない tabérarenài; (poisonous) 食用に適さない shokúyō ni tekísanaì

ineffective [inifek'tiv] *adj* (policy, government) 効果のない kóka no naì

ineffectual [inifek'tʃu:əl] *adj* = **ineffective**

inefficiency [inifiʃ'ənsi:] *n* 非能率 hinō-ritsu

inefficient [inifiʃ'ənt] *adj* (person, machine, system) 能率の悪い nōritsu no waruì

inept [inept'] *adj* (politician, management) 無能な munō na

inequality [inikwɑ:l'iti:] *n* (of system) 不平等 fubyōdō; (of amount, share) 不等 futó

inert [inərt'] *adj* (immobile) 動かない ugókanaì; (gas) 不活性の fukássei no

inertia [inər'ʃə] *n* (apathy) 物臭 monógusa; (PHYSICS) 惰性 daséi

inescapable [inəskei'pəbəl] *adj* (conclusion, impression) 避けられない sakérarenaì

inevitable [inev'itəbəl] *adj* (outcome, result) 避けられない sakérarenaì, 必然的な hitsúzenteki na

inevitably [inev'itəbli:] *adv* 必然的に hitsúzenteki ni

inexcusable [inikskju:'zəbəl] *adj* (behavior, error) 許されない yurúsarenaì

inexhaustible [inigzɔ:s'təbəl] *adj* (wealth, resources) 無尽蔵の mujíñzō no

inexorable [inek'sə:rəbəl] *adj* (progress, decline) 止め様のない tomḗyō no naí

inexpensive [inikspen'siv] *adj* (cheap) 安い yasúi

inexperience [inikspi:'ri:əns] *n* (of person) 不慣れ fúnàre

inexperienced [inikspi:'ri:ənst] *adj* (swimmer, worker) 不慣れの fúnàre no

inexplicable [ineks'plikəbəl] *adj* (decision, mistake) 不可解な fukákài na

inextricably [ineks'trikəbli:] *adv* (entangled, linked) 分けられない程 wakérarenái hodo

infallible [infæl'əbəl] *adj* (person, guide) 間違いのない machígaì no náì

infamous [in'fəməs] *adj* (crime, murderer) 悪名高い akúmeidakaì

infamy [in'fəmi:] *n* (notoriety) 悪評 akúhyō

infancy [in'fənsi:] *n* (of person) 幼年時代 yōnenjidài

infant [in'fənt] *n* (baby) 赤ちゃん ákāchan; (young child) 幼児 yōji

infantile [in'fəntail] *adj* (disease) 幼児の yōji no; (foolish) 幼稚な yōchì na

infantry [in'fəntri:] *n* (MIL) 歩兵隊 hohéitai

infant school (*BRIT*) *n* 幼稚園 yōchien

infatuated [infæt∫'u:eitid] *adj*: **to be infatuated with** ...にのぼせている ...ni nobósete irù

infatuation [infæt∫u:ei'∫ən] *n* (passion) ...にのぼせる事 ...ni nobóseru koto

infect [infekt'] *vt* (person, animal) ...に感染させる ...ni kañsen saserù; (food) 汚染する osén suru

infection [infek'∫ən] *n* (MED: disease) 感染 kañsen; (contagion) 伝染 deñsen

infectious [infek'∫əs] *adj* (person, animal) 伝染病にかかった deńsenbyō ni kakáttà; (disease) 伝染性の deńsensei no; (*fig*: enthusiasm, laughter) 移りやすい utsúriyasuì

infer [infə:r'] *vt* (deduce) 推定する suítei suru; (imply) ...の意味を含む ...no ímì wo fukúmù

inference [in'fə:rəns] *n* (deduction) 推定 suítei; (implication) 含み fukúmi

inferior [infi:'ri:ə:r] *adj* (in rank) 下級の kakyū no; (in quality, quantity) 劣った otóttà

♦*n* (subordinate) 下の者 shitá no monò; (junior) 年下の者 toshíshita no monò

inferiority [infi:ri:ə:r'iti:] *n* (in rank) 下級である事 kakyū de arù kotó; (in quality) 品質の悪さ hiñshitsu nò wárùsa

inferiority complex *n* (PSYCH) 劣等感 rettōkan

infernal [infə:r'nəl] *adj* (racket, temper) ひどい hidóì

inferno [infə:r'nou] *n* (blaze) 大火事 ōkaji

infertile [infə:r'təl] *adj* (soil) 不毛の fumō no; (person, animal) 不妊の funín no

infertility [infə:rtil'əti:] *n* (of soil) 不毛 fumō; (of person, animal) 不妊症 funínshō

infested [infes'tid] *adj*: **infested with** (vermin, pests) ...がうじゃうじゃいる ...ga újàuja irú

infidelity [infidel'iti:] *n* (unfaithfulness) 浮気 uwáki

in-fighting [in'faitiŋ] *n* 内紛 naífun, 内ゲバ uchígeba

infiltrate [infil'treit] *vt* ...に潜入する ...ni seńnyū suru

infinite [in'fənit] *adj* (very great: variety, patience) ばく大な bakúdai na; (without limits: universe) 無限の mugén no

infinitive [infin'ətiv] *n* (LING) 不定詞 futéishi

infinity [infin'əti:] *n* (infinite number) 無限大 mugéndai; (infinite point) 無限 mugén

infirm [infə:rm'] *adj* (weak) 虚弱な kyojáku na; (ill) 病弱な byōjaku na

infirmary [infə:r'mə:ri:] *n* (hospital) 病院 byōin

infirmity [infə:r'miti:] *n* (weakness) 虚弱さ kyojákusa; (being ill) 病弱さ byōjakusa; (specific illness) 病気 byōki

inflamed [infleimd'] *adj* (tongue, appendix) 炎症を起した eńshō no okóshità

inflammable [inflæm'əbəl] *adj* (fabric, chemical) 可燃性の kanénsei no, 燃えや

すい moéyasuî

inflammation [infləmei'ʃən] *n* (of throat, appendix etc) 炎症 eńshoó

inflatable [inflei'təbəl] *adj* (life jacket, dinghy, doll) 膨らます事のできる fukúramasu kotó no dekírù

inflate [infleit'] *vt* (tire, balloon) 膨らます fukúramasù; (price) つり上げる tsurí-agerù

inflation [inflei'ʃən] *n* (ECON) インフレ ińfure

inflationary [inflei'ʃəneːri:] *adj* (spiral) インフレの ińfure no; (demand) インフレを引起こす ińfure wò hikíokosù

inflexible [inflek'səbəl] *adj* (rule, timetable) 融通が利かない yúzū ga kikánai; (person) 譲らない yuzúranaî

inflict [inflikt'] *vt*: **to inflict something on someone** (damage, suffering) ...に...を加える ...ni ...wo kuwáerù

influence [in'flu:əns] *n* (power) 実力 jitsúryoku; (effect) 影響 eíkyō
♦*vt* (person, situation, choice etc) 左右する sáyū suru
under the influence of alcohol 酒に酔って saké ni yottè

influential [influ:en'tʃəl] *adj* (politician, critic) 有力な yúryoku na

influenza [influ:en'zə] *n* (MED) 流感 ryúkan

influx [in'flʌks] *n* (of refugees, funds) 流入 ryúnyū

inform [infɔːrm'] *vt*: **to inform someone of something** (tell) ...に...を知らせる ...ni ...wo shiráserù
♦*vi*: **to inform on someone** (to police, authorities) ...を密告する ...wo mikkóku suru

informal [infɔːr'məl] *adj* (manner, discussion, party) 寛いだ kutsúroidà; (clothes) 普段の fúdan no; (unofficial: visit, meeting) 非公式の hikóshiki no

informality [infɔːrmæl'iti:] *n* (of manner, party etc) 寛いだ雰囲気 kutsúroida fuń-iki

informant [infɔːr'mənt] *n* (source) 情報提供者 jóhōteikyòsha, インフォーマント ińfōmañto

information [infəːrmei'ʃən] *n* 情報 jóhō
a piece of information 1つの情報 hitótsù no jóhō

information office *n* 案内所 ańnaijo

informative [infɔːr'mətiv] *adj* (report, comment) 有益な yúeki na

informer [infɔːr'məːr] *n* (*also:* **police informer**) 密告者 mikkókusha, スパイ supáî

infra-red [in'frəred] *adj* (rays, light) 赤外線の sekígaisen no

infrastructure [in'frəstrʌk'tʃəːr] *n* (of system etc) 下部構造 kabúkōzō, インフラストラクチャー ińfurasutorakùchā

infrequent [infriː'kwint] *adj* (visits) 間遠な madó na; (buses) 本数の少ない hoń-sū nò sukúnaî

infringe [infrindʒ'] *vt* (law) 破る yabúrù
♦*vi*: **to infringe on** (rights) ...を侵す ...wo okásù

infringement [infrindʒ'mənt] *n* (of law) 違反 ihán; (of rights) 侵害 shińgai

infuriating [infju:'ri:eitiŋ] *adj* (habit, noise) いらいらさせる íraira saséru

ingenious [indʒi:n'jəs] *adj* (idea, solution) 巧妙な kómyō na

ingenuity [indʒənu:'iti:] *n* (cleverness, skill) 才能 saínō

ingenuous [indʒen'ju:əs] *adj* (innocent, trusting) 無邪気な mújàki na

ingot [iŋ'gət] *n* (of gold, platinum) 延べ棒 nobébō, インゴット ińgotto

ingrained [ingreind'] *adj* (habit, belief) 根深い nebúkaî

ingratiate [ingrei'ʃi:eit] *vt*: **to ingratiate oneself with** ...に取入る ...ni toríiru

ingratitude [ingræt'ətuːd] *n* (of beneficiary, heir) 恩知らず ońshiràzu

ingredient [ingriː'diːənt] *n* (of cake) 材料 zaíryō; (of situation) 要素 yóso

inhabit [inhæb'it] *vt* (town, country) ...に住む ...ni súmù

inhabitant [inhæb'ətənt] *n* (of town, street, house, country) 住民 júmin

inhale [inheil'] *vt* (breathe in: smoke, gas etc) 吸込む suíkomù
♦*vi* (breathe in) 息を吸う íkì wo suu; (when smoking) 煙を吸込む kemúri wò

suíkomù

inherent [inhe:r'ent] *adj*: **inherent in**
...に固有の ...ni koyú no

inherit [inhe:r'it] *vt* (property, money)
相続する sōzoku suru; (characteristic)
遺伝で受継ぐ idén de ukétsugù

inheritance [inhe:r'itəns] *n* (property,
money etc) 相続財産 sōzoku zaisàn;
(characteristics etc) 遺伝 idén

inhibit [inhib'it] *vt* (growth: *also*
PSYCH) 抑制 yokúsei

inhibited [inhib'itid] *adj* (PSYCH) 抑制
の多い yokúsei no ói

inhibition [inibiʃ'ən] *n* 抑制 yokúsei

inhospitable [inha:spit'əbəl] *adj* (person) もてなしの悪い moténashi nò waru-
i; (place, climate) 住みにくい sumínikuì

inhuman [inhju:'mən] *adj* (behavior) 残
忍な zańnin na; (appearance) 非人間的な
hiníngenteki na

inimitable [inim'itəbəl] *adj* (tone, style)
まねのできない mané no dekinài

iniquity [inik'witi:] *n* (wickedness) 悪á-
kù; (injustice) 不正 fuséi

initial [iniʃ'əl] *adj* (stage, reaction) 最初
の saísho no
♦*n* (letter) 頭文字 kashíramojì
♦*vt* (document) ...に頭文字で署名する
...ni kashíramojì de shoméi surù

initials [iniʃ'əlz] *npl* (of name) 頭文字 kashíramojì; (as signature) 頭文字の署名
kashíramojì no shoméi

initially [iniʃ'əli:] *adv* (at first) 最初は saísho wa; (first) まず最初に mázù saísho ni

initiate [iniʃ'i:it] *vt* (begin: talks, process) 始める hajímerù; (new member) 入
会させる nyúkai saseru
to initiate someone into a secret ...に
秘密を教える ...ni himítsu wò oshíerù
*to initiate proceedings against
someone* (LAW) ...を起訴する ...wo kisó
suru

initiation [iniʃi:ei'ʃən] *n* (beginning) 開始
kaíshi; (into organization etc) 入会式
nyúkaìshiki; (into secret etc) 伝授 déñju

initiative [iniʃ'i:ətiv] *n* (move) 企画 kikáku; (enterprise) 進取の気 shíñshu no kí
to take the initiative 先手を打つ señte

wò útsù

inject [indʒekt'] *vt* (drugs, poison) 注射す
る chúsha suru; (patient): *to inject
someone with something* ...に...を注射
する ...ni ...wo chúsha suru; (funds) つぎ
込む tsugíkomù

injection [indʒek'ʃən] *n* (of drugs, medicine) 注射 chúsha; (of funds) つぎ込む事
tsugíkomù kotó

injunction [indʒʌŋk'ʃən] *n* (LAW) 差止
め命令 sashítomemeìrei

injure [in'dʒə:r] *vt* (hurt: person, leg etc)
傷付ける kizútsukerù; (: feelings, reputation) 害する gaí surù

injured [in'dʒə:rd] *adj* (person, arm) 傷付
いた kizútsuità; (feelings) 害された gaí-
saretà; (tone) 感情を害された kañjō wò
gaí saretà

injury [in'dʒə:ri:] *n* (wound) 傷 kizú, けが
kegá

injury time *n* (SPORT) 延長時間 eñchōjikàn ◇傷の手当てなどに使った分の延長
時間 kizú no teàte nádò ni tsukátta buñ
no eñchōjikàn

injustice [indʒʌs'tis] *n* (unfairness) 不公
平 fukóhei

ink [iŋk] *n* (in pen, printing) インク íñku

inkling [iŋk'liŋ] *n* (idea, clue) 薄々と気付
く事 usúusu tò kizúku kotð

inlaid [in'leid] *adj* (with gems, wood etc)
...をちりばめた ...wo chiríbametà

inland [in'lænd] *adj* (port, sea, waterway) 内陸の naíriku no
♦*adv* (travel) 内陸へ naíriku e

Inland Revenue (*BRIT*) *n* 国税庁 kokúzeichò

in-laws [in'lɔːz] *npl* 義理の親せき girí nò
shíñseki, 姻せき íñseki

inlet [in'let] *n* (GEO) 入江 irîe

inmate [in'meit] *n* (in prison) 受刑者 ju-
kéisha; (in asylum) 入院患者 nyúinkañja

inn [in] *n* 旅館 ryokán

innate [ineit'] *adj* (skill, quality, characteristic) 生来の seírai no

inner [in'ə:r] *adj* (office, courtyard) 内側
の uchígawa no; (calm, feelings) 内心の
naíshin no

inner city *n* インナーシティー íñnāshīti ◇スラム化した都心部を指す súramu-ka shita toshínbu wo sásù

inner tube n (of tire) チューブ chùbu

inning [in'iŋ] n (BASEBALL) イニング íníngu

innings [in'iŋz] n (CRICKET) イニング íníngu

innocence [in'əsəns] n (LAW) 無罪 múzài; (naivety: of child, person) 純真さ juńshinsa

innocent [in'əsənt] adj (not guilty: of crime etc) 無罪の múzài no, 潔白な keppáku na; (naive: child, person) 純真な juńshin na; (not involved: victim) 罪のない tsúmì no nái; (remark, question) 無邪気な mújàki na

innocuous [inɑːk'juːəs] adj (harmless) 無害の múgài no

innovation [inəvei'ʃən] n (change) 刷新 sasshín

innuendo [injuːen'dou] (pl **innuendoes**) n (insinuation) 当てこすり atékosuri

innumerable [inuː'məːrəbəl] adj (countless) 無数の musú no

inoculation [inɑːkjəlei'ʃən] n (MED) 接種 sesshú

inopportune [inɑːpəːrtuːn'] adj (event, moment) 都合の悪い tsugó no warùi

inordinately [inɔːr'dənitiː] adv (proud, long, large etc) 極度に kyokúdò ni

in-patient [in'peiʃənt] n (in hospital) 入院患者 nyúinkanja

input [in'put] n (information) 情報 jóhò; (resources etc) つぎ込む事 tsugíkomù kotó; (COMPUT) 入力 nyúryoku, インプット ínputtò

inquest [in'kwest] n (on someone's death) 検死審問 keńshishimòn

inquire [inkwaiə:r'] vi (ask) 尋ねる tazúnerù, 聞く kíkù
♦vt (ask) ...に尋ねる ...ni tazúnerù, ...に聞く ...ni kíkù

to inquire about (person, fact) ...について問い合せする ...ni tsúìte tofawase surù

inquire into vt fus (death, circumstances) 調べる shiráberù

inquiry [inkwaiə:r'iː] n (question) 質問 shitsúmon; (investigation) 調査 chósa

inquiry office (BRIT) n 案内所 ańnaijò

inquisitive [inkwiz'ətiv] adj (curious) せん索好きな seńsakuzuki na

inroads [in'roudz] npl: **to make inroads into** (savings, supplies) ...を消費する ...wo shóhi suru

ins abbr = **inches**

insane [insein'] adj (foolish, crazy) 気違い染みた kichígaijimità; (MED) 狂気の kyóki no

insanity [insæn'itiː] n (foolishness) 狂気のさた kyóki nò satá; (MED) 狂気 kyóki

insatiable [insei'ʃəbəl] adj (greed, appetite) 飽く事のない akú kotò no nái

inscription [inskrip'ʃən] n (on gravestone, memorial etc) 碑文 hibún; (in book) 献呈の言葉 keńtei no kotòba

inscrutable [inskruː'təbəl] adj (comment, expression) 不可解な fukákài na

insect [in'sekt] n 虫 mushi, 昆虫 końchū

insecticide [insek'tisaid] n 殺虫剤 satchúzài

insecure [insikjuːr'] adj (structure, lock, door: weak) 弱い yówài; (: unsafe) 安全でない ańzen de naì; (person) 自信のない jishín no naì

insecurity [insikjuːr'itiː] n (of structure, lock etc: weakness) 弱さ yówàsa; (: lack of safety) 安全でない事 ańzen de naì kotó; (of person) 自信欠如 jishínketsujò

insemination [inseminei'ʃən] n: **artificial insemination** (AGR, MED) 人工授精 jińkōjùsei

insensible [insen'səbəl] adj (unconscious) 意識を失った íshìki wo ushínattà

insensitive [insen'sətiv] adj (uncaring, indifferent) 思いやりのない omóiyarì no nái

inseparable [insep'əːrəbəl] adj (ideas, elements) 分離できない buńri dekinài; (friends) いつも一緒の ítsùmo isshó no

insert [insəːrt'] vt (between two things) ...の間に入れる ...no aídà ni irérù; (into something) 差込む sashíkomù, 挿入する sónyū suru

insertion [insəːr'ʃən] n (of needle, comb, peg etc) 差込む事 sashíkomù kotó, 挿入 sónyū

in-service [in'sə:r'vis] *adj* (training, course) 現職の geñshoku no

inshore [in'ɔ:r] *adj* (fishing, waters) 近海の kíñkai no
♦*adv* (be) 岸の近くに kishí no chikakù ni; (move) 岸の近くへ kishí no chikakù e

inside [in'said'] *n* (interior) 中 nákà, 内側 uchígawa
♦*adj* (interior) 中〔内側〕nákà〔uchígawa〕no
♦*adv* (go) 中〔内側〕へ nákà〔uchígawa〕e; (be) 中〔内側〕に nákà〔uchígawa〕ni
♦*prep* (of location) ...の中へ〔に〕...no nákà e(ni); (of time): *inside 10 minutes* 10分以内に juppún inài ni

inside forward *n* (SPORT) インサイドフォワード iñsaidofowàdo

inside information *n* 内部情報 naíbujōhò

inside lane *n* (AUT) 内側車線 uchígawashaseñ

inside out *adv* (be, turn) 裏返しで urágaèshi de; (know) すっかり sukkárì

insides [in'saidz] *npl* (*inf*: stomach) おなか onáka

insidious [insid'i:əs] *adj* (effect, power) 潜行的な señkōteki na

insight [in'sait] *n* (into situation, problem) 洞察 dōsatsu

insignia [insig'ni:ə] *npl* 記章 kishṓ

insignificant [insignif'ikənt] *adj* (extent, importance) ささいな sasái na

insincere [insinsi:r'] *adj* (smile, welcome) 偽りの itsúwarì no

insinuate [insin'ju:eit] *vt* (imply) 当てこする atékosurù

insipid [insip'id] *adj* (person, activity, color) 面白くない omóshirokunài; (food, drink) 風味のない fūmi no naí

insist [insist'] *vi* (maintain) 主張する shuchṓ suru, 言い張る iíharù
to insist on (demand) ...を要求する ...wo yōkyū suru
to insist that (demand) ...する様要求する ...surú yō yṓkyū suru; (claim) ...だと言い張る ...da to iíharù

insistence [insis'təns] *n* (determination) 強要 kyṓyō

insistent [insis'tənt] *adj* (determined: person) しつこい shitsúkoì; (continual: noise, action) 絶間ない taémanaì

insole [in'soul] *n* (of shoe) 敷皮 shikíkawa

insolence [in'sələns] *n* (rudeness) 横柄さ ōheisa

insolent [in'sələnt] *adj* (attitude, remark) 横柄な ōhei na

insoluble [insɑːl'jəbəl] *adj* (problem) 解決のできない kaíketsu nò dekínaì

insolvent [insɑːl'vənt] *adj* (bankrupt) 破産した hasán shita

insomnia [insɑːm'ni:ə] *n* 不眠症 fumíñshō

inspect [inspekt'] *vt* (examine: *gen*) 調べる shiráberù; (premises) 捜査する sṓsa suru; (equipment) 点検する teñken suru; (troops) 査閲する saétsu suru; (*BRIT*: ticket) 改札する kaísatsu suru

inspection [inspek'ʃən] *n* (examination: *gen*) 検査 keñsa; (of premises) 捜査 sṓsa; (of equipment) 点検 teñken; (of troops) 査閲 saétsu; (*BRIT*: of ticket) 改札 kaísatsu

inspector [inspek'tə:r] *n* (ADMIN) 検査官 keñsakàn; (*BRIT*: on buses, trains) 車掌 shashṓ; (: POLICE) 警部 keibu

inspiration [inspərei'ʃən] *n* (encouragement) 発憤 happún; (influence, source) 発憤させる happún saserù mono; (idea) 霊感 reíkan, インスピレーション iñsupirḕshon

inspire [inspaiə:r'] *vt* (workers, troops) 奮い立たせる furúitataserù; (confidence, hope etc) 持たせる motáserù

instability [instəbil'əti:] *n* (of place, person, situation) 不安定 fuáñtei

install [instɔ:l'] *vt* (machine) 取付ける torítsukerù; (official) 就任させる shúnin saserù

installation [instəlei'ʃən] *n* (of machine, equipment) 取付け torítsuke, 設置 sétchì; (plant: INDUSTRY) 工場施設 kōjōshisètsu, プラント puráñto; (: MIL) 基地 kichí

installment [instɔ:l'mənt] (*BRIT* **instalment**) *n* (of payment, story, TV

serial etc) 1回分 ikkáîbun
in installments (pay, receive) 分割払い
で bunkatsubarài de
instance [in'stəns] *n* (example) 例 réî
for instance 例えば tatôeba
in the first instance まず最初に mázù
saîsho ni
instant [in'stənt] *n* (moment) 瞬間 shuǹ-
kan
♦*adj* (reaction, success) 瞬間的な shuǹ-
kanteki na; (coffee, food) 即席の sokúseki no, インスタントの îǹsutanto no
instantaneous [instəntei'ni:əs] *adj*
(immediate) 即時の sokújì no
instantly [in'stəntli:] *adv* (immediately)
即時に sokújì ni
instead [insted'] *adv* (in place of) (そ
の) 代りに (sonó) kawári ni
instead of ...の代りに ...no kawári ni
instep [in'step] *n* (of foot) 足の甲 ashí no
kồ; (of shoe) 靴の甲 kutsú no kồ
instigate [in'stəgeit] *vt* (rebellion etc) 起
させる okósaserù; (talks etc) 始めさせる
hajímesaserù
instil(l) [instil'] *vt*: *to instil something
into* (confidence, fear etc) ...を...に吹込
む ...wo ...ni fukíkomù
instinct [in'stiŋkt] *n* 本能 hońnō
instinctive [instiŋk'tiv] *adj* (reaction,
feeling) 本能的な hońnōteki na
institute [in'stitu:t] *n* (for research,
teaching) 施設 shisétsu; (professional
body: of architects, planners etc) 協会
kyồkai
♦*vt* (system, rule, course of action) 設け
る mốkerù; (proceedings, inquiry) 始める
hajímerù
institution [institu:'ʃən] *n* (of system
etc) 開設 kaísetsu; (custom, tradition) 伝
統 deńtō; (organization: financial, religious, educational) 協会 kyồkai; (hospital, mental home) 施設 shisétsu
instruct [instrʌkt'] *vt*: *to instruct
someone in something* (teach) ...に...を
教える ...ni ...wo oshíerù
to instruct someone to do something
(order) ...する様に...に命令する ...surú yồ
...ni meírei suru

instruction [instrʌk'ʃən] *n* (teaching) 教
育 kyồiku
instructions [instrʌk'ʃənz] *npl* (orders)
命令 meírei
instructions (for use) 取扱い説明 toríatsukai setsúmei
instructive [instrʌk'tiv] *adj* (lesson,
response) 有益な yū́eki na
instructor [instrʌk'tə:r] *n* (teacher) 先
生 seńsei; (for skiing, driving etc) 指導者
shidồshà
instrument [in'strəmənt] *n* (tool) 道具
dồgu; (measuring device etc) 計器 keíki;
(MUS) 楽器 gakkí
instrumental [instrəmen'təl] *adj* (MUS)
器楽の kígàku no
to be instrumental in ...に大きな役割
を果す ...ni ồkina yakúwari wo hatasù
instrument panel *n* 計器盤 keíkiban
insubordination [insəbɔ:rdənei'ʃən] *n*
(disobedience) 不服従 fufúkujū̀
insufferable [insʌf'ə:rəbəl] *adj* (arrogance, laziness) 耐えがたい taégataì;
(person) 我慢のならない gámàn no naránaì
insufficient [insəfiʃ'ənt] *adj* (funds,
data, research) 不十分な fujūbùn na
insular [in'sələ:r] *adj* (outlook, person)
狭量な kyốryō na
insulate [in'səleit] *vt* (protect: person,
group) 孤立させる korítsu saserù;
(against cold: house, body) 断熱する dań-
netsu suru; (against sound) 防音にする
bồon ni suru; (against electricity) 絶縁す
る zetsúen suru
insulating tape [in'səleitiŋ-] *n* (ELEC)
絶縁テープ zetsúentēpu
insulation [insəlei'ʃən] *n* (of person,
group) 孤立させる事 korítsu saserù ko-
tồ; (against cold) 断熱材 dańnetsuzaì;
(against sound) 防音材 bồonzài; (against
electricity) 絶縁材 zetsúenzai
insulin [in'səlin] *n* (MED) インシュリン iń-
shurin
insult [*n* in'sʌlt *vb* insʌlt'] *n* (offence) 侮
辱 bujóku
♦*vt* (offend) 侮辱する bujóku suru
insulting [insʌl'tiŋ] *adj* (attitude, lan-

guage) 侮辱的な bujōkuteki na

insuperable [insu:'pərəbəl] *adj* (obstacle, problem) 乗越えられない noríkoerarenaí

insurance [inʃəːr'əns] *n* (on property, car, life etc) 保険 hokén
fire/ life insurance 火災〔生命〕保険 kasái〔seímei〕hokén

insurance agent *n* 保険代理店 hokéndairitèn

insurance policy *n* 保険証書 hokénshòsho

insure [inʃuːr'] *vt* (life, property): *to insure (against)* ...に (...の) 保険を掛ける ...ni (...no) hokén wò kakérù
to insure (oneself) against (disappointment, disaster) ...に備える ...ni sonáerù

insurrection [insərek'ʃən] *n* (uprising) 反乱 haǹran

intact [intæk't] *adj* (whole) 元のままの mótò no mamá no; (unharmed) 無傷の múkizu no

intake [in'teik] *n* (gen) 取込み toríkomi; (of food etc) 摂取 sésshù; (of air) 吸入 kyúnyū; (BRIT: SCOL): *an intake of 200 a year* 毎年の新入生は200人 maítoshi nò shifinyūsei wa nihyákunìn

intangible [intæn'dʒəbəl] *adj* (quality, idea, benefit) ばく然とした bakúzen to shita

integral [in'təgrəl] *adj* (feature, element) 不可欠な fukákètsu na

integrate [in'təgreit] *vt* (newcomer) 溶け込ませる tokékomaserù; (ideas, systems) 取入れる toríirerù
♦*vi* (groups, individuals) 溶け込む tokékomù

integrity [integ'riti:] *n* (morality: of person) 誠実さ seíjitsusa

intellect [in'təlekt] *n* (intelligence) 知性 chiséi; (cleverness) 知能 chinō

intellectual [intəlek'tʃuːəl] *adj* (activity, interest, pursuit) 知的な chitéki na
♦*n* (intelligent person) 知識人 chishíkijìn, インテリ iǹteri

intelligence [intel'idʒəns] *n* (cleverness, thinking power) 知能 chinō; (MIL etc) 情報 jōhō

intelligence service *n* 情報部 jōhōbu

intelligent [intel'idʒənt] *adj* (person) 知能の高い chinō no takaí; (decision) 利口な rikō na; (machine) インテリジェントの iǹterijèǹto no

intelligentsia [intelidʒen'tsi:ə] *n* 知識階級 chishíkikaìkyū, インテリ階級 iǹterikaíkyū

intelligible [intel'idʒəbəl] *adj* (clear, comprehensible) 分かりやすい wakáriyasuí

intend [intend'] *vt* (gift etc): *to intend something for* ...を...に上げようと思っている ...wo ...ni agéyò to omótte irù
to intend to do something (mean) ...する決心でいる ...suru kesshíǹ de irú; (plan) ...するつもりである ...suru tsumóri de arù

intended [inten'did] *adj* (effect, insult) 意図した ítò shita; (journey) 計画した keíkaku shita; (victim) ねらった nerátta

intense [intens'] *adj* (heat, effort, anger, joy) 猛烈な mōretsu na; (person) 情熱的な jōnetsuteki na

intensely [intens'li:] *adv* (extremely) 激しく hagéshikù

intensify [inten'səfai] *vt* (efforts, pressure) 増す másù

intensity [inten'siti:] *n* (of heat, anger, effort) 激しさ hagéshisa

intensive [inten'siv] *adj* (concentrated) 集中的な shūchūteki na

intensive care unit *n* (MED) 集中治療室 shūchūchiryòshitsu, ICU aishíyū

intent [intent'] *n* (intention) 意図 ítò; (LAW) 犯意 háñ-i
♦*adj* (absorbed): *intent (on)* (...しようとして) 余念がない (...shíyò to shite) yonén ga naî; (attentive) 夢中な muchú na
to all intents and purposes 事実上 jijítsujō
to be intent on doing something (determined) ...しようとして余念がない ...shíyò to shite yonén ga naî

intention [inten'tʃən] *n* (purpose) 目的 mokúteki; (plan) 意図 ítò

intentional [inten't∫ənəl] adj (deliber- ate) 意図的な ítóteki na

intentionally [inten't∫ənəli:] adv (delib- erately) 意図的に ítóteki ni, わざと wázà to

intently [intent'li:] adv (listen, watch) 熱 心に nesshín ni

inter [intər'] vt (bury) 埋葬する maísō suru

interact [intə:rækt'] vi: **to interact (with)** (people, things, ideas) (...と) 相 互に反応し合う (...to) sōgo ni hañnō shiaù

interaction [intə:ræk'∫ən] n 相互反応 sōgohañnō

intercede [intə:rsi:d'] vi: **to intercede (with)** (...に) 取りなしをする (...ni) to- rínashi wo surù

intercept [intə:rsept'] vt (person, car) 途 中で捕まえる tochū de tsukamaerù; (message) 傍受する bōju suru

interchange [in'tə:rt∫eindʒ] n (ex- change) 交換 kōkan; (on motorway) イン ターチェンジ íñtāchieñji

interchangeable [intə:rtʃein'dʒəbəl] adj (terms, ideas, things) 置換えられる okí- kaerarerù

intercom [in'tə:rkɑ:m] n (in office etc) インターホーン íñtāhōn

intercourse [in'tə:rkɔ:rs] n (also: **sexual intercourse**) 性交 seíkō

interest [in'trist] n (in subject, idea, per- son etc) 興味 kyōmi; (pastime, hobby) 趣 味 shúmì; (advantage, profit) 利益 rfèki; (COMM: in company) 株 kábù; (: sum of money) 利息 risóku

◆vt (subj: work, subject, idea etc) ...の興 味をそそる ...no kyōmi wo sosórù

to be interested in ...に興味がある ...ni kyōmi ga árù

interesting [in'tristiŋ] adj (idea, place, person) 面白い omóshiroì

interest rate n 利率 rirítsu

interface [in'tə:rfeis] n (COMPUT) イン ターフェース íñtāfèsu

interfere [intə:rfi:r'] vi: **to interfere in** (quarrel, other people's business) ...に干 渉する ...ni kañshō suru

to interfere with (object) ...をいじる

...wo ijírù; (plans, career, duty, decision) ...を邪魔する ...wo jamá suru

interference [intə:rfi:r'əns] n (in someone's affairs etc) 干渉 kañshō; (RADIO, TV) 混信 koñshin

interim [in'tə:rim] adj (agreement, gov- ernment) 暫定的な zañteiteki na

◆n: **in the interim** (meanwhile) その間 sonó aìda

interior [inti:'ri:ər] n (of building, car, box etc) 内部 náibu; (of country) 内陸 naí- riku

◆adj (door, window, room etc) 内部の náibu no; (minister, department) 内務の náimu no

interior designer n インテリアデザイ ナー íñteriadezaìnā

interjection [intə:rdʒek'∫ən] n (interrup- tion) 野次 yájì; (LING) 感嘆詞 kañtañshi

interlock [in'tə:rlɑ:k] vi かみ合う kamí- aù

interloper [intə:rlou'pər] n (in town, meeting etc) ちん入者 chíñnyūsha

interlude [in'tə:rlu:d] n (break) 休憩 kyūkei; (THEATER) 休憩時間 kyūkeiji- kàn

intermarry [intə:rmær'i:] vi 交婚する kōkon suru

intermediary [intə:rmi:'di:e:ri:] n 仲介 者 chūkaìsha

intermediate [intə:rmi:'di:it] adj (stage, student) 中間の chúkan no

interminable [intə:r'mənəbəl] adj (proc- ess, delay) 果てし無い hatéshinaì

intermission [intə:rmiʃ'ən] n (pause) 休 止 kyūshi; (THEATER, CINEMA) 休憩 時間 kyūkeijikàn

intermittent [intə:rmit'ənt] adj (noise, publication etc) 断続的な dañzokuteki na

intern [in'tə:rn] vt (imprison) 拘置する kōchi suru

◆n (US: houseman) 研修医 keñshūī

internal [intə:r'nəl] adj (layout, struc- ture, memo etc) 内部の náibu no; (pipes etc) 埋め込みの umékomi no; (bleeding, injury) 体内の táinai no; (security, poli- tics) 国内の kokúnài no

internally [intə:r'nəli:] *adv*:「*not to be taken internally*」内服外用薬 naffuku-gaiyòyaku

Internal Revenue Service (*US*) *n* 国税庁 kokúzeichò

international [intə:rnæʃ'ənəl] *adj* (trade, agreement etc) 国際的な kokúsaiteki na, 国際... kokúsai...
♦*n* (*BRIT*: SPORT: match) 国際試合 kokúsaijiài

interplay [in'tə:rplei] *n*: *interplay (of/between)* (...の) 相互反応 (...no) sōgohañnō

interpret [intə:r'prit] *vt* (explain, understand) 解釈する kaíshaku suru; (translate) 通訳する tsúyaku suru
♦*vi* (translate) 通訳する tsúyaku suru

interpretation [intə:rpritei'ʃən] *n* (explanation) 解釈 kaíshaku; (translation) 通訳 tsúyaku

interpreter [intə:r'pritə:r] *n* (translator) 通訳 (者) tsúyaku(sha)

interrelated [intə:rilei'tid] *adj* (causes, factors etc) 相互関係のある sōgokankèi no aru

interrogate [inte:r'əgeit] *vt* (question: witness, prisoner, suspect) 尋問する jiñmon suru

interrogation [inte:rəgei'ʃən] *n* (of witness, prisoner etc) 尋問 jiñmon

interrogative [intərɑ:g'ətiv] *adj* (LING) 疑問の gímòn no

interrupt [intərʌpt'] *vt* (speaker) ...の話に割込む ...no hanáshi nì waríkomù; (activity) 邪魔する jamá suru
♦*vi* (during someone's conversation etc) 話に割込む hanáshi ni waríkomù; (during activity) 邪魔する jamá suru

interruption [intərʌp'ʃən] *n* (act) 邪魔する事 jamá suru kotò; (instance) 邪魔jamá

intersect [intə:rsekt'] *vi* (roads) 交差する kōsa suru

intersection [intə:rsek'ʃən] *n* (of roads) 交差点 kōsatèn

intersperse [intə:rspə:rs'] *vt*: *to intersperse with* ...を所々に入れる ...wo tokórodokòro ni irérù

intertwine [intə:rtwain'] *vi* 絡み合う karámiaù

interval [in'tə:rvəl] *n* (break, pause) 間隔 kañkaku; (*BRIT*: SCOL: also THEATER, SPORT) 休憩時間 kyúkeijikàn
at intervals (periodically) 時々 tokídoki

intervene [intə:rvi:n'] *vi* (person: in situation: interfere) 介入する kaínyu suru; (: : to help) 仲裁に入る chúsai ni hairù; (: in speech) 割込む waríkomù; (event) 間に起る aída ni okorù; (time) 経つ tátsu

intervention [intə:rven'tʃən] *n* (of person: interference) 介入 kaínyu; (help) 仲裁 chúsai

interview [in'tə:rvju:] *n* (for job etc) 面接 meñsetsu; (RADIO, TV etc) インタビュー íñtabyū
♦*vt* (for job etc) ...と面接する ...to meñsetsu suru; (RADIO, TV etc) ...にインタビューする ...ni íñtabyū suru

interviewer [in'tə:rvju:ə:r] *n* (of candidate, job applicant) 面接者 meñsetsushà; (RADIO, TV etc) インタビューア íñtabyūa

intestine [intes'tin] *n* 腸 chō

intimacy [in'təməsi:] *n* (closeness) 親しみ shitáshimi

intimate [*adj* in'təmit *vb* in'təmeit] *adj* (friendship, relationship) 親しい shitáshiì; (detail) 知られざる shirárezarù; (restaurant, dinner, atmosphere) こじんまりした kojiñmarì shita; (knowledge) 詳しい kuwáshiì
♦*vt* (announce) ほのめかす honómekasù

intimidate [intim'ideit] *vt* (frighten) 脅す odósu

intimidation [intimidei'ʃən] *n* 脅し odóshi

KEYWORD

---

into [in'tu:] *prep* **1** (indicating motion or direction) ...の中に〔へ〕...no nàka ni(e)
come into the house/garden 家〔庭〕に入って来て下さい ié(niwà)nì haítte kité kudasaì
go into town 町に出掛ける machí ni dekakerù

he got into the car 彼は車に乗った kárè wa kurúma ni nottá

throw it into the fire 火の中へ捨てて下さい hí no nakâ e sutéte kudasaî

research into cancer がんの研究 gáñ no keñkyū

he worked late into the night 彼は夜遅くまで働いた kárè wa yórù osóku madè hataráìta

the car bumped into the wall 車は塀にぶつかった kurúma wà heî nî butsúkattà

she poured tea into the cup 彼女は紅茶をカップについだ kánòjo wa kôcha wò káppù ni tsuîdà

2 (indicating change of condition, result): *she burst into tears* 彼女は急に泣き出した kánòjo wa kyū̂ nî nakídashîta

he was shocked into silence 彼はショックで物も言えなかった kárè wa shókkù de monô mò iênakattâ

it broke into pieces ばらばらに割れた barábara nî warétà

she translated into French 彼女はフランス語に訳した kánòjo wa furánsugo nî yakúshità

they got into trouble 彼らは問題を起した kárèra wa moñdai wò okóshità

---

intolerable [intə:l'ə:rəbəl] *adj* (extent, quality) 我慢できない gámàn dekínaî

intolerance [intə:l'ə:rəns] *n* (bigotry, prejudice) 偏狭さ heñkyōsa

intolerant [intə:l'ə:rənt] *adj*: **intolerant (of)** (...に対して) 偏狭な (...ni tâîshite) heñkyō na

intonation [intounei'ʃən] *n* (of voice, speech) 抑揚 yokúyō, イントネーション iñtonêshon

intoxicated [intɑ:k'sikeitid] *adj* (drunk) 酔っ払った yoppáràtta

intoxication [intɑ:ksikei'ʃən] *n* 泥酔 deísui

intractable [intræk'təbəl] *adj* (child, problem) 手に負えない té ni oenâi

intransigent [intræn'sidʒənt] *adj* (attitude) 頑固な gañko na

intransitive [intræn'sətiv] *adj* (LING): **intransitive verb** 自動詞 jidôshì

intravenous [intrəvi:'nəs] *adj* (injection, drip) 静脈内の jōmyakunâi no

in-tray [in'trei] *n* (in office) 着信のトレー chakúshin nò torê

intrepid [intrep'id] *adj* (adventurer, explorer) 勇敢な yūkan na

intricate [in'trəkit] *adj* (pattern, design) 複雑な fukúzatsu na

intrigue [intri:g'] *n* (plotting) 策略 sakúryàku

♦*vt* (fascinate) ...の好奇心をそそる ...no kôkishin wò sosôrù

intriguing [intri:'giŋ] *adj* (fascinating) 面白い omóshiroî

intrinsic [intrin'sik] *adj* (quality, nature) 本質的な hoñshitsuteki na

introduce [intrədu:s'] *vt* (new idea, measure etc) 導入する dōnyū suru; (speaker, TV show etc) 紹介する shôkai suru

to introduce someone (to someone) (...に) ...を紹介する (...ni) ...wo shôkai suru

to introduce someone to (pastime, technique) ...に...を初めて経験させる ...ni ...wo hajímète keñken saserù

introduction [intrədʌk'ʃən] *n* (of new idea, measure etc) 導入 dōnyū; (of person) 紹介 shôkai; (to new experience) 初めて経験させる事 hajímète keñken saserù kotô; (to book) 前書 maêgaki

introductory [intrədʌk'tə:ri:] *adj* (lesson) 導入の dōnyū no; (offer) 初回の shokái no

introspective [intrəspek'tiv] *adj* (person, mood) 内省的な naîseiteki na

introvert [in'trəvə:rt] *n* 内向性の人 naîkosei no hitô

♦*adj* (*also*: **introverted**: behavior, child etc) 内向性の naîkosei no

intrude [intru:d'] *vi* (person) 邪魔する jamá suru

to intrude on (conversation, grief, party etc) ...のところを邪魔する ...no tokôro wò jamá suru

intruder [intru:'də:r] *n* (into home, camp) 侵入者 shiñnyūshà

intrusion [intru:'ʒən] *n* (of person, outside influences) 邪魔 jamá

intuition [intu:iʃ'ən] *n* (feeling, hunch) 直感 chokkán

intuitive [intu:'ətiv] *adj* (instinctive) 直感的な chokkánteki na

inundate [in'ʌndeit] *vt*: **to inundate with** (calls, letters etc) ...が殺到する ...ga sattō suru

invade [inveid'] *vt* (MIL) ...を侵略する ...wo shińryaku suru

invalid [*n* in'vəlid *adj* invæ'lid] *n* (MED: disabled person) 身障者 shińshōsha; (: sick and weak person) 病弱な人 byōjaku na hitō
♦*adj* (not valid) 無効の mukō no

invaluable [invæl'ju:əbəl] *adj* (person, thing) 貴重な kichō na

invariable [inve:r'i:əbəl] *adj* 変らない kawáranai, 不変の fuhén no

invariably [inve:r'i:əbli:] *adv* 必ず kanárazù

invasion [invei'ʒən] *n* (MIL) 侵略 shińryaku

invent [invent'] *vt* (machine, game, phrase etc) 発明する hatsúmei suru; (fabricate: lie, excuse) でっち上げる detchíagerù

invention [inven'tʃən] *n* (machine, system) 発明品 hatsúmeihin; (untrue story) 作り話 tsukúribanàshi; (act of inventing: machine, system) 発明 hatsúmei

inventor [inven'tər] *n* (of machines, systems) 発明家 hatsúmeika

inventory [in'vəntɔ:ri:] *n* (of house, ship etc) 物品目録 buppínmokùroku

inverse [invə:rs'] *adj* (relationship) 逆の gyakú no

invert [in'və:rt] *vt* (turn upside down) 逆さにする sakása ni surù

invertebrate [invə:r'təbrit] *n* 無せきつい動物 musékitsuidòbutsu

inverted commas [invə:r'tid-] (BRIT) *npl* 引用符 ińyōfù

invest [invest'] *vt* (money) 投資する tōshi suru; (fig: time, energy) つぎ込む tsugíkomù
♦*vi*: **invest in** (COMM) ...に投資する

...ni tōshi suru; (fig: something useful) 購入する kōnyū suru

investigate [inves'təgeit] *vt* (accident, crime, person) 取調べる toríshiraberù, 捜査する sōsa suru

investigation [inves'təgeiʃən] *n* 取調べ toríshirabe, 捜査 sōsa

investigator [inves'təgeitə:r] *n* (of events, situations, people) 捜査官 sōsakàn

investiture [inves'titʃə:r] *n* (of chancellor) 就任式 shúniñshiki; (of prince) たい冠式 taíkañshiki

investment [invest'mənt] *n* (activity) 投資額 tōshigàku; (amount of money) 投資額 tōshigàku

investor [inves'tə:r] *n* (COMM) 投資者 tōshishà

inveterate [invet'ə:rit] *adj* (liar, cheat etc) 常習的な jōshūteki na

invidious [invid'i:əs] *adj* (task, job: unpleasant) 憎まれ役の nikúmareyàku no; (comparison, decision: unfair) 不公平な fukōhei na

invigilator [invidʒ'əleitə:r] (BRIT) *n* (in exam) 試験監督 shikéñkañtoku

invigorating [invig'ə:reitiŋ] *adj* (air, breeze etc) さわやかな sawáyàka na; (experience etc) 元気が出る様な geñki ga deru yō na

invincible [invin'səbəl] *adj* (army, team: unbeatable) 無敵の mútèki no

invisible [inviz'əbəl] *adj* 目に見えない mé ni mienài

invitation [invitei'ʃən] *n* (to party, meal, meeting etc) 招待 shōtai; (written card, paper) 招待状 shōtaijō

invite [in'vait] *vt* (to party, meal, meeting etc) 招く manékù, 招待する shōtai suru; (encourage: discussion, criticism) 求める motómerù
to invite someone to do ...に...するよう求める ...ni ...surú yō motómerù

inviting [invai'tiŋ] *adj* (attractive, desirable) 魅力的な miryókuteki na

invoice [in'vɔis] *n* (COMM) 請求書 seíkyùsho
♦*vt* ...に請求書を送る ...ni seíkyùsho wo

okúrù

invoke [invouk'] *vt* (law, principle) ...に訴える ...ni uttáerù

involuntary [inva:l'ənte:ri:] *adj* (action, reflex etc) 反射的な hanshateki na

involve [inva:lv'] *vt* (person, thing: include, use) 伴う tomónaù, 必要とする hitsuyō to surù; (: concern, affect) ...に関係する ...ni kankei suru

  to involve someone (in something) (...に) ...を巻込む (...ni) ...wo makíkomù

involved [inva:lvd'] *adj* (complicated) 複雑な fukúzatsu na

  to be involved in (take part in activity etc) ...にかかわる ...ni kakáwarù; (be engrossed) ...に夢中になっている ...ni muchū ni nattè irú

involvement [inva:lv'mənt] *n* (participation) 参加 sańka; (concern, enthusiasm) 感情的かかわり合い kanjōteki nà kakáwariaì

inward [in'wə:rd] *adj* (thought, feeling) 内心の naíshin no; (movement) 中の方への nákà no hố e no

inward(s) [in'wə:rd(z)] *adv* (move, face) 中の方へ nákà no hố e

I/O [ai'ou'] *abbr* (COMPUT: = input/output) 入出力 nyūshutsuryòku

iodine [ai'ədain] *n* (chemical element) ヨウ素 yốso, ヨード yồdo; (disinfectant) ヨードチンキ yốdochiǹki

ion [ai'ən] *n* イオン fòn

iota [aiou'tə] *n*: *not one/an iota* 少しも ...ない sukóshì mo ...naî

IOU [aioujuː'] *n abbr* (= I owe you) 借用証 shakúyồshō

IQ [aikjuː'] *n abbr* (= intelligence quotient) 知能指数 chinốshisù, IQ aikyū

IRA [aia:rei'] *n abbr* (= Irish Republican Army) アイルランド共和国軍 aírurando kyōwakakugùn

Iran [iræn'] *n* イラン fràn

Iranian [irei'niːən] *adj* イランの fràn no

  ♦*n* イラン人 iránjìn

Iraq [iræk'] *n* イラク fràku

Iraqi [ira:k'iː] *adj* イラクの fràku no

  ♦*n* イラク人 irákujìn

irascible [iræs'əbəl] *adj* 怒りっぽい okó-

rippoî

irate [aireit'] *adj* 怒っている okótte irù

Ireland [aiə:r'lənd] *n* アイルランド aírurando

iris [ai'ris] (*pl* **irises**) *n* (ANAT) こう彩 kốsai; (BOT) アヤメ ayáme, アイリス áirisu

Irish [ai'riʃ] *adj* アイルランドの aírurando no

  ♦*npl*: *the Irish* アイルランド人 aírurandojìn ◇総称 sōshō

Irishman/woman [ai'riʃmən/wumən] (*pl* **Irishmen/women**) *n* アイルランド人男性〔女性〕aírurandojìn dańsei〔joséi〕

Irish Sea *n*: *the Irish Sea* アイリッシュ海 aírisshukài

irksome [ə:rk'səm] *adj* いらいらさせる í-ràira saséru

iron [ai'ə:rn] *n* (metal) 鉄 tetsú; (for clothes) アイロン aíron

  ♦*cpd* (bar, railings) 鉄の tetsú no; (will, discipline etc) 鉄の様な tetsú no yỗ na

  ♦*vt* (clothes) ...にアイロンを掛ける ...ni aíron wò kakérù

Iron Curtain *n*: *the Iron Curtain* 鉄のカーテン tetsú no kàten

ironic(al) [aira:n'ik(əl)] *adj* (remark, gesture, situation) 皮肉な hínìku na

ironing [ai'ə:rniŋ] *n* (activity) アイロン掛け aíron kàke; (clothes) アイロンを掛けるべき衣類 aíron wò kakérubeki irùi

ironing board *n* アイロン台 aírondai

ironmonger [ai'ə:rnmʌŋgə:r] (BRIT) *n* 金物屋 kanámonoya ◇人を指す hitố wò sásù

ironmonger's (shop) [ai'ə:rnmʌŋgə:rz-] *n* 金物屋 kanámonoya ◇店を指す mise wò sásù

iron out *vt* (fig: problems) 打開する dakái suru

irony [ai'rəni:] *n* 皮肉 hínìku

irrational [iræʃ'ənəl] *adj* (feelings, behavior) 不合理な fugỗri na

irreconcilable [irek'ənsailəbəl] *adj* (ideas, views) 両立しない ryőritsu shinaì; (disagreement) 調和不可能な chốwafukanồ na

irrefutable [irifjuː'təbəl] *adj* (fact) 否め

られない inámerarenaî; (argument) 反ば
くできない hañbaku dekínai

irregular [ireg'jələr] *adj* (surface) 凸凹
の dekóboko no; (pattern, action, event
etc) 不規則な fukísoku na; (not acceptable: behavior) 良くない yókùnai; (verb,
noun, adjective) 不規則変化の fukísoku-
heñka no

irregularity [iregjələr'iti:] *n* (of surface) 凸凹 dekóboko; (of pattern, action
etc) 不規則 fukísoku; (instance of behavior) 良くない行為 yókunai kôi

irrelevant [irel'əvənt] *adj* (fact, information) 関係のない kañkei no naî

irreparable [irep'ə:rəbəl] *adj* (harm,
damage etc) 取返しの付かない toríkae-
shi no tsukanâi

irreplaceable [iriplei'səbəl] *adj* 掛替え
のない kakégae no naî

irrepressible [iripres'əbəl] *adj* 陽気な
yôki na

irresistible [irizis'təbəl] *adj* (force) 抵抗
できない teíkô dekínai; (urge, desire) 抑
えきれない osáekirenaî; (person, thing)
とても魅惑的な totémô miwákuteki na

irresolute [irez'əlu:t] *adj* 決断力のない
ketsúdanryòku no naî

irrespective [irispek'tiv]: *irrespective
of prep* …と関係なく …to kañkei nakù

irresponsible [irispɑn'səbəl] *adj* (person, action) 無責任な muségkinin na

irreverent [irev'ə:rənt] *adj* 不敬な fukéi
na

irrevocable [irev'əkəbəl] *adj* (action,
decision) 変更できない heñkô dekínai

irrigate [ir'igeit] *vt* (AGR) かんがいする
kañgai suru

irrigation [irigei'ʃən] *n* (AGR) かんがい
kañgai

irritable [ir'itəbəl] *adj* 怒りっぽい okó-
rippoî

irritate [ir'əteit] *vt* (annoy) いらいらさ
せる írâira saséru; (MED) 刺激する shigéki suru

irritating [ir'əteitiŋ] *adj* (person, sound
etc) いらいらさせる íraira saséru

irritation [iritei'ʃən] *n* (feeling of annoyance) いら立ち irádachi; (MED) 刺激 shi-

géki; (annoying thing) いら立ちの元 irádachi no motò

IRS [aiɑːres'] (*US*) *n abbr* = **Internal
Revenue Service**

is [iz] *vb see* **be**

Islam [iz'lɑːm] *n* イスラム教 isúramukyō

Islamic [izlɑːm'ic] *adj* イスラム教の isúramukyō no

island [ai'lənd] *n* (GEO) 島 shimá

islander [ai'ləndəːr] *n* 島の住民 shimá no
júmin

isle [ail] *n* (GEO) 島 shimá

isn't [iz'ənt] = **is not**

isolate [ai'sətout] *vt* (physically, socially:
set apart) 孤立させる korítsu saserù;
(substance) 分離する buñri suru; (sick
person, animal) 隔離する kakúri suru

isolated [ai'səleitid] *adj* (place) へんぴな
heñpi na; (person) 孤立した korítsu shita; (incident) 単独の tañdoku no

isolation [aisəlei'ʃən] *n* 孤立 korítsu

isotope [ai'sətoup] *n* (PHYSICS) 同位体
dôitai, アイソトープ aísotôpu

Israel [iz'reiəl] *n* イスラエル isúraeru

Israeli [izrei'li:] *adj* イスラエルの isúraeru
ru no
♦*n* イスラエル人 isúraerujîn

issue [iʃ'u:] *n* (problem, subject, most
important part) 問題 moñdai; (of newspaper, magazine etc) 号 gô; (of book) 版
hañ; (of stamp) 発行部数 hakkôbûsu
♦*vt* (statement) 発表する happyô suru;
(rations, equipment, documents) 配給す
る kaíkyu suru

at issue 問題は〔の〕moñdai wa〔no〕

to take issue with someone (over)
(…について) …と争う (…ni tsúite) …to
arásoù

isthmus [is'məs] *n* (GEO) 半島 hañtō

KEYWORD

it [it] *pron* **1** (specific: subject) それは
〔が〕soré wà〔gà〕; (: direct object) それ
を soré wò; (: indirect object) それに soré
nî 通常日本語では表現しない tsújō ni-
hongo de wa hyōgen shínai

where's my book? - it's on the table
私の本はどこですか-テーブルにあります

watákushi no hoñ wa dókò desu ká - tébùru ni arímàsù

I can't find it 見当りません miátarimaseñ

give it to me それを私に渡して下さい soré wò watákushi nì watáshite kudasaí

about/from/in/of/to it それについて〔から、の中に、の、の方へ〕 soré ni tsuíte〔kárá, no nákà ni, nó, no hô è〕

I spoke to him about it その件について私は彼に話しました sono keñ ni tsuíte watákushi wa kárè ni hanáshimashìta

what did you learn from it? その事からあなたは何を学びましたか sonó kotò kara anátà wa nánì wo manábimashìta ká

what role did you play in it? その件に関してあなたはどんな役割をしましたか sonó keñ ni kañ shite anátà wa doñna yakùwari wo shimáshìta ká

I'm proud of it それを誇りに思っています soré wò hokóri nì omótte imasù

did you go to it? (party, concert etc) 行きましたか ikímashìta ká

2 (impersonal): *it's raining* 雨が降っている ámè ga futté irù

it's cold today 今日は寒い kyố wà samúì

it's Friday tomorrow 明日は金曜日です asú wà kiñ-yòbi desu

it's 6 o'clock/the 10th of August 6時〔8月10日〕です rokújì〔hachígàtsu tố-kà〕desu

how far is it? - it's 10 miles/2 hours on the train そこまでどのぐらいありますか-10マイルあります〔列車で2時間です〕sokó madè donó gurai arimasù ká - júmaìru arímàsù〔ressha dè nijíkàn desu〕

who is it? - it's me どなたですか-私です dónàta desu ká - watákushi desù

Italian [itæl'jən] *adj* イタリアの itária no; (LING) イタリア語の itáriago no
♦*n* (person) イタリア人 itáriajìn; (LING) イタリア語 itáriago

italics [itæl'iks] *npl* (TYP) 斜体文字 shatáimòji, イタリック体 itárikkutai

Italy [it'əli:] *n* イタリア itária

itch [itʃ] *n* (irritation) かゆみ kayúmi
♦*vi* (person) かゆがる kayúgarù; (part of body) かゆい kayúì
to itch to do something …をしたくてむずむずしている …wo shitákutè múzùmuzu shité irù

itchy [itʃ'i:] *adj* (person) かゆがっている kayúgatte irù; (skin etc) かゆい kayúì

it'd [it'əd] = **it would; it had**

item [ai'təm] *n* (one thing: of list, collection) 品目 hiñmoku; (on agenda) 項目 kốmoku; (*also*: **news item**) 記事 kíji

itemize [ai'təmaiz] *vt* (list) 明細に書く meísai ni kakù, リストアップする risútoappù suru

itinerant [aitin'ə:rənt] *adj* (laborer, salesman, priest etc) 巡回する juñkai suru

itinerary [aitin'əre:ri:] *n* 旅程 ryotéi

it'll [it'əl] = **it will; it shall**

its [its] *adj* それ〔あれ〕の soré〔aré〕no

it's [its] = **it is; it has**

itself [itself'] *pron* それ〔あれ〕自身 soré〔aré〕jishiñ

ITV [ait:vi:'] *n abbr* (BRIT: = *Independent Television*) 民間テレビ放送 miñkan terebi hồsō

IUD [aiju:di:'] *n abbr* (= *intra-uterine device*) 子宮内避妊具 shikyűnaihininñgu, IUD aiyúdī

I've [aiv] = **I have**

ivory [ai'və:ri:] *n* (substance) 象げ zồge; (color) アイボリー áibòrī

ivory tower *n* (fig) 象げの塔 zồge no tồ

ivy [ai'vi:] *n* (BOT) キヅタ kízùta, アイビー áibī

J

jab [dʒæb] *vt* (poke: with elbow, stick) 突く tsukú
♦*n* (inf: injection) 注射 chúsha
to jab something into something …を…に突っ込む …wo…ni tsukkómù

jabber [dʒæb'ə:r] *vi* (*also*: **jabber away**) ぺちゃくちゃしゃべる péchàkucha shabérù

jack [dʒæk] n (AUT) ジャッキ jákkì; (CARDS) ジャック jákkù

jackal [dʒæk'əl] n ジャッカル jákkàru

jackdaw [dʒæk'dɔ:] n コクマルガラス kokúmarugàrasu

jacket [dʒæk'it] n (garment) ジャケット jákètto; (of book) ジャケット jákètto, カバー kábà

potatoes in their jackets 皮ごと料理したジャガイモ kawágòto ryōri shita jagáimo

jack-knife [dʒæk'naif] vi (trailer truck) ジャックナイフ現象を起す jakkúnaifu genshō wo okósù ◇鋭角に折り曲って動けなくなる efkaku ni orímagatte ugokenáku nárù

jack plug n (ELEC: for headphones etc) プラグ purágù

jackpot [dʒæk'pɑ:t] n 大賞金 daíshōkin

to hit the jackpot 大賞金を当てる daíshōkin wo atérù, 大当りする ōatàri suru

jack up vt (AUT) ジャッキで持上げる jákkì de mochíagerù

jade [dʒeid] n (stone) ひすい hisúi

jaded [dʒei'did] adj (tired) 疲れ切った tsukárekittà; (fed-up) うんざりした uñzaríshita

jagged [dʒæg'id] adj (outline, edge) ぎざぎざの gízàgiza no

jail [dʒeil] n 刑務所 keímusho
◆vt 刑務所に入れる keímusho ni irérù

jam [dʒæm] n (food) ジャム jámù; (also: **traffic jam**) 交通渋滞 kōtsūjūtai; (inf: difficulty): *to be in a jam* 困っている komátte irù
◆vt (passage etc) ふさぐ fuságù; (mechanism, drawer etc) 動けなくする ugokenáku suru; (RADIO) 妨害する bōgai suru
◆vi (mechanism, drawer etc) 動けなくなる ugokenàku nárù

to jam something into something (cram, stuff) ...に...を押込む ...ni...wo oshíkomù

Jamaica [dʒəmei'kə] n ジャマイカ jámaìka

jangle [dʒæŋ'gəl] vi (keys, bracelets etc) じゃらじゃら鳴る járàjara narú

janitor [dʒæn'itər] n (caretaker: of building) 管理人 kañrinin

January [dʒæn'ju:we:ri:] n 1月 ichígatsu

Japan [dʒəpæn'] n 日本 nihóñ(nippóñ)

Japanese [dʒæpəni:z'] adj 日本の nihóñ (nippóñ) no; (LING) 日本語の nihóngo no
◆n inv (person) 日本人 nihóñ(nippóñ)jiñ; (LING) 日本語 nihóngo

jar [dʒɑ:r] n (container: glass with wide mouth) 瓶 bíñ; (: stone, earthenware) つぼ tsubó, かめ kamé
◆vi (sound) 耳ざわりである mimízawàri de aru, きしる kishírù; (colors) 釣合わない tsuríawanài

jargon [dʒɑ:r'gən] n 専門用語 señmonyōgo, 隠語 iñgo

jasmine [dʒæz'min] n ジャスミン jásùmin

jaundice [dʒɔ:n'dis] n (MED) 黄だん ōdan

jaundiced [dʒɔ:n'dist] adj *to view with a jaundiced eye* 白い目で見る shiróì me de mírù

jaunt [dʒɔ:nt] n (trip, excursion) 遠足 eñsoku

jaunty [dʒɔ:n'ti:] adj (attitude, tone) 陽気な yōki na; (step) 軽やかな karóyàka na

javelin [dʒæv'lin] n (SPORT) やり投げ yarínage

jaw [dʒɔ:] n (ANAT) あご agó

jay [dʒei] n カケス kakésu

jaywalker [dʒei'wɔ:kər] n ◇交通規則を無視して道路を横断する人 kōtsūkisòku wo mushíˈ shite dōro wo ōdan surù hitó

jazz [dʒæz] n (MUS) ジャズ jázù

jazz up vt (liven up: party) 活気付ける kakkízukeru; (: taste) ぴりっとさせる pi ríttò saséru; (: image) 派手にする hadé ni surù

jazzy [dʒæz'i:] adj (shirt, pattern) 派手な hadé na

jealous [dʒel'əs] adj (suspicious: husband etc) 嫉妬深い shittóbukài; (envious: person) うらやましい uráyamashìi, うらやましがっている uráyamashigatte irù; (look etc) うらやましそうな uráyamashisōna

jealousy [dʒel'əsi:] n (resentment) ねた

み netámi; (envy) うらやむ事 uráyamù kotó

jeans [dʒiːnz] *npl* (trousers) ジーパン jíːpaň

jeep [dʒiːp] *n* (AUT, MIL) ジープ jíːpù

jeer [dʒiːr] *vi* (mock, scoff): **to jeer (at)** 野次る yajírù

jelly [dʒɛlˈiː] *n* (CULIN) ゼリー zérì

jellyfish [dʒɛlˈiːfiʃ] *n* クラゲ kuráge

jeopardize [dʒɛpˈəːrdaiz] *vt* 危険にさらす kikén ni sarásù

jeopardy [dʒɛpˈəːrdiː] *n*: **to be in jeopardy** 危険にさらされる kikén ni sarásarerù

jerk [dʒəːrk] *n* (jolt, wrench) ◇急な動き kyū́ na ugóki; (*inf*: idiot) 間抜け manúke
♦*vt* (pull) ぐいと引っ張る guí to hippárù
♦*vi* (vehicle, person, muscle) 急に動く kyū́ ni ugóku

jerkin [dʒəːrˈkin] *n* チョッキ chokkí

jersey [dʒəːrˈziː] *n* (pullover) セーター sḗtā; (fabric) ジャージー jā́jī

jest [dʒɛst] *n* 冗談 jṓdaň

Jesus [dʒiːˈzəs] *n* イエス iésù

jet [dʒɛt] *n* (of gas, liquid) 噴射 fuńsha, ジェット jéttò; (AVIAT) ジェット機 jéttokì

jet-black [dʒɛtˈblækˈ] *adj* 真っ黒な makkúrò na

jet engine *n* ジェットエンジン jétto eňjin

jet lag *n* 時差ぼけ jisábòke

jettison [dʒɛtˈəsən] *vt* (fuel, cargo) 捨てる sutéru

jetty [dʒɛtˈiː] *n* 波止場 hatóba

Jew [dʒuː] *n* ユダヤ人 yudáyajìn

jewel [dʒuːˈəl] *n* (*also fig*) 宝石 hṓseki; (in watch) 石 ishí

jeweler [dʒuːˈələr] (*BRIT* **jeweller**) *n* (dealer in jewelery) 宝石商 hōsekishṓ; (dealer in watches) 時計屋 tokéiya

jeweler's (shop) [dʒuːˈələrz-] *n* (jewelery shop) 宝石店 hōsekitèn; (watch shop) 時計店 tokéiten

jewelery [dʒuːˈəlriː] (*BRIT* **jewellery**) *n* 装身具 sṓshiňgu

Jewess [dʒuːˈis] *n* ユダヤ人女性 yudáyajin jòsei

Jewish [dʒuːˈiʃ] *adj* ユダヤ人の yudáyajiň no

jibe [dʒaib] *n* 野次 yájì

jiffy [dʒifˈiː] (*inf*) *n*: **in a jiffy** 直ぐ súgù

jig [dʒig] *n* (dance) ジグ jígù ◇動きの早い活発なダンス ugóki nò hayáì kappátsu na dáňsu

jigsaw [dʒigˈsɔː] *n* (*also*: **jigsaw puzzle**) ジグソーパズル jígùsō-pazuru

jilt [dʒilt] *vt* (lover etc) 振る furú

jingle [dʒinˈgəl] *n* (for advert) コマーシャルソング komásharu soňgu
♦*vi* (bells, bracelets) ちりんちりんと鳴る chírìnchirin to narú

jinx [dʒiŋks] *n* ジンクス jíňkusu

jitters [dʒitˈəːrz] (*inf*) *npl*: **to get the jitters** びびる bibírù

job [dʒɑːb] *n* (chore, task) 仕事 shigóto; (post, employment) 職 shokú

it's not my job (duty, function) それは私の仕事ではない soré wà watákushi nò shigóto de wa naì

it's a good job that ... (*BRIT*) ...して良かったね ...shite yókàtta né

just the job! (*BRIT*: *inf*) おあつらえ向きだ o-átsurae muki da, 丁度いい chṓdo iì

job centre (*BRIT*) *n* 公共職業安定所 kṓkyōshokugyō anteishò

jobless [dʒɑːbˈlis] *adj* (ECON) 失業の shitsúgyō no

jockey [dʒɑːkˈiː] *n* (SPORT) 騎手 kíshù
♦*vi*: **to jockey for position** (rivals, competitors) 画策する kakúsaku suru

jocular [dʒɑːkˈjələr] *adj* (person, remark) ひょうきんな hyṓkiň na

jog [dʒɑːg] *vt* (bump) 小突く kozúku
♦*vi* (run) ジョギングする jógiňgu suru
to jog someone's memory ...に...を思い起させる ...ni...wo omóì okosaserù

jog along *vi* (person, vehicle) のんびりと進む noňbiri to susúmù

jogging [dʒɑːgˈiŋ] *n* ジョギング jógiňgu

join [dʒɔin] *vt* (queue) ...に加わる ...ni kuwáwarù; (party) ...に参加する ...ni sańka suru; (club etc) ...に入会する ...ni nyū́kai suru; (put together: things, places) つなぐ tsunágu; (meet: group of people) 一緒

になる isshó ni narù

joiner [dʒɔi'nə:r] (*BRIT*) n 建具屋 tatéguya

joinery [dʒɔi'nə:ri:] n 建具職 tatégushóku

join in vi 参加する sañka suru
♦vt fus (work, discussion etc) ...に参加する ...ni sañka surù

joint [dʒɔint] n (TECH: in woodwork, pipe) 継ぎ目 tsugíme; (ANAT) 関節 kañsetsu; (of meat) ブロック肉 búròkku niku; (inf: nightclub, pub, cheap restaurant etc) 店 misé; (: of cannabis) マリファナタバコ marífana tabakó
♦adj (common) 共通の kyótsū no; (combined) 共同の kyódō no

joint account n (at bank etc) 共同預金口座 kyódō yokin kôza

join up vi (meet) 一緒になる isshó ni narù; (MIL) 入隊する nyútai suru

joist [dʒɔist] n はり harí

joke [dʒouk] n (gag) 冗談 jódañ; (also: **practical joke**) いたずら itázura
♦vi 冗談を言う jódañ wo iú
to play a joke on ...をからかう ...wo karákaù

joker [dʒou'kə:r] n (inf) 冗談を言う人 jódañ wo iu hitó; (pej: person) 野郎 yáró; (cards) ジョーカー jôkā

jolly [dʒɑ:l'i:] adj (merry) 陽気な yóki na; (enjoyable) 楽しい tanóshiì
♦adv (BRIT: inf) とても totémo

jolt [dʒoult] n (physical) 衝撃 shógeki; (emotional) ショック shókkù
♦vt (physically) ...に衝撃を与える ...ni shógeki wò atáerù; (emotionally) ショックを与える shókkù wo atáerù

Jordan [dʒɔːr'dʌn] n ヨルダン yórùdan

jostle [dʒɑ:s'əl] vt: *to be jostled by the crowd* 人込みにもまれる hitógomi ni momárerù

jot [dʒɑ:t] n: *not one jot* 少しも...ない sukóshì mo ...nâî

jot down vt (telephone number etc) 書留める kakítomerù

jotter [dʒɑːt'ə:r] (BRIT) n (notebook, pad) ノート（ブック）nôto(búkkù), メモ帳 memóchō

journal [dʒə:r'nəl] n (magazine, periodical) 雑誌 zasshí; (diary) 日記 nikkí

journalese [dʒəːrnəli:z'] n (pej) 大衆新聞調 taíshūshinbunchō

journalism [dʒə:r'nəlizəm] n ジャーナリズム jánarizūmu

journalist [dʒə:r'nəlist] n ジャーナリスト jánarisùto

journey [dʒə:r'ni:] n (trip, route) 旅行 ryokó; (distance covered) 道のり michínori

jovial [dʒou'vi:əl] adj (person, air) 陽気な yóki na

joy [dʒɔi] n (happiness, pleasure) 喜び yorókobi

joyful [dʒɔi'fəl] adj (news, event) うれしい uréshiì; (look) うれしそうな uréshisô na

joyride [dʒɔi'raid] n (AUT: US) 無謀運転のドライブ mubôuñten no doráibù; (: BRIT) 盗難車でのドライブ tônansha de no doráibù

joystick [dʒɔi'stik] n (AVIAT) 操縦かん sójūkan; (COMPUT) 操縦レバー sójū rebâ, ジョイスティック jofsūtikku

JP [dʒeipi:'] n abbr = **Justice of the Peace**

Jr abbr = **junior**

jubilant [dʒu:'bələnt] adj 大喜びの óyorokobi no

jubilee [dʒu:'bəli:] n (anniversary) ...周年記念日 ...shúnen kineñbi

judge [dʒʌdʒ] n (LAW) 裁判官 saíbankan; (in competition) 審査員 shiñsa-in; (fig: expert) 通 tsû
♦vt (LAW) 裁く sabákù; (competition) 審査する shiñsa suru; (person, book etc) 評価する hyóka suru; (consider, estimate) 推定する suítei suru

judg(e)ment [dʒʌdʒ'mənt] n (LAW) 判決 hañketsu; (REL) 審判 shiñpan; (view, opinion) 意見 ikén; (discernment) 判断力 hañdañryoku

judicial [dʒuːdiʃ'əl] adj (LAW) 司法の shihó no

judiciary [dʒuːdiʃ'i:e:ri:] n 司法部 shihóbù

judicious [dʒuːdiʃˈəs] *adj* (action, decision) 分別のある fuñbetsu no árù

judo [dʒuːˈdou] *n* 柔道 jūdō

jug [dʒʌg] *n* 水差し mizúsashi

juggernaut [dʒʌgˈəːrnɔːt] (*BRIT*) *n* (huge truck) 大型トラック ōgata torakkù

juggle [dʒʌgˈəl] *vi* 玉をする shinádama wo surù ◇幾つもの玉などを投上げて受止める曲芸 íkùtsu mo no tamá nadò wo nagéagetè ukétomerù kyokúgei

juggler [dʒʌgˈləːr] *n* 玉をする曲芸師 shinádama wo suru kyokúgeishì

Jugoslav [juːˈgouslɑːv] *etc* = **Yugoslav** *etc*

juice [dʒuːs] *n* (of fruit, plant, meat) 汁 shírù; (beverage) ジュース jūsu

juicy [dʒuːˈsiː] *adj* (food) 汁の多い shírù no ōi; (*inf*: story, details) エッチな étchì na

jukebox [dʒuːkˈbɑːks] *n* ジュークボックス júkùbokkusu

July [dʒʌlaiˈ] *n* 7月 shichí gatsu

jumble [dʒʌmˈbəl] *n* (muddle) ごたまぜ gotámaze
♦*vt* (*also*: **jumble up**) ごたまぜにする gotámaze ni suru

jumble sale (*BRIT*) *n* 慈善バザー jizén bazá

jumbo (jet) [dʒʌmˈbou] *n* ジャンボジェット機 jánbo jettókì

jump [dʒʌmp] *vi* (into air) 飛び上る tobíagarù; (with fear, surprise) ぎくっとする gíkùtto suru; (increase: price etc) 急上昇する kyújōshō suru; (: population etc) 急増する kyúzō suru
♦*vt* (fence) 飛び越える tobíkoeru
♦*n* (into air etc) 飛び上る事 tobíagarù kotó; (increase: in price etc) 急上昇 kyújōshō; (: in population etc) 急増 kyúzō

to jump the queue (*BRIT*) 列に割込む rétsu ni waríkomù

jumper [dʒʌmˈpəːr] *n* (*BRIT*: pullover) セーター sētā; (*US*: dress) ジャンパースカート jañpásukàto

jumper cables *npl* (*US*) ブースターケーブル búsutākèburu ◇外のバッテリーから

電気を得るために用いるコード hoká nò báttèrī kara déñki wo érù tamé nì mochíirù kōdo

jump leads (*BRIT*) [-liːdz] *npl* = **jumper cables**

jumpy [dʒʌmˈpiː] *adj* (nervous) びくびくしている bíkùbiku shité ìrù

Jun. *abbr* = **junior**

junction [dʒʌŋkˈʃən] *n* (*BRIT*: of roads) 交差点 kōsatèn; (RAIL) 連絡駅 reñraku-eki

juncture [dʒʌŋkˈtʃəːr] *n*: *at this juncture* この時 konó tokì

June [dʒuːn] *n* 6月 rokúgatsu

jungle [dʒʌŋˈgəl] *n* ジャングル jáñguru; (*fig*) 弱肉強食の世界 jakúniku kyōshoku nò sékai

junior [dʒuːnˈjəːr] *adj* (younger) 年下の toshíshita no; (subordinate) 下位の kái no; (SPORT) ジュニアの jùnia no
♦*n* (office junior) 後輩 kōhai; (young person) 若者 wakámono

he's my junior by 2 years 彼は私より2才年下です kárè wa watákushi yorí nísaì toshíshita desu

junior school (*BRIT*) *n* 小学校 shōgakkō

junk [dʒʌŋk] *n* (rubbish, cheap goods) がらくた garákuta; (ship) ジャンク jáñku

junk food *n* ジャンクフード fūdo ◇ポテトチップス，ファーストフードなど高カロリーだが低栄養のスナック食品 potétochippùsu, fásuto fūdo nádò kōkarorī da ga teíeiyō no sunákku shokùhin

junkie [dʒʌŋˈkiː] (*inf*) *n* ペイ中 peichū

junk shop *n* 古物商 kobútsushò

Junr. *abbr* = **junior**

jurisdiction [dʒuːrisdikˈʃən] *n* (LAW) 司法権 shihōkèn; (ADMIN) 支配権 shiháikèn

juror [dʒuːˈrəːr] *n* (person on jury) 陪審員 baíshiñ-in

jury [dʒuːˈriː] *n* (group of jurors) 陪審員 baíshiñ-in

just [dʒʌst] *adj* (fair: decision) 公正な kōsei na; (: punishment) 適切な tekísetsu na

♦*adv* (exactly) 丁度 chôdo; (only) ただ tádà; (barely) ようやく yôyaku

he's just done it ついさっきそれをやったばかりだ tsuí sakkí sore wo yatta bákàri da

he's just left ついさっき出た〔帰った〕ばかりだ tsuí sakkí détà 〔káèttà〕 bákàri da

just right 丁度いい chôdo iî

just two o'clock 丁度2時 chôdo nîji

she's just as clever as you 彼女はあなたに負けないぐらい頭がいい kánòjo wa anátà ni makénai gurài atáma ga iî

just as well that ... ...して良かった ...shîte yokátta

just as he was leaving 丁度出掛けるところに chôdo dekákèrù tokóro ni

just before 丁度前に chôdo máe ni

just enough 辛うじて間に合って kárôjite ma nî attè

just here ぴったりここに pittárî kokó ni

he just missed わずかの差で外れた wázùka no sá dè hazúreta

just listen ちょっと聞いて chottó kiite

justice [dʒʌs'tis] *n* (LAW: system) 司法 shihô; (rightness: of cause, complaint) 正当さ seítòsa; (fairness) 公正さ kôseisa; (*US*: judge) 裁判官 saíbankan

to do justice to (*fig*: task) ...をやりこなす ...wo yaríkonasù; (: meal) ...を平らげる ...wo taíragerù; (: person) ...を正当に扱う ...wo seftô ni atsúkaù

Justice of the Peace *n* 治安判事 chián hañji

justifiable [dʒʌs'tifaiəbəl] *adj* (claim, statement etc) 正当な seítò na

justification [dʒʌstəfəkei'ʃən] *n* (reason) 正当とする理由 seftô to suru riyû

justify [dʒʌs'təfai] *vt* (action, decision) 正当である事を証明する seftô de arù kotô wo shômei suru; (text) 行の長さをそろえる gyô no nágàsa wo soróerù

justly [dʒʌst'li:] *adv* (with reason) 正当に seftô ni; (deservedly) 当然 tôzen

jut [dʒʌt] *vi* (*also*: **jut out**: protrude) 突出る tsukíderù

juvenile [dʒu:'vənəl] *adj* (court) 未成年の

miséînen no; (books) 少年少女向きの shônen shôjo mukí no; (humor, mentality) 子供っぽい kodômoppoî

♦*n* (LAW, ADMIN) 未成年者 miséîneñsha

juxtapose [dʒʌkstəpouz'] *vt* (things, ideas) 並べておく narábete okù

K

K [kei] *abbr* (= *one thousand*) 1000 séñ = **kilobyte**

kaleidoscope [kəlai'dəskoup] *n* 万華鏡 mañgekyô

Kampuchea [kæmpu:tʃi:'ə] *n* カンプチア káñpuchia

kangaroo [kæŋgəru:'] *n* カンガルー kañgarù

karate [kərɑ:'ti:] *n* 空手 karáte

kebab [kəbɑ:b'] *n* くし刺の焼肉 kushísashi nò yakíniku, シシカバブ shishikababu

keel [ki:l] *n* 竜骨 ryûkotsu

on an even keel (*fig*) 安定して antei shite

keen [ki:n] *adj* (eager) やりたがっている yarítagattè írù; (intense: interest, desire) 熱心な nesshín na; (acute: eye, intelligence) 鋭い surúdoî; (fierce: competition) 激しい hagéshiî; (sharp: edge) 鋭い surúdoî

to be keen to do/on doing something (eager, anxious) ...をやりたがっている ...wo yarítagattè írù

to be keen on something/someone ...に熱を上げている ...ni netsú wò agéte irù

keep [ki:p] (*pt, pp* **kept**) *vt* (retain: receipt etc) 保管する hokán suru; (: money etc) 自分の物にする jíbùn no monó ni surù; (: job etc) なくさない様にする nakúsanai yô ni suru, 守る mamórù; (preserve, store) 貯蔵する chozô suru; (maintain: house, garden etc) 管理する káñri suru; (detain) 引留める hikítomerù; (run: shop etc) 経営する keíei suru; (chickens, bees etc) 飼育する shíîku suru; (accounts, diary etc) ...を付ける ...wo tsukérù; (support: family etc) 養う yashínaù; (fulfill: promise) 守る mamórù; (prevent): **to keep someone from doing something** ...が...をできない様に阻止する ...ga ...wo dekínài yō ni soshí surù

♦*vi* (remain: in a certain state) ...でいる 〔ある〕 ...de irú 〔árù〕; (: in a certain place) ずっと ...にいる zuttő ...ni irú; (last: food) 保ちがきく hozón ga kikú

♦*n* (cost of food etc) 生活費 seíkatsuhì; (of castle) 本丸 hońmaru

to keep doing something ...をし続ける ...wo shitsúzukerù

to keep someone happy ...の期限をとる ...no kígèn wo torú

to keep a place tidy ある場所をきちんとさせておく árù bashó wo kichíñ to saséte okù

to keep something to oneself ...について黙っている ...ni tsúite damátte irú

to keep something (back) from someone ...の事を...に隠す ...no kotő wo ...ni kakúsù

to keep time (clock) 時間を正確に計る jíkàn wo seíkaku ni hakárù

for keeps (*inf*) 永久に eíkyū ni

keeper [ki:'pər] *n* (in zoo, park) 飼育係 shi-íkugakàri, キーパー kípà

keep-fit [ki:p'fit'] *n* (*BRIT*) 健康体操 keńkōtaìsō

keeping [ki:'piŋ] *n* (care) 保管 hokán

in keeping with ...に合って ...ni áttè, ...に従って ...ni shitagatte

keep on *vi* (continue): **to keep on doing** ...し続ける ...shitsúzukerù

to keep on (about something) (...を話題に) うるさくしゃべる (...wo wadái ni) urúsakù shabérù

keep out *vt* (intruder etc) 締出す shimédasù

「**keep out**」立入禁止 tachíiri kinshi

keepsake [ki:p'seik'] *n* 形見 katámi

keep up *vt* (maintain: payments etc) 続ける tsuzúkerù; (: standards etc) 保持する hojí suru

♦*vi*: **to keep up (with)** (match: pace)

(...と)速度を合せる (...to) sókùdo wo awáserù; (: level) (...に) 遅れない様にする (...ni) okúrenai yő ni suru

keg [keg] *n* たる tarú

kennel [ken'əl] *n* イヌ小屋 inúgoya

kennels [ken'əlz] *npl* (establishment) イヌ屋 inúya

Kenya [ken'jə] *n* ケニア kénìa

Kenyan [ken'jən] *adj* ケニアの kénìa no
♦*n* ケニア人 keníajìn

kept [kept] *pt, pp of* **keep**

kerb [kə:rb] (*BRIT*) *n* = **curb**

kernel [kə:r'nəl] *n* (BOT: of nut) 実 mi; (*fig*: of idea) 核 kákù

kerosene [ker:'əsi:n] *n* 灯油 tőyu

ketchup [ketʃ'əp] *n* ケチャップ kecháppù

kettle [ket'əl] *n* やかん yakán

kettle drum *n* ティンパニ tíñpani

key [ki:] *n* (for lock etc) かぎ kagí; (MUS: scale) 調 chő; (of piano, computer, typewriter) キー kí
♦*adj* (issue etc) 重要な jūyő na
♦*vt* (*also*: **key in**: into computer etc) 打込む uchíkomù, 入力する nyúryoku suru

keyboard [ki:'bɔ:rd] *n* (of computer, typewriter) キーボード kíbòdo; (of piano) けん盤 keńban, キーボード kíbòdo

keyed up [ki:d-] *adj* (person) 興奮している kőfun shite irú

keyhole [ki:'houl] *n* 鍵穴 kagíana

keynote [ki:'nout] *n* (MUS) 主音 shúòn; (of speech) 基調 kichő

key ring *n* キーホルダー kíhorùdā

kg *abbr* = **kilogram**

khaki [kæk'i:] *n* (color) カーキ色 kákì iro; (*also*: **khaki cloth**) カーキ色服地 kákì iro fukùji

kibbutz [kibuts'] *n* キブツ kíbùtsu ◇イスラエルの農業共同体 ísùraeru no nőgyō kyōdōtai

kick [kik] *vt* (person, table, ball) ける kérù; (*inf*: habit, addiction) やめる yamérù
♦*vi* ける kérù
♦*n* (from person, animal) けり kéri; (to ball) キック kíkkù; (thrill): **he does it for kicks** 彼はそんな事をやるのはスリ

ルのためだ kárè wa sońna kotó wo yárù no wa surfrù no tamé dà

kick off vi (FOOTBALL, SOCCER) 試合を開始する shiái wò kaíshi suru

kick-off [kik'ɔːf] n (FOOTBALL, SOCCER) 試合開始時 shiái kaishi, キックオフ kíkkùofu

kid [kid] n (inf: child) がき gakí, じゃりjarí; (animal) 子ヤギ koyágì; (also: **kid leather**) キッド革 kíddògawa
♦vi (inf) 冗談を言う jódàń wo iú

kidnap [kid'næp] vt 誘拐する yúkai suru

kidnapper [kid'næpəːr] n 誘拐犯人 yúkai hańnin

kidnapping [kid'næpiŋ] n 誘拐事件 yúkai jikèn

kidney [kid'ni:] n (ANAT) じん臓 jińzō; (CULIN) キドニー kíddònī

kill [kil] vt (person, animal) 殺す korósu; (plant) 枯らす karásù; (murder) 殺す korosu, 殺害する satsúgai suru
♦n koróshi

to kill time 時間をつぶす jíkàn wo tsubúsù

killer [kil'əːr] n 殺し屋 koróshiya

killing [kil'iŋ] n (action) 殺す事 korósu kotó; (instance) 殺人事件 satsújin jikèn

to make a killing (inf) 大もうけする ōmōke suru

killjoy [kil'dʒɔi] n 白けさせる人 shirákesaserù hitó

kiln [kiln] n 窯 kamá

kilo [ki:'lou] n キロ kíro

kilobyte [kil'əbait] n (COMPUT) キロバイト kiróbaìto

kilogram(me) [kil'əgræm] n キログラムkirógurầmu

kilometer [kil'əmi:təːr] (BRIT **kilometre**) n キロメーター kirómēta

kilowatt [kil'əwɑːt] n キロワット kirówattò

kilt [kilt] n キルト kirúto

kimono [kimou'nou] n 着物 kimóno, 和服 wafúku

kin [kin] n see **kith; next-of-kin**

kind [kaind] adj 親切な shíñsetsu na
♦n (type, sort) 種類 shúrùi; (species) 種 shú

to pay in kind 現物で支払う geńbutsu de shiháraú

a kind of ...の一種 ...no ísshù

to be two of a kind 似たり寄ったりする nitárì yottárì suru, 似た者同志である nitá mono dṓshi de árù

kindergarten [kin'dəːrgɑːrtən] n 幼稚園 yōchièn

kind-hearted [kaind'hɑːr'tid] adj 心の優しい kokóro no yasáshiì

kindle [kin'dəl] vt (light: fire) たく takú, つける tsukeru; (arouse: emotion) 起す okósù, そそる sosórù

kindly [kaind'li:] adj 親切な shíñsetsu na
♦adv (smile) 優しく yasáshikù; (behave) 親切に shíñsetsu ni

will you kindly ... ...して下さいませんか ...shítè kudásaìmasen ká

kindness [kaind'nis] n (personal quality) 親切 shíñsetsu; (helpful act) 親切な行為 shíñsetsu na kṓi

kindred [kin'drid] adj: **kindred spirit** 自分と気の合った人 jíbùn to kí no attà hitó

kinetic [kinet'ik] adj 動的な dṓteki na

king [kiŋ] n (monarch) 国王 kokúṓ; (CARDS, CHESS) キング kíñgu

kingdom [kiŋ'dəm] n 王国 ṓkoku

kingfisher [kiŋ'fiʃəːr] n カワセミ kawásemi

king-size [kiŋ'saiz] adj 特大の tokúdai no

kinky [kiŋ'ki:] (pej) adj (person, behavior) へんてこな heńteko na, 妙な myṓ na; (sexually) 変態気味の heńtaigimi no

kiosk [ki:ɑːsk'] n (shop) キオスク kiósùku; (BRIT: TEL) 電話ボックス deńwa bokkùsu

kipper [kip'əːr] n 薫製ニシン kuńsei nishìn

kiss [kis] n キス kísù
♦vt ...にキスする ...ni kísù suru

to kiss (each other) キスする kísù suru

kiss of life n 口移しの人工呼吸 kuchíutsushi no jińkōkokyū

kit [kit] n (clothes: sports kit etc) 運動服一式 uńdōfuku isshíki; (equipment, set of tools: also MIL) 道具一式 dṓgu isshíki; (for assembly) キット kíttò

kitchen [kitʃ'ən] *n* 台所 daídokoro, キッチン kítchìn

kitchen sink *n* 台所の流し daídokoro no nagáshi

kite [kait] *n* (toy) たこ takó

kith [kiθ] *n*: **kith and kin** 親せき知人 shiñsekichijin

kitten [kit'ən] *n* 子ネコ konékò

kitty [kit'i:] *n* (pool of money) お金の蓄え o-káne no takúwae; (CARDS) 総掛金 sókakekìn

kleptomaniac [kleptəmei'ni:æk] *n* 盗癖のある人 tóheki no árù hitó

km *abbr* = **kilometer**

knack [næk] *n*: **to have the knack of doing something** ...をするのが上手である ...wo suru nò ga jôzu de arù

knapsack [næp'sæk] *n* ナップサック nappúsakkù

knead [ni:d] *vt* (dough, clay) 練る nérù

knee [ni:] *n* ひざ hizá

kneecap [ni:'kæp] *n* ひざ頭 hizágashìra, ひざ小僧 hizákozò

kneel [ni:l] (*pt, pp* **knelt**) *vi* (*also:* **kneel down**) ひざまずく hizámazukù

knelt [nelt] *pt, pp of* **kneel**

knew [nu:] *pt of* **know**

knickers [nik'ə:rz] (*BRIT*) *npl* パンティー pántì

knife [naif] (*pl* **knives**) *n* ナイフ náìfu

♦*vt* ナイフで刺す náìfu de sásù

knight [nait] *n* (HISTORY) 騎士 kishí; (*BRIT*) ナイト náìto; (CHESS) ナイト náìto

knighthood [nait'hud] (*BRIT*) *n* (title): **to get a knighthood** ナイト爵位を与えられる naíto shakùi wo atáerarerù

knit [nit] *vt* (garment) 編む ámù

♦*vi* (with wool) 編物をする amímòno wo suru; (broken bones) 治る naôru

to knit one's brows まゆをひそめる máyù wo hisómerù

knitting [nit'iŋ] *n* 編物 amímòno

knitting machine *n* 編機 amíkì

knitting needle *n* 編棒 amíbò

knitwear [nit'we:r] *n* ニット・ウェアー nittó ueà

knives [naivz] *npl of* **knife**

knob [nɑ:b] *n* (handle: of door) 取っ手 tottê, つまみ tsumámi; (: of stick) 握り nigíri; (on radio, TV etc) つまみ tsumámi

knock [nɑ:k] *vt* (strike) たたく tatákù; (*inf*: criticize) 批判する hihán suru

♦*vi* (at door etc): **to knock at/on** ...にノックする ...ni nôkku surù

♦*n* (blow, bump) 打撃 dagéki; (on door) ノック nôkkù

knock down *vt* (subj: person) 殴り倒す nagúritaosù; (: car) ひき倒す hikítaosù

knocker [nɑ:k'ə:r] *n* (on door) ノッカー nokkâ

knock-kneed [nɑ:k'ni:d] *adj* X脚の ekúsukyaku no

knock off *vi* (*inf*: finish) やめる yamérù, 終りにする owári ni surù

♦*vt* (from price) 値引する nebíki suru; (*inf*: steal) くすねる kusúnerù

knock out *vt* (subj: drug etc) 気絶させる kizétsu saserù, 眠らせる nemúraserù; (BOXING etc, *also fig*) ノックアウトする nokkúaùto suru; (defeat: in game, competition) ...に勝つ ...ni kátsù, 敗退させる haítai saserù

knockout [nɑ:k'aut] *n* (BOXING) ノックアウト nokkúaùto

♦*cpd* (competition etc) 決定的な kettéiteki na

knock over *vt* (person, object) 倒す taósù

knot [nɑ:t] *n* (in rope) 結び目 musúbime; (in wood) 節目 fushíme; (NAUT) ノット nóttò

♦*vt* 結ぶ musúbù

knotty [nɑ:t'i:] *adj* (*fig*: problem) 厄介な yakkái na

know [nou] (*pt* **knew**, *pp* **known**) *vt* (facts, dates etc) 知っている shitté irù; (language) できる dekírù; (be acquainted with: person, place, subject) 知っている shitté irù; (recognize: by sight) 見て分かる mítè wakárù; (: by sound) 聞いて分かる kiíte wakaru

to know how to swim 泳げる oyógerù

to know about/of something/some-

one ...の事を知っている ...no kotó wò
shitté irù

know-all [nou'ɔ:l] n 知ったか振りの人
shittákaburi no hitó

know-how [nou'hau] n 技術知識 gijútsu-
chishìki, ノウハウ nóuháù

knowing [nou'iŋ] adj (look: of complicity) 意味ありげな imírige na

knowingly [nou'iŋli:] adv (purposely) 故
意に kòí ni; (smile, look) 意味ありげに
imírige ni

knowledge [nɑ:l'idʒ] n (understanding,
awareness) 認識 nínshiki; (learning,
things learnt) 知識 chíshìki

knowledgeable [nɑ:l'idʒəbəl] adj 知識の
ある chíshìki no árù

known [noun] pp of know

knuckle [nʌk'əl] n 指関節 yubí kañsetsu ◇特に指の付根の関節を指す tókù ni
yubí no tsukéne no kañsetsu wò sásù

KO [kei'ou'] n abbr = knockout

Koran [kɔːrɑːn'] n コーラン kôran

Korea [kɔːri:'ə] n 韓国 káñkoku, 朝鮮
chôseñ

Korean [kɔːri:'ən] adj 韓国の káñkoku
no, 朝鮮の chôseñ no; (LING) 韓国語の
kañkokugo no, 朝鮮語の chôseñgo no
◆n (person) 韓国人 kañkokujìn, 朝鮮人
chôseñjìn; (LING) 韓国語 kañkokugo, 朝
鮮語 chôseñgo

kosher [kou'ʃəːr] adj 適法の tekíhō no ◇
ユダヤ教の戒律に合った食物などについ
て言う yudáyakyð no kaíritsu ni attà
shokúmòtsu nádò ni tsuîte iú

L

L (BRIT) abbr = learner driver

l. abbr = liter

lab [læb] n abbr = laboratory

label [lei'bəl] n (on suitcase, merchandise etc) ラベル rábèru
◆vt (thing) ...にラベルを付ける ...ni rábèru wo tsukérù

labor [lei'bəːr] (BRIT **labour**) n (hard
work) 労働 rôdō; (work force) 労働者 rōdósha ◇総称 sōshō; (work done by work

force) 労働 rôdō; (MED): **to be in labor**
陣痛が始まっている jiñtsù ga hajímatte
irù
◆vi: **to labor (at something)** (...に)
苦心する (...ni) kushíñ suru
◆vt: **to labor a point** ある事を余計に強
調する árù kotó wò yokéi nì kyôchō
suru

laboratory [læb'rətɔːri:] n (scientific:
building, institution) 研究所 keñkyūjo;
(: room) 実験室 jikkéñshitsu; (school) 理
科教室 rikákyòshitsu

labored [lei'bəːrd] adj (breathing: one's
own) 苦しい kurúshiì; (: someone else's)
苦しそうな kurúshisò na

laborer [lei'bəːrəːr] n (industrial) 労働者
rōdósha
farm laborer 農場労務者 nójōrōmushà

laborious [ləbɔːr'i:əs] adj 骨の折れる honé no orérù

labour [lei'bəːr] etc n = **labor** etc
Labour, the Labour Party (BRIT) 労
働党 rôdōtō

labyrinth [læb'ə:rinθ] n 迷路 mêìro

lace [leis] n (fabric) レース rèsu; (of shoe
etc) ひも himó
◆vt (shoe etc: also: **lace up**) ...のひもを結
ぶ ...no himó wo musúbù

lack [læk] n (absence) 欠如 kétsùjo
◆vt (money, confidence) ...が無い ...ga
naí; (intelligence etc) 欠いている kaíte
irù
through/for lack of ...が無いために
...ga naí tamé ni
to be lacking ...がない ...ga naí
to be lacking in (intelligence, generosity etc) ...を欠いている ...wo kaíte iru

lackadaisical [lækədei'zikəl] adj (lacking interest, enthusiasm) 気乗りしない
kinóri shinaí

laconic [ləkɑ:n'ik] adj 言葉数の少ない
kotóbakazù no sukúnaì

lacquer [læk'əːr] n (paint) ラッカー rák-
kà; (also: **hair lacquer**) ヘアスプレー he-
ásupurề

lad [læd] n (boy) 少年 shônen; (young
man) 若者 wakámonò

ladder [læd'əːr] n (metal, wood, rope) は

しご子 hashígo; (*BRIT*: in tights) 伝線
defísen

laden [lei'dən] *adj*: **laden (with)** (ship,
truck etc) (...を) たっぷり積んだ (...wo)
tappúrí tsuñda; (person) (...を) 沢山抱
えている (...wo) takúsañ kakáete irú
laden with fruit (tree) 実をたわわに付
けている mi wo tawáwa ni tsukéte irú

ladle [lei'dəl] *n* 玉じゃくし tamájakushi

lady [lei'di:] *n* (woman) 女性 joséi; (:
dignified, graceful etc) 淑女 shukújò, レディ
ー rédì; (in address): **ladies and gentlemen** ... 紳士淑女の皆様 shíñshishukujò
no minásàma
young lady 若い女性 wakái joséi
the ladies' (room) 女性用トイレ joséi-
yōtòíre

ladybird [lei'di:bə:rd] *n* テントウムシ te-
ñtōmushi

ladybug [lei'debag] (*US*) *n* = **ladybird**

ladylike [lei'di:laik] *adj* (behavior) レデ
ィーらしい rédìrashii

ladyship [lei'di:ʃip] *n*: **your ladyship** 奥
様 ókùsama

lag [læg] *n* (period of time) 遅れ okúre
♦*vi* (*also*: **lag behind**: person, thing) ...に
遅れる ...ni okúrerù; (: trade, investment
etc) ...の勢いが衰える ...no ikíoi ga otóroerù
♦*vt* (pipes etc) ...に断熱材を巻く ...ni dañ-
netsuzài wo makú

lager [lɑ:'gə:r] *n* ラガービール ragábìru

lagoon [ləgu:n] *n* 潟 katá, ラグーン rá-
gūn

laid [leid] *pt*, *pp* of **lay**[3]

laid back (*inf*) *adj* のんびりした noñbirī
shitá

laid up *adj*: **to be laid up (with)**
(...で) 寝込んでいる (...de) nekónde irú

lain [lein] *pp* of **lie**

lair [le:r] *n* (*ZOOL*) 巣穴 suána

lake [leik] *n* 湖 mizú-umì

lamb [læm] *n* (animal) 子ヒツジ kohítsu-
jì; (meat) ラム rámù

lamb chop *n* ラムチャップ ramúchappù,
ラムチョップ ramúchoppù

lambswool [læmz'wul] *n* ラムウール ra-
múùru

lame [leim] *adj* (person, animal) びっこの
bíkkò no; (excuse, argument, answer) 下
手な hetá na

lament [ləment'] *n* 嘆き nagéki
♦*vt* 嘆く nagékù

laminated [læm'əneitid] *adj* (metal,
wood, glass) 合板の gőhan no; (covering,
surface) プラスチック張りの purásu-
chikkubari no

lamp [læmp] *n* (electric, gas, oil) 明りa-
kári, ランプ ráñpu

lamppost [læmp'poust] *n* 街灯 gaítō

lampshade [læmp'ʃeid] *n* ランプの傘 ráñpu no kasá, シェード shēdo

lance [læns] *n* やり yarí
♦*vt* (*MED*) 切開する sekkái suru

land [lænd] *n* (area of open ground) 土地
tochí; (property, estate) 土地 tochí, 所有
地 shoyúchì; (as opposed to sea) 陸 rikú;
(country, nation) 国 kuní
♦*vi* (from ship) 上陸する jóriku suru;
(*AVIAT*) 着陸する chakúriku suru; (*fig*:
fall) 落ちる ochírù
♦*vt* (passengers, goods) 降ろす orósù
to land someone with something
(*inf*) ...に...を押付ける ...ni ...wo oshítsukerù

landing [læn'diŋ] *n* (of house) 踊り場 o-
dóriba; (*AVIAT*) 着陸 chakúriku

landing gear *n* (*AVIAT*) 着陸装置 cha-
kúrikusōchi

landing strip *n* 滑走路 kassórò

landlady [lænd'leidi:] *n* (of rented house,
flat, room) 女大家 oñnaðya; (of pub) 女
主人 oñnashujìn, おかみ okámi

landlocked [lænd'lɑ:kt] *adj* 陸地に囲ま
れた rikúchi ni kakómareta

landlord [lænd'lɔ:rd] *n* (of rented house,
flat, room) 大家 ðya; (of pub) 主人 shujìn

landmark [lænd'mɑ:rk] *n* (building, hill
etc) 目標 mokúhyõ; (*fig*) 歴史的な事件
rekíshiteki na jíkèn

landowner [lænd'ounə:r] *n* 地主 jinúshi

landscape [lænd'skeip] *n* (view over
land, buildings etc) 景色 késhìki; (*ART*)
風景画 fúkeiga

landscape gardener *n* 造園家 zőenka

landslide [lænd'slaid] *n* (*GEO*) 地滑り jisúberi; (*fig*: electoral) 圧勝 asshṓ

land up *vi*: *to land up in/at* 結局...に
行くはめになる kekkyóku ...ni ikú hame
ni narú

lane [lein] *n* (in country) 小道 komíchi;
(AUT: of carriageway) 車線 shasén; (of
race course, swimming pool) コース kṓ-
su

language [læŋ'gwidʒ] *n* (national
tongue) 国語 kokúgo; (ability to communicate verbally) 言語 géñgo; (specialized
terminology) 用語 yṓgo; (style: of written piece, speech etc) 言葉遣 kotóbazu-
kài; (SCOL) 語学 gógaku

bad language 下品な言葉 gehíñ na kotóba

he is studying languages 彼は外国語
を勉強している kare wa gaikokugo wo
benkyṓ shite iru

language laboratory *n* ランゲージラ
ボラトリー rañgḗjiraboratòrì, エルエル
éruèru

languid [læŋ'gwid] *adj* (person, movement) 元気のない géñki no náì

languish [læŋ'gwiʃ] *vi* 惨めに生きる míjìme ni ikírù

lank [læŋk] *adj* (hair) 長くて手入れしな
い nagákutè teíre shinai

lanky [læŋ'ki:] *adj* ひょろっとした hyo-
rottó shita

lantern [læn'tə:rn] *n* カンテラ kañtera

lap [læp] *n* (of person) ひざの上 hizá nò
ué; (in race) 1周 ísshū, ラップ ráppù

◆*vt* (*also*: **lap up**: drink) ぴちゃぴちゃ飲
む pichápìcha nómu

◆*vi* (water) ひたひたと打寄せる hitáhìta
to uchíyoserù

lapel [ləpel'] *n* 折えり oríeri, ラペル rápè-
ru

Lapland [læp'lənd] *n* ラップランド ráp-
pùrando

lapse [læps] *n* (bad behavior) 過失 kashí-
tsu; (of memory) 喪失 sṓshitsu; (of time)
経過 keíka

◆*vi* (law) 無効になる mukṓ ni narú; (contract, membership, passport) 切れる kirérù

a lapse of concentration 不注意 fu-

chū̀i

to lapse into bad habits (of behavior)
堕落する daráku suru

lap up *vt* (*fig*: flattery etc) 真に受ける
ma ni ukérù

larceny [lɑːr'səni:] *n* (LAW) 窃盗罪 set-
tōzai

larch [lɑːrtʃ] *n* (tree) カラマツ karámà-
tsu

lard [lɑːrd] *n* ラード rádo

larder [lɑːr'də:r] *n* 食料貯蔵室 shokúryò-
chozòshitsu

large [lɑːrdʒ] *adj* (big: house, person,
amount) 大きい ōkii

at large (as a whole) 一般に ippán ni;
(at liberty) 捕まらないで tsukámaranaì-
de ¶ *see also* **by**

largely [lɑːrdʒ'li:] *adv* (mostly) 大体 daítai; (mainly: introducing reason) 主に ó-
mō ni

large-scale [lɑːrdʒ'skeil'] *adj* (action,
event) 大規模な daíkibo no; (map, diagram) 大縮尺の daíshukùshaku no

largesse [lɑːrdʒes'] *n* (generosity) 気前の
さ kimáeyosà; (money etc) 贈り物 okúrimonò

lark [lɑːrk] *n* (bird) ヒバリ hibári; (joke)
冗談 jṓdañ

lark about *vi* ふざけ回る fuzákemawa-
ru

larva [lɑːr'və] (*pl* **larvae**) *n* 幼虫 yṓchū

larvae [lɑːr'vi:] *npl of* **larva**

laryngitis [lærəndʒai'tis] *n* こうとう炎
kṓtòen

larynx [lær'iŋks] *n* (ANAT) こうとう
kṓtō

lascivious [ləsiv'i:əs] *adj* (person, conduct) みだらな midára na

laser [lei'zə:r] *n* レーザー rḕzā

laser printer *n* レーザープリンター rḗ-
zāpurìñtā

lash [læʃ] *n* (eyelash) まつげ mátsùge;
(blow of whip) むち打ち muchíuchi

◆*vt* (whip) むち打つ muchíutsù; (subj:
rain) 激しくたたく hagéshikù tatákù;
(: wind) 激しく揺さぶる hagéshikù yusáburù; (tie): *to lash to/together* ...を...に
〔...と一緒に〕縛る ...wo ...ni〔...to isshó ni〕

shibárù

lash out *vi: to lash out (at someone)*
(hit) (...に) 打ち掛る (...ni) uchíkakarù

to lash out against someone (criticize) ...を激しく非難する ...wo hageshikù hínàn suru

lass [læs] *n* (girl) 少女 shốjo; (young woman) 若い女性 wakáì joséi

lasso [læs'ou] *n* 投縄 nagénawa

last [læst] *adj* (latest: period of time, event, thing) 前の máè no; (final: bus, hope etc) 最後の sáìgo no; (end: of series, row) 一番後の ichíban atò no; (remaining: traces, scraps etc) 残りの nokórì no

♦*adv* (most recently) 最近 saíkin; (finally) 最後に sáìgo ni

♦*vi* (continue) 続く tsuzúkù; (: in good condition) もつ mótsù; (money, commodity) ...に足りる ...ni taríru

last week 先週 senshū

last night 昨晩 sakúbàn, 昨夜 sakúyà

at last (finally) とうとう tốtō

last but one 最後から2番目 sáìgo kara nibánme

last-ditch [læst'ditʃ'] *adj* (attempt) 絶体絶命の zettáizetsumei no

lasting [læs'tin] *adj* (friendship, solution) 永続的な eízokuteki na

lastly [læst'li:] *adv* 最後に sáìgo ni

last-minute [læst'min'it] *adj* (decision, appeal etc) 土壇場の dotánba no

latch [lætʃ] *n* (on door, gate) 掛け金 kakégàne, ラッチ rátchi

late [leit] *adj* (far on in time, process, work etc) 遅い osóì; (not on time) 遅れた okúreta; (former) 前の máè no, 前... zến...

♦*adv* (far on in time, process, work etc) 遅く osóku; (behind time, schedule) 遅れて okúrete

of late (recently) 最近 saíkin

in late May 5月の終り頃 gógàtsu no owári gorò

the late Mr X (deceased) 故Xさん ko ékusu san

latecomer [leit'kʌmə:r] *n* 遅れて来る人 okúrete kurù hitó

lately [leit'li:] *adv* 最近 saíkin

latent [lei'tənt] *adj* (energy, skill, abil-

ity) 表に出ない omóte nì dénài

later [lei'tə:r] *adj* (time, date, meeting etc) もっと後の móttò átò no; (version etc) もっと新しい móttò atárashiì

♦*adv* 後で átò de

later on 後で átò de

lateral [læt'ə:rəl] *adj* (position) 横の yokṍ no; (direction) 横への yokṍ e no

latest [lei'tist] *adj* (train, flight etc) 最後の sáìgo no; (novel, film, news etc) 最新の saíshin no

at the latest 遅くとも osókùtomo

lathe [leið] *n* (for wood, metal) 旋盤 seńban

lather [læð'ə:r] *n* 石けんの泡 sekkén nò awá

♦*vt* ...に石けんの泡を塗る ...ni sekkén nò awá wò nurú

Latin [læt'in] *n* (LING) ラテン語 raténgo

♦*adj* ラテン語の raténgo no

Latin America *n* ラテンアメリカ raténamèrika

Latin American *adj* ラテンアメリカの ratén-amèrika no

♦*n* ラテンアメリカ人 ratén-amerikajìn

latitude [læt'ətu:d] *n* (GEO) 緯度 ído; (*fig*: freedom) 余裕 yoyú

latrine [lətri:n'] *n* 便所 beñjo

latter [læt'ə:r] *adj* (of two) 後者の kṍsha no; (recent) 後の saíkin no; (later) 後の方の átò no hṍ no

♦*n: the latter* (of two people, things, groups) 後者 kṍsha

latterly [læt'ə:rli:] *adv* 最近 saíkin

lattice [læt'is] *n* (pattern, structure) 格子 kṍshi

laudable [lɔ:'dəbəl] *adj* (c o n d u c t, motives etc) 感心な kańshin na

laugh [læf] *n* 笑い warái

♦*vi* 笑う waráù

(to do something) for a laugh 冗談として (...をする) jṍdaǹ toshitè (...wo suru)

laugh at *vt fus* ...をばかにする ...wo bakấ ni surù

laughable [læf'əbəl] *adj* (attempt, quality etc) ばかげた bakágeta

laughing stock [læf'iŋ-] n: *to be the laughing stock of* ...の笑い者になる ...no waráimono ni narú

laugh off vt (criticism, problem) 無視す る mushí suru

laughter [læf'tər] n 笑い声 waráigoe

launch [lɔːntʃ] n (of rocket, missile) 発射 hasshá; (of satellite) 打上げ uchíage; (COMM) 新発売 shiñhatsubai; (motor-boat) ランチ ráñchi
♦vt (ship) 進水させる shiñsui saséru; (rocket, missile) 発射する hasshá suru; (satellite) 打上げる uchíagerù; (fig: start) 開始する kaíshi suru; (COMM) 発売する hatsúbai suru

launch into vt fus (speech, activity) 始 める hajímerù

launch(ing) pad [lɔːn'tʃ(iŋ)-] n (for missile, rocket) 発射台 hasshádai

launder [lɔːn'dər] vt (clothes) 洗濯する señtaku suru

launderette [lɔːndəret'] (BRIT) n コイ ンランドリー koíñrañdorī

Laundromat [lɔːn'drəmæt] (® US) n コ インランドリー koíñrañdorī

laundry [lɔːn'driː] n (dirty, clean) 洗濯物 señtakumono; (business) 洗濯屋 señtaku-ya ◊ドライクリーニングはしない doráikurīningu wa shináî; (room) 洗濯場 señtakuba

laureate [lɔː'riːit] adj see **poet laureate**

laurel [lɔːr'əl] n (tree) ゲッケイジュ gek-kéîju

lava [læv'ə] n 溶岩 yógan

lavatory [læv'ətɔːriː] n お手洗い otéaraî

lavender [læv'əndər] n (BOT) ラベンダ ー rabéñdā

lavish [læv'iʃ] adj (amount) たっぷりの tappúrī no, 多量の taryō no; (person): *lavish with* ...を気前良く与える ...wo kimáeyokù atáerù
♦vt: *to lavish something on someone* ...に...を気前よく与える ...ni ...wo kimáe-yokù atáerù

law [lɔː] n (system of rules: of society, government) 法 hō; (a rule) 法律 hōritsu; (of nature, science) 法則 hōsoku; (lawyers' profession) 弁護士の職 beñgoshì no shokú; (police) 警察 keísatsu; (SCOL) 法学 hōgaku

law-abiding [lɔː'əbaidiŋ] adj 法律を遵守 する hōritsu wò júñshu suru

law and order n 治安 chíañ

law court n 法廷 hōtei

lawful [lɔː'fəl] adj 合法の gōhō no

lawless [lɔː'lis] adj (action) 不法の fuhō no

lawn [lɔːn] n 芝生 shibáfu

lawnmower [lɔːn'mouər] n 芝刈機 shi-bákarikî

lawn tennis n ローンテニス rōntenisu

law school (US) n (SCOL) 法学部 hōga-kùbu

lawsuit [lɔː'suːt] n 訴訟 soshó

lawyer [lɔː'jər] n (gen) 弁護士 beñgoshì; (solicitor) 事務弁護士 jimúbeñgoshi; (barrister) 法廷弁護士 hōteibeñgoshi

lax [læks] adj (behavior, standards) いい加減な iíkagen na

laxative [læk'sətiv] n 下剤 gezái

lay¹ [lei] pt of **lie**

lay² [lei] adj (REL) 俗人の zokújin no; (not expert) 素人の shíroto no

lay³ [lei] (pt, pp **laid**) vt (place) 置く okú; (table) ...に食器を並べる ...ni shokkî wo nárabèrù; (carpet etc) 敷く shikú; (cable, pipes etc) 埋設する maísetsu suru; (ZOOL: egg) 産む úmù

layabout [lei'əbaut] (BRIT: inf) n のら くら者 norákuramono

lay aside vt (put down) わきに置く wakí ni okù; (money) 貯蓄する chochíku suru; (belief, prejudice) 捨てる sutérù

lay by vt = **lay aside**

lay-by [lei'bai] (BRIT) n 待避所 taíhijo

lay down vt (object) 置く okú; (rules, laws etc) 設ける mōkerù
to lay down the law (pej) 威張り散らす ibárichirasu
to lay down one's life (in war etc) 命を捨てる inóchi wo sutérù

layer [lei'ər] n 層 só

layman [lei'mən] (pl **laymen**) n (non-expert) 素人 shíroto

lay off vt (workers) 一時解雇にする ichíjikaîko ni suru, レイオフにする reíofù ni suru

lay on *vt* (meal, entertainment etc) 提供
する teíkyō suru

lay out *vt* (spread out: things) 並べて置
く narábete okù

layout [lei'aut] *n* (arrangement: of garden, building) 配置 haíchi; (: of piece of
writing etc) レイアウト reíaùto

laze [leiz] *vi* (*also*: **laze about**) ぶらぶら
する búrabura suru

laziness [lei'zi:nis] *n* 怠惰 taída

lazy [lei'zi:] *adj* (person) 怠惰な taída na;
(movement, action) のろい noróì

lb *abbr* = **pound (weight)**

lead¹ [li:d] *n* (front position: SPORT, *fig*)
先頭 seńtō; (piece of information) 手掛り
tegákàri; (in play, film) 主演 shuén; (for
dog) 引綱 hikízùna, ひも himó; (ELEC)
リード線 rīdosen

◆*vb* (*pt*, *pp* **led**)

◆*vt* (walk etc in front) 先導する seńdō
suru; (guide): *to lead someone somewhere* ...を...に案内する ...wo ...ni afinaì
suru; (group of people, organization)
...のリーダーになる ...no rídà ni nárù;
(start, guide: activity) ...の指揮を取る
...no shikí wo torù

◆*vi* (road, pipe, wire etc) ...に通じる ...ni
tsújiru; (SPORT) 先頭に立つ seńtō ni tatsù

in the lead (SPORT, *fig*) 先頭に立って
seńtō ni tatte

to lead the way (*also fig*) 先導する seńdō suru

lead² [led] *n* (metal) 鉛 namári; (in pencil) しん shíñ

lead away *vt* 連れ去る tsurésarù

lead back *vt* 連れ戻す tsurémodosù

leaden [led'ən] *adj* (sky, sea) 鉛色の na-
máriiro no

leader [li:'də:r] *n* (of group, organization) 指導者 shidóshà, リーダー rīdà;
(SPORT) 先頭を走る選手 seńtō wo hashírù seńshù

leadership [li:'də:rʃip] *n* (group, individual) 指導権 shidókèn; (position, quality)
リーダーシップ rídāshìppu

lead-free [ledfri:'] *adj* (petrol) 無鉛の

muén no

leading [li:'diŋ] *adj* (most important:
person, thing) 主要な shuyó na; (role) 主
演の shuén no; (first, front) 先頭の seńtō
no

leading lady *n* (THEATER) 主演女優
shuénjoyù

leading light *n* (person) 主要人物 shu-
yójinbùtsu

leading man (*pl* **leading men**) *n* (THE-
ATER) 主演男優 shuéndañ-yū

lead on *vt* (tease) からかう karákaù

lead singer *n* (in pop group) リードシン
ガー rīdoshìñgā, リードボーカリスト rí-
dobōkarìsuto

lead to *vt fus* ...の原因になる ...no geń-in
ni narù

lead up to *vt fus* (events) ...の原因にな
る ...no geń-in ni narù; (in conversation)
話題を...に向ける wadái wo ...ni mukérù

leaf [li:f] (*pl* **leaves**) *n* (of tree, plant) 葉
ha

◆*vi*: *to leaf through* (book, magazine)
...にさっと目を通す ...ni sátto me wò tṓ-
sù

to turn over a new leaf 心を入れ換え
る kokórò wo irékaerù

leaflet [li:f'lit] *n* ビラ birá, 散らし chirá-
shi

league [li:g] *n* (group of people, clubs,
countries) 連盟 reńmei, リーグ rīgu

to be in league with someone ...と手を
組んでいる ...to te wo kuńdè irú

leak [li:k] *n* (of liquid, gas) 漏れ moré;
(hole: in roof, pipe etc) 穴 aná; (piece of
information) 漏えい róei

◆*vi* (shoes, ship, pipe, roof) ...から...が漏
れる ...kara ...ga moreru; (liquid, gas) 漏
れる morérù

◆*vt* (information) 漏らす morásù

the news leaked out そのニュースが漏
れた sonó nyūsu ga moréta

lean [li:n] *adj* (person) やせた yaséta;
(meat) 赤身の akámi no

◆*vb* (*pt*, *pp* **leaned** *or* **leant**)

◆*vt*: *to lean something on something*
...を...にもたせかける ...wo ...ni motáse-
kakeru

♦*vi* (slope) 傾く katámukù

to lean against ...にもたれる ...ni motárerù

to lean on ...に寄り掛る ...ni yoríkakerù

lean back *vi* 後ろへもたれる ushíro e motárerù

lean forward *vi* 前にかがむ máe ni kagámù

leaning [li:'niŋ] *n*: *leaning (towards)* (tendency, bent) (...する) 傾向 (...surú) keíkō

lean out *vi* ...から体を乗出す ...kara karáda wò norídasù

lean over *vi* ...の上にかがむ ...no ué nì kagámù

leant [lent] *pt, pp of* **lean**

leap [li:p] *n* (jump) 跳躍 chóyaku; (in price, number etc) 急上昇 kyúūjōshō

♦*vi* (*pt, pp* **leaped** *or* **leapt**) (jump: high) 跳ね上がる hanéagarù; (: far) 跳躍する chóyaku suru; (price, number etc) 急上昇する kyúūjōshō suru

leapfrog [li:p'frɔːg] *n* 馬跳び umátobi

leapt [lept] *pt, pp of* **leap**

leap year *n* うるう年 urúūdoshi

learn [lə:rn] (*pt, pp* **learned** *or* **learnt**) *vt* (facts, skill) 学ぶ manábù; (study, repeat: poem, play etc) 覚える obóerù, 暗記する añki suru

♦*vi* 習う naráù

to learn about something (hear, read) ...を知る ...wo shírù

to learn to do something ...の仕方を覚える ...no shikáta wò obóerù

learned [lə:r'nid] *adj* (person) 学識のある gakúshiki no arù; (book, paper) 学術の gakújùtsu no

learner [lə:r'nə:r] (*BRIT*) *n* (*also*: **learner driver**) 仮免許運転者 karímenkyo unteñsha

learning [lə:r'niŋ] *n* (knowledge) 学識 gakúshiki

learnt [lə:rnt] *pt, pp of* **learn**

lease [li:s] *n* (legal agreement, contract: to borrow something) 賃借契約 chiñshakukeīyaku, リース rīsu; (: to lend something) 賃貸契約 chiñtaikeīyaku, リース rīsu

♦*vt* (borrow) 賃借する chiñshaku suru; (lend) 賃貸する chiñtai suru

leash [li:ʃ] *n* (for dog) ひも himó

least [li:st] *adj*: *the least* (+noun: smallest) 最も小さい móttòmo chiísaì; (: smallest amount of) 最も少ない móttòmo sukúnaì

♦*adv* (+verb) 最も...しない móttòmo ...shinâì; (+adjective): *the least* 最も...でない móttòmo ...de nâì

the least possible effort 最小限の努力 saíshōgen no dóryòku

at least 少なくとも sukúnakùtomo

you could at least have written 少なくとも手紙をくれたら良かったのに sukúnakùtomo tegámi wò kurétara yokattà no ni

not in the least ちっとも...でない chíttò mo ...de nâì

leather [leð'ə:r] *n* なめし革 naméshigawa, 革 kawá

leave [li:v] (*pt, pp* **left**) *vt* (place: go away from) 行ってしまう itté shimaù, 帰る kaérù; (place, institution: permanently) 去る sárù, 辞める yamérù; (leave behind: person) 置去りにする okízari ni surù, 見捨てる mísuterù; (: thing: accidentally) 置忘れる okíwasurerù; (: deliberately) 置いて行く oíte ikù; (husband, wife) ...と別れる ...to wakárerù; (allow to remain: food, space, time etc) 残す nokósù

♦*vi* (go away) 去る sárù, 行ってしまう itté shimaù; (: permanently) 辞める yamérù; (bus, train) 出発する shuppátsu suru, 出る dérù

♦*n* 休暇 kyúka

to leave something to someone (money, property etc) ...に...を残して死ぬ ...ni ...wo nokóshite shinù; (responsibility etc) ...に...を任せる ...ni ...wo makáserù

to be left 残る nokórù

there's some milk left over ミルクは少し残っている mírùku wa sukóshì nokôtte irù

on leave 休暇中で kyúkachū de

leave behind *vt* (person, object) 置いて

行く oíte ikú; (object: accidentally) 置忘れる okíwasurerù

leave of absence n 休暇 kyúka, 暇 himá

leave out vt 抜かす nukásù

leaves [li:vz] npl of **leaf**

Lebanon [leb'ənən] n レバノン rebánòn

lecherous [letʃ'ə:rəs] (pej) adj 助平な sukébè na

lecture [lek'tʃə:r] n (talk) 講演 kóen; (SCOL) 講義 kógi
♦vi (talk) 講演する kóen suru; (SCOL) 講義する kógi sùru
♦vt (scold): **to lecture someone on/about something** ...の事で...をしかる ...no kotó de ...wo shikárù
to give a lecture on ...について講演する ...ni tsúite kóen suru

lecturer [lek'tʃə:rə:r] (BRIT) n (at university) 講師 kóshi

led [led] pt, pp of **lead¹**

ledge [ledʒ] n (of mountain) 岩棚 iwádana; (of window) 桟 sáñ; (on wall) 棚 taná

ledger [ledʒ'ə:r] n (COMM) 台帳 dáichō

lee [li:] n 風下 kazáshimo

leech [li:tʃ] n ヒル hírù

leek [li:k] n リーキ ríki, リーク ríku

leer [li:r] vi: **to leer at someone** ..をいん乱な目で見る ...wo iñran na me de mirù

leeway [li:'wei] n (fig): **to have some leeway** 余裕がある yoyú ga arù

left [left] pt, pp of **leave**
♦adj (direction, position) 左の hidári no
♦n (direction, side, position) 左 hidári
♦adv (turn, look etc) 左に〔へ〕 hidári ni〔e〕
on the left 左に〔で〕 hidári ni〔de〕
to the left 左に〔へ〕 hidári ni〔e〕
the Left (POL) 左翼 sáyòku

left-handed [left'hæn'did] adj 左利きの hidárikiki no, ぎっちょの gítchò no

left-hand side [left'hænd'-] n 左側 hidárigawa

left-luggage (office) [leftlʌg'idʒ-] (BRIT) n 手荷物預かり所 tenímotsu azukarishò

leftovers [left'ouvə:rz] npl (of meal) 残り物 nokórimono

left-wing [left'wiŋ] adj (POL) 左翼の sáyòku no

leg [leg] n (gen) 脚 ashí; (CULIN: of lamb, pork, chicken) もも mómò; (part: of journey etc) 区切り kugíri

legacy [leg'əsi] n (of will: also fig) 遺産 isán

legal [li:'gəl] adj (of law) 法律の hóritsu no; (action, situation) 法的な hóteki na

legal holiday (US) n 法定休日 hóteikyújitsu

legality [li:gæl'iti:] n 合法性 góhōsei

legalize [li:'gəlaiz] vt 合法化する góhōka suru

legally [li:'gəli:] adv (by law) 法的に hóteki ni

legal tender n (currency) 法定通貨 hóteitsūka, 法貨 hóka

legend [ledʒ'ənd] n (story) 伝説 deñsetsu; (fig: person) 伝説的人物 deñsetsutekijinbutsu

legendary [ledʒ'əndeːri:] adj (of legend) 伝説の deñsetsu no; (very famous) 伝説的な deñsetsuteki na

legible [ledʒ'əbəl] adj 読める yomérù

legion [li:'dʒən] n (MIL) 軍隊 guñtai

legislation [ledʒislei'ʃən] n 法律 hóritsu

legislative [ledʒ'isleitiv] adj 立法の rippō no

legislature [ledʒ'isleitʃə:r] n (POL) 議会 gíkài

legitimate [lidʒit'əmit] adj (reasonable) 正当な seítō na; (legal) 合法な góhō na

leg-room [leg'ru:m] n (in car, plane etc) 脚を伸ばせる空間 ashí wo nobáserù kúkan

leisure [li:'ʒə:r] n (period of time) 余暇 yoká, レジャー rejā
at leisure ゆっくり yukkúrì

leisure centre (BRIT) n レジャーセンター rejásentà ◇スポーツ施設, 図書室, 会議室, 喫茶店など各種文化施設 supótsushisetsù, toshóshitsu, kaígishìtsu, kissáteñ nádò wo fukúnda buñkashisetsù

leisurely [li:'ʒə:rli:] adj (pace, walk) ゆっくりした yukkúrì shitá

lemon [lem'ən] n (fruit) レモン rémòn

lemonade [leməneid'] n (BRIT: fizzy drink) ラムネ rámùne; (with lemon juice) レモネード remónêdo

lemon tea n レモンティー remóntī

lend [lend] (pt, pp **lent**) vt: **to lend something to someone** (money, thing) ...に...を貸す ...ni ...wo kásù

lending library [len'diŋ-] n 貸出し図書館 kashídashitoshokàn

length [leŋkθ] n (measurement) 長さ nagása; (distance): **the length of** ...の端から端まで ...no hashí kara hashi madè; (of swimming pool) プールの長さ pùru no nagása; (piece: of wood, string, cloth etc) 1本 ippón; (amount of time) 時間 jikáñ

at length (at last) とうとう tótō; (for a long time) 長い間 nagáì aída

lengthen [leŋk'θən] vt 長くする nágàku suru

♦vi 長くなる nágàku naru

lengthways [leŋkθ'weiz] adv (slice, fold, lay) 縦に táte ni

lengthy [leŋk'θi:] adj (meeting, explanation, text) 長い nagáì

lenient [li:'ni:ənt] adj (person, attitude) 寛大な kañdai na

lens [lenz] n (of spectacles, camera) レンズ rêñzu; (telescope) 望遠鏡 bôenkyō

Lent [lent] n 四旬節 shijúñsetsu

lent [lent] pt, pp of **lend**

lentil [len'təl] n ヒラマメ hirámame

Leo [li:'ou] n (ASTROLOGY) しし座 shishíza

leopard [lep'ə:rd] n (ZOOL) ヒョウ hyô

leotard [li:'ətɑ:rd] n レオタード reótàdo

leprosy [lep'rəsi:] n らい病 raíbyō, ハンセン病 hañsenbyō

lesbian [lez'bi:ən] n 女性同性愛者 joséidōseiaishà, レスビアン resúbìan

less [les] adj (in size, degree) ...より小さい ...yórì chísaì; (in amount, quality) ...より少ない ...yórì sukúnaì

♦pron ...より少ないもの ...yórì sukúnaì monó

♦adv ...より少なく ...yórì sukúnakù

♦prep: **less tax/10% discount** ...から税金〔1割り〕を引いて ...kara zeíkin(ichí-

wàri)wo hiíte

less than half 半分以下 hañbùn íkà

less than ever 更に少なく sárà ni sukúnàku

less and less ますます少なく masúmàsu sukúnàku

the less he talks the better ... 彼はできるだけしゃべらない方がいい kárè wa dekíru dake shabéranai hô ga íi

lessen [les'ən] vi 少なくなる sukúnaku narù

♦vt 少なくする sukúnàku suru

lesser [les'ə:r] adj (smaller: in degree, importance, amount) 小さい〔少ない〕方の chísaì(sukúnaì)hô no

to a lesser extent それ程ではないが ...mo soré hodò de wa naî ga

lesson [les'ən] n (class: history etc) 授業 jugyô; (: ballet etc) けいこ kéìko, レッスン réssùn; (example, warning) 見せしめ miséshime

to teach someone a lesson (fig) ...に思い知らせてやる ...ni omóishiraseté yarù

lest [lest] conj ...しない様に ...shinái yô ni

let [let] (pt, pp **let**) vt (allow) 許す yurúsù; (BRIT: lease) 賃貸する chíntai suru

to let someone do something ...に...するのを許す ...ni ...surú no wò yurúsù

to let someone know something ...に...を知らせる ...ni ...wo shiráserù

let's go 行きましょう ikímashò

let him come (permit) 彼が来るのを邪魔しないで下さい kárè ga kúrù no wo jamá shinàide kudásaì

「to let」貸し家 kashíyà

let down vt (tire etc) ...の空気を抜く ...no kûki wo nuku; (person) がっかりさせる gakkárì saséru

let go vi (stop holding: thing, person) 手を放す te wo hanásù

♦vt (release: person, animal) 放す hanásu

lethal [li:'θəl] adj (chemical, dose etc) 致命的な chiméiteki na

a lethal weapon 凶器 kyôki

lethargic [ləθɑ:r'dʒik] adj 無気力の mukíryòku no

let in vt (water, air) ...が漏れる ...ga morérù; (person) 入らせる haíraserù

let off *vt* (culprit) 許す yurúsù; (firework, bomb) 爆発させる bakúhatsu saseru; (gun) 撃つ útsù

let on *vi* 漏らす morásù

let out *vt* (person, dog) 外に出す sótò ni dásù; (breath) 吐く háků; (water, air) 抜く núků; (sound) 出す dásù

letter [let'əːr] *n* (correspondence) 手紙 tegámi; (of alphabet) 文字 mójì

letter bomb *n* 手紙爆弾 tegámibakùdan

letterbox [let'əːrbɑːks] *n* (BRIT) (for receiving mail) 郵便受け yúbìn-uke; (for sending mail) 郵便ポスト yúbinposùto, ポスト pósùto

lettering [let'əːriŋ] *n* 文字模様 mójì

lettuce [let'is] *n* レタス rétàsu

let up *vi* (cease) やむ yámù; (diminish) 緩む yurúmù

let-up [let'ʌp] *n* (of violence, noise etc) 減少 geńshō

leukemia [luːkiː'miːə] (BRIT **leukaemia**) *n* 白血病 hakkétsubyò

level [lev'əl] *adj* (flat) 平らな taíra na

♦*adv*: **to draw level with** (person, vehicle) ...に追い付く ...ni oítsukù

♦*n* (point on scale, height etc) 高さ tákàsa, レベル rébèru; (of lake, river) 水位 súì

♦*vt* (land: make flat) 平らにする taíra ni suru; (building, forest etc: destroy) 破壊する hakái suru

to be level with ...と同じぐらいである ...to onáji gurài de árù

"A" levels (BRIT) 学科の上級試験 gakká no jōkyū shikén ◇大学入学資格を得るための試験 daígakunyūgaku shikakù wo érù tamé nò shikén

"O" levels (BRIT) 学科の普通級試験 gakká no futsūkyū shikén ◇中等教育を5年受けた後に受ける試験 chūtōkyoiku wo gonén ukéta nochi ni ukérù shikén

on the level (fig: honest) 正直で shōjiki de

level crossing (BRIT) *n* 踏切 fumíkiri

level-headed [lev'əlhed'id] *adj* (calm) 分別のある fúňbetsu no árù

level off *vi* (prices etc) 横ばい状態にな

る yokóbaijōtai ni nárù

level out *vi* = **level off**

lever [lev'əːr] *n* (to operate machine) レバー rébà; (bar) バール bárù; (fig: 人を動かす手段 hitð wo ugókasù shúdàn, てこ tékò

leverage [lev'əːridʒ] *n* (using bar, lever) てこの作用 tékò no sáyò; (fig: influence) 影響力 eíkyōryòku

levity [lev'iti:] *n* (frivolity) 不真面目さ fumájimesa

levy [lev'i:] *n* (tax, charge) 税金 zeíkin

♦*vt* 課する ka súrù

lewd [luːd] *adj* (look, remark etc) わいせつな waísetsu na

liabilities [laiəbil'əti:z] *npl* (COMM) 債務 sáìmu

liability [laiəbil'əti:] *n* (person, thing) 負担 fután; (LAW: responsibility) 責任 sekínin

liable [lai'əbəl] *adj* (subject): **liable to** ...の罰則が適用される ...no bassóku ga tekíyō sarerù; (responsible): **liable for** ...の責任を負うべきである ...no sekínin wð oúbeki de arù; (likely): **liable to do** ...しがちである ...shigáchi de arù

liaise [liːeiz'] *vi*: **to liaise (with)** (...と) 連携する (...to) reńkei suru

liaison [liːei'zɑːn] *n* (cooperation, coordination) 連携 reńkei; (sexual relationship) 密通 mittsū

liar [lai'əːr] *n* うそつき usótsùki

libel [lai'bəl] *n* 名誉棄損 meíyokisòn

♦*vt* 中傷する chūshō suru

liberal [lib'əːrəl] *adj* (tolerant) 開放的な kaíhōteki na; (large: offer, amount etc) 寛大な kańdai na

liberate [lib'əːreit] *vt* 解放する kaíhō suru

liberation [libərei'ʃən] *n* 解放 kaíhō

liberty [lib'əːrti:] *n* (gen) 自由 jiyú; (criminal): **to be at liberty** 捕まらないでいる tsukámaranàide írù, 逃走中である tősō-chū de arù

to be at liberty to do 自由に...できる jiyú ni ...dekírù

to take the liberty of doing something 勝手に...する katté ni ...surú

Libra [li:'brə] n (ASTROLOGY) 天びん座 teñbinza

librarian [laibre:r'i:ən] n (worker) 図書館員 toshókañ-in; (qualified) 司書 shísho

library [lai'breri:] n (institution, SCOL: building) 図書館 toshókàn; (: room) 図書室 toshóshìtsu; (private collection) 蔵書 zósho

libretto [libret'ou] n (OPERA) 脚本 kyakúhon

Libya [lib'i:ə] n リビア ríbìa

Libyan [lib'i:ən] adj リビアの ríbìa no
♦n リビア人 ribíajìn

lice [lais] npl of **louse**

licence [lai'səns] (US also: **license**) n (official document) 免許 méñkyo; (AUT) 運転免許証 uñtenmenkyoshò

license [lai'səns] n (US) = **licence**
♦vt (person, organization, activity) 認可する níñka suru

licensed [lai'sənst] adj (driver, pilot etc) 免許を持った méñkyo wo mottá; (for alcohol) 酒類販売許可を持った sakéruihanbaikyòka wo mottá

license plate (US) n ナンバープレート nañbāpurèto

licentious [laisen'tʃəs] adj いん乱な iñran na

lichen [lai'kən] n 地衣 chíi

lick [lik] vt (stamp, fingers etc) なめる namérù; (inf: defeat) ...に楽勝する ...ni rakúshò suru
  to lick one's lips (also fig) 舌なめずりする shitánamèzuri suru

licorice [lik'ə:ris] (US) n カンゾウあめ kañzóame

lid [lid] n (of box, case, pan) ふた futá; (eyelid) まぶた mábùta

lie [lai] (pt **lay**, pp **lain**) vi (person) 横になる yokó ni narù; (be situated: place, object: also fig) ...にある ...ni árù; (be placed: in race, league etc) 第...位である dái ...i de arù; (tell lies: pt, pp **lied**) うそをつく usó wo tsúkù
♦n (untrue statement) うそ usó
  to lie low (fig) 人目を避ける hitóme wo sakérù

lie about/around vi (things) 散らばっ

ている chirábatte iru; (people) ごろりと寝ている gorórì to neté iru

lie-down [lai'daun] (BRIT) n: *to have a lie-down* 昼寝する hirúne suru

lie-in [lai'in] (BRIT) n: *to have a lie-in* 寝坊する nebó suru

lieu [lu:]: *in lieu of* prep ...の代りに ...no kawári ni

lieutenant [lu:ten'ənt] n (MIL) (also: **first lieutenant**) 中財 chùi; (also: **second lieutenant**) 小尉 shòi

life [laif] (pl **lives**) n (quality of being alive) 生命 seímeì; (live things) 生物 seíbùtsu; (state of being alive) 命 ínòchi; (lifespan) 一生 isshó; (events, experience, activities) 生活 seíkatsu
  to come to life (fig: person, party etc) 活気付く kakkízukù

life assurance (BRIT) n = **life insurance**

lifebelt [laif'belt] n 救命具 kyúmeìgu

lifeboat [laif'bout] n (rescue launch) 巡視艇 juñshitèi; (on ship) 救命ボート kyúmeibòto

lifeguard [laif'gɑ:rd] n (at beach, swimming pool) 看視員 kañshiìn

life imprisonment n 無期懲役 mukíchòeki

life insurance n 生命保険 seímeihokèn

life jacket n 救命胴衣 kyúmeidòi

lifeless [laif'lis] adj (dead: person, animal) 死んだ shiñda; (fig: person) 元気のない géñki no nàì; (: party etc) 活気のない kakkí no naì

lifelike [laif'laik] adj (model, dummy, robot etc) 生きている様な íkìte irú yòna; (realistic: painting, performance) 写実的な shajítsuteki na

lifeline [laif'lain] n (means of surviving) 命綱 inóchizùna

lifelong [laif'lɔ:ŋ] adj (friend, ambition etc) 一生の isshó no

life preserver (US) n = **lifebelt; life jacket**

life sentence n 無期懲役 mukíchòeki

life-size(d) [laif'saiz(d)] adj (painting, model etc) 実物大の jitsúbutsudaì no

life-span [laif'spæn] n (of person, animal, plant: *also fig*) 寿命 jumyṓ

life style *n* 生き方 ikíkata, ライフスタイル raífusutaíru

life support system *n* (MED) 生命維持装置 seímeiijisṓchi

lifetime [laif'taim] *n* (of person) 生涯 shṓgai; (of thing) 寿命 jumyṓ

lift [lift] *vt* (raise: thing, part of body) 上げる agérù; (end: ban, rule) 撤廃する teppái suru

♦*vi* (fog) 晴れる harérù

♦*n* (*BRIT*: machine) エレベーター erébētā

to give someone a lift (AUT) ...を車に乗せて上げる ...wo kurúma ni nosête agerù

lift-off [lift'ɔːf] *n* (of rocket) 離昇 rishṓ

ligament [lig'əmənt] *n* じん帯 jíntai

light [lait] *n* (brightness: from sun, moon, lamp, fire) 光 hikári; (ELEC) 電気 deńki; (AUT) ライト raíto; (for cigarette etc): *have you got a light?* 火をお持ちですか hí wò o-móchi desu ká

♦*vt* (*pt, pp* **lit**) (fire) たく takú; (candle, cigarette) ...に火を付ける ...ni hí wo tsukérù; (room): *to be lit by* ...で照明されている ...de shṓmei sarête irù

♦*adj* (pale) 淡い awáì; (not heavy: object) 軽い karúì; (: rain) 細かい komákaì; (: traffic) 少ない sukúnaì; (not strenuous: work) 軽い karúì; (bright: building, room) 明るい akáruì; (graceful, gentle: movement, action) 軽やかな karóyàka na; (not serious: book, play, film, music) 肩の凝らない katá no korónaì

to come to light 明るみに出る akárumi ni derù

in the light of (discussions, new evidence etc) ...を考慮して ...wo kṓryo shite

light bulb *n* 電球 deńkyū

lighten [lai'tən] *vt* (make less heavy) 軽くする karúku surù

lighter [lai'tər] *n* (*also:* **cigarette lighter**) ライター raítā

light-headed [lait'hed'id] *adj* (dizzy) 頭がふらふらする atáma ga fúràfura suru; (excited) 浮わついた uwátsuita

light-hearted [lait'hɑːr'tid] *adj* (person)

陽気な yṓki na; (question, remark etc) 気楽な kiráku na

lighthouse [lait'haus] *n* 燈台 tṓdai

lighting [lai'tiŋ] *n* (system) 照明 shṓmei

lightly [lait'li:] *adv* 軽く karúku; (thoughtlessly) 軽率に keísotsu ni; (slightly) 少し sukóshì

to get off lightly 軽い罰だけで逃れる karúi bátsù dáke de nogárerù

lightness [lait'nis] *n* (in weight) 軽さ karúsa

lightning [lait'niŋ] *n* (in sky) 稲妻 inázùma

lightning conductor (*BRIT*) *n* = **lightning rod**

lightning rod (*US*) *n* 避雷針 hiráìshin

light pen *n* ライトペン raítopeñ

lights [laits] *npl* (AUT: traffic lights) (交通)信号 (kṓtsū)shíngō

light up *vi* (face) 輝く kagáyakù

♦*vt* (illuminate) 明るくする akáruku suru

lightweight [lait'weit] *adj* (suit) 薄いusúi

♦*n* (BOXING) ライト級のボクサー raítokyū no bókùsā

light year *n* (PHYSICS) 光年 kṓnen

like [laik] *vt* (find pleasing, attractive, acceptable: person, thing) ...が好きである ...ga sukí de arù

♦*prep* (similar to) ...の様な ...no yṓ na; (in comparisons) ...の様に ...no yṓ ni; (such as) 例えば...などの様な(に) tatóeba ...nádò no yṓ na(ni)

♦*adj* 似た nitá

♦*n: and the like* など nádò

his likes and dislikes 彼の好きな物と嫌いな物 kárè no sukí na monò to kirái na monò

I would like, I'd like ...が欲しいのですが ...ga hoshíi no desu gà

would you like a coffee? コーヒーはいかがですか kṓhī wa ikágà desu ká

to be/look like someone/something ...に似ている ...ni nité irù

what does it look/taste/sound like? どんな格好[味, 音]ですか dónna kákkō [ají, otó]dèsu ká *that's just like him* 彼らしいね karé rashìi né

do it like this やり方はこうです yarikata wa kṓ desu

it is nothing like ... ...とは全く違います ...to wa mattáku chigaìmasu

likeable [laiˈkəbəl] *adj* (person) 人好きのする hitózukì no surú

likelihood [laikˈliːhud] *n* 可能性 kanṓsei

likely [laikˈliː] *adj* (probable) ありそうな arísō na

to be likely to do ...しそうである ...shisṓ de arù

not likely! 何があっても...しない nánì ga atté mo ...shínài, とんでもない tondemonài

likeness [laikˈnis] *n* (similarity) 似ている事 nité irù kotó

that's a good likeness (photo, portrait) 実物そっくりだ jitsúbùtsu sokkúrì da

likewise [laikˈwaiz] *adv* (similarly) 同じく onájìku

to do likewise 同じ様にする onáji yṓ ni suru

liking [laiˈkiŋ] *n*: *to have a liking for* (person, thing) ...が好きである ...ga sukí de arù

to be to someone's liking ...の気に入っている ...no kí ni itte irù

lilac [laiˈlək] *n* (BOT: tree, flower) ライラック raírakkù, リラ rírà

lily [lilˈiː] *n* (plant, flower) ユリ yurí

lily of the valley *n* スズラン suzúrań

limb [lim] *n* (ANAT) 手足 téashi, 肢 shí

limber up [limˈbəːr-] *vi* (SPORT) 準備運動をする juñbiuñdō wo suru, ウォーミングアップをする u̯ṓminguappù suru

limbo [limˈbou] *n*: *to be in limbo* (*fig*) 忘れ去られている wasúresararete irù

lime [laim] *n* (fruit) ライム raímu; (*also*: **lime tree**) ライムの木 raímu no ki; (*also*: **lime juice**) ライムジュース raímujùsu; (for soil) 石灰 sékkài; (rock) 石灰岩 sekkáìgan

limelight [laimˈlait] *n*: *to be in the limelight* 注目を浴びている chúmoku wò abíte irù

limerick [limˈəːrik] *n* 五行わい歌 gogyṓwaìka

limestone [laimˈstoun] *n* 石灰岩 sekkáìgan

limit [limˈit] *n* (greatest amount, extent, degree) 限界 geñkai; (restriction: of time, money etc) 制限 seígen; (of area) 境界 kyṓkai

♦*vt* (production, expense etc) 制限する seígen suru

limitation [limiteiˈʃən] *n* (control, restriction) 制限 seígen; (of person, thing) 限界 geñkai

limited [limˈitid] *adj* (small: choice, resources etc) 限られた kagírareta

to be limited to ...に限られる ...ni kagírarerù

limited (liability) company (*BRIT*) *n* 有限会社 yūgengaìsha

limousine [limˈəziːn] *n* リムジン rímùjin

limp [limp] *n*: *to have a limp* びっこを引く bíkkò wo hikú

♦*vi* (person, animal) びっこを引く bíkkò wo hikú

♦*adj* (person) ぐにゃぐにゃの gúnyàgunya no

limpet [limˈpit] *n* カサガイ kaságai

line [lain] *n* (long thin mark) 線 séń; (wrinkle: on face) しわ shiwá; (row: of people, things) 列 rétsù; (of writing, song) 行 gyṓ; (rope) 綱 tsuná, ロープ rōpu; (*also*: **fishing line**) 釣糸 tsurîito; (*also*: **power line**) 送電線 sṓdensen; (*also*: **telephone line**) 電話線 deñwasen; (TEL) 回線 kaísen; (railway track) 線路 séńro; (bus, coach, train route) ...線 ...séń; (*fig*: attitude, policy) 方針 hṓshin; (: business, work) 分野 búń-ya; (COMM: of product(s)) シリーズ shírìzu

♦*vt* (road, room) ...に並ぶ ...ni narábù; (subj: person: container) ...の内側に...を張る ...no uchigawa ni ...wo harú; (: clothing) ...に裏地を付ける ...ni uráji wo tsukérù

to line something with ...に...の裏を付ける ...ni ...no urá wo tsukérù

to line the streets 道路の両側に並ぶ dōro no ryṓgawa ni narábù

in line (in a row) 1列に ichíretsu ni

in line with (according to) ...に従って ...ni shitágatte

linear [lin'i:ər] *adj* (process, sequence) 一直線の itchókusen no; (shape, form) 線形の sefíkei no

lined [laind] *adj* (face) しわのある shiwá no árù; (paper) 線を引いた séñ wo hiíta

linen [lin'ən] *n* (cloth) リンネル rínneru, リネン rínèn; (tablecloths, sheets etc) リネン rínèn

liner [lai'nə:r] *n* (ship) 豪華客船 gókakyakùsen; (for bin) ごみ袋 gomíbùkuro

linesman [lainz'mən] (*pl* **linesmen**) *n* (SPORT) 線審 séñshin, ラインズマン raíñzuman

line up *vi* 列を作る rétsù wo tsukúrù

♦*vt* (people) 1列に並ばせる ichíretsu ni narábaserù; (prepare: event, celebration) 手配する tehái suru

line-up [lain'ʌp] *n* (*US:* queue) 行列 gyóretsu; (SPORT) ラインアップ raíñ-appù

linger [liŋ'gə:r] *vi* (smell, tradition etc) 残る nokórù; (person) ぐずぐずする gúzuguzu suru

lingerie [lɑːn'dʒərei] *n* 女性下着類 joséishitagìru, ランジェリー ráñjerī

lingo [liŋ'gou] (*pl* **lingoes**: *inf*) *n* (language) 言葉 kotóba

linguist [liŋ'gwist] *n* (person who speaks several languages) 数カ国語を話せる人 sūkakokùgo wo hanáserù hitò

linguistic [liŋgwis'tik] *adj* (studies, developments, ideas etc) 語学の gógàku no

linguistics [liŋgwis'tiks] *n* 語学 gógàku

lining [lai'niŋ] *n* (cloth) 裏地 uráji; (ANAT) 粘膜 néñmaku

link [liŋk] *n* (relationship) 関係 kañkei; (of a chain) 輪 wá

♦*vt* (join) つなぐ tsunágu; (associate: *to link with/to* ...と関連付ける ...to kañren-zukerù

links [liŋks] *npl* (GOLF) ゴルフ場 gorúfujō

link up *vt* (machines, systems) つなぐ tsunágu

♦*vi* 合流する góryū suru

lino [lai'nou] *n* = **linoleum**

linoleum [linou'li:əm] *n* リノリウム rínòriumu

lion [lai'ən] *n* (ZOOL) ライオン raíon

lioness [lai'ənis] *n* 雌ライオン mesúràion

lip [lip] *n* (ANAT) 唇 kuchíbiru

lip-read [lip'ri:d] *vi* 読唇する dokúshin suru

lip salve *n* 唇の荒れ止め kuchíbiru no arédome

lip service *n*: *to pay lip service to something* (*pej*) 上辺だけ...に賛成する u-wábe dake ...ni sañsei suru

lipstick [lip'stik] *n* 口紅 kuchíbeni

liqueur [likə:r] *n* リキュール ríkyùru

liquid [lik'wid] *adj* 液体の ekítai no

♦*n* 液 ékì, 液体 ekítai

liquidate [lik'wideit] *vt* (opponents, rivals) 消す kesú, 殺す korósù; (company) つぶす tsubúsù

liquidize [lik'widaiz] *vt* (CULIN) ミキサーに掛ける míkìsa ni kakérù

liquidizer [lik'widaizə:r] (*BRIT*) *n* ミキサー míkìsa

liquor [lik'ə:r] *n* 酒 sake

liquorice [lik'ə:ris] (*BRIT*) *n* = **licorice**

liquor store (*US*) *n* 酒屋 sákaya

Lisbon [liz'bən] *n* リスボン rísùbon

lisp [lisp] *n* 舌足らずの発音 shitátaràzu no hatsúon

♦*vi* 舌足らずに発音する shitátaràzu ni hatsúon suru

list [list] *n* (catalog: of things) 目録 mokúroku, リスト rísùto; (: of people) 名簿 meíbo, リスト rísùto

♦*vt* (mention) 並べてあげる narábete agerù; (put on list) ...のリストを作る ...no rísùto wo tsukúrù

listed building [lis'tid-] (*BRIT*) *n* 指定建造物 shitéikenzòbutsu

listen [lis'ən] *vi* 聞く kikú

to listen to someone/something ...を〔...の言う事を〕聞く ...wo〔...no iú kotò wo〕kikú

listener [lis'ənə:r] *n* (person listening to speaker) 聞いている人 kiíte irù hitò; (RADIO) 聴取者 chōshusha

listless [list'lis] *adj* 物憂い monóuì

lit [lit] *pt, pp of* **light**

liter [li:'tər] *(US) n* (unit of volume) リットル ríttòru

literacy [lit'ə:rəsi:] *n* 識字 shikíji

literal [lit'ə:rəl] *adj* (exact: sense, meaning) 厳密な genmitsu na; (word for word: translation) 逐語的な chikúgoteki na

literally [lit'ə:rəli:] *adv* (in fact) 本当に hontō ni; (really) 文字通りに mojídōri ni

literary [lit'əre:ri:] *adj* 文学の bungàku no

literate [lit'ə:rit] *adj* (able to read etc) 読み書きできる yomíkaki dekirù; (educated) 教養のある kyōyō no arù

literature [lit'ə:rətʃə:r] *n* (novels, plays, poetry) 文学 bungàku; (printed information: scholarly) 文献 bunken; (: brochures etc) 印刷物 insatsubùtsu, カタログ katárogu

lithe [laið] *adj* (person, animal) しなやかな shináyàka na

litigation [litəgei'ʃən] *n* 訴訟 soshō

litre [li:'tə:r] *(BRIT) n =* **liter**

litter [lit'ə:r] *n* (rubbish) 散らばっているごみ chirábatte irù gomi; (young animals) 一腹 hitóhara

litter bin *(BRIT) n* ごみ入れ gomíìre

littered [lit'ə:rd] *adj: littered with* (scattered) ...を散らかされた ...wo chirákasareta

little [lit'əl] *adj* (small: thing, person) 小さい chiísài; (young: child) 幼い osánài; (short: distance) 近い chikáì; (time, event) 短い mijíkaì

♦*adv* 少ししか...ない sukóshì shika ...náì

a little (amount) 少し(の) sukóshì (no)

a little bit 少し sukóshì

little brother/sister 弟〔妹〕otóto〔imóto〕

little by little 少しずつ sukóshizùtsu

little finger *n* 小指 koyúbi

live [*vb* liv *adj* laiv] *vi* (reside: in house, town, country) 住む súmù; (lead one's life) 暮す kurásù; (be alive) 生きている ikíte irù

♦*adj* (animal, plant) 生きている ikíte irù; (TV, RADIO) 生の namá no, ライブの ráibu no; (performance) 実演の jitsúen no; (ELEC) 電流が通じている denryū ga tsūjite irù, 生きている ikíte irù; (bullet, bomb, missile) 使用可能状態の shiyōkanōjōtai no, 実の jitsú no

to live with someone (cohabit) ...と同せいする ...to dōsei suru

live down *vt* (defeat, error, failure): *I'll never live it down* 一生の恥だ isshō no hájì da

livelihood [laiv'li:hud] *n* (income source) 生計 seíkei

lively [laiv'li:] *adj* (person) 活発な kappátsu na; (interesting: place etc) 活気に満ちた kakkí ni michítà; (: event) にぎやかな nigíyaka na; (: book) 面白い omóshiròì; (enthusiastic: interest, admiration etc) 熱心な nesshín na

liven up [laiv'ən-] *vt* (person) ...に元気を付ける ...ni génki wo tsukérù; (discussion, evening etc) 面白くする omóshirokù suru

♦*vi* (person) 元気になる génki ni nárù; (discussion, evening etc) 面白くなる omóshirokù nárù

live on [laiv-] *vt fus* (food) ...を食べて暮す ...wo tábète kurásu

liver [liv'ə:r] *n* (ANAT) 肝臓 kanzō; (CULIN) レバー rébà

livery [liv'ə:ri:] *n* (of servant) お仕着せ o-shíkise

lives [laivz] *npl of* **life**

livestock [laiv'sta:k] *n* (AGR) 家畜 kachíku

live together *vi* (cohabit) 同せいする dōsei suru

live up to *vt fus* (fulfil) 守る mamórù

livid [liv'id] *adj* (color: of bruise) 青黒い aóguroì; (: of angry face) どす黒い dosúguroì; (: of sky) 鉛色の namáiiro no; (furious: person) 激怒した gékìdo shitá

living [liv'iŋ] *adj* (alive: person, animal) 生きている ikíte iru

♦*n: to earn/make a living* 生計を立てる seíkei wo tatérù

living conditions *npl* 暮しの状況 kuráshi no jōkyō

living room *n* 居間 imá

living standards *npl* 生活水準 seíkatsusuijùn

living wage n 生活賃金 seíkatsuchiǹgin

lizard [liz'ə:rd] n トカゲ tokáge

load [loud] n (thing carried: of person) 荷物 nímòtsu; (: of animal) 荷 ní; (: of vehicle) 積荷 tsumíni; (weight) 負担 fután
♦vt (also: **load up**: vehicle, ship etc): **to load (with)** (...を...) ...に積む ...ni tsúmù; (COMPUT: program) メモリーに読込む mémòrī ni yomíkomù, ロードする rōdo suru; (gun) ...に弾丸を込める ...ni dangan wo kométe; (camera) ...にフィルムを入れる ...ni fírùmu wo iréru; (tape recorder) ...にテープを入れる ...ni tếpu wo iréru
a load of rubbish (inf) でたらめ detárame
loads of/a load of (fig) 沢山の takúsaǹ no

loaded [lou'did] adj (vehicle): **to be loaded with** ...を積んでいる ... wo tsuǹde iru; (question) 誘導的な yúdòteki na; (inf: rich) 金持の kanémochi na

loaf [louf] (pl **loaves**) n 一かたまりのパン hitókàtamari no pan

loan [loun] n (sum of money) 貸付金 kashítsukekin, ローン ròn
♦vt (money, thing) 貸す kasú
on loan (borrowed) 借りている karíte irù

loath [louθ] adj: **to be loath to do something** ...をしたくない ...wo shitáku naì

loathe [louð] vt (person, activity) ...が大嫌いである ...ga daíkiraì de árù

loaves [louvz] npl of **loaf**

lobby [lɑ:b'i:] n (of building) ロビー robī; (POL: pressure group) 圧力団体 atsúryokudaǹtai
♦vt (POL) ...に圧力を掛ける ...ni atsúryoku wò kakérù

lobe [loub] n (also: **earlobe**) 耳たぶ mimítabù

lobster [lɑ:b'stə:r] n ロブスター róbùsutā

local [lou'kəl] adj (council, paper, police station) 地元の jimóto no
♦n (BRIT: pub) 地元のパブ jimóto no

pábù

local anesthetic n (MED) 局部麻酔 kyokúbumasùi

local authority n 地方自治体 chihójichìtai

local call n (TEL) 市内通話 shináitsùwa

local government n 地方自治体 chihójichìtai

locality [loukæl'iti:] n 場所 basho

locally [lou'kəli:] adv 地元で jimóto de

locals [lou'kəlz] npl: **the locals** (local inhabitants) 地元の住民 jimóto no júmiǹ

locate [lou'keit] vt (find: person, thing) 見付ける mitsúkeru; (situate): **to be located in** ...にある〔いる〕 ...ni árù〔irú〕

location [loukei'ʃən] n (particular place) 場所 basho
on location (CINEMA) ロケで rokè de

loch [lɑːk] n 湖 mizúumì

lock [lɑːk] n (of door, drawer, suitcase) 錠 jō; (on canal) こう門 kōmon; (also: **lock of hair**) 髪の一房 kamí no hitófùsa
♦vt (door, drawer, suitcase: with key) ...のかぎを掛ける ...no kagí wo kakérù
♦vi (door etc) かぎが掛る kagí ga kakárù; (wheels) 回らなくなる mawáranaku narù

locker [lɑːk'ə:r] n (in school, railway station etc) ロッカー rókkà

locket [lɑːk'it] n ロケット rokéttð

lock in vt 閉じ込める tojíkomerù

lock out vt (person) 閉出す shimédasu

locksmith [lɑːk'smiθ] n 錠前師 jōmaeshì

lock up vt (criminal) 刑務所に入れる keímushò ni iréru; (mental patient) 施設に預ける shisétsu ni azúkerù; (house) ...のかぎを掛ける ...no kagí wo kakérù
♦vi ...のかぎが掛ける ...no kagí wo kakérù

lockup [lɑːk'ʌp] n (jail) 刑務所 keímushò

locomotive [loukəmou'tiv] n 機関車 kikáñsha

locum tenens [lou'kəm ti:'nenz] (BRIT **locum**) n (MED) 代診 daíshin

locust [lou'kəst] n イナゴ inágo

lodge [lɑːdʒ] n (small house) 守衛室 shuéishìtsu; (hunting lodge) 山小屋 yamágoya

♦*vi* (person): *to lodge (with)* (...の家に) 下宿する (...no iè ni) geshúku suru; (bullet, bone etc) ...に支える ...ni tsukáerù

♦*vt* (complaint, protest etc) 提出する teíshutsu suru

lodger [lɑ:dʒˈəːr] *n* 下宿人 geshúkunin

lodgings [lɑːdʒˈiŋz] *npl* 下宿 geshúku

loft [lɔːft] *n* (attic) 屋根裏部屋 yanéurabèya

lofty [lɔːfˈtiː] *adj* (noble: ideal, aim) 高尚な kôshō na; (self-important: manner) 横柄な ôhei na

log [lɔːg] *n* (piece of wood) 丸太 marúta; (written account) 日誌 nisshí

♦*vt* (event, fact) 記録する kiróku suru

logarithm [lɔːgˈəriðəm] *n* (MATH) 対数 taísū

logbook [lɔːgˈbuk] *n* (NAUT) 航海日誌 kôkainisshì; (AVIAT) 航空日誌 kôkūnisshi; (BRIT: of car) 登録帳 tôrokuchō

loggerheads [lɔːgˈəːrhedz] *npl*: *to be at loggerheads* 対立している taíritsu shite iru

logic [lɑːdʒˈik] *n* (method of reasoning) 論理学 roñrigàku; (process of reasoning) 論理 rôñri

logical [lɑːdʒˈikəl] *adj* (argument, analysis) 論理的な roñriteki na; (conclusion, result) 当然な tôzen na; (course of action) 合理的な gôriteki na

logistics [loudʒisˈtiks] *n* (planning and organization) 仕事の計画と実行 shigóto nò keíkaku tò jikkô

logo [lou'gou] *n* (of firm, organization) シンボルマーク shíñborumāku, ロゴ rôgò

loin [lɔin] *n* (of meat) 腰肉 koshíniku

loiter [lɔiˈtəːr] *vi* (linger) ぶらつく burátsuku

loll [lɑːl] *vi* (person: *also*: **loll about**) ごろ寝する goróne suru

lollipop [lɑːlˈiːpɑːp] *n* 棒あめ bôame

lollipop lady (BRIT) *n* 緑のおばさん midóri no obasàn ◇学童道路横断監視員 gakúdō dōroōdan kañshiin

lollipop man (BRIT: *pl* **lollipop men**) *n* ◇緑のおばさんの仕事をする男性 midó-

ri no obasàn no shigóto wò suru dansei

London [lʌnˈdən] *n* ロンドン róñdon

Londoner [lʌnˈdənəːr] *n* ロンドンっ子 roñdonkko

lone [loun] *adj* (person) たったひとりのtattá hitóri no; (thing) たったひとつの tattá hitótsu no

loneliness [loun'li:nis] *n* 孤独 kodóku

lonely [loun'li:] *adj* (person) 寂しい sabíshiì; (situation) 孤独な kodóku na; (place) 人気のない hitóke no naì

long [lɔːŋ] *adj* 長い nagáì

♦*adv* 長く nágaku

♦*vi*: *to long for something* ...を恋しがる ...wo koíshigarù

so/as long as ...さえすれば ...sáè suréba

don't be long! 早く帰って来て下さいね háyàku kaétte kite kudàsai né

how long is the street? この道の端から端までどのぐらいありますか konó michí no hashí kara hashí madè donó guraí arímasù ká

how long is the lesson? レッスンの時間はどのぐらいですか réssùn no jíkàn wa donó guraì desu ká

6 meters long 長さは6メーター nágàsa wa rokú mētā

6 months long 期間は6か月 kíkàn wa rokkágetsu

all night long ひと晩中 hitóbanjū

he no longer comes 彼はもう来ない kárè wa mô kônài

long before ずっと前に zuttó máè ni

before long (+future, +past) まもなく mamónàku

at long last やっと yattô

long-distance [lɔːŋˈdisˈtəns] *adj* (travel, phone call) 長距離の chôkyori no

longevity [lɑːndʒevˈitiː] *n* 長生き nagáiki

long-haired [lɔːŋˈheːrd] *adj* (person) 長髪の chôhatsu no

longhand [lɔːŋˈhænd] *n* 普通の書き方 futsū no kakíkata

longing [lɔːŋˈiŋ] *n* あこがれ akôgare

longitude [lɑːnˈdʒətuːd] *n* 経度 keído

long jump *n* 走り幅跳び hashírihabàtobi

long-life [lɔ:ŋ'laif] *adj* (batteries etc) 寿命の長い jumyŏ no nagáì; (milk) ロングライフの roṅguraìfu no

long-lost [lɔ:ŋ'lɔ:st] *adj* (relative, friend) 長年会わなかった nagánen awánakattà

long-playing record [lɔ:ŋ'plei'iŋ-] *n* L Pレコード erúpírekòdo

long-range [lɔ:ŋ'reindʒ] *adj* (plan, forecast) 長期の chóki no; (missile, plane etc) 長距離の chókyori no

long-sighted [lɔ:ŋ'saitid] *adj* (MED) 遠視の eńshi no

long-standing [lɔ:ŋ'stæn'diŋ] *adj* 長年にわたる nagánen ni watárù

long-suffering [lɔ:ŋ'sʌf'ə:riŋ] *adj* (person) 忍耐強い niñtaizuyoi

long-term [lɔ:ŋ'tə:rm'] *adj* (project, solution etc) 長期の chóki no

long wave *n* (RADIO) 長波 chŏha

long-winded [lɔ:ŋ'win'did] *adj* (speech, text) 長たらしい nagátarashiì

loo [lu:] (*BRIT: inf*) *n* トイレ tóìre

look [luk] *vi* (see) 見る mírù; (seem, appear) ...に見える ...ni miérù; (building etc): **to look south/(out) onto the sea** 南〔海〕に面している mínami〔úmi〕ni méñ shite irú
♦*n* (*gen*): **to have a look** 見る mírù; (glance: expressing disapproval etc) 目付き métsùki; (appearance, expression) 様子 yŏsu
look (here)! (expressing annoyance etc) おい ôì
look! (expressing surprise: male language) 見てくれ mítè kurê; (: female language) 見て mítè

look after *vt fus* (care for) ...の面倒を見る ...no meñdo wo mírù; (deal with) 取扱う toríatsukaù

look at *vt fus* (see) ...を見る ...wo mírù; (read quickly) ...にさっと目を通す ...ni sattó me wo tŏsù; (study: problem, subject etc) 調べる shiráberù

look back *vi* (remember) 振返ってみる furíkaette mirù

look down on *vt fus* (*fig*) 軽べつする keíbetsu suru

look for *vt fus* (person, thing) 捜す sagásu

look forward to *vt fus* ...を楽しみにする ...wo tanóshimi ni suru; (in letters): **we look forward to hearing from you** ご返事をお待ちしております go-héñji wo o-máchi shitè orímasù

look into *vt* (investigate) ...を調べる ...wo shiráberù

look on *vi* (watch) 傍観する bŏkan suru

look out *vi* (beware): **to look out (for)** (...に) 注意する (...ni) chúì suru

lookout [luk'aut] *n* (tower etc) 看視所 kañshìjò; (person) 見張り人 mihárinìn
to be on the lookout for something ...を警戒する ...wo keíkai suru

look out for *vt fus* (seek) 捜す sagásu

look round *vi* 見回す mimáwasù

looks [luks] *npl* (good looks) 容ぼう yŏbō

look through *vt fus* (examine) ...を調べる ...wo shiráberù

look to *vt fus* (rely on) ...を頼りにする ...wo tayóri ni surù

look up *vi* (with eyes) 見上げる miágerù; (situation) ...の見通しがよくなる ...no mitŏshi ga yokù naru
♦*vt* (piece of information) 調べる shiráberù

look up to *vt fus* (hero, idol) ...を尊敬する ...wo soñkei suru

loom [lu:m] *vi* (*also*: **loom up**: object, shape) ぼんやりと姿を現す boñ-yarì to sugáta wò aráwasù; (: event: approach) 迫っている semátte irú
♦*n* (for weaving) 機織機 hatáorikì

loony [lu:'ni:] (*inf*) *adj* 狂っている kurútte irú
♦*n* 気違い kichígaì

loop [lu:p] *n* (in string, ribbon etc) 輪 wá
♦*vt*: **to loop something round something** ...に...を巻付ける ...ni ...wo makítsukerù

loophole [lu:p'houl] *n* (*fig*) 抜け穴 nukéana

loose [lu:s] *adj* (not firmly fixed) 緩い yurúì; (not close fitting: clothes etc) ゆったりした yuttárì shita; (not tied back: long hair) 縛ってない shibátte naì; (promiscuous: life, morals) ふしだらな fushídàra na

♦*n*: **to be on the loose** (prisoner, maniac) 逃亡中である tôbōchū de arù

loose change *n* 小銭 kozéni

loose chippings [-tʃíp'iŋz] *npl* (on road) 砂利 jarí

loose end *n*: **to be at loose ends** (US) *or* **a loose end** (BRIT) 暇を持て余している himá wo motéamashite irù

loosely [luːsˈliː] *adv* 緩く yúrùku

loosen [luːˈsən] *vt* 緩める yurúmerù

loot [luːt] *n* (*inf*) 分捕り品 buńdorihìn

♦*vt* (steal from: shops, homes) 略奪する ryakúdatsu suru

lop off [lɑːp-] *vt* (branches etc) 切り落す kiríotosù

lopsided [lɑːpˈsaiˈdid] *adj* (crooked) 偏った katáyottà

lord [lɔːrd] *n* (BRIT: peer) 貴族 kízòku

Lord Smith スミス卿 sumísukyō

the Lord (REL) 主 shú

my lord (to bishop, noble, judge) 閣下 kákkà

good Lord! えっ Ét

the (House of) Lords (BRIT) 上院 jóin

lordship [lɔːrdˈʃip] *n*: **your Lordship** 閣下 kákkà

lore [lɔːr] *n* (of particular culture) 伝承 deńshō

lorry [lɔːrˈiː] (BRIT) *n* トラック torákkù

lorry driver (BRIT) *n* トラック運転手 torákkù unteńshu

lose [luːz] (*pt*, *pp* **lost**) *vt* (object) 紛失する fuńshitsu suru, なくす nakúsù; (job) 失う ushínaù; (weight) 減らす herásù; (friend, relative through death) 失う ushínaù, なくす nakusu; (waste: time) 無駄にする mudá ni surù; (: opportunity) 逃す nogásù; (money) 損する sóň suru

♦*vi* (competition, argument) ...に負ける ...ni makérù

to lose (time) (clock) 遅れる okúrerù

loser [luːˈzəːr] *n* (in game, contest) 敗者 háìsha; (*inf*: failure: person, thing) 出来損ない dekísokonai

loss [lɔːs] *n* (act of losing something) 紛失 fuńshitsu; (occasion of losing some-

thing) 喪失 sōshitsu; (death) 死亡 shibō; (COMM): **to make a loss** 損する sóň suru

heavy losses (MIL) 大きな損害 ōkina sońgai

to be at a loss 途方に暮れる tohō ni kurérù

lost [lɔːst] *pt*, *pp of* **lose**

♦*adj* (person, animal: in unknown place) 道に迷った michí ni mayótta; (: missing) 行方不明の yukúe fumèi no; (object) なくした nakúshàta

lost and found (US) *n* 遺失物 ishítsubùtsu

lost property (BRIT) *n* = **lost and found**

lot [lɑːt] *n* (set, group: of things) ひと組 hitōkùmi; (at auctions) ロット róttò

the lot (everything) 全部 zéňbu

a lot (large number, amount) 沢山 takúsan

a lot of 沢山の takusan no

lots of (things, people) 沢山の takúsan no

I read a lot 私は沢山の本を読みます watákushi wa takúsàn no hoň wò yomímasù

to draw lots (for something) (...のために) くじを引く (...no tamé nì) kújì wo híkù

lotion [louˈʃən] *n* (for skin, hair) ローション rōshon

lottery [lɑːtˈəːriː] *n* (game) 宝くじ takárakùji

loud [laud] *adj* (noise, voice, laugh) 大きい ōkii; (support, condemnation) 強い tsuyói; (clothes) 派手な hadé na

♦*adv* (speak etc) 大きな声で ōkina kôè de

out loud (read, laugh, pray etc) 声を出して kôè wo dáshìte

loudhailer [laudˈheiləːr] (BRIT) *n* = **bullhorn**

loudly [laudˈliː] *adv* 大きな声で ōkina kôè de

loudspeaker [laudˈspiːkəːr] *n* 拡声器 kakúseìki, スピーカー súpìkā

lounge [laundʒ] *n* (BRIT: in house) 居間

imá; (in hotel, at airport, station) ロビーróbì; (*BRIT*: also: **lounge bar**) ラウンジバー raúnjibā

♦*vi* ぐったりもたれる guttárì motárerù

lounge about *vi* ぶらぶらする búràbura suru

lounge around *vi* = **lounge about**

lounge suit (*BRIT*) *n* 背広 sebíro、スーツ sūtsu

louse [laus] (*pl* **lice**) *n* (insect) シラミ shirámi

lousy [lau'zi:] *adj* (*inf*: bad quality: show, meal etc) 最低の saítei no; (: ill) 気持が悪い kimóchi gà warúî

lout [laut] *n* ちんぴら chíñpira

lovable [lʌv'əbəl] *adj* 愛らしい aírashiî

love [lʌv] *n* (*gen*) 愛 áî, 愛情 aíjō; (romantic) 恋愛 reñ-ai; (sexual) 性愛 seíai; (strong liking: for music, football, animals etc) 愛着 aíchaku、好み konómi

♦*vt* (*gen*) 愛する aí surù; (thing, activity etc) ...が大好きである ...ga daísuki de arù

love (from) Anne (on letter) 愛を込めて、アン（より）âî wo kométe, áñ (yórì)

to love to do ...するのが大好きである ...surú nò ga daísuki de arù

to be in love with ...にほれている ...ni horéte irù, ...が好きである ...ga sukí de arù

to fall in love with ...と恋に落ちる ...to koî ni ochírù, ...が好きになる ...ga sukí ni narù

to make love (have sex) 性交する seíkō suru、セックスする sékkùsu suru

15 love (TENNIS) 15対0 jū̀go taî zérò, フィフティーンラブ ffūtîn rabu

I love chocolate 私はチョコレートが大好きです watákushi wà chokórèto ga daísuki desù

love affair *n* 情事 jōji

love letter *n* ラブレター rábùretā

love life *n* 性生活 seíseikàtsu

lovely [lʌv'li:] *adj* (beautiful) 美しい utsúkushiî; (delightful) 楽しい tanóshiî

lover [lʌv'ə:r] *n* (sexual partner) 愛人 aíjin; (person in love) 恋人 koíbito

a lover of art/music 美術〔音楽〕の愛

好者 bíjùtsu〔óñgaku〕no áikōsha

loving [lʌv'iŋ] *adj* (person) 愛情深い aíjōbukaî; (actions) 愛情のこもった aíjō no komótta

low [lou] *adj* (*gen*) 低い hikuî; (income, price etc) 安い yasúî; (quality) 粗悪な soáku na; (sound: deep) 深い fukáî; (: quiet) 低い hikúî

♦*adv* (sing) 低音で teíon de; (fly) 低く hikúkù

♦*n* (METEOROLOGY) 低気圧 teíkìatsu

to be low on (supplies etc) ...が少なくなっている ...ga sukúnàku natté irù

to feel low (depressed) 元気がない géñki ga náî

low-alcohol [lou'æl'kəhɔ:l] *adj* (wine, beer) 度の低い do no hikúî

low-cut [lou'kʌt'] *adj* (dress) 襟ぐりの深い eríguri no fukáî, ローカットの rōkattò no

lower [lou'ə:r] *adj* (bottom, less important) 下の shitá no

♦*vt* (object, price etc) 下げる sagérù; (voice) 低くする hikúkù suru; (eyes) 下に向ける shitá ni mukéru

low-fat [lou'fæt'] *adj* 低脂肪の teíshibō no, ローファットの rōfattò no

lowlands [lou'ləndz] *npl* (GEO) 低地 teíchi

lowly [lou'li:] *adj* (position, origin) 卑しい iyáshiî

loyal [lɔi'əl] *adj* (friend, support etc) 忠実な chújitsu na

loyalty [lɔi'əltiː] *n* 忠誠 chúsei

lozenge [la:z'indʒ] *n* (MED) ドロップ dóròppu

LP [el'piː'] *n abbr* = **long-playing record**

L-plates [el'pleits] (*BRIT*) *npl* 仮免許運転中の表示プレート karímenkyo unten-chū no hyōjipurèto

Ltd *abbr* (COMM) = **limited (liability) company**

lubricate [lu:b'rikeit] *vt* (part of machine, chain etc) ...に油を差す ...ni a-búra wo sásù

lucid [luː'sid] *adj* (writing, speech) 分かりやすい wakáriyasuî; (able to think clearly) 正気な shṓki na

luck [lʌk] n (also: **good luck**) 運 úǹ
bad luck 悪運 akúùn
good luck! 成功を祈るよ seíkō wò inórì yo
bad/hard/tough luck! 残念だね zaňneň da né

luckily [lʌk'ili:] adv 幸いに saíwai ni

lucky [lʌk'i:] adj (person: fortunate) 運の良い úǹ no yói; (: at cards etc) ...に強い ...ni tsuyóì; (situation, event) まぐれの magúrè no; (object) 好運をもたらす kṓuǹ wo motárasù

lucrative [lu:'krətiv] adj もうかる mṓkarù

ludicrous [lu:'dəkrəs] adj (feeling, situation, price etc) ばかばかしい bakábakashii

lug [lʌg] (inf) vt (heavy object, suitcase etc) 引きずる hikízuru

luggage [lʌg'idʒ] n 手荷物 tenímòtsu

luggage rack n (on car) ルーフラック rǘfurakkù; (in train) 網棚 amidana

lukewarm [lu:k'wɔ:rm] adj (liquid) ぬるい nurúî; (person, reaction etc) 気乗りしない kinóri shinai

lull [lʌl] n (break: in conversation, fighting etc) 途切れる事 togírerù kotó
♦vt: *to lull someone to sleep* ゆすって ...を寝付かせる yusútte ...wo netsúkaserù
to be lulled into a false sense of security 油断する yudán suru

lullaby [lʌl'əbai] n 子守歌 komóriùta

lumbago [lʌmbei'gou] n (MED) 腰痛 yṓtsū

lumber [lʌm'bə:r] n (wood) 材木 zaímoku; (BRIT: junk) 粗大ごみ sodáigomi

lumberjack [lʌm'bə:rdʒæk] n きこり kikóri

lumber with vt: *to be lumbered with something* ...を押付けられる ...wo oshítsukerarerù

luminous [lu:'minəs] adj (fabric, color, dial, instrument etc) 蛍光の keíkō no

lump [lʌmp] n (of clay, butter etc) 塊 katámari; (on body) しこり shikóri; (on head) こぶ kobú; (also: **sugar lump**) 角砂

糖 kakúzatō
♦vt: *to lump together* 一緒くたに扱う isshṓkuta ni atsúkaù
a lump sum 一時払い金額 ichíjibaraikiǹgaku

lumpy [lʌm'pi:] adj (sauce) 塊だらけの katámaridaràke no; (bed) ごつごつの gotsúgotsuno

lunar [lu:'nə:r] adj (landscape, module, landing etc) 月の tsukí no

lunatic [lu:'nətik] adj (behavior) 気違い染みた kichígaijimità

lunch [lʌntʃ] n 昼食 chúshoku

luncheon [lʌn'tʃən] n (formal meal) 昼食会 chúshokukài

luncheon meat n ランチョンミート raňchonmìto

luncheon voucher (BRIT) n 昼食券 chúshokukèn

lunch time n 昼食時 chúshokudoki

lung [lʌŋ] n (ANAT) 肺 haí

lunge [lʌndʒ] vi (also: **lunge forward**) 突進する tosshín suru
to lunge at ...を目掛けて突っ掛る ...wo megákete tsukkákarù

lurch [lə:rtʃ] vi (person) よろめく yorómekù; (vehicle) 揺れる yurérù
♦n (movement: of person) よろめき yorómeki; (: of vehicle) 揺れる事 yurérù kotó
to leave someone in the lurch 見捨てる misúterù

lure [lu:r] n (attraction) 魅惑 miwáku
♦vt (entice, tempt) 魅惑する miwáku suru

lurid [lu:'rid] adj (violent, sexually graphic: story etc) どぎつい dogítsuì; (pej: brightly colored: dress etc) けばけばしい kebákebashiî

lurk [lə:rk] vi (animal, person) 待ち伏せする machíbuse surù

luscious [lʌʃ'əs] adj (attractive: person, thing) 魅力的な miryókuteki na; (food) おいしそうな oíshisō na

lush [lʌʃ] adj (fields, gardens) 生茂った oíshigettà

lust [lʌst] (pej) n (sexual desire) 性欲 sefyoku; (desire for money, power etc) 欲望

yokúbō

lust after *vt fus* (desire: strongly) ...の欲に駆られる ...no yokú ni karárerù; (: sexually) ...とセックスをしたがる ...to sekkúsù wo shitágarù

luster [lʌk'stər] (*BRIT* lustre) *n* (shining: of metal, polished wood etc) つや tsuyá

lust for *vt fus* = **lust after**

lusty [lʌs'tiː] *adj* (healthy, energetic) 元気一杯の geñkiippaî no

Luxembourg [lʌk'səmbəːrg] *n* ルクセンブルク rukúseňburuku

luxuriant [lʌgʒuːr'iːənt] *adj* (plants, trees) 生茂った oíshigettà; (gardens) 植込みの生茂った uékomi no oíshigettà; (hair) 豊富な hôfu na

luxurious [lʌgʒuːr'iːəs] *adj* (hotel, surroundings etc) 豪華な gôka na

luxury [lʌk'ʃəriː] *n* (great comfort) ぜいたく zeítaku; (expensive extra) ぜいたく品 zeítakuhìn; (infrequent pleasure) 得難い楽しみ egátaî tanóshimî

◆*cpd* (hotel, car etc) 豪華... gôka...

lying [lai'iŋ] *n* うそをつく事 usó wo tsúkù kotó

◆*adj* うそつきの usótsuki no

lynch [lintʃ] *vt* (prisoner, suspect) 勝手に絞り首にする katté ni shibárikùbi ni suru

lyrical [lir'ikəl] *adj* (poem) 叙情の jojô no; (*fig*: praise, comment) 叙情的な jojôteki na

lyrics [lir'iks] *npl* (of song) 歌詞 káshì

M

m. *abbr* = **meter**; **mile**; **million**

M.A. [emei'] *abbr* = **Master** *of* **Arts**

mac [mæk] (*BRIT*) *n* = **mackintosh**

macabre [məkɑː'brə] *adj* 背筋の凍る様なsesúji no kôru yo na

macaroni [mækərou'niː] *n* マカロニ makároni

machine [məʃiːn'] *n* (piece of equipment) 機械 kikáî; (*fig*: party machine, war machine etc) 組織 sôshìki

◆*vt* (TECH) 機械で作る kikáî de tsukúrù; (dress etc) ミシンで作る míshìn de tsukúrù

machine gun *n* 機関銃 kikánjū

machine language *n* (COMPUT) 機械語 kikáigò

machinery [məʃiː'nəriː] *n* (equipment) 機械類 kikáirùi; (*fig*: of government) 組織 sôshìki

macho [mɑː'tʃou] *adj* (man, attitude) 男っぽい otôkoppoi

mackerel [mæk'əːrəl] *n inv* サバ sabá

mackintosh [mæk'intɑːʃ] (*BRIT*) *n* レーンコート rêňkōto

mad [mæd] *adj* (insane) 気の狂った ki no kurúttà; (foolish) ばかげた bakágetà; (angry) 怒っている okôtte irù; (keen): **to be mad about** (person, football etc) ...に夢中になっている ...ni muchû ni nátte iru

madam [mæd'əm] *n* (form of address) 奥様 ôkùsama

madden [mæd'ən] *vt* 怒らせる okóraserù

made [meid] *pt, pp of* **make**

Madeira [mədei'rə] *n* (GEO) マデイラ madéira; (wine) マデイラ madéira

made-to-measure [meid'təmeʒ'əːr] (*BRIT*) *adj* = **made-to-order**

made-to-order [meid'tuːɔːr'dəːr] (*US*) *adj* オーダーメードの ôdāmêdo no

madly [mæd'liː] *adv* (frantically) 死物狂いで shinímonogurùi de

madly in love ぞっこんほれ込んで zokkôn horékoňde

madman [mæd'mæn] (*pl* **madmen**) *n* 気違い kichígaî

madness [mæd'nis] *n* (insanity) 狂気 kyôki; (foolishness) 気違い沙汰 kichígaizata

Madrid [mədrid'] *n* マドリード madôrìdo

Mafia [mɑː'fiːə] *n* マフィア máfìa

magazine [mægəziːn'] *n* (PRESS) 雑誌 zasshí; (RADIO, TV) 放送ジャーナル hôsō jānarù

maggot [mæg'ət] *n* ウジムシ ujímùshi

magic [mædʒ'ik] *n* (supernatural power) 魔法 mahô; (conjuring) 手品 téjìna, マジック májìkku

♦*adj* (powers, ritual) 魔法の mahō no

magical [mædʒˈikəl] *adj* (powers, ritual) 魔法の mahō no; (experience, evening) 夢の様な yumé no yō na

magician [mədʒíʃˈən] *n* (wizard) 魔法使い mahōtsukaì; (conjurer) マジシャン májìshan

magistrate [mædʒˈistreit] *n* 軽犯罪判事 keíhanzai hanji

magnanimous [mægnænˈəməs] *adj* (person, gesture) 寛大な kańdai na

magnate [mægˈneit] *n* 大立者 ōdatemono, ...王 ...ō

magnesium [mægniːˈziːəm] *n* マグネシウム magúneshiùmu

magnet [mægˈnit] *n* 磁石 jíshàku

magnetic [mægnetˈik] *adj* (PHYSICS) 磁石の jíshàku no; (personality) 魅力的な miryōkuteki na

magnetic tape *n* 磁気テープ jikí tèpu

magnetism [mægˈnitizəm] *n* 磁気 jíkì

magnificent [mægnifˈəsənt] *adj* 素晴らしい subárashiì

magnify [mægˈnəfai] *vt* (enlarge: object) 拡大する kakúdai suru; (increase: sound) 大きくする ōkiku suru

magnifying glass [mægˈnəfaiiŋ-] *n* 拡大鏡 kakúdaikyō

magnitude [mægˈnətuːd] *n* (size) 大きさ ōkisa; (importance) 重要性 jūyōsei

magnolia [mægnoulˈjə] *n* マグノリア magúnorìa ◇モクレン, コブシ, タイサンボクを含む植物の類 mókùren, kóbùshi, taísañboku wo fukúmù shokúbùtsu no ruí

magpie [mægˈpai] *n* カササギ kasásagi

mahogany [məhɑːgˈəni:] *n* マホガニー mahógànī

maid [meid] *n* (servant) メイド meídò
   old maid (pej: spinster) ハイミス haímìsu

maiden [meidˈən] *n* (literary: girl) 少女 shōjo
   ♦*adj* (aunt etc) 未婚の mikōn no; (speech, voyage) 処女... shōjò ...

maiden name *n* 旧姓 kyūsei ◇既婚女性について使う kikónjòsei ni tsuíte tsukáù

mail [meil] *n* (postal service) 郵便 yūbin;

(letters etc) 郵便物 yūbiñbutsu
   ♦*vt* (post) 投かんする tōkan suru

mailbox [meilˈbɑːks] (*US*) *n* ポスト pósùto

mailing list [meilˈiŋ-] *n* 郵送先名簿 yūsōsaki meìbo

mail-order [meilˈɔːrdəːr] *n* (system) 通信販売 tsūshinhañbai

maim [meim] *vt* 重傷を負わせる jūshō wo owáserù ◇その結果不具になる場合について言う sonō kekká fúgù ni nárù baái ni tsuíte iú

main [mein] *adj* 主な ōmò na, 主要な shuyō na, メーンの mēn no
   ♦*n* (pipe) 本管 hofikan
   in the main (in general) 概して gáì shite

mainframe [meinˈfreim] *n* (COMPUT) メインフレーム meínfurèmu

mainland [meinˈlənd] *n* 本土 hóñdo

mainly [meinˈliː] *adv* 主に ōmò ni

main road *n* 幹線道路 kañsendōro

mains [meinz] *npl*: *the mains* (gas, water) 本管 hofikan; (ELEC) 本線 hofisen

mainstay [meinˈstei] *n* (fig: prop) 大黒柱 daíkokubàshira

mainstream [meinˈstriːm] *n* (fig) 主流 shuryū

maintain [meintein´] *vt* (preserve: contact, friendship, system) 続ける tsuzúkeru, 保持する hojí suru; (keep up: momentum, output) 維持する ijf suru; (provide for: dependant) 養う yashínaù; (look after: building) 管理する káñri suru; (affirm: belief, opinion) 主張する shuchō suru

maintenance [meinˈtənəns] *n* (of contact, friendship, system) 保持 hojí; (of momentum, output) 維持 ijf; (provision for dependent) 扶養 fuyō; (looking after building) 管理 káñri; (affirmation: of belief, opinion) 主張する事 shuchō suru koto; (*BRIT*: LAW: alimony) 離婚手当 rikónteate

maize [meiz] *n* トウモロコシ toúmorðkoshi

majestic [mədʒesˈtik] *adj* (splendid: scenery etc) 壮大な sodái na; (dignified)

堂々とした dōdō to shitá

majesty [mædʒ'isti:] *n* (title): *Your Majesty* 陛下 hêîka; (sovereignty) 王位 ôî; (splendor) 威厳 igén

major [mei'dʒəːr] *n* (MIL) 少佐 shôsa
♦*adj* (important, significant: event, factor) 重要な jûyō na; (MUS: key) 長調の chôchō no

Majorca [məjɔːr'kə] *n* マジョルカ majórūka

majority [mədʒɔːr'iti:] *n* (larger group: of people, things) 過半数 kahánsū; (margin: of votes) 得票差 tokúhyōsa

make [meik] (*pt*, *pp* **made**) *vt* (produce, form: object, clothes, cake) 作る tsukúrù; (: noise) 立てる tatérù; (: speech, mistake) する surú; (: remark) 言う iú; (manufacture: goods) 作る tsukúrù, 製造する seízō suru; (cause to be): *to make someone sad* ...を悲しくさせる ...wo kanáshikù saséru; (force): *to make someone do something* ...に...をさせる ...ni ...wo saseru; (earn: money) もうける mốkerù; (equal): *2 and 2 make 4* 2足す2は4 2 tásù 2 wà 4
♦*n* (brand): *it's a Japanese make* 日本製です nihônsei desu

to make the bed ベッドを整える béddò wo totónoerù

to make a fool of someone ...をばかにする ...wo bákà ni suru

to make a profit 利益を得る riéki wò érù

to make a loss 損をする sốn wo suru

to make it (arrive on time) 間に合う ma ní aù; (achieve success) 成功する seíkō suru

what time do you make it? 今何時ですか imá nánji desu ká

to make do with ...で間に合せる ...de ma ní awaserù

make-believe [meik'bili:v] *n* (pretense) 見せ掛け misékake

make for *vt fus* (place) ...に向かう ...ni mukáù

make out *vt* (decipher) 解読する kaídoku suru; (understand) 分かる wakárù; (see) 見る mírù; (write: cheque) 書く ká-

kù

maker [mei'kəːr] *n* (of program, film etc) 制作者 seísakushà; (manufacturer) 製造者 seízōshà, メーカー mêkā

makeshift [meik'ʃift] *adj* (temporary) 間に合せの ma ní awase no

make up *vt* (constitute) 構成する kôsei suru; (invent) でっち上げる detchíagerù; (prepare: bed) 用意する yôi suru; (: parcel) 包む tsutsúmù
♦*vi* (after quarrel) 仲直りする nakánaori suru; (with cosmetics) 化粧する keshô suru

make-up [meik'ʌp] *n* (cosmetics) メーキャップ mêkyappù

make up for *vt fus* (loss, disappointment) ...の埋め合せをする ...no uméawase wò suru

make-up remover *n* 化粧落し keshô otôshi

making [mei'kiŋ] *n* (*fig*): *a doctor etc in the making* 医者の卵 ishá no tamágo

to have the makings of ...の素質がある ...no soshítsu ga arù

malaise [mæleiz'] *n* 倦怠 keńtai

malaria [mələːr'iːə] *n* マラリア marária

Malaya [məlei'jə] *n* マラヤ máràya

Malaysia [məlei'ʒə] *n* マレーシア maréshìa

male [meil] *n* (BIOL: not female) 雄 osú
♦*adj* (animal) 雄の osú no; (human) 男の otôko no, 男性の dańsei no; (attitude etc) 男性的な dańseiteki na

malevolent [məlev'ələnt] *adj* (evil, harmful: person, intention) 悪魔の様な ákùma no yố na

malfunction [mælfʌŋk'ʃən] *n* (of computer, machine) 故障 koshô

malice [mæl'is] *n* (ill will) 悪意 ákùi; (rancor) 恨み urámi

malicious [məlɪʃ'əs] *adj* (spiteful: person, gossip) 悪意に満ちた ákùi no michíta

malign [məlain'] *vt* (slander) 中傷する chûshō suru

malignant [məlig'nənt] *adj* (MED: tumor, growth) 悪性の ákúsei no

mall [mɔːl] *n* (*also*: **shopping mall**) ショ

ッピング・モール shoppíngu mòru

mallet [mæl'it] *n* 木づち kízuchi

malnutrition [mælnu:triʃ'ən] *n* 栄養失調 eíyōshìtchō

malpractice [mælpræk'tis] *n* (MED) 医療過誤 iryōkagò; (LAW) 不正行為 fuséikòi

malt [mɔ:lt] *n* (grain) もやし moyáshi, モルト mórùto; (*also*: **malt whisky**) モルトウイスキー morúto uisùkī

Malta [mɔ:l'tə] *n* マルタ márùta

Maltese [mɔ:lti:z'] *adj* マルタの márùta no

◆*n inv* マルタ人 marútajìn

maltreat [mæltri:t'] *vt* (treat badly, violently: child, animal) 虐待する gyakútai suru

mammal [mæm'əl] *n* ほ乳類 honyūrùi

mammoth [mæm'əθ] *n* (animal) マンモス mánmosu

◆*adj* (colossal, enormous: task) ばく大な bakúdai na

man [mæn] (*pl* **men**) *n* (adult male) 男 otóko, 男性 dañsei; (mankind) 人類 jíñrui

◆*vt* (NAUT: ship) 乗組ませる norîkumaserù; (MIL: gun, post) 配置につく haîchi ni tsúkù; (operate: machine) 操作する sōsa suru

an old man 老人 rōjiñ

man and wife 夫婦 fūfu

manage [mæn'idʒ] *vi* (succeed) うまくなんとかする úmàku náñtoka suru; (get by financially) なんとかして暮す náñtoka shite kurásù

◆*vt* (be in charge of: business, shop, organization) 管理する káñri suru; (control: ship) 操縦する sṓjū suru; (: person) うまくあしらう úmàku ashíraù

manageable [mæn'idʒəbəl] *adj* (task, number) 扱いやすい atsúkaiyasuī

management [mæn'idʒmənt] *n* (of business etc: control, organization) 管理 káñri; (: persons) 管理職 kañrishòku

manager [mæn'idʒər] *n* (of business etc) 支配人 shiháinin; (of pop star) マネージャー manèjā; (SPORT) 監督 kañtoku

manageress [mæn'idʒə:ris] *n* (of business etc) 女性支配人 joséishihaìnin; (of pop star) 女性マネージャー josei manèjā; (SPORT) 女性監督 joséi kañtoku

managerial [mænidʒi:'ri:əl] *adj* (role, skills) 管理職の kañrishòku no

managing director [mæn'idʒiŋ-] *n* 専務取締役 sēnmutorīshimariyàku

mandarin [mæn'də:rin] *n* (*also*: **mandarin orange**) みかん míkàn; (high-ranking bureaucrat) 高級官僚 kṓkyū kañryō

mandate [mæn'deit] *n* (authority) 権限 keñgen; (task) 任務 níñmu

mandatory [mæn'dətɔ:ri:] *adj* (obligatory) 義務的な gimúteki na

mane [mein] *n* (of horse, lion) たてがみ tatégami

maneuver [mənu:'və:r] (*US*) *vt* (move: car, bulky, object) 巧みに動かす tákùmi ni ugókasù; (manipulate: person, situation) 操る ayátsuru

◆*vi* (move: car, plane) 巧みに動く tákùmi ni ugókù; (MIL) 軍事演習を行う guñjieñshū wo okonau

◆*n* 巧みな動き tákùmi na ugóki

manfully [mæn'fəli:] *adv* (valiantly) 勇ましく isámashikù

mangle [mæŋ'gəl] *vt* (crush, twist) めちゃくちゃにする mechákucha ni suru

mango [mæŋ'gou] (*pl* **mangoes**) *n* マンゴー máñgō

mangy [mein'dʒi:] *adj* (animal) 汚らしい kitánarashiī

manhandle [mæn'hændəl] *vt* (mistreat) 手荒に扱う teára ni atsúkaù

manhole [mæn'houl] *n* マンホール mañhōru

manhood [mæn'hud] *n* (age) 成人時代 seíjin jidài; (state) 成人である事 seíjin de arù kotó ◇男性のみについて言う dañsei nomi ni tsúite iú

man-hour [mæn'auə:r] *n* (time) 人時 níñji

manhunt [mæn'hʌnt] *n* (POLICE) 人間狩り niñgeñgari

mania [mei'ni:ə] *n* (craze) ...狂 ...kyò; (illness) そう病 sōbyō

maniac [mei'ni:æk] *n* (lunatic) 狂人 kyōjin; (*fig*) 無謀な人 mubō na hitò

manic [mæn'ik] *adj* (behavior, activity) 猛烈な mṓretsu na

manic-depressive [mæn'ikdipres'iv] *n* そううつ病患者 sṓutsubyō kaṅja

manicure [mæn'əkju:r] *n* マニキュア maníkyùa

manicure set *n* マニキュア・セット maníkyua settō

manifest [mæn'əfest] *vt* (show, display) 表す aráwasù

◆*adj* (evident, obvious) 明白な meíhaku na

manifestation [mænəfestei'ʃən] *n* 現れ aráware

manifesto [mænəfes'tou] *n* 声明書 seímeisho

manipulate [mənip'jəleit] *vt* (people) 操る ayátsurù; (system, situation) 操作する sṓsa suru

mankind [mæn'kaind'] *n* (human beings) 人類 jíñrui

manly [mæn'li:] *adj* (masculine) 男らしい otókorashiì

man-made [mæn'meid] *adj* (environment, satellite etc) 人工の jiñkō no; (fiber, lake etc) 人造の jiñzō no

manner [mæn'ə:r] *n* (way) やり方 yaríkata; (behavior) 態度 taído; (type, sort): *all manner of things* あらゆる物 aráyuru monò

mannerism [mæn'ə:rizəm] *n* 癖 kusé

manners [mæn'ə:rz] *npl* (conduct) 行儀 gyốgi, マナー mánā

bad manners 行儀の悪い事 gyốgi no warúî kotò

manoeuvre [mənu:'və:r] (*BRIT*) = **maneuver**

manor [mæn'ə:r] *n* (*also:* **manor house**) 屋敷 yashíki

manpower [mæn'pauə:r] *n* (workers) 人手 hitóde

mansion [mæn'tʃən] *n* 豪邸 gṓtei

manslaughter [mæn'slɔ:tə:r] *n* (LAW) 殺意なき殺人 satsúinaki satsújin

mantelpiece [mæn'təlpi:s] *n* マントルピース maňtorupīsu

manual [mæn'ju:əl] *adj* (work, worker) 肉体の nikútai no; (controls) 手動の shu-

dṓ no

◆*n* (book) マニュアル mányùaru

manufacture [mænjəfæk'tʃə:r] *vt* (make, produce: goods) 製造する seízō suru

◆*n* (making) 製造 seízō

manufacturer [mænjəfæk'tʃə:rə:r] *n* 製造業者 seízōgyṓsha, メーカー mḗkā

manure [mənu:r'] *n* 肥やし koyáshi

manuscript [mæn'jəskript] *n* (of book, report) 原稿 geñkō; (old document) 写本 shahóñ

many [men'i:] *adj* (a lot of: people, things, ideas) 沢山の takúsañ no

◆*pron* (several) 多数 tasū

a great many 非常に沢山の hijō ni takúsañ no

many a time 何回も nañkai mo

map [mæp] *n* (of town, country) 地図 chízù

maple [mei'pəl] *n* (tree) カエデ kaéde; (wood) カエデ材 kaédezài

map out *vt* (plan, task) 計画する keíkaku suru

mar [mɑ:r] *vt* (spoil: appearance) 損なう sokónaù; (: day, event) ぶち壊す buchí kowasù

marathon [mær'əθɑ:n] *n* (race) マラソン marásoñ

marauder [mərɔ:d'ə:r] *n* (robber, killer) ◇殺人、略奪などを繰返しながら荒し回る無法者 satsújin, ryakúdatsu nado wo kuríkaeshinagara arashimawarù muhṓmòno

marble [mɑ:r'bəl] *n* (stone) 大理石 daíriseki; (toy) ビー玉 bídama

March [mɑ:rtʃ] *n* 3月 sáñgatsu

march [mɑ:rtʃ] *vi* (MIL: soldiers) 行進する kṓshin suru; (*fig*: protesters) デモ行進をする demō kṓshin wo suru; (walk briskly) 足音も高く歩く ashíoto mo takakù arúkù

◆*n* (MIL) 行進 kṓshin; (demonstration) デモ行進 demō kṓshin

mare [me:r] *n* 牝ウマ mesú uma

margarine [mɑ:r'dʒə:rin] *n* マーガリン mágarin

margin [mɑ:r'dʒin] *n* (difference: of

votes) 差 sa; (extra amount) 余 裕 yoyú; (COMM: profit) 利ざや rizáya, マージン májin; (space: on page) 余 白 yoháku; (edge: of area, group) 外れ hazúre

marginal [mɑːˈdʒɪnəl] adj (unimportant) 二次的な nijíteki na

marginal (seat) n (POL) 不安定な議席 fuántei na giséki ◇わずかな票の差で得たので、次の選挙で失う可能性のある議席 wázùka na hyõ nò sá de età node, tsugí nò seńkyo de ushínaù kanõsei no arù giséki

marigold [ˈmærəgould] n マリーゴールド maríğorudo

marijuana [mærəwɑːˈnə] n マリファナ marífầna

marina [məˈriːˈnə] n (harbor) マリーナ marínầ

marinate [ˈmærəneit] vt (CULIN) マリネにする márĭne ni suru

marine [məriːˈn] adj (life, plant, biology) 海の umí no; (engineer, engineering) 船舶の seńpaku no
◆n (US: sailor) 海兵隊員 kaíheitaìin; (BRIT: soldier) 海兵隊員 kaíheitaìin

marital [ˈmærˈitəl] adj (problem, relations) 夫婦の fúfu no
marital status ◇未婚、既婚、離婚を尋ねる時に使う言葉 mikón, kikón, ríkon wo tazúnerù tokí ni tsukaù kotóba

maritime [ˈmærˈitaim] adj 海事の kấĭji no

marjoram [mɑːˈdʒəˈrəm] n マヨラナ mayónầra, マージョラム májòramu

mark [mɑːrk] n (symbol: cross, tick etc) 印 shirúshi; (stain) 染み shimí; (of shoes, fingers, tires: in snow, mud etc) 跡 átò; (sign: of friendship, respect etc) 印 shirúshi; (SCOL) 成績 seíseki; (level, point): **the halfway mark** 中間点の目印 chúkanteñ no mejírùshi; (currency) マルク márùku
◆vt (make a mark on: with pen etc) 印を書く shirúshi wo kákù; (: with shoes, tires etc) 跡を残す átò wo nokósù; (damage: furniture etc) 傷を付ける kizú wo tsukérù; (stain: clothes, carpet etc) 染みを付ける shimí wo tsukérù; (indicate:

place, time, price) 示す shimésù; (commemorate: event) 記念する kinén suru; (BRIT: SCOL) 成績をつける seíseki wò tsukérù
to mark time (MIL, fig) 足踏みする a-shífumi suru

marked [mɑːrkt] adj (obvious) 著しい i-chíjirushiî

marker [mɑːˈkəːr] n (sign) 目印 mejírùshi; (bookmark) しおり shiórí
marker pen サインペン saínpen

market [mɑːˈkit] n (for fish, cattle, vegetables etc) 市場 íchìba; (in proper names) 市場 íchìba, 市場 shijõ; (COMM: business and trading activity) 市場 shijõ; (: demand) 需要 juyõ
◆vt (COMM: sell) 市場に出す shijõ ni dásù

market garden (BRIT) n 野菜農園 ya-sáinðen ◇主に市場向けの野菜や果物を栽培する小規模農場 ómò ni shijõmuke nò yasái ya kudámono wò saíbai surù shõkibo nõjõ

marketing [mɑːˈkitiŋ] n (COMM) 販売 hańbai

marketplace [mɑːˈkitpleis] n (area, site: also マーケット) 市場 íchìba

market research n 市場調査 shijõchõ-sa

marksman [mɑːrksˈmən] (pl **marksmen**) n 射撃の名手 shagéki no meíshu

marmalade [mɑːrˈməleid] n マーマレード mãmarềdo

maroon [məruːˈn] vt: **to be marooned** (shipwrecked) 遭難で置去りになる sõnan dè okízari ni narù; (fig: abandoned) 置去りにされる okízari ni saréru
◆adj (color) クリ色 kuríiro

marquee [mɑːrki:ˈ] n (tent) テント téñto ◇運動会、野外パーティなどで使う物を指す uńdõkai, yagái pãti nádð de tsukáù monõ wo sásù

marquess [mɑːrˈkwis] n 侯爵 kõshaku

marquis [mɑːrˈkwis] n = **marquess**

marriage [ˈmærˈidʒ] n (relationship, institution) 結婚 kekkón; (wedding) 結婚式 kekkốnshiki

marriage bureau n 結婚相談所 kekkónsōdanjo

marriage certificate n 結婚証明書 kekkónshōmeishō

married [mǽr'i:d] adj (man, woman) 既婚の kikón no; (life, love) 結婚の kekkón no

marrow [mǽr'ou] n (vegetable) セイヨウカボチャ seíyōkabòcha; (also: **bone marrow**) 骨髄 kotsúzui

marry [mǽr'i:] vt (man, woman) …と結婚する …to kekkón surù; (subj: father, priest etc) …の結婚式を行う …no kekkónshiki wo okónaù
♦vi (also: **get married**) 結婚する kekkón suru

Mars [mɑːrz] n (planet) 火星 kaséi

marsh [mɑːrʃ] n (bog) 沼沢地 shōtakúchi; (also: **salt marsh**) 塩性沼沢地 eñsei shōtakuchi

marshal [mɑːr'ʃəl] n (MIL: also: **field marshal**) 陸軍元帥 rikúgun geñsui; (official: at sports meeting etc) 役員 yakúìn; (US: of police, fire department) 長官 chōkan
♦vt (organize: thoughts) 整理する seíri suru; (: support) 集める atsúmerù; (: soldiers) 整列させる seíretsu saserù

marshy [mɑːr'ʃi:] adj 沼沢の多い shōtaku nò ōì

martial [mɑːr'ʃəl] adj (military) 軍の gúñ no

martial arts npl 武術 bújùtsu

martial law n 戒厳令 kaígeñrei

martyr [mɑːr'tər] n (for beliefs) 殉教者 juñkyōsha

martyrdom [mɑːr'tərdəm] n 殉教 juñkyō

marvel [mɑːr'vəl] n (wonder) 驚異 kyōi
♦vi: **to marvel (at)** 驚嘆する kyōtan suru

marvelous [mɑːr'vələs] (BRIT **marvellous**) adj 素晴らしい subárashiî

Marxism [mɑːrk'sizəm] n マルクス主義 marúkushùgi

Marxist [mɑːr'ksist] adj マルクス主義の marúkushùgi no
♦n マルクス主義者 marúkushùgisha

marzipan [mɑːr'zəpæn] n マジパン majípan

mascara [mæskæːr'ə] n マスカラ masúkara

mascot [mǽs'kɔːt] n マスコット masúkòtto

masculine [mǽs'kjəlin] adj (male: characteristics, pride) 男性の dañsei no; (: atmosphere) 男性的な dañseiteki na; (woman) 男の様な otóko no yō na; (LING: noun, pronoun etc) 男性の dañsei no

mash [mǽʃ] vt つぶす tsubúsu

mashed potatoes [mǽʃt-] npl マッシュポテト masshú potèto

mask [mǽsk] n (disguise) 覆面 fukúmen; (shield: gas mask, face mask) マスク másùku
♦vt (cover: face) 覆い隠す óikakùsu; (hide: feelings) 隠す kakúsù

masochist [mǽs'əkist] n マゾヒスト mazóhisùto

mason [mei'sən] n (also: **stone mason**) 石屋 ishíya; (also: **freemason**) フリーメーソン furímèson

masonic [məsɑːn'ik] adj (lodge, dinner) フリーメーソンの furímèson no

masonry [mei'sənri:] n (stonework) 石造部 sekízōbu ◊建物の石やれんがなどで造られた部分 tatémòno no ishí yà reñga nadò de tsukúrarèta búbùn

masquerade [mæskəreiˈd] vi: **to masquerade as** …を装う …wo yosóoù

mass [mǽs] n (large number: of papers, people etc) 多数 tasū; (large amount: of detail, hair etc) 大量 taíryō; (amount: of air, liquid, land) 集団 shūdan; (PHYSICS) 物量 butsúryō; (REL) ミサ聖祭 misá seisāi
♦cpd (communication, unemployment etc) 大量の taíryō no
♦vi (troops, protesters) 集合する shūgō suru

massacre [mǽs'əkər] n 大虐殺 daígyakùsatsu

massage [məsɑːʒ'] n マッサージ massájì
♦vt (rub) マッサージする massájì suru

masses [mǽs'iz] npl: **the masses** (ordinary people) 大衆 taíshū

ーベーション masutābēshon, オナニー o-náni

masses of (*inf*: food, money, people) 一杯の ippái no

masseur [mæsəːrʰ] *n* マッサージ師 massájishì

masseuse [məsuːsʰ] *n* マッサージ嬢 massájijō

massive [mæsʰiv] *adj* (large and heavy: furniture, door, person) どっしりした dosshírì shita; (huge: support, changes, increase) 膨大な bōdai na

mass media [-miːˈdiːə] *npl* マスメディア masúmèdia

mass production (*BRIT* **mass-production**) *n* 大量生産 taíryōseisan, マスプロ masúpuro

mast [mæst] *n* (NAUT) マスト másùto; (RADIO etc) 放送アンテナ hōsō àñtena

master [mæsˈtəːr] *n* (of servant, slave) 主人 shujíñ; (in secondary school) 先生 señsèī; (title for boys): **Master X** X君 ékusu kùn

♦*vt* (control: situation) 掌握する shōaku suru; (: one's feelings etc) 抑える osáerù; (learn: skills, language) 修得する shútoku suru, マスターする masútā suru

to be master of the situation (*fig*) 事態を掌握している jítai wo shōaku shite irù

master key *n* マスターキー masútā kī

masterly [mæsˈtəːrliː] *adj* あっぱれな appárè na

mastermind [mæsˈtəːrmaind] *n* (of crime etc) 首謀者 shubōshà, 黒幕 kurómaku

♦*vt* 計画を練って実行させる keíkaku wò néttè jikkō saserù

Master of Arts/Science *n* (person) 文学〔理学〕修士 buñgaku〔rígaku〕shùshi; (qualification) 文学〔理学〕修士号 buñgaku〔rígaku〕shùshigō

masterpiece [mæsˈtəːrpiːs] *n* 傑作 kessáku

mastery [mæsˈtəːriː] *n* (of skill, language) 修得 shútoku

masturbate [mæsˈtəːrbeit] *vi* マスターベーション〔オナニー〕をする masútābēshon〔onáni〕wo suru

masturbation [mæstəːrbeiˈʃən] *n* マスタ

ーベーション masutābēshon, オナニー o-náni

mat [mæt] *n* (on floor) マット máttò; (at door: *also*: **doormat**) ドアマット doá-mattò; (on table: *also*: **table mat**) テーブルマット tēburumattò

♦*adj* = **matt**

match [mætʃ] *n* (game: of football, tennis etc) 試合 shiái, マッチ mátchì; (for lighting fire, cigarette) マッチ mátchì; (equal) 力が同等な人 chikára ga dōtō na hitò

♦*vt* (go well with: subj: colors, clothes) ...に合う ...ni áù; (equal) ...と同等である ...to dōtō de arù; (correspond to) ...に合う ...ni áù; (pair: *also*: **match up**) ...と合せる ...to awáserù, ...と組ませる ...to kumáserù

♦*vi* (colors, materials) 合う áù

to be a good match (colors etc) よく合う yokú áù; (couple) 似合いの...である niáì no ...de árù

matchbox [mætʃˈbɑːks] *n* マッチ箱 mat-chíbàko

matching [mætʃˈiŋ] *adj* (clothes etc) そろいの soróì na

mate [meit] *n* (workmate) 仲間 nakáma; (*inf*: friend) 友達 tomódachi; (animal) 相手 aîte; (in merchant navy: first, second) ...等航海士 ...tō kōkaishì

♦*vi* (animals) 交尾する kōbi suru

material [mətiːˈriəl] *n* (substance) 物質 busshítsu; (cloth) 生地 kijí; (information, data) 情報 jōhō

♦*adj* (possessions, existence) 物質的な busshítsuteki na

materialistic [mətiːriːəlisˈtik] *adj* 唯物主義的な yuíbutsushugiteki na

materialize [mətiːrˈiəlaiz] *vi* (happen) 起る okórù; (appear) 現れる aráwarerù

materials [mətiːˈriːəlz] *npl* (equipment) 材料 zaíryō

maternal [mətəːrˈnəl] *adj* (feelings, role) 母性の boséi no

maternity [mətəːrˈnitiː] *n* 母性 boséi

maternity dress *n* マタニティドレス matánitidorèsu

maternity hospital *n* 産院 sañ-in

math [mæθ] (BRIT **maths**) n 数学 súgaku

mathematical [mæθəmǽtˈikəl] adj (formula) 数学の súgaku no; (mind) 数学的な súgakuteki na

mathematician [mæθəmətiʃˈən] n 数学者 súgakushà

mathematics [mæθəmǽtˈiks] n 数学 súgaku

maths [mæθs] (BRIT) n = **math**

matinée [mætənei'] n マチネー machínē

mating call [mei'tiŋ-] n (of animals) 求愛の声 kyúai nò kóè

matrices [meit'risiːz] npl of **matrix**

matriculation [mətrikjəlei'ʃən] n (enrollment) 大学入学 daígakunyúgaku

matrimonial [mætrəmou'niːəl] adj 結婚の kekkón no

matrimony [mæt'rəmouniː] n (marriage) 結婚 kekkón

matrix [mei'triks] (pl **matrices**) n (context, environment) 環境 kańkyō

matron [mei'trən] n (in hospital) 婦長 fuchó; (in school) 養護員 yógoin

mat(t) [mæt] adj つや消しの tsuyákeshi no

matted [mæt'id] adj もつれた motsúretà

matter [mæt'əːr] n (event) 事件 jikén; (situation) 事情 jijó; (problem) 問題 mońdai; (PHYSICS) 物質 busshítsu; (substance, material) 素材 sozái; (written material: reading matter etc) 印刷物 íñsatsubùtsu, 本 hóñ; (MED: pus) うみ umí
♦vi (be important: family, job etc) 大切である taísetsu de arù

it doesn't matter 構わない kamáwanài

what's the matter? どうしましたか dô shimashita ká

no matter what (whatever happens) 何があっても nánì ga atté mo

as a matter of course (automatically) 当然ながら tôzen nagara

as a matter of fact 実は jitsú wa

matter-of-fact [mæt'əːrʌvfækt'] adj 無味乾燥な mumíkañsō na

matters [mæt'əːrz] npl (affairs) 物事 monógòto; (situation) 状況 jókyō

mattress [mæt'ris] n マットレス mattóresu

mature [mətuːr'] adj (person) 成熟した seíjuku shita; (cheese, wine etc) 熟成した jukúsei shita
♦vi (develop: child, style) 成長する seíchō suru; (grow up: person) 成熟する seíjuku suru; (ripen, age: cheese, wine etc) 熟成する jukúsei suru

maturity [mətuːr'ritiː] n (adulthood) 成熟 seíjuku; (wisdom) 分別 fúñbetsu

maul [mɔːl] vt ...に大けがをさせる ...ni ōkega wò saséru

mausoleum [mɔːsəliː'əm] n 納骨堂 nókotsudò

mauve [mouv] adj フジ色の fujíiro no

maverick [mæv'əːrik] n 一匹オオカミ ippíki ōkami

maxim [mæk'sim] n 格言 kakúgen

maximum [mæk'səməm] (pl **maxima**) adj (efficiency, speed, dose) 最大の saídai no
♦n 最大限 saídaìgen

May [mei] n 5月 gógàtsu

may [mei] (conditional: **might**) vi (indicating possibility): *he may come* 彼は来るかも知れない kárè wa kurú ka mo shirenai; (be allowed to): *may I smoke?* タバコをすってもいいですか tabáko wo sutté mò íi desu ká; (wishes): *may God bless you!* 神の祝福をあなたに！ kamí nò shukúfuku wò anáta no
♦vi *you may as well go* 行ってもいいかも知れない itté mò íi ka mo shirenai; (dismissive) 行った方がいいかも知れない itta hō ga íi ka mo shirénai

maybe [mei'biː] adv 事によると kotó ni yorù to

May Day n メーデー mēdē

mayhem [mei'hem] n 混乱 kofran

mayonnaise [meiəneiz'] n マヨネーズ mayónèzu

mayor [mei'əːr] n (of city, town) 市〔町, 村〕長 shi〔chō, son〕chó

mayoress [mei'əːris] n (partner) 市〔町, 村〕長夫人 shi〔chō, son〕chó fujín

maze [meiz] n (labyrinth, puzzle) 迷路 meíro

M.D. [emdi:'] *abbr* = **Doctor of Medicine**

KEYWORD
---

me [mi:] *pron* **1** (direct) 私 を watákushi wo

can you hear me? 私の声が聞えますか watákushi no koè ga kikóemasù ká

he heard me 彼は私の声を聞いた kárè wa watákushi no koè wo kiíta

he heard ME! (not anyone else) 彼が聞いたのは私の声だった kárè ga kiítá no wa watákushi no koè dáttà

it's me 私です watákushi desù

2 (indirect) 私に watákushi nì

he gave me the money, he gave the money to me 彼は私に金を渡した kárè wa watákushi nì kané wò watáshità

give them to me それらを私に下さい sorérà wo watákushi nì kudásaì

3 (after prep): *the letter's for me* 手紙は私宛てです tegámi wà watákushi ate dèsu

with me 私と一緒に watákushi tò isshó nì

without me 私抜きで watákushi nukí de

---

meadow [med'ou] *n* 草原 kusáhara

meager [mi:'gər] (*BRIT* **meagre**) *adj* 乏しい tobóshiì

meal [mi:l] *n* (occasion, food) 食事 shokúji; (flour) 粉 koná

mealtime [mi:l'taim] *n* 食事時 shokúji-dòki

mean [mi:n] *adj* (with money) けちな kechí na; (unkind: person, trick) 意地悪な ijíwarù na; (shabby: street, lodgings) 見すぼらしい misúborashiì; (average: height, weight) 中位の chúgurai no

♦*vt* (*pt, pp* **meant**) (signify) 意味する ímì suru; (refer to): *I thought you meant her* あなたは彼女の事を言っていると私は思った anátà wa kanójò no kotó wò itté irù to watákushi wà omótta; (intend): *to mean to do something* ...をするつもりでいる ...wo suru tsumóri de irú

♦*n* (average) 平均 heíkin

do you mean it? 本当ですか hoñtó desù ká

what do you mean? それはどういう事ですか soré wa dó iú kotò desu ká

to be meant for someone/something ...に当てた物である ...ni atéta monò de árù

meander [mi:æn'dər] *vi* (river) 曲がりくねって流れる magárikunettè nagárerù

meaning [mi:'niŋ] *n* (of word, gesture, book) 意味 ímì; (purpose, value) 意義 ígì

meaningful [mi:'niŋfəl] *adj* (result) 意味のある ímì no árù; (explanation) 納得できる nattóku dekirù; (glance, remark) 意味ありげな imírige na; (relationship, occasion) 意味深い imíbùkai

meaningless [mi:'niŋlis] *adj* 無意味な muímì na

meanness [mi:n'nis] *n* (with money) けちkechí; (unkindness) 意地悪 ijíwarù; (shabbiness) 見すぼらしさ misúborashisà

means [mi:nz] *npl* (way) 方法 hóhō; (money) 財産 zaísan

by means of ...を使って ...wo tsukátte

by all means! ぜひどうぞ zéhì dózò

meant [ment] *pt, pp of* **mean**

meantime [mi:n'taim] *adv* (*also:* **in the meantime**) その間に sonó aìda ni

meanwhile [mi:n'wail] *adv* (meantime) その間に sonó aìda ni

measles [mi:'zəlz] *n* はしか hashíka

measly [mi:z'li:] (*inf*) *adj* ちっぽけなchippókè na

measure [meʒ'əːr] *vt* (size, weight, distance) 計る hakárù

♦*vi* (room, person) ...だけの寸法がある ...daké nò suñpō ga arù

♦*n* (amount: of protection etc) ある程度árù teídò; (: of whisky etc) 定量 teíryō; (ruler, *also:* **tape measure**) 巻尺 makíjaku, メジャー mejáa; (action) 処置 shochí

measured [meʒ'əːrd] *adj* 慎重な shiñchō na

measurements [meʒ'əːrmənts] *npl* (size) 寸法 suñpō

meat [mi:t] *n* 肉 nikú

cold meat コールドミート kórudomìto

meatball [mi:t'bɔ:l] *n* ミートボール mítobòru

meat pie *n* ミートパイ mítopài

Mecca [mek'ə] *n* (city) メッカ mékkà; (*fig*) あこがれの地 akógare nò chí

mechanic [məkæn'ik] *n* 自動車整備士 jidósha seíbishi

mechanical [məkæn'ikəl] *adj* 機械仕掛の kikáijikakè no

mechanics [məkæn'iks] *n* (PHYSICS) 力学 rikígaku
♦*npl* (of reading, government etc) 機構 kikó

mechanism [mek'ənizəm] *n* (device) 装置 sóchi; (procedure) 方法 hóhò; (automatic reaction) 反応 hañnò

mechanization [mekənizei'ʃən] *n* 機械化 kikáika

medal [med'əl] *n* (award) メダル médaru

medallion [mədæl'jən] *n* メダリオン medáriòn

medalist [med'list] (*BRIT* **medallist**) *n* (SPORT) メダリスト medárisùto

meddle [med'əl] *vi*: **to meddle in** ...にちょっかいを出す ...ni chokkáì wo dásù
to meddle with something ...をいじる ...wo ijírù

media [mi:'di:ə] *npl* マスメディア masúmedìa

mediaeval [mi:di:i:'vəl] *adj* = **medieval**

median [mi:'di:ən] (*US*) *n* (*also*: **median strip**) 中央分離帯 chūō buñritai

mediate [mi:'di:it] *vi* (arbitrate) 仲裁する chūsai suru

mediator [mi:'di:eitə:r] *n* 仲裁者 chūsaishà

Medicaid [med'əkeid] (*US*) *n* メディケイド medíkeìdo ◇低所得者への医療扶助 teíshotòkusha e no iryófujo

medical [med'ikəl] *adj* (treatment, care) 医学的な igákuteki na
♦*n* (*BRIT*: examination) 健康診断 keñkōshìndan

Medicare [med'əke:r] (*US*) *n* メディケア medíkèa ◇高齢者への医療扶助 kóreishà no iryófujo

medicated [med'ikeitid] *adj* 薬用の ya-

kúyo no

medication [medikei'ʃən] *n* (drugs etc) 薬 kusúri

medicinal [mədis'ənəl] *adj* 薬効のある yakkó no arù

medicine [med'isin] *n* (science) 医学 ígaku; (drug) 薬 kusúri

medieval [mi:di:i:'vəl] *adj* 中世の chūsei no

mediocre [mi:'di:oukə:r] *adj* (play, artist) 粗末な sómatsu na

mediocrity [mi:di:ɑ:k'riti:] *n* (poor quality) 粗末さ somátsusà

meditate [med'əteit] *vi* (think carefully) 熟考する jukkó suru; (REL) めい想する meísō suru

meditation [meditei'ʃən] *n* (thinking) 熟考 jukkó; (REL) めい想 meísō

Mediterranean [meditərei'ni:ən] *adj* 地中海の chichúkai no
the Mediterranean (Sea) 地中海 chichúkai

medium [mi:'di:əm] *adj* (average: size, color) 中位の chūgurai no
♦*n* (*pl* **media**: means) 手段 shúdàn; (*pl* **mediums**: people) 霊媒 reíbai

medium wave *n* 中波 chūha

medley [med'li:] *n* (mixture) ごったまぜ gottámaze; (MUS) メドレー médòrē

meek [mi:k] *adj* 穏和な oñwa na

meet [mi:t] (*pt, pp* **met**) *vt* (friend: accidentally) ...に出会う ...ni deáù; (: by arrangement) ...に会う ...ni áù; (stranger: for the first time) ...と知合いになる ...to shíriai ni naru; (go and fetch: at station, airport) 出迎える demúkaerù; (opponent) ...と試合をする ...to shíái wo surù; (obligations) 果す hatásù; (problem, need) 解決する kaíketsu suru
♦*vi* (friends: accidentally) 出会う deáù; (: by arrangement) 会う áù; (strangers: for the first time) 知合いになる shiríai ni narù; (for talks, discussion) 会合する kaígō suru; (join: lines, roads) 合流する góryū suru

meeting [mi:'tiŋ] *n* (assembly: of club, committee etc) 会合 kaígō; (: of people) 集会 shúkai; (encounter: with friend) 出

会い deaî; (COMM) 会議 kaîgi; (POL) 集会 shúkai

meet with *vt fus* (encounter: difficulty) 合う aû
to meet with success 成功する seîkō suru

megabyte [meg'əbait] *n* (COMPUT) メガバイト megábaìto

megaphone [meg'əfoun] *n* メガホン megáhòn

melancholy [mel'ənkɑ:li:] *n* (sadness) 憂うつ yúutsu, メランコリー meránkorī
◆*adj* (sad) 憂鬱な yúutsu na

mellow [mel'ou] *adj* (sound, light, color) 柔らかい yawárakaî; (wine) 芳じゅんな hōjun na
◆*vi* (person) 角が取れる kádò ga torérù

melodrama [mel'ədræmə] *n* メロドラマ meródòrama

melody [mel'ədi:] *n* 旋律 seńritsu, メロディー méròdī

melon [mel'ən] *n* メロン méròn

melt [melt] *vi* (metal, snow) 溶ける tokérù
◆*vt* (metal, snow, butter) 溶かす tokásù

melt down *vt* (metal) 溶かす tokásù

meltdown [melt'daun] *n* (in nuclear reactor) メルトダウン merútodàun

melting pot [melt'iŋ-] *n* (*fig*: mixture) るつぼ rútsùbo

member [mem'bəːr] *n* (of group, family) 一員 ichî-in; (of club) 会員 kaîin, メンバー méñbā; (ANAT) 体の一部 karáda no íchìbu
Member of Parliament (BRIT) 国会議員 kokkái gìin
Member of the European Parliament (BRIT) 欧州議会議員 óshūgikai gìin

membership [mem'bəːrʃip] *n* (members) 会員一同 kaîin ichidô; (state) 会員である事 kaîin de arù kotô

membership card *n* 会員証 kaîiñshō

membrane [mem'brein] *n* 膜 makú

memento [məmen'tou] *n* 記念品 kinéñhin

memo [mem'ou] *n* 覚書 obóegaki, メモ mémò

memoirs [mem'wɑːrz] *npl* 回顧録 kaîko-

roku

memorable [mem'əːrəbəl] *adj* 記念すべき kinénsubeki

memorandum [meməræn'dəm] (*pl* **memoranda**) *n* (official note) 覚書 obóegaki; (order to employees etc) 社内通達 shanái tsùtatsu

memorial [məmɔːr'iːəl] *n* (statue, monument) 記念碑 kinéñhi
◆*adj* (service) 追悼の tsuítō no; (prize) 記念の kinén no

memorize [mem'əːraiz] *vt* (learn) 暗記する añki suru

memory [mem'əːriː] *n* (ability to remember) 記憶 kióku; (things one remembers) 思い出 omóide; (instance) 思い出 omóide; (of dead person): *in memory of* ...を記念して ...wo kinén shite; (COMPUT) 記憶装置 kiókusòchi, メモリー mémòrī

men [men] *pl of* **man**

menace [men'is] *n* (threat) 脅威 kyóī; (nuisance) 困り者 komárimono
◆*vt* (threaten) 脅かす odókasu; (endanger) 危険にさらす kikén ni sarásu

menacing [men'isiŋ] *adj* (person, gesture) 脅迫的な kyóhakuteki na

mend [mend] *vt* (repair) 修理する shúri suru; (darn: socks etc) 繕う tsukúroù, 修繕する shúzen suru
◆*n*: *to be on the mend* 回復に向かっている kaîfuku nì mukátte irù
to mend one's ways 心を入替える kokórò wo irékaerù

mending [mend'iŋ] *n* (repairing) 修繕 shúzen; (clothes) 繕い物 tsukúroimòno

menial [miː'niːəl] *adj* (lowly: often *pej*) 卑しい iyáshiì

meningitis [menindʒai'tis] *n* 脳膜炎 nómakuèn

menopause [men'əpɔːz] *n* 更年期 kóneñki

menstruation [menstruːei'ʃən] *n* 月経 gekkéi, 生理 seîri, メンス méñsu

mental [men'təl] *adj* (ability, effort) 精神的な seîshinteki na; (illness, health) 精神の seîshin no
mental arithmetic/calculation 暗算 añzan

mentality [mentæl'iti:] n (attitude) 考え方 kañgaekàta

menthol [men'θɔ:l] n メントール meñtōru

mention [men'tʃən] n (reference) 言及 geñkyū
♦vt (speak of) ...に言及する ...ni geñkyū suru
don't mention it! どういたしまして dō itáshimashitè

mentor [men'tɔːr] n 良き指導者 yokí shidōsha

menu [men'juː] n (set menu) 献立 koñdate; (printed) 献立表 koñdatehyō, メニュー mēnyū; (COMPUT) メニュー mēnyū

MEP [emi:pi:'] (BRIT) n abbr = **Member of the European Parliament**

mercenary [məːr'sɛnəri:] adj 金銭ずくの kiñsenzuku no
♦n (soldier) よう兵 yōhei

merchandise [məːr'tʃəndais] n 商品 shōhin

merchant [məːr'tʃənt] n (trader) 貿易商 bōekishō

merchant bank (BRIT) n マーチャントバンク māchantobañku

merchant marine (BRIT **merchant navy**) n 商船 shōsen ◇一国の全商船を集合的に指す ikkóku no zeñshōsen wò shūgōteki ni sasù

merciful [məːr'sifəl] adj (kind, forgiving) 情け深い nasákebukaì; (fortunate): *merciful release* 苦しみからの解放 kurúshimi kara no kaíhō ◇重病人などの死亡について言う jūbyōnin nado no shibō ni tsuitè iú

merciless [məːr'silis] adj (person, regime) 冷酷な reíkoku na

mercury [məːr'kjəːri:] n 水銀 suígin

mercy [məːr'si:] n (clemency: also REL) 情け nasáke, 慈悲 jihí
at the mercy of ...のなすがままになって ...no násù ga mamá ni nattè

mere [miːr] adj (emphasizing insignificance: child, trifle, amount) ほんの hoñ no; (emphasizing significance): *his mere presence irritates her* 彼がそこにいるだけで彼女は頭に来る kárè ga sokó ni

irù daké de kánòjo wa atáma ni kurù

merely [miːr'li:] adv ただ ...だけ tádà ...dake

merge [məːrdʒ] vt (combine: companies, institutions etc) 合併させる gappéi saserù
♦vi (COMM) 合併する gappéi suru; (colors, sounds, shapes) 次第に溶け合う shidái ni tokéaù; (roads) 合流する gōryū suru

merger [məːr'dʒəːr] n (COMM) 合併 gappéi

meringue [məræŋ'] n メレンゲ meréñge

merit [meːr'it] n (worth, value) 価値 kachí; (advantage) 長所 chōsho, 利点 ritén
♦vt ...に値する ...ni atái suru

mermaid [məːr'meid] n 人魚 níñgyo

merry [meːr'i:] adj (happy: laugh, person) 陽気な yōki na; (cheerful: music) 活気ある kakkí arù
Merry Christmas! メリークリスマス merí kurisùmasu

merry-go-round [meːr'i:gouraund] n 回転木馬 kaíteñmokuba

mesh [meʃ] n (net) メッシュ mésshù

mesmerize [mez'məːraiz] vt 魅惑する miwáku suru

mess [mes] n (muddle: in room) 散らかしっ放し chirákashippanashi, めちゃくちゃ mechákucha; (: of situation) 混乱 koñran; (dirt) 汚れ yogóre; (MIL) 食堂 shokúdō

mess about/around (inf) vi (fool around) ぶらぶらする búràbura suru

mess about/around with vt fus (play around with) いじる ijírù

message [mes'idʒ] n (piece of information) 伝言 deñgon, メッセージ mésséji; (meaning: of play, book etc) 教訓 kyókun

messenger [mes'indʒəːr] n 使者 shíshà, メッセンジャー messéñjā

Messrs. [mes'əːrz] abbr (on letters) ◇Mr. の複数形 Mr. no fukúsūkei

mess up vt (spoil) 台無しにする daínashi ni suru; (dirty) 汚す yogósù

messy [mes'i:] adj (dirty) 汚れた yogóreta; (untidy) 散らかした chirákashita

met [met] pt, pp of **meet**

metabolism [mətæb'əlizəm] n 新陳代謝 shiñchintaîsha

metal [met'əl] n 金属 kiñzoku

metallic [mitæl'ik] adj (made of metal) 金属の kiñzoku no; (sound, color) 金属的な kiñzokuteki na

metallurgy [met'ələːrdʒiː] n や金学 yakiñgaku

metamorphosis [metəmɔːr'fəsis] (pl **metamorphoses**) n 変態 heñtai

metaphor [met'əfɔːr] n 隠ゆ iñ-yu, メタファー metáfā

mete [miːt] vt: **to mete out** (punishment, justice) 与える atáerù, 加える kuwáerù

meteor [miː'tiːour] n 流れ星 nagárebòshi

meteorite [miː'tiːərait] n いん石 iñseki

meteorology [miːtiːərɑːl'ədʒiː] n 気象学 kishṓgàku

meter [miː'təːr] n (instrument: gas meter, electricity meter) ...計 ...kéi, メーター mḗtā; (also: **parking meter**) パーキングメーター pákingumètā; (US: unit) メートル mḗtòru

method [meθ'əd] n (way) 方法 hṓhō

methodical [məθɑːd'ikəl] adj (careful, thorough) 慎重な shiñchō na

Methodist [meθ'ədist] n メソジスト教徒 mesṓjisuto kyṓto

methodology [meθədɑːl'ədʒiː] n 方法論 hṓhōron

meths [meθs] (BRIT) n = **methylated spirit**

methylated spirit [meθ'əleitid-] (BRIT) n 変性アルコール heñsei arukṓru

meticulous [mətik'jələs] adj 厳密な geñmitsu na

metre [miː'təːr] (BRIT) n (unit) = **meter**

metric [met'rik] adj メートル法の mḗtoruhō no

metropolis [mitrɑːp'əlis] n 大都会 daîtokai

metropolitan [metrəpɑːl'itən] adj 大都会の daîtokai no

Metropolitan Police (BRIT) n: **the Metropolitan Police** ロンドン市警察 roñdon shikeîsatsu

mettle [met'əl] n (spirit, courage): **to be on one's mettle** 張切っている haríkitte

irù

mew [mjuː] vi (cat) にゃあと鳴く nyã to nakú

mews [mjuːz] n (BRIT): **mews flat** アパート apâto ◇昔の馬屋をアパートに改造した物を指す mukáshi nò umáya wò apâtò ni kaîzō shita monò wo sásù

Mexican [mek'səkən] adj メキシコの mekíshiko no
♦n メキシコ人 mekíshikojìn

Mexico [mek'səkou] n メキシコ mekíshiko

Mexico City n メキシコ市 mekíshiko-shi

miaow [miau'] vi (cat) にゃあと鳴く nyã to nakú

mice [mais] pl of **mouse**

micro- [mai'krou] prefix 微小... bishṓ ...

microbe [mai'kroub] n 細菌 saîkin

microchip [mai'krətʃip] n マイクロチップ maîkurochippù

micro(computer) [maikrou(kəmpjuː'təːr)] n マイクロコンピュータ maîkuro-kompyùta, パソコン pasŏkòn

microcosm [mai'krəkɑːzəm] n 小宇宙 shóuchū, ミクロコスモス mikúrokosumòsu

microfilm [mai'krəfilm] n マイクロフィルム maîkurofirùmu

microphone [mai'krəfoun] n マイクロホン maîkurohòn

microprocessor [maikrouprɑːs'esəːr] n マイクロプロセッサー maîkuropuroses-så

microscope [mai'krəskoup] n 顕微鏡 keñbikyŏ

microscopic [mai'krəskɑːp'ik] adj 微小の bishṓ no

microwave [mai'krouweiv] n (also: **microwave oven**) 電子レンジ deñshi reñji

mid [mid] adj: **in mid May** 5月半ばに gogátsu nakàba ni
in mid afternoon 昼下がりに hirúsagari ni
in mid air 空中に kúchū ni

midday [mid'dei] n 正午 shṓgo

middle [mid'əl] n (center) 真ん中 mañnaka, 中央 chǔ̄ō; (half-way point) 中間 chǔ̄kan; (waist) ウエスト uésùto

♦*adj* (of place, position) 真ん中の mañnaka no; (average: quantity, size) 中位の chǔgurai no

in the middle of the night 真夜中に mayónaka ni

middle-aged [mid'əleid3d'] *adj* 中年の chǔnen no

Middle Ages *npl*: *the Middle Ages* 中世 chǔsei

middle-class [mid'əlklæs] *adj* 中流の chǔ̄ryū no

middle class(es) [mid'əlklæs(iz)] *n(pl)*: *the middle class(es)* 中流階級 chǔ̄ryū-kaīkyū

Middle East *n*: *the Middle East* 中東 chǔ̄tō

middleman [mid'əlmæn] (*pl* **middlemen**) *n* 仲買人 nakágainin

middle name *n* ミドルネーム midórunēmu

middle-of-the-road [mid'əlʌvðəroud'] *adj* (politician, music) 中道の chǔ̄dō no

middleweight [mid'əlweit] *n* (BOX-ING) ミドル級の midórukyū no

middling [mid'liŋ] *adj* 中位の chǔgurai no

midge [mid3] *n* ブヨ bǔyō ◇ブヨの様な小さい虫の総称 bǔyō no yō na chíísaī mushí no sō̄shō

midget [mid3'it] *n* 小人 kobíto

Midlands [mid'ləndz] (BRIT) *npl*: *the Midlands* イングランド中部地方 íngurañdo chǔ̄bu chihō̄

midnight [mid'nait] *n* 真夜中 mayónaka

midriff [mid'rif] *n* おなか onáka ◇ウエストから胸までの部分を指す uésùto kara munē madè no bǔbùn wo sásù

midst [midst] *n*: *in the midst of* (crowd, group) ...の中に〔で〕...no nákà ni 〔de〕; (situation, event) ...のさなかに ...no sanáka ni; (action) ...をしている所 ...wo shité irù tokóro

midsummer [mid'sʌm'ə:r] *n* 真夏 manátsu

midway [mid'wei] *adj*: *midway (between/through)* ...の途中で ...no to-

chū de

♦*adv*: *midway (between/through)* ...の途中に〔で〕 ...no tochū ni 〔de〕

midweek [mid'wi:k] *adv* 週半ば shū nakabà

midwife [mid'waif] (*pl* **midwives**) *n* 助産婦 josáñpu

midwinter [mid'win'tə:r] *n*: *in midwinter* 真冬に mafúyu ni

might[1] [mait] *see* **may**

might[2] [mait] *n* (power) 力 chikára

mighty [mai'ti:] *adj* 強力な kyōryoku na

migraine [mai'grein] *n* 偏頭痛 heñzutsū

migrant [mai'grənt] *adj*: *migrant bird* 渡り鳥 watáridòri

migrant worker 渡り季節労働者 watári kisetsurō̄dōshà

migrate [mai'greit] *vi* (bird etc) 移動する idō̄ suru; (person) 移住する ijū̄ suru

migration [maigrei'ʃən] *n* (bird etc) 移動 idō̄; (person) 移住 ijū̄

mike [maik] *n abbr* = **microphone**

Milan [milæn'] *n* ミラノ miránò

mild [maild] *adj* (gentle: character) 大人しい otónashiī; (climate) 穏やかな odáyàka na; (slight: infection, illness) 軽い karúi; (: interest) 少しの sukóshī no; (taste) 甘口の amákuchi no

mildew [mil'du:] *n* かび kabí

mildly [maild'li:] *adv* (gently) 優しく yasáshìku; (somewhat) 少し sukóshī

to put it mildly 控え目に言って hikáeme ni ittè

mile [mail] *n* (unit) マイル maírù

mileage [mai'lid3] *n* (number of miles) マイル数 maírùsū

mileometer [maila:m'itə:r] (BRIT) *n* = **odometer**

milestone [mail'stoun] *n* (marker) 一里塚 ichírizùka; (fig: important event) 画期的な出来事 kakkíteki na dekígòto

milieu [mi:lju:'] *n* 環境 kañkyō

militant [mil'ətənt] *adj* 戦闘的な señtō̄teki na

military [mil'ite:ri:] *adj* 軍隊の gúntai na

militate [mil'əteit] *vi*: *to militate against* (prevent) 邪魔する jamá suru

militia [mili'ʃə] *n* 民兵 miñpei

milk [milk] n (of any mammal) 乳 chichí; (of cow) 牛乳 gyúnyū, ミルク mírùku
♦vt (cow, goat) ...の乳を搾る ...no chichí wŏ shibórù; (fig: situation, person) 食い物にする kuímonò ni suru

milk chocolate n ミルクチョコレート mirúkuchokorēto

milkman [milk'mæn] (pl **milkmen**) n 牛乳配達人 gyúnyūhaitatsunìn

milkshake [milk'ʃeik] n ミルクセーキ mirúkusèki

milky [mil'ki:] adj (color) 乳白色の nyúhakùshoku no; (drink) ミルク入りの mirúku iri no

Milky Way n 銀河 gínga

mill [mil] n (windmill etc: for grain) 製粉機 seífùnki; (also: **coffee mill**) コーヒーひき kŏhìhikì; (factory: steel mill, saw mill) 製...工場 seî...kòjō
♦vt (grind: grain, flour) ひく híkù
♦vi (also: **mill about**: people, crowd) 右往左往する uósaò suru
woolen mill 織物工場 orímonokòjō

miller [mil'ər] n 製粉業者 seífungyòsha

milligram(me) [mil'əgræm] n ミリグラム miríguràmu

millimeter [mil'əmi:tər] (BRIT **millimetre**) n ミリメートル mirímètoru

millinery [mil'əne:ri:] n 婦人帽子店 fujínbòshiten

million [mil'jən] n 100万 hyakúmàn
a million times 何回も nánkai mo

millionaire [miljəne:r'] n 大富豪 daífugò

milometer [mai'loumi:tər] n = **mileometer**

mime [maim] n (action) パントマイム pantomaìmu; (actor) パントマイム役者 pantomaìmu yakùsha
♦vt (act) 身振り手振りでまねる mibúritebùri de manérù
♦vi (act out) パントマイムを演ずる pantomaìmu wo enzurù

mimic [mim'ik] n 物まね師 monómaneshì
♦vt (imitate) ...のまねをする ...no manê wo surú

min. abbr **minute(s)**; **minimum**

minaret [minəret'] n ミナレット minárètto ◇モスクのせん塔 mósùku no sentō arukù

mince [mins] vt (meat) ひく híkù
♦vi (in walking) 気取って歩く kidótte arukù
♦n (BRIT: CULIN) ひき肉 hikíniku

mincemeat [mins'mi:t] n (fruit) ミンスミート minsumìto ◇ドライフルーツなどの細切り doráifurùtsu nádò no komágiri; (US: meat) ひき肉 hikíniku

mincemeat pie (US) n (sweet) ミンスミートパイ minsumītopaì

mince pie (BRIT) n (sweet) = **mincemeat pie**

mincer [min'sər] n 肉ひき器 nikúhikikì

mind [maind] n (thoughts) 考え kangáe; (intellect) 頭脳 zunŏ; (opinion): **to my mind** 私の意見では watákushi no iken de wa; (sanity): **to be out of one's mind** 気が狂っている ki ga kurútte irù
♦vt (attend to, look after: shop, home etc) ...の番をする ...no bán wo suru; (: children, pets etc) ...の面倒を見る ...no mendō wo mírù; (be careful of) ...に注意する ...ni chúi suru; (object to): **I don't mind the noise** その音を気にしません sonó otó wo kì ni shimásen
it is on my mind 気に掛っている ki ni kakátte irù
to keep/bear something in mind ...を気にする ...wo kì ni suru
to make up one's mind 決心する kesshín suru
I don't mind 構いませんよ kamáimasèn yó
mind you, ... でもこれだけ言っておく ...de mo koré dakè itté okù ...
never mind! (it makes no odds) 気にしないで下さいよ kì ni shináide kudásaì; (don't worry) ほうっておきなさい hótte oki nasaì, 心配しないで下さい shinpai shinaìde kudásaì
「**mind the step**」階段に注意 kaídan ni chúi

minder [maind'ər] n (childminder) ベビーシッター bebíshittà; (BRIT inf: bodyguard) ボディーガード bodígàdo

mindful [maind'fəl] adj: **mindful of** ...を気に掛ける ...wo kì ni kakérù

mindless [maind'lis] *adj* (violence) 愚かな órokà na, 愚かな gurétsu na; (boring: job) 退屈な taíkutsu na

---
KEYWORD
---

mine[1] [main] *pron* 私の物 watákushi no monò

that book is mine その本は私のです sonó hoǹ wa watákushi no dèsu

these cases are mine それらのケースは私のです sorérà no kèsu wa watákushi no dèsu

this is mine これは私の物です koré wà watákushi no monò desu

yours is red, mine is green あなたのは赤いが, 私のは緑色です anátà no wa akái ga, watákushi no wà midóri irò desu

a friend of mine 私のある友達 watákushi nò árù tomódachi

---

mine[2] [main] *n* (*gen*) 鉱山 kózan; (*also:* land mine) 地雷 jirái; (bomb in water) 機雷 kírái

♦*vt* (coal) 採掘する saíkutsu suru; (beach) 地雷を敷設する jirái wo fusétsu suru; (harbor) 機雷を敷設する kírái wo fusétsu suru

coal mine 炭坑 taňkō

gold mine 金坑 kiňkō

minefield [main'fi:ld] *n* (area: land) 地雷原 jiráigeň; (: water) 機雷敷設水域 kírái-fusetsu suíiki; (*fig*: situation) 危険をはらんだ事態 kíkeň wò haráňda jítai

miner [main'ə:r] *n* 鉱山労働者 kózanrōdōshà

mineral [min'ə:rəl] *adj* (deposit, resources) 鉱物の kóbutsu no

♦*n* (in earth) 鉱物 kóbutsu no; (in food) ミネラル mínérarù

minerals [min'ə:rəlz] (*BRIT*) *npl* (soft drinks) 炭酸飲料水 tańsan-inryōsui

mineral water *n* ミネラルウォーター mínéraru uòtā

mingle [miŋ'gəl] *vi*: *to mingle with* ...と交わる ...to majíwaru ◇特にパーティなどで多くの人に声を掛けて回るなどの意味で使う tôkù ni pátì nádò de ốkù no

hitó ni kôè wo kakétè mawárù nádò no ímì de tsukáù

miniature [min'i:ətʃə:r] *adj* (small, tiny) ミニチュアの mínichùa no

♦*n* ミニチュア mínichùa

minibus [min'i:bʌs] *n* マイクロバス maíkurobasu

minim [min'əm] *n* (MUS) 二分音符 níbun oňpu

minimal [min'əməl] *adj* 最小限(度)の saíshōgen(do) no

minimize [min'əmaiz] *vt* (reduce: risks, disease) 最小限(度)に抑える saíshōgen (do) ni osáerù; (play down: role) 見くびる mikúbirù; (: weakness) 小さく見せる chíisaku mísèru

minimum [min'əməm] (*pl* **minima**) *n* 最小限(度) saíshōgeň(do)

♦*adj* 最小限(度)の saíshōgeň(do) no

mining [mai'niŋ] *n* 鉱業 kógyō

miniskirt [min'i:skə:rt] *n* ミニスカート mínísukàto

minister [min'istə:r] *n* (POL) 大臣 dáijin; (REL) 牧師 bókùshi

♦*vi*: *to minister to* (people, needs) ...に仕える ...ni tsukáerù

ministerial [ministə:ri'əl] (*BRIT*) *adj* (POL) 大臣の dáijin no

ministry [min'istri:] *n* (POL) ...省 ...shò; (REL) 聖職 seíshoku

mink [miŋk] *n* (fur) ミンクの毛皮 míňku no kegáwa; (animal) ミンク míňku

mink coat *n* ミンクのコート míňku no kōto

minnow [min'ou] *n* 小魚 kozákàna

minor [mai'nə:r] *adj* (unimportant: repairs) ちょっとした chottó shitá; (: injuries) 軽い karúi; (: poet) 二流の niryū no; (MUS) 短調の tanchō no

♦*n* (LAW) 未成年 miséinen

minority [minə:r'iti:] *n* (less than half: of group, society) 少数派 shōsūha

mint [mint] *n* (plant) ハッカ hakká; (sweet) ハッカあめ hakká amè

♦*vt* (coins) 鋳造する chūzō suru

the (US) Mint (US), the (Royal) Mint (BRIT) 造幣局 zóheìkyoku

in mint condition 新品同様で shinpindòyò de

minus [mai'nəs] *n* (*also*: **minus sign**) マイナス記号 maínasu kigò
♦*prep*: **12 minus 6 equals 6** 12引く6は 6 jǔni hikù rokú wà rokú; (temperature): **minus 24** 零下24度 reíka nijǔyoň do

minuscule [min'əskjuːl] *adj* 微々たる bíbìtaru

minute [min'it] *n* (unit) 分 fúñ; (*fig*: short time) ちょっと chottó
♦*adj* (search, detail) 細かい komákaì
at the last minute 土壇場に dotáñba ni

minutes [min'its] *npl* (of meeting) 会議録 kaígìròku

miracle [mir'əkəl] *n* (REL, *fig*) 奇跡 kiséki

miraculous [miræk'jələs] *adj* 奇跡的な kisékiteki na

mirage [mirɑ:ʒ'] *n* しん気楼 shíñkirò

mirror [mir'ər] *n* (in bedroom, bathroom) 鏡 kagámi, ミラー mírà; (in car) バックミラー bakkúmirà

mirth [mə:rθ] *n* (laughter) 笑い warái

misadventure [misədven'tʃər] *n* 災難 saínaň

misapprehension [misæprihen'tʃən] *n* 誤解 gokái

misappropriate [misəprou'pri:eit] *vt* (funds, money) 横領する óryō suru

misbehave [misbiheiv'] *vi* 行儀悪くする gyógiwarukù suru

miscalculate [miskæl'kjəleit] *vt* 見込み違いする mikómichigaì suru

miscarriage [miskær'idʒ] *n* (MED) 流産 ryūzan; (failure): *miscarriage of justice* 誤審 goshíñ

miscellaneous [misəlei'ni:əs] *adj* (collection, group: of tools, people) 雑多な zattá na; (subjects, items) 種々の shujú no

mischance [mistʃæns'] *n* (misfortune) 不運 fúuñ

mischief [mis'tʃif] *n* (naughtiness: of child) いたずら itázura; (playfulness, fun) いたずら itázura; (maliciousness) 悪さ wárùsa

mischievous [mis'tʃəvəs] *adj* (naughty, playful) いたずらな itázura na

misconception [miskənsep'ʃən] *n* 誤解 gokái

misconduct [miskɑ:n'dʌkt] *n* (behavior) 非行 hikò
professional misconduct 背任 haínin, 職権乱用 shokkéñ rañyò

misdemeanor [misdimi:'nə:r] (*BRIT* **misdemeanour**) *n* 軽犯罪 keíhañzai

miser [mai'zə:r] *n* けちん坊 kéchìnbō, 守銭奴 shuséñdo

miserable [miz'ə:rəbəl] *adj* (unhappy: person, expression) 惨めな míjìme na, 不幸な fukò na; (wretched: conditions) 哀れな áwàre na; (unpleasant: weather, person) いやな iyá na; (contemptible: offer, donation) ちっぽけな chippókè na; (: failure) 情けない nasákenaì

miserly [mai'zə:rli:] *adj* けちな kechí na

misery [miz'ə:ri:] *n* (unhappiness) 惨めさ mijímesà, 不幸せ fushíawase; (wretchedness) 哀れな状態 áwàre na jòtai

misfire [misfair'] *vi* (plan etc) 失敗する shippái suru

misfit [mis'fit] *n* (person) 適応不能者 tekíōfunòsha

misfortune [misfɔ:r'tʃən] *n* (bad luck) 不運 fúuñ

misgiving [misgiv'iŋ] *n* (apprehension) 心もとなさ kokóromotonasà, 疑念 ginéñ
to have misgivings about something ...を疑問に思う ...wo gimóñ ni omóù

misguided [misgai'did] *adj* (opinion, view) 心得違いの kokóroechigaì no

mishandle [mishæn'dəl] *vt* (mismanage: problem, situation) ...の処置を誤る ...no shóchì wo ayámarù

mishap [mis'hæp] *n* 事故 jíkò

misinform [misinfɔ:rm'] *vt* ...にうそを伝える ...ni úsò wo tsutáerù

misinterpret [misintər'prit] *vt* 誤解する gokái suru

misjudge [misdʒʌdʒ'] *vt* ...の判断を誤る ...no hañdañ wo ayámarù

mislay [mislei'] (*pt, pp* **mislaid**) *vt* (lose) なくす nakúsù, 置忘れる okíwasurerù

mislead [misli:d'] (*pt, pp* **misled**) *vt* うそを信じ込ませる úsò wo shíñjikomaserù

misleading [misli:'diŋ] *adj* (information)

誤解させる gokái saserù

mismanage [mismæn'idʒ] *vt* (manage badly: business, institution)下手な管理をする hetà na kánri wo surù; (: problem, situation) ...の処置を誤る ...no shóchì wo ayámarù

misnomer [misnou'mə:r] *n* (term) 誤った名称 ayámattà mefshō

misogynist [misɑːdʒ'ənist] *n* 女嫌い onnágirai

misplace [mispleis'] *vt* (lose) なくす nakúsù, 置忘れる okíwasurerù

misprint [mis'print] *n* 誤植 goshóku

Miss [mis] *n* ...さん ...sán ◇未婚の女性に対する敬称 míkòn no josei ni taí surù kefshō

miss [mis] *vt* (train, bus etc) ...に乗遅れる ...ni norfokurerù; (: fail to hit: target) ...に当て損なう ...ni atésokonaù; (: fail to see): **you can't miss it** 見落しっこない miótoshikkonài; (: regret the absence of) ...が恋しい ...ga koíshiì, ...が懐かしい ...ga natsúkashiì; (: chance, opportunity) 逃す nigásù, のがす nogásù; (: class, meeting) ...に欠席する ...ni kesséki suru
♦*vi* (fail to hit) 当り損なう atárisokonaù, それる sorérù
♦*n* (failure to hit) 当て損ない atésokonài, ミス mísù

misshapen [misʃei'pən] *adj* 不格好な bukákkō na

missile [mis'əl] *n* (weapon: MIL) ミサイル misáiru; (: object thrown) 飛道具 tobídōgu

missing [mis'iŋ] *adj* (lost: person, pupil) 行方不明の yukúefumèi no; (: object) なくなっている nakúnatte irù; (removed: tooth) 抜かれた nukáretà; (: wheel) 外された hazúsaretà; (MIL) 行方不明の yukúefumèi no
to be missing 行方不明である yukúefumèi de aru

mission [miʃ'ən] *n* (task) 任務 nínmu; (official representatives) 代表団 daíhyōdan; (MIL) 出撃 shutsúgeki ◇特に爆撃機について言う tókù ni bakúgekikì ni tsuíte iú; (REL: activity) 伝道 deńdō; (: building) 伝道所 deńdōjò

missionary [miʃ'əne:ri:] *n* 伝道師 deńdōshi

miss out (*BRIT*) *vt* (leave out) 落す otósù

misspent [misspent'] *adj*: **his misspent youth** 浪費した彼の青春 rōhi shitá kárè no seíshun

mist [mist] *n* (light) もや móyà; (heavy) 濃霧 nōmu
♦*vi* (*also*: **mist over**, **mist up**) (eyes) 涙ぐむ namídagùmu; (windows) 曇る kumórù

mistake [misteik'] *n* (error) 間違い machígaì
♦*vt* (*pt* **mistook**, *pp* **mistaken**) (be wrong about) 間違える machígaerù
by mistake 間違って machígattè
to make a mistake 間違いをする machígaì wo suru
to mistake A for B AをBと間違える A wo B to machígaerù

mistaken [mistei'kən] (*pp of* **mistake**) *adj* (idea, belief etc) 間違った machígattà
to be mistaken 間違っている machígattè irú

mister [mis'tə:r] (*inf*) *n* ◇男性への呼び掛け dańsei e no yobíkake ¶ *see* **Mr.**

mistletoe [mis'əltou] *n* ヤドリギ yadórigì

mistook [mistuk'] *pt of* **mistake**

mistress [mis'tris] *n* (lover) 愛人 aíjin; (of house, servant) 女主人 oñna shùjin; (in primary, secondary schools) 先生 seńsei
to be mistress of the situation (*fig*) 事態を掌握している jítài wo shōaku shite irù

mistrust [mistrʌst'] *vt* 信用しない shińyō shinài

misty [mis'ti:] *adj* (day etc) もやった moyáttà; (glasses, windows) 曇った kumóttà

misunderstand [misʌndə:rstænd'] (*irreg*) *vt* (fail to understand: person, book) 誤解する gokái suru
♦*vi* (fail to understand) 誤解する gokái suru

misunderstanding [misʌndə:rstæn'diŋ]

n (failure to understand) 誤解 gokái; (disagreement) 口げんか kuchígeñka

misuse [misjuːs'] *n* (of power) 乱用 rañyō; (of funds) 悪用 akúyō
♦*vt* (power) 乱用する rañ-yō suru; (funds) 悪用する akúyō suru

mitigate [mit'əgeit] *vt* 和らげる yawáragerù

mitt(en) [mit'(ən)] *n* ミトン mítòn

mix [miks] *vt* (combine: liquids, ingredients, colors) 混ぜる mazérù; (cake, cement) こねる konérù; (drink, sauce) 作る tsukúrù
♦*vi* (people): **to mix (with)** ...と交わる ...to majíwarù ◇特にパーティなどで多くの人に声を掛けて回るなどの意味で使う tóku ni pấti nádò de ōku no hitó nì kôè wo kakétè máwarù nádò no ímì de tsukáù
♦*n* (combination) 混合物 koñgōbùtsu; (powder) ミックス míkkùsu

mixed [mikst] *adj* (salad) コンビネーションの koñbinēshon no; (grill) 盛り合せの moríawase no; (feelings, reactions) 複雑な fukúzatsu na; (school, education etc) 共学の kyốgaku no
a mixed marriage (religion) 異なった宗教の信徒間の結婚 kotónatta shūkyō no shinto kan no kekkon; (race) 異なった人種間の結婚 kotónatta jiñshu kan no kekkon

mixed-up [mikst'ʌp] *adj* (confused) 混乱している koñran shite irù

mixer [mik'səːr] *n* (for food) ミキサー míkìsā; (person): *to be a good mixer* 付合い上手である tsukíaijồzu de aru

mixture [miks't'ʃəːr] *n* (combination) 混合物 koñgōbùtsu; (MED: for cough etc) 飲薬 nomígusùri

mix up *vt* (confuse: people, things) 混同する koñdō suru

mix-up [miks'ʌp] *n* (confusion) 混乱 koñran

mm *abbr* = millimeter

moan [moun] *n* (cry) うめき umḗki
♦*vi* (*inf*: complain): *to moan (about)* (...について) 愚痴を言う (...ni tsúite) guchí wo iù

moat [mout] *n* 堀 horí

mob [mɑ:b] *n* (crowd) 群衆 guñshū
♦*vt* (person) ...の回りにわっと押し寄せる ...no mawárì ni wáttò oshíyoserù

mobile [mou'bəl] *adj* (able to move) 移動式の idṓshiki no
♦*n* (decoration) モビール mồbìru

mobile home *n* モビールハウス mobíruhaùsu

mobility [moubil'əti:] *n* 移動性 idṓsei

mobilize [mou'bəlaiz] *vt* (friends, work force) 動員する dṓin suru; (MIL: country, army) 戦時態勢を取らせる señji taísei wo toráserù

moccasin [mɑ:k'əsin] *n* モカシン mokáshìn

mock [mɑ:k] *vt* (ridicule) ばかにする bákà ni suru; (laugh at) あざ笑う azáwaraù
♦*adj* (fake) 見せ掛けの misḗkake no; (exam, battle) 模擬の mógì no

mockery [mɑ:k'əːri:] *n* (derision) あざけり azákeri
to make a mockery of ...をばかにする ...wo bákà ni suru

mock-up [mɑ:k'ʌp] *n* (model) 模型 mokḗi

mod [mɑ:d kɑ:nz] *adj see* **convenience**

mode [moud] *n* (form: of life) 様式 yốshiki; (: of transportation) 手段 shùdan

model [mɑ:d'əl] *n* (representation: of boat, building etc) 模型 mokḗi; (fashion model, artist's model) モデル mṓdèru; (example) 手本 tḗhòn
♦*adj* (excellent) 模範的な mohánteki na
♦*vt* (clothes) ...のモデルをする ...no mṓdèru wo suru; (with clay etc) ...の模型を作る ...no mokḗi wo tsukúrù; (copy): *to model oneself on* ...の模範に習う ...no mṓhàn ni naráù
♦*vi* (for designer, photographer etc) モデルをする mṓdèru wo suru

model railway *n* 模型鉄道 mokḗi tetsudṓ

modem [mou'dem] *n* (COMPUT) モデム mṓdèmu

moderate [*adj* mɑ:d'əːrit *vb* mɑ:d'əːreit] *adj* (views, opinion) 穏健な oñken na; (amount) 中位の chūgurai no; (change)

ある程度の arú teĩdo no

♦vi (storm, wind etc) 弱まる yawámarù

♦vt (tone, demands) 和らげる yawárage-rù

moderation [mɑ:dərei'ʃən] n 中庸 chúyō

modern [mɑ:d'ərn] adj 現代的な geńdaiteki na, 近代的な kińdaiteki na, モダンな modáń na

modernize [mɑ:d'ə:rnaiz] vt 現代的にする geńdaiteki ni suru

modest [mɑ:d'ist] adj (small: house, budget) 質素な shíssò na; (unassuming: person) 謙虚な keńkyo na

modesty [mɑ:d'isti:] n 慎み tsutsúshimi

modicum [mɑ:d'əkəm] n: a modicum of ちょっとだけの... chóttò dake no ...

modification [mɑ:dəfəkei'ʃən] n (alteration: of law) 改正 kaísei; (: of building) 改修 kaíshū; (: of car, engine etc) 改造 kaízō

modify [mɑ:d'əfai] vt (law) 改正する kaísei suru; (building, car, engine) 改造する kaízō suru

module [mɑ:dʒ'u:l] n (unit, component, SPACE) モジュール mojúrù

mogul [mou'gəl] n (fig) 大立者 ốdatemồno

mohair [mou'he:r] n モヘア móheà

moist [mɔist] adj (slightly wet: earth, eyes, lips) 湿った shiméttà

moisten [mɔis'ən] vt (lips, sponge) 湿らす shimérasù

moisture [mɔis'tʃə:r] n 湿り気 shimérike

moisturizer [mɔis'tʃə:raizə:r] n (cream) モイスチュアクリーム moísuchua kurímu; (lotion) モイスチュアローション moísuchua rồshon

molar [mou'lə:r] n きゅう歯 kyūshi

mold [mould] (BRIT **mould**) n (cast: for jelly, metal) 型 katá; (mildew) かび kabí

♦vt (shape: plastic, clay etc) ...で...の形を作る ...de ...no katáchi wò tsukúrù; (fig: influence: public opinion, character) 作り上げる tsukúriagerù

moldy [moul'di:] (BRIT **mouldy**) adj (bread, cheese) かびた kabítà; (smell) かび臭い kabíkusaì

mole [moul] n (spot) ほくろ hokúro; (ani-

mal) モグラ mogúra; (fig: spy) 秘密工作員 himítsukōsakuiñ

molecule [mɑ:l'əkju:l] n 分子 búnshi

molest [məlest'] vt (assault sexually) ...にいたずらをする ...ni itázura wo surù; (harass) いじめる ijímerù

mollycoddle [mɑ:l'i:kɑ:dəl] vt (pamper) 甘やかす amáyakasù

molt [moult] (BRIT **moult**) vi (animal, bird) 換毛する kańmō suru

molten [moul'tən] adj (metal, rock) 溶解の yốkai no

mom [mɑ:m] (US: inf) n かあちゃん kā-chan, ママ mámà

moment [mou'mənt] n (period of time): for a moment ちょっと chóttò; (point in time): at that moment 丁度その時 chốdò sonó tokì

at the moment 今の所 imá no tokòro

momentary [mou'mənte:ri:] adj (brief: pause, glimpse) 瞬間的な shuńkanteki na

momentous [moumen'təs] adj (occasion, decision) 重大な jūdai na

momentum [moumen'təm] n (PHYSICS) 運動量 uńdōryố; (fig: of events, movement, change) 勢い ikíòi, 惰性 daséi

to gather momentum (lit, fig) 勢いが付く ikíòi ga tsúkù

mommy [mɑ:m'i:] (US) n ママ mámà ◊幼児用語 yốjiyồgo

Monaco [mɑ:n'əkou] n モナコ mónàko

monarch [mɑ:n'ə:rk] n 君主 kúñshu

monarchy [mɑ:n'ə:rki:] n (system) 王制 ốsei; (royal family) 王室 ốshitsu, 王族 ố-zoku

monastery [mɑ:n'əste:ri:] n 修道院 shúdồin

Monday [mʌn'dei] n 月曜日 getsúyồbi

monetary [mɑ:n'ite:ri:] adj (system, policy, control) 金融の kiń-yū no

money [mʌn'i:] n (coins and notes) 金 ka-nế; (currency) 通貨 tsūka

to make money (earn) 金をもうける ka-nế wo mốkerù

money order n 郵便為替 yǘbinkawàse

money-spinner [mʌn'i:spinə:r] (BRIT:

inf) *n* (person, idea, business) ドル箱 do-rúbako

mongol [mɑːŋˈɡəl] *adj* モンゴルの móñgoru no
♦*n* (MED) ダウン症候群患者 daúnshōkōgun kañja

mongrel [mʌŋˈɡrəl] *n* (dog) 雑種 zasshú

monitor [mɑːnˈitər] *n* (machine) モニター装置 monítāsōchi; (screen: *also*: **television monitor**) ブラウン管 buráuñkan; (of computer) モニター móñītā
♦*vt* (broadcasts) 傍受する bốju suru; (heartbeat, pulse) モニターする móñītā suru; (progress) 監視する kañshi suru

monk [mʌŋk] *n* 修道師 shúdōshi

monkey [mʌŋˈkiː] *n* (animal) サル sarú

monkey nut (*BRIT*) *n* ピーナッツ pínattsu

monkey wrench *n* モンキーレンチ moñkīrenchi

mono [mɑːnˈou] *adj* (recording) モノラルの mónōraru no

monochrome [mɑːnˈəkroum] *adj* (film, photograph) 白黒の shírðkuro no, モノクロの monókùro no

monogram [mɑːnˈəɡræm] *n* モノグラム monóguramu

monologue [mɑːnˈəlɔːɡ] *n* 会話の独占 kaíwa no dokúsen; (THEATER) 独白 dokúhaku, モノローグ monórðgu

monopolize [mənɑːpˈəlaiz] *vt* 独占する dokúsen suru

monopoly [mənɑːpˈəliː] *n* (domination) 独占 dokúsen; (COMM) 専売 señbai, モノポリー monópðrī

monosyllable [mɑːnˈəsiləbəl] *n* 単音節語 tañ-onsetsugð

monotone [mɑːnˈətoun] *n*: **to speak in a monotone** 単調な声で話す tañchō na kôè de hanásù

monotonous [mənɑːtˈənəs] *adj* (life, job etc) 退屈な taíkutsu na; (voice, tune) 単調な tañchō na

monotony [mənɑːtˈəniː] *n* 退屈 taíkutsu

monsoon [mɑːnsuːn] *n* モンスーン móñsūn

monster [mɑːnˈstər] *n* (animal, plant: misshapen) 奇形 kikéi; (: enormous) 怪物

kaíbùtsu, お化け obáke; (imaginary creature) 怪物 kaíbùtsu; (person: cruel, evil) 怪物 kaíbùtsu

monstrosity [mɑːnstrɑːsˈəti:] *n* (hideous object, building) 見るに堪えない代物 mírù ni taénài shirómòno

monstrous [mɑːnˈstrəs] *adj* (huge) 巨大な kyodái na; (ugly) 見るに堪えない mírù ni taénài; (atrocious) 極悪な gokúaku na

month [mʌnθ] *n* 月 tsukí

monthly [mʌnθˈliː] *adj* (ticket etc) 一カ月の ikkágètsu no; (magazine) 月刊 gekkán no; (payment etc) 毎月の maítsuki no; (meeting) 月例の getsúrei no
♦*adv* 毎月 maítsuki

monument [mɑːnˈjəmənt] *n* (memorial) 記念碑 kinéñhi; (historical building) 史的記念物 shitékikinéñbutsu

monumental [mɑːnjəmenˈtəl] *adj* (large and important: building, statue) 歴史的な rekíshiteki na; (important: book, piece of work) 画期的な kakkíteki na; (terrific: storm, row) すごい sugóî, すさまじい susámajiî

moo [muː] *vi* (cow) もーと鳴く mố tò nakú

mood [muːd] *n* (humor: of person) 機嫌 kigén; (: of crowd, group) 雰囲気 fuñ-ikī, ムード mûdo
to be in a good/bad mood (temper) 機嫌がいい〔悪い〕kigén gà íî〔warûî〕

moody [muːˈdiː] *adj* (variable) むら気な muráki na; (sullen) 不機嫌な fukígèn na

moon [muːn] *n* 月 tsukí

moonlight [muːnˈlait] *n* 月光 gekkố

moonlighting [muːnˈlaitiŋ] *n* (work) アルバイト arúbàito ◇本職の外にする仕事で、特に規定、規則違反の仕事を指す hoñshòku no hoká nì suru shigóto dè, tôkù ni kitéî, kisóku ihàn no shigóto wò sásù

moonlit [muːnˈlit] *adj*: **a moonlit night** 月夜 tsukíyò

moor [muːr] *n* (heath) 荒れ野 aréno
♦*vt* (ship) つなぐ tsunágù
♦*vi* 停泊する teíhaku suru

moorland [muːrˈlænd] *n* 荒れ野 aréno

moose [muːs] *n inv* アメリカヘラジカ a-mérikaherajīka

mop [mɑːp] *n* (for floor) モップ moppú; (for dishes) スポンジたわし supónjitawá-shi ◇短い柄の付いた皿洗い用を指す mijíkaī e no tsúīta saráarai yō wo sásù
♦*vt* (floor) モップでふく moppú de fukú; (eyes, face) ぬぐう nugúú
a mop of hair もじゃもじゃ頭 mojá-moja atáma

mope [moup] *vi* ふさぎ込む fuságikomù

moped [mou'ped] *n* モペット mopéttò ◇ペダルで動かす事も出来る小型オートバイ pedárù de ugókasù kotó mo dekirù kogáta ótobài

mop up *vt* (liquid) ふく fukú

moral [mɔːr'əl] *adj* 倫理的な rínriteki na
♦*n* (of story etc) 教訓 kyōkun
moral support (encouragement) 精神的支え seíshinteki sasáe

morale [məræl'] *n* (of army, staff) 士気 shikí

morality [məræl'iti:] *n* (good behavior) 品行 hínkō; (system of morals: *also* correctness, acceptability) 倫理 rínri

morals [mɔːr'əlz] *npl* (principles, values) 倫理 rínri

morass [məræs'] *n* (*lit, fig*) 泥沼 dorónu-ma

morbid [mɔːr'bid] *adj* (imagination, ideas) 陰気な ínki na

KEYWORD

---

more [mɔːr] *adj* **1** (greater in number etc) より多くの yorí ōku no
more people/work/letters than we expected 私たちが予定していたより多くの人々〔仕事，手紙〕watákushitàchi ga yotéi shite ita yorí ōku no hítòbito〔shigóto, tegámi〕
I have more books/money than you 私はあなたより沢山の本〔金〕を持っています watákushi wà anátà yorí takúsan nò hón〔kané〕wo mótte imasù
this store has more wine than beer この店はビールよりワインが沢山あります konó mise wà bírù yori wáīn ga takúsan arimasù

2 (additional) もっと móttò
do you want (some) more tea? もっと紅茶をいかがですか móttò kōcha wò ikága desù ká
is there any more wine? ワインはまだありますか wáīn wa mádà arímasù ká
I have no/I don't have any more money お金はもうありません o-káne wa mō arímaseñ
it'll take a few more weeks あと数週間掛かります átò sūshūkàn kakárimasù
♦*pron* **1** (greater amount) もっと沢山 móttò takúsan
more than 10 10以上 jūijō ◇この成句の英語には「10」が含まれないが，日本語の場合「10」も含まれる konó seīku no éigo ni wà "jū" gà fukúmarenaī ga, nihóngo no baái "jū" mō fukúmarerù. (Note: the English phrase indicates a quantity of 11 and above, but the Japanese indicates 10 and above.)
it cost more than we expected 予想以上に金が掛けました yosō ijò ni kané gà kakárimashìta
2 (further or additional amount) もっと沢山 móttò takúsan
is there any more? まだありますか mádà arímasù ká
there's no more もうありません mō arímaseñ
a little more もう少し mō sukoshì
many/much more ...よりずっと沢山 ...yorí zuttó takúsañ
♦*adv* ...よりもっと... ...yorí mottò...
more dangerous/difficult etc (than) ...より危ない〔難しい〕...yorí abúnai〔muzúkashiī〕
more easily/economically/quickly (than) ...よりたやすく〔経済的に，早く〕...yorí tayasukù〔keizaiteki ni, hayákù〕
more and more excited/friendly/expensive ますます興奮して〔親しくなって，高くなって〕masúmàsu kōfun shitè〔shitáshiku nattè, tákàku natte〕
he grew to like her more and more 彼はますます彼女が好きになった kárè wa masúmàsu kánòjo ga sukí ni nattà

more or less 大体 daítai, 大よそ őyoso

the job's more or less finished 仕事は大体できています shigóto wà daítai dékìte imasu

it should cost £ 500, more or less 大よそ500ポンド掛りそうです őyoso gohyákupoñdo kakárisȏ desu

more than ever ますます masúmàsu, より一層 yorí issȏ

more beautiful than ever ますます美しい masúmàsu utsúkushìì

more quickly than ever ますます早く masúmàsu háyàku

he loved her more than ever 彼はより一層彼女を愛する様になった kárè wa yorí issȏ kánòjo wo aí suru yȏ ni náttà

moreover [mɔːrou'vəːr] *adv* なお náȏ

morgue [mɔːrg] *n* 死体保管所 shitáihokañjo, モルグ morúgȗ

moribund [mɔːr'əbʌnd] *adj* (organization, industry) 斜陽の shayȏ no

Mormon [mɔːr'mən] *n* モルモン教徒 morúmon kyȏto

morning [mɔːr'niŋ] *n* (period after daybreak) 朝 asá; (from midnight to noon) 午前 gózeñ

in the morning 朝に asá ni, 午前中に gozéñchū ni

7 o'clock in the morning 午前7時 gózen shichíji

morning paper 朝刊 chȏkan

morning sun 朝日 ásàhi

morning walk 朝の散歩 ásà no sañpo

morning sickness *n* つわり tsuwári

Morocco [mərɑːk'ou] *n* モロッコ morókkò

moron [mɔːr'ɑːn] (*inf*) *n* ばか bákà

morose [mərous'] *adj* (miserable) 陰気な íñki na

morphine [mɔːr'fiːn] *n* モルヒネ morúhine

Morse [mɔːrs] *n* (*also*: **Morse code**) モールス信号 mȏrusu shiñgȏ

morsel [mɔːr'səl] *n* (of food) 一口 hitókùchi

mortal [mɔːr'təl] *adj* (man) いつか死ぬ ítsùka shinú; (wound) 致命的な chiméitekì na; (danger) 命にかかわる ínòchi ni kakáwarù

♦*n* (human being) 人間 niñgen

mortal combat 死闘 shitȏ

mortal enemy 宿敵 shukúteki

mortal remains 遺骨 ikótsu

mortal sin 大罪 taízai

mortality [mɔːrtæl'itiː] *n* いつか死ぬ事 ítsùka shinú kotȏ; (number of deaths) 死亡率 shibȏritsu

mortar [mɔːr'təːr] *n* (cannon) 迫撃砲 hakúgekihȏ; (CONSTR) モルタル mȏrùtaru; (bowl) 乳鉢 nyȗbachi

mortgage [mɔːr'gidʒ] *n* 住宅ローン jȗtakuroñ

♦*vt* (house, property) 抵当に入れて金を借りる teítȏ ni irète kané wo karírù

mortify [mɔːr'təfai] *vt*: *to be mortified* 恥を感じる hají wo kañjirù

mortuary [mɔːr'tʃuːeːriː] *n* 霊安室 reíañshitsu

mosaic [mouzei'ik] *n* モザイク mozáìku

Moscow [mɑːs'kau] *n* モスクワ mosúkuwa

Moslem [mɑːz'ləm] *adj, n* = **Muslim**

mosque [mɑːsk] *n* イスラム教寺院 isúramukyȏ jìin, モスク mósùku

mosquito [məski:'tou] (*pl* **mosquitoes**) *n* 蚊 ká

moss [mɔːs] *n* (plant) コケ koké

KEYWORD

---

most [moust] *adj* **1** (almost all: people, things etc) ほとんどの hotóñdo no

most people ほとんどの人 hotóñdo no hitó

most men/dogs behave like that ほとんどの男性〔イヌ〕はそういう振舞をする hotóñdo no dañsei〔inú〕wà sȏ iȗ furúmaì wo surú

most houses here are privately owned ここのほとんどの家は個人所有の物です kokó nò hotóñdo no íè wà kojíñshoyȗ nò monȏ desù

2 (largest, greatest: interest, money etc) 最も沢山の mottómò takúsañ no

who has (the) most money? 最も多くの金を持っているのは誰でしょう mottó-

mò ōku no kane wo motte iru no wa
dare deshō

*he derived the most pleasure from
her visit* 最も彼を喜ばせたのは彼女の
訪問だった mottómò kárè wo yorókoba-
seta no wà kánòjo no hōmon dattà

♦*pron* (greatest quantity, number) ほと
んど hotóndo

most of it/them それ〔それら〕のほとん
ど soré〔sorérà〕no hotóndo

most of his/her friends 金〔彼
女の友達〕のほとんど kané〔kánòjo no to-
módachi〕nò hotóndo

most of the time ほとんどの場合 hotóndo no baái

do the most you can できるだけの事を
して下さい dekíru dakè no kotó wò shité kudasaì

I saw the most 私が一番沢山見ました
watákushi gà ichíban takùsan mimáshīta

to make the most of something ...を
最大限に利用する ...wò saídaìgen ni riyō
surù

at the (very) most 最大に見積っても
saídaì nì mitsúmotte mò

♦*adv* (+ verb: spend, eat, work etc) 最も
多く mottómò ōkù; (+ adjective: *the
most intelligent/expensive etc* 最も利
口〔高価〕な mottómò rikō〔kōka〕nà; (+
adverb: carefully, easily etc) 最も注意深
く〔たやすく〕mottómò chúibukakù〔ta-
yásukù〕; (very: polite, interesting etc) と
ても totémo

a most interesting book とても面白い
本 totémo omoshiroī hón

---

mostly [moust'li:] *adv* (chiefly) 主に ōmo
ni; (usually) 普段は fúdàn wa, 普通は futsū wa

MOT [emouti:'] *n abbr* = Ministry of
Transport: *the MOT (test)* (*BRIT*) 車
検 shakén

motel [moutel'] *n* モーテル mōteru

moth [mɔ:θ] *n* (insect) ガ gá; (clothes
moth) イガ igá

mothball [mɔ:θ'bɔ:l] *n* 防虫剤 bōchūzai

mother [mʌð'ə:r] *n* 母 háhà, 母親 haháo-

---

ya, お母さん o-káasan

♦*adj*: *mother country* 母国 bókòku

♦*vt* (act as mother to) 母親として育てる
haháoya toshitè sodáterù; (pamper, protect) 甘やかす amáyakasù

mother company 親会社 oyágaìsha

motherhood [mʌð'ə:rhud] *n* 母親である
事 haháoya de arù kotó

mother-in-law [mʌð'ə:rinlɔ:] (*p l*
mothers-in-law) *n* しゅうと shūto

motherly [mʌð'ə:rli:] *adj* 母の様な háhà
no yō na

mother-of-pearl [mʌð'ə:rəvpə:rl'] *n* 真
珠母 shińjùbo

mother-to-be [mʌð'ə:rtəbi:'] (*p l*
mothers-to-be) *n* 妊婦 nínpu

mother tongue *n* 母国語 bokókugò

motif [mouti:f'] *n* (design) 模様 moyō

motion [mou'ʃən] *n* (movement) 動き u-
gókì; (gesture) 合図 aízù; (at meeting) 動
議 dōgi

♦*vt*: *to motion (to) someone to do
something* ...する様に...に合図をする
...surú yō ni ...ni aízù wo suru

motionless [mou'ʃənlis] *adj* 動かない u-
gókanài

motion picture *n* (film) 映画 eígà

motivated [mou'təveitid] *adj* (enthusiastic) 張切っている haríkitte irù; (+
impelled): *motivated by* (envy, desire)
...の動機で ...no dōki de

motivation [moutəvei'ʃən] *n* (drive) 動
機 dōki

motive [mou'tiv] *n* (aim, purpose) 目標
mokúhyō

motley [mɑ:t'li:] *adj* 雑多で奇妙な zattá
dè kimyō na

motor [mou'tə:r] *n* (of machine) 原動機
geńdòki, モーター mōtā; (of vehicle) エ
ンジン éǹjin; (*BRIT*: *inf*: vehicle) 車 kurúma

♦*cpd* (industry, trade) 自動車の jídòsha
no

motorbike [mou'tə:rbaik] *n* オートバイ
ōtòbai

motorboat [mou'tə:rbout] *n* モーターボ
ート mōtābòto

motorcar [mou'tə:rkɑ:r] (*BRIT*) *n* 自動

車 jídōsha

motorcycle [mou'tə:rsai'kəl] n オートバイ ōtóbai

motorcycle racing n オートバイレーシング ōtóbairēshingu

motorcyclist [mou'tə:rsaiklist] n オートバイのライダー ōtóbai no raídā

motoring [mou'tə:riŋ] (BRIT) n 自動車運転 jidósha uñten

motorist [mou'tə:rist] n 運転者 uñteñsha

motor racing (BRIT) n カーレース kárēsu

motor vehicle n 自動車 jídōsha

motorway [mou'tə:rwei] (BRIT) n ハイウェー haíuē

mottled [mɑːt'əld] adj ぶちの buchí no

motto [mɑːt'ou] (pl mottoes) n 標語 hyógo, モットー mottő

mould [mould] (BRIT) n, vt = **mold**

mouldy [moul'diː] (BRIT) adj = **moldy**

moult [moult] (BRIT) vi = **molt**

mound [maund] n (heap: of blankets, leaves, earth etc) 一山 hitóyàma

mount [maunt] n (mountain in proper names): *Mount Carmel* カルメル山 karúmeruzàn

♦vt (horse) ...に乗る ...ni norú; (exhibition, display) 開催する kaísai suru; (fix: jewel) 台座にはめる daíza ni hamérù; (: picture) 掛ける kakérù; (staircase) 昇る nobórù

♦vi (increase: inflation) 上昇する jóshō suru; (: tension) つのる tsunoru; (: problems) 増える fuérù

mountain [maun'tən] n (GEO) 山 yamá

♦cpd (road, stream) 山の yamá no

mountaineer [mauntəni:r'] n 登山家 tozáñka

mountaineering [mauntəni:'riŋ] n 登山 tózàn

mountainous [maun'tənəs] adj (country, area) 山の多い yamá no ōi

mountain rescue team n 山岳救助隊 sañgaku kyūjotai

mountainside [maun'tənsaid] n 山腹 sañpuku

mount up vi (bills, costs, savings) たまる tamárù

mourn [mɔːrn] vt (death) 悲しむ kanáshimù

♦vi: *to mourn for* (someone) ...の死を悲しむ ...no shí wo kanáshimù

mourner [mɔːr'nər] n 会葬者 kaísōsha

mournful [mɔːrn'fəl] adj (sad) 悲しそうな kanáshisō na

mourning [mɔːr'niŋ] n 喪 mo
in mourning 喪中で mochú de

mouse [maus] (pl **mice**) n (animal) ハツカネズミ hatsúkanezùmi; (COMPUT) マウス máùsu

mousetrap [maus'træp] n ネズミ取り nezúmitòri

mousse [muːs] n (CULIN) ムース mūsu; (also: **hair mousse**) ヘアムース heámūsu

moustache [məstæʃ'] (BRIT) n = **mustache**

mousy [mau'siː] adj (hair) 薄汚い茶色の usugitanai cha-íro no

mouth [mauθ] (pl **mouths**) n (ANAT) 口 kuchí; (of cave, hole) 入口 iríguchi; (of river) 河口 kakố

mouthful [mauθ'ful] n (amount) 口一杯 kuchí ippaì

mouth organ n ハーモニカ hámonika

mouthpiece [mauθ'piːs] n (of musical instrument) 吹口 fukígùchi; (spokesman) スポークスマン supókusumàn

mouthwash [mauθ'wɔːʃ] n マウスウォッシュ máùsu uósshù ◊口臭防止洗口液 kóshūbōshi senkōeki

mouth-watering [mauθ'wɔːtəriŋ] adj おいしそうな oíshisō na

movable [muː'vəbəl] adj 可動な kadố na

move [muːv] n (movement) 動き ugóki; (in game: change of position) 手 té; (: turn to play) 番 báñ; (change: of house) 引っ越し hikkóshi; (: of job) 転職 teñshoku

♦vt (change position of: furniture, car, curtains etc) 動かす ugókasù; (chessmen etc: in game) 動かす ugókasù; (emotionally) 感動させる kañdō saserù; (POL: resolution etc) 提議する teígi suru

♦vi (person, animal) 動く ugókù; (traffic) 流れる nagárerù; (also: **move house**)

引っ越す hikkósù; (develop: situation, events) 進展する shińten suru

to get a move on 急ぐ isógù

to move someone to do something ...に ...をする気を起こさせる ...ni ...wo suru ki wò okósaserù

moveable [muːˈvəbəl] *adj* = **movable**

move about/around *vi* (change position) そわそわする sówàsowa suru; (travel) 頻繁に旅行する hińpan ni ryokó suru; (change: residence) 頻繁に引っ越す hińpan ni hikkósù; (: job) 頻繁に転職する hińpan ni teńshoku suru

move along *vi* 立ち去る tachísarù

move along! 立ち止まるな tachídomarù ná

move away *vi* (leave: town, area) よそ へ引っ越す yosó e hikkósù

move back *vi* (return) 元の所へ引っ越す mótò no tokóro e hikkósù

move forward *vi* (advance) 前進する zeńshin suru

move in *vi* (to a house) 入居する nyúkyo suru; (police, soldiers) 攻撃を加える kố-geki wò kuwáerù

movement [muːˈvmənt] *n* (action: of person, animal) 動き ugóki, 動作 dòsa; (: of traffic) 流れ nagáre; (gesture) 合図 aízù; (transportation: of goods etc) 運輸 úñ-yu; (shift: in attitude, policy) 変化 heñ-ka; (group of people: esp REL, POL) 運動 uñdò; (MUS) 楽章 gakúshò

move on *vi* 立ち去る tachísarù

move on! 立ち止まるな tachídomarù ná

move out *vi* (of house) 引っ越す hikkó-sù

move over *vi* (to make room) 横へどい て場所を空ける yokó è doíte bashó wò akérù

move up *vi* (employee, deputy) 昇進する shóshin suru; (pupil) 進級する shińkyù suru

movie [muːˈviː] *n* 映画 eígà

to go to the movies 映画を見に行く eígà wo mí ni ikù

movie camera *n* 映画カメラ eígà kámèra

moving [muːˈviŋ] *adj* (emotional) 感動的

に kańdōteki ni; (that moves) 動く ugó-kù

mow [mou] (*pt* **mowed**, *pp* **mowed** *or* **mown**) *vt* (grass, corn) 刈る karú

mow down *vt* (kill) なぎ払う様に殺す nagíharaù yố nì korósù

mower [mouˈəːr] *n* (*also:* **lawnmower**) 芝 刈機 shibákarikì

MP [empiː] (*BRIT*) *n abbr* = **Member of Parliament**

m.p.h. [empieitʃ] *abbr* (= *miles per hour*) 時速...マイル jísoku ...máìru

Mr, Mr. [misˈtəːr] *n*: *Mr. Smith* スミス さん sumisu sán ◇男性の敬称 dańsei no keíshō

Mrs, Mrs. [misˈiz] *n*: *Mrs Smith* スミ スさん sumisu sán ◇既婚女性の敬称 kí-kònjoséi no keíshō

Ms, Ms. [miz] *n*: *Ms. Smith* スミスさん sumisu sán ◇既婚・未婚を問わず女性の 敬称 kíkòn, míkòn wo towázù joséi no keíshō

M.Sc. [emessiː] *abbr* = **Master of Science**

KEYWORD

much [mʌtʃ] *adj* (time, money, effort) 沢 山の takúsañ no, 多くの ốkù no

we haven't got much time/money あ まり多くの時間〔金〕はありません amári ốku no jikán〔kané〕wà arímaseñ

much effort was expended on the project その企画に多くの努力を費やし た sonó kikáku ni ốkù no dóryòku wo tsufyashìta

how much money/time do you need? お金〔時間〕はどのぐらい必要ですか o-káne〔jikán〕wà dóño gurai hitsúyō desù ká

he's done so much work for the charity その慈善事業のために彼は様々 な仕事をしてくれました sonó jizénjigyò no tamé nì kárè wa samázàma na shigó-to wò shité kuremashìta

it's too much あんまりだ añmarì da

it's not much 大した事じゃない táìshi-ta kotó jà nai

to have too much money/free time 金

〔暇〕が有り余る kané〔himá〕gà aríamarù
as much as ...と同じぐらい ...to onáji gurài

I have as much money/intelligence as you 私はあなたと同じぐらいの金〔知識〕を持っています watákushi wà anátà to onáji gurài no kané〔chíshiki〕wò móttè imasu

◆*pron* 沢山の物 takúsan no monò

there isn't much to do あまりする事はありません amári suru kotò wa arímaseñ

much has been gained from our discussions 我々の話し合いは多くの成果を産みました waréwarè no hanáshiai wà ókù no seíka wò umímashìta

how much does it cost? - too much 値段はいくらですか-べらぼうさ nedán wà íkùra desu ká - berábō sà

how much is it? いくらですか íkùra desu ká

◆*adv* 1 (greatly, a great deal) とても totémo

thank you very much 大変有難うございます taíhen arígatò gozáimasu

much bigger (than) (...より) はるかに大きい (...yori) haruka ni ōkii

we are very much looking forward to your visit あなたが来られるのを首を長くして待っております anátà ga korárerù no wo kubí wò nágàku shite mattè orimasù

he is very much the gentleman/politician 彼はれっきとした紳士〔政治家〕です kárè wa rekkí tò shita shíñshi〔seíjika〕desu

however much he tries 彼はどんなに努力しても kárè wa dóñna ni doryóku shite mò

as much as ...と同じぐらい沢山 ...tò onáji gurài takúsañ

I read as much as ever 私はいつもと同じぐらい沢山の本を読んでいます watákushi wà ítsùmo to onáji gurài takúsañ no hốn wo yóñde imásù

I read as much as possible/as I can 私はできるだけ沢山の本を読む事にしています watákushi wà dekíru dakè takúsañ no hốn wo yómù koto ni shité imasù

he is as much a part of the community as you 彼はあなたと同様ここの社会の一員です kárè wa anátà to dốyō kokó no shakài no ichíin desu

2 (by far) ずっと zúttò

I'm much better now 私はずっと元気になっています watákushi wà zúttò géñki ni natté imasu

much reduced in price ずっと安くなって zuttó yasúku natte

it's much the biggest publishing company in Europe あれは断然ヨーロッパ最大の出版社です aré wà dañzen yốroppasaidài no shuppáñsha desu

3 (almost) ほとんど hotóñdo

the view is much as it was 10 years ago 景色は10年前とほとんど変っていません késhìki wa júnen maè to hotóñdo kawátte imaseñ

the 2 books are much the same その2冊の本はどちらも同じ様な物です sonó nisàtsu no hốn wa dóchìra mo onáji yố na monó desù

how are you feeling? - much the same ご気分はいかがですか-大して変りません go-kíbùn wa ikága dèsu ká - taíshite kawárimaseñ

---

muck [mʌk] *n* (dirt) 泥 doró; (excrement) くそ kusó

muck about/around *vi* (*inf*: fool about) ぶらぶらする búràbura suru

muck up *vt* (*inf*: ruin) 台無しにする daínashi ni suru

mucus [mjuːˈkəs] *n* 粘液 néñ-eki

mud [mʌd] *n* 泥 doró

muddle [mʌdˈəl] *n* (mess, mix-up) めちゃくちゃ mechákucha, 混乱 koñran

◆*vt* (*also*: **muddle up**) (confuse: person, things) 混乱させる koñran saserù; (: story, names) ごちゃごちゃにする gochágocha ni suru

muddle through *vi* (get by) どうにかして切抜ける dố ni ka shite kirínukerù

muddy [mʌdˈiː] *adj* (floor, field) どろどろの doródoro no

mudguard [mʌdˈgɑːrd] *n* フェンダー féñdā

muesli [mjuːzˈliː] n ムースリ mùsuri ◇朝食用のナッツ，ドライフルーツ，穀物の混合 chōshoku yō no náttsu, doráifurūtsu, kokúmotsu no kongō

muffin [mʌfˈin] n (US) マドレーヌ madórēnu; (BRIT) マフィン máfīn

muffle [mʌfˈəl] vt (sound) 弱める yowámerù; (against cold) ...に防寒具を付ける ...ni bōkangu wo tsukérù

muffled [mʌfˈəld] adj (sound) 弱い yowáì

muffler [mʌfˈlər] (US) n (AUT) マフラー máfūrā

mug [mʌg] n (cup) マグ mágù; (for beer) ジョッキ jókkì; (inf: face) 面 tsurá; (: BRIT: fool) ばか bákà
♦vt (assault) 襲う osóù ◇特に強盗行為について言う tókù ni gōtōkōì ni tsúite iú

mugging [mʌgˈin] n 強盗事件 gōtōjikèn

muggy [mʌgˈiː] adj (weather, day) 蒸暑い mushíatsuì

mule [mjuːl] n ラバ rábà

mull [mʌl] vt: to mull over ...について考え込む ...ni tsúite kañgaekomù

multi... [mʌltˈiː] prefix 複数の ... fukúsū no ...

multicolored [mʌltˈikʌlərd] (BRIT **multicoloured**) adj 多色の tashóku no

multilateral [mʌltilætˈərəl] adj (disarmament, talks) 多国間の takōkukan no

multi-level [mʌltiːlevˈəl] (US) adj = **multistory**

multinational [mʌltənæsˈənəl] adj (company, business) 多国籍の takōkuseki no

multiple [mʌlˈtəpəl] adj (collision) 玉突きの tamátsuki no; (interests) 複数のfukúsū no
♦n (MATH) 倍数 baísū

multiple sclerosis [-sklirouˈsis] n 多発性硬化症 tahátsusei kōkashō

multiplication [mʌltəpləkeiˈʃən] n (MATH) 掛算 kakézàn; (increase) 増加 zōka

multiply [mʌlˈtəplai] vt (MATH): 4 multiplied by 2 is 8 4掛ける2は8 yón kakérù ní wa hachí
♦vi (increase) 増える fuérù

multistory [mʌltiːstɔːrˈiː] (BRIT **multistorey**) adj (building etc) 高層の kōsō no

multitude [mʌlˈtətuːd] n (crowd) 群衆 guńshū; (large number): a multitude of (reasons, ideas) 沢山の takúsañ no

mum [mʌm] (BRIT: inf) n = **mom**
♦adj: to keep mum 黙っている damátte irù

mumble [mʌmˈbəl] vt (speak indistinctly) もぐもぐ言う mógùmogu iú
♦vi ぶつぶつ言う bútsùbutsu iú

mummy [mʌmˈiː] n (embalmed) ミイラ míira; (BRIT: mother) = **mommy**

mumps [mʌmps] n おたふく風邪 otáfukukàze

munch [mʌntʃ] vt (chew) かむ kámù
♦vi かむ kámù

mundane [mʌndeinˈ] adj (task, life) 平凡な heíbon na

municipal [mjuːnisˈəpəl] adj 市の shí no

munitions [mjuːnisˈənz] npl 兵器弾薬 heíkidañ-yaku

mural [mjurˈəl] n 壁画 hekíga

murder [məːrˈdər] n (killing) 殺人 satsújin
♦vt (kill) 殺す korósù

murderer [məːrˈdərər] n 人殺し hitógoroshi

murderous [məːrˈdərəs] adj (person) 殺人も辞さない satsújin mo jisanài; (attack) 殺しを目的とする koróshi wò mokúteki to surù

murky [məːrˈkiː] adj (street, night) 暗い kurái; (water) 濁った nigótta

murmur [məːrˈmər] n: a murmur of voices かすかな人声 kásùkana hitógòe; (of wind, waves) さざめき sazámeki
♦vt (speak quietly) 声をひそめて言う kóè wo hisómetè iú
♦vi 声をひそめて話す kóè wo hisómetè hanásù

muscle [mʌsˈəl] n (ANAT) 筋肉 kiñniku; (fig: strength) 力 chikára

muscle in vi 割込む warfkomù

muscular [mʌsˈkjələr] adj (pain) 筋肉の kiñniku no; (build) たくましい takúmashiì; (person) 強そうな tsuyósō na

muse [mju:z] *vi* (think) 考え込む kañgae-komù
♦*n* (MYTHOLOGY) ミューズ myũzu ◊ 人間の知的活動をつかさどるという女神 niñgen no chitékikatsudõ wo tsukásadorù to iú mégami

museum [mju:zi:'əm] *n* 博物館 hakúbùtsukan

mushroom [mʌʃ'ru:m] *n* (fungus: edible, poisonous) キノコ kínòko
♦*vi* (*fig*: town, organization) 急速に成長する kyũsoku ni seíchõ suru

music [mju:'zik] *n* (sound, art) 音楽 oñgaku; (written music, score) 楽譜 gakúfu

musical [mju:'zikəl] *adj* (career, skills, person) 音楽の oñgaku no; (sound, tune) 音楽的な oñgakuteki na
♦*n* (show, film) ミュージカル myũjikaru

musical instrument *n* 楽器 gakkí

music hall *n* (place) ボードビル劇場 bõdobiru gekijõ

musician [mju:ziʃ'ən] *n* ミュージシャン myũjishàn

musk [mʌsk] *n* じゃ香 jakõ

Muslim [mʌz'lim] *adj* イスラム教の isúramukyõ no
♦*n* イスラム教徒 isúramukyõto

muslin [mʌz'lin] *n* モスリン mósùrin

mussel [mʌs'əl] *n* ムールガイ mũrugai

must [mʌst] *aux vb* (necessity, obligation): *I must do it* 私はそれをしなければならない watákushi wa soré wò shinákereba naranài; (probability): *he must be there by now* もう彼はあそこに着いているでしょね kãre wa asóko ni tsúite írù deshõ; (suggestion, invitation): *you must come and see me soon* そのうち是非遊びに来て下さい sonó uchi zéhi asóbi ni kíte kudasaì; (indicating something unwelcome): *why must he behave so badly?* どうしてまたあの子はそんなに行儀悪くするのだろう dõshite mata ánò ko wa soñna ni gyõgiwarukù suru no darõ
♦*n* (necessity): *it's a must* 必需品だ hitsújuhin da

mustache [məstæʃ'] (*US*) *n* 鼻ひげ hanáhige

mustard [mʌs'tə:rd] *n* (Japanese) 辛子 karáshi, 和辛子 wagárashi; (Western) 辛子 karáshi, 洋辛子 yõgaràshi, マスタード masútàdo

muster [mʌs'tə:r] *vt* (support) 求める motómerù; (energy, strength) 奮い起す furúiokosù; (MIL) 召集する shõshū suru

mustn't [mʌs'ənt] = **must not**

musty [mʌs'ti:] *adj* かび臭い kabíkusaì

mutation [mju:tei'ʃən] *n* (alteration) 変化 heñka

mute [mju:t] *adj* (silent) 無言の mugón no

muted [mju:'tid] *adj* (color) 地味な jimí na; (reaction) ひそめた hisómeta

mutilate [mju:'təleit] *vt* (person, thing) 傷付ける kizútsukerù ◊特に体の部分を切断する場合に使う tókù ni karáda no búbùn wo setsúdan suru baái ni tsukáu

mutiny [mju:'təni:] *n* (rebellion: of soldiers, sailors) 反乱 hañran
♦*vi* 反乱を起す hañran wð okósù

mutter [mʌt'ə:r] *vt* (speak quietly) つぶやく tsubúyakù
♦*vi* ぶつぶつ不平を言う bútsùbutsu fuhéi wð iú

mutton [mʌt'ən] *n* (meat) マトン máton

mutual [mju:'tʃu:əl] *adj* (shared: benefit, interest) 共通の kyõtsū no; (reciprocal: feeling, attraction) 相互の sõgo no

mutually [mju:'tʃu:əli:] *adv* 相互に sõgo ni

muzzle [mʌz'əl] *n* (mouth: of dog) ふん fún, 鼻づら hanázura; (: of gun) 銃口 jũkō; (guard: for dog) 口輪 kuchíwa
♦*vt* (dog) ...に口輪をはめる ...ni kuchíwa wo hamérù

KEYWORD

my [mai] *adj* 私の watákushi nð
this is my house/car/brother これは私の家〔車、兄〕です koré wà watákushi nð ié〔kurúma, ání〕desù
I've washed my hair/cut my finger 私は髪を洗いました〔指を切りました〕watákushi wà kamí wð aráimashìta〔yubí wð kiríwashìta〕
is this my pen or yours? これは私の

ペンですか，それともあなたのですか
koré wà watákushi nò péñ desu ká,
sorétomò anátá no desu ká

Myanmar [mai'ænmɑ:r] *n* ミャンマー
myáñmā

myopic [maiə'pik] *adj* 近眼の kiñgan no

myriad [mir'i:əd] *n* (of people, things) 無
数 musú

myself [maiself'] *pron* 私自身 watákushi-
jishìn ¶ *see also* **oneself**

mysterious [misti:r'i:əs] *adj* (strange) な
ぞの nazó no

mystery [mis'tə:ri:] *n* (puzzle) なぞ nazó
shrouded in mystery (place) なぞに包
まれた nazó nì tsutsúmaréta

mystic [mis'tik] *n* (person) 神秘主義者
shíñpishùgisha

mystic(al) [mis'tik(əl)] *adj* 神秘的な shíñ-
piteki na

mystify [mis'təfai] *vt* (perplex) ...の理解
を越える ...no rikái wò koérù

mystique [misti:k'] *n* 神秘 shíñpi

myth [miθ] *n* (legend, story) 神話 shíñ-
wa; (fallacy) 俗信 zokúshin

mythology [miθɑ:l'ədʒi:] *n* 神話集 shíñ-
wàshū

N

n/a *abbr* (= *not applicable*) ◇申請用紙な
どで空欄にしておく場合に書く shiñsei
yòshi nádò de kū̀ran ni shite oku baài ni
kákù

nag [næg] *vt* (scold) がみがみ言う gámì-
gami iú

nagging [næg'iŋ] *adj* (doubt) 晴れない
harénaì; (pain) しつこい shitsúkoì

nail [neil] *n* (on fingers, toes) つめ tsumé;
(metal) くぎ kugí

♦*vt*: *to nail something to something*
...を...にくぎで留める ...wo ...ni kugí dè
toméru

*to nail someone down to doing some-
thing* 強制的に...に...をさせる kyṓseiteki-
ki ni ...ni ...wò sasérù

nailbrush [neil'brʌʃ] *n* つめブラシ tsu-

méburàshi

nailfile [neil'fail] *n* つめやすり tsuméyasùri

nail polish *n* マニキュア maníkyùa

nail polish remover *n* 除光液 jokṓeki,
マニキュア落し maníkyua otòshi

nail scissors *npl* つめ切りばさみ tsumé-
kiribasàmi

nail varnish (*BRIT*) *n* = **nail polish**

naive [naii:v'] *adj* (person, ideas) 無邪気
な mújàki na, ナイーブな naíbù na

naked [nei'kid] *adj* 裸の hadáka no

name [neim] *n* (of person, animal, place)
名前 namáe; (surname) 名字 myṓjì, 姓 sé-
ì; (reputation) 評判 hyṓban

♦*vt* (child) ...に名前を付ける ...ni namáe
wò tsukérù; (identify: accomplice, criminal) 名指す nazásù; (specify: price, date
etc) 指定する shitéi suru

what's your name? お名前は何とおっ
しゃいますか o-námae wà náñto osshái-
masù ká

by name 名指しで nazáshi dè

in the name of (*fig*) ...の名において
...no ná ni oìte

to give one's name and address (to
police etc) 名前と住所を知らせる namáe
tò jū́shò wo shiráserù

nameless [neim'lis] *adj* (unknown) 無名
の muméi no; (anonymous: witness, contributor) 匿名の tokúmei no

namely [neim'li:] *adv* 即ち sunáwàchi

namesake [neim'seik] *n* 同姓同名の人
dṓseidṓmei no hitó

nanny [næn'i:] *n* 養育係 yṓikugakàri

nap [næp] *n* (sleep) 昼寝 hirúne

to be caught napping (*fig*) 不意を突か
れる fuí wò tsukárerù

napalm [nei'pɑ:m] *n* ナパーム napámù

nape [neip] *n*: *nape of the neck* えり首
eríkùbi

napkin [næp'kin] *n* (*also*: **table napkin**)
ナプキン nápùkin

nappy [næp'i:] (*BRIT*) *n* おむつ o-mútsù

nappy rash (*BRIT*) *n* おむつかぶれ o-
mútsukabùre

narcissus [nɑ:rsis'əs] (*pl* **narcissi**) *n*
(BOT) スイセン suísen

narcotic [nɑːrkɑːtˈik] *adj* 麻酔性の
masúisei no
♦*n* 麻薬 mayáku

narrative [nærˈətiv] *n* 物語 monógatàri

narrator [nærˈeitər] *n* (in book) 語り手
katárite; (in film etc) ナレーター narétā

narrow [nærˈou] *adj* (space, road etc) 狭
い semái; (fig: majority, advantage) ぎり
ぎりの girígiri no; (: ideas, attitude) 狭量
な kyóryō na
♦*vi* (road) 狭くなる semáku naru; (gap,
difference: diminish) 小さくなる chíisaku naru

to have a narrow escape 間一髪で逃れ
る kán-ippátsu dè nogárerù

to narrow something down to (choice,
possibility) ...を...に絞る ...wo ...ni shibórù

narrowly [nærˈouli] *adv* (miss) 辛うじ
て karōjîte, 間一髪で kán-ippátsu dè

narrow-minded [nærˈoumin'did] *adj*
狭量な kyóryō na

nasal [neiˈzəl] *adj* (of the nose) 鼻の haná
no; (voice, sound) 鼻にかかった haná ni
kakattá

nasty [næsˈtiː] *adj* (unpleasant: remark,
person) いやな iyá nà; (malicious) 腹黒い
haráguroî; (rude) 無礼な búrei na;
(revolting: taste, smell) むかつかせる
mukátsukaserù; (wound, disease etc) ひ
どい hidóî

nation [neiˈʃən] *n* (country) 国 kuní, 国家
kókkà; (people) 国民 kokúmin

national [næˈʃənəl] *adj* 国の kuní no
♦*n: a foreign national* 外国人 gaíkokujîn

national dress *n* 民族衣装 mínzokuishṓ

National Health Service (*BRIT*) *n*
国民医療制度 kokúmin iryōseîdo

National Insurance (*BRIT*) *n* 国民保
険 kokúminhokèn

nationalism [næˈʃənəlizəm] *n* 国家主義
kokkáshugì, 民族主義 mínzokushugì

nationalist [næsˈʃənəlist] *adj* 国家主義の
kokkáshugì no, 民族主義の mínzokushugì
no
♦*n* 国家主義者 kokkáshugishà, 民族主義
者 mínzokushugishà

nationality [næʃənælˈətiː] *n* 国籍 kokú-
seki

nationalization [næʃnələzeiˈʃən] *n* 国有
化 kokúyūka, 国営化 kokúeika

nationalize [næʃˈnəlaiz] *vt* 国営にする
kokúei ni surù

nationally [næʃˈnəli] *adv* (nationwide)
全国的に zeńkokuteki ni; (as a nation) 国
として kuní toshite

nationwide [neiˈʃənwaid'] *adj* (problem,
campaign) 全国的な zeńkokuteki na
♦*adv* (campaign, search) 全国的に zeńkokuteki ni

native [neiˈtiv] *n* (local inhabitant) 地元
の人 jimóto no hitð; (of tribe etc) 原住民
geńjūmin
♦*adj* (indigenous) 地元の jimóto no, 地元
生れの jimóto umàre no; (of one's birth)
生れの umáre no; (innate) 生れつきの u-
máretsuki no

a native of Russia ロシア生れの人 roshía umare no hitð

a native speaker of French フランス
語を母国語とする人 furánsugo wð bokókugo to suru hitð

native language *n* 母国語 bokókugo

Nativity [nətivˈətiː] *n: the Nativity* キ
リストの降誕 kirísuto nð kótan

NATO [neiˈtou] *n abbr* (= *North Atlantic Treaty Organization*) 北大西洋条
約機構 kitátaiseiyō jōyaku kikō

natural [nætʃˈərəl] *adj* (gen) 自然の shizén no; (innate) 生れつきの umáretsuki
no

natural gas *n* 天然ガス teńnengasù

naturalist [nætʃˈərəlist] *n* 博物学者 ha-
kúbutsugakushà

naturalize [nætʃˈəːrəlaiz] *vt: to become
naturalized* (person, plant) 帰化する ki-
ká suru

naturally [nætʃˈəːrəli] *adv* (gen) 自然に
shizén ni; (of course) もちろん mochíròn,
当然 tōzen

nature [neiˈtʃər] *n* (*also:* **Nature**) 自然
shizén, 大自然 daíshizèn; (character) 性
質 seíshitsu; (type, sort) 種類 shúrui
by nature 生れつき umáretsuki

naught [nɔːt] *n* 零 reî, ゼロ zérò

naughty [nɔː'tʲiː] adj (child) 行儀の悪い gyṓgi no waruĩ

nausea [nɔː'ziːə] n 吐気 hakĩke

nauseate [nɔː'ziːeit] vt むかつかせる mukátsukaserù, 吐気を起させる hakĩke wò okósaserù; (fig) いやな感じを与える iyá na kañji wo atáerù

nautical [nɔː'tikəl] adj (uniform) 船員の señ-in no; (people) 海洋の kaíyō no
a nautical mile 海里 kaíri

naval [nei'vəl] adj (uniform, academy) 海軍の káigun no
a naval battle 海戦 kaísen
naval forces 海軍力 kaígunryòku

naval officer n 海軍将校 kaígunshōkō

nave [neiv] n 外陣 gaíjin

navel [nei'vəl] n へそ hesó

navigate [næv'əgeit] vi (NAUT, AVIAT) 航行する kṓkō suru; (AUT) 道案内する michíannai suru

navigation [nævəgei'ʃən] n (action) 航行 kṓkō; (science) 航海術 kōkaíjutsu

navigator [næv'əgeitər] n (NAUT) 航海長 kōkaíchō; (AVIAT) 航空士 kōkū-shi; (AUT) 道案内をする人 michíannai wo suru hitŏ

navvy [næv'iː] (BRIT) n 労働者 rṓdōsha

navy [nei'viː] n 海軍 kaígun

navy(-blue) adj 濃紺の nṓkon no

Nazi [nɑːt'siː] n ナチ náchì

NB [enbiː'] abbr (= nota bene) 注 chū ◇脚注などに使う略語 kyakúchū nadò ni tsukáù ryakúgo

near [niːr] adj (place, time, relation) 近い chikáì
◆adv 近く chikákù
◆prep (also: near to: space, time) ...の近くに ...no chikákù ni
◆vt (place, event) ...に近づく ...ni chikázukù

nearby [niːr'bai'] adj 近くの chikákù no
◆adv 近くに chikákù ni

nearly [niːr'liː] adv (not totally) ほとんど hotóndo; (on the point of) 危うく ayáukù
I nearly fell 危うく転ぶところだった ayáukù koróbu tokoro dattá

near miss n (narrow escape) ニアミス niámisù; (of planes) 異常接近 ijṓsekkìn,

ニアミス niámisù; (of cars etc): *that was a near miss!* 危ないところだった abúnai tokoro dattá

nearside [niːr'said] n (AUT: in Britain, Japan) 左側 hidárigawa; (: in US, Europe etc) 右側 migígawa

near-sighted [niːr'saitid] adj 近眼の kíngan no, 近視の kíñshi no

neat [niːt] adj (place, person) きちんとした kichĩn to shita; (skillful: work, plan) 上手な jṓzu na; (spirits) ストレートの sutórēto no

neatly [niːt'liː] adv (tidily) きちんと kichĩn to; (skillfully) 上手に jṓzu nĩ

necessarily [nesəsər'ili:] adv (inevitably) 必然的に hitsúzenteki ni
not necessarily (not automatically) 必ずしも...でない kanárazushìmo ...de nái

necessary [nes'ise:ri:] adj (required: skill, quality, measure) 必要な hitsúyō na; (inevitable: result, effect) 必然の hitsúzen no
it is necessary to/that ...する必要がある ...suru hitsúyō ga arù

necessitate [nəses'əteit] vt 必要とする hitsúyō to surù

necessities [nəses'iti:z] npl (essentials) 必需品 hitsújuhin

necessity [nəses'iti:] n (thing needed) 必需品 hitsújuhin; (compelling circumstances) 必然 hitsúzen

neck [nek] n (of person, animal, garment, bottle) 首 kubí
◆vi (inf) ペッティングする pettíñgu suru
neck and neck 接戦して sessén shite

necklace [nek'lis] n ネックレス nékkùresu

neckline [nek'lain] n ネックライン nekkúraìn

necktie [nek'tai] (US) n ネクタイ nékùtai

née [nei] adj: *née Scott* 旧姓スコット kyúsei sukóttò

need [niːd] n (lack) 欠乏 ketsúbō; (necessity) 必要 hitsúyō; (thing needed) 必需品 hitsújuhin
◆vt (require) ...を必要とする ...wo hitsú-

yō to surù

I need to do it 私はそれをしなければならない watákushi wà soré wò shinákereba naranaî, 私はそれをする必要がある watákushi wà soré wò suru hitsuyō ga arù

you don't need to go 行かなくてもいい ikánakute mo iî

needle [niːdəl] *n* (gen) 針 hárî; (for knitting) 編棒 amíbō

♦*vt* (fig: inf) からかう karákaù

needless [niːdlis] *adj* (criticism, risk) 不必要な fuhítsuyō na

needless to say 言うまでもなく iú made mo nakù

needlework [niːdəlwəːrk] *n* (item(s) of needlework) 縫い物 nuímonò; (activity) 針仕事 haríshigòto

needn't [niːdənt] = **need not**

needy [niːdiː] *adj* 貧しい mazúshiî

negation [nigeiʃən] *n* 否定 hitéi

negative [negʻətiv] *adj* (answer) 否定の hitéi no; (attitude) 否定的な hitéiteki na; (reaction) 消極的な shókyokuteki na; (ELEC) 陰極の iñkyoku no, マイナスの maĩnasu no

♦*n* (LING) 否定形 hitéikei; (PHOT) 陰画 iñga, ネガ négà

neglect [niglektʻ] *vt* (child) 放任する hónin suru, ほったらかす hottárakasù; (one's duty) 怠る okótaru

♦*n* (of child) 放任 hónin; (of area, house, garden) ほったらかす事 hottárakasu kotò; (of duty) 怠る事 okótaru kotò

negligee [negʻləʒei] *n* (dressing gown) ネグリジェ negúrijè

negligence [negʻlidʒəns] *n* (carelessness) 不注意 fuchûi

negligible [negʻlidʒəbəl] *adj* (cost, difference) わずかな wázùka na

negotiable [nigouʻʃəbəl] *adj* (check) 譲渡できる jôto dekirù

negotiate [nigouʻʃiːeit] *vi*: *to negotiate (with)* (...と) 交渉する (...to) kôshō su-ru

♦*vt* (treaty, transaction) 協議して決める kyôgi shite kimerù; (obstacle) 乗越える norîkoerù; (bend in road) 注意して通る

negotiation [nigouʃiːeiʻʃən] *n* 交渉 kôshō

negotiator [nigouʻʃiːeitəːr] *n* 交渉する人 kôshō suru hitò

Negress [niːgʻris] *n* 黒人女性 kokújinjoseì

Negro [niːgʻrou] *adj* 黒人の kokújin no

♦*n* 黒人 kokújin

neigh [nei] *vi* いななく inánakù

neighbor [neiʻbəːr] (*BRIT* **neighbour**) *n* (next door) 隣の人 tonári no hitò; (in vicinity) 近所の人 kíñjo no hitò

neighborhood [neiʻbəːrhud] *n* (place) 近所 kíñjo, 界隈 káìwai; (people) 近所の人々 kíñjo no hitòbito

neighboring [neiʻbəːriŋ] *adj* (town, state) 隣の tonári no

neighborly [neiʻbəːrliː] *adj* (person, attitude) 親切な shíñsetsu na

neighbour [neiʻbəːr] *etc* (*BRIT*) *n* = **neighbor** *etc*

neither [niːʻðəːr] *adj* どちらの...も...でない dóchìra no ...mo ...de naî

neither story is true どちらの話も本当ではない dóchìra no hanáshi mò hoñtō de wa naî

♦*conj*: *I didn't move and neither did John* 私も動かなかったしジョンも動かなかった watákushi mò ugókanakattà shi, jóñ mo ugókanakattà

♦*pron* どちらも...でない dóchìra mo ...de naî

neither is true どちらも本当でない dóchìra mo hoñtō de naî

♦*adv*: *neither good nor bad* よくも悪くもない yókù mo warúkù mo naî

neon [niːʻɑːn] *n* ネオン néòn; (*also*: **neon sign**) ネオンサイン neóñsaìn

neon light *n* ネオン灯 neóntō

nephew [nefʻjuː] *n* おい oí

nerve [nəːrv] *n* (ANAT) 神経 shíñkei; (courage) 勇気 yúkî; (impudence) 厚かましさ atsúkamashisà, 図々しさ zúzùshisà

to have a fit of nerves 神経質になる shiñkeishitsu ni narù

nerve-racking [nəːrvʻrækiŋ] *adj* いらいらさせる íraira saserù

nervous [nəːr'vəs] adj (ANAT) 神経の shínkei no; (anxious) 神経質な shínkeishitsu na; (timid: person) 気の小さい ki no chíisai; (: animal) おく病な okúbyō na

nervous breakdown n 神経衰弱 shínkeisuíjàku

nest [nest] n 巣 sú
♦vi 巣を作る sú wò tsukúrù

nest egg n (fig) へそくり hesôkuri

nestle [nes'əl] vi: **to nestle in a valley/ the mountains** (village etc) 谷間[山あい]に横たわる taníma〔yamá-ai〕nî yokótawarù

net [net] n (gen) 網 amí; (fabric) レース rēsù; (TENNIS, VOLLEYBALL etc) ネット nèttò; (fig) わな wánā
♦adj (COMM) 正味の shómi no
♦vt (fish, game) 網で取る amí dè tórù; (profit) 得る érù

netball [net'bɔːl] n ネットボール nettóbòru ◇英国で行われるバスケットボールに似た球技 eīkoku de okonawarerù basúkettobòru ni nítà kyûgî

net curtains npl レースのカーテン rēsù no kâten

Netherlands [neð'əːrləndz] npl: **the Netherlands** オランダ oránda

nett [net] (BRIT) adj = **net**

netting [net'iŋ] n 網 amí

nettle [net'əl] n イラクサ irákusa

network [net'wəːrk] n (of roads, veins, shops) ネットワーク nettówàku; (TV, RADIO) 放送網 hôsômô, ネットワーク nettówàku

neurotic [nurɑːt'ik] adj 神経過敏な shínkeikabìn na, ノイローゼの noíròze no
♦n ノイローゼの人 noíròze no hitô

neuter [nuː'təːr] adj (LING) 中性の chúsei no
♦vt (cat etc) 去勢する kyoséi suru

neutral [nuː'trəl] adj (person) 中立の chúritsu no; (color etc) 中間色の chúkañshoku no; (ELEC) 中性の chúsei no
♦n (AUT) ニュートラル nyûtoraru

neutrality [nuːtræl'iti:] n 中立 chúritsu

neutralize [nuː'trəlaiz] vt (acid, poison etc) 中和する chúwa suru; (campaign, goodwill) 台無しにする daínashi ni surù

never [nev'əːr] adv どんな時でも…ない dónna toki de mo …náî
I never went 行かなかった ikánakattâ
never in my life …したことがない …shitá kotò ga náî ¶ see also **mind**

never-ending [nev'əːren'diŋ] adj 終りのない owári no naî, 果てしない hatéshinaî

nevertheless [nevəːrðəles'] adv それにもかかわらず soré ni mò kakáwarazù, それでもやはり soré de mò yahárì

new [nuː] adj (brand new) 新しい atárashiî; (recent) 最近の saíkin no; (different) 今までになかった imá madè ni nákàtta; (inexperienced) 新入りの shín-iri no

newborn [nuː'bɔːrn] adj 生れたばかりの umáreta bakàri no

newcomer [nuː'kʌməːr] n 新顔 shíngao, 新入り shín-iri

new-fangled [nuː'fæŋ'gəld] (pej) adj 超モダンな chômodàn na

new-found [nuː'faund] adj (enthusiasm, confidence) 新たに沸いた áràta ni waîta; (friend) 新しくできた atárashikù dékìta

newly [nuː'liː] adv 新しく atárashikù

newly-weds [nuː'liːwedz] npl 新婚者 shínkoñsha

new moon n 新月 shíngetsu

news [nuːz] n ニュース nyûsu
a piece of news ニュース項目 nyûsukômoku, ニュース nyûsu
the news (RADIO, TV) ニュース nyûsu

news agency n 通信社 tsûshiñsha

newsagent [nuːz'eidʒənt] (BRIT) n = **newsdealer**

newscaster [nuːz'kæstəːr] n ニュースキャスター nyûsukyasùtā

newsdealer [nuːz'diːləːr] (US) n (shop) 新聞販売店 shíñbunhanbaitèn; (person) 新聞販売業者 shíñbunhanbaigyòsha

newsflash [nuːz'flæʃ] n ニュース速報 nyûsusokuhô

newsletter [nuːz'letəːr] n ニュースレター nyûsuretå

newspaper [nuːz'peipəːr] n 新聞 shíñbun

newsprint [nuːz'print] n 新聞印刷用紙 shíñbun insatsuyôshi

newsreader [nuːz'riːdəːr] n = **newscaster**

newsreel [nuːzˈriːl] *n* ニュース映画 nyūsuēīga

newsstand [nuːzˈstænd] *n* (in station etc) 新聞スタンド shiñbun sutañdo

newt [nuːt] *n* イモリ imóri

New Year *n* 新年 shíñnen

New Year's Day *n* 元旦 gañtan, 元日 gañjitsu

New Year's Eve *n* 大みそ日 ōmísòka

New York [-jɔːrk] *n* ニューヨーク nyūyōku

New Zealand [-ziː'lənd] *n* ニュージーランド nyūjīrando

New Zealander [-ziː'ləndər] *n* ニュージーランド人 nyūjīrandojìn

next [nekst] *adj* (in space) 隣の tonári no; (in time) 次の tsugí no

♦*adv* (place) 隣に tonári ni; (time) 次に tsugí ni, 今度 kóñdo

the next day 次の日 tsugí no hì, 翌日 yokújitsu

next time 次回に jíkài ni, 今度 kóñdo

next year 来年 raínen

next to ...の隣に ...no tonári ni

to cost next to nothing ただ同然である tádà dōzen de arù

to do next to nothing ほとんど何もしない hotóñdo naní mo shinàí

next please! (at doctor's etc) 次の方 tsugí no katà

next door *adv* 隣の家に tonári nò ié nì

♦*adj* (neighbor, flat) 隣の tonári no

next-of-kin [nekstʾəvkin'] *n* 最も近い親せき mottómo chikaì shiñseki

NHS [eniteʃes'] *n abbr* = **National Health Service**

nib [nib] *n* ペン先 peñsakì

nibble [nib'əl] *vt* 少しずつかじる sukóshizutsù kajírù, ちびちび食べる chíbìchibi tabérù

Nicaragua [nikərɑːgˈwə] *n* ニカラグア nikáragua

nice [nais] *adj* (likeable) 感じのよい kañji no yoì; (kind) 親切な shíñsetsu na; (pleasant) 天気のよい téñki no yoì; (attractive) 魅力的な miryókuteki na

nicely [nais'liː] *adv* (pleasantly) 気持よく kimóchi yokù; (kindly) 親切に shíñsetsu

ni; (attractively) 魅力的に miryókuteki ni

niceties [nai'sətiːz] *npl* 細かい点 komákaì teñ

nick [nik] *n* (wound) 切傷 kiríkìzu; (cut, indentation) 刃の跡 há no atò

♦*vt* (*BRIT inf*: steal) かっ払う kappáraù

in the nick of time 際どい時に kiwádoì tókì ni, 危ういところで ayáui tokoro dè

nickel [nik'əl] *n* (metal) ニッケル nikkéru; (*US*) 5セント玉 5 señto dama

nickname [nik'neim] *n* あだ名 adána, 愛称 aíshō, ニックネーム nikkúnēmu

♦*vt* ...に...のあだ名をつける ...ni ...no adána wo tsukérù

nicotine [nik'ətiːn] *n* ニコチン nikóchin

niece [niːs] *n* めい meí

Nigeria [naidʒiːˈriːə] *n* ナイジェリア naíjeria

Nigerian [naidʒiːˈriːən] *adj* ナイジェリアの naíjeria no

♦*n* ナイジェリア人 naíjeriajìn

nigger [nig'əːr] (*inf*) *n* (highly offensive) 黒ん坊 kurónbō

niggling [nig'liŋ] *adj* (trifling) つまらない tsumáranaì; (annoying) いらいらさせる íraìra sasérù

night [nait] *n* (period of darkness) 夜 yórù; (evening) 夕方 yúgata

the night before last おとといの夜 otótoì no yórù

at night 夜(に) yórù (ni)

by night 夜に yórù ni

nightcap [nait'kæp] *n* (drink) 寝酒 nezáke, ナイトキャップ naítokyappù

nightclub [nait'klʌb] *n* ナイトクラブ naítokuràbu

nightdress [nait'dres] *n* 寝巻 nemáki ◇女性用のを指す joséiyō no wò sásù

nightfall [nait'fɔːl] *n* 夕暮 yūgure

nightgown [nait'gaun] *n* = **nightdress**

nightie [nai'tiː] *n* = **nightdress**

nightingale [nai'təngeil] *n* ヨナキウグイス yonákiuguìsu, サヨナキドリ sayónakidòri, ナイチンゲール naíchingèru

nightlife [nait'laif] *n* 夜の生活 yórù no seíkatsu

nightly [nait'li:] *adj* 毎晩の máiban no
♦*adv* 毎晩 máiban

nightmare [nait'me:r] *n* 悪夢 ákùmu

night porter *n* 夜間のフロント係 yákàn no furóntogakàri

night school *n* 夜間学校 yakángakkò

night shift *n* 夜間勤務 yakánkiǹmu

night-time [nait'taim] *n* 夜 yórù

night watchman *n* 夜警 yakéi

nil [nil] *n* ゼロ zérò; (*BRIT: SPORT*) 零点 reíteǹ, ゼロ zérò

Nile [nail] *n*: *the Nile* ナイル川 naírugàwa

nimble [nim'bəl] *adj* (agile) 素早い subáyaì, 軽快な keíkai na; (skillful) 器用な kíyò na

nine [nain] *num* 9 (の) kyū́ (no), 九つ (の) kokónòtsu (no)

nineteen [nain'ti:n] *num* 19 (の) jū́ku (no)

ninety [nain'ti:] *num* 90 (の) kyū́jū̀ (no)

ninth [nainθ] *adj* 第9 (の) dáìku (no)

nip [nip] *vt* (pinch) つねる tsunérù; (bite) かむ kámù

nipple [nip'əl] *n* (ANAT) 乳首 chikúbì

nitrogen [nai'trədʒən] *n* 窒素 chíssò

KEYWORD

no [nou] (*pl* **noes**) *adv* (opposite of "yes") いいえ iíe

are you coming? - no (I'm not) 一緒に来ませんか-いいえ (行きません) isshó ni kimaseñ ká - iíe (ikímaseñ)

would you like some? - no thank you いりませんか-いいえ, 結構です irímaseñ ká - iíe, kékkò desu

♦*adj* (not any) 何も...ない naní mò ...nái
I have no money/time/books 私には金(時間, 本)がありません watákushi ni wà kanè(jíkan, hóñ)ga arimaseñ

no other man would have done it 他の人ならだれもそれをしてくれなかったでしょう hoká no hitò nara daré mò soré wò shité kurenakatta deshò

「*no entry*」立入禁止 tachíirikiǹshi

「*no smoking*」禁煙 kiñ-en

♦*n* 反対意見 hañtai ikèn, 反対票 hañtaihyð

there were 20 noes and one "don't know" 反対意見20に対し、「分からない」は1つだった hañtai ikèn nijū̀ ni tai shi, "wakáranaì" wa hitótsu dattà

nobility [noubil'əti:] *n* (dignity) 気高さ kedákasà; (social class) 貴族 kízòku

noble [nou'bəl] *adj* (person, character: worthy) 気高い kedákaì; (title, family: of high social class) 貴族の kízòku no

nobody [nou'bɑ:di:] *pron* だれも...ない daré mò ...nái

nocturnal [nɑ:ktə:r'nəl] *adj* (tour, visit) 夜の yórù no, 夜間の yákàn no; (animal) 夜行性の yakṓsei no

nod [nɑ:d] *vi* (gesture) 頭で合図する atáma dè áìzu suru; (*also*: *nod in agreement*) うなずく unázukù; (doze) うとうとする útòuto suru
♦*vt*: *to nod one's head* うなずく unázukù
♦*n* うなずき unazuki

nod off *vi* 居眠りする inémuri suru

noise [nɔiz] *n* (sound) 音 otð; (din) 騒音 sõon

noisy [nɔi'zi:] *adj* (audience, child, machine) うるさい urúsaì

nomad [nou'mæd] *n* 遊牧民 yū́bokumìn

nominal [nɑ:m'ənəl] *adj* (leader) 名目上の meímokujõ no; (rent, price) わずかな wázùka na

nominate [nɑ:m'əneit] *vt* (propose) 推薦する suíseñ suru; (appoint) 任命する nifímei suru

nomination [nɑ:mənei'ʃən] *n* (proposal) 推薦 suíseñ; (appointment) 任命 nifímei

nominee [nɑ:məni:'] *n* (proposed person) 推薦された人 suíseñ sareta hitð; (appointed person) 任命された人 nifímei sareta hitð

non... [nɑ:n] *prefix* 非... hī́..., 無... mū́..., 不... fū́...

non-alcoholic [nɑ:nælkəhɔ:l'ik] *adj* アルコールを含まない arúkòru wò fukúmanaì

non-aligned [nɑ:nəlaind'] *adj* 非同盟の hidṓmei no

nonchalant [nɑːnʃələɑːnt] *adj* 平然とした heízen to shitá

noncommittal [nɑːnkəmit'əl] *adj* (person, answer) どっちつかずの dotchí tsukazú no

nondescript [nɑːn'diskript] *adj* (person, clothes, color) 特徴のない tokúchō no naí

none [nʌn] *pron* (person) だれも...ない daré mò ...naí; (thing) どれも...ない dóre mo ...naí

none of you あなたたちの1人も...ない anátatàchi no hitóri mò ...naí

I've none left 何も残っていません naní mò nokótte imaseñ

he's none the worse for it それでも彼は大丈夫です soré de mò kare wa daíjōbu desu

nonentity [nɑːnen'titiː] *n* 取るに足らない人 tórù ni taránai hitò

nonetheless [nʌn'ðəles'] *adv* それにもかかわらず soré ni mò kakáwarazù, それでもやはり soré de mò yahárì

non-existent [nɑːnigzis'tənt] *adj* 存在しない soñzai shinaí

non-fiction [nɑːnfik'ʃən] *n* ノンフィクション noñfikùshon

nonplussed [nɑːnplʌst'] *adj* 困惑した koñwaku shita, 困った kómattà

nonsense [nɑːn'sens] *n* でたらめ detárame, ナンセンス náñsensu

nonsense! そんな事はない soñna koto wà naí, ナンセンス náñsensu

non-smoker [nɑːn'smou'kəːr] *n* タバコを吸わない人 tabáko wò suwánai hitò, 非喫煙者 híkitsueñsha

non-stick [nɑːnstik'] *adj* (pan, surface) こげつかない kogétsukanaí

non-stop [nɑːn'stɑːp'] *adj* (conversation) 止らない tomáranaì; (flight, train) 直行の chokkō no, ノンストップの noñsutoppù no

♦*adv* 止らずに tomárazu ni

noodles [nuː'dəlz] *npl* ヌードル nūdòru

nook [nuk] *n: every nook and cranny* 隅々 sumízùmi

noon [nuːn] *n* 正午 shōgò

no one (*BRIT* **no-one**) *pron* = **nobody**

noose [nuːs] *n* (loop) 引結び hikímusùbi

hangman's noose 絞首刑用の縄 kōshukeíyō no nawà

nor [nɔːr] *conj* = **neither**

♦*adv see* **neither**

norm [nɔːrm] *n* (convention) 慣習 kañshū; (rule, requirement) ノルマ nórùma

normal [nɔːr'məl] *adj* (usual, ordinary: life, behavior, result) 普通の futsū no; (child: not abnormal) 異常のない ijō no naí, ノーマルな nōmàru na

normally [nɔːr'məliː] *adv* 普通は futsū wa, 普通に futsū ni

north [nɔːrθ] *n* 北 kitá

♦*adj* 北の kitá no

♦*adv* 北へ kitá e

North America *n* 北米 hokúbei

north-east [nɔːrθiːst'] *n* 北東 hokútō

northerly [nɔːr'ðəːrliː] *adj* (point) 北方の hoppō no; (direction) 北方への hoppō e nò

a northerly wind 北からの風 kitá kara nò kaze

northern [nɔːr'ðəːrn] *adj* 北の kitá no

the northern hemisphere 北半球 kitá-hañkyū

Northern Ireland *n* 北アイルランド kitá airurañdo

North Pole *n* 北極 hokkyókù

North Sea *n* 北海 hokkái

northward(s) [nɔːr'θwəːrd(z)] *adv* 北へ kitá e

north-west [nɔːrθwest'] *n* 北西 hokúsei

Norway [nɔːr'wei] *n* ノルウェー norúuē

Norwegian [nɔːrwiː'dʒən] *adj* ノルウェーの norúuē no; (LING) ノルウェー語の norúuēgo no

♦*n* (person) ノルウェー人 norúuējìn; (LING) ノルウェー語 norúuēgo

nose [nouz] *n* (ANAT, ZOOL) 鼻 haná; (sense of smell) きゅう覚 kyúkaku

♦*vi: nose about* せん索する señsaku suru

nosebleed [nouz'bliːd] *n* 鼻血 hanáji

nose-dive [nouz'daiv] *n* (of plane) 急降下 kyúkōka

nosey [nou'ziː] (*inf*) *adj* = **nosy**

nostalgia [nəstæl'dʒə] *n* 郷愁 kyōshū, ノ

スタルジア nosútarùjia

nostalgic [nəstæl'dʒik] *adj* (person, book, film) 懐かしい natsúkashiì

nostril [nɑːs'trəl] *n* (of person, animal) 鼻のあな haná no anà, 鼻孔 bikố

nosy [nou'zi:] (*inf*) *adj* せん索好きな señsakuzùki na

KEYWORD

not [nɑːt] *adv* ...でない ...de naì

he is not/isn't here 彼はいません kárè wa imáseñ

you must not/you mustn't do that それをしてはいけません soré wò shité wà ikémaseñ

it's too late, isn't it? 遅過ぎますよね ososúgimasù yo né, 遅過ぎるでしょう ososúgirù deshō

he asked me not to do it それをしないで下さいと彼に頼まれました soré wò shináide kudasaì to kárè ni tanómaremashìta

not that I don't like him/he isn't interesting 彼を嫌い〔面白くない〕というのではないが kárè wo kiráì〔omóshirokùnaì〕to iú no de wa naì gá

not yet まだ mádà

not now 今は駄目 ímà wa damé ¶ *see also* **all; only**

---

notably [nou'təbli:] *adv* (particularly) 特に tókù ni; (markedly) 著しく ichíjirushikù

notary [nou'tə:ri:] *n* 公証人 kốshōnin

notch [nɑːtʃ] *n* (in wood, blade, saw) 刻み目 kizámime, ノッチ notchí

note [nout] *n* (record) 覚書 obóegaki, ノート nồto, メモ mémò; (letter) 短い手紙 mijíkaì tegámi; (banknote) 紙幣 shíhèi, 札 satsú; (MUS) 音符 oñpu; (tone) 音 otó
♦*vt* (observe) ...に気が付く ...ni ki gá tsukù; (write down) 書留める kakítomerù

notebook [nout'buk] *n* 帳面 chốmen, ノート nồto

noted [nou'tid] *adj* (famous) 有名な yū́mei na

notepad [nout'pæd] *n* メモ用紙 memóyòshi ◇糊などでつづった物を指す norí

notepaper [nout'peipər] *n* 便せん biñsen

nothing [nʌθ'iŋ] *n* (not anything) 何も ...ない naní mò ...naì; (zero) ゼロ zérò

he does nothing 彼は何もしない kárè wa naní mò shinái

nothing new/much/special 目新しい〔大した、特別な〕ことはない meátarashiì〔táìshita, tokúbetsu nà〕kotó wa naì

for nothing (free) 無料で muryố de, ただで tádà de; (in vain) 無駄に mudá ni

notice [nou'tis] *n* (announcement) 通知 tsúchi; (warning) 通告 tsúkoku; (dismissal) 解雇通知 kaíkotsùchi; (resignation) 辞表 jihyố; (period of time) 予告 yokóku
♦*vt* (observe) ...に気が付く ...ni ki gá tsukù

to bring something to someone's notice (attention) ...を...に知らせる ...wo ...ni shiráserù

to take notice of ...に気が付く ...ni ki gá tsukù

at short notice 急に kyū́ ni

until further notice 追って通知があるまで otté tsúchi ga aru madè

to hand in one's notice 辞表を出す jihyố wò dásù

noticeable [nou'tisəbəl] *adj* (mark, effect) はっきりした hakkírì shita

noticeboard [nou'tisbɔːrd] (*BRIT*) *n* 掲示板 keíjiban

notify [nou'təfai] *vt*: *to notify someone (of something)* (...を) ...に知らせる (...wo) ...ni shiráserù

notion [nou'ʃən] *n* (idea) 考え kañgaè, 概念 gáìnen; (opinion) 意見 íkèn

notorious [noutɔːr'iːəs] *adj* (criminal, liar, place) 悪名高い akúmeitakaì

notwithstanding [nɑːtwiθstæn'diŋ] *adv* ...にもかかわらず ...níì mò kakáwarazù
♦*prep* ...にもかかわらず ...níì mò kakáwarazù

nougat [nuː'gət] *n* ヌガー núgằ ◇クルミなどの入ったキャラメル風のお菓子 kurúmi nadò no haíttà kyarámerufū̀ no okáshì

nought [nɔːt] n = **naught**

noun [naun] n 名詞 meíshi

nourish [nəːˈriʃ] vt (feed) 養 う yashínaù; (fig: foster) 心中にはぐくむ shíñchū ni hagúkumù

nourishing [nəːˈriʃiŋ] adj (food) 栄養のある eíyō no arù

nourishment [nəːˈriʃmənt] n (food) 栄養 eíyō

novel [nɑːˈvəl] n 小説 shōsetsu
♦adj (new, fresh: idea, approach) 目新しい meátarashiì, 新鮮な shiñsen na

novelist [nɑːˈvəlist] n 小説家 shōsetsuka

novelty [nɑːˈvəltiː] n (newness) 新鮮さ shiñsensa; (object) 変ったもの kawátta monò

November [nouvemˈbəːr] n 11月 júichigatsu

novice [nɑːˈvis] n (beginner) 初心者 shoshíñsha; (REL) 修練者 shúreñsha

now [nau] adv 今 imá
♦conj: **now (that)** ...であるから ...de árù kara
right now (immediately) 今すぐ imá súgù; (at the moment) 今の所 imá no tokoro
by now 今ごろはもう imágoro wà mő
just now 今の所 imá no tokoro
now and then, now and again 時々 tokídoki
from now on 今後 kóñgo

nowadays [nauˈədeiz] adv このごろ(は) konőgoro (wa)

nowhere [nouˈweːr] adv どこにも...ない dókò ni mo ...naì

nozzle [nɑːˈzəl] n (of hose, fire extinguisher etc) ノズル nózùru; (of vacuum cleaner) 吸口 suíkuchi

nuance [nuːˈɑːnts] n ニュアンス nyúansu

nubile [nuːˈbail] adj (woman) セクシーな sékùshī na

nuclear [nuːˈkliːər] adj (fission, weapons) 核... kákù...
the nuclear industry 原子力産業界 geñshiryoku sangyōkai
nuclear physics 原始物理学 geñshibutsurigàku, 核物理学 kakúbutsurigàku
nuclear power 原子力 geñshiryoku

nucleus [nuːˈkliːəs] (pl **nuclei**) n (of atom, cell) 核 kákù; (of group) 中心 chúshin

nude [nuːd] adj 裸の hadáka no
♦n ヌード nűdo
in the nude (naked) 裸で hadáka de

nudge [nʌdʒ] vt (person) 小突く kozúkù

nudist [nuːˈdist] n 裸体主義者 ratáishugishà, ヌーディスト núdisùto

nudity [nuːˈditiː] n 裸 hadáka

nuisance [nuːˈsəns] n (state of affairs) 厄介な事情 yákkài na jijő; (thing) 厄介な物 yákkài na monò; (person: irritating) 迷惑な人 meíwaku na hitő
what a nuisance! 困ったもんだ komátta moñ da

null [nʌl] adj: **null and void** (contract, agreement) 無効な mukő na

numb [nʌm] adj: **numb (with)** (with cold etc) ...でしびれた ...de shibíretà; (fig: with fear etc) ...で気が動転した ...de ki ga dőten shità

number [nʌmˈbəːr] n (MATH) 数字 sújì; (quantity) 数 kázù; (of house, bank account etc) 番号 bañgő
♦vt (pages etc) ...に番号を付ける ...ni bañgő wo tsukérù; (amount to) 総数は...である sősū wa ...de árù
to be numbered among ...の1人である ...no hitőrì de árù
a number of (several) 数...の sū... no
they were ten in number (people) 彼らは10人だった kárèra wa júnin datta; (things) 10個あった júkkò atta

number plate (BRIT) n (AUT) ナンバープレート nañbápurèto

numeral [nuːˈməːrəl] n 数詞 súshi

numerate [nuːˈməˈreit] adj 数学ができる súgaku gà dekírù

numerical [nuːmeːrˈikəl] adj (value) 数字で表した sújì dè aráwashità; (order) 数字の sújì no

numerous [nuːˈməːrəs] adj (many, countless) 多くの őkù no, 多数の tasú no

nun [nʌn] n (Christian) 修道女 shúdōjo; (Buddhist) 尼 ámá

nurse [nəːrs] n (in hospital) 看護婦 kañgofù; (also: **nursemaid**) 保母 hőbo

♦ vt (patient) 看護する kángo suru; (baby) ...に乳を飲ませる ...ni chichí wò nomáserù

nursery [nə:r'sə:ri:] n (institution) 保育園 hoíkuèn; (room) 育児室 ikújishìtsu; (for plants: commercial establishment) 種苗園 shubyóèn

nursery rhyme n 童謡 dóyō

nursery school n 保育園 hoíkuèn

nursery slope (BRIT) n (SKI) 初心者用ゲレンデ shoshínshayō gerènde

nursing [nə:rs'iŋ] n (profession) 看護職 kańgoshòku; (care) 看病 kánbyō

nursing home n (gen) 療養所 ryōyōjo; (for old people) 老人ホーム rōjinhòmu

nursing mother n 授乳している母親 junyū shite irù hahàoya

nurture [nə:r't∫ə:r] vt (child, plant) 育てる sodáterù

nut [nʌt] n (TECH) ナット náttò; (BOT) 木ノ実 kínomì(kónomi)、ナッツ náttsù

nutcracker [nʌt'kræk:ər] npl クルミ割り kurúmiwarì

nutmeg [nʌt'meg] n ニクズク nikúzuku、ナツメッグ natsúmeggù ◇香辛料の一種 kóshinryō no ísshù

nutrient [nu:'tri:ənt] n 養分 yóbùn

nutrition [nu:tri∫'ən] n (diet, nourishment) 栄養 eíyō; (proteins, vitamins etc) 養分 yóbùn

nutritious [nu:tri∫'əs] adj (food) 栄養価の高い eíyōka no takáì

nuts [nʌts] (inf) adj 頭がおかしい atáma gà okáshiì

nutshell [nʌt'∫el] n クルミの殻 kurúmi no karà

in a nutshell (fig) 簡単に言えば kańtan nì iébà

nylon [nai'lɑ:n] n ナイロン náìron

♦ adj ナイロンの náìron no

O

oak [ouk] n オーク ōkù

♦ adj (table) オークの ōkù no

O.A.P. [oueipi:'] (BRIT) n abbr = **old-age pensioner**

oar [ɔ:r] n かい kaî、オール ōrú

oasis [ouei'sis] (pl **oases**) n (in desert) オアシス oáshìsu

oath [ouθ] n (promise) 誓い chikái; (swear word) 悪態 akútaì

under or **on** (BRIT) **oath** 宣誓して señsei shite

oatmeal [out'mi:l] n オートミール ōtómìru

oats [outs] n カラスムギ karásumugì

obedience [oubi:'di:əns] n 服従 fukújū

obedient [oubi:'di:ənt] adj (child, dog etc) 素直な sunào na、よく言う事を聞く yokù iú koto wo kikù

obesity [oubi:'siti:] n 肥満 himán

obey [oubei'] vt (instructions, person) ...に従う ...ni shitágau; (regulations) 守る mamóru

obituary [oubit∫'u:e:ri:] n 死亡記事 shibō-kijì

object [n ɑ:b'dʒikt vt əbdʒekt'] n (thing) 物 monó; (aim, purpose) 目的 mokuteki; (of affection, desires) 対象 taishō; (LING) 目的語 mokútekigo

♦ vi: **to object to** ...に反対する ...ni hańtai suru

to object that ...だと言って反対する ...da to itté hańtai suru

expense is no object 費用にはこだわらない hiyō ni wa kodáwaranaì

I object! 反対です hańtai dèsu

objection [əbdʒek'∫ən] n 異議 igì

I have no objection to ... ...には異議はありません ...ni igì wa arímasèn

objectionable [ədʒek'∫ənəbəl] adj (person, language, conduct) いやな iyá na

objective [əbdʒek'tiv] adj (impartial: person, information) 客観的な kyakúkanteki na

♦ n (aim, purpose) 目的 mokúteki

obligation [ɑ:bləgei'∫ən] n (duty, commitment) 義務 gimù

without obligation (COMM) 買う義務なしで kaú gimù nashi de

obligatory [əblig'ətɔ:ri:] adj 強制的な kyōseiteki na

oblige [əblaidʒ'] vt (force): **to oblige someone to do something** 強制的に

...に..をさせる kyṓseiteki ni ...ni ...wo saserù; (do a favor for) ...の頼みを聞く ...no tanómi wo kikú

to be obliged to someone for something (grateful) ...の事で...に感謝している ...no kotó de ...ni kañsha shité irù

obliging [əblai'dʒiŋ] *adj* (helpful) 親切な shíñsetsu na

oblique [əbli:k'] *adj* (line) 斜めの nanáme no; (comment, reference) 間接的な kañsetsuteki na

obliterate [əblit'əreit] *vt* 跡形もなくする atókata mo nakúsuru

oblivion [əbliv'i:ən] *n* (unawareness) 無意識 muíshìki; (being forgotten) 忘却 bṓkyaku

oblivious [əbliv'i:əs] *adj*: **oblivious of / to** ...を意識していない ...wo ishíki shité inai

oblong [ɑ:b'lɔ:ŋ] *adj* 長方形の chṓhṓkei no
♦*n* 長方形 chṓhṓkei

obnoxious [əbnɑ:k'ʃəs] *adj* (unpleasant: behavior, person) 不愉快な fuyúkài na; (: smell) いやな iyá na

oboe [ou'bou] *n* オーボエ ōbòe

obscene [əbsi:n'] *adj* (gesture, remark, behavior) わいせつな waísetsu na

obscenity [əbsen'iti:] *n* (of book, behavior etc) わいせつ waísetsu; (offensive word) 卑語 higo

obscure [əbskju:r'] *adj* (little known: place, author etc) 無名の muméi no; (difficult to understand) 難解な nañkai na
♦*vt* (obstruct: view, sun etc) 覆い隠す ōīkakusù; (conceal: truth, meaning etc) 隠す kakúsù

obsequious [əbsi:'kwi:əs] *adj* ぺこぺこする pekópeko suru

observance [əbzə:r'vəns] *n* (of law) 遵守 juñshu; (of custom) 守る事 mamóru koto

observant [əbzə:r'vənt] *adj* (person) 観察力の優れた kañsatsuryòku no sugureta; (remark) 鋭い surúdòi

observation [ɑ:bzə:rvei'ʃən] *n* (remark) 意見 ikèn; (act of observing) 観察 kañsatsu; (MED) 監視 kañshi

observatory [əbzə:r'vətɔ:ri:] *n* 観測所 kañsokujo

observe [əbzə:rv'] *vt* (watch) 観察する kañsatsu suru; (comment) 意見を述べる ikèn wo nobérù; (abide by: rule) 守る mamórù, 遵守する juñshu suru

observer [əbzə:r'və:r] *n* 観察者 kañsatsushà

obsess [əbses'] *vt* ...に取付く ...ni toritsuku

obsession [əbseʃ'ən] *n* 強迫観念 kyṓhakukannen

obsessive [əbses'iv] *adj* (person, tendency, behavior) 妄想に取付かれた様な mōsō ni toritsukareta yō na

obsolescence [ɑ:bsəles'əns] *n* 旧式化 kyūshikika

obsolete [ɑ:bsəli:t'] *adj* (out of use: word etc) 廃れた sutáreta; (: machine etc) 旧式の kyūshiki no

obstacle [ɑ:b'stəkəl] *n* (obstruction) 障害物 shōgaibutsù; (*fig*: problem, difficulty) 障害 shōgai

obstacle race *n* 障害物競走 shōgaibutsukyōsō

obstetrics [əbstet'riks] *n* 産科 sañka

obstinate [ɑ:b'stənit] *adj* (determined: person, resistance) 頑固な gañko na

obstruct [əbstrʌkt'] *vt* (block) ふさぐ fuságu; (*fig*: hinder) 妨害する bōgai suru

obstruction [əbstrʌk'ʃən] *n* (action) 妨害 bōgai; (object) 障害物 shōgaibutsu

obtain [əbtein'] *vt* (get) 手に入れる te nī iréru, 獲得する kakútoku suru; (achieve) 達成する tasséi suru

obtainable [əbtein'əbəl] *adj* (object) 入手できる nyūshu dekírù

obvious [ɑ:b'vi:əs] *adj* (clear) 明かな akíràka na; (self-evident) 分かり切った wakárikitta

obviously [ɑ:b'vi:əsli:] *adv* 明らかに akíràka ni

obviously not 明らかに...でない akíràka ni ...de nai

occasion [əkei'ʒən] *n* (point in time) 時 tokí, 時点 jitén; (event, celebration etc) 行事 gyōji, イベント ibénto; (opportunity) 機会 kikái, チャンス chañsu

occasional [əkei'ʒənəl] *adj* (infrequent)

時々の tokídokì no

occasionally [əkei'ʒənəli:] adv 時々 to-kídokì

occult [əkʌlt'] n: the occult 超自然 chṓshizen, オカルト okárùto

occupant [ɑ:k'jəpənt] n (long-term: of house etc) 居住者 kyojūshà; (of office etc) テナント tenánto; (temporary: of car, room etc) 中にいる人 nakà ni iru hitó

occupation [ɑ:kjəpei'ʃən] n (job) 職業 shokúgyò; (pastime) 趣味 shumì; (of building, country etc) 占領 sefiryō

occupational hazard [ɑ:kjəpei'ʃənəl-] n 職業上の危険 shokúgyōjō no kikén

occupier [ɑ:k'jəpaiər] n 居住者 kyojūshà

occupy [ɑ:k'jəpai] vt (inhabit: house) ...に住む ...ni sumù; (take: seat, place etc) ...に居る ...ni irú; (take over: building, country etc) 占領する sefiryō suru; (take up: time) ...が掛る ...ga kakárù; (: attention) 奪う ubáù; (: space) 取る torù

to occupy oneself in doing (to be busy with) ...に専念する ...ni sénnen suru

occur [əkə:r'] vi (event: take place) 起る okórù; (phenomenon: exist) 存在する sofizai suru

to occur to someone ...の頭に浮ぶ ...no atáma ni ukábu

occurrence [əkə:r'əns] n (event) 出来事 dekígoto; (existence) 存在 sofizai

ocean [ou'ʃən] n 海 umì

Indian Ocean インド洋 iñdoyò ¶ see also **Atlantic**; **Pacific**

ocean-going [ou'ʃəngouiŋ] adj 外洋の gaíyō no

ocher [ou'kər] (BRIT: **ochre**) adj (color) 黄土色の ōdōiro no, オークルの ōkùru no

o'clock [əklɑ:k'] adv: it is 5 o'clock 5時です gojì desu

OCR [ousi:ɑ:r'] n abbr (COMPUT: = optical character recognition) 光学読取り kṓgakuyomitorì (: = optical character reader) 光学読取り装置 kṓgakuyomisōchì

octagonal [ɑ:ktæg'ənəl] adj 八角形の hákkakukeì no

octave [ɑ:k'tiv] n (MUS) オクターブ o-kútàbu

October [ɑ:ktou'bər] n 10月 jűgatsu

octopus [ɑ:k'təpəs] n タコ takò

odd [ɑ:d] adj (strange: person, behavior, expression) 変な heñ na, 妙な myṑ na; (uneven: number) 奇数の kísù no; (not paired: sock, glove, shoe etc) 片方の kátahō no

60-odd 60幾つ rokújū ikutsu

at odd times 時々 tokídokì

to be the odd one out 例外である reígai de aru

oddity [ɑ:d'iti:] n (person) 変り者 kawarimono; (thing) 変った物 kawatta mono

odd-job man [ɑ:ddʒɑ:b'-] n 便利屋 beñriya

odd jobs npl 雑用 zatsúyō

oddly [ɑ:d'li:] adv (strangely: behave, dress) 変な風に heñ na fū ni ¶ see also **enough**

oddments [ɑ:d'mənts] npl (COMM) 残り物 nokórimono

odds [ɑ:dz] npl (in betting) かけ率 kakéritsu, オッズ ozzù

it makes no odds 構いません kamáímasen

at odds 仲たがいして nakátagàishite

odds and ends npl 半端物 hañpamono

ode [oud] n しょう歌 shōkà, オード ōdò

odious [ou'di:əs] adj 不快な fukái na

odometer [oudɑ:m'itər] n 走行距離計 sōkōkyorikeì

odor [ou'dər] (BRIT **odour**) n (smell) におい niòi; (: unpleasant) 悪臭 akúshū

KEYWORD

of [ʌv] prep 1 (gen) ...の ...nò

the history of France フランスの歴史 furánsu nò rekíshi

a friend of ours 私たちのある友達 watákushitàchi no árù tomódachi

a boy of 10 10才の少年 jússài no shṓnen

that was kind of you ご親切にどうも go-shíñsetsu ni dṓmo

a man of great ability 才能抜群の人 saínō batsugùn no hitó

the city of New York ニューヨーク市 nyǔyōkushī

south of Glasgow グラスゴーの南 gurásugǒ no mínámi

2 (expressing quantity, amount, dates etc): *a kilo of flour* 小麦粉1キロ komúgiko ichíkiro

how much of this do you need? これはどのぐらい要りますか koré wà donó gurai irimasù ká

there were 3 of them (people) 3人いました sannín imáshīta; (objects) 3個ありました sánko arímáshīta

3 of us went 私たちの内から3人行きました watákushitàchi no uchí karà sánnin ikímashìta

the number of road accidents is increasing 交通事故の数が増えています kótsūjikò no kázǔ ga fúète imásù

a cup of tea お茶1杯 o-chá ippài

a vase of flowers 花瓶に生けた花 kabín nì íkèta haná

the 5th of July 7月5日 shichígàtsu itsúká

the winter of 1987 1987年の冬 señkyûhyakuhachíjûnánàneñ no fuyú

3 (from, out of): *a bracelet of solid gold* 純金の腕輪 junkín nò udéwa

a statue of marble 大理石の彫像 daírisèki no chǒzō

made of wood 木製の mokúsei no

KEYWORD

off [ɔːf] *adv* **1** (referring to distance, time) 離れて hanárète

it's a long way off あれは遠い aré wà tǒi

the game is 3 days off 試合は3日先です shíai wà mikká saki desù

2 (departure) 出掛けて dekákete

to go off to Paris/Italy パリ〔イタリア〕へ出掛ける parì〔itária〕e dekákerù

I must be off そろそろ出掛けます soròsoro dekákemasù

3 (removal) 外しての hazúshìte

to take off one's hat/coat/clothes 帽子〔コート，服〕を脱ぐ bǒshi〔kǒto, fu-

kú〕wo núgù

the button came off ボタンが取れた botán gà tórèta

10% off (COMM) 10パーセント引き juppásentobiki

4 (not at work: on holiday) 休暇中で kyúkachū dě; (: due to sickness) 欠勤して kekkín shite

I'm off on Fridays 私の休みは金曜日です watákushi nò yasúmi wa kiń-yōbi desu

he was off on Friday (on holiday) 金曜日には彼は休みでした kiń-yōbi ni wa kárè wa yasúmi deshìta; (sick etc) 金曜日には彼は欠勤しました kiń-yōbi ni wa kárè wa kékkin shimashìta

to have a day off (from work) 1日の休みを取る ichínichi nò yasúmi wò tórù

to be off sick 病欠する byǒketsu suru

◆*adj* **1** (not turned on: machine, engine, water, gas etc) 止めてある tométe arù; (: tap) 締めてある shiméte arù; (: light) 消してある keshíte arù

2 (cancelled: meeting, match, agreement) 取消された toríkesàreta

3 (BRIT: not fresh: milk, cheese, meat etc) 悪くなった warúku natta

4: *on the off chance* (just in case) …の場合に備えて …no baái ni sonaete

to have an off day (not as good as usual) 厄日である yakúbì de árù

◆*prep* **1** (indicating motion, removal etc) …から …kárà

to fall off a cliff 崖から落ちる gake karà ochírù

the button came off my coat コートのボタンが取れた kǒtò no botán gà tórèta

to take a picture off the wall 壁に掛けてある絵を降ろす kabé nì kákète aru é wò orósù

2 (distant from) …から離れて …kárà hanárète

it's just off the M1 国道M1を降りて直ぐの所にあります kokúdò emúwaň wo órìte súgù no tokórò ni arímasù

it's 5 km off the main road 幹線道路から5キロの所にあります kańsendòro

kara gókìro no tokórò ni arímasù

an island off the coast 沖合の島 okíai nò shimá

to be off meat (no longer eat it) 肉をやめている nikú wò yaméte irù; (no longer like it) 肉が嫌いになっている nikú gà kirái nì natté irù

offal [ɔːˈfəl] *n* (CULIN) もつ motsù

off-color [ɔːˈfkʌlˈəːr] (*BRIT* **off-colour**) *adj* (ill) 病気の byóki no

offend [əfendˈ] *vt* (upset: person) 怒らせる okóraseru

offender [əfenˈdəːr] *n* (criminal) 犯罪者 hañzaìsha, 犯人 hañnin, ...犯 ...hañ

offense [əfensˈ] (*BRIT* **offence**) *n* (crime) 犯罪 hañzaì

to take offense at ...に怒る ...ni okóru

offensive [əfenˈsiv] *adj* (remark, gesture, behavior) 侮辱的な bujókuteki na; (smell etc) いやな iyá na; (weapon) 攻撃用の kógekiyō no

♦ *n* (MIL) 攻撃 kógeki

offer [ɔːˈfəːr] *n* (proposal: to help etc) 申出 mòshide; (: to buy) 申込み mòshikomi

♦ *vt* (advice, help, information) ...すると申出る ...surú to mòshideru; (opportunity, service, product) 提供する teíkyō suru

on offer (*BRIT*: COMM) 値下げ品で neságehin de

offering [ɔːˈfəriŋ] *n* (of a company: product) 売物 urímono; (REL) 供物 sonáemono

off-hand [ɔːˈfhændˈ] *adj* (behavior) いい加減な iíkagen na

♦ *adv* 即座に sokúza ni

office [ɔːˈfis] *n* (place) 事務所 jimúshò, オフィス ofìsu; (room) 事務室 jimúshìtsu; (position) 職 shokú

doctor's office (US) 医院 iìn

to take office 職に就く shokú ni tsuku

office automation *n* オフィスオートメーション ofìsu ōtómèshon

office building (*BRIT* **office block**) *n* オフィスビル ofìsubiru

office hours *npl* (COMM) 業務時間 gyòmujikan; (US: MED) 診察時間 shiñ-

satsujikan

officer [ɔːˈfisəːr] *n* (MIL etc) 将校 shókò; (*also*: **police officer**) 警官 keíkan; (of organization) 役員 yakúin

office worker *n* 事務員 jimúin

official [əfiʃˈəl] *adj* (authorized) 公認の kóniñ no; (visit, invitation, letter etc) 公式の kóshiki no

♦ *n* (in government) 役人 yakúnin; (in trade union etc) 役員 yakúin

official residence 官邸 kañtei

officialdom [əfiʃˈəldəm] (*pej*) *n* 官僚の世界 kañryō no sekài

officiate [əfiʃˈieit] *vi* 司会する shikái suru

officious [əfiʃˈəs] *adj* (person, behavior) 差出がましい sashídegamashiì

offing [ɔːˈfiŋ] *n*: *in the offing* (*fig*: imminent) 差迫って sashísematte

off-licence [ɔːˈflaisəns] *BRIT n* (shop selling alcohol) 酒屋 sakáya

off-line [ɔːˈflaínˈ] *adj* (COMPUT) オフラインの ofúrain no

♦ *adv* オフラインで ofúrain de

off-peak [ɔːˈfpiːkˈ] *adj* (heating) オフピークの ofúpīku no; (train, ticket) 混んでいない時の koñde inai tokí no

off-putting [ɔːˈfput'iŋ] (*BRIT*) *adj* (person, remark etc) 気を悪くさせる kì wo warúku saseru

off-season [ɔːˈfsiːzən] *adj* (holiday, ticket) オフシーズンの ofúshīzun no

♦ *adv* (travel, book etc) オフシーズンに ofúshīzun ni

offset [ɔːˈfset'] (*pt, pp* **offset**) *vt* (counteract) 補う ogínaù

offshoot [ɔːˈfʃuːt] *n* (*fig*) 副産物 fukúsañbutsu

offshore [ɔːˈfʃɔːr] *adj* (breeze) 陸からの rikú kara no; (oilrig, fishing) 沖合の okíai no

offside [ɔːˈfsaidˈ] *adj* (SPORT) オフサイドの ofúsaido no; (AUT: with right-hand drive) 右の migí no; (: with left-hand drive) 左の hidári no

offspring [ɔːˈfspriŋ] *n inv* 子孫 shisòn

offstage [ɔːˈfsteidʒˈ] *adv* 舞台裏に〔で〕 butáiura ni〔de〕

off-the-rack [ɔːf'ðəræk'] (*BRIT* **off-the-peg**) *adj* (clothing) 出来合いの dekíai no, 既製の kiséi no

off-white [ɔːf'wait'] *adj* (grayish white) 灰色がかった白の haírogakatta shirō no; (yellowish white) 黄色がかった白の kiírogakatta shirō no

often [ɔːf'ən] *adv* (frequently) よく yokù, しょっちゅう shotchū, 度々 tabítabi
how often do you go? どのぐらい行きますか donō gurai ikímasu ká

ogle [ou'gəl] *vt* 色目で見る irómè de mirù

oh [ou] *excl* あっ át

oil [ɔil] *n* (*gen*) 油 abúra, オイル oírù; (CULIN) サラダ油 sarádayu; (petroleum) 石油 sekíyu; (crude) 原油 geñyu; (for heating) 石油 sekíyu, 灯油 tōyu
♦*vt* (lubricate: engine, gun, machine) ...に油を差す ...ni abúra wo sasù

oilcan [ɔil'kæn] *n* 油差し abúrasashi

oilfield [ɔil'fiːld] *n* 油田 yudén

oil filter *n* (AUT) オイルフィルター oírufirutā

oil painting *n* 油絵 abúrae

oil refinery [-riːfain'əːriː] *n* 精油所 seíyujo

oil rig *n* 石油採削装置 sekíyu kússakusōchi

oilskins [ɔil'skinz] *npl* 防水服 bōsuifuku

oil tanker *n* (ship) オイルタンカー oírutankā; (truck) タンクローリー tañkurōrī

oil well *n* 油井 yuséi

oily [ɔi'liː] *adj* (rag) 油染みた abúrajimitā; (substance) 油の様な abúra no yō na; (food) 脂っこい abúrakkoi

ointment [ɔint'mənt] *n* 軟こう nañkō

O.K., okay [oukei'] (*inf*) *excl* (agreement: alright) よろしい yoróshii, オーケー ōkē; (: don't fuss) 分かったよ wakáttá yo
♦*adj* (average: film, book, meal etc) まあまあの mā́mā no
♦*vt* (approve) 承認する shōnin suru

old [ould] *adj* (aged: person) 年寄の toshíyori no; (: thing) 古い furúì; (former: school, home etc) 元の motò no, 前の maè no

how old are you? お幾つですか o-íkutsu desu ká
he's 10 years old 彼は10才です karè wa jussái desu
older brother (one's own) 兄 ani; (of person spoken to) お兄さん o-nīsan; (of third party) 兄さん nīsan

old age *n* 老齢 rōrei

old-age pensioner [ould'eidʒ-] (*BRIT*) *n* 年金で生活する老人 nefíkin dè seíkatsu surù rōjín, 年金暮しの人 nefíkingurāshi no hitò

old-fashioned [ould'fæʃ'ənd] *adj* (style, design) 時代遅れの jidáiokûre no, 古くさい furúkusai; (person, values) 保守的な hoshúteki na

olive [ɑːl'iv] *n* (fruit) オリーブ orībù; (*also*: **olive tree**) オリーブの木 orībù no ki
♦*adj* (*also*: **olive-green**) オリーブ色の oríbùiro no

olive oil *n* オリーブ油 oríbùyu

Olympic [oulim'pik] *adj* 五輪の gorín no, オリンピックの orínpikkù no

Olympic Games *npl: the Olympic Games* 五輪 gorín, オリンピック orínpikkù
the Olympics 五輪 gorín, オリンピック orínpikkù

omelet(te) [ɑːm'lit] *n* オムレツ omúretsu

omen [ou'mən] *n* (sign) 兆し kizáshi, 前触れ maébure

ominous [ɑːm'ənəs] *adj* (worrying) 不気味な bukími na

omission [oumiʃ'ən] *n* 省略 shōryaku

omit [oumit'] *vt* (deliberately) 省略する shōryaku suru; (by mistake) うっかりして抜かす ukkárì shite nukásu

---

| KEYWORD |

on [ɑːn] *prep* **1** (indicating position) ...(の上)に〔で〕...(no ué) nî [de]
on the wall 壁に kabé ni
it's on the table テーブル(の上)にあります tēburu (no ué) nî arímasù
on the left 左に hidári nì
the house is on the main road 家は幹線道路に面しています ié wà kańsendòro

ni méñ shite imásù

2 (indicating means, method, condition etc) ...で ...dè

on foot (go, be) 歩いて aruíte

on the train/plane (go) 電車〔飛行機〕で déñsha(hikóki)de; (be) 電車〔飛行機〕に乗って déñsha(hikóki)ni notté

on the telephone/radio/television 電話〔ラジオ, テレビ〕で déñwa(rájìo, térèbi)de

she's on the telephone 彼女は電話に出ています〔電話中です〕kánòjo wa déñwa ni détè imasu(deñwachū desù)

I heard it on the radio/saw him on television 私はラジオで聞きました〔テレビで彼を見ました〕watákushi wa rájìo de kikimashìta(térèbi de kárè wo mimáshìta)

to be on drugs 麻薬をやっている mayáku wò yatté irú

to be on holiday 休暇中である kyúkachū de arù

to be away on business 商用で出掛けている shóyò dè dekákete irù

3 (referring to time) ...に ...ni

on Friday 金曜日に kiń-yóbi ni

on Fridays 金曜日に kiń-yóbi ni, 毎週金曜日に maíshù kiń-yòbi ni, 金曜日毎に kiń-yóbi gótò ni

on June 20th 6月20日に rokúgatsu hatsúka ni

on Friday, June 20th 6月20日金曜日に rokúgatsu hatsúka kiń-yóbi ni

a week on Friday 来週の金曜日に raíshù ni kiń-yóbi ni

on arrival he went straight to his hotel 到着すると彼は真っ直ぐにホテルへ行きました tóchaku suru tò kárè wa massúgù ni hótèru e ikímashita

on seeing this これを見ると koré wò mírù to

4 (about, concerning) ...について ...ni tsúìte, ...に関して ...ni káñ shite

information on train services 列車に関する情報 resshá nì kañ surù jóhò

a book on physics 物理の本 bútsùri no hóñ

♦*adv* **1** (referring to dress) 身につけて

mi ní tsukète

to have one's coat on コートを着ている kóto wo kité irú

what's she got on? 彼女は何を着ていますか kánòjo wa nánì wo kité imasù ká

she put her boots/gloves/hat on 彼女はブーツを履いた〔手袋をはめた, 帽子をかぶった〕kánòjo wa bútsu wo haíta(tebúkuro wò haméta, bóshì wo kabúttà)

2 (referring to covering): *screw the lid on tightly* ふたをしっかり締めて下さい futá wò shikkárì shímète kudasaì

3 (further, continuously) 続けて tsuzúkète

to walk/drive/go on 歩き〔車で走り, 行き〕続ける arúki(kuruma dè hashíri, ikí)tsuzukèru

to read on 読み続ける yomítsuzukèru

♦*adj* **1** (functioning, in operation: machine) 動いている ugóite irù; (: radio, TV, light) ついている tsúíte iru; (: faucet) 水が出ている mízú ga deté irù; (: brakes) かかっている kakátte irù; (: meeting) 続いている tsuzúíte irù

is the meeting still on? (in progress) まだ会議中ですか mádà kaígichū desù ká; (not cancelled) 会議は予定通りにやるんですか kaígi wa yotéi dòri ni yarún desù ká

there's a good film on at the cinema 映画館で今いい映画をやっています eígakàn de ímà ìí eíga wò yatté imasù

2: *that's not on!* (*inf*: of behavior) それはいけません sorè wà ikémaseñ

---

once [wʌns] *adv* (on one occasion) 一度 ichídò, 一回 ikkái; (formerly) 前 は maè wa, かつて katsùte

♦*conj* (immediately afterwards) ...した後 ...shitá ato, ...してから ...shité kara

once he had left/it was done 彼が出て〔事が済んで〕から kare ga detè(kotó ga suñde)kara

at once (immediately) 直ちに tadáchi ni, 直ぐに sugù ni; (simultaneously) 同時に dójì ni

once a week 週一回 shū ikkái

once more もう一度 mố ichído

once and for all 断念 dañzen

once upon a time 昔々 mukáshi mukashi

oncoming [aːnˈkʌmiŋ] *adj* (approaching: traffic etc) 向ってくる mukátte kurù

KEYWORD

one [wʌn] *num* 一（の） ichí (no), 1つ（の） hitótsù (no)

one hundred and fifty 150 hyakúgojū

I asked for two coffees, not one 注文したのは1つじゃなくて2つのコーヒーです chúmon shita no wà hitótsu jànakutè futátsu nò kōhī desu

one day there was a sudden knock at the door ある日突然だれかがドアをノックした árù hi totsúzen dárèka ga dóà wo nókkù shita

one by one 1つずつ hitótsu zùtsu

♦*adj* **1** (sole) ただ一つの tádà hitótsù no, 唯一の yúìtsu no

it's the one book which interests me 私が興味を感じる唯一の本です watákushi gà kyốmi wo kañjiru yúìtsu no hốñ desu

that is my one worry 私が心配しているのはそれだけです watákushi gà shiñpai shite iru nò wa soré dake dèsu

the one man who ... する唯一の人 ...suru yúìtsu no hitó

2 (same) 同じ onájì

they came in the one car 彼らは皆同じ車で来ました kárèra wa mínà onáji kurùma de kimáshìta

they all belong to the one family 彼らは皆身内です kárèra wa mínà miúchi desù

♦*pron* **1** 物 monó

this one これ koré

that one それ soré, あれ aré

I've already got one/a red one 私は既に1つ〔赤いの〕を持っています watákushi wà súdè ni hitótsù〔akái nò wo〕 móttè imasu

2: *one another* お互いに o-tágai nì

do you two ever see one another? お二人は付合っていますか o-fútàri wa tsu-

kíattè imasu ká

the boys didn't dare look at one another 少年たちはあえて顔を合せる事ができなかった shốnentàchi wa áète kaô wo awáseru kotò ga dekínakattà

3 (impersonal): *one never knows* どうなるか分かりませんね dố naru ka wakárimaseñ né

to cut one's finger 指を切る yubí wò kírù

one needs to eat 人は食べる必要がある hitó wà tabérù hitsúyō ga arù

one-day excursion [wʌnˈdeiˌ] (US) *n* (day return) 日帰り往復券 higáeri ōfukuken

one-man [wʌnˈmæn] *adj* (business) 1人だけの hitóri dake no, ワンマンの wañman no

one-man band *n* ワンマンバンド wañmanbando

one-off [wʌnˈɔːf] (BRIT: inf) *n* 一つだけの物 hitótsù dake no mono

KEYWORD

oneself [wʌnsɛlf] *pron* (reflexive) 自分自身を jibúnjishín wo; (after prep) 自分自身に jibúnjishín ni; (alone: often after prep) 自分一人で jibún hitòri de; (emphatic) 自分で jibún dè

to hurt oneself けがする kegá surù

to keep something for oneself 自分のために...を取って置く jibún no tamè ni ...wò tóttè oku

to talk to oneself 独り言を言う hitórigotò wo iú

one-sided [wʌnˈsaidid] *adj* (argument) 一方的な ippôteki na

one-to-one [wʌnˈtəwʌnˈ] *adj* (relationship) 一対一の ittáiichi no

one-upmanship [wʌnʌpˈmənʃip] *n* 自分の方が一枚上だと見せ付ける事 jibún no hō ga ichímài ué da to misétsukerù koto

one-way [wʌnˈwei] *adj* (street, traffic) 一方通行の ippôtsūkō no

ongoing [aːnˈgouiŋ] *adj* (project, situation etc) 進行中の shiñkōchū no

onion [ʌn'jən] n タマネギ tamánegì

on-line [ɑːn'lain] adj (COMPUT) オンラインの ofraìn no
♦adv (COMPUT) オンラインで ofraìn de

onlooker [ɑːn'lukəːr] n 見物人 kenbutsunìn

only [oun'li:] adv ...だけ ...dake
♦adj (sole, single) ただ一つ〔一人〕の tada hitótsù〔hitòrì〕no
♦conj (but) しかし shikáshì
an only child 一人っ子 hitórikkò
not only ... but also ... ...ばかりでなく...も ...bakàri de naku ...mo

onset [ɑːn'set] n (beginning: of war, winter, illness) 始まり hajímari, 始め hajíme

onshore [ɑːn'jɔːr] adj (wind) 海からの umì kara no

onslaught [ɑːn'slɔːt] n 攻撃 kógeki

onto [ɑːn'tuː] prep = on to

onus [ou'nəs] n 責任 sekínin

onward(s) [ɑːn'wəːrd(z)] adv (forward: move, progress) 先へ sakî e
from that time onward(s) それ以後 soré igo

onyx [ɑːn'iks] n オニキス onîkisu

ooze [uːz] vi (mud, water, slime) にじみでる nijímideru

opal [ou'pəl] n オパール opárù

opaque [oupeik'] adj (substance) 不透明な futómèka na

OPEC [ou'pek] n abbr (= Organization of Petroleum-Exporting Countries) 石油輸出国機構 sekíyu yushutsukoku kikō

open [ou'pən] adj (not shut: window, door, mouth etc) 開いた aíta; (: shop, museum etc) 営業中の eígyōchū no, 開いている aíte iru; (unobstructed: road) 開通している kaítsū shite iru; (: view) 開けた hiráketa; (not enclosed: land) 囲いのない kakói no nai; (fig: frank: person, manner, face) 率直な sótchoku na; (unrestricted: meeting, debate, championship) 公開の kókai no
♦vt 開ける akéru, 開く hiráku
♦vi (flower, eyes, door, shop) 開く akú, 開く hiráku; (book, debate etc: commence) 始まる hajímaru

in the open (air) 野外に yagài ni
an open car オープンカー ôpunkā

opening [ou'pəniŋ] adj (commencing: speech, remarks etc) 開会の kaíkai no, 冒頭の bôtō no
♦n (gap, hole) 穴 anâ; (start: of play, book etc) 始め hajíme, 冒頭 bôtō; (opportunity) 機会 kikái, チャンス chañsu

openly [ou'pənli:] adv (speak, act) 公然と kôzen to; (cry) 人目をはばからず hitóme wo habákarazu

open-minded [ou'pənmain'did] adj 偏見のない henkén no nai

open-necked [ou'pənnekt'] adj (shirt) 開きんの kaíkin no

open on to vt fus (subj: room, door) ...に面している ...ni mén shite iru

open-plan [ou'pənplæn'] adj 間仕切のない majîkiri no nai

open up vt (building, room: unlock) 開ける akéru; (blocked road) ...の障害物を取除く ...no shôgaìbutsu wo torínozokù
♦vi (COMM: shop, business) 開く akú

opera [ɑːp'rə] n 歌劇 kagèki, オペラ opèra

opera singer n オペラ歌手 opèrakashu

operate [ɑːp'əːreit] vt (machine) 操作する sôsa suru; (vehicle) 運転する uñten suru
♦vi (machine) 動く ugòkù; (vehicle) 走る hashiru, 動く ugòkù; (company, organization) 営業する eígyō suru
to operate on someone (for) (MED) ...に (...の) 手術をする ...ni (...no) shujùtsu wo suru

operatic [ɑːpəræt'ik] adj 歌劇の kagèki no, オペラの opèra no

operating [ɑːp'əːreitiŋ] adj: **operating table** 手術台 shujùtsudai
operating theater 手術室 shujùtsushitsu

operation [ɑːpəːrei'jən] n (of machine etc) 操作 sôsà; (of vehicle) 運転 uñten; (MIL, COMM etc) 作戦 sakúsen; (MED) 手術 shujùtsu
to be in operation (law, regulation) 実施されている jisshî sarete iru
to have an operation (MED) 手術を受

ける shujútsu wo ukérù

operational [ɑːpəreiʃ'ənəl] *adj* (working: machine, vehicle etc) 使用可能な shíyōkanō na

operative [ɑːp'ərətiv] *adj* (law, measure, system) 実施されている jisshí sarete iru

operator [ɑːp'əreitər] *n* (TEL) 交換手 kốkanshu, オペレーター opérētā; (of machine) 技師 gishī

ophthalmic [ɑːfθæl'mik] *adj* 眼科の gañka no

opinion [əpin'jən] *n* (point of view, belief) 意見 ikén

in my opinion 私の意見では watákushi no ikèn de wa

opinionated [əpin'jəneitid] (*pej*) *adj* 独善的な dokúzenteki na

opinion poll *n* 世論調査 yorónchōsa

opium [ou'piːəm] *n* あへん ahén

opponent [əpou'nənt] *n* (person not in favor) 反対者 hañtaisha; (MIL) 敵 tekí; (SPORT) 相手 aíte

opportunism [ɑːpəːrtu'nizəm] (*pej*) *n* 日和見主義 hiyórimishugī

opportunist [ɑːpəːrtu'nist] (*pej*) *n* 日和見主義者 hiyórimishugìsha

opportunity [ɑːpəːrtju:'niti:] *n* 機会 kikái, チャンス chañsu

to take the opportunity of doing 折角の機会を利用して...する sekkáku no kikái wo riyố shite ...suru

oppose [əpouz'] *vt* (object to: wish, opinion, plan) ...に反対する ...ni hañtai suru

to be opposed to something ...に反対である ...ni hañtai de aru

as opposed to ...ではなくて ...de wa nakutè

opposing [əpouz'iŋ] *adj* (side, ideas) 反対の hañtai no; (team) 相手の aíte no

opposite [ɑːp'əzit] *adj* (house) 向かい側の mukáigawa no; (end, direction, side) 反対の hañtai no; (point of view, effect) 逆の gyakú no

♦*adv* (live, stand, work, sit) 向い側に〔で〕mukáigawa ni〔de〕

♦*prep* (in front of) ...の向い側に〔で〕...no mukáigawa ni〔de〕

♦*n: the opposite* (say, think, do etc) 反対 hañtai

the opposite sex 異性 iséi

opposition [ɑːpəziʃ'ən] *n* (resistance) 反対 hañtai; (those against) 反対勢力 hañtaiseiryokù; (POL) 野党 yatố

oppress [əpres'] *vt* 抑圧する yokúatsu suru

oppression [əpreʃ'ən] *n* 抑圧 yokúatsu

oppressive [əpres'iv] *adj* (political regime) 抑圧的な yokúatsuteki na; (weather, heat) 蒸し暑い mushíatsuì

opt [ɑːpt] *vi: to opt for* ...を選ぶ...wo erábù

to opt to do ...する事にする ...surú koto ni suru

optical [ɑːp'tikəl] *adj* (instrument, device etc) 光学の kốgaku no

optical illusion *n* 目の錯覚 mé no sakkáku

optician [ɑːptiʃ'ən] *n* 眼鏡屋 megáneya

optimism [ɑːp'təmizəm] *n* 楽観 rakkán, 楽天主義 rakútenshugī

optimist [ɑːp'təmist] *n* 楽天家 rakútenka

optimistic [ɑːptəmis'tik] *adj* 楽観的な rakkánteki na

optimum [ɑːp'təməm] *adj* (conditions, number, size) 最良の saíryō no, 最善の saízen no

option [ɑːp'ʃən] *n* (choice) 選択 señtaku, オプション opúshon

optional [ɑːp'ʃənəl] *adj* (not obligatory) 自由選択の jiyúsentakuno

opt out *vi: to opt out of* ...から手を引く ...kara te wò hiku

opulent [ɑːp'jələnt] *adj* (very wealthy: person, society etc) 大金持の ốganèmochi no

or [ɔːr] *conj* (linking alternatives: up or down, in or out etc) それとも sorétomò, または matá wa; (otherwise) でないと de naī to, さもないと sa mò naì to; (with negative): *he hasn't seen or heard anything* 彼は何一つ見ても聞いてもいない karè wa nanī hitótsu mitè mo kiíte mo inaì

or else (otherwise) でないと de naī to

oracle [ɔːrˈəkəl] n 予言者 yogénsha

oral [ɔːrˈəl] adj (spoken: test, report) 口頭の kōtō no; (MED: vaccine, medicine) 経口の keíkō no
♦n (spoken examination) 口頭試問 kōtō-shimon

orange [ɔːrˈindʒ] n (fruit) オレンジ orénji
♦adj (color) だいだい色の daídaiiro no, オレンジ色の orénjiiro no

orator [ɔːrˈətər] n 雄弁家 yūbenka

orbit [ɔːrˈbit] n (SPACE) 軌道 kidō
♦vt (circle: earth, moon etc) ...の周囲を軌道を描いて回る ...no shūi wo kidō wo egaite mawaru

orchard [ɔːrˈtʃərd] n 果樹園 kajúen

orchestra [ɔːrˈkistrə] n (MUS) 楽団 gakúdan, オーケストラ ōkesùtora; (US: THEATER: seating) 舞台前の特等席 butáimae no tokútòseki

orchestrate [ɔːrˈkistreit] vt (stage-manage) 指揮する shikí suru

orchid [ɔːrˈkid] n ラン rañ

ordain [ɔːrdeinˈ] vt (REL) 聖職に任命する seíshoku ni niñmei suru

ordeal [ɔːrdiːlˈ] n 試練 shíren

order [ɔːrˈdəːr] n (command) 命令 meírei; (COMM: from shop, company etc: also in restaurant) 注文 chúmon; (sequence) 順序 juñjo; (good order) 秩序 chitsújò; (law and order) 治安 chiàn
♦vt (command) 命ずる mèizuru; (COMM: from shop, company etc: also in restaurant) 注文する chúmon suru; (also: put in order) 整理する seíri suru
in order (gen) 規定通りで kitéidòri de; (of document) 規定通りで kitéidòri de
in (working) order 整備されて seíbi sarete
in order to do/that ...するために ...surú tame ni
on order (COMM) 発注してあって hatchú shite atte
out of order (not in correct order) 順番が乱れて juñban ga midáretè; (not working) 故障して koshō shite
to order someone to do something ...に...する様に命令する ...ni ...suru yō ni meírei suru

order form n 注文用紙 chúmon yōshi

orderly [ɔːrˈdəːliː] n (MIL) 当番兵 tōbanhei; (MED) 雑役夫 zatsúekifù
♦adj (well-organized: room) 整とんされた seíton sareta; (: person, situation etc) 規則正しい kisòkutadashii

ordinary [ɔːrˈdəneriː] adj (everyday, usual) 普通の futsú no; (pej: mediocre) 平凡な heíbon na
out of the ordinary (exceptional) 変った kawátta

Ordnance Survey [ɔːrdˈnəns-] (BRIT) n 英国政府陸地測量局 eíkokuseifù rikúchi sokuryōkyoku

ore [ɔːr] n 鉱石 kōseki

organ [ɔːrˈgən] n (ANAT: kidney, liver etc) 臓器 zōki; (MUS) オルガン orúgan

organic [ɔːrgænˈik] adj (food, farming etc) 有機の yūkì no

organism [ɔːrˈgənizəm] n 有機体 yūkìtai, 生物 seíbutsu

organist [ɔːrˈgənist] n オルガン奏者 orúgansòsha, オルガニスト orúganisuto

organization [ɔːrgənəzeiˈʃən] n (business, club, society) 組織 soshìki, 機構 kikō, オーガニゼーション ōganizēshon

organize [ɔːrˈgənaiz] vt (arrange: activity, event) 企画する kikáku suru

organizer [ɔːrˈgənaizər] n (of conference, party etc) 主催者 shusáisha

orgasm [ɔːrˈgæzəm] n オルガズム orúgazumù

orgy [ɔːrˈdʒiː] n 乱交パーティ rañkōpàti

Orient [ɔːrˈiːənt] n: **the Orient** 東洋 tōyō

oriental [ɔːriːenˈtəl] adj 東洋の tōyō no

orientate [ɔːrˈiːenteit] vt: **to orientate oneself** (in place) 自分の居場所を確認する jibún no ibásho wo kakúnin suru; (in situation) 環境になれる kañkyō ni narérù

origin [ɔːrˈidʒin] n (beginning, source) 起源 kigén; (of person) 生れ umare

original [əridʒˈənəl] adj (first: idea, occupation) 最初の saísho no; (genuine: work of art, document etc) 本物の hoñmono no; (fig: imaginative: thinker, writer, artist) 独創的な dokúsōteki na

♦*n* (genuine work of art, document) 本物 hoñmono

originality [əridʒənæl'iti:] *n* (imagination: of artist, writer etc) 独創性 dokúsōsei

originally [əridʒ'ənəli:] *adv* (at first) 最初は saísho wa, 当初 tōsho

originate [əridʒ'əneit] *vi*: *to originate from* (person, idea, custom etc) ...から始まる ...karà hajímaru

to originate in ...で始まる ...dè hajímaru

Orkneys [ɔːrk'niːz] *npl*: *the Orkneys* (*also*: *the Orkney Islands*) オークニー諸島 ōkūnīshotō

ornament [ɔːr'nəmənt] *n* (gen) 飾り kazári, 装飾 sōshoku; (to be worn) 装身具 sōshiñgu

ornamental [ɔːrnəmen'təl] *adj* (decorative: garden, pond) 装飾的な sōshokuteki na

ornate [ɔːrneit'] *adj* (highly decorative: design, style) 凝った kottà

ornithology [ɔːrnəθɑːl'ədʒiː] *n* 鳥類学 chōruigaku

orphan [ɔːr'fən] *n* 孤児 kojì

orphanage [ɔːr'fənidʒ] *n* 孤児院 kojìin

orthodox [ɔːr'θədɑːks] *adj* (REL: *also fig*) 正統派の seítōha no

orthodoxy [ɔːr'θədɑːksiː] *n* (traditional beliefs) 正統思想 seítōshisō

orthopedic [ɔːrθəpiː'dik] (*BRIT* **orthopaedic**) *adj* 整形外科の seíkeigeka no

oscillate [ɑːs'əleit] *vi* (ELEC) 発振する hasshín suru; (PHYSICS) 振動する shiñdō suru; (*fig*: mood, person, ideas) 頻繁に変る hiñpan ni kawáru

ostensibly [ɑːsten'səbliː] *adv* 表面上 hyōmeñjō

ostentatious [ɑːstentei'ʃəs] *adj* (showy: building, car etc) 派手な hadé na; (: person) 万事に派手な bañji ni hadé na

osteopath [ɑːs'tiːəpæθ] *n* 整骨療法医 seíkotsuryōhōì

ostracize [ɑːs'trəsaiz] *vt* のけ者にする nokémono ni suru

ostrich [ɔːs'tritʃ] *n* ダチョウ dachō

other [ʌð'əːr] *adj* (that which has not been mentioned: person, thing) 外の hoká no; (second of 2 things) もう一つの mō hitotsu no

♦*pron*: *the other (one)* 外の物 hoká no mono

♦*adv*: *other than* ...を除いて ...wo nozóite

others (other people) 他人 tanín

the other day (recently) 先日 señjitsu, この間 konó aida

otherwise [ʌð'əːrwaiz] *adv* (in a different way) 違ったやり方で chígatta yarikata dè; (apart from that) それを除けば soré wo nozókeba

♦*conj* (if not) そうでないと sō dè nai to

otter [ɑːt'əːr] *n* カワウソ kawáuso

ouch [autʃ] *excl* 痛い itái

ought [ɔːt] (*pt* **ought**) *aux vb*: *she ought to do it* 彼女はそれをやるべきです kanòjo wa soré wo yarubeki desu

this ought to have been corrected これは直すべきだった koré wa naósubeki datta

he ought to win (probability) 彼は勝つはずです karè wa katsù hazu desu

ounce [auns] *n* (unit of weight) オンス oñsu

our [au'əːr] *adj* 私たちの watákushitachi no ¶ *see also* **my**

ours [au'əːrz] *pron* 私たちの物 watákushitachi no mono ¶ *see also* **mine**

ourselves [auəːrselvz'] *pron* 私たち自身 watákushitachi jishiñ ¶ *see also* **oneself**

oust [aust] *vt* (forcibly remove: government, MP etc) 追放する tsuíhō suru

─────────
| KEYWORD |

out [aut] *adv* 1 (not in) 外に〔で，へ〕 sótò ni〔de, e〕

they're out in the garden 彼らは庭にいます kárèra wa niwá ni imasù

(to stand) out in the rain/snow 雨〔雪〕の降る中に立っている áme〔yukí〕no fúrù nákà ni tátte irù

it's cold out here/out in the desert 外〔砂漠〕は寒い sótò〔sabáku〕wa samúi

out here/there ここ〔あそこ〕だ・外の方に kokó〔asóko〕dà - sótò no hṓ nì *to go/come etc out* 出て行く〔来る〕détè iku(kuru)

(to speak) out loud 大きな声で言う ókina koè de iú

2 (not at home, absent) 不在で fuzái de, 留守で rúsu de

Mr Green is out at the moment グリーンさんはただ今留守ですが gurín san wa tadáìma rúsu desu ga

to have a day/night out 1日〔1晩〕外出して遊ぶ ichínichì〔hitóbàn〕gaíshutsu shitè asóbù

3 (indicating distance): *the boat was 10 km out* 船は10キロ沖にあった fúnè wa jukkíró okí ni attá

3 days out from Plymouth プリマスを出港して3日の所 purímàsu wo shukkó shitè mikká no tokorò

4 (SPORT) アウトで áùto de

the ball is/has gone out ボールはアウトだ(出た) bóru wa áùto da〔détá〕

out! (TENNIS etc) アウト áùto

♦*adj* **1**: *to be out* (person: unconscious) 気絶〔失神〕している kizétsu〔shisshín〕shite irù; (: SPORT) アウトである áùto de árù; (out of fashion: style) 流行遅れである ryūkóokùre de árù, 廃れている sutárete irù; (: singer) 人気がなくなった nínki gà nakúnattà

2 (have appeared: flowers): *to be out* 咲いている saíte irù; (: news) 報道されている hódó sarete irù; (: secret) ばれた bárèta, 発覚した hakkáku shità

3 (extinguished: fire, light, gas) 消えた kiétà

before the week was out (finished) その週が終らない内に sonó shū ga owáranai uchi nì

4: *to be out to do something* (intend) ...しようとしている ...shiyó tò shité irù

to be out in one's calculations (wrong) 計算が間違っている keísan gà machígatte irù

---

out-and-out [aut'əndaut'] *adj* (liar, thief etc) 全くの mattáku no, 根っからの nekkára no

outback [aut'bæk] *n* (in Australia) 奥地 okùchi

outboard [aut'bɔ:rd] *adj*: *outboard motor* アウトボードエンジン aùtobōdo-enjin

outbreak [aut'breik] *n* (of war, disease, violence etc) ぼっ発 boppátsu

outburst [aut'bə:rst] *n* (sudden expression of anger etc) 爆発 bakúhatsu

outcast [aut'kæst] *n* のけ者 nokémono

outcome [aut'kʌm] *n* (result) 結果 kekká

outcrop [aut'krɑ:p] *n* (of rock) 露頭 rotó

outcry [aut'krai] *n* 反発 hañpatsu

outdated [autdei'tid] *adj* (old-fashioned) 時代遅れの jidáiokùre no

outdo [autdu:'] (*pt* **outdid** *pp* **outdone**) *vt* しのぐ shinógu

outdoor [aut'dɔ:r] *adj* (open-air: activities, games etc) 野外の yagái no, 屋外の okùgài no; (clothes) 野外用の yagáiyō no

outdoors [autdɔ:rz'] *adv* (play, stay, sleep: in the open air) 野外に〔で〕yagái ni〔de〕

outer [aut'ə:r] *adj* (exterior: door, wrapping, wall etc) 外側の sotógawa no

outer space *n* 宇宙空間 uchūkūkan

outfit [aut'fit] *n* (set of clothes) 衣装 ishó

outgoing [aut'gouiŋ] *adj* (extrovert) 外向性の gaíkōsei no; (retiring: president, mayor etc) 退陣する taíjin suru

outgoings [aut'gouiŋz] *npl* (*BRIT*) 出費 shuppí

outgrow [autgrou'] (*pt* **outgrew** *pp* **outgrown**) *vt* (one's clothes) 大きくなって ...が着られなくなる ōkiku natte ...ga kirárenaku naru

outhouse [aut'haus] *n* 納屋 nayà; (*US*) 屋外便所 okùgaibenjo

outing [au'tiŋ] *n* (excursion: family outing, school outing) 遠足 eñsoku

outlandish [autlæn'diʃ] *adj* (strange: looks, behavior, clothes) 奇妙な kimyó na

outlaw [aut'lɔ:] *n* 無法者 muhómono

♦*vt* (person, activity, organization) 禁止する kiñshi suru

outlay [aut'lei] *n* (expenditure) 出費

shuppī

outlet [aut'let] n (hole, pipe) 排水口 haísuīkō; (US: ELEC) コンセント koñseñto; (COMM: also: **retail outlet**) 販売店 hañbaīten

outline [aut'lain] n (shape: of object, person etc) 輪郭 riñkaku, アウトライン aútoraiñ; (brief explanation: of plan) あらまし arámashi, アウトライン aútoraiñ; (rough sketch) 略図 ryakúzu

♦vt (fig: theory, plan etc) ...のあらましを説明する ...no arámashi wo setsúmei suru

outlive [autliv'] vt (survive: person) ...より長生きする ...yorí naga-ikí suru; (: war, era) 生き延びる ikínobiru

outlook [aut'luk] n (view, attitude) 見方 mikáta; (: prospects) 見通し mitōshi; (: for weather) 予報 yohō

outlying [aut'laiiŋ] adj (away from main cities: area, town etc) 中心部を離れた chū́shinbu wo hanáreta

outmoded [autmou'did] adj (old-fashioned: custom, theory) 時代遅れの jidáiokùre no

outnumber [autnʌm'bə:r] vt ...より多い ...yorí ōī

KEYWORD

out of prep **1** (outside, beyond) ...の外へ〔に, で〕 ..no sóto e(ni, de)

to go out of the house 家から外へ出る ié kará sótò e dérù

to look out of the window 窓から外を見る mádò kara sótò wo mírù

to be out of danger (safe) 危険がなくなった kikén gà nakúnattà

2 (cause, motive) ...に駆られて ...ni karáretè

out of curiosity/fear/greed 好奇心〔恐怖, どん欲〕に駆られて kốkishìn〔kyốfu, dóñ-yoku〕ni karáretè

3 (origin) ...から ...kara

to drink something out of a cup カップから...を飲む káppù kara ...wo nomù

to copy something out of a book 本から...を写す hóñ kara ...wð utsúsù

4 (from among) ...の中から ...no nákà

kara, ...の内 ...no uchí

1 out of every 3 smokers 喫煙者3人に1人 kitsúeñsha sañnin nì hitórì

out of 100 cars sold, only one had any faults 売れた100台の車の内, 1台だけに欠陥があった uréta hyakúdài no kurúma no uchi, íchidai dake ni kekkán ga atta

5 (without) ...が切れて ...ga kírète, ...がなくなって ...ga nakúnattè

to be out of milk/sugar/gas (US)/petrol (BRIT) etc ミルク〔砂糖, ガソリン〕が切れている mírùku〔satő, gasórin〕ga kírète iru

out-of-date [autəvdeit'] adj (passport) 期限の切れた kigén no kiréta; (clothes etc) 時代遅れの jidáiokùre no

out-of-the-way [autəvðəwei'] adj (place) へんぴな heñpi na

outpatient [aut'peiʃənt] n (MED) 外来患者 gaíraikanja

outpost [aut'poust] n (MIL, COMM) 前しょう zeñshō; (COMM) 前進基地 zeñshinkichi

output [aut'put] n (production: of factory, mine etc) 生産高 seísañdaka; (: of writer) 作品数 sakúhinsū; (COMPUT) 出力 shutsúryoku, アウトプット aùtoputto

outrage [aut'reidʒ] n (action: scandalous) 不法行為 fuhókōī; (: violent) 暴力行為 bố ryokukōī; (anger) 激怒 gekído

♦vt (shock, anger) 激怒させる gekído saseru

outrageous [autrei'dʒəs] adj 非難すべき hiñánsubeki

outright [adv autrait' adj aut'rait] adv (absolutely: win) 圧倒的に attőteki ni; (at once: kill) 即座に sokúza ni; (openly: ask, deny, refuse) はっきりと hakkíri to

♦adj (absolute: winner, victory) 圧倒的な attőteki na; (open: refusal, denial, hostility) 明白な meíhaku na

outset [aut'set] n (start) 始め hajíme

outside [aut'said'] n (exterior: of container, building) 外側 sotðgawa

♦adj (exterior) 外側の sotðgawa no

♦adv (away from the inside: to be, go,

wait) 外に〔で〕sotó ni〔de〕

◆*prep* (not inside) ...の外に〔で〕...no sotó ni〔de〕; (not included in) ...の外に ...no hoká ni; (beyond) ...を越えて ...wo koéte

at the outside (*fig*) せいぜい seízei

outside lane *n* (AUT) 追越し車線 oíkoshishaseñ

outside line *n* (TEL) 外線 gaíseñ

outsider [autsai'dər] *n* (stranger) 部外者 bugáisha

outside-left/-right [aut'saidleft'/'rait] *n* (SOCCER) レフト〔ライト〕ウイング refúto〔raíto〕uíñgu

outsize [aut'saiz] *adj* (clothes) キングサイズの kíñgusaìzu no

outskirts [aut'skə:rts] *npl* (of city, town) 外れ hazúre

outspoken [aut'spou'kən] *adj* (statement, opponent, reply) 遠慮のない eñryo no naí

outstanding [autstæn'diñ] *adj* (exceptional) 並外れた namíhazureta, 優れた sugúretà; (remaining: debt, work etc) 残っている nókottè iru

outstay [autstei'] *vt*: *to outstay one's welcome* 長居して嫌われる nagái shite kiráwareru

outstretched [autstretʃt'] *adj* (hand) 伸ばした nobáshìta; (arms) 広げた hirógetà

outstrip [autstrip'] *vt* (competitors, demand) 追抜く oínuku

out-tray [aut'trei] *n* 送信のトレー sôshin no torè

outward [aut'wə:rd] *adj* (sign, appearances) 外部の gaíbu no; (journey) 行きの ikí no

outwardly [aut'wə:rdli:] *adv* 外部的に gaíbuteki ni

outweigh [autwei'] *vt* ...より重要である ...yorí jūyô de aru

outwit [autwit'] *vt* ...の裏をかく ...no urá wo káku

oval [ou'vəl] *adj* (table, mirror, face) だ円形の daéñkei no

◆*n* だ円形 daéñkei

ovary [ou'və:ri:] *n* 卵巣 rañsō

ovation [ouvei'ʃən] *n* 大喝さい daíkassai

oven [ʌv'ən] *n* (CULIN) 天火 teñpi, オーブン ōbùn; (TECH) 炉 ro

ovenproof [ʌv'ənpru:f] *adj* (dish etc) オーブン用の ōbùn yō no

KEYWORD

over [ou'və:r] *adv* 1 (across: walk, jump, fly etc) ...を越えて ...wò koétè

to cross over to the other side of the road 道路を横断する dóro wo ôdan suru

over here/there ここ〔あそこ〕に〔で〕kokó〔asóko〕nì〔dè〕

to ask someone over (to one's house) ...を家に招く ...wò ié nì manékù

2 (indicating movement from upright: fall, knock, turn, bend etc) 下へ shitá è, 地面へ jímen e

3 (excessively: clever, rich, fat etc) 余り amári, 過度に kádò ni

she's not over intelligent, is she? 彼女はあまり頭が良くないね kánòjo wa amári atáma gà yôkùnai né

4 (remaining: money, food etc) 余って amáttè, 残って nokóttè

there are 3 over 3個が残っている sáñko ga nokóttè irù

is there any cake (left) over? ケーキが残っていませんか kêki ga nokótte imaseñ ká

5: *all over* (everywhere) 至る所に〔で〕itáru tokoro ni〔de〕, どこもかしこも dókò mo káshikò mo

over and over (again) (repeatedly) 何度〔何回、何返〕も nâñdo〔náñkai, nâñben〕mo

◆*adj* (finished): *to be over* (game, life, relationship etc) 終りである owári de arù

◆*prep* 1 (on top of) ...の上に〔で〕...no ué nì〔de〕; (above) ...の上方に〔で〕...no jôhō nì〔de〕

to spread a sheet over something ...の上にシーツを掛ける ...no ué nì shítsu wo kakérù

there's a canopy over the bed ベッドの上に天蓋がある béddò no ué nì teñgai ga arù

2 (on the other side of) ...の向こう側に

〔で〕 ...no mukṓgawa nī(dè)

the pub over the road 道路の向こう側
にあるパブ dṓrò no mukṓgawa ni arù
pábù

he jumped over the wall 彼は塀を飛
越えた kárè wa heí wò tobíkoèta

3 (more than) 以上 ijō

over 200 people came 200人以上の人
が来ました nihyákunìn íjò no hitó gà
kimáshìta

over and above ...の外に ...no hóka ni,
...に加えて ...ni kuwáetè

*this order is over and above what
we have already ordered* この注文は
これまでの注文への追加です konó chū-
mon wa koré madè no chūmòn e no
tsuíka desù

4 (during) ...の間 ...no áida

over the last few years 過去数年の間
kákò sūnèn no áida

over the winter 冬の間 fuyú nò aída

let's discuss it over dinner 夕食をし
ながら話し合いましょう yūshoku wò
shinágàra hanáshiaimashṓ

overall [*adj, n* ou'vǝ:rɔ:l *adv* ouvǝ:rɔ:l']
adj (length, cost etc) 全体の zeńtai no;
(general: study, survey) 全面的な zeńmenteki na

◆*adv* (view, survey etc) 全面的に zeńmenteki ni; (measure, paint) 全体に zeńtai ni

◆*n* (BRIT: woman's, child's, painter's)
上っ張り uwáppàri

overalls [ou'vǝ:rɔ:lz] *npl* オーバーオール
ōbāōrù

overawe [ouvǝ:rɔ:'] *vt* 威圧する iátsu suru

overbalance [ouvǝ:rbæl'ǝns] *vi* バラン
スを失う baránsu wo ushínau

overbearing [ouvǝ:rbe:'riŋ] *adj* (person,
behavior, manner) 横柄な ōhei na

overboard [ou'vǝ:rbɔ:rd] *adv* (NAUT):
to fall overboard 船から水に落ちる fu-
nè kara mizú ni ochírù

overbook [ou'vǝ:rbuk] *vt* 予約を取り過
ぎる yoyáku wo torísugiru

overcast [ou'vǝ:rkæst] *adj* (day, sky) 曇
った kumóttà

overcharge [ou'vǝ:rtʃɑ:rdʒ] *vt* ...に不当
な金額を請求する ...ni futṓ na kińgaku
wo seíkyū suru

overcoat [ou'vǝ:rkout] *n* オーバーコー
ト ōbākoto, オーバー ōbā

overcome [ouvǝ:rkʌm'] (*pt* **overcame** *pp*
overcome) *vt* (defeat: opponent, enemy)
...に勝つ ...ni katsù; (fig: difficulty, problem) 克服する kokúfuku suru

overcrowded [ouvǝ:rkrau'did] *adj*
(room, prison) 超満員の chṓman-in no;
(city) 過密な kamítsu na

overdo [ouvǝ:rdu:'] (*pt* **overdid** *pp* **over-
done**) *vt* (exaggerate: concern, interest)
誇張する kochṓ suru; (overcook) 焼き過
ぎる yakísugiru

to overdo it (work etc) やり過ぎる yarí-
sugirù

overdose [ou'vǝ:rdous] *n* (MED: dangerous dose) 危険量 kikénryō; (: fatal dose)
致死量 chíshìryō

overdraft [ou'vǝ:rdræft] *n* 当座借越 tṓ-
zakarikoshi

overdrawn [ouvǝ:rdrɔ:n'] *adj* (account)
借越した karíkoshi shita

overdue [ouvǝ:rdu:'] *adj* (late: person,
bus, train) 遅れている okúrete iru;
(change, reform etc) 待望の taíbō no

overestimate [ouvǝ:res'tǝmeit] *vt* (cost,
importance, time) 高く見積りすぎる ta-
kàku mitsúmorisugirù; (person's ability,
skill etc) 買いかぶる kaíkaburu

overexcited [ouvǝ:riksaí'tid] *adj* 過度に
興奮した kadò ni kṓfun shita

overflow [*vb* ouvǝ:rflou' *n* ou'vǝ:rflou]
vi (river) はん濫する hańran suru; (sink,
vase etc) あふれる afúrèru

◆*n* (also: **overflow pipe**) 放出パイプ hṓ-
shutsupaipu

overgrown [ouvǝ:rgroun'] *adj* (garden)
草がぼうぼうと生えた kusa ga bṓbō to
haèta

overhaul [*vb* ouvǝ:rhɔ:l' *n* ou'vǝ:rhɔ:l]
vt (engine, equipment etc) 分解検査する
buńkaikensa suru, オーバーホールする
ōbāhōru suru

◆*n* オーバーホール ōbāhōru

overhead

[adv ouvə:rhed' adj, n ou'və:rhed] adv
(above) 頭上に〔で〕zujô ni〔de〕; (in the
sky) 上空に〔で〕jôkû ni〔de〕
♦adj (lighting) 上からの ué kara no;
(cables, railway) 高架の kôka no
♦n (US) = **overheads**

overheads [ou'və:rhedz] npl (expenses)
経費 keíhi

overhear [ouvə:rhiə:r'] (pt, pp **over-heard**) vt 耳にする mimí ni suru

overheat [ouvə:rhi:t'] vi (engine) 過熱す
る kanétsu suru, オーバーヒートする ô-
bâhîto suru

overjoyed [ouvə:rdʒɔid'] adj 大喜びした
ôyôrokobi shita

overkill [ou'və:rkil] n やり過ぎ yarísugi

overland [ou'və:rlænd] adj (journey) 陸
路の rikúro no
♦adv (travel) 陸路で rikúro de

overlap [ouvə:rlæp'] vi (edges) 部分的に
重なる bubúnteki ni kasánaru, オーバー
ラップする ôbârappu suru; (fig: ideas,
activities etc) 部分的に重複する bubúnteki ni chôfuku suru, オーバーラップす
る ôbârappu suru

overleaf [ou'və:rli:f] adv ページの裏に
péji no urá ni

overload [ou'və:rloud] vt (vehicle) ...に積
み過ぎる ...ni tsumísugiru; (ELEC) ...に負
荷を掛け過ぎる ...ni fuká wo kakésugi-
ru; (fig: with work, problems etc) ...に負
担を掛け過ぎる ...ni fután wo kakésugi-
ru

overlook [ou'və:rluk] vt (have view
over) 見下ろす miórosu; (miss: by mistake) 見落す miótosu; (excuse, forgive)
見逃す minógasu

overnight [adv ouvə:rnait' adj ou'və:r-
nait] adv (during the whole night) 一晩中
hitóbànjū; (fig: suddenly) いつの間にか
itsù no ma ni ka
♦adj (bag, clothes) 1泊用の ippákuyô no
to stay overnight 一泊する ippáku suru

overpass [ou'və:rpæs] n 陸橋 ríkkyô

overpower [ouvə:rpau'ə:r] vt (person) 腕
力で抑え込む wañryoku de osáekomù;
(subj: emotion, anger etc) 圧倒する attô

suru

overpowering [ouvə:rpau'ə:riŋ] adj
(heat, stench) 圧倒する様な attô suru yô
na

overrate [ouvə:rreit'] vt (person, film,
book) 高く評価し過ぎる takáku hyôka
shisúgiru

override [ouvə:raid'] (pt **overrode** pp
overridden) vt (order) 無効にする mukô-
ni suru; (objection) 無視する mushî suru

overriding [ouvə:raid'iŋ] adj (importance) 最大の saídai no; (factor, consideration) 優先的な yūsénteki na

overrule [ouvə:ru:l'] vt (decision, claim,
person) 無効にする mukô ni suru; (per-
son) ...の提案を退ける ...no teían wo shirízokerù

overrun [ou'və:rʌn] (pt **overran** pp
overrun) vt (country) 侵略する shiñryaku suru; (time limit) 越える koéru

overseas [adv ouvə:rsi:z' adj ou'və:r-
si:z] adv (live, travel, work: abroad) 海外
に〔で〕kaígai ni〔de〕
♦adj (market, trade) 海外の kaígai no;
(student, visitor) 外国人の gaíkokujîn no

overshadow [ouvə:rʃæd'ou] vt (throw
shadow over: place, building etc) ...の上
にそびえる ...no ué ni sobíerù; (fig) ...の
影を薄くさせる ...no kagê wo usúku saseru

overshoot [ouvə:rʃu:t'] (pt, pp **overshot**)
vt (subj: plane, train, car etc) ...に止らず
に行き過ぎる ...ni tomárazu ni ikísugirù

oversight [ou'və:rsait] n 手落ち teôchi

oversleep [ouvə:rsli:p'] (pt, pp **overslept**)
vi 寝過ごす nesúgòsu, 寝坊する nebô su-
ru

overstate [ouvə:rsteit'] vt (exaggerate:
case, problem, importance) 誇張する ko-
chô suru

overstep [ouvə:rstep'] vt: to overstep
the mark (go too far) 行き過ぎをやる
ikísugi wo yaru

overt [ouvə:rt'] adj あからさまな akárasama na

overtake [ouvə:rteik'] (pt **overtook** pp
overtaken) vt (AUT) 追越す oíkòsu

overthrow [ouvə:rθrou'] vt (government, leader) 倒す taósù

overtime [ou'vəːrtaim] n 残業 zańgyō

overtone [ou'vəːrtoun] n (fig) 含み fukúmì

overture [ou'vəːrtʃəːr] n (MUS) 序曲 jokyōku; (fig) 申出 mōshìde

overturn [ouvəːrtəːrn'] vt (car, chair) 引っ繰り返す hikkúrikaèsu; (fig: decision, plan, ruling) 翻す hirúgaèsu; (: government, system) 倒す taósù

♦vi (car, train, boat etc) 転覆する teńpuku suru

overweight [ouvəːrweit'] adj (person) 太り過ぎの futórìsugi no

overwhelm [ouvəːrwelm'] vt 圧倒する attō suru

overwhelming [ouvəːrwel'miŋ] adj (victory, heat, feeling) 圧倒的な attōteki na

overwork [ouvəːrwəːrk'] n 働き過ぎ határakisugì, 過労 karō

overwrought [ou'vəːrɔːt'] adj 神経が高ぶった shińkei ga tákabuttà

owe [ou] vt: to owe someone something, to owe something to someone (money) ...に...を借りている ...ni ...wo karíte iru, ...に...を払う義務がある ...ni ...wo haráū gimù ga aru; (fig: gratitude, respect, loyalty) ...に...しなければならない ...ni ...shinákereba naranaì; (: life, talent, good looks etc) ...は...のおかげである ...wa ...no o-kagé de aru

owing to [ou'iŋ tuː] prep (because of) ...のために ...no tamé nì

owl [aul] n フクロウ fukúrō, ミミズク mìmìzuku

own [oun] vt (possess: house, land, car etc) 所有する shoyū suru, 保有する hoyū suru

♦adj (house, work, style etc) 自分の jibún no, 自分自身の jubúnjishìn no

a room of my own 自分の部屋 jibún no heyá

to get one's own back (take revenge) 復しゅうする fukushū suru

on one's own (alone) 自分で jibun de, 自分の力で jibún no chikára de

owner [ou'nəːr] n (gen) 所有者 shoyūsha, 持主 mōchìnushi, オーナー ōnā; (of shop)

主人 shujìn, 経営者 kéieìsha; (of pet) 飼主 kaínushi

ownership [ou'nəːrʃip] n (possession) 所有 shoyū

own up vi (admit: guilt, error) ...を認める ...wo mitómeru

ox [ɑːks] (pl oxen) n ウシ ushí◇通常去勢した牡ウシを指す tsujō kyoséi shita oùshi wo sasu

oxtail [ɑːks'teil] n: oxtail soup オックステールスープ okkùsutērusūpu

oxygen [ɑːk'sidʒən] n 酸素 sańso

oxygen mask/tent n 酸素マスク〔テント〕 sańsomasuku(tento)

oyster [ɔis'təːr] n カキ kaki

oz. abbr = ounce(s)

ozone [ou'zoun] n オゾン ozòn

ozone layer n オゾン層 ozònsō

P

p [piː] abbr = penny; pence

P.A. [piːei'] n abbr = personal assistant; public address system

p.a. abbr = per annum

pa [pɑː] (inf) n 父ちゃん tōchan, パパ pápà

pace [peis] n (step) 1歩 íppò; (distance) 歩幅 hohába; (speed) 早さ háyàsa, 速度 sókùdo, ペース pêsu

♦vi: to pace up and down (walk around angrily or impatiently) うろうろする úrờuro suru

to keep pace with (person) ...と足並をそろえる ...to ashínami wð soróerù

pacemaker [peis'meikəːr] n (MED) ペースメーカー pêsumèkā; (SPORT: also: pacesetter) ペースメーカー pêsumèkā

Pacific [pəsif'ik] n: the Pacific (Ocean) 太平洋 taíheìyō

pacifist [pæs'əfist] n 平和主義者 heíwashugìsha

pacify [pæs'əfai] vt (soothe: person) なだめる nadámerù; (: fears) 鎮める shizúmerù

pack [pæk] n (packet) 包み tsutsúmi; (US: of cigarettes) 1箱 hitóhàko; (group:

of hounds) 群れ muré; (: of people) グループ gúrūpu; (back pack) リュックサック ryukkúsakkù; (of cards) 1組 hitókùmi

♦*vt* (fill: box, container, suitcase etc) ...に詰込む ...ni tsumékomù; (cram: people, objects): **to pack into** ...を...に詰込む ...wo ...ni tsumékomù

to pack (one's bags) 荷造りをする nizúkuri wo suru

to pack someone off ...を追出す ...wo oídasù

pack it in! (*inf*: stop it!) やめなさい! yaménasai!

package [pæk'idʒ] *n* (parcel) 小包 kozútsumi; (*also*: **package deal**) 一括取引 ikkátsutorihìki

package holiday *n* = **package tour**

package tour *n* パッケージツアー pakkéjitsuà, パックツアー pakkútsuà

packed lunch [pækt-] *n* 弁当 beńtō

packet [pæk'it] *n* (box) 1箱 hitóhàko; (bag) 1袋 hitófùkuro

packing [pæk'iŋ] *n* (act) 詰込む事 tsumékomù kotó; (external: paper, plastic etc) 包装 hōsō

packing case *n* 木箱 kíbàko

pact [pækt] *n* 協定 kyōtei

pad [pæd] *n* (block of paper) 一つづり hitótsùzuri; (to prevent friction, damage) こん包材 koñpōzài; (in shoulders of dress, jacket etc) パッド páddò; (*inf*: home) 住い súmài

♦*vt* (SEWING: cushion, soft toy etc) ...に詰物をする ...ni tsumémòno wo suru

padding [pæd'iŋ] *n* (material) 詰物 tsumémòno

paddle [pæd'əl] *n* (oar) かい kâi, パドル pádòru; (*US*: for table tennis) ラケット rakéttò

♦*vt* (boat, canoe etc) こぐ kógù

♦*vi* (with feet) 水の中を歩く mizú no nakà wo arúkù

paddle steamer *n* (on river) 外輪船 gaírinsen

paddling pool [pæd'liŋ-] (*BRIT*) *n* (children's) 子供用プール kodómoyō pūru

paddock [pæd'ək] *n* (for horse: small field) 放牧場 hōbokujō; (: at race course)

パドック pádòkku

paddy field [pæd'i:-] *n* 水田 suíden, 田んぼ tañbo

padlock [pæd'lɑ:k] *n* (on door, bicycle etc) 錠 (前) jō(mae)

paediatrics [pi:di:æt'riks] (*BRIT*) *n* = **pediatrics**

pagan [pei'gən] *adj* (gods, festival, worship) 異教の ikyō no ◇キリスト教、ユダヤ教、イスラム教以外の宗教をさげすんで言う語 kirísutokyō, yudáyakyō, isúramukyō igài no shūkyō wo sagésuñde iú go

♦*n* (worshipper of pagan gods) 異教徒 ikyōto

page [peidʒ] *n* (of book, magazine, newspaper) ページ péji; (*also*: **page boy**) 花嫁付添いの少年 hanáyòmetsukisoi no shōnen

♦*vt* (in hotel etc) ボーイ bōi

pageant [pædʒ'ənt] *n* (historical procession, show) ページェント péjento

pageantry [pædʒ'əntri:] *n* 見世物 misémono

paid [peid] *pt, pp of* **pay**

♦*adj* (work) 有料の yūryo no; (staff, official) 有給の yūkyū no; (gunman, killer) 雇われた yatówaretà

a paid holiday 有給休暇 yūkyūkyūka

to put paid to (*BRIT*: end, destroy) ...を台無しにする ...wo daínashi ni surù

pail [peil] *n* (for milk, water etc) バケツ bakétsu

pain [pein] *n* (unpleasant physical sensation) 痛み itámi, 苦痛 kutsū; (*fig*: unhappiness) 苦しみ kurúshimi, 心痛 shiñtsū

to be in pain (person, animal) 苦痛を感じている kutsū wo kañjite irù, 苦しんでいる kurúshinde irù

to take pains to do something (make an effort) 苦心して...する kushín shite ...surù

pained [peind] *adj* (expression) 怒った okôttà

painful [pein'fəl] *adj* (back, wound, fracture etc) 痛い itái, 痛む itámù; (upsetting, unpleasant: sight etc) 痛々しい itáitashii; (memory) 不快な fukái na; (decision) 苦しい kurúshiî; (laborious: task, progress etc) 骨の折れる honé no orerù

painfully [pein'fəli:] adv (fig: very) 痛い程 itáihodo

painkiller [pein'kilər] n (aspirin, paracetamol etc) 鎮痛剤 chíntsūzai

painless [pein'lis] adj (operation, childbirth) 無痛の mutsū no

painstaking [peinz'teikiŋ] adj (work) 骨折れの honéore no; (person) 勤勉な kínben na

paint [peint] n (decorator's: for walls, doors etc) 塗料 toryố, ペンキ peñki, ペイント peínto; (artist's: oil paint, watercolor paint etc) 絵の具 e nó gu

♦vt (wall, door, house etc) ...にペンキを塗る ...ni peñki wo nurù; (picture, portrait) 描く kákù

to paint the door blue ドアに水色のペンキを塗る dóa ni mizúiro nò peñki wò nurù

paintbrush [peint'brʌʃ] n (decorator's) 刷毛 hakê, ブラシ búrashi; (artist's) 絵筆 éfùde

painter [pein'tər] n (artist) 画家 gaká; (decorator) ペンキ屋 peñkiya

painting [pein'tiŋ] n (activity: decorating) ペンキ塗り peñkinùri; (: art) 絵描き ekáki; (picture) 絵画 káìga

an oil painting 油絵 abúraè

paintwork [peint'wəːrk] n (painted parts) 塗装の部分 tosố no bubùn

pair [pe:r] n (of shoes, gloves etc) 対 tsuí

a pair of scissors はさみ hasámi

a pair of trousers ズボン zubóñ

pajamas [pədʒɑːm'əz] (US) npl パジャマ pájàma

Pakistan [pæk'istæn] n パキスタン pakísùtan

Pakistani [pæk'əstæn'iː] adj パキスタンの pakísùtan no

♦n パキスタン人 pakísutanjìn

pal [pæl] (inf) n (friend) 友達 tomódachi

palace [pæl'is] n (residence: of monarch) 宮殿 kyúden; (: of president etc) 官邸 kañtei; (: of Japanese emperor) 皇居 kōkyo, 御所 gósho

palatable [pæl'ətəbəl] adj (food, drink)

おいしい oíshiî

palate [pæl'it] n 口がい kốgai

palatial [pəlei'ʃəl] adj (surroundings, residence) 豪華な gốka na

palaver [pəlæv'əːr] n (US) 話し合い hanáshiai; (BRIT: inf: fuss) 大騒ぎ ốsawàgi

pale [peil] adj (whitish: color) 白っぽい shíroppoî; (: face) 青白い aójiroî, 青ざめた aốzametà; (: light) 薄暗い usúguraî

♦n: **beyond the pale** (unacceptable) 容認できない yốnin dekinài

Palestine [pæl'istain] n パレスチナ parésùchina

Palestinian [pælistin'iːən] adj パレスチナの parésùchina no

♦n パレスチナ人 parésuchinajìn

palette [pæl'it] n (ART: paint mixing board) パレット paréttð

palings [pei'liŋz] npl (fence) さく sakú

pall [pɔːl] n: **a pall of smoke** 一面の煙 ichímen no kemuri

♦vi ...が詰まらなくなる ...ga tsumáranakù naru, ...に飽きる ...ni akírù

pallet [pæl'it] n (for goods) パレット paréttð

pallid [pæl'id] adj (person, complexion) 青白い aójiroî

pallor [pæl'əːr] n そう白 sốhaku

palm [pɑːm] n (also: **palm tree**) ヤシ yáshì; (of hand) 手のひら tenóhìra

♦vt: **to palm something off on someone** (inf) ...に...をつかませる ...ni ...wo tsukámaserù

Palm Sunday n 枝の主日 edá nò shujítsu

palpable [pæl'pəbəl] adj (obvious: lie, difference etc) 明白な méhaku na

palpitations [pælpitei'ʃənz] npl (MED) 動き dốki

paltry [pɔːl'triː] adj (amount: tiny, insignificant) ささいな sásai na

pamper [pæm'pəːr] vt (cosset: person, animal) 甘やかす amáyakasù

pamphlet [pæm'flit] n (political, literary etc) 小冊子 shốsasshî, パンフレット páñfuretto

pan [pæn] n (CULIN: also: **saucepan**) 片

手なべ katátenabè; (: also: **frying pan**)
フライパン furáipan

panacea [pænəsi:'ə] n 万能薬 bańnōyàku

panache [pənǽʃ] n 気取り kidóri

Panama [pǽnəmɑː] n パナマ pánama

Panama Canal n: **the Panama Canal**
パナマ運河 panáma uṅga

pancake [pǽn'keik] n パンケーキ paṅ-
kēki, ホットケーキ hottókēki

pancreas [pǽn'kriːəs] n すい臓 suízō

panda [pǽn'də] n (ZOOL) ジャイアント
パンダ jaíantopaǹda

panda car (BRIT) n (police car) パトカ
ー patóka

pandemonium [pændəmou'niːəm] n
(noisy confusion) 大混乱 daíkoṅran

pander [pǽn'dəːr] vi: **to pander to** (person, whim, desire etc) ...に迎合する ...ni
geígo suru

pane [pein] n (of glass) 窓ガラス madó-
garàsu

panel [pǽn'əl] n (oblong piece: of wood,
metal, glass etc) 羽目板 haméita, パネル
pánèru; (group of judges, experts etc)
...の一団 ...no ichídàn, パネル pánèru

paneling [pǽn'əliŋ] (BRIT **panelling**) n
羽目板 haméita ◇総称 sōshō

pang [pæŋ] n: **a pang of regret** 悔恨の
情 kaíkon nò jō
hunger pangs (physical pain) 激しい空
腹感 hagéshiì kúfukukan

panic [pǽn'ik] n (uncontrollable terror,
anxiety) パニック pánìkku
♦vi (person) うろたえる urótaerù;
(crowd) パニック状態になる paníkkujō-
tai ni nárù

panicky [pǽn'iki] adj (person) うろたえ
る urótaerù

panic-stricken [pǽn'ikstrikən] adj
(person, face) パニックに陥った pánìkku
ni ochíttà

panorama [pænəræm'ə] n (view) 全景
zeíkei, パノラマ panórama

pansy [pǽn'ziː] n (BOT) サンシキスミレ
sańshikisumìre, パンジー páǹjī; (inf:
pej) 弱虫 yowámushi

pant [pænt] vi (gasp: person, animal) あ
えぐ aégù

panther [pǽn'θəːr] n ヒョウ hyō

panties [pǽn'tiːz] npl パンティー páǹtī

pantomime [pǽn'təmaim] (BRIT) n ク
リスマスミュージカル kurísumasu myū-
jikaru

pantry [pǽn'triː] n 食料室 shokúryōshì-
tsu, パントリー páǹtorī

pants [pænts] n (BRIT: underwear:
woman's) パンティー páǹtī; (: man's) パ
ンツ páǹtsu; (US: trousers) ズボン zubóǹ

panty hose n パンティーストッキング paǹ-
tísutokkiǹgu

papal [pei'pəl] adj ローマ法王の rōmahō-
ṑ no

paper [pei'pəːr] n (gen) 紙 kamí; (also:
newspaper) 新聞 shiǹbun; (exam) 試験
shikén; (academic essay) 論文 roǹbun, ペ
ーパー pēpā; (also: **wallpaper**) 壁紙 kabégami
♦adj (made from paper: hat, plane etc)
紙の kamí no
♦vt (room: with wallpaper) ...に壁紙を張
る ...ni kabégami wò hárù

paperback [pei'pəːrbæk] n ペーパーバッ
ク pēpábakku

paper bag n 紙袋 kamíbukùro

paper clip n クリップ kuríppù

paper hankie n ティッシュ tísshù

papers [pei'pəːrz] npl (documents) 書類
shórùi; (also: **identity papers**) 身分証明
書 mibúnshōmeishò

paperweight [pei'pəːrweit] n 文鎮 buń-
chin

paperwork [pei'pəːrwəːrk] n (in office:
dealing with letters, reports etc) 机上の
事務 kijō no jimù, ペーパーワーク pēpā-
wàku

papier-mâché [pei'pəːrməʃei'] n 張り子
haríko

paprika [pɑːpriː'kə] n パプリカ papúrìka

par [pɑːr] n (equality of value) 同等 dōtō;
(GOLF) 基準打数 kijúndasù, パー pá
to be on a par with (be equal with)
...と同等である ...to dōtō de arù

parable [pær'əbəl] n たとえ話 tatóeba-
nàshi

parachute [pær'əʃuːt] n 落下傘 rakkásàn,
パラシュート paráshūto

parade [pəreid'] n (public procession) パレード parédð
♦vt (show off: wealth, knowledge etc) 見せびらかす misébirakasù
♦vi (MIL) 行進する kốshin suru

paradise [pær'ədais] n (REL: heaven, nirvana etc: also fig) 天国 téñgoku, 極楽 gokúraku

paradox [pær'əda:ks] n (thing, statement) 逆説 gyakúsetsu

paradoxically [pærəda:k'sikli:] adv 逆説的に言えば gyakúsetsuteki nì iébà

paraffin [pær'əfin] (BRIT) n (also: paraffin oil) 灯油 tốyu

paragon [pær'əga:n] n (of honesty, virtue etc) 模範 mohán, かがみ kagámi

paragraph [pær'əgræf] n 段落 dañrakù, パラグラフ parágùrafu

Paraguay [pær'əgwei] n パラグアイ parágùai

parallel [pær'əlel] adj (lines, walls, streets etc) 平行の heíkô no; (fig: similar) 似た nitá
♦n (line) 平行線 heíkôsen; (surface) 平行面 heíkômen; (GEO) 緯度線 idósèn; (fig: similarity) 似た所 nitá tokoro

paralysis [pəræl'isis] n (MED) 麻ひ máhì

paralyze [pær'əlaiz] vt (MED) 麻ひさせる máhì saséru; (fig: organization, production etc) 麻ひ状態にする mahíjðtai ni suru

parameters [pəræm'itə:rz] npl (fig) 限定要素 geñteiyôso

paramilitary [pærəmil'ite:ri:] adj (organization, operations) 準軍事的な juñguñjiteki na

paramount [pær'əmaunt] adj: of paramount importance 極めて重要な kiwámète júyô na

paranoia [pærənɔi'ə] n 被害妄想 higáimôsð

paranoid [pær'ənɔid] adj (person, feeling) 被害妄想の higáimôsô no

parapet [pær'əpit] n 欄干 rañkan

paraphernalia [pærəfə:rneil'jə] n (gear) 道具 dôgu

paraphrase [pær'əfreiz] vt (poem, article etc) やさしく言替える yasáshikù iíkaerù

paraplegic [pærəpli:'dʒik] n 下半身麻ひ患者 kahánshinmahi kañja

parasite [pær'əsait] n (insect: also fig: person) 寄生虫 kiséichū; (plant) 寄生植物 kiséishokùbutsu

parasol [pær'əsɔ:l] n 日傘 higasa, パラソル páràsoru

paratrooper [pær'ətru:pə:r] n (MIL) 落下傘兵 rakkásanhei

parcel [pɑ:r'səl] n (package) 小包 kozútsùmi
♦vt (object, purchases: also: parcel up) 小包にする kozútsùmi ni suru

parch [pɑ:rtʃ] vt (land) 干上がらす hiágarasu; (crops) からからに枯らす karákara ni karasù

parched [pɑ:rtʃt] adj (person) のどがからからの nódð ga karákara no

parchment [pɑ:rtʃ'mənt] n (animal skin) 羊皮紙 yôhishì; (thick paper) 硫酸紙 ryūsanshì

pardon [pɑ:r'dən] n (LAW) 赦免 shamén
♦vt (forgive: person, sin, error etc) 許す yurúsù

pardon me!, I beg your pardon! (I'm sorry) 済みません sumímaseñ, 失礼しました shitsúrèi shimashita, ご免なさい gomén nasaì

(I beg your) pardon?, pardon me? (what did you say?) もう一度言って下さい mố ichido ittè kudásaì

parent [pe:r'ənt] n (mother or father) 親 oyá; (mother) 母親 haháoya; (father) 父親 chichíoya

parental [pəren'təl] adj (love, control, guidance etc) 親の oyá no

parenthesis [pəren'θəsis] (pl parentheses) n 括弧 kákkð

parents [pe:r'ənts] npl (mother and father) 両親 ryôshin

Paris [pær'is] n パリ párì

parish [pær'iʃ] n (REL) 教区 kyốkù; (BRIT: civil) 行政教区 gyôseikyôku

Parisian [pəriʒ'ən] adj パリの párì no
♦n パリっ子 paríkkð

parity [pær'iti:] n (equality: of pay, conditions etc) 平等 byódō

park [pɑːrk] *n* (public) 公園 kṓen

♦*vt* (AUT) 駐車させる chūsha saséru

♦*vi* (AUT) 駐車する chūsha suru

parka [pɑːrkə] *n* パーカ pákà, アノラック anórakkù

parking [pɑːrkiŋ] *n* 駐車 chūsha

「*no parking*」駐車禁止 chūshakinshi

parking lot (*US*) *n* 駐車場 chūshajō

parking meter *n* パーキングメーター pākingumḗtā

parking ticket *n* (fine) 駐車違反切符 chūshaihan kippù

parlance [pɑːrləns] *n* 用語 yṓgo

parliament [pɑːrləmənt] (*BRIT*) *n* (institution) 議会 gíkài

parliamentary [pɑːrləmenˈtəriː] *adj* (business, behavior etc) 議会の gíkài no

parlor [pɑːrləːr] (*BRIT* **parlour**) *n* (in house) 居間 imá, 応接間 ṓsetsuma

parochial [pərouˈkiːəl] (*pej*) *adj* (person, attitude) 偏狭な heñkyō na

parody [pærˈədiː] *n* (THEATER, LITERATURE, MUS) パロディー párōdī

parole [pəroulˈ] *n*: **on parole** (LAW) 仮釈放で karíshakuhō de

paroxysm [pærˈəksizəm] *n* (of rage, jealousy, laughter) 爆発 bakúhatsu

parquet [pɑːrkeiˈ] *n*: **parquet floor(ing)** 寄せ木張りの床 yoségibari nò yuká

parrot [pærˈət] *n* オウム ṓmu

parry [pærˈiː] *vt* (blow) かわす kawásu

parsimonious [pɑːrsəmouˈniːəs] *adj* けちな kechí na

parsley [pɑːrzˈliː] *n* パセリ páseri

parsnip [pɑːrsˈnip] *n* 白にんじん shironinjin, パースニップ pásunippù

parson [pɑːrˈsən] *n* (REL) 牧師 bókùshi

part [pɑːrt] *n* (section, division) 部分 búbùn; (of machine, vehicle) 部品 buhín; (THEATER, CINEMA etc: role) 役 yakú; (PRESS, RADIO, TV: of serial) 第 ...部 dáì...bù; (*US*: in hair) 分け目 wakéme

♦*adv* = **partly**

♦*vt* (separate: people, objects, hair) 分ける wakérù

♦*vi* (people: leave each other) 別れる wákarerù; (crowd) 道を開ける michí wo akerù

to take part in (participate in) ...に参加する ...ni sañka suru

to take something in good part ...を怒らない ...wo okóranaì

to take someone's part (support) ...の肩を持つ ...no kátà wo mótsù

for my part 私としては watákushi toshite wà

for the most part (usually, generally) ほとんどは hotóndo wa

part exchange *n*: **in part exchange** (*BRIT*: COMM) 下取りで shitádòri de

partial [pɑːrʃəl] *adj* (not complete: victory, support, solution) 部分的な bubúnteki na

to be partial to (like: person, food, drink etc) ...が大好きである ...ga daísuki de arù

participant [pɑːrtisˈəpənt] *n* (in competition, debate, campaign etc) 参加者 sañkashà

participate [pɑːrtisˈəpeit] *vi*: **to participate in** (competition, debate, campaign etc) ...に参加する ...ni sañka suru

participation [pɑːrtisəpeiˈʃən] *n* (in competition, debate, campaign etc) 参加 sañka

participle [pɑːrˈtisipəl] *n* (LING) 分詞 búnshi

particle [pɑːrˈtikəl] *n* (tiny piece: *gen*) 粒子 ryúshi; (: of dust) 一片 ippéñ; (of metal) 砕片 saíhen; (of food) 粒 tsúbù

particular [pərtikˈjələːr] *adj* (distinct from others: person, time, place etc) 特定の tokútei no; (special) 特別な tokúbetsu na; (fussy, demanding) やかましい yakámashiì

in particular 特に tókù ni

particularly [pərtikˈjələːrliː] *adv* 特に tókù ni

particulars [pərtikˈjələːrz] *npl* (facts) 詳細 shōsai; (personal details) 経歴 keíreki

parting [pɑːrtiŋ] *n* (action) 分ける事 wakérù kotó; (farewell) 別れ wakáre;

(*BRIT*: hair) 分け目 wakéme

♦*adj* (words, gift etc) 別れの wakáre no

partisan [pɑ:r'tizən] *adj* (politics, views) 党派心の tóhashìn no

♦*n* (supporter) 支援者 shiénsha; (fighter) パルチザン parúchizàn

partition [pɑːrtíʃən] *n* (wall, screen) 間仕切 majíkìri; (POL: of country) 分割 buñkatsu

partly [pɑːrt'liː] *adv* (to some extent) 幾分か ikúbun ka

partner [pɑːrt'nəːr] *n* (wife, husband) 配偶者 haígùsha; (girlfriend, boyfriend) 交際の相手 kōsai nò aíte; (COMM) 共同経営者 kyódōkeieìsha; (SPORT) パートナー pátonā; (at dance) 相手 aíte

partnership [pɑːrt'nəːrʃip] *n* (COMM) 共同経営事業 kyódōkeieijigyò; (POL etc) 協力 kyốryoku

partridge [pɑːr'tridʒ] *n* ウズラ uzúra

part-time [pɑːrt'taim] *adj* (work, staff) 非常勤の hijōkin no, パートタイムの pátotaìmu no

♦*adv* (work, study) パートタイムで pátotaìmu de

part with *vt fus* (money, possessions) ...を手放す ...wo tebánasù

party [pɑːr'tiː] *n* (POL) 政党 seftō; (celebration, social event) パーティ pấti; (group of people) 一行 ikkṓ, パーティ pấti; (LAW) 当事者 tōjìsha; (individual) 人 hitó

♦*cpd* (POL) 党の tō no

party dress *n* パーティドレス pấtidòresu

party line *n* (TEL) 共同線 kyódōsen

pass [pæs] *vt* (spend: time) 過ごす sugósù; (hand over: salt, glass, newspaper etc) 渡す watásù; (go past: place) 通り過ぎる tōrisugirù; (overtake: car, person etc) 追越す oíkosù; (exam) ...に合格する ...ni gṓkaku suru; (approve: law, proposal) 可決する kakétsu suru

♦*vi* (go past) 通る tōrù; (in exam) 合格する gṓkaku suru, パスする pásù suru

♦*n* (permit) 許可証 kyokáshṓ; (membership card) 会員証 kaíinshṓ; (in mountains) 峠 tṓge; (SPORT) パス pásù;

(SCOL: *also*: **pass mark**): **to get a pass in** ...で及第する ...de kyūdai suru, ...でパスする ...de pásù suru

to pass something through something ...を...に通す ...wo ...ni tōsu

to make a pass at someone (*inf*) ...にモーションを掛ける ...ni mōshon wo kakérù

passable [pæs'əbəl] *adj* (road) 通行できる tsūkō dekirù; (acceptable: work) まずまずの mázùmazu no

passage [pæs'idʒ] *n* (*also*: **passageway**: indoors) 廊下 rōka; (: outdoors) 通路 tsūro; (in book) 一節 issétsu; (ANAT): **the nasal passages** 鼻こう道 bikṓdō; (act of passing) 通過 tsūka; (journey: on boat) 船旅 funátabi

pass away *vi* (die) 死ぬ shinú

passbook [pæs'buk] *n* 銀行通帳 giñkōtsūchō

pass by *vi* (go past) ...のそばを通る ...no sóbà wo tōrù

♦*vt* (ignore) 無視する múshì suru

passenger [pæs'indʒəːr] *n* (in car, boat, plane etc) 乗客 jōkyaku

passer-by [pæsəːrbai'] *n* 通行人 tsūkōnin

pass for *vt fus* ...で通る ...de tōru

passing [pæs'iŋ] *adj* (fleeting: moment, glimpse, thought etc) 束の間の tsuká no ma no

in passing (incidentally) ついでに tsuíde ni

passing place *n* (AUT) 待避所 taíhijo

passion [pæʃ'ən] *n* (love: for person) 情欲 jōyoku; (*fig*: for cars, football, politics etc) 熱狂 nekkyṓ, マニア mánìa

passionate [pæʃ'ənit] *adj* (affair, embrace, person etc) 情熱的な jōnetsuteki na

passive [pæs'iv] *adj* (person, resistance) 消極的な shōkyokuteki na; (LING) 受動態の judṓtai no, 受け身の ukémi no

pass on *vt* (news, object) 伝える tsutáerù; (illness) 移す utsúsù

pass out *vi* (faint) 気絶する kizétsu suru

Passover [pæs'ouvəːr] *n* 過越し祭 sugíkòshisai

passport [pæs'pɔːrt] *n* (official document) 旅券 ryokén, パスポート pasúpôto

passport control n 出入国管理所 shutsúnyūkoku kañrijo

pass up vt (opportunity) 逃す nogásù

password [pǽs'wərd] n (secret word, phrase) 合言葉 aíkotòba, パスワード pasúwâdo

past [pǽst] prep (drive, walk, run: in front of) ...を通り過ぎて ...wo tôrisugite; (: beyond: also in time: later than) ...を過ぎて ...wo sugíte

◆adj (previous: government, monarch etc) 過去の kákò no; (: week, month etc) この前の konó maè no, 先... señ...

◆n (period and events prior to the present: also of person) 過去 kákò

he's past forty (older than) 彼は40才を過ぎている kárè wa yoñjussaí wo sugíte irù

ten/quarter past eight 8時10分〔15分〕過ぎ hachíji juppùn〔jûgofun〕sugí

for the past few/3 days この数日〔3日〕の間 konó sûjitsu(mikkà) no aída

pasta [pɑːs'tə] n パスタ pásùta

paste [peist] n (wet mixture) 練り物 nerímòno; (glue) のり norí; (CULIN: fish, meat, tomato etc paste) ペースト pêsuto

◆vt (stick: paper, label, poster etc) 張る harú

pastel [pæstel'] adj (color) パステルの pásùteru no

pasteurized [pǽs'tʃəraizd] adj (milk, cream) 低温殺菌された teíonsakkìn sareta

pastille [pǽsti:l'] n (sweet) ドロップ dôrõppu

pastime [pǽs'taim] n (hobby) 趣味 shúmì

pastoral [pǽs'tə:rəl] adj (REL: duties, activities) 牧師としての bókùshi toshite no

pastry [peis'tri:] n (dough) 生地 kíjî; (cake) 洋菓子 yôgashi, ケーキ kêki

pasture [pǽs'tʃə:r] n (grassland) 牧場 bokújõ

pasty [n pæs'ti: adj peis'ti:] n (meat and vegetable pie) ミートパイ mítopài

◆adj (complexion, face) 青ざめた aóza-

metã

pat [pǽt] vt (with hand: dog, someone's back etc) 軽くたたく karúku tatákù

patch [pǽtʃ] n (piece of material) 継ぎ tsugí; (also: **eye patch**) 眼帯 gañtai; (area: damp, bald, black etc) 一部 ichíbu; (repair: on tire etc) 継ぎはぎ tsugíhagi

◆vt (clothes) ...に継ぎを当てる ...ni tsugí wo aterù

to go through a bad patch 不運の時期に合う fúùn no jíkì ni áù

patch up vt (mend temporarily) 応急的に直す ôkyūteki ni naosù; (quarrel) ...をやめて仲直りする ...wo yamétè nakánaori surù

patchwork [pǽtʃ'wə:rk] n (SEWING) パッチワーク patchíwâku

patchy [pǽtʃ'i:] adj (uneven: color) むらの多い murá no ôi; (incomplete: information, knowledge etc) 不完全な fukánzen na

pâté [pɑːtei'] n パテ pátê ◇肉、魚などを香辛料とすり合せて蒸焼きにして冷ました物 nikú, sakana nadò wo kôshiñryō to suríawasetè mushíyaki ni shitè samáshita monò

patent [pǽt'ənt] n (COMM) 特許 tôkkyo

◆vt (COMM) ...の特許を取る ...no tôkkyo wo tôrù

◆adj (obvious) 明白な meíhaku na

patent leather n: **patent leather shoes** エナメル靴 enámerugùtsu

paternal [pətər'nəl] adj (love, duty) 父親の chichíoya no; (grandmother etc) 父方の chichígata no

paternity [pətər'niti:] n (of child) 父親である事 chichíoya de arù kotó

path [pǽθ] n (trail, track) 小道 kómìchi; (concrete path, gravel path etc) 道 michí; (of planet, missile) 軌道 kidô

pathetic [pəθet'ik] adj (pitiful: sight, cries) 哀れな áwàre na; (very bad) 哀れな程悪い áwàre na hódò warui

pathological [pæθəlɑ:dʒ'ikəl] adj (liar, hatred) 病的な byôteki na; (of pathology: work) 病理の byôri no

pathology [pəθɑ:l'ədʒi:] n (medical field) 病理学 byôrigàku

pathos [peiˈθɑːs] n 悲哀 hiái

pathway [pæθˈwei] n (path) 歩道 hodố

patience [peiˈʃəns] n (personal quality) 忍耐 níntai; (BRIT: CARDS) 一人トランプ hitóritoraṅpu

patient [peiˈʃənt] n (MED) 患者 kañja
♦adj (person) 忍耐強い níñtaizuyoỉ

patio [pætˈiːou] n テラス tếrasu

patriot [peiˈtriːət] n 愛国者 aíkokushà

patriotic [peitriːɑːtˈik] adj (person) 愛国心の強い aíkokushìn no tsuyoỉ; (song, speech etc) 愛国の aíkoku no

patriotism [peiˈtriːətizəm] n 愛国心 aíkokushìn

patrol [pətroulˈ] n (MIL, POLICE) 巡回 juñkai, パトロール patốrồru
♦vt (MIL, POLICE: city, streets etc) 巡回する juñkai suru, パトロールする patốrồru suru

patrol car n (POLICE) パトカー patókằ

patrolman [pətroulˈmən] (pl patrolmen: US) n (POLICE) 巡査 júñsa

patron [peiˈtrən] n (customer, client) 客 kyakú; (benefactor: of charity) 後援者 kốeñsha
patron of the arts 芸術のパトロン geíjùtsu no pátòron

patronage [peiˈtrənidʒ] n (of artist, charity etc) 後援 kốen

patronize [peiˈtrənaiz] vt (pej: look down on) 尊大にあしらう soñdai nì ashíraừ; (artist, writer, musician) 後援する kốen suru; (shop, club, firm) ひいきにする hiíki ni surù

patron saint n (REL) 守護聖人 shugố-seijìn

patter [pætˈəːr] n (sound: of feet) ぱたぱたという音 pátàpata to iú oto; (of rain) パラパラという音 páràpara to iú otò; (sales talk) 売込み口上 uríkomikòjò
♦vi (footsteps) ぱたぱたと歩く pátàpata to arúkừ; (rain) ぱらぱらと降る páràpara to fúrù

pattern [pætˈəːrn] n (design) 模様 moyố; (SEWING) 型紙 katágami, パターン patấñ

paunch [pɔːntʃ] n 太鼓腹 taíkobara

pauper [pɔːˈpəːr] n 貧乏人 biñbốnin

pause [pɔːz] n (temporary halt) 休止 kyúshi, ポーズ pồzu
♦vi (stop temporarily) 休止する kyúshi suru; (: while speaking) 間を置く má wò okú

pave [peiv] vt (street, yard etc) 舗装する hosố suru
to pave the way for (fig) ...を可能にする ...wo kanố ni suru

pavement [peivˈmənt] n (US) 路面 romén; (BRIT) 歩道 hodố

pavilion [pəvilˈjən] n (BRIT: SPORT) 選手更衣所 señshukồijò

paving [peiˈviŋ] n (material) 舗装材 hosố-zai

paving stone n 敷石 shikíishi

paw [pɔː] n (of animal) 足 ashí

pawn [pɔːn] n (CHESS) ポーン pồn; (fig) 操り人形 ayátsuriniñgyò
♦vt 質に入れる shichí ni irerù

pawnbroker [pɔːnˈbroukəːr] n 質屋 shi-chíyà

pawnshop [pɔːnˈʃɑːp] n 質屋 shichíyà

pay [pei] n (wage, salary etc) 給料 kyū́ryō
♦vb (pt, pp paid)
♦vt (sum of money, debt, bill, wage) 払う haraú
♦vi (be profitable) 利益になる ríèki ni nárù
to pay attention (to) (...に) 注意する (...ni) chū́i suru
to pay someone a visit ...を訪問する ...wo hốmon suru
to pay one's respects to someone ...にあいさつをする ...ni aísatsu wo suru

payable [peiˈəbəl] adj (sum of money) 支払うべき shiháraubeki
payable to bearer (check) 持参人払いの jisáñninbaraỉ no

pay back vt (money) 返す kaésù; (person) ...に仕返しをする ...ni shikáeshi wò suru

payday [peiˈdei] n 給料日 kyúryòbi

payee [peiiːˈ] n (of check, postal order) 受取人 ukétorinìn

pay envelope (US) n 給料袋 kyúryòbu-kùro

pay for vt fus (purchases) ...の代金を払う ...no daíkin wò haráù; (fig) 償う tsugúnaù

pay in vt (money, check etc) 預け入れる azúkeirerù, 入金する nyúkin suru

payment [pei'mənt] n (act) 支払い shiháraì; (amount of money) 支払い金額 sihárikiñgaku

a monthly payment 月賦 géppù

pay off vt (debt) 返済する heñsai suru; (person: with bribe etc) 買収する baíshū suru

♦vi (scheme, decision) 成功する seíkō suru

pay packet (BRIT) n = **pay envelope**

pay phone n 公衆電話 kōshūdeñwa

payroll [pei'roul] n 従業員名簿 jūgyōinmeìbo

pay slip n 給料明細書 kyūryōmeisaishò

pay up vt 払う haráù

PC [pi:si:'] n abbr = **personal computer**; (BRIT: = _police constable_) 巡査 júñsa

p.c. abbr = **per cent**

pea [pi:] n エンドウマメ eñdōmame

peace [pi:s] n (not war) 平和 heíwa; (calm: of place, surroundings) 静けさ shizúkesà; (: personal) 心の平和 kokórò no heíwa

peaceful [pi:s'fəl] adj (calm: place, time) 静寂な seíjaku na; (: person) 穏和な o-ñwa na

peach [pi:tʃ] n モモ momó

peacock [pi:'kɑːk] n クジャク kujáku

peak [pi:k] n (of mountain: top) 頂上 chōjō; (of cap) つば tsúbà; (fig: physical, intellectual etc) 頂点 chōten, ピーク pīku

peak hours npl ピーク時 pīkujì

peak period n ピーク時 pīkuji

peal [pi:l] n (of bells) 響き hibíki

peal of laughter 大きな笑い声 ōkina waráigoè

peanut [pi:'nʌt] n 落花生 rakkásèi, ピーナッツ pínattsù

peanut butter n ピーナッツバター pínattsubatà

pear [pe:r] n セイヨウナシ seíyōnashì

pearl [pə:rl] n 真珠 shíñju, パール pāru

peasant [pez'ənt] n 百姓 hyakúshò, 農夫 nōfu

peat [pi:t] n 泥炭 deítan

pebble [peb'əl] n 小石 koíshi

peck [pek] vt (also: **peck at**: subj: bird) つつく tsutsúkù

♦n (of bird) つつく事 tsutsúkù kotó; (kiss) 軽いキス karúi kísù

pecking order [pek'iŋ-] n (fig: hierarchy) 序列 jorétsu

peckish [pek'iʃ] (BRIT: inf) adj (hungry): _to be peckish_ おなかがすいた onáka ga suità

peculiar [pikju:l'jə:r] adj (strange: person, taste, shape etc) 変った kawátta; (belonging exclusively): _peculiar to_ 独特な dokútoku na

peculiarity [pikju:li:ær'iti:] n (strange habit, characteristic) 癖 kusé; (distinctive feature: of person, place etc) 特徴 tokúchō

pedal [ped'əl] n (on bicycle, car, machine) ペダル pédàru

♦vi (on bicycle) こぐ kógù

pedantic [pədæn'tik] adj げん学的な geñgakuteki na

peddler [ped'lə:r] n (also: **drug peddler**) 麻薬の売人 mayáku nò baínin

pedestal [ped'istəl] n 台座 daíza

pedestrian [pədes'tri:ən] n 歩行者 hokōshà

♦adj 歩行者の hokōshà no

pedestrian crossing (BRIT) n 横断歩道 ōdanhodō

pediatrics [pi:di:æt'riks] (BRIT **paediatrics**) n (hospital department) 小児科 shōnika; (subject) 小児科学 shōnikagàku

pedigree [ped'əgri:] n (of animal) 血統 kettō; (fig: background) 経歴 keíreki

♦cpd (animal) 純血の juñketsu no

pee [pi:] (inf) vi おしっこする o-shíkkò suru

peek [pi:k] vi のぞく nozóku

peel [pi:l] n (of orange, apple, potato) 皮 kawá

♦vt (vegetables, fruit) ...の皮をむく ...no kawá wo mukú

♦vi (paint, wallpaper) はげる hagérù; (skin) むける mukérù

peep [pi:p] *n* (look) のぞき見 nozōkimi; (sound) 鳴き声 nakígoè
♦*vi* (look) のぞく nozóku

peephole [pi:p'houl] *n* のぞき穴 nozōkiàna

peep out *vi* (be visible) のぞく nozóku

peer [pi:r] *vi*: **to peer at** ...をじっと見る ...wo jíttŏ mírŭ
♦*n* (noble) 貴族 kízŏku; (equal) 同等の人 dốtŏ nŏ hitŏ; (contemporary) 同輩 dốhai

peerage [pi:'ridʒ] *n* (rank) 貴族の地位 kízŏku no chíi

peeved [pi:vd] *adj* (annoyed) 怒った okóttà

peevish [pi:'viʃ] *adj* (bad-tempered) 機嫌の悪い kigén nŏ warúì

peg [peg] *n* (hook, knob: for coat etc) フック fúkkù; (BRIT: also: **clothes peg**) 洗濯ばさみ seńtakubasàmi

pejorative [pidʒɔːr'ətiv] *adj* (word, expression) 軽べつ的な keíbetsuteki na

Peking [pi:kiŋ'] *n* 北京 pékìn

Peking(g)ese [pi:kəni:z'] *n* (dog) ペキニーズ pekínìzu

pelican [pel'ikən] *n* (ZOOL) ペリカン perîkàn

pelican crossing (BRIT) *n* (AUT) 押しボタン式信号 oshíbotanshiki shíñgō

pellet [pel'it] *n* (of paper, mud etc) 丸めた球 marúmeta tamà; (also: **shotgun pellet**) 散弾銃の弾 sańdañjū no tamá

pelt [pelt] *vt*: **to pelt someone with something** ...に...を浴びせ掛ける ...ni ...wo abísekakerù
♦*vi* (rain) 激しく降る hagéshikù fúrù; (inf: run) 駆ける kakérù
♦*n* (animal skin) 毛皮 kegáwa

pelvis [pel'vis] *n* 骨盤 kotsúbàn

pen [pen] *n* (for writing: fountain pen, ballpoint pen) ペン péń; (: felt-tip pen etc) サインペン saínpen; (enclosure: for sheep, pigs etc) 囲い kakói

penal [pi:'nəl] *adj* (colony, institution) 刑罰の keíbatsu no; (system, code, reform) 刑法の keíhō no

penalize [pi:'nəlaiz] *vt* (punish) 罰する bassúrù; (: SPORT) ...にペナルティーを科する ...ni penárutī wo kasúrù

penalty [pen'əlti:] *n* (punishment) 罰 bátsù; (fine) 罰金 bakkín; (SPORT) ペナルティー penárutī

penalty (kick) *n* (RUGBY, SOCCER) ペナルティーキック penárutī kikkù

penance [pen'əns] *n* 償い tsugúnai

pence [pens] *pl of* **penny**

pencil [pen'səl] *n* (for writing, drawing) 鉛筆 eńpitsu

pencil case *n* 筆入れ fudéîre

pencil sharpener *n* 鉛筆削り eńpitsukezùri, シャープナー shāpunà

pendant [pen'dənt] *n* ペンダント péñdanto

pending [pen'diŋ] *prep* ...を待つ間 ...wo mátsù aída
♦*adj* (business) 未決の mikétsu no; (lawsuit) 審理中の shińrichū no; (exam) 差迫った sashísemattà

pendulum [pen'dʒələm] *n* (of clock) 振子 furíko

penetrate [pen'itreit] *vt* (subj: person: enemy territory) ...に侵入する ...ni shińnyū suru; (forest etc) ...に入り込む ...ni haírikomù; (: water etc) 染込む shimíkomù; (: light) 通る tŏru

penetrating [pen'itreitiŋ] *adj* (sound, glance, mind, observation) 鋭い surúdoì

penetration [penitrei'ʃən] *n* (action) 入り込む事 haírikomù kotó

penfriend [pen'frend] (BRIT) *n* = **pen pal**

penguin [pen'gwin] *n* ペンギン péñgin

penicillin [penisil'in] *n* ペニシリン peníshirin

peninsula [pənin'sələ] *n* 半島 hańtō

penis [pi:'nis] *n* 陰茎 ińkei, ペニス pénìs

penitent [pen'itənt] *adj* (person: very sorry) 後悔している kốkai shite irù

penitentiary [peniten'tʃɔːri:] (US) *n* 刑務所 keímushò

penknife [pen'naif] *n* ペンナイフ peńnaìfu

pen name *n* ペンネーム peńnèmu

penniless [pen'i:lis] *adj* (person) 一文なしの ichímoñnashi no

penny [pen'i:] (*pl* **pennies** or BRIT **pence**) *n* (US) ペニ pénì, セント séñto;

(*BRIT*: after 1971: = one hundredth of a pound) ペニ péni

pen pal *n* ペンパル pénparu, ペンフレンド penfuréndo

pension [pen'tʃən] *n* (state benefit) 年金 nénkin; (company pension etc) 恩給 oñkyū

pensioner [pen'tʃənəːr] (*BRIT*) *n* (old-age pensioner) 年金で生活する老人 nénkin dè sefkatsu surù rōjin, 年金暮らしの人 nefkinguràshi no hitó

pension fund *n* 年金基金 nénkinkikìn

pensive [pen'siv] *adj* (person, expression etc) 考え込んだ kañgaekoñda

pentagon [pen'təgɑːn] *n*: *the Pentagon* (*US*: POL) 国防総省 kokúbōsōshō, ペンタゴン peftágon

Pentecost [pen'təkɔːst] *n* 聖霊降臨祭 seĩreikōrìnsai

penthouse [pent'haus] *n* (flat) 屋上階 okújōkai

pent-up [pent'ʌp'] *adj* (feelings) たまった tamátta

penultimate [pinʌl'təmit] *adj* 最後から2番目の saĩgo kara nibánme no

people [piː'pəl] *npl* (persons) 人々 hitóbìto; (inhabitants) 住民 júmin; (citizens) 市民 shímin; (POL): *the people* 国民 kokúmin

♦*n* (nation) 国民 kokúmin; (race) 民族 mínzoku

several people came 数人来ました súnin kimashità

people say that ... ...だと言われている ...da to iwárete irù, ...だそうだ ...da sō dà

pep [pep] (*inf*) *n* (energy, vigor) 元気 geñki

pepper [pep'əːr] *n* (spice) こしょう koshō; (hot pepper) トウガラシ tōgarashi; (sweet pepper) ピーマン pìman

♦*vt* (*fig*): *to pepper with* ...を振掛ける ...wo furíkakerù

peppermint [pep'əːrmint] *n* (sweet) ハッカあめ hakkáamè

peptalk [pep'tɔːk] (*inf*) *n* (encouraging talk) 激励演説 gekíreienzetsù

pep up *vt* (enliven) 活気付ける kakkízukerù

per [pəːr] *prep* (of amounts, prices etc: for each) ...につき ...ni tsukí

per day/person 1日〔1人〕につき... ichínichi〔hitórì〕ni tsukí...

per annum 1年につき... ichínèn ni tsukí...

per capita [-kæp'itə] *adj* (income) 一人当りの hitóri atarì no

♦*adv* 一人当り hitóri atarì

perceive [pəːrsiːv'] *vt* (sound) 聞く kíkù; (light) 見る mírù; (difference) 認識する nifshiki suru; (notice) ...に気が付く ...ni ki gá tsukù; (realize, understand) 分かる wakárù

per cent *n* パーセント pásento

percentage [pəːrsen'tidʒ] *n* (amount) 割合 waríai, 率 rítsù

perception [pəːrsep'ʃən] *n* (insight) 洞察力 dōsatsuryòku; (opinion, understanding) 理解 rikái; (faculty) 知覚 chikáku

perceptive [pəːrsep'tiv] *adj* (person) 洞察力のある dōsatsuryòku no árù, 鋭敏な eíbin na; (analysis, assessment) 鋭い surúdoi

perch [pəːrtʃ] *n* (for bird) 止り木 tomárigì; (fish) パーチ pāchi とスズキに似た淡水魚 suzúki ni nità tañsuigyò

♦*vi*: *to perch (on)* (bird) (...に) 止る (...ni) tomárù; (person) (...に) 腰掛ける (...ni) koshíkakerù

percolator [pəːr'kəleitəːr] *n* (*also*: **coffee percolator**) パーコレーター pākorētā

percussion [pəːrkʌʃ'ən] *n* 打楽器 dagákkì ◇総称 sōshō

peremptory [pəːremp'təːriː] (*pej*) *adj* (person) 横柄な ōhei na; (order, instruction) 断固たる dañkotarù

perennial [pəren'iːəl] *adj* (flower, plant) 多年生の tanénsei no; (*fig*: problem, feature etc) ありがちな arígachi na

perfect [*adj, n* pəːr'fikt *vb* pəːrfekt'] *adj* (without fault: person, weather, behavior etc) 完璧な kañpeki na; (utter: nonsense, stranger etc) 全くの mattáku no

♦*n* (*also*: **perfect tense**) 完了形 kañryōkei

♦*vt* (technique) 仕上げる shiágerù

perfection [pəːrfek'ʃən] *n* (faultlessness) 完璧さ kañpekisa

perfectionist [pəːrfek'ʃənist] *n* 完璧主義者 kañpekishugishà

perfectly [pəːr'fiktli:] *adv* (emphatic) 全く mattáku; (faultlessly: perform, do etc) 完璧に kañpeki ni; (completely: understand etc) 完全に kañzen ni

perforate [pəːr'fəːreit] *vt* ...に穴を開ける ...ni aná wò akérù

perforations [pəːrfərei'ʃənz] *npl* (series of small holes) ミシン目 mishíñme

perform [pəːrfɔːrm'] *vt* (carry out: task, operation, ceremony etc) 行う okónaù, する surú; (piece of music) 演奏する eñsō suru; (play etc) 上演する jóen suru
♦*vi* (well, badly) する surú, やる yarú

performance [pəːrfɔːr'məns] *n* (of actor) 演技 eñgi; (of dancer) 踊り odóri; (of musician) 演奏 eñsō; (of singer) 歌い方 utáikata; (of play, show) 上演 jóen; (of car, engine) 性能 seínō; (of athlete, company, economy) 成績 seíseki

performer [pəːrfɔːr'məːr] *n* (actor, dancer, singer etc) 芸能人 geínōjìn

perfume [pəːr'fjuːm] *n* (cologne, toilet water, essence) 香水 kốsui; (pleasant smell: of flowers etc) 香り kaốrì

perfunctory [pəːrfʌŋk'təːri:] *adj* (kiss, remark etc) いい加減な iíkagen na

perhaps [pəːrhæps'] *adv* (maybe) たぶん ...だろう tábùn ...darố

peril [peːr'əl] *n* (great danger) 危険 kikén

perimeter [pərim'itəːr] *n* 周辺 shúhen

period [piːr'iːəd] *n* (length of time) 期間 kikáñ; (SCOL) 時限 jigéñ; (full stop) 終止符 shúshifù, ピリオド pírìodo; (MED) 月経 gekkéi, メンス méñsu, 生理 seíri
♦*adj* (costume, furniture) 時代の jidái no

periodic(al) [piːriːɑːd'ik(əl)] *adj* (event, occurrence) 周期的な shúkiteki na, 定期的な teíkiteki na

periodical [piːriːɑːd'ikəl] *n* (magazine) 雑誌 zasshí

periodically [piːriːɑːd'ikliː] *adv* 定期的に teíkiteki ni

peripheral [pərif'əːrəl] *adj* 二次的な nijíteki na; (on the edge: also COMPUT) 周辺の shúhen no
♦*n* (COMPUT) 周辺機器 shúhenkikì

periphery [pərif'əːriː] *n* (edge) 周辺 shúhen

periscope [peːr'iskoup] *n* 潜望鏡 señbōkyō

perish [peːr'iʃ] *vi* (die) 死ぬ shinú; (die out) 滅びる horóbirù; (rubber, leather etc) 腐る kusárù

perishable [peːr'iʃəbəl] *adj* (food) いたみやすい itámiyasuì

perjury [pəːr'dʒəːriː] *n* (LAW) 偽証 gishő

perk [pəːrk] (*inf*) *n* (extra) 役得 yakútoku

perk up *vi* (cheer up) 元気を出す géñki wo dásù

perky [pəːr'kiː] *adj* (cheerful) 朗らかな hogáraka na

perm [pəːrm] *n* (for hair) パーマ pầma

permanent [pəːr'mənənt] *adj* 永久的な eíkyūteki na

permeate [pəːr'miːeit] *vi* (pass through) 浸透する shiñtō suru; (*fig*: spread) 広がる hirógarù
♦*vt* (subj: liquid) ...に染込む ...ni shimíkomù; (: idea) ...に広まる ...ni hirómarù

permissible [pəːrmis'əbəl] *adj* (action, behavior) 許される yurúsarerù

permission [pəːrmiʃ'ən] *n* (consent, authorization) 許可 kyőka

permissive [pəːrmis'iv] *adj* (person, behavior, society) 甘い amáì

permit [*n* pəːr'mit *vb* pəːrmit'] *n* (official authorization) 許可証 kyokáshô
♦*vt* (allow) 許可する kyőkà suru; (make possible) 可能にする kanő ni surù

permutation [pəːrmjətei'ʃən] *n* 置換え o-kíkae

pernicious [pəːrniʃ'əs] *adj* (very harmful: attitude, influence etc) 有害な yűgai na; (MED) 悪性の akúsei no

perpendicular [pəːrpəndik'jələːr] *adj* (line, surface) 垂直の suíchoku no; (cliff, slope) 険しい kewáshiì

perpetrate [pəːr'pitreit] *vt* (commit: crime) 犯す okásù

perpetual [pəːrpetʃ'uːəl] *adj* (constant:

motion, darkness) 永久の eíkyū no; (: noise, questions) 年がら年中の neñgaraneñjū no

perpetuate [pə:rpetʃ'u:eit] vt (situation, custom, belief etc) 永続させる eízoku saserù

perplex [pə:rpleks'] vt (person) まごつかせる magótsukaserù

persecute [pə:'səkju:t] vt (harass, oppress: minorities etc) 迫害する hakúgai suru

persecution [pə:rsəkju:'ʃən] n (of minorities etc) 迫害 hakúgai

perseverance [pə:rsəvi:r'əns] n 根気 koñki

persevere [pə:rsəvi:r'] vi 辛抱強く続ける shiñbōzuyokù tsuzúkerù

Persian [pə:r'ʒən] adj ペルシアの pérùshia no
♦n ペルシア人 perúshiajìn
the (Persian) Gulf ペルシア湾 perúshiawàn

persist [pə:rsist'] vi: *to persist (in doing something)* (...をし) 続ける (...wo shi)tsuzúkerù

persistence [pə:rsis'təns] n (determination) 根気強さ koñkizuyòsa

persistent [pə:rsis'tənt] adj (noise, smell, cough etc) いつまでも続く ítsùmademo tsuzúku; (person: determined) 根気強い koñkizuyoì

person [pə:r'sən] n 人 hitó
in person (appear, sing, recite etc) 本人が hofínin ga

personal [pə:r'sənəl] adj (belongings, phone etc) 個人の kojín no; (opinion, life, habits etc) 個人的な kojínteki na; (in person: visit) 本人自身の hofíninjishìñ no

personal assistant n 秘書 hishó

personal call n (TEL) 私用の電話 shiyó no deñwa

personal column n 私信欄 shishínrañ

personal computer n パーソナルコンピュータ pāsonarukoñpyùta, パソコン pasókòn

personality [pə:rsənæl'iti:] n (character) 人格 jíñkaku; (famous person) 有名人 yūmeijìn

personally [pə:r'sənəli:] adv (for my etc part) 個人的には kojínteki ni wà; (in person) 本人が hofínin ga
to take something personally ...を個人攻撃と受止める ...wo kojínkōgeki to ukétomerù

personal organizer n 予定帳 yotéichò

personify [pə:rsɑ:n'əfai] vt (evil) ...の権化である ...no góñge de árù; (good) ...の化身である ...no késhìn de árù

personnel [pə:rsənel'] n 職員 shokúin ◇総称 sōshō

perspective [pə:rspek'tiv] n (ARCHIT, ART) 遠近法 eñkinhō; (way of thinking) 見方 mikáta
to get something into perspective (fig) 事情を考えて...を見る jijó wò kañgaetè ...wo mírù

Perspex [pə:rs'peks] ® n アクリル ákùriru

perspiration [pə:rspərei'ʃən] n 汗 áse

persuade [pə:rsweid'] vt: *to persuade someone to do something* ...する様に...を説き伏せる ...surú yò ni ...wo tokífuserù

persuasion [pə:rswei'ʒən] n (act) 説得 settóku; (creed) 信条 shiñjō

persuasive [pə:rswei'siv] adj (person, argument) 説得力のある settókuryòku no árù

pertaining [pə:rtein'iŋ]: *pertaining to* prep (relating to) ...に関する ...ni kañ suru

pertinent [pə:r'tənənt] adj (answer, remark) 適切な tekísetsu na

perturb [pə:rtə:rb'] vt (person) 不安にする fuán ni surù

Peru [pəru:'] n ペルー pérù

peruse [pəru:z'] vt (newspaper, documents etc) ...に目を通す ...ni mé wo tòsù

Peruvian [pəru:'vi:ən] adj ペルーの pérù no
♦n ペルー人 perújìn

pervade [pə:rveid'] vt (subj: smell, feeling) ...に充満する ...ni júman suru

perverse [pə:rvə:rs'] adj (contrary: behavior) 天のじゃくの amá no jàku no

perversion [pə:rvə:r'ʒən] n (sexual) 変態

pervert [*n* pəːrˈvəːrt *vb* pəːrˈvəːrt] *n* (sexual pervert) 変態 heńtai
♦*vt* (person, mind) 堕落させる daráku saseru; (truth, someone's words) 曲解する kyokkái suru

pessimism [pesˈəmizəm] *n* 悲観主義 hikánshùgi, ペシミズム peshímizùmu

pessimist [pesˈəmist] *n* 悲観主義者 hikánshugisha, ペシミスト peshímisùto

pessimistic [pesəmisˈtik] *adj* (person) 悲観的な hikánteki na, ペシミスティックな peshímisutikkù na

pest [pest] *n* (insect) 害虫 gaíchū; (*fig*: nuisance) うるさいやつ urúsai yatsù

pester [pesˈtəːr] *vt* (bother) 悩ませる naýámaserù

pesticide [pesˈtisaid] *n* 殺虫剤 satchū́zai

pet [pet] *n* (domestic animal) 愛がん動物 aígandōbùtsu, ペット péttð
♦*cpd* (theory, hate etc) 十八番の oháko no
♦*vt* (stroke: person, animal) 愛ぶする aíbu suru
♦*vi* (*inf*: sexually) ペッティングする pettíngu suru

teacher's pet (favorite) 先生のお気に入り seńsei nð o-kí ni irì

petal [petˈəl] *n* 花びら hanábira

peter [piːˈtəːr]: *peter out vi* (road, stream etc) だんだんなくなる dańdań nakúnarù; (conversation, meeting) しりすぼまりに終る shirísubomarì ni owárù

petite [pətiːtˈ] *adj* (referring to woman: small) 小柄な kogára na

petition [pətiʃˈən] *n* (signed document) 陳情書 chińjōshò; (LAW) 請願 seígan

petrified [petˈrəfaid] *adj* (*fig*: terrified) 恐怖に駆られた kyōfu ni karáretà

petrol [petˈrəl] (BRIT) *n* (fuel) ガソリン gasórin

two/four-star petrol レギュラー〔ハイオク〕ガソリン regyúrà〔haíoku〕gasórin

petrol can *n* ガソリン缶 gasórińkan

petroleum [pətrouˈliːəm] *n* 石油 sekíyu

petrol pump (BRIT) *n* (in garage) ガソリンポンプ gasórinpoñpu

petrol station (BRIT) *n* ガソリンスタンド gasórinsutañdo

petrol tank (BRIT) *n* ガソリンタンク gasórintañku

petticoat [petˈiːkout] *n* (underskirt) ペチコート péchìkōto

petty [petˈiː] *adj* (small, unimportant) さいさな sásài na; (small-minded) 狭量な kyōryō na

petty cash *n* (in office) 小口現金 kogúchigeñkin

petty officer *n* (in navy) 下士官 kashíkaǹ

petulant [petʃˈələnt] *adj* せっかちな sekkáchi na

pew [pjuː] *n* (in church) 長いす nagáisu

pewter [pjuːˈtəːr] *n* しろめ shíròme

phallic [fælˈik] *adj* (object, symbol) 陰茎状の iñkeijō no

phantom [fænˈtəm] *n* (ghost) お化け o-báke

pharmaceutical [fɑːrməsuːˈtikəl] *adj* 製薬の seíyaku no

pharmacist [fɑːrˈməsist] *n* 薬剤師 yakúzaishì

pharmacy [fɑːrˈməsiː] *n* 薬局 yakkyóku

phase [feiz] *n* (stage) 段階 dańkai
♦*vt*: *to phase something in/out* ...を段階的に取入れる〔なくす〕 ...wo dańkaiteki nì toríirerù〔nakúsù〕

Ph.D. [piːˈeitʃˈdiːˈ] *abbr* = Doctor of Philosophy

pheasant [fezˈənt] *n* キジ kijí

phenomena [finɑːmˈənə] *npl of* **phenomenon**

phenomenal [finɑːmˈənəl] *adj* 驚異的な kyōiteki na

phenomenon [finɑːmˈənɑːn] (*pl* **phenomena**) *n* 現象 geńshō

philanthropist [filænˈθrəpist] *n* 慈善家 jizénka

Philippines [filˈipiːnz] *npl*: *the Philippines* フィリピン fírìpin

philosopher [filɑːsˈəfəːr] *n* (scholar) 哲学者 tetsúgakushà

philosophical [filəsɑːfˈikəl] *adj* (ideas, conversation etc) 哲学的な tetsúgakuteki na; (*fig*: calm, resigned) 冷静な reísei na

philosophy [filɑːsˈəfiː] n (SCOL) 哲学 tetsúgàku; (set of ideas: of philosopher) ...の哲学 ...no tetsúgàku; (theory: of any person) 考え方 kángaekatà, 思想 shisō

phlegm [flem] n (substance) たん tañ

phlegmatic [flegmætˈik] adj (person) のろまな norōma na

phobia [fouˈbiːə] n (irrational fear: of insects, flying, water etc) 恐怖症 kyốfushō

phone [foun] n (system) 電話 deñwa; (apparatus) 電話器 deñwakì
♦vt ...に電話を掛ける ...ni deñwa wò kakérù
to be on the phone (BRIT: possess a phone) 電話を持っている deñwa wò mottē irù; (be calling) 電話中である deñwachū de arù

phone back vt ...に電話を掛け直す ...ni deñwa wò kakénaosù
♦vi 電話を掛け直す deñwa wò kakénaosù

phone book n (directory) 電話帳 deñwachō

phone booth n 電話ボックス deñwabokkùsu

phone box (BRIT) n 電話ボックス deñwabokkùsu

phone call n 電話 deñwa

phone-in [founˈin] (BRIT) n (RADIO, TV) 視聴者が電話で参加する番組 shichōsha ga deñwa dè sañka suru bañgumi

phonetics [fənetˈiks] n 音声学 oñseigàku

phone up vt ...に電話を掛ける ...ni deñwa wò kakérù
♦vi 電話を掛ける deñwa wò kakérù

phoney [founˈiː] adj (false: address) うその úsò no; (: accent) 偽の nisè no; (person) 信用できない shiñ-yō dekinài

phonograph [founˈəgræf] (US) n 蓄音機 chikúonkì

phosphorus [fɑːsˈfɔːrəs] n りん ríñ

photo [fouˈtou] n (photograph) 写真 shashín

photocopier [fouˈtəkɑːpiːər] n (machine)

写真複写機 shashínfukushakì, コピー機 kopíkì

photocopy [fouˈtəkɑːpiː] n コピー kópì
♦vt (picture, document etc) ...のコピーを取る ...no kópì wo tórù

photogenic [foutədʒenˈik] adj (person) 写真写りの良い shashín-utsurì no yoì

photograph [fouˈtəgræf] n 写真 shashín
♦vt (person, object, place etc) 撮影する satsúei suru

photographer [fətɑːgˈrəfəːr] n カメラマン kaméramàn

photographic [foutəgræfˈik] adj (equipment etc) 写真の shashín no

photography [fətɑːgˈrəfiː] n (art, subject) 写真撮影 shashínsatsùei

phrase [freiz] n (group of words, expression) 言方 iíkatà; (LING) 句 kú
♦vt (express) 表現する hyốgen suru

phrase book n (foreign language aid) 表現集 hyốgenshū

physical [fizˈikəl] adj (of the body: needs, punishment, exercise etc) 肉体的な nikútaiteki na; (geography, properties) 物理的な butsúriteki na; (world, universe, object) 自然の shizén no; (sciences) 物理学の butsúrigàku no

physical education n 体育 taíku

physically [fizˈikliː] adv (fit, attractive) 肉体的に nikútaiteki ni

physician [fiziˈʃən] n (doctor) 医者 ishá

physicist [fizˈəsist] n 物理学者 butsúrigakushà

physics [fizˈiks] n 物理学 butsúrigàku

physiology [fiziɑːlˈədʒiː] n (science) 生理学 seírigàku; (functioning: of animal, plant) 生理 seíri

physiotherapy [fiziːouθeːrˈəpiː] n (MED) 物理療法 butsúriryòhō

physique [fiziˈkˈ] n (build: of person) 体格 taíkaku

pianist [piˈænist] n (MUS) ピアニスト piánisùto

piano [piˈænˈou] n (MUS) ピアノ piáno

piccolo [pikˈəlou] n (MUS) ピッコロ pikkóro

pick [pik] n (tool: also: **pick-axe**) つるはし tsurúhàshi

♦*vt* (select) 選ぶ erábù; (gather: fruit, flowers) 摘む tsúmù; (remove, take) 取る tórù; (lock) こじ開ける kojíakerù

take your pick (choose) 選ぶ erábù

the pick of (best) ...からえり抜かれた物 ...kara erínukaretà mónò

to pick one's nose/teeth 鼻〔歯〕をほじる hanà[há]wò hojírù

to pick a quarrel (with someone) (...に) けんかを売る (...ni) keñka wò urú

pick at *vt fus* (food) ちびちび食べる chíbichibi tabérù

picket [pik'it] *n* (in strike) ピケ piké
♦*vt* (factory, workplace etc) ...にピケを張る ...ni piké wò hárù

pickle [pik'əl] *n* (*also*: **pickles**: as condiment) ピクルス píkurusu; (*fig*: mess) 苦境 kukyố
♦*vt* (CULIN: in vinegar) 酢漬にする suzúke ni surú; (: in salt water) 塩漬にする shiózuke ni surú

pick on *vt fus* (person: criticize) 非難する hinán suru; (: treat badly) いじめる ijímerù

pick out *vt* (distinguish) 識別する shikíbetsu ni suru; (choose from a group) 選び出す erábidasù, ピックアップする pikkúappù suru

pickpocket [pik'pɑ:kit] *n* すり súrì

pick up *vi* (improve: health, economy, trade) 良くなる yókù naru
♦*vt* (object: from floor) 拾う hirốu; (POLICE: arrest) 逮捕する taího suru; (collect: person, parcel etc) 引取る hikítorù; (AUT: passenger) 乗せる nosérù; (person: for sexual encounter) 引っ掛ける hikkákerù; (learn: language, skill etc) 覚える obóerù; (RADIO) 受信する jushín suru

to pick up speed 加速する kasóku suru

to pick oneself up (after falling etc) 起き上る okíagarù

pickup [pik'ʌp] *n* (small truck) ピックアップ pikkúappù

picnic [pik'nik] *n* (outdoor meal) ピクニック pikunikku

picture [pik'tʃər] *n* (painting, drawing, print) 絵 é; (photograph) 写真 shashín;

(TV) 画像 gazố; (film) 映画 éìga; (*fig*: description) 描写 byốsha; (: situation) 事態 jítài
♦*vt* (imagine) 想像する sốzo suru

picture book *n* 絵本 ehốñ

pictures [pik'tʃərz] (*BRIT*) *npl*: **the pictures** (cinema) 映画 éìga

picturesque [piktʃəresk'] *adj* (place, building) 風情のある fúzèi no árù

pie [pai] *n* (CULIN: vegetable, meat, fruit) パイ pâî

piece [pi:s] *n* (bit or part of larger thing) かけら kakéra; (portion: of cake, chocolate, bread etc) 一切れ hitókìre; (length: of string, ribbon) 一本 íppòn; (item): *a piece of clothing/furniture/advice* 1 つ hitótsù
♦*vt*: *to piece together* (information) 総合する sốgō suru; (parts of a whole) 継ぎ合せる tsugíawaserù

to take to pieces (dismantle) 分解する buñkai suru

piecemeal [pi:s'mi:l] *adv* (irregularly) 少しずつ sukóshizutsù

piecework [pi:s'wə:rk] *n* 出来高払いの仕事 dekídakabarài no shigóto

pie chart *n* 円形グラフ eñkeigurầfu

pier [pi:r] *n* 桟橋 sañbashi

pierce [pi:rs] *vt* (puncture: surface, material, skin etc) 貫通する kañtsū suru

piercing [pi:rs'iŋ] *adj* (*fig*: cry) 甲高い kañdakaì; (: eyes, stare) 鋭い surúdoì; (wind) 刺す様な sásù yō na

piety [pai'əti:] *n* (REL) 信心 shiñjìn

pig [pig] *n* (ZOOL) ブタ butá; (*pej*: unkind person) 畜生 chikúshồ; (: greedy person) 欲張り目 yokúbarimè

pigeon [pidʒ'ən] *n* (bird) ハト hátò

pigeonhole [pidʒ'ənhoul] *n* (for letters, messages) 小仕切り kojíkìri

piggy bank [pig'i:-] *n* (money box) 貯金箱 chokíñbako

pigheaded [pig'hedid] (*pej*) *adj* (stubborn) 頑固な gañko na

piglet [pig'lit] *n* 子ブタ kobúta

pigment [pig'mənt] *n* 色素 shikíso

pigskin [pig'skin] *n* ブタのなめし革 butá no naméshigàwa

pigsty [pig'stai] n (on farm) ブタ小屋 butágoya

pigtail [pig'teil] n (plait) お下げ o-ságe

pike [paik] n (fish) カワカマス kawákamàsu

pilchard [pil'tʃərd] n (fish) イワシ iwáshi

pile [pail] n (heap, stack) 山 yamá; (of carpet, cloth) 毛足 keáshi, パイル pâìru
♦vt (also: **pile up**: objects) 積上げる tsumíagerù
♦vi (also: **pile up**: objects) 積重なる tsumíkasanarù; (problems, work) たまる tamárù

pile into vt fus (car) ...に乗込む ...ni noríkomù

piles [pailz] npl (MED) じ ji

pile-up [pail'ʌp] n (AUT) 衝突事故 shốtotsujikò

pilfering [pil'fə:riŋ] n (petty thieving) くすねる事 kusúnerù kotó

pilgrim [pil'grim] n (REL) 巡礼者 juńreishà

pilgrimage [pil'grəmidʒ] n (REL) 巡礼 juńreì

pill [pil] n (MED: tablet) 錠剤 jōzai
the pill (contraceptive pill) 経口避妊薬 keíkòhinìn-yaku, ピル pírù

pillage [pil'idʒ] vt (loot: house, town etc) 略奪する ryakúdatsu suru

pillar [pil'ə:r] n (ARCHIT) 柱 hashíra

pillar box (BRIT) n (MAIL) ポスト pósùto

pillion [pil'jən] n: *to ride pillion* (on motorcycle) 後ろに相乗りする ushíro nì aínori surù

pillory [pil'ə:ri:] vt (criticize strongly) 非難する hínan suru

pillow [pil'ou] n (cushion: for head) まくら makùra

pillowcase [pil'oukeis] n (cover: for pillow) 枕カバー makúrakabà, ピロケース píròkèsu

pilot [pai'lət] n (AVIAT) 操縦士 sốjùshi, パイロット pâìrotto
♦cpd (scheme, study etc) 試験的な shikénteki na
♦vt (aircraft) 操縦する sốjù suru

pilot light n (on cooker, boiler, fire) 口火 kuchíbi

pimp [pimp] n ポン引き poñbiki, ひも himó

pimple [pim'pəl] n にきび níkìbi

pin [pin] n (metal: for attaching, fastening) ピン píñ
♦vt (fasten with pin) ピンで止める píñ de tomérù
pins and needles (in arms, legs etc) しびれが切れる事 shibíre gà kirérù kotó
to pin someone down (fig) ...に約束させる ...ni yakúsoku saserù, ...にくぎを刺す ...ni kugí wò sásù
to pin something on someone (fig) ...に...のぬれぎぬを着せる ...ni ...no nuréginù wo kiserù

pinafore [pin'əfɔ:r] n (also: **pinafore dress**) エプロンドレス epúrondorèsu

pinball [pin'bɔ:l] n (game) スマートボール sumátobòru; (machine) スマートボール機 sumátobòruki

pincers [pin'sə:rz] npl (TECH) やっとこ yattóko, ペンチ peńchi; (of crab, lobster etc) はさみ hasámi

pinch [pintʃ] n (small amount: of salt etc) 一つまみ hitótsùmami
♦vt (person: with finger and thumb) つねる tsunérù; (inf: steal) くすねる kusúnerù
at a pinch 緊急の場合 kiñkyù nò baái

pincushion [pin'kuʃən] n (SEWING) 針刺し harísashì

pine [pain] n (also: **pine tree**) マツ mátsù; (wood) マツ材 matsúzài
♦vi: *to pine for* (person, place) 思い焦がれる omóikogarerù

pineapple [pain'æpəl] n (fruit) パイナップル paínappùru

pine away vi (gradually die) 衰弱して死ぬ suíjaku shite shinù

ping [piŋ] n (noise) ぴゅーんという音 pyūn to iú otò

ping-pong [piŋ'pɔ:ŋ] ® n (sport) 卓球 takkyū, ピンポン píñpon

pink [piŋk] adj ピンク色の píñkuiro no
♦n (color) ピンク色 píñkuiro; (BOT) ナデシコ nadéshìko

pinnacle [pin'əkəl] n (of building, mountain) 天辺 teppén; (fig) 頂点 chōteń

pinpoint [pin'point] vt (discover) 発見する hakkén suru; (explain) 説明する setsúmei suru; (position of something) 正確に示す seíkaku nì shimésù

pint [paint] n (US: = 473 cc; BRIT: = 568 cc) パイント paíñto

a pint of beer, (BRIT: inf) a pint ビール1パイント bíru ichípaiñto

pin-up [pin'ʌp] n (picture) ピンナップ写真〔絵〕 piñnappushashiñ〔e〕

pioneer [paiəni:r'] n (initiator: of scheme, science, method) 先駆者 señkushà, パイオニア paíonià; (early settler) 開拓者 kaítakushà

pious [pai'əs] adj (person) 信心深い shiñjiñbukai

pip [pip] n (seed of fruit) 種 tanế; (BRIT: time signal on radio) 時報 jihố

pipe [paip] n (gen, also for smoking) パイプ paípu; (also: **water pipe**) 水道管 suídōkan; (also: **gas pipe**) ガス管 gasúkan

♦vt (water, gas, oil) パイプで運ぶ paípu de hakóbù

pipes [paipz] npl (also: **bagpipes**) バグパイプ bagúpaipu

pipe cleaner n パイプクリーナー paípukurīnà

pipe down (inf) vi (be quiet) 黙る damárù

pipe dream n (hope, plan) 夢想 musố

pipeline [paip'lain] n (for oil, gas) パイプライン paípurain

piper [pai'pə:r] n (bagpipe player) バグパイプ奏者 bagúpaipu sōsha

piping [pai'piŋ] adv: *piping hot* (water, food, coffee) うんと熱い úñto atsúi

piquant [pi:'kənt] adj (food: spicy) ぴりっとした piríttò shitá; (fig: interesting, exciting) 興味深い kyōmibùkai

pique [pi:k] n 立腹 rippúku

pirate [pai'rit] n (sailor) 海賊 kaízoku

♦vt (book, video tape, cassette etc) …の海賊版を作る …no kaízokubań wo tsukúrù

pirate radio (BRIT) n 海賊放送 kaízokuhōsō

pirouette [piru:et'] n つま先旋回 tsumásakiseñkai

Pisces [pai'si:z] n (ASTROLOGY) 魚座 uózà

piss [pis] (inf!) vi (urinate) おしっこする oshíkkð suru

pissed [pist] (inf!) adj (US) 怒った okóttà; (BRIT: drunk) 酔っ払った yoppárattà

pistol [pis'təl] n けん銃 keñjū, ピストル písutoru

piston [pis'tən] n ピストン písùton

pit [pit] n (hole in ground) 穴 aná; (in surface of something) くぼみ kubómi; (also: **coal pit**) 炭坑 tañkō; (quarry) 採石場 saísekijō

♦vt: *to pit one's wits against someone* …と知恵比べをする …to chiékuràbe wo suru

pitch [pitʃ] n (BRIT: SPORT: ground) グラウンド guráundo; (MUS) 調子 chốshi, ピッチ pitchi; (fig: level, degree) 度合 doai; (tar) ピッチ pítchî

♦vt (throw) 投げる nagérù

♦vi (fall forwards) つんのめる tsuñnomerù

to pitch a tent (erect) テントを張る téñto wo hárù

pitch-black [pitʃ'blæk'] adj (night, place) 真っ暗な makkúra na

pitched battle [pitʃt-] n (violent fight) 激戦 gekísen

pitchfork [pitʃ'fɔ:rk] n ホーク hőku

piteous [pit'i:əs] adj (sight, sound etc) 悲惨な hisán na

pitfall [pit'fɔ:l] n (difficulty, danger) 落し穴 otóshiàna, 危険 kikén

pith [piθ] n (of orange, lemon etc) わた watá

pithy [piθ'i:] adj (comment, saying etc) 中身の濃い nakámí no kôî

pitiful [pit'ifəl] adj (touching: appearance, sight) 哀れな awáre na

pitiless [pit'ilis] adj (person) 冷酷な reíkoku na

pits [pits] npl (AUT) ピット pitto

pittance [pit'əns] n (very small income) スズメの涙 suzúme no namída

pity [pit'i:] n (compassion) 哀れみ awáremì

♦vt 哀れむ awáremù

what a pity! (expressing disappointment) 残念だ zańnen da

pivot [piv'ət] n (TECH) 旋回軸 seńkaijìku, ピボット píbòtto; (*fig*) 中心 chūshin

pizza [pi:t'sə] n ピッツァ píttsà, ピザ pízà

placard [plæk'ɑːrd] n (sign: in public place) 看板 kańban; (: in march etc) プラカード purákàdo

placate [plei'keit] vt (person, anger) なだめる nadámerù

place [pleis] n (in general: point, building, area) 所 tokóro, 場所 bashó; (position: of object) 位置 íchì; (seat) 席 sékì; (job, post etc) 職 shokú, ポスト pósùto; (home): *at/to his place* 彼の家で[へ] kárè no iê de(e); (role: in society, system etc) 役割 yakúwarì

♦vt (put: object) 置く okú; (identify: person) 思い出す omóidasù

to take place (happen) 起る okórù

out of place (not suitable) 場違いの bachígai no

in the first place (first of all) まず第一に mázù dáìchi nì

to change places with someone ...と交代する ...to kótai suru

to be placed (in race, exam) 入賞する nyūshō suru

place of birth n 出生地 shusséichì

placenta [pləsen'tə] n 胎盤 taíban

placid [plæs'id] adj (person) 穏和な ońwa na

plagiarism [plei'dʒə:rizəm] n ひょう窃 hyōsetsu, 盗作 tōsaku

plague [pleig] n (MED) 伝染病 deńsenbyō; (*fig*: of locusts etc) 異常発生 ijōhassèi

♦vt (*fig*: subj: problems, difficulties) 悩ます nayámasù

plaice [pleis] n inv (fish) カレイ kárèi

plaid [plæd] n (cloth) チェックの生地 chékkù no kíjì

plain [plein] adj (unpatterned) 無地の mújì no; (simple: dress, food) 質素な shísùsò na; (clear, easily understood) 明白な meíhaku na; (not beautiful) 不器量な bukíryō na

♦adv (wrong, stupid etc) 全く mattáku

♦n (area of land) 平原 heígen

plain chocolate n ブラックチョコレート burákku chokorèto

plain-clothes [plein'klouz] adj (police officer) 私服の shifúku no

plainly [plein'li:] adv (obviously) 明白に meíhaku ni; (hear, see, smell: easily) はっきりと hakkírì to; (state: clearly) ざっくばらんに zákkùbaran ni

plaintiff [plein'tif] n (LAW) 原告 geńkoku

plaintive [plein'tiv] adj (cry, voice) 哀れっぽい awáreppoì

plait [plæt] n (of hair) お下げ o-ságe; (of rope, leather) 編みひも状の物 amíhimojō no monó

plan [plæn] n (scheme, project) 計画 keíkaku, プラン púràn; (drawing) 図面 zúmèn; (schedule) 予定表 yotéihyō

♦vt (work out in advance: crime, holiday, future etc) 計画する keíkaku suru

♦vi (think ahead) 計画する keíkaku suru

to plan to do ...しようと計画する ...shiyō tò keíkaku suru

plane [plein] n (AVIAT) 飛行機 hikōki; (MATH) 面 méñ; (*fig*: level) 段階 dańkai; (tool) かんな kanna; (*also*: **plane tree**) スズカケノキ suzúkake no ki, プラタナス purátanàsu

planet [plæn'it] n 惑星 wakúsei

plank [plæŋk] n (of wood) 板 ítà

planner [plæn'əːr] n (*gen*) 計画をする人 keíkaku wo suru hitò; (*also*: **town planner**) 都市計画担当者 toshíkeikaku tantōshà; (of TV program, project) 計画者 keíkakushà

planning [plæn'iŋ] n (of future, project, event etc) 計画 keíkaku; (*also*: **town planning**) 都市計画 toshíkeìkaku

family planning 家族計画 kazókukeìkaku

planning permission n 建築許可 keńchikukyokà

plant [plænt] n (BOT) 植物 shokúbùtsu;

(machinery) 設 備 sétsùbi; (factory) プラント puránto

♦vt (seed, plant, sapling) 植 え る uérù; (field, garden) ...に植える ...ni uérù; (secretly: microphone, bomb, incriminating evidence etc) 仕掛ける shikákerù

plantation [plænteiˈʃən] n (of tea, rubber, sugar etc) 農園 nốen; (area planted out with trees) 植林地 shokúrìnchi

plaque [plæk] n (commemorative plaque: on building etc) 銘板 meíban; (on teeth) 歯こう shíkô

plasma [plæzˈmə] n 血清 kesséi

plaster [plæsˈtəːr] n (for walls) しっくい shikkúì; (also: plaster of Paris) 石こう sekkố; (BRIT: also: sticking plaster) ばんそうこう bańsồkō

♦vt (wall, ceiling) ...にしっくいを塗る ...ni shikkúì wo nurú; (cover: to plaster with ...に...をべったり張る ...ni ...wo bettárì hárù

plastered [plæsˈtəːrd] (inf) adj 酔っ払った yopparáttà

plasterer [plæsˈtərəːr] n (of walls, ceilings) 左官屋 sakáñ-ya

plastic [plæsˈtik] n 合成樹脂 gőseijushì, プラスチック purásuchikkù

♦adj (made of plastic: bucket, chair, cup etc) プラスチック製の purásuchikkusei no

plastic bag n ポリ袋 poríbùkuro

Plasticine [plæsˈtisiːn] Ⓡ n 合成粘土 gőseineñdo

plastic surgery n 整形手術 seíkeishujùtsu

plate [pleit] n (dish) 皿 sará; (plateful: of food, biscuits etc) 一皿 hitósàra; (in book: picture, photograph) 1ページ大の挿絵 ichípèjidai nò sashíè, プレート púrèto; (dental plate) 入れ歯 iréba

gold/silver plate n 貴金属の食器類 kikínzoku no shokkírùi

plateau [plætouˈ] (pl plateaus or plateaux) n (GEO) 高原 kốgen

plate glass n (for window, door) 板ガラス itágaràsu

platform [plætˈfɔːrm] n (at meeting, for band) 演壇 eñdan; (raised structure: for landing, loading on etc) 台 dáì; (RAIL) ホーム hốmu; (BRIT: of bus) 踏段 fumídan, ステップ sutéppù; (POL) 綱領 kốryō

platinum [plætˈənəm] n 白金 hakkín, プラチナ puráchina

platitude [plætˈətuːd] n 決り文句 kimárimoñku

platonic [plətɑˈnik] adj 純粋に精神的な juńsui nì seíshinteki na, プラトニックな purátonikkù na

platoon [plətuːnˈ] n 小隊 shốtai

platter [plætˈəːr] n 盛皿 morízara

plausible [plɔːˈzəbəl] adj (theory, excuse, statement) もっともらしい mottómorashiî; (person) 口先のうまい kuchísaki nò umaî

play [plei] n (THEATER, RADIO, TV) 劇 gékì

♦vt (subj: children: game) ...して遊ぶ ...shite asóbù; (football, tennis, chess) やる yarú; (compete against) ...と試合をする ...to shiái wo suru; (part, role: in play, film etc) 演ずる eñzurù, ...にふんする ...ni funsuru; (instrument, tune) 演奏する eñsō suru; (listen to: tape, record) 聞く kíkù

♦vi (children: on beach, swings etc) 遊ぶ asóbù; (MUS: orchestra, band) 演奏する eñsō suru; (: record, tape, radio) かかる kakárù

to play safe 大事を取る daíji wò tórù

playboy [pleiˈbɔi] n プレーボーイ purébòi

play down vt 軽く扱う karúku atsukaù

player [pleiˈəːr] n (SPORT) 選手 sénshu, プレーヤー purêyà; (MUS) 奏者 sốsha; (THEATER) 役者 yakúsha

playful [pleiˈfəl] adj (person, animal) 遊び好きの asóbizuki no

playground [pleiˈgraund] n (in park) 遊び場 asóbiba; (in school) 校庭 kốtei, 運動場 uñdōjō

playgroup [pleiˈgruːp] (BRIT) n 保育園 hoíkuèn

playing card [pleiˈiŋ-] n トランプ toráñpu

playing field n グラウンド guráundo

playmate [pleiˈmeit] n 遊び友達 asóbitomòdachi

play-off [plei'ɔːf] n (SPORT) 優勝決定戦 yūshōketteĩsen、プレーオフ purḗofù

playpen [plei'pen] n ベビーサークル bebísàkuru

plaything [plei'θiŋ] n おもちゃ omóchà

playtime [plei'taim] n (SCOL) 休み時間 yasúmijikàn

play up vi (cause trouble: machine) 調子が悪くなる chốshi gà wáruku naru; (: children) 行儀を悪くする gyốgi wò wárùku suru

playwright [plei'rait] n 劇作家 gekísakka

plc [pi:elsi:'] abbr (= public limited company) 有限株式会社 yūgen kabushikigaishà

plea [pli:] n (request) 懇願 koñgan; (LAW) 申立て mōshitate

plead [pli:d] vt (LAW) 申立てる mōshitaterù; (give as excuse: ignorance, ill health etc) ...だと言い訳する ...dá tò iíwake surù

♦vi (LAW) 申立てる mōshitaterù; (beg): **to plead with someone** ...に懇願する ...ni koñgan suru

pleasant [plez'ənt] adj (agreeable, nice: weather, chat, smile etc) 気持の良い kimóchi no yoì; (agreeable: person) 愛想の良い aísò no yoì

pleasantries [plez'əntri:z] npl: **to exchange pleasantries** あいさつを交わす aísatsu wo kawásù

please [pli:z] excl (polite request) どうぞ dốzo、どうか dốka; (polite acceptance): **yes, please** ええ、有難 eế、arígàtō; (to attract someone's attention) 済みません sumímaseñ

♦vt (give pleasure or satisfaction to) 喜ばす yorókobasu

♦vi (give pleasure, satisfaction) 人を喜ばす hitó wò yorókobasu; (think fit): **do as you please** お好きな様にして下さい o-súki na yố ni shité kudasaĩ

please yourself! (inf) ご勝手に go-kátte nĩ

pleased [pli:zd] adj (happy, satisfied): **pleased (with)** (...で) 満足している

(...de) mañzoku shite irù

pleased to meet you 初めまして hajímemashīte

pleasing [pli:'ziŋ] adj (remark etc) 愉快な yúkai na、うれしい uréshiĩ; (picture) 楽しい tanóshiĩ; (person) 愛敬のある aíkyō no arù

pleasure [pleʒ'əːr] n (happiness, satisfaction) 快楽 kaíraku; (activity of enjoying oneself, enjoyable experience) 楽しみ tanóshimi

it's a pleasure どういたしまして dố itáshimashitè

pleasure boat n 遊覧船 yúransen

pleat [pli:t] n ひだ hĩda、プリーツ purītsù

pledge [pledʒ] n (promise) 約束 yakúsoku

♦vt (promise: money, support, help) 約束する yakúsoku suru

plentiful [plen'tifəl] adj (food, supply, amount) 豊富な hốfù na

plenty [plen'ti:] n: **plenty of** (much, many) 沢山の takúsan no; (sufficient) 十分な jūbun na

pleurisy [plur'isi:] n ろく膜炎 rokúmakuèn

pliable [plai'əbəl] adj (material) しなやかな shináyàka na; (fig: person) 素直な súnào na

pliant [plai'ənt] adj = **pliable**

pliers [plai'əːrz] npl ペンチ péñchi

plight [plait] n (of person, country) 苦境 kukyṓ

plimsolls [plim'səlz] (BRIT) npl 運動靴 uñdṓgutsu、スニーカー suníkà

plinth [plinθ] n 台座 daíza

plod [plɑːd] vi (walk) とぼとぼ歩く tóbòtobo arúkù; (fig) 何とかやる nañ to ka yárù

plonk [plɑːŋk] (inf) n (BRIT: wine) 安ワイン yasúwaìn

♦vt: **to plonk something down** たたきつける様に...を置く tatákitsukeru yố ni ...wo ókù

plot [plɑːt] n (secret plan) 陰謀 iñbō; (of story, play, film) 筋 sújì、プロット purót-tò; (of land) 区画 kukáku

♦vt (sb's downfall etc) たくらむ takúramù; (AVIAT, NAUT: position on chart) 地図に書込む chízù ni kakíkomù; (MATH: point on graph) グラフにする gúrafu ni suru

plotter [plɑ:t'ə:r] n (instrument) 製図道具 seízudōgu

plough [plau] (US also: **plow**) n (AGR) すき sukí

♦vt (earth) 耕す tagáyasù

to plough money into (company, project etc) ...に金をつぎ込む ...ni kané wo tsugíkomù

ploughman's lunch [plau'mənz-] (BRIT) n 軽食 keíshoku ◊ パブのランチで, パン, チーズ, ピクルスからなる pábù no ránchi de, páñ, chízu, píkùrusu kara nárù

plough through vt fus (crowd) ...をかき分けて歩く ...wo kakíwakete arukù

plow [plau] (US) = **plough**

ploy [plɔi] n 策略 sakúryaku

pluck [plʌk] vt (fruit, flower, leaf) 摘む tsúmù; (musical instrument) つま弾く tsumábikù; (bird) ...の羽をむしる ...no hané wo mushírù; (remove hairs from: eyebrow) ...の毛を抜く ...no ké wo nukú

♦n (courage) 勇気 yúki

to pluck up courage 勇気を出す yúki wo dásù

plug [plʌg] n (ELEC) 差込み sashíkomi, プラグ púràgu; (stopper: in sink, bath) 栓 sén; (AUT: also: **spark(ing) plug**) スパークプラグ supákupuràgu

♦vt (hole) ふさぐ fuságù; (inf: advertise) 宣伝する señden suru

plug in vt (ELEC) ...のプラグを差込む ...no púragu wo sashíkomù

plum [plʌm] n (fruit) プラム púràmu

♦cpd (inf): **plum job** 甘い汁を吸える職 amái shirù wo suérù shokú

plumage [plu:'midʒ] n 羽 hané ◊ 鳥の体を覆う羽の総称 torí nò karáda wo ōù hané no sōshō

plumb [plʌm] vt: **to plumb the depths** (fig) (of unpleasant emotion) 辛酸をなめ尽す shiñsan wò namétsukusù; (of un-

pleasant expression) ...を極端に表現する ...wo kyokútan nì hyōgen suru

plumber [plʌm'ə:r] n 配管工 haíkankō

plumbing [plʌm'iŋ] n (piping) 水道設備 suídōsetsubì; (trade, work) 配管業 haíkangyō

plume [plu:m] n (of bird) 羽 hané; (on helmet, horse's head) 前立 maédate

plummet [plʌm'it] vi: **to plummet (down)** (bird, aircraft) 真っ直ぐに落下する massúgù ni rakká surù; (price, amount, rate) 暴落する bóraku suru

plump [plʌmp] adj (person) ぽっちゃりした potchárì shita

♦vi: **to plump for** (inf: choose) 選ぶ erábù

plump up vt (cushion, pillow) 膨らませる fukúramaserù

plunder [plʌn'dər] n (activity) 略奪 ryakúdatsu; (stolen things) 分捕り品 buñdorihìñ

♦vt (steal from: city, tomb) 略奪する ryakúdatsu suru

plunge [plʌndʒ] n (dive: of bird, person) 飛込み tobíkomi; (fig: of prices, rates etc) 暴落 bóraku

♦vt (hand, knife) 突っ込む tsukkómù

♦vi (fall: person, thing) 落ちる ochírù; (dive: bird, person) 飛込む tobíkomù; (fig: prices, rates etc) 暴落する bóraku suru

to take the plunge 冒険する bóken suru

plunger [plʌn'dʒə:r] n (for sink) プランジャー puráñjà ◊ 長い棒の付いたゴムカップ nagáì bō no tsuitá gomúkappù

plunging [plʌn'dʒiŋ] adj (neckline) 切込みの深い kiríkomi no fukaí

pluperfect [plu:pə:r'fikt] n 過去完了形 kakókanryōkei

plural [plu:r'əl] adj 複数の fukúsū no

♦n 複数形 fukúsūkei

plus [plʌs] n (also: **plus sign**) 加符号 kafúgō, プラス púràsu

♦prep (MATH) ...に ...を加算して ...ni ...wo kasán shite, ...に ...を足して ...ni ...wo tashíte; (in addition to) ...に加えて ...ni kuwáete

2 plus 2 is 4 2足す2は4 ní tasù ní wà yóň

ten/twenty plus (more than) 10(20)以上 jū(nìjú)ijō

plush [plʌʃ] *adj* (car, hotel etc) 豪華な gṓka na

plutonium [plu:tou'ni:əm] *n* プルトニウム purútoníùmu

ply [plai] *vt* (a trade) 営む itónamù
♦*vi* (ship) 往復する ṓfuku suru
♦*n* (of wool, rope) 太さ futósa

to ply someone with drink ...に強引に酒を勧める ...ni gṓin nì saké wò susúmerù

plywood [plai'wud] *n* ベニヤ板 beníyaità

P.M. [pi:'em'] *abbr* = **Prime Minister**

p.m. [pi:'em'] *adv abbr* (= *post meridiem*) 午後 gógò

pneumatic [nu:mæt'ik] *adj* (air-filled) 空気で膨らませた kūki dè fukúramasetà; (powered by air) 空気... kūki...

pneumatic drill *n* 空気ドリル kū́kidorìru

pneumonia [nu:moun'jə] *n* 肺炎 haîen

poach [poutʃ] *vt* (steal: fish) 密漁する mitsúryō suru; (: animals, birds) 密猟する mitsúryō suru; (cook: egg) 落し卵にする otóshitamagò ni suru, ポーチエッグにする pṓchitoeggù ni suru; (: fish) 煮る nirú
♦*vi* (steal: fish) 密漁する mitsúryō suru; (: animals, birds) 密猟する mitsúryō suru

poached [poutʃt] *adj*: *poached egg* 落し卵 otóshitamagò, ポーチエッグ pṓchitoeggù

poacher [pou'tʃəːr] *n* (of fish) 密漁者 mitsúryōshà; (of animals, birds) 密猟者 mitsúryōshà

P.O. Box [pi:'ou-] *n abbr* = **Post Office Box**

pocket [pɑːk'it] *n* (on jacket, trousers, suitcase, car door etc) ポケット pokéttò; (*fig*: small area) 孤立地帯 korítsuchitài
♦*vt* (put in one's pocket) ポケットに入れる pokéttò ni irérù; (steal) くすねる kusúnerù

to be out of pocket (*BRIT*) 損する sóň suru

pocketbook [pɑːk'itbuk] (*US*) *n* (wallet) 財布 sáīfu; (handbag) ハンドバッグ hańdobaggù

pocket calculator *n* 電卓 deńtaku

pocket knife *n* ポケットナイフ pokéttonaìfu

pocket money *n* 小遣い kózùkai

pod [pɑːd] *n* さや sáyà

podgy [pɑːdʒ'i:] *adj* 小太りの kobútòri no

podiatrist [pədai'ətrist] (*US*) *n* 足治療医 ashíchiryòi

poem [pou'əm] *n* 詩 shi

poet [pou'it] *n* 詩人 shijín

poetic [pouet'ik] *adj* (relating to poetry) 詩の shi no; (like poetry) 詩的な shitéki na

poet laureate *n* 桂冠詩人 keikanshijin

poetry [pou'itri:] *n* (LITERATURE) 詩歌 shíika

poignant [pɔin'jənt] *adj* (emotion, look, grief etc) 痛ましい itámashiì

point [pɔint] *n* (*gen*) 点 teń, ポイント poîňto; (sharp end: of needle, knife etc) せん端 seńtan; (purpose) 目的 mokúteki; (significant part) 要点 yṓteń; (detail, aspect, quality) 特徴 tokúchō; (particular place or position) 地点 chíteń; (moment) 時点 jíteń; (stage in development) 段階 dańkai; (score: in competition, game, sport) 得点 tokúten, 点数 tensū́; (*BRIT*: ELEC: socket) コンセント kóňsento; (*also*: **decimal point**) 小数点 shṓsūten; (in numbers): *2 point 3 (2.3)* 2点3 ní teň sań
♦*vt* (show, mark) 指す sásù; (gun etc): *to point something at someone* ...に...を向ける ...ni ...wo mukérù
♦*vi*: *to point at* (with finger, stick etc) ...を指す ...wo sásù

to be on the point of doing something ...をする所である ..wo suru tokorò de árù

to make a point of doing 努めて...する tsutómete ...surù

to get/miss the point 相手が言わんとする事が分かる〔分からない〕 aîte gà iwáň to suru kotò ga wakárù〔wakáranaì〕

to come to the point 要点を言う yṓteń

wǒ iú

there's no point (in doing) (...するの
は) 無意味だ (...surú no wà) muími dà

point-blank [pɔint'blæŋk'] *adv* (say,
ask) ずばり zubárí; (refuse) あっさり as-
sárí; (*also:* **at point-blank range**) 至近距
離で shikínkyori de

pointed [pɔin'tid] *adj* (stick, pencil, chin,
nose etc) とがった togátta; (*fig:* remark)
辛らつな shifíratsu na

pointedly [pɔin'tidli:] *adv* (reply etc) 意
味深長に ímìshinchô ni

pointer [pɔin'tər] *n* (on chart, machine)
針 hárî; (*fig:* piece of information or
advice) ヒント hífito

pointless [pɔint'lis] *adj* (useless, senseless) 無意味な muími na

point of view *n* (opinion) 観点 kańten

point out *vt* (in debate etc) ...を指摘する
...wo shitéki suru

points [pɔints] *npl* (AUT) ポイント poífito; (RAIL) 転てつ機 teńtetsukî, ポイント
poífito

point to *vt fus* (*fig*) ...を指摘する ...wo
shitéki suru

poise [pɔiz] *n* (composure) 落ち着き ochítsuki

poison [pɔi'zən] *n* (harmful substance)
毒 dokú

♦*vt* (person, animal: kill with poison) 毒
殺する dokúsatsu suru; (: give poison to)
...に毒を飲ませる ...ni dokú wò nomáserù

poisonous [pɔi'zənəs] *adj* 有毒な yúdoku
na, 毒... dokú...

poke [pouk] *vt* (jab with finger, stick etc)
つつく tsutsúkù; (put): ***to poke something in(to)*** ...の中へ...を突っ込む ...no
nákà e ...wo tsukkómù

poke about *vi* (search) 物色する busshóku suru

poker [pou'kər] *n* (metal bar) 火かき棒
hikákibô; (CARDS) ポーカー pôkā

poky [pou'ki:] *adj* (room, house) 狭苦し
い semákurushiî

Poland [pou'lənd] *n* ポーランド pôrando

polar [pou'lə:r] *adj* (GEO, ELEC) 極地の
kyókùchi no

polar bear *n* 北極グマ hokkyókugùma

polarize [pou'lə:raiz] *vt* 分裂させる buń-
retsu saserù

Pole [poul] *n* ポーランド人 pôrandojîn

pole [poul] *n* (post, stick) 棒 bô, さお sáò;
(GEO, ELEC) 極 kyókù

flag pole 旗ざお hatázao

telegraph/telephone pole 電柱 deńchū

pole bean (*US*) *n* (runner bean) インゲ
ン íñgen

pole vault *n* 棒高飛び bôtakàtobi

police [pəlis'] *n* (organization) 警察 keísatsu; (members) 警官 keíkan

♦*vt* (street, area, town) ...の治安を維持す
る ...no chián wò fji suru

police car *n* パトカー patókà

policeman [pəli:s'mən] (*pl* **policemen**) *n*
警官 keíkan

police state *n* (POL) 警察国家 keísatsu-
kokkà

police station *n* 警察署 keísatsusho

policewoman [pəli:s'wumən] (*pl* **police-
women**) *n* 婦人警官 fujínkeìkan, 婦警 fukéi

policy [pɑ:l'isi:] *n* (POL, ECON: set of
ideas, plans) 政策 seísaku; (*also:* **insurance policy**) 保険証券 hokéñshōken

polio [pou'li:ou] *n* 小児麻ひ shőnimahî,
ポリオ pőrìo

Polish [pou'liʃ] *adj* ポーランドの pôrando no; (LING) ポーランド語の pôrando-
go no

♦*n* (LING) ポーランド語 pôrandogo

polish [pɑ:l'iʃ] *n* (*also:* **shoe polish**) 靴墨
kutsúzùmi; (for furniture, floors etc) 光
沢剤 kốtakuzài; (shine: on shoes, floors,
furniture etc) 光沢 kốtaku; (*fig:* refinement) 洗練 señren

♦*vt* (put polish on, make shiny) 磨く
migáku

polished [pɑ:l'iʃt] *adj* (*fig:* person, style)
洗練された señren sareta

polish off *vt* (work) 仕上げる shiágerù;
(food) 平らげる taíragerù

polite [pəlait'] *adj* (person: well-
mannered) 礼儀正しい reígitadashiî;
(socially superior: company, society) 上
流の jôryū no

politeness [pəlait'nis] *n* 礼儀正しさ reígitadashisa

political [pəlit'ikəl] *adj* (relating to politics) 政治の seíji no; (person) 政治に関心ある seíji ní kańshin arú

politically [pəlit'ikli:] *adv* 政治的に seíjiteki ni

politician [pɑ:litiʃ'ən] *n* 政治家 seíjika

politics [pɑ:l'itiks] *n* (activity) 政治 seíji; (subject) 政治学 seíjigàku
♦*npl* (beliefs, opinions) 政治的思想 seíjitekishisō

poll [poul] *n* (*also*: **opinion poll**) 世論調査 yorónchòsa; (political election) 選挙 séñkyo
♦*vt* (in opinion poll) ...の意見を聞く ...no íkèn wo kikú; (number of votes) 獲得する kakútoku suru

pollen [pɑ:l'ən] *n* 花粉 kafún

polling day [pou'liŋ-] (*BRIT*) *n* 投票日 tóhyòbi

polling station (*BRIT*) *n* 投票所 tóhyòjo

pollute [pəlu:t'] *vt* (air, water, land) 汚染する osén suru

pollution [pəlu:'ʃən] *n* (process) 汚染 osén; (substances) 汚染物質 osénbusshìtsu

polo [pou'lou] *n* (sport) ポロ pórò

polo-necked [pou'lounekt] *adj* (sweater) とっくりえりの tokkúrierì no

poltergeist [poul'tə:rgaist] *n* けん騒霊 keńsōrei, ポルターガイスト porútāgaìsuto

polyester [pɑ:li:es'tə:r] *n* ポリエステル porésutèru

polyethylene [pɑ:li:eθ'əli:n] (*US*) *n* ポリエチレン poríechìren

polystyrene [pɑ:li:stai'ri:n] *n* ポリスチレン porísuchìren

polytechnic [pɑ:li:tek'nik] *n* 科学技術専門学校 kagákugijutsu senmongakkō ◇英国では大学レベルの高等教育機関 eíkoku de wà daígakurebèru no kōtōkyōìku kikañ

polythene [pɑ:l'əθi:n] (*BRIT*) *n* = **polyethylene**

pomegranate [pɑ:m'əgrænit] *n* ザクロ zákùro

pomp [pɑ:mp] *n* 華やかさ hanáyàkasa

pompom [pɑ:m'pɑ:m] *n* ポンポン póñpon

pompon [pɑ:m'pɑ:n] *n* = **pompom**

pompous [pɑ:m'pəs] (*pej*) *adj* (person, piece of writing) もったい振った mottáibuttà

pond [pɑ:nd] *n* (natural, artificial) 池 iké

ponder [pɑ:n'də:r] *vt* 熟考する jukkō suru

ponderous [pɑ:n'də:rəs] *adj* (large and heavy) 大きくて重い ōkikute omóì; (speech, writing) 重苦しい omókurushiì

pong [pɔ:ŋ] (*BRIT*: *inf*) *n* 悪臭 akúshū

pontificate [pɑ:ntif'ikeit] *vi* (*fig*): **to pontificate (about)** (...について) もったい振って話す (...ni tsúìte) mottáibuttè hanásù

pontoon [pɑ:ntu:n'] *n* (platform) ポンツーン poñtsūn; (for seaplane etc) フロート fúròto

pony [pou'ni:] *n* ポニー pónì

ponytail [pou'ni:teil] *n* (person's hairstyle) ポニーテール ponítèru

pony trekking [-trek'iŋ] (*BRIT*) *n* 乗馬旅行 jōbaryokō

poodle [pu:'dəl] *n* プードル pūdoru

pool [pu:l] *n* (*also*: **pool of water**) 水たまり mizútamari; (pond) 池 iké; (*also*: **swimming pool**) プール pūru; (*fig*: of light, liquid) たまり tamári; (SPORT) 玉突 tamátsuki, ビリヤード biríyàdo
♦*vt* (money, knowledge, resources) 出し合う dashíaù, プールする pūru suru

typing pool タイピストのプール taípisùto no púru

pools [pu:lz] *npl* (football pools) トトカルチョ totókarùcho

poor [pu:r] *adj* (not rich: person, place, country) 貧しい mazúshiì, 貧乏な bíñbō na; (bad) 粗末な sómàtsu na
♦*npl*: **the poor** 貧乏人 biñbōnin ◇総称 sōshō

poor in (resources etc) ...が不足している ...ga fusóku shite irù

poorly [pu:r'li:] *adj* (ill) 病気の byókì no
♦*adv* (badly: designed) 粗末に sómàtsu ni; (paid, furnished) 不十分に fujúbùn ni

pop [pɑ:p] *n* (MUS) ポップス póppùsu;

(fizzy drink) 炭酸飲料 tansan-iñryō, ソーダ水 sōdasuì; (*inf*: father) 父ちゃん tōchan, パパ pápà; (sound) ぽんという音 póñ to iú otò

♦*vt* (put quickly) 突っ込む tsukkómù

♦*vi* (balloon) 破裂する harétsu suru; (cork) 飛出す tobídasù

popcorn [pɑːˈkɔːrn] *n* ポップコーン poppúkōn

pope [poup] *n* 法王 hōō

pop in *vi* 立寄る tachíyorù

poplar [pɑˈplɑːr] *n* ポプラ pópùra

poplin [pɑpˈlin] *n* ポプリン pópùrin

pop out *vi* 飛出る tobíderù

popper [pɑpˈəːr] (*BRIT*) *n* (for fastening) スナップ sunáppù

poppy [pɑpˈiː] *n* ケシ keshí

Popsicle [pɑpˈsikəl] (® *US*) *n* (ice lolly) アイスキャンディー aísukyandī

pop star *n* ポップスター poppúsutà

populace [pɑpˈjələs] *n* 大衆 taíshū

popular [pɑpˈjələːr] *adj* (well-liked: person, place, thing) 人気のある niñki no arù; (of ordinary people: idea, belief) 一般の ippán no, 流行の ryūkō no; (non-academic) 一般向けの ippánmuke no; (POL) 国民の kokúmin no

popularity [pɑːpjəlærˈitiː] *n* (of person, thing, activity) 人気 niñki

popularize [pɑpˈjələraiz] *vt* (sport, music, fashion) 普及させる fukyū saserù; (science, ideas) 分かりやすくする wakáriyasukù suru

population [pɑpjəleiˈʃən] *n* (inhabitants: of country, area) 住民 júmin; (number of inhabitants) 人口 jiñkō

populous [pɑpˈjələs] *adj* (country, city, area) 人口の多い jiñkō no ōì

pop up *vi* 現れる aráwarerù

porcelain [pɔːrˈsəlin] *n* 磁器 jíkì

porch [pɔːrtʃ] *n* (ARCHIT: entrance) 玄関 genkan; (*US*) ベランダ beránda

porcupine [pɔːrˈkjəpain] *n* ヤマアラシ yamáarashi

pore [pɔːr] *n* (ANAT) 毛穴 keána; (BOT) 気孔 kikō; (GEO) 小穴 koána

♦*vi*: **to pore over** (book, article etc) 熟読する jukúdoku suru

pork [pɔːrk] *n* 豚肉 butániku

pornographic [pɔːrnəgræfˈik] *adj* (film, book, magazine) わいせつな waísetsuna, ポルノの poruno no

pornography [pɔːrnɑːˈgrəfiː] *n* (films, books, magazines) ポルノ pórùno

porous [pɔːrˈəs] *adj* (soil, rock, clay etc) 小穴の多い koána nò ōì

porpoise [pɔːrˈpəs] *n* イルカ irúka

porridge [pɔːrˈidʒ] *n* オートミール ōtomīru

port [pɔːrt] *n* (harbor) 港 mínáto; (NAUT: left side) 左げん sagén; (wine) ポートワイン pōtowaìn

port of call 寄港地 kikōchì

portable [pɔːrˈtəbəl] *adj* (television, typewriter, telephone etc) 携帯用の keítai yō no, ポータブルの pōtaburu no

porter [pɔːrˈtəːr] *n* (for luggage) 赤帽 akábō, ポーター pōtà; (doorkeeper) 門番 moñban

portfolio [pɔːrtfouˈliːou] *n* (case) かばん kabán; (POL) 大臣の職 dáìjin no shokú; (FINANCE) ポートフォリオ pōtoforìo; (of artist) 代表作品集 daíhyōsakuhiñshū

porthole [pɔːrtˈhoul] *n* げん窓 geñsō

portion [pɔːrˈʃən] *n* (part) 部分 búbùn; (helping of food) 一人前 ichíninmaè

portly [pɔːrtˈliː] *adj* (man) 太った futóttà

portrait [pɔːrˈtrit] *n* (picture) 肖像 shōzō, ポートレート pōtorèto

portray [pɔːrtreiˈ] *vt* (subj: artist) 描く egákù; (: actor) 演じる eñjirù

portrayal [pɔːrtreiˈəl] *n* (artist's: *also* representation in book, film etc) 描写 byōsha; (actor's) 演技 eñgi

Portugal [pɔːrˈtʃəgəl] *n* ポルトガル porútogàru

Portuguese [pɔːrtʃəgiːzˈ] *adj* ポルトガルの porútogàru no; (LING) ポルトガル語の porútogarugò no

♦*n inv* ポルトガル人 porútogarujìn; (LING) ポルトガル語 porútogarugò

pose [pouz] *n* (posture) ポーズ pōzu

♦*vi* (pretend): **to pose as** ...を装う ...wo yosóoù, ...の名をかたる ...no ná wò katárù

♦*vt* (question) 持出す mochídasù; (problem, danger) ...である ...de árù

to pose for (painting etc) ...のためにポーズを取る ...no tamé nì pōzu wo tórù

posh [pɑːʃ] (*inf*) *adj* (smart: hotel, restaurant etc) 高級な kốkyū na; (upper class: person, behavior) 上流階級の jốryūkaì-kyū no

position [pəziʃ'ən] *n* (place: of house, thing, person) 位置 íchì; (of person's body) 姿勢 shiséi; (social status) 地位 chíi; (in race, competition) 第...位 dáì ...i; (attitude) 態度 táìdo; (situation) 立場 tachíba
♦*vt* (person, thing) 置く okú

positive [pɑːz'ətiv] *adj* (certain) 確かな táshìka na; (hopeful, confident) 確信している kakúshin shite irù; (definite: decision, action, policy) 積極的な sekkyókuteki na

posse [pɑːs'iː] (*US*) *n* 捜索隊 sốsakutai

possess [pəzes'] *vt* (have, own: car, watch, radio etc) 所有する shoyū suru, 保有する hoyū suru; (quality, ability) ...がある ...ga árù, ...を持っている ...wo mốttè irù; (subj: feeling, belief) 支配する shíhaì suru

possession [pəzeʃ'ən] *n* (state of possessing) 所有 shoyū

to take possession of 占領する seńryō suru

possessions [pəzeʃ'ənz] *npl* (belongings) 持物 mochímòno

possessive [pəzes'iv] *adj* (of another person) ...の愛情を独占したがる ...no aíjō wo dokúsen shitagarù; (of things) 他人に使わせたがらない tanín nì tsukáwasetagaranài; (LING) 所有を表す shoyū wo aráwasù

possibility [pɑːsəbil'əti:] *n* 可能性 kanố-sei; (possible event) 可能な事 kanố na kotò

possible [pɑːs'əbəl] *adj* (which can be done) 可能な kanố na; (event, reaction) 有り得る arígurù; (candidate, successor) 成り得る narígurù

it's possible (may be true) そうかも知れない số ka mò shirénaì

as fast as possible できるだけ早く de-

kíru dakè hayákù

possibly [pɑːs'əbliː] *adv* (perhaps) あるいは arúìwa; (expressing surprise, shock, puzzlement) ...が考えられない ...ga kañ-gaerarenài; (emphasizing someone's efforts) できる限り dekíru kagirì

I cannot possibly come どう合っても私は行かれません dốatté mo watákushi wà ikáremaseñ

post [poust] *n* (*BRIT*: service, system) 郵便 yū́bin; (: letters) 郵便(物) yū́bin (bùtsu); (delivery) 配達 haítatsu ◊1回分の配達郵便を指す ikkáìbun no haítatsu-yū́bin wo sásù; (pole) 柱 hashíra; (situation) 職務(MIL) 持場 mochíba
♦*vt* (*BRIT*: send by post) 郵送する yū́sō suru; (: put in mailbox) 投かんする tốkan suru; (: appoint): *to post someone to* ...を...へ配置する ...wo ...e haíchi suru

postage [pous'tidʒ] *n* (charge) 郵便料金 yū́bin ryṓkin

postage stamp *n* 〔郵便〕切手 (yū́bin) kitté

postal [pous'təl] *adj* (charges, service, strike) 郵便の yū́bin no

postal order *n* 郵便為替 yū́bin kawàse

postbox [poust'bɑːks] (*BRIT*) *n* (郵便) ポスト (yū́bin) pósùto

postcard [poust'kɑːrd] *n* (郵便) 葉書 (yū́bin) hagáki

postcode [poust'koud] (*BRIT*) *n* 郵便番号 yū́bin bañgō

postdate [poust'deit] *vt* (check) ...に先の日付を付ける ...ni sakí nò hizúke wò tsukérù

poster [pous'tər] *n* ポスター pósùtā

poste restante [poust res'tɑːnt] (*BRIT*) *n* 局留 kyokúdome

posterity [pɑːster'itiː] *n* 後世 kốsei

postgraduate [poustgrædʒ'uːit] *n* 大学院生 daígakuiñsei

posthumous [pɑːs'tʃəməs] *adj* (award, publication) 死後の shígo no

postman [poust'mən] (*pl* **postmen**) *n* 郵便屋 yū́bin-ya

postmark [poust'mɑːrk] *n* 消印 keshíin

post-mortem [poustmɔːr'təm] *n* 司法解剖 shihốkaibō, 検死解剖 keñshikaibố

post office n (building) 郵便局 yūbiñkyoku; (organization): **the Post Office** 郵政省 yūseĩshō

Post Office Box n 私書箱 shishōbáko

postpone [poustpoun'] vt 延期する eñki suru

postscript [poust'skript] n 追伸 tsuíshin

posture [pɑːs'tʃəːr] n (position of body) 姿勢 shiséi; (fig) 態度 táĩdo

postwar [poust'wɔːr'] adj (building, period, politics) 戦後の séñgo no

posy [pou'ziː] n 花束 hanátaba ◇小さい花束を指す chíīsaī hanátaba wo sásù

pot [pɑt] n (for cooking) なべ nábè; (also: **teapot**) ティーポット tíːpottò; (also: **coffeepot**) コーヒーポット kōhīpottò; (tea/coffee in pot) ティー[コーヒー]ポット一杯 tíː[kōhī]pottò íppai; (bowl, container: for paint etc) つぼ tsubó; (flowerpot) 植木鉢 uékibáchi; (inf: marijuana) マリファナ marífàna

♦vt (plant) 鉢に植える hachí nì uérù

to go to pot (inf: work, performance) 駄目になる damé ni narù

potato [pətei'tou] (pl **potatoes**) n ジャガイモ jagáimo

potato peeler [-piː'ləːr] n 皮むき器 kawámukikì

potent [pout'ənt] adj (powerful: weapon, argument, drink) 強力な kyōryoku na; (man) 性的能力のある seítekinōryoku no árù

potential [pəten'tʃəl] adj (candidate) 成り得る naríurù; (sales, success) 可能な kanō na; (danger etc) 潜在する señzai suru

♦n (talents, abilities) 潜在能力 señzaiñōryoku; (promise, possibilities) 将来性 shōraisei

potentially [pəten'tʃəliː] adv 潜在的に señzaiteki ni

pothole [pɑt'houl] n (in road) 穴ぼこ anábòko; (BRIT: underground) 洞くつ dókutsu

potholing [pɑt'houliŋ] (BRIT) n: **to go potholing** 洞くつを探検する dókutsu wò tañken suru

potion [pou'ʃən] n (of medicine, poison etc) 水薬 mizúgusùri

potluck [pɑt'lʌk] n: **to take potluck** 有り合せの物で間に合せる aríawase no monò de ma ní awaserù

potted [pɑt'id] adj (food) つぼ詰めの tsubōzume no; (plant) 鉢植えの hachíue no; (abbreviated: account, biography etc) 要約した yōyaku shita

potter [pɑt'əːr] n (pottery maker) 陶芸家 tōgeika

♦vi: **to potter around/about in the garden** (BRIT) ぶらぶらと庭いじりをする búràbura to niwáijìri wo suru

pottery [pɑt'əːriː] n (pots, dishes etc) 陶器 tōki; (factory, workshop) 陶器製造所 tōkiseizōjo

potty [pɑt'iː] adj (inf: mad) 狂った kurúttā

♦n (for child) おまる o-máru

pouch [pautʃ] n (for tobacco, coins etc) 小袋 kobúkuro; (ZOOL) 袋 fukúro

poultry [poul'triː] n (live chickens, ducks etc) 家きん kakíñ; (meat from chickens etc) 鳥肉 toríniku

pounce [pauns] vi: **to pounce on** (animal, person) ...に襲い掛る ...ni osóikakarù; (fig: mistake, idea etc) 攻撃する kōgeki suru

pound [paund] n (unit of weight) ポンド póñdo; (BRIT: unit of money) ポンド póñdo

♦vt (beat: table, wall etc) 強くたたく tsúyòku tatákù; (crush: grain, spice etc) 砕く kudákù

♦vi (heart) どきどきする dókìdoki suru

pound sterling n ポンド póñdo

pour [pɔːr] vt (tea, wine, cereal etc) つぐ tsugú

♦vi (water, blood, sweat etc) 流れ出る nagárederù

to pour someone a drink ...に酒をついでやる ...ni sakê wð tsuíde yarù

pour away/off vt 流して捨てる nagáshite suterù

pour in vi (people) ぞろぞろと入って来る zórðzoro to haítte kurù; (information) 続々と入る zókùzoku to haírù

pouring [pɔːr'iŋ] adj: **pouring rain** 土砂

降りの雨 dosháburi no amè

pour out vi (people) ぞろぞろと出て来る zórózoro to deté kurù

♦vt (tea, wine etc) つぐ tsugú; (fig: thoughts, feelings, etc) せきを切った様に吐き出す sékì wo kittá yổ ni hakídasù

pout [paut] vi 膨れっ面をする fukúrettsura wo suru

poverty [pɑːvˈəːrtiː] n 貧乏 bínbō

poverty-stricken [pɑːvˈəːrtiːstrikən] adj (people, town, country) 非常に貧しい hijổ nì mazúshiì

powder [pauˈdəːr] n (tiny particles of solid substance) 粉 koná; (face powder) おしろい oshíroi, パウダー páudā

♦vt: *to powder one's face* 顔におしろいをつける kaó nì oshíroi wò tsukérù

powder compact n コンパクト kônpakuto

powdered milk [pauˈdəːrd-] n 粉ミルク konámirùku

powder puff n パフ páfù

powder room n 化粧室 keshóshìtsu

power [pauˈəːr] n (control: over people, activities) 権力 kéñryoku; (ability, opportunity) 能力 nổryoku; (legal right) 権利 kéñri; (of explosion, engine) 威力 íryòku; (electricity) 電力 déñryoku

to be in power (POL etc) 権力を握っている kéñryoku wo nigítte irù

power cut (BRIT) n 停電 teíden

powered [pauˈəːrd] adj: *powered by* ...で動く ...de ugókù

power failure n 停電 teíden

powerful [pauˈəːrfəl] adj (person, organization) 有力な yúryoku na; (body) 力強い chikárazuyoì; (blow, kick etc) 強力な kyóryoku na; (engine) 馬力のある baríki no tsuyoì; (speech, piece of writing) 力強い chikárazuyoì

powerless [pauˈəːrlis] adj (without control or influence) 無力な múryòku na

powerless to do ...する力がない ...súrù chikára ga naì

power point (BRIT) n コンセント kôñsento

power station n 発電所 hatsúdensho

p.p. [piːˈpiːˈ] abbr (= *per procurationem*):

p.p. J. Smith J.Smithの代理として jē sumísù no daíri tòshité; (= *pages*) ページ péji

PR [piːˈɑːrˈ] abbr = **public relations**

practicable [prækˈtikəbəl] adj (scheme, task, idea) 実用的な jitsúyōteki na

practical [prækˈtikəl] adj (not theoretical: difficulties, experience etc) 実際の jissái no; (person: sensible) 現実的な geñjitsuteki na; (: good with hands) 器用な kíyồ na; (ideas, methods) 現実的な geñjitsuteki na; (clothes, things: sensible) 実用的な jitsúyōteki na

practicality [præktikælˈitiː] n (no pl) 現実主義 geñjitsushùgi; (of situation etc) 現実 geñjitsu

practical joke n 悪ふざけ warúfuzàke

practically [prækˈtikliː] adv (almost) ほとんど hotóndo

practice [prækˈtis] n (habit) 習慣 shúkan; (of profession) 業務 gyổmu; (REL) おきてを守る事 okíte wò mamóru kotò; (exercise, training) 練習 reñshū; (MED, LAW: business) 開業 kaígyō

♦vt (train at: musical instrument, sport etc) 練習する reñshū suru; (carry out: custom, craft etc) 行う okónaù; (religion) ...のおきてを守る ...no okite wo mamoru; (profession) ...に従事する ...ni jūji suru

♦vi (train) 練習する reñshū suru; (lawyer, doctor etc) ...の業務をする ...no gyổmu wo suru

in practice (in reality) 実際には jissái ni wà

out of practice 腕が鈍って udé gà nibúttè

practicing [prækˈtisiɳ] (BRIT **practising**) adj (Christian etc) おきてを守っている okíte wò mamótte irù; (doctor, lawyer) 業務をしている gyổmu wo shité irù

practise [prækˈtis] vt, vi (BRIT) = **practice**

practitioner [præktiˈənəːr] n (MED): *medical practitioner* 医者 ishá

pragmatic [prægmætˈik] adj (person, reason etc) 現実的な geñjitsuteki na

prairie [preˈriː] n 草原 sổgen

praise [preiz] n (expression of approval, admiration) 賞賛 shōsan

♦vt (express approval, admiration: of person, thing, action etc) ほめる homérù

praiseworthy [preiz'wɔːrði] adj (person, act etc) ほめるべき homérùbeki

pram [præm] (BRIT) n 乳母車 ubágurùma

prance [præns] vi (person) 威張って歩く ibátte arúku; (horse) 躍る様に歩く odóru yō ni arúkù

prank [præŋk] n いたずら itázura

prawn [prɔːn] n エビ ebí

pray [prei] vi (REL) 祈る inórù; (fig) 祈る inórù, 願う negáù

prayer [pre:r] n (REL: activity, words) 祈り inóri

preach [priːtʃ] vi (REL) 説教する sékkyō suru; (pej: moralize) お説教する o-sékkyō suru

♦vt (peace, doctrine etc) 説く tókù

to preach a sermon 説教する sékkyō suru

preacher [priː'tʃəːr] n (REL) 説教者 sekkyōshà

preamble [priː'æmbəl] n (to spoken words) 前置き maéoki; (to written words) 前書 maégaki

precarious [prike:r'iːəs] adj (dangerous: position, situation) 不安定な fuántei na; (fig) 危険な kikén na

precaution [prikɔː'ʃən] n 用心 yōjin

precede [prisiː'd] vt (event, period of time) ...の前に起る ...no máè ni okórù; (person) ...の前を歩く ...no máè wo arúkù; (sentence, paragraph, chapter) ...の前にある ...no máè ni árù

precedence [pres'idəns] n (priority) 優先 yúsen

precedent [pres'idənt] n (action, official decision) 判例 hafírei; (something that has happened before) 先例 sefírei

preceding [prisiː'diŋ] adj (chapter, programme, day) 前の máè no

precept [priː'sept] n おきて okíte

precinct [priː'siŋkt] n (US: part of city) 管区 kánku

pedestrian precinct (BRIT) 歩行者天

国 hokōshatengoku

shopping precinct (BRIT) ショッピングセンター shóppìngu séñtā ◇車が閉出される kuróma gà shimédasarerù

precincts [priː'siŋkts] npl (of a large building) 構内 kōnai

precious [preʃ'əs] adj (commodity: valuable, useful) 貴重な kichō na; (object, material) 高価な kōka na

precious stone n 宝石 hōseki

precipice [pres'əpis] n 断崖 dañgai

precipitate [prisip'iteit] vt (hasten) 早める hayámerù

precise [prisais'] adj (exact: time, nature etc) 正確な seíkaku na; (detailed: instructions, plans etc) 細かい komákaì

precisely [prisais'liː] adv (accurately) 正確に seíkaku ni; (exactly) その通り sonó tòri

precision [prisiʒ'ən] n 正確さ seíkakusa

preclude [prikluːd'] vt (action, event) 不可能にする fukánō ni suru

precocious [prikou'ʃəs] adj (child, talent) 早熟な sōjuku na

preconceived [priːkənsiːvd'] adj:
preconceived idea 先入観 señnyūkan

precondition [priːkəndiʃ'ən] n 前提条件 zeñteijōken

precursor [prikəːr'səːr] n (person) 先駆者 señkushà; (thing) 前触れ maébure

predator [pred'ətəːr] n 捕食者 hoshókushà

predecessor [pred'isesəːr] n (person) 前任者 zeñíñsha

predestination [priːdestinei'ʃən] n 予定説 yotéisètsu

predicament [pridik'əmənt] n 苦境 kukyō

predict [pridikt'] vt 予言する yogén suru

predictable [pridikt'əbəl] adj (event, behavior etc) 予知できる yóchì dekírù

prediction [pridik'ʃən] n 予言 yogén

predominantly [pridɑm'ənəntliː] adv 圧倒的に attóteki ni

predominate [pridɑm'əneit] vi (person, thing) ...が圧倒的に多い ...ga attóteki ni ōì; (feature, quality) 目立つ medátsù

pre-eminent [priːem'ənənt] adj (person,

thing) 優れた sugúretà

pre-empt [pri:empt] *vt* (decision, action, statement) 先取りする sakídori suru

preen [pri:n] *vt*: *to preen itself* (bird) 羽繕いをする hazúkùroi wo suru
to preen oneself 得意がる tokúîgaru

prefab [pri:ˈfæb] *n* プレハブ住宅 puréhabujûtaku

prefabricated [pri:fæbˈrikeitid] *adj* (buildings) プレハブの puréhabu no

preface [prefˈis] *n* (in book) 前書 maégaki

prefect [pri:ˈfekt] (*BRIT*) *n* (in school) 監督生 kantokusei

prefer [prifəˈr] *vt* (like better: person, thing, activity) ...の方を好む ...no hô wò konómù
to prefer doing/to do ...する方が好きである ...suru hô gà sukí de arù

preferable [prefˈə:rəbəl] *adj* ...が望ましい ...ga nozómashiì

preferably [prifəˈr'əbli:] *adv* できれば dekírèba

preference [prefˈə:rəns] *n* (liking) 好み konómi
to give preference to ...を優先的に扱う ...wo yûsenteki nì atsúkaù

preferential [prefəren'tʃəl] *adj*: *preferential treatment* 優先的な取扱い yûsenteki nà toríatsukai

prefix [pri:ˈfiks] *n* 接頭辞 settôjì

pregnancy [pregˈnənsi:] *n* (of woman, female animal) 妊娠 nínshin

pregnant [pregˈnənt] *adj* (woman, female animal) 妊娠している nínshin shite irù

prehistoric [pri:histɔ:rˈik] *adj* (person, dwelling, monster etc) 有史以前の yúshiizèn no

prejudice [predʒˈədis] *n* (unreasonable dislike) 偏見 henken; (bias in favor) ひいき hîiki

prejudiced [predʒˈədist] *adj* (person: prejudiced against) ...に対して偏見のある ...ni táishite henken no arù; (: prejudiced in favor) ...をひいきにした ...wo hîiki ni shitá

preliminary [prilimˈə:ne:ri:] *adj* (action,

discussion) 予備的な yobíteki na

prelude [preiˈlu:d] *n* (preliminary event) 前兆 zenchō; (MUS) 序曲 jôkyòku

premarital [pri:mærˈitəl] *adj* 婚前の konzen no

premature [pri:mətʃuˈr] *adj* (earlier than expected: baby) 早産の sôzan no; (death, arrival) 早過ぎた hayásugita; (too early: action, event etc) 時期尚早の jíkìshōsō no
premature aging 早老 sôrō

premeditated [primedˈəteitid] *adj* 計画的な keíkakuteki na

premier [primjiːˈr] *adj* (best) 最良の saíryō no
♦*n* (POL) 総理大臣 sôridaìjin, 首相 shushô

première [primjiːˈr] *n* (of film) 初公開 hatsúkôkai; (of play) 初演 shoén

premise [premˈis] *n* 前提 zentei

premises [premˈisiz] *npl* (of business, institution) 構内 kônai
on the premises 構内で kônai de

premium [pri:ˈmiəm] *n* (COMM: extra sum of money) 割増金 warímashikin, プレミアム purémìamu; (: sum paid for insurance) 掛金 kakékin
to be at a premium (expensive) 高価である kôka de arù; (hard to get) 手に入りにくい té nì haírinikùi

premium bond (*BRIT*) *n* 割増金付き債券 warímashikintsukisaìken ◇抽選による賞金が付く chûsen ni yorù shôkin ga tsukù

premonition [premoni'ʃən] *n* 予感 yokán

preoccupation [pri:ɑ:kjəpei'ʃən] *n* (obsession) 専念する事 sefìnen surù kotó; (worry) 気掛りな事 kigákàri na kotó

preoccupied [pri:ɑ:k'jəpaid] *adj* (person) 上の空になった uwánosorà ni náttà

prep [prep] *n* (SCOL: study) 勉強 benkyō

prepaid [pri:peid'] *adj* (paid in advance) 支払い済みの shiháraizumi no

preparation [prepərei'ʃən] *n* (activity) 準備 júnbi; (food) 料理 ryôri; (medicine) 薬品 yakúhin; (cosmetic) 化粧品 keshôhin

preparations [prepərei'ʃənz] *npl* (arrangements) 準備 júnbi

preparatory [pripǽr'ətɔːri:] *adj* (report) 予備の yóbi no; (training) 準備の júnbi no

preparatory school *n* (*US*) 予備校 yobíkō; (*BRIT*) 私立小学校 shirítsu shōgakkō

prepare [pripe:r'] *vt* (make ready: plan, speech, room etc) 準備する júnbi suru; (CULIN) 調理する chōri suru

♦*vi*: **to prepare for** (event, action) ...の準備をする ...no júnbi wo suru

prepared to (willing) ...する用意がある ...surú yōi ga árù

prepared for (ready) ...の用意ができている ...no yōi ga dékìte irú

preponderance [pripɑ:n'dərəns] *n* (of people, things) 大多数 daítasū

preposition [prepəzíʃ'ən] *n* 前置詞 zeńchishi

preposterous [pripɑ:s'tərəs] *adj* (suggestion, idea, situation) 途方もない tohōmonáì

prep school *n* = **preparatory school**

prerequisite [prirek'wizit] *n* 必要条件 hitsúyōjōken

prerogative [prərɑ:g'ətiv] *n* (of person, group) 特権 tokkén

Presbyterian [prezbiti:r'i:ən] *adj* 長老派の chōrōha no

♦*n* 長老派の信者 chōrōha no shiñja

preschool [pri:'sku:l'] *adj* (age, child, education) 就学前の shūgakumaè no

prescribe [priskraib'] *vt* (MED: medicine) 処方する shohō suru; (treatment) 命ずる meízurù

prescription [priskríp'ʃən] *n* (MED: slip of paper) 処方せん shohōsen; (: medicine) 処方薬 shohōyàku

presence [prez'əns] *n* (state of being somewhere) ...に居る事 ...ni irú kotò; (*fig*: strong personal quality) 風さい fúsai; (spirit, invisible influence) 霊界 reí

in someone's presence ...の居る前で ...no irú maè de

presence of mind *n* 機転 kitén

present [*adj, n* prez'ənt *vb* prizent'] *adj* (current: person, thing) 現在の geñzai no; (in attendance) 出席している shussé-ki shite irú

♦*n* (actuality): **the present** 現在 geñzai; (gift) 贈り物 okúrimono, プレゼント purézento

♦*vt* (give: prize, award etc) 贈る okúrù; (cause, provide: difficulty, threat etc) ...になる ...ni nárù; (information) 与える atáerù; (describe: person, thing) 描写する byōsha suru; (RADIO, TV) 提供する teíkyō suru; (formally introduce: person) 紹介する shōkai suru

to give someone a present ...にプレゼントを上げる ...ni purézento wo agérù

at present 今の所 imá no tokoro

presentable [prizen'təbəl] *adj* (person) 人前に出られる hitómae nì derárerù

presentation [prezəntei'ʃən] *n* (of plan, proposal, report etc) 提出 teíshutsu; (appearance) 体裁 teísai; (formal ceremony) 贈呈式 zōteishìki

present-day [prez'əntdei'] *adj* 現代の geñdai no

presenter [prizen'tə:r] *n* (RADIO, TV) 司会者 shikáìsha

presently [prez'əntli:] *adv* (soon) 間もなく mamónàku; (now) 現在 geñzai

preservation [prezə:rvei'ʃən] *n* (act of preserving) 保存 hozón; (state of being preserved) 保存状態 hozónjōtai

preservative [prizə:r'vətiv] *n* (for food, wood, metal etc) 保存剤 hozónzài

preserve [prizə:rv'] *vt* (maintain: situation, condition) 維持する íjì suru; (: building, manuscript) 保存する hozón suru; (food) 保存する hozón suru

♦*n* (*often pl*: jam, marmalade) ジャム jámù

preside [prizaid'] *vi*: **to preside (over)** (meeting, event etc) (...の) 議長をする (...no) gichō wò suru

presidency [prez'idənsi:] *n* (POL: post) 大統領職 daítōryōshoku; (: time in office) 大統領の任期 daítōryō no niñki

president [prez'idənt] *n* (POL) 大統領 daítōryō; (of organization) ...長 ...chō

presidential [preziden'tʃəl] *adj* 大統領の daítōryō no

press [pres] *n*: **the Press** (newspapers)

報道機関 hōdōkikàn; (journalists) 報道陣 hōdōjìn; (printing press) 印刷機 iṅsatsukì; (of switch, button, bell) 押す事 osú kotò

♦vt (hold one thing against another) 押付ける oshítsukerù; (button, switch, bell etc) 押す osú; (iron: clothes) ...にアイロンを掛ける ...ni aíron wò kakérù; (put pressure on: person) せき立てる sekítaterù; (insist): **to press something on someone** ...に...を押付ける ...ni ...wo oshítsukerù

♦vi (squeeze) 押える osáerù; (pressurize): **to press for** (improvement, change etc) ...のために働く ...no tamé nì határakù; (forcibly) 強要する kyōyō suru

we are pressed for time/money 時間〔金〕が足りない jíkàn〔kanè〕ga tarínai

press agency n 通信社 tsūshìnsha

press conference n 記者会見 kishákaìken

pressing [pres'iŋ] adj (engagement, decision etc) 緊急の kiṅkyū no

press on vi (despite problems etc) ひるまずに続ける hirúmazù ni tsuzúkerù

press stud [pres'stʌd] (BRIT) n スナップ sunáppù

press-up [pres'ʌp] (BRIT) n 腕立て伏せ udétatefùse

pressure [preʃ'əːr] n (physical force: also fig) 圧力 atsúryòku; (also: **air pressure**) 気圧 kiátsu; (also: **water pressure**) 水圧 suíatsu; (also: **oil pressure**) 油圧 yuátsu; (stress) 圧迫 appáku, プレッシャー puréssha

to put pressure on someone (to do) (...する様に) ...に圧力を掛ける (...surú yồ ni) ...ni atsúryòku wo kakérù

pressure cooker n 圧力ガマ atsúryokugàma

pressure gauge n 圧力計 atsúryokukei

pressure group n (POL) 圧力団体 atsúryokudaǹtai, プレッシャーグループ purésshāgurùpu

pressurized [preʃ'əraizd] adj (cabin, container, spacesuit) 気圧を一定に保った kiátsu wò ittéi ni tamottà

prestige [presti:ʒ'] n 名声 meísei

prestigious [prestidʒ'əs] adj (prestigious job, reputation: person, organization) 著名な cho-

méi na

presumably [prizu:'məbliː] adv たぶん tábùn, おそらく osóràku

presume [prizu:m'] vt: **to presume (that)** (suppose) (...だと) 推定する (...dá tò) suítei suru

presumption [prizʌmp'ʃən] n (supposition) 推定 suítei

presumptuous [prizʌmp'tʃuːəs] adj せん越な señ-etsu na

presuppose [priːsəpouz'] vt ...を前提とする ...wo zeñtei tò suru

pretence [pritens'] (US also: **pretense**) n (false appearance) 見せ掛け misékake

under false pretences うそを言って úsò wo itté

pretend [pritend'] vt (feign) ...の振りをする ...no furí wò suru

♦vi (feign) 見せ掛ける misékakerù

to pretend to do ...する振りをする ...suru furí wò suru

pretense [pritens'] (US) n = **pretence**

pretentious [priten'tʃəs] adj (claiming importance, significance: person, play, film etc) うぬぼれた unúboreta

pretext [pri:'tekst] n 口実 kōjitsu

pretty [prit'iː] adj (person, thing) きれいな kírèi na

♦adv (quite) かなり kánàri

prevail [priveil'] vi (be current: custom, belief) はやる hayárù; (gain acceptance, influence: proposal, principle) 勝つ kátsù

prevailing [privei'liŋ] adj (wind) 卓越風 takúetsufù; (dominant: fashion, attitude etc) 一般の ippán no

prevalent [prev'ələnt] adj (common) 一般的な ippántekì na

prevent [privent'] vt: **to prevent someone from doing something** ...が...をするのを妨げる ...ga ...wo suru no wò samátagerù

to prevent something from happening ...が起るのを防ぐ ...ga okórù no wo fuségù

preventative [priven'tətiv] adj = **preventive**

prevention [priven'tʃən] n 予防 yobó

preventive [priven'tiv] *adj* (measures, medicine) 予防の yobố no

preview [pri:'vju:] *n* (of film) 試写会 shishākai; (of exhibition etc) 招待展示内覧 shốtaitenjinairan

previous [pri:'vi:əs] *adj* (earlier: event, thing, period of time) 前の mâe no

previously [pri:'vi:əsli:] *adv* 前に mâe ni

pre-war [pri:'wɔ:r'] *adj* 戦前の senzen no

prey [prei] *n* 獲物 emóno
♦*vi*: **to prey on** (animal: feed on) ...を捕食する ...wo hoshóku suru
it was preying on his mind 彼はそれを気にしていた kárè wa soré wò ki ní shite itá

price [prais] *n* (amount of money) 値段 nedán; (*fig*) 代償 daíshō
♦*vt* (goods) ...に値段を付ける ...ni nedán wò tsukérù

priceless [prais'lis] *adj* 非常に貴重な hijố nì kichó na

price list *n* 値段表 nedánhyồ

prick [prik] *n* (short, sharp pain) ちくっとする痛み chikúttò suru itámi
♦*vt* (make hole in) 鋭い物で刺す surúdoi monồ dè sásù; (cause pain) ちくっと刺す chikúttô sásù
to prick up one's ears (listen eagerly) 耳を澄まして聞く mimí wò sumáshite kikù

prickle [prik'əl] *n* (of plant) とげ togè; (sensation) ちくちくする痛み chíkuchiku suru itámi

prickly [prik'li:] *adj* (plant) とげだらけの togédarakè no; (fabric) ちくちくする chíkuchiku suru

prickly heat *n* 汗も asémo

pride [praid] *n* (satisfaction) 誇り hokóri; (dignity, self-respect) 自尊心 jisónshin, プライド puráido; (*pej*: feeling of superiority) 高慢 kốman
♦*vt*: **to pride oneself on** ...を誇りとする ...wo hokóri tò suru

priest [pri:st] *n* (Christian: Catholic, Anglican etc) 司祭 shisái; (non-Christian) 僧侶 sốryo

priestess [pri:s'tis] *n* (non-Christian) みこ míkò

priesthood [pri:st'hud] *n* (position) 司祭職 shisáishokù

prig [prig] *n* 気取り屋 kidóriyà

prim [prim] (*pej*) *adj* (formal, correct) 堅苦しい katákurushiî; (easily shocked) 上品ぶった jốhiñbutta

primarily [praime:r'ili:] *adv* (above all) 主に ồmò ni

primary [prai'me:ri:] *adj* (first in importance) 主要な shuyố na
♦*n* (*US*: election) 予備選挙 yobísenkyo

primary school *n* 小学校 shốgakkồ

primate [prai'meit] *n* (ZOOL) 霊長類 refchốrui

prime [praim] *adj* (most important) 最も重要な mottómò jūyố na; (best quality) 最上の saíjō no
♦*n* (of person's life) 盛り sakári
♦*vt* (wood) ...に下塗りをする ...ni shitánuri wò suru; (*fig*: person) ...に教え込む ...ni oshíekomù
prime example (typical) 典型的な例 teñkeiteki nà reí

Prime Minister *n* 総理大臣 sốridaìjin, 首相 shushố

primeval [praimi:'vəl] *adj* (existing since long ago): *primeval forest* 原生林 geñseírin; (feelings, tribe) 原始的な geñshiteki na

primitive [prim'ətiv] *adj* 原始的な geñshiteki na

primrose [prim'rouz] *n* サクラソウ tsukímiso

primus (stove) [prai'məs-] (*BRIT*) *n* 石油こんろ sekíyukoñro

prince [prins] *n* (son of king etc) 王子 ốji; (son of Japanese emperor) 親王 shiñnố

princess [prin'sis] *n* (daughter of king etc) 王女 ồjo; (daughter of Japanese emperor) 内親王 naíshinnồ

principal [prin'səpəl] *adj* (most important: reason, character, aim etc) 主要な shuyố na
♦*n* (of school) 校長 kốchō; (of college) 学長 gakúchō

principle [prin'səpəl] *n* (moral belief) 信念 shiñnen; (general rule) 原則 geñsoku; (scientific law) 法則 hốsoku *in principle* (theoretically) 原則として geñsoku tòshité

on principle (morally) 主義として shugí tòshité

print [print] n (letters and numbers on page) 印刷文字 iñsatsumojì; (ART) 版画 hañga; (PHOT) 陽画 yóga, プリント purínto; (footprint) 足跡 ashíatò; (fingerprint) 指紋 shimón
♦vt (produce: book, newspaper, leaflet) 印刷する iñsatsu suru; (publish: story, article etc) 記載する kisái suru; (cloth) ...になっ染する ...ni nassén suru; (write in capitals) 活字体で書く katsújitai dè kákù

out of print 絶版で zeppán de

printed matter [prin'tid-] n 印刷物 iñsatsubùtsu

printer [prin'tər] n (person, firm) 印刷屋 iñsatsuyà; (machine) 印刷機 iñsatsukì

printing [prin'tiŋ] n (act, art) 印刷 iñsatsu

printout [print'aut] n (COMPUT) プリントアウト puríntoaùto

prior [prai'ə:r] adj (previous: knowledge, warning, consent etc) 事前の jizén no; (more important: claim, duty) より重要な yorí jûyô na

prior to ...の前に ...no máè ni

priority [praiɔ:r'iti:] n (most urgent task) 優先課題 yúsenkadài; (most important thing, task) 最重要課題 saíjûyôkadài

to have priority (over) (...に) 優先する (...ni) yûsen suru

prise [praiz] vt: *to prise open* こじ開ける kojíakerù

prism [priz'əm] n プリズム purízumu

prison [priz'ən] n (building) 刑務所 keímusho
♦cpd 刑務所の keímusho no

prisoner [priz'ənə:r] n (in prison) 囚人 shújin; (captured person) 捕虜 hóryò

prisoner of war n 戦争捕虜 señsōhoryò

pristine [pris'ti:n] adj (condition: new) 真新しい maátarashiì; (: like new) 新品同様の shiñpindoyò no

privacy [prai'vəsi:] n プライバシー puráibashi

private [prai'vit] adj (not public: property, club etc) 私有の shiyû no, プライベートの puráibēto no; (not state-owned: industry, service) 民間の miñkan no; (discussion, sitting etc) 非公開の hikôkai no; (personal: activities, belongings) 個人の kójìn no; (: thoughts, plans) 心の中の kokóro no naka no; (quiet: place) 奥まった okúmattà; (: person) 内気な uchíki na; (confidential) 内密の naímitsu no; (intimate) 部外者立入禁止の bugáisha tachíirikinshi no
♦n (MIL) 兵卒 heísotsu

「*private*」(on envelope) 親展 shiñten; (on door) 部外者立入禁止 bugáishà tachíirikinshi

in private 内密に naímitsu ni

private enterprise n (not state owned) 民間企業 miñkan kigyô; (owned by individual) 個人企業 kójin kigyô

private eye n 私立探偵 shirítsutaǹtei

private property n 私有地 shiyûchì

private school n (fee-paying) 私立学校 shirítsugakkô

privatize [prai'vətaiz] vt (government-owned company etc) 民間に払い下げる miñkan nì harái sagerù

privet [priv'it] n イボタノキ ibótanoki

privilege [priv'əlidʒ] n (advantage) 特権 tokkén; (opportunity) 光栄な機会 kôei na kikaì

privileged [priv'əlidʒd] adj (having advantages) 特権のある tokkén no arù; (having special opportunity) 光栄な機会を得た kôei na kikaì wo etá

privy [priv'i:] adj: *to be privy to* 内々に関知している naínai nì kánchi shité irù

prize [praiz] n (reward) 賞 shô
♦adj (first class) 典型的な teñkeiteki na
♦vt 重宝する chôhô suru

prize-giving [praiz'giviŋ] n 表彰式 hyôshôshìki

prizewinner [praiz'winə:r] n 受賞者 jushôshà

pro [prou] n (SPORT) 職業選手 shokúgyôseñshu, プロ púrò

♦*prep* (in favor of) ...に賛成して ...ni sansei shite

the pros and cons 賛否両論 sánpiryōron

probability [prɑːbəbilʾəti:] *n* (likelihood): *probability of/that* ...の〔...が起る〕公算 ...no 〔...ga okórù〕kốsan

in all probability たいてい taítei

probable [prɑːbʾəbəl] *adj* (likely to happen) 起りそうな okórisō na; (likely to be true) ありそうな arísō na

probably [prɑːbʾəbli:] *adv* た ぶ ん tábùn, おそらく osóraku

probation [prəbeiʾʃən] *n*: *on probation* (LAW) 保護観察 hogókaǹsatsu de; (employee) 見習いで minárai de

probe [proub] *n* (MED) ゾンデ zóǹde; (SPACE) 探査衛星 tañsaeisèi; (enquiry) 調査 chốsa

♦*vt* (investigate) 調査する chṓsa suru; (poke) つついて探る tsutsúite sagúrù

problem [prɑːbʾləm] *n* 問題 moǹdai

problematic(al) [prɑːbləmætʾik(əl)] *adj* 問題になる moǹdai ni narú

procedure [prəsiːʾdʒəːr] *n* (way of doing something) や り 方 yaríkata; (ADMIN, LAW) 手続 tetsúzuki

proceed [prəsiːdʾ] *vi* (do afterwards): *to proceed to do something* ...をし始める ...wo shihájimerù; (continue): *to proceed (with)* (...を) 続ける (...wo) tsuzúkerù; (activity, event, process: carry on) 続ける tsuzúkerù; (person: go) 行く ikú

proceedings [prəsiːʾdiŋz] *npl* (organized events) 行事 gyṓji; (LAW) 訴訟手続き soshṓtetsuzùki

proceeds [prouʾsiːdz] *npl* 収益 shúeki

process [prɑːsʾes] *n* (series of actions: *also* BIOL, CHEM) 過程 katéi, プロセス purósèsu

♦*vt* (raw materials, food) 加工する kakṓ suru; (information) 処理する shóri suru

processing [prɑːsʾesiŋ] *n* (PHOT) 現像 geńzō

procession [prəseʾʃən] *n* 行列 gyṓretsu

proclaim [prəkleimʾ] *vt* (announce) 宣言する señgen suru

proclamation [prɑːkləmeiʾʃən] *n* 宣言 señgen

procrastinate [prəkræsʾtəneit] *vi* 先に延ばす sakí nī nobásù

procreation [proukri:eiʾʃən] *n* 生殖 seíshoku

procure [prəkjuːrʾ] *vt* 調達する chṓtatsu suru

prod [prɑːd] *vt* (push: with finger, stick, knife etc) つつく tsutsúkù

♦*n* (with finger, stick, knife etc) 一突き hitótsuki

prodigal [prɑːdʾəgəl] *adj*: *prodigal son/daughter* 放とう息子〔娘〕hṓtōmusùko 〔musùme〕

prodigious [prədidʒʾəs] *adj* 巨大な kyódai na

prodigy [prɑːdʾədʒi:] *n* 天才 teńsai

produce [*n* prouʾduːs *vb* prəduːsʾ] *n* (AGR) 農産物 nṓsanbùtsu

♦*vt* (cause: effect, result etc) 起す okósù; (make, create: object) 作 る tsukúrù; (BIOL: fruit, seeds) つける tsukérù, ...には...がなる ...nî wà ...ga nárù; (: young) 産む umú; (CHEM) 作り出す tsukúridasù; (fig: evidence, argument) 示す shimésù; (: bring or take out) 取出す torídasù; (play, film, program) 製作する seísaku suru

producer [prəduːʾsəːr] *n* (of film, play, program, record) 製作者 seísakushà, プロデューサー puródyūsā; (country: of food, material) 生産国 seísankòku; (company: of food, material) 生産会社 seísangaìsha

product [prɑːdʾəkt] *n* (thing) 産物 sańbutsu; (result) 結果 kekká

production [prədʌkʾʃən] *n* (process of manufacturing, growing) 生産 seísan; (amount of goods manufactured, grown) 生産高 seísandaka; (THEATER) 上演 jṓen

electricity production 発電 hatsúden

production line *n* 工程ライン kṓteiraìn, ライン ráìn

productive [prədʌkʾtiv] *adj* (person, thing: *also fig*) 生産的な seísanteki na

productivity [prɑːdəktivʾəti:] *n* 生産性

力 seísannòryoku

profane [prəfeɪn'] adj (secular, lay) 世俗的な sezōkuteki na; (language etc) 下品な gehín na

profess [prəfes'] vt (claim) 主張する shuchō suru; (express: feeling, opinion) 明言する meígen suru

profession [prəfeʃ'ən] n (job requiring special training) 知的職業 chitékishokugyò; (people) 同業者仲間 dōgyōshanakàma

professional [prəfeʃ'ənəl] adj (skill, organization, advice) 専門職の senmonshoku no; (not amateur: photographer, musician etc) プロの púrò no; (highly trained) 専門家の senmonka no; (of a high standard) 本職らしい hoñshokurashiì
♦n (doctor, lawyer, teacher etc) 知的職業者 chitékishokugyòshà; (SPORT) プロ púrò; (skilled person) 玄人 kúrðto

professor [prəfes'ər] n (US) 教師 kyōshi, 先生 seńsei; (BRIT) 教授 kyōju

proficiency [prəfiʃ'ənsi:] n 熟練 jukúren

proficient [prəfiʃ'ənt] adj 熟練した jukúren shita

profile [prou'faɪl] n (of person's face) 横顔 yokógaò; (fig: article) 経歴 keíreki

profit [prɑ:f'it] n (COMM) 利益 ríèki
♦vi: to profit by/from (fig) …がために なる …ga tamé nì nárù

profitability [prɑ:fitəbil'əti:] n (ECON) 収益性 shúekisei

profitable [prɑ:f'itəbəl] adj (ECON) 利益になる ríèki ni nárù

profound [prəfaund'] adj (great: shock, effect) 強い tsuyóì; (intellectual: idea, work) 深遠な shiń-en na

profusely [prəfju:s'li:] adv (bleed) 多量に taryő ni; (thank) 重ね重ね kasánegasàne

profusion [prəfju:'ʒən] n 大量 taíryō

prognoses [prɑ:gnou'si:z] npl of **prognosis**

prognosis [prɑ:gnou'səs] (pl **prognoses**) n (forecast) 予想 yosō; (of illness) 予後 yógò

program [prou'græm] (BRIT **programme**) n (of actions, events) 計画 keíkaku; (RADIO, TV) 番組 bañgumi; (leaflet) プログラム puróguràmu; (COMPUT) プログラム puróguràmu
♦vt (machine, system) …にプログラムを入れる …ni puróguràmu wo irérù

programing [prou'græmiŋ] (BRIT **programming**) n (COMPUT) プログラム作成 puróguramu sakuséì, プログラミング puróguramiñgu

programmer [prou'græmər] n (COMPUT) プログラマー puróguràmā

progress [n prɑ:g'res vb prəgres'] n (process of getting nearer to objective) 前進 zeńshin; (changes, advances in society) 進歩 shíñpo; (development) 発展 hattén
♦vi (become more advanced, skilled) 進歩する shíñpo suru; (become higher in rank) 昇進する shōshin suru; (continue) 続く tsuzúkù

in progress (meeting, battle, match) 進行中で shiñkōchū de

progression [prəgreʃ'ən] n (gradual development) 進展 shiñten; (series) 連続 reñzoku

progressive [prəgres'iv] adj (person) 進歩的な shiñpoteki na; (change) 段階的な dañkaiteki na

prohibit [prouhib'it] vt (forbid, make illegal) 禁じる kiñjirù

prohibition [prouəbiʃ'ən] n (law, rule) 禁則 kiñsoku; (forbidding: of strikes, alcohol etc) 禁止 kiñshi; (US): **Prohibition** 禁酒法時代 kiñshuhōjidài

prohibitive [prouhib'ətiv] adj (price etc) 法外な hōgai na, 手が出ない様な té gà dénài yō na

project [n prɑ:dʒ'ekt vb prədʒekt'] n (large-scale plan, scheme) 計画 keíkaku; (SCOL) 研究テーマ keñkyūtèma
♦vt (plan) 計画する keíkaku suru; (estimate: figure, amount) 見積る mitsúmorù; (light) 投射する tōsha suru; (film, picture) 映写する eísha suru
♦vi (stick out) 突出る tsukíderù

projectile [prədʒek'təl] n 弾丸 dañgan

projection [prədʒek'ʃən] n (estimate) 見積り mitsúmori; (overhang) 突起 tokkí;

(CINEMA) 映写 eísha

projector [prədʒek'tə:r] n 映写機 eíshaki

proletarian [prouliteːr'iːən] adj 無産階級の musánkaìkyū no, プロレタリアの puróretarìa no

proletariat [prouliteːr'iːət] n 無産階級 musánkaìkyū, プロレタリア puróretarìa

proliferate [proulif'əːreit] vi 急増する kyúzo suru

prolific [proulif'ik] adj (artist, composer, writer) 多作の tasáku no

prologue [prou'lɔːg] n (of play) 序幕 jomáku, プロローグ purórògu; (of book) 序言 jogén

prolong [prəlɔːŋ'] vt (life, meeting, holiday) 引延ばす hikínobasù, 延長する eńchō suru

prom [prɑːm] n abbr = **promenade;** (US: ball) 学生舞踏会 gakúseibutòkai

promenade [prɑːməneid'] n (by sea) 海岸の遊歩道 kaígan nò yúhodò

promenade concert (BRIT) n 立見席のある音楽会 tachímisèki no árù oñgakukài

prominence [prɑːm'ənəns] n (importance) 重要性 júyōsei

prominent [prɑːm'ənənt] adj (important) 重要な júyō na; (very noticeable) 目立つ medátsù

promiscuous [prəmis'kjuːəs] adj (person) 相手構わずにセックスをする aíte kamawazù ni sékkùsu wo suru

promise [prɑːm'is] n (vow) 約束 yakúsoku; (talent) 才能 saínō; (hope) 見込み mikómi

♦vi (vow) 約束する yakúsoku suru

♦vt: **to promise someone something, promise something to someone** ...に...を約束する ...ni ...wo yakúsoku suru

to promise (someone) to do something/that (...に) ...すると約束する (...ni) ...surú tò yakúsoku suru

promising [prɑːm'isiŋ] adj (person, thing) 有望な yūbō na

promote [prəmout'] vt (employee) 昇進させる shōshin saserù; (product, pop star) 宣伝する señden suru; (ideas) 促進

する sokúshin suru

promoter [prəmou'təːr] n (of event) 興業主 kōgyōshù, プロモーター purómōtā; (of cause, idea) 推進者 suíshinsha

promotion [prəmou'ʃən] n (at work) 昇進 shōshin; (of product, event, idea) 宣伝 señden

prompt [prɑːmpt] adj (rapid: reaction, response etc) 迅速な jińsoku na

♦adv (exactly) 丁度 chōdo

♦n (COMPUT) プロンプト puróñputo

♦vt (cause) ...の原因となる ...no geñ·in tò nárù; (when talking) ...に水を向ける ...ni mizú wò mukérù

to prompt someone to do something ...が...をするきっ掛けとなる ...ga ...wo suru kikkáke to narù

promptly [prɑːmpt'liː] adv (immediately) 直ちに tádàchi ni; (exactly) 丁度 chōdo

prone [proun] adj (lying face down) うつ伏せの utsúbuse no

prone to (inclined to) ...しがちな ...shigáchi na

prong [prɔːŋ] n (of fork) 歯 há

pronoun [prou'naun] n 代名詞 daímeìshi

pronounce [prənauns'] vt (word) 発音する hatsúon suru; (declare) 宣言する señgen suru; (give verdict, opinion) 言渡す iíwatasù

pronounced [prənaunst'] adj (marked) 著しい ichíjirushiì

pronunciation [prənʌnsiːei'ʃən] n 発音 hatsúon

proof [pruːf] n (evidence) 証拠 shōko; (TYP) 校正刷り kōseizuri, ゲラ gerá

♦adj: **proof against** ...に耐えられる ...ni taérarerù

prop [prɑːp] n (stick, support: also fig) 支え sasáe

♦vt (also: **prop up**) 支える sasáerù; (lean): **to prop something against** ...を...に立掛ける ...wo ...ni tatékakerù

propaganda [prɑːpəgæn'də] n 宣伝 señden, プロパガンダ purópaganda

propagate [prɑːp'əgeit] vt (idea, information) 普及させる fukyū saserù

propel [prəpel'] vt (vehicle, boat,

machine) 推進する suíshin suru; (*fig:* person) 駆立てる karítaterù

propeller [prəpel'ə:r] *n* プロペラ puròperà

propensity [prəpen'siti:] *n* 傾向 keíkō

proper [prɑ:p'ə:r] *adj* (real, authentic) ちゃんとした chánto shita; (correct) 正しい tadáshiì; (suitable) 適 当 な tekítō na; (socially acceptable) 社会の通念にかなった shákài no tsūnen ni kanáttà; (referring to place): *the village proper* 村その ものの murá sonò monò

properly [prɑ:p'ə:rli:] *adv* (adequately: eat, study) 充分に júbun ni; (decently: behave) 正しく tadáshiku

proper noun *n* 固有名詞 koyúmeìshi

property [prɑ:p'ə:rti:] *n* (possessions) 財産 zaísan; (building and its land) 物件 bukkén; (land owned) 所有地 shoyúchì; (quality: of substance, material etc) 特性 tokúsei

property owner *n* 地主 jinúshi

prophecy [prɑ:f'isi:] *n* 予言 yogén

prophesy [prɑ:f'isai] *vt* (predict) 予言する yogén suru

prophet [prɑ:f'it] *n* (REL) 予言者 yogénsha

prophetic [prəfet'ik] *adj* (statement, words) 予言的な yogénteki na

proportion [prəpɔ:r'ʃən] *n* (part: of group, amount) 割合 waríai; (number: of people, things) 数 kázù; (ratio) 率 rítsu

proportional [prəpɔ:r'ʃənəl] *adj: proportional (to)* (...に) 比例する (...ni) hiréi suru

proportional representation *n* 比例代表制 hiréidaihyōsei

proportionate [prəpɔ:r'ʃənit] *adj: proportionate (to)* (...に) 比例する (...ni) hiréi suru

proposal [prəpou'zəl] *n* (plan) 提案 teían

a proposal (of marriage) 結婚の申込み kekkón nò mōshikomi, プロポーズ purópòzu

propose [prəpouz'] *vt* (plan, idea) 提案する teían suru; (motion) 提出する teíshutsu suru; (toast) ...の音頭を取る ... no ón̄do wo tórù

♦*vi* (offer marriage) 結婚を申込む kekkón wò mōshikomù, プロポーズする purópòzu suru

to propose to do ...するつもりでいる ...suru tsumóri de irù

proposition [prɑ:pəziʃ'ən] *n* (statement) 主張 shuchō; (offer) 申出 mōshide

proprietor [prəprai'ətə:r] *n* (of hotel, shop, newspaper etc) 持主 mochínùshi, オーナー ōnā

propriety [prəprai'əti:] *n* (seemliness) 礼儀正しさ reígitadashìsa

pro rata [-rɑ:'tə] *adv* 比例して hiréi shite

prosaic [prouzei'ik] *adj* (person, piece of writing) 散文的な sañbunteki na

prose [prouz] *n* (not poetry) 散文 sañbun

prosecute [prɑ:s'əkju:t] *vt* (LAW) 訴追する sotsúi suru

prosecution [prɑ:səkju:'ʃən] *n* (action) 訴追 sotsúi; (accusing side) 検察側 keñsatsugàwa

prosecutor [prɑ:s'əkju:tə:r] *n* (*also:* **public prosecutor**) 検察官 keñsatsukàn

prospect [prɑ:s'pekt] *n* (possibility) 可能性 kanōsei; (outlook) 見込み mikómi

♦*vi: to prospect (for)* (gold etc) (...を) 探鉱する (...wo) tañkō suru

prospecting [prɑ:s'pektiŋ] *n* (for gold, oil etc) 探鉱 tañkō

prospective [prəspek'tiv] *adj* (son-in-law, customer, candidate etc) ...になろうとしている ...ni narō tò shité irù

prospects [prɑ:s'pekts] *npl* (for work etc) 見込み mikómi

prospectus [prəspek'təs] *n* (of college, school, company) 要綱 yōkō

prosper [prɑ:s'pə:r] *vi* (person, business, city etc) 繁栄する hañ-ei suru

prosperity [prɑ:sper'iti:] *n* 繁栄 hañ-ei

prosperous [prɑ:s'pə:rəs] *adj* (person, city etc) 裕福な yúfuku na; (business etc) 繁盛している hañjō shite irù

prostitute [prɑ:s'titu:t] *n* (female) 売春婦 baíshuñfu; (male) 男娼 dañshō

prostrate [prɑ:s'treit] *adj* (face down) うつ伏せの utsúbuse no

protagonist [proutæg'ənist] *n* (sup-

protect [prətɛkt'] *vt* (person, thing) 守る mamórù, 保護する hógò suru

protection [prətɛk'ʃən] *n* 保護 hógò

protective [prətɛk'tiv] *adj* (clothing, layer, etc) 防護の bǒgo no; (gesture) 防衛の bǒei no; (person) 保護的な hogóteki na

protégé [prou'təʒei] *n* 偉い人のひいきを受ける人 erái hitó nò hiíki wò ukérù hitó

protein [prou'ti:n] *n* たんぱく質 tañpakushītsu

protest [*n* prou'tɛst *vb* prətɛst'] *n* (strong expression of disapproval, opposition) 抗議 kǒgi

♦*vi*: **to protest about/against/at** ...に抗議する ...ni kǒgi suru

♦*vt* (insist): **to protest (that)** (...だと)主張する (...dá tò) shuchǒ suru

Protestant [prɑt'istənt] *adj* 新教の shíñkyo no, プロテスタントの purótesùtanto no

♦*n* 新教徒 shíñkyoto, プロテスタント教徒 purótesùtanto kyóto

protester [prətɛs'tə:r] *n* 抗議者 kǒgishà

protocol [prou'təkɔ:l] *n* 外交儀礼 gaíkǒgirèi

prototype [prou'tətaip] *n* 原型 geñkei

protracted [proutræk'tid] *adj* (absence, meeting etc) 長引いた nagábiità

protrude [proutru:d'] *vi* (rock, ledge, teeth etc) 突出る tsukéderù

proud [praud] *adj* (pleased): **proud of** ...を誇りとする ...wo hokóri tò suru; (dignified) プライドのある puráido no arù; (arrogant) 尊大な soñdai na

prove [pru:v] *vt* (verify) 立証する risshǒ suru

♦*vi*: **to prove (to be) correct** *etc* 結局...が正しいと判明する kekkyóku ...ga tadáshiì to hañmei suru

to prove oneself 自分の才能を立証する jibún nò saínō wò risshǒ suru

proverb [prɑ'və:rb] *n* ことわざ kotówaza

proverbial [prəvə:r'bi:əl] *adj* ことわざの kotówaza no

provide [prəvaid'] *vt* (give) 与える atáerù; (make available) 供給する kyǒkyū suru

to provide someone with something ...に...を供給する ...ni ...wo kyǒkyō suru

provided (that) [prəvai'did-] *conj* ...という条件で ...tò iù jǒken de

provide for *vt fus* (person) ...の面倒を見る ...no meñdō wò mírù

♦*vt* (future event) ...に備える ...ni sonáerù

Providence [prɑːv'idəns] *n* 摂理 sétsùri

providing [prəvai'diŋ] *conj*: **providing (that)** ...という条件で ...tò iù jǒken de

province [prɑːv'ins] *n* (of country) 県 kéñ; (*fig*) 管轄 kañkatsu

provincial [prəvin'tʃəl] *adj* (town, newspaper etc) 地方の chihǒ no; (*pej*) 田舎みた ináka jimità

provision [prəviʒ'ən] *n* (supplying) 供給 kyǒkyū; (of contract, agreement) 規定 kitéi

provisional [prəviʒ'ənəl] *adj* (government, agreement, arrangement etc) 暫定的な zañteiteki na

provisions [prəviʒ'ənz] *npl* (food) 食料 shokúryō

proviso [prəvai'zou] *n* 規定 kitéi

provocation [prɑːvəkei'ʃən] *n* 挑発 chǒhatsu

provocative [prəvɑːk'ətiv] *adj* (remark, article, gesture) 挑発的な chǒhatsuteki na; (sexually stimulating) 扇情的な señjōteki na

provoke [prəvouk'] *vt* (annoy: person) 怒らせる okóraserù; (cause: fight, argument etc) 引起こす hikíokosù

prow [prau] *n* へさき hesáki, 船首 séñshu

prowess [prau'is] *n* (outstanding ability) 手腕 shúwan

prowl [praul] *vi* (*also*: **prowl about**, **prowl around**) うろつく urótsukù

♦*n*: **on the prowl** あさり歩いて asáriaruìte

prowler [prau'lə:r] *n* うろつく人 urótsuku hitó

proximity [prɑːksimˈitiː] *n* 近さ chikása

proxy [prɑːkˈsiː] *n*: **by proxy** 代理を通じて dáiri wò tsūjite

prude [pruːd] *n* 上品ぶる人 jōhiñburu hitō

prudence [pruːˈdəns] *n* (care, sense) 慎重さ shiñchōsa

prudent [pruːˈdənt] *adj* (careful, sensible) 慎重な shiñchō na

prune [pruːn] *n* 干しプラム hoshípurâmu
♦*vt* (bush, plant, tree) せん定する señtei suru

pry [prai] *vi*: **to pry (into)** (...を) せん索する (...wo) señsaku suru

PS [piːˈes] *abbr* = **postscript**

psalm [sɑːm] *n* 詩編 shihén

pseudo- [suːˈdou] *prefix* 偽... nisé...

pseudonym [suːˈdənim] *n* 筆名 hitsúmei, ペンネーム peñnêmu

psyche [saiˈkiː] *n* 精神 seíshin

psychiatric [saikiˈætˈrik] *adj* (hospital, problem, treatment) 精神科の seíshinka no

psychiatrist [sikaiˈətrist] *n* 精神科医 seíshinka-ì

psychiatry [sikaiˈətriː] *n* 精神医学 seíshin-igàku

psychic [saiˈkik] *adj* (person: *also*: **psychical**) 霊媒の reíbai no; (of the mind) 精神の seíshin no

psychoanalysis [saikouənælˈisis] *n* 精神分析 seíshinbuñseki

psychoanalyst [saikouænˈəlist] *n* 精神分析医 seíshinbuñseki-ì

psychoanalyze [saikouænˈəlaiz] *vt* ...の精神分析をする ...no seíshinbuñseki wo suru

psychological [saikəlɑːdʒˈikəl] *adj* (related to the mind: difference, problem etc) 精神的な seíshinteki na; (related to psychology: test, treatment etc) 心理的な shiñriteki na

psychologist [saikɑːlˈədʒist] *n* 心理学者 shiñrigakùsha

psychology [saikɑːlˈədʒiː] *n* (study) 心理学 shiñrigàku; (mind) 心理 shiñri

psychopath [saiˈkəpæθ] *n* 精神病質者 seíshinbyōshitsushà

psychosomatic [saikousoumætˈik] *adj* 精神身体の seíshinshiñtai no

psychotic [saikɑːtˈik] *adj* 精神病の seíshinbyō no

PTO [piːˈtiːˈou] *abbr* (= *please turn over*) 裏面に続く rímen ni tsuzukù

pub [pʌb] *n* *abbr* (= *public house*) 酒場 sakába, パブ pábù

puberty [pjuːˈbəːrtiː] *n* 思春期 shishúñki

pubic [pjuːˈbik] *adj*: **pubic hair** 陰毛 iñmō

public [pʌbˈlik] *adj* (of people: support, opinion, interest) 国民の kokúmin no; (for people: building, service) 公共の kōkyō no; (for people to see: statement, action etc) 公の ōyake no
♦*n*: **the public** (all people of country, community) 公衆 kōshū; (particular set of people) ...層 ...sō; (fans, supporters) 支持者 shijísha
in public 公に ōyake ni, 人前で hitómaè de
to make public 公表する kōyō suru

public address system *n* 場内放送 (装置) jōnaihōsō(sōchi)

publican [pʌbˈlikən] *n* パブの亭主 pábù no teíshu

publication [pʌblikeiˈʃən] *n* (act) 出版 shuppán; (book, magazine) 出版物 shuppáñbutsu

public company *n* 株式会社 kabúshiki-gaìsha

public convenience (*BRIT*) *n* 公衆便所 kōshūbeñjo

public holiday *n* 休日 kyújitsu

public house (*BRIT*) *n* 酒場 sakába, パブ pábù

publicity [pʌblisˈətiː] *n* (information) 宣伝 señden; (attention) 広く知られる事 híròku shiráreru kotò

publicize [pʌbˈləsaiz] *vt* (fact, event) 報道する hōdō suru

publicly [pʌbˈlikliː] *adv* 公に ōyake ni, 人前で hitómaè de

public opinion *n* 世論 yóron

public relations *n* 広報活動 kōhōkatsu-dō, ピーアール píàru

public school *n* (*US*) 公立学校 kōritsugakkō̃; (BRIT) 私立学校 shirítsugakkō̃

public-spirited [pʌb'likspir'itid] adj 公心のある kốkyōshin nò árù

public transport n 公共輸送機関 kốyō-yusōkikaǹ

publish [pʌb'liʃ] vt (book, magazine) 出版する shuppán suru, 発行する hakkố suru; (letter etc: in newspaper) 記載する kisái suru; (subj: person: article, story) 発表する happyố suru

publisher [pʌb'liʃə:r] n (person) 発行者 hakkố̃shà; (company) 出版社 shuppáǹsha

publishing [pʌb'liʃiŋ] n (profession) 出版業 shuppangyō̃

puce [pju:s] adj 暗かっ色の aǹkasshoku no

pucker [pʌk'ə:r] vt (part of face) ...をしかめる ...wo shikámerù; (fabric etc) ...にしわを寄せる ...ni shiwá wò yosérù

pudding [pud'iŋ] n (cooked sweet food) プディング púdìngu; (BRIT: dessert) デザート dezáto
　　black pudding ブラッドソーセージ buráddosōsēji

puddle [pʌd'əl] n (also: **a puddle of water**) 水溜まり mizutamari; (of blood etc) 溜まり tamari

puff [pʌf] n (of cigarette, pipe) 一服 ippúku; (gasp) あえぎ aégi; (of air, smoke) 一吹き hitófuki
　　◆vt: **to puff one's pipe** パイプをふかす páĩpu wo fukásù
　　◆vi (breathe loudly) あえぐ aégù

puffed [pʌft] (inf) adj (out of breath) 息を切らせた íkì wo kírasetà

puff out vt (fill with air: one's chest, cheeks) 膨らます fukúramasù

puff pastry n パイ皮 paíkawa

puffy [pʌf'i:] adj (eye) はれぼったい harébottaì; (face) むくんだ mukúǹda

pull [pul] n (tug): **to give something a pull** ...を引っ張る ...wo hippárù
　　◆vt (gen) 引く hikú; (tug: rope, hair etc) 引っ張る hippárù
　　◆vi (tug) 引く hikú, 引っ張る hippárù
　　to pull to pieces 引裂く hikísakù
　　to pull one's punches 手加減する teká-

gen suru
　　to pull one's weight 仲間同様に働く nakámadòyō ni határakù
　　to pull oneself together 落着きを取り戻す ochítsuki wò torímodosù
　　to pull someone's leg (fig) ...をからかう ...wo karákaù

pull apart vt (break) ばらばらにする barábara nì suru

pull down vt (building) 取壊す toríkowasù

pulley [pul'i:] n 滑車 kasshá

pull in vi (AUT: at the curb) ...に停車する ...ni teísha suru; (RAIL) 到着する tố̃chaku suru

pull off vt (take off: clothes etc) 脱ぐ núgù; (fig: difficult thing) ...に成功する ...ni seíkō suru

pull out vi (AUT: from curb) 発進する hasshín suru; (RAIL) 出発する shuppátsu suru
　　◆vt (extract) 取出す torídasù

pull over vi (AUT) 道路わきに寄せて停車する dốrowaki ni yosétè teísha suru

pullover [pul'ouvə:r] n セーター sếtā

pull through vi (MED) 治る naórù

pull up vi (AUT, RAIL: stop) 停車する teísha suru
　　◆vt (raise: object, clothing) 引上げる hikíagerù; (uproot) 引抜く hikínukù

pulp [pʌlp] n (of fruit) 果肉 kaníku

pulpit [pul'pit] n 説教壇 sekkyố̃daǹ

pulsate [pʌl'seit] vi 脈動する myakúdō suru

pulse [pʌls] n (ANAT) 脈拍 myakúhaku; (rhythm) 鼓動 kodố̃; (BOT) 豆類 mamé-rùi

pulverize [pʌl'və:raiz] vt (crush to a powder) 砕く kudákù; (fig: destroy) 破壊する hakái suru

puma [pu:'mə] n ピューマ pyū̃ma

pummel [pʌm'əl] vt 続け様にげんこつで打つ tsuzúkezama nì geńkotsu de utsù

pump [pʌmp] n (for water, air, petrol) ポンプ póǹpu; (shoe) パンプス páǹpusu
　　◆vt (force: in certain direction: liquid, gas) ポンプで送る póǹpu de okúrù; (obtain supply of: oil, water, gas) ポンプ

で汲む pónpu de kúmù

pumpkin [pʌmpˈkin] n カボチャ kabócha

pump up vt (inflate) ポンプで膨らます pónpu de fukúramasù

pun [pʌn] n しゃれ sharé

punch [pʌntʃ] n (blow) げんこつで打つ事 geñkotsu dè útsù kotó, パンチ páñchi; (tool: for making holes) パンチ páñchi; (drink) ポンチ póñchi

♦vt (hit): **to punch someone/something** げんこつで…を打つ geñkotsu de …wo útsù

punchline [pʌntʃˈlain] n 落ち ochí

punch-up [pʌntʃˈʌp] n (BRIT: inf) けんか keñka

punctual [pʌŋkˈtʃuːəl] adj 時間を厳守する jíkàn wo geñshu suru

punctuation [pʌŋktʃuːeiˈʃən] n 句読法 kutóhō

puncture [pʌŋkˈtʃəːr] n パンク pañku
♦vt …に穴を開ける …ni aná wo akérù

pundit [pʌnˈdit] n 物知り monóshiri

pungent [pʌnˈdʒənt] adj (smell, taste) 刺激的な shigékiteki na

punish [pʌnˈiʃ] vt (person, crime) 罰する bassúrù

punishment [pʌnˈiʃmənt] n (act) 罰する事 bassúrù kotó; (way of punishing) 罰 bátsù

punk [pʌŋk] n (also: **punk rock**) パンクロック pañkurokkù; (also: **punk rocker**) パンクロッカー pañkurokkà; (US: inf: hoodlum) ちんぴら chíñpira

punt [pʌnt] n (boat) ボート bòto ◇底が平らでさおで川底を突いて進める物を指す sokó ga taira dè sáò de kawázoko wo tsuité susúmeru mono wò sásù

punter [pʌnˈtəːr] n (BRIT: gambler) ばくち打ち bakúchiuchì; (inf: client, customer) 客 kyakú

puny [pjuːˈniː] adj (person, effort) ちっぽけな chippókè na

pup [pʌp] n (young dog) 子イヌ koínu

pupil [pjuːˈpəl] n (SCOL) 生徒 seíto; (of eye) 瞳孔 dōkō

puppet [pʌpˈit] n (doll) 操り人形 ayátsurinìñgyō; (fig: person) かいらい kaírai

puppy [pʌpˈiː] n 子イヌ koínu

purchase [pəːrˈtʃis] n (act of buying) 購入 kónyū; (item bought) 買い物 kaímono
♦vt (buy: house, book, car etc) 買う káù

purchaser [pəːrˈtʃisəːr] n 買い手 kaíte

pure [pjuːr] adj (not mixed with anything: silk, gold etc) 純粋な juñsui na; (clean, healthy: water, air etc) 清潔な seíketsu na; (fig: woman, girl) 純潔な juñketsu na; (complete, total: chance, bliss) 全くの mattáku no

purée [pjuːreiˈ] n (of tomatoes, potatoes, apples etc) ピューレ pyūre

purely [pjuːrˈliː] adv 単に táñ ni

purgatory [pəːrˈgətɔːriː] n (REL) れん獄 reñgoku; (fig) 地獄 jigóku

purge [pəːrdʒ] n (POL) 粛正 shukúsei, パージ pāji
♦vt (organization) 粛正する shukúsei suru, パージする pāji suru

purify [pjuːrˈəfai] vt (air, water etc) 浄化する jōka suru

purist [pjuːrˈist] n 純正主義者 juñseishugishà

puritan [pjuːrˈitən] n 禁欲主義者 kiñyokuku shugishà

purity [pjuːrˈitiː] n (of silk, gold etc) 純粋さ juñsuisa; (of water, air etc) 清潔 seíketsu; (fig: of woman, girl) 純潔 juñketsu

purple [pəːrˈpəl] adj 紫色の murásakiiro no

purport [pəːrˈpɔːrt] vi: **to purport to be/do** …である〔…をする〕と主張する …de árù〔…ga dekírù〕to shuchō suru

purpose [pəːrˈpəs] n (reason) 目的 mokúteki; (objective: of person) 目標 mokúhyō

on purpose 意図的に itóteki ni, わざと wáza to

purposeful [pəːrˈpəsfəl] adj (person, look, gesture) 果敢な kakán na

purr [pəːr] vi (cat) ごろごろとのどを鳴らす górògoro to nódò wo narásù

purse [pəːrs] n (for money) 財布 saífu; (US: handbag) ハンドバッグ hañdobaggù
♦vt (lips) すぼめる subómerù

purser [pəːr'səːr] n (NAUT) 事務長 jimúchō, パーサー pāsā

pursue [pəːrsuː'] vt (follow: person, thing) 追う óù, 追跡する tsuíseki suru; (fig: activity, interest) 行う okonau; (: plan) 実行する jikkō suru; (: aim, result) 追求める oímotomerù

pursuer [pəːrsuː'əːr] n 追跡者 tsuísekishà

pursuit [pəːrsuːt'] n (chase: of person, thing) 追跡 tsuíseki; (fig: of happiness, pleasure etc) 追求 tsuíkyū; (pastime) 趣味 shúmì

pus [pʌs] n うみ umí

push [puʃ] n 押す事 osú kotò
♦vt (press, shove) 押す osú; (promote) 宣伝する señden suru
♦vi (press, shove) 押す osú; (fig: demand urgently): **to push for** 要求する yōkyū suru

push aside vt 押しのける oshínokerù

pushchair [puʃ'tʃeːr] (BRIT) n いす型ベビーカー isúgata bebíkā

pusher [puʃ'əːr] n (drug pusher) 売人 baínin

push off (inf) vi: **push off!** 消えうせろ kiéuserò

push on vi (continue) 続ける tsuzúkerù

pushover [puʃ'ouvəːr] (inf) n: **it's a pushover** 朝飯前だ asámeshimaè da

push through vi (crowd etc) ...を押し分けて進む ...wo oshíwakete susumù
♦vt (measure, scheme etc) 押し通す oshítōsu

push up vt total, prices 押し上げる oshíagerù

push-up [puʃ'ʌp] (US) n (press-up) 腕立て伏せ udétatefùse

pushy [puʃ'iː] (pej) adj 押しの強い oshí no tsuyoì

puss [pus] (inf) n ネコちゃん nékòchan

pussy(cat) [pus'iː(kæt)] (inf) n ネコちゃん nékòchan

put [put] (pt, pp **put**) vt (place: thing) 置く okú; (: person: in institution etc) 入れる irérù; (express: idea, remark etc) 表現する hyōgen suru; (present: case, view) 説明する setsúmei suru; (ask: question) する súrù; (place: person: in state, situation) 追込む oíkomù, 置く okú; (estimate) 推定する suítei suru; (write, type: word, sentence etc) 書く kákù

put about/around vt (rumor) 広める hirómerù

put across vt (ideas etc) 分からせる wakáraserù

put away vt (store) 仕舞っておく shimátte okù

put back vt (replace) 戻す modósù; (postpone) 延期する eñki suru; (delay) 遅らせる okúraserù

put by vt (money, supplies etc) 蓄えておく takúwaete okù

put down vt (on floor, table) 下ろす orósù; (in writing) 書く kákù; (riot, rebellion) 鎮圧する chiñ-atsu suru; (kill: animal) 安楽死させる añrakushi saserù; (attribute): **to put something down to** ...を...のせいにする ...wo ...no seí ni surù

put forward vt (ideas, proposal) 提案する teían suru

put in vt (application, complaint) 提出する teíshutsu suru; (time, effort) つぎ込む tsugíkomù

put off vt (delay) 延期する eñki suru; (discourage) いやにさせる iyá ni saserù

put on vt (shirt, blouse, dress etc) 着る kírù; (hat etc) かぶる kabúrù; (shoes, pants, skirt etc) はく hakú; (gloves etc) はめる hamérù; (make-up, ointment etc) つける tsukérù; (light etc) つける tsukérù; (play etc) 上演する jōen suru; (brake) かける kakérù; (record, tape, video) かける kakérù; (kettle, dinner etc) 火にかける hí nì kakérù; (assume: look, behavior etc) 装う yosóòu; (gain): **to put on weight** 太る futórù

put out vt (fire, candle, cigarette, light) 消す kesú; (take out: rubbish, cat etc) 出す dásù; (one's hand) 伸ばす nobásù; (inf: person): **to be put out** 怒っている okótte irù

putrid [pjuː'trid] adj 腐った kusáttà

putt [pʌt] n (GOLF) パット pátto

put through vt (TEL: person, call) つなぐ tsunágù; (plan, agreement) 成功させる seíkō saserù

putting green [pʌt'iŋ-] n (GOLF: smooth area around hole) グリーン gurín; (: for practice) パット練習場 páttòreñshūjō

putty [pʌt'i:] n パテ pátè

put up vt (build) 建てる tatérù; (raise: umbrella) 広げる hirógerù; (: tent) 張る hárù; (: hood) かぶる kabúrù; (poster, sign etc) 張る harú; (increase: price, cost) 上げる agérù; (accommodate) 泊める tomérù

put-up [put'ʌp] n: *put-up job* (BRIT) n 八百長 yaôchō

put up with vt fus 我慢する gáman suru

puzzle [pʌz'əl] n (question, game) なぞなぞ nazónazo; (toy) パズル pázùru; (mystery) なぞ nazó
♦vt 当惑させる tôwaku saserù
♦vi: *to puzzle over something* ...を思案する ...wo shían suru

puzzling [pʌz'liŋ] adj (thing, action) 訳の分からない wákè no wakáranaì

pyjamas [pədʒɑːm'əz] (BRIT) npl = **pajamas**

pylon [pai'lɑːn] n (for electric cables) 鉄塔 tettô

pyramid [pir'əmid] n (ARCHIT) ピラミッド pirámiddò; (shape, object, pile) ピラミッド状の物 pirámiddojô no monó

Pyrenees [pir'əni:z] npl: *the Pyrenees* ピレネー山脈 pírēnè sáñmyaku

python [pai'θɑːn] n ニシキヘビ nishíkihebì

Q

quack [kwæk] n (of duck) がーがー gàgā; (pej: doctor) やぶ医者 yabúisha

quad [kwɑːd] abbr = **quadrangle**; **quadruplet**

quadrangle [kwɑːd'ræŋgəl] n (courtyard) 中庭 nakániwa

quadruple [kwɑːdru:'pəl] vt (increase fourfold) 4倍にする yoñbai ni suru
♦vi 4倍になる yoñbai ni naru

quadruplets [kwɑːdrʌ'plits] npl 四つ子

yotsúgo

quagmire [kwæg'maiə:r] n (bog) 湿地 shitchî; (muddy place) ぬかるみ nukárumi

quail [kweil] n (bird) ウズラ uzúra
♦vi: *to quail at/before* (anger, prospect) ...の前でおじけづく ...no maè de ojíkezùku

quaint [kweint] adj (house, village) 古風で面白い kofú de omóshiroì; (ideas, customs) 奇妙な kimyõ na

quake [kweik] vi (with fear) 震える furúeru
♦n abbr = **earthquake**

Quaker [kwei'kə:r] n クエーカー教徒 kuēkākyōto

qualification [kwɑːləfəkei'(ən] n (often pl: training, degree, diploma) 資格 shikáku; (skill, quality) 能力 nōryòku; (reservation, modification) 限定 geñtei, 条件 jôken

qualified [kwɑːl'əfaid] adj (trained) 資格のある shikáku no aru; (fit, competent): *qualified to* ...する能力がある ...suru nōryòku ga aru; (limited) 条件付きの jôkentsuki no

qualify [kwɑːl'əfai] vt (make competent) ...に資格を与える ...ni shikáku wo ataerù; (modify) 限定する gentei suru
♦vi (pass examination(s)): *to qualify (as)* ...の資格を取る ...no shikáku wo torù; (be eligible): *to qualify (for)* (...の) 資格がある (...no) shikáku ga aru; (in competition): *to qualify (for)* (...に進む) 資格を得る ...ni susúmu shikáku wo eru

quality [kwɑːl'iti:] n (standard: of work, product) 品質 hiñshitsu; (characteristic: of person) 性質 seíshitsu; (: of wood, stone etc) 特徴 tokúchō

qualm [kwɑːm] n (doubt) 疑問 gimón
qualms of conscience 良心のか責 ryôshin nò kasháku

quandary [kwɑːn'dri:] n: *to be in a quandary* 途方に暮れる tohô ni kuréru

quantity [kwɑːn'titi:] n (amount: of uncountable thing) 量 ryõ; (: of countable things) 数 kazù

quantity surveyor n 積算士 sekísanshi ◇工事などの費用を見積りで計算する人 kōji nadò no hīyō wo mitsúmori dè keísan suru hitò

quarantine [kwɔːrˈəntiːn] n (isolation) 隔離 kakúri

quarrel [kwɔːrˈəl] n (argument) けんか kenka

♦vi: **to quarrel (with)** (...と) けんかする (...to) kenka suru

quarrelsome [kwɔːrˈəlsəm] adj けんかっ早い kénkappayaì

quarry [kwɔːrˈiː] n (for stone) 石切り場 ishíkiriba, 採石場 saísekijō; (animal) 獲物 emóno

quart [kwɔːrt] n クォート kwóto

quarter [kwɔːrˈtəːr] n (fourth part) 4分の1 yoñbun no ichi; (US: coin) 25セント玉 nijūgosentodamà; (of year) 四半期 shihánki; (district) 地区 chikú

♦vt (divide by four) 4等分する yoñtōbun suru; (MIL: lodge) 宿泊させる shukúhaku saseru

a quarter of an hour 15分 jūgófun

quarter final n 準々決勝 juñjunkesshō

quarterly [kwɔːrˈtəːrliː] adj (meeting, payment) 年4回の nèn-yonkai no

♦adv (meet, pay) 年4回に nèn-yonkai ni

quarters [kwɔːrˈtəːrz] npl (barracks) 兵舎 heīsha; (living quarters) 宿舎 shúkusha

quartet(te) [kwɔːrtet'] n (group: of instrumentalists) 四重奏団 shijūsōdan, カルテット karùtetto; (: of singers) 四重唱団 shijūshōdan, カルテット karùtetto; (piece of music) 四重奏曲 shijūsōkyokù

quartz [kwɔːrts] n 水晶 suíshō

quash [kwɑːʃ] vt (verdict, judgement) 破棄する hakì suru

quasi- [kwei'zai] prefix 疑似... gijí...

quaver [kwei'vəːr] n (BRIT: MUS) 八分音符 hachíbùn ofipu

♦vi (voice) 震える furúeru

quay [kiː] n (also: **quayside**) 岸壁 gañpeki

queasy [kwiː'ziː] adj (nauseous) 吐気がする hakíkè ga suru

queen [kwiːn] n (monarch) 女王 joò; (king's wife) 王妃 ōhì; (ZOOL: also:

queen bee) 女王バチ joòbachi; (CARDS, CHESS) クイーン kuíñ

queen mother n 皇太后 kōtaigò

queer [kwiːr] adj (odd) 変な heñ na

♦n (inf: homosexual) ホモ homó

quell [kwel] vt (opposition) 鎮める shizúmeru; (unease, fears) なだめる nadámeru, 静める shizúmeru

quench [kwentʃ] vt: **to quench one's thirst** のどの乾きをいやす nodò no kawákì wo iyásu

querulous [kwerˈələs] adj (person, voice) 愚痴っぽい guchíppòi

query [kwiərˈiː] n (question) 質問 shitsúmon

♦vt (question) ...に聞く ...ni kikú, ...に質問する ...ni shitsúmon suru

quest [kwest] n 探求 tañkyū

question [kwesˈtʃən] n (query) 質問 shitsúmon; (doubt) 疑問 gimón; (issue) 問題 moñdai; (in test: problem) 問 toî

♦vt (ask) ...に聞く ...ni kikú, ...に質問する ...ni shitsúmon suru; (interrogate) 尋問する jiñmon suru; (doubt) ...に疑問を投げ掛ける ...ni gimón wo nagékakeru

beyond question 疑いもなく utágai mo naku

out of the question 全く不可能で mattáku fúkanò de

questionable [kwesˈtʃənəbəl] adj (doubtful) 疑わしい utágawashii

question mark n 疑問符 gimónfu

questionnaire [kwestʃənəːr'] n 調査票 chōsàhyō, アンケート añkēto

queue [kjuː] n (BRIT) 列 retsù

♦vi (also: **queue up**) 列を作る retsù wo tsukúru

quibble [kwib'əl] vi 詰まらない議論をする tsumáranaì giròn wo suru

quiche [kiːʃ] n キッシュ kisshū ◇パイの一種 paî no isshū

quick [kwik] adj (fast: person, movement, action etc) 早い hayáì; (agile) 素早い subáyai; (: mind) 理解の早い rikài no hayáì; (brief: look, visit) 短い mijíkài, ちょっとした chottó shita

♦n: **cut to the quick** (fig) ...の感情を害する ...no kañjō wo gaí sùru

be quick! 急いで isóÍde

quicken [kwík'ən] vt (pace, step) 早める hayámeru
♦vi (pace, step) 早くなる hayáku naru

quickly [kwík'li:] adv 早く hayáku

quicksand [kwík'sænd] n 流土砂 ryúdo-sha, クイックサンド kuíñkkùsando

quick-witted [kwík'wit'id] adj (alert) 機敏な kibín na

quid [kwid] (BRIT: inf) n inv ポンド poñdo

quiet [kwái'it] adj (not loud or noisy) 静かな shizúka na; (silent) 何も言わない naní mo iwánai; (peaceful: place) 平和な heiwa na; (calm: person) もの静かな mo-nóshizuka na; (without fuss etc: ceremony) 簡単な kañtan na
♦n (peacefulness) 静けさ shizúkesa; (silence) 静かにする事 shizúka ni suru koto
♦vi (US: also: quiet down) (grow calm) 落着く ochitsuku; (grow silent) 静かになる shizúka ni naru
♦vt (person, animal) 落着かせる ochítsu-kaserù

quieten [kwái'itən] (BRIT) = quiet vi, vt

quietly [kwái'itli:] adv (speak, play) 静かに shizúka ni; (silently) 黙って damáttè

quietness [kwái'itnis] n (peacefulness) 静けさ shizúkesa; (silence) 静かにする事 shizúka ni suru koto

quilt [kwilt] n (covering) ベッドカバー beddôkabà; (also: continental quilt) 掛布団 kakébuton, キルト kirúto

quin [kwin] n abbr = quintuplet

quinine [kwái'nain] n キニーネ kiníñè

quintet(te) [kwintet'] n (group) 五重奏団 gojúsòdan, クインテット kuíñtetto; (piece of music) 五重奏曲 gojúsòkyoku

quintuplets [kwintʌ'plits] npl 五つ子 i-tsútsugo

quip [kwip] n 警句 keíku

quirk [kwə:rk] n (unusual characteristic) 癖 kusé; (accident: of fate, nature) 気まぐれ kimágure

quit [kwit] (pt, pp quit or quitted) vt (smoking, grumbling) やめる yaméru;

(job) 辞める yaméru; (premises) ...から出ていく ...kara detè iku
♦vi (give up) やめる yaméru; (resign) 辞める yaméru

quite [kwait] adv (rather) かなり kanàri; (entirely) 全く mattáku, 完全に kañzen ni; (following a negative: almost): **that's not quite big enough** それはちょっと小さい soré wa chottô chiisai
I saw quite a few of them 私はそれらをかなり沢山見ました watákushi wa soréra wo kanàri takúsan mimashita
quite (so)! 全くその通り mattáku sonó tōri

quits [kwits] adj: **quits (with)** (...と) おあいこである (...to) o-áiko de aru
let's call it quits (call it even) おあいこにしましょう o-aíko ni shimáshò; (stop working etc) やめましょう yamé-mashō

quiver [kwiv'ə:r] vi (tremble) 震える fu-rúerù

quiz [kwiz] n (game) クイズ kuízu; (US: short test) 小テスト shótesùto
♦vt (question) 尋問する jiñmon suru

quizzical [kwiz'ikəl] adj (look, smile) なぞめいた nazómeìta

quorum [kwɔːr'əm] n (of members) 定足数 teísokusū

quota [kwou'tə] n 割当数〔量〕waríatesū〔ryō〕

quotation [kwoutei'ʃən] n (from book, play etc) 引用文 iñ-yobuñ; (estimate) 見積り mitsúmori

quotation marks npl 引用符 iñyófù

quote [kwout] n (from book, play etc) 引用文 iñyóbuñ; (estimate) 見積り mitsú-mori
♦vt (sentence, proverb etc) 引用する iñ-yō suru; (figure, example) 引合いに出す hikíai ni dasù; (price) 見積る mitsúmorù
♦vi: **to quote from** (book, play etc) ...から引用する ...kara iñ-yō suru

quotes [kwouts] npl (quotation marks) 引用符 iñ-yófù

quotient [kwou'ʃənt] n (factor) 指数 shi-sū

R

rabbi [ræb'ai] *n* ラビ rábì ◊ユダヤ教の聖職者 yudáyakyō nò séfshokushà

rabbit [ræb'it] *n* ウサギ usági

rabbit hutch *n* ウサギ小屋 uságigoyà

rabble [ræb'əl] (*pej*) *n* 群衆 guńshū

rabies [rei'bi:z] *n* 恐犬病 kyōkeǹbyō

RAC [ɑːreisi:'] *n abbr* (= *Royal Automobile Club*) 英国自動車連盟 eŕkoku jídōsha reǹmei

raccoon [ræku:n'] *n* アライグマ aráigùma

race [reis] *n* (species) 人種 jińshu; (competition: for speed) 競走 kyōsō, レース rēsù; (: for power, control) 競争 kyōsō; (public gambling event: *also*: **horse race**) 競馬 keíba, (: *also*: **bicycle race**) 競輪 keírin; (: *also*: **motorboat race**) 競艇 kyótei

◆*vt* (horse) 競馬に出場させる keíba nì shutsújō saserù; (compete against: person) ...と競走する ...to kyōsō suru

◆*vi* (compete: for speed) 競走する kyōsō suru; (: for power, control) 競争する kyōsō suru; (hurry) 急いで行く isóide ikù; (pulse) どきどきする dókìdoki suru; (engine) 空回りする karámawarì suru

race car (*US*) *n* レーシングカー rḗshingukā

race car driver (*US*) *n* レーサー rḗsā

racecourse [reis'kɔ:rs] *n* 競馬場 keíbajō

racehorse [reis'hɔ:rs] *n* 競走馬 kyṓsōba

racetrack [reis'træk] *n* (for people) トラック torákkù; (for cars) サーキット sā́kitto

racial [rei'ʃəl] *adj* 人種の jińshu no, 人種... jińshu...

racing [rei'siŋ] *n* (horses) 競馬 keíba; (bicycles) 競輪 keírin; (motorboats) 競艇 kyótei; (cars) 自動車レース jídōsharḕsu; (motorcycles) オートレース ōtorḕsu

racing car (*BRIT*) *n* = **race car**

racing driver (*BRIT*) *n* = **race car driver**

racism [rei'sizəm] *n* 人種差別 jińshusabètsu

racist [rei'sist] *adj* (statement, policy) 人種差別的な jińshusabetsuteki na

◆*n* 人種差別主義者 jińshusabetsushugishà

rack [ræk] *n* (*also*: **luggage rack**) 網棚 amídana; (shelf) 棚 taná; (*also*: **roof rack**) ルーフラック rūfurakkù; (dish rack) 水切りかご mizúkirikago

◆*vt*: **racked by** (pain, anxiety) ...でもだえ苦しんで ...de modáekurushiǹde

to rack one's brains 知恵を絞る chié wò shibórù

racket [ræk'it] *n* (for tennis, squash etc) ラケット rakéttò; (noise) 騒音 sōon; (swindle) 詐欺 sági

racoon [ræku:n'] *n* = **raccoon**

racquet [ræk'it] *n* (for tennis, squash etc) ラケット rakéttò

racy [rei'si:] *adj* きびきびした kíbìkibi shita

radar [rei'dɑ:r] *n* レーダー rēdā

radial [rei'di:əl] *adj* (*also*: **radial-ply**) ラジアルの rájìaru no

radiance [rei'di:əns] *n* (glow) 光 hikári

radiant [rei'di:ənt] *adj* (happy, joyful) 輝く kagáyakù

radiate [rei'di:eit] *vt* (heat) 放射する hōsha suru; (emotion) ...で輝く ...de kagáyakù

◆*vi* (lines) 放射状に広がる hōshajō nì hirógarù

radiation [reidi:ei'ʃən] *n* (radioactive) 放射能 hōshanò; (from sun etc) 放射 hōsha

radiator [rei'di:eitər] *n* ラジエーター rajiḗtā

radical [ræd'ikəl] *adj* (change etc) 抜本的な bappónteki na; (person) 過激な kagéki na; (organization) 過激派の kagékiha no, 過激派... kagékiha...

radii [rei'di:ai] *npl of* **radius**

radio [rei'di:ou] *n* (broadcasting) ラジオ放送 rajíohōsō; (device: for receiving broadcasts) ラジオ rájìo; (: for transmitting and receiving signals) 無線通信機 muséntsūshìnki

◆*vt* (person) ...と無線で通信する ...to musén dè tsūshin suru

on the radio ラジオで rájìo de

radioactive [reidiːouæk'tiv] *adj* 放射性
の hōshasei no

radiography [reidiːɑːg'rəfiː] *n* レントゲ
ン撮影 reńtogensatsuèi

radiology [reidiːɑːl'ədʒiː] *n* 放射線医学
hōshasen-igàku

radio station *n* ラジオ放送局 rajío hō-
sōkyòku

radiotherapy [reidiːouθeːr'əpiː] *n* 放射
線療法 hōshasenryòhō

radish [ræd'iʃ] *n* はつかだいこん hatsú-
kadaikon

radius [rei'diːəs] (*pl* **radii**) *n* (of circle) 半
径 hańkei; (from point) 半径内の範囲 hań-
keinai no hań-i

RAF [ɑːrieief'] *n abbr* = **Royal Air
Force**

raffle [ræf'əl] *n* 宝くじ takárakùji ◇当る
と金ではなく賞品をもらえる物を指す a-
tárù to kané de wa nakù shōhin wò
moráerù monó wò sásù

raft [ræft] *n* (craft) いかだ ikáda; (*also*:
life raft) 救命いかだ kyúmei ikáda

rafter [ræf'təːr] *n* はり harí

rag [ræg] *n* (piece of cloth) ぞうきん zō-
kin; (torn cloth) ぼろ bórò; (*pej*: newspaper) 三流紙 sańryūshi; (*BRIT*: UNI-
VERSITY: for charity) 慈善募金運動 ji-
zénbokin-uńdō

rag-and-bone man [rægənboun'-]
(*BRIT*) *n* = **ragman**

rag doll *n* 縫いぐるみ人形 nuíguruminiñ-
gyō

rage [reidʒ] *n* (fury) 憤怒 fúñdo

♦*vi* (person) 怒り狂う ikárikuruù;
(storm) 荒れ狂う arékuruù; (debate) 荒れ
る arérù

it's all the rage (very fashionable) 大
流行している daíryūkō shite irù

ragged [ræg'id] *adj* (edge) ぎざぎざの gi-
zágiza no; (clothes) ぼろぼろの boróboro
no; (appearance) 不ぞろいの fuzóròi no

ragman [ræg'mæn] (*pl* **ragmen**) *n* くず
屋 kuzúyà

rags [rægz] *npl* (torn clothes) ぼろぼろの
衣服 boróboro no ifùku

raid [reid] *n* (MIL) 襲撃 shúgeki; (criminal) 不法侵入 fuhōshiñnyū; (by police) 手

入れ teíre

♦*vt* (MIL) 襲撃する shúgeki suru; (crimi-
nally) ...に不法侵入する ...ni fuhōshiñnyū
suru; (subj: police) 手入れする teíre suru

rail [reil] *n* 手すり tesúri

by rail (by train) 列車で resshá de

railing(s) [rei'liŋ(z)] *n(pl)* (fence) さく
sakú

railroad [reil'roud] (*US*) *n* (track) 線路
séñro; (company) 鉄道 tetsúdō

railroader [reil'roudəːr] (*US*) *n* 鉄道員
tetsúdōin

railroad line (*US*) *n* 鉄道線 tetsúdōsen

railroad station (*US*) *n* 駅 ékì

rails [reilz] *npl* (for train) レール rèru

railway [reil'wei] (*BRIT*) *n* = **railroad**
etc

railwayman [reil'weimən] (*BRIT*: *pl*
railwaymen) *n* = **railroader**

rain [rein] *n* 雨 ámè

♦*vi* 雨が降る ámè ga fúrù

in the rain 雨の中で ámè no nákà de

it's raining 雨が降っている ámè ga futté irù

rainbow [rein'bou] *n* にじ nijí

raincoat [rein'kout] *n* レーンコート réñ-
kòto

raindrop [rein'drɑːp] *n* 雨の一滴 ámè no
ittéki

rainfall [rein'fɔːl] *n* 降雨量 kóuryò

rainy [rei'niː] *adj* 雨模様の amémoyò no

raise [reiz] *n* (payrise) 賃上げ chíñ-age

♦*vt* (lift) 持上げる mochíagerù;
(increase: salary) 上げる agérù; (: production) 増やす fuyásù; (improve:
morale) 高める takámerù; (: standards)
引上げる hikíagerù; (produce: doubts,
question) 引起こす hikíokosù; (rear: cattle) 飼育する shiíku suru; (: family) 育て
る sodáterù; (cultivate: crop) 栽培する
saíbai suru; (get together: army, funds,
loan) 集める atsúmerù

to raise one's voice 声を大きくする
kôè wo ókiku suru

raisin [rei'zin] *n* 干しぶどう hoshíbudò,
レーズン rèzun

rake [reik] *n* (tool) レーキ rèki

♦*vt* (garden) レーキで...の土をならす rèki de ...no tsuchí wo narásù; (leaves) かき集める kakíatsumerù; (with machine gun) 掃射する sósha suru

rally [ræl'iː] n (POL etc) 集会 shúkai; (AUT) ラリー rarī; (TENNIS etc) ラリー rárī
♦vt (support) 集める atsúmerù
♦vi (sick person, Stock Exchange) 持直す mochínaosù

rally round vt fus (fig: give support to) ...の支援に駆け付ける ...no shién nǐ kakétsukerù

RAM [ræm] n abbr = **(random access memory)** ラム rámù

ram [ræm] n (ZOOL) 雄ヒツジ osúhitsùji
♦vt (crash into) ...に激突する ...ni gekítotsu suru; (push: bolt, fist etc) 押込む oshíkomù

ramble [ræm'bəl] n (walk) ハイキング háikingu
♦vi (walk) ハイキングする háikingu suru; (talk: also: **ramble on**) だらだらしゃべる dárǎdara shabérù

rambler [ræm'blə:r] n (walker) ハイカー háikā; (BOT) ツルバラ tsurúbara

rambling [ræm'bliŋ] adj (speech) 取留めのない torítome no naī; (house) だだっ広い dadáppiroì; (BOT) つる性の tsurúsei no

ramp [ræmp] n 傾斜路 keísharo
on/off ramp (US: AUT) 入口[出口]ランプ iríguchi(degúchi)ráñpu

rampage [ræm'peidʒ] n: **to be on the rampage** 暴れ回っている abáremawatte irù
♦vi: **they went rampaging through the town** 彼らは町中暴れ回った kárèra wa machíjū abaremawattà

rampant [ræm'pənt] adj (crime) はびこる habíkorù; (disease) まん延する mañ-en suru

rampart [ræm'pɑːrt] n (fortification) 城壁 jōheki

ramshackle [ræm'ʃækəl] adj (house, car, table) がたがたの gatágata no

ran [ræn] pt of **run**

ranch [ræntʃ] n 牧場 bokújō

rancher [ræn'tʃəːr] n 牧場主 bokújōshu

rancid [ræn'sid] adj (butter, bacon etc) 悪くなった wárùku natta

rancor [ræŋ'kəːr] (BRIT **rancour**) n 恨み urámi

random [ræn'dəm] adj (arrangement, selection) 手当り次第の teátarishidài no; (COMPUT, MATH) 無作為の musákùi no
♦n: **at random** 手当り次第に teátarishidài ni

random access n (COMPUT) ランダムアクセス rañdamuakùsesu

randy [ræn'diː] (inf) adj セックスをしたがっている sékkùsu wo shitágatte irù

rang [ræŋ] pt of **ring**

range [reindʒ] n (also: **mountain range**) 山脈 sañmyaku; (of missile) 射程距離 shatéikyorì; (of voice) 声域 seíiki; (series: of proposals, offers, products) 一連の... ichíren no ...; (MIL: also: **shooting range**) 射撃場 shagékijō; (also: **kitchen range**) レンジ réñji
♦vt (place) 歩き回る arúkimawarù; (arrange) 並べる naráberù
♦vi: **to range over** (extend) ...にわたる ...ni watárù
to range from ... to ... ...から...までにわたる ...kárà ...mádè ni watárù

ranger [rein'dʒəːr] n 森林警備隊員 shiñrinkeibitaiin, レーンジャー rḗñjā

rank [ræŋk] n (row) 列 rétsù; (MIL) 階級 kaíkyū; (status) 地位 chíi; (BRIT: also: **taxi rank**) タクシー乗場 takúshīnorĭba
♦vi: **to rank among** ...のうちに数えられる ...no uchí nǐ kazóerarerù
♦adj (stinking) 臭い kusái
the rank and file (fig: ordinary members) 一般の人 ippáñ no hitó, 一般人 ippáñjin

rankle [ræŋ'kəl] vi (insult) わだかまる wadákamarù

ransack [ræn'sæk] vt (search) 物色する busshóku suru; (plunder) 略奪する ryakúdatsu suru

ransom [ræn'səm] n (money) 身代金 mínòshirokiñ
to hold to ransom (fig: nation, company, individual) ...に圧力を掛ける ...ni

atsúryòku wo kakérù

rant [rænt] vi (rave) わめく wamékù

rap [ræp] vt (on door, table) たたく tatákù

rape [reip] n (of woman) 強かん gókan; (BOT) アブラナ abúranà
♦vt (woman) 強かんする gókan suru

rape(seed) oil [reip'(si:d)-] n ナタネ油 natáneabùra

rapid [ræp'id] adj (growth, development, change) 急速な kyúsoku na

rapidity [rəpid'iti:] n (speed) 速さ háyàsa

rapidly [ræp'idli:] adv (grow, develop, change) 急速に kyúsoku ni

rapids [ræp'idz] npl (GEO) 早瀬 hayáse

rapist [rei'pist] n 強かん者 gókaǹsha

rapport [ræpɔːr'] n 親和関係 shiǹwaka-ǹkei

rapture [ræp'tʃəːr] n (delight) 歓喜 kánki

rapturous [ræp'tʃəːrəs] adj (applause) 熱狂的な nekkyóteki na

rare [re:r] adj (uncommon) まれな maré na; (unusual) 珍しい mezúrashiî; (CULIN: steak) レアの réa no

rarely [re:r'li:] adv (seldom) めったに ...ない méttà ni ...náî

raring [re:r'iŋ] adj: **raring to go** (inf: keen) 意気込んでいる ikígonde irù

rarity [re:r'iti:] n (exception) 希有な物 kéû na monó; (scarcity) 希少性 kishósei

rascal [ræs'kəl] n (rogue) ごろつき gorótsuki; (mischievous child) いたずらっ子 itázurakkò

rash [ræʃ] adj (person) 向こう見ずの mukómizu no; (promise, act) 軽率な keísotsu na
♦n (MED) 発しん hasshín; (spate: of events, robberies) 多発 tahátsu

rasher [ræʃ'əːr] n (of bacon) 一切れ hitókìre

raspberry [ræz'be:ri:] n キイチゴ kíìchìgo

rasping [ræs'piŋ] adj: **a rasping noise** きしむ音 kishímù otó

rat [ræt] n ネズミ nezúmi

rate [reit] n (speed) 速度 sókùdo; (of change, inflation) 進行度 shiǹkòdo;

(ratio: also of interest) 率 rítsù; (price: at hotel etc) 料金 ryókin
♦vt (value, estimate) 評価する hyóka suru

to rate someone/something as ...を ...と評価する ...wo ...to hyóka suru

rateable value [rei'təbəl-] (BRIT) n 課税評価額 kazéi hyókagàku

ratepayer [reit'peiər-] (BRIT) n 納税者 nózeîsha ◇固定資産税の納税者について言う kotéishisàzei no nózeîsha ni tsuíte iú

rates [reits] npl (BRIT: property tax) 固定資産税 kotéishisàzei; (fees) 料金 ryókin

rather [ræð'əːr] adv (quite, somewhat) かなり kánari; (to some extent) 少し sukóshî; (more accurately): **or rather** 正確に言えば seíkaku ni iébà

it's rather expensive (quite) かなり値段が高い kánari nedán gà takáî; (too) 値段が高過ぎる nedán gà takásugirù

there's rather a lot かなり沢山ある kánari takúsan arù

I would rather go どちらかというと行きたいと思う dóchìra ka to iú to ikítaî to omóù

ratify [ræt'əfai] vt (agreement, treaty) 批准する hijún suru

rating [rei'tiŋ] n (assessment) 評価 hyóka; (score) 評点 hyóten; (NAUT: BRIT: sailor) 海軍兵卒 kaígunheîsotsu

ratings [rei'tiŋz] npl (RADIO, TV) 視聴率 shichórìtsu

ratio [rei'ʃou] n 率 rítsù

in the ratio of 100 to 1 100に1つという割合で hyaku ni hitotsu to iu waríai de

ration [ræʃ'ən] n (allowance: of food, petrol etc) 配給分 haíkyùbun
♦vt (food, petrol etc) 配給する haíkyù suru

rational [ræʃ'ənəl] adj (solution, reasoning) 合理的な góriteki na; (person) 訳の分かる wákè no wakárù

rationale [ræʃənæl'] n 根拠 kóňkyo

rationalize [ræʃ'ənəlaiz] vt (justify) 正当化する seítòka suru

rationally [ræʃ'ənəli:] adv (sensibly) 合理的に gōriteki ni

rationing [ræʃ'əniŋ] n (of food, petrol etc) 配給 haíkyū

rations [rei'ʃənz] npl (MIL) 兵糧 hyōrō

rat race n 競争の世界 kyōsō nō sékai

rattle [ræt'əl] n (of door, window) がたがたという音 gátàgata to iú oto; (of train, car, engine etc) ごう音 gṓon; (of coins) じゃらじゃらという音 járàjara to iú oto; (of chain) がらがらという音 gáràgara to iú oto; (object: for baby) がらがら garágarà

♦vi (small objects) がらがら鳴る gáràgara narú; (car, bus): **to rattle along** がたがた走る gatagata hashírù

♦vt (unnerve) どぎまぎさせる dógìmagi sasérù

rattlesnake [ræt'əlsneik] n ガラガラヘビ garágarahebì

raucous [rɔː'kəs] adj しゃがれ声の shagáregoè no

ravage [ræv'idʒ] vt (damage) 荒す arásù

ravages [ræv'idʒiz] npl (of time, weather) 荒廃 kōhai

rave [reiv] vi (in anger) わめく wamékù; (with enthusiasm) ...をべたほめする ...wo betábòme suru; (MED) うわごとを言う uwágoto wò iú

raven [rei'vən] n ワタリガラス watárigaràsu

ravenous [ræv'ənəs] adj 猛烈におなががすいた mōretsu nì onáka ga suìta

ravine [rəvin'] n 渓谷 keíkoku

raving [rei'viŋ] adj: **raving lunatic** ど気違い dokíchigaì

ravishing [ræv'iʃiŋ] adj (beautiful) 悩殺する nōsatsu suru

raw [rɔː] adj (uncooked) 生の námà no; (not processed: cotton, sugar etc) 原料のままの geñryō no mamá no; (sore) 赤むけした akámuke shità; (inexperienced) 青二才の aónisài no; (weather, day) 肌寒い hadázamuì

raw deal (inf) n ひどい仕打 hidóì shiúchi

raw material n (coal, oil, gas etc) 原料 geñryò

ray [rei] n (also: **ray of light**) 光線 kōsen; (also: **ray of heat**) 熱線 nessén

the rays of the sun 太陽の光線 táiyō no kōsen

a ray of hope 希望のひらめき kibṓ nò hirámeki

rayon [rei'ɑːn] n レーヨン rèyon

raze [reiz] vt 根こそぎ破壊する nekósògi hakái suru

razor [rei'zəːr] n (open razor) かみそり kamísorì; (safety razor) 安全かみそり añzenkamisòri; (electric razor) 電気かみそり deñkikamisòri

razor blade n かみそりの刃 kamísorì no há

Rd n abbr = **road**

re [rei] prep (with regard to) ...に関して ...ni káñ shite

reach [riːtʃ] n (range: of arm) 手が届く範囲 té gà todōkù háñ-i; (scope: of imagination) 範囲 háñ-i; (stretch: of river etc) 区域 kúìki

♦vt (arrive at: place) ...に到着する ...ni tṓchaku suru; (: conclusion, agreement, decision, end) ...に達する ...ni tassúrù; (be able to touch) ...に手が届く ...ni té gà todōkù; (by telephone) ...に連絡する ...ni refiraku suru

♦vi (stretch out one's arm) 手を伸ばす té wò nobásù

within reach 手の届く所に té nò todōkù tokórò ni

out of reach 手の届かない所に té nò todōkanaì tokórò ni

within reach of the shops/station 商店街[駅]の近くに shōteñgai[éki]no chikákù ni

「**keep out of the reach of children**」子供の手が届かない所に保管して下さい kodómo nò té gà todōkanaì tokórò ni hokán shitè kudásaì

reach out vt (hand) 伸ばす nobásù

♦vi 手を伸ばす té wò nobásù

to reach out for something ...を取ろうとして手を伸ばす ...wo toró tò shite té wò nobásù

react [riːækt'] vi (CHEM): **to react (with)** (...と) 反応する (...to) hañnō su-

ru; (MED): *to react (to)* (...に対して)
副作用が起る (...ni táishite) fukúsayő ga
okórù; (respond): *to react (to)* (...に)
反応する (...ni) hañnō suru; (rebel): *to
react (against)* (...に) 反発する (...ni)
hañpatsu suru

reaction [ri:ǽk'ʃən] *n* (response): *reaction (to)* (...に対する) 反応 (...ni taísu-
rù) hañnō; (rebellion): *reaction
(against)* (...に対する) 反発 (...ni taí-
surù) hañpatsu; (belief in conservatism)
反動 hañdő; (CHEM) 反応 hañnō; (MED)
副作用 fukúsayő

reactionary [ri:ǽk'ʃəne:ri:] *adj* (forces,
attitude) 反動的な hañdōteki na

reactions [ri:ǽk'ʃənz] *npl* (reflexes) 反
応 hañnō

reactor [ri:ǽk'tə:r] *n* (*also*: **nuclear
reactor**) 原子炉 geñshirő

read [ri:d] (*pt, pp* **read**) *vi* (person, child)
...を読む ...wo yómù; (piece of writing,
letter etc) ...と書いてある ...to káìte árù
♦*vt* (book, newspaper, music etc) 読む
yómù; (mood, thoughts) 読取る yomíto-
rù; (meter, thermometer etc) 読む yómù;
(study: at university) 学ぶ manábù

readable [ri:'dəbəl] *adj* (writing) 読める
yomérù; (book, author etc) 読ませる yo-
máserù

reader [ri:'də:r] *n* (of book, newspaper
etc) 読者 dókùsha; (book) リーダー rīdà;
(*BRIT*: at university) 助教授 jokyőjù
an avid reader 読書家 dokúshòka

readership [ri:'də:rʃip] *n* (of newspaper
etc) 読者 dókùsha ◇総称 sősho

readily [red'əli:] *adv* (willingly) 快く ko-
kőroyokù; (easily) たやすく tayásukù;
(quickly) 直ぐに súgù ni

readiness [red'i:nis] *n* (preparedness) 用
意ができている事 yői ga dekite iru koto;
(willingness) ...する意志 ...suru ishi
in readiness (prepared) 用意ができて
yői ga dekite

reading [ri:d'iŋ] *n* (of books, newspapers
etc) 読書 dokusho; (in church, as entertainment) 朗読 rōdoku; (on meter, thermometer etc) 記録 kiroku

readjust [ri:ədʒʌst'] *vt* (alter: position,

knob, mirror etc) 調節する chōsetsu suru
♦*vi* (adapt): *to readjust (to)* (...に)な
れる (...ni) nareru

read out *vt* 朗読する rődoku suru

ready [red'i:] *adj* (prepared) 用意ができ
ている yői ga dekite iru; (willing) ...する
意志がある ...surú ishi ga árù; (available)
用意されている yői saréte irù
♦*n: at the ready* (MIL) 銃を構えて jù
wo kamáetè
to get ready
♦*vi* 支度する shitáku suru
♦*vt* 準備する júñbi suru

ready-made [red'i:meid'] *adj* 既製の kiséi no

ready money *n* 現金 geñkiñ

ready reckoner [-rek'ənə:r] *n* 計算表
keísañhyō

ready-to-wear [red'i:təwe:r'] *adj* 既製
の kiséi no

reaffirm [ri:əfə:rm'] *vt* 再び言明する futátabi geñmei suru

real [ri:l] *adj* (actual, true: reason, interest, result etc) 本当の hoñtō no; (not artificial: leather, gold etc) 本物の hoñmono
no; (not imaginary: life, feeling) 実際の
jissái no; (for emphasis): *a real idiot/
miracle* 正真正銘のばか〔奇跡〕shőshin-
shőmei no bákà 〔kiséki〕
in real terms 事実は jífìtsu wa

real estate *n* 不動産 fudősan

realism [ri:'əlizəm] *n* (practicality) 現実
主義 geñjitsushugī; (ART) リアリズム ri-
árizùmu

realist [ri:'əlist] *n* 現実的な人 geñjitsuteki nà hitő

realistic [ri:əlis'tik] *adj* (practical) 現実
的な geñjitsuteki na; (true to life) 写実的
な shajítsuteki na

reality [ri:ǽl'iti:] *n* (actuality, truth) 事
実 jífìtsu
in reality 事実は jífìtsu wa

realization [ri:ələzei'ʃən] *n* (understanding: of situation) 実感 jikkáñ; (fulfilment: of dreams, hopes) 実現 jitsúgen;
(of asset) 現金化 geñkiñka

realize [ri:'əlaiz] *vt* (understand) 実感す

る jikkán suru; (fulfil: a dream, hope, project etc) 実現する jitsúgen suru; (COMM: asset) 現金に替える geñkiñ ni kaérù

really [ri:'əli:] adv (for emphasis) 実に jitsú ni, とても totémo; (actually): *what really happened* 実際に起った事は jissái nì okótta kotó wa

really? (indicating interest) そうですか sô desu ka; (expressing surprise) 本当ですか hoñtô desu kà

really! (indicating annoyance) うんもう! úñ mô!

realm [relm] n (of monarch) 王国 ôkoku; (*fig*: area of activity or study) 分野 búñya

realtor [ri:'əltə:r] (*US*) n 不動産業者 fudôsangyôsha

reap [ri:p] vt (crop) ...の刈り入れをする ...no karfire wð suru; (*fig*: benefits, rewards) 収穫する shúkaku suru

reappear [ri:əpi:r'] vi 再び現れる futátabi arawarerù

rear [ri:r] adj (back) 後ろの ushíro no
♦n (back) 後ろ ushíro
♦vt (cattle) 飼育する shiíku suru; (family) 育てる sodáterù
♦vi (*also*: **rear up**: animal) 後足で立ち上る atôashi de tachíagarù

rearguard [ri:r'gɑ:rd] n (MIL) 後衛 kôei

rearmament [ri:ɑ:rm'əmənt] n 再軍備 saíguñbi

rearrange [ri:əreindʒ'] vt 並べ直す narábenaosù

rear-view mirror [ri:r'vju:'-] n (AUT) バックミラー bakkúmirà

reason [ri:'zən] n (cause) 理由 riyú; (ability to think) 理性 riséi
♦vi: *to reason with someone* ...の説得に当る ...no settóku nì atárù
it stands to reason that ...という事は当然である ...to iú kotð wa tôzen de arù

reasonable [ri:'zənəbəl] adj (sensible) 訳の分かる wáke no wakárù; (fair: number, amount) 程々の hodóhodo no; (: quality) まあまあの mámà no; (: price) 妥当な datô na

reasonably [ri:'zənəbli:] adv (sensibly)

常識的に jôshikiteki ni; (fairly) 程々に hodóhodo ni

reasoned [ri:'zənd] adj (argument) 筋の通った sújì no tôttà

reasoning [ri:'zəniŋ] n (process) 推理 suíri

reassurance [ri:əʃu:r'əns] n 安心 áñdo

reassure [ri:əʃu:r'] vt (comfort) 安心させる añshin saserù
to reassure someone of ...に...だと安心させる ...ni ...dá tò añshin saserù

reassuring [ri:əʃu:r'iŋ] adj (smile, manner) 安心させる añshin saserù

rebate [ri:'beit] n (on tax etc) リベート ribétò

rebel [n reb'əl vb ribel'] n (against political system) 反逆者 hañgyakushà; (against society, parents etc) 反抗分子 hañkôbuñshi
♦vi (against political system) 反乱を起す hañran wð okósù; (against society, parents etc) 反抗する hañkô suru

rebellion [ribel'jən] n (against political system) 反乱 hañran; (against society, parents etc) 反抗 hañkô

rebellious [ribel'jəs] adj (subject) 反逆者の hañgyakushà no; (child, behavior) 反抗的な hañkôteki na

rebirth [ri:bə:rθ'] n 復活 fukkátsu

rebound [vb ribaund' n ri:'baund] vi (ball) 跳ね返る hanékaerù
♦n: *on the rebound* (ball) 跳ね返った所を hanékaettà tokórð wo; (*fig*: person) ...した反動で ...shíta handô de

rebuff [ribʌf'] n 拒絶 kyozétsu

rebuild [ri:bild'] (*pt, pp* rebuilt) vt (town, building etc) 建直す taténaosù; (economy, confidence) 立直す taténaosù

rebuke [ribju:k'] vt しかる shikárù

rebut [ribʌt'] vt しりぞける shirízokerù

recalcitrant [rikæl'sitrənt] adj (child, behavior) 反抗的な hañkôteki na

recall [ri:kɔ:l'] vt (remember) 思い出す omóidasù; (parliament, ambassador etc) 呼戻す yobímodosù
♦n (ability to remember) 記憶 kióku; (of ambassador etc) 召還 shôkan

recant [rikænt'] vi 自説を取消す jisétsu

wò toríkesù

recap [ri:'kæp] *vt* (summarize) 要約する yōyaku suru

♦*vi* ...を要約する ...wo yōyaku su ru

recapitulate [ri:kəpitʃ'u:leit] *vt, vi* = **recap**

recapture [ri:kæp'tʃər] *vt* (town, territory etc) 奪還する dakkán suru; (atmosphere, mood etc) 取戻す torímodosù

rec'd *abbr* = **received**

recede [risi:d'] *vi* (tide) ひく hikú; (lights etc) 遠のく tōnokù; (memory) 薄らぐ usúragù; (hair) はげる hagérù

receding [risi:'diŋ] *adj* (hair) はげつつある hagétsutsu arù; (chin) 無いに等しい naî ni hitóshiì

receipt [risi:t'] *n* (document) 領収書 ryō-shūsho; (from cash register) レシート reshítò; (act of receiving) 受取る事 ukétorù kotó

receipts [risi:ts'] *npl* (COMM) 収入 shū-nyū

receive [risi:v'] *vt* (get: money, letter etc) 受け取る ukétorù; (criticism, acclaim) 受ける ukérù; (visitor, guest) 迎える mukáerù

to receive an injury けがする kegá surù

receiver [risi:'vər] *n* (TEL) 受話器 juwá-kì; (RADIO, TV) 受信機 jushínkì; (of stolen goods) 故買屋 kobáìya; (COMM) 管財人 kañzainiñ

recent [ri:'sənt] *adj* (event, times) 近ごろの chikágòro

recently [ri:'səntli:] *adv* 近ごろ chikágòro

receptacle [risep'təkəl] *n* 容器 yōkì

reception [risep'ʃən] *n* (in hotel, office, hospital etc) 受付 ukétsuke; (party) レセプション resépùshon; (welcome) 歓迎 kañ-gei; (RADIO, TV) 受信 jushín

reception desk *n* 受付 ukétsuke, フロント furóhto

receptionist [risep'ʃənist] *n* 受付係 ukétsukegàkari

receptive [risep'tiv] *adj* (person, attitude) 前向きの maémuki no

recess [ri:'ses] *n* (in room) 壁のくぼみ

kabé nò kubómi; (secret place) 奥深い所 okúfukaì tokórò; (POL etc: holiday) 休憩時間 kyūkeijikan

recession [rise'ʃən] *n* 景気後退 keíkikō-tai

recharge [ri:tʃɑ:rdʒ'] *vt* (battery) 充電する jūden suru

recipe [res'əpi:] *n* (CULIN) 調理法 chōri-hō; (*fig*: for success) 秘けつ hikétsu; (: for disaster) やり方 yaríkata

recipient [risip'i:ənt] *n* (of letter, payment etc) 受取人 ukétorinìn

reciprocal [risip'rəkəl] *adj* (arrangement, agreement) 相互の sōgò no

recital [risait'əl] *n* (concert) リサイタル risáìtaru

recite [risait'] *vt* (poem) 暗唱する añshō suru

reckless [rek'lis] *adj* (driving, driver) 無謀な mubō na; (spending) 無茶な múchà na

recklessly [rek'lisli:] *adv* (drive) 無謀に mubō ni; (spend) むやみに múyàmi ni

reckon [rek'ən] *vt* (calculate) 計算する keísan suru; (think): *I reckon that ...* ...だと思う ...dá tò omóù

reckoning [rek'əniŋ] *n* (calculation) 計算 keísan

reckon on *vt fus* (expect) 当てにする a-té nì suru

reclaim [rikleim'] *vt* (demand back) ...の返還を要求する ...no heñkan wò yōkyū suru; (land: by filling in) 埋め立てる umétaterù; (: by draining) 干拓する kañtaku suru; (waste materials) 再生する saísei suru

reclamation [rekləmei'ʃən] *n* (of land: by filling in) 埋め立て umétate; (: by draining) 干拓 kañtaku

recline [riklain'] *vi* (sit or lie back) もたれる motárerù

reclining [riklain'iŋ] *adj*: *reclining seat* リクライニングシート rikúrainingushìto

recluse [rek'lu:s] *n* 隠とん者 iñtoñsha

recognition [rekəgni'ʃən] *n* (of person, place) 認識 niñshiki; (of problem, fact) 意識 íshìki; (of achievement) 認める事

mitómeru kotǒ

transformed beyond recognition 見分けが付かない程変化した miwáke ga tsukanái hodo hénka shita

recognizable [rekəgnai'zəbəl] *adj*: **recognizable (by)** (...で) 見分けが付く (...de) miwáke ga tsukù

recognize [rek'əgnaiz] *vt* (person, place, attitude, illness) ...だ と 分かる ...dá tò wakárù; (problem, need) 意識する íshìki suru; (qualification, achievement) 認める mitómerù; (government) 承認する shónin suru

to recognize by/as ...で〔として〕分かる ...de 〔toshítè〕 wakárù

recoil [rikɔil'] *vi* (person): **to recoil from doing something** ...するのをいやがる ...surú no wò iyágarù
♦*n* (of gun) 反動 handō

recollect [rekəlekt'] *vt* (remember) 思い出す omóidasù

recollection [rekəlek'ʃən] *n* (memory) 思い出 omóide; (remembering) 思い出す事 omóidasu kotò

recommend [rekəmend'] *vt* (book, shop, person) 推薦する suísen suru; (course of action) 勧める susúmerù

recommendation [rekəmendei'ʃən] *n* (of book, shop, person) 推薦 suísen; (of course of action) 勧告 kaňkoku

recompense [rek'əmpens] *n* (reward) 報酬 hóshū

reconcile [rek'ənsail] *vt* (two people) 仲直りさせる nakánaòri saserù; (two facts, beliefs) 調和させる chówa saserù

to reconcile oneself to something (unpleasant situation, misery etc) ...だとあきらめる ...dá tò akíramerù

reconciliation [rekənsili:ei'ʃən] *n* (of people etc) 和解 wakái; (of facts etc) 調和 chówa

recondition [ri:kəndi'ʃən] *vt* (machine) 修理する shūri suru

reconnaissance [rikɑ:n'isəns] *n* (MIL) 偵察 teísatsu

reconnoiter [ri:kənɔi'tə:r] (*BRIT* **reconnoitre**) *vt* (MIL: enemy territory) 偵察する teísatsu suru

reconsider [ri:kənsid'ə:r] *vt* (decision, opinion etc) 考え直す kaňgaenaosù

reconstruct [ri:kənstrʌkt'] *vt* (building) 建直す taténaosù; (policy, system) 練り直す nerínaosù; (event, crime) 再現する saígen suru

reconstruction [ri:kənstrʌk'ʃən] *n* (of building, country) 再建 saíken; (of crime) 再現 saígen

record [*n* rek'ə:rd *vb* rekɔ:rd'] *n* (gen) 記録 kiróku; (MUS: disk) レコード rekódò; (history: of person, company) 履歴 riréki; (*also*: **criminal record**) 前科 zénka
♦*vt* (write down) 記録する kiróku suru; (temperature, speed etc) 表示する hyóji suru; (MUS: song etc) 録音する rokúon suru

in record time 記録的速さで kirókuteki hayàsa de

off the record *adj* (remark) オフレコの ofúreko no
♦*adv* (speak) オフレコで ofúreko de

record card *n* (in file) ファイルカード faírukàdo

recorded delivery [rikɔ:r'did-] (*BRIT*) *n* (MAIL) 簡易書留 kaň-i kakítome

recorder [rikɔ:r'də:r] *n* (MUS: instrument) リコーダー rikódà

record holder *n* (SPORT) 記録保持者 kiróku hojìsha

recording [rikɔ:r'diŋ] *n* 録音 rokúon

record player *n* レコードプレーヤー rekódopurèya

recount [rikaunt'] *vt* (story, event etc) 述べる nobérù

re-count [*n* ri:'kaunt *vb* ri:kaunt'] *n* (POL: of votes) 数え直し kazóenaoshi
♦*vt* (votes etc) 数え直す kazóenaosù

recoup [riku:p'] *vt*: **to recoup one's losses** 損失を取戻す soňshitsu wò torímodosù

recourse [ri:'kɔ:rs] *n*: **to have recourse to** ...を用いる ...wo mochíirù

recover [rikʌv'ə:r] *vt* (get back: stolen goods, lost items, financial loss) 取戻す torímodosù
♦*vi*: **to recover (from)** (illness) (...が)

治る (...ga) naórù; (operation, shock, experience) (...から) 立直る (...kará) tachínaorù

recovery [rikʌv'əri:] n (from illness, operation: in economy etc) 回復 kaífuku; (of stolen, lost items) 取戻し torímodoshi

re-create [ri:kri:eit'] vt 再現する saígen suru

recreation [rekri:ei'ʃən] n (play, leisure activities) 娯楽 goráku

recreational [rekri:ei'ʃənəl] adj 娯楽の goráku no

recrimination [rikrimənei'ʃən] n 責合い seméai

recruit [rikru:t'] n (MIL) 新兵 shiñpei; (in company, organization) 新入社〔会〕員 shiñnyūsha〔kai〕īn
♦vt 募集する boshū suru

recruitment [rikru:t'mənt] n 募集 boshū

rectangle [rek'tæŋgəl] n 長方形 chốhōkei

rectangular [rektæŋ'gjələr] adj (shape, object etc) 長方形の chốhōkei no

rectify [rek'təfai] vt (correct) 正す tadásù

rector [rek'tər] n (REL) 主任司祭 shuníñshisài

rectory [rek'tə:ri:] n (house) 司祭舘 shisáikan

recuperate [riku:'pə:reit] vi (recover: from illness etc) 回復する kaífuku suru

recur [rikə:r'] vi (error, event) 繰返される kuríkaesarerù; (illness, pain) 再発する saíhatsu suru

recurrence [rikə:r'əns] n (of error, event) 繰返し kuríkaeshi; (of illness, pain) 再発 saíhatsu

recurrent [rikə:r'ənt] adj 頻繁に起る hiñpan ni okórù

red [red] n (color) 赤 ákà; (pej: POL) 過激派 kagékiha
♦adj 赤い akáì

to be in the red (bank account, business) 赤字になっている akáji ni natté irù

red carpet treatment n 盛大な歓迎式 seídai nà kañgeishìki

Red Cross n 赤十字 sekíjūji

redcurrant [red'kʌr'ənt] n アカフサスグリ akáfusasugùri

redden [red'ən] vt (turn red) 赤くする a-kákù suru
♦vi (blush) 赤面する sekímen suru

reddish [red'iʃ] adj 赤っぽい akáppòi

redeem [ridi:m'] vt (fig: situation, reputation) 救う sukúù; (something in pawn, loan) 請出す ukédasù; (REL: rescue) 救う sukúù

redeeming [ridi:'miŋ] adj: *redeeming feature* 欠点を補う取柄 kettén wò ogínaù toríe

redeploy [ri:diploi'] vt (resources) 配置し直す haíchi shinaosù

red-haired [red'he:rd] adj 赤毛の akáge no

red-handed [red'hæn'did] adj: *to be caught red-handed* 現行犯で捕まる geñkōhan de tsukámarù

redhead [red'hed] n 赤毛の人 akáge no hitò

red herring n (fig) 本論から注意をそらす物 hoñron karà chúì wo sorásù monó

red-hot [red'hɑ:t'] adj (metal) 真っ赤に焼けた makká nì yakétà

redirect [ri:dərekt'] vt (mail) 転送する teñsō suru

red light n: *to go through a red light* (AUT) 信号無視をする shiñgōmùshi wo suru

red-light district [red'lait-] n 赤線地区 akásenchikù

redo [ri:du:'] (pt redid pp redone) vt やり直す yarínaosù

redolent [red'ələnt] adj: *redolent of* (smell: also fig) ...臭い ...kusái

redouble [ri:dʌb'əl] vt: *to redouble one's efforts* 一層努力する issố doryòku suru

redress [ridres'] n (compensation) 賠償 baíshō
♦vt (error, wrong) 償う tsugúnaù

Red Sea n: *the Red Sea* 紅海 kốkai

redskin [red'skin] n (pej) インディアン ín-dian

red tape n (fig) 形式的手続き keíshikiteki tetsuzùki

reduce [ridu:s'] vt (decrease: spending, numbers etc) 減らす herásù

to reduce someone to (begging, stealing) ...を余儀なくさせる ...wo yogínaku saserù

to reduce someone to tears 泣かせる nakáserù

to reduce someone to silence 黙らせる damáraserù

「*reduce speed now*」(AUT) 徐行 jokő

at a reduced price (goods) 割引でwaríbiki de

reduction [ridʌk'ʃən] n (in price) 値下げ neságe; (in numbers etc) 減少 geñshō

redundancy [ridʌn'dənsi:] n (dismissal) 解雇 kái̇ko; (unemployment) 失業 shitsúgyō

redundant [ridʌn'dənt] adj (worker) 失業中の shitsúgyōchū no; (detail, object) 余計な yokéi na

to be made redundant 解雇される káí̇ko sarérù

reed [ri:d] n (BOT) アシ ashí; (MUS: of clarinet etc) リード rído

reef [ri:f] n (at sea) 暗礁 añshō

reek [ri:k] vi: *to reek (of)* (...の) においがぷんぷんする (...no) niói ga púñpun suru

reel [ri:l] n (of thread, string) 巻 makí; (of film, tape: also on fishing-rod) リール rīru; (dance) リール rīru

♦vi (sway) よろめく yorómekù

reel in vt (fish, line) 手繰り寄せる tagúriyoserù

ref [ref] (inf) n abbr = referee

refectory [rifek'tə:ri:] n 食堂 shokúdō

refer [rifəːr'] vt (person, patient): *to refer someone to* ...を...に回す ...wo ...ni mawásù; (matter, problem): *to refer something to* ...を...に委託する ...wo ...ni itáku suru

♦vi: *to refer to* (allude to) ...に言及する ...ni geñkyū suru; (consult) ...を参照する ...wo sañshō suru

referee [refəri:'] n (SPORT) 審判員 shiñpañ-in, レフェリー réfèrī; (BRIT: for job application) 身元保証人 mimótohoshōnìn

♦vt (football match etc) ...のレフェリーをやる ...no réfèrī wo yárù

reference [ref'əːrəns] n (mention) 言及 geñkyū; (in book, paper) 引用文献 iñ-yō buñken; (for job application: letter) 推薦状 suíseñjō

with reference to (COMM: in letter) ...に関しては ...ni kañshite wa

reference book n 参考書 sañkòsho

reference number n 整理番号 seíribañgō

referenda [refəren'də] npl of **referendum**

referendum [refəren'dəm] (pl **referenda**) n 住民投票 jūmintōhyō

refill [vb ri:fil' n ri:'fil] vt (glass etc) ...にもう一杯つぐ ... ni mő ippaì tsugú; (pen etc) ...に...を詰替える ...ni ...wo tsumékaerù

♦n (of drink etc) お代り o-káwari; (for pen etc) スペアー supéà

refine [rifain'] vt (sugar, oil) 精製する seísei suru; (theory, idea) 洗練する sefren suru

refined [rifaind'] adj (person, taste) 洗練された sefren saretà

refinement [rifain'mənt] n (of person) 優雅さ yűgasa; (of system) 精度 seído

reflect [riflekt'] vt (light, image) 反射する hañsha suru; (situation, attitude) 反映する hañ-ei suru

♦vi (think) じっくり考える jikkúrì kañgaerù

it reflects badly/well on him それは彼の悪い(いい)所を物語っている soré wa kárè no warúì (íì) tokórò wo monógatatte irù

reflection [riflek'ʃən] n (of light, heat) 反射 hañsha; (image) 影 kágè; (of situation, attitude) 反映する物 hañ-ei suru monò; (criticism) 非難 hínàn; (thought) 熟考 jukkő

on reflection よく考えると yőkù kañgaerù to

reflector [riflek'tə:r] n 反射器 hañshakí

reflex [ri:'fleks] adj (action, gesture) 反射的な hañshateki na

♦n (PHYSIOLOGY, PSYCH) 反射 hañsha

reflexive [riflek'siv] adj (LING) 再帰の saíki no

reform [rifɔːrm'] n (of sinner, character) 改心 kaíshin; (of law, system) 改革 kaíkaku
♦vt (sinner) 改心させる kaíshin saserù; (law, system) 改革する kaíkaku suru

Reformation [refɔrmei'ʃən] n: **the Reformation** 宗教改革 shúkyōkaìkaku

reformatory [rifɔːr'mətɔːri:] (US) n 感化院 kaŕkaìn

refrain [rifrein'] vi: **to refrain from doing** ...をしない様にする ...wo shinái yō ni suru
♦n (of song) 繰返し kuríkaeshi, リフレイン rifúreìn

refresh [rifreʃ'] vt (subj: sleep, drink) 元気付ける geñkizukerù
to refresh someone's memory ...に思い出させる ...ni omóidasaserù

refresher course [rifreʃ'əːr-] (BRIT) n 研修会 keñshūkaì

refreshing [rifreʃ'iŋ] adj (drink) 冷たくておいしい tsumétakùte oíshiì; (sleep) 気分をさわやかにする kíbùn wo sawáyàka ni suru

refreshments [rifreʃ'mənts] npl (food and drink) 軽食 keíshoku

refrigeration [rifridʒərei'ʃən] n (of food) 冷蔵 reízō

refrigerator [rifridʒ'əːreitəːr] n 冷蔵庫 reízōko

refuel [ri:fju:'əl] vi 燃料を補給する neńryō wo hokyú suru

refuge [ref'ju:dʒ] n (shelter) 避難場所 hináñbasho
to take refuge in ...に避難する ...ni hínàn suru

refugee [refjudʒi:'] n 難民 nañmin

refund [n ri:'fʌnd vb rifʌnd'] n 払い戻し haráimodoshi
♦vt (money) 払い戻す haráimodosù

refurbish [ri:fəːr'biʃ] vt (shop, theater) 改装する kaísō suru

refusal [rifju:'zəl] n 断り kotówari, 拒否 kyóhì
first refusal (option) オプション権 o-

púshoñken

refuse[1] [rifju:z'] vt (request, offer, gift) 断る kotówarù; (invitation) 辞退する jítài suru; (permission, consent) 拒む kobámù
♦vi (say no) 断る kotówarù; (horse) 飛越を拒否する hiétsu wò kyóhì suru
to refuse to do something ...するのを拒む ...surú no wò kobámù

refuse[2] [ref'ju:s] n (rubbish) ごみ gomí

refuse collection n ごみ収集 gomíshū-shū

refute [rifju:t'] vt (argument) 論破する roñpa suru

regain [rigein'] vt (power, position) 取戻す torímodosù

regal [ri:'gəl] adj 堂々とした dṓdō to shitā

regalia [rigei'li:ə] n (costume) 正装 seísō

regard [rigɑːrd'] n (gaze) 視線 shisén; (attention, concern) 関心 kañshin; (esteem) 尊敬 soñkei
♦vt (consider) 見なす minásù
to give one's regards to ...から...によろしく伝える ...kará ...nì yoróshìku tsutáerù
with kindest regards 敬具 keígu
regarding, as regards, with regard to (with reference to, concerning) ...に関して ...ni kañshitè

regardless [rigɑːrd'lis] adv (carry on, continue) 構わずに kamáwazù ni
regardless of (danger, consequences) ...を顧みず ...wo kaёrimizù

regatta [rigɑːt'ə] n ヨット〔ボート〕競技会 yottó〔bốto〕kyōgikài

regenerate [ri:dʒen'əːreit] vt (inner cities, arts) よみがえらせる yomígaera-serù

regent [ri:'dʒənt] n 摂政 sesshṓ

regime [reiʒi:m'] n (system of government) 政治体制 seíjitaìsei

regiment [redʒ'əmənt] n (MIL) 連隊 reñtai

regimental [redʒəmen'təl] adj 連隊の reñtai no

region [ri:'dʒən] n (area: of land) 地区 chíkù; (: of body) ...部 ...bù; (administrative division of country) 行政区 gyóseí-ku

in the region of (*fig*: approximately) 約 yákù

regional [ri:'dʒənəl] *adj* (organization, wine, geography) 地元の jimóto no; (provincial) 地方の chihô no

register [redʒ'istə:r] *n* (list: of births, marriages, deaths, voters) 登録簿 tórokùbo; (SCOL: of attendance) 出席簿 shussékibò; (MUS: of voice) 声域 seíìki; (: of instrument) 音域 oń-iki

♦*vt* (birth, death, marriage) 届出る todókederù; (car) 登録する tóroku suru; (MAIL: letter) 書留にする kakítome nì suru; (subj: meter, gauge) 示す shimésù

♦*vi* (at hotel) チェックインする chekkúìn suru; (for work) 登録する namáè wo tóroku suru; (as student) 入学手続きをする nyúgakutetsuzuki wò suru; (make impression) ぴんと来る píñ tò kúrù

registered [redʒ'istə:rd] *adj* (MAIL: letter, parcel) 書留の kakítome no

registered trademark *n* 登録商標 tórokushôhyò

registrar [redʒ'istrɑ:r] *n* (official) 戸籍係 kosékìgakàri; (in college, university) 教務係 kyómugakàri; (*BRIT*: in hospital) 医務吏員 imúrìn

registration [redʒistrei'ʃən] *n* (*gen*) 登録 tóroku; (of birth, death) 届出 todókede; (AUT: *also*: **registration number**) ナンバー náñbā

registry [redʒ'istri:] *n* 登記所 tókisho

registry office (*BRIT*) *n* 戸籍登記所 kosékitôkisho

to get married in a registry office 戸籍登記所で結婚する kosékitôkisho dè kekkóñ suru

regret [rigret'] *n* (sorrow) 悔み kuyámi

♦*vt* (decision, action) 後悔する kôkai suru; (loss, death) 悔む kuyámù; (inability to do something) 残念に思う zaňnen nì omóù; (inconvenience) 済まないと思う sumánài to omóù

regretfully [rigret'fəli:] *adv* (sadly) 残念ながら zaňnen nagàra

regrettable [rigret'əbəl] *adj* (unfortunate: mistake, incident) あいにくの aínìku no

regular [reg'jələ:r] *adj* (even: breathing, pulse etc) 規則的な kisôkuteki na; (evenly-spaced: intervals, meetings etc) 定期的な teíkìteki na; (symmetrical: features, shape etc) 対称的な taíshôteki na; (frequent: raids, exercise etc) 頻繁な híñpan na; (usual: time, doctor, customer etc) 通常の tsújô no; (soldier) 正規の seíki no; (LING) 規則変化の kisôkuheñka no

♦*n* (client etc) 常連 jôren

regularity [regjəlær'iti:] *n* (frequency) 高頻度 kôhìñdo

regularly [reg'jələ:rli:] *adv* (at evenly-spaced intervals) 規則的に kisôkuteki ni; (symmetrically: shaped etc) 対称的に taíshôteki ni; (often) 頻繁に híñpan ni

regulate [reg'jəleit] *vt* (conduct, expenditure) 規制する kiséi suru; (traffic, speed) 調整する chôsei suru; (machine, oven) 調節する chôsetsu suru

regulation [regjəlei'ʃən] *n* (of conduct, expenditure) 規制 kiséi; (of traffic, speed) 調整 chôsei; (of machine, oven) 調節 chôsetsu; (rule) 規則 kisôku

rehabilitation [ri:həbilətei'ʃən] *n* (of criminal, addict) 社会復帰 shakáifukkì, リハビリテーション rihábiritèshon

rehearsal [rihər'səl] *n* リハーサル rihâsàru

rehearse [rihə:rs'] *vt* (play, dance, speech etc) ...のリハーサルをする ...no rihâsàru wo suru

reign [rein] *n* (of monarch) 治世 chiséi; (: of terror etc) 支配 shíhai

♦*vi* (monarch) 君臨する kuñrin suru; (*fig*: violence, fear etc) はびこる habíkorù; (: peace, order etc) 行渡る ikíwatarù

reimburse [ri:imbə:rs'] *vt* (pay back) ...に弁償する ...ni beñshô suru

rein [rein] *n* (for horse) 手綱 tazúna

reincarnation [ri:inkɑ:rnei'ʃən] *n* (belief) 輪ね rîñne

reindeer [rein'di:r] *n inv* トナカイ tonákài

reinforce [ri:info:rs'] vt (strengthen: object) 補強する hokyō suru; (: situation) 強化する kyōka suru; (support: idea, statement) 裏付ける urázukerù

reinforced concrete [ri:info:rst'-] n 鉄筋コンクリート tekkín konkurīto

reinforcement [ri:info:rs'mənt] n (strengthening) 補強 hokyō

reinforcements [ri:info:rs'mənts] npl (MIL) 援軍 efigun

reinstate [ri:insteit'] vt (worker) 復職させる fukúshoku saserù; (tax, law, text) 元通りにする motódòri ni surù

reiterate [ri:it'əreit] vt (repeat) 繰返す kuríkaesù

reject [n ri:'dʒekt vb ridʒekt'] n (COMM) 傷物 kizúmono
♦vt (plan, proposal etc) 退ける shirízokerù; (offer of help) 断る kotówarù; (belief, political system) 拒絶する kyozétsu suru; (candidate) 不採用にする fusáìyō ni suru; (coin) 受付けない ukétsukenài; (goods, fruit etc) 傷物として処分する kizúmono toshitè shóbùn suru

rejection [ridʒek'ʃən] n (of plan, proposal, offer of help etc) 拒否 kyóhì; (of belief etc) 拒絶 kyozétsu; (of candidate) 不採用 fusáìyō

rejoice [ridʒɔis'] vi: to rejoice at/over ...を喜ぶ ...wo yorókobù

rejuvenate [ridʒu:'vəneit] vt (person) 若返らせる wakágaeraserù

relapse [rilæps'] n (MED) 再発 saíhatsu

relate [rileit'] vt (tell) 話す hanásù; (connect) 結び付ける musúbitsukerù
♦vi: to relate to (person, subject, thing) ...に関係がある ...ni kañkei ga arù

related [rilei'tid] adj (person) 血縁がある ketsúen ga arù; (animal, language) 近縁の kiñ-en no
related to ...に関係がある ...ni kañkei ga arù

relating [rilei'tiŋ]: relating to prep ...に関する ...ni kañ suru

relation [rilei'ʃən] n (member of family) 親せき shiñseki; (connection) 関係 kañkei

relations [relei'ʃənz] npl (dealings) 関係 kañkei; (relatives) 親せき shiñseki

relationship [rilei'ʃənʃip] n (between two people, countries, things) 関係 kañkei; (also: **family relationship**) 親族関係 shiñzokukañkei

relative [rel'ətiv] n (member of family) 親類 shiñrui, 親せき shiñseki
♦adj (comparative) 相対的な sōtaiteki na; (connected): relative to ...に関する ...ni kañ suru

relatively [rel'ətivli:] adv (comparatively) 比較的な hikákuteki

relax [rilæks'] vi (person: unwind) くつろぐ kutsúrogù; (muscle) 緩む yurúmù
♦vt (one's grip) 緩める yurúmerù; (mind, person) くつろがせる kutsúrogaserù; (rule, control etc) 緩める yurúmerù

relaxation [ri:lækseí'ʃən] n (rest) 休み yasúmi; (of muscle, grip) 緩み yurúmi; (of rule, control etc) 緩和 kañwa; (recreation) 娯楽 goráku

relaxed [rilækst'] adj (person) 落着いた ochítsuità; (discussion, atmosphere) くつろいだ kutsúroìda

relaxing [rilæks'iŋ] adj (holiday, afternoon) くつろいだ kutsúroìda

relay [ri:'lei] n (race) リレー rírè
♦vt (message, question) 伝える tsutáerù; (programme, signal) 中継する chúkei suru

release [rilis'] n (from prison) 釈放 shakúhō; (from obligation) 免除 méñjo; (of gas, water etc) 放出 hōshutsu; (of film) 封切 fúkiri; (of book, record) 発売 hatsúbai
♦vt (prisoner: from prison) 釈放する shakúhō suru; (: from captivity) 解放する kaíhō suru; (gas etc) 放出する hōshutsu suru; (free: from wreckage etc) 救出する kyúshutsu suru; (TECH: catch, spring etc) 外す hazúsù; (book, record) 発売する hatsúbai suru; (film) 公開する kōkai suru; (report, news) 公表する kōhyō suru

relegate [rel'əgeit] vt (downgrade) 格下げする kakúsage suru; (BRIT: SPORT): to be relegated 格下げされる kakúsage sarerù

relent [rilent'] vi (give in) ...の態度が軟化し

する ...no táido ga nañka suru

relentless [rilent'lis] *adj* (unceasing) 絶間ない taémanaì; (determined) 執念深い shúneñbukai

relevance [rel'əvəns] *n* (of remarks, information) 意義 ígì; (of question etc) 関連 kañren

relevant [rel'əvənt] *adj* (fact, information, question) 意義ある ígì árù

relevant to (situation, problem etc) ...に関連のある ...ni kañren no arù

reliability [rilaiəbil'əti:] *n* (of person, machine) 信頼性 shiñraisei; (of information) 信ぴょう性 shiñpyōsei

reliable [rilai'əbəl] *adj* (person, firm) 信頼できる shiñrai dekirù; (method, machine) 信頼性のある shiñraisei no arù; (news, information) 信用できる shiñyō dekirù

reliably [rilai'əbli:] *adv*: *to be reliably informed that ...* 確かな情報筋による と... táshìka na jōhōsùji ni yorú tò ...

reliance [rilai'əns] *n*: *reliance (on)* (...への) 依存 (...é nò) izón

relic [rel'ik] *n* (REL) 聖遺物 seíbùtsu; (of the past) 遺物 ibútsu

relief [rili:f'] *n* (from pain, anxiety etc) 緩和 kañwa; (help, supplies) 救援物資 kyúenbusshì; (ART) 浮彫 ukíbori, レリーフ rerífù; (GEO) 際立つ事 kiwádatsu kotó

relieve [rili:v'] *vt* (pain, fear, worry) 緩和する kañwa suru; (patient) 安心させる afishin saserù; (bring help to: victims, refugees etc) ...に救援物資を届ける ...ni kyúenbusshì wo todókerù; (take over from: colleague, guard) ...と交替する ...to kótai suru

to relieve someone of something (load) ...の...を持って上げる ...no ...wo móttè agérù; (duties, post) ...を解任する ...wo kaínin suru

to relieve oneself 小便する shóben suru

religion [rilidʒ'ən] *n* 宗教 shúkyō

religious [rilidʒ'əs] *adj* (activities, faith) 宗教の shúkyō no; (person) 信心深い shíñjiñbukai

relinquish [riliŋ'kwiʃ] *vt* (authority) ...から手を引く ...kara té wò hikú; (plan, habit) やめる yamérù

relish [rel'iʃ] *n* (CULIN) レリッシュ rerísshù; (enjoyment) 楽しみ tanóshimi

♦*vt* (enjoy: food, competition) 楽しむ tanóshimù

to relish the thought/idea/prospect of something/doing something ...を〔...するのを〕心待ちに待つ ...wo〔... surú nò wo〕kokóromachi nì mátsù

relocate [ri:lou'keit] *vt* 移動させる idó saserù

♦*vi* 移動する idó suru

reluctance [rilʌk'təns] *n* (unwillingness) 気が進まない事 kí gà susúmanai kotó

reluctant [rilʌk'tənt] *adj* (unwilling) 気が進まない kí gà susúmanai

reluctantly [rilʌk'təntli:] *adv* (unwillingly) いやいやながら iyáiyanagàra

rely on [rilai'-] *vt fus* (be dependent on) ...に頼る ...ni tayórù; (trust) ...を信用する ...wo shiñ-yō suru

remain [rimein'] *vi* (survive, be left) 残る nokórù; (continue to be) 相変らず...である kawarazù ...de árù; (stay) とどまる todómarù

remainder [rimein'də:r] *n* (rest) 残り nokóri

remaining [rimein'niŋ] *adj* 残りの nokóri no

remains [rimeinz'] *npl* (of meal) 食べ残り tabénokori; (of building) 廃虚 haíkyo; (corpse) 遺体 itái

remand [rimænd'] *n*: *on remand* 拘置中で kóchichū de

♦*vt*: *to be remanded in custody* 拘置される kóchi sarerù

remand home (BRIT) *n* 少年院 shónen-ìn

remark [rimɑːrk'] *n* (comment) 発言 hatsúgen

♦*vt* (comment) 言う iú

remarkable [rimɑːr'kəbəl] *adj* (outstanding) 著しい ichíjirushi

remarry [ri:mær'i:] *vi* 再婚する saíkon suru

remedial [rimi:'di:əl] *adj* (tuition, classes) 補修の hoshū no; (exercise) 矯正の kyōsei no

remedy [rem'idi:] n (cure) 治療法 chiryō-hō
♦vt (correct) 直す naósù

remember [rimem'bə:r] vt (call back to mind) 思い出す omóidasù; (bear in mind) 忘れない様にする wasúrenai yō ni suru; (send greetings): **remember me to him** 彼によろしくお伝え下さい kárè ni yoró-shikù o-tsútae kudasái

remembrance [rimem'brəns] n (memory: of dead person) 思い出 omóide; (souvenir: of place, event) 記念品 kinénhin

remind [rimaind'] vt: **to remind someone to do something** ...するのを忘れない様に...に注意する ...surú no wò wasúrenai yō ni ...ni chūī suru
to remind someone of something ...に...を思い出させる ...ni ...wo omóidasasè-ru
she reminds me of her mother 彼女を見ると彼女の母親を思い出す kánòjo wo mírù to kánòjo no haháoya wò omóidasù

reminder [rimaind'ə:r] n (souvenir) 記念品 kinénhin; (letter) 覚書 obóegaki

reminisce [remənis'] vi (about the past) 追憶する tsuíoku suru

reminiscent [remənis'ənt] adj: **to be reminiscent of something** ...を思い出させる ...wo omóidasaserù

remiss [rimis'] adj (careless) 不注意な fu-chūī na
it was remiss of him 彼は不注意だった kárè wa fuchūì dáttà

remission [rimiʃ'ən] n (of debt) 免除 ménjo; (of prison sentence) 減刑 geñkei; (of illness) 緩解 kañkai; (REL: of sins) 許し yurúshi

remit [rimit'] vt (send: money) 送金する sōkin suru

remittance [rimit'əns] n (payment) 送金 sōkin

remnant [rem'nənt] n (small part remaining) 残り nokóri; (of cloth) 切れ端 kiréhashi

remnants [rem'nənts] npl (COMM) 端切れ hagíre

remorse [rimɔːrs'] n (guilt) 後悔 kōkai

remorseful [rimɔːrs'fəl] adj (guilty) 後悔している kōkai shite irù

remorseless [rimɔːrs'lis] adj (fig: noise, pain) 絶間ない taémanaì

remote [rimout'] adj (distant: place, time) 遠い tōì; (person) よそよそしい yo-sóyososhiì; (slight: possibility, chance) かすかな kásùka na

remote control n 遠隔操作 eñkakusō-sa, リモートコントロール rimōtokonto-rōru

remotely [rimout'li:] adv (distantly) 遠くに tōku ni; (slightly) かすかに kásùka ni

remould [ri:'mould] (BRIT) n (tire) 再生タイヤ saíseitaiya

removable [rimu:'vəbəl] adj (detachable) 取外しのできる toríhazushi nò dekírù

removal [rimu:'vəl] n (taking away) 取除く事 torínozoku kotò; (of stain) 消し取る事 keshítoru kotò; (BRIT: from house) 引っ越し hikkóshi; (from office: dismissal) 免職 meñshoku; (MED) 切除 sétsùjo

removal van (BRIT) n 引っ越しトラック hikkóshi torakkù

remove [rimu:v'] vt (gen) 取除く toríno-zokù; (clothing) 脱ぐ núgù; (bandage etc) 外す hazúsù; (stain) 消し取る keshítorù; (employee) 解雇する káìko suru; (MED: lung, kidney, appendix etc) 切除する sé-tsùjo suru

removers [rimu:'və:rz] (BRIT) npl (company) 引っ越し屋 hikkóshiyà

remuneration [rimju:nərei'ʃən] n (payment) 報酬 hōshū

Renaissance [ren'isɑ:ns] n: **the Renaissance** ルネッサンス runéssànsu

render [ren'də:r] vt (give: thanks, service) する surú; (make) させる sasérù

rendering [ren'də:riŋ] n (MUS: instrumental) 演奏 eñsō; (: song) 歌い方 utáikatà

rendez-vous [rɑːn'deivu:] n (meeting) 待ち合せ machíawase; (place) 待ち合せの

場所 machíawase nò báshò

renegade [ren'əgeid] n 裏切者 urágirimono

renew [rinu:'] vt (resume) 再び始める futátabi hajimerù; (loan, contract etc) 更新する kóshin suru; (negotiations) 再開する saíkai suru; (acquaintance, relationship) よみがえらせる yomígaeraserù

renewal [rinu:'əl] n (resumption) 再開 saíkai; (of license, contract etc) 更新 kóshin

renounce [rinauns'] vt (belief, course of action) 捨てる sutérù; (claim, right, peerage) 放棄する hóki suru

renovate [ren'əveit] vt (building, machine) 改造する kaízō suru

renovation [renəvei'∫ən] n 改造 kaízō

renown [rinaun'] n (fame) 名声 meísei

renowned [rinaund'] adj (famous) 有名な yúmei na

rent [rent] n (for house) 家賃 yáchìn

♦vt (take for rent: house) 賃借する chíñshaku suru; (: television, car) レンタルで借りる rêñtaru de karírù; (also: **rent out**: house) 賃貸する chíñtai suru; (: television, car) 貸出す kashídasù

rental [ren'təl] n (for television, car) レンタル rêñtaru

renunciation [rinʌnsiːei'∫ən] n 放棄 hóki

reorganize [riːɔːr'gənaiz] vt 再編成する saíhensei suru

rep [rep] n abbr (COMM) = **representative**; (THEATER) = **repertory**

repair [riper'] n (of clothes, shoes) 修繕 shúzen; (of car, road, building etc) 修理 shúri

♦vt (clothes, shoes) 修繕する shúzen suru; (car, engine, road, building) 修理する shúri suru

in good/bad repair 整備が行届いている〔いない〕seíbi gà ikítodoite irù〔ínài〕

repair kit n 修理キット shúrikittò

repatriate [ri:pei'tri:eit] vt (refugee, soldier) 送還する sókan suru

repay [ripei'] (pt, pp **repaid**) vt (money, debt, loan) 返済する heñsai suru; (person) ...に借金を返済する ...ni shakkín wo

heñsai suru; (sb's efforts) ...に答える ...ni kotáerù; (favor) ...の恩返しをする ...no oñgaeshi wò suru

repayment [ripei'mənt] n (amount of money) 返済金 heñsaikiñ; (of debt, loan etc) 返済 heñsai

repeal [ripiː'l] n (of law) 廃止する haíshi suru

♦vt (law) 廃止 haíshi

repeat [ripiːt'] n (RADIO, TV) 再放送 saíhōsō

♦vt (say/do again) 繰返す kuríkaesù; (RADIO, TV) 再放送する saíhōsō surù

♦vi 繰返す kuríkaesù

repeatedly [ripiːt'idliː] adv (again and again) 再三 saísan

repel [ripel'] vt (drive away: enemy, attack) 撃退する gekítai suru; (disgust: subj: appearance, smell) ...に不快な感じを与える ...ni fukái na kañji wò atáerù

repellent [ripel'ənt] adj いやな iyá nà

♦n: *insect repellent* 虫よけ mushíyoke

repent [ripent'] vi: *to repent (of)* (sin, mistake) (...を) 後悔する (...wo) kókai suru

repentance [ripen'təns] n 後悔 kókai

repercussions [riːpərkʌ∫'ənz] npl 反響 hañkyō

repertoire [rep'əːrtwɑːr] n レパートリー repátòrī

repertory [rep'əːrtɔːriː] n (also: **repertory theater**) レパートリー演劇 repátòrīeñgeki

repetition [repiti∫'ən] n (repeat) 繰返し kuríkaeshi

repetitive [ripet'ətiv] adj (movement, work) 単純反復の tañjunhañpuku no; (speech) くどい kudóì; (noise) 反復される hañpuku sarerù

replace [ripleis'] vt (put back) 元に戻す mótò ni modósù; (take the place of) ...に代る ...ni kawárù

replacement [ripleis'mənt] n (substitution) 置き換え okíkae; (substitute) 代りの物 kawári no monò

replay [ri:plei'] n (of match) 再試合 saíshiai; (of tape, film) 再生 saísei

replenish [riplen'i∫] vt (glass) ...にもう一

杯つぐ ...ni mố ippài tsugú; (stock etc) 補充する hojú suru

replete [ripli:t'] *adj* (well-fed) 満腹の mańpuku no

replica [rep'ləkə] *n* (copy) 複製 fukúsei, レプリカ repúrīka

reply [riplai'] *n* (answer) 答え kotáè
♦*vi* (to question, letter) 答える kotáèrù

reply coupon *n* 返信券 heńshìñken ◇切手と交換できる券 kitté tò kốkan dekirù kèñ

report [ripə:rt'] *n* (account) 報告書 hốkokushò; (PRESS, TV etc) 報道 hốdō; (BRIT: also: **school report**) レポート repốtò; (of gun) 銃声 jūsei
♦*vt* (give an account of: event, meeting) 報告する hốkoku suru; (PRESS, TV etc) 報道する hốdō suru; (theft, accident, death) 届け出る todőkederù
♦*vi* (make a report) 報告する hốkoku suru; (present oneself): **to report (to someone)** (...に) 出頭する (...ni) shuttố suru; (be responsible to): **to report to someone** ...が直属の上司である ...ga chokúzoku nò jốshi de arù

report card (*US, SCOTTISH*) *n* 通知表 tsúchihyò

reportedly [ripə:r'tidli:] *adv* うわさによると uwása ni yoru tò

reporter [ripə:r'tər] *n* (PRESS, TV etc) 記者 kishá

repose [ripouz'] *n*: **in repose** (face, mouth) 平常で heíjō de

reprehensible [reprihen'səbəl] *adj* (behavior) 不届きな futódòki na

represent [reprizent'] *vt* (person, nation) 代表する daíhyō suru; (view, belief) ...の典型的な例である ...no teńkeiteki nà reí de arù; (symbolize: idea, emotion) ...のシンボルである ...no shíñboru de árù; (constitute) ...である ...de árù; (describe): **to represent something as** ...を...として描写する ...wo ...toshite byősha suru; (COMM) ...のセールスマンである ...no sếrusumàn de árù

representation [reprizentei'ʃən] *n* (state of being represented) 代表を立てている事 daíhyō wò tátète irú kotð; (pic-

ture) 絵 é; (statue) 彫像 chốzō; (petition) 陳情 chíñjō

representations [reprizentei'ʃənz] *npl* (protest) 抗議 kốgi

representative [reprizen'tətiv] *n* (of person, nation) 代表者 daíhyōsha; (of view, belief) 典型 teñkei; (COMM) セールスマン sếrusumàn; (*US*: POL) 下院議員 kaíñgììn
♦*adj* (group, survey, cross-section) 代表的な daíhyōteki na

repress [ripres'] *vt* (people, revolt) 抑圧する yokúatsu suru; (feeling, impulse) 抑制する yokúsei suru

repression [ripreʃ'ən] *n* (of people, country) 抑圧 yokúatsu; (of feelings) 抑制 yokúsei

repressive [ripres'iv] *adj* (society, measures) 抑圧的な yokúatsuteki na

reprieve [ripri:v'] *n* (LAW) 執行延期 shikkốeñki ◇特に死刑について言う tókù ni shikéi ni tsuitè iú; (*fig*: delay) 延期 eñki

reprimand [rep'rəmænd] *n* (official rebuke) 懲戒 chốkai
♦*vt* 懲戒する chốkai suru

reprint [*n* ri:'print *vb* ri:print'] *n* 復刻版 fukkốkuban
♦*vt* 復刻する fukkốku suru

reprisal [riprai'zəl] *n* 報復 hốfuku

reprisals [riprai'zəlz] *npl* (acts of revenge) 報復行為 hốfukukði

reproach [riproutʃ'] *n* (rebuke) 非難 hínàn
♦*vt*: **to reproach someone for something** ...の...を非難する ...no ...wo hínàn suru

reproachful [riproutʃ'fəl] *adj* (look, remark) 非難めいた hinánmeìta

reproduce [ri:prədu:s'] *vt* (copy: document etc) 複製する fukúsei suru; (sound) 再生する saísei suru
♦*vi* (mankind, animal, plant) 繁殖する hañshoku suru

reproduction [ri:prədʌk'ʃən] *n* (copy: of document, report etc) 複写 fukúsha; (of sound) 再生 saísei; (of painting, furniture) 複製品 fukúseìhin; (of mankind, animal etc) 繁殖 hańshoku

reproductive [ri:prədʌk'tiv] adj (system, process) 繁殖の hańshoku no

reproof [ripru:f'] n し責 shisséki

reprove [ripru:v'] vt: **to reprove someone for something** ...の事で...をしっ責する ...no kotó dè ...wo shisséki suru

reptile [rep'tail] n は虫類 hachūrùi

republic [ripʌb'lik] n 共和国 kyówakòku

republican [ripʌb'likən] adj (system, government etc) 共和国の kyówakòku no; (US: POL): **Republican** 共和党の kyówatò no

repudiate [ripju:'di:eit] vt (accusation, violence) 否定する hitéi suru

repugnant [ripʌg'nənt] adj 不愉快な fuyúkài na

repulse [ripʌls'] vt (enemy, attack) 撃退する gekítai suru

repulsive [ripʌl'siv] adj (sight, idea) 不愉快な fuyúkài na

reputable [rep'jətəbəl] adj 評判の良い hyóban no yoî

reputation [repjətei'ʃən] n 評判 hyóban

reputed [ripju:'tid] adj (supposed) ...とされる ...to sarérù

reputedly [ripju:'tidli:] adv (supposedly) 人の言うには hitő nò iú ni wà

request [rikwest'] n (polite demand) 願い negái; (formal demand) 要望 yőbō; (RADIO, TV) リクエスト rikúesùto

♦vt: **to request something of/from someone** (politely) ...に ...をお願いする ...ni ...wo o-négai suru; (formally) ...に ...を要望する ...ni ...wo yőbō suru; (RADIO, TV) リクエストする rikúesùto suru

request stop (BRIT) n 随時停留所 zuíjiteiryùjo ◇乗降客がいる時だけバスが留る停留所 jőkòkyaku ga irú toki dakè básù ga tomárù teíryùjo

requiem [rek'wi:əm] n (REL) 死者のためのミサ shísha no tamé nò mísa; (MUS) 鎮魂曲 chínkoǹkyoku, レクイエム rekúîemu

require [rikwaiə:r'] vt (need) ...が必要である ...ga hitsúyō de arù; (order): **to**

require someone to do something ...に...する事を要求する ...ni ...surú kotó wo yőkyū suru

requirement [rikwaiə:r'mənt] n (need) 必要条件 hitsúyőjōken; (want) 要求 yőkyū

requisite [rek'wizit] n (requirement) 必要条件 hitsúyőjōken

♦adj (required) 必要な hitsúyō na

requisition [rekwiziʃ'ən] n: **requisition (for)** (demand) (...の) 請求 (...no) seíkyū

♦vt (MIL) 徴発する chőhatsu suru

resale [ri:'seil] n 転売 teńbai

rescind [risind'] vt (law) 廃止する haíshi suru; (contract, order etc) 破棄する hákì suru

rescue [res'kju:] n (help) 救援 kyúen; (from drowning, accident) 人命救助 jínmeikyùjo

♦vt: **to rescue (from)** (person, animal) (...から) 救う (...kara) sukúù; (company) 救済する kyúsai suru

rescue party n 救援隊 kyúentai, レスキュー隊 resúkyūtai

rescuer [res'kju:ə:r] n 救助者 kyújoshà

research [risə:rtʃ'] n 研究 keńkyū

♦vt (story, subject) 研究する keńkyū suru; (person) ...について情報を集める ...ni tsuíte jőhō wò atsúmerù

researcher [risə:r'tʃə:r] n 研究者 keńkyūsha

resemblance [rizem'bləns] n (likeness) 似ている事 nité iru kotó

resemble [rizem'bəl] vt ...に似ている ...ni nité irù

resent [rizent'] vt ...に対して腹を立てる ...ni táìshite hará wò tatérù

resentful [rizent'fəl] adj 怒っている okőtte irú

resentment [rizent'mənt] n 恨み urámi

reservation [rezə:rvei'ʃən] n (booking) 予約 yoyáku; (doubt) 疑い utágai; (for tribe) 居留地 kyoryűchì

reserve [rizə:rv'] n (store) 備蓄 bichíku, 蓄え takúwae; (SPORT) 補欠 hokétsu; (game reserve) 保護区 hogőkù; (restraint) 遠慮 eńryo

♦vt (keep) 取って置く tóttè oku; (seats, table etc) 予約する yoyáku suru

in reserve 蓄えてあって takúwaete attè

reserved [rizəːrvd'] adj (restrained) 遠慮深い eñryobùkai

reserves [rizəːrvz'] npl (MIL) 予備軍 yobígùn

reservoir [rez'əːrvwɑːr] n (of water) 貯水池 chosúichi

reshuffle [riːʃʌf'əl] n: *Cabinet reshuffle* (POL) 内閣改造 naíkakukaizō

reside [rizaid'] vi (person: live) 住む súmù

residence [rez'idəns] n (formal: home) 住い sumáì; (length of stay) 滞在 taízai

residence permit (BRIT) n 在留許可 zaíryūkyokà

resident [rez'idənt] n (of country, town) 住民 jūmin; (in hotel) 泊り客 tomárikyakù

♦adj (population) 現住の geñjū no; (doctor) レジデントの réjìdento no

residential [reziden'tʃəl] adj (area) 住宅の jútaku no; (course) 住込みの sumíkomi no; (college) 全寮制の zeñryōsei no

residue [rez'iduː] n (remaining part) 残留物 zañryūbutsu

resign [rizain'] vt (one's post) 辞任する jinín suru

♦vi (from post) 辞任する jinín suru

to resign oneself to (situation, fact) あきらめて...を認める akírametè ...wo mitómerù

resignation [rezignei'ʃən] n (post) 辞任 jinín; (state of mind) あきらめ akírame

resigned [rizaind'] adj (to situation etc) あきらめている akírame irù

resilience [rizil'jəns] n (of material) 弾力 dañryoku; (of person) 回復力 kaífukuryòku

resilient [rizil'jənt] adj (material) 弾力のある dañryoku no arù; (person) 立直りの速い tachínaori nò hayáì

resin [rez'in] n 樹脂 júshì

resist [rizist'] vt 抵抗する teíkō suru

resistance [rizis'təns] n (gen) 抵抗 teíkō; (to illness, infection) 抵抗力 teíkōryoku

resolute [rez'əluːt] adj (person) 意志の強

い íshì no tsuyóì; (refusal) 断固とした dáñko to shitá

resolution [rezəluː'ʃən] n (decision) 決心 kesshín; (determination) 決意 kétsùi; (of problem, difficulty) 解決 kaíketsu

resolve [rizɑːlv'] n (determination) 決意 kétsùi

♦vt (problem, difficulty) 解決する kaíketsu suru

♦vi: **to resolve to do** ...しようと決心する ...shiyō tò kesshín suru

resolved [rizɑːlvd'] adj (determined) 決心している kesshín shité irù

resonant [rez'ənənt] adj 朗朗たる rórō taru

resort [rizɔːrt'] n (town) リゾート rizótò; (recourse) 利用 riyó

♦vi: **to resort to** ...を利用する ...wo riyó suru

in the last resort 結局 kekkyókù

resound [rizaund'] vi: **to resound (with)** (...の音が...中に) 鳴り響く (...no otô ga ...jū ni) naríhibikù

resounding [rizaun'diŋ] adj (noise) 響き渡る hibíkiwatarù; (fig: success) 完全な kañzen na

resource [riː'sɔːrs] n (raw material) 資源 shígèn

resourceful [risɔːrs'fəl] adj (quick-witted) やり手の yaríte no

resources [riː'sɔːrsiz] npl (coal, iron, oil etc) 天然資源 teñnenshigèn; (money) 財産 zaísan

respect [rispekt'] n (consideration, esteem) 尊敬 soñkei

♦vt 尊敬する soñkei suru

with respect to ...に関して ...ni káñ shite

in this respect この点では konó ten de wà

respectability [rispektəbil'əti:] n 名声 meísei

respectable [rispek'təbəl] adj (morally correct) 道理にかなった dóri nì kanáttà; (large: amount) かなりの kánàri no; (passable) まあまあの mǎmǎ no

respectful [rispekt'fəl] adj (person, behavior) 礼儀正しい reígitadashiì

respective [rispek'tiv] adj (separate) そ
れぞれの sorézòre no

respectively [rispek'tivli:] adv それぞれ
sorézòre

respects [rispekts'] npl (greetings) あい
さつ áîsatsu

respiration [respərei'∫ən] n see **artificial respiration**

respite [res'pit] n (rest) 休息 kyúsoku

resplendent [risplen'dənt] adj 華やかな
hanáyàka na

respond [rispɑːnd'] vi (answer) 答える
kotáerù; (react: to pressure, criticism)
反応する hañnō suru

response [rispɑːns'] n (answer) 答え ko-
tâè; (reaction) 反応 hañnō

responsibility [rispɑːnsəbil'əti:] n (liability) 責任 sekínin; (duty) 義務 gímù

responsible [rispɑːn'səbəl] adj (liable):
responsible (for) (...の) 責任がある
(...no) sekínin gà árù; (character, person)
責任感のある sekíniñkan no aru; (job) 責
任の重い sekínin nò omóî

responsive [rispɑːn'siv] adj (child, gesture) 敏感な biñkan na; (to demand,
treatment) よく応じる yókù ōjìrù

rest [rest] n (relaxation) 休み yasúmi;
(pause) 休止 kyúshi; (remainder) 残り nokóri; (object: to support something) 台
dâî; (MUS) 休止符 kyúshifù

♦vi (relax) 休む yasúmù; (stop) 休止する
kyúshi suru: **to rest on** (idea) ...に基づく
...ni motózukù; (weight, object) ...に置か
れている ...ni okárete irù

♦vt (head, eyes, muscles) 休ませる yasú-
maserù; (lean): **to rest something on/
against** ...を...に置く〔寄り掛ける〕...wo
...ni okú (yoríkakerù)

the rest of them (people) 残りの人たち
nokóri nò hitótàchi; (objects) 残りの物
nokóri no monò

it rests with him to ... ...するのは彼の
責任だ ...surú no wà kárè no sekínin dà

restaurant [res'tɔːrənt] n レストラン résùtoran

restaurant car (BRIT) n 食堂車 shokúdòsha

restful [rest'fəl] adj 心を落着かせる ko-

kórð wo ochítsukaserù

rest home n 養老院 yốroîn

restitution [restitu:'∫ən] n: **to make
restitution to someone for something**
(compensate) ...に対して...の弁償をする
...ni táîshite ...no beñshō wo surù

restive [res'tiv] adj (person, crew) 反抗
的な hañkōteki na; (horse) 言う事を聞か
ない iú kotò wo kikánaî

restless [rest'lis] adj (person, audience)
落着かない ochítsukanaî

restoration [restərei'∫ən] n (of building
etc) 修復 shúfuku; (of law and order,
faith, health) 回復 kaífuku; (of something stolen) 返還 heñkan; (to power,
former state) 復旧 fukkyû

restore [ristɔːr'] vt (building) 修復する
shúfuku suru; (law and order, faith,
health) 回復する kaífuku suru; (something stolen) 返す káèsu; (to power, former state) 元に戻す mótò ni modósù

restrain [ristrein'] vt (feeling, growth,
inflation) 抑制する yokúsei suru; (person): **to restrain (from doing)** (...し
ない様に) 抑える (...shinái yô ni) osáerù

restrained [ristreind'] adj (style, person)
控え目な hikáeme na

restraint [ristreint'] n (restriction) 抑制
yokúsei; (moderation) 程々 hodóhodo;
(of style) 控え目な調子 hikáeme nà chôshi

restrict [ristrikt'] vt (limit: growth,
numbers etc) 制限する seígen suru;
(: vision) 邪魔をする jámà suru; (confine:
people, animals) ...の動きを制限する
...no ugókì wò seígen suru; (: activities,
membership) 制限する seígen suru

restriction [ristrik'∫ən] n (gen) 制限 seígen; (of vision) 妨げ samátagè; (limitation): **restriction (on)** (...の) 制限
(...no) seígen

restrictive [ristrik'tiv] adj (environment) 束縛的な sokúbakuteki na; (clothing) きつい kitsúî

restrictive practices npl (INDUS-
TRY) 制限的慣行 seígentekikañkō

rest room (US) n お手洗い o-téàrài

restructure [riːstrʌk't∫əːr] vt (business,

economy) 再編成する saíheñsei suru

result [rizʌlt'] n (of event, action) 結果 kekká; (of match) スコア sukóà; (of exam, competition) 成績 seíseki

♦vi: **to result in** ...に終る ...ni owárù

as a result of ...の結果 ...no kekká

resume [rizuːm'] vt (work, journey) 続ける tsuzúkerù

♦vi (start again) また始まる matá hàjimaru

résumé [rez'uːmei] n (summary) 要約 yóyaku; (US: curriculum vitae) 履歴書 rirékishò

resumption [rizʌmp'ʃən] n (of work, activity) 再開 saíkai

resurgence [risəːr'dʒəns] n 復活 fukkátsu

resurrection [rezərek'ʃən] n (of hopes, fears) よみがえらせる事 yomígaeraserù kotó; (REL): **the Resurrection** キリストの復活 kirísuto no fukkátsu

resuscitate [risʌs'əteit] vt (MED) そ生させる soséi saserù

resuscitation [risʌsətei'ʃən] n そ生 soséi

retail [riːteil] adj (trade, department, shop, goods) 小売の koúri no

♦adv 小売で koúri de

retailer [riː'teilər] n (trader) 小売業者 koúrigyòsha

retail price n 小売価格 koúrikakàku

retain [ritein'] vt (keep) 保つ tamótsù

retainer [ritei'nəːr] n (fee) 依頼料 iráiryò

retaliate [ritæl'iːeit] vi: **to retaliate (against)** (attack, ill-treatment) (...に対して) 報復する (...ni taíshite) hófuku suru

retaliation [ritæliːei'ʃən] n 報復 hófuku

retarded [ritɑːr'did] adj (child) 知恵遅れの chiéokùre no; (development, growth) 遅れた okúretà

retch [retʃ] vi むかつく mukátsukù

retentive [riten'tiv] adj (memory) 優れた sugúretà

reticent [ret'isənt] adj 無口な múkùchi na

retina [ret'ənə] n (ANAT) 網膜 mómaku

retire [ritaiər'] vi (give up work: gen) 引

退する iñtai suru; (: at a certain age) 定年退職する teínentaìshoku suru; (withdraw) 引下がる hikísagarù; (go to bed) 寝る nérù

retired [ritaiəːrd'] adj (person: gen) 引退した iñtai shita; (: at certain age) 定年退職した teínentaìshoku shita

retirement [ritaiəːr'mənt] n (giving up work: gen) 隠退 iñtai; (: at certain age) 定年退職 teínentaìshoku

retiring [ritaiəːr'iŋ] adj (leaving) 退職する taíshoku suru; (shy) 内気な uchíki na

retort [ritɔːrt'] vi しっぺ返しをする shippégaèshi wo suru

retrace [riːtreis'] vt: **to retrace one's steps** 来た道を戻る kitá michì wo modórù

retract [ritrækt'] vt (statement, offer) 撤回する tekkái suru; (claws, aerial etc) 引っ込める hikkómerù

retrain [riːtrein'] vt 再訓練する saíkuñren suru

retraining [riːtrei'niŋ] n 再訓練 saíkuñren

retread [riː'tred] n (tire) 再生タイヤ saíseitaìya

retreat [ritriːt'] n (place) 隠れ家 kakúregà; (withdrawal) 避難 hínàn; (MIL) 退却 taíkyaku

♦vi (from danger, enemy) 避難する hínàn suru; (MIL) 退却する taíkyaku suru

retribution [retrəbjuː'ʃən] n 天罰 teñbatsu

retrieval [ritriː'vəl] n (of object) 回収 kaíshū; (of situation) 繕う事 tsukúrou kotó; (of honor) ばん回 bañkai; (of error) 償い tsugúnaì; (loss) 取返し toríkaeshi

retrieve [ritriːv'] vt (object) 回収する kaíshū suru; (situation) 繕う tsukúroù; (honor) ばん回する bañkai suru; (error) 償う tsugúnaù; (loss) 取返す toríkaesù

retriever [ritriː'vəːr] n (dog) リトリーバ犬 ritóríbàken

retrograde [ret'rəgreid] adj 後戻りの atómodòri no

retrospect [ret'rəspekt] n: **in retrospect** 振返ってみると furíkaette miru tò

retrospective [retrəspek'tiv] adj (exhibition) 回顧的な kaíkoteki na; (feeling, opinion) 過去にさかのぼる kákò ni sakánoborù; (law, tax) そ及する sokyū́ suru

return [ritə:rn'] *n* (going or coming back) 帰り kaéri; (of something stolen, borrowed etc) 返還 heñkan; (FINANCE: from land, shares, investment) 利回り rimáwari

♦*cpd* (journey) 帰りの kaéri no; (BRIT: ticket) 往復の őfuku no; (match) 雪辱の setsújoku no

♦*vi* (person etc: come or go back) 帰る kaérù; (feelings, symptoms etc) 戻る modórù; (regain): **to return to** (consciousness) ...を回復する ...wo kaífuku suru; (power) ...に返り咲く ...ni kaérizakù

♦*vt* (favor, love etc) 返す kaésù; (something borrowed, stolen etc) 返却する heñkyaku suru; (LAW: verdict) ...と答申する ...to tőshin suru; (POL: candidate) 選出する señshutsu suru; (ball) 返す kaésù

in return (for) (...の) お返しに (...no) o-káèshi ni

by return of post 折返し郵便で oríkaeshiyùbin de

many happy returns (of the day)! お誕生日おめでとう o-táñjòbi omédetò

returns [ritə:rnz'] *npl* (COMM) 利益 ríèki

reunion [ri:ju:n'jən] *n* (of family) 集い tsudói; (of school, class etc) 同窓会 dősōkai; (of two people) 再会 saíkai

reunite [ri:ju:nait'] *vt* (bring or come together again) 元のさやに収めさせる mótò no sáyà ni osámesaserù; (reconcile) 和解させる wakái saserù

rev [rev] *n abbr* (AUT: = *revolution*) 回転 kaíten

♦*vt* (also: **rev up**: engine) ふかす fukásù

revamp [ri:væmp'] *vt* (organization, company, system) 改革する kaíkaku suru

reveal [rivi:l'] *vt* (make known) 明らかにする akíràka ni suru; (make visible) 現す aráwasù

revealing [rivi:'liŋ] *adj* (action, statement) 手の内を見せる té nò uchí wò misérù; (dress) 肌をあらわにする hádà

wo arawa ni suru

reveille [rev'əli:] *n* (MIL) 起床らっぱ kishő rappà

revel [rev'əl] *vi*: **to revel in something/ in doing something** (enjoy) ...を (...する のを) 楽しむ ...wo (...surú no wò) tanóshimù

revelation [revəlei'jən] *n* (fact, experience) 意外な新知識 igái nà shiñchishìki

revelry [rev'əlri:] *n* どんちゃん騒ぎ doñchan sawàgi

revenge [rivend3'] *n* (for injury, insult) 復しゅう fukúshū

to take revenge on (enemy) ...に復しゅうする ...ni fukúshū suru

revenue [rev'ənu:] *n* (income: of individual, company, government) 収入 shúnyū

reverberate [rivə:r'bə:reit] *vi* (sound, thunder etc: also *fig*) 響く hibíkù

reverberation [rivə:rbərei'jən] *n* (of sound, etc: also *fig*) 響き hibíki

revere [rivi:r'] *vt* 敬愛する keíai suru

reverence [rev'ə:rəns] *n* 敬愛 keíai

Reverend [rev'ə:rənd] *adj* (in titles) ...師 ...shī ◇聖職者の名前に付ける敬称 seíshokushà no namáè ni tsukérò keíshō

reversal [rivə:r'səl] *n* (of order) 反転 hañten; (of direction) 逆戻り gyakúmodòri; (of decision, policy) 逆転 gyakúten; (of roles) 入れ代り iríkawari

reverse [rivə:rs'] *n* (opposite) 反対 hañtai; (back) 裏 urá; (AUT: also: **reverse gear**) バック bákkù; (setback, defeat) 失敗 shippái

♦*adj* (opposite: order, direction, process) 反対の hañtai no, 逆の gyakú no; (: side) 裏の urá no

♦*vt* (order, position, direction) 逆にする gyakú ni surù; (process, policy, decision) 引っ繰り返す hikkúrikaèsu; (roles) 入れ替える iríkaerù; (car) バックさせる bákkù saserù

♦*vi* (BRIT: AUT) バックする bákkù suru

reverse-charge call [rivə:rs'tjɑːrd3-] (BRIT) *n* 受信人払い電話 jushíñninbarai deñwa

reversing lights [rivə:r'siŋ-] (BRIT)

npl (AUT) バックライト bakkúraìto

revert [rivəːrt'] *vi*: *to revert to* (former state) ...に 戻る ...ni modóru; (LAW: money, property) ...に帰属する ...ni kizóku suru

review [rivju:'] *n* (magazine) 評論雑誌 hyóronzasshì; (of book, film etc) 批評 hihyő; (examination: of situation, policy etc) 再検討 saíkeñtō

♦*vt* (MIL) 閲兵する eppéi suru; (book, film etc) ...の批評を書く ...no hihyő wò kákù; (situation, policy etc) 再検討する saíkeñtō suru

reviewer [rivju:'əːr] *n* (of book, film etc) 批評者 hihyőshà

revile [rivail'] *vt* (insult) 侮辱する bujóku suru

revise [rivaiz'] *vt* (manuscript) 修正する shūsei suru; (opinion, price, procedure) 変える kaérù

♦*vi* (BRIT: study) 試験勉強する shikénbeñkyō suru

revision [riviʒ'ən] *n* (amendment) 修正 shūsei; (for exam) 試験勉強 shikénbeñkyō

revitalize [ri:vai'təlaiz] *vt* ...に新しい活力を与える ...ni atárashiì katsúryòku wo atáerù

revival [rivai'vəl] *n* (recovery) 回復 kaífuku; (of interest, faith) 復活 fukkátsu; (THEATER) リバイバル ribáìbaru

revive [rivaiv'] *vt* (person) ...の意識を回復させる ...no íshìki wo kaífuku saserù; (economy, industry) 復興させる fukkő saserù; (custom, hope, courage) 復活させる fukkátsu saserù; (play) 再上演する saíjōèn suru

♦*vi* (person: from faint) 意識を取戻す í-shìki wo torímodosù; (: from ill-health) 元気になる géñki ni nárù; (activity, economy etc) 回復する kaífuku suru; (faith, interest etc) 復活する fukkátsu suru

revoke [rivouk'] *vt* 取消す toríkesù

revolt [rivoult'] *n* (rebellion) 反逆 hañgyaku

♦*vi* (rebel) 反逆する hañgyaku suru

revolting [rivoul'tiŋ] *adj* (disgusting) むかつかせる mukátsukaserù

revolution [revəlu:'ʃən] *n* (POL) 革命 kakúmei; (rotation: of wheel, earth etc: *also* AUT) 回転 kaíten

revolutionary [revəlu:'ʃəneːri:] *adj* (method, idea) 革命的な kakúmeiteki na; (leader, army) 革命の kakúmei no

♦*n* (POL: person) 革命家 kakúmeika

revolutionize [revəlu:'ʃənaiz] *vt* (industry, society etc) ...に大変革をもたらす ...ni daíhenkaku wò motárasù

revolve [riva:lv'] *vi* (turn: wheel, earth etc) 回転する kaíten suru; (life, discussion): *to revolve (a)round* ...を中心に展開する ...wo chūshin nì teñkai suru

revolver [riva:l'vəːr] *n* けん銃 keñjū、リボルバー ribórùbā ◇回転式の物を指す kaíteñshiki no monő wò sásù

revolving [riva:l'viŋ] *adj* (chair etc) 回転式の kaíteñshiki no

revolving door *n* 回転ドア kaíten doà

revue [rivju:'] *n* (THEATER) レビュー rébyù

revulsion [rivʌl'ʃən] *n* (disgust) 嫌悪 kéño

reward [riwɔ:rd'] *n* (for service, merit, work) 褒美 hőbi; (money for capture of criminal, information etc) 賞金 shőkin

♦*vt*: *to reward (for)* (effort) (...のために) 褒美を与える (... no tamé nì) hőbi wò atáerù

rewarding [riwɔ:rd'iŋ] *adj* (*fig*: worthwhile) やりがいのある yarígai no arù

rewind [ri:waind'] (*pt*, *pp* **rewound**) *vt* (tape, cassette) 巻戻す makímodosù

rewire [ri:waiəːr'] *vt* (house) ...の電気配線をし直す ...no deñki haìsen wo shínaosù

rewrite [ri:rait'] (*pt* **rewrote**, *pp* **rewritten**) *vt* 書き直す kakínaosù

rhapsody [ræp'sədi:] *n* (MUS) 狂詩曲 kyőshikyòku、ラプソディー rápùsodī

rhetorical [ritɔːr'ikəl] *adj* (question, speech) 修辞的な shűjiteki na

rheumatic [ru:mæt'ik] *adj* リューマチの ryúmachi no

rheumatism [ruːˈmətizəm] n リューマチ ryûmachi

Rhine [rain] n: **the Rhine** ライン川 raíñgawa

rhinoceros [rainɑːˈsɛˈəˈrəs] n サイ sáí

rhododendron [roudəden'drən] n シャクナゲ shakúnage

Rhone [roun] n: **the Rhone** ローヌ川 rő-nùgawa

rhubarb [ruːˈbɑːrb] n ルバーブ rubábù

rhyme [raim] n (of two words) 韻 iñ; (verse) 詩 shi; (technique) 韻を踏む事 iñ wò fumú kotò

rhythm [riðˈəm] n リズム rízùmu

rhythmic(al) [riðˈmik(əl)] adj リズミカ ルな rizúmìkàru na

rib [rib] n (ANAT) ろっ骨 rokkótsu
♦vt (tease) からかう karákaù

ribbon [rib'ən] n リボン ríbòn
in ribbons (torn) ずたずたになって zu-tázuta ni nattè

rice [rais] n (grain) 米 komé; (cooked) 御飯 gőhàn

rice pudding n ライスプディング raísu pudìngu◇御飯にミルク, 卵, 砂糖などを加えたデザート góhàn ni mírùku, ta-mágo, satő nadò wo kuwáetà dezátò

rich [ritʃ] adj (person, country) 金持の kanémochi no; (clothes, jewels) 高価な kőka na; (soil) 肥えた koétà, 肥よくな hi-yőku na; (food, diet) 濃厚な nőkò na; (color, voice, life) 豊かな yútàka na; (abundant): **rich in** (minerals, resources etc) ...に富んだ ...ni tőnda
♦npl: **the rich** 金持 kanémochi◇総称 sőshō

riches [ritʃ'iz] npl (wealth) 富 tőmì

richly [ritʃ'liː] adv (dressed, decorated) 豪華に gőka ni; (rewarded, deserved, earned) 十分に júbuñ ni

rickets [rik'its] n くる病 kurúbyō

rickety [rik'əti:] adj (shaky) がたがたの gatágata no

rickshaw [rik'ʃɔː] n 人力車 jiñrikìshà

ricochet [rikəʃei'] vi (bullet, stone) 跳ね飛ぶ hanétobù

rid [rid] (pt, pp **rid**) vt: **to rid someone of something** ...の...を取除く ...no ...wo torínozokù
to get rid of (something no longer required) 捨てる sutérù; (something unpleasant or annoying) ...を取除く ...wo torínozokù

ridden [rid'ən] pp of **ride**

riddle [rid'əl] n (conundrum) なぞなぞ nazónazo; (mystery) なぞ nazó
♦vt: **to be riddled with** ...だらけである ...dáràke de árù

ride [raid] n (in car, on bicycle, horse) 乗る事 norú kotò; (distance covered) 道のり michínori
♦vb (pt **rode**, pp **ridden**)
♦vi (as sport) 乗馬をする jőba wo suru; (go somewhere: on horse, bicycle, bus) 乗って行く notté ikù
♦vt (a horse, bicycle, motorcycle) ...に乗る ...ni norú; (distance) 行く ikú
to take someone for a ride (fig: deceive) ぺてんに掛ける petéñ nì kakérù
to ride a bicycle 自転車に乗る jitéñsha ni norú
to ride at anchor (NAUT) 停泊する teíhaku suru

rider [rai'dər] n (on horse) 乗り手 norí-te; (on bicycle, motorcycle) 乗る人 norú hitò, ライダー ráìdā

ridge [ridʒ] n (of hill) 尾根 őnè; (of roof) 天辺 teppéñ; (wrinkle) うね uné

ridicule [rid'əkjuːl] n あざけり azákerì
♦vt あざける azákerù

ridiculous [ridik'jələs] adj (foolish) ばかげた bakágetà

riding [rai'diŋ] n (sport, activity) 乗馬 jőba

riding school n 乗馬学校 jőbagakkő

rife [raif] adj: **to be rife** (bribery, corruption, superstition) はびこる habíkorù
to be rife with (rumors, fears) ...がはびこっている ...ga habíkotte irù

riffraff [rif'ræf] n (rabble) ろくでなしの連中 rokúdenashi nò reñchū

rifle [rai'fəl] n (gun) ライフル ráìfuru
♦vt (steal from: wallet, pocket etc) ...の中身を盗む ...no nakámi wò nusúmù

rifle range n (for sport) 射撃場 shagé-kijō; (at fair) 射的 shatéki

rifle through vt fus (papers) ...をかき
回して捜す ...wo kakímawashite sagásù

rift [rift] n (split: in ground) 亀裂 kirétsu;
(: in clouds) 切れ間 kiréma; (fig: disagreement) 仲たがい nakátagaì

rig [rig] n (also: **oil rig**) 油井掘削装置 yuséi kussaku sôchi

♦vt (election, game etc) 不正操作する fu-
séisôsa suru

rigging [rig'iŋ] n (NAUT) 索具 sakúgù

right [rait] adj (correct: answer, solution, size etc) 正しい tadáshiì; (suitable:
person, clothes, time) 適当な tekítō na;
(: decision etc) 適切な tekísetsu na; (morally good) 正しな seítō na; (fair, just) 公
正な kôsei na; (not left) 右の migí no

♦n (what is morally right) 正義 seígi;
(entitlement) 権利 keńri; (not left) 右 migí

♦adv (correctly: answer etc) 正しく ta-
dáshìku; (properly, fairly: treat etc) 公正
に kôsei ni; (not on the left) 右に migí ni;
(directly, exactly): **right now** 今すぐ í-
mà súgù

♦vt (put right way up: ship, car etc) 起す
okósù; (correct: fault, situation, wrong)
正す tadásù

♦excl では dé wà

to be right (person) ...の言う事が合って
いる ...no iú kotò ga atté irù; (answer) 正
解である seíkai de arù; (clock, reading
etc) 合っている atté irù

by rights 当然 tôzen

on the right 右に migí ni

to be in the right ...の方が正しい ...no
hô gà tadáshiì

right away すぐに súgù ni

right in the middle 丁度真ん中に chôdo maǹnaka ni

right angle n (MATH) 直角 chokkáku

righteous [rait'ʃəs] adj (person) 有徳な
yútoku na; (anger) 当然な tôzen na

rightful [rait'fəl] adj (heir, owner) 合法
の gôhō no; (place, share) 正当な seítō na

right-handed [rait'hændid] adj (person)
右利きの migíkikì no

right-hand man [rait'hænd'-] n 右腕
migíude

right-hand side n 右側 migígawa

rightly [rait'li:] adv (with reason) 当然
tôzen

right of way n (on path etc) 通行権 tsú-
kōken; (AUT) 先行権 seńkōken

right-wing [rait'wiŋ] adj (POL) 右翼の
úyòku no

rigid [ridʒ'id] adj (structure, back etc) 曲
らない magáranaì; (attitude, views etc)
厳格な geńkaku na; (principle, control
etc) 厳しい kibíshiì

rigmarole [rig'məroul] n (procedure) 手
続 tetsúzùki

rigor [rig'ə:r] (BRIT **rigour**) n (strict-
ness) 厳格さ geńkakusa; (severity):
rigors of life/winter 生活〔冬〕の厳し
さ seíkatsu[fuyú]nò kibíshisa

rigorous [rig'ə:rəs] adj (control, test) 厳
密な geńmitsu na; (training) 厳しい kibíshiì

rig out (BRIT) vt: **to rig out as** ...の仮
装をする ...no kasô wò suru

to rig out in ...を着る ...wo kírù

rig up vt 作り上げる tsukúriagerù

rile [rail] vt (annoy) ...を怒らせる ...wo o-
kóraserù

rim [rim] n (of glass, dish) 縁 fuchí; (of
spectacles) フレーム furému; (of wheel)
リム rímù

rind [raind] n (of bacon, fruit, cheese) 皮
kawá

ring [riŋ] n (of metal, light, smoke) 輪
wá; (for finger) 指輪 yubíwà; (of spies,
drug-dealers etc) 組織 sóshìki; (for boxing, of circus) リング ríǹgu; (bullring) 闘
牛場 tôgyújō; (sound of bell) ベルの音 bérù no otó

♦vb (pt **rang**, pp **rung**)

♦vi (person: by telephone) 電話を掛ける
deńwa wo kakérù; (telephone, bell, doorbell) 鳴る narú; (also: **ring out**: voice,
words) 鳴り響く naríhibikù

♦vt (BRIT: TEL) ...に電話を掛ける ...ni
deńwa wò kakérù; (bell etc) 鳴らす narásù

a ring of people 車座になった人々 ku-
rúmaza ni nattá hitóbìto

a ring of stones 環状に並んだ石 kańjō

ni naranda ishí
to give someone a ring (BRIT: TEL)
...に電話を掛ける ...ni denwa wò kakérù
my ears are ringing 耳鳴りがする mimínari ga surù

ring back (BRIT) vt (TEL) ...に電話を
掛け直す ...ni denwa wò kakénaosù
♦vi (TEL) 電話を掛け直す denwa wò kakénaosù

ringing [riŋ'iŋ] n (of telephone, bell) 鳴
る音 narú otò; (in ears) 耳鳴り mimínari

ringing tone n (TEL) ダイヤルトーン
daíyarutòn

ringleader [riŋ'li:dər] n (of gang) 主犯
shuhán

ringlets [riŋ'lits] npl (of hair) 巻毛 makíge

ring off (BRIT) vi (TEL) 電話を切る
denwa wò kírù

ring road (BRIT) n 環状線 kanjōsen

ring up (BRIT) vt (TEL) ...に電話を掛け
る ...ni denwa wò kakérù

rink [riŋk] n (also: **ice rink**) スケートリ
ンク sukétorìnku

rinse [rins] n (of dishes, hands) すすぎ
susúgi; (of hair) リンスする事 ríñsu suru
kotò; (dye: for hair) リンス ríñsu
♦vt (dishes, hands etc) すすぐ susúgù;
(hair etc) リンスする ríñsu suru; (also:
rinse out: clothes) すすぐ susúgù;
(: mouth) ゆすぐ yusúgù

riot [rai'ət] n (disturbance) 騒動 sōdō
♦vi (crowd, protestors etc) 暴動を起す
bōdō wò okósù
a riot of colors 色取り取り irótoridòri
to run riot (children, football fans etc)
大騒ぎをする ōsawàgi wo suru

riotous [rai'ətəs] adj (mob, assembly
etc) 暴動的な bōdōteki na; (behavior, living) 遊とうざんまい yūtōzañmai; (party)
どんちゃん騒ぎの dońchan sawàgi no

rip [rip] n (tear) 破れ目 yabúremè
♦vt (paper, cloth) 破る yabúrù
♦vi (paper, cloth) 破れる yabúrerù

ripcord [rip'kɔːrd] n (on parachute) 引き
網 hikízùna

ripe [raip] adj (fruit, grain, cheese) 熟し
た jukú shità

ripen [rai'pən] vt (subj: sun) 熟させる jukú saserù
♦vi (fruit, crop) 熟する jukú suru

ripple [rip'əl] n (of water) さざ波 sazánami;
(of laughter, applause) ざわめき zawá-
meki
♦vi (water) さざ波が立つ sazánami gà
tátsù

rise [raiz] n (slope) 上り坂 nobórizaka;
(hill) 丘 oká; (increase: in wages: BRIT)
賃上げ chíñ-age; (: in prices, temperature) 上昇 jōshō; (fig: to power etc) 出世
shussé
♦vi (pt **rose**, pp **risen**) (prices, numbers)
上がる agárù; (waters) 水かさが増す mi-
zúkasa gà masú; (sun, moon) 昇る nobórù; (person: from bed etc) 起きる okírù;
(sound, voice) 大きくなる ōkiku nárù;
(also: **rise up**: tower, building) そびえる
sobíerù; (: rebel) 立ち上がる tachíagarù;
(in rank) 昇進する shōshin suru
to give rise to ...を起す ...wo okósù
to rise to the occasion 腕前を見せる
udémaè wo misérù

risen [riz'ən] pp of **rise**

rising [rai'ziŋ] adj (increasing: number,
prices) 上がる agárù; 満ちる michí-
rù; (sun, moon) 昇る nobórù

risk [risk] n (danger) 危険 kikén;
(INSURANCE) リスク rísùku
♦vt (endanger) 危険にさらす kikén nì sarásù; (chance) ...の危険を冒す ...no kinén
wò okásù
to take/run the risk of doing ...する
危険を冒す ...súrù kikén wò okásù
at risk 危険にさらされて kikén nì sara-
sáretè
at one's own risk 自分の責任で jibún
nò sekínin de

risky [ris'ki:] adj (dangerous) 危険な kikén na

risqué [riskei'] adj (joke) わいせつがかっ
た waísetsugakattà

rissole [ris'ɑ:l] n (of meat, fish etc) メン
チカツ meńchikatsù

rite [rait] n 儀式 gíshìki
last rites (REL) 終油の秘蹟 shūyu nò
hiséki

ritual [rit'u:əl] *adj* (law, dance) 儀式的な
gishíkiteki na
♦*n* 儀式 gíshìki

rival [rai'vəl] *n* ライバル ráibaru
♦*adj* ライバルの ráibaru no
♦*vt* (match) ...に匹敵する ...ni hittéki suru

rivalry [rai'vəlri:] *n* (competition) 競争
kyósō

river [riv'ə:r] *n* 川 kawá
♦*cpd* (port, traffic) 川の kawá no
up/down river 川上〔下〕へ kawákami
〔shimo〕e

riverbank [riv'ə:rbæŋk] *n* 川岸 kawágishi

riverbed [riv'ə:rbed] *n* 河原 kawára

rivet [riv'it] *n* (bolt) リベット ribéttò
♦*vt* (*fig*): *to rivet one's eyes/attention on* ...に注目する ...ni chūmoku suru

Riviera [rivi:e:r'ə] *n*: *the (French) Riviera* リビエラ ribíèra
the Italian Riviera イタリアのリビエラ itária nò ribíèra

road [roud] *n* (*gen*) 道 michí, 道路 dòro
♦*cpd* (accident, sense) 交通の kôtsū no
major/minor road 優先〔非優先〕道路
yúsen〔hìyūsen〕dòro

roadblock [roud'bla:k] *n* 検問所 keñmonjo

roadhog [roud'hɔ:g] *n* マナーの悪いドライバー máñā no warúì doráibā

road map *n* 道路地図 dórochizù

road safety *n* 交通安全 kôtsūañzen

roadside [roud'said] *n* 道路脇 dórowaki

roadsign [roud'sain] *n* 道路標識 dórohyóshiki

road user *n* ドライバー doráibā

roadway [roud'wei] *n* 車道 shadó

roadworks [roud'wə:rks] *npl* 道路工事
dórokòji

roadworthy [roud'wə:rði:] *adj* (car) 整備状態のいい seíbijòtai no íi

roam [roum] *vi* (wander) さまよう samáyoù

roar [rɔ:r] *n* (of animal) ほえ声 hoégoè;
(of crowd) どよめき doyómeki; (of vehicle, storm) とどろき todóroki
♦*vi* (animal) ほえる hoérù; (person) どな

る donárù; (crowd) どよめく doyómekù;
(engine, wind etc) とどろく todórokù
a roar of laughter 大笑い ówarài
to roar with laughter 大笑いする ó-
warài suru
to do a roaring trade ...の商売が繁盛す
る ...no shóbai gà hañjō suru

roast [roust] *n* (of meat) ロースト rósuto
♦*vt* (meat, potatoes) オーブンで焼く ó-
bun de yakú; (coffee) いる írù

roast beef *n* ローストビーフ rósutobìfu

rob [ra:b] *vt* (person, house, bank) ...から
盗む ...kara nusúmù
to rob someone of something ...から
...を盗む ...kará ...wo nusúmù; (*fig*:
deprive) 奪う ubáù

robber [ra:b'ə:r] *n* 泥棒 doróbō

robbery [ra:b'ə:ri:] *n* (theft) 盗み nusúmi

robe [roub] *n* (for ceremony etc) ローブ
róbu; (*also*: **bath robe**) バスローブ basú-
robu; (*US*) ひざ掛け hizákake

robin [ra:b'in] *n* コマドリ komádòri

robot [rou'bət] *n* ロボット robóttò

robust [roubʌst'] *adj* (person) たくましい
takúmashiì; (economy) 健全な keñzen
na; (appetite) おう盛な ósei na

rock [ra:k] *n* (substance) 岩石 gañseki;
(boulder) 岩 iwá; (*US*: small stone, pebble) 小石 koíshi; (*BRIT*: sweet) 氷砂糖
kórizatò
♦*vt* (swing gently: cradle) 優しく揺する
yasáshiku yusurù; (: child) あやす ayásù;
(shake: subj: explosion, waves etc) 激し
く揺すぶる hagéshiku yusuburù
♦*vi* (object) 揺れる yurérù; (person) 震え
る furúerù
on the rocks (drink) オンザロックで oñ-
zarokkù de; (marriage etc) 危ぶまれて
ayábumaretè

rock and roll *n* ロックンロール rokkún-
rōru

rock-bottom [ra:k'ba:t'əm] *adj* (*fig*:
lowest point) 最低の saítei no

rockery [ra:k'ə:ri:] *n* (in garden) 庭石 ni-
wá-ishi ◇綜称 sóshō

rocket [ra:k'it] *n* (space rocket) ロケッ
ト rokéttò; (missile) ロケット弾 rokétto-
dañ; (firework) ロケット花火 rokétto ha-

nàbi

rocking chair [rɑːkʼiŋ-] *n* 揺りいす yurîisu

rocking horse *n* 揺り木馬 yurímokùba

rocky [rɑːkʼiː] *adj* (covered with rocks) 岩だらけの iwádaràke no; (unsteady: table) 不安定な fuáñtei na; (unstable: business, marriage) 危ぶまれている ayábumarete irù

rod [rɑːd] *n* (pole) さお saô; (*also*: **fishing rod**) 釣ざお tsurízao

rode [roud] *pt of* **ride**

rodent [rouʼdənt] *n* げっ歯類 gesshírùi

rodeo [rouʼdiːou] *n* ロデオ ródèo

roe [rou] *n* (species: *also*: **roe deer**) ノロジカ norójìka; (of fish) 卵 tamágò
   hard roe 腹子 haráko
   soft roe 白子 shirákò

rogue [roug] *n* 野郎 yarô

role [roul] *n* 役 yakú

roll [roul] *n* (of paper, cloth etc) 巻き makí; (of banknotes) 札束 satsútabà; (*also*: **bread roll**) ロールパン rôrupàn; (register, list) 名簿 meíbo; (sound: of drums etc) とどろき todóroki

♦*vt* (ball, stone etc) 転がす korógasù; (*also*: **roll up**: string) 巻く makú; (: sleeves) まくる makúrù; (cigarette) 巻く makú; (eyes) 白黒させる shírðkuro sasérù; (*also*: **roll out**: pastry) 延ばす nobásù; (flatten: lawn, road, surface) ならす narásù

♦*vi* (ball, stone etc) 転がる korógarù; (drum) 鳴り響く narîhibikù; (vehicle: *also*: **roll along**) 走る hashírù; (ship) 揺れる yurérù

roll about/around *vi* 転がる korógarù

roll by *vi* (time) 過ぎる sugírù

roll call *n* 点呼 teñko

roller [rouʼlər] *n* (*gen*) ローラー rôrā; (for hair) カーラー kârā

roller coaster [-kouʼstəːr] *n* ジェットコースター jettôkōsutà

roller skates *npl* ローラースケート rôrāsukèto

roll in *vi* (mail, cash) 大量に入る taíryð nì haírù

rolling [rouʼliŋ] *adj* (landscape) うねりの

多い unéri no ðì

rolling pin *n* めん棒 meñbō

rolling stock *n* (RAIL) 車両 sharyô ◇総称 sôshō

roll over *vi* 寝返りを打つ negáeri wò útsù

roll up *vi* (*inf*: arrive) やって来る yattê kurù

♦*vt* (carpet, newspaper, umbrella etc) 巻く makú

ROM [rɑːm] *n abbr* (*COMPUT*: = *read only memory*) ロム rômù

Roman [rouʼmən] *adj* ローマの rôma no

Roman Catholic *adj* ローマカトリックの rômakatorikkù no
♦*n* ローマカトリック信者 rômakatorikku shìnja

romance [roumæns'] *n* (love affair) 恋愛 reñ-ai; (charm) ロマンス rômànsu; (novel) 恋愛小説 reñ-ai shôsetsu

Romania [roumei'niːə] *n* = **Rumania**

Roman numeral *n* ローマ数字 rômasùji

romantic [roumæn'tik] *adj* ロマンチックな románchikkù na

Rome [roum] *n* ローマ rôma

romp [rɑːmp] *n* 騒々しい遊び sôzōshiî asôbi
♦*vi* (*also*: **romp about**: children, dogs etc) はしゃぎ回る hashágimawarù

rompers [rɑːmʼpəːrz] *npl* ロンパース roñpàsu

roof [ruːf] (*pl* **roofs**) *n* 屋根 yánè, ルーフ rûfu
♦*vt* (house, building etc) 屋根を付ける yánè wo tsukérù
   the roof of one's mouth 口がい kôgai

roofing [ruːʼfiŋ] *n* 屋根ふき材 yanéfukizài

roof rack *n* (AUT) ルーフラック rûfurakkù

rook [ruk] *n* (bird) ミヤマガラス miyámagaràsu; (CHESS) ルック rúkkù

room [ruːm] *n* (in house, hotel etc) 部屋 heyá; (space) 空間 kúkan, 場所 bashô; (scope: for improvement, change etc) 余地 yóchì
   「*rooms for rent*」, 「*rooms to let*」賃間

あり kashíma arí

single/double room シングル〔ダブル〕部屋 shínguru〔dabúru〕beyà

rooming house [ru:'miŋ] (*US*) *n* 下宿屋 geshúkuya

roommate [ru:m'meit] *n* ルームメート rúmumēto ◇寄宿舎などで同室に泊まる人 kishúkushà nádò de dóshitsu nì tomárù hitó

rooms [ru:mz] *npl* (lodging) 下宿 geshúku

room service *n* (in hotel) ルームサービス rúmusābisu

roomy [ru:'mi:] *adj* (building, car) 広々とした hiróbiro to shità; (garment) ゆったりした yuttári shità

roost [ru:st] *vi* (birds) ねぐらにつく negúra ni tsukú

rooster [ru:s'tə:r] *n* オンドリ ońdóri

root [ru:t] *n* (BOT) 根 né; (MATH) 根 kóñ; (of problem, belief) 根源 kóñgen
◆*vi* (plant) 根を下ろす né wò orósù; (belief) 定着する teíchaku suru

the root of a hair 毛根 mókon

the root of a tooth 歯根 shikón

root about *vi* (fig: search) かき回す kakímawasù

root for *vt fus* (support) ...を応援する ...wo óen surù

root out *vt* (find) 捜し出す sagáshidasù

roots [ru:ts] *npl* (family origins) ルーツ rútsu

rope [roup] *n* (thick string) ロープ rópu; (NAUT) 綱 tsuná; (for climbing) ザイル záiru
◆*vt* (tie) 縛る shibárù; (climbers: *also*: **rope together**) ザイルでつなぐ záiru de tsunágù; (an area: *also*: **rope off**) 縄で仕切る nawá dè shikírù

to know the ropes (fig: know how to do something) こつが分かっている kotsú gà wakátte irù

rope in *vt* (fig: person) 誘い込む sasóikomù

rope ladder *n* 縄ばしご nawábashigo

rosary [rou'zə:ri:] *n* ロザリオ rozárìo

rose [rouz] *pt of* **rise**
◆*n* (single flower) バラ bará; (shrub) バ

ラの木 bará nò kí; (on watering can) はす口 hasúkuchi

rosé [rouzei'] *n* ロゼワイン rozéwaìn

rosebud [rouz'bʌd] *n* バラのつぼみ bará nò tsubómi

rosebush [rouz'buʃ] *n* バラの木 bará no ki

rosemary [rouz'me:ri:] *n* ローズマリー rózumarī

rosette [rouzet'] *n* ロゼット rozéttò

roster [rɑːs'tə:r] *n*: *duty roster* 勤務当番表 kíñmutōbañhyō

rostrum [rɑːs'trəm] *n* 演壇 eńdan

rosy [rou'zi:] *adj* (color) バラ色の bará-iro no; (face, cheeks) 血色のいい kesshóku no iĩ; (situation) 明るい akáruĩ

a rosy future 明るい見通し akáruĩ mitŏshi

rot [rɑːt] *n* (decay) 腐敗 fuhái; (fig: pej: rubbish) でたらめ detárame
◆*vt* (cause to decay: teeth, wood, fruit etc) 腐らす kusárasù
◆*vi* (decay: teeth, wood, fruit etc) 腐る kusárù

rota [rou'tə] (*BRIT*) *n* 勤務当番表 kíñmutōbañhyō

rotary [rou'tə:ri:] *adj* 回転式の kaíteñshiki no

rotate [rou'teit] *vt* (revolve) 回転させる kaíten saserù; (change round: jobs) 交替でやる kŏtai de yarù
◆*vi* (revolve) 回転する kaíten suru

rotating [rou'teitiŋ] *adj* (movement) 回転する kaíten suru

rotation [routei'ʃən] *n* (revolving) 回転 kaíten; (changing round: jobs) 交替 kŏtai; (of crops) 輪作 rińsaku

rote [rout] *n*: *by rote* 暗記で ańki de

rotor [rou'tə:r] *n* (*also*: **rotor blade**) 回転翼 kaíteñyoku, ローター rŏta

rotten [rɑːt'ən] *adj* (decayed: fruit, meat, wood, eggs etc) 腐った kusáttà; (fig: person, situation) いやな iyá nà; (inf: bad) ひどい hidóĩ

a rotten tooth 虫歯 mushíba

to feel rotten (ill) 気分が悪い kíbùn ga warúĩ

rotund [routʌnd'] *adj* (person) 丸々と太

った marúmarù to futóttà

rouble [ru:'bəl] (*BRIT*) n = **ruble**

rouge [ru:ʒ] n ほお紅 hóbeni

rough [rʌf] adj (skin, surface, cloth) 粗い aráì; (terrain, road) 凸凹の dekóboko no; (voice) しゃがれた shagáretà; (person, manner: violent) 荒っぽい araȁpoꜝ; (: brusque) ぶっきらぼうな bukkírabò na; (treatment) 荒い aráì; (weather, sea) 荒れた arétà; (town, area) 治安の悪い chiánnò warúì; (plan, sketch) 大まかな ȍmaka na; (guess) 大よその ȍyoso no

♦n (GOLF): **in the rough** ラフに ráfù ni

to rough it 原始的な生活をする geńshiteki nà seíkatsu wò suru

to sleep rough (*BRIT*) 野宿する nójùku suru

roughage [rʌf'idʒ] n 繊維 séñ-i

rough-and-ready [rʌf'ənred'i:] adj 原始的な geńshiteki na

roughcast [rʌf'kæst] n (for wall) 小石を混ぜたしっくい koíshi wò mazétà shikkúì

rough copy n 下書き shitágaki

rough draft n 素案 soán

roughly [rʌf'li:] adv (handle) 荒っぽく a-ráppokù; (make) 大まかに ȍmaka ni; (speak) ぶっきらぼうに bukkírabò ni; (approximately) 大よそ ȍyoso

roughness [rʌf'nis] n (of surface) 荒さ arása; (of manner) がさつさ gasátsusa

roulette [ru:let'] n ルーレット rūretto

Roumania [ru:mei'ni:ə] n = **Rumania**

round [raund] adj 丸い marúì; (figures, sum) 概数の gaísū no

♦n (*BRIT*: of toast) 一切 hitókire; (of policeman, milkman, doctor) 巡回 juńkai; (game: of cards) 一勝負 ichíshòbu; (: in competition) ...回戦 ...kaísen; (of ammunition) 一発 ippátsu; (BOXING) ラウンド raúndo; (*also*: **round of golf**) ラウンド raúndo; (of talks) 一連 ichíren

♦vt (corner) 回る mawárù

♦prep (surrounding): **round his neck/the table** 首〔家〕の回りに kubí(ié)no mawári ni; (in a circular movement): **to move round the room** 部屋の中を一回りする heyá no nakà wo hitómawarì

suru: **to sail round the world** 世界一周の航海をする sékàisshū nò kōkai wò suru; (in various directions): **to move round a room/house** 部屋〔家〕の中を動き回る heyá〔ié〕no nakà wo ugókimawarù; (approximately): **round about 300** 大よそ300 ȍyoso sańbyaku

♦adv: **all round** 回りに mawári ni

a round of golf ゴルフのワンラウンド górùfu no wańraundo

the long way round 遠回り tōmawari

all the year round 一年中 ichínenjū

it's just round the corner (fig) 直ぐそこまで来ている súgù sokó madè kitè irù

round the clock 24時間 nijū-yo jíkan

to go round to someone's (house) ...のうちへ行く ...no uchí è ikú

to go round the back 裏に回る urá nì mawárù

to go round a house ある家を訪ねる árù ié wò tazúnerù

enough to go round みんなに足りる程 mínna nì tarírù hodô

a round of applause 拍手 hákùshu

a round of drinks/sandwiches みんなに一通りの飲み物〔サンドウィッチ〕をおごる事 mínna nì hitótòri nò nomímòno〔sańdouicchì〕wo ogórù kotó

roundabout [raund'əbaut] (*BRIT*) n (AUT) ロータリー rōtarî; (at fair) メリーゴーラウンド merígòraundo

♦adj (route) 遠回りの tȍmawàri no; (means) 遠回しの tȍmawàshi no

rounders [raun'dɔ:rz] npl (game) ラウンダーズ raúndazu ◊野球に似た英国のゲーム yakyū ni nità eíkoku no gȅmu

roundly [raund'li:] adv (fig: criticize) 厳しく kibíshisà

round off vt (speech etc) 終える oérù

round-shouldered [raund'ʃouldə:rd] adj ねこ背の nekózè no

round trip n 往復旅行 ōfukuryokȍ

round up vt (cattle, people) 駆集める karíatsumerù; (price, figure) 概数にする gaísū ni suru

roundup [raund'ʌp] n (of news, information) まとめ matóme; (of animals) 駆集め karíatsume; (of criminals) 一斉逮捕

isséitaīho

rouse [rauz] *vt* (wake up) 起す okósù; (stir up) 引起す hikíokosù

rousing [rau'ziŋ] *adj* (cheer, welcome) 熱狂的な nekkyōteki na

rout [raut] *n* (MIL) 敗走 haísō
♦*vt* (defeat) 敗走させる saserù

route [ru:t] *n* (way) ルート rúto; (of bus, train) 路線 rosén; (of shipping) 航路 kōro; (of procession) 通り道 tōrimíchi

route map (BRIT) *n* (for journey) 道路地図 dōrochizú

routine [ru:ti:n'] *adj* (work) 日常の nichíjō no; (procedure) お決りの o-kímari no
♦*n* (habits) 習慣 shūkan; (drudgery) 反復作業 hañpukusagyō; (THEATER) お決りの演技 o-kímari nò éñgi

rove [rouv] *vt* (area, streets) はいかいする haíkai suru

row[1] [rou] *n* (line of people, things) 列 rétsù; (KNITTING) 段 dáñ; (in boat) こぐ事 kogú kotò
♦*vi* (in boat) こぐ kogú
♦*vt* (boat) こぐ kogú
in a row (fig) 一列に ichíretsu ni

row[2] [rau] *n* (racket) 騒ぎ sáwàgi; (noisy quarrel) 口論 kóron; (dispute) 論争 roñsō; (BRIT inf: scolding): *to give someone a row* ...に大目玉を食らわす ...ni ōmedàma wo kuráwasù
♦*vi* (argue) 口論する kóron suru

rowboat [rou'bout] (US) *n* ボート bōto

rowdy [rau'di:] *adj* (person: noisy) 乱暴な rañbō na; (occasion) 騒々しい sōzōshiī

rowing [rou'iŋ] *n* (sport) ボートレース bōtorēsu

rowing boat (BRIT) *n* = **rowboat**

royal [rɔi'əl] *adj* 国王〔女王〕の kokúō〔jóō〕 no

Royal Air Force (BRIT) *n* 英国空軍 eíkokukūgun

royalty [rɔi'əlti:] *n* (royal persons) 王族 ōzoku; (payment to author) 印税 iñzei

rpm [a:rpi:em'] *abbr* (= *revolutions per minute*) 毎分回転数 maffunkaiteñsū

RSVP [a:resvi:pi:'] *abbr* (= *répondez s'il vous plaît*) 御返事を請う go-héñji wò kóù

Rt Hon. (BRIT) *abbr* (= *Right Honourable*) 閣下 kákkà

rub [rʌb] *vt* こする kosúrù
♦*n*: *to give something a rub* こする kosúrù
to rub one's hands (together) もみ手をする momíde wò suru
to rub someone the wrong way (US) or to rub someone up the wrong way (BRIT) 怒らせる okóraserù

rubber [rʌb'ə:r] *n* (substance) ゴム gómù; (BRIT: eraser) 消しゴム keshígomu

rubber band *n* 輪ゴム wagómu

rubber plant *n* ゴムの木 gómù no ki

rubbery [rʌb'ə:ri:] *adj* (material, substance) ゴムの様な gómù no yō na; (meat, food) 固い katáī

rubbish [rʌb'iʃ] *n* (waste material) ごみ gomí; (junk) 廃品 haíhin; (fig: pej: nonsense) ナンセンス náñsensu

rubbish bin (BRIT) *n* ごみ箱 gomíbako

rubbish dump *n* ごみ捨て場 gomísuteba

rubble [rʌb'əl] *n* (debris) がれき garéki; (CONSTR) バラス bárāsu

ruble [ru:'bəl] (BRIT **rouble**) *n* (currency) ルーブル rūburu

rub off *vi* (paint) こすり取る kosúritorù

rub off on *vt fus* ...に移る ...ni utsúrù

rub out *vt* (erase) 消す késù

ruby [ru:'bi:] *n* ルビー rúbī

rucksack [rʌk'sæk] *n* リュックサック ryukkúsakkù

rudder [rʌd'ə:r] *n* (of ship) かじ kají; (of plane) 方向かじ hōkōda

ruddy [rʌd'i:] *adj* (face, complexion) 血色の良い kesshóku no yoī; (BRIT: inf: damned) くそったれの kusóttarè no

rude [ru:d] *adj* (impolite: person, manners, word) 無礼な buréi na; (shocking: word, behavior) 下品な gehín na

rudeness [ru:d'nis] *n* (impoliteness) 無礼 buréi

rudimentary [ru:dəmen'tə:ri:] *adj* (equipment, knowledge) 原始的な geñshiteki na

rudiments [ru:'dəmənts] *npl* (basics) 基本 kihón

rueful [ru:'fəl] *adj* 悲しい kanáshiī

ruffian [rʌf'i:ən] n ごろつき gorótsuki

ruffle [rʌf'əl] vt (hair) 乱す midásù; (clothes) しわくちゃにする shiwákucha ni surù; (fig: person) 怒らせる okóraserù

rug [rʌg] n (on floor) じゅうたん jūtan; (BRIT: blanket) ひざ掛け hizákake

rugby [rʌg'bi:] n (also: **rugby football**) ラグビー rágùbī

rugged [rʌg'id] adj (landscape) 岩だらけの iwádaràke no; (features) ごつい gotsúì; (character) 無愛想な buáisō na

rugger [rʌg'əːr] (BRIT: inf) n ラグビー rágùbī

ruin [ruː'in] n (destruction: of building) 破壊 hakái; (: of hopes, plans) ざ折 zasétsu; (downfall) 失墜 shittsúi; (bankruptcy) 破産 hasán; (remains: of building) 廃墟 haíkyo
♦vt (destroy: building) 破壊する hakái suru; (: hopes, plans, health) 壊す kowásù; (: future) 台無しにする daínashi ni surù; (: person) 失墜させる shittsúi saserù; (: financially) 破産に追込む hasán ni oikomù

ruinous [ruː'inəs] adj (expense, interest) 破滅的な hamétsuteki na

ruins [ruː'inz] npl (of building, castle etc) 廃墟 haíkyo

rule [ruːl] n (norm, regulation) 規則 kisóku; (government) 君臨 kuñrin; (ruler) 物差し monósashi
♦vt (country, person) 支配する shíhai suru
♦vi (leader, monarch etc) 君臨する kuñrin suru; (LAW) 裁定する saítei suru
as a rule 普通は futsū wà

ruled [ruːld] adj (paper) けい紙 keíshi

rule out vt (idea, possibility etc) 除外する jogái suru

ruler [ruː'ləːr] n (sovereign) 元首 géñshu; (for measuring) 物差し monósashi

ruling [ruː'liŋ] adj 支配する shíhai suru
♦n (LAW) 決定 kettéi
ruling party 与党 yótò
ruling class 支配階級 shiháikaìkyū

rum [rʌm] n ラム酒 ramúshu

Rumania [ruːmei'niːə] n ルーマニア rúmania

Rumanian [ruːmei'niːən] adj ルーマニアの rúmania no; (LING) ルーマニア語の rúmaniagò no
♦n (person) ルーマニア人 rúmaniajìn; (LING) ルーマニア語 rúmaniagò

rumble [rʌm'bəl] n ごう音 gốon, とどろき todóroki
♦vi (make rumbling noise: heavy truck) ごう音を響かせて走る gốon wò hibíkasète hashírù; (: stomach) 鳴る narú; (: pipes) ゴボゴボいう góbogobo iù; (: thunder) とどろく todórokù

rummage [rʌm'idʒ] vi (search) 引っかき回して捜す hikkákimawashitè sagásù

rumor [ruː'məːr] (BRIT **rumour**) n うわさ uwása
♦vt: **it is rumored that ...** ...だとうわさされている ...dá tò uwása sarete irù

rump [rʌmp] n (of animal) しり shirí; (of group, political party) 残党 zañtō

rump steak n ランプステーキ rañpusutēki

rumpus [rʌm'pəs] n 騒ぎ sawági

run [rʌn] n (fast pace) 駆け足 kakéashi; (for exercise) ジョギング jogíñgu; (in car) ドライブ dóraìbu; (distance traveled) 行程 kōtei; (journey) 区間 kukán; (series) 継続 keízoku; (SKI) ゲレンデ gerénde; (CRICKET, BASEBALL) 得点 tokúten; (THEATER) 上演期間 jōenkikàn; (in tights, stockings) ほころび hokórobi
♦vb (pt **ran**, pp **run**)
♦vt (race, distance) 走る hashírù; (operate: business, hotel) 経営する keíei suru; (: competition, course) 行う okónaù; (: house) ...の切盛りをする ...no kirímori wò surù; (COMPUT) 走らせる hashírasserù; (pass: hand) 通す tōsu; (water) 出す dásù; (bath) ...に水をはる ...ni mizú wò hárù; (PRESS: feature) 載せる nosérù
♦vi (move quickly) 走る hashírù; (flee) 逃げる nigérù; (work: machine) 作動する sadō suru; (bus, train: operate) 動く ugókù; (: travel) 走る hashírù; (continue: play) 上演される jōen sarerù; (: contract) 継続する keízoku suru; (flow: river, liquid) 流れる nagárerù; (colors) 落ちる o-

chírù; (washing) 色落ちする iróochi suru; (in election) 立候補する rikkóho suru; (nose) 鼻水が出る hanámizu ga dérù

there was a run on ... (meat, tickets) 人々は...を買いに殺到した hitóbito wa ...wo kaí nì sattó shità

in the long run 行く行く（は）yukú-yuku (wà)

on the run 逃亡中で tóbochū de

I'll run you to the station 駅まで車で送ろう kurúma dè okúró

to run a risk 危険を冒す kikén wò okásù

run about/around *vi* (children) はしゃぎ回る hashágimawarù

run across *vt fus* (find) 偶然に見付ける gúzen nì mitsúkerù

run away *vi* (from home, situation) 逃げる nigérù

runaway [rʌn'əwei] *adj* (horse, truck) 暴走の bóso no; (person) 逃走中の tósochū no

run down *vt* (production, factory) ...の規模を縮小する ...no kíbò wo shukúshō suru; (AUT: person) ひく hikú; (criticize) けなす kenásù

to be run down (person: tired) へとへとになっている hetóheto nì natté irù

rung [rʌŋ] *pp of* **ring**

♦*n* (of ladder) 一段 ichídàn

run in (*BRIT*) *vt* (car) ...のならし運転をする ...no naráshiùnten wo suru

run into *vt fus* (meet: person, trouble) ...に出会う ...ni deáù; (collide with) ...にぶつかる ...ni butsúkarù

runner [rʌn'əːr] *n* (in race: person) 競走の選手 kyóso nò senshu, ランナー ráñnā; (: horse) 競走馬 kyósoba; (on sledge) 滑り木 subérigi, ランナー ráñnā; (for drawer etc) レール rēru

runner bean (*BRIT*) *n* サヤインゲン sayáingèn

runner-up [rʌnəːrʌp'] *n* 第2位入賞者 daí ni-i nyūshōsha

running [rʌn'iŋ] *n* (sport) ジョギング jogíngu; (of business, organization) 経営 keíei

♦*adj* (water) 水道の suídō no

to be in/out of the running for something ...の候補者である〔でなくなっている〕...no kóhosha de árù 〔de nakúnatte irù〕

6 days running 連続6日間 reñzoku muikakàn

running commentary *n* 生中継 namáchūkei

running costs *npl* (of car, machine etc) 維持費 ijíhi

runny [rʌn'i:] *adj* (honey, egg) 緩い yurúi; (nose) 垂れる tarérù; (eyes) 目やにの出る meyáni nò dérù

run off *vt* (water) ...から流れ落ちる ...kara nagáreochirù; (copies) 印刷する iñsatsu suru

♦*vi* (person, animal) 逃げる nigérù

run-of-the-mill [rʌnəvðəmil'] *adj* (ordinary) ごく普通の gókù futsú no

run out *vi* (person) 走って出る hashítte derù; (liquid) 流れ出る nagárederù; (lease, passport) 切れる kirérù; (money) なくなる nakúnarù

run out of *vt fus* (money, time, ideas) ...がなくなる ...ga nakúnarù

run over *vt* (AUT) ひく hikú

♦*vt fus* (revise) おさらいする o-sárai suru

runt [rʌnt] *n* (animal) 未熟児 mijúkujì; (*pej*) どちび dochíbi

run through *vt fus* (instructions) ...に目を通す ...ni mé wo tósu; (rehearse, practice: play) 一通り練習する hitótori reñshū suru

run up *vt* (debt) ...がかさむ ...ga kasámù

to run up against (difficulties) ...にぶつかる ...ni butsúkarù

run-up [rʌn'ʌp] *n* (*BRIT*): *run-up to* (election etc) ...への準備期間 ...é nò juñbikikàn

runway [rʌn'wei] *n* (AVIAT) 滑走路 kassóro

rupee [ru:'pi:] *n* (currency) ルピー rúpì

rupture [rʌp'tʃəːr] *n* (MED) ヘルニア herúnia

rural [ru:r'əl] *adj* (area) 田舎の ináka no; (economy) 地方の chihó no

ruse [ru:z] *n* 策略 sakúryaku

rush [rʌʃ] n (hurry) 大急ぎ ōisogi; (COMM: sudden demand) 急激な需要 kyūgeki na juyō; (of water, current) 奔流 honryū; (of feeling, emotion) 高まり takámari; (BOT) イグサ igúsa
♦vt (hurry) 急がせる isógaserù
♦vi (person) 急ぐ isógù; (air, water) 速く流れる háyaku nagárerù

rush hour n ラッシュアワー rasshúawà

rusk [rʌsk] n (biscuit) ラスク rásùku

Russia [rʌʃʻə] n ロシア róshìa

Russian [rʌʃʻən] adj ロシアの róshìa no; (LING) ロシア語の roshíagò no
♦n (person) ロシア人 roshíajìn; (LING) ロシア語 roshíagò

rust [rʌst] n さび sabí
♦vi (iron, machine etc) さびる sabírù

rustic [rʌs'tik] adj (style, furniture) 田舎風の inákafū no

rustle [rʌs'əl] vi (leaves) かさかさいう kásàkasa iú
♦vt (paper) かさかさ動かす kásàkasa ugókasù; (US: cattle) 盗む nusúmù

rustproof [rʌst'pru:f] adj (car, machine) さびない sabínaì

rusty [rʌs'ti:] adj (car) さびた sábìta; (fig: skill) …の勘が鈍くなった …no kań gà níbùku natta

rut [rʌt] n (groove) わだち wadáchi; (ZOOL: season) 発情期 hatsújòki
to be in a rut 型にはまっている katá nì hamátte irù

ruthless [ru:θ'lis] adj (person) 血も涙もない chí mò namída mò náì; (action) 残酷な zańkoku na

rye [rai] n (cereal) ライ麦 raímugì

rye bread n ライパン raípaǹ

S

Sabbath [sæb'əθ] n (Jewish) 土曜日 doyōbì; (Christian) 日曜日 nichíyòbi

sabbatical [səbæt'ikəl] n (also: **sabbatical year**) 一年休暇 ichínen kyúka ◊7年置きに大学教授に与えられる1年の長期有給休暇 nanánèn okí nì daígakukyòju nádò ni atáerarerù ichínen no chōkyū-

kyūkyūka

sabotage [sæb'əta:ʒ] n 破壊工作 hakái-kōsaku
♦vt (machine, building) 破壊する hakái suru; (plan, meeting) 妨害する bōgai suru

saccharin(e) [sæk'ə:rin] n サッカリン sakkárìn

sachet [sæʃei'] n (of shampoo, sugar, etc) 小袋 kobúkùro ◊一回分ずつのシャンプー、砂糖などを入れた小さな包 ikkáibun zutsu no sháňpu, satō nádò wo iréta chiísana tsutsúmi

sack [sæk] n (bag: for flour, coal, grain, etc) 袋 fukúro
♦vt (dismiss) 首にする kubí ni surù; (plunder) 略奪する ryakúdatsu suru
to get the sack 首になる kubí ni narù

sacking [sæk'iŋ] n (dismissal) 解雇 kái-ko; (material) ズック zúkkù

sacrament [sæk'rəmənt] n (ceremony: Protestant) 聖礼典 seíreitèn; (: Catholic) 秘跡 hiséki

sacred [sei'krid] adj (of religion: music, history, writings) 宗教の shūkyō no; (holy: animal, building, memory) 神聖な shińsei na

sacrifice [sæk'rəfais] n (offering of someone/something) 犠牲 giséi; (thing/person offered) いけにえ ikénie
♦vt (animal) 殺す korósu; (fig: human lives, health, career) 犠牲にする giséi ni surù

sacrilege [sæk'rəlidʒ] n 冒とく bōtoku

sacrosanct [sæk'rousæŋkt] adj (also fig) 神聖な shińsei na

sad [sæd] adj (unhappy: person, day, story, news) 悲しい kanáshii; (: look) 悲しそうな kanáshisō na; (deplorable: state of affairs) 嘆かわしい nagékawashī

saddle [sæd'əl] n (for horse) くら kurá; (of bicycle) サドル sadoru
♦vt (horse) …にくらを付ける …ni kurá wò tsukérù
to be saddled with (inf) …の重荷を負わされる …no omóni wò owásarerù

saddlebag [sæd'əlbæg] n (on bicycle) サ

ドルバッグ sadórubaggù

sadism [sei'dizəm] *n* サディズム sadízu-mu

sadistic [sədis'tik] *adj* サディスティック な sadísutikkù na

sadly [sæd'li:] *adv* (unhappily) 悲しそう に kanáshisō ni; (unfortunately) 残念なが ら zaňneňnagara; (seriously: mistaken, neglected) ひどく hídòku

 sadly lacking (in) 残念ながら (...が) ない zaňneňnagara (...ga) náî

sadness [sæd'nis] *n* 悲しみ kanáshimi

sae [eseii:'] *abbr* (= *stamped addressed envelope*) 返信用封筒 heňshin-yō fútō ◇ 宛先を書き、切手を張った物を指す até-saki wò kákî, kitté wò hattá mono wò sásù

safari [səfɑ:'ri:] *n* サファリ sáfàri

safe [seif] *adj* (out of danger) 安全な場所 にいる〔ある〕 aňzen na bashò ni irú 〔árù〕; (not dangerous, sure: place) 安全 な aňzen na; (unharmed: return, journey) 無事な bují na; (without risk: bet, subject, appointment) 安全な aňzen na, 安心 できる aňshin dekirù; (: seat in parliament) 落選する恐れのない rakúsen suru osore nò náî

 ◆*n* (for valuables, money) 金庫 kíñko

 safe from (attack) ...される心配のない 場所にいる〔ある〕...saréru shiňpai no náî bashò ni irú 〔árù〕

 safe and sound (return, sleep, etc) 無事 で bují de

 (just) to be on the safe side 念のため に neň no tame nì

safe-conduct [seif'kɑ:n'dʌkt] *n* (right to pass) 通行許可 tsúkōkyokà

safe-deposit [seif'dipɑ:zit] *n* (vault) 貸 金庫室 kashíkiňkoshitsu; (*also:* **safe deposit box**) 貸金庫 kashíkiňko

safeguard [seif'gɑ:rd] *n* 保護手段 hogó-shudàn

 ◆*vt* 保護する hógò suru

safekeeping [seifki:'piŋ] *n* 保管 hokáñ

safely [seif'li:] *adv* (without risk: assume, say) 安心して aňshin shite; (without mishap: drive) 安全に aňzen ni; (arrive) 無事に bují ni

safety [seif'ti:] *n* 安全 aňzen

safety belt *n* 安全ベルト aňzenberùto, シートベルト shítoberùto

safety pin *n* 安全ピン aňzeňpin

safety valve *n* 安全弁 aňzeňben

saffron [sæf'rən] *n* (powder) サフラン sáfùran

sag [sæg] *vi* (breasts, hem) 垂れ下がる tarésagarù; (roof) 凹む kubómu

saga [sæg'ə] *n* (long story, *also fig*) 長編 物語 chōheňmonogatàri

sage [seidʒ] *n* (herb) セージ sēji; (wise man) 賢人 keňjiň

Sagittarius [sædʒiteːr'iːəs] *n* (sign of Zodiac) 射手座 itéza

Sahara [səheːr'ə] *n*: **the Sahara (Desert)** サハラ砂漠 sahára sabàku

said [sed] *pt, pp of* **say**

sail [seil] *n* (on boat) 帆 hố; (trip): **to go for a sail** ヨットに乗る yőttò ni noru

 ◆*vt* (boat) 操縦する sőjū suru

 ◆*vi* (travel: ship) 航海する kốkai suru; (SPORT) ヨットに乗る yőttò ni norú; (begin voyage: ship) 出航する shukkố suru; (: passenger) 船で出発する fúnè de shuppátsu suru

 they sailed into Copenhagen 彼らはコ ペンハーゲンに入港した kárèra wa ko-péňhàgen ni nyúkō shitá

sailboat [seil'bout] (*US*) *n* ヨット yőttò

sailing [sei'liŋ] *n* (SPORT) ヨット遊び yottőasòbi

 to go sailing ヨットに乗る yőttò ni no-rú, ヨット遊びをする yottőasòbi wo suru

sailing boat *n* ヨット yőttò

sailing ship *n* 帆船 haňsen

sailor [sei'lə:r] *n* (seaman) 船乗り funá-nòri

sail through *vt fus* (*fig*: exams, interview etc) ...に楽々と合格する ...ni rakú-rakù to gốkaku suru

saint [seint] *n* (*also fig*) 聖人 séijin

saintly [seint'li:] *adj* (person, life, expression) 聖人の様な séijin no yố nà

sake [seik] *n*: **for the sake of some-one/something** ...のために ...no tamé nì

salad [sæl'əd] *n* サラダ sáràda

salad bowl *n* サラダボール sarádaboru

salad cream (*BRIT*) *n* マヨネーズ mayónēzu

salad dressing *n* サラダドレッシング sarádadoresshìngu

salami [səlɑːˈmiː] *n* サラミ sárāmi

salary [sælˈəːriː] *n* 給料 kyúryō

sale [seil] *n* (act of selling: commercial goods etc) 販売 hañbai; (: house, land etc) 売却 baíkyaku; (at reduced prices) 安売り yasúuri, セール sēru; (auction) 競売 kyóbai

「*for sale*」売物 urímono

on sale 発売中 hatsúbaichū

on sale or return (goods) 委託販売で itákuhañbai de

saleroom [seilˈruːm] *BRIT* *n* = **salesroom**

sales [seilz] *npl* (total amount sold) 売上 uríage

sales clerk (*BRIT* **sales assistant**) *n* 店員 teñ-in

salesman [seilzˈmən] (*pl* **salesmen**) *n* (in shop) 男子店員 dañshiteñ-in; (representative) セールスマン sērusumàn

salesroom [seilzˈruːm] (*US*) *n* 競売場 kyóbaijō

saleswoman [seilzˈwumən] (*pl* **saleswomen**) *n* 女子店員 joshíteñ-in

salient [seiˈliːənt] *adj* (features, points) 重要な júyō na

saliva [səlaivˈə] *n* だ液 daéki

sallow [sælˈou] *adj* (complexion) 血色の悪い kesshóku nò warúī

salmon [sæmˈən] *n inv* サケ sákè

salon [səlɑːnˈ] *n* (hairdressing salon, beauty salon) 美容院 biyóīn

saloon [səluːnˈ] *n* (*US*: bar) 酒場 sakába; (*BRIT*: AUT) セダン sédàn; (ship's lounge) 広間 hírōma

salt [sɔːlt] *n* 塩 shió

♦*vt* (preserve: fish, beef, etc) 塩漬にする shiózukè ni suru; (put salt on) ...に塩を掛ける ...ni shió wò kakérù

salt cellar *n* 塩入れ shió-ire

saltwater [sɔːltˈwɔːtəːr] *adj* (fish, plant) 海水の kaísui no

salty [sɔːlˈtiː] *adj* しょっぱい shoppáī

salutary [sælˈjətəːriː] *adj* (lesson,

reminder) ためになる tamé ni narù

salute [səluːtˈ] *n* (MIL) 敬礼 keírei; (with guns) 礼砲 reíhō; (*gen*: greeting) あいさつ aísatsu

♦*vt* (MIL) ...に敬礼する ...ni keírei suru; (*fig*) ...に敬意を現す ...ni kéīi wo aráwasù

salvage [sælˈvidʒ] *n* (action: *gen*) 救助作業 kyújo sagyò; (: of shipwreck) 海難救助作業 kaínan kyújo sagyò; (things saved) サルベージ sarúbēji, 救助された物 kyújo sareta monó

♦*vt* 救助する kyújò suru; (*fig*: situation etc) 収拾する shúshū suru

salvation [sælveiˈʃən] *n* (REL) 霊魂の救い reíkon no sukúi; (economic etc) 救済 kyúsai

Salvation Army *n* 救世軍 kyúseigùn

salvo [sælˈvou] *n* (in battle) 一斉射撃 isséishagèki; (ceremonial) 一斉祝砲 isséishukùhō

same [seim] *adj* 同じ onáji

♦*pron*: *the same* 同じ物 onáji monò

the same book as ...と同じ本 ...to onáji hoñ

at the same time (at the same moment) 同時に dójī ni; (yet) とはいえ tó wà ie

all/just the same それにしても soré ni shite mò

to do the same (as someone) (...と) 同じ事をする (...to) onáji koto wò suru

the same to you! お前もだ omáe mo dà ◇侮辱を返す時に言う bujóku wò kaésu toki nì iú

sample [sæmˈpəl] *n* (MED: blood/urine sample) 検体 keñtai, サンプル sáñpuru; (of work, merchandise) 見本 mihón, サンプル sáñpuru

♦*vt* (food) 試食する shishóku suru; (drink) 試飲する shíīn suru

sanatoria [sænətɔːrˈiːə] *npl of* **sanatorium**

sanatorium [sænətɔːrˈiːəm] (*pl* **sanatoria**) *n* = **sanitarium**

sanctify [sæŋkˈtəfai] *vt* 神聖にする shiñsei ni surù

sanctimonious [sæŋktəmouˈniːəs] *adj*

(person, remarks) 宗教心を装う shúkyō-shìn wo yosóoù

sanction [sæŋk'ʃən] n (approval) お墨付き osúmitsùki, 認可 nínka

♦vt (give approval to) 認可する nínka suru

sanctions [sæŋk'ʃənz] npl (severe measures) 制裁処置 seísaishochì

sanctity [sæŋk'titi:] n 神聖さ shínseisa

sanctuary [sæŋk'tʃue:ri:] n (also: **bird sanctuary**) 鳥類保護区 chōruihogokù, サンクチュアリ sañkuchùari; (place of refuge) 避難所 hínànjo; (REL: in church) 内陣 naíjin

sand [sænd] n (material, fine grains) 砂 suná; (beach: also: **sands**) 砂浜 sunáhama

♦vt (piece of furniture: also: **sand down**) 紙やすりで磨く kamíyasùri de migáku

sandal [sæn'dəl] n (shoe) サンダル sañdaru

sandbox [sænd'bɑːks] US n (for children) 砂場 sunába

sandcastle [sænd'kæsəl] n 砂の城 suná no shirò

sand dune n 砂丘 sakyū

sandpaper [sænd'peipəːr] n 紙やすり kamíyasùri, サンドペーパー sañdopēpā

sandpit [sænd'pit] (BRIT) n = **sandbox**

sandstone [sænd'stoun] n 砂岩 ságan

sandwich [sænd'witʃ] n サンドイッチ sañdoitchì

♦vt: **sandwiched between** ...の間に挟まれて ...no aída nì hasámarète

cheese/ham sandwich チーズ〔ハム〕サンドイッチ chízu〔hámù〕sañdoitchì

sandwich course (BRIT) n サンドイッチコース sañdoitchikòsu ◊勉強と現場実習を交互に行う課程 beñkyō tò geñbajisshū wo kōgō ni okónaù katéi

sandy [sæn'di:] adj (beach) 砂の suná no; (color) 砂色の suná-iro no

sane [sein] adj (person) 正気の shōki no; (sensible: action, system) 合理的な gōriteki na

sang [sæŋ] pt of **sing**

sanitarium [sæniteːr'iːəm] (US) n 療養所 ryōyōjo, サナトリウム sanátoriùmu

sanitary [sæn'iteːri:] adj (system, arrangements, inspector) 衛生の eísei no; (clean) 衛生的な eíseiteki na

sanitary napkin (BRIT **sanitary towel**) n 生理用ナプキン seíriyō napùkin

sanitation [sænitei'ʃən] n (in house) 衛生設備 eíseisetsùbi; (in town) 下水道設備 gesúidōsetsùbi

sanitation department (US) n 清掃局 seísōkyòku

sanity [sæn'iti:] n (quality of being sane: of person) 正気 shōki; (common sense: of suggestion etc) 合理性 gōrisei

sank [sæŋk] pt of **sink**

Santa Claus [sæn'tə klɔːz] n サンタクロース sañtakurōsu

sap [sæp] n (of plants) 樹液 juéki

♦vt (strength, confidence) 失わせていく ushínawasete ikù

sapling [sæp'liŋ] n 苗木 naégi

sapphire [sæf'aiəːr] n サファイア safáia

sarcasm [sɑːr'kæzəm] n 皮肉 hínìku

sarcastic [sɑːrkæs'tik] adj (person) いやみ好きな iyámizùki na; (remark, smile) 皮肉な hiníku na

sardine [sɑːrdiːn'] n イワシ iwáshi

Sardinia [sɑːrdin'i:ə] n サルディニア島 sarúdiniatò

sardonic [sɑːrdɑːn'ik] adj (smile) あざける様な azákeru yō na

sari [sɑː'riː] n サリー sárì

sash [sæʃ] n (Western) サッシュ sásshù; (Japanese) 帯 ōbì

sat [sæt] pt, pp of **sit**

Satan [sei'tən] n 大魔王 daímaò, サタン sátàn

satchel [sætʃ'əl] n (child's) かばん kabán

satellite [sæt'əlait] n (body in space) 衛星 eísei; (communications satellite) 通信衛星 tsūshin-eisei

satellite dish n パラボラアンテナ parábora añtena

satin [sæt'ən] n サテン sátèn

♦adj サテンの sátèn no

satire [sæt'aiəːr] n (form of humor) 風刺 fūshi; (novel) 風刺小説 fūshishōsetsu; (play) 風刺劇 fūshigekì

satirical [sətir'ikəl] adj (remarks, drawings etc) 風刺の fúshi no

satisfaction [sætisfæk'ʃən] n (pleasure) 満足 mánzoku; (refund, apology etc) 謝罪 shazái

satisfactory [sætisfæk'tə:ri:] adj (patient's condition) 良い yóî; (results, progress) 満足できる mánzoku dekíru

satisfy [sæt'isfai] vt (please) 満足させる mánzoku saserù; (meet: needs, demand) ...に応じる ...ni ójirù; (convince) 納得させる nattóku saserù

satisfying [sæt'isfaiɪŋ] adj (meal, job, feeling) 満足な mánzoku na

saturate [sætʃ'əreit] vt: **to saturate (with)** (also fig) (...で)一杯にする (...de) ippái ni surù

saturation [sætʃərei'ʃən] n (also fig) 飽和状態 hówajōtai

Saturday [sæt'ə:rdei] n 土曜日 doyóbì

sauce [sɔ:s] n (sweet, savory) ソース sósù

saucepan [sɔ:s'pæn] n ソースパン sósupaǹ

saucer [sɔ:'sə:r] n 受皿 ukézàra, ソーサー sósà

saucy [sɔ:'si:] adj (cheeky) ずうずうしい zúzūshiî

Saudi [sau'di:] n: **Saudi Arabia** n サウジアラビア saújiaràbia

Saudi (Arabian) adj サウジアラビアの saújiaràbia no

sauna [sɔ:'nə] n サウナ sáùna

saunter [sɔ:n'tə:r] vi のんびりと歩く noǹbiri to árùku

sausage [sɔ:'sidʒ] n ソーセージ sósèji

sausage roll n ソーセージパン sósèjipaǹ

sauté [sɔ:tei'] adj: **sauté potatoes** フライポテト furáipotèto

savage [sæv'idʒ] adj (cruel, fierce: dog) どうもうな dómō na; (: attack) 残忍な zaǹnin na; (primitive: tribe) 未開な mikái na

♦n 野蛮人 yabánjiǹ

savagery [sæv'idʒri:] n 残忍さ zannínsa

save [seiv] vt (rescue: someone, someone's life, marriage) 救う sukúu; (economize on: money, time) 節約する setsúyaku suru; (put by: receipts etc) 取って置く tóttè oku; (: money) 蓄える takúwaeru;

(COMPUT) 格納する kakúnō suru, セーブする sèbu suru; (avoid: work, trouble) 省く habúkù; (keep: seat) 確保する kákùho suru; (SPORT: shot, ball) セーブする sèbu suru

♦vi (also: **save up**) 貯金する chokín suru

♦n (SPORT) セーブ sèbu

♦prep (except) (...を)除いて (...wo) nozóite

saving [sei'viŋ] n (on price etc) 節約 setsúyaku

♦adj: **the saving grace of something** ...の唯一の長所 ...no yúîtsu no chósho

savings [sei'viŋz] npl (money) 貯金 chokín

savings account n 普通預金口座 futsúyokinkòza

savings bank n 普通銀行 futsúginkò

savior [seiv'jə:r] (BRIT **saviour**) n (gen) 救い主 sukúinùshi; (REL) 救世主 kyúseishu

savor [sei'və:r] (BRIT **savour**) vt (food, drink, experience) 味わう ajíwaù

savory [sei'və:ri:] (BRIT **savoury**) adj (dish: not sweet: spicy) ぴりっとした piríttò shita; (: salt-flavored) 塩味の shióaji no

saw [sɔ:] n (tool) のこぎり nokógirì

♦vt (pt **sawed**, pp **sawed** or **sawn**) のこぎりで切る nokógirì de kírù

♦pt of **see**

sawdust [sɔ:'dʌst] n のこくず nokókuzù

sawed-off [sɔ:d'ɔ:f] n (US): **sawed-off shotgun** 短身散弾銃 tañshin sandanjù ◇のこぎりで銃身を短く切った散弾銃 nokógirì de júshin wò mijíkaku kittà sandanjù

sawmill [sɔ:'mil] n 製材所 seízaisho

sawn-off [sɔ:n'ɔ:f] adj (BRIT) = **sawed-off**

saxophone [sæk'səfoun] n サキソホーン sakísohòn

say [sei] n: **to have one's say** 意見を言う íkèn wo iú

♦vt (pt, pp **said**) 言う iú

to have a/some say in something ...について ある程度の発言権がある ...ni tsúite áru teidò no hatsúgeǹken ga árù

to say yes/no 承知する〔しない〕shōchi suru〔shinaì〕

could you say that again? もう一度言ってくれませんか mō ichidò itté kuremaseñ ka

that is to say つまり tsúmari

that goes without saying それは言うまでもない soré wà iú made mo naì

saying [sei'iŋ] n (proverb) ことわざ kotówaza; (words of wisdom) 格言 kakúgen; (often repeated phrase) 愛用の言葉 aíyō no kotoba

scab [skæb] n (on wound) かさぶた kasábuta; (pej: strike-breaker) スト破り sutó-yabùri

scaffold [skæf'əld] n (for execution) 死刑台 shikéidai; (for building etc) = **scaffolding**

scaffolding [skæf'əldiŋ] n 足場 ashíba

scald [skɔ:ld] n やけど yakédo ◇熱湯や蒸気などによるやけどを指す nettó yà jókì nado ni yórù yakédo wò sásù
   ◆vt (burn: skin) やけどさせる yakédo saserù

scale [skeil] n (gen: set of numbers) 目盛 memóri; (of salaries, fees etc) 表 hyő; (of fish) うろこ uróko; (MUS) 音階 ofíkai; (of map, model) 縮小率 shukúshōrìtsu; (size, extent) 規模 kíbò
   ◆vt (mountain, tree) 登る nobórù

on a large scale 大規模で daíkibò de

scale of charges 料金表 ryőkinhyò

scale down vt 縮小する shukúshō suru

scales [skeilz] npl (for weighing) 量り hakári

scallop [skɑ:l'əp] n (ZOOL) ホタテガイ hotátegài; (SEWING) スカラップ sukárappù

scalp [skælp] n 頭の皮膚 atáma no hifù, 頭皮 tōhi
   ◆vt ...の頭皮をはぐ ...no tōhì wo hágù

scalpel [skæl'pəl] n メス mésù

scamper [skæm'pəːr] vi: **to scamper away/off** (child, animal) ぱたぱた走って行く pátàpata hashítte ikù

scampi [skæm'pi:] npl エビフライ ebífurài

scan [skæn] vt (examine: horizon) 見渡す

miwátasu; (glance at quickly: newspaper) ...にさっと目を通す ...ni sáttò mé wò tósù; (TV, RADAR) 走査する sősa suru
   ◆n (MED) スキャン sukyán

scandal [skæn'dəl] n (shocking event) 醜聞 shűbun, スキャンダル sukyáñdaru; (defamatory: reports, rumors) 陰口 kagégùchi; (gossip) うわさ uwása; (fig: disgrace) 恥ずべき事 hazúbeki kotò

scandalize [skæn'dəlaiz] vt 憤慨させる fuñgai saserù

scandalous [skæn'dələs] adj (disgraceful, shocking: behavior etc) 破廉恥な haréñchi na

Scandinavian [skændənei'vi:ən] adj スカンディナビアの sukándinabìa no

scant [skænt] adj (attention) 不十分な fujúbùn na

scanty [skæn'ti:] adj (meal) ささやかな sasáyàka na; (underwear) 極めて小さい kiwámète chíisaì

scapegoat [skeip'gout] n 身代り migáwari

scar [skɑːr] n (on skin: also fig) 傷跡 kizúato
   ◆vt (also fig) 傷跡を残す kizúato wò nokósù

scarce [skeːrs] adj (rare, not plentiful) 少ない sukúnaì
   to make oneself scarce (inf) 消えうせる kiéuserù

scarcely [skeːrs'li:] adv (hardly) ほとんど...ない hotóñdo ...naì; (with numbers: barely) わずかに wázùka ni

scarcity [skeːr'siti:] n (shortage) 不足 fusóku

scare [skeːr] n (fright) 恐怖 kyőfu; (public fear) 恐慌 kyőkō
   ◆vt (frighten) 怖がらす kowágarasù
   bomb scare 爆弾騒ぎ bakúdan sawàgi
   to scare someone stiff ...に怖い思いをさせる ...ni kowái omoì wo saserù

scarecrow [skeːr'krou] n かかし kakáshi

scared [skeːrd] adj: **to be scared** 怖がる kowágarù

scare off/away vt おどかして追払う odōkashite oiharaù

scarf [skɑ:rf] (*pl* **scarfs** *or* **scarves**) *n* (long) マフラー máfūrā; (square) スカーフ sukáfù

scarlet [skɑ:r'lit] *adj* (color) ひ色 hiíro

scarlet fever *n* しょう紅熱 shōkōnetsu

scarves [skɑ:rvz] *npl of* **scarf**

scary [sker'i:] (*inf*) *adj* 怖い kowáî

scathing [skei'ðiŋ] *adj* (comments, attack) 辛らつな shiñratsu na

scatter [skæt'ə:r] *vt* (spread: seeds, papers) まき散らす makíchirasù; (put to flight: flock of birds, crowd of people) 追散らす oíchirasù
♦*vi* (crowd) 散る chirú

scatterbrained [skæt'ə:rbreind] (*inf*) *adj* (forgetful) おつむの弱い o-tsúmù no yowáî

scavenger [skæv'indʒə:r] *n* (person) くず拾い kuzúhiròi

scenario [sine:r'i:ou] *n* (THEATER, CINEMA) 脚本 kyakúhon, シナリオ shinário; (*fig*) 筋書 sujígaki

scene [si:n] *n* (THEATER, *fig*) 場 ba, シーン shîn; (of crime, accident) 現場 geñba; (sight, view) 景色 késhìki; (fuss) 騒ぎ sáwàgi

scenery [si:'nə:ri:] *n* (THEATER) 大道具 ṓdṑgu; (landscape) 景色 késhìki

scenic [si:'nik] *adj* (picturesque) 景色の美しい késhìki no utsúkushiî

scent [sent] *n* (pleasant smell) 香り kaóri; (track) 通った後のにおい tōtta átò no nióî; (*fig*) 手がかり tegákàri; (liquid perfume) 香水 kōsui

scepter [sep'tə:r] (*BRIT* **sceptre**) *n* しゃく shaku

sceptic [skep'tik] (*BRIT*) *n* = **skeptic** *etc*

schedule [skedʒ'u:l] *n* (of trains, buses) 時間割 jikánwari; (list of events and times) 時刻表 jikókuhyō; (list of prices, details etc) 表 hyố
♦*vt* (timetable, visit) 予定する yotéi suru
on schedule (trains, buses) 定刻通りに teíkokudòri ni; (project etc) 予定通りに yotéidòri ni
to be ahead of schedule 予定時間より

早い yotéijikàn yórì hayáî
to be behind schedule 予定時間に遅れる yotéijikàn ni okúrerù

scheduled flight [skedʒ'u:ld-] *n* 定期便 teíkibin

schematic [ski:mæt'ik] *adj* (diagram etc) 模式的な moshíkiteki na

scheme [ski:m] *n* (personal plan, idea) もくろみ mokúromi; (dishonest plan, plot) 陰謀 iñbō; (formal plan: pension plan etc) 計画 keíkaku, 案 áñ; (arrangement) 配置 haíchi
♦*vi* (intrigue) たくらむ takúramù

scheming [ski:'miŋ] *adj* 腹黒い haráguroì
♦*n* たくらみ事 takúramì kotó

schism [skiz'əm] *n* 分裂 buñretsu

schizophrenic [skitsəfren'ik] *adj* 精神分裂症の seíshinbunretsushō no

scholar [skɑ:l'ə:r] *n* (pupil) 学習者 gakúshùsha; (learned person) 学者 gakúsha

scholarly [skɑ:l'ə:rli:] *adj* (text, approach) 学問的な gakúmonteki na; (person) 博学的な hakúgakuteki na

scholarship [skɑ:l'ə:rʃip] *n* (academic knowledge) 学問 gakúmòn; (grant) 奨学金 shōgakukìn

school [sku:l] *n* (place where children learn: *gen*) 学校 gakkṓ; (*also:* **elementary school**) 小学校 shōgakkō; (*also:* **secondary school**: lower) 中学校 chúgakkō; (: higher) 高(等学)校 kṓ(tōgak)kō; (*US:* university) 大学 daígaku
♦*cpd* 学校の gakkō no

school age *n* 学齢 gakúrei

schoolbook [sku:l'buk] *n* 教科書 kyōkashò

schoolboy [sku:l'bɔi] *n* 男子生徒 dañshiseìto

schoolchildren [sku:l'tʃildrən] *npl* 生徒 seíto

schooldays [sku:l'deiz] *npl* 学校時代 gakkōjidài

schoolgirl [sku:l'gə:rl] *n* 女子生徒 joshíseìto

schooling [sku:'liŋ] *n* (education at school) 学校教育 gakkōkyòiku

schoolmaster [sku:l'mæstə:r] *n* 教師

kyōshi, 教員 kyōin, 先生 seńsei ◇男子教
員 dańshikyōin

schoolmistress [sku:l'mistris] *n* 教師
kyōshi, 教員 kyōin, 先生 seńsei ◇女子教
員 joshíkyōin

schoolteacher [sku:l'ti:tʃər] *n* 教師 kyōshi, 教員 kyōin, 先生 seńsei ◇男女を問わ
ず使う dáñjo wo tówazu tsukáù

schooner [sku:'nər] *n* (ship) 帆船 hańsen

sciatica [saiæt'ikə] *n* 座骨神経痛 zakó-
tsushinkeìtsū

science [sai'əns] *n* (study of natural
things) 科学 kágaku; (branch of such
knowledge) ...学 ...gàku

science fiction *n* 空想科学物語 kūsōka-
gakumonogatàri, SF esuefu

scientific [saiəntif'ik] *adj* (research,
instruments) 科学の kágaku no

scientist [sai'əntist] *n* 科学者 kagáku-
shà

scintillating [sin'təleitiŋ] *adj* (fig: conversation, wit, smile) 輝く様な kagáya-
kù yō na

scissors [siz'ə:rz] *npl* (also: **a pair of
scissors**) はさみ hasámi

scoff [skɑ:f] *vt* (BRIT: inf: eat) がつがつ
食う gátsùgatsu kúù
◆*vi*: **to scoff (at)** (mock) ...をあざける
...wo azákerù

scold [skould] *vt* しかる shikárù

scone [skoun] *n* スコーン sukóñ ◇小さな
ホットケーキの一種 chíisa na hottókèki
no ísshù

scoop [sku:p] *n* (measuring scoop: for
flour etc) スコップ sukóppù; (for ice
cream) サーバー sábà; (PRESS) スクー
プ sukúpù

scoop out *vt* すくい出す sukúidasù

scoop up *vt* すくい上げる sukúiagerù

scooter [sku:'tə:r] *n* (also: **motor
scooter**) スクーター sukútà; (toy) スクー
ター sukútà ◇片足を乗せて走る遊び道具
katáashi wo nosete hashírù asóbidògu

scope [skoup] *n* (opportunity) 機会 kikáì;
(range: of plan, undertaking) 範囲 háñ-i;
(: of person) 能力 nōryoku

scorch [skɔ:rtʃ] *vt* (clothes) 焦がす kogásù; (earth, grass) 枯らす karásù

score [skɔ:r] *n* (total number of points
etc) 得点 tokúteñ, スコア sukóà; (MUS)
楽譜 gakúfu; (twenty) 20 níjù
◆*vt* (goal, point, mark) 取る tórù;
(achieve: success) 収める osámerù
◆*vi* (in game) 得点する tokúten suru;
(FOOTBALL etc) トライする toráì suru;
(keep score) 得点を記録する tokúteñ wo
kirókù suru

scores of (very many) 多数の tasū no

on that score その点に関して sonó teñ
ni kańshitè

to score 6 out of 10 10回中6回成功す
る jukkáichū rokkaì seíkō suru

scoreboard [skɔ:r'bɔ:rd] *n* スコアボード
sukóabòdo

score out *vt* 線を引いて消す séñ wo hif-
te kesù

scorn [skɔ:rn] *n* 軽べつ keíbetsu
◆*vt* 軽べつする keíbetsu suru

scornful [skɔ:rn'fəl] *adj* (laugh, disregard) 軽べつ的な keíbetsuteki na

Scorpio [skɔ:r'pi:ou] *n* (sign of Zodiac)
さそり座 sasórizà

scorpion [skɔ:r'pi:ən] *n* サソリ sasóri

Scot [skɑ:t] *n* スコットランド人 sukótto-
randojìn

Scotch [skɑ:tʃ] *n* (whisky) スコッチ su-
kótchì

scotch [skɑ:tʃ] *vt* (end: rumor) 消し止め
る keshítomerù; (plan, idea) 没にする bó-
tsu ni suru

scot-free [skɑ:t'fri:'] *adv*: **to get off
scot-free** (unpunished) 何の罰も受けな
い náñ no bátsù mo ukénaì

Scotland [skɑ:t'lənd] *n* スコットランド
sukóttoràndo

Scots [skɑ:ts] *adj* (accent, people) スコッ
トランドの sukóttoràndo no

Scotsman [skɑ:ts'mən] (*pl* **Scotsmen**) *n*
スコットランドの男性 sukóttoràndo no
dansei

Scotswoman [skɑ:ts'wumən] (*pl* **Scots-
women**) *n* スコットランドの女性 sukóttoràndo no joséi

Scottish [skɑ:t'iʃ] *adj* (history, clans,
people) スコットランドの sukóttoràndo
no

scoundrel [skaun'drəl] n 悪党 akútō

scour [skaur] vt (search: countryside etc) くまなく捜し回る kumánaku sagáshimawarù

scourge [skə:rdʒ] n (cause of trouble: also fig) 悩みの種 nayámi no tanè

scout [skaut] n (MIL) 斥候 sekkő; (also: **boy scout**) ボーイスカウト bőisukaùto
girl scout (US) ガールスカウト gárusukaùto

scout around vi 捜し回る sagáshimawarù

scowl [skaul] vi 顔をしかめる káò wo shikámerù
to scowl at someone しかめっつらをして ...をにらむ shikámettsura wò shité ...wo nirámù

scrabble [skræb'əl] vi (claw): **to scrabble (at)** (...を)引っかく (...wo) hikkákù; (also: **scrabble around**: search) 手探りで探す teságuri de sagásù
♦n: **Scrabble** ⑧ スクラッブル sukúrabbùru◇単語作りゲーム tañgozukurigèmu

scraggy [skræg'i:] adj (animal, body, neck etc) やせこけた yasékoketà

scram [skræm] (inf) vi (get away fast) うせる usérù

scramble [skræm'bəl] n (difficult climb) よじ上り yojínobori; (struggle, rush) 奪い合い ubáiai
♦vi: **to scramble out/through** 慌てて出る〔通る〕awátete derù 〔tőru〕
to scramble for ...の奪い合いをする ...no ubáiai wo surù

scrambled eggs [skræm'bəld-] npl いり卵 iritamago, スクランブルエッグ sukúranburu eggù

scrap [skræp] n (bit: of paper, material etc) 切れ端 kiréhashi; (: of information) 少し sukóshì; (fig: of truth) 欠けら kakéra; (fight) けんか keñka; (also: **scrap iron**) くず鉄 kuzútetsu
♦vt (discard: machines etc) くず鉄にする kuzútetsu ni surù; (fig: plans etc) 捨てる sutérù
♦vi (fight) けんかする keñka suru

scrapbook [skræp'buk] n スクラップブック sukúrappubukkù

scrap dealer n くず鉄屋 kuzútetsuyà

scrape [skreip] n (fig: difficult situation) 窮地 kyűchi
♦vt (scrape off: potato skin etc) むく mukú; (scrape against: hand, car) こする kosúrù
♦vi: **to scrape through** (exam etc) ...をどうにか切抜ける ...wo dő ni ka kirínukerù

scrape together vt (money) かき集める kakíatsumerù

scrap heap n (fig): **on the scrap heap** 捨てられて sutérarete

scrap merchant n (BRIT) = **scrap dealer**

scrap paper n 古い紙 furúî kamí, 古紙 kőshì, ほご hőgò

scrappy [skræp'i:] adj (piece of work) 雑な zatsú na

scraps [skræps] npl (leftovers: food, material etc) くず kúzù

scratch [skrætʃ] n (cut: on body, furniture: also from claw) かき傷 kakíkizu
♦cpd: **scratch team** 寄集めチーム yosé-atsumechīmu
♦vt (rub: one's nose etc) かく kákù; (damage: paint, car) 傷付ける kizútsukerù; (with claw, nail) ひっかく hikkákù
♦vi (rub one's body) ...をかく ...wo kákù
to start from scratch 何もない所から始める naní mo naî tokóro karà hajímerù
to be up to scratch いい線をいってる íì sen wo itté irù

scrawl [skrɔ:l] n なぐり書き nagúrigaki
♦vi なぐり書きする nagúrigaki suru

scrawny [skrɔ:'ni:] adj (person, neck) やせこけた yasékoketà

scream [skri:m] n 悲鳴 himéi
♦vi 悲鳴を上げる himéi wo agerù

scree [skri:] n 岩くず iwákuzu◇崩れ落ちてたい積した岩くずを指す kuzúreochitè taíseki shità iwákuzu wo sasù

screech [skri:tʃ] vi (person) 金切り声を出す kanákirigoè wo dásù; (bird) きーきー声で鳴く kíkigoè de náku; (tires, brakes) きーきーと鳴る kíkī to nárù

screen [skri:n] n (CINEMA) スクリーン

sukúrìn; (TV, COMPUT) ブラウン管bu-ráunkan; (movable barrier) ついたてtsuítate; (fig: cover) 幕makú

♦vt (protect, conceal) 覆い隠すóikakusù; (from the wind etc) ...の...よけになる...no...yoké ni narù; (film) 映写するeísha suru; (television program) 放映するhõei suru; (candidates etc) 審査するshíñsa suru

screening [skri:'niŋ] n (MED) 健康診断keñkōshìndan

screenplay [skri:n'plei] n 映画脚本eígakyakùhon

screw [skru:] n (for fixing something) ねじnéjì

♦vt (fasten) ねじで留める neji de tomérù

screwdriver [skru:'draivər] n ねじ回しnejímawashì

screw up vt (paper etc) くしゃくしゃにする kushákùsha ni suru

to screw up one's eyes 目を細める mé wò hosómerù

scribble [skrib'əl] n 走り書き hashírigakì

♦vt (write carelessly: note etc) 走り書きする hashírigaki suru

♦vi (make meaningless marks) 落書するrakúgaki suru

script [skript] n (CINEMA etc) 脚本kyakúhon, スクリプト sukúripùto; (system of writing) 文字mójì

scripture(s) [skrip'tʃər(z)] n(pl) (holy writing(s) of a religion) 聖典seíten

scroll [skroul] n (official paper) 巻物makímono

scrounge [skraundʒ] vt (inf): to scrounge something off/from someone ...に...をねだる ...ni...wo nedárù

♦n: on the scrounge たかって takátte

scrub [skrʌb] n (land) 低木地帯 teíbokuchitài

♦vt (rub hard: floor, hands, pan, washing) ごしごし洗う góshìgoshi aráù; (inf: reject: idea) 取り止める toríyamerù

scruff [skrʌf] n: by the scruff of the neck 首筋をつかんで kubísuji wò tsukáñde

scruffy [skrʌf'i:] adj (person, object,

appearance) 薄汚い usúgitanaì

scrum(mage) [skrʌm('idʒ)] n (RUGBY) スクラム sukúràmu

scruple [skru:'pəl] n (gen pl) 良心のとがめ ryōshìn no togáme

scrupulous [skru:'pjələs] adj (painstaking: care, attention) 細心の saíshin no; (fair-minded: honesty) 公正な kōsei na

scrutinize [skru:'tənaiz] vt (examine closely) 詳しく調べる kuwáshikù shiráberù

scrutiny [skru:'təni:] n (close examination) 吟味 gíñmi

to keep someone under scrutiny ...を監視する ...wo kañshi suru

scuff [skʌf] vt (shoes, floor) すり減らす suríherasù

scuffle [skʌf'əl] n (fight) 乱闘 rañtō

sculptor [skʌlp'tər] n 彫刻家 chōkokuka

sculpture [skʌlp'tʃər] n 彫刻 chōkoku

scum [skʌm] n (on liquid) 汚い泡 kitánaì awá; (pej: people) 人間のくず niñgen nò kúzù

scupper [skʌp'əːr] (BRIT: inf) vt (plan, idea) 邪魔して失敗させる jamá shitè shippái saserù

scurrilous [skəːr'ələs] adj 口汚い kuchígitanaì

scurry [skəːr'iː] vi ちょこちょこ走る chókòchoko hashírù

scurry off vi ちょこちょこ走って行く chókòchoko hashítte ikù

scuttle [skʌt'əl] n (also: coal scuttle) 石炭入れ sekítan-ire

♦vt (ship) 沈没させる chiñbotsu saserù

♦vi (scamper): to scuttle away/off ちょこちょこ走っていく chókòchoko hashítte ikù

scythe [saið] n 大がま ōgàma ◇柄も刃も長いかま é mò há mò nagáì káma

sea [siː] n 海 úmì; (fig: very many) 多数 tasū; (: very much) 多量 taryō

♦cpd (breeze, bird, air etc) 海の úmì no

by sea (travel) 海路で kaíro de

on the sea (boat) 海上で kaíjō de; (town) 海辺の umíbe no

out to/at sea 沖に okí ni

to be all at sea (fig) 頭が混乱している atáma gà konran shite irù

a sea of faces (fig) 顔の海 kaó nò úmì

seaboard [siːˈbɔːrd] *n* 海岸 kaígan

seafood [siːˈfuːd] *n* 魚介類 gyokáirùi, シーフード shíífùdo ◇料理に使う魚介類を指す ryōrí ni tsukáù gyokáirùi wo sásù

seafront [siːˈfrʌnt] *n* 海岸 kaígan ◇海辺の町などの海沿いの部分を指す umíbe nò machí nadò no umízoi no bubùn wo sásù

sea-going [siːˈɡouiŋ] *adj* (ship) 遠洋航海用の eñ-yōkōkaiyō no

seagull [siːˈɡʌl] *n* カモメ kamóme

seal [siːl] *n* (animal) アザラシ azárashi ◇セイウチを除いて全てのひれ足類を含む seíuchì wo nozóìte súbète no hiréashirùi wo fúkumù; (official stamp) 印章 íñshō; (closure) 封印 fūin

◆*vt* (close: envelope) ...の封をする ...no fū wò suru; (: opening) 封じる fūjirù

sea level *n* 海抜 kaíbatsu

sea lion *n* トド tódò

seal off *vt* (place) 封鎖する fūsa suru

seam [siːm] *n* (line of stitches) 縫い目 nuíme; (where edges meet) 継ぎ目 tsugíme, 合せ目 awáseme; (of coal etc) 薄層 hakúsō

seaman [siːˈmən] (*pl* **seamen**) *n* 船乗り funánòri

seamy [siːˈmiː] *adj*: *the seamy side of* ...の汚い裏面 ...no kitánaì rímèn, ...の恥部 ...no chíbù

seance [seiˈɑːns] *n* 降霊会 kōreīkai

seaplane [siːˈplein] *n* 水上飛行機 suíjōhikōki

seaport [siːˈpɔːrt] *n* 港町 minátomachi

search [səːrtʃ] *n* (hunt: for person, thing) 捜索 sōsaku, 探索 tañsaku, 検索 keñsaku; (inspection: of someone's home) 家宅捜査 katákusōsa

◆*vt* (look in: place) ...の中を捜す ...no nákà wo sagásù; (examine: memory) 捜す sagásù; (person) ...の身体検査をする ...no shiñtaikeñsa wo suru

◆*vi*: *to search for* ...を捜す ...wo sagásù

in search of ...を求めて ...wo motómete

searching [səːrˈtʃiŋ] *adj* (question, look) 鋭い surúdoì

searchlight [səːrtʃˈlait] *n* サーチライト sáchiraìto

search party *n* 捜索隊 sōsakutai

search through *vt fus* ...の中をくまなく捜す ...no nákà wo kumánaku sagásù

search warrant *n* 捜査令状 sōsareijō

seashore [siːˈʃɔːr] *n* 海岸 kaígan

seasick [siːˈsik] *adj* 船酔いになった funáyòi ni nattà

seaside [siːˈsaid] *n* 海辺 umíbe

seaside resort *n* 海辺の行楽地 umíbe nò kōrakuchì

season [siːˈzən] *n* (of year) 季節 kisétsù; (time of year for something: football season etc) シーズン shízun; (series: of films etc) シリーズ shírīzu

◆*vt* (food) ...に味を付ける ...ni ají wò tsukérù

in season (fruit, vegetables) しゅんで shúñ de

out of season (fruit, vegetables) 季節外れで kisétsuhàzure de

seasonal [siːˈzənəl] *adj* (work) 季節的な kisétsuteki na

seasoned [siːˈzənd] *adj* (fig: traveler) 経験豊かな keíken yutàka na

seasoning [siːˈzəniŋ] *n* 調味料 chōmiryò, 薬味 yakúmi

season ticket *n* (RAIL) 定期券 teíkikèn; (THEATER) シーズン入場券 shízun nyūjōken

seat [siːt] *n* (chair) いす isú; (in vehicle, theater: place) 席 sékì; (PARLIAMENT) 議席 giséki; (buttocks: *also* of trousers) しり shirí

◆*vt* (place: guests etc) 座らせる suwáraserù; (subj: table, theater: have room for) ...人分の席がある ...niñbun no sékì ga árù

to be seated 座る suwárù

seat belt *n* シートベルト shítoberùto

sea water *n* 海水 kaísui

seaweed [siːˈwiːd] *n* 海草 kaísō

seaworthy [siːˈwəːrðiː] *adj* (ship) 航海に耐えられる kōkai nì taérarerù

sec. *abbr* = **second(s)**

secluded [sikluˈdid] *adj* (place) 人里離れた hitózato hanaretà; (life) 隠とんの íñton no

seclusion [sîklu:'ʒən] n 隔離 kákuri

second [sek'ənd] adj (after first) 第 二 (の) dái ní (no)

♦adv (come, be placed: in race etc) 二番 に níban ni; (when listing) 第二に dái ní ni

♦n (unit of time) 秒 byǒ; (AUT: also: **second gear**) セカンド sekándo; (COMM: imperfect) 二 流品 niryūhìn; (BRIT: SCOL: degree) 2級優等卒業学位 níkyū yūtō sotsugyō gakùi ¶ see also **first**

♦vt (motion) ...に支持を表明する ...ni shíjî wo hyōmei suru; (BRIT: worker) 派遣 する hakén suru

secondary [sek'əndeːriː] adj (less important) 二次的な nijíteki na

secondary school n 中等高等学校 chútōkōtōgakkō

second-class [sek'əndklæs'] adj (hotel, novel, work) 二 流 の niryū no; (tickets, transport) 2等の nitó no

♦adv (travel) 2等で nitó de

secondhand [sek'əndhænd'] adj (clothing, car) 中古の chūkó no

second hand n (on clock) 秒針 byōshìn

secondly [sek'əndliː] adv 2番目に nibánme ni

secondment [sek'əndmənt] (BRIT) n 派 遣 hakén

second-rate [sek'əndreit'] adj (film etc) 二流の niryū no

second thoughts npl ためらい tamérai *on second thought* (US) *or* *thoughts* (BRIT) 気が変って ki gá kawattè

secrecy [siː'krisiː] n: *to swear someone to secrecy* ...に秘密を誓わせる ...ni himítsu wò chikáwaserù

secret [siː'krit] adj (plan, passage, agent) 秘密の himítsu no; (admirer, drinker) ひ そかな hisókà na

♦n 秘密 himítsu

in secret 内密に naímitsu ni

secretarial [sekriteːr'iːəl] adj (w o r k , course, staff, studies) 秘書の hishò no

secretariat [sekriteːr'iːət] n 事務局 jimúkyòku

secretary [sek'riteːriː] n (COMM) 秘書 hishǒ; (of club) 書記 shokî

Secretary of State (for) (BRIT: POL) (...)大臣 (...)dáîjin

secretion [sikriː'ʃən] n (substance) 分 泌 物 buńpitsubùtsu

secretive [siː'kritiv] adj 秘密主義の hi-mítsushùgi no

secretly [siː'kritliː] adv (tell, marry) 内密 に naímitsu ni

sect [sekt] n 宗派 shūha

sectarian [sekteːr'iːən] adj (riots etc) 宗 派間の shūhakàn no

section [sek'ʃən] n (part) 部 分 búbun; (department) ...部 ...bù; (of document) 章 shǒ; (of opinion) 一 部 ichíbù; (cross-section) 断面図 dańmenzù

sector [sek'təːr] n (part) 部 門 búmon; (MIL) 戦闘地区 seńtōchikù

secular [sek'jələːr] adj (music, society etc) 世俗 の sezóku no; (priest) 教 区 の kyǒku no

secure [sikjuːr'] adj (safe: person) 安全な 場所にいる   ańzen na bashò ni irú; (: money) 安全な場所にある ańzen na bashò ni árù; (: building) 防犯対策完備の bǒhantaisakukaǹbi no; (firmly fixed, strong: rope, shelf) 固定された kotéi saretà

♦vt (fix: rope, shelf etc) 固定する kotéi suru; (get: job, contract etc) 確保する kákùho suru

security [sikjuːr'itiː] n (protection) 警 備 kéîbi; (for one's future) 保証 hoshǒ; (FINANCE) 担保 táñpo

sedan [sidæn'] (US) n (AUT) セダン sé-dàn

sedate [sideit'] adj (person, pace) 落着い た ochítsuità

♦vt (MED: with injection) ...に鎮静剤を 注射する ...ni chíñseizai wo chūshà suru; (: with pills etc) ...に鎮静剤を飲ませる ...ni chíñseizai wo nomáserù

sedation [sidei'ʃən] n (MED): *under sedation* 薬で鎮静されて kusúri dè chíñsei saretè

sedative [sed'ətiv] n 鎮静剤 chíñseizài

sedentary [sed'əɒteːriː] adj (occupation,

work) 座ってする suwátte surù

sediment [sed'əmənt] n (in bottle) おり orí; (in lake etc) 底のたい積物 sokó nò taísekibùtsu

seduce [sidu:s'] vt (entice: gen) 魅了する miryṓ suru; (: sexually) 誘惑する yūwaku suru, たらし込む taráshikomù

seduction [sidʌk'ʃən] n (attraction) 魅惑 miwáku; (act of seducing) 誘惑 yūwaku

seductive [sidʌk'tiv] adj (look, voice, also fig offer) 誘惑的な yūwakuteki na

see [si:] (pt **saw**, pp **seen**) vt (gen) 見る mírù; (accompany): **to see someone to the door** ...を戸口まで送る ...wo tógùchi máde okúrù; (understand) 分かる wakárù

◆vi (gen) 見える miérù; (find out) 調べる shiráberù

◆n (REL) 教区 kyōkù

to see that someone does something ...が...する様に気を付ける ...ga...surú yṓ ni kí wo tsukérù

see you soon! またね matá nè

see about vt fus ...の問題を調べて片付ける ...no mońdai wò shirábete katazùkeru

seed [si:d] n (of plant, fruit) 種 tánè; (sperm) 精液 seféki; (fig: gen pl) 種 tánè; (TENNIS) シード shído

to go to seed (plant) 種ができる tánè ga dekírù; (fig) 衰える otóroerù

seedling [si:d'liŋ] n 苗 náè

seedy [si:'di:] adj (shabby: person, place) 見すぼらしい misúborashiì

seeing [si:'iŋ] conj: **seeing (that)** ...だから ...dákàra

seek [si:k] (pt, pp **sought**) vt (truth, shelter, advice, post) 求める motómerù

seem [si:m] vi ...に見える ...ni miérù

there seems to be ... ...がある様です ...ga árù yṓ desù

seemingly [si:'miŋli:] adv ...らしく ...rashíkù

seen [si:n] pp of **see**

see off vt ...を見送る ...wo miókurù

seep [si:p] vi (liquid, gas) 染み透る shimítòru

seesaw [si:'sɔ:] n シーソー shísò

seethe [si:ð] vi (place: with people/things) 騒然としている sōzen to shite irù

to seethe with anger 怒りで煮え繰り返る ikári dè niékurikaerù

see through vt 最後までやり通す sáigo made yarítōsu

◆vt fus 見抜く minúkù

see-through [si:'θru:] adj (blouse etc) すけすけルックの sukésukerukkù no

see to vt fus ...の世話をする ...no sewá wò suru

segment [seg'mənt] n (part: gen) 一部 ichíbù; (of orange) ふさ fusá

segregate [seg'rəgeit] vt 分ける wakérù

seismic [saiz'mik] adj (activity) 地震の jishín no

seize [si:z] vt (grasp) つかむ tsukámù; (take possession of: power, control, territory) 奪う ubáù; (: hostage) 捕まえる tsukámaerù; (opportunity) 捕える toráerù

seize up vi (TECH: engine) 焼き付く yakétsukù

seize (up)on vt fus ...に飛付く ...ni tobítsukù

seizure [si:'ʒə:r] n (MED) 発作 hossá; (LAW) 没収 bosshū́; (: of power) 強奪 gṓdatsu

seldom [sel'dəm] adv めったに...ない méttà ni...náî

select [silekt'] adj (school, group, area) 一流の ichíryū no

◆vt (choose) 選ぶ erábù

selection [silek'ʃən] n (being chosen) 選ばれる事 erábareru kotò; (COMM: range available) 選択 seńtaku

selective [silek'tiv] adj (careful in choosing) 選択的な seńtakuteki na; (not general: strike etc) 限られた範囲の kagírareta hán-i no

self [self] (pl **selves**) n: **the self** 自我 jígà

◆prefix 自分で〔の〕 jibún de〔no〕...

self-assured [self'əʃu:rd'] adj 自信のある jishín no arù

self-catering [self'kei'tə:riŋ] adj (BRIT: holiday, apartment) 自炊の jisúi no

self-centered [self'sen'tə:rd] (BRIT **self-centred**) adj 自己中心の jikóchūshinno

self-colored [self'kʌl'ə:rd] (BRIT **self-coloured**) adj (of one color) 単色の tañshoku no

self-confidence [self'kɑːn'fidəns] n 自信 jishín

self-conscious [self'kɑːn'tʃəs] adj (nervous) 照れる terérù

self-contained [self'kənteind'] (BRIT) adj (flat) 設備完備の setsúbikañbi no

self-control [self'kəntroul'] n 自制 jiséi

self-defense [self'difens'] (BRIT **self-defence**) n 自己防衛 jikóbōei

in self-defense 自己防衛で jikóbōei de

self-discipline [self'dis'əplin] n 気力 kíryòku

self-employed [self'imploid'] adj 自営業の jiéigyō no

self-evident [self'ev'idənt] adj 自明の jiméi no

self-governing [self'gʌv'ə:rniŋ] adj 独立の dokúritsu no

self-indulgent [self'indʌl'dʒənt] adj 勝手気ままな kattékimama na

self-interest [self'in'trist] n 自己利益 jikórièki

selfish [sel'fiʃ] adj 身勝手な migátte na

selfishness [sel'fiʃnis] n 利己主義 rikóshùgi

selfless [self'lis] adj 献身的な keñshinteki na

self-made [self'meid'] adj: *self-made man* 自力でたたき上げた人 jiríki dè tatákiageta hitò

self-pity [self'pit'i:] n 自己れんびん jikóreñbin

self-portrait [self'pɔ:r'trit] n 自画像 jigázō

self-possessed [self'pəzest'] adj 落着いた ochítsuità

self-preservation [self'prezə:rvei'ʃən] n 本能的の自衛 hoñnōtekijièi

self-respect [self'rispekt'] n 自尊心 jisóñshin

self-righteous [self'rai'tʃəs] adj 独善的な dokúzenteki na

self-sacrifice [self'sæk'rəfais] n 献身 keñshin

self-satisfied [self'sæt'isfaid] adj 自己満足の jikómañzoku no

self-service [self'sə:r'vis] adj (shop, restaurant, service station) セルフサービスの serúfusābisu no

self-sufficient [self'səfiʃ'ənt] adj (farm, country) 自給自足の jikyūjisòku no; (person) 独立独歩の dokúritsudoppò no

self-taught [self'tɔ:t'] adj 独学の dokúgàku no

sell [sel] (pt, pp **sold**) vt (gen) 売る urú; (fig: idea) 売込む uríkomù
   ♦vi (goods) 売れる urérù

to sell at/for $10 値段は10ドルである nedán wà 10 dórù de arú

sell-by date [sel'bai-] (BRIT) n 賞味期限 shōmikigèn

seller [sel'ə:r] n 売手 uríte

selling price [sel'iŋ-] n 値段 nedán

sell off vt 売払う uríharaù

sell out vi (use up stock): *to sell out (of something)* (...が) 売切れる (...ga) uríkirerù

the tickets are sold out 切符は売切れだ kippú wà uríkire da

sellotape [sel'əteip] ® (BRIT) n セロテープ serótēpu

selves [selvz] pl of **self**

semaphore [sem'əfɔ:r] n 手旗 tebáta

semblance [sem'bləns] n 外観 gaíkan

semen [si:'mən] n 精液 seíeki

semester [simes'tə:r] (US) n 学期 gakkí

semi... [sem'i:] prefix 半分の... hañbùn no ...

semicircle [sem'i:sə:rkəl] n 半円形 hañeñkei

semicolon [sem'i:koulən] n セミコロン semíkoròn

semiconductor [semi:kəndʌk'tə:r] n 半導体 hañdōtai

semidetached (house) [sem:ditætʃt'] (BRIT) n 二戸建て住宅 nikódate jūtaku

semifinal [semi:fai'nəl] n 準決勝 juñkesshō

seminar [sem'ənɑ:r] n セミナー sémìnā

seminary [sem'əne:ri:] n (REL) 神学校 shiñgakkō

semiskilled [semi:skild'] adj (work,

worker) 半熟練の hañjukùren no

senate [sen'it] n 上院 jōin

senator [sen'ətə:r] n 上院議員 jōingìin

send [send] (pt, pp **sent**) vt (dispatch) 送る okúrù; (transmit: signal) 送信する sōshin suru

send away vt (letter, goods) 送る okúrù; (unwelcome visitor) 追払う oíharaù

send away for vt fus 郵便で注文する yūbin dè chūmon suru

send back vt 送り返す okúrikaesù

sender [send'ə:r] n 差出人 sashídashinìn

send for vt fus (thing) 取寄せる toríyoseru; (person) 呼寄せる yobíyoserù

send off vt (goods) 送る okúrù; (BRIT: SPORT: player) 退場させる taíjō saserù

send-off [send'ɔːf] n: a good send-off 素晴らしい送別 subárashiì sōbetsu

send out vt (invitation) 送る okúrù; (signal) 発信する hasshín suru

send up vt (price, blood pressure) 上昇させる jōshō saserù; (astronaut) 打上げる uchíagerù; (BRIT: parody) 風刺する fūshi suru

senile [si:'nail] adj 老いぼれた oíboretà, ぼけた bōketà; (MED) 老人性の rōjinsei no

senior [si:n'jə:r] adj (older) 年上の toshíue no; (on staff: position, officer) 幹部の kánbu no; (of higher rank: partner) 上級の jōkyū no

senior citizen n 老人 rōjin, 高齢者 kōreisha

seniority [si:njɔ:r'iti:] n (in service) 年功 nefíkō

sensation [sensei'ʃən] n (feeling) 感覚 kañkaku; (great success) 大成功 daíseikō

sensational [sensei'ʃənəl] adj (wonderful) 素晴らしい subárashiì; (causing much interest: headlines) 扇情的な señjōteki na; (: result) センセーショナルな señsēshònaru na

sense [sens] n (physical) 感覚 kañkaku; (feeling: of guilt, shame etc) 感じ kañji; (good sense) 常識 jōshiki; (meaning: of word, phrase etc) 意味 ímì

◆vt (become aware of) 感じる kañjirù

it makes sense (can be understood) 意味が分かる ímì ga wakáru; (is sensible) 賢明だ kefímei dà

sense of humor ユーモアを解する心 yūmòa wo kaí surù kokórò, ユーモアのセンス yūmòa no sénsu

senseless [sens'lis] adj (pointless: murder) 無意味な muími na; (unconscious) 気絶した kizétsu shità

sensible [sen'səbəl] adj (person) 利口な ríkō na; (reasonable: price, advice) 合理的な gōriteki na; (: decision, suggestion) 賢明な kefímei na

sensitive [sen'sətiv] adj (understanding) 理解のある ríkai no árù; (nerve, skin) 敏感な bíñkan na; (instrument) 高感度の kōkando no; (fig: touchy: person) 怒りっぽい okórippòi; (: issue) 際どい kiwádoì

sensitivity [sensətiv'əti:] n (understanding) 理解 ríkai; (responsiveness: to touch etc) 敏感さ bíñkansa; (: of instrument) 感度 kándo; (touchiness: of person) 怒りっぽさ okórippòsa; (delicate nature: of issue etc) 際どさ kiwádosà

sensual [sen'ʃu:əl] adj (of the senses: rhythm etc) 官能的な kafínōteki na; (relating to sexual pleasures) 肉感的な nikkánteki na

sensuous [sen'ʃu:əs] adj (lips, material etc) 官能的な kafínōteki na

sent [sent] pt, pp of **send**

sentence [sen'təns] n (LING) 文 búñ; (LAW) 宣告 señkoku

◆vt: *to sentence someone to death/to 5 years in prison* ...に死刑〔懲役5年〕の判決を言渡す ...ni shikéi 〔chōeki gonèn〕nò hañketsu wò iíwatasù

sentiment [sen'təmənt] n (tender feelings) 感情 kañjō; (opinion, also pl) 意見 íkèn

sentimental [sentəmen'təl] adj (song) 感傷的な kafíshōteki na, センチメンタルな señchimentaru na; (person) 情にもろい jō nì moróì

sentry [sen'tri:] n 番兵 bañpei

separate [adj sep'rit vb sep'əreit] adj (distinct: piles, occasions, ways, rooms) 別々の betsúbetsu no

♦vt (split up: people, things) 分けるwakérù; (make a distinction between: twins) 見分けるmiwákerù; (: ideas etc) 区別するkubétsu suru

♦vi (split up, move apart) 分かれるwakárerù

separately [sep'ritli:] adv 別々にbetsúbetsu ni

separates [sep'rits] npl (clothes) セパレーツ sepárētsu

separation [səperei'ʃən] n (being apart) 分離bunri; (time spent apart) 別れ別れになっている期間 wakárewakàre ni natté irù kikáñ; (LAW) 別居 bekkyó

September [septem'bə:r] n 9月 kúgatsu

septic [sep'tik] adj (wound, finger etc) 感染したkañsen shita

septic tank n 浄化槽 jókasò

sequel [si:'kwəl] n (follow-up) 後日談 gojítsudàn; (of film, story) 続編 zokúhen

sequence [si:'kwins] n (ordered chain) 連続 refizoku; (also: **dance sequence, film sequence**) 一場面 ichíbamèn, シークエンス shíkueñsu

sequin [si:'kwin] n シークイン shíkuìn, スパンコール supáñkòru

serene [səri:n'] adj (smile, expression etc) 穏やかな odáyàka na

serenity [səren'iti:] n 穏やかさ odáyàkasa

sergeant [sɑːr'dʒənt] n (MIL etc) 軍曹 gúñsò; (POLICE) 巡査部長 juñsabùchō

serial [si:r'i:əl] n 連続物 refizokumono

serialize [si:r'i:əlaiz] vt (in newspaper, magazine) 連載する refisai suru; (on radio, TV) 連続物として放送する refizokumono toshitè hōsō suru

serial number n 製造番号 seízōbañgō

series [si:r'i:z] n inv (group) 一連 ichíren; (of books, TV programs) シリーズ shirízù

serious [si:r'i:əs] adj (person, manner) 真剣な shiñken na; (important: matter) 大事な daíji na; (grave: illness, condition) 重い omóì

seriously [si:r'i:əsli:] adv (talk, take) 真剣に shiñken ni; (hurt) ひどく hídòku

seriousness [si:r'i:əsnis] n (of person,

manner) 真剣さ shiñkensa; (importance) 重大さ júdaisa; (gravity) 重さ omósa

sermon [sə:r'mən] n (also fig) 説教 sekkyó

serrated [se:rei'tid] adj (edge, knife) のこぎり状の nokógirijō no

serum [si:r'əm] n 血清 kesséi

servant [sə:r'vənt] n (gen) 召使い meshítsukài; (fig) 人に仕える物 hitó nì tsukáerù monó

serve [sə:rv] vt (gen: company, country) 仕える tsukáerù; (in shop: goods) 売る urú; (: customer) ...の用をうかがう ...no yó wò ukágaù; (subj: train) ...の足になる ...no ashí nì naru; (apprenticeship) 務める tsutómerù

♦vi (at table) 給仕する kyúji suru; (TENNIS) サーブする sábu suru; (be useful):
to serve as/for ...として役に立つ ...toshítè yakú ni tatsù

♦n (TENNIS) サーブ sábu

to serve to do ...をするのに役に立つ ...wo suru nò ni yakú ni tatsù

it serves him right 自業自得だ jigójitòku da

to serve a prison term 服役する fukúeki suru

serve out/up vt (food) 出す dásù

service [sə:r'vis] n (gen: help) 役に立つ事 yakú ni tatsù koto; (in hotel) サービス sábisu; (REL) 式 shikí; (AUT) 整備 seíbi; (TENNIS) サーブ sábu; (plates, dishes etc) 一そろい hitósoroì; (also: **train service**) 鉄道 の便 tetsúdō no bén; (also: **plane service**) 空の便 sórà no bén

♦vt (car, washing machine) 整備する seíbi suru

military/national service 兵役 heíeki

to be of service to someone ...に役に立つ ...ni yakú ni tatsù

serviceable [sə:r'visəbəl] adj 役に立つ yakú ni tatsù

service area n (on motorway) サービスエリア sábisu erìa

service charge (BRIT) n サービス料 sábisuryò

serviceman [sə:r'vismæn] (pl **servicemen**) n (MIL) 軍人 guñjin

Services [səːr'visiz] *npl*: *the Services* (army, navy etc) 軍隊 gúntai

service station *n* ガソリンスタンド gasórinsutàndo; (*BRIT*: on motorway) サービスエリア sábisu erìa

serviette [səːrviːet'] (*BRIT*) *n* 紙ナプキン kamínapùkin

servile [səːr'vail] *adj* (person, obedience) おもねる様な omóneru yǒ na

session [seʃ'ən] *n* (period of activity: recording/drinking session) ...する為に集まる事 ...surú tame nì atsúmaru kotð

to be in session (court) 開廷中である kaíteichū de arù; (Parliament etc) 開会中である kaíkaichū de arù

set [set] *n* (collection of things) 一そろい hitósoroì, 一式 isshíki, セット séttð; (radio set) ラジオ rájìo; (TV set) テレビ térèbi; (TENNIS) セット séttð; (group of people) 連中 reńchū; (MATH) セット séttð; (CINEMA, THEATER) 舞台装置 butáisòchi, セット séttð; (HAIRDRESSING) セット séttð

◆*adj* (fixed: rules, routine) 決りの kimári no; (ready) 用意ができた yối ga dekíta

◆*vb* (*pt*, *pp* **set**)

◆*vt* (place) 置く ðkù; (fix, establish: time, price, rules etc) 決める kimérù; (: record) 作る tsukúrù; (adjust: alarm, watch) セットする séttð suru; (impose: task) 命ずる meízurù; (: exam) 作る tsukúrù

◆*vi* (sun) 沈む shizúmù; (jam, jelly, concrete) 固まる katámarù; (broken bone) 治る náðru

to set the table 食卓の用意をする shokútaku nò yối wo suru

to be set on doing something どうしても...をすると決めている dǒshite mo ... wo suru tð kiméte irù

to set to music ...に曲を付ける ...ni kyokú wò tsukérù

to set on fire ...に火を付ける ...ni hí wð tsukérù

to set free 放してやる hanáshite yarù, 自由にする jiyú ni surù

to set something going ...を始めさせる

...wo hajímesaserù

to set sail 出航する shukkő suru

set about *vt fus* (task) 始める hajímerù

set aside *vt* (money etc) 取って置く tóttè oku; (time) 空けておく akétè okù

set back *vt* (cost): *to set someone back $5* 5ドル払わなければならない go dőru haráwànakereba naránaì; (in time): *to set someone back (by)* ...を (...) 遅らせる ...wo (...) okúraserù

setback [set'bæk] *n* (hitch) 苦難 kúnan

set menu *n* 定食メニュー teíshokumenyū

set off *vi* 出発する shuppátsu suru

◆*vt* (bomb) 爆発させる bakúhatsu saserù; (alarm) 鳴らす narásù; (chain of events) ...の引金となる ...no hikígane to narù; (show up well: jewels) 引立たせる hikítataserù

set out *vi* (depart) 出発する shuppátsu suru

◆*vt* (arrange: goods etc) 並べて置く narábete okù; (state: arguments) 述べる nobérù

to set out to do something ...をするつもりである ...wo suru tsumori de arù

settee [seti:'] *n* ソファー sófà

setting [set'iŋ] *n* (background) 背景 haíkei; (position: of controls) セット séttð; (of jewel) はめ込み台 hamékomidaì

the setting of the sun 日没 nichíbotsu

settle [set'əl] *vt* (argument, matter) ...に決着を付ける ...ni ketcháku wð tsukérù; (accounts) 清算する seísan suru; (MED: calm: person) 落着かせる ochítsukaserù

◆*vi* (*also*: **settle down**) 一カ所に落着く ikkáshò ni ochítsukù; (bird) 降りる orírù; (dust etc) つく tsukú; (calm down: children) 静まる shizúmarù

to settle for something ...で我慢する ...de gáman suru

to settle on something ...に決める ...ni kimérù

settle in *vi* 新しい所に落着く atárashiì tokórò ni ochítsukù

settle up *vi*: *to settle up with someone* ...に借金を返す ...ni shakkín wo kǎèsu

settlement [set'əlmənt] n (payment) 清算 seísan; (agreement) 和解 wakái; (village etc) 集落 shūraku

settler [set'lə:r] n 入植者 nyūshokushà

set up vt (organization) 設立する setsúritsu suru

setup [set'ʌp] n (organization) 機構 kikō; (situation) 様子 yōsu, 状況 jōkyō

seven [sev'ən] num 七(の) nánà (no), 七つ(の) nanátsù (no)

seventeen [sev'əntiːn'] num 十七 (の) júnanà (no)

seventh [sev'ənθ] num 第七(の) dái nanà (no)

seventy [sev'əntiː] num 七十 (の) nanájū (no)

sever [sev'ə:r] vt (artery, pipe) 切断する setsúdan suru; (relations) 切る kírù, 断つ tátsù

several [sev'ə:rəl] adj (things) 幾つかの íkùtsu ka no; (people) 幾人かの íkùnin ka no

♦pron 幾つか íkùtsu ka

several of us 私たちの中から幾人か watákushitàchi no nákà kara íkùnin ka

severance [sev'ə:rəns] n (of relations) 断交 dańkō

severance pay n 退職金 taíshokukìn

severe [sivir'] adj (serious: pain) 激しい hagéshiî; (: damage) 大きな ōki na; (: shortage) 深刻な shiñkoku na; (hard: winter, climate) 厳しい kibíshiî; (stern) 厳格な geñkaku na; (plain: dress) 簡素な kánso na

severity [siver'itiː] n (seriousness: of pain) 激しさ hagéshisa; (: of damage) 大きさ ōkisa; (: of shortage) 深刻さ shiñkokusa; (bitterness: of winter, climate) 厳しさ kibíshisa; (sternness) 厳格さ geñkakusa; (plainness: of dress) 簡素さ kańsosa

sew [sou] (pt sewed, pp sewn) vt 縫う núù

sewage [suː'idʒ] n (waste) 汚水 osúì

sewer [suː'ə:r] n 下水道 gesúidō

sewing [sou'iŋ] n (activity) 裁縫 saíhō; (items being sewn) 縫物 nuímono

sewing machine n ミシン míshìn

sewn [soun] pp of **sew**

sew up vt (item of clothing) 縫い合せる nuíawaserù

sex [seks] n (gender) 性別 seíbetsu; (love-making) セックス sékkùsu

to have sex with someone ...とセックスをする ...to sékkùsu wo suru

sexist [seks'ist] adj 性差別の seísabetsu no

sextet [sekstet'] n (group) セクステット sekúsutettò

sexual [sek'ʃuːəl] adj (of the sexes: reproduction) 有性の yūsei no; (: equality) 男女の dáñjo no; (of sex: attraction) 性的な seíteki na; (: relationship) 肉体の nikútai no

sexy [sek'siː] adj (pictures, underwear etc) セクシーな sékùshī na

shabby [ʃæb'iː] adj (person, clothes) 見すぼらしい misúborashiî; (trick, treatment) 卑劣な hirétsu na

shack [ʃæk] n バラック barákkù

shackles [ʃæk'əlz] npl (on foot) 足かせ ashíkasè; (on hands) 手かせ tékàse; (fig) 束縛 sokubaku

shade [ʃeid] n (shelter) 日陰 hikáge; (also: lampshade) ランプのかさ ráñpu no kásà; (of colour) 色合 iróaî; (small quantity): *a shade too large* ちょっと大き過ぎる chottó ōkisugirù

♦vt (shelter) ...の日よけになる ...no hiyóke ni narù; (eyes) ...に手をかざす ...ni té wò kazásù

in the shade 日陰に hikáge ni

a shade more もうちょっと mō chottó

shadow [ʃæd'ou] n 影 kágè

♦vt (follow) 尾行する bikō suru

shadow cabinet (BRIT) n (POL) 影の内閣 kágè no náikaku

shadowy [ʃæd'ouiː] adj (in shadow) 影の多い kágè no ōî; (dim: figure, shape) 影の様な kágè no yō nà

shady [ʃei'diː] adj (place) 日陰のある hikáge no arù; (trees) 日よけになる hiyóke ni narù; (fig: dishonest: person, deal) いかがわしい ikágawashiî

shaft [ʃæft] n (of arrow) 矢柄 yagára; (of spear) 柄 e; (AUT, TECH) 回転軸 kaíteñjiku, シャフト sháfùto; (of mine) 縦坑 ta-

tékò; (of elevator) 通路 tsúrò
a shaft of light 一条 の 光 ichíjō no hikarí

shaggy [ʃægˈiː] *adj* (appearance, beard, dog) ぼさぼさの bosábosa no

shake [ʃeik] (*pt* **shook**, *pp* **shaken**) *vt* (gen) 揺すぶる yusúburù; (bottle) 振る fúrù; (cocktail) シェイクする shéìkù suru; (building) 揺るがす yurúgasù; (weaken: beliefs, resolve) ぐらつかせる gurátsukaserù; (upset, surprise) ...にショックを与える ...ni shókkù wo atáerù
♦*vi* (tremble) 震える furúerù
to shake one's head (in refusal, dismay) 頭を振る atáma wò fúrù
to shake hands with someone ...と握手をする ...to ákùshu wo suru

shaken [ʃeiˈkən] *pp* of **shake**

shake off *vt* (lit) 振り落す furíotosù; (*fig*: pursuer) まくmakú

shake up *vt* (lit: ingredients) よく振る yókù furu; (*fig*: organization) 一新する isshín suru

shaky [ʃeiˈkiː] *adj* (hand, voice) 震える furúerù; (table, building) ぐらぐらする gúragura suru

shall [ʃæl] *aux vb*: **I shall go** 行きます ikímasù
shall I open the door? ドアを開けましょうか dóà wo akémashò ka
I'll get some, shall I? 少し取ってきましょうか sukóshì totté kimashò ka

shallow [ʃælˈou] *adj* (water, box, breathing) 浅い asáì; (*fig*: ideas etc) 浅薄な señpaku na

sham [ʃæm] *n* いんちき ínchiki
♦*vt* ...の振りをする ...no furí wò suru

shambles [ʃæmˈbəlz] *n* 大混乱 daíkoñran

shame [ʃeim] *n* (embarrassment) 恥 hají; (disgrace) 不面目 fuméñboku
♦*vt* 辱める hazúkashimerù
it is a shame that ... ...であるのは残念だ ...de árù no wa zañneñ da
it is a shame to do ... ...するのはもったいない ...surú no wà mottáinaí
what a shame! 残念だ zañneñ da

shamefaced [ʃeimˈfeist] *adj* 恥ずかしそうな hazúkashisō na

shameful [ʃeimˈfəl] *adj* (disgraceful) 恥ずべき hazúbeki

shameless [ʃeimˈlis] *adj* (liar, deception) 恥知らずの hajíshirazù no

shampoo [ʃæmpuːˈ] *n* シャンプー sháñpū
♦*vt* シャンプーする sháñpū suru
shampoo and set シャンプーとセット sháñpū to séttò

shamrock [ʃæmˈrɑːk] *n* ツメクサ tsumékusa, クローバー kurōbā

shandy [ʃænˈdiː] *n* シャンディー shándì ◇ビールをレモネードで割った飲物 bírù wo remónèdo de wattá nomimonò

shan't [ʃænt] = **shall not**

shanty town [ʃænˈtiː-] *n* バラック集落 barákkushūraku

shape [ʃeip] *n* (form, outline) 形 katáchi
♦*vt* (fashion, form) 形作る katáchizukurù; (someone's ideas, life) 方向付ける hôkōzukerù
to take shape (painting) 段々格好がつく dañdañ kakkô ga tsukú; (plan) 具体化してくる gutáika shite kurú

-shaped [ʃeipt] *suffix*: **heart-shaped** ハート形の hâtogata no

shapeless [ʃeipˈlis] *adj* 不格好な bukákkō na

shapely [ʃeipˈliː] *adj* (woman, legs) 美しい utsúkushiì

shape up *vi* (events) 具体化してくる gutáika shite kurù; (person) 期待通りに進歩する kitáidòri ni shiñpo suru

share [ʃeːr] *n* (part received) 分け前 wakémaè; (part contributed) 持分 mochíbun, 負担分 futáñbun; (COMM) 株 kabú
♦*vt* (books, toys, room) 共用する kyôyō suru; (cost) 分担する buñtan suru; (one's lunch) 分けてやる wakéte yarù; (have in common: features, qualities etc) ...の点で似ている ...no téñ de nité irù

shareholder [ʃeːrˈhouldər] *n* 株主 kabúnùshi

share out *vi* 分配する buñpai suru

shark [ʃɑːrk] *n* サメ samé

sharp [ʃɑːrp] *adj* (razor, knife) よく切れる yókù kirérù; (point, teeth) 鋭い surúdoì; (nose, chin) とがった togáttà; (outline) くっきりした kukkírì shità; (pain)

鋭い surúdoì; (cold) 身を切る様な mí wò kírù yō na; (taste) 舌を刺す様な shitá wò sásù yō na; (MUS) ピッチが高過ぎる pítchì ga takásugirù; (contrast) 強い tsuyóì; (increase) 急な kyū na; (voice) 甲高い kańdakaì; (person: quick-witted) 抜け目のない nukéme no naì; (dishonest: practice etc) 不正な fuséi na

♦**n** (MUS) えい音記号 eíonkigò, シャープ sháppù

♦**adv** (precisely): **at 2 o'clock sharp** 2時きっかりに nijí kikkárì ni

sharpen [ʃɑːr'pən] vt (stick etc) とがらせる togáraserù; (pencil) 削る kezúrù; (fig: appetite) そそる sosórù

sharpener [ʃɑːr'pənəːr] n (also: **pencil sharpener**) 鉛筆削り eńpitsukezùri

sharp-eyed [ʃɑːrp'aid] adj 目の鋭い mé nò surudoì

sharply [ʃɑːrp'liː] adv (turn, stop) 急に kyū ni; (stand out) くっきりと kukkírì to; (contrast) 強く tsuyókù; (criticize, retort) 辛らつに shińratsu ni

shatter [ʃæt'əːr] vt (break) 割る warú, 木っ端みじんにする kóppàmijin ni suru; (fig: ruin) 台無しにする daínashi ni surù; (: upset) がっくりさせる gakkúrî saserù

♦**vi** (break) 割れる warérù

shave [ʃeiv] vt (person, face, legs etc) そる sórù

♦**vi** ひげをそる higé wò sórù

♦**n**: **to have a shave** (at barber's) ひげをそってもらう higé wò sóttè moráù; (oneself) ひげをそる higé wò sórù

shaver [ʃei'vəːr] n (also: **electric shaver**) 電気かみそり deńkikamìsori

shaving [ʃei'viŋ] n (action) ひげをそる事 higé wò sórù kótó

shaving brush n シェービングブラシ shébinguburàshi

shaving cream, shaving foam n シェービングクリーム shébingukurìmu

shavings [ʃei'viŋz] npl (of wood etc) かんなくず kańnakuzù

shawl [ʃɔːl] n 肩掛 katákàke, ショール shórù

she [ʃiː] pron 彼女は〔が〕 kánòjo wa 〔ga〕

sheaf [ʃiːf] (npl **sheaves**) n (of corn, papers)

shear [ʃiːr] (pt **sheared**, pp **shorn**) vt (sheep) ...の毛を刈る ...no ké wò karú

shear off vi 折れる orérù

shears [ʃiːr'əːrz] npl (for hedge) はさみ hasámi

sheath [ʃiːθ] n (of knife) さや sáyà; (contraceptive) コンドーム końdômu, スキン sukíñ

sheaves [ʃiːvz] npl of **sheaf**

she-cat [ʃiː'kæt] n 雌ネコ mesúneko

shed [ʃed] n 小屋 koyá

♦**vt** (pt, pp **shed**) (leaves, fur, hair etc) 落す otósù; (skin) 脱皮する dappí suru; (tears) 流す nagásù

to shed blood 人を殺す hitó wò korósù

to shed a load (subj: truck etc) 荷崩れを起す nikúzure wò okósù

she'd [ʃiːd] = **she had; she would**

sheen [ʃiːn] n つや tsuyá

sheep [ʃiːp] n inv ヒツジ hitsúji

sheepdog [ʃiːp'dɔːg] n 牧用犬 bokúyōken

sheepish [ʃiː'piʃ] adj 恥ずかしそうな hazúkashisô na

sheepskin [ʃiːp'skin] n ヒツジの毛皮 hitsúji nò kegáwa, シープスキン shípusukìñ

sheer [ʃiːr] adj (utter) 全くの mattáku no; (steep) 垂直の suíchoku no; (almost transparent) ごく薄手の gókù usúde no

♦**adv** (straight up: rise) 垂直に suíchoku ni

sheet [ʃiːt] n (on bed) シーツ shítsù; (of paper, glass, metal) 一枚 ichímaì

a sheet of ice アイスバーン aísubàn

sheik(h) [ʃiːk] n 首長 shuchō

shelf [ʃelf] (pl **shelves**) n 棚 taná

shell [ʃel] n (on beach) 貝殻 kaígara; (of egg, nut etc) 殻 kará; (explosive) 弾丸 dańgan; (of building) 外壁 sotókabe

♦**vt** (peas) むく múkù; (MIL: fire on) 砲撃する hôgeki suru

she'll [ʃiːl] = **she will; she shall**

shellfish [ʃel'fiʃ] n inv (crab) カニ kaní; (prawn, shrimp etc) エビ ebí; (lobster) ロブスター robúsùtà; (scallop, clam etc) 貝 kái ◇料理用語として殻のある海の生物を指す ryóriyōgo toshite kará no arù úmí no séíbutsu wo sásù

shelter [ʃelˈtər] n (building) シェルター shérùtā; (protection: for hiding) 隠れ場 所 kakúrebashò; (: from rain) 雨宿りの 場所 amáyàdori no bashó
♦vt (protect) 守る mamórù; (give lodging to: homeless, refugees) ...に避難の場 所を提供する ...ni hínàn no bashó wò teíkyō suru; (: wanted man) かくまう kakúmaù
♦vi (from rain etc) 雨宿りをする amáyàdori wo surù; (from danger) 避難する hínàn suru; (hide) 隠れる kakúrerù

sheltered [ʃelˈtərd] adj (life) 世間の荒波 から守られた sékèn no aránami karà mamóraretà; (spot) 雨風を避けられる á-mèkaze wo sakérarerù
sheltered housing 老人・身障者用住宅 rójìn, shíńshòshayō jútakù

shelve [ʃelv] vt (fig: plan) 棚上げにする taná-age ni surù

shelves [ʃelvz] npl of shelf

shepherd [ʃepˈərd] n ヒツジ飼い hitsúji-kài
♦vt (guide) 案内する afnai suru

shepherd's pie (BRIT) n シェパードパ イ shepádopaì ◇ひき肉にマッシュポテト を乗せて焼いた料理 hikíniku nì masshú-potèto wo nosète yaità ryórì

sheriff [ʃerˈif] (US) n 保安官 hoáňkan

sherry [ʃerˈiː] n シェリー酒 sheríshù

she's [ʃiːz] = she is; she has

Shetland [ʃetˈlənd] n (also: the Shetlands, the Shetland Isles) シェットラン ド諸島 shettórando shotò

shield [ʃiːld] n (MIL) 盾 tátè; (SPORT: trophy) 盾型トロフィー tatégata toròfì; (protection) ...よけ ...yoké
♦vt: to shield (from) ...の(...) よけにな る ...no (...) yoké ni narù

shift [ʃift] n (change) 変更 heñkō; (work-period) 交替 kòtai; (group of workers) 交 替組 kótaigùmi
♦vt (move) ...の位置を変える ...no íchì wo kaérù; (remove: stain) 抜く nukú
♦vi (move: wind, person) 変る kawárù

shiftless [ʃiftˈlis] adj (person) ろくでなし の rokúdenashi no

shift work n 交替でする作業 kótai de suru sagyō

shifty [ʃifˈtiː] adj (person, eyes) うさん臭 い usáňkusaì

shilling [ʃilˈiŋ] (BRIT) n シリング shíríňgu ◇かつての英国の硬貨でポンドの1/20 kátsùte no eíkoku no kòka de póndo no nijúbùn no ichí

shilly-shally [ʃilˈiːʃæliː] vi ぐずぐずする gúzùguzu suru

shimmer [ʃimˈər] vi ちらちら光る chírà-chira hikárù

shin [ʃin] n 向こうずね mukòzune

shine [ʃain] n つや tsuyá
♦vb (pt, pp shone)
♦vi (sun) 照る térù; (torch, light, eyes) 光 る hikárù; (fig: person) 優れる sugúrerù
♦vt (glasses) ふく fukú; (shoes) 磨く mi-gákù
to shine a torch on something ...を懐 中電燈で照す ...wo kaíchūdeñtō de terá-sù

shingle [ʃiŋˈgəl] n (on beach) 砂利 jarí

shingles [ʃiŋˈgəlz] n (MED) 帯状ヘルペス taíjōherupèsu

shiny [ʃaiˈniː] adj (coin) ぴかぴかの pikápika no; (shoes, hair, lipstick) つやつや の tsuyátsuya no

ship [ʃip] n 船 fúnè
♦vt (transport by ship) 船で運ぶ fúnè de hakóbù; (send: goods) 輸送する yusó suru

shipbuilding [ʃipˈbildiŋ] n 造船 zósen

shipment [ʃipˈmənt] n (goods) 輸送貨物 yusókamòtsu

shipper [ʃipˈər] n 送り主 okúrinùshi

shipping [ʃipˈiŋ] n (transport of cargo) 運送 uñsō; (ships collectively) 船舶 séñpaku

shipshape [ʃipˈʃeip] adj きちんとした ki-chíñ to shita

shipwreck [ʃipˈrek] n (event) 難破 nañpa; (ship) 難破船 nañpasen
♦vt: to be shipwrecked 難破する nañpa suru

shipyard [ʃipˈjɑːrd] n 造船所 zósenjo

shire [ʃaiəˈr] (BRIT) n 郡 gúñ

shirk [ʃəːrk] vt (work, obligations) 怠る

okótarù

shirt [ʃəːrt] n (man's) ワイシャツ waíshatsu; (woman's) シャツブラウス shatsúburaùsu

in (one's) shirt sleeves 上着を脱いで uwági wò núìde

shit [ʃit] (*inf!*) excl くそっ kusót

shiver [ʃivʹəːr] n (act of shivering) 身震い mibúruì

♦vi 震える furúerù

shoal [ʃoul] n (of fish) 群れ muré; (*fig: also*: **shoals**) 大勢 ózeì

shock [ʃɑːk] n (start, impact) 衝撃 shógeki; (ELEC) 感電 kańden; (emotional) 打撃 dagéki, ショック shókkù; (MED) ショック shókkù

♦vt (upset, offend) ...にショックを与える ...ni shókkù wo atáerù

shock absorber n 緩衝器 kańshōkì

shocking [ʃɑːkʹiŋ] adj (awful: standards, accident) ひどい hidóì; (outrageous: play, book) 衝撃的な shógekiteki na

shod [ʃɑːd] pt, pp of **shoe**

shoddy [ʃɑːdʹiː] adj (goods, workmanship) 粗雑な sozátsu na

shoe [ʃuː] n (for person) 靴 kutsú; (for horse) てい鉄 teítetsu

♦vt (pt, pp **shod**) (horse) ...にてい鉄を付ける ...ni teítetsu wò tsukérù

shoebrush [ʃuːʹbrʌʃ] n 靴ブラシ kutsúburàshi

shoelace [ʃuːʹleis] n 靴ひも kutsúhìmo

shoe polish n 靴磨き kutsúmigàki

shoeshop [ʃuːʹʃɑːp] n 靴屋 kutsúyà

shoestring [ʃuːʹstriŋ] n (*fig*): *on a shoestring* わずかの金で wázùka no kané de

shone [ʃoun] pt, pp of **shine**

shoo [ʃuː] excl しっ shítt ◇動物を追払う時に言う言葉 dóbutsu wò oíharaù toki ni iú kotoba

shook [ʃuk] pt of **shake**

shoot [ʃuːt] n (on branch, seedling) 若枝 wakáèda

♦vb (pt, pp **shot**)

♦vt (gun) 撃つ útsù; (arrow) 射る írù; (kill: bird, robber etc) 撃ち殺す uchíkorosù; (wound) そ撃する sogéki suru; (execute) 銃殺する júsatsu suru; (film) 撮影する satsúei suru

♦vi (with gun/bow): *to shoot (at)* (...を目掛けて)撃つ〔射る〕 (...wo megákete) útsù 〔írù〕; (SOCCER) シュートする shúto suru

shoot down vt (plane) 撃ち落とす uchíotosù

shoot in/out vi (rush) 飛込む〔飛出す〕 tobíkomù 〔tobídasù〕

shooting [ʃuːʹtiŋ] n (shots) 発砲事件 happójikèn; (HUNTING) 狩猟 shuryó

shooting star n 流れ星 nagárebòshi

shoot up vi (*fig*) 急上昇する kyújōshō suru

shop [ʃɑːp] n (selling goods) 店 misé; (*also*: **workshop**) 作業場 sagyóbà

♦vi (*also*: **go shopping**) 買物する kaímono suru

shop assistant (*BRIT*) n 店員 teń-in

shop floor (*BRIT*) n 労働側 ródōgawa

shopkeeper [ʃɑːpʹkiːpəːr] n 店主 teńshu

shoplifting [ʃɑːpʹliftiŋ] n 万引 mańbìki

shopper [ʃɑːpʹəːr] n (person) 買物客 kaímonokỳaku

shopping [ʃɑːpʹiŋ] n (goods) 買物 kaímono

shopping bag n ショッピングバッグ shoppíngubaggù

shopping center (*BRIT* **shopping centre**) n ショッピングセンター shoppíngusentà

shop-soiled [ʃɑːpʹsɔild] adj (goods) 棚ざらしの tanázarashi no

shop steward (*BRIT*) n (INDUSTRY) 職場代表 shokúbadaihyò

shop window n ショーウインドー shóuiňdò

shore [ʃɔːr] n 岸 kishí

♦vt: *to shore up* 補強する hokyó suru

on shore 陸に rikú ni

shorn [ʃɔːrn] pp of **shear**

short [ʃɔːrt] adj (not long) 短い mijíkaì; (person: not tall) 背の低い sé nò hikúì; (curt) ぶっきらぼうな bukkírabò na; (insufficient) 不足している fusóku shite irù

to be short of something ...が不足している ...ga fusóku shite irù

in short 要するに yó surù ni

short of doing ... ...をしなければ ...wo shinákereba

it is short for それは...の短縮形です soré wà ... no tañshukukei desu

to cut short (speech, visit) 予定より短くする yotéi yorì mijíkakù suru

everything short of ... ...を除いて何でも ...wo nozóìte náñ de mo

to fall short of ...に達しない ...ni tasshínaì

to run short of ...が足りなくなる ...ga tarínakunarù

to stop short (while walking etc) 急に立ち止まる kyū ni tachidomarù; (while doing something) 急にやめる kyū ni yamerù

to stop short of ...まではしない ...mádè wa shináì

shortage [ʃɔːrˈtidʒ] *n*: *a shortage of* ...不足 ...busóku

shortbread [ʃɔːrtˈbred] *n* ショートブレッド ♢小麦粉，バター，砂糖で作った菓子 komúgiko, bátà, sató dè tsukútta kashì

short-change [ʃɔːrtˈtʃeindʒ] *vt* ...に釣銭を少なく渡す ...ni tsurísen wò sukúnakù watásù

short-circuit [ʃɔːrtsəːrˈkit] *n* (ELEC) ショート shóto

shortcoming [ʃɔːrtˈkʌmiŋ] *n* 欠点 kettéñ

short(crust) pastry [ʃɔːrt(ˈkrʌst)-] *(BRIT)* *n* パイ生地 páikijì

shortcut [ʃɔːrtˈkʌt] *n* 近道 chikámichi

shorten [ʃɔːrˈtən] *vt* (clothes, visit) 短くする mijíkakù suru

shortfall [ʃɔːrtˈfɔːl] *n* 不足 fusóku

shorthand [ʃɔːrtˈhænd] *n* 速記 sokkí

shorthand typist *(BRIT)* *n* 速記もできるタイピスト sokkí mo dekirù taípisùto

shortlist [ʃɔːrtˈlist] *(BRIT)* *n* (for job) 予備審査の合格者リスト yobíshiñsa no gókakusha risùto

short-lived [ʃɔːrtˈlivd] *adj* つかの間の tsuká no ma no

shortly [ʃɔːrtˈliː] *adv* 間もなく ma mó nàku

shorts [ʃɔːrts] *npl*: *(a pair of) shorts* (short trousers) 半ズボン hañzùbon; (men's underwear) パンツ páñtsu

short-sighted [ʃɔːrtˈsaiˈtid] *(BRIT)* *adj* 近眼の kiñgan no; *(fig)* 先見の明のない señken no meì no nai

short-staffed [ʃɔːrtˈstæft] *adj*: *to be short-staffed* 人手不足である hitódebùsoku de aru

short story *n* 短編小説 tañpeñshòsetsu

short-tempered [ʃɔːrtˈtempəːrd] *adj* 短気な táñki na

short-term [ʃɔːrtˈtəːrm] *adj* (effect, borrowing) 短期の táñki no

shortwave [ʃɔːrtˈweiv] *n* (RADIO) 短波 táñpa

shot [ʃɑːt] *pt, pp of* **shoot**
♦*n* (of gun) 発砲 happó; (try, *also* SOCCER etc) シュート shūto; (injection) 注射 chūsha; (PHOT) ショット shóttò

a good/poor shot (person) 射撃のうまい〔下手な〕人 shagéki no umaì〔hetà na〕hitó

like a shot (without any delay) 鉄砲玉の様に teppódama no yò ni

shotgun [ʃɑːtˈgʌn] *n* 散弾銃 sañdañjū

should [ʃud] *aux vb*: *I should go now* もうおいとましなくては mő o-ítoma shinákute wà

he should be there now 彼は今あそこにいるはずです kárè wa ímà asóko nì irú hazù desu

I should go if I were you 私だったら，行きますよ watákushi dattàra, ikímasù yó

I should like to ...をしたいと思いますが ...wo shitái tò omóimasù ga

shoulder [souˈldəːr] *n* (ANAT) 肩 kátà
♦*vt* (*fig*: responsibility, blame) 負う óù

shoulder bag *n* ショルダーバッグ shorúdābaggù

shoulder blade *n* 肩甲骨 keñkókotsu

shoulder strap *n* ショルダーストラップ shorúdasutorappù

shouldn't [ʃudˈənt] = **should not**

shout [ʃaut] *n* 叫び声 sakébigoè
♦*vt* 大声で言う őgoè de iú
♦*vi* (*also*: **shout out**) 叫ぶ sakébù

shout down *vt* (speaker) どなって黙らせる donátte damáraserù

shouting [ʃaut'iŋ] n 叫び声 sakébigoè

shove [ʃʌv] vt 押す osú; (inf: put): **to shove something in** ...を...に押込む ...wo...ni oshíkomù

shovel [ʃʌv'əl] n (gen) スコップ sukóppù, シャベル shábèru; (mechanical) パワーシャベル pawáshabèru
♦vt (snow) かく kákù; (coal, earth) すくう sukúù

shove off vi: **shove off!** (inf) うせろ uséro

show [ʃou] n (demonstration: of emotion) 表現 hyṓgen; (semblance) 見せ掛け misékake; (exhibition: flower show etc) 展示会 teñjikài, ショー shṓ; (THEATER, TV) ショー shṓ
♦vb (pt **showed**, pp **shown**)
♦vt (indicate) 示す shimésù, 見せる misérù; (exhibit) 展示する teñji suru; (courage etc) 示す shimésù; (illustrate, depict) 描写する byṓsha suru; (film: in movie theater) 上映する jṓei suru; (program, film: on television) 放送する hṓsō suru
♦vi (be evident) 見える miérù; (appear) 現れる aráwarerù
for show 格好だけの kakkṓ dake no
on show (exhibits etc) 展示中 teñjichū

show business n 芸能界 geínōkài

showdown [ʃou'daun] n 対決 taíketsu

shower [ʃau'əːr] n (of rain) にわか雨 niwákaamè; (of stones etc) ...の雨 ...no áme; (for bathing in) シャワー sháwà
♦vi 降ってくる futté kurù
♦vt: **to shower someone with** ...の上に...を降らす ...no ué nì...wo furásù
to have a shower シャワーを浴びる sháwà wo abírù

showerproof [ʃau'əːrpruːf] adj 防水の bṓsui no ◇にわか雨程度なら耐えられるが強い雨にはぬれてしまうコートなどについて言う niwákaamè teído nara taérarerù ga tsuyói amè ni wa nuréteshimau kṓto nado ni tsúite iú

show in vt (person) 中へ案内する nákà e añnai suru

showing [ʃou'iŋ] n (of film) 上映 jṓei

show jumping [-dʒʌmp'iŋ] n (of horses) 障害飛越 shṓgaihìetsu

shown [ʃoun] pp of **show**

show off vi (pej) 気取る kidóru
♦vt (display) 見せびらかす misébirakasù

show-off [ʃou'ɔːf] (inf) n (person) 自慢屋 jimáñ-ya

show out vt (person) 出口へ案内する dégùchi e añnai suru

showpiece [ʃou'piːs] n (of exhibition etc) 立派な見本 rippá nà mihón

showroom [ʃou'ruːm] n ショールーム shṓrūmu

show up vi (stand out) 目立つ medátsù; (inf: turn up) 現れる aráwarerù
♦vt (uncover: imperfections etc) 暴露する bákùro suru

shrank [ʃræŋk] pt of **shrink**

shrapnel [ʃræp'nəl] n 弾丸の破片 dañgan nò hahén

shred [ʃred] n (gen pl) 切れ端 kiréhashi
♦vt (gen) ずたずたにする zutázuta ni surù; (CULIN) 刻む kizámù

shredder [ʃred'əːr] n (vegetable shredder) 削り器 kezúrikì; (document shredder) シュレッダー shurédḍà

shrewd [ʃruːd] adj (businessman) 抜け目のない nukéme no naì; (assessment) 賢明な keñmei na

shriek [ʃriːk] n 金切り声 kanákirigoè
♦vi 金切り声を出す kanákirigoè wo dásù

shrill [ʃril] adj (cry, voice) 甲高い kañdakaì

shrimp [ʃrimp] n (shellfish) えび ebí

shrine [ʃrain] n (place of worship) 礼拝堂 reíhaidō; (for relics) 聖遺物容器 seíbutsuyōki; (fig: building) 殿堂 deñdō; (: place) 聖地 seíchi

shrink [ʃriŋk] (pt **shrank**, pp **shrunk**) vi (cloth) 縮む chijímù; (be reduced: profits, audiences) 減る herú; (move: also: **shrink away**) 縮こまって逃げる chijíkomattè nigérù
♦vt (cloth) 縮める chijímerù
♦n (inf: pej: psychiatrist) 精神科医 seíshinka-ì
to shrink from (doing) something ...を(するのを)いやがる ...wo (surú no wò) iyágarù

shrinkage [ʃriŋk'idʒ] *n* 縮まる分 chijímarù bún

shrinkwrap [ʃriŋk'ræp] *vt* ラップで包む ráppù de tsutsúmù

shrivel [ʃriv'əl] (*also*: **shrivel up**) *vt* しおれさせる shióresaserù

♦*vi* しおれる shiórerù

shroud [ʃraud] *n* 覆い ōí

♦*vt*: **shrouded in mystery** なぞに包まれて nazó nì tsutsúmaretè

Shrove Tuesday [ʃrouv-] *n* 謝肉祭の火曜日 shaníkusaì no kayóbi

shrub [ʃrʌb] *n* 低木 teíboku

shrubbery [ʃrʌb'əːri:] *n* 植込み uékomi

shrug [ʃrʌg] *n* 肩をすくめる事 kátà wo sukúmerù kotó

♦*vt, vi*: **to shrug (one's shoulders)** 肩をすくめる kátà wo sukúmerù

shrug off *vt* (criticism) 受流す ukénagasù; (illness) 無視する múshì suru

shrunk [ʃrʌŋk] *pp of* shrink

shudder [ʃʌd'əːr] *n* 身震い mibúrùi

♦*vi* (person: with fear, revulsion) 身震いする mibúrùi suru

shuffle [ʃʌf'əl] *vt* (cards) 混ぜる mazérù

♦*vt* (walk) 足を引きずって歩く ashí wò hikízuttè arukú

to shuffle (one's feet) (while standing, sitting) 足をもぞもぞ動かす ashí wò mózòmozo ugókasù

shun [ʃʌn] *vt* (publicity, neighbors etc) 避ける sakérù

shunt [ʃʌnt] *vt* (train) 分岐線に入れる buńkisen ni irerù; (object) 動かす ugókasù

shut [ʃʌt] (*pt, pp* **shut**) *vt* (door) 閉める shimérù; (shop) しまう shimáù; (mouth, eyes) 閉じる tojírù

♦*vi* (door, eyes, shop) 閉る shimárù

shut down *vt* (for a time) 休業させる kyúgyō saserù; (forever) 閉鎖する heísa suru

♦*vi* (for a time) 休業する kyúgyō surù; (forever) 閉鎖になる heísa ni narù

shut off *vt* (supply etc) 遮断する shadán suru

shutter [ʃʌt'əːr] *n* (on window: *also* PHOT) シャッター sháttà

shuttle [ʃʌt'əl] *n* (plane etc) シャトル

shátòru; (*also*: **space shuttle**) スペースシャトル supésushatòru; (*also*: **shuttle service**) 折り返し運転 oríkaeshi uñten

shuttlecock [ʃʌt'əlkɑːk] *n* シャットルコック shattórukokkù

shut up *vi* (*inf*: keep quiet) 黙る damárù

♦*vt* (close) しまう shimau; (silence) 黙らせる damáraserù

shy [ʃai] *adj* (timid: animal) 臆病な okúbyō na; (reserved) 内気な uchíki na

shyness [ʃai'nis] *n* (timidity: of animal) 臆病 okúbyō; (reservedness) 内気 uchíki na

Siamese [saiəmiːz'] *adj*: **Siamese cat** シャムネコ shamúneko

Siberia [saibi:'ri:ə] *n* シベリア shibéria

sibling [sib'liŋ] *n* 兄弟 kyódai ◇男兄弟にも女兄弟（姉妹）にも使う otókokyōdai ni mo onnákyōdai (shímài) ni mo tsukáù

Sicily [sis'ili:] *n* シチリア shichíria

sick [sik] *adj* (ill) 病気の byóki no; (nauseated) むかついた mukátsuita; (humor) 病的な byóteki na; (vomiting):

to be sick 吐く hákù

to feel sick むかつく mukátsukù

to be sick of (*fig*) ...にうんざりしている ...ni uñzari shite irú

sick bay *n* (on ship) 医務室 imúshitsu

sicken [sik'ən] *vt* むかつかせる mukátsukaserù

sickening [sik'əniŋ] *adj* (*fig*) 不快な fukái na

sickle [sik'əl] *n* かま kámà

sick leave *n* 病気休暇 byókikyūka

sickly [sik'li:] *adj* (child, plant) 病気がちな byókigachi na; (causing nausea: smell) むかつかせる mukátsukaserù

sickness [sik'nis] *n* (illness) 病気 byóki; (vomiting) おう吐 óto

sick pay *n* 病気手当 byókiteàte

side [said] *n* (of object) 横 yokó; (of body) 脇腹 wakíbara; (of lake) 岸 kishí; (aspect) 側面 sokúmen; (team) 側 gawá

♦*adj* (door, entrance) 横の yokó no

♦*vi*: **to side with someone** ...の肩を持つ ...no kátà wo mótsù

the side of the road 路肩 rokáta

the side of a hill 山腹 sañpuku

by the side of ...の横に ...no yokó ni

side by side 横に並んで yokó ni naráñde

from side to side 左右に sáyū ni

from all sides 四方八方から shihôhappô kara

to take sides (with) (...に)味方する (...ni) mikáta suru

sideboard [said'bɔ:rd] *n* 食器戸棚 shokkítodāna, サイドボード saídobōdo

sideboards [said'bɔ:rdz] (*BRIT*) *npl* = **sideburns**

sideburns [said'bə:rnz] *npl* もみあげ momîage

side drum *n* (*MUS*) 小太鼓 kodáīko

side effect *n* (*MED, fig*) 副作用 fukúsayō

sidelight [said'lait] *n* (*AUT*) 車幅灯 shafúkutō

sideline [said'lain] *n* (*SPORT*) サイドライン saídorain; (*fig*: supplementary job) 副業 fukúgyō

sidelong [said'lɔ:ŋ] *adj*: *to give someone/something a sidelong glance* ...を横目で見る ...wo yokóme de mirù

sidesaddle [said'sædəl] *adv*: *to ride sidesaddle* 馬に横乗りする umá nì yokónori surù

side show *n* (stall at fair, circus) 見世物屋台 misémonoyatâi

sidestep [said'step] *vt* (*fig*) 避けて通る sakétetorù

side street *n* わき道 wakímichi

sidetrack [said'træk] *vt* (*fig*) ...の話を脱線させる ...no hanáshi wo dassén saserù

sidewalk [said'wɔ:k] (*US*) *n* 歩道 hodô

sideways [said'weiz] *adv* (go in) 横向きに yokómuki ni; (lean) 横へ yokó e

siding [sai'diŋ] *n* (*RAIL*) 側線 sokúsen

sidle [sai'dəl] *vi*: *to sidle up (to)* (...に) こっそり近寄る (...ni) kossórì chikáyorù

siege [si:dʒ] *n* (*gen, MIL*) 包囲 hôi

siesta [si:es'tə] *n* 昼寝 hirúne

sieve [siv] *n* ふるい furúi

♦*vt* ふるう furúu

sift [sift] *vt* (*fig*: *also*: **sift through**: information) ふるい分ける furúiwakerù; (sieve) ふるう furúu

sigh [sai] *n* ため息 taméikì

♦*vi* ため息をつく taméikì wo tsukú

sight [sait] *n* (faculty) 視覚 shikáku; (spectacle) 光景 kôkei; (on gun) 照準器 shôjunki

♦*vt* 見掛ける mikákerù

in sight 見える所に mierù tokórò ni

on sight (shoot) 見付け次第 mitsúkeshidài

out of sight 見えない所に mienaí tokórò ni

sightseeing [sait'si:iŋ] *n* 名所見物 meíshokenbutsu

to go sightseeing 名所見物に行く meíshokenbutsu ni ikú

sign [sain] *n* (with hand) 合図 áizu; (indication: of present condition) しるし shirúshi; (: of future condition) 兆し kizáshi; (notice) 看板 kañban; (written) 張り紙 harígami

♦*vt* (document) ...に署名〔サイン〕する ...ni shoméi〔sáin〕suru; (player) 雇う yatôu

to sign something over to someone ...を...に譲渡する ...wo...ni jôtò suru

signal [sig'nəl] *n* (*gen*) 信号 shiñgō; (equipment on highway, railway) 信号機 shiñgōki

♦*vi* (make signs: *also AUT*) 合図をする áizu wo suru

♦*vt* (person) ...に合図をする ...ni áizu wo suru; (message) ...する様に合図をする ...suru yô ni aizu wo suru

signalman [sig'nəlmən] (*pl* **signalmen**) *n* (*RAIL*) 信号手 shiñgōshu

signature [sig'nətʃər] *n* 署名 shoméi, サイン sáin

signature tune *n* テーマ音楽 têmaoñgaku

signet ring [sig'nit-] *n* 印章指輪 iñshōyubiwà

significance [signif'əkəns] *n* (importance) 重要性 jûyōsei

significant [signif'ikənt] *adj* (full of meaning: look, smile) 意味深い imíbukài; (important: amount, discovery) 重要な jûyō na

signify [sig'nəfai] *vt* 意味する ímì suru

sign language *n* 手話 shúwà

sign on *vi* (MIL) 入隊する nyū́tai surù; (*BRIT*: as unemployed) 失業手当を請求する shitsúgyōteàte wo seíkyū suru; (for course) 受講手続をする jukṓtetsuzuki wo suru

♦*vt* (MIL: recruits) 入隊させる nyū́tai saserù; (employee) 雇う yatóù

signpost [sain'poust] *n* 案内標識 añnai-hyṓshiki

sign up *vi* (MIL) 入隊する nyū́tai suru; (for course) 受講手続をする jukṓtetsuzuki wo suru

silence [sai'ləns] *n* (of person) 沈黙 chi-ńmoku; (of place) 静けさ shizúkesà

♦*vt* (person, opposition) 黙らせる damá-raserù

silencer [sai'lənsər] *n* (on gun) 消音器 shōóñki, サイレンサー saíreñsà; (*BRIT*: AUT) 消音器 shōóñki, マフラー máfūrà

silent [sai'lənt] *adj* (person) 黙っている damátte irù; (place) しんとした shíñto shitá; (machine) 音のない otő no naì; (film) 無声の muséi no

to remain silent 黙っている damátte irù

silent prayer 黙とう mokútō

silent partner *n* (COMM) 出資者 shus-shíshà ◇資本金の一部を出すが，業務に直接関与しない社員について言う shihóñ-kin no ichíbù wo dásù ga, győmù ni chokúsetsu kañyo shináì shá-iñ ni tsuite iú

silhouette [silu:et'] *n* シルエット shírù-etto

silicon chip [sil'ikən-] *n* シリコンチップ shírikonchippù

silk [silk] *n* 絹 kínù

♦*adj* (scarf, shirt) 絹の kínù no

silky [sil'ki:] *adj* (material, skin) 絹の様な kínù no yő nà

silly [sil'i:] *adj* (person, idea) ばかな bákà na

silo [sai'lou] *n* (on farm, for missile) サイロ sáĩro

silt [silt] *n* (in harbor, river etc) 沈泥 chiń-dei

silver [sil'vər] *n* (metal) 銀 gíñ; (coins) 硬貨 kőkà; (items made of silver) 銀製品 gińseîhin

♦*adj* (color) 銀色の giń-iro no; (made of silver) 銀の gíñ no

silver paper (*BRIT*) *n* 銀紙 gíñgami

silver-plated [sil'və:rplei'tid] *adj* 銀めっきの giñmekkî no

silversmith [sil'və:rsmiθ] *n* 銀細工師 giń-zaikushī

silvery [sil'və:ri:] *adj* (like silver) 銀の様な gíñ no yő nà

similar [sim'ələr] *adj*: **similar (to)** (...に) 似た (...ni) nitá

similarity [siməlær'iti:] *n* 似ている事 ni-té irù kotő

similarly [sim'ələ:rli:] *adv* 同じ様に oná-ji yő ni

simile [sim'əli:] *n* 例え tatőè

simmer [sim'ə:r] *vi* (CULIN) ぐつぐつ煮える gútsùgutsu niérù

simpering [sim'pə:riŋ] *adj* (person) ばかみたいな作り笑いをする bákàmitai na tsukúriwarài wo suru

a simpering smile ばかみたいな作り笑い bákàmitai na tsukúriwarài

simple [sim'pəl] *adj* (easy) 簡単な kañtan na; (plain: dress, life) 素朴な sobóku na, シンプルな shíñpuru na; (foolish) ばかな bákà na; (COMM: interest) 単純な tañ-jun na

simplicity [simplis'əti:] *n* (ease) 簡単さ kañtansa; (plainness) 素朴さ sobőkusa; (foolishness) 白痴 hakuchi

simplify [sim'pləfai] *vt* 簡単にする kañ-tan ni surù

simply [sim'pli:] *adv* (in a simple way: live) 素朴に sobóku ni; (talk) 平易に hêíi ni; (just, merely) 単に táñ ni

simulate [sim'jəleit] *vt* (enthusiasm, innocence) 装う yosóoù

simulated [sim'jəleitid] *adj* (hair, fur) 偽の nisé no, 人工の jiñkō no; (nuclear explosion) 模擬の mógĩ no

simultaneous [saiməltei'ni:əs] *adj* (translation, broadcast) 同時の dőji no

simultaneously [saiməltei'ni:əsli:] *adv* 同時に dőji ni

sin [sin] *n* 罪 tsúmì

♦*vi* 罪を犯す tsúmì wo okásù

since [sins] *adv* それ以来 soré irái
♦*prep* ...以来 ...írài
♦*conj* (time) ...して以来 ...shité irái;
(because) ...ので ...nódè
since then, ever since それ以来 soré irái

sincere [sinsi:r] *adj* 誠実な seíjitsu na

sincerely [sinsi:r'li:] *adv*: *yours sincerely* (in letters) 敬具 keígu

sincerity [sinse:r'iti:] *n* 誠実さ seíjitsusa

sinew [sin'ju:] *n* (of person, animal) けん kéñ, 筋 sújì

sinful [sin'fəl] *adj* (thought, person) 罪深い tsumíbukaì

sing [siŋ] (*pt* **sang**, *pp* **sung**) *vt* 歌う utáù
♦*vi* (*gen*) 歌う utáù; (bird) 鳴く nakú

Singapore [siŋ'gəpɔːr] *n* シンガポール shíñgapòru

singe [sindʒ] *vt* 焦がす kogásù

singer [sin'əːr] *n* 歌手 káshù

singing [sin'iŋ] *n* (noise: of people) 歌声 utágoè; (: of birds) 鳴声 nakígoè; (art) 声楽 seígaku

single [sin'gəl] *adj* (individual) 一つ一つの hitótsuhitotsu no; (unmarried) 独身の dokúshin no; (not double) 一つだけの hitótsu dake nò
♦*n* (*BRIT*: *also*: **single ticket**) 片道乗車券 katámichijōshakèn; (record) シングル盤 shíñguruban

single-breasted [sin'gəlbres'tid] *adj* (jacket, suit) シングルの shíñguru no

single file *n*: *in single file* 一列縦隊で ichíretsujūtai de

single-handed [sin'gəlhæn'did] *adv* (sail, build something) 一人で hitóri de

single-minded [sin'gəlmain'did] *adj* 一つだけの目的を追う hitótsu dake nò mokúteki wò oú

single out *vt* (choose) 選び出す erábidasù; (distinguish) 区別する kúbetsu suru

single room *n* シングル部屋 shíñgurubeya

singles [sin'gəlz] *n* (TENNIS) シングルス shíñgurusu

singly [sin'gli:] *adv* (alone, one by one: people) 一人ずつ hitóri zutsu; (: things) 一つずつ hitótsu zutsu

singular [sin'gjələːr] *adj* (odd: occurrence) 変った kawátta; (outstanding: beauty) 著しい ichíjirushiì; (LING) 単数の tañsū no
♦*n* (LING) 単数 tañsū

sinister [sin'istəːr] *adj* 怪しげな ayáshige na

sink [siŋk] *n* 流し nagáshi
♦*vb* (*pt* **sank**, *pp* **sunk**)
♦*vt* (ship) 沈没させる chíñbotsu saserù; (well, foundations) 掘る hórù
♦*vi* (ship) 沈没する chíñbotsu suru; (heart, spirits) しょげる shogérù, がっかりする gakkárì suru; (ground) 沈下する chíñka suru; (*also*: **sink back**, **sink down**: into chair) 身を沈める mí wò shizúmerù; (: to one's knees etc) しゃがみ込む shágamikomù; (: head etc) うなだれる unádarerù
to sink something into (teeth, claws etc) ...に...を食込ませる ...ni...wo kuíkomaserù

sink in *vi* (*fig*: words) 理解される ríkài sarérù, 身にしみる mí nì shimírù

sinner [sin'əːr] *n* 罪人 tsumíbìto

sinus [sai'nəs] *n* (ANAT) 副鼻こう fukúbikò

sip [sip] *n* 一口 hitókùchi
♦*vt* ちびりちびり飲む chibírichibiri nómù

siphon [sai'fən] *n* サイホン sáíhon

siphon off *vt* (liquid) サイホンで汲み出す sáíhon de kumídasù; (money etc) ほかへ回す hoká è mawásù

sir [səːr] *n* ◇男性に対する丁寧な呼び掛け。日本語では表現しない dañsei ni taí surù teínei na yobíkake. nihóngo de wa hyṓgen shinaì
Sir John Smith ジョン・スミス卿 jóñ sumísukyō
yes sir はい háì

siren [sai'rən] *n* サイレン sáíren

sirloin [səːr'lɔin] *n* (*also*: **sirloin steak**) サーロインステーキ sāroinsutēki

sissy [sis'i:] (*inf*) *n* 弱虫 yowámushi

sister [sis'təːr] *n* (relation: *gen*) 女きょうだい ofínakyōdai, 姉妹 shímài; (*also*: **older sister**) 姉 ané, 姉さん nēēsan; (*also*:

younger sister) 妹 imóto; (nun) 修道女 shúdōjo; (BRIT: nurse) 婦長 fuchō

sister-in-law [sis'tə:rinlɔ:] n (pl **sisters-in-law)** n (older) 義理の姉 girí nð ané; (younger) 義理の妹 girí nð imóto

sit [sit] (pt, pp **sat**) vi (sit down) 座る suwárù, 腰掛ける koshíkakerù; (be sitting) 座っている suwátte irù, 腰掛けている koshíkakete irù; (assembly) 会期中である kaíkichū de arù; (for painter) モデルになる módèru ni nárù

♦vt (exam) 受ける ukérù

sitcom [sit'kɑ:m] n abbr (= situation comedy) 連続放送コメディー reñzoku hōsōkomèdī

sit down vi 座る suwárù, 腰掛ける ko-shíkakerù

site [sait] n (place) 場所 bashó; (also: **building site)** 用地 yóchi

♦vt (factory, cruise missiles) 置く ókù

sit-in [sit'in] n (demonstration) 座り込み suwárikomi

sit in on vt fus (meeting) 傍聴する bố-chō suru

sitting [sit'iŋ] n (of assembly etc) 開会 kaíkai; (in canteen) 食事の時間 shokúji nð jikan

we have two sittings for lunch 昼食は2交代で出されます chúshoku wà nikôtài de dasáremasù

sitting room n 居間 imá

situated [sitʃ'u:eitid] adj ...にある ...ni árù

situation [sitʃu:ei'ʃən] n (state) 状況 jố-kyō; (job) 職業 shokú; (location) 立地条件 ritchíjōken

「**situations vacant**」 (BRIT) 求人 kyújin ◇新聞などの求人欄のタイトル shiñ-bun nadð no kyújiñrañ no táìtoru

sit up vi (after lying) 上体を起す jốtai wð okósù; (straight) きちんと座る kichíñto suwárù; (not go to bed) 起きている ókìte irú

six [siks] num 六 (の) rokú (no), 六つ (の) múttsù (no)

sixteen [siks'ti:n'] num 十六 (の) júroku (no)

sixth [siksθ] num 第六(の) daí roku (no)

sixty [siks'ti:] num 六十 (の) rokújū (no)

size [saiz] n (gen) 大きさ ốkisa; (extent: of project etc) 規模 kíbò; (of clothing, shoes) サイズ sáìzu; (glue) サイズ sáìzu ◇紙のにじみ止め kamí nð nijímidome

sizeable [sai'zəbəl] adj (crowd, income etc) かなり大きい kánàri ốkiì

size up vt (person, situation) 判断する hañdan suru

sizzle [siz'əl] vi (sausages etc) じゅうじ ゅうと音を立てる jújù to otó wð tatérù

skate [skeit] n (ice skate) スケート sukḗ-tð; (roller skate) ローラースケート rốrā-sukèto; (fish) エイ éì

♦vi スケートをする sukḗto wo suru

skateboard [skeit'bɔ:rd] n スケートボー ド sukḗtobòdo

skater [skei'tə:r] n スケートをする人 su-kḗto wo suru hito, スケーター sukḗtà

skating [skei'tiŋ] n (SPORT) スケート sukḗtð

skating rink n スケートリンク sukḗto-riñku

skeleton [skel'itən] n (bones) がい骨 gáì-kotsu; (TECH: framework) 骨組 honé-gumi; (outline) 骨子 kósshì

skeleton staff n 最小限度の人員 saí-shōgeñdo no jiń-in

skeptic [skep'tik] (US) n 疑い深い人 utá-gaibukaì hitó

skeptical [skep'tikəl] (US) adj 疑ってい る utagátte irù, 信用しない shiñ-yō shi-naì

skepticism [skep'tisizəm] (US) n 疑問 gimón

sketch [sketʃ] n (drawing) スケッチ su-kḗtchì; (outline) 骨子 kósshì; (THEA-TER, TV) 寸劇 suñgeki, スキット sukít-tð

♦vt スケッチする sukḗtchì suru; (also: **sketch out**: ideas) ...のあらましを言う ...no arámashi wð iú

sketchbook [sketʃ'buk] n スケッチブッ ク sukḗtchibukkù

sketchy [sketʃ'i:] adj (coverage, notes etc) 大雑把な ózappà na

skewer [skju:'ə:r] n くし kushí

ski [ski:] *n* スキー sukī
♦*vi* スキーをする sukī wo surù

ski boot *n* スキー靴 sukígutsu

skid [skid] *n* (AUT) スリップ suríppù
♦*vi* (*gen*, AUT) スリップする suríppù suru

skier [ski:'ə:r] *n* スキーヤー sukīyà

skiing [ski:'iŋ] *n* スキー sukī

ski jump *n* スキージャンプ sukījañpu

skilful [skil'fəl] (*BRIT*) *adj* = **skillful**

ski lift *n* スキーリフト sukírifùto

skill [skil] *n* (ability, dexterity) 熟練 jukúreñ; (work requiring training: computer skill etc) 技術 gíjùtsu

skilled [skild] *adj* (able) 上手な jōzu na; (worker) 熟練の jukúreñ no

skillful [skil'fəl] (*BRIT*: **skilful**) *adj* 上手な jōzu na

skim [skim] *vt* (milk) ...の上澄みをすくい取る ...no uwázumi wò sukúitorù; (glide over) ...すれすれに飛ぶ ...surésure nì tobú
♦*vi*: **to skim through** (book) ...をざっと読む ...wo záttò yómù

skimmed milk [skimd-] *n* 脱脂乳 dasshínyū

skimp [skimp] *vt* (*also*: **skimp on**: work) いいかげんにする iíkagen nì suru; (: cloth etc) けちる kechírù

skimpy [skim'pi:] *adj* (meager: meal) 少な過ぎる sukúnasugirù; (too small: skirt) 短過ぎる mijíkasugirù

skin [skin] *n* (*gen*: of person, animal) 皮膚 hífù; (: of fruit) 皮 kawá; (complexion) 顔の肌 kaó nò hádà
♦*vt* (fruit etc) ...の皮をむく ...no kawá wò múkù; (animal) ...の皮を剥ぐ ...no kawá wò hágù

skin-deep [skin'di:p'] *adj* (superficial) 表面だけの hyṓmeñ daké no

skin-diving [skin'daiviŋ] *n* スキンダイビング sukíndaìbingu

skinny [skin'i:] *adj* (person) やせた yasétà

skintight [skin'tait] *adj* (jeans etc) 体にぴったりの karáda nì pittárì no

skip [skip] *n* (movement) スキップ sukíppù; (*BRIT*: container) ごみ箱 gomíbàko

♦*vi* (jump) スキップする sukíppù suru; (with rope) 縄跳びする nawátobì suru
♦*vt* (pass over: boring parts) とばす tobásù; (miss: lunch) 抜く nukú; (: lecture) すっぽかす suppókasù

ski pants *npl* スキーズボン sukízubòn

ski pole *n* スキーストック sukísutokkù

skipper [skip'ə:r] *n* (NAUT) 船長 señchō; (SPORT) 主将 shushṓ, キャプテン kyápùten

skipping rope [skip'iŋ-] (*BRIT*) *n* 縄跳びの縄 nawátobi nò nawá

skirmish [skə:r'miʃ] *n* (*also* MIL) こぜりあい kozérìai

skirt [skə:rt] *n* スカート sukátò
♦*vt* (*fig*: go round) 避けて通る sákète tṓrù

skirting board [skə:r'tiŋ-] (*BRIT*) *n* 幅木 habáki

ski slope *n* ゲレンデ geréñde

ski suit *n* スキー服 sukífùku

skit [skit] *n* スキット sukíttò

skittle [skit'əl] *n* スキットルのピン sukíttòru no píñ

skittles [skit'əlz] *n* (game) スキットル sukíttòru ◇9本のピンを木のボールで倒すボーリングに似た遊び kyūhòn no píñ wo kí no bōru de taosu bōringu ni nita asobī

skive [skaiv] (*BRIT*: *inf*) *vi* サボる sabórù

skulk [skʌlk] *vi* うろつく urótsukù

skull [skʌl] *n* (ANAT) 頭がい骨 zugáìkotsu

skunk [skʌŋk] *n* (animal) スカンク sukáñku

sky [skai] *n* 空 sórà

skylight [skai'lait] *n* 天窓 teñmado

skyscraper [skai'skreipə:r] *n* 摩天楼 matéñrō

slab [slæb] *n* (stone) 石板 sekíban; (of cake, cheese) 厚い一切れ atsúì hitokìre

slack [slæk] *adj* (loose: rope, trousers etc) たるんでいる tarúnde irù; (slow: period) 忙しくない isógashikunaì; (careless: security, discipline) いい加減な iíkagen na

slacken [slæk'ən] (*also*: **slacken off**) *vi*

(demand) 減る herú; (speed) 落ちる ochírù

♦vt (trousers) 緩める yurúmeru; (speed) 緩める yurúmerù, 落す otósù

slacks [slæks] npl ズボン zubóñ, スラックス surákkùsu

slag heap [slæg-] n ぼた山 botáyama

slag off (BRIT: inf) vt (criticize) ...の悪口を言う ...no warúgùchi wo iú

slain [slein] pp of **slay**

slalom [slɑ:'ləm] n 回転競技 kaítenkyògi, スラローム surárōmu

slam [slæm] vt (door) ばたんと閉める batáñ to shimérù; (throw) 投付ける nagétsukerù; (criticize) 非難する hínàn suru

♦vi (door) ばたんと閉まる batáñ to shimárù

slander [slæn'də:r] n 中傷 chúshō

slang [slæŋ] n (informal language) 俗語 zokúgo, スラング suráñgu; (jargon: prison slang etc) 符丁 fuchó

slant [slænt] n (sloping: position) 傾斜 keísha; (fig: approach) 見方 mikáta

slanted [slæn'tid] adj (roof) 傾斜のある keísha no aru; (eyes) つり上った tsuríagattà

slanting [slæn'tiŋ] adj = **slanted**

slap [slæp] n (hit) 平手打ち hiráteuchi, びんた bíñta

♦vt (child, face) ぴしゃりと打つ pishárì to útsù

♦adv (directly) まともに matómo nì

to slap something on something (paint etc) ...を...にいい加減に塗り付ける ...wo ...ni ikágen nì nurítsukerù

slapdash [slæp'dæʃ] adj (person, work) いい加減な ikágen na

slapstick [slæp'stik] n (comedy) どたばた喜劇 dotábata kigèki

slap-up [slæp'ʌp] adj: *a slap-up meal* (BRIT) 御馳走 gochísō

slash [slæʃ] vt (cut: upholstery, wrists etc) 切る kírù ◊特に長くて深い切傷を付けるという意味で使う tókù ni nágakute fukái kiríkìzu wo tsukérù to iú imì de tsukáù; (fig: prices) 下げる sagérù

slat [slæt] n (of wood, plastic) 板 ítà ◊百葉箱に使われる様な薄くて細い板を指す

hyakúyōbàko ni tsukáwareru yò na usúkùte hosóî ítà wo sásù

slate [sleit] n (material) 粘板岩 neñbangan; (piece: for roof) スレート surétò

♦vt (fig: criticize) けなす kenásù

slaughter [slɔ:'tə:r] n (of animals) と殺 tosátsu; (of people) 虐殺 gyakúsatsu

♦vt (animals) と殺する tosátsu suru; (people) 虐殺する gyakúsatsu suru

slaughterhouse [slɔ:'tə:rhaus] n と殺場 tosátsujō

Slav [slɑ:v] adj スラブ民族の surábumiñzoku no

slave [sleiv] n 奴隷 doréi

♦vi (also: **slave away**) あくせく働く ákùseku határakù

slavery [slei'və:ri:] n (system) 奴隷制度 doréiseìdo; (condition) 奴隷の身分 doréi no míbùn

slavish [slei'viʃ] adj (obedience) 卑屈な hikútsu na; (copy) 盲目的な mómokuteki na

slay [slei] (pt **slew**, pp **slain**) vt 殺す korósù

sleazy [sli:'zi:] adj (place) 薄汚い usúgitanaî

sledge [sledʒ] n そり sóri

sledgehammer [sledʒ'hæmə:r] n 大づち ōzúchi

sleek [sli:k] adj (shiny, smooth: hair, fur etc) つやつやの tsuyátsuyà no; (car, boat etc) 優雅な yūga na

sleep [sli:p] n 睡眠 suímin

♦vi (pt, pp **slept**) (gen) 眠る nemúrù, 寝る nerú; (spend night) 泊る tomárù

to go to sleep (person) 眠る nemúrù, 寝る neru

sleep around vi 色々な人とセックスをする iróiro na hito tò sékkùsu wo suru

sleeper [sli:'pə:r] (BRIT) n (RAIL: on track) まくら木 makúragi; (: train) 寝台列車 shíndairesshà

sleep in vi (oversleep) 寝坊する nebó suru

sleeping bag [sli:'piŋ-] n 寝袋 nebúkùro

sleeping car n (RAIL) 寝台車 shíndaishà

sleeping partner (BRIT) n (COMM)

= **silent partner**

sleeping pill n 睡眠薬 suímiñ-yaku

sleepless [sli:p'lis] adj: *a sleepless night* 眠れない夜 nemúrenai yorù

sleepwalker [sli:p'wɔːkər] n 夢遊病者 muyűbyōshà

sleepy [sli:'pi:] adj (person) 眠い nemúi; (fig: village etc) ひっそりとした hissórì to shita

sleet [sli:t] n みぞれ mizóre

sleeve [sli:v] n (of jacket etc) そで sodé; (of record) ジャケット jákètto

sleeveless [sli:v'lis] adj (garment) そでなしの sodénashi no, スリーブレスの suríburèsu no

sleigh [slei] n そり sórì

sleight [slait] n: *sleight of hand* 奇術 kíjùtsu

slender [slen'dəːr] adj (slim: figure) ほっそりした hossórì shita, スリムな súrìmu na; (small: means, majority) わずかな wázùka na

slept [slept] pt, pp of **sleep**

slew [slu:] vi (BRIT) = **slue**
♦pt of **slay**

slice [slais] n (of meat, bread, lemon) スライス suráìsu; (utensil: fish slice) フライ返し furáigaèshi; (: cake slice) ケーキサーバー kékisābā
♦vt (bread, meat etc) スライスする suráìsu suru

slick [slik] adj (skillful: performance) 鮮やかな azáyàka na; (clever: salesman, answer) 抜け目のない nukéme no naí
♦n (also: **oil slick**) 油膜 yumáku

slid [slid] pt, pp of **slide**

slide [slaid] n (downward movement) 下落 geráku; (in playground) 滑り台 subéridài; (PHOT) スライド suráìdo; (BRIT: also: **hair slide**) 髪留 kamídòme, ヘアクリップ heákurìppu
♦vb (pt, pp **slid**)
♦vt 滑らせる subéraserù
♦vi (slip) 滑る subérù; (glide) 滑る様に動く subéru yō ni ugókù

slide rule n 計算尺 kefsanjaku

sliding [slai'diŋ] adj: **sliding door** 引戸 hikídò

sliding scale n スライド制 suráidosei

slight [slait] adj (slim: figure) やせ型の yaségata no; (frail) か弱い kayőwaì; (small: increase, difference) わずかな wázùka na; (error, accent, pain etc) ちょっとした chóttò shita; (trivial) ささいな sásài na
♦n (insult) 侮辱 bujóku

not in the slightest 少しも...ない sukóshì mo ...náì

slightly [slait'li:] adv (a bit, rather) 少し sukóshì

slim [slim] adj (person, figure) ほっそりした hossórì shita; (chance) わずかな wázùka na
♦vi (lose weight) やせる yasérù

slime [slaim] n ぬるぬるした物 núrùnuru shita monő

slimming [slim'iŋ] n (losing weight) そう身 sőshin

slimy [slai'mi:] adj (pond) ぬるぬるした物に覆われた núrùnuru shita monő nì ōwaretà

sling [sliŋ] n (MED) 三角きん sañkakùkin; (for baby) 子守り帯 komóriobì; (weapon) 石投げ器 ishínagekì
♦vt (pt, pp **slung**) (throw) 投げる nagérù

slip [slip] n (while walking) 踏外し fumíhazushi; (of vehicle) スリップ suríppù; (mistake) 過ち ayámachì; (underskirt) スリップ suríppù; (also: **slip of paper**) 一枚の紙 ichímài no kamí ◇通常メモ用紙, 伝票などの様な小さい紙を指す tsújō memoyōshi, deñpyō nadð no yố nà chíísaì kamí wð sásù
♦vt (slide) こっそり...を...にやる kossórì ...wo ...ni yarú
♦vi (slide) 滑る subérù; (lose balance) 踏外す fumíhazusù; (decline) 悪くなる wárùku nárù; (move smoothly): *to slip into/out of* (room etc) そっと入る〔出て行く〕sóttò háìru〔détè iku〕

to give someone the slip ...をまく ...wo mákù

a slip of the tongue うっかり言ってしまう事 ukkárì itté shimaù kotó

to slip something on/off さっと...を着る〔脱ぐ〕sáttò ...wo kírù〔nugu〕

slip away vi (go) そっと立ち去る sóttŏ tachísaru

slip in vt (put) こっそり入れる kossórĭ irérŭ

♦vi (errors) いつの間にか入ってしまう itsú no ma ni kà haítte shimaù

slip out vi (go out) そっと出て行く sóttŏ détě ikú

slipped disc [slipt-] n つい間板ヘルニア tsuíkaňbanherunìa

slipper [slip'ɔːr] n (carpet slipper) スリッパ suríppà

slippery [slip'əːri:] adj (road) 滑りやすい subériyasuì; (fish etc) つかみにくい tsukáminikuì

slip road (BRIT) n (on motorway: access road) 入路 nyúro; (: exit road) 出口 deguchi

slipshod [slip'ʃɑːd] adj いい加減な iíkagen na

slip up vi (make mistake) 間違いをする machígai wŏ suru

slip-up [slip'ʌp] n (error) 間違い machígaì

slipway [slip'wei] n 造船台 zōsendài

slit [slit] n (cut) スリット suríttŏ; (opening) すき間 sukíma

♦vt (pt, pp slit) 切り開く kiríhirakù

slither [sliŏ'əːr] vi (person) 足を取られながら歩く ashí wŏ torárenagara arukù; (snake etc) はう háù

sliver [sliv'əːr] n (of glass, wood) 破片 hahén; (of cheese etc) 一切れ hitókìre

slob [slɑːb] (inf) n (man) だらしない野郎 daráshinai yarō; (woman) だらしないあま daráshinai áma

slog [slɑːg] (BRIT) vi (work hard) あくせく働く ákùseku határakù

♦n: **it was a hard slog** 苦労した kuró shita

slogan [slou'gən] n スローガン surōgàn

slop [slɑːp] vi (also: **slop over**) こぼれる kobórerù

♦vt こぼす kobósù

slope [sloup] n (gentle hill) 坂道 sakámĭchi; (side of mountain) 山腹 sañpuku; (ski slope) ゲレンデ gerénde; (slant) 傾斜 keísha

♦vi: **to slope down** 下り坂になる kudárizaka ni narù

slope up vi 上り坂になる nobórizaka ni narù

sloping [slou'piŋ] adj (ground, roof) 傾斜になっている keísha ni natte irù; (handwriting) 斜めの nanáme no

sloppy [slɑːp'i:] adj (work, appearance) だらしない daráshinaì

slot [slɑːt] n (in machine) 投入口 tónyūguchi, スロット suróttŏ

♦vt: **to slot something into** ... (のスロットなど) に...を入れる ... (no suróttŏ nado) ni ...wo irérŭ

sloth [slɔːθ] n (laziness) 怠惰 taída

slot machine n (BRIT: vending machine) 自動販売機 jidóhanbaikì; (for gambling) スロットマシーン suróttomashìn

slouch [slautʃ] vi (person) だらしない姿勢で...する daráshinai shiséi dè ... suru

slovenly [slʌv'ənli:] adj (dirty: habits, conditions) 汚い kitánaĭ; (careless: work) だらしない daráshinaĭ

slow [slou] adj (music, journey) ゆっくりした yukkúrĭ shita; (service) 遅い osóĭ, のろい noróĭ; (person: not clever) 物覚えの悪い monóobðe no warúĭ; (watch, clock): **to be slow** 遅れている okúrete irù

♦adv ゆっくりと yukkúrĭ to, 遅く osóku

♦vt (also: **slow down, slow up**: vehicle) ...のスピードを落す ...no supídŏ wo otósù; (: business etc) 低迷させる teímei saserù

♦vi (also: **slow down, slow up**: vehicle) スピードを落す supídŏ wo otósù; (: business etc) 下火になる shitábi nǐ narù

「**slow**」(road sign) 徐行 jokō

slowly [slou'li:] adv ゆっくりと yukkúrĭ to, 遅く osóku

slow motion n: **in slow motion** スローモーションで surōmŏshon de

sludge [slʌdʒ] n (mud) ヘどろ hedóro

slue [sluː] (US **veer**) vi スリップする suríppú suru

slug [slʌg] n (creature) なめくじ namékujì; (bullet) 弾丸 dañgan, 鉄砲玉 teppódama

sluggish [slʌg'iʃ] *adj* (stream, engine, person) 緩慢な kañman na; (COMM: trading) 不活発な fukáppatsu na

sluice [slu:s] *n* (*also*: **sluicegate**) 水門 suímon; (channel) 水路 suíro

slum [slʌm] *n* (house) 汚い家 kitánaì ié; (area) 貧民街 hiñmiñgai, スラム súràmu

slump [slʌmp] *n* (economic) 不景気 fukéìki; (COMM) スランプ suráñpu

♦*vi* (fall: person) 崩れ落ちる kuzúreochirù; (: prices) 暴落する bóraku suru

slung [slʌŋ] *pt, pp of* **sling**

slur [slə:r] *n* (*fig*): **slur (on)** (...の)悪口 (...no) warúkuchi

♦*vt* (words) 口ごもって言う kuchígomottè iú

slush [slʌʃ] *n* (melted snow) 溶けかかった雪 tokékakattà yukí

slush fund *n* 裏金用資金 uráganeyōshikiñ

slut [slʌt] (*inf!*) *n* ばいた baíta

sly [slai] *adj* (smile, expression, remark) 意味ありげな imíarige na; (person: clever, wily) ずるい zurúì

smack [smæk] *n* (slap) 平手打ち hiráteuchi; (on face) びんた bíñta

♦*vt* (hit: *gen*) 平手で打つ hiráte dè útsù; (: child) ぶつ bútsù; (: on face) ...にびんたを食らわす ...ni bíñta wo kuráwasù

♦*vi*: **to smack of** (smell of) ...くさい ...kusáì; (remind one of) ...を思わせる ...wo omówaserù

small [smɔ:l] *adj* (person, object) 小さい chíìsaì; (child: young) 幼い osánaì; (quantity, amount) 少しの sukóshì no

small ads (*BRIT*) *npl* 分類広告 buñruikōkoku

small change *n* 小銭 kozéni

small fry *npl* (unimportant people) 下っ端 shitáppa

smallholder [smɔ:l'houldə:r] (*BRIT*) *n* 小自作農 shójisakunò

small hours *npl*: **in the small hours** 深夜に shíñya ni

smallpox [smɔ:l'pɑ:ks] *n* 天然痘 teñnentō

small talk *n* 世間話 sekénbanàshi

smart [smɑ:rt] *adj* (neat, tidy) きちんとした kichíñ to shitá; (fashionable: clothes etc) しゃれた sharéta, いきな ikí na, スマートな sumáto na; (: house, restaurant) しゃれた shareta, 高級な kốkyū na; (clever) 頭がいい atáma ga iî; (quick) 早い hayáì

♦*vi* しみる shimírù; (*fig*) 悔しがる kuyáshigarù

smarten up [smɑ:r'tən-] *vi* 身なりを直す mínàri wo naósù

♦*vt* きれいにする kírèi ni suru

smash [smæʃ] *n* (collision: *also*: **smash-up**) 衝突 shốtotsu; (smash hit) 大ヒット daíhittồ

♦*vt* (break) めちゃめちゃに壊す mechámecha nì kowásù; (car etc) 衝突してめちゃめちゃにする shốtotsu shitè mechámecha ni surù; (SPORT: record) 破る yabúrù

♦*vi* (break) めちゃめちゃに壊れる mechámecha nì kowárerù; (against wall etc) 激突する gekítotsu suru

smashing [smæʃ'iŋ] (*inf*) *adj* 素晴らしい subárashiî

smattering [smæt'ə:riŋ] *n*: **a smattering of** ...をほんの少し ...wo hoñno sukoshì

smear [smi:'ə:r] *n* (trace) 染み shimí; (MED) スミア sumíà

♦*vt* (spread) 塗る nurú; (make dirty) 汚す yogósù

smear campaign *n* 中傷作戦 chûshōsakuseñ

smell [smel] *n* (odor) におい nióî; (sense) 臭覚 kyúkaku

♦*vb* (*pt, pp* **smelt** *or* **smelled**)

♦*vt* (become aware of: odor) ...のにおいがする ...no nioi ga suru; (sniff) かぐ kagú

♦*vi* (*pej*) におう nióù, 臭い kusáî; (food etc) ...においがする ...nióî ga suru

to smell of ...のにおいがする ...no nióî ga suru

smelly [smel'i:] *adj* (cheese, socks) 臭い kusáî

smile [smail] *n* ほほえみ hohóemi

♦*vi* ほほえむ hohóemù

smirk [smə:rk] n にやにや笑い niyániya warái

smithy [smiθ'i:] n 鍛冶屋の仕事場 kajíya no shigótobà

smock [sma:k] n (gen) 上っ張り uwáppari; (children's) スモック sumókkù; (US: overall) 作業着 sagyógì

smog [sma:g] n スモッグ sumóggù

smoke [smouk] n 煙 kemúri

♦vi (person) タバコを吸う tabáko wò súù; (chimney) 煙を出す kemúri wò dásù

♦vt (cigarettes) 吸う súù

smoked [smoukt] adj (bacon etc) 薫製の kuńsei no; (glass) いぶした ibúshita

smoker [smou'kə:r] n (person) タバコを吸う人 tabáko wò súù hito, 喫煙者 kitsúeñsha; (RAIL) 喫煙車 kitsúeñsha

smokescreen [smouk'skri:n] n (also fig) 煙幕 éñmaku

smoking [smou'kiŋ] n (act) 喫煙 kitsúen
「no smoking」(sign) 禁煙 kiń-en

smoky [smou'ki:] adj (atmosphere, room) 煙い kemúî; (taste) 薫製の（様な）kuńsei no (yō na)

smolder [smoul'də:r] (US) vi (fire: also fig: anger, hatred) くすぶる kusúburù

smooth [smu:ð] adj (gen) 滑らかな naméràka na; (sauce) つぶつぶのない tsubútsubu no nai; (flat: sea) 穏やかな odáyaka na; (flavor, whisky) まろやかな maróyàka na; (movement) 滑らかな naméràka na; (pej: person) 口先のうまい kuchísaki nò umáî

♦vt (also: smooth out: skirt, piece of paper etc) …のしわを伸ばす …no shiwá wò nobásù; (: creases) 伸ばす nobásù; (: difficulties) 取除く torínozokù

smother [smʌð'ə:r] vt (fire) …に…をかぶせて消す …ni …wo kabúsete kesù; (suffocate: person) 窒息させる chissóku sasérù; (repress: emotions) 抑える osáerù

smoulder [smoul'də:r] (BRIT) vi = smolder

smudge [smʌdʒ] n 汚れ yogóre

♦vt 汚す yogósù

smug [smʌg] adj 独り善がりの hitóriyogarì no

smuggle [smʌg'əl] vt (diamonds etc) 密

輸する mitsúyu suru; (refugees) 密入国させる mitsúnyūkoku sasérù

smuggler [smʌg'lə:r] n 密輸者 mitsúyushà

smuggling [smʌg'liŋ] n (traffic) 密輸 mitsúyu

smutty [smʌt'i:] adj (fig: joke, book) わいせつな waísetsu na

snack [snæk] n (light meal) 軽食 keíshoku; (food) スナック sunákkù

snack bar n スナックバー sunákkubà, スナック sunákkù

snag [snæg] n 障害 shógai

snail [sneil] n カタツムリ katátsumùri ◇一般に水生の巻貝をも指す ippán nì suísei nò makígai wo mo sásù

snake [sneik] n (gen) ヘビ hébì

snap [snæp] n (sound) ぱちっという音 pachíttò iú otò; (photograph) 写真 shashín

♦adj (decision etc) 衝動的な shódōteki na

♦vt (break) 折る órù; (fingers) 鳴らす narásù

♦vi (break) 折れる orérù; (fig: person: speak sharply) 辛らつな事を言う shiñratsu na kotò wo iú

to snap shut (trap, jaws etc) がちゃっと閉まる gachíttò shimárù

snap at vt fus (subj: dog) かみつこうとする kamítsukò to suru

snap off vi (break) 折れる orérù ◇折れて取れる場合に使う órète torérù baái nì tsukáù

snappy [snæp'i:] (inf) adj (answer, slogan) 威勢のいい iséi no iì

make it snappy (hurry up) 早くしなさい háyàku shinásaî

snapshot [snæp'ʃɑ:t] n 写真 shashín

snap up vt (bargains) すぐ買う súgù káù

snare [sne:r] n わな wánà

snarl [snɑ:rl] vi (animal) うなる unárù; (person) どなる donárù

snatch [snætʃ] n (small piece: of conversation, song etc) 断片 dañpeñ

♦vt (snatch away: handbag, child etc) ひったくる hittákurù; (fig: opportunity) 利用する riyō suru; (: look, some sleep etc)

急いでやる isóide yarù

sneak [sni:k] *(pt, pp* **sneaked** *also US* **snuck)** *vi:* **to sneak in/out** こっそり入る(出る) kossórì háiru (deru)

♦*n (inf)* 告げ口するひと tsugéguchi suru hitò

to sneak up on someone ...に忍び寄る ...ni shinóbiyorù

sneakers [sni:'kərz] *npl* 運動靴 uñdṓgutsu, スニーカー suníkā

sneer [sni:r] *vi (laugh nastily)* 冷笑する reíshō suru; *(mock):* **to sneer at** ...をあざわらう ...wo azáwaraù

sneeze [sni:z] *n* くしゃみ kushámì

♦*vi* くしゃみをする kushámì wo suru

sniff [snif] *n (sound)* 鼻をくんくん鳴らす音 haná wò kúñkun narásù otó; *(smell: by dog, person)* くんくんかぐ事 kúñkun kagú kotò

♦*vi (person: when crying etc)* 鼻をくんくん鳴らす haná wò kúñkun narásù

♦*vt (gen)* かぐ kagú; *(glue, drugs)* 鼻で吸う haná dè súù

snigger [snig'ər] *vi* くすくす笑う kúsùkusu waráù

snip [snip] *n (cut)* はさみで切る事 hasámi dè kírù koto; *(BRIT: inf: bargain)* 掘出し物 horídashimonò

♦*vt (cut)* はさみで切る hasámi dè kírù

sniper [snai'pər] *n* 狙撃兵 sogékihèi

snippet [snip'it] *n (of information, news)* 断片 dañpen

snivelling [sniv'əliŋ] *adj (whimpering)* めそめそ泣く mésòmeso nakú

snob [snɑːb] *n* 俗物 zokúbutsu

snobbery [snɑːb'ə:ri:] *n* 俗物根性 zokúbutsukoñjō

snobbish [snɑːb'iʃ] *adj* 俗物的な zokúbutsuteki na

snooker [snuk'ə:r] *n* ビリヤード biríyādo

snoop [snu:p] *vi:* **to snoop about** こっそりのぞき回る kossórì nozókimawarù

snooty [snu:'ti:] *adj (person, letter, reply)* 横柄な ṓhei na

snooze [snu:z] *n* 昼寝 hirúne

♦*vi* 昼寝する hirúne suru

snore [snɔːr] *n* いびき ibíki

snorkel [snɔːr'kəl] *n (for swimming)* シュノーケル shunókèru

snort [snɔːrt] *n* 鼻を鳴らす事 haná wò narásù koto

♦*vi (animal, person)* 鼻を鳴らす haná wò narásù

snout [snaut] *n* ふん fúñ

snow [snou] *n* 雪 yukí

♦*vi* 雪が降る yukí gà fúrù

snowball [snou'bɔːl] *n* 雪のつぶて yukí nò tsubúte

♦*vi (fig: problem, campaign)* どんどん大きくなる dóñdon ṓkiku nárù

snowbound [snou'baund] *adj (people)* 雪に閉じ込められた yukí ni tojíkomerarèta; *(vehicles)* 雪で立ち往生した yukí dè tachíōjō shita

snowdrift [snou'drift] *n* 雪の吹きだまり yukí nò fukídamarì

snowdrop [snou'drɑːp] *n* 雪の花 yukínohanà

snowfall [snou'fɔːl] *n (amount)* 降雪量 kṓsetsuryò; *(a fall of snow)* 降雪 kṓsetsu

snowflake [snou'fleik] *n* 雪のひとひら yukí nò hitóhìra

snowman [snou'mæn] *(pl* **snowmen)** *n* 雪だるま yukídaruma

snowplow [snou'plau] *(BRIT* **snowplough)** *n* 除雪車 josétsushà

snowshoe [snou'ʃu:] *n* かんじき kañjiki

snowstorm [snou'stɔːrm] *n* 吹雪 fúbùki

snub [snʌb] *vt (person)* 鼻であしらう haná dè ashíraù

♦*n* 侮辱 bujóku

snub-nosed [snʌb'nouzd] *adj* 鼻先の反った hanásaki no sottá

snuck [snʌk] *(US) pt, pp of* sneak

snuff [snʌf] *n* かぎタバコ kagítabàko

snug [snʌg] *adj (sheltered: person, place)* こじんまりした kojínmarī shita; *(person)* 心地好い kokóchiyoì; *(well-fitting)* ぴったりした pittárì shita

snuggle [snʌg'əl] *vi:* **to snuggle up to someone** ...に体を擦り付ける ...ni karáda wò surítsukerù

KEYWORD

so [sou] adv 1 (thus, likewise) そう sṓ, その通り sonṓ tòri

so saying he walked away そう言って彼は歩き去った sṓ itté kárè wa arúkisattà

while she was so doing, he ... 彼女がそれをやっている間彼は... kánòjo ga sorè wò yatté iru aìda kárè wa...

if so だとすれば dá tò surèba

do you enjoy soccer? if so, come to the game フットボールが好きですか, だったら試合を見に来て下さい futtbṓru ga sukí desù ká, dáttàra shiái wò mi ní kite kudasaì

I didn't do it -you did so! やったのは私じゃない -いや, お前だ yattá no wà watákushi ja naì -iyá, omáe dà

so do I, so am I etc 私もそうです watákushi mò sṓ desù

I like swimming -so do I 私は水泳が好きです -私もそうです watákushi wà suíei gà sukí desù -watákushi mò sṓ desù

I'm still at school -so am I 私はまだ学生です -私もそうです watákushi wà mádà gakúsei desù -watákushi mò sṓ desù

I've got work to do -so has Paul 私には仕事がありますから -ポールもそうですよ watákushi ni wà shigóto gà arímasu karà -pṑru mo sṓ desù yó

it's 5'o'clock -so it is! 5時です -あっ, そうですね gójì desu -át, sṓ desù nè

I hope so そう希望します sṓ kibṓ shimasù

I think so そうだと思います sṓ da tò omóimasù

so far これまで korè madè

how do you like the book so far? これまでその本はどうでしたか korè madè sonó hoǹ wa dṓ deshìta ka

so far I haven't had any problems ここまでは問題はありません kokó madè wa moǹdai wa arímaseǹ

2 (in comparisons etc: to such a degree) そんなに soǹna nì

so quickly (that) (...がある程) 素早く (...ga árù hodo) subáyàku, とても素早く (...したので ...) totémo subáyàku (...shitá no dè ...)

so big (that) (...がある程) 大きな (...ga árù hodo) ōkina, とても大きい (ので...) totémo ōkii (nó dè ...)

she's not so clever as her brother 彼女は兄さん程利口ではない kánòjo wa niísaǹ hodo ríkṓ dè wa naì

we were so worried 私たちはとても心配していましたよ watákushitàchi wa totémo shiǹpai shite imashìta yó

I wish you weren't so clumsy あなたの不器用さはどうにかなりませんかね anáta no bukíyòsa wa dṓ ni kà narímaseǹ kà nè

I'm so glad to see you あなたを見てほっとしました anátà wo mítè hóttò shimáshità

3: **so much** adv そんなに沢山で soǹna nì takúsaǹ de

♦adj そんなに沢山の soǹna nì takúsaǹ de

I've got so much work 私は仕事が山程あります watákushi wà shigóto gà yamá hodð arímasù

I love you so much あなたを心から愛しています anátà wo kokórð kara áì shite imasu

so many そんなに沢山 (の) soǹna nì takúsaǹ (no)

there are so many things to do する事が山程あります surú kotð ga yamá hodð arímasù

there are so many people to meet 私が会うべき人たちは余りにも大勢です watákushi ga áùbeki hitótàchi wa amári ni mð ōzei desù 4 (phrases): **10 or so** 10個ぐらい júkkð gurai

so long! (inf: goodbye) じゃねじゃ ね, また又ね jₐné já nè, matá né

♦conj 1 (expressing purpose): **so as to do** ...する様〔ため〕に ...surú yṓ〔tamè〕ni

we hurried so as not to be late 遅れない様に急いで行きました okúrenai yṓ ni isóìde ikímashìta

so (that) ...する様〔ため〕に ...surú yṓ

〔tamè〕ni

I brought it so (that) you could see it あなたに見せるために持ってきました anátà ni misérù tame ni mottè kimashìta

2 (expressing result) ...であるから...de árù kara ..., ...ので...nó dè ...

he didn't arrive so I left 彼が来なかったので私は帰りました káre ga kónakatta nó de watákushi wà kaérimashìta

so I was right after all 結局私の言った通りでした kekkyókù watákushi nò ittá tōri deshita

so you see, I could have gone ですかろね、行こうと思えば行けたんです désu kara né, ikō tò omóebà ikétán desu

---

soak [souk] vt (drench) ずぶぬれにする zubúnure nì suru; (steep in water) 水に漬ける mizú nì tsukéru

♦vi (dirty washing, dishes) 漬かる tsukárù

soak in vi (be absorbed) 染み込む shimíkomù

soak up vt (absorb) 吸収する kyūshū surù

soap [soup] n 石けん sekkén

soapflakes [soup'fleiks] npl フレーク石けん furékusekkèn ◇洗濯用の固形石けんをフレークにした物を指す señtakuyō no kokéisekkèn wo furékù ni shitá monò wo sásù

soap opera n メロドラマ meródoràma ◇テレビやラジオの連続物を指す térèbi ya rájìo no reñzokumonò wo sásù

soap powder n 粉石けん konásekkèn

soapy [sou'pi:] adj (hands etc) 石けんのついた sekkén no tsuità

soapy water 石けん水 sekkéñsui

soar [sɔːr] vi (on wings) 舞上がる maîagarù; (rocket) 空中に上がる kūchū nì agárù; (price, production, temperature) 急上昇する kyūjōshō suru; (building etc) そびえたつ sobíetatsù

sob [sɑːb] n しゃくり泣き shakúrinaki

♦vi 泣きじゃくる nakíjakurù

sober [sou'bərr] adj (serious) まじめな majíme na; (dull: color, style) 地味な ji-

mí na; (not drunk) しらふの shírafu no

sober up vt ...の酔いを覚ます ...no yoî wò samásù

♦vi 酔いが覚める yoî gà samérù

so-called [sou'kɔːld'] adj (friend, expert) いわゆる iwáyurù ◇多くの場合不信や軽べつなどを表す ốkù no baái fushín yà keíbetsu nadò wo aráwasù

soccer [sɑːk'əːr] n サッカー sákkầ

sociable [sou'ʃəbəl] adj 愛想の良い aíso no yoî

social [sou'ʃəl] adj (gen: history, structure, background) 社会の shákài no; (leisure: event, life) 社交的な shakóteki na; (sociable: animal) 社会性のある shakáisei no arù

♦n (party) 懇親会 koñshinkai

social club n 社交クラブ shakókurabu

socialism [sou'ʃəlizəm] n 社会主義 shakáishugì

socialist [sou'ʃəlist] adj 社会主義の shakáishugì no

♦n 社会主義者 shakáishugishà

socialize [sou'ʃəlaiz] vi: ***to socialize (with)*** (...と) 交際する (...to) kốsai suru

socially [sou'ʃəli:] adv (visit) 社交的に shakóteki ni; (acceptable) 社会的に shakáiteki ni

social security (BRIT) n 社会保障 shakáihoshō

social work n ソーシャルワーク sōsharuwằku

social worker n ソーシャルワーカー sōsharuwằkầ

society [səsai'əti:] n (people, their lifestyle) 社会 shákaì; (club) 会 kâì; (also: **high society**) 上流社会 jōryūshakài

sociologist [sousi:ɑːl'ədʒist] n 社会学者 shakáigakùsha

sociology [sousi:ɑːl'ədʒi:] n 社会学 shakáigàku

sock [sɑːk] n 靴下 kutsúshita

socket [sɑːk'it] n (gen: cavity) 受け口 ukéguchi; (ANAT: of eye) 眼か gáñka; (ELEC: for light bulb) ソケット sokéttò; (BRIT: ELEC: wall socket) コンセント kốñsento

sod [sɑ:d] n (of earth) 草の生えた土 kusá nò háeta tsuchí; (BRIT: inf!) くそ kusó

soda [sou'də] n (CHEM) ナトリウム化合物 natóriùmu kagóbutsu◇一般にか性ソーダ, 重曹などを指す ippán nì kaséisòda, júsō nadò wo sásù; (also: **soda water**) ソーダ水 sódasui; (US: also: **soda pop**) 清涼飲料 seíryoìnryō

sodden [sɑ:d'ən] adj びしょぬれの bishónure no

sodium [sou'di:əm] n ナトリウム natóriùmu

sofa [sou'fə] n ソファー sófà

soft [sɔ:ft] adj (not hard) 柔らかい yawárakaì; (gentle, not loud: voice, music) 静かな shízùka na; (not bright: light, color) 柔らかな yawárakà na; (kind: heart, approach) 優しい yasáshii

soft drink n 清涼飲料水 seíryoìnryōsui

soften [sɔ:f'ən] vt (gen: make soft) 柔らかくする yawárakàku suru; (effect, blow, expression) 和らげる yawárageru
♦vi (gen: become soft) 柔らかくなる yawárakaku narù; (voice, expression) 優しくなる yasáshiku narù

softly [sɔ:ft'li:] adv (gently) 優しく yasáshiku; (quietly) 静かに shízùka ni

softness [sɔ:ft'nis] n (gen) 柔らかさ yawárakasa; (gentleness) 優しさ yasáshisa

soft spot n: **to have a soft spot for someone** ...が大好きである ...ga dáìsuki de árù

software [sɔ:ft'we:r] n (COMPUT) ソフトウエア sofútoueà

soggy [sɑ:g'i:] adj (ground, sandwiches etc) ぐちゃぐちゃの guchágucha no

soil [sɔil] n (earth) 土壌 dójò; (territory) 土地 tochí
♦vt 汚す yogósù

solace [sɑ:l'is] n 慰め nagúsame

solar [sou'lə:r] adj (eclipse, power etc) 太陽の taíyō no

sold [sould] pt, pp of **sell**

solder [sɑ:d'ə:r] vt はんだ付けにする hañdazuke nì suru
♦n はんだ hañda

soldier [soul'dʒə:r] n (in army) 兵隊 heítai; (not a civilian) 軍人 guñjin

sold out adj (COMM: goods, tickets, concert etc) 売切れで uríkire de

sole [soul] n (of foot) 足の裏 ashí nò urá; (of shoe) 靴の底 kutsú nò sokó; (fish: pl inv) シタビラメ shitábiràme
♦adj (unique) 唯一の yuíitsu no

solely [soul'li:] adv ...だけ ...dáke

solemn [sɑ:l'əm] adj (person) 謹厳な kiñgen na; (music) 荘重な sốchō na; (promise) 真剣な shiñken na

sole trader n (COMM) 自営業者 jiéigyòsha

solicit [səlis'it] vt (request) 求める motómerù
♦vi (prostitute) 客引きする kyakúbiki suru

solicitor [səlis'itə:r] (BRIT) n (for wills etc, in court) 弁護士 beñgoshì

solid [sɑ:l'id] adj (not hollow) 中空でない chūkū de naì; (not liquid) 固形の kokéi no; (reliable: person, foundations etc) しっかりした shikkári shita; (entire) 全ての...marú...; (pure: gold etc) 純粋の juñsui no
♦n (solid object) 固体 kotái

solidarity [sɑ:lidær'iti:] n 団結 dañketsu

solidify [səlid'əfai] vi (fat etc) 固まる katámarù

solids [sɑ:l'idz] npl (food) 固形食 kokéishòku

solitaire [sɑ:l'ite:r] n (gem) 一つはめの宝石 hitótsuhame nò hốseki; (game) 一人遊び hitóriasòbi

solitary [sɑ:l'ite:ri:] adj (person, animal, life) 単独の tañdoku no; (alone: walk) 一人だけでする hitórì dake de suru; (isolated) 人気のない hitóke no naì; (single: person) 一人だけの hitórì dake no; (: animal, object) 一つだけの hitótsu dake no

solitary confinement n 独房監禁 dokúbō kàñkin

solitude [sɑ:l'ətu:d] n 人里を離れている事 hitózato wò hanárete iru kotò

solo [sou'lou] n (piece of music, performance) 独奏 dokúsō
♦adv (fly) 単独で tañdoku de

soloist [sou'louist] n 独奏者 dokúsōshà

soluble [sɑ:l'jəbəl] adj (aspirin etc) 溶けて tokérù

solution [səluːˈʃən] n (of puzzle, problem, mystery: answer) 解決 kaíketsu; (liquid) 溶液 yōeki

solve [sɑːlv] vt (puzzle, problem, mystery) 解決する kaíketsu suru

solvent [sɑːˈlvənt] adj (COMM) 支払い能力のある shiháriroryoku no aru
♦n (CHEM) 溶剤 yōzai

somber [sɑːˈmbəːr] (BRIT **sombre**) adj (dark: color, place) 暗い kuráî; (serious: person, view) 陰気な íñki na

---

KEYWORD

---

some [sʌm] adj 1 (a certain amount or number of) 幾らかの íkuraka no, 幾つかの íkutsuka no, 少しの sukóshî no

some tea/water/biscuits お茶(水, ビスケット) o-chá(mízu, bisúkettð) ◇この用法では日本語で表現しない場合が多い konó yōhō de wa nihóngo dè hyógen shinaî baái gà ōi

some children came 何人かの子供が来た nánninka no kodómo gà kítà

there's some milk in the fridge 冷蔵庫にミルクがあります reízōko ni mírùku ga arímasu

he asked me some questions 彼は色々な事を聞きました kárè wa iróiro na kotò wo kikímashita

there were some people outside 数人の人が外に立っていた súnìn no hitó gà sótò ni tatté ità

I've got some money, but not much 金はあるにはありますが, 少しだけです kané wà árù ni wa arímasù gá, sukóshî dake désù

2 (certain: in contrasts) ある árù

some people say that ... ... と言っている人がいます ...tð itté irù hitó ga imasù

some people hate fish, while others love it 魚の嫌いな人もいれば大好きな人もいます sakána no kirái na hitó mo iréba daísuki na hitó mo imásù

some films were excellent, but most were mediocre 中には優れた映画もあったが, 大半は平凡な物だった nákà ni wa sugúreta eîga mo attá gà, taíhan wa heíbon na monò dáttà

3 (unspecified) 何かの nánìka no, だれかの dárèka no

some woman was asking for you だれか女の人があなたを訪ねていましたよ dárèka ońna no hitò ga anátà wo tazúnete imashìta yò

he was asking for some book (or other) 彼は何かの本を捜していました kárè wa nánìka no hoñ wo sagáshite imashìta

some day いつか ítsùka, そのうち sonó uchì

we'll meet again some day そのうちまた会うチャンスがあるでしょう sonó uchì matá aû châñsu ga árù deshō

shall we meet some day next week? 来週のいつかに会いましょうか raíshū nò ítsùka ni aímashð ká

♦pron 1 (a certain number) 幾つか íkùtsuka

I've got some (books etc) 私は幾つか持っています watákushi wà íkùtsuka móttè imasu

some (of them) have been sold 数個は売れてしまいました súkð wa uréte shimaimashìta

some went for a taxi and some walked 何人かはタクシーを拾いに行ったが, 残りの人は歩いた nâñninka wa tákùshì wo hirói ni itta gà, nokóri nò hitð wà arúîta

2 (a certain amount) 幾分か ikúbun kà

I've got some (money, milk) 私は幾分か持っています watákushi wà ikúbun kà móttè imasu

some was left 少し残っていた sukóshî nokótte ità

could I have some of that cheese? そのチーズを少しもらっていいかしら sonó chīzu wo sukóshî morátte ii kashìra

I've read some of the book その本の一部を読みました sonó hoñ no ichíbù wo yomímashìta

♦adv: *some 10 people* 10人ぐらい júnìn gurai

---

somebody [sʌmˈbɑːdiː] pron = someone
somehow [sʌmˈhau] adv (in some way)

何とかして náñ to ka shite; (for some reason) どういう訳か dô iu wákè ka

KEYWORD

someone [sʌm'wʌn] *pron* だれか dárèka, 人 hitó
there's someone coming 人が来ます hitó gà kimásù
I saw someone in the garden だれか 庭にいました dárèka niwà nì imáshìta

someplace [sʌm'pleis] (*US*) *adv* = **somewhere**

somersault [sʌm'ə:rsɔ:lt] *n* とんぼ返り toñbogaèri
♦*vi* (person, vehicle) とんぼ返りする toñbogaèri suru

KEYWORD

something [sʌm'θiŋ] *pron* 何か nánìka
something nice 何かいい物 nánìka fí mono
something to do 何かする事 nánìka suru kotò
there's something wrong 何かおかし い nánìka okáshìî
would you like something to eat/ drink? 何か食べません〔飲みません〕か nánìka tabémaseñ〔nomímaseñ〕ká

sometime [sʌm'taim] *adv* (in future) い つか ítsùka; (in past): *sometime last month* 先月のいつか señgetsu no ítsùka
sometimes [sʌm'taimz] *adv* 時々 tokído-ki
somewhat [sʌm'wʌt] *adv* 少し sukóshì

KEYWORD

somewhere [sʌm'we:r] *adv* (be) どこか に〔で〕dókòka ni〔de〕; (go) どこかへ dó-kòka e
I must have lost it somewhere どこか に落とした様です dókòka ni otóshìta yò desu
it's somewhere or other in Scotland スコットランドのどこかにあります su-kóttorañdo no dókòka ni arímasù
somewhere else (be) どこか外の所に

〔で〕dókòka hoká no tokorò ni〔de〕; (go) どこか外の所へ dókòka hoká no tokorò e

son [sʌn] *n* 息子 musúko
sonar [sou'na:r] *n* ソナー sónà
song [sɔːŋ] *n* (MUS) 歌 utá; (of bird) さえ ずり saézurì
sonic [sɑːn'ik] *adj*: *sonic boom* ソニック ブーム soníkkubùmu
son-in-law [sʌn'inlɔː] (*pl* **sons-in-law**) *n* 義理の息子 girí no musuko
sonnet [sɑːn'it] *n* ソネット sonéttò
sonny [sʌn'i:] (*inf*) *n* 坊や bôya
soon [suːn] *adv* (in a short time) もうすぐ mô sugù; (a short time after) 間もなく mamónàku; (early) 早く hayákù
soon afterwards それから間もなく so-ré karà mamónàku ¶ *see also* **as**
sooner [suː'nɔːr] *adv* (time) もっと早く móttò háyàku; (preference): *I would sooner do that* 私はむしろあれをやりた い watákushi wà múshìro aré wò yarí-tàî
sooner or later 遅かれ早かれ osókare hayákàre
soot [sut] *n* すす súsù
soothe [suːð] *vt* (calm: person, animal) 落 着かせる ochítsukaserù; (reduce: pain) 和らげる yawáragerù
sophisticated [səfis'tikeitid] *adj* (woman, lifestyle, audience) 世慣れた yonáréta; (machinery) 精巧な seíkō na; (arguments) 洗練された señren sarèta
sophomore [sɑːf'əmɔːr] (*US*) *n* 2年生 ni-néñsei
soporific [sɑːpərif'ik] *adj* (speech) 眠気 を催させる nemúke wo moyóosaserù; (drug) 睡眠の suímin no
sopping [sɑːp'iŋ] *adj*: *sopping (wet)* (hair, clothes etc) びしょぬれの bishónure no
soppy [sɑːp'iː] (*pej*) *adj* (sentimental) セ ンチな séñchi na
soprano [səpræn'ou] *n* (singer) ソプラノ sopúrano
sorcerer [sɔːr'sərəːr] *n* 魔法使い mahô-tsukài

sordid [sɔːr'did] *adj* (dirty: bed-sit etc) 汚らしい kitánarashiì; (wretched: story etc) 浅ましい asámashiì, えげつない egétsunaì

sore [sɔːr] *adj* (painful) 痛い itáì
♦*n* (shallow) ただれ tadáre; (deep) かいよう kaíyō

sorely [sɔːr'liː] *adv*: *I am sorely tempted to* よほど...しようと思っている yohódo ...shiyō to omótte irù

sorrow [sɑːr'ou] *n* (regret) 悲しみ kanáshimi

sorrowful [sɑːr'oufəl] *adj* (day, smile etc) 悲しい kanáshiì

sorrows [sɑːr'ouz] *npl* (causes of grief) 不幸 fúkō

sorry [sɑːr'iː] *adj* (regretful) 残念な zańneň na; (condition, excuse) 情けない nasákenaì
sorry! (apology) 済みません sumímaseń
sorry? (pardon) はい？ haî? ◇相手の言葉を聞取れなかった時に言う aîte no kotòba wo kíkitorenakatta tokî ni iú
to feel sorry for someone ...に同情する ...ni dōjō suru

sort [sɔːrt] *n* (type) 種類 shúrui
♦*vt* (*also*: **sort out**: papers, mail, belongings) より分ける yoríwakerù; (: problems) 解決する kaíketsu suru

sorting office [sɔːr'tiŋ-] *n* 郵便物振分け場 yūbinbutsufuriwakejō

SOS [esoues'] *n* エスオーエス esú ō esù

so-so [sou'sou'] *adv* (average) まあまあ maámaà

soufflé [suːflei'] *n* スフレ súfure

sought [sɔːt] *pt*, *pp* of **seek**

soul [soul] *n* (spirit etc) 魂 támashii; (person) 人 hitó

soul-destroying [soul'distrɔiŋ] *adj* (work) ぼけさせる様な bokésaseru yō na

soulful [soul'fəl] *adj* (eyes, music) 表情豊かな hyōjō yútàka na

sound [saund] *adj* (healthy) 健康な keńkō na; (safe, not damaged) 無傷の múkìzu no; (secure: investment) 安全な ańzen na; (reliable, thorough) 信頼できる shifrai dekirù; (sensible: advice) 堅実な keńjitsu na

♦*adv*: *sound asleep* ぐっすり眠って gussúrì nemútte
♦*n* (noise) 音 otó; (volume on TV etc) 音声 ôńsei; (GEO) 海峡 kaíkyo
♦*vt* (alarm, horn) 鳴らす narásù
♦*vi* (alarm, horn) 鳴る narú; (*fig*: seem) ...の様である ...no yō de árù
to sound like ...の様に聞える ...no yō ni kikóerù

sound barrier *n* 音速障害 ońsokushṓgai

sound effects *npl* 音響効果 ońkyōkṓka

soundly [saund'liː] *adv* (sleep) ぐっすり gussúrì; (beat) 手ひどく tehídokù

sound out *vt* (person, opinion) 打診する dashín suru

soundproof [saund'pruːf] *adj* (room etc) 防音の bốon no

soundtrack [saund'træk] *n* (of film) サウンドトラック saúndotorakkù

soup [suːp] *n* スープ súpu
in the soup (*fig*) 困って komáttè

soup plate *n* スープ皿 sûpuzarà

soupspoon [suːp'spuːn] *n* スープスプーン sûpusupûn

sour [sau'əːr] *adj* (bitter) 酸っぱい suppáì; (milk) 酸っぱくなった suppáku náttà; (*fig*: bad-tempered) 機嫌の悪い kigén no waruì
it's sour grapes (*fig*) 負け惜しみだ makéoshimi da

source [sɔːrs] *n* (*also fig*) 源 minámoto

south [sauθ] *n* 南 minámi
♦*adj* 南の minámi no
♦*adv* (movement) 南へ minámi e; (position) 南に minámi ni

South Africa *n* 南アフリカ minámi afúrika

South African *adj* 南アフリカの minámi afúrika no
♦*n* 南アフリカ人 minámi afurikajîn

South America *n* 南米 nańbei

South American *adj* 南米の nańbei nò
♦*n* 南米人 nańbeijîn

south-east [sauθiːst'] *n* 南東 nańtō

southerly [sʌð'əːrliː] *adj* (to/towards the south: aspect) 南への minámi e nò; (from the south: wind) 南からの minámi kara nò

southern [sʌð'ə:rn] *adj* (in or from the south of region) 南の minámi no; (to/towards the south) 南向きの minámimuki no

the southern hemisphere 南半球 mínámihañkyū

South Pole *n* 南極 nańkyoku

southward(s) [sauθ'wə:rd(z)] *adv* 南 へ minámi e

south-west [sauθwest'] *n* 南西 nańsei

souvenir [su:vəni:r'] *n* (memento) 記念品 kinéñhin

sovereign [sɑ:v'rin] *n* (ruler) 君主 kúñshu

sovereignty [sɑ:v'rənti:] *n* 主権 shukéñ

soviet [sou'vi:it] *adj* ソビエトの sobíetð no

the Soviet Union ソ連 sórèn

sow[1] [sau] *n* (pig) 牝豚 mesúbùta

sow[2] [sou] (*pt* **sowed**, *pp* **sown**) *vt* (*gen*: seeds) まく mákù; (*fig*: spread: suspicion etc) 広める hirómerù

soy [sɔi] (*BRIT* **soya**) *n*: **soy bean** 大豆 dáìzu

soy sauce しょう油 shóyù

spa [spɑ:] *n* (*also*: **spa town**) 鉱泉町 kõseñmachi; (*US*: *also*: **health spa**) ヘルスセンター herúsuseñtà

space [speis] *n* (gap) すき間 sukíma, ギャップ gyáppù; (place) 空所 kûsho, 余白 yoháku; (room) 空間 kûkan; (beyond Earth) 宇宙空間 uchūkūkan, スペース supèsu; (interval, period) 間 ma

♦*cpd* 宇宙... úchù...

♦*vt* (*also*: **space out**: text, visits, payments) 間隔を置く kańkaku wò okú

spacecraft [speis'kræft] *n* 宇宙船 uchūsen

spaceman [speis'mæn] (*pl* **spacemen**) *n* 宇宙飛行士 uchūhikōshi

spaceship [speis'ʃip] *n* = **spacecraft**

spacewoman [speis'wumən] (*pl* **spacewomen**) *n* 女性宇宙飛行士 joséi uchūhikōshi

spacing [spei'siŋ] *n* (between words) スペース supèsu

spacious [spei'ʃəs] *adj* (car, room etc) 広

spade [speid] *n* (tool) スコップ sukóppù; (child's) おもちゃのスコップ omóchà no sukóppù

spades [speidz] *npl* (CARDS: suit) スペード supèdo

spaghetti [spəget'i:] *n* スパゲッティ supágettì

Spain [spein] *n* スペイン supéìn

span [spæn] *n* (of bird, plane) 翼長 yokúchō; (of arch) スパン supáñ; (in time) 期間 kikáñ

♦*vt* (river) ...にまたがる ...ni matágarù; (*fig*: time) ...に渡る ...ni watárù

Spaniard [spæn'jə:rd] *n* スペイン人 supéinjìn

spaniel [spæn'jəl] *n* スパニエル supánièru

Spanish [spæn'iʃ] *adj* スペインの supéìn no; (LING) スペイン語の supéingo no

♦*n* (LING) スペイン語 supéingo

♦*npl*: *the Spanish* スペイン人 supéinjìn ◇総称 sóshō

spank [spæŋk] *vt* (someone, someone's bottom) ...のしりをたたく ...no shirí wð tatákù

spanner [spæn'ə:r] (*BRIT*) *n* スパナ supánà

spar [spɑ:r] *n* (pole) マスト másùto

♦*vi* (BOXING) スパーリングする supárìngu suru

spare [spe:r] *adj* (free) 空きの akí no; (surplus) 余った amáttà

♦*n* = **spare part**

♦*vt* (do without: trouble etc) ...なしで済ます ...náshì de sumásù; (make available) 与える atáerù; (refrain from hurting: person, city etc) 助けてやる tasúkete yarù

to spare (surplus: time, money) 余った amáttà

spare part *n* 交換用部品 kōkan-yōbuhiñ

spare time *n* 余暇 yókà

spare wheel *n* (AUT) スペアタイア supéataià

sparing [spe:r'iŋ] *adj*: *to be sparing with* ...を倹約する ...wo keñ-yaku suru

sparingly [spe:r'iŋli:] *adv* (use) 控え目に

hikáeme ni

spark [spɑːrk] *n* 火花 híbàna, スパーク supákù; (*fig*: of wit etc) ひらめき hirámekì

spark(ing) plug [spɑːrk'(iŋ)-] *n* スパークプラグ supākupuràgu

sparkle [spɑːr'kəl] *n* きらめき kirámekì
♦*vi* (shine: diamonds, water) きらめく kirámekù

sparkling [spɑːr'kliŋ] *adj* (wine) 泡立つ awádatsù; (conversation, performance) きらめく様な kirámeku yố na

sparrow [spær'ou] *n* スズメ suzúme

sparse [spɑːrs] *adj* (rainfall, hair, population) 少ない sukúnaì

spartan [spɑːr'tən] *adj* (*fig*) 簡素な kánso na

spasm [spæz'əm] *n* (MED) けいれん keíren

spasmodic [spæzmɑːd'ik] *adj* (*fig*: not continuous, irregular) 不規則な fukísoku na

spastic [spæs'tik] *n* 脳性麻ひ患者 nốseimahikàňja

spat [spæt] *pt, pp of* spit

spate [speit] *n* (*fig*): *a spate of* (letters, protests etc) 沢山の takúsaň no

spatter [spæt'əːr] *vt* (liquid, surface) ...を...にはねかす ...wo ...ni hanékasù

spatula [spætʃ'ələ] *n* (CULIN, MED) へら hérà

spawn [spɔːn] *vi* (fish etc) 産卵する saňran suru
♦*n* (frog spawn etc) 卵 tamágò

speak [spiːk] (*pt* spoke, *pp* spoken) *vt* (language) 話す hanásù; (truth) 言う iú
♦*vi* (use voice) 話す hanásù; (make a speech) 演説する eňzetsu suru
to speak to someone ...に話し掛ける ...ni hanáshikakerù
to speak to someone of/about something ...に...のことを話す ...ni ...no kotó wò hanásù
speak up! もっと大きな声で話しなさい móttò ốkìna kôè de hanáshi nasaì

speaker [spiː'kəːr] *n* (in public) 演説者 eňzetsushà; (*also*: **loudspeaker**) スピーカー supíkà; (POL): *the Speaker* (US,

BRIT) 下院議長 ka-íngichồ

spear [spi'əːr] *n* (weapon) やり yarí
♦*vt* 刺す sásù

spearhead [spi'ːhed] *vt* (attack etc) ...の先頭に立つ ...no señtō nì tátsù

spec [spek] (*inf*) *n*: *on spec* 山をかけて yamá wo kakète

special [speʃ'əl] *adj* 特別な tokúbetsu na
special delivery 速達 sokútatsu
special school (BRIT) 特殊学校 tokúshugakkồ
special adviser 特別顧問 tokúbetsukomòn
special permission 特別許可 tokúbetsukyokà

specialist [speʃ'əlist] *n* (*gen*) 専門家 señmonka; (MED) 専門医 señmoñ-i

speciality [speʃiːæl'əti:] *n =* specialty

specialize [speʃ'əlaiz] *vi*: *to specialize (in)* (...を) 専門的にやる (...wo) seňmonteki ni yarù

specially [speʃ'əliː] *adv* (especially) 特に tókù ni; (on purpose) 特別に tokúbetsu ni

specialty [speʃ'əlti:] *n* (dish) 名物 meíbutsu; (study) 専門 seňmon

species [spiː'ʃiːz] *n inv* 種 shú

specific [spisif'ik] *adj* (fixed) 特定の tokútei no; (exact) 正確な seíkaku na

specifically [spisif'ikliː] *adv* (especially) 特に tókù ni; (exactly) 明確に meíkaku ni

specification [spesəfəkei'ʃən] *n* (TECH) 仕様 shiyố; (requirement) 条件 jốkeň

specifications [spesəfəkei'ʃənz] *npl* (TECH) 仕様 shiyố

specify [spes'əfai] *vt* (time, place, color etc) 指定する shitéi suru

specimen [spes'əmən] *n* (single example) 見本 mihóñ; (sample for testing, *also* MED) 標本 hyốhon

speck [spek] *n* (of dirt, dust etc) 粒 tsúbù

speckled [spek'əld] *adj* (hen, eggs) 点々模様の teñteñmoyồ no

specs [speks] (*inf*) *npl* 眼鏡 mégàne

spectacle [spek'təkəl] *n* (scene) 光景 kốkei; (grand event) スペクタクル supékùtakuru

spectacles [spek'təkəlz] *npl* 眼 鏡 mégàne

spectacular [spektæk'jələr] *adj* (dramatic) 劇的な gekíteki na; (success) 目覚しい mezámashiî

spectator [spek'teitər] *n* 観 客 kañkyaku

specter [spek'tər] (*US*) *n* (ghost) 幽 霊 yûrei

spectra [spek'trə] *npl of* **spectrum**

spectre [spek'tər] (*BRIT*) = **specter**

spectrum [spek'trəm] (*pl* **spectra**) *n* (color/radio wave spectrum) スペクトル supékùtoru

speculate [spek'jəleit] *vi* (FINANCE) 投機をする tôki wo suru; (try to guess): **to speculate about** ...についてあれこれと憶測する ...ni tsúîte arékòre to okúsoku suru

speculation [spekjəlei'ʃən] *n* (FINANCE) 投機 tôki; (guesswork) 憶測 okúsoku

speech [spi:tʃ] *n* (faculty) 話す能力 hanásu nôryoku; (spoken language) 話し言葉 hanáshikotòba; (formal talk) 演説 eñzetsu, スピーチ supíchi; (THEATER) せりふ serífu

speechless [spi:tʃ'lis] *adj* (be, remain etc) 声も出ない kóè mo denáî

speed [spi:d] *n* (rate, fast travel) 速度 sókùdo, スピード supídò; (haste) 急ぎ isógi; (promptness) 素早さ subáyasà

at full/top speed 全速力で zeñsokuryôku de

speed boat *n* モーターボート môtābòto

speedily [spi:'dili:] *adv* 素早く subáyakù

speeding [spi:'diŋ] *n* (AUT) スピード違反 supído-ihàn

speed limit *n* 速度制限 sokúdoseîgen

speedometer [spi:da:m'itər] *n* 速 度 計 sokúdokèi

speed up *vi* (*also fig*) 速度を増す sókùdo wo masú
♦*vt* (*also fig*) ...の速度を増す ...no sókùdo wo masú, 速める hayámerù

speedway [spi:d'wei] *n* (sport) オートレース ôtorèsu

speedy [spi:'di:] *adj* (fast: car) スピードの出る supídò no dérù; (prompt: reply, recovery, settlement) 速い hayáî

spell [spel] *n* (*also:* **magic spell**) 魔法 mahô; (period of time) 期間 kikáñ
♦*vt* (*pt, pp* **spelled** *or* (*Brit*) **spelt**) (*also:* **spell out**) ...のつづりを言う ...no tsuzúri wò iú; (*fig:* advantages, difficulties) ...の兆しである ...no kizáshi de arù

to cast a spell on someone ...に魔法を掛ける ...ni mahô wò kakérù

he can't spell 彼はスペルが苦手だ kárè wa supérù ga nigáte dà

spellbound [spel'baund] *adj* (audience etc) 魅せられた miséraretà

spelling [spel'iŋ] *n* つづり tsuzúri, スペリング supériñgu

spend [spend] (*pt, pp* **spent**) *vt* (money) 使う tsukáù; (time, life) 過す sugósù

spendthrift [spend'θrift] *n* 浪費家 rôhikà

spent [spent] *pt, pp of* **spend**

sperm [spə:rm] *n* 精子 sêîshi

spew [spju:] *vt* 吐き出す hakídasù

sphere [sfi:r] *n* (round object) 球 kyû; (area) 範囲 hấn-i

spherical [sfe:r'ikəl] *adj* (round) 丸 い marúî

sphinx [sfiŋks] *n* スフィンクス suffíñkusu

spice [spais] *n* 香辛料 kốshiñryō, スパイス supáîsu
♦*vt* (food) ...にスパイスを入れる ...ni supáîsu wo irérù

spick-and-span [spik'ənspæn'] *adj* きちんときれいな kichíñ to kírèi na

spicy [spai'si:] *adj* (food) スパイスの利いた supáîsu no kíîta

spider [spai'dər] *n* クモ kúmò

spike [spaik] *n* (point) くい kuí; (BOT) 穂 hồ

spill [spil] (*pt, pp* **spilt** *or* **spilled**) *vt* (liquid) こぼす kobósù
♦*vi* (liquid) こぼれる kobórerù

spill over *vi* (liquid: *also fig*) あふれる afúrerù

spin [spin] *n* (trip in car) ドライブ doráîbu; (AVIAT) きりもみ kirímomi; (on ball) スピン supíñ
♦*vb* (*pt, pp* **spun**)

♦*vt* (wool etc) 紡ぐ tsumúgù; (ball, coin) 回転させる kaíten saserù

♦*vi* (make thread) 紡ぐ tsumúgù; (person, head) 目が回る mé gà mawárù

spinach [spin'it∫] *n* (plant, food) ホウレンソウ hōreñsō

spinal [spin'nəl] *adj* (injury etc) 背骨の sebóne no

spinal cord *n* せき髄 sekízùi

spindly [spind'li:] *adj* (legs, trees etc) か細い kabósoì

spin-dryer [spindrai'ə:r] (*BRIT*) *n* 脱水機 dassúikì

spine [spain] *n* (ANAT) 背骨 sebóne; (thorn: of plant, hedgehog etc) とげ togé

spineless [spain'lis] *adj* (*fig*) 意気地なしの ikújinashi no

spinning [spin'iŋ] *n* (art) 紡績 bōseki

spinning top *n* こま kómà

spinning wheel *n* 紡ぎ車 tsumúgigurùma

spin-off [spin'ɔːf] *n* (*fig*: by-product) 副産物 fukúsañbutsu

spin out *vt* (talk, job, money, holiday) 引延ばす hikínobasù

spinster [spin'stə:r] *n* オールドミス ōrudomisù

spiral [spai'rəl] *n* ら旋形 rasénkei

♦*vi* (*fig*: prices etc) うなぎ登りに上る unáginobòri ni nobórù

spiral staircase *n* ら旋階段 rasénkaidàn

spire [spai'ə:r] *n* せん塔 señtō

spirit [spir'it] *n* (soul) 魂 támàshii; (ghost) 幽霊 yūrei; (energy) 元気 géñki; (courage) 勇気 yūki; (frame of mind) 気分 kíbùn; (sense) 精神 seíshin

in good spirits 気分上々で kíbùn jōjō de

spirited [spir'itid] *adj* (performance, retort, defense) 精力的な seíryokuteki na

spirit level *n* 水準器 suíjuñki

spirits [spir'its] *npl* (drink) 蒸留酒 jōryūshu

spiritual [spir'it∫uəl] *adj* (of the spirit: home, welfare, needs) 精神的な seíshinteki na; (religious: affairs) 霊的な reíteki

♦*n* (*also*: **Negro spiritual**) 黒人霊歌 kokújinreìka

spit [spit] *n* (for roasting) 焼きぐし yakígushi; (saliva) つばき tsubáki

♦*vi* (*pt, pp* **spat**) (throw out saliva) つばを吐く tsubá wo hákù; (sound: fire, cooking) じゅうじゅういう jūjū iu; (rain) ぱらつく parátsukù

spite [spait] *n* 恨み urámi

♦*vt* (person) ...に意地悪をする ...ni ijíwarù wo suru

in spite of ...にもかかわらず ...ní mò kakáwarazù

spiteful [spait'fəl] *adj* (child, words etc) 意地悪な ijíwarù na

spittle [spit'əl] *n* つばき tsubáki

splash [splæʃ] *n* (sound) ざぶんという音 zabúñ to iú otò; (of color) 派手なはん点 hadé nà hañten

♦*vt* はね掛ける hanékakerù

♦*vi* (*also*: **splash about**) ぴちゃぴちゃ水をはねる pichápìcha mízù wò hanérù

spleen [spli:n] *n* (ANAT) ひ臓 hizó

splendid [splen'did] *adj* (excellent: idea, recovery) 素晴らしい subárashiǐ; (impressive: architecture, affair) 立派な rippá nà

splendor [splen'də:r] (*BRIT* **splendour**) *n* (impressiveness) 輝き kagáyakî

splendors [splen'də:rz] *npl* (features) 特色 tokúshoku

splint [splint] *n* 副木 fukúboku

splinter [splin'tə:r] *n* (of wood, glass) 破片 hahéñ; (in finger) とげ togé

♦*vi* (bone, wood, glass etc) 砕ける kudákerù

split [split] *n* (crack) 割れ目 waréme; (tear) 裂け目 sakéme; (*fig*: division) 分裂 buñretsu; (: difference) 差異 sá-ì

♦*vb* (*pt, pp* **split**)

♦*vt* (divide) 割る wárù, 裂く sákù; (party) 分裂させる buñretsu saserù; (share equally: work) 手分けしてやる tewáke shite yarù; (: profits) 山分けする yamáwake suru

♦*vi* (divide) 割れる warérù

split up *vi* (couple) 別れる wakárerù;

(group, meeting) 解散する kaísan suru

splutter [splʌt'ər] *vi* (engine etc) ぱちぱち音を立てる páchìpachi otó wò tatérù; (person) どもる domórù

spoil [spɔil] (*pt, pp* **spoilt** *or* **spoiled**) *vt* (damage, mar) 台無しにする daínashi ni surù; (child) 甘やかす amáyakasù

spoils [spɔilz] *npl* (loot: *also fig*) 分捕り品 buńdorihìn

spoilsport [spɔil'spɔːrt] *n* 座を白けさせる人 zá wò shirákesaserù hitó

spoke [spouk] *pt of* **speak**
♦*n* (of wheel) スポーク supókù

spoken [spou'kən] *pp of* **speak**

spokesman [spouks'mən] (*pl* **spokesmen**) *n* スポークスマン supókusumàn

spokeswoman [spouks'wumən] (*pl* **spokeswomen**) *n* 女性報道官 joséi hōdōkan, 女性スポークスマン joséi supōkusumàn

sponge [spʌndʒ] *n* (for washing with) スポンジ supóñji; (*also*: **sponge cake**) スポンジケーキ supóñjikèki
♦*vt* (wash) スポンジで洗う supóñji de aráù
♦*vi*: **to sponge off/on someone** ...にたかる ...ni takárù

sponge bag (*BRIT*) *n* 洗面バッグ señmenbaggù ◊洗面道具を入れて携帯するバッグ señmendōgu wo iréte keitai surù bággù

sponsor [spɑn'sər] *n* (of player, event, club, program) スポンサー supóñsā; (of charitable event etc) 協賛者 kyósaǹsha; (for application) 保証人 hoshōnin; (for bill in parliament etc) 提出者 teíshutsushà
♦*vt* (player, event, club, program etc) ...のスポンサーになる ...no supóñsā ni nárù; (charitable event etc) ...の協賛者になる ...no kyósaǹsha ni nárù; (applicant) ...の保証人になる ...no hoshōnin ni nárù; (proposal, bill etc) 提出する teíshutsu suru

sponsorship [spɑn'sərʃip] *n* (financial support) 金銭的の援助 kińsentekieñjo

spontaneous [spɑntei'niːəs] *adj* (unplanned: gesture) 自発的な jihátsuteki na

spooky [spuː'kiː] (*inf*) *adj* (place, atmosphere) お化けが出そうな o-báke gà desó nà

spool [spuːl] *n* (for thread) 糸巻 itómàki; (for film, tape etc) リール rīru

spoon [spuːn] *n* さじ sají, スプーン supūn

spoon-feed [spuːn'fiːd] *vt* (baby, patient) スプーンで食べさせる supūn de tabésaserù; (*fig*: students etc) ...に一方的に教え込む ...ni ippóteki nì oshíekomù

spoonful [spuːn'ful] *n* スプーン一杯分 supūn ippáibun

sporadic [spɔːræd'ik] *adj* (glimpses, attacks etc) 散発的な sañpatsuteki na

sport [spɔːrt] *n* (game) スポーツ supótsu; (person) 気さくな人 kisáku nà hitó
♦*vt* (wear) これみよがしに身に付ける korémiyogashi ni mi ni tsukérù

sporting [spɔːr'tiŋ] *adj* (event etc) スポーツの supótsù no; (generous) 気前がいい kimáe ga íi
to give someone a sporting chance ...にちゃんとしたチャンスを与える ...ni chańtò shita cháňsu wo atáerù

sport jacket (*US*) *n* スポーツジャケット supótsujakettò

sports car [spɔːrts-] *n* スポーツカー supótsukà

sports jacket (*BRIT*) *n* = **sport jacket**

sportsman [spɔːrts'mən] (*pl* **sportsmen**) *n* スポーツマン supótsumàn

sportsmanship [spɔːrts'mənʃip] *n* スポーツマンシップ supótsumanshippù

sportswear [spɔːrts'weər] *n* スポーツウエア supótsuueà

sportswoman [spɔːrts'wumən] (*pl* **sportswomen**) *n* スポーツウーマン supótsuùman

sporty [spɔːr'tiː] *adj* (good at sports) スポーツ好きの supótsuzuki no

spot [spɑːt] *n* (mark) 染み shimí; (on pattern, skin etc) はん点 hañten; (place) 場所 bashó; (RADIO, TV) コーナー kòna; (small amount): **a spot of** 少しの sukóshi no
♦*vt* (notice: person, mistake etc) ...に気

が付く ...ni kí gà tsúkù

on the spot (in that place) 現場に genba ni; (immediately) その場で sonó ba de, 即座に sókùza ni; (in difficulty) 困って komántte

spot check n 抜取り検査 nukítorikeñsa

spotless [spɑ:t'lis] adj (shirt, kitchen etc) 清潔な seíketsu na

spotlight [spɑ:t'lait] n スポットライト supóttoraìto

spotted [spɑ:t'id] adj (pattern) はん点模様の hañtenmoyō no

spotty [spɑ:t'i:] adj (face, youth: with freckles) そばかすだらけの sobákasudaràke no; (: with pimples) にきびだらけの nikíbidaràke no

spouse [spaus] n (male/female) 配偶者 haígūsha

spout [spaut] n (of jug) つぎ口 tsugígùchi; (of pipe) 出口 dégùchi
◆vi (flames, water etc) 噴出す fukídasù

sprain [sprein] n ねんざ neñza
◆vt: to sprain one's ankle/wrist 足首 〔手首〕をねんざする ashíkubì〔tékùbi〕wo neñza suru

sprang [spræŋ] pt of **spring**

sprawl [sprɔ:l] vi (person: lie) 寝そべる nesóberù; (: sit) だらしない格好で座る daráshinai kakkò de suwárù; (place) 無秩序に広がる muchítsujo ni hirógarù

spray [sprei] n (small drops) 水煙 mizúkemùri; (sea spray) しぶき shíbuki; (container: hair spray etc) スプレー supúrè; (garden spray) 噴霧器 fuñmukì; (of flowers) 小枝 koéda
◆vt (sprinkle) 噴霧器で...に...を掛ける fuñmukì de ...ni ...wo kakérù; (crops) 消毒する shódoku suru

spread [spred] n (range, distribution) 広がり hirógari; (CULIN: for bread) スプレッド supúreddò; (inf: food) ごちそう gochísō
◆vb (pt, pp spread)
◆vt (lay out) 並べる naráberù; (butter) 塗る núrù; (wings, arms, sails) 広げる hirógerù; (workload, wealth) 分配する buñpai suru; (scatter) まく mákù
◆vi (disease, news) 広がる hirógarù;

(also: **spread out**: stain) 広がる hirógarù

spread-eagled [spred'i:gəld] adj 大の字に寝た daí no jì ni netá

spread out vi (move apart) 散らばる chirábarù

spreadsheet [spred'ʃi:t] n (COMPUT) スプレッドシート supúreddoshìto

spree [spri:] n: to go on a spree ...にふける ...ni fukérù

sprightly [sprait'li:] adj (old person) かくしゃくとした kakúshaku to shitá

spring [spriŋ] n (leap) 跳躍 chóyaku; (coiled metal) ばね bánè; (season) 春 hárù; (of water) 泉 izúmi
◆vi (pt sprang, pp sprung) (leap) 跳ぶ tobú

in spring (season) 春に hárù ni

springboard [spriŋ'bɔ:rd] n スプリングボード supúriñgubōdo

spring-cleaning [spriŋ'kli:'niŋ] n 大掃除 ōsōji ◇春とは関係なく言う hárù to wa kañkeinakù iú

springtime [spriŋ'taim] n 春 hárù

spring up vi (thing: appear) 現れる aráwarerù

sprinkle [spriŋ'kəl] vt (scatter: liquid) まく mákù; (: salt, sugar) 振り掛ける furíkakerù

to sprinkle water on, sprinkle with water ...に水をまく ...ni mizú wò mákù

sprinkler [spriŋ'klər] n (for lawn, to put out fire) スプリンクラー supúriñkurā

sprint [sprint] n (race) 短距離競走 tañkyorikyōsō, スプリント supúriñto
◆vi (gen: run fast) 速く走る háyàku hashírù; (SPORT) スプリントする supúriñto suru

sprinter [sprin'tər] n スプリンター supúriñtā

sprout [spraut] vi (plant, vegetable) 発芽する hatsúga suru

sprouts [sprauts] npl (also: **Brussels sprouts**) 芽キャベツ mekyábètsu

spruce [spru:s] n inv (BOT) トウヒ tóhì
◆adj (neat, smart) スマートな sumátò na

sprung [sprʌŋ] pp of **spring**

spry [sprai] adj (old person) かくしゃく

とした kakúshaku to shitá

spun [spʌn] *pt, pp of* **spin**

spur [spə:r] *n* 拍車 hakúsha; (*fig*) 刺激 shigéki

♦*vt* (*also*: **spur on**) 激励する gekírei suru

on the spur of the moment とっさに tossá ni

spurious [spju:'ri:əs] *adj* (false: attraction) 見せ掛けの misékake no; (: argument) 間違った machígattá

spurn [spə:rn] *vt* (reject) はねつける hanétsukerù

spurt [spə:rt] *n* (of blood etc) 噴出 fuńshutsu; (of energy) 奮発 fuńpatsu

♦*vi* (blood, flame) 噴出す fukídasù

spy [spai] *n* スパイ supáí

♦*vi*: *to spy on* こっそり見張る kossóri mihárù

♦*vt* (see) 見付ける mitsúkerù

spying [spai'iŋ] *n* スパイ行為 supáikòi

sq. *abbr* = **square**

squabble [skwɑ:b'əl] *vi* 口げんかする kuchígeňka suru

squad [skwɑ:d] *n* (MIL, POLICE) 班 háñ; (SPORT) チーム chímu

squadron [skwɑ:d'rən] *n* (MIL) 大隊 daítai

squalid [skwɑ:'lid] *adj* (dirty, unpleasant: conditions) 汚らしい kitánarashiî; (sordid: story etc) えげつない egétsunaí

squall [skwɔ:l] *n* (stormy wind) スコール sukóru

squalor [skwɑ:'lə:r] *n* 汚い環境 kitánai kaňkyō

squander [skwɑ:n'də:r] *vt* (money) 浪費 する rṓhi suru; (chances) 逃す nogásù

square [skwe:r] *n* (shape) 正方形 seíhṓkei; (in town) 広場 hírðba; (*inf*: person) 堅物 katábutsu

♦*adj* (in shape) 正方形の seíhṓkei no; (*inf*: ideas, tastes) 古臭い furúkusaî

♦*vt* (arrange) ...を...に一致させる ...wo ...ni itchí saserù; (MATH) 2乗する nijṓ suru; (reconcile) ...を...と調和させる ...wo ...to chṓwa saserù

all square 貸し借りなし kashíkàri náshī

a square meal 十分な食事 júbùn na shokúji

2 meters square 2メーター平方 ni métā heíhō

2 square meters 2平方メーター ni heíhō métā

squarely [skwe:r'li:] *adv* (directly: fall, land etc) まともに matómo nì; (fully: confront) きっぱりと kippárī to

squash [skwɑ:ʃ] *n* (*US*: marrow etc) カボチャ kabócha; (*BRIT*: drink): *lemon/ orange squash* レモン〔オレンジ〕スカッシュ remón〔orénji〕sukasshù; (SPORT) スカッシュ sukásshù

♦*vt* つぶす tsubúsu

squat [skwɑ:t] *adj* ずんぐりした zuńgurí shita

♦*vi* (*also*: **squat down**) しゃがむ shagámù

squatter [skwɑ:t'ə:r] *n* 不法居住者 fuhṓkyojūsha

squawk [skwɔ:k] *vi* (bird) ぎゃーぎゃー 鳴く gyáagyā nakú

squeak [skwi:k] *vi* (door etc) きしむ ki-shímù; (mouse) ちゅーちゅー鳴く chū-chū nakú

squeal [skwi:l] *vi* (children) きゃーきゃー 言う kyákyā iú; (brakes etc) キーキー言 う kĩkĩ iú

squeamish [skwi:'miʃ] *adj* やたら...に弱 い yatára ...ni yowáî

squeeze [skwi:z] *n* (*gen*: of hand) 握り締 める事 nigírishimerù kotó; (ECON) 金融 引締め kiń-yūhikishime

♦*vt* (*gen*) 絞る shibórù; (hand, arm) 握り 締める nigírishimerù

squeeze out *vt* (juice etc) 絞り出す shibóridasù

squelch [skweltʃ] *vi* ぐちゃぐちゃ音を立 てる gúchàgucha otó wò tatérù

squid [skwid] *n* イカ iká

squiggle [skwig'əl] *n* のたくった線 notá-kuttà séñ

squint [skwint] *vi* (have a squint) 斜視で ある sháshì de árù

♦*n* (MED) 斜視 sháshì

squire [skwai'ə:r] *n* (*BRIT*) 大地主 ṓjinù-shi

squirm [skwə:rm] *vi* 身もだえする mimōdàe suru

squirrel [skwəːrˈəl] *n* リス rísù

squirt [skwəːrt] *vi* 噴出す fukídasù

♦*vt* 噴掛ける fukíkakerù

Sr *abbr* = **senior**

St *abbr* = **saint; street**

stab [stæb] *n* (with knife etc) ひと刺し hitóshashi; (*inf*: try): *to have a stab at (doing) something* ...をやってみる ...wo yatté mirù

♦*vt* (person, body) 刺す sásù

a stab of pain 刺す様な痛み sásù yō na itámi

stability [stəbílˈətiː] *n* 安定 aǹtei

stabilize [steiˈbəlaiz] *vt* (prices) 安定させる aǹtei saserù

♦*vi* (prices, one's weight) 安定する aǹtei suru

stable [steiˈbəl] *adj* (prices, patient's condition) 安定した aǹtei shita; (marriage) 揺るぎない yurúgi naì

♦*n* (for horse) 馬小屋 umágoya

staccato [stəkɑːˈtou] *adv* スタッカート sutákkàto

stack [stæk] *n* (pile) ...の山 ...no yamá

♦*vt* (pile) 積む tsumú

stadium [steiˈdiːəm] *n* 競技場 kyōgijō, スタジアム sutájìamu

staff [stæf] *n* (work force) 職員 shokúìn; (*BRIT*: SCOL) 教職員 kyōshokuìn

♦*vt* ...の職員として働く ...no shokúìn toshite határaku

stag [stæg] *n* 雄ジカ ójìka

stage [steidʒ] *n* (in theater etc) 舞台 bútai; (platform) 台 dái; (profession): *the stage* 俳優業 haíyūgyō; (point, period) 段階 daṅkai

♦*vt* (play) 上演する jōen suru; (demonstration) 行う okónaù

in stages 少しずつ sukóshi zutsu

stagecoach [steidʒˈkoutʃ] *n* 駅馬車 ekíbashà

stage manager *n* 舞台監督 butáikaǹtoku

stagger [stægˈəːr] *vi* よろめく yorómekù

♦*vt* (amaze) 仰天させる gyōten saserù; (hours, holidays) ずらす zurásù

staggering [stægˈəːriŋ] *adj* (amazing) 仰天させる gyōten saserù

stagnant [stægˈnənt] *adj* (water) よどんだ yodóǹda; (economy etc) 停滞した teítai shita

stagnate [stægˈneit] *vi* (economy, business, person) 停滞する teítai suru; (person) だれる darérù

stag party *n* スタッグパーティ sutággupàti

staid [steid] *adj* (person, attitudes) 古めかしい furúmekashiì

stain [stein] *n* (mark) 染み shimí; (coloring) 着色剤 chakúshokuzài, ステイン sutéiǹ

♦*vt* (mark) 汚す yogósù; (wood) ...にステインを塗る ...ni sutéiǹ wo núrù

stained glass window [steind-] *n* ステンドグラスの窓 suténdoguràsu no mádò

stainless steel [steinˈlis-] *n* ステンレス suténresu

stain remover [-rimuːˈvəːr] *n* 染み抜き shimínuki

stair [steːr] *n* (step) 段 dáǹ, ステップ sutéppù

staircase [steːrˈkeis] *n* 階段 kaídan

stairs [steːrz] *npl* (flight of steps) 階段 kaídan

stairway [steːrˈwei] *n* = **staircase**

stake [steik] *n* (post) くい kúì; (COMM: interest) 利害関係 rigáikaṅkei; (BETTING: *gen pl*) 賞金 shōkin

♦*vt* (money, life, reputation) かける kakérù

to stake a claim to ...に対する所有権を主張する ...ni taí surù shoyúken wò shuchō suru

to be at stake 危ぶまれる ayábumarerù

stalactite [stəlækˈtait] *n* しょう乳石 shōnyūseki

stalagmite [stəlægˈmait] *n* 石じゅんせき sekíjun

stale [steil] *adj* (bread) 固くなった katáku nattà; (food, air) 古くなった fúrùku natta; (air) よどんだ yodóǹda; (smell) かび臭い kabíkusaì; (beer) 気の抜けた kí nò nukétà

stalemate [steil'meit] n (CHESS) ステールメート sutérumèto; (fig) 行き詰り ikízumari

stalk [stɔːk] n (of flower, fruit) 茎 kukí
♦vt (person, animal) ...に忍び寄る ...ni shinóbiyorù

stalk off vi 威張って行く ibátte ikù

stall [stɔːl] n (in market) 屋台 yátai; (in stable) 馬房 babó
♦vt (AUT: engine, car) エンストを起す eńsuto wò okósù; (fig: delay: person) 引止める hikítomerù; (: decision etc) 引延ばす hikínobasù
♦vi (AUT: engine, car) エンストを起す eńsuto wò okósù; (fig: person) 時間稼ぎをする jikánkasegi wò suru

stallion [stæl'jən] n 種ウマ tanéùma

stalls [stɔːlz] (BRIT) npl (in cinema, theater) 特別席 tokúbetsusèki

stalwart [stɔːl'wəːrt] adj (worker, supporter, party member) 不動の fudó no

stamina [stæm'inə] n スタミナ sutámina

stammer [stæm'əːr] n どもり dómòri
♦vi どもる domórù

stamp [stæmp] n (postage stamp) 切手 kitté; (rubber stamp) スタンプ sutáñpu; (mark, also fig) 特徴 tokúchōu
♦vi (also: stamp one's foot) 足を踏み鳴らす ashí wò fumínarasù
♦vt (letter) ...に切手を張る ...ni kitté wò harú; (mark) 特徴付ける tokúchōzukerù; (with rubber stamp) ...にスタンプを押す ...ni sutáñpu wo osú

stamp album n 切手帳 kittéchōu

stamp collecting [-kəlek'tiŋ] n 切手収集 kittéshūshū

stampede [stæmpi:d'] n (of animal herd) 暴走 bósōu; (fig: of people) 殺到 sattóu

stance [stæns] n (way of standing) 立っている姿勢 tatté irù shiséi; (fig) 姿勢 shiséi

stand [stænd] n (position) 構え kámàe; (for taxis) 乗場 noríba; (hall, music stand) 台 dái; (SPORT) スタンド sutáñdo; (stall) 屋台 yátai
♦vb (pt, pp stood)
♦vi (be: position, unemployment etc) ...になっている ...ni natté irù; (be on foot) 立

つ tátsù; (rise) 立ち上る tachíagarù; (remain: decision, offer) 有効である yúkō de arù; (in election etc) 立候補する rikkóho suru
♦vt (place: object) 立てる tatérù; (tolerate, withstand: person, thing) ...に耐える ...ni taérù; (treat, invite to) ...におごる ogórù

to make a stand (fig) 立場を執る tachíba wò tórù

to stand for parliament (BRIT) 議員選挙に出馬する giíñsenkyo ni shutsúba suru

standard [stæn'dəːrd] n (level) 水準 suíjun; (norm, criterion) 基準 kijún; (flag) 旗 hatá
♦adj (normal: size etc) 標準的な hyójunteki na; (text) 権威のある kéñ-i no árù

standardize [stæn'dəːrdaiz] vt 規格化する kikákuka suru

standard lamp (BRIT) n フロアスタンド furóasutañdo

standard of living n 生活水準 seíkatsusuijùn

standards [stæn'dəːrdz] npl (morals) 道徳基準 dótoku kijùn

stand by vi (be ready) 待機する táiki suru
♦vt fus (opinion, decision) 守る mamórù; (person) ...の力になる ...no chikára ni narù

stand-by [stænd'bai] n (reserve) 非常用の物 hijóyō no monó

to be on stand-by 待機している táiki shité irù

stand-by ticket n (AVIAT) キャンセル待ちの切符 kyáñserumachi nò kippú

stand down vi (withdraw) 引下がる hikísagarù

stand for vt fus (signify) 意味する ímì suru; (represent) 代表する daíhyō suru; (tolerate) 容認する yóniñ suru

stand-in [stænd'in] n 代行 daíkō

stand in for vt fus (replace) ...の代役を務める ...no daíyaku wò tsutómerù

standing [stæn'diŋ] adj (on feet: ovation) 立ち上っている tachíagatte surù; (permanent: invitation) 持続の jizóku no, 継続の keízoku no

♦n (status) 地位 chíi

of many years' standing 数年前から続いている sǔnen maè kara tsuzúite irù

standing joke n お決りの冗談 o-kímari nò jôdaǹ

standing order (BRIT) n (at bank) 自動振替 jidṓfurǐkae ◇支払額が定額である場合に使う shiháraǐgaku ga teígaku de arú báai ni tsukáù

standing room n 立見席 tachímiséki

stand-offish [stændɔːfíʃ] adj 無愛想な buáǐsō na

standout vi (be prominent) 目立つ medátsù

standpoint [stǽndpɔint] n 観点 kaǹteǹ

standstill [stǽndstil] n: at a standstill (also fig) 滞って todókòtte

to come to a standstill 止ってしまう tomátte shimaù

stand up vi (rise) 立ち上る tachíagarù

stand up for vt fus (defend) 守る mamórù

stand up to vt fus (withstand: also fig) ...に立向かう ...ni tachímukaù

stank [stæŋk] pt of stink

staple [stéipəl] n (for papers) ホチキスの針 hóchìkisu no hárí

♦adj (food etc) 主要の shuyṓ no

♦vt (fasten) ホチキスで留める hóchìkisu de tomérù

stapler [stéiplər] n ホチキス hóchìkisu

star [stɑːr] n (in sky) 星 hoshí; (celebrity) スター sutá

♦vi: to star in ...で主演する ...de shuén suru

♦vt (THEATER, CINEMA) 主役とする shuyáku to surù

starboard [stɑːrbərd] n 右げん úgeǹ

starch [stɑːrtʃ] n (for shirts etc) のりrí; (CULIN) でんぷん deǹpun

stardom [stɑːrdəm] n スターの身分 sutá no mibùn

stare [steːr] n じろじろ見る事 jíròjiro mírù koto

♦vi: to stare at じろじろ見る jíròjiro mírù

starfish [stɑːrfiʃ] n ヒトデ hitode

stark [stɑːrk] adj (bleak) 殺風景な sap-

pǔkèi na

♦adv: stark naked 素っ裸の suppádàka no

starling [stɑːrliŋ] n ムクドリ mukúdòri

starry [stɑːriː] adj (night, sky) 星がよく見える hoshí gà yókù miérù

starry-eyed [stɑːriːaid] adj (innocent) 天真らん漫な teǹshinranman na

stars [stɑːrz] npl: the stars (horoscope) 星占い hoshíuranaì

start [stɑːrt] n (beginning) 初め hajíme; (departure) 出発 shuppátsu; (sudden movement) ぎくっとする事 gikúttð suru kotð; (advantage) リード rǐdo

♦vt (begin) 始める hajímerù; (cause) 引起こす hikíokosù; (found: business etc) 創立する sṓritsu suru; (engine) かける kakérù

♦vi (begin) 始まる hajímarù; (with fright) ぎくっとする gikúttð suru; (train etc) 出発する shuppátsu suru

to start doing/to do something ...をし始める ...wo shihájimerù

starter [stɑːrtər] n (AUT) スタータースutấtā; (SPORT: official) スタータースutấtā; (BRIT: CULIN) 最初の料理 saíshò no ryốri

starting point [stɑːrtiŋ-] n 出発点 shuppátsutèn

startle [stɑːrtəl] vt 驚かす odórokasù

startling [stɑːrtliŋ] adj (news etc) 驚く様な odóroku yố na

start off vi (begin) 始める hajímerù; (begin moving) 出発する shuppátsu suru

start up vi (business etc) 開業する kaígyō suru; (engine) かかる kakárù; (car) 走り出す hashíridasù

♦vt (business etc) 創立する sṓritsu suru; (engine) かける kakérù; (car) 走らせる hashíraserù

starvation [stɑːrveiʃən] n 飢餓 kígà

starve [stɑːrv] vi (inf: be very hungry) おなかがぺこぺこである onáka gà pekópeko dè árù; (also: starve to death) 餓死する gáshǐ suru

♦vt (person, animal: not give food to) 飢えさせる uésaserù; (: to death) 餓死させる gáshǐ saserù

state [steit] *n* (condition) 状態 jōtai; (government) 国 kuní

♦*vt* (say, declare) 明言する meígen suru

to be in a state 取乱している torímidashite irù

stately [steit'li:] *adj* (home, walk etc) 優雅な yūga na

statement [steit'mənt] *n* (declaration) 陳述 chíñjutsu

States [steits] *npl*: *the States* 米国 beíkoku

statesman [steits'mən] (*pl* **statesmen**) *n* リーダー格の政治家 rídākaku nò seíjikà

static [stæt'ik] *n* (RADIO, TV) 雑音 zatsúon

♦*adj* (not moving) 静的な seíteki na

static electricity *n* 静電気 seídeñki

station [stei'ʃən] *n* (RAIL) 駅 ékì; (police station etc) 署 shó; (RADIO) 放送局 hōsōkyoku

♦*vt* (position: guards etc) 配置する haíchi suru

stationary [stei'ʃəne:ri:] *adj* (vehicle) 動いていない ugóite inaì

stationer [stei'ʃənə:r] *n* 文房具屋 buñbōguya

stationer's (shop) [stei'ʃənə:rz-] *n* 文房具店 buñbōguteñ

stationery [stei'ʃəne:ri:] *n* 文房具 buñbōgu

stationmaster [stei'ʃənmæstə:r] *n* (RAIL) 駅長 ekíchō

station wagon (*US*) *n* ワゴン車 wagóñsha

statistic [stətis'tik] *n* 統計値 tōkeichì

statistical [stətis'tikəl] *adj* (evidence, techniques) 統計学的な tōkeigakuteki na

statistics [stətis'tiks] *n* (science) 統計学 tōkeigàku

statue [stætʃ'uː] *n* 像 zō

stature [stætʃ'ɔːr] *n* 身長 shíñchō

status [stei'təs] *n* (position) 身分 míbùn; (official classification) 資格 shikáku; (importance) 地位 chíi

the status quo 現状 geñjō

status symbol *n* ステータスシンボル sutētasushiñboru

statute [stætʃ'uːt] *n* 法律 hōritsu

statutory [stætʃ'uːtɔːri:] *adj* (powers, rights etc) 法定の hōtei no

staunch [stɔːntʃ] *adj* (ally) 忠実な chūjitsu na

stave off [steiv-] *vt* (attack, threat) 防ぐ fuségù

stay [stei] *n* (period of time) 滞在期間 taízaikikàn

♦*vi* (remain) 居残る inókorù; (with someone, as guest) 泊る tomárù; (in place: spend some time) とどまる todómarù

to stay put とどまる todómarù

to stay the night 泊る tomárù

stay behind *vi* 居残る inókorù

stay in *vi* (at home) 家にいる ié nì irù

staying power [stei'iŋ-] *n* 根気 końki

stay on *vi* 残る nokórù

stay out *vi* (of house) 家に戻らない ié nì modóranaì

stay up *vi* (at night) 起きている ókìte i-ru

stead [sted] *n*: *in someone's stead* ...の代りに ...no kawári ni

to stand someone in good stead ...の役に立つ ...no yakú ni tatsù

steadfast [sted'fæst] *adj* 不動の fudō no

steadily [sted'ili:] *adv* (firmly) 着実に chakújitsu ni; (constantly) ずっと zuttó; (fixedly) じっと jittó; (walk) しっかりと shikkárì to

steady [sted'i:] *adj* (constant: job, boyfriend, speed) 決った kimátta, 変らない kawáranaì; (regular: rise in prices) 着実な chakújitsu na; (person, character) 堅実な keñjitsu na; (firm: hand etc) 震えない furúenaì; (calm: look, voice) 落着いた ochítsuita

♦*vt* (stabilize) 安定させる añtei saserù; (nerves) 静める shizúmerù

steak [steik] *n* (*also*: **beefsteak**) ビーフステーキ bífusutèki; (beef, fish, pork etc) ステーキ sutékì

steal [stiːl] (*pt* **stole**, *pp* **stolen**) *vt* 盗む nusúmu

♦*vi* (thieve) 盗む nusúmù; (move secretly) こっそりと行く kossórì to ikú

stealth [stelθ] *n*: *by stealth* こっそりと kossóri to

stealthy [stel'θi:] *adj* (movements, actions) ひそかな hisókà na

steam [sti:m] *n* (mist) 水蒸気 suíjōki; (on window) 曇り kumóri
♦*vt* (CULIN) 蒸す músù
♦*vi* (give off steam) 水蒸気を立てる suíjōki wo tatérù

steam engine *n* 蒸気機関 jōkikikàn

steamer [sti:'mər] *n* 汽船 kisén

steamroller [sti:m'roulə:r] *n* ロードローラー rōdorōrā

steamship [sti:m'ʃip] *n* = **steamer**

steamy [sti:'mi:] *adj* (room) 湯気でもうもうした yúgè de mōmō no; (window) 湯気で曇った yúgè de kumóttà; (heat, atmosphere) 蒸暑い mushíatsuì

steel [sti:l] *n* 鋼鉄 kōtetsu
♦*adj* 鋼鉄の kōtetsu no

steelworks [sti:l'wə:rks] *n* 製鋼所 seíkōjo

steep [sti:p] *adj* (stair, slope) 険しい kewáshiī; (increase) 大幅の ōhaba na; (price) 高い takáī
♦*vt* (fig: soak) 浸す hitásù

steeple [sti:'pəl] *n* せん塔 seńtō

steeplechase [sti:'pəltʃeis] *n* 障害レース shōgairēsu

steer [sti:r] *vt* (vehicle) 運転する uńten suru; (person) 導く michíbikù
♦*vi* (maneuver) 車を操る kurúma wò ayátsurù

steering [sti:r'iŋ] *n* (AUT) ステアリング sutéarìngu

steering wheel *n* ハンドル hańdòru

stem [stem] *n* (of plant) 茎 kukí; (of glass) 足 ashí
♦*vt* (stop: blood, flow, advance) 止める tomérù

stem from *vt fus* (subj: condition, problem) ...に由来する ...ni yurái suru

stench [stentʃ] *n* 悪臭 akúshū

stencil [sten'səl] *n* (lettering) ステンシルで書いた文字 sutéñshiru de káità mójī; (pattern used) ステンシル sutéñshiru
♦*vt* (letters, designs etc) ステンシルで書く sutéñshiru de kákù

stenographer [stənɑ:g'rəfə:r] (US) *n* 速記者 sokkíshà

step [step] *n* (footstep, *also fig*) 一歩 íppò; (sound) 足音 ashíoto; (of stairs) 段 dáñ, ステップ sutéppù
♦*vi*: *to step forward* 前に出る máe ni dérù *to step back* 後ろに下がる ushíro nì sagárù

in/out of step (with) (...と) 歩調が合って〔ずれて〕(...to) hochō ga attè〔zurète〕

stepbrother [step'brʌðə:r] *n* 異父〔異母〕兄弟 ffù〔íbò〕kyōdài

stepdaughter [step'dɔ:tə:r] *n* まま娘 mamámusùme

step down *vi* (fig: resign) 辞任する jinín suru

stepfather [step'fɑ:ðə:r] *n* まま父 mamáchichi

stepladder [step'lædə:r] *n* 脚立 kyatátsu

stepmother [step'mʌðə:r] *n* まま母 mamáhaha

step on *vt fus* (something: walk on) 踏む fumú

stepping stone [step'iŋ-] *n* 飛石 tobíishi

steps [steps] *npl* = **stepladder**

stepsister [step'sistə:r] *n* 異父〔異母〕姉妹 ffù〔íbò〕shímài

stepson [step'sʌn] *n* まま息子 mamámusùko

step up *vt* (increase: efforts, pace etc) 増す masú

stereo [ster'i:ou] *n* (system) ステレオ sutéreo; (record player) レコードプレーヤー rekódopurèyà
♦*adj* (*also*: **stereophonic**) ステレオの sutéreo no

stereotype [ster'i:ətaip] *n* 固定概念 kotéigaìnen

sterile [ster'əl] *adj* (free from germs: bandage etc) 殺菌した sakkín shita; (barren: woman, female animal) 不妊の funín no; (: man, male animal) 子供を作れない kodómo wò tsukúrenaì; (land) 不毛の fumō no

sterilize [ster'əlaiz] *vt* (thing, place) 殺菌する sakkín suru; (woman) ...に避妊手術をする ...ni hinínshujùtsu wo suru

sterling [stəːrˈliŋ] *adj* (silver) 純銀の juńgin no
♦*n* (ECON) 英国通貨 eíkokutsūka
one pound sterling 英貨1ポンド eíka ichí poǹdo

stern [stəːrn] *adj* (father, warning etc) 厳しい kibíshiì
♦*n* (of boat) 船尾 séǹbi

stethoscope [steθˈəskoup] *n* 聴診器 chóshiǹki

stew [stuː] *n* シチュー shichū
♦*vt* (meat, vegetables) 煮込む nikómù; (fruit) 煮る nirú

steward [stuːˈərd] *n* (on ship, plane, train) スチュワード suchúwàdo

stewardess [stuːˈəːrdis] *n* (especially on plane) スチュワーデス suchúwàdesu

stick [stik] *n* (gen: of wood) 棒 bṑ; (as weapon) こん棒 końbō; (walking stick) つえ tsúè
♦*vb* (*pt, pp* **stuck**)
♦*vt* (with glue etc) 張る harú; (*inf*: put) 置く okú; (: tolerate) ...の最後まで我慢する ...no sâigo made gámàn suru; (thrust): *to stick something into* ...の中へ...を突っ込む ...no nákà e ...wo tsukkómù
♦*vi* (become attached) くっつく kuttsúkù; (be immovable) 引っ掛る hikkákarù; (in mind etc) 焼付く yakítsukù
a stick of dynamite ダイナマイト1本 dainamaito ippon

sticker [stikˈəːr] *n* ステッカー sutékkà

sticking plaster [stikˈiŋ-] *n* ばんそうこう bańsōkō

stickler [stikˈləːr] *n*: *to be a stickler for* ...に関してやかましい ...ni káǹ shite yakámashiì

stick out *vi* (ears etc) 突出る tsukíderù

stick up *vi* (hair etc) 立つ tátsù

stick-up [stikˈʌp] (*inf*) *n* ピストル強盗 pisútoru gótò

stick up for *vt fus* (person) ...の肩をもつ ...no kátà wo mótsù; (principle) 守る mamórù

sticky [stikˈiː] *adj* (messy: hands etc) べたべたしている bétàbeta shité irù; (label) 粘着の neńchaku no; (*fig*: situation) 厄介な yákkài na

stiff [stif] *adj* (hard, firm: brush) 堅い katáì; (hard: paste, egg-white) 固まった katámattà; (moving with difficulty: arms, legs, back) こわばった kowábattà; (: door, zip etc) 堅い katáì; (formal: manner, smile) 堅苦しい katágurushiì; (difficult: competition, sentence) 厳しい kibíshiì; (strong: drink, breeze) 強い tsuyóì; (high: price) 高い takáì
♦*adv* (bored, worried, scared) ひどく hídòku

stiffen [stifˈən] *vi* (body, muscles, joints) こわばる kowábarù

stiff neck *n* 首が回らない事 kubí ga mawáranaì kotó

stifle [staiˈfəl] *vt* (cry, yawn) 抑える osáerù; (opposition) 抑圧する yokúatsu suru

stifling [staifˈliŋ] *adj* (heat) 息苦しい ikígurushiì

stigma [stigˈmə] *n* (*fig*: of divorce, failure, defeat etc) 汚名 ómèi

stile [stail] *n* 踏段 fumídan ◇牧場のさくの両側に設けられ、人間が越えられるが家畜が出られない様にした物 bokújō nò sakú nò ryógawa nì mókerarè, niňgen gà koérarerù ga kachíku gà derárenai yò ni shitá monò

stiletto [stiletˈou] (*BRIT*) *n* (*also*: **stiletto heel**) ハイヒール haíhìru

still [stil] *adj* (person, water, air) 動かない ugókanaì; (place) 静寂な seíjaku na
♦*adv* (up to this time, yet) まだ mádà; (even) 更に sárà ni; (nonetheless) それにしても soré ni shite mò

stillborn [stilˈbɔːrn] *adj* 死産の shízàn no

still life *n* 静物画 seíbutsugà

stilt [stilt] *n* (pile) 脚柱 kyakúchū; (for walking on) 竹馬 takéuma

stilted [stilˈtid] *adj* (behavior, conversation) 堅苦しい katákurushiì

stimulant [stimˈjələnt] *n* 覚せい剤 kakúseizài

stimulate [stimˈjəleit] *vt* (person, demand) 刺激する shigéki suru

stimulating [stimˈjəleitiŋ] *adj* (conversation, person, experience) 刺激的な shigékiteki na

stimuli [stim'jəlai] *npl of* **stimulus**

stimulus [stim'jələs] (*pl* **stimuli**) *n* (encouragement, *also* MED) 刺激 shigé-ki

sting [stiŋ] *n* (wound) 虫刺され mushísasaré; (pain) 刺す様な痛み sásù yō na itámi; (organ) 針 hárì
♦*vb* (*pt, pp* **stung**)
♦*vt* (insect, plant etc) 刺す sásù; (*fig*) 傷付ける kizútsukerù
♦*vi* (insect, plant etc) 刺す sásù; (eyes, ointment etc) しみる shimírù

stingy [stin'dʒi:] *adj* けちな kéchì na

stink [stiŋk] *n* (smell) 悪臭 akúshū
♦*vi* (*pt* **stank**, *pp* **stunk**) (smell) におう nióù

stinking [stiŋ'kiŋ] (*inf*) *adj* (*fig*) くそったれの kusóttare no

stint [stint] *n* 仕事の期間 shigóto no kikañ
♦*vi*: **to stint on** (work, ingredients etc) ...をけちる ...wo kechírù

stipulate [stip'jəleit] *vt* ...の条件を付ける ...no jóken wò tsukérù

stir [stə:r] *n* (*fig*: agitation) 騒ぎ sáwàgi
♦*vt* (tea etc) かき混ぜる kakímazerù; (*fig*: emotions) 刺激する shigéki suru
♦*vi* (move slightly) ちょっと動く chóttò ugókù

stirrup [stə:r'əp] *n* あぶみ abúmi

stir up *vt* (trouble) 引起こす hikíokosù

stitch [stitʃ] *n* (SEWING, MED) 一針 hitóhàri; (KNITTING) ステッチ sutétchì; (pain) わき腹のけいれん wakíbara nò keíren
♦*vt* (sew: *gen*, MED) 縫う núù

stoat [stout] *n* てん téñ

stock [sta:k] *n* (supply) 資源 shígèn; (COMM) 在庫品 zaíkohìn; (AGR) 家畜 kachíku; (CULIN) 煮出し汁 nidáshijìru, ストック sutókkù; (descent) 血統 kettó; (FINANCE: government stock etc) 株式 kabúshìki
♦*adj* (*fig*: reply, excuse etc) お決りの okímàri no
♦*vt* (have in stock) 常備する jóbì suru
stocks and shares 債券 saíken
in/out of stock 在庫がある〔ない〕 zaí-

ko gà árù 〔nai〕
to take stock of (*fig*) 検討する keñtō suru

stockbroker [sta:k'broukə:r] *n* 株式仲買人 kabúshikinakagainìn

stock cube (*BRIT*) *n* 固形スープの素 kokéi sùpu no moto

stock exchange *n* 株式取引所 kabúshikitorihikijò

stocking [sta:k'iŋ] *n* ストッキング sutókkiñgu

stockist [sta:k'ist] (*BRIT*) *n* 特約店 tokúyakutèn

stock market *n* 株式市場 kabúshikishijò

stock phrase *n* 決り文句 kimárimoñku

stockpile [sta:k'pail] *n* 備蓄 bichíku
♦*vt* 貯蔵する chozó suru

stocktaking [sta:k'teikiŋ] (*BRIT*) *n* (COMM) 棚卸し tanáoroshi

stock up with *vt* ...を仕入れる ...wo shiírérù

stocky [sta:k'i:] *adj* (strong, short) がっしりした gasshírì shita; (short, stout) ずんぐりした zuñgurì shita

stodgy [sta:dʒ'i:] *adj* (food) こってりした kottérì shita

stoical [stou'ikəl] *adj* 平然とした heízen tò shita

stoke [stouk] *vt* (fire, furnace, boiler) ...に燃料をくべる ...ni neñryō wo kubérù

stole [stoul] *pt of* **steal**
♦*n* ストール sutórù

stolen [stou'lən] *pp of* **steal**

stolid [sta:l'id] *adj* (person, behavior) 表情の乏しい hyójō no tobóshìì

stomach [stʌm'ək] *n* (ANAT) 胃 i; (belly) おなか onáka
♦*vt* (*fig*) 耐える taérù

stomachache [stʌm'əkeik] *n* 腹痛 fukútsu

stone [stoun] *n* (rock) 石 ishí; (pebble) 小石 koíshi; (gem) 宝石 hóseki; (in fruit) 種 tánè; (MED) 結石 kesséki; (*BRIT*: weight) ストーン sutóñ ◇体重の単位、約 6.3 kg taíjū no tañ-i, yákù 6.3 kg
♦*adj* (pottery) ストーンウエアの sutóñ-ueà no

♦*vt* (person) ...に石を投付ける ...ni ishi wo nagetsukeru; (fruit) ...の種を取る ...no táne wo tórù

stone-cold [stoun'kould'] *adj* 冷え切った hiékittà

stone-deaf [stoun'def'] *adj* かなつんぼの kanátsuñbo no

stonework [stoun'wə:rk] *n* (stones) 石造りの物 ishízukùri no mono

stony [stou'ni:] *adj* (ground) 石だらけの ishídaràke no; (*fig*: glance, silence etc) 冷淡な reítan na

stood [stud] *pt, pp* of **stand**

stool [stu:l] *n* スツール sutsúrù

stoop [stu:p] *vi* (*also*: **stoop down**: bend) 腰をかがめる koshí wò kagámerù; (*also*: **have a stoop**) 腰が曲っている koshí gà magátte irù

stop [sta:p] *n* (halt) 停止 teíshi; (short stay) 立寄り tachíyori; (in punctuation: *also*: **full stop**) ピリオド píriòdo; (bus stop etc) 停留所 teíryūjo

♦*vt* (break off) 止める tomérù; (block: pay, check) ...の支払を停止させる ...no shiharai wò teíshi saserù; (prevent: *also*: **put a stop to**) やめさせる yamésaserù

♦*vi* (halt: person) 立ち止る tachídomarù; (: watch, clock) 止る tomárù; (end: rain, noise etc) やむ yamú

to stop doing something ...するのをやめる ...surú no wò yamérù

stop dead *vi* 急に止る kyū ni tomárù

stopgap [sta:p'gæp] *n* (person/thing) 間に合せの人[物] ma ní awase nò hitó [monó]

stop off *vi* 立寄る tachíyorù

stopover [sta:p'ouvə:r] *n* (*gen*) 立寄って泊る事 tachíyottè tomáru kotò; (AVIAT) 給油着陸 kyúyuchakùriku

stoppage [sta:p'idʒ] *n* (strike) ストライキ sutóraìki; (blockage) 停止 teíshi

stopper [sta:p'ə:r] *n* 栓 séñ

stop press *n* 最新ニュース saíshinnyùsu

stopwatch [sta:p'wa:tʃ] *n* ストップウオッチ sutóppuuotchì

storage [stɔːr'idʒ] *n* 保管 hokán

storage heater *n* 蓄熱ヒーター chikú-

netsuhìtā ◇深夜など電気需要の少ない時に熱を作って蓄え、昼間それを放射するヒーター shíñ-ya nádò deñkíjuyò no sukúnai tokî ni netsú wo tsukuttè takúwaè, hirúma sorê wò hōsha suru hítā

store [stɔːr] *n* (stock) 蓄え takúwaè; (depot) 倉庫 sōko; (*BRIT*: large shop) デパート depā́to; (*US*) 店 misé; (reserve) 備蓄 bichíku

♦*vt* (provisions, information etc) 蓄える takúwaerù

in store 未来に待構えて mírai ni machí-kamaetè

storeroom [stɔːr'ruːm] *n* 倉庫 sōko

stores [stɔːrz] *npl* (provisions) 物資 bússhì

store up *vt* (nuts, sugar, memories) 蓄える takúwaerù

storey [stɔːr'iː] (*BRIT*: floor) *n* = **story**

stork [stɔːrk] *n* コウノトリ kōnotòri

storm [stɔːrm] *n* (bad weather) 嵐 áràshi; (*fig*: of criticism, applause etc) 爆発 bakúhatsu

♦*vi* (*fig*: speak angrily) どなる donárù

♦*vt* (attack: place) 攻撃する kōgeki suru

stormy [stɔːr'miː] *adj* (weather) 荒れ模様の arémoyò no; (*fig*: debate, relations) 激しい hagéshìì

story [stɔːr'iː] *n* (*gen*: *also*: **history**) 物語 monógatàri; (lie) うそ úsò; (*US*) 階 kaî

storybook [stɔːr'iːbuk] *n* 童話の本 dōwa no hoñ

stout [staut] *adj* (strong: branch etc) 丈夫な jōbu na; (fat) 太った futóttà; (resolute: friend, supporter) 不動の fudō no

♦*n* (beer) スタウト sutáùto

stove [stouv] *n* (for cooking) レンジ réñji; (for heating) ストーブ sutōbù

stow [stou] *vt* (*also*: **stow away**) しまう shimáù

stowaway [stou'əwei] *n* 密航者 mikkō-sha

straddle [stræd'əl] *vt* (chair, fence etc: *also fig*) ...にまたがる ...ni matágarù

straggle [stræg'əl] *vi* (houses etc) 散在する sañzai suru; (people etc) 落ごする rakúgo suru

straggly [stræg'liː] *adj* (hair) ぼさぼさし

た bósàbosa shita

straight [streit] *adj* (line, road, back, hair) 真っ直ぐの massúgù no; (honest: answer) 正直な shójiki na; (simple: choice, fight) 簡潔な kańketsu na
♦*adv* (directly) 真っ直ぐに massúgù ni; (drink) ストレートで sutórèto de
to put/get something straight (make clear) 明らかにする akíràka ni suru
straight away, straight off (at once) 直ちに tádàchi ni

straighten [streitən] *vt* (skirt, bed etc) 整える totónoerù

straighten out *vt* (*fig*: problem, situation) 解決する kańketsu suru

straight-faced [streit'feist] *adj* まじめな顔をした majíme nà kaó wo shità

straightforward [streitfɔːr'wəːrd] *adj* (simple) 簡単な kantan na; (honest) 正直な shójiki na

strain [strein] *n* (pressure) 負担 fután; (TECH) ひずみ hizúmi; (MED: tension) 緊張 kińchō; (breed) 血統 kettō
♦*vt* (back etc) 痛める itámerù; (stretch: resources) ...に負担をかける ...ni fután wò kakérù; (CULIN: food) こす kosú
back strain (MED) ぎっくり腰 gikkúrigòshi

strained [streind] *adj* (back, muscle) 痛めた itámetà; (relations) 緊迫した kińpaku shità
a strained laugh 作り笑い tsukúriwarài

strainer [strei'nəːr] *n* (CULIN) こし器 koshíkì

strains [streinz] *npl* (MUS) 旋律 señritsu

strait [streit] *n* (GEO) 海峡 kaíkyō

strait-jacket [streit'dʒækit] *n* 拘束衣 kósokuì

strait-laced [streit'leist] *adj* しかつめらしい shikátsumerashiì

straits [streits] *npl*: **to be in dire straits** (*fig*) 困り果てている komárihatete irù

strand [strænd] *n* (of thread, hair, rope) 一本 íppòn

stranded [stræn'did] *adj* (holiday-makers) 足留めされた ashídome saretà

strange [streindʒ] *adj* (not known) 未知の míchì no; (odd) 変な hén na

strangely [streindʒ'liː] *adv* (act, laugh) 変った風に kawátta fú ni ¶ *see also* **enough**

stranger [strein'dʒəːr] *n* (unknown person) 知らない人 shíranai hitò; (from another area) よそ者 yosómono

strangle [stræŋ'gəl] *vt* (victim) 絞殺する shimékorosù; (*fig*: economy) 圧迫する appáku suru

stranglehold [stræŋ'gəlhould] *n* (*fig*) 抑圧 yokúatsu

strap [stræp] *n* 肩ひも katáhimo, ストラップ sutórappù

strapping [stræp'iŋ] *adj* たくましい takúmashiì

strata [stræt'ə] *npl of* **stratum**

stratagem [stræt'ədʒəm] *n* 策略 sakúryàku

strategic [strəti'dʒik] *adj* (positions, withdrawal, weapons etc) 戦略的な señryakuteki na

strategy [stræt'idʒiː] *n* (plan, *also* MIL) 作戦 sakúsen

stratum [strei'təm] (*pl* **strata**) *n* (*gen*) 層 sṓ; (in earth's surface) 地層 chisṓ; (in society) 階層 kaísō

straw [strɔː] *n* (dried stalks) わら wárà; (drinking straw) ストロー sutórō
that's the last straw! もう我慢できない mṓ gáman dekínaì

strawberry [strɔː'beriː] *n* イチゴ ichígo

stray [strei] *adj* (animal) のら ... norá...; (bullet) 流れ ... nagáre...; (scattered) 点在する teñzai suru
♦*vi* (children, animals) はぐれる hagúrerù; (thoughts) 横道にそれる yokómichi ní sorérù

streak [striːk] *n* (stripe: *gen*) 筋 sújì
♦*vt* ...に筋を付ける ...ni sújì wo tsukérù
♦*vi*: **to streak past** 猛スピードで通り過ぎる mōsupídò de tōrisugirù

stream [striːm] *n* (small river) 小川 ogáwa; (of people, vehicles, smoke) 流れ nagáre; (of questions, insults etc) 連続 reñzoku

♦*vt* (SCOL: students) 能力別に分ける nō-ryokubètsu ni wakérù

♦*vi* (water, oil, blood) 流れる nagárerù

to stream in/out (people) 流れ込む〔出る〕 nagárekomù(derù)

streamer [stri:'mə:r] *n* 紙テープ kamítēpu

streamlined [stri:m'laind] *adj* 流線形の ryūsénkei no

street [stri:t] *n* 道 michí

streetcar [stri:t'kɑ:r] (*US*) *n* 路面電車 roméndeṅsha

street lamp *n* 街灯 gaítō

street plan *n* 市街地図 shigáichizù

streetwise [stri:t'waiz] (*inf*) *adj* 裏町の悪知恵を持っている urámàchi no warújie wò motté irù

strength [streŋkθ] *n* (physical) 体力 taíryoku; (of girder, knot etc) 強さ tsúyòsa; (*fig*: power, number) 勢力 seíryoku

strengthen [streŋk'θən] *vt* (building, machine) 補強する hokyō suru; (*fig*: group, argument, relationship) 強くする tsúyòku suru

strenuous [stren'ju:əs] *adj* (energetic: exercise) 激しい hagéshiì; (determined: efforts) 精力的な seíryokuteki na

stress [stres] *n* (force, pressure, *also* TECH) 圧力 atsúryòku; (mental strain) ストレス sutórèsu; (emphasis) 強調 kyōchō

♦*vt* (point, importance etc) 強調する kyōchō suru; (syllable) ...にアクセントを置く ...ni ákùsento wo okú

stretch [stretʃ] *n* (area: of sand, water etc) 一帯 ittái

♦*vi* (person, animal) 背伸びする sénòbi suru; (extend): *to stretch to/as far as* ...まで続く ...màde tsuzúkù

♦*vt* (pull) 伸ばす nobásù; (subj: job, task: make demands of) ...に努力を要求する ...ni dóryòku wo yōkyū suru

stretcher [stretʃ'ə:r] *n* 担架 táṅka

stretch out *vi* 体を伸ばす karáda wò nobásù

♦*vt* (arm etc) 伸ばす nobásù; (spread) 広げる hirógerù

strewn [stru:n] *adj*: *strewn with* ...が散らばっている ...ga chírábatte irù

stricken [strik'ən] *adj* (person) 打ちひしがれた uchíhishigaretà; (city, industry etc) 災いに見舞われた wazáwai nì mimáwaretà

stricken with (arthritis, disease) ...にかかっている ...ni kakátte irù

strict [strikt] *adj* (severe, firm: person, rule) 厳しい kibíshiì; (precise: meaning) 厳密な geñmitsu na

strictly [strikt'li:] *adv* (severely) 厳しく kibíshikù; (exactly) 厳密に geñmitsu ni

stridden [strid'ən] *pp of* **stride**

stride [straid] *n* (step) 大また の一歩 ṓmàta no íppò

♦*vi* (*pt* **strode**, *pp* **stridden**) 大またに歩く ōmàta ni arúkù

strident [straid'ənt] *adj* (voice, sound) 甲高い kañdakaì

strife [straif] *n* 反目 hañmoku

strike [straik] *n* (of workers) ストライキ sutóraìki; (of oil etc) 発見 hakkén; (MIL: attack) 攻撃 kōgeki

♦*vb* (*pt*, *pp* **struck**)

♦*vt* (hit: person, thing) 打つ útsù; (*fig*: subj: idea, thought) ...の心に浮ぶ ...no kókorò ni ukábù; (oil etc) 発見する hakkén suru; (bargain, deal) 決める kimérù

♦*vi* (go on strike) ストライキに入る sutóraìki ni haírù; (attack: soldiers) 攻撃する kōgeki suru; (: illness) 襲う osóu; (: disaster) 見舞う mimáù; (clock) 鳴る narú

on strike (workers) ストライキ中で sutóraikichū de

to strike a match マッチを付ける mátchì wo tsukérù

strike down *vt* (kill) 殺す korósù; (harm) 襲う osóù

striker [strai'kə:r] *n* (person on strike) ストライキ参加者 sutóraikisankashà; (SPORT) 攻撃選手 kōgekiseñshu

strike up *vt* (MUS) 演奏し始める eñsō shihajimerù; (conversation) 始める hajímerù; (friendship) 結ぶ musúbù

striking [strai'kiŋ] *adj* (noticeable) 目立つ medátsù; (attractive) 魅力的な miryōkuteki na

string [striŋ] n (thin rope) ひも himó; (row: of beads etc) 数珠つなぎの物 juzútsunági no monó; (: of disasters etc) 一連 ichíren; (MUS) 弦 gén

♦vt (pt, pp **strung**): to string together つなぐ tsunágù

a string of islands 列島 rettó

to pull strings (fig) コネを利用する kónè wo riyó suru

to string out 一列に並べる ichíretsu nì naráberù

string bean n さや豆 sayámame

string(ed) instrument [striŋ(d)-] n (MUS) 弦楽器 geñgakkì

stringent [strin'dʒənt] adj (rules, measures) 厳しい kibíshiì

strings [striŋz] npl: *the strings* (MUS: section of orchestra) 弦楽器 geñgakkì

strip [strip] n (gen) 細長い切れ hosónagaì kiré; (of land, water) 細長い一帯 hosónagaì ittái

♦vt (undress) 裸にする hadáka ni surù; (paint) はがす hagásù; (also: **strip down**: machine) 分解する buñkai suru

♦vi (undress) 裸になる hadáka ni narù

strip cartoon n 四こま漫画 yoñkoma mañga

stripe [straip] n (gen) しま shima; (MIL, POLICE) そで章 sodéshò

striped [straipt] adj しま模様の shimámoyò no

strip lighting n 蛍光灯 keíkōtō

stripper [strip'ə:r] n ストリッパー sutórippà

striptease [strip'ti:z] n ストリップショー sutórippushò

strive [straiv] (pt **strove**, pp **striven**) vi: *to strive for something/to do something* ...しようと努力する ...shiyó tò dóryòku suru

striven [striv'ən] pp of **strive**

strode [stroud] pt of **stride**

stroke [strouk] n (blow) 一撃 ichígeki; (SWIMMING) ストローク sutórōku; (MED) 脳卒中 nósotchū; (of paintbrush) 筆の運び fudé no hakóbi

♦vt (caress) なでる nadérù

at a stroke 一気に íkkì ni

stroll [stroul] n 散歩 sañpo

♦vi 散歩する sañpo suru

stroller [strou'lə:r] (US) n (pushchair) いす型ベビーカー isúgata bebíkā

strong [strɔːŋ] adj (person, arms, grasp) 強い tsuyóì; (stick) 丈夫な jóbu na; (wind) 強い tsuyóì; (imagination) 想像力のある sózòryoku no árù; (personality) 気性の激しい kishó nò hagéshiì; (influence) 強い tsuyóì; (nerves) 頑丈な gañjō na; (smell) 強烈な kyóretsu na; (coffee) 濃い kóì; (taste) 際立った kiwádattà

they are 50 strong 50人いる gojúnìn irú

stronghold [strɔːŋ'hould] n とりで toríde; (fig) 根城 néjiro

strongly [strɔːŋ'liː] adv (solidly: construct) 頑丈に gañjō ni; (with force: push, defend) 激しく hagéshikù; (deeply: feel, believe) 強く tsuyóku

strongroom [strɔːŋ'ruːm] n 金庫室 kiñkoshìtsu

strove [strouv] pt of **strive**

struck [strʌk] pt, pp of **strike**

structural [strʌk'tʃəːrəl] adj (damage, defect) 構造的な kózòteki na

structure [strʌk'tʃəːr] n (organization) 組織 sóshìki; (building) 構造物 kózōbùtsu

struggle [strʌg'əl] n 闘争 tósò

♦vi (try hard) 努力する dóryòku suru; (fight) 戦う tatákaù

strum [strʌm] vt (guitar) つま弾く tsumábikù

strung [strʌŋ] pt, pp of **string**

strut [strʌt] n (wood, metal) 支柱 shichú

♦vi 威張って歩く ibátte arukù

stub [stʌb] n (of check, ticket etc) 控え hikáè; (of cigarette) 吸殻 suígara

♦vt: *to stub one's toe* つま先をぶつける tsumásaki wò butsúkerù

stubble [stʌb'əl] n (AGR) 切株 kiríkàbu; (on chin) 不精ひげ bushóhìge

stubborn [stʌb'əːrn] adj (child, determination) 頑固な gáñko na

stub out vt (cigarette) もみ消す momíkesù

stuck [stʌk] pt, pp of **stick**

♦*adj* (jammed) 引っ掛かっている hikkákatte iru

stuck-up [stʌk'ʌp'] (*inf*) *adj* 天ぐになっている teñgu nǐ natté irù

stud [stʌd] *n* (on clothing etc) 飾りボタン kazáribotàn; (earring) 丸玉 marúdamà (on sole of boot) スパイク supáĭku; (*also*: **stud farm**) 馬の繁殖牧場 umá nò hañshokubokujò; (*also*: **stud horse**) 種馬 tanéùma

♦*vt* (*fig*): **studded with** ...をちりばめた ...wo chiríbametà

student [stu:'dənt] *n* (at university) 学生 gakúsei; (at lower schools) 生徒 seíto

♦*adj* (nurse, life, union) 学生の gakúsei no

student driver (*US*) *n* 仮免許運転者 karímenkyo unteñsha

studies [stʌd'iz] *npl* (subjects studied) 勉強の科目 beñkyō nò kamóku

studio [stu:'di:ou] *n* (TV etc) スタジオ sutájîo; (sculptor's etc) アトリエ atórìè

studio apartment (*BRIT* **studio flat**) *n* ワンルームマンション wañrûmu mánshon

studious [stu:'di:əs] *adj* (person) 勉強家の beñkyòka no; (careful: attention) 注意深い chûibukaì

studiously [stu:'di:əsli:] *adv* (carefully) 注意深く chûibukakù

study [stʌd'i:] *n* (activity) 勉強 beñkyō; (room) 書斎 shosái

♦*vt* (learn about: subjects) 勉強する beñkyō suru; (examine: face, evidence) 調べる shiráberù

♦*vi* 勉強する beñkyō suru

stuff [stʌf] *n* (thing(s)) 物 monó, 事 kotó; (substance) material 素質 soshítsu

♦*vt* (soft toy: *also* CULIN) ...に詰める ...ni tsumérù; (dead animals) はく製にする hakúsei ni surù; (*inf*: push: object) 差込む sashíkomù

stuffing [stʌf'iŋ] *n* (gen, CULIN) 詰物 tsumémòno

stuffy [stʌf'i:] *adj* (room) 空気の悪い kúki nò warúì; (person, ideas) 古臭い furúkusaì

stumble [stʌm'bəl] *vi* つまづく tsumázukù

to stumble across/on (*fig*) ...に出くわす ...ni dekúwasù

stumbling block [stʌm'bliŋ-] *n* 障害 shōgai

stump [stʌmp] *n* (of tree) 切株 kiríkàbu; (of limb) 断端 dañtan

♦*vt*: **to be stumped** まごつく magótsukù

stun [stʌn] *vt* (subj: news) あ然とさせる azen to saserù; (: blow on head) 気絶させる kizetsu saserù

stung [stʌŋ] *pt, pp of* **sting**

stunk [stʌŋk] *pp of* **stink**

stunning [stʌn'iŋ] *adj* (*fig*: news, event) 仰天させる gyóten saserù; (: girl, dress) 美しい utsúkushiì

stunt [stʌnt] *n* (in film) スタント sutáñto; (: **publicity stunt**) 宣伝用のトリック señden-yò no toríkkù

stunted [stʌn'tid] *adj* (trees, growth etc) 成長を阻害された seíchō wò sogái saretà

stuntman [stʌnt'mən] (*pl* **stuntmen**) *n* スタントマン sutáñtoman

stupefy [stu:'pəfai] *vt* ぼう然とさせる bṓzen to saserù

stupendous [stu:pen'dəs] *adj* 途方もない tohōmonaì

stupid [stu:'pid] *adj* (person, question etc) ばかな bákà na

stupidity [stu:pid'iti:] *n* 愚かさ orókasà

stupor [stu:'pər] *n* 前後不覚 zeñgofukáku

sturdy [stə:r'di:] *adj* (person, thing) がっちりした gatchírì shita

stutter [stʌt'ə:r] *n* どもり dómòri

♦*vi* どもる domórù

sty [stai] *n* (*also*: **pigsty**) 豚小屋 butágoya

stye [stai] *n* (MED) ものもらい monómorài

style [stail] *n* (way, attitude) やり方 yaríkata; (elegance) 優雅さ yū́gàsa; (design) スタイル sutáĭru

stylish [stai'liʃ] *adj* 優雅な yū́gà na

stylus [stai'ləs] *n* (of record player) 針 harí

suave [swɑːv] *adj* 物腰の丁寧な monógoshi no teínei na

subconscious [sʌbkəːn'tʃəs] *adj* (desire etc) 潜在意識の señzaiishĭki no

subcontract [sʌbkəntrækt'] *vt* 下請に出す shitáuke nǐ dásù

subdivide [sʌbdivaid'] *vt* 小分けする kowáke suru

subdue [səbduː'] *vt* (rebels etc) 征服する seífuku suru; (passions) 抑制する yokúsei suru

subdued [səbduːd'] *adj* (light) 柔らかな yawárakà na; (person) 落込んだ ochíkoǹda

subject [*n* sʌb'dʒikt *vb* səbjekt'] *n* (matter) 話題 wadái; (SCOL) 学科 gakká; (of kingdom) 臣民 shifimiǹ; (GRAMMAR) 主語 shúgò

♦*vt*: *to subject someone to something* …を…にさらす …wo …ni sarásù

to be subject to (law) …に服従しなければならない …ni fukújū shinakerèba naránaì; (heart attacks) …が起りやすい …ga okóriyasuǐ

to be subject to tax 課税される kazéi sarerù

subjective [səbdʒek'tiv] *adj* 主観的な shukánteki na

subject matter *n* (content) 内容 naíyò

subjugate [sʌb'dʒəgeit] *vt* (people) 征服する seífuku suru

subjunctive [səbdʒʌŋk'tiv] *n* 仮定法 katéihō

sublet [sʌb'let] *vt* また貸しする matágashi suru

sublime [səblaim'] *adj* 素晴らしい subárashiǐ

submachine gun [sʌbməʃiːn'-] *n* 軽機関銃 keíkikaǹjū

submarine [sʌb'məːriːn] *n* 潜水艦 señsuikan

submerge [səbməːrdʒ'] *vt* 水中に沈める suíchū nǐ shizúmerù

♦*vi* (submarine, sea creature) 潜る mogúrù

submission [səbmiʃ'ən] *n* (state) 服従 fukújū; (claim) 申請書 shiñseishò; (of plan) 提出 teíshutsu

submissive [səbmis'iv] *adj* 従順な jújun na

submit [səbmit'] *vt* (proposal, application etc) 提出する teíshutsu suru

♦*vi*: *to submit to something* …に従う …ni shitágaù

subnormal [sʌbnɔːr'məl] *adj* (below average: temperatures) 通常以下の tsújōikà no

subordinate [səbɔːr'dənit] *adj* 二次的な nijíteki na

♦*n* 部下 búkà

subpoena [səpiː'nə] *n* (LAW) 召喚状 shókaǹjō

subscribe [səbskraib'] *vi*: *to subscribe to* (opinion) …に同意する …ni dóǐ suru; (fund) …に寄付する …ni kifú suru; (magazine etc) …を購読する …wo kódoku suru

subscriber [səbskraib'əːr] *n* (to periodical, telephone) 購読者 kódokushà; (to telephone) 加入者 kanyúshà

subscription [səbskrip'ʃən] *n* (to magazine etc) 購読契約 kódokukeiyáku

subsequent [sʌb'səkwənt] *adj* (following) その後の sonó atò no; (resulting) その結果として起る sonó kekkà toshite okórù

subsequently [sʌb'səkwəntliː] *adv* その後 sonó atò

subside [səbsaid'] *vi* (feeling) 収る osámarù; (flood) ひく hikú; (wind) やむ yamú

subsidence [səbsaid'əns] *n* (in road etc) 陥没 kañbotsu

subsidiary [səbsid'iːeːriː] *adj* (question, details) 二次的な nijíteki na

♦*n* (also: **subsidiary company**) 子会社 kogáisha

subsidize [sʌb'sidaiz] *vt* (education, industry etc) …に補助金を与える …ni hojókìn wo atáerù

subsidy [sʌb'sidiː] *n* 補助金 hojókìn

subsistence [səbsis'təns] *n* (ability to live) 最低限度の生活水準 saíteigeǹdo no seíkatsusuijùn

subsistence allowance (*BRIT*) *n* (advance payment) 支度金 shitákukin;

(for expenses etc) 特別手当 tokúbetsu teáte

substance [sʌb'stəns] *n* (product, material) 物質 busshítsu

substantial [səbstæn'tʃəl] *adj* (solid) 頑丈な ganjō na; (fig: reward, meal) 多い ōi

substantially [səbstæn'tʃəli:] *adv* (by a large amount) 大いに ōi ni; (in essence) 本質的に honshitsuteki ni

substantiate [səbstæn'tʃi:eit] *vt* 裏付ける urázukerù

substitute [sʌb'stitu:t] *n* (person) 代人 daínin; (thing) 代用品 daíyōhìn
♦*vt*: to substitute A for B B の代りに A を置く B nò kawári nì A wò okú

substitution [sʌbstitu:'ʃən] *n* (act of substituting) 置換え okíkae; (SOCCER) 選手交代 seńshukōtai

subterfuge [sʌb'tə:rfju:dʒ] *n* 策略 sakúryàku

subterranean [sʌbtərei'ni:ən] *adj* 地下の chiká no

subtitle [sʌb'taitəl] *n* 字幕スーパー jimákusūpā

subtle [sʌt'əl] *adj* (slight: change) 微妙な bimyō na; (indirect: person) 腹芸のうまい harágei no umái

subtlety [sʌt'əlti:] *n* (small detail) 微妙な所 bimyō nà tokórò; (art of being subtle) 腹芸 harágei

subtotal [sʌbtou'təl] *n* 小計 shōkei

subtract [səbtrækt'] *vt* ...から ...を引く ...kárà ...wò hikú

subtraction [səbtræk'ʃən] *n* 引算 hikízan

suburb [sʌb'ə:rb] *n* 都市周辺の自治体 toshíshūhen no jichítai

suburban [səbə:r'bən] *adj* (train, lifestyle etc) 郊外の kōgai no

suburbia [səbə:r'bi:ə] *n* 郊外 kōgai

suburbs [sʌb'ə:rbz] *npl*: the suburbs (area) 郊外 kōgai

subversive [səbvə:r'siv] *adj* (activities, literature) 破壊的な hakáiteki na

subway [sʌb'wei] *n* (US: underground railway) 地下鉄 chikátetsu; (BRIT: underpass) 地下道 chikádō

succeed [səksi:d'] *vi* (plan etc) 成功する seíkō suru; (person: in career etc) 出生する shusshō suru
♦*vt* (in job) ...の後任になる ...no kōnin ni narù; (in order) ...の後に続く ...no átò ni tsuzúkù

to succeed in doing ...する事に成功する ...surú kotò ni seíkō suru

succeeding [səksi:'diŋ] *adj* (following) その後の sonó átò no

success [səkses'] *n* (achievement) 成功 seíkō; (hit, *also* person) 大ヒット daíhittò

successful [səkses'fəl] *adj* (venture) 成功した seíkō shita; (writer) 出生した shusshō shita

to be successful 成功する seíkō suru

to be successful in doing ...する事に成功する ...surú kotò ni seíkō suru

successfully [səkses'fəli:] *adv* (complete, do) うまく úmàku

succession [səkseʃ'ən] *n* (series) 連続 reńzoku; (to throne etc) 継承 keíshō

in succession 立続けに tatétsuzuke ni

successive [səkses'iv] *adj* 連続の reńzoku no

successor [səkses'ə:r] *n* 後任 kōnin

succinct [səksiŋkt'] *adj* 簡潔な kańketsu na

succulent [sʌk'jələnt] *adj* 汁が多くておいしい shírù ga ōkùte oíshiì

succumb [səkʌm'] *vi* (to temptation) 負ける makérù; (to illness: become very ill) ...で倒れる ...de taórerù; (: die) ...で死ぬ ...de shinú

such [sʌtʃ] *adj* (emphasizing similarity) この〔その, あの〕様な konó〔sonó, anó〕yō na; (of that kind): such a book そんな本 sofina hoñ; (so much): such courage そんな勇気 sofina yūki
♦*adv* こんな〔そんな, あんな〕に kofina〔sofina, afina〕ni

such books そんな本 sofina hoñ

such a long trip あんなに長い旅行 afina nì nagái ryokō

such a lot of そんなに沢山の sofina nì takúsan no

such as (like) ...の様な ...no yō na

as such その物 sonó monò

such-and-such [sʌtʃ'ənsʌtʃ] *adj* しかじ かの shikájìka no

suck [sʌk] *vt* (gen: ice-lolly etc) なめる namérù; (bottle, breast) 吸う súù

sucker [sʌk'əːr] *n* (ZOOL) 吸盤 kyúban; (inf: easily cheated person) かも kámò

suction [sʌk'ʃən] *n* 吸引 kyúin

Sudan [suːdæn'] *n* スーダン súdan

sudden [sʌd'ən] *adj* (unexpected, rapid: increase, shower, change) 突然の totsúzen no

　all of a sudden (unexpectedly) 突然 totsúzen

suddenly [sʌd'ənliː] *adv* (unexpectedly) 突然 totsúzen

suds [sʌdz] *npl* 石けんの泡 sekkén no a-wà

sue [suː] *vt* ...を相手取って訴訟を起す ...wo aítedottè soshó wò okósù

suede [sweid] *n* スエード suédò

suet [suː'it] *n* 脂肪 shibó ◊料理に使うウ シやヒツジの堅い脂肪を指す ryórì ni tsukáù ushí yà hitsúji nò katáì shibó wò sásù

Suez [suː'ez] *n*: **the Suez Canal** スエズ 運河 suézu unga

suffer [sʌf'əːr] *vt* (undergo: hardship etc) 経験する keíken suru; (bear: pain, rude-ness) 我慢する gámàn suru

　◆*vi* (be harmed: person, results etc) 苦し む kurúshimù; (results etc) 悪くなる wá-rùku narù

　to suffer from (illness etc) ...の病気にか かっている ...no byókì ni kakátte irù

sufferer [sʌf'əːrəːr] *n* (MED) 患者 kańja

suffering [sʌf'əːriŋ] *n* (hardship) 苦しみ kurúshimi

suffice [səfais'] *vi* 足りる tarírù

sufficient [səfiʃ'ənt] *adj* 十分な júbùn na

sufficiently [səfiʃ'əntliː] *adv* 十分に jú-bùn ni

suffix [sʌf'iks] *n* 接尾辞 setsúbìjì

suffocate [sʌf'əkeit] *vi* 窒息する chissó-ku suru

suffocation [sʌfəkei'ʃən] *n* 窒息 chissó-ku

suffrage [sʌf'ridʒ] *n* (right to vote) 参政 権 sańseikèn

suffused [səfjuːzd'] *adj*: **suffused with** (light, color, tears) ...で満たされた ...de mitásaretà

sugar [ʃug'əːr] *n* 砂糖 satő

　◆*vt* (tea etc) ...に砂糖を入れる ...ni satő wò irérù

sugar beet *n* サトウダイコン satődaìkon

sugar cane *n* サトウキビ satőkìbi

suggest [səgdʒest'] *vt* (propose) 提案する teían suru; (indicate) 示唆する shísà suru

suggestion [səgdʒes'tʃən] *n* (proposal) 提案 teían; (indication) 示唆 shísà

suggestive [səgdʒes'tiv] (*pej*) *adj* (re-marks, looks) 卑わいな hiwái na

suicide [suː'isaid] *n* (death, *also fig*) 自殺 jisátsu; (person) 自殺者 jisátsushà ¶ *see also* **commit**

suit [suːt] *n* (man's) 背広 sebíro; (woman's) スーツ sútsu; (LAW) 訴訟 soshő; (CARDS) 組札 kumífùda

　◆*vt* (gen: be convenient, appropriate) ...に都合がいい ...ni tsugő ga iî; (color, clothes) ...に似合う ...ni niáù; (adapt): **to suit something to** ...を...に合せる ...wo ...ni awáserù

　well suited (well matched: couple) お似 合いの o-níaì no

suitable [suː'təbəl] *adj* (convenient: time, moment) 都合のいい tsugő no iî; (appro-priate: person, clothes etc) 適当な tekítö na

suitably [suː'təbliː] *adv* (dressed) 適当に tekítö ni; (impressed) 期待通りに kitái-dőri ni

suitcase [suːt'keis] *n* スーツケース sútsu-kèsu

suite [swiːt] *n* (of rooms) スイートルーム suítorùmu; (MUS) 組曲 kumíkyòku; (furniture): **bedroom / dining room suite** 寝室〔食堂〕用家具の一そろい shiń-shitsu(shokúdō)yő kágù no hitósòroi

suitor [suː'təːr] *n* 求婚者 kyúkoǹsha

sulfur [sʌl'fəːr] (*US*) *n* 硫黄 iő

sulk [sʌlk] *vi* すねる sunérù

sulky [sʌl'kiː] *adj* (child, silence) すねた sunétà

sullen [sʌl'ən] *adj* (person, silence) すね た sunétà

sulphur [sʌl'fə:r] *n* = sulfur

sultan [sʌl'tən] *n* サルタン sárùtan ◇ イスラム教国の君主 isúramukyōkoku no kúǹshu

sultana [sʌltæn'ə] *n* (fruit) 白いレーズン shiróî rēsùn

sultry [sʌl'tri:] *adj* (weather) 蒸暑い mushîfatsuî

sum [sʌm] *n* (calculation) 計算 keísan; (amount) 金額 kíngaku; (total) 合計 gōkei

summarize [sʌm'ə:raiz] *vt* 要約する yōyaku suru

summary [sʌm'ə:ri:] *n* 要約 yōyaku

summer [sʌm'ə:r] *n* 夏 natsú
♦*adj* (dress, school) 夏の natsú no
in summer 夏に natsú ni

summer holidays *npl* 夏休み natsúyasùmi

summerhouse [sʌm'ə:rhaus] *n* (in garden) 東屋 azúmayà

summertime [sʌm'ə:rtaim] *n* (season) 夏 natsú

summer time *n* (by clock) サマータイム samátaìmu

summer vacation (*US*) *n* 夏休み natsúyasùmi

summit [sʌm'it] *n* (of mountain) 頂上 chōjō; (*also:* **summit conference/meeting**) 首脳会議 shunōkaîgi, サミット samíttò

summon [sʌm'ən] *vt* (person, police, help) 呼ぶ yobú; (to a meeting) 召集する shōshū suru; (LAW: witness) 召喚する shōkan suru

summons [sʌm'ənz] *n* (LAW) 召喚書 shōkaǹsho; (*fig*) 呼出し yobídashi
♦*vt* (JUR) 召喚する shōkan suru

summon up *vt* (strength, energy, courage) 奮い起す furúiokosù

sump [sʌmp] (*BRIT*) *n* (AUT) オイルパン oírupaǹ

sumptuous [sʌmp'tʃu:əs] *adj* 豪華な gōkà na

sum up *vt* (describe) 要約する yōyaku suru
♦*vi* (summarize) 要約する yōyaku suru

sun [sʌn] *n* (star) 太陽 taíyō; (sunshine)

日光 níkkò

sunbathe [sʌn'beið] *vi* 日光浴する nikkōyòku suru

sunburn [sʌn'bə:rn] *n* (painful) 日焼け hiyáke

sunburnt [sʌn'bə:rnt] *adj* (tanned) 日に焼けた hi ní yaketà; (painfully) ひどく日焼けした hídòku hiyáke shita

Sunday [sʌn'dei] *n* 日曜日 nichíyòbi

Sunday school *n* 日曜学校 nichíyōgakkò

sundial [sʌn'dail] *n* 日時計 hidōkèi

sundown [sʌn'daun] *n* 日没 nichíbotsu

sundries [sʌn'dri:z] *npl* (miscellaneous items) その他 sonó tà

sundry [sʌn'dri:] *adj* (various) 色々な iróiro na
all and sundry だれもかも dárè mo kámò

sunflower [sʌn'flauə:r] *n* ヒマワリ himáwàri

sung [sʌŋ] *pp of* **sing**

sunglasses [sʌn'glæsiz] *npl* サングラス sańguràsu

sunk [sʌŋk] *pp of* **sink**

sunlight [sʌn'lait] *n* 日光 níkkò

sunlit [sʌn'lit] *adj* 日に照らされた hi ní terasaretà

sunny [sʌn'i:] *adj* (weather, day) 晴れた háreta; (place) 日当りの良い hiátari no yoì

sunrise [sʌn'raiz] *n* 日の出 hí nó de

sun roof *n* (AUT) サンルーフ sańrùfu

sunset [sʌn'set] *n* 日没 nichíbotsu

sunshade [sʌn'ʃeid] *n* (over table) パラソル páràsoru

sunshine [sʌn'ʃain] *n* 日光 níkkò

sunstroke [sʌn'strouk] *n* 日射病 nisshábyō

suntan [sʌn'tæn] *n* 日焼け hiyáke

suntan lotion *n* 日焼け止めローション hiyákedome rōshon

suntan oil *n* サンタンオイル sańtan oirù

super [su:'pə:r] (*inf*) *adj* 最高の saíkō no

superannuation [su:pə:rænju:ei'ʃən] *n* 年金の掛金 neńkin nò kakékìn

superb [su:pə:rb'] *adj* 素晴しい subárashiî

supercilious [su:pə:rsil'i:əs] adj (disdainful, haughty) 横柄な ōhei na

superficial [su:pə:rfíʃ'əl] adj (wound) 浅い asái; (knowledge) 表面的な hyōmenteki na; (shallow: person) 浅はかな asáhaka na

superfluous [su:pə:r'flu:əs] adj 余計な yokéi na

superhuman [su:pə:rhju:'mən] adj 超人的な chōjinteki na

superimpose [su:pə:rimpouz'] vt 重ね合せる kasáneawaserù

superintendent [su:pə:rinten'dənt] n (of place, activity) …長 …chō; (POLICE) 警視 keíshi

superior [səpi:r'i:ə:r] adj (better) (より) すぐれた (yorí) sugúretà; (more senior) 上位の jōi no; (smug) 偉ぶった erábuttà
♦n 上司 jōshì

superiority [səpi:ri:ɔ:r'iti:] n 優位性 yūisei

superlative [səpə:r'lətiv] n (LING) 最上級 saíjōkyū

superman [su:'pə:rmæn] (pl **supermen**) n 超人 chōjin

supermarket [su:'pə:rmɑ:rkit] n スーパー sūpā

supernatural [su:pə:rnætʃ'ə:rəl] adj (creature, force etc) 超自然の chōshizen no
♦n: **the supernatural** 超自然の現象 chōshizen no geńshō

superpower [su:pə:rpau'ə:r] n (POL) 超大国 chōtaikoku

supersede [su:pə:rsi:d'] vt …に取って代る …ni tóttè kawárù

supersonic [su:pə:rsɑ:n'ik] adj (flight, aircraft) 超音速の chōonsoku no

superstar [su:'pə:rstɑ:r] n (CINEMA, SPORT etc) スーパースター sūpāsutā

superstition [su:pə:rstiʃ'ən] n 迷信 meíshin

superstitious [su:pə:rstiʃ'əs] adj (person) 迷信深い meíshinbùkai; (practices) 迷信的な meíshinteki na

supertanker [su:'pə:rtæŋkə:r] n スーパータンカー sūpātaǹkā

supervise [su:'pə:rvaiz] vt (person, activity) 監督する kaǹtoku suru

supervision [su:pə:rviʒ'ən] n 監督 kaǹtoku

supervisor [su:'pə:rvaizə:r] n (of workers, students) 監督 kaǹtoku

supine [su:'pain] adj 仰向きの aōmuki no

supper [sʌp'ə:r] n (early evening) 夕食 yūshoku; (late evening) 夜食 yashóku

supplant [səplænt'] vt (person, thing) …に取って代る …ni tóttè kawárù

supple [sʌp'əl] adj (person, body, leather etc) しなやかな shináyàka na

supplement [n sʌp'ləmənt vb sʌp'ləment] n (additional amount, e.g. vitamin supplement) 補給品 hokyūhìn; (of book) 補遺 hōì; (of newspaper, magazine) 付録 furóku
♦vt 補足する hosóku suru

supplementary [sʌpləmen'tə:ri:] adj (question) 補足的な hosókuteki na

supplementary benefit (BRIT) n 生活保護 seíkatsuhogò

supplier [səplai'ə:r] n (COMM: person, firm) 供給業者 kyōkyūgyōsha

supplies [səplaiz'] npl (food) 食料 shokúryō; (MIL) 軍需品 guǹjuhìn

supply [səplai'] vt (provide) 供給する kyōkyū suru; (equip): **to supply (with)** (…を) 支給する (…wo) shikyū suru
♦n (stock) 在庫品 zaíkohìn; (supplying) 供給 kyōkyū

supply teacher (BRIT) n 代行教師 daíkōkyōshi

support [səpɔ:rt'] n (moral, financial etc) 支援 shién; (TECH) 支柱 shichū
♦vt (morally: football team etc) 支援する shién suru; (financially: family etc) 養う yashínaù; (TECH: hold up) 支える saérù; (sustain: theory etc) 裏付ける urázukerù

supporter [səpɔ:r'tə:r] n (POL etc) 支援者 shiénshà; (SPORT) ファン faǹ

suppose [səpouz'] vt (think likely) …だと思う …dá tò omóù; (imagine) 想像する sōzō suru; (duty): **to be supposed to do something** …する事になっている …surú kotò ni natté irù

supposedly [səpou'zidli:] adv …だとされ

て ...dá tò saréte

supposing [səpou'ziŋ] *conj* もし ... móshì

suppress [səpres'] *vt* (revolt) 鎮圧する chín-atsu suru; (information) 隠す kakúsù; (feelings, yawn) 抑える osáerù

suppression [səpreʃ'ən] *n* (of revolt) 鎮圧 chín-atsu; (of information) 隠ぺい iñpei; (of feelings etc) 抑制 yokúsei

supremacy [səprem'əsi:] *n* 優越 yúetsu

supreme [səpri:m'] *adj* (in titles: court etc) 最高の saíkō no; (effort, achievement) 最上の saíjō no

surcharge [sər'tʃɑːrdʒ] *n* (extra cost) 追加料金 tsuíkaryōkin

sure [ʃuːr] *adj* (definite, convinced) 確信している kakúshin shite irù; (aim, remedy) 確実な kakújitsu na; (friend) 頼りになる táyòri ni nárù

to make sure of something ...を確かめる ...wo tashíkamerù

to make sure that ...だと確かめる ...dá tò tashíkamerù

sure! (of course) いいとも íi to mo

sure enough 案の定 añ no jō

sure-footed [ʃuːr'fut'id] *adj* 足のしっかりした ashí nò shikkárì shita

surely [ʃuːr'li:] *adv* (certainly: *US: also:* **sure**) 確かに táshìka ni

surety [ʃuːr'əti:] *n* (money) 担保 táñpo

surf [səːrf] *n* 打寄せる波 uchíyoseru namì

surface [səːr'fis] *n* (of object) 表面 hyōmen; (of lake, pond) 水面 suímen

♦*vt* (road) 舗装する hosō suru

♦*vi* (fish, person in water: *also fig*) 浮上する fujō suru

surface mail *n* 普通郵便 futsúyùbin

surfboard [səːrf'bɔːrd] *n* サーフボード sáfubōdo

surfeit [səːr'fit] *n*: **a surfeit of** ...の過剰 ...no kajō

surfing [səːr'fiŋ] *n* サーフィン sáfìn

surge [səːrdʒ] *n* (increase: *also fig*) 高まり takámarì

♦*vi* (water) 波打つ namíutsù; (people, vehicles) 突進する tosshín suru; (emotion) 高まる takámarù

surgeon [səːr'dʒən] *n* 外科医 gekái-ì

surgery [səːr'dʒəri:] *n* (treatment) 手術 shújutsu; (*BRIT*: room) 診察室 shiñsatsushìtsu; (: *also:* **surgery hours**) 診療時間 shiñryō jikàn

surgical [səːr'dʒikəl] *adj* (instrument, mask etc) 外科用の gekáyō no; (treatment) 外科の gekā no

surgical spirit (*BRIT*) *n* 消毒用アルコール shōdokuyō arúkòru

surly [səːr'li:] *adj* 無愛想な buáìsō na

surmount [səːrmaunt'] *vt* (*fig*: problem, difficulty) 乗越える noríkoerù

surname [səːr'neim] *n* 名字 myōji

surpass [səːrpæs'] *vt* (person, thing) しのぐ shinógù

surplus [səːr'pləs] *n* (extra, *also* COMM, ECON) 余剰分 yojōbùn

♦*adj* (stock, grain etc) 余剰の yojō no

surprise [səːrpraiz'] *n* (unexpected) 思い掛け無い物 omóigakenaì monó; (astonishment) 驚き odóroki

♦*vt* (astonish) 驚かす odórokasù; (catch unawares: army, thief) ...の不意を突く ...no fuí wò tsukú

surprising [səːrpraiz'iŋ] *adj* 驚くべき odórokubèki

surprisingly [səːrpraiz'iŋli:] *adv* (easy, helpful) 驚く程 odóroku hodò

surrealist [səːri:'əlist] *adj* (paintings etc) 超現実主義の chōgenjitsushùgi no

surrender [səren'dəːr] *n* 降伏 kōfuku

♦*vi* (army, hijackers etc) 降伏する kōfuku suru

surreptitious [səːrəptiʃ'əs] *adj* ひそかな hisōkà na

surrogate [səːr'əgit] *n* 代理の daíri no

surrogate mother *n* 代理母 daírihahà

surround [səraund'] *vt* (subj: walls, hedge etc) 囲む kakómù; (MIL, POLICE etc) 包囲する hōì suru

surrounding [səraun'diŋ] *adj* (country-side) 周囲の shūì no

surroundings [səraun'diŋz] *npl* 周辺 shūhen

surveillance [səːrvei'ləns] *n* 監視 kañshi

survey [*n* səːr'vei *vb* səːrvei'] *n* (examination: of land, house) 測量 sokúryō;

surveyor [sə:rvei'ə:r] n (of land, house) 測量技師 sokúryōgishi

survival [sə:rvai'vəl] n (continuation of life) 生存 seízon; (relic) 遺物 ibútsu

survive [sə:rvaiv'] vi (person, thing) 助かる tasúkarù; (custom etc) 残る nokórù
♦vt (outlive: person) ...より長生きする ...yórì nagáikì suru

survivor [sə:rvai'və:r] n (of illness, accident) 生存者 seízonsha

susceptible [səsep'təbəl] adj: **susceptible (to)** (affected by: heat, injury) (...に) 弱い (...ni) yowáì; (influenced by: flattery, pressure) (...に) 影響されやすい (...ni) eíkyō sareyasuì

suspect [adj, n sʌs'pekt vb səspekt']
adj 怪しい ayáshiì
♦n 容疑者 yōgìsha
♦vt (person) ...が怪しいと思う ...ga ayáshiì to omóù; (think) ...ではないかと思う ...dé wà náì ka to omóù

suspend [səspend'] vt (hang) つるす tsurúsù; (delay, stop) 中止する chūshi suru; (from employment) 停職処分にする teíshokushobùn ni suru

suspended sentence [səspen'did-] n (LAW) 執行猶予付きの判決 shikkṓyūyotsuki no haṅketsu

suspender belt [səspen'də:r-] n ガーターベルト gátāberùto

suspenders [səspen'də:rz] npl (US) ズボンつり zubóṅtsuri; (BRIT) ガーターベルトのストッキング留め gátāberùto no sutókkingudòme

suspense [səspens'] n (uncertainty) 気掛り kigakárì; (in film etc) サスペンス sásūpensu
to keep someone in suspense はらはらさせる hárahara sasérù

suspension [səspen'tʃən] n (from job, team) 停職 teíshoku; (AUT) サスペンション sasúpeṅshon; (of driver's license, payment) 停止 teíshi

suspension bridge n つり橋 tsuríbàshi

suspicion [səspiʃ'ən] n (distrust) 疑いutágai; ((bad) feeling) 漠然とした感じ bakúzen to shità kaṅji

suspicious [səspiʃ'əs] adj (suspecting: look) 疑い深い utágaibukaì; (causing suspicion: circumstances) 怪しげな ayáshigè na

sustain [səstein'] vt (continue: interest etc) 維持する íjì suru; (subj: food, drink) ...に力を付ける ...ni chikára wò tsukérù; (suffer: injury) 受ける ukérù

sustained [səsteind'] adj (effort, attack) 絶間ない taémanaì

sustenance [sʌs'tənəns] n 食物 shokúmòtsu

swab [swɑːb] n (MED) 綿球 meṅkyū

swagger [swæg'ə:r] vi 威張って歩く ibátte arukù

swallow [swɑːl'ou] n (bird) ツバメ tsubáme
♦vt (food, pills etc) 飲込む nomíkomù; (fig: story) 信じ込む shíṅjikomù; (: insult) ...に黙って耐える ...ni damátte taérù; (one's pride, one's words) 抑える osáerù

swallow up vt (savings etc) 飲込む nomíkomù

swam [swæm] pt of **swim**

swamp [swɑːmp] n 沼地 numáchi
♦vt (with water etc) 水没させる suíbotsu saserù; (fig: person) 圧倒する attṓ suru

swan [swɑːn] n ハクチョウ hakúchō

swap [swɑːp] n 交換 kṓkan
♦vt: **to swap (for)** (exchange (for)) (...) と交換する (...to) kṓkan suru; (replace (with)) (...と) 取替える (...to) toríkaerù

swarm [swɔːrm] n (of bees) 群れ muré; (of people) 群衆 guṅshū
♦vi (bees) 群れで巣別れする muré dè suwákare suru; (people) 群がる murágarù; (place): **to be swarming with** ...で...がうじゃうじゃいる ...ni ...ga újàuja irú

swarthy [swɔːr'ðiː] adj 浅黒い aságuroì

swastika [swɑːs'tikə] n かぎ十字 kagíjūji

swat [swɑːt] vt (insect) たたく tatákù

sway [swei] vi (person, tree) 揺れる yuré-

rù
♦vt (influence) 揺さぶる yusáburù

swear [swe'ə:r] (pt **swore**, pp **sworn**) vi (curse) 悪態をつく akútai wo tsukú
♦vt (promise) 誓う chikáu

swearword [swe:r'wə:rd] n 悪態 akútai

sweat [swet] n 汗 áse
♦vi 汗をかく áse wo kákù

sweater [swet'ə:r] n セーター sétā

sweatshirt [swet'ʃə:rt] n トレーナー torénā

sweaty [swet'i:] adj (clothes, hands) 汗ばんだ asébañda

Swede [swi:d] n スウェーデン人 suédenjìn

swede [swi:d] (BRIT) n スウェーデンカブ suédeñkabu

Sweden [swi:d'ən] n スウェーデン suéden

Swedish [swi:'diʃ] adj スウェーデンの suéden no; (LING) スウェーデン語の suédeñgo no
♦n (LING) スウェーデン語 suédeñgo

sweep [swi:p] n (act of sweeping) 掃く事 hákù kotó; (also: **chimney sweep**) 煙突掃除夫 eñtotsusójifù
♦vb (pt, pp **swept**)
♦vt (brush) 掃く hákù; (with arm) 払う haráù; (subj: current) 流す nagásù
♦vi (hand, arm) 振る furú; (wind) 吹きまくる fukímakurù

sweep away vt 取除く torínozokù

sweeping [swi:'piŋ] adj (gesture) 大振りな ōburi na; (generalized: statement) 十把一からげの jíppàhitókàrage no

sweep past vi (at great speed) 猛スピードで通り過ぎる mósupìdo de tórisugirù; (majestically) 堂々と通り過ぎる dódò tò tórisuguru

sweep up vi 掃き取る hakítorù

sweet [swi:t] n (candy) あめ amé; (BRIT: pudding) デザート dezátò
♦adj (not savory: taste) 甘い amái; (fig: air, water, smell, sound) 快い kokóroyoì; (: kind) 親切な shíñsetsu na; (attractive: baby, kitten) かわいい kawáiì

sweetcorn [swi:t'kɔ:rn] n トウモロコシ tómorðkoshi

sweeten [swi:t'ən] vt (add sugar to) 甘くする amáku surù; (soften: temper) なだめる nadámerù

sweetheart [swi:t'hɑ:rt] n (boyfriend/girlfriend) 恋人 koíbito

sweetness [swi:t'nis] n (amount of sugar) 甘さ amása; (fig: of air, water, smell, sound) 快さ kokóroyosà; (kindness) 親切 shíñsetsu; (attractiveness: of baby, kitten) かわいさ kawáisà

sweetpea [swi:t'pi:] n スイートピー suítopì

swell [swel] n (of sea) うねり unéri
♦adj (US: inf: excellent) 素晴らしい subárashiì
♦vi (pt **swelled**, pp **swollen** or **swelled**) (increase: numbers) 増える fuérù; (get stronger: sound, feeling) 増す masú; (also: **swell up**: face, ankle etc) はれる harérù

swelling [swel'iŋ] n (MED) はれ haré

sweltering [swel'tə:riŋ] adj (heat, weather, day) うだる様な udáru yō na

swept [swept] pt, pp of **sweep**

swerve [swə:rv] vi (person, animal, vehicle) それる sorérù

swift [swift] n (bird) アマツバメ amátsubàme
♦adj (happening quickly: recovery) じん速な jiñsoku na; (moving quickly: stream, glance) 早い hayáì

swiftly [swift'li:] adv (move, react, reply) 早く háyàku

swig [swig] (inf) n (drink) がぶ飲み gabúnomi

swill [swil] vt (also: **swill out**, **swill down**) がぶがぶ飲む gábùgabu nómù

swim [swim] n: **to go for a swim** 泳ぎに行く oyógì ni ikú
♦vb (pt **swam**, pp **swum**)
♦vi (person, animal) 泳ぐ oyógù; (head, room) 回る mawárù
♦vt (the Channel, a length) 泳いで渡る oyóide watárù

swimmer [swim'ə:r] n 泳ぐ人 oyógù hitó

swimming [swim'iŋ] n 水泳 suíei

swimming cap n 水泳用の帽子 suíeiyō no bốshi

swimming costume (*BRIT*) *n* 水着 mizúgi

swimming pool *n* 水泳プール suíeipùru

swimming trunks *npl* 水泳パンツ suíeipañtsu

swimsuit [swim'su:t] *n* 水着 mizúgi

swindle [swin'dəl] *n* 詐欺 sági
♦*vt* ぺてんにかける petén nì kakérù

swine [swain] (*inf!*) *n* 畜生め chikúshòme

swing [swiŋ] *n* (in playground) ぶらんこ búranko; (movement) 揺れ yuré; (change: in opinions etc) 変動 heñdō; (MUS: also **rhythm**) スイング suíñgu
♦*vb* (*pt, pp* **swung**)
♦*vt* (arms, legs) 振る furú; (also: **swing round**: vehicle etc) 回す mawásù
♦*vi* (pendulum) 揺れる yurérù; (on a swing) ぶらんこに乗る búranko ni norú; (also: **swing round**: person, animal) 振向く furímukù; (: vehicle) 向きを変える múkì wo kaérù

to be in full swing (party etc) たけなわである takénawa de arù

swing bridge *n* 旋回橋 señkaikyō

swingeing [swin'dʒiŋ] (*BRIT*) *adj* (blow, attack) 激しい hageshiì; (cuts) 法外な hōgai na

swinging door [swiŋ'iŋ-] (*BRIT* **swing door**) *n* 自在ドア jizáidòa

swipe [swaip] *vt* (hit) たたく tatákù; (*inf*: steal) かっ払う kappáraù

swirl [swə:rl] *vi* (water, smoke, leaves) 渦巻く uzúmakù

swish [swiʃ] *vt* (tail etc) 音を立てて振る otó wò tátète furú
♦*vi* (clothes) 衣ずれの音を立てる kinúzure nò otó wò tatérù

Swiss [swis] *adj* スイスの suísu no
♦*n inv* スイス人 suísujìn

switch [switʃ] *n* (for light, radio etc) スイッチ suítchì; (change) 取替え toríkae
♦*vt* (change) 取替える toríkaerù

switchboard [switʃ'bɔ:rd] *n* (TEL) 交換台 kōkandai

switch off *vt* (light, radio) 消す kesú; (engine, machine) 止める tomérù

switch on *vt* (light, radio, machine) つ

ける tsukérù; (engine) かける kakérù

Switzerland [swit'sə:rlənd] *n* スイス suísu

swivel [swiv'əl] *vi* (also: **swivel round**) 回る mawárù

swollen [swou'lən] *pp of* **swell**

swoon [swu:n] *vi* 気絶する kizétsu suru

swoop [swu:p] *n* (by police etc) 手入れ te-íre
♦*vi* (also: **swoop down**: bird, plane) 舞降りる maíoririrù

swop [swɑ:p] = **swap**

sword [sɔ:rd] *n* 刀 katána

swordfish [sɔ:rd'fiʃ] *n* メカジキ mekájìki

swore [swɔ:r] *pt of* **swear**

sworn [swɔ:rn] *pp of* **swear**
♦*adj* (statement, evidence) 宣誓付きの señseitsuki no; (enemy) 年来の néñrai no

swot [swɑ:t] *vi* がり勉する garíben suru

swum [swʌm] *pp of* **swim**

swung [swʌŋ] *pt, pp of* **swing**

sycamore [sik'əmɔ:r] *n* カエデ kaéde

syllable [sil'əbəl] *n* 音節 oñsetsu

syllabus [sil'əbəs] *n* 講義概要 kōgigaìyō

symbol [sim'bəl] *n* (sign, abbreviation) 記号 kigō; (representation) 象徴 shōchō

symbolic(al) [simbɑ:l'ik(əl)] *adj* 象徴的な shōchōteki na

symbolism [sim'bəlizəm] *n* 象徴的な意味 shōchōteki imì

symbolize [sim'bəlaiz] *vt* 象徴する shōchō suru

symmetrical [simet'rikəl] *adj* 対称的な taíshōteki na

symmetry [sim'itri:] *n* 対称 taíshō

sympathetic [simpəθet'ik] *adj* (showing understanding) 同情的な dōjōteki na; (likeable: character) 人好きのする hitózuki no surù; (showing support): *sympathetic to(wards)* ...に好意的である ...ni kōiteki de arù

sympathies [sim'pəθi:z] *npl* (support, tendencies) 支援 shién

sympathize [sim'pəθaiz] *vi*: *to sympathize with* (person) ...に同情する ...ni dōjō suru; (feelings, cause) ...に共感する ...ni kyōkan suru

sympathizer [sim'pəθaizər] n (POL) 支援者 shiénsha

sympathy [sim'pəθi:] n (pity) 同情 dṓjō

with our deepest sympathy 心からお悔みを申上げます kokórò kara o-kúyami wò mõshiagemasù

in sympathy (workers: come out) 同情して dṓjō shite

symphony [sim'fəni:] n 交響曲 kṓkyòkyoku

symposia [simpou'zi:ə] npl of **symposium**

symposium [simpou'zi:əm] (pl **symposiums** or **symposia**) n シンポジウム shiñpojiùmu

symptom [simp'təm] n (indicator: MED) 症状 shṓjō; (: gen) しるし shirúshi

synagogue [sin'əgɑːg] n ユダヤ教会堂 yudáyakyòkaidō

synchronize [siŋ'krənaiz] vt (watches, sound) 合せる awáserù

syncopated [siŋ'kəpeitid] adj (rhythm, beat) シンコペートした shiñkopèto shita

syndicate [sin'dəkit] n (of people, businesses, newspapers) シンジケート shiñjikèto

syndrome [sin'droum] n (also MED) 症候群 shṓkõgun

synonym [sin'ənim] n 同意語 dṓigò

synopses [sinɑːp'si:z] npl of **synopsis**

synopsis [sinɑːp'sis] (pl **synopses**) n 概要 gaíyō

syntax [sin'tæks] n (LING) 統語法 tṓgohò, シンタックス shiñtakkùsu

syntheses [sin'θəsi:z] npl of **synthesis**

synthesis [sin'θəsis] (pl **syntheses**) n (of ideas, styles) 総合する sṓgõ suru

synthetic [sinθet'ik] adj (man-made: materials) 合成の gṓsei no

syphilis [sif'əlis] n 梅毒 báidoku

syphon [sai'fən] = **siphon**

Syria [si:r'i:ə] n シリア shírìa

Syrian [si:r'i:ən] adj シリアの shírìa no
♦n シリア人 shiríàjin

syringe [sərindʒ'] n 注射器 chúshakì

syrup [sir'əp] n シロップ shiróppù

system [sis'təm] n (organization) 組織 sōshìki; (POL): *the system* 体制 taísei;

(method) やり方 yaríkata; (the body) 身体系 shíñtai

the digestive system (MED) 消化器系 shṓkakikèi

the nervous system (MED) 神経系 shiñkeikèi

systematic [sistəmæt'ik] adj (methodical) 組織的な soshíkiteki na

system disk n (COMPUT) システムディスク shisútemu disùku

systems analyst [sis'təmz-] n システムアナリスト shisútemu anarisùto

T

ta [tɑ:] (BRIT: inf) excl (thanks) どうも dōmo

tab [tæb] n (on file etc) 耳 mimí; (on drinks can etc) プルタブ purútàbu, プルトップ purútoppù; (label: name tab) 名札 nafúda

to keep tabs on (fig) 監視する kañshi suru

tabby [tæb'i:] n (also: **tabby cat**) とら毛のネコ torágè nò nékò

table [tei'bəl] n (piece of furniture) テーブル tḕburu; (MATH, CHEM etc) 表 hyṓ
♦vt (BRIT: motion etc) 上程する jṓtei suru; (US: put off: proposal etc) 棚上げにする taná-age ni surù

to lay/set the table 食卓に皿を並べる shokútaku nì sará wo naráberù

tablecloth [tei'bəlklɔ:θ] n テーブルクロス tḕburukurosù

table d'hôte [tæb'əl dout'] adj (menu, meal) 定食の teíshoku no

table lamp n 電気スタンド deñki sutañdo

tablemat [tei'bəlmæt] n (for plate) テーブルマット tḕburumattò; (for hot dish) なべ敷 nabéshìki

table of contents n 目次 mokúji

tablespoon [tei'bəlspu:n] n (type of spoon) テーブルスプーン tḕburusupūn; (also: **tablespoonful**: as measurement) 大さじ一杯 ṓsaji ippài

tablet [tæb'lit] n (MED) 錠剤 jṓzai

a stone tablet 石板 sekíban

table tennis n 卓球 takkyū

table wine n テーブルワイン tḗburuwaìn

tabloid [tǽb'lɔid] n (newspaper) タブロイド新聞 tabúroido shiñbun

taboo [tæbu:'] n (religious, social) タブー tabū

♦adj (subject, place, name etc) タブーの tabū no

tabulate [tǽb'jəleit] vt (data, figures) 表にする hyō ni surù

tacit [tǽs'it] adj (agreement, approval etc) 暗黙の añmoku no

taciturn [tǽs'itəːrn] adj (person) 無口な múkùchi na

tack [tæk] n (nail) びょう byō; (fig) やり方 yaríkata

♦vt (nail) びょうで留める byō de tomérù; (stitch) 仮縫する karínui suru

♦vi (NAUT) 間切る magírù

tackle [tǽk'əl] n (gear: fishing tackle etc) 道具 dōgù; (for lifting) ろくろ rōkùro, 滑車 kásshà; (FOOTBALL, RUGBY) タックル tákkùru

♦vt (deal with: difficulty) …と取組む …to toríkumù; (challenge: person) …に掛合う …ni kakéaù; (grapple with: person, animal) …と取組む …to toríkumù; (FOOTBALL, RUGBY) タックルする tákkùru suru

tacky [tǽk'i:] adj (sticky) べたべたする bétàbeta suru; (pej: of poor quality) 安っぽい yasúppoi

tact [tækt] n 如才なさ josáinasà

tactful [tǽkt'fəl] adj 如才ない josáinaì

tactical [tǽk'tikəl] adj (move, withdrawal, voting) 戦術的な señjutsuteki na

tactics [tǽk'tiks] n 用兵学 yōheigàku

♦npl 駆引き kakéhìki

tactless [tǽkt'lis] adj 気転の利かない kitén no kikanaì

tadpole [tǽd'poul] n オタマジャクシ otámajakùshi

taffy [tǽf'i:] (US) n (toffee) タフィー táfì ◇あめの一種 amé nò ísshù

tag [tæg] n (label) 札 fudá

tag along vi ついて行く tsúìte ikú

tail [teil] n (of animal) しっ尾 shíppò; (of plane) 尾部 bíbù; (of shirt, coat) すそ susó

♦vt (follow: person, vehicle) 尾行する bikō suru

tail away/off vi (in size, quality etc) 次第に減る shidái ni herù

tailback [teil'bæk] (BRIT) n (AUT) 交通渋滞 kōtsūjūtai

tail end n 末端 mattán

tailgate [teil'geit] n (AUT: of hatchback) 後尾ドア kōbidòa

tailor [tei'ləːr] n 仕立屋 shitáteya

tailoring [tei'ləːriŋ] n (cut) 仕立て方 shitátekata; (craft) 仕立職 shitáteshòku

tailor-made [tei'ləːrmeid] adj (suit) あつらえの atsúraè no; (fig: part in play, person for job) おあつらえ向きの o-átsuraemuki no

tails [teilz] npl (formal suit) えん尾服 eñbifùku

tailwind [teil'wind] n 追風 oíkàze

tainted [teint'id] adj (food, water, air) 汚染された osén saretà; (fig: profits, reputation etc) 汚れた yogóretà

Taiwan [tai'wɑːn'] n 台湾 taíwañ

take [teik] (pt took, pp taken) vt (photo, notes, holiday etc) とる tórù; (shower, walk, decision etc) する surú; (grab: someone's arm etc) 取る tórù; (gain: prize) 得る érù; (require: effort, courage, time) …が必要である …ga hitsúyō de arù; (tolerate: pain etc) 耐える taérù; (hold: passengers etc) 収容する shūyō suru; (accompany, bring, carry: person) 連れて行く tsuréte ikù; (: thing) 持って行く motté ikù; (exam, test) 受ける ukérù

to take something from (drawer etc) …を…から取出す …wo …kárà torídasù; (steal from: person) …を…から盗む …wo …kárà nusúmù

I take it that ... …だと思っていいですね …dá tò omótte iǐ desu né

take after vt fus (resemble) …に似ている …ni nité irù

take apart vt 分解する buñkai suru

take away vt (remove) 下げる sagérù; (carry off) 持って行く motté ikù; (MATH) 引く hikú

takeaway [tei'kəwei] (*BRIT*) *n* = **take-out**

take back *vt* (return) 返す kaésù; (one's words) 取消す toríkesù

take down *vt* (dismantle: building) 解体 する kaítai suru; (write down: letter etc) 書き取る kakítorù

take in *vt* (deceive) だます damásù; (understand) 理解する rikái suru; (include) 含む fukúmù; (lodger) 泊める tomérù

take off *vi* (AVIAT) 離陸する ríríku su-ru; (go away) 行ってしまう itté shimaù
♦*vt* (remove) 外す hazúsù

takeoff [teik'ɔːf] *n* (AVIAT) 離陸 ríríku

take on *vt* (work) 引受ける hikíukerù; (employee) 雇う yatóù; (opponent) ...と戦 う ...to tatákaù

take out *vt* (invite) 外食に連れて行く gaíshoku nì tsurété ikù; (remove) 取出す torídasù

takeout [teik'aut] (*US*) *n* (shop, restaurant) 持帰り料理店 mochíkaeriryōritèn; (food) 持帰り料理 mochíkaeriryòri

take over *vt* (business, country) 乗っ取る nottórù
♦*vi*: **to take over from someone** ...と交替する ...to kótai suru

takeover [teik'ouvə:r] *n* (COMM) 乗っ取り nottóri

take to *vt fus* (person, thing, activity) 気に入る ki ní irù, 好きになる sukí ni narù; (engage in: hobby etc) やり出す yarídasù

take up *vt* (a dress) 短くする mijíkakù suru; (occupy: post, time, space) ...につく ...ni tsukù; (: time) ...がかかる ...ga kakárù; (engage in: hobby etc) やり出す yarídasù
  to take someone up on something (offer, suggestion) ...に応じる ...ni ōjirù

takings [tei'kiŋz] *npl* 売上 uríage

talc [tælk] *n* (*also*: **talcum powder**) タル カムパウダー tarúkamupaùdā

tale [teil] *n* (story, account) 物語 monógatàri
  to tell tales (*fig*: to teacher, parents etc) 告げ口する tsugéguchi suru

talent [tæl'ənt] *n* 才能 saínō

talented [tæl'əntid] *adj* 才能ある saínō arù

talk [tɔːk] *n* (a (prepared) speech) 演説 eñzetsu; (conversation) 話 hanáshi; (gossip) うわさ uwása
♦*vi* (speak) 話す hanásù; (give information) しゃべる shabérù
  to talk about ...について話す ...ni tsuíte hanásù
  to talk someone into doing something ...する様に...を説得する ...surú yò ni ...wo settóku suru
  to talk someone out of doing something ...しない様に...を説得する ...shinái yò ni ...wo settóku suru
  to talk shop 仕事の話をする shigóto nò hanáshi wo surù

talkative [tɔː'kətiv] *adj* おしゃべりな o-shábèri na

talk over *vt* (problem etc) 話し合う hanáshiaù

talks [tɔːks] *npl* (POL etc) 会談 kaídan

talk show *n* おしゃべり番組 o-shábèri bañgumi

tall [tɔːl] *adj* (person) 背が高い sé gà takáî; (object) 高い takáî
  to be 6 feet tall (person) 身長が6フィ ートである shiñchō gà 6 fítò de árù

tall story *n* ほら話 horábanàshi

tally [tæl'iː] *n* (of marks, amounts of money etc) 記録 kiróku
♦*vi*: **to tally (with)** (subj: figures, stories etc) (...と) 合う (...to) áù

talon [tæl'ən] *n* かぎづめ kagízume

tambourine [tæm'bəriːn] *n* タンバリン táñbarin

tame [teim] *adj* (animal, bird) なれた ná-rèta; (*fig*: story, style) 平凡な heíbon na

tamper [tæm'pə:r] *vi*: **to tamper with something** ...をいじる ...wo ijírù

tampon [tæm'pɑn] *n* タンポン táñpon

tan [tæn] *n* (*also*: **suntan**) 日焼け hiyáke
♦*vi* (person, skin) 日に焼ける hi ní yake-rù
♦*adj* (color) 黄かっ色の ókasshòku no

tandem [tæn'dəm] *n*: **in tandem** (together) 2人で futári dè

tang [tæŋ] *n* (smell) 鼻をつくにおい haná wò tsukú nioî; (taste) ぴりっとした味 piríttò shita ajî

tangent [tænˈdʒənt] *n* (MATH) 接線 sessén

to go off at a tangent (*fig*) わき道へそ れる wakímìchi e soréru

tangerine [tændʒəriːnʹ] *n* ミカン míkàn

tangible [tænʹdʒəbəl] *adj* (proof, bene- fits) 具体的な gutáiteki na

tangle [tæŋʹgəl] *n* もつれ motsúre

to get in(to) a tangle (*also fig*) もつれ る motsúrerù

tank [tæŋk] *n* (*also*: **water tank**) 貯水タ ンク chosúitàñku; (for fish) 水槽 suísō; (MIL) 戦車 séñsha

tanker [tæŋkˈəːr] *n* (ship) タンカー táñ- kā; (truck) タンクローリー tañkurōrī

tanned [tænd] *adj* (skin) 日に焼けた hi ní yaketá

tantalizing [tænˈtəlaiziŋ] *adj* (smell, possibility) 興味をそそる kyőmi wò so- sóru

tantamount [tænˈtəmaunt] *adj*: *tanta- mount to* ...も同然である ...mo dőzen de arû

tantrum [tænˈtrəm] *n* かんしゃく kañ- shaku

tap [tæp] *n* (on sink etc) 蛇口 jagúchi; (*also*: **gas tap**) ガスの元栓 gásù no motó- sen; (gentle blow) 軽くたたく事 karúku tatakú kotó

♦*vt* (hit gently) 軽くたたく karúku tata- kù; (resources) 利用する riyő suru; (tele- phone) 盗聴する tőchō suru

on tap (*fig*: resources) いつでも利用でき る ítsùdemo riyő dekírù

tap-dancing [tæpʹdænsiŋ] *n* タップダン ス tappúdàñsu

tape [teip] *n* (*also*: **magnetic tape**) 磁気 テープ jikítēpu; (cassette) カセットテー プ kaséttotēpu; (sticky tape) 粘着テープ nefíchakutēpu; (for tying) ひも himó

♦*vt* (record: sound) 録音する rokúon su- ru; (: image) 録画する rokúga suru; (stick with tape) テープで張る tēpu de harú

tape deck *n* テープデッキ tēpudekkî

tape measure *n* メジャー méjā

taper [teiʹpəːr] *n* (candle) 細いろうそく hosóî rősokù

♦*vi* (narrow) 細くなる hósòku narù

tape recorder *n* テープレコーダー tē- purekődā

tapestry [tæpʹistri] *n* (object) タペスト リー tapésutòrī; (art) ししゅう shishū

tar [tɑːr] *n* コールタール kőrutàru

tarantula [tərænʹtʃələ] *n* タランチュラ táráñchura

target [tɑːrʹgit] *n* (thing aimed at, *also fig*) 的 matő

tariff [tærʹif] *n* (tax on goods) 関税 kañ- zei; (*BRIT*: in hotels, restaurants) 料金 表 ryőkiñhyō

tarmac [tɑːrʹmæk] *n* (*BRIT*: on road) ア スファルト asúfarùto; (AVIAT) エプロ ン épùron

tarnish [tɑːrʹniʃ] *vt* (metal) さびさせる sabísaserù; (*fig*: reputation etc) 汚す yo- gósù

tarpaulin [tɑːrpɔːʹlin] *n* シート shîto

tarragon [tærʹəgən] *n* タラゴン táràgon ◇香辛料の一種 kőshiñryō no ísshù

tart [tɑːrt] *n* (CULIN) タルト tárùto ◇菓 子の一種 káshî no ísshù; (*BRIT*: *inf*: prostitute) ばいた bâita

♦*adj* (flavor) 酸っぱい suppáî

tartan [tɑːrʹtən] *n* タータンチェック tā- tanchekkû

♦*adj* (rug, scarf etc) タータンチェックの tātanchekkû no

tartar [tɑːrʹtəːr] *n* (on teeth) 歯石 shiséki

tartar(e) sauce [tɑːrʹtəːr-] *n* タルタルソ ース tarútarusősu

tart up (*BRIT*) *vt* (*inf*: object) 派手にす る hadé nî suru

to tart oneself up おめかしをする o-mékashi wò suru

task [tæsk] *n* 仕事 shigóto

to take to task ...の責任を問う ...no sekínin wò tóù

task force *n* (MIL, POLICE) 機動部隊 kidőbutai

Tasmania [tæzmeiʹniːə] *n* タスマニア ta- súmanìa

tassel [tæsʹəl] *n* 房 fusá

taste [teist] n (also: **sense of taste**) 味覚 mikáku; (flavor: also: **aftertaste**) 味 ajî; (sample) 一口 hitókùchi; (fig: glimpse, idea) 味わい ajîwaì

♦vt (get flavor of) 味わう ajîwaù; (test) 試食する shishóku suru

♦vi: **to taste of / like** (fish etc) ...の味がする ...no ajî ga surù

you can taste the garlic (in it) (含まれている) ニンニクの味がする (fukúmarete irù) nínniku nò ajî ga surù

in good/bad taste 趣味がいい〔悪い〕 shúmì ga íì〔warúì〕

tasteful [teist'fəl] adj (furnishings) 趣味の良い shúmì no yóì

tasteless [teist'lis] adj (food) 味がない ajî ga naî; (remark, joke, furnishings) 趣味の悪い shúmì no warúì

tasty [teis'ti:] adj (food) おいしい oíshiì

tatters [tæt'ə:rz] npl: **in tatters** (clothes, papers etc) ずたずたになって zutázuta ni natté

tattoo [tætu:'] n (on skin) 入れ墨 irézumi; (spectacle) パレード parêdò

♦vt (name, design) ...の入れ墨をする ...no irézumi wò suru

tatty [tæt'i:] (BRIT: inf) adj (inf) 薄汚い usúgitanaì

taught [tɔ:t] pt, pp of **teach**

taunt [tɔ:nt] n あざけり azákerì

♦vt あざける azákerù

Taurus [tɔ:r'əs] n 牡牛座 oúshizà

taut [tɔ:t] adj ぴんと張った pín tò hattá

tavern [tæv'ə:rn] n (old) 酒場 sakába

tax [tæks] n 税金 zeíkin

♦vt (earnings, goods etc) ...に税金をかける ...ni zeíkin wò kakérù; (fig: test: memory) 最大限に使う saídaìgen ni tsukáù; (patience) 試練にかける shírèn ni kakérù

taxable [tæk'səbəl] adj (income) 課税される kazéi sarerù

taxation [tæksei'ʃən] n (system) 課税 kazéi; (money paid) 税金 zeíkin

tax avoidance [-əvɔi'dəns] n 節税 setsúzei

tax disc (BRIT) n (AUT) 納税ステッカー nôzeisutekkà

tax evasion n 脱税 datsúzei

tax-free [tæks'fri:'] adj (goods, services) 免税の meñzei no

taxi [tæk'si:] n タクシー tákùshì

♦vi (AVIAT: plane) 滑走する kassô suru

taxi driver n タクシーの運転手 tákùshì no uñtenshu

taxi rank (BRIT) n = **taxi stand**

taxi stand n タクシー乗場 takúshinorìba

tax payer [-pei'ə:r] n 納税者 nôzeishà

tax relief n 減税 geñzei

tax return n 確定申告書 kakúteishinkokushò

TB [ti:bi:'] n abbr = **tuberculosis**

tea [ti:] n (drink: Japanese) お茶 o-chá; (: English) 紅茶 kôchà; (BRIT: meal) おやつ o-yátsù

high tea (BRIT) 夕食 yúshoku ◇夕方早目に食べる食事 yúgata hayáme nì tabérù shokúji

tea bag n ティーバッグ tíbaggù

tea break (BRIT) n 休憩 kyúkei

teach [ti:tʃ] (pt, pp taught) vt (gen) 教える oshíerù; (be a teacher of) ...(の) 教師をする ...(no)kyôshi wò suru

♦vi (be a teacher: in school etc) 教師をする kyôshi wò suru

teacher [ti:'tʃə:r] n 教師 kyôshi, 先生 señseì

teaching [ti:'tʃiŋ] n (work of teacher) 教職 kyôshoku

tea cosy n お茶帽子 o-chábòshi

tea cup n (Western) ティーカップ tíkappù; (Japanese) 湯飲み茶碗 yunómijàwan, 湯飲み yunómi

teak [ti:k] n チーク chìku

tea leaves npl 茶殻 chagára

team [ti:m] n (of people: gen, SPORT) チーム chìmu; (of animals) 一組 hitókumi

teamwork [ti:m'wə:rk] n チームワーク chìmuwàku

teapot [ti:'pɑ:t] n きゅうす kyúsu

tear¹ [te:r] n (hole) 裂け目 sakéme

♦vb (pt tore, pp torn)

♦vt (rip) 破る yabúrù

♦vi (become torn) 破れる yabúrerù

tear² [tir] n (in eye) 涙 námìda

in tears 泣いている naíte irù

tear along vi (rush) 猛スピードで走って行く mṓsupídò de hashítte ikù

tearful [tiːrˈfəl] adj (family, face) 涙ぐんだ namídagundà

tear gas n 催涙ガス saíruigasù

tearoom [tiːˈruːm] n 喫茶店 kissáteñ

tear up vt (sheet of paper etc) ずたずたに破る zutázuta nì yabúrù

tease [tiːz] vt からかう karákaù

tea set n 茶器セット chakísettò

teaspoon [tiːˈspuːn] n (type of spoon) ティースプーン tísupùn; (also: **teaspoonful**: as measurement) 小さじ一杯 kosáji ippaì

teat [tiːt] n (ANAT) 乳首 chikúbì; (also: **bottle teat**) ほ乳瓶の乳首 honyúbìn no chikúbì

teatime [tiːˈtaim] n おやつの時間 o-yátsù no jikán

tea towel (BRIT) n ふきん fukín

technical [tekˈnikəl] adj (terms, advances) 技術の gíjùtsu no

technical college (BRIT) n 高等専門学校 kótōsenmongakkṑ

technicality [teknikælˈiti] n (point of law) 法律の専門的細目 hṓritsu nò señmonteki saimòku; (detail) 細かい事 komákaì kotó

technically [tekˈnikliː] adv (strictly speaking) 正確に言えば seíkaku nì iébà; (regarding technique) 技術的に gíjùtsuteki ni

technician [tekniˈʃən] n 技術者 gijútsushà

technique [tekniˈkʲ] n 技術 gíjùtsu

technological [teknəlɑːˈdʒikəl] adj 技術的な gijútsuteki na

technology [teknɑːˈlədʒiː] n 科学技術 kagákugijùtsu

teddy (bear) [tedˈiː-] n クマのぬいぐるみ kumá nò nuígùrumi

tedious [tiːˈdiːəs] adj (work, discussions etc) 退屈な taíkutsu na

tee [tiː] n (GOLF) ティー tí

teem [tiːm] vi: **to teem with** (visitors, tourists etc) ...がぞろぞろ来ている ...ga zṓrozoro kité irù

it is teeming (with rain) 雨が激しく降っている ámè ga hagéshikù futté irù

teenage [tiːnˈeidʒ] adj (children, fashions etc) ティーンエージャーの tín-èjā no

teenager [tiːnˈeidʒər] n ティーンエージャー tín-èjā

teens [tiːnz] npl: **to be in one's teens** 年齢は10代である neñrei wà júdaì de árù

tee-shirt [tiːˈʃərt] n = **T-shirt**

teeter [tiːˈtər] vi (also fig) ぐらつく gurátsukù

teeth [tiːθ] npl of **tooth**

teethe [tiːð] vi (baby) 歯が生える há gà haérù

teething ring [tiːˈðiŋ-] n おしゃぶりリング o-shábùri リング状の物を指す riñgujṓ no monó wò sásù

teething troubles npl (fig) 初期の困難 shóki no kóñnan

teetotal [tiːtoutˈəl] adj (person) 酒を飲まない saké wò nománaì

telecommunications [teləkəmjuːnikeíʃɔnz] n 電気通信 deñkitsūshin

telegram [telˈəgræm] n 電報 deñpō

telegraph [telˈəgræf] n (system) 電信 deñshin

telegraph pole n 電柱 deñchū

telepathic [teləpæθˈik] adj テレパシーの terépàshī no

telepathy [təlepˈəθiː] n テレパシー terépàshī

telephone [telˈəfoun] n 電話 deñwa
♦vt (person) ...に電話をかける ...ni deñwa wò kakérù; (message) 電話で伝える deñwa dè tsutáerù

on the telephone (talking) 電話中で deñwachū de; (possessing phone) 電話を持っている deñwa wò mótte irù

telephone booth n 電話ボックス deñwabokkùsu

telephone box (BRIT) n = **telephone booth**

telephone call n 電話 deñwa

telephone directory n 電話帳 deñwachō

telephone number n 電話番号 deñwabañgō

telephonist [teləˈfounist] (BRIT) n 電話交換手 deñwakōkañshu

telescope [tel'əskoup] n 望遠鏡 bóenkyō

telescopic [teliskɑːp'ik] adj (lens) 望遠の bóen no; (collapsible: tripod, aerial) 入れ子式の irékoshïki no

television [tel'əviʒən] n (all senses) テレビ térebi

on television テレビで térebi de

television set n テレビ受信機 terébijuzóki

telex [tel'eks] n テレックス terékkùsu
♦vt (company) ...にテレックスを送る ...ni terékkùsu wo okúrù; (message) テレックスで送る terékkùsu de okúrù

tell [tel] (pt, pp told) vt (say) ...に言う ...ni iú; (relate: story) 述べる nobérù; (distinguish): *to tell something from* ...から...を区別する ...kará ...wò kúbètsu suru
♦vi (talk): *to tell (of)* ...について話す ...ni tsúite hanásù; (have an effect) 効果的である kókateki de arù

to tell someone to do something ...に...する様に言う ...ni ...surú yõ ni iú

teller [tel'ər] n (in bank) 出納係 suítōgakàri

telling [tel'iŋ] adj (remark, detail) 意味深い imíbukài

tell off vt: *to tell someone off* しかる shikáru

telltale [tel'teil] adj (sign) 証拠の shóko no

telly [tel'iː] (BRIT: inf) n abbr = **television**

temerity [təmeːr'itiː] n ずうずうしさ zúzūshisà

temp [temp] n abbr (= temporary) 臨時職員 riñjishokuiñ

temper [tem'pər] n (nature) 性質 seíshitsu; (mood) 機嫌 kigén; (fit of anger) かんしゃく kañshaku
♦vt (moderate) 和らげる yawáragerù

to be in a temper 怒っている okótte irù

to lose one's temper 怒る okórù

temperament [tem'pə:rəmənt] n (nature) 性質 sefshitsu

temperamental [tempə:rəmen'təl] adj (person, fig: car) 気まぐれな kimágùre na

temperate [tem'pə:rit] adj (climate, country) 温暖な oñdan na

temperate zone n 温帯 oñtai

temperature [tem'pə:rətʃəːr] n (of person, place) 温度 óñdo

to have/run a temperature 熱がある netsú ga arù

tempest [tem'pist] n 嵐 árashi

tempi [tem'piː] npl of **tempo**

temple [tem'pəl] n (building) 神殿 shiñden; (ANAT) こめかみ kométakami

tempo [tem'pou] (pl tempos or tempi) n (MUS) テンポ téñpo; (fig: of life etc) ペース pèsu

temporarily [tempə:reːr'iliː] adv 一時的に ichíjiteki ni

temporary [tem'pə:reːriː] adj (passing) 一時的な ichíjiteki na; (worker, job) 臨時の riñji no

tempt [tempt] vt 誘惑する yúwaku suru

to tempt someone into doing something ...する様に...を誘惑する ...surú yõ ni ...wo yúwaku suru

temptation [temptei'ʃən] n 誘惑 yúwaku

tempting [temp'tiŋ] adj (offer) 魅惑的な miwákuteki na; (food) おいしそうな ofshisō na

ten [ten] num 十 (の) jú (no)

tenacity [tənæs'itiː] n (of person, animal) 根気強さ koñkizúyosa

tenancy [ten'ənsiː] n (possession of room, land etc) 賃借 chiñshaku; (period of possession) 賃借期間 chiñshakukikàn

tenant [ten'ənt] n (rent-payer) 店子 tanáko, テナント tenáñto

tend [tend] vt (crops, sick person) ...の世話をする ...no sewá wo suru
♦vi: *to tend to do something* ...しがちである ...shigáchi de arù

tendency [ten'dənsiː] n (of person, thing) 傾向 keíkō

tender [ten'dəːr] adj (person, heart, care) 優しい yasáshiì; (sore) 触ると痛い sawáru tò itái; (meat) 柔らかい yawárakaì; (age) 幼い osánaì
♦n (COMM: offer) 見積り mitsúmori; (money): *legal tender* 通貨 tsúka

♦*vt* (offer, resignation) 提出する teíshutsu suru

to tender an apology 陳謝する chínsha suru

tenderness [ten'də:rnis] *n* (affection) 優しさ yasáshisà; (of meat) 柔らかさ yawárakasà

tendon [ten'dən] *n* けん kén

tenement [ten'əmənt] *n* 安アパート yasúapàto

tenet [ten'it] *n* 信条 shínjō

tennis [ten'is] *n* テニス ténìsu

tennis ball *n* テニスボール tenísubòru

tennis court *n* テニスコート tenísukòto

tennis player *n* テニス選手 tenísuseñshu

tennis racket *n* テニスラケット tenísurakettò

tennis shoes *npl* テニスシューズ tenísushūzu

tenor [ten'ə:r] *n* (MUS) テノール tenórù

tenpin bowling [ten'pin-] *n* ボウリング bóriñgu

tense [tens] *adj* (person, smile, muscle) 緊張した kiñchō shita; (period) 緊迫した kiñpaku shita

♦*n* (LING) 時制 jiséi

tension [ten'ʃən] *n* (nervousness) 緊張 kiñchō; (between ropes etc) 張力 chóryoku

tent [tent] *n* テント téñto

tentacle [ten'təkəl] *n* (of octopus etc) あし ashí

tentative [ten'tətiv] *adj* (person, step, smile) 自信のない jishín no naì; (conclusion, plans) 差し当っての sashíatattè no

tenterhooks [ten'tə:rhuks] *npl*: *on tenterhooks* はらはらして hárahara shite

tenth [tenθ] *num* 第十（の）dáijū (no)

tent peg *n* テントのくい téñto no kuí

tent pole *n* テントの支柱 téñto no shichū

tenuous [ten'ju:əs] *adj* (hold, links, connection etc) 弱い yowái

tenure [ten'jə:r] *n* (of land, buildings etc) 保有権 hoyúken; (of office) 在職期間 zaíshokukikàn

tepid [tep'id] *adj* (tea, pool etc) ぬるい

nurúi

term [tə:rm] *n* (word, expression) 用語 yógo; (period in power etc) 期間 kikán; (SCOL) 学期 gakkí

♦*vt* (call) ...と言う ...to iú

in the short/long term 短〔長〕期間で tañ(chó)kikàn de

terminal [tə:r'mənəl] *adj* (disease, cancer, patient) 末期の mákkì no

♦*n* (ELEC) 端子 táñshi; (COMPUT) 端末機 tañmatsukì; (*also*: **air terminal**) ターミナルビル tāminarubìru; (*BRIT: also*: **coach terminal**) バスターミナル basútāminaru

terminate [tə:r'məneit] *vt* (discussion, contract, pregnancy) 終らせる owáraserù, 終える oérù; (contract) 破棄する hákì suru; (pregnancy) 中絶する chūzetsu suru

termini [tə:r'məni:] *npl of* **terminus**

terminology [tə:rmənɑ:l'ədʒi:] *n* 用語 yógo ◊総称 sōshō

terminus [tə:r'mənəs] (*pl* **-mini**) *n* (for buses, trains) ターミナル tāminaru

terms [tə:rmz] *npl* (conditions: *also* COMM) 条件 jōken

to be on good terms with someone ...と仲がいい ...to nákà ga íi

to come to terms with (problem) ...と折合いがつく ...to oríaì ga tsukú

terrace [te:r'əs] *n* (*BRIT*: row of houses) 長屋 nagáyà; (patio) テラス téràsu; (AGR) 段々畑 dañdanbatàke

terraced [te:r'əst] *adj* (house) 長屋の nagáyà no; (garden) ひな壇式の hinádañshiki no

terraces [te:r'əsiz] (*BRIT*) *npl* (SPORT): *the terraces* 立見席 tachímisèki

terracotta [te:rəkɑ:t'ə] *n* テラコッタ terácottà

terrain [tərein'] *n* 地面 jímèn

terrible [te:r'əbəl] *adj* ひどい hidóì

terribly [te:r'əbli:] *adv* (very) とても totémo; (very badly) ひどく hídòku

terrier [te:r'i:ə:r] *n* テリア térià

terrific [tərif'ik] *adj* (very great: thunderstorm, speed) 大変な taíhen na; (wonderful: time, party) 素晴らしい subárashiî

terrify [ter'əfai] *vt* おびえさせる obíesaserù

territorial [te:ritə:r'i:əl] *adj* (waters, boundaries, dispute) 領土の ryódò no

territory [ter'ətə:ri:] *n* (*gen*) 領土 ryódò; (*fig*) 縄張り nawábarî

terror [ter'ə:r] *n* (great fear) 恐怖 kyôfu

terrorism [ter'ə:rizəm] *n* テロ térò

terrorist [ter'ə:rist] *n* テロリスト terórisùto

terrorize [ter'ə:raiz] *vt* おびえさせる o-bíesaserù

terse [tə:rs] *adj* (style) 簡潔な kańketsu na; (reply) そっけない sokkénaî ◇言葉数が少なく無愛想な返事などについて言う kotóbakazù ga sukúnakù buáîso na heñji nadò ni tsúîte iú

Terylene [ter'əli:n]® *n* テリレン térìren ◇人工繊維の一種 jíñkòseñ-i no ísshù

test [test] *n* (trial, check: *also* MED, CHEM) テスト tésùto; (of courage etc) 試練 shíren; (SCOL) テスト tésùto; (*also*: **driving test**) 運転免許の試験 uñtenmeñkyo no shíken
♦*vt* (*gen*) テストする tésùto suru

testament [tes'təmənt] *n* 証拠 shôko
the Old/New Testament 旧〔新〕約聖書 kyú〔shíñ〕yaku seishò

testicle [tes'tikəl] *n* こう丸 kôgan

testify [tes'təfai] *vi* (LAW) 証言する shôgen suru
to testify to something ...が...だと証言する ...ga ...dá tò shôgen suru

testimony [tes'təmouni:] *n* (LAW: statement) 証言 shôgen; (clear proof) 証拠 shôko

test match *n* (CRICKET, RUGBY) 国際戦 kokúsaisen, 国際試合 kokúsaijìài

test pilot *n* テストパイロット tesútopairottò

test tube *n* 試験管 shikéñkan

tetanus [tet'ənəs] *n* 破傷風 hashôfù

tether [teð'ə:r] *vt* (animal) つなぐ tsunágù
♦*n*: *at the end of one's tether* 行き詰って ikízumattè

text [tekst] *n* 文書 bûñsho

textbook [tekst'buk] *n* 教科書 kyôkasho

textiles [teks'tailz] *npl* (fabrics) 織物 o-rímòno; (textile industry) 織物業界 orímonogyôkai

texture [teks'tʃə:r] *n* (of cloth, skin, soil, silk) 手触り tezáwàri

Thailand [tai'lənd] *n* タイ tâî

Thames [temz] *n*: *the Thames* テムズ川 témùzugawa

KEYWORD

than [ðæn] *conj* (in comparisons) ...より(も) ...yórì(mo)
you have more than 10 あなたは10個以上持っています anátà wa júkkò íjò móttè imasu
I have more than you/Paul 私はあなた〔ポール〕より沢山持っています watákushi wà anátà〔pórù〕yori takúsan móttè imasu
I have more pens than pencils 私は鉛筆よりペンを沢山持っています watákushi wà eñpitsu yorì péñ wo takúsan móttè imasu
she is older than you think 彼女はあなたが思っているより年ですよ kánòjo wa anátà ga omótte irù yórì toshí desù yó
more than once 数回 sûkài

thank [θæŋk] *vt* (person) ...に感謝する ...ni káñsha suru
thank you (very much) （大変）有難うございました (taíhen) arígatò gozáimashità
thank God! ああ良かった ã yókàtta

thankful [θæŋk'fəl] *adj*: *thankful (for)* (...を) 有難く思っている (...wo) arígatakù omôtte irù

thankless [θæŋk'lis] *adj* (task) 割の悪い warí no waruî

thanks [θæŋks] *npl* 感謝 káñsha
♦*excl* (*also*: **many thanks**, thanks a lot) 有難う arígatò

Thanksgiving (Day) [θæŋksgiv'iŋ-] *n* 感謝祭 kañshasaî

thanks to *prep* ...のおかげで ...no o-kâge dè

that [ðæt] (demonstrative adj, pron: pl
those) adj (demonstrative) その sonó、あ
の anó

that man/woman/book その〔あの〕男
性〔女性, 本〕 sonó〔anó〕daňsei〔josei,
hoň〕

leave those books on the table その本
をテーブルの上に置いていって下さい so-
nó hoň wo tḕburu no ué nǐ oíte ittě
kudásaǐ

that one それ soré、あれ aré

that one over there あそこにある物
asóko nǐ árù monó

I want this one, not that one 欲しい
のはこれです、あれは要りません hoshíi
no wà koré desù、aré wà irímaseň

◆*pron* 1 (demonstrative) それ soré、あれ
aré

who's/what's that? あれはだれですか
〔何ですか〕aré wà dárè desu ká〔náň
desu ká〕

is that you? あなたですか anátà desu
ká

I prefer this to that あれよりこちらの
方が好きです aré yorǐ kochíra no hǒ ga
sukí desù

will you eat all that? あれを全部食
べるつもりですか aré wò zéňbu tabérù
tsumóri desù ká

that's my house 私の家はあれです watákushi nò ié wà aré desù

that's what he said 彼はそう言いまし
たよ kárè wa số iimashǐta yó

what happened after that? それから
どうなりましたか soré karà dố narima-
shǐta ká

that is (to say) つまり tsúmàri、すなわ
ち sunáwàchi

2 (relative): *the book (that) I read* 私
の読んだ本 watákushi nò yóňda hoň

the books that are in the library 図
書館にある本 toshókàn ni árù hoň

the man (that) I saw 私の見た男 watákushi no mǐta otóko

all (that) I have 私が持っているだけ
watákushi gà móttè irú dàke

the box (that) I put it in それを入れ
た箱 soré wò iréta hakó

the people (that) I spoke to 私が声を
掛けた人々 watákushi gà kốè wo kákèta hitóbìto

3 (relative: of time): *the day (that) he
came* 彼が来た日 kárè ga kitá hǐ

*the evening/winter (that) he came
to see us* 彼が私たちの家に来た夜〔冬〕
kárè ga watákushitàchi no ié ni kitá
yorù〔fuyù〕

◆*conj* ...だと ...dá tò

he thought that I was ill 私が病気だ
と彼は思っていました watákushi gà
byốkǐ dá tò kárè wa omótte imashìta

she suggested that I phone you あな
たに電話する様にと彼女は私に勧めまし
た anátà ni deňwa suru yố ni to kánòjo
wa watákushi nǐ susúmemashìta

◆*adv* (demonstrative) それ程 soré hodò、
あれ程 aré hodò、そんなに soňna nǐ、あん
なに aňna nǐ

I can't work that much あんなに働け
ません aňna nǐ határakemaseň

I didn't realize it was that bad 事態
があれ程悪くなっているとは思いま
せんでした jítai ga aré hodò wárùku
natté irù to wa omótte imasen deshìta

that high あんなに高い aňna nǐ takáǐ

*the wall's about that high and that
thick* 塀はこれぐらい高くてこれぐらい
厚い heí wà koré gurài tákàkute koré
gurài atsúi

thatched [θætʃt] adj (roof, cottage) わら
ぶきの warábuki no

thaw [θɔ:] n 雪解けの陽気 yukídokè no
yốkǐ

◆*vi* (ice) 溶ける tokérù; (food) 解凍され
る kaítō sarerù

◆*vt* (food: *also*: **thaw out**) 解凍する kaítō suru

the [ðə] def art 1 (gen) その sonó ◇ 通常
日本語では表現しない tsújō nihóngo de
wà hyốgen shinaǐ

the history of France フランスの歴史

furánsu nò rekíshi

the books/children are in the library 本〔子供たち〕は図書館にあります〔います〕hón〔kodómotàchi〕wa toshókàn ni arímasù〔imásù〕

she put it on the table/gave it to the postman 彼女はテーブルに置きました〔郵便屋さんにあげました〕kánòjo wa tèburu ni okímashìta〔yūbin-yasan nî agémashìta〕

he took it from the drawer 彼は引出しから取り出しました kárè wa hikídashi karà torídashimashìta

I haven't the time/money 私にはそれだけの時間〔金〕がありません watákushi ni wà soré dakè no jikan〔kanè〕gà arímaseñ

to play the piano/violin ピアノ〔バイオリン〕をひく piáno〔baíorin〕wo hikú

the age of the computer コンピュータの時代 koñpyùta no jidái

I'm going to the butcher's/the cinema 肉屋に〔映画を見に〕行って来ます nikúyà ni〔eíga wò mí nì〕itté kimasù

2 (+ adjective to form noun)

the rich and the poor 金持と貧乏人 kanémochì to biñbóniñ

the wounded were taken to the hospital 負傷者は病院に運ばれた fushóshà wa byóìn ni hakóbaretà

to attempt the impossible 不可能な事をやろうとする fukánò na kotò wo yaró to surù

3 (in titles): *Elizabeth the First* エリザベス1世 erízabèsu íssèi

Peter the Great ピョートル大帝 pyótòru taítei

4 (in comparisons): *the more he works the more he earns* 彼は働けば働く程うかる kárè wa határakèba hataraku hodò mòkarù

the more I look at it the less I like it 見れば見る程いやになります mírèba míru hodò iyá ni narimasù

---

theater [θi:'ətər] *n* (*BRIT* **theatre**) *n* (building with stage) 劇場 gekíjò; (art form) 演劇 eñgeki; (*also*: **lecture thea-**

---

ter) 講義室 kõgishìtsu; (*MED*: *also*: **operating theater**) 手術室 shujútsushìtsu

theater-goer [θi:'ətərgouə:r] *n* 芝居好き shibáizùki

theatrical [θi:æt'rikəl] *adj* (event, production) 演劇の eñgeki no; (gestures) 芝居染みた shibáijimìta

theft [θeft] *n* 窃盗 settő

their [ðe:r] *adj* 彼らの kárèra no ¶ *see also* **my**

theirs [ðe:rz] *pron* 彼らの物 kárèra no monő ¶ *see also* **mine**

them [ðem] *pron* (direct) 彼らを kárèra wo; (indirect) 彼らに kárèra ni; (stressed, after prep) 彼ら kárèra ¶ *see also* **me**

theme [θi:m] *n* (main subject) 主題 shudái, テーマ tèma; (*MUS*) テーマ tèma

theme park *n* テーマ遊園地 témayüeñchi

theme song *n* 主題歌 shudáika

themselves [ðəmselvz'] *pl pron* (reflexive) 彼ら自身を karéra jishìn wo; (after prep) 彼ら自身 karéra jishìn ¶ *see also* **oneself**

then [ðen] *adv* (at that time) その時(に) sonó tokì (ni); (next, later, and also) それから soré karà

♦*conj* (therefore) だから dá kàra

♦*adj*: *the then president* 当時の大統領 tõjì no daítòryõ

by then (past) その時 sonó tokì; (future) その時になったら sonó tokì ni nattárà

from then on その時から sonó tokì kara

theology [θi:ɑ:l'ədʒi:] *n* 神学 shiñgaku

theorem [θi:r'əm] *n* 定理 teíri

theoretical [θi:əret'ikəl] *adj* (biology, possibility) 理論的な riróñteki na

theorize [θi:'ə:raiz] *vi* 学説を立てる gakúsetsu wò tatérù

theory [θi:ər'i:] *n* (all senses) 理論 ríròn

in theory 理論的には riróñteki ni wà

therapeutic(al) [θe:rəpju:'tik(əl)] *adj* 治療の chiryő no

therapist [θe:r'əpist] *n* セラピスト serápisùto

therapy [θerˈəpiː] n 治療 chiryō

KEYWORD

there [δeːr] adv 1: **there is, there are** …があるいる …ga árù(irú)
there are 3 of them (things) 3つあります míttsu arímasù; (people) 3人います saññíñ imásù
there is no one here だれもいません dáre mo imáseñ
there is no bread left パンがなくなりました páñ ga nakúnarimashìta
there has been an accident 事故がありました jíkò ga arímashìta
there will be a meeting tomorrow 明日会議があります asú káìgi ga arímasù
2 (referring to place) そこに〔で、へ〕sokó nì(dè, e), あそこに〔で、へ〕asokó nì (dè, e)
where is the book? - it's there 本はどこにありますか-あそこにあります hóñ wa dókò ni arímasù ká - asókò nì arímasù
put it down there そこに置いて下さい sokó nì oíte kudasaì
he went there on Friday 彼は金曜日に行きました kárè wa kiñ-yōbi ni ikímashìta
I want that book there そこの本が欲しい sokó nò hóñ ga hoshíì
there he is! いました imáshìta
3: **there, there** (especially to child) よしよし yóshì yóshì
there, there, it's not your fault/don't cry よしよし、お前のせいじゃないから(泣かないで) yóshì yóshì, omáe nò seí ja naì kara(nakánaìde)

thereabouts [δeːrˈəbauts] adv (place) そこら辺 sokórahèñ; (amount) それぐらい soré gurai

thereafter [δeːræfˈtəːr] adv それ以来 soré iraì

thereby [δeːrbaiˈ] adv それによって soré ni yottè

therefore [δeːrˈfɔːr] adv だから dá kàra

there's [δeːrz] = **there is; there has**

thermal [θəːrˈməl] adj (underwear) 防寒

用の bōkan-yō no; (paper) 感熱の kańnetsu no; (printer) 熱式の netsúshìki no

thermal spring n 温泉 ońseñ

thermometer [θəːrmɑːmˈitəːr] n (for room/body temperature) 温度計 ońdokèi

Thermos [θəːrˈməs]® n (also: **Thermos flask**) 魔法瓶 mahōbìn

thermostat [θəːrˈməstæt] n サーモスタット sāmosutattò

thesaurus [θisɔːrˈəs] n シソーラス shisōrāsu

these [δiːz] pl adj これらの korérà no
◆pl pron これらは(を) korérà wa(wo)

theses [θiːˈsiːz] npl of **thesis**

thesis [θiːˈsis] (pl **theses**) n (for doctorate etc) 論文 rońbun

they [δei] pl pron 彼らは(が) kárèra wa (ga)
they say that … (it is said that) …と言われている …to iwárete irù

they'd [δeid] = **they had; they would**

they'll [δeil] = **they shall, they will**

they're [δeːr] = **they are**

they've [δeiv] = **they have**

thick [θik] adj (in shape: slice, jersey etc) 厚い atsúì; (line) 太い futóì; (in consistency: sauce, mud, fog etc) 濃い kóì; (: forest) 深い fukáì; (stupid) 鈍い nibúì
◆n: **in the thick of the battle** 戦いのさなかに tatákai nò sánàka ni
it's 20 cm thick 厚さは20センチだ atsúsa wà nijússeñchi da

thicken [θikˈən] vi (fog etc) 濃くなる kókù naru; (plot) 込入ってくる komíitte kurù
◆vt (sauce etc) 濃くする kókù suru

thickness [θikˈnis] n 厚み atsúmi

thickset [θikˈset] adj (person, body) がっちりした gatchírì shita

thickskinned [θikˈskind] adj (fig: person) 無神経な mushíñkei na

thief [θiːf] (pl **thieves**) n 泥棒 doróbō

thieves [θiːvz] npl of **thief**

thigh [θai] n 太もも futómomo

thimble [θimˈbəl] n 指抜き yubínuki

thin [θin] adj (gen) 薄い usúì; (line) 細い hosóì; (person, animal) やせた yasétà;

(crowd) まばらな mabára na

♦vt: **to thin (down)** (sauce, paint) 薄める usúmerù

thing [θiŋ] n (gen) 物事 monógòto; (physical object) 物 monõ; (matter) 事 kotõ:
to have a thing about someone/something (mania) ...が大嫌いである ...ga dáikirai de árù; (fascination) ...が大好きである ...ga dáisuki de árù
poor thing かわいそうに kawáisō ni
the best thing would be to ... ...するのが一番いいだろう ...surú no gà ichíban iî darõ
how are things? どうですか dõ desu ká

things [θiŋz] npl (belongings) 持物 mochímòno

think [θiŋk] (pt, pp **thought**) vi (reflect) 考える kañgaerù; (believe) 思う omóù
♦vt (imagine) ...だと思う ...dá tò omóù
what did you think of them? 彼らの事をどう思いましたか kárèra no kotó wo dõ omóimashità ka
to think about something/someone ...について考える ...ni tsúîte kañgaerù
I'll think about it 考えておくね kañgaete okù né
to think of doing something ...しようと思う ...shiyõ tò omóù
I think so/not そうだ〔違う〕と思う sõ dà 〔chígáù〕to omóù
to think well of someone ...に対して好感を持つ ...ni táishite kõkan wò mótsù

think over vt (offer, suggestion) よく考える yókù kañgaerù

think tank n シンクタンク shiñkutañku

think up vt (plan, scheme, excuse) 考え出す kañgaedasù

thinly [θin'li:] adv (cut, spread) 薄く usúkù

third [θə:rd] num 第三（の）dáî san (no)
♦n (fraction) 3分の1 sañbun no ichí; (AUT: also: **third gear**) サードギヤ sā́dogiyà; (BRIT: SCOL: degree) 3級優等卒業学位 sañkyū yūtō sotsugyō gakùi
¶ see also **first**

thirdly [θə:rd'li:] adv 第三に dáî san ni

third party insurance (BRIT) n 損害倍償保険 soñgaibaishōhoken

third-rate [θə:rd'reit'] adj 三流の sañryū no

Third World n: **the Third World** 第三世界 dáî san sékài

thirst [θə:rst] n 渇き kawáki

thirsty [θə:rs'ti:] adj (person, animal) のどが渇いた nódò ga kawáità; (work) のどが渇く nódò ga kawákù
to be thirsty (person, animal) のどが渇いている nódò ga kawáite irù

thirteen [θə:r'ti:n'] num 十三（の）jū́san (no)

thirty [θə:r'ti:] num 三十（の）sáñjū (no)

KEYWORD

this [ðis] (pl **these**) adj (demonstrative) この konõ
this man/woman/book この男性〔女性, 本〕konõ dansei〔josei, hon〕
these people/children/records この人たち〔子供たち, レコード〕konõ hitótàchi〔kodomotàchi, rekõdo〕
this one これ korế
it's not that picture but this one that I like 私が好きなのはあの絵ではなくて, この絵です watákushi gà sukí na no wà anõ e de wa nakùte, konõ e desù
♦pron (demonstrative) これ korế
what is this? これは何ですか korế wà náñ desu ká
who is this? この方はどなたですか konõ katà wa dónàta desu ká
I prefer this to that 私はあれよりこの方が好きです watákushi wà arế yorí konõ hõ ga sukí desù
this is where I live 私の住いはここです watákushi no sumáì wa kokố desù
this is what he said 彼はこう言いました kárè wa kõ iimashìta
this is Mr Brown (in introductions/photo) こちらはブラウンさんです kochíra wà buráûnsan desu; (on telephone) こちらはブラウンですが kochíra wà burá-

ùn desu ga

♦*adv* (demonstrative): *this high/long*
高さ(長さ)はこれぐらいで tákàsa(nágàsa)wa koré gùrài de

it was about this big 大きさはこれぐらいでした ókìsa wa korégùrài deshita

the car is this long 車の長さはこれぐらいです kurúma no nagàsa wa koré gùrài desu

we can't stop now we've gone this far ここまで来たらやめられません kokó madè kitára yaméraremaseñ

---

thistle [θis'əl] *n* アザミ azámi

thong [θɔːŋ] *n* バンド bándo

thorn [θɔːrn] *n* とげ togé

thorny [θɔːr'niː] *adj* (plant, tree) とげの多い togé no òi; (problem) 厄介な yákkài na

thorough [θəːr'ou] *adj* (search, wash) 徹底的な tettéiteki na; (knowledge, research) 深い fukáì; (person: methodical) きちょうめんな kichómen na

thoroughbred [θəːr'oubred] *adj* (horse) サラブレッド sarábureddò

thoroughfare [θəːr'oufeːr] *n* 目抜き通り menúkidòri

「*no thoroughfare*」通行禁止 tsúkōkìnshi

thoroughly [θəːr'ouliː] *adv* (examine, study, wash, search) 徹底的に tettéiteki ni; (very) とても totémo

those [ðouz] *pl adj* それらの sorérà no, あれらのarérà no

♦*pl pron* それらを sorérà wo, あれらを arérà wo

though [ðou] *conj* ...にもかかわらず ...ní mò kakáwarazù

♦*adv* しかし shikáshì

thought [θɔːt] *pt, pp of* **think**

♦*n* (idea, reflection) 考え kañgaè; (opinion) 意見 íkèn

thoughtful [θɔːt'fəl] *adj* (person: deep in thought) 考え込んでいる kañgaekonde irù; (: serious) 真剣な shiñken na; (considerate: person) 思いやりのある omóiyari no arù

thoughtless [θɔːt'lis] *adj* (inconsiderate:

behavior, words, person) 心ない kokóronaì

thousand [θau'zənd] *num* 千(の) séñ (no)

two thousand 二千(の) niséñ (no)

thousands of 何千もの... nañzeñ mo no ...

thousandth [θau'zəndθ] *num* 第千(の) dáì sen (no)

thrash [θræʃ] *vt* (beat) たたく tatákù; (defeat) ...に快勝する ...ni kaíshō suru

thrash about/around *vi* のたうつ notáutsù

thrash out *vt* (problem) 討議する tógi suru

thread [θred] *n* (yarn) 糸 ítò; (of screw) ねじ山 nejíyama

♦*vt* (needle) ...に糸を通す ...ni ítò wo tósù

threadbare [θred'beːr] *adj* (clothes, carpet) 擦切れた suríkiretà

threat [θret] *n* (*also fig*) 脅し odóshi; (*fig*) 危険 kíkèn

threaten [θret'ən] *vi* (storm, danger) 迫る semárù

♦*vt: to threaten someone with/to do* ...で(...すると言って)...を脅す ...de (...surú tò itté)...wò odósù

three [θriː] *num* 三(の) sañ (no)

three-dimensional [θriː'dimen'tʃənəl] *adj* 立体的 rittái no

three-piece suit [θriː'piːs-] *n* 三つぞろい mitsúzorði

three-piece suite *n* 応接三点セット ósetsu santensettò

three-ply [θriː'plai] *adj* (wool) 三重織りの sañjūori no

thresh [θreʃ] *vt* (AGR) 脱穀する dakkóku suru

threshold [θreʃ'ould] *n* 敷居 shikíi

threw [θruː] *pt of* **throw**

thrift [θrift] *n* 節約 setsúyaku

thrifty [θrif'tiː] *adj* 節約家の setsúyakukà no

thrill [θril] *n* (excitement) スリル súrìru; (shudder) ぞっとする事 zottó suru kotò

♦*vt* (person, audience) わくわくさせる wákùwaku sasérù

to be thrilled (with gift etc) 大喜びである ōyorókobi de árù

thriller [θríl'əːr] n (novel, play, film) スリラー surírā

thrilling [θríl'iŋ] adj (ride, performance, news etc) わくわくさせる wákùwaku sasérù

thrive [θraiv] (pt **throve**, pp **thrived** or **thriven**) vi (grow: plant) 生茂る oíshigerù; (: person, animal) よく育つ yókù sodátsù; (: business) 盛んになる sakán ni narù; (do well): **to thrive on something** ...で栄える ...de sakáerù

thriven [θráivən] pp of **thrive**

thriving [θráiviŋ] adj (business, community) 繁盛している hánjō shité irù

throat [θrout] n のど nódò

to have a sore throat のどが痛い nódò ga itáí

throb [θrɑːb] n (of heart) 鼓動 kodō; (of wound) うずき uzúki; (of engine) 振動 shíndō

♦vi (heart) どきどきする dókìdoki suru; (head, arm: with pain) ずきずきする zúkìzuki suru; (machine: vibrate) 振動する shíndō suru

throes [θrouz] npl: **in the throes of** (war, moving house etc) ...と取組んでいるさなかに ...to toríkunde irù sánàka ni

thrombosis [θrɑːmbou'sis] n 血栓症 kessénshō

throne [θroun] n 王座 ōzà

throng [θrɔːŋ] n 群衆 gunshū

♦vt (streets etc) ...に殺到する ...ni sattō suru

throttle [θrɑːt'əl] n (AUT) スロットル suróttòru

♦vt (strangle) ...ののどを絞める ...no nódò wo shimérù

through [θruː] prep (space) ...を通って ...wo tőttè; (time) ...の間中 ...no áìda jū; (by means of) ...を使って ...wo tsukáttè; (owing to) ...が原因で ...ga geń-in dè

♦adj (ticket, train) 直通の chokútsū no

♦adv 通して tőshìte

to put someone through to someone (TEL) ...を...につなぐ ...wo ...ni tsunágù

to be through (TEL) つながれる tsuná-

garerù; (relationship: finished) 終る owárù

「**no through road**」(BRIT) 行き止り ikídomarì

throughout [θruːaut'] prep (place) ...の至る所に ...no itárù tokoro ni; (time) ...の間中 ...no áìda jū

♦adv 至る所に itárù tokoro ni

throve [θrouv] pt of **thrive**

throw [θrou] n (gen) 投げる事 nagéru kotò

♦vt (pt **threw**, pp **thrown**) (object) 投げる nagérù; (rider) 振り落す furíotosù; (fig: person: confuse) 迷わせる mayówaserù

to throw a party パーティをやる pátì wo yárù

throw away vt (rubbish) 捨てる sutérù; (money) 浪費する rōhi suru

throwaway [θrou'əwei] adj (toothbrush) 使い捨ての tsukáisùte no; (line, remark) 捨てぜりふ染みた sutézerifujimìta

throw-in [θrou'in] n (SPORT) スローイン suróìn

throw off vt (get rid of: burden, habit) かなぐり捨てる kanágurisuterù; (cold) ...が治る ...ga naórù

throw out vt (rubbish, idea) 捨てる sutérù; (person) ほうり出す hōridasù

throw up vi (vomit) 吐く hákù

thru [θruː] (US) = **through**

thrush [θrʌʃ] n (bird) つぐみ tsugúmi

thrust [θrʌst] n (TECH) 推進力 suíshinryoku

♦vt (pt, pp **thrust**) (person, object) 強く押す tsuyőku osú

thud [θʌd] n ばたんという音 batán to iú otő

thug [θʌg] n (pej) ちんぴら chíñpira; (criminal) 犯罪者 hañzaìsha

thumb [θʌm] n (ANAT) 親指 oyáyubi

♦vt: **to thumb a lift** ヒッチハイクする hitchíhaìku suru

thumbtack [θʌm'tæk] (US) n 画びょう gabyō

thumb through vt fus (book) 拾い読みする hiróiyomi suru

thump [θʌmp] n (blow) 一撃 ichígeki; (sound) どしんという音 doshín to iú otó
♦vt (person, object) たたく tatákú
♦vi (heart etc) どきどきする dókìdoki suru

thunder [θʌn'də:r] n 雷 kamínari
♦vi 雷が鳴る kamínari ga narù; (fig: train etc): **to thunder past** ごう音を立てて通り過ぎる góon wò tátète tṓrisugirù

thunderbolt [θʌn'də:rboult] n 落雷 rakúrai

thunderclap [θʌn'də:rklæp] n 雷鳴 raímei

thunderstorm [θʌn'də:rstɔ:rm] n 雷雨 ráīu

thundery [θʌn'də:ri:] adj (weather) 雷が鳴る kamínarì ga narù

Thursday [θə:rz'dei] n 木曜日 mokúyòbi

thus [ðʌs] adv (in this way) こうして kṓshìte; (consequently) 従って shitágattè

thwart [θwɔ:rt] vt (person, plans) 邪魔する jamá suru

thyme [taim] n タイム táīmu

thyroid [θai'rɔid] n (also: **thyroid gland**) 甲状腺 kōjōsen

tiara [ti:ær'ə] n ティアラ tíàra

Tibet [tibet'] n チベット chibéttò

tic [tik] n チック chíkkù

tick [tik] n (sound of clock) かちかち káchìkachi; (mark) 印 shirúshi; (ZOOL) だに danī; (BRIT: inf): **in a tick** もうすぐ mō sugù
♦vi (clock, watch) かちかちいう káchìkachi iú
♦vt (item on list) ...に印を付ける ...ni shirúshi wò tsukérù

ticket [tik'it] n (for public transport, theater etc) 切符 kippú; (in shop: on goods) 値札 nefúda; (for raffle, library etc) チケット chikéttò; (also: **parking ticket**) 駐車違反のチケット chūsha-ihàn no chikéttò

ticket collector n 改札係 kaísatsugakàri

ticket office n (RAIL, theater etc) 切符売場 kippú urìba

tickle [tik'əl] vt (person, dog) くすぐる kusúguru
♦vi (feather etc) くすぐったい kusúguttai

ticklish [tik'liʃ] adj (person) くすぐったがる kusúguttagàru; (problem) 厄介な yákkai na

tick off vt (item on list) ...に印を付ける ...ni shirúshi wò tsukérù; (person) しかる shikárù

tick over vi (engine) アイドリングする aídoriñgu suru; (fig: business) 低迷する teímei suru

tidal [taid'əl] adj (force) 潮の shió no; (estuary) 干満のある kañman no arù

tidal wave n 津波 tsunámi

tidbit [tid'bit] (US) n (food) うまいもの一口 umái monò hitókùchi; (news) 好奇心をあおり立てるうわさ話 kṓkishìn wo aóritaterù uwásabanàshi

tiddlywinks [tid'li:wiŋks] n おはじき ohájìki

tide [taid] n (in sea) 潮 shió; (fig: of events, fashion, opinion) 動向 dṓkō
high/low tide 満(干)潮 mañ(kañ)chō

tide over vt (help out) ...の一時的な助けになる ...no ichíjiteki nà tasúke ni narù

tidy [tai'di:] adj (room, dress, desk, work) きちんとした kichín to shita; (person) きれい好きな kiréïzuki na
♦vt (also: **tidy up**: room, house etc) 片付ける katázukerù

tie [tai] n (string etc) ひも himó; (BRIT: also: **necktie**) ネクタイ nékùtai; (fig: link) 縁 éñ; (SPORT: even score) 同点 dṓten
♦vt (fasten: parcel) 縛る shibárù; (: shoelaces, ribbon) 結ぶ musúbù
♦vi (SPORT etc) 同点になる dṓten nì narù
to tie in a bow ちょう結びにする chṓmusùbi ni suru
to tie a knot in something ...に結び目を作る ...ni musúbime wò tsukúrù

tie down vt (fig: person: restrict) 束縛する sokúbaku suru; (: to date, price etc) 縛り付ける shibáritsukerù

tier [ti:r] n (of stadium etc) 列 rétsù; (of cake) 層 sṓ

tie up vt (parcel) ...にひもを掛ける ...ni himó wo kakérù; (dog, boat) つなぐ tsunagu; (prisoner) 縛る shibárù; (arrangements) 整える totónoerù

to be tied up (busy) 忙しい isógashiì

tiger [tai'gə:r] n トラ torá

tight [tait] adj (firm: rope) ぴんと張った piñ tò hattá; (scarce: money) 少ない sukúnaì; (narrow: shoes, clothes) きつい kitsúì; (bend) 急な kyū na; (strict: security, budget, schedule) 厳しい kibíshiì; (inf: drunk) 酔っ払った yoppárattà

♦adv (hold, squeeze, shut) 堅く katákù

tighten [tait'ən] vt (rope, screw) 締める shimérù; (grip) 固くする katáku suru; (security) 厳しくする kibíshiku suru

♦vi (grip) 固くなる katáku narù; (rope) 締る shimárù

tightfisted [tait'fis'tid] adj けちな kéchi na

tightly [tait'li:] adv (grasp) 固く katáku

tightrope [tait'roup] n 綱渡りの綱 tsunáwatàri no tsuná

tights [taits] npl タイツ táìtsu

tile [tail] n (on roof) かわら kawára; (on floor, wall) タイル táìru

tiled [taild] adj (roof) かわらぶきの kawárabuki no; (floor, wall) タイル張りの taírubari no

till [til] n (in shop etc) レジの引出し réjì no hikídashi

♦vt (land: cultivate) 耕す tagáyasù

♦prep, conj = **until**

tiller [til'ə:r] n (NAUT) だ柄 dahéi, チラー chírà

tilt [tilt] vt 傾ける katámukerù

♦vi 傾く katámukù

timber [tim'bə:r] n (material) 材木 zaímoku; (trees) 材木用の木 zaímokuyò no kí

time [taim] n (gen) 時間 jíkàn; (epoch: often pl) 時代 jidái; (by clock) 時刻 jíkòku; (moment) 瞬間 shuñkan; (occasion) 回 kái; (MUS) テンポ téñpo

♦vt (measure time of: race, boiling an egg etc) ...の時間を計る ...no jíkàn wo hakárù; (fix moment for: visit etc) ...の時間を選ぶ ...no jíkì wo erábù; (remark etc) ...のタイミングを合せる ...no taímiñgu wo awáserù

a long time 長い間 nagái aìda

for the time being 取りあえず toríaezù

4 at a time 4つずつ yottsú zùtsu

from time to time 時々 tokídoki

at times 時には tokí ni wà

in time (soon enough) 間に合って ma ní attè; (after some time) やがて yagáte; (MUS) ...のリズムに合せて ...no rízùmu ni awásetè

in a week's time 1週間で isshúkan de

in no time 直ぐに súgù ni

any time いつでも ítsù de mo

on time 間に合って ma ní attè

5 times 5 5かける5 gó kakerù gó

what time is it? 何時ですか náñji desu ká

to have a good time 楽しむ tanóshimù

time bomb n 時限爆弾 jigénbakùdan

time lag n 遅れ okúre

timeless [taim'lis] adj 普遍的な fuhénteki na

time limit n 期限 kígèn

timely [taim'li:] adj (arrival, reminder) 時機を得た jígì wo étà, 丁度いい時の chōdo ii tokí no, タイムリーな taímurī na

time off n 休暇 kyúka

timer [taim'ə:r] n (time switch) タイムスイッチ taímusuitchì; (in cooking) タイマー táìmā

time scale (BRIT) n 期間 kíkàn

time-share [taim'ʃe:r] n リゾート施設の共同使用権 rizótoshisètsu no kyódòshiyōken

time switch n タイムスイッチ taímusuitchì, タイマー taima

timetable [taim'teibəl] n (RAIL etc) 時刻表 jikókuhyō; (SCOL etc) 時間割 jikánwari

time zone n 時間帯 jikántai

timid [tim'id] adj (shy) 気が小さい ki gá chiìsai; (easily frightened) 臆病な okúbyō na

timing [tai'miŋ] n (SPORT) タイミング taímingu

the timing of his resignation 彼の辞

退のタイミング kárè no jítài no taímingu

timpani [tim'pəni:] npl ティンパニー tíñpanī

tin [tin] n (material) すず súzù; (also: **tin plate**) ブリキ buríki; (container: biscuit tin etc) 箱 hakó; (: BRIT: can) 缶 káñ

tinfoil [tin'fɔil] n ホイル hóiru

tinge [tindʒ] n (of color) 薄い色合 usúî iróaî; (of feeling) 気味 kimí

♦vt: **tinged with** (color) ...の色合を帯びた ...no iróaî wo óbìta; (feeling) ...の気味を帯びた ...no kimí wò óbìta

tingle [tiŋ'gəl] vi (person, arms etc) ぴりぴりする bíríbiri suru

tinker [tiŋk'əːr]: **to tinker with** vt fus いじくる ijíkurù

tinned [tind] (BRIT) adj (food, salmon, peas) 缶詰の kañzume no

tin opener [-ou'pənəːr] (BRIT) n 缶切り kañkirì

tinsel [tin'səl] n ティンセル tíñseru

tint [tint] n (color) 色合い iróaî; (for hair) 染毛剤 señmôzai

tinted [tin'tid] adj (hair) 染めた sométa; (spectacles, glass) 色付きの irótsuki no

tiny [tai'ni:] adj 小さな chíisa na

tip [tip] n (end: of paintbrush etc) 先端 sefitan; (gratuity) チップ chíppù; (BRIT: for rubbish) ごみ捨て場 gomí suteba; (advice) 助言 jogén

♦vt (waiter) ...にチップをあげる ...ni chíppù wo agérù; (tilt) 傾ける katámukerù; (overturn: also: **tip over**) 引っ繰り返す hikkúrikaesù; (empty: also: **tip out**) 空ける akérù

tip-off [tip'ɔːf] n (hint) 内報 naíhō

tipped [tipt] (BRIT) adj (cigarette) フィルター付きの firútātsuki no

Tipp-Ex [tip'eks] ® BRIT n 修正ペン shūseipeñ ◇白い修正液の出るフェルトペン shiróî shúseieki no derù ferútopeñ

tipsy [tip'si:] (inf) adj 酔っ払った yoppárattà

tiptoe [tip'tou] n: **on tiptoe** つま先立って tsumásakidatte

tiptop [tip'tɑːp] adj: **in tiptop condition** 状態が最高で jôtai gà saíkō dè

tire [taiəːr] n (BRIT **tyre**) タイヤ táiya

♦vt (make tired) 疲れさせる tsukáresaserù

♦vi (become tired) 疲れる tsukárerù; (become wearied) うんざりする uñzarí suru

tired [taiəːrd] adj (person, voice) 疲れた tsukáretà

to be tired of something ...にうんざりしている ...ni uñzarî shité irù

tireless [taiəːr'lis] adj (worker) 疲れを知らない tsukáre wò shiránaî; (efforts) たゆまない tayúmanaî

tire pressure n タイヤの空気圧 táiya no kûkiatsù

tiresome [taiəːr'səm] adj (person, thing) うんざりさせる uñzarí saserù

tiring [taiəːr'iŋ] adj 疲れさせる tsukáresaserù

tissue [tiʃ'uː] n (ANAT, BIO) 組織 sóshìki; (paper handkerchief) ティッシュ tísshù

tissue paper n ティッシュペーパー tisshúpêpā

tit [tit] n (bird) シジュウカラ shijúkàra

to give tit for tat しっぺ返しする shippégaèshi suru

titbit [tit'bit] = **tidbit**

titillate [tit'əleit] vt 刺激する shigéki suru ◇特に性的描写などについて言う tókù ni seíteki byôsha nádò ni tsúîte iú

title [tait'əl] n (of book, play etc) 題 dâî; (personal rank etc) 肩書 katágaki; (BOXING etc) タイトル táîtoru

title deed n (LAW) 権利証書 keñrishôsho

title role n 主役 shuyáku

titter [tit'əːr] vi くすくす笑う kusúkusu waraù

TM [tiːem'] abbr = **trademark**

to [tuː] prep 1 (direction) ...へ ...é

to go to France/London/school/the station フランス〔ロンドン，学校，駅〕へ行く furánsu(róñdon, gakkô, êkî) i-kù

to go to Claude's/the doctor's クロー

ドの家〔医者〕へ行く kuródò no ié〔ishá〕e ikú

the road to Edinburgh エジンバラへの道 ejínbara é nò michí

to the left/right 左〔右〕へ hidári〔migí〕e

2 (as far as) ...まで ...mádè

from here to London ここからロンドンまで kokó karà róndon madè

to count to 10 10まで数える jú madè kazóerù

from 40 to 50 people 40ないし50人の人 yónjū nàishi gojúnìn no hitó

3 (with expressions of time): *a quarter to 5* 5時15分前 gójì júgofun máè

it's twenty to 3 3時20分前です sánji nijúppun máè desu

4 (for, of) ...の ...no

the key to the front door 玄関のかぎ génkan no kagí

she is secretary to the director 彼女は所長の秘書です kánjo wa shochó nò hishó desù

a letter to his wife 妻への手紙 tsúmà e no tegámi

5 (expressing indirect object) ...に ...ni

to give something to someone ...に...を与える ...ni ...wò atáerù

to talk to someone ...に話す ...ni hanásù

I sold it to a friend 友達にそれを売りました tomódachi nì soré wò urímashìta

to cause damage to something ...に損害を与える ...ni sóngai wò atáerù

to be a danger to someone/something ...を危険にさらす ...wò kikén nì sarásù

to carry out repairs to something ...を修理する ...wò shúrì suru

you've done something to your hair あなたは髪型を変えましたね anátà wa kamígata wò kaémashìta né

6 (in relation to) ...に対して ...ni táìshite

A is to B as C is to D A対Bの関係はC対Dの関係に等しい A táì B no kánkei wà C táì D no kánkei nì hitóshìì

3 goals to 2 スコアは3対2 sukóà wa san táì ní

30 miles to the gallon ガソリン1ガロンで30マイル走れる gasórin ichígaròn de sanjūmaìru hashírerù

7 (purpose, result): *to come to someone's aid* ...を助けに来る ...wò tasúke nì kúrù

to sentence someone to death ...に死刑の宣告を下す ...ni shikéi nò senkoku wò kudásù

to my surprise 驚いた事に odóroita kotò ni

◆*with vb* **1** (simple infinitive): *to go/eat* 行く〔食べる〕事 ikú〔tabérù〕kotò

2 (following another verb): *to want to do* ...したい ...shitái

to try to do ...をしようとする ...wò shiyó tò suru

to start to do ...をし始める ...wò shihájimerù

3 (with vb omitted): *I don't want to* それをしたくない soré wò shitákùnai

you ought to あなたはそうすべきです anátà wa só sùbeki desu

4 (purpose, result) ...するために ...surú tamè ni, ...する様に ...surú yó ni, ...しに ...shí nì

I did it to help you あなたを助け様と思ってそれをしました anátà wo tasúkeyó to omóttè soré wò shimáshìta

he came to see you 彼はあなたに会いに来ました kárè wa anátà ni áì ni kimáshìta

I went there to meet him 彼に会おうとしてあそこへ行きました kárè wa anátà ni áó ni shite asóko e ikimashìta

5 (equivalent to relative clause): *I have things to do* 色々とする事があります iróiro tò suru kotò ga arímasù

he has a lot to lose if ... ...が起れば、彼は大損をするだろう ...gà okóreba, kárè wa ō suru darò

the main thing is to try 一番大切なのは努力です ichíban taìsetsu ná no wà dóryòku desu

6 (after adjective etc): *ready to go* 行く準備ができた ikú junbi ga dékìta

too old/young to ... ...するのに年を取り過ぎている〔若過ぎる〕...surú no nì to-

shī wò torísugite irù〔wakásugirù〕
it's too heavy to lift 重くて持上げられ
ません omókùte mochíageraremaseǹ

♦*adv: push/pull the door to* ドアを閉
める dôawo shimérù ◇ぴったり閉めない
場合に使う pittárì shiménai baái nì tsukáù

toad [toud] *n* ヒキガエル hikígaeru

toadstool [toud'stu:l] *n* キノコ kínoko

toast [toust] *n* (CULIN) トースト tôsuto;
(drink, speech) 乾杯 kañpai
♦*vt* (CULIN: bread etc) 焼く yákù;
(drink to) ...のために乾杯する ...no tamé
nì kañpai suru

toaster [tous'tə:r] *n* トースター tôsutā

tobacco [təbæk'ou] *n* タバコ tabáko

tobacconist [təbæk'ənist] *n* タバコ売り
tabákòuri

tobacconist's (shop) [təbæk'ənists-] *n*
タバコ屋 tabákoya

toboggan [təba:g'ən] *n* (*also* child's) ト
ボガン tobógaǹ

today [tədei'] *adv* (*also fig*) 今日(は) kyố
(wà)
♦*n* 今日 kyố; (*fig*) 現在 géñzai

toddler [ta:d'lə:r] *n* 幼児 yốjì

to-do [tədu:'] *n* (fuss) 騒ぎ sáwàgi

toe [tou] *n* (of foot) 足指 ashíyùbi; (of
shoe, sock) つま先 tsumásaki
♦*vt: to toe the line* (*fig*) 服従する fukújū suru

toenail [tou'neil] *n* 足のつめ ashí no tsu-
mè

toffee [tɔːf'iː] *n* = *taffy*

toffee apple (*BRIT*) *n* タフィー衣のり
んご tafígoromo no riǹgo

toga [tou'gə] *n* トーガ tôga

together [tu:geð'ə:r] *adv* (to/with each
other) 一緒に ísshò ni; (at same time) 同
時に dôji ni
together with ...と一緒に ...to ísshò ni

toil [tɔil] *n* 労苦 rốkù
♦*vi* あくせく働く ákùseku határakù

toilet [tɔi'lit] *n* (apparatus) 便器 béñki,
トイレ tôire; (room with this apparatus)
便所 beñjo, お手洗い o-téarài, トイレ tôire

toilet bag (for woman) 化粧バッグ ke-
shốbaggù; (for man) 洗面バッグ señmenbaggù

toilet paper *n* トイレットペーパー toírettopēpā

toiletries [tɔi'litri:z] *npl* 化粧品 keshốhìn

toilet roll *n* トイレットペーパーのロー
ル toírettopēpā no rôru

toilet soap *n* 化粧石けん keshốsekkèn

toilet water *n* 化粧水 keshốsùi

token [tou'kən] *n* (sign, souvenir) 印 shirúshi; (substitute coin) コイン kôiǹ
♦*adj* (strike, payment etc) 名目の meí-
moku no
book/record/gift token (*BRIT*) 商品
券 shốhiǹken

Tokyo [tou'ki:jou] *n* 東京 tốkyō

told [tould] *pt, pp of* **tell**

tolerable [ta:l'ə:rəbəl] *adj* (bearable) 我
慢できる gámàn dekírù; (fairly good) ま
あまあの mǎmā no

tolerance [ta:l'ə:rəns] *n* (patience) 寛容
kañ-yō; (TECH) 耐久力 taíkyūryòku

tolerant [ta:l'ə:rənt] *adj: tolerant (of)*
(...に) 耐えられる (...ni) taérarerù

tolerate [ta:l'ə:reit] *vt* (pain, noise, injustice) 我慢する gámàn suru

toll [toul] *n* (of casualties, deaths) 数 kázù; (tax, charge) 料金 ryốkin
♦*vi* (bell) 鳴る narú

tomato [təmei'tou] (*pl* **tomatoes**) *n* トマ
ト tómàto

tomb [tu:m] *n* 墓 haká

tomboy [ta:m'bɔi] *n* お転婆 o-téǹba

tombstone [tu:m'stoun] *n* 墓石 haká-ishi

tomcat [ta:m'kæt] *n* 雄ネコ osúneko

tomorrow [təmɔ:r'ou] *adv* (*also fig*) 明
日 asú, あした ashíta
♦*n* (*also fig*) 明日 asu, あした ashíta
the day after tomorrow あさって a-
sáttè
tomorrow morning あしたの朝 ashíta
nò ásà

ton [tʌn] *n* トン tôǹ ◇*BRIT* = 1016 kg;
US = 907 kg
tons of (*inf*) ものすごく沢山の monósu-
gòku takúsan no

tone [toun] *n* (of voice) 調子 chốshi; (of

instrument) 音色 ne-íro; (of color) 色調 shikíchō

♦vi (colors: also: **tone in**) 合う áù

tone-deaf [toun'def] adj 音痴の ónchi no

tone down vt (color, criticism, demands) 和らげる yawáragerù; (sound) 小さくする chiísakù suru

tone up vt (muscles) 強くする tsúyòku suru

tongs [tɔːŋz] npl (also: **coal tongs**) 炭ばさみ sumíbasàmi; (curling tongs) 髪ごて kamígote

tongue [tʌŋ] n (ANAT) 舌 shitá; (CULIN) タン táñ; (language) 言語 géñgo

tongue in cheek (speak, say) からかって karákattè

tongue-tied [tʌŋ'taid] adj (fig) ものも言えない monó mò iénaì

tongue-twister [tʌŋ'twistə:r] n 早口言葉 hayákuchi kotobà

tonic [tɑːn'ik] n (MED, also fig) 強壮剤 kyōsōzai; (also: **tonic water**) トニックウオーター toníkkuuōtā

tonight [tənait'] adv (this evening) 今日の夕方 kyō no yūgata; (this night) 今夜 kóñ-ya

♦n (this evening) 今日の夕方 kyō no yūgata; (this night) 今夜 kóñ-ya

tonnage [tʌn'idʒ] n (NAUT) トン数 tóñsū

tonsil [tɑːn'səl] n へんとうせん heñtōsen

tonsillitis [tɑːnsəlai'tis] n へんとうせん炎 heñtōsen-èn

too [tuː] adv (excessively) あまりに...過ぎる amári nì ...sugírù; (also) ...も (また) ...mo (matá)

too much adv あまり沢山で amári takusaǹ de

♦adj あまり沢山の amári takusaǹ no

too many adv あまり沢山の amári takusaǹ no

♦pron あまり沢山 amári takusaǹ

took [tuk] pt of **take**

tool [tuːl] n 道具 dṓgù

tool box n 道具箱 dṓgubàko

toot [tuːt] n (of horn) ぷーぷー pū́pū; (of whistle) ぴーぴー pī́pī

♦vi (with car-horn) クラクションを鳴らす kurákùshon wo narásù

tooth [tuːθ] (pl **teeth**) n (ANAT, TECH) 歯 há

toothache [tuːθ'eik] n 歯の痛み há nò itámi, 歯痛 shitsū

toothbrush [tuːθ'brʌʃ] n 歯ブラシ habúràshi

toothpaste [tuːθ'peist] n 歯磨き hamigaki

toothpick [tuːθ'pik] n つまようじ tsumáyòji

top [tɑːp] n (of mountain, tree, head, ladder) 天辺 teppéñ; (page) 頭 atáma; (of cupboard, table, box) ...の上 ...no ué; (of list etc) 筆頭 hittṓ; (lid: of box, jar, bottle) ふた futá; (blouse etc) トップ tóppù; (toy) こま kómà

♦adj (highest: shelf, step) 一番上の ichíban ue no; (: marks) 最高の saíkō no; (in rank: salesman etc) ぴか一の piká-ìchi no

♦vt (be first in: poll, vote, list) ...の首位に立つ ...no shúì ni tátsù; (exceed: estimate etc) 越える koérù

on top of (above) ...の上に ...no ué nì; (in addition to) ...に加えて ...ni kuwáetè

from top to bottom 上から下まで ué karà shitá madè

top floor n 最上階 saíjōkai

top hat n シルクハット shirúkuhattò

top-heavy [tɑːp'hevi:] adj (object) 不安定な fuáñtei na; (administration) 幹部の多過ぎる káñbu no ōsugírù

topic [tɑːp'ik] n 話題 wadái

topical [tɑːp'ikəl] adj 時事問題の jijímoñdai no

topless [tɑːp'lis] adj (bather, waitress, swimsuit) トップレスの tóppùresu no

top-level [tɑːp'lev'əl] adj (talks, decision) 首脳の shunṓ no

topmost [tɑːp'moust] adj (branch etc) 一番上の ichíban ue no

top off (US) vt = **top up**

topple [tɑːp'əl] vt (government, leader) 倒す taósù

♦vi (person, object) 倒れる taórerù

top-secret [tɑːp'si:'krit] adj 極秘の gokúhi no

topsy-turvy [tɑːpˈsiːtərˈviː] *adj* (world) はちゃめちゃの háchàmecha no

♦*adv* (fall, land etc) 逆様に sakásama ni

top up *vt* (bottle etc) 一杯にする ippái ni surú

torch [tɔːrtʃ] *n* (with flame) たいまつ tái-matsu; (*BRIT:* electric) 懐中電とう kaíchūdentō

tore [tɔːr] *pt of* **tear**

torment [*n* tɔːrˈment *vb* tɔːrˈment'] *n* 苦しみ kurúshimì

♦*vt* (subj: feelings, guilt etc) 苦しませる kurúshimaserù, 悩ませる nayámaserù; (*fig:* annoy: subj: person) いじめる ijímerù

torn [tɔːrn] *pp of* **tear**

tornado [tɔːrneiˈdou] (*pl* **tornadoes**) *n* 竜巻 tatsúmaki

torpedo [tɔːrpiˈdou] (*pl* **torpedoes**) *n* 魚雷 gyorái

torrent [tɔːrˈənt] *n* (flood) 急流 kyúryū; (*fig*) 奔流 hoñryū

torrential [tɔːrenˈtʃəl] *adj* (rain) 土砂降りの doshábùri no

torrid [tɔːrˈid] *adj* (sun) しゃく熱の shakúnetsu no; (love affair) 情熱的な jónetsuteki na

torso [tɔːrˈsou] *n* 胴 dṓ

tortoise [tɔːrˈtəs] *n* カメ kámè

tortoiseshell [tɔːrˈtəsʃel] *adj* べっ甲の bekkṓ no

tortuous [tɔːrˈtʃuːəs] *adj* (path) 曲りくねった magárikunettà; (argument) 回りくどい mawárikudoì; (mind) 邪悪な jaáku na

torture [tɔːrˈtʃəːr] *n* (*also fig*) 拷問 gṓmon

♦*vt* (*also fig*) 拷問にかける gṓmon nì kakérù

Tory [tɔːrˈiː] (*BRIT*) *adj* 保守党の hoshútō no

♦*n* 保守党員 hoshútòin

toss [tɔːs] *vt* (throw) 投げる nagérù; (one's head) 振る furú

to toss a coin コインをトスする kóìn wo tósù suru

to toss up for something コインをトスして...を決める kóìn wo tósù shité ...wò

kimérù

to toss and turn (in bed) ころげ回る korógemawarù

tot [tɑːt] *n* (*BRIT:* drink) おちょこ一杯 ochókò íppài; (child) 小さい子供 chiísai kodómo

total [touˈtəl] *adj* (complete: number, workforce etc) 全体の zeñtai no; (: failure, wreck etc) 完全な kañzen na

♦*n* 合計 gṓkei

♦*vt* (add up: numbers, objects) 合計する gṓkei suru; (add up to: X dollars/pounds) 合計は...になる gṓkei wà ...ni nárù

totalitarian [toutæliteːrˈiːən] *adj* 全体主義の zeñtaishùgi no

totally [touˈtəliː] *adv* (agree, write off, unprepared) 全く mattáku

totter [tɑːtˈəːr] *vi* (person) よろめく yorómekù

touch [tʌtʃ] *n* (sense of touch) 触覚 shokkáku; (contact) 触る事 sawárù kotó

♦*vt* (with hand, foot) ...に触る ...ni sawárù; (tamper with) いじる ijíru; (make contact with) ...に接触する ...ni sesshóku suru; (emotionally) 感動させる kañdō saserù

a touch of (*fig:* frost etc) 少しばかり sukóshi bakàri

to get in touch with someone ...に連絡する ...ni refíraku suru

to lose touch (friends) ...との連絡が途絶える ...tó nò refíraku gà todáerù

touch-and-go [tʌtʃˈəngouˈ] *adj* 危ない abúnai

touchdown [tʌtʃˈdaun] *n* (of rocket, plane: on land) 着陸 chakúriku; (: on water) 着水 chakúsui; (US FOOTBALL) タッチダウン tatchídaùn

touched [tʌtʃt] *adj* (moved) 感動した kañdō shita

touching [tʌtʃˈiŋ] *adj* 感動的な kañdōteki na

touchline [tʌtʃˈlain] *n* (SPORT) サイドライン saídoraìn

touch on *vt fus* (topic) ...に触れる ...ni furérù

touch up *vt* (paint) 修正する shū́sei suru

touchy [tʌtʃ'iː] *adj* (person) 気難しい kimúzukashii

tough [tʌf] *adj* (strong, hard-wearing: material) 丈夫な jốbu na; (meat) 固い katái; (person: physically) 頑丈な gañjō na; (: mentally) 神経が太い shiñkei gã futối; (difficult: task, problem, way of life) 難しい muzúkashiì; (firm: stance, negotiations, policies) 譲らない yuzúranaì

toughen [tʌf'ən] *vt* (someone's character) 強くする tsúyoku suru; (glass etc) 強化する kyốka suru

toupée [tuːpei'] *n* かつら katsúra ◇男性のはげを隠す小さな物を指す dañsei no hagè wo kakúsù chíisa na monð wo sásù

tour [tuːr] *n* (journey) 旅行 ryokố; (*also*: **package tour**) ツアー tsúā; (of town, factory, museum) 見学 keñgaku; (by pop group etc) 巡業 juñgyō
♦*vt* (country, city, factory etc) 観光旅行する kañkōryokố suru; (city) 見物する keñbutsu suru; (factory etc) 見学する keñgaku suru

tourism [tuːr'izəm] *n* (business) 観光 kañkō

tourist [tuːr'ist] *n* 観光客 kañkốkyaku
♦*cpd* (attractions etc) 観光の kañkō no

tourist class (on ship, plane) ツーリストクラス tsúrisutokuràsu

tourist office *n* 観光案内所 kañkōannaisho

tournament [tuːr'nəmənt] *n* トーナメント tốnàmento

tousled [tau'zəld] *adj* (hair) 乱れた midáretà

tout [taut] *vi*: **to tout for business** (business) 御用聞きする goyókìki suru
♦*n* (*also*: **ticket tout**) だふ屋 dafúyà

tow [tou] *vt* (vehicle, caravan, trailer) 引く hikú, けん引する keñ-in suru
「*in* (US) *or* (BRIT) *on tow*」(AUT) けん引中 keñ-iñchū

toward(s) [tɔːrd(z)] *prep* (direction) ...の方へ ...no hố è; (attitude) ...に対して ...ni táishite; (purpose) ...に向かって ...ni mukátte; (in time) ...のちょっと前に ...no chốttò maè ni

towel [tau'əl] *n* (hand/bath towel) タオル tâoru

towelling [tau'əliŋ] *n* (fabric) タオル地 taốrujì

towel rack (*BRIT*: **towel rail**) *n* タオル掛け taốrukàke

tower [tau'əːr] *n* 塔 tố

tower block (*BRIT*) *n* 高層ビル kốsōbirù

towering [tau'əːriŋ] *adj* (buildings, trees, cliffs) 高くそびえる tákàku sobèrù; (figure) 体の大きな karáda nò ốkì na

town [taun] *n* 町 machí
to go to town 町に出掛ける machí ni dekákerù; (*fig*: on something) 思い切りやる omóikiri yarù, 派手にやる hadé ni yárù

town center *n* 町の中心部 machí nò chúshiňbu

town council *n* 町議会 chốgikài

town hall *n* 町役場 machíyakùba

town plan *n* 町の道路地図 machí nò dốrochizù

town planning *n* 開発計画 kaíhatsukeikàku

towrope [tou'roup] *n* けん引用ロープ keñin-yố rốpù

tow truck (*US*) *n* (breakdown lorry) レッカー車 rekkáshà

toxic [tɑk'sik] *adj* (fumes, waste etc) 有毒の yúdoku no

toy [tɔi] *n* おもちゃ omóchà

toyshop [tɔi'ʃɑːp] *n* おもちゃ屋 omóchayà

toy with *vt fus* (object, food) いじくり回す ijíkurimawasù; (idea) ...しようかなと考えてみる ...shiyố kà na to kañgaete mirù

trace [treis] *n* (sign) 跡 átð; (small amount) 微量 biryố
♦*vt* (draw) トレースする torésù suru; (follow) 追跡する tsuíseki suru; (locate) 見付ける mitsúkerù

tracing paper [trei'siŋ-] *n* トレーシングペーパー torếshingupèpā

track [træk] *n* (mark) 跡 átò; (path: *gen*) 道 michí; (: of bullet etc) 弾道 dáñdō; (: of suspect, animal) 足跡 ashíatò; (RAIL) 線路 sếnro; (on tape, record: *also* SPORT)

トラック torákkù

♦vt (follow: animal, person) 追跡する tsuíseki suru

to keep track of ...を監視する ...wo kañshi suru

track down vt (prey) 追詰める oítsumerù; (something lost) 見付ける mitsúkerù

tracksuit [træk'su:t] n トレーニングウエア torḗningu ueà

tract [trækt] n (GEO) 地帯 chitái; (pamphlet) 論文 roñbun

traction [træk'ʃən] n (power) けん引力 keñ-iñryoku; (MED): **in traction** けん引療法中 keñ-iñryōhōchū

tractor [træk'tər] n トラクター toráku-tā

trade [treid] n (activity) 貿易 bóeki; (skill) 技術 gíjùtsu; (job) 職業 shokúgyò

♦vi (do business) 商売する shóbai suru

♦vt (exchange): **to trade something (for something)** (...と) ...を交換する (...to) ...wo kókan suru

trade fair n トレードフェアー torḗdo-feà

trade in vt (old car etc) 下取に出す shi-tádori ni dásù

trademark [treid'mɑ:rk] n 商標 shóhyō

trade name n 商品名 shóhiñmei

trader [trei'də:r] n 貿易業者 bóekigyò-sha

tradesman [treidz'mən] (pl **tradesmen**) n 商人 shóniñ

trade union n 労働組合 ródōkumìai

trade unionist [-ju:n'jənist] n 労働組合員 ródōkumiaìñ

tradition [trədiʃ'ən] n 伝統 deñtō

traditional [trədiʃ'ənəl] adj (dress, costume, meal) 伝統的な deñtōteki na

traffic [træf'ik] n (movement: of people, vehicles) 往来 órai; (: of drugs etc) 売買 báibai; (air traffic, road traffic etc) 交通 kótsū

♦vi: **to traffic in** (liquor, drugs) 売買する báibai suru

traffic circle (US) n ロータリー rōtarī

traffic jam n 交通渋滞 kótsūjūtai

traffic lights npl 信号(機) shiñgō(kì)

traffic warden n 違反駐車取締官 ihán-

chūsha toríshimarikàn

tragedy [trædʒ'idi:] n 悲劇 higéki

tragic [trædʒ'ik] adj (death, consequences) 悲劇的な higékiteki na; (play, novel etc) 悲劇の higéki no

trail [treil] n (path) 小道 kómìchi; (track) 足跡 ashíatò; (of smoke, dust) 尾 ó

♦vt (drag) 後に引く átò ni hikú; (follow: person, animal) 追跡する tsuíseki suru

♦vi (hang loosely) 後ろに垂れる ushíro-nì tarérù; (in game, contest) 負けている makéte irù

trail behind vi (lag) 遅れる okúrerù

trailer [trei'lə:r] n (AUT) トレーラー to-rḗrā; (US: caravan) キャンピングカー kyañpingukā; (CINEMA) 予告編 yokó-kuheñ

trailer truck (US) n トレーラートラック torḗrātorakkù

train [trein] n (RAIL) 列車 resshá; (underground train) 地下鉄 chikátetsu; (of dress) トレイン toréiñ

♦vt (educate: mind) 教育する kyóiku su-ru; (teach skills to: apprentice, doctor, dog etc) 訓練する kuñren suru; (athlete) 鍛える kitáerù; (point: camera, hose, gun etc): **to train on** 向ける mukérù

♦vi (learn a skill) 訓練を受ける kuñren wò ukérù; (SPORT) トレーニングする torḗniñgu suru

one's train of thought 考えの流れ kañ-gaè no nagáre

trained [treind] adj (worker, teacher) 技術が確かな gíjùtsu ga táshika na; (animal) 訓練された kuñren saretà

trainee [treini:'] n (apprentice: hairdresser etc) 見習 mínārai; (teacher etc) 実習生 jisshúsei

trainer [trei'nə:r] n (SPORT: coach) コーチ kóchi; (: shoe) スニーカー suníkā; (of animals) 訓練師 kuñreñshi

training [trei'niŋ] n (for occupation) 訓練 kuñren; (SPORT) トレーニング torḗ-niñgu

in training トレーニング中 torḗningu-chū

training college n (gen) 職業大学 sho-kúgyōdaigàku; (for teachers) 教育大学

kyŏikudaigàku

training shoes npl スニーカー suníkà

traipse [treips] vi 足を棒にして歩き回る ashí wò bŏ ni shitè arúkimawarù

trait [treit] n 特徴 tokúchō

traitor [trei'tə:r] n 裏切者 urágirimòno

tram [træm] (BRIT) n (also: **tramcar**) 路面電車 roméndeǹsha

tramp [træmp] n (person) ルンペン rúǹpen; (inf: pej: woman) 浮気女 uwákioǹna

♦vi どしんどしん歩く doshíǹdoshin arúkù

trample [træm'pəl] vt: **to trample (underfoot)** 踏み付ける fumítsukerù

trampoline [træmpəli:n'] n トランポリン toráǹporin

trance [træns] n (gen) こん睡状態 koǹsuijŏtai; (fig) ぼう然とした状態 bŏzen to shitá jŏtai

tranquil [træŋ'kwil] adj (place, old age) 平穏な heíon na; (sleep) 静かな shízùka na

tranquillity [træŋkwil'iti:] n 平静さ heíseisà

tranquillizer [træŋ'kwəlaizə:r] n (MED) 鎮静剤 chiǹseìzai

transact [trænsækt'] vt: **to transact business** 取引する toríhìki suru

transaction [trænsæk'ʃən] n (piece of business) 取引 toríhìki

transatlantic [trænsətlæn'tik] adj (trade, phone-call etc) 英米間の eíbeíkan no

transcend [trænsend'] vt 越える koérù

transcript [træn'skript] n (of tape recording etc) 記録文書 kiróku buǹsho

transfer [træns'fə:r] n (moving: of employees etc) 異動 idŏ; (: of money) 振替 furíkaè; (POL: of power) 引継ぎ hikítsugi; (SPORT) トレード torédò; (: picture, design) 写し絵 utsúshiè

♦vt (move: employees) 転任させる teǹnin saserù; (: money) 振替える furíkaerù; (: power) 譲る yuzúrù

to transfer the charges (BRIT: TEL) コレクトコールにする korékutokòru ni suru

transform [træn'sfɔ:rm] vt 変化させる

héǹka saserù

transformation [trænsfə:rmei'ʃən] n 変化 héǹka

transfusion [trænsfju:'ʒən] n (also: **blood transfusion**) 輸血 yukétsu

transient [træn'ʃənt] adj 一時的な ichíjiteki na

transistor [trænzis'tə:r] n (ELEC) トランジスタ toránjisùta; (also: **transistor radio**) トランジスタラジオ toránjisuta rajìo

transit [træn'sit] n: **in transit** (people, things) 通過中の tsúkachū no

transition [trænzij'ən] n 移行 ikŏ

transitional [trænzij'ənəl] adj (period, stage) 移行の ikŏ no

transitive [træn'sətiv] adj (LING): **transitive verb** 他動詞 tadŏshì

transit lounge n (at airport etc) トランジットラウンジ toránjitto raùnji

transitory [træn'sitɔ:ri:] adj つかの間の tsuká no ma no

translate [trænz'leit] vt (word, book etc) 翻訳する hoǹ-yaku suru

translation [trænzlei'ʃən] n (act/result of translating) 訳 yákù

translator [trænslei'tə:r] n 訳者 yákùsha

transmission [trænsmiʃ'ən] n (of information, disease) 伝達 deǹtatsu; (TV: broadcasting, program broadcast) 放送 hŏsō; (AUT) トランスミッション toránsumisshòn

transmit [trænsmit'] vt (message, signal, disease) 伝達する deǹtatsu suru

transmitter [trænsmit'ə:r] n (piece of equipment) トランスミッタ toránsumittà

transparency [trænsper'ənsi:] n (of glass etc) 透明度 tŏmeìdo; (PHOT: slide) スライド suráìdo

transparent [trænspe:r'ənt] adj (seethrough) 透明の tŏmei no

transpire [trænspaiə:r'] vi (turn out) 明らかになる akíràka ni nárù; (happen) 起る okŏrù

transplant [vb trænzplænt' n træn'zplænt] vt (seedlings: also: MED: organ)

移植する ishóku suru
◆n (MED) 移植 ishóku

transport [n trænsˈpɔːrt vb trænsˈpɔːrtˈ] n (moving people, goods) 輸送 yusō; (also: **road/rail transport** etc) 輸送機関 yusōkikàn; (car) 車 kurúma
◆vt (carry) 輸送する yusō suru

transportation [trænspɔːrteiˈʃən] n (transport) 輸送 yusō; (means of transport) 輸送機関 yusōkikàn

transvestite [trænsvesˈtait] n 女装趣味の男性 josōshùmi no dañsei

trap [træp] n (snare, trick) わな wánà; (carriage) 軽馬車 keíbashà
◆vt (animal) わなで捕まえる wánà de toraérù; (person: trick) わなにかける wánà ni kakérù; (: confine: in bad marriage, burning building): **to be trapped** 逃げられなくなっている nigérarenakù natté irù

trap door n 落し戸 otóshidò

trapeze [træpiːzˈ] n 空中ぶらんこ kūchūburañko

trappings [træpˈiŋz] npl 飾り kazári

trash [træʃ] n (rubbish: also pej) ごみ gomí; (: nonsense) でたらめ detárame

trash can (US) n ごみ入れ gomíìre

trauma [trɔːˈmə] n 衝撃 shōgeki, ショック shókkù

traumatic [trɔːmætˈik] adj 衝撃的な shōgekiteki na

travel [trævˈəl] n (traveling) 旅行 ryokō
◆vi (person) 旅行する ryokō suru; (news, sound) 伝わる tsutáwarù; (wine etc): **to travel well/badly** 運搬に耐えられる〔耐えられない〕 uñpan nì taérarerù〔taérarenaì〕
◆vt (distance) 旅行する ryokō suru

travel agency n 旅行代理店 ryokōdaìritèn

travel agent n 旅行業者 ryokōgyòsha

traveler [trævˈələr] (BRIT **traveller**) n 旅行者 ryokōshà

traveler's check [trævˈələrz-] (BRIT **traveller's cheque**) n トラベラーズチェ

ック torāberāzuchekkù

traveling [trævˈəliŋ] (BRIT **travelling**) n 旅行 ryokō

travels [trævˈəlz] npl (journeys) 旅行 ryokō

travel sickness n 乗物酔い norímono-yoì

travesty [trævˈisti] n パロディー páròdi

trawler [trɔːˈlər] n トロール漁船 torōrugyòsen

tray [trei] n (for carrying) お盆 o-bóñ; (on desk) デスクトレー desúkutorè

treacherous [tretʃˈəːrəs] adj (person, look) 裏切り者の urágirimòno no; (ground, tide) 危険な kikén na

treachery [tretʃˈəːri] n 裏切り urágirì

treacle [triːˈkəl] n 糖みつ tōmitsu

tread [tred] n (step) 歩調 hochō; (sound) 足音 ashíotò; (of stair) 踏面 fumízùra; (of tire) トレッド toréddò
◆vi (pt **trod**, pp **trodden**) 歩く arúkù

tread on vt fus 踏む fumú

treason [triːˈzən] n 反逆罪 hañgyakuzài

treasure [treʒˈəːr] n (gold, jewels etc) 宝物 takáramono; (person) 重宝な人 chōhō nà hitó
◆vt (value: object) 重宝する chōhō suru; (: friendship) 大事にしている daíji nì shité irù; (: memory, thought) 心に銘記する kokórò ni meíki suru

treasurer [treʒˈəːrər] n 会計 kaíkei

treasures [treʒˈəːrz] npl (art treasures etc) 貴重品 kichōhìn

treasury [treʒˈəːri] n: (US) **the Treasury Department**, (BRIT) **the Treasury** 大蔵省 ōkurashō

treat [triːt] n (present) 贈物 okúrimono
◆vt (handle, regard: person, object) 扱う atsúkaù; (MED: patient, illness) 治療する chiryō suru; (TECH: coat) 処理する shórì suru

to treat someone to something ...に...をおごる ...ni ...wo ogórù

treatment [triːtˈmənt] n (attention, handling) 扱い方 atsúkaikata; (MED) 治療 chiryō

treaty [triːˈti] n 協定 kyōtei

treble [trebˈəl] adj 3倍の sañbai no;

(MUS) 高音部の kóonbu no
♦vt 3倍にする sañbai nǐ suru
♦vi 3倍になる sañbai ni narù

treble clef n (MUS) 高音部記号 kóonbu-kigǒ

tree [tri:] n 木 kí

tree trunk n 木の幹 kí nò míkì

trek [trek] n (long difficult journey: on foot) 徒歩旅行 tohóryokǒ; (: by car) 自動車旅行 jidósharyokǒ; (tiring walk) 苦しい道のり kurúshiì michínori

trellis [trel'is] n (for climbing plants) 棚 taná

tremble [trem'bəl] vi (voice, body, trees: with fear, cold etc) 震える furúerù; (ground) 揺れる yurérù

tremendous [trimen'dəs] adj (enormous: amount etc) ばく大な bakúdai na; (excellent: success, holiday, view etc) 素晴らしい subárashiì

tremor [trem'ə:r] n (trembling: of excitement, fear: in voice) 震え furúe; (also: **earth tremor**) 地震 jishín

trench [trentʃ] n (channel) 溝 mizó; (for defense) ざんごう zañgǒ

trend [trend] n (tendency) 傾向 keíkō; (of events) 動向 dókō; (fashion) トレンド toréñdo

trendy [tren'di:] adj (idea, person, clothes) トレンディな toréñdi na

trepidation [trepidei'ʃən] n (apprehension) 不安 fuán

trespass [tres'pæs] vi: **to trespass on** (private property) ...に不法侵入する ...ni fuhóshiñnyū suru
「**no trespassing**」立入禁止 tachíirikiñshi

trestle [tres'əl] n (support for table etc) うま umá

trial [trail] n (LAW) 裁判 saíban; (test: of machine etc) テスト tésùto
on trial (LAW) 裁判に掛けられて saíban ni kakérarete
by trial and error 試行錯誤で shikósakùgo de

trial period n テスト期間 tesúto kikàn

trials [trailz] npl (unpleasant experiences) 試練 shírèn

triangle [trai'æŋgəl] n (MATH) 三角 sáñkaku; (MUS) トライアングル toráiañguru

triangular [traiæŋ'gjələ:r] adj 三角形の sañkakkèi no

tribal [trai'bəl] adj (warrior, warfare, dance) 種族の shúzòku no

tribe [traib] n 種族 shúzòku

tribesman [traibz'mən] (pl **tribesmen**) n 種族の男性 shúzòku no dañsei

tribulations [tribjəlei'ʃənz] npl 苦労 kúrō, 苦難 kúnàn

tribunal [traibju:'nəl] n 審判委員会 shiñpan iiñkai

tributary [trib'jəte:ri:] n 支流 shiryū

tribute [trib'ju:t] n (compliment) ほめの言葉 homé no kotobà
to pay tribute to ...をほめる ...wò homérù

trice [trais] n: **in a trice** あっという間に áttò iú ma nǐ

trick [trik] n (magic trick) 手品 tejína; (prank, joke) いたずら itázura; (skill, knack) こつ kotsú; (CARDS) トリック toríkkù
♦vt (deceive) だます damásù
to play a trick on someone ...にいたずらをする ...ni itázura wò suru
that should do the trick これでいいはずだ koré de iǐ hazú dà

trickery [trik'ə:ri:] n 計略 keíryaku

trickle [trik'əl] n (of water etc) 滴り shitátari
♦vi (water, rain etc) 滴る shitátarù

tricky [trik'i:] adj (job, problem, business) 厄介な yákkài na

tricycle [trai'sikəl] n 三輪車 sañríñsha

trifle [trai'fəl] n (small detail) ささいな事 sásài na kotó; (CULIN) トライフル toráifuru ◊カステラにゼリー, フルーツ, プリンなどをのせたデザート kasútera nǐ zérǐ, furútsù, púrìn nádò wo nosétà dezátò
♦adv: **a trifle long** ちょっと長い chóttò nagáì

trifling [traif'liŋ] adj (detail, matter) ささいな sásài na

trigger [trig'ə:r] n (of gun) 引金 hikígane

trigger off *vt* (reaction, riot) ...の引金
となる ...no hikígane tò nárù

trigonometry [trigənɑ:'mətri:] *n* 三角法
sańkakuhō

trill [tril] *vi* (birds) さえずる saézurù

trim [trim] *adj* (house, garden) 手入れの
行届いた teíre nò ikítodoità; (figure) す
らっとした suráttò shitá
♦*n* (haircut etc) 刈る事 karú kotò; (on
car) 飾り kazári
♦*vt* (cut: hair, beard) 刈る karú; (decorate): *to trim (with)* (...で) 飾る (...de)
kazárù; (NAUT: a sail) 調節する chốse-
tsu suru

trimmings [trim'iŋz] *npl* (CULIN) お決
りの付け合せ o-kímari no tsukéawase

trinket [triŋ'kit] *n* (ornament) 安い置物
yasúi okímono; (piece of jewellery) 安い
装身具 yasúi sṓshiňgu

trio [tri:'ou] *n* (gen) 三つ組 mitsúgumi;
(MUS) トリオ tório

trip [trip] *n* (journey) 旅行 ryokṓ; (outing) 遠足 eńsoku; (stumble) つまずき tsu-
mázuki
♦*vi* (stumble) つまずく tsumázukù; (go
lightly) 軽快に歩く keíkai nì arúkù
on a trip 旅行中で ryokṓchù de

tripe [traip] *n* (CULIN) トライプ toráî-
pu ◇ウシ, ブタなどの胃の料理 ushí, bu-
tá nadò no i no ryṓri; (*pej*: rubbish) 下ら
ない物 kudaranai mono ◇特に人の発言
や文書について言う tōkù ni hitó nò hatsúgen yà búnsho ni tsuítè iú

triple [trip'əl] *adj* (ice cream, somersault
etc) トリプルの toríþuru no

triplets [trip'lits] *npl* 三つ子 mitsúgo

triplicate [trip'ləkit] *n*: *in triplicate* 三
通で sańtsū de

tripod [trai'pɑːd] *n* 三脚 sańkyaku

trip up *vi* (stumble) つまずく tsumázukù
♦*vt* (person) つまずかせる tsumázukase-
rù

trite [trait] *adj* 陳腐な chíňpu na

triumph [trai'əmf] *n* (satisfaction) 大満
足 daímaňzoku; (great achievement) 輝
かしい勝利 kagáyakashiî shṓrì

♦*vi*: *to triumph (over)* (...に) 打勝つ
(...ni) uchíkatsù

triumphant [traiʌm'fənt] *adj* (team,
wave, return) 意気揚々とした íkiyōyō to
shitá

trivia [triv'i:ə] *npl* 詰まらない事 tsumá-
ranai kotò

trivial [triv'i:əl] *adj* (unimportant) 詰ま
らない tsumáranaî; (commonplace) 平凡
な heíbon na

trod [trɑːd] *pt of* **tread**

trodden [trɑːd'ən] *pp of* **tread**

trolley [trɑːl'i:] *n* (for luggage, shopping,
also in supermarkets) 手車 tegúruma;
(table on wheels) ワゴン wágòn; (*also*:
trolley bus) トロリーバス toróríbàsu

trombone [trɑːmboun'] *n* トロンボーン
toróňbōn

troop [tru:p] *n* (of people, monkeys etc)
群れ muré

troop in/out *vi* ぞろぞろと入って来る
〔出て行く〕zórðzoro to haítte kurù
〔détè iku〕

trooping the color [tru:p'iŋ-] (*BRIT*)
n (ceremony) 軍旗敬礼の分列行進 kuňki-
keírei no buňretsu kṓshin

troops [tru:ps] *npl* (MIL) 兵隊 heítai

trophy [trou'fi:] *n* トロフィー tórðfī

tropic [trɑːp'ik] *n* 回帰線 kaíkisèn
the tropics 熱帯地方 nettái chihṓ

tropical [trɑːp'ikəl] *adj* (rain forest etc)
熱帯 (地方) の nettái(chihṓ) no

trot [trɑːt] *n* (fast pace) 小走り kobáshìri; (of horse) 速足 hayáashi, トロット toróttò
♦*vi* (horse) トロットで駆ける toróttò de
kakérù; (person) 小走りで行く kobáshìri
de ikù
on the trot (*BRIT*: *fig*) 立続けに tatétsuzuke ni

trouble [trʌb'əl] *n* (difficulty) 困難 koń-
nan; (worry) 心配 shińpai; (bother,
effort) 苦労 kúrō; (unrest) トラブル torábùru; (MED): *heart etc trouble* ...病
...byṓ
♦*vt* (worry) ...に心配を掛ける ...ni shińpai wò kakérù; (person: disturb) 面倒を
かける meńdō wo kakérù

♦*vi: to trouble to do something* わざ
わざ...する wázawaza ...suru

to be in trouble (gen)困っている komátte irù; (ship, climber etc) 危険にあっ
ている kikén ni atte irù

it's no trouble! 迷惑ではありませんか
ら mêlwaku de wa arímàsen kará

what's the trouble? (with broken television etc) どうなっていますか dô natté
imasù ká; (doctor to patient) いかがです
か ikága desù ká

troubled [trʌb'əld] *adj* (person, country,
life, era) 不安な fuáñ na

troublemaker [trʌb'əlmeikə:r] *n* トラブ
ルを起す常習犯 torábùru wo okósù jô-
shûhan; (child) 問題児 moñdaìji

troubles [trʌb'əlz] *npl* (personal, POL
etc) 問題 moñdai

troubleshooter [trʌb'əlʃu:tə:r] *n* (in conflict) 調停人 chôteiniñ

troublesome [trʌb'əlsəm] *adj* (child,
cough etc) 厄介な yákkài na

trough [trɔːf] *n* (*also*: **drinking trough**)
水入れ mizúirè; (feeding trough) えさ入
れ esá-irè; (depression) 谷間 taníma

troupe [tru:p] *n* (of actors, singers,
dancers) 団 dáñ

trousers [trau'zə:rz] *npl* ズボン zubóñ

short trousers 半ズボン hañzubòn

trousseau [tru:'sou] (*pl* **trousseaux** *or*
trousseaus) *n* 嫁入り道具 yomé-iri dògu

trout [traut] *n inv* マス masu

trowel [trau'əl] *n* (garden tool) 移植ごて
ishókugòte; (builder's tool) こて koté

truant [tru:'ənt] (*BRIT*) *n: to play truant* 学校をサボる gakkô wo sabórù

truce [tru:s] *n* 休戦 kyûsen

truck [trʌk] *n* (*US*) トラック torákkù;
(RAIL) 台車 daísha

truck driver *n* トラック運転手 torákku
unteñshu

truck farm (*US*) *n* 野菜農園 yasáinòen

trudge [trʌdʒ] *vi* (*also*: **trudge along**) と
ぼとぼ歩く tóbòtobo arúkù

true [tru:] *adj* (real: motive) 本当の hoñtô
no; (accurate: likeness) 正確な seíkaku
na; (genuine: love) 本物の hoñmono no;
(faithful: friend) 忠実な chûjitsu na

to come true (dreams, predictions) 実現
される jitsúgen sarerù

truffle [trʌf'əl] *n* (fungus) トリュフ tó-
ryùfu; (sweet) トラッフル toráffùru ◇菓
子の一種 káshì no ísshū

truly [tru:'li:] *adv* (really) 本当に hoñtô
ni; (truthfully) 真実に shíñjitsu ni; (faithfully) *yours truly* (in letter) 敬具 keígu

trump [trʌmp] *n* (*also*: **trump card**: *also
fig*) 切札 kirífùda

trumped-up [trʌmpt'ʌp'] *adj* (charge,
pretext) でっち上げた detchíagetà

trumpet [trʌm'pit] *n* トランペット toráñ-
petto

truncheon [trʌn'tʃən] *n* 警棒 keíbo

trundle [trʌn'dəl] *vt* (push chair etc) ご
ろごろ動かす górògoro ugókasù

♦*vi: to trundle along* (vehicle) 重そう
に動く omósō ni ugókù; (person) ゆっく
り行く yukkúrì ikú

trunk [trʌŋk] *n* (of tree, person) 幹 míkì;
(of person) 胴 dô; (of elephant) 鼻 haná;
(case) トランク toráñku; (*US*: AUT) ト
ランク toráñku

trunks [trʌŋks] *npl* (*also*: **swimming
trunks**) 水泳パンツ suíei pañtsu

truss [trʌs] *n* (MED) ヘルニアバンド herúnia bañdo

truss (up) *vt* (CULIN) 縛る shibárù

trust [trʌst] *n* (faith) 信用 shíñ-yò;
(responsibility) 責任 sekínin; (LAW) 信
託 shíñtaku

♦*vt* (rely on, have faith in) 信用する shíñ-
yō suru; (hope) きっと...だろうね kittô
...dárô nê; (entrust): *to trust something
to someone* ...を...に任せる ...wo ...ni
makáserù

to take something on trust (advice,
information) 証拠なしで...を信じる shôko nashî de ...wo shiñjirù

trusted [trʌs'tid] *adj* (friend, servant) 信
用された shiñ-yō saretà

trustee [trʌsti:'] *n* (LAW) 受託者 jutáku-
shà; (of school etc) 理事 ríjì

trustful/trusting [trʌst'fəl/trʌs'tiŋ]
adj (person, nature, smile) 信用する shíñ-
yō suru

trustworthy [trʌst'wə:rði:] *adj* (person,

report) 信用できる shiń-yō dekirù

truth [truːθ] *n* (true fact) 真 実 shíñjitsu; (universal principle) 真理 shíñri

truthful [truːθfəl] *adj* (person, answer) 正直な shōjiki na

try [trai] *n* (attempt) 努 力 dóryòku; (RUGBY) トライ toráì

♦*vt* (attempt) やってみる yatté mirù; (test: something new: *also*: **try out**) 試す tamésù; (LAW: person) 裁判にかける sáìban ni kakérù; (strain: patience) ぎりぎりまで追込む girígiri madè oíkomù

♦*vi* (make effort, attempt) 努力する dóryòku suru

to have a try やってみる yatté mirù

to try to do something (seek) ...をしようとする ...wo shíyò to suru

trying [traiiŋ] *adj* (person) 気難しい kimúzukashiî; (experience) 苦しい kurúshiî

try on *vt* (dress, hat, shoes) 試着する shicháku suru

tsar [zɑːr] *n* ロシア皇帝 roshía kòtei

T-shirt [tiːʃəːrt] *n* Tシャツ tíshatsu

T-square [tiːskweːr] *n* T定規 tíjôgi

tub [tʌb] *n* (container: shallow) たらい taráì; (: deeper) おけ òke; (bath) 湯舟 yúbùne

tuba [tuːbə] *n* チューバ chùba

tubby [tʌbiː] *adj* 太った futóttà

tube [tuːb] *n* (pipe) 管 kúdà; (container, in tire) チューブ chùbu; (BRIT: underground) 地下鉄 chikátetsu

tuberculosis [tuːbəːrkjəlouˈsis] *n* 結核 kekkáku

tube station (BRIT) *n* 地下鉄の駅 chikátetsu nò ékì

tubular [tuːbjələːr] *adj* (furniture, metal) 管状の kańjō no; (furniture) パイプ製の paípusei nò

TUC [tiːjuːsiː] *n abbr* (BRIT: = Trades Union Congress) 英国労働組合会議 eíkoku rōdōkumiai kaìgi

tuck [tʌk] *vt* (put) 押込む oshíkomù

tuck away *vt* (money) 仕舞い込む shimáikomù; (building): *to be tucked away* 隠れている kakúrete irù

tuck in *vt* (clothing) 押込む oshíkomù;

(child) 毛布にくるんで寝かせる mófù ni kurúñde nekáserù

♦*vi* (eat) かぶりつく kabúritsukù

tuck shop (BRIT) *n* 売店 baíten ◇学校内でお菓子などを売る売店を指す gakkṑnaì de o-káshi nadò wo urú baíten wò sásù

tuck up *vt* (invalid, child) 毛布にくるんで寝かせる mófù ni kurúñde nekáserù

Tuesday [tuːzˈdei] *n* 火曜日 kayōbi

tuft [tʌft] *n* (of hair, grass etc) 一房 hitófùsa

tug [tʌg] *n* (ship) タグボート tagúbòto

♦*vt* 引っ張る hippárù

tug-of-war [tʌgˈəvwɔːr] *n* (SPORT) 綱引き tsunáhiki; (fig) 競り合い seríaì ◇二者間の競り合いを指す nishákàn no seríaì wo sásù

tuition [tuːiʃˈən] *n* (BRIT) 教授 kyōju; (: private tuition) 個人教授 kojíñkyòju; (US: school fees) 授業料 jugyōryò

tulip [tuːˈlip] *n* チューリップ chūrippu

tumble [tʌmˈbəl] *n* (fall) 転ぶ事 koróbu kotò

♦*vi* (fall: person) 転ぶ koróbù; (water) 落ちる ochírù

to tumble to something (inf) ...に気が付く ...ni ki gá tsukù

tumbledown [tʌmˈbəldaun] *adj* (building) 荒れ果てた aréhatetà

tumble dryer (BRIT) *n* 乾燥機 kańsōki

tumbler [tʌmˈbləːr] *n* (glass) コップ koppú

tummy [tʌmˈiː] (inf) *n* (belly, stomach) おなか onákà

tumor [tuːˈməːr] (BRIT **tumour**) *n* しゅよう shuyō

tumult [tuːˈmʌlt] *n* 大騒ぎ ōsawàgi

tumultuous [tuːmʌlˈtʃuːəs] *adj* (welcome, applause etc) にぎやかな nigíyàka na

tuna [tuːˈnə] *n inv* (also: **tuna fish**) マグロ maguro; (in can, sandwich) ツナ tsúnà

tune [tuːn] *n* (melody) 旋律 seńritsu

♦*vt* (MUS) 調律する chōritsu suru; (RADIO, TV) 合せる awáserù; (AUT) チューンアップする chūn-appù suru

to be in/out of tune (instrument, singer)

調子が合って〔外れて〕いる chôshi gà atte〔hazúrete〕irù

to be in/out of tune with (fig) …と気が合っている〔いない〕 …to ki gá atte irù〔ináî〕

tuneful [tuːnˈfəl] adj (music) 旋律のきれいな señritsu nò kírei na

tuner [tuːˈnəːr] n: **piano tuner** 調律師 chôritsushì

tune in vi (RADIO, TV): **to tune in (to)** (…を) 聞く (…wo) kikú

tune up vi (musician, orchestra) 調子を合せる chôshi wò awáserù

tunic [tuːˈnik] n チュニック chuníkkù

Tunisia [tuːniˈʒə] n チュニジア chuníjìa

tunnel [tʌnˈəl] n (passage) トンネル toñnèru; (in mine) 坑道 kôdo
♦vi トンネルを掘る toñnèru wo hórù

turban [təːrˈbən] n ターバン tâbàn

turbine [təːrˈbain] n タービン tâbìn

turbulence [təːrˈbjələns] n (AVIAT) 乱気流 rañkiryû

turbulent [təːrˈbjələnt] adj (water) 荒れ狂う arékuruù; (fig: career) 起伏の多い kífùku no ôì

tureen [təriːnˈ] n スープ鉢 sûpubàchi, チューリン chûrìn

turf [təːrf] n (grass) 芝生 shibáfu; (clod) 芝土 shibátsuchì
♦vt (area) 芝生を敷く shibáfu wò shikú

turf out (inf) vt (person) 追出す ofdasù

turgid [təːrˈdʒid] adj (speech) 仰々しい gyôgyôshiì

Turk [təːrk] n トルコ人 torúkojìn

Turkey [təːrˈkiː] n トルコ tôrùko

turkey [təːrˈkiː] n (bird, meat) 七面鳥 shichímenchò, ターキー tâkî

Turkish [təːrˈkiʃ] adj トルコの tôrùko no; (LING) トルコ語の torúkogò no
♦n (LING) トルコ語 torúkogò

Turkish bath n トルコ風呂 torúkobùro

turmoil [təːrˈmɔil] n 混乱 koñran

in turmoil 混乱して koñran shitè

turn [təːrn] n (change) 変化 héñka; (in road) カーブ kâbu; (tendency: of mind, events) 傾向 keíkō; (performance) 出し物 dashímòno; (chance) 番 báñ; (MED) 発作 hossá

♦vt (handle, key) 回す mawásù; (collar, page) めくる mekúrù; (steak) 裏返す urágaesù; (change): **to turn something into …** を…に変える …wo …ni kaérù

♦vi (object) 回る mawárù; (person: look back) 振向く furímukù; (reverse direction: in car) Uターンする yūtân suru; (: wind) 向きが変る múkì ga kawárù; (milk) 悪くなる wárùku nárù; (become) なる nárù

a good turn 親切 shíñsetsu

it gave me quite a turn ああ, 怖かったあ, kowákattà

「no left turn」 (AUT) 左折禁止 sasétsukiñshi

it's your turn あなたの番です anáta nò báñ desu

in turn 次々と tsugítsugi tò

to take turns (at) 交替で (…を) する kôtai dè (…wo) suru

turn away vi 顔をそむける kaó wò somúkerù
♦vt (applicants) 門前払いする moñzenbarài suru

turn back vi 引返す hikíkaesù
♦vt (person, animal) 引返させる hikíkaesaserù; (clock) 遅らせる okúraserù

turn down vt (refuse: request) 断る kotówarù; (reduce: heating) 弱くする yówàku suru; (fold: bedclothes) 折返す oríkaesù

turn in vi (inf: go to bed) 寝る nerú
♦vt (fold) 折込む oríkomù

turning [təːrˈniŋ] n (in road) 曲り角 magárikadò

turning point n (fig) 変り目 kawárime

turnip [təːrˈnip] n カブ kábu

turn off vi (from road) 横道に入る yokómichi nì hâìru
♦vt (light, radio etc) 消す kesú; (tap) …の水を止める …no mizú wò tomérù; (engine) 止める tomérù

turn on vt (light, radio etc) つける tsukérù; (tap) …の水を出す …no mizú wò dasù; (engine) かける kakérù

turn out vt (light, gas) 消す kesú; (produce) 作る tsukúrù
♦vi (voters) 出る dérù

to turn out to be (prove to be) 結局...で あると分かる kekkyóku ...de arú to wa- karu

turnout [təːrn'aut] *n* (of voters etc) 人出 hitóde

turn over *vi* (person) 寝返りを打つ ne- gáeri wò utsù

♦*vt* (object) 引っ繰り返す hikkúrikaesu; (page) めくる mekúrù

turnover [təːrn'ouvəːr] *n* (COMM: amount of money) 売上高 ur「agedàka; (: of goods) 回転率 kaíteñritsu; (: of staff) 異動率 idóritsu

turnpike [təːrn'paik] (*US*) *n* 有料道路 yúryòdòro

turn round *vi* (person) 振向く furímu- kù; (vehicle) Uターンする yútàn suru; (rotate) 回転する kaíten suru

turnstile [təːrn'stail] *n* ターンスタイル táñsutàiru

turntable [təːrn'teibəl] *n* (on record player) ターンテーブル táñtèburu

turn up *vi* (person) 現れる aráwarerù; (lost object) 見付かる mitsúkarù

♦*vt* (collar) 立てる tatérù; (radio, stereo etc) ...のボリュームを上げる ...no boryú- mu wò agérù; (heater) 強くする tsúyòku suru

turn-up [təːrn'ʌp] (*BRIT*) *n* (on trousers) 折返し orīkaeshi

turpentine [təːr'pəntain] *n* (*also*: **turps**) テレビン油 terébiñ-yu

turquoise [təːr'kɔiz] *n* (stone) トルコ石 torúkoìshi

♦*adj* (color) 青みどりの aómidòri no

turret [təːr'it] *n* (on building) 小塔 shótō; (on tank) 旋回砲塔 señkaihōtō

turtle [təːr'təl] *n* カメ kámè

turtleneck (sweater) [təːr'təlnek-] *n* タートルネック tátorunekkù

tusk [tʌsk] *n* きば kíbà

tussle [tʌs'əl] *n* (fight, scuffle) 取っ組み 合い tokkúmiaì

tutor [tuː'təːr] *n* (SCOL) チューター chū- tā; (private tutor) 家庭教師 katéikyòshi

tutorial [tuːtɔːr'iːəl] *n* (SCOL) 討論授業 tóronjugyò

tuxedo [tʌksiː'dou] (*US*) *n* タキシード ta-

kíshìdo

TV [tiː'viː] *n abbr* = **television**

twang [twæŋ] *n* (of instrument) びゅん という音 byùn to iú otò; (of voice) 鼻声 hanágoè

tweed [twiːd] *n* ツイード tsuídò

tweezers [twiː'zəːrz] *npl* ピンセット píñ- setto

twelfth [twelfθ] *num* 第十二の dái jūni no

twelve [twelv] *num* 十二 (の) júnì (no)

at twelve (o'clock) (midday) 正午に shốgò ni; (midnight) 零時に reiji ni

twentieth [twen'tiːiθ] *num* 第二十の dái nījū no

twenty [twen'tiː] *num* 二十 (の) níjū (no)

twice [twais] *adv* 2回 nikáì

twice as much ...の二倍 ...no nibái

twiddle [twid'əl] *vt* いじくる ijíkurù

♦*vi*: *to twiddle (with) something* ...を いじくる ...no ijíkurù

to twiddle one's thumbs (*fig*) 手をこま ねく tê wò kománekù

twig [twig] *n* 小枝 koéda

♦*vi* (*inf*: realize) 気が付く ki gá tsukù

twilight [twai'lait] *n* 夕暮 yúgure

twin [twin] *adj* (sister, brother) 双子の futágo no; (towers, beds etc) 対の tsuí no, ツインの tsuíñ no

♦*n* 双子の一人 futágo nò hitórì

♦*vt* (towns etc) 姉妹都市にする shimái- toshì ni suru

twin-bedded room [twin'bedid-] *n* ツイ ンルーム tsuíñrūmu

twine [twain] *n* ひも himó

♦*vi* (plant) 巻付く makítsukù

twinge [twindʒ] *n* (of pain) うずき uzúki; (of conscience) かしゃく kasháku; (of regret) 苦しみ kurúshimì

twinkle [twiŋ'kəl] *vi* (star, light, eyes) き らめく kirámekù

twirl [twəːrl] *vt* くるくる回す kúrùkuru mawásù

♦*vi* くるくる回る kúrùkuru mawárù

twist [twist] *n* (action) ひねり hinéri; (in road, coil, flex) 曲り magári; (in story) ひねり hinéri

◆*vt* (turn) ひ ね る hinérù; (injure: ankle etc) ねんざする neñza suru; (weave) より合さる yoríawasarù; (roll around) 巻付ける makítsukerù; (*fig*: meaning, words) 曲げる magérù

◆*vi* (road, river) 曲り くね る magárikunerù

twit [twit] (*inf*) *n* ばか bákà

twitch [twitʃ] *n* (pull) ぐいと引く事 guí tò hikú kotò; (nervous) 引きつり hikítsuri

◆*vi* (muscle, body) 引きつる hikítsurù

two [tu:] *num* 二 （の） ní (no), 二つ （の） futátsù (no)

to put two and two together (*fig*) あ れ これ を総合してなぞを解く arékòre wo sṓgō shitè nazó wò tókù

two-door [tu:'dɔ:r] *adj* (AUT) ツー ド ア の tsúdoà no

two-faced [tu:'feist] (*pej*) *adj* (person) 二枚舌の nimáɪjita no

twofold [tu:'fould] *adv*: *to increase twofold* 倍になる bai ni narù

two-piece (suit) [tu:'pi:s-] *n* ツーピースの服 tsúpīsu no fukú

two-piece (swimsuit) *n* ツーピースの水着 tsúpīsu no mizúgi

twosome [tu:'səm] *n* (people) 二 人 組 futárigùmi

two-way [tu:'wei'] *adj*: *two-way traffic* 両方向交通 ryṓhōkōtsū

tycoon [taiku:n'] *n*: *(business) tycoon* 大物実業家 ṓmonojitsugyōka

type [taip] *n* (category, model, example) 種類 shúruì; (TYP) 活字 katsúji

◆*vt* (letter etc) タイプする táɪpu suru

type-cast [taip'kæst] *adj* (actor) はまり役の hamáriyaku no

typeface [taip'feis] *n* 書体 shotái

typescript [taip'skript] *n* タイプライターで打った原稿 taípuraɪtā de úttà geñkō

typewriter [taip'raitə:r] *n* タイプライター taípuraɪtā

typewritten [taip'ritən] *adj* タイプライターで打った taípuraɪtā de úttà

typhoid [tai'fɔid] *n* 腸チフス chōchifùsu

typhoon [taifu:n'] *n* 台風 taffū

typical [tip'ikəl] *adj* 典型的な teñkeiteki na

typify [tip'əfai] *vt* ...の典型的な例である ...no teñkeiteki nà reí de arù

typing [tai'piŋ] *n* タイプライターを打つ事 taípuraɪtā wo útsù kotó

typist [tai'pist] *n* タイピスト taípisùto

tyranny [ti:r'əni:] *n* 暴政 bṓsei

tyrant [tai'rənt] *n* 暴君 bṓkun

tyre [taiə:r] (*BRIT*) *n* = **tire**

tzar [zɑ:r] *n* = **tsar**

U

U-bend [ju:'bend] *n* (in pipe) トラップ toráppù

ubiquitous [ju:bik'witəs] *adj* いたる所にある itáru tokoro nì aru

udder [ʌd'ə:r] *n* 乳房 chibúsa ◇ ウ シ, ヤ ギなどについて言う ushí, yagí nado ni tsuite iú

UFO [ju:efou'] *n abbr* (= *unidentified flying object*) 未確認飛行物体 mikákunin hikōbuttài, ユーフォー yūfṓ

Uganda [ju:gæn'də] *n* ウガンダ ugáǹda

ugh [ʌ] *excl* おえっ oét

ugliness [ʌg'li:nis] *n* 醜さ miníkusà

ugly [ʌg'li:] *adj* (person, dress etc) 醜い miníkuì; (dangerous: situation) 物騒な bussṓ nà

UK [ju:'kei'] *n abbr* = **United Kingdom**

ulcer [ʌl'sə:r] *n* かいよう kaíyō

Ulster [ʌl'stə:r] *n* アルスター arùsutā

ulterior [ʌlti:r'i:ə:r] *adj*: *ulterior motive* 下心 shitágokòro

ultimate [ʌl'təmit] *adj* (final: aim, destination, result) 最後の saígo no; (greatest: insult, deterrent, authority) 最大の saídai no

ultimately [ʌl'təmitli:] *adv* (in the end) やがて yagáte; (basically) 根本的に koñponteki ni

ultimatum [ʌltimei'təm] *n* 最後通ちょう saígotsūchō

ultrasound [ʌl'trəsaund] *n* (MED) 超音波 chṓoñpa

ultraviolet [ʌltrəvai'əlit] *adj* (rays, light) 紫外線の shigáisen no

umbilical cord [ʌmbil'ikəl-] *n* へその緒 hesó no o

umbrella [ʌmbrel'ə] *n* (for rain) 傘 kasà, 雨 傘 ámagàsà; (for sun) 日 傘 higása, パ ラソル parásoru

umpire [ʌm'paiər] *n* (TENNIS, CRICKET) 審判 shinpan, アンパイア añpaìa

♦*vt* (game) ...のアンパイアをする ...no añpaìa wo suru

umpteen [ʌmp'tiːn'] *adj* うんと沢山の uñto takusan no

umpteenth [ʌmp'tiːnθ'] *adj*: **for the umpteenth time** 何回目か分からないが nañkaime kà wakáranaì ga

UN [juː'en'] *n abbr* = **United Nations**

unable [ʌnei'bəl] *adj*: **to be unable to do something** ...する事ができない ...surú koto gà dekínai

unaccompanied [ʌnəkʌm'pəniːd] *adj* (child, woman) 同伴者のいない dōhaǹsha no inai; (luggage) 別送の bessó no; (song) 無伴奏の mubáǹso no

unaccountably [ʌnəkaunt'əbliː] *adv* 妙 に myō nì

unaccustomed [ʌnəkʌs'təmd] *adj*: **to be unaccustomed to** (public speaking, Western clothes etc) ...になれていない ...ni narète inai

unanimous [juːnæn'əməs] *adj* (vote) 満 場一致の mañjōitchi no; (people) 全員同 意の zeñ-indòi no

unanimously [juːnæn'əməsliː] *adv* (vote) 満場一致で mañjōitchi de

unarmed [ʌnɑːrmd'] *adj* 武器を持たない búkì wo motánaì, 丸腰の marúgoshi no **unarmed combat** 武器を使わない武術 búkì wo tsukáwanaì bújùtsu

unashamed [ʌnəʃeimd'] *adj* (greed) 恥 知 らずの hajíshìràzu no; (pleasure) 人目を はばからない hitóme wo habákaranaì

unassuming [ʌnəsuː'miŋ] *adj* (person, manner) 気取らない kidóranai

unattached [ʌnətætʃt'] *adj* (person) 独身 の dokúshin no; (part etc) 遊んでいる a-sónde iru

unattended [ʌnəten'did] *adj* (car, luggage, child) ほったらかしの hottárakaー

shi no

unattractive [ʌnətræk'tiv] *adj* (person, character) いや な iyá na; (building, appearance, idea) 魅力のない miryóku no nai

unauthorized [ʌnɔː'θ'əːraizd] *adj* (visit, use, version) 無許可の mukyóka no

unavoidable [ʌnəvɔi'dəbəl] *adj* (delay) 避けられない sakérarenaì

unaware [ʌnəweːr'] *adj*: **to be unaware of** ...に気が付いていない ...ni ki gá tsuìte inai

unawares [ʌnəweːrz'] *adv* (catch, take) 不意に fuí ni

unbalanced [ʌnbæl'ənst] *adj* (report) 偏った katáyottà; (mentally) 狂った kurút-tà

unbearable [ʌnbeːr'əbəl] *adj* (heat, pain) 耐えられない taérarenaì; (person) 我慢で きない程いやな gamàn dekínaì hodo iyá na

unbeatable [ʌnbiː'təbəl] *adj* (team) 無 敵 の mutéki no; (quality) 最高の saíkō no; (price) 最高に安い saíkō ni yasuì

unbeknown(st) [ʌnbinoun(st)'] *adv*: **unbeknown(st) to me/Peter** 私〔ピ ー タ ー〕に 気付かれずに watákushi〔pítà〕ni kizúkarezù ni

unbelievable [ʌnbiliː'vəbəl] *adj* 信じられ ない shiñjirarenàì

unbend [ʌnbend'] (*pt, pp* **bent**) *vi* (relax) くつろぐ kutsúrogù

♦*vt* (wire) 真っ直ぐにする massúgù ni suru

unbiased [ʌnbai'əst] *adj* (person, report) 公正な kősei na

unborn [ʌnbɔːrn'] *adj* (child, young) おな かの中の onáka no nakà no

unbreakable [ʌnbrei'kəbəl] *adj* (glass-ware, crockery etc) 割れない warénai; (other objects) 壊れない kowárenai

unbroken [ʌnbrou'kən] *adj* (seal) 開けて ない akéte naì; (silence, series) 続く tsu-zúku; (record) 破られていない yabúrare-te inai; (spirit) くじけない kujíkenài

unbutton [ʌnbʌt'ən] *vt* ...のボタンを外す ...no botán wo hazúsu

uncalled-for [ʌnkɔːld'fɔːr] *adj* (remark)

余計な yokéi na; (rudeness etc) いわれのない iwáre no nai

uncanny [ʌnkǽn'i:] adj (silence, resemblance, knack) 不気味な bukími na

unceasing [ʌnsi:'siŋ] adj 引っ切り無しの hikkírinashi no

unceremonious [ʌnseːrəmouni:əs] adj (abrupt, rude) ぶしつけな bushítsuke na

uncertain [ʌnsəːr'tən] adj (hesitant: voice, steps) 自信のない jishín no nai; (unsure) 不確実な fukákùjitsu na

uncertainty [ʌnsəːr'tənti:] n (not knowing) 不確実さ fukákùjitsusa; (also pl: doubts) 疑問 gimón

unchanged [ʌntʃeind͡ʒd'] adj (condition) 変っていない kawátte inai

unchecked [ʌntʃekt'] adv (grow, continue) 無制限に muséigen ni

uncivilized [ʌnsiv'ilaizd] adj (gen: country, people) 未開の mikái no; (fig: behavior, hour etc) 野蛮な yabán na

uncle [ʌŋ'kəl] n おじ ojí

uncomfortable [ʌnkʌmf'təbəl] adj (physically, also furniture) 使い心地の悪い tsukáigokochi nò warúì; (uneasy) 不安な fuán na; (unpleasant: situation, fact) 厄介な yakkái na

uncommon [ʌnkɑːm'ən] adj (rare, unusual) 珍しい mezúrashii

uncompromising [ʌnkɑːm'prəmaiziŋ] adj (person, belief) 融通の利かない yūzú no kikánai

unconcerned [ʌnkənsəːrnd'] adj (indifferent) 関心がない kańshin ga naì; (not worried) 平気な heíki na

unconditional [ʌnkəndiʃ'ənəl] adj 無条件の mujōkèn no

unconscious [ʌnkɑːn'tʃəs] adj (in faint, also MED) 意識不明の ishíkifumei no; (unaware): **unconscious of** ...に気が付かない ...ni kí ga tsukanaì
◆n: **the unconscious** 潜在意識 señzaii-shìki

unconsciously [ʌnkɑːn'tʃəsli:] adv (unawares) 無意識に muíshikì ni

uncontrollable [ʌnkəntrou'ləbəl] adj (child, animal) 手に負えない te nì oénai; (temper) 抑制のきかない yokúsei no ki-

kánai; (laughter) やめられない yaméra-renài

unconventional [ʌnkənven'tʃənəl] adj 型破りの katáyabùri no

uncouth [ʌnku:θ'] adj 無様な buzáma na

uncover [ʌnkʌv'əːr] vt (take lid, veil etc off) ...の覆いを取る ...no ōi wo torù; (plot, secret) 発見する hakkén suru

undecided [ʌndisai'did] adj (person) 決定していない kettéi shite inai; (question) 未決定の mikettéi no

undeniable [ʌndinai'əbəl] adj (fact, evidence) 否定できない hitéi dekínaì

under [ʌn'dəːr] prep (beneath) ...の下に ...no shitá ni; (in age, price: less than) ...以下に ...ikà ni; (according to: law, agreement etc) ...によって ...ni yottè; (someone's leadership) ...のもとに ...no motò ni
◆adv (go, fly etc) ...の下に〔で〕...no shitá ni〔de〕
under there あそこの下に〔で〕asóko no shitá ni〔de〕
under repair 修理中 shūrìchū

under... prefix 下の... shitá no...

under-age [ʌn'dəːr] adj (person, drinking) 未成年の miséìnen no

undercarriage [ʌn'dəːrkær'idʒ] (BRIT) n (AVIAT) 着陸装置 chakúrikusòchi

undercharge [ʌn'dəːrtʃɑːrdʒ] vt ...から正当な料金を取らない ...kara séitō na ryōkìn wo toránài

underclothes [ʌn'dəːrklouz] npl 下着 shitági

undercoat [ʌn'dəːrkout] n (paint) 下塗り shitánuri

undercover [ʌn'dəːrkʌv'əːr] adj (work, agent) 秘密の himítsu no

undercurrent [ʌn'dəːrkəːrənt] n (fig: of feeling) 底流 teíryū

undercut [ʌn'dəːrkʌt'] (pt, pp **undercut**) vt (person, prices) ...より低い値段で物を売る ...yorì hikúì nedán de monò wo urú

underdog [ʌn'dəːrdɔːg] n 弱者 jakùsha

underdone [ʌndəːrdʌn'] adj (CULIN) 生焼けの namáyake na

underestimate [ʌndəːres'təmeit] vt (person, thing) 見くびる mikúbiru

underexposed [ʌndərikspouzd'] adj
(PHOT) 露出不足の roshútsubusoku no

underfed [ʌndərfed'] adj (person, animal) 栄養不足の eíyōbusóku no

underfoot [ʌndərfut'] adv (crush, trample) 脚の下に〔で〕ashí no shitá ni(de)

undergo [ʌndərgou'] (pt **underwent** pp **undergone**) vt (test, operation, treatment) 受ける ukéru
to undergo change 変る kawáru

undergraduate [ʌndərgrædʒ'uːit] n 学部の学生 gakúbu no gakúsei

underground [ʌn'dərgraund] n (BRIT: railway) 地下鉄 chikátetsu; (POL) 地下組織 chikásoshiki
♦adj (car park) 地下の chiká no; (newspaper, activities) 潜りの mogúrì no
♦adv (work) 潜りで mogúrì de; (fig): *to go underground* 地下に潜る chiká ni mogúrù

undergrowth [ʌn'dərgrouθ] n 下生え shitábae

underhand [ʌndərhænd] adj (fig) ずるい zurúi

underhanded [ʌndərhæn'did] adj = **underhand**

underlie [ʌndərlai'] (pt **underlay** pp **underlain**) vt (fig: be basis of) ...の根底になっている ...no koñtei ni nattè iru

underline [ʌndərlain'] vt 下線をひく kasén suru, ...にアンダーラインを引く ...ni añdārain wo hikú; (fig) 強調する kyóchō suru

underling [ʌn'dərliŋ] (pej) n 手下 teshítà

undermine [ʌn'dərmain] vt (confidence) 失わせる ushínawaseru; (authority) 弱める yowámerù

underneath [ʌndərni:θ'] adv 下に〔で〕shitá ni(de)
♦prep ...の下に〔で〕...no shitá ni(de)

underpaid [ʌndərpeid'] adj 安給料の yasúkyūryō no

underpants [ʌn'dərpænts] npl パンツ pañtsu

underpass [ʌn'dərpæs] (BRIT) n 地下道 chikádō

underprivileged [ʌndərpriv'əlidʒd] adj

(country, race, family) 恵まれない megúmarenai

underrate [ʌndəreit'] vt (person, power etc) 見くびる mikúbirù; (size) 見誤る miáyamarù

undershirt [ʌn'dərʃərt] (US) n アンダーシャツ añdāshatsù

undershorts [ʌn'dərʃɔːrts] (US) npl パンツ pañtsu

underside [ʌn'dərsaid] n (of object) 下側 shitágawa; (of animal) おなか onáka

underskirt [ʌn'dərskərt] (BRIT) n アンダースカート añdāsukātò

understand [ʌndərstænd'] (pt, pp **understood**) vt 分かる wakárù, 理解する rikái suru
♦vi (believe): *I understand that* ...だそうですね ...da sõdesù ne, ...だと聞いていますが ...da tò kíite imasu gà

understandable [ʌndərstæn'dəbəl] adj (behavior, reaction, mistake) 理解できる rikái dekírù

understanding [ʌndərstæn'diŋ] adj (kind) 思いやりのある omóiyari no aru
♦n (gen) 理解 rikái; (agreement) 合意 góì

understatement [ʌn'dərsteit'mənt] n (of quality) 控えめな表現 hikáeme na hyógen
that's an understatement! それは控え目過ぎるよ sore wa hikáemesugírù yo

understood [ʌndərstud'] pt, pp of **understand**
♦adj (agreed) 合意された góì sareta; (implied) 暗黙の añmoku no

understudy [ʌn'dərstʌdi:] n (actor, actress) 代役 daíyaku

undertake [ʌndərteik'] (pt **undertook** pp **undertaken**) vt (task) 引受ける hikíukerù
to undertake to do something ...する事を約束する ...surú koto wo yakúsoku suru

undertaker [ʌn'dərteikə:r] n 葬儀屋 sógiyà

undertaking [ʌn'dərteikiŋ] n (job) 事業 jigyò; (promise) 約束 yakúsoku

undertone [ʌn'dərtoun] n: *in an undertone* 小声 kogóe

underwater [ʌn'dəːrwɔːt'əːr] *adv* (use) 水中に〔で〕 suíchū ni(de); (swim) 水中に潜って suíchū ni mogútte

♦*adj* (exploration) 水中の suíchū no; (camera etc) 潜水用の sēnsuiyō no

underwear [ʌn'dəːrweːr] *n* 下着 shítagi

underworld [ʌn'dəːrwəːrld] *n* (of crime) 暗黒街 ańkokugai

underwriter [ʌn'dəːraitəːr] *n* (INSUR-ANCE) 保険業者 hokéngyōshà

undesirable [ʌndizaiəːr'əbəl] *adj* (person, thing) 好ましくない konómashiku-nai

undies [ʌn'diːz] (*inf*) *npl* 下着 shítagi ◇女性用を指す joséiyō wo sasù

undisputed [ʌndispjuː'tid] *adj* (fact) 否定できない hitéi dekinaî; (champion etc) 断トツの dańtotsu no

undo [ʌndu:'] (*pt* **undid** *pp* **undone**) *vt* (unfasten) 外す hazúsu; (spoil) 台無しにする daínashi ni suru

undoing [ʌndu:'iŋ] *n* 破滅 hamétsu

undoubted [ʌndau'tid] *adj* 疑う余地のない utágau yochî no naî

undoubtedly [ʌndau'tidli:] *adv* 疑う余地なく utágau yochî naku

undress [ʌndres'] *vi* 服を脱ぐ fukú wo nugù

undue [ʌndu:'] *adj* (excessive) 余分な yo-bún na

undulating [ʌn'dʒəleitiŋ] *adj* (country-side, hills) 起伏の多い kifúku no ōî

unduly [ʌndu:'li:] *adv* (excessively) 余分に yobún ni

unearth [ʌnəːrθ'] *vt* (skeleton etc) 発掘する hakkútsu suru; (*fig*: secrets etc) 発見する hakkén suru

unearthly [ʌnəːrθ'li:] *adj* (hour) とんでもない tońde mo naî

uneasy [ʌniː'ziː] *adj* (person: not comfortable) 窮屈な kyūkutsu na; (: worried: *also* feeling) 不安な fuán na; (peace, truce) 不安定な fuántei na

uneconomic(al) [ʌniːkənəːm'ik(əl)] *adj* 不経済な fukéizai na

uneducated [ʌnedʒu:'keitid] *adj* (person) 教育のない kyōiku no nai

unemployed [ʌnemplɔid'] *adj* (worker)

失業中の shitsúgyōchū no

♦*npl*: **the unemployed** 失業者 shitsú-gyōshà ◇総称 sōshō

unemployment [ʌnemplɔi'mənt] *n* 失業 shitsúgyō

unending [ʌnen'diŋ] *adj* 果てし無い ha-téshi naî

unerring [ʌnəːr'iŋ] *adj* (instinct etc) 確実な kakújitsu na

uneven [ʌniː'vən] *adj* (not regular: teeth) 不ぞろいの fuzôròi no; (performance etc) むらのある murá no aru; (road etc) 凸凹の dekóboko no

unexpected [ʌnikspek'tid] *adj* (arrival) 不意の fuî no; (success etc) 思い掛けない omóigakenaî, 意外な igâi na

unexpectedly [ʌnikspek'tidli:] *adv* (arrive) 不意に fuî ni; (succeed) 意外に igâi ni

unfailing [ʌnfei'liŋ] *adj* (support, energy) 尽きる事のない tsukíru koto no naî

unfair [ʌnfeːr'] *adj*: **unfair (to)** (...に対して) 不当な (...ni taishite) futô na

unfaithful [ʌnfeiθ'fəl] *adj* (lover, spouse) 浮気な uwâki na

unfamiliar [ʌnfəmil'jəːr] *adj* (place, person, subject) 知らない shiránai

to be unfamiliar with ...を知らない ...wo shiránai

unfashionable [ʌnfæʃ'ənəbəl] *adj* (clothes, ideas, place) はやらない hayáranaî

unfasten [ʌnfæs'ən] *vt* (undo) 外す hazúsu; (open) 開ける akéru

unfavorable [ʌnfei'vəːrəbəl] (*BRIT* **unfavourable**) *adj* (circumstances, weather) 良くない yokûnai; (opinion, report) 批判的な hihánteki na

unfeeling [ʌnfiː'liŋ] *adj* 冷たい tsumétai, 冷酷な reîkoku na

unfinished [ʌnfin'iʃt] *adj* (incomplete) 未完成の mikáňsei no

unfit [ʌnfit'] *adj* (physically) 運動不足の uñdōbusoku no; (incompetent): **unfit (for)** (...に) 不向きな fumúki na

to be unfit for work 仕事に不向きである shigóto ni fumúki de aru

unfold [ʌnfould'] *vt* (sheets, map) 広げる hirógeru

♦*vi* (situation) 展開する teñkai suru

unforeseen [ʌnfɔːrsiːn'] *adj* (circumstances etc) 予期しなかった yokì shinákatta, 思い掛けない omóigakenaì

unforgettable [ʌnfəːrget'əbəl] *adj* 忘れられない wasúrerarenaì

unforgivable [ʌnfəːrgiv'əbəl] *adj* 許せない yurúsenaì

unfortunate [ʌnfɔːr'tʃənit] *adj* (poor) 哀れな awàre na; (event) 不幸な fukô na; (remark) まずい mazùi

unfortunately [ʌnfɔːr'tʃənitli] *adv* 残念ながら zañneñnagara

unfounded [ʌnfaun'did] *adj* (criticism, fears) 根拠のない koñkyo no nài

unfriendly [ʌnfrend'liː] *adj* (person, behavior, remark) 不親切な fushíñsetsu na

ungainly [ʌngein'liː] *adj* ぎこちない gikóchinaì

ungodly [ʌngɑːd'liː] *adj* (hour) とんでもない toñdemonaì

ungrateful [ʌngreit'fəl] *adj* (person) 恩知らずの oñshírazu no

unhappiness [ʌnhæp'iːnis] *n* 不幸せ fushíawàse, 不幸 fukô

unhappy [ʌnhæp'iː] *adj* (sad) 悲しい kanáshiì; (unfortunate) 不幸な fukô na; (childhood) 恵まれない megúmarenaì; (dissatisfied): **unhappy about/with** (arrangements etc) ...に不満がある ...ni fumán ga aru

unharmed [ʌnhɑːrmd'] *adj* 無事な bují na

unhealthy [ʌnhel'θiː] *adj* (person) 病弱な byôjaku na; (place) 健康に悪い keñkô ni warùi; (*fig*: interest) 不健全な fukéñzen na

unheard-of [ʌnhəːrd'əv] *adj* (shocking) 前代未聞の zeñdaimimon no; (unknown) 知られていない shirárete inaì

unhurt [ʌnhəːrt'] *adj* 無事な bují na

unidentified [ʌnaiden'təfaid] *adj* 未確定の mikákùtei no ¶*see also* **UFO**

uniform [juː'nəfɔːrm] *n* 制服 seífuku, ユニフォーム yunífòmù

♦*adj* (length, width etc) 一定の ittéi no

uniformity [juːnəfɔːr'miti] *n* 均一性 kiñitsusei

unify [juː'nəfai] *vt* 統一する tôitsu suru

unilateral [juːnəlæt'əːrəl] *adj* (disarmament etc) 一方的な ippôteki na

uninhabited [ʌninhæb'itid] *adj* (island etc) 無人の mujín no; (house) 空き家になっている akíya ni nattè iru

unintentional [ʌninten'tʃənəl] *adj* 意図的でない itôteki de naì

union [juːn'jən] *n* (joining) 合併 gappéi; (grouping) 連合 reñgô; (*also*: **trade union**) 組合 kumíai

♦*cpd* (activities, leader etc) 組合の kumíai no

Union Jack *n* 英国国旗 eíkokukòkki, ユニオンジャック yunîonjakkù

unique [juːniːk'] *adj* 独特な dokútoku na, ユニークな yunîkù na

unisex [juː'niseks] *adj* (clothes, hairdresser etc) ユニセックスの yunísekkusu no

unison [juː'nisən] *n*: **in unison** (say) 一同に ichídô ni; (sing) 同音で dôon de, ユニゾンで yuníxon de

unit [juː'nit] *n* (single whole, *also* measurement) 単位 tañ-i; (section: of furniture etc) ユニット yunítto; (team, squad) 班 hàn

    kitchen unit 台所用ユニット daídokoroyô yunítto

unite [juːnait'] *vt* (join: *gen*) 一緒にする isshô ni suru, 一つにする hitótsù ni suru; (: country, party) 結束させる kessoku saseru

♦*vi* 一緒になる isshò ni naru, 一つになる hitótsù ni naru

united [juːnai'tid] *adj* (*gen*) 一緒になった isshò ni natta, 一つになった hitótsù ni natta; (effort) 団結した dañketsu shita

United Kingdom *n* 英国 eíkoku

United Nations (Organization) *n* 国連 kokúren

United States (of America) *n* (アメリカ) 合衆国 (américa)gasshûkoku

unit trust (*BRIT*) *n* ユニット型投資信託 yuníttogata tôshishiñtaku

unity [ju:'niti:] *n* 一致 itchí

universal [ju:nəvər'səl] *adj* 普遍的な fu-hénteki na

universe [ju:'nəvə:rs] *n* 宇宙 uchū

university [ju:nəvər'siti:] *n* 大学 daígaku

unjust [ʌndʒʌst'] *adj* 不当な futō na

unkempt [ʌnkempt'] *adj* (appearance) だらしのない daráshi no naí; (hair, beard) もじゃもじゃの mojàmoja no

unkind [ʌnkaind'] *adj* (person, behavior, comment etc) 不親切な fushínsetsu na

unknown [ʌnnoun'] *adj* 知られていない shiráretè inái

unlawful [ʌnlɔ:'fəl] *adj* (act, activity) 非合法な higōhō na

unleash [ʌnli:ʃ'] *vt* (*fig:* feeling, forces etc) 爆発させる bakúhatsu saseru

unless [ʌnles'] *conj* ...しなければ〔でなければ〕 ...shinákereba〔denákereba〕
unless he comes 彼が来なければ karè ga konàkereba

unlike [ʌnlaik'] *adj* (not alike) 似ていない nitè inái; (not like) 違った chigátta
♦*prep* (different from) ...と違って ...to chigátte

unlikely [ʌnlaik'li:] *adj* (not likely) ありそうもない arísò mo naí; (unexpected: combination etc) 驚くべき odórokubeki

unlimited [ʌnlim'itid] *adj* (travel, wine etc) 無制限の muséigen na

unlisted [ʌnlis'tid] (*BRIT* **ex-directory**) *adj* (ex-directory) 電話帳に載っていない deñwachō ni notté inaí

unload [ʌnloud'] *vt* (box, car etc) ...の積荷を降ろす ...no tsumíni wo orósù

unlock [ʌnlɑ:k'] *vt* ...のかぎを開ける ...no kagí wo akéru

unlucky [ʌnlʌk'i:] *adj* (person) 運の悪い uñ no warúì; (object, number) 縁起の悪い eñgi no warúì
to be unlucky (person) 運が悪い uñ ga warúì

unmarried [ʌnmær'i:d] *adj* (person) 独身の dokúshin no; (mother) 未婚の mikón no

unmask [ʌnmæsk'] *vt* (reveal: thief etc) ...の正体を暴く ...no shōtaì wo abákù

unmistakable [ʌnmistei'kəbəl] *adj* (voice, sound, person) 間違え様のない machígaeyō no naí

unmitigated [ʌnmit'əgeitid] *adj* (disaster etc) 紛れもない magíre mò naí

unnatural [ʌnnætʃ'ə:rəl] *adj* 不自然な fushízèn na

unnecessary [ʌnnes'ise:ri:] *adj* 不必要な fuhítsuyō na

unnoticed [ʌnnou'tist] *adj:* (*to go/pass*) *unnoticed* 気付かれない kizúkàrenai

UNO [u:'nou] *n abbr* = **United Nations Organization**

unobtainable [ʌnəbtei'nəbəl] *adj* (item) 手に入らない te nì haíranaì; (TEL): *this number is unobtainable* この電話番号は現在使用されていません konó deñwabangō wa geñzai shiyō sarete imásèn

unobtrusive [ʌnəbtru:'siv] *adj* (person) 遠慮がちな eñryogachi na; (thing) 目立たない medátanaí

unofficial [ʌnəfiʃ'əl] *adj* (news) 公表されていない kōhyō sarete inaí; (strike) 公認されていない kōnin sarete inaí

unorthodox [ʌnɔ:r'θədɑ:ks] *adj* (treatment) 通常でない tsújò de nai; (REL) 正統でない seítō de nai

unpack [ʌnpæk'] *vi* 荷物の中身を出して片付ける nimòtsu no nakàmi wo dashìte katázukerù
♦*vt* (suitcase etc) ...の中身を出して片付ける ...no nakamì wo dashìte katázuke-rù

unpalatable [ʌnpæl'ətəbəl] *adj* (meal) まずい mazúì; (truth) 不愉快な fuyúkài na

unparalleled [ʌnpær'əleld] *adj* (unequalled) 前代未聞の zeñdaimimon no

unpleasant [ʌnplez'ənt] *adj* (disagreeable: thing) いやな iyà na; (: person, manner) 不愉快な fuyúkài na

unplug [ʌnplʌg'] *vt* (iron, TV etc) ...のプラグを抜く ...no puràgu wo nukú

unpopular [ʌnpɑ:p'jələ:r] *adj* (person, decision etc) 不評の fuhyō no

unprecedented [ʌnpres'identid] *adj* 前代未聞の zeñdaimimon no

unpredictable [ʌnpridik'təbəl] *adj*

(weather, reaction) 予測できない yosóku dekínaî; (person): *he is unpredictable* 彼のする事は予測できない karè no suru koto wa yosóku dekínaî

unprofessional [ʌnprəfeʃˈənəl] *adj* (attitude, conduct) 職業倫理に反する shokúgyōrìhri ni hañ suru

unqualified [ʌnkwɑːlˈɪfaid] *adj* (teacher, nurse etc) 資格のない shikáku no nai; (complete: disaster) 全くの mattáku no, 大... daî...; (: success) 完全な kañzen na, 大... daî...

unquestionably [ʌnkwesˈtʃənəbliː] *adv* 疑いもなく utágai mò naku

unravel [ʌnrævˈəl] *vt* (ball of string) ほぐす hogúsù; (mystery) 解明する kaímei suru

unreal [ʌnriˈəl] *adj* (not real) 偽の nisé no; (extraordinary) うその様な usð no yð na

unrealistic [ʌnriˈəlisˈtik] *adj* (person, project) 非現実的な higénjitsuteki na

unreasonable [ʌnriˈzənəbəl] *adj* (person, attitude) 不合理な fugðri na; (demand) 不当な futð na; (length of time) 非常識な hijðshìki na

unrelated [ʌnrileiˈtid] *adj* (incident) 関係のない kañkei no naî, 無関係な mukáñkei na; (family) 親族でない shiñzoku de naî

unrelenting [ʌnrilenˈtiŋ] *adj* 執念深い shûnenbukai

unreliable [ʌnrilaiˈəbəl] *adj* (person, firm) 信頼できない shiñrai dekinaî; (machine, watch, method) 当てにならない atè ni naranaî

unremitting [ʌnrimitˈiŋ] *adj* (efforts, attempts) 絶間ない taéma naî

unreservedly [ʌnrizəːrˈvidliː] *adv* 心から kokórð kara

unrest [ʌnrestˈ] *n* (social, political, industrial etc) 不安 fuán

unroll [ʌnroulˈ] *vt* 広げる hirógeru

unruly [ʌnruːˈliː] *adj* (child, behavior) 素直でない sunào de nai, 手に負えない te nî oénaî; (hair) もじゃもじゃの mojámoja no

unsafe [ʌnseifˈ] *adj* (in danger) 危険にさ

らされた kinkén ni sarásareta; (journey, machine, bridge etc) 危険な kikén na, 危ない abúnai

unsaid [ʌnsedˈ] *adj*: *to leave something unsaid* ...を言わないでおく ...wo iwánaide okù

unsatisfactory [ʌnsætisfækˈtəːri:] *adj* (progress, work, results) 不満足な fumáñzoku na

unsavory [ʌnseiˈvəːri:] (*BRIT* **unsavoury**) *adj* (*fig*: person, place) いかがわしい ikágawashiî

unscathed [ʌnskeiðdˈ] *adj* 無傷の mukízu no

unscrew [ʌnskruːˈ] *vt* (bottletop etc) ねじって開ける nejítte akéru; (sign, mirror etc) ...のねじを抜く ...no nejî wo nukú

unscrupulous [ʌnskruːˈpˈjələs] *adj* (person, behavior) 悪徳... akútoku...

unsettled [ʌnsetˈəld] *adj* (person) 落付かない ochítsukanài; (weather) 変りやすい kawáriyasuî

unshaven [ʌnʃeiˈvən] *adj* 不精ひげの bushðhìge no

unsightly [ʌnsaitˈli:] *adj* (mark, building etc) 醜い miníkuî, 目障りな mezáwàri na

unskilled [ʌnskildˈ] *adj* (work, worker) 未熟練の mijúkuren no

unspeakable [ʌnspiːˈkəbəl] *adj* (indescribable) 言語に絶する geñgo ni zéssuru, 想像を絶する sðzō wo zéssurù; (awful) ひどい hidðî

unstable [ʌnsteiˈbəl] *adj* (piece of furniture) ぐらぐらする gurágura suru; (government) 不安定な fuáñtei na; (mentally) 情緒不安定な jðchofuántei na

unsteady [ʌnstedˈi:] *adj* (step, legs) ふらふらする furáfura suru; (hands, voice) 震える furúeru; (ladder) ぐらぐらする gurágura suru

unstuck [ʌnstʌkˈ] *adj*: *to come unstuck* (label etc) 取れてしまう toréte shimaù; (*fig*: plan, idea etc) 失敗する shippái suru

unsuccessful [ʌnsəkses'fəl] *adj* (attempt) 失敗した shippái shita; (writer) 成功しない seíkō shinaî, 売れない urénai; (proposal) 採用されなかった saíyō sarènakatta

to be unsuccessful (in attempting something) 失敗する shippai suru; (application) 採用されない saíyō sarènai

unsuccessfully [ʌnsəksesˈfəliː] adv (try) 成功せずに seíkō sezu ni

unsuitable [ʌnsuːˈtəbəl] adj (inconvenient: time, moment) 不適当な futékìtō na; (inappropriate: clothes) 場違いの bachígaì no; (: person) 不適当な futékìtō na

unsure [ʌnʃuːr] adj (uncertain) 不確実な fukákùjitsu na

unsure about ...について確信できない ...ni tsuìte kakúshin dekinaì

to be unsure of oneself 自信がない jishín ga nai

unsuspecting [ʌnsəspekˈtiŋ] adj 気付いていない kizúite inai

unsympathetic [ʌnsimpəθetˈik] adj (showing little understanding) 同情しない dōjō shinai; (unlikeable) いやな iyá na

untapped [ʌntæptˈ] adj (resources) 未開発の mikáìhatsu no

unthinkable [ʌnθiŋkˈəbəl] adj 考えられない kańgaerarenaì

untidy [ʌntaiˈdiː] adj (room) 散らかった chírakatta; (person, appearance) だらしない daráshi nai

untie [ʌntaiˈ] vt (knot, parcel, ribbon) ほどく hodókù; (prisoner) ...の縄をほどく ...no nawá wo hodókù; (parcel, dog) ...のひもをほどく ...no himó wo hodókù

until [ʌntilˈ] prep ...まで ...madè
♦conj ...するまで ...suru madè

until he comes 彼が来るまで karè ga kurù made

until now 今まで imámadè

until then その時まで sonó toki madè

untimely [ʌntaimˈliː] adj (inopportune: moment, arrival) 時機の悪い jikì no warúì

an untimely death 早死に hayájini, 若死に wakájini

untold [ʌntouldˈ] adj (story) 明かされていない akásarete inai; (joy, suffering, wealth) 想像を絶する sōzō wo zessúru

untoward [ʌntɔːrdˈ] adj 困った komáttà

unused [ʌnjuːzdˈ] adj (not used: clothes, portion etc) 未使用の mishíyō no

unusual [ʌnjuːˈʒuːəl] adj (strange) 変った kawátta; (rare) 珍しい mezúrashiì; (exceptional, distinctive) 並外れた namíhazureta

unveil [ʌnveilˈ] vt (statue) ...の除幕式を行う ...no jomákushìki wo okónau

unwanted [ʌnwɔːnˈtid] adj (clothing etc) 不要の fuyō no; (child, pregnancy) 望まれなかった nozómarenakatta

unwavering [ʌnweiˈvəːriŋ] adj (faith) 揺るぎ無い yurúginaì; (gaze) じっとした jittó shita

unwelcome [ʌnwelˈkəm] adj (guest) 歓迎されない kańgeisarenaì; (news) 悪い warúì

unwell [ʌnwelˈ] adj: **to feel unwell** 気分が悪い kibùn ga warúì

to be unwell 病気である byóki de aru

unwieldy [ʌnwiːlˈdiː] adj (object, system) 大きくて扱いにくい ōkìkute atsúkaìnikuì

unwilling [ʌnwilˈiŋ] adj: **to be unwilling to do something** ...するのをいやがっている ...surú no wo iyagatte iru

unwillingly [ʌnwilˈiŋliː] adv いやがって iyágatte

unwind [ʌnwaindˈ] (pt, pp **unwound**) vt (undo) ほどく hodókù
♦vi (relax) くつろぐ kutsúrogù

unwise [ʌnwaizˈ] adj (person) 思慮の足りない shiryō no tarínai; (decision) 浅はかな asáhàka na

unwitting [ʌnwitˈiŋ] adj (victim, accomplice) 気付かない kizúkànai

unworkable [ʌnwəːrˈkəbəl] adj (plan) 実行不可能な jikkófukanō nà

unworthy [ʌnwəːrˈðiː] adj ...の値打がない ...no neúchi ga naì

unwrap [ʌnræpˈ] vt 開ける akéru

unwritten [ʌnritˈən] adj (law) 慣習の kańshū no; (agreement) 口頭での kótō de no

---
KEYWORD

---

up [ʌp] prep: **to go up something** ...を登る ...wo nobóru

to be up something ...の上に(登って)いる ...no ué ni nobotte iru *he went up the stairs/the hill* 彼は階段(坂)を登った karè wa kaídan〔sakà〕wo nobótta

the cat was up a tree ネコは木の上にいた nekò wa ki nò ué ni ita

we walked/climbed up the hill 私たちは丘を登った watákushitachi wa oká wo nobótta

they live further up the street 彼らはこの道をもう少し行った所に住んでいます karèra wa konó michi wo mố sukoshi ittá tokoro ni suñde imasu

go up that road and turn left この道を交差点まで行って左に曲って下さい konố michi wo kốsaten màde itte hidári ni magátte kudásaì

♦*adv* 1 (upwards, higher) 上に〔で, へ〕ué ni〔de, e〕

up in the sky/the mountains 空〔山の上〕に sorà〔yamá no ué〕ni

put it a bit higher up もう少し高い所に置いて下さい mố sukoshì takái tokoro ni oíte kudásaì

up there あの上に anố ue ni

what's the cat doing up there? ネコは何であの上にいるのかしら nekò wa nañde anố ue nì irú no kashira

up above 上の方に〔で〕ué no hō nì〔de〕

there's a village and up above, on the hill, a monastery 村があって、その上の丘に修道院がある murá ga atte, sonó ue no oká ni shūdóìn ga aru

2: *to be up* (out of bed) 起きている okíte iru; (prices, level) 上がっている agátte iru; (building) 建ててある tatète aru, 立っている tattè iru; (tent) 張ってある hatté aru

3: *up to* (as far as) …まで …made

I've read up to p.60 私は60ページまで読みました watákushi wa rokújupēji madè yomímashita

the water came up to his knees 水深は彼のひざまでだった suíshin wa karè no hizá madè datta

up to now 今〔これ〕まで imà〔korè〕madè

I can spend up to $10 10ドルまで使えます júdòru made tsukáemasu

4: *to be up to* (depending on) …の責任である …no sekínin de aru, …次第である …shidái de aru

it's up to you あなた次第です anàta shidái desu

it's up to me to decide 決めるのは私の責任ではない kimèru no wa watákushi no sekínin de wa naì

5: *to be up to* (equal to) …に合う …ni aù

he's not up to it (job, task etc) 彼にはその仕事は無理です karè ni wa sonó shigoto wa murì desu

his work is not up to the required standard 彼の仕事は基準に合いません karè no shigoto wa kijūn ni aìmasen

6: *to be up to* (inf: be doing) やっている yatté iru

what is he up to? (showing disapproval, suspicion) あいつは何をやらかしているんだろうね aítsu wa nanì wo yarákashite irún darō nè

♦*n*: *ups and downs* (in life, career) 浮き沈み ukíshizumi

we all have our ups and downs だれだっていい時と悪い時がありますよ darè datte iì toki to warùi toki ga arimasu yo

his life had its ups and downs, but he died happy 彼の人生には浮き沈みが多かったが、死ぬ時は幸せだった karè no jiñsei ni wa ukíshizumi ga ōkattà ga, shinú toki wa shiáwase datta

upbringing [ʌp'briŋiŋ] *n* 養育 yốiku

update [ʌpdeit'] *vt* (records, information) 更新する kốshin suru

upgrade [ʌp'greid] *vt* (improve: house) 改築する kaíchiku suru; (job) 格上げする kakúage suru; (employee) 昇格させる shốkaku saseru

upheaval [ʌphi:'vəl] *n* 変動 héndō

uphill [*adj* ʌp'hil *adv* ʌp'hil'] *adj* (climb) 上りの nobòri no; (*fig*: task) 困難な koñnan na

♦*adv*: *to go uphill* 坂を上る sakà wo nobóru

uphold [ʌphould'] (*pt, pp* **upheld**) *vt* (law, principle, decision) 守る mamórù

upholstery [ʌphoul'stə:ri:] *n* いすに張っ

た生地 isú ni hattá kijí

upkeep [ʌpˈkiːp] *n* (maintenance) 維持 ijí

upon [əpɑːnˈ] *prep* ...の上に〔で〕 ...no ué ni〔de〕

upper [ʌpˈər] *adj* 上の方の ué no hō nò

♦*n* (of shoe) 甲皮 kōhí

upper-class [ʌpˈərklæs] *adj* (families, accent) 上流の jōryū no

upper hand *n*: **to have the upper hand** 優勢である yūsei de aru

uppermost [ʌpˈərmoust] *adj* 一番上の i-chíbàn ué no

what was uppermost in my mind 私が真っ先に考えたのは watákushi ga massákì ni kañgaèta no wa

upright [ʌpˈrait] *adj* (straight) 直立の chokúritsu no; (vertical) 垂直の suíchoku no; (fig: honest) 正直な shōjiki na

uprising [ʌpˈraiziŋ] *n* 反乱 hañran

uproar [ʌpˈrɔːr] *n* (protests, shouts) 大騒ぎ ōsawàgi

uproot [ʌpruːtˈ] *vt* (tree) 根こそぎにする nekősogi ni suru; (fig: family) 故郷から追出す kokyō kara oídasù

upset [*n* ʌpˈset *vb* ʌpsetˈ] (*pt*, *pp* **upset**) *n* (to plan etc) 失敗 shippái

♦*vt* (knock over: glass etc) 倒す taósù; (routine, plan) 台無しにする daínashi ni suru; (person: offend, make unhappy) 動転させる dőten saseru

♦*adj* (unhappy) 動転した dőten shita

to have an upset stomach 胃の具合が悪い i nò gúai ga warúi

upshot [ʌpˈʃɑt] *n* 結果 kekka

upside down [ʌpˈsaid-] *adv* (hang, hold) 逆様に〔で〕 sakásama ni〔de〕

to turn a place upside down (fig) 家中を引っかき回す iéjū wo híkkakìmawasu

upstairs [ʌpˈsteːrz] *adv* (be) 2階に〔で〕 nikái ni〔de〕; (go) 2階へ nikái e

♦*adj* (window, room) 2階の nikái no

♦*n* 2階 nikái

upstart [ʌpˈstɑrt] *n* 横柄な奴 ōhèi na yatsù

upstream [ʌpˈstriːm] *adv* 川上に〔で，へ〕 kawákami ni〔de, e〕，上流に〔で，へ〕 jōryū ni〔de, e〕

uptake [ʌpˈteik] *n*: *to be quick/slow on*

the uptake 物分かりがいい〔悪い〕mo-nówakàri ga ií〔warui〕

uptight [ʌpˈtait] *adj* ぴりぴりした pirí-piri shita

up-to-date [ʌpˈtədeitˈ] *adj* (most recent: information) 最新の saíshin no; (person) 最新の情報に通じている saíshin no jōhō ni tsūjíte irù

upturn [ʌpˈtəːrn] *n* (in luck) 好転 kőten; (COMM: in market) 上向き uwámuki

upward [ʌpˈwəːrd] *adj* (movement, glance) 上への ué e no

upwards [ʌpˈwəːrdz] *adv* (move, glance) 上の方へ ué no hō è; (more than): *upwards(s) of* ...以上の...ijō no

uranium [jureiˈniːəm] *n* ウラン uràn, ウラニウム uránìumù

urban [əːrˈbən] *adj* 都会の tokái no

urbane [əːrbeinˈ] *adj* 上品な jōhìn na

urchin [əːrˈtʃin] *n* (child) がき gakí; (waif) 浮浪児 furőjì

urge [əːrdʒ] *n* (need, desire) 衝動 shődō

♦*vt*: *to urge someone to do something* ...する様に...に...を説得する ...surú yō ni ...settőku suru

urgency [əːrˈdʒənsiː] *n* (importance) 緊急性 kiñkyūseì; (of tone) 緊迫した調子 kiñpaku shita chőshi

urgent [əːrˈdʒənt] *adj* (need, message) 緊急な kiñkyū na; (voice) 切迫した seppáku shita

urinal [juːrˈənəl] *n* 小便器 shōbeñki

urinate [juːrˈəneit] *vi* 小便をする shōbeñ wo suru

urine [juːrˈin] *n* 尿 nyő, 小便 shőbeñ

urn [əːrn] *n* (container) 骨つぼ kotsútsubo; (*also*: **coffee/tea urn**) 大型コーヒー〔紅茶〕メーカー ōgatakōhī〔kőcha〕mèkà

Uruguay [juːrˈəgwei] *n* ウルグアイ urùguai

us [ʌs] *pron* 私たちを〔に〕watákushitachi wo〔ni〕 ¶ *see also* **me**

US(A) [juːes'(ei')] *n abbr* = **United States (of America)**

usage [juːˈsidʒ] *n* (LING) 慣用 kañyō

use [*n* juːs *vb* juːz] *n* (using) 使用 shíyō; (usefulness, purpose) 役に立つ事 yakú ni tatsu koto 利益 rîeki

♦*vt* (object, tool, phrase etc) 使う tsukáu, 用いる mochíirù, 使用する shíyō suru

in use 使用中 shíyōchū

out of use 廃れて sutáretè

to be of use 役に立つ yakú ni tatsu

it's no use (not useful) 使えません tsukáemasen; (pointless) 役に立ちません yakú ni tachimasen, 無意味です muímì desu

she used to do it 前は彼女はそれをする習慣でした maè wa kanòjo wa soré wo suru shūkan deshita

to be used to ...に慣れている ...ni narète iru

used [juːzd] *adj* (object) 使われた tsukáwareta; (car) 中古の chūkò no

useful [juːsʹfəl] *adj* 役に立つ yakú ni tatsu, 有益な yūeki na, 便利な beñri na

usefulness [juːsʹfəlnis] *n* 実用性 jitsúyōsei

useless [juːsʹlis] *adj* (unusable) 使えない tsukáenai; (pointless) 役に立たない yakú ni tatanai; (pointless) 無意味な múimì na, 無駄な mudá na; (person: hopeless) 能無しの nōnashi no, 役に立たない yakú ni tatanai

user [juːzʹr] *n* 使用者 shiyōsha

user-friendly [juːzʹzəːrfrendʹliː] *adj* (computer) 使いやすい tsukáiyasuì, ユーザーフレンドリーな yūzáfureńdorī na

use up *vt* 全部使ってしまう zeñbu tsukátte shimaù, 使い尽す tsukáitsukusù

usher [ʌʃʹəːr] *n* (at wedding) 案内係 añnaigakàri

usherette [ʌʃəretʹ] *n* (in cinema) 女性案内係 joséi añnaigakàri

USSR [juːesesaːrʹ] *n*: *the USSR* ソ連 sorèn

usual [juːʹʒuːəl] *adj* (time, place etc) いつもの itsùmo no

as usual いつもの様に itsùmo no yō ni

usually [juːʹʒuːəliː] *adv* 普通は futsū wa

usurp [juːsəːrpʹ] *vt* (title, position) 強奪する gōdatsu suru

utensil [juːtenʹsəl] *n* 用具 yōgu

kitchen utensils 台所用具 daídokoro yōgu

uterus [juːʹtəːrəs] *n* 子宮 shikyū

utility [juːtilʹitiː] *n* (usefulness) 有用性 yūyōsei, 実用性 jitsúyōsei; (also: **public utility**) 公益事業 kōekijigyō

utility room *n* 洗濯部屋 señtakubeya

utilize [juːʹtəlaiz] *vt* (object) 利用する riyō suru, 使う tsukáu

utmost [ʌtʹmoust] *adj* 最大の saídai no

♦*n*: *to do one's utmost* 全力を尽す zeñryoku wo tsukusù

utter [ʌtʹəːr] *adj* (total: amazement, fool, waste, rubbish) 全くの mattáku no

♦*vt* (sounds) 出す dasù, 発する hassúru; (words) 口に出す kuchí ni dasù, 言う iù

utterance [ʌtʹəːrəns] *n* 発言 hatsúgen, 言葉 kotóba

utterly [ʌtʹəːrliː] *adv* 全く mattáku

U-turn [juːʹtəːrn] *n* Uターン yūtāñ

V

v. *abbr* = **verse**; **versus**; **volt**; (= **vide**) ...を見よ ...wo mìyo

vacancy [veiʹkənsiː] *n* (BRIT: job) 欠員 ketsúin; (room) 空き部屋 akíbeya

vacant [veiʹkənt] *adj* (room, seat, toilet) 空いている afte iru; (look, expression) うつろの utsúro no

vacant lot (US) *n* 空き地 akíchi

vacate [veiʹkeit] *vt* (house, one's seat) 空ける akéru; (job) 辞める yaméru

vacation [veikeiʹʃən] *n* (esp US: holiday) 休暇 kyūka; (SCOL) 夏休み natsúyasùmi

vaccinate [vækʹsəneit] *vt*: *to vaccinate someone (against something)* ...に (...の) 予防注射をする ...ni (...no) yobō-chūshà wo suru

vaccine [væksiːnʹ] *n* ワクチン wakùchin

vacuum [vækʹjuːm] *n* (empty space) 真空 shiñkū

vacuum cleaner *n* (真空) 掃除機 (shiñkū)sōjikì

vacuum-packed [vækʹjuːmpæktʹ] *adj* 真空パックの shiñkūpakkù no

vagabond [vægʹəbaːnd] *n* 浮浪者 furōshà, ルンペン ruñpen

vagina [vədʒaiʹnə] *n* ちつ chitsú

vagrant [veiʹgrənt] *n* 浮浪者 furōshà, ルンペン ruñpen

vague [veig] *adj* (blurred: memory, outline) ぼんやりとした boń-yarí to shita; (uncertain: look, idea, instructions) 漠然とした bakúzen to shita; (person: not precise) 不正確な fuseíkaku na; (: evasive) 煮え切らない niékiranái

vaguely [veig'li:] *adv* (not clearly) ぼんやりとして boń-yarí to shite; (without certainty) 漠然と bakúzen to, 不正確に fuseíkaku ni; (evasively) あいまいに aímai ni

vain [vein] *adj* (conceited) うぬぼれた unúboreta; (useless: attempt, action) 無駄な mudá na

in vain 何のかいもなく nań no kaí mo nakù

valentine [væl'əntain] *n* (*also*: **valentine card**) バレンタインカード baréntaiñkàdo; (person) バレンタインデーの恋人 baréntaiñdè no koíbito

valet [vælei'] *n* 召使い meshítsukài

valiant [væl'jənt] *adj* (attempt, effort) 勇敢な yúkan na

valid [væl'id] *adj* (ticket, document) 有効な yúkō na; (argument, reason) 妥当な datō na

validity [vəlid'iti:] *n* (of ticket, document) 有効性 yúkōseî; (of argument, reason) 妥当性 datōseî

valley [væl'i:] *n* 谷(間) taní(ma)

valor [væl'ə:r] (*BRIT* **valour**) *n* 勇ましさ isámashisà

valuable [væl'ju:əbəl] *adj* (jewel etc) 高価な kōka na; (time, help, advice) 貴重な kichō na

valuables [væl'ju:əbəlz] *npl* (jewellery etc) 貴重品 kichōhin

valuation [vælju:ei'ʃən] *n* (worth: of house etc) 価値 kachî; (judgment of quality) 評価 hyōka

value [væl'ju:] *n* (financial worth) 価値 kachî, 価格 kakáku; (importance, usefulness) 価値 kachî
♦*vt* (fix price or worth of) ...に値を付ける ...ni ne wó tsukérù; (appreciate) 大切にする taísetsu ni suru, 重宝する chōhō suru

values [væl'ju:z] *npl* (principles, beliefs)

価値観 kachîkañ

value added tax [-æd'id-] (*BRIT*) *n* 付加価値税 fukákachizèi

valued [væl'ju:d] *adj* (appreciated: customer, advice) 大切な taísetsu na

valve [vælv] *n* 弁 beñ, バルブ barúbu

vampire [væm'paiə:r] *n* 吸血鬼 kyúketsùki

van [væn] *n* (AUT) バン bañ

vandal [væn'dəl] *n* 心無い破壊者 kokóronaî hakáisha

vandalism [væn'dəlizəm] *n* 破壊行動 hakáikōdō

vandalize [væn'dəlaiz] *vt* 破壊する hakái suru

vanguard [væn'gɑ:rd] *n* (*fig*): *in the vanguard of* ...の先端に立って ...no señtan ni tattè

vanilla [vənil'ə] *n* バニラ banîra

vanilla ice cream *n* バニラアイスクリーム banîra aísukurīmu

vanish [væn'iʃ] *vi* (disappear suddenly) 見えなくなる miénaku narù, 消える kiéru

vanity [væn'iti:] *n* (of person: unreasonable pride) 虚栄心 kyoéishiñ

vantage point [væn'tidʒ-] *n* (lookout place) 観察点 kañsatsuten; (viewpoint) 有利な立場 yūri na tachîba

vapor [vei'pə:r] (*BRIT* **vapour**) *n* (gas) 気体 kitái; (mist, steam) 蒸気 jōki

variable [ve:r'i:əbəl] *adj* (likely to change: mood, quality, weather) 変りやすい kawáriyasuî; (able to be changed: temperature, height, speed) 調節できる chōsetsu dekírù

variance [ve:r'i:əns] *n*: *to be at variance (with)* (people) (...と) 仲たがいしている (...to) nakátagaì shité iru; (facts) (...と) 矛盾している (...to) mujúnshité iru

variation [ve:ri:ei'ʃən] *n* (change in level, amount, quantity) 変化 heñka, 変動 heñdō; (different form: of plot, musical theme etc) 変形 heñkai

varicose [vær'əkous] *adj*: *varicose veins* 拡張蛇行静脈 kakúchōdakōjōmyakù

varied [veːrˈiːd] *adj* (diverse: opinions, reasons) 様々な sámàzama na; (full of changes: career) 多彩な tasái na

variety [vərʌiˈəti:] *n* (degree of choice, diversity) 変化 heńka, バラエティー baráetī; (varied collection, quantity) 様々な物 sámàzama na mono; (type) 種類 shurùi

variety show *n* バラエティーショー baráetīshò

various [veːrˈi:əs] *adj* 色々な iróiro na

varnish [vɑːrˈniʃ] *n* (product applied to surface) ニス nisù

  ♦*vt* (apply varnish to: wood, piece of furniture etc) ...にニスを塗る ...ni nisù wo nuru; (: nails) ...にマニキュアをする ...ni manîkyua wo suru

  nail varnish マニキュア manîkyua

vary [veːrˈi:] *vt* (make changes to: routine, diet) 変える kaéru

  ♦*vi* (be different: sizes, colors) ...が色々ある ...ga iróiro aru; (become different): *to vary with* (weather, season etc) ...によって変る ...ni yótte kawáru

vase [veis] *n* 花瓶 kabín

Vaseline [vǽsˈəliːn]® *n* ワセリン wasérin

vast [vǽst] *adj* (wide: area, knowledge) 広い hirôi; (enormous: expense etc) ばく大な bakúdai na

VAT [vǽt] *n abbr* = **value added tax**

vat [vǽt] *n* 大おけ ōokè

Vatican [vǽtˈikən] *n*: *the Vatican* (palace) バチカン宮殿 bachîkan kyûdeñ; (authority) ローマ法王庁 rôma hōōchō

vault [vɔːlt] *n* (of roof) 丸天井 marúteñjō; (tomb) 地下納骨堂 chikánōkotsudō; (in bank) 金庫室 kiñkoshitsú

  ♦*vt* (*also*: **vault over**) 飛越える tobíkoerù

vaunted [vɔːnˈtid] *adj*: *much-vaunted* ご自慢の go-jíman no

VCR [viːsiːɑːrˈ] *n abbr* = **video cassette recorder**

VD [viːdiːˈ] *n abbr* = **venereal disease**

VDU [viːdiːjuːˈ] *n abbr* = **visual display unit**

veal [viːl] *n* 子ウシ肉 koúshiniku

veer [viːr] *vi* (vehicle, wind) 急に向きを変える kyû ni mukî wo kaéru

vegetable [vedʒˈtəbəl] *n* (BOT) 植物 shokúbùtsu; (edible plant) 野菜 yasái

  ♦*adj* (oil etc) 植物性の shokubutsusei no

vegetarian [vedʒiteːrˈiːən] *n* 菜食主義者 saíshokushugishà

  ♦*adj* (diet etc) 菜食主義の saíshokushugi no

vegetate [vedʒˈiteit] *vi* 無為に暮す muì ni kurásu

vegetation [vedʒiteiˈʃən] *n* (plants) 植物 shokúbutsu ◇総称 sóshō

vehement [viːˈəmənt] *adj* (strong: attack, passions, denial) 猛烈な mõretsu na

vehicle [viːˈikəl] *n* (machine) 車 kurúma; (*fig*: means of expressing) 手段 shudàn

veil [veil] *n* ベール bèru

veiled [veild] *adj* (*fig*: threat) 隠された kakúsareta

vein [vein] *n* (ANAT) 静脈 jômyaku; (of ore etc) 脈 myakú

  vein of a leaf 葉脈 yômyaku

velocity [vəlɑːsˈitiː] *n* 速度 sokúdo

velvet [velˈvit] *n* ビロード birôdo, ベルベット berúbetto

  ♦*adj* ビロードの birôdo no, ベルベットの berúbettò no

vendetta [vendetˈə] *n* 復しゅう fukúshū

vending machine [venˈdiŋ-] *n* 自動販売機 jidôhanbaiki

vendor [venˈdəːr] *n* (of house, land) 売手 urîte; (of cigarettes, beer etc) 売子 urîko

veneer [vəniːrˈ] *n* (on furniture) 化粧張り keshôbari; (*fig*: of person, place) 虚飾 kyoshóku

venereal [vəniːrˈiːəl] *adj*: *venereal disease* 性病 seíbyō

Venetian blind [vəniːˈʃən-] *n* ベネシャンブラインド benéshanburaindò

Venezuela [venizweiˈlə] *n* ベネズエラ benézuèra

vengeance [venˈdʒəns] *n* (revenge) 復しゅう fukúshū

  with a vengeance (*fig*: to a greater extent) 驚く程 odôrokù hodo

venison [venˈisən] *n* シカ肉 shikániku

venom [ven'əm] n (of snake, insect) 毒 dokú; (bitterness, anger) 悪意 ákui

venomous [ven'əməs] adj (poisonous: snake, insect) 毒... dokú...; (full of bitterness: look, stare) 敵意に満ちた tekíi ni michíta

vent [vent] n (also: **air vent**) 通気孔 tsúkikō; (in jacket) ベンツ beñtsu
♦vt (fig: feelings, anger) ぶちまける buchímakeru

ventilate [ven'təleit] vt (room, building) 換気する kañki suru

ventilation [ventəlei'ʃən] n 換気 kañki

ventilator [ven'təleitər] n (TECH) 換気装置 kañkisōchi, ベンチレーター beñchirētā; (MED) 人工呼吸器 jiñkōkokyūkì, レスピレタ resúpiretà

ventriloquist [ventril'əkwist] n 腹話術師 fukúwajùtsushi

venture [ven'tʃər] n (risky undertaking) 冒険 bōken
♦vt (opinion) おずおず言う ozúozu iú
♦vi (dare to go) おずおず行く ozúozu i-kú
business venture 投機 tōki

venue [ven'juː] n (place fixed for something) 開催地 kaísaichi

veranda(h) [vəræn'də] n ベランダ beránda

verb [vəːrb] n 動詞 dōshi

verbal [vəːr'bəl] adj (spoken: skills etc) 言葉の kotóba no; (: translation etc) 口頭の kōtō no; (of a verb) 動詞の dōshi no

verbatim [vəːrbei'tim] adj 言葉通りの kotóbadòri no
♦adv 言葉通りに kotóbadōri ni

verbose [vəːrbous'] adj (person) 口数の多い kuchíkazu no ōi; (speech, report etc) 冗長な jōchō na

verdict [vəːr'dikt] n (LAW) 判決 hañketsu; (fig: opinion) 判断 hañdan

verge [vəːrdʒ] n (BRIT: of road) 路肩 rokáta
「soft verges」(BRIT: AUT) 路肩軟弱 rokáta nanjaku
to be on the verge of doing something ...する所である ...surú tokoro dè arù

verge on vt fus ...同然である ...dōzen de arù

verify [ver'əfai] vt (confirm, check) 確認する kakúnin suru

veritable [ver:'itəbəl] adj (reinforcer: = real) 全くの mattáku no

vermin [vəːr'min] npl (animals) 害獣 gaíjū; (fleas, lice etc) 害虫 gaíchū

vermouth [vəːrmuː'θ] n ベルモット berúmottò

vernacular [vəːrnæk'jələr] n (language) その土地の言葉 sonó tochi no kotóba

versatile [vəːr'sətəl] adj (person) 多才の tasái no; (substance, machine, tool etc) 使い道の多い tsukáimichi no ōi

verse [vəːrs] n (poetry) 詩 shi; (one part of a poem: also in bible) 節 setsù

versed [vəːrst] adj: **(well-)versed in** ...に詳しい ...ni kuwáshii

version [vəːr'ʒən] n (form: of design, production) 型 katá; (: of book, play etc) ...版 ...bañ; (account: of events, accident etc) 説明 setsúmei

versus [vəːr'səs] prep ...対... ...tai ...

vertebra [vəːr'təbrə] n (pl **vertebrae**) n せきつい sekítsuìi

vertebrae [vəːr'təbrei] npl of **vertebra**

vertebrate [vəːr'təbreit] n せきつい動物 sekítsuidōbutsu

vertical [vəːr'tikəl] adj 垂直の suíchoku no

vertigo [vəːr'təgou] n めまい memáî

verve [vəːrv] n (vivacity) 気迫 kiháku

very [ver'iː] adv (+ adjective, adverb) とても totémo, 大変 taíhen, 非常に hijō ni
♦adj: *it's the very book he'd told me about* 彼が話していたのは正にその本だ karè ga hanáshite ita no wà masá ni sonó hon dà
the very last 正に最後の masá ni saígo no
at the very least 少なくとも sukunàkutomo
very much 大変 taíhen

vessel [ves'əl] n (NAUT) 船 funè; (container) 容器 yōki see **blood**

vest [vest] n (US: waistcoat) チョッキ chôkki; (BRIT) アンダーシャツ añdāshatsù

vested interests [ves'tid-] *npl* 自分の利
益 jibún no rièki, 私利 shirì

vestige [ves'tidʒ] *n* 残り nokóri

vet [vet] (*BRIT*) *n abbr* = **veterinary
surgeon**

♦*vt* (examine: candidate) 調べる shiráberù

veteran [vet'ərən] *n* (of war) ...戦争で戦
った人 ...seńsō de tatákatta hito; (former soldier) 退役軍人 taíekigunjin; (old
hand) ベテラン betéran

veterinarian [vetə:rənə:r'i:ən] (*US*) *n* 獣
医 jūi

veterinary [vet'ə:rənə:ri:] *adj* (practice,
care etc) 獣医の jūi no

veterinary surgeon (*BRIT*) *n* = **veterinarian**

veto [vi:'tou] (*pl* **vetoes**) *n* (right to forbid) 拒否権 kyohìken; (act of forbidding)
拒否権の行使 kyohìken no kōshì

♦*vt* ...に拒否権を行使する ...ni kyohìken
wo kōshì suru

vex [veks] *vt* (irritate, upset) 怒らせる o-
kòraserù

vexed [vekst] *adj* (question) 厄介な yak-
kài na

via [vai'ə] *prep* (through, by way of) ...を
経て ...wo hetè, ...経由 ...keìyu

viable [vai'əbəl] *adj* (project) 実行可能な
jikkòkanō na; (company) 存立できる soñ-
ritsu dekirù

viaduct [vai'ədʌkt] *n* 陸橋 rikkyō

vibrant [vai'brənt] *adj* (lively) 力強い
chikárazuyoì; (bright) 生き生きした ikíikì shita; (full of emotion: voice) 感情の
こもった kańjō no komótta

vibrate [vai'breit] *vi* (house, machine
etc) 振動する shińdō suru

vibration [vaibrei'ʃən] *n* 振動 shińdō

vicar [vik'ə:r] *n* 主任司祭 shuńnshisaì

vicarage [vik'ə:ridʒ] *n* 司祭館 shisáikaǹ

vicarious [vaike:r'i:əs] *adj* (pleasure) 他
人の身になって感じる tanín no mi nì
nattè kañjirù

vice [vais] *n* (moral fault) 悪徳 akútoku;
(TECH) 万力 mańriki

vice- [vais] *prefix* 副... fukú...

vice-president [vais'prez'idənt] *n* (*US*
POL) 副大統領 fukúdaitòryð

vice squad *n* 風俗犯罪取締班 fùzokuhań-
zai toríshimarihaǹ

vice versa [vais'və:r'sə] *adv* 逆の場合も
同じ gyakú no baái mo onáji

vicinity [visin'əti:] *n* (area): **in the
vicinity (of)** (...の) 近所に (...no) kiñ-
jo ni

vicious [viʃ'əs] *adj* (violent: attack, blow)
猛烈な mōretsu na; (cruel: words, look)
残酷な zańkoku na; (horse, dog) どう猛
な dōmō na

vicious circle *n* 悪循環 akújuǹkan

victim [vik'tim] *n* (person, animal, business) 犠牲者 giséisha

victimize [vik'təmaiz] *vt* (strikers etc)
食い物にする kuímono nì suru

victor [vik'tə:r] *n* 勝利者 shōrìsha

Victorian [viktour'i:ən] *adj* ヴィクトリア
朝の bikútoriachō no

victorious [viktɔ:r'i:əs] *adj* (triumphant:
team, shout) 勝ち誇る kachíhokoru

victory [vik'tə:ri:] *n* 勝利 shōrì

video [vid'i:ou] *cpd* ビデオの bideo no

♦*n* (video film) ビデオ映画, ビデオ映画
bideo éiga; (also: **video cassette**) ビデオ
カセット bidéokasettð; (also: **video cassette recorder**) ビデオテープレコーダー
bidéo tēpùrekōdằ, VTR buitìāru

video tape *n* ビデオテープ bidéotēpù

vie [vai] *vi*: **to vie (with someone)(for
something)** (...のために) (...と) 競り
合う ...no tamè ni) (...to) seríaù

Vienna [vi:en'ə] *n* ウィーン uíń

Vietnam [vi:etna:m'] *n* ベトナム betónamu

Vietnamese [vi:etna:mi:z'] *adj* ベトナム
の betónamu no; (LING) ベトナム語の
betónamugð no

♦*n inv* (person) ベトナム人 betónamujiǹ;
(LING) ベトナム語 betónamugð

view [vju:] *n* (sight) 景色 keshìki; (outlook) 見方 mikáta; (opinion) 意見 ikèn

♦*vt* (look at: also fig) 見る mirù

on view (in museum etc) 展示中 teñjichū

in full view (of) (...の) 見ている前で
(...no) mitè iru maè de

in view of the weather こういう天気だから kō fu teñki da karà

in view of the fact that ...だという事を考えて ...da tó iu koto wo kañgaetè

in my view 私の考えでは watákushi no kañgae de wà

viewer [vju:'ə:r] n (person) 見る人 mirù hito

viewfinder [vju:'faində:r] n ファインダー faíndā

viewpoint [vju:'pɔint] n (attitude) 考え方 kañgaekata, 見地 keñchi; (place) 観察する地点 kañsatsu suru chíteñ

vigil [vidʒ'əl] n 不寝番 fushíñban

vigilance [vidʒ'ələns] n 用心 yōjiñ

vigilant [vidʒ'ələnt] adj 用心する yōjiñ suru

vigor [vig'ə:r] (BRIT **vigour**) n (energy: of person, campaign) 力強さ chikárazuyosà

vigorous [vig'ə:rəs] adj (full of energy: person) 元気のいい geñki no íi; (: action, campaign) 強力な kyőryoku na; (: plant) よく茂った yokù shigéttà

vile [vail] adj (evil: action) 下劣な gerétsu na; (: language) 下品な gehiñ na; (unpleasant: smell, weather, food, temper) ひどい hidoì

villa [vil'ə] n (country house) 別荘 besső; (suburban house) 郊外の屋敷 kōgài no yashikí

village [vil'idʒ] n 村 murá

villager [vil'idʒə:r] n 村民 soñmin

villain [vil'in] n (scoundrel) 悪党 akútō; (in novel) 悪役 akúyaku; (BRIT: criminal) 犯人 hañnin

vindicate [vin'dikeit] vt (person: free from blame) ...の正しさを立証する ...no tadashìsa wo risshősuru; (action: justify) ...が正当である事を立証する ...ga seítő de arù koto wo risshő suru

vindictive [vindik'tiv] adj (person) 執念深い shúneñbukaì; (action etc) 復しゅう心による fukúshūshiñ ni yoru

vine [vain] n (climbing plant) ツル tsurù; (grapevine) ブドウの木 budő no ki

vinegar [vin'əgə:r] n 酢 su

vineyard [vin'jə:rd] n ブドウ園 budően

vintage [vin'tidʒ] n (year) ブドウ収穫年 budő shúkakuneñ

◆cpd (classic: comedy, performance etc) 典型的な teñkeiteki na

vintage car n クラシックカー kurashìkku kā

vintage wine n 当り年のワイン atáridoshi no waìn

vinyl [vai'nil] n ビニール binírù

viola [vi:ou'lə] n (MUS) ビオラ biòra

violate [vai'əleit] vt (agreement, peace) 破る yaburù; (graveyard) 汚す kegasù

violation [vaiəlei'ʃən] n (of agreement etc) 違反 ihán

violence [vai'ələns] n (brutality) 暴力 bōryòku; (strength) 乱暴 rañbō

violent [vai'ələnt] adj (brutal: behavior) 暴力の bōryòku no, 乱暴な rañbō na; (intense: debate, criticism) 猛烈な mōrétsu na

a violent death 変死 heñshi

violet [vai'əlit] adj 紫色の murásaiiro no

◆n (color) 紫 murasàki; (plant) スミレ sumíre

violin [vaiəlin'] n バイオリン baíorin

violinist [vaiəlin'ist] n バイオリン奏者 baíorinsōsha, バイオリニスト baíorinisuto

VIP [vi:aipi:'] n abbr (= very important person) 要人 yōjiñ, 貴賓 kihíñ, ブイアイピー bufaipī, ビップ bippù

viper [vai'pə:r] n クサリヘビ kusárihebì

virgin [və:r'dʒin] n (person) 処女 shojò, バージン bājiñ

◆adj (snow, forest etc) 処女... shojò...

virginity [və:rdʒin'əti:] n (of person) 処女 shojò

Virgo [və:r'gou] n (sign) 乙女座 otomèza

virile [vir'əl] adj 男らしい otőkorashiì

virility [vəril'əti:] n (sexual power) 性的能力 seítekinőryoku; (fig: masculine qualities) 男らしさ otőkorashisà

virtually [və:r'tʃu:əli:] adv (almost) 事実上 jijítsujō

virtue [və:r'tʃu:] n (moral correctness) 徳 tokú, 徳行 tokkő; (good quality) 美徳 bitőku; (advantage) 利点 ritéñ, 長所 chōshō

by virtue of ...である事で... de arù kotō de

virtuosi [vəːrtʃuːouˈziː] *npl of* **virtuoso**

virtuoso [vəːrtʃuːouˈzou] (*pl* **virtuosos** *or* **virtuosi**) *n* 名人 meíjin

virtuous [vəːrˈtʃuːəs] *adj* (displaying virtue) 良心的な ryōshínteki na, 高潔な kōkétsu na, 敬けんな keíken na

virulent [virˈjələnt] *adj* (disease) 悪性の akúsei no 危険な kiken na; (actions, feelings) 憎悪に満ちた zōō ni michíta

virus [vaiˈrəs] *n* ウイルス uírusu

visa [viːˈzə] *n* 査証 sashō, ビザ bizà

vis-à-vis [viːzɑːviːˈ] *prep* (compared to) ...と比べて ...to kurábete; (in regard to) ...に関して ...ni kań shite

viscose [visˈkouz] *n* ビスコース人絹 bisúkōsùjíñkeñ, ビスコースレーヨン bisúkōsùrēyòn

viscous [visˈkəs] *adj* ねばねばした nebá-neba shita

visibility [vizəbilˈətiː] *n* 視界 shikái

visible [vizˈəbəl] *adj* (able to be seen or recognized: *also fig*) 目に見える me nì mierú

vision [viʒˈən] *n* (sight: ability) 視力 shiryòku; (: sense) 視覚 shikáku; (foresight) ビジョン bijòn; (in dream) 幻影 geń-ei

visit [vizˈit] *n* (to person, place) 訪問 hőmon

♦*vt* (person: *US also*: visit with) 訪問する hőmon suru, 訪ねる tazúnerù, ...の所へ遊びに行く ...no tokòro e asóbi ni ikú; (place) 訪問する hőmon suru, 訪ねる tazúneru

visiting hours [vizˈitiŋ-] *npl* (in hospital etc) 面会時間 meńkaijikan

visitor [vizˈitəːr] *n* (person visiting, invited) 客 kyakú; (tourist) 観光客 kańkōkyàku

visor [vaiˈzəːr] *n* (of helmet etc) 面 meñ; (of cap etc) ひさし hisáshi; (AUT: *also*: **sun visor**) 日よけ hiyőke

vista [visˈtə] *n* (view) 景色 keshíki

visual [viʒˈuːəl] *adj* (arts etc) 視覚の shikáku no

visual aid *n* 視覚教材 shikákukyōzai

visual display unit *n* モニター monítā, ディスプレー disúpurè

visualize [viʒˈuːəlaiz] *vt* (picture, imagine) 想像する sőzō suru

vital [vaitˈəl] *adj* (essential, important, crucial) 重要な júyō na; (full of life: person) 活発な kappátsu na; (necessary for life: organ) 生命に必要な seímei ni hitsúyō na

vitality [vaitælˈitiː] *n* (liveliness) 元気 geńki

vitally [vaitˈəliː] *adv*: *vitally important* 極めて重要な kiwámete júyō na

vital statistics *npl* (of population) 人口動態統計 jiñkōdōtaitōkei; (*inf*: woman's measurements) スリーサイズ surísaizù

vitamin [vaiˈtəmin] *n* ビタミン bitámin

vivacious [viveiˈʃəs] *adj* にぎやかな nigiyàka na

vivid [vivˈid] *adj* (clear: description, memory) 鮮明な señmei na; (bright: color, light) 鮮やかな azáyàka na; (imagination) はつらつとした hatsúratsu to shitá

vividly [vivˈidliː] *adv* (describe) 目に見える様に me ni mierù yō ni; (remember) はっきりと hakkírì to

vivisection [vivisekˈʃən] *n* 生体解剖 seítaikaibō

V-neck [viːˈnek] *n* (*also*: **V-neck jumper/pullover**) Vネックセーター buínekkusétā

vocabulary [voukæbˈjələːriː] *n* (words known) 語い goî

vocal [vouˈkəl] *adj* (of the voice) 声の koè no; (articulate) はっきり物を言う hakkírì monò wo iú

vocal c(h)ords *npl* 声帯 seítai

vocation [voukeiˈʃən] *n* (calling) 使命感 shiméikan; (chosen career) 職業 shokugyō

vocational [voukeiˈʃənəl] *adj* (training etc) 職業の shokugyō no

vociferous [vousifˈəːrəs] *adj* (protesters, demands) やかましい yakámashii, しつこい shitsúkoî

vodka [vɑdˈkə] *n* ウォッカ uőkkà

vogue [voug] *n* 流行 ryūkō

in vogue 流行して ryūkṓ shite

voice [vɔis] *n* (of person) 声 koè
♦*vt* (opinion) 表明する hyṓmei suru

void [vɔid] *n* (emptiness) 空 虚 kūkyò; (hole) 穴 aná, 空間 kūkan
♦*adj* (invalid) 無効の mukṓ no; (empty): *void of* ...が全くない ...ga mattáku naì

volatile [vɑːlətəl] *adj* (liable to change: situation) 不安定な fuántei na; (: person) 気まぐれな kimágure na; (: liquid) 揮発性の kihátsusei no

volcanic [vɑːlkǽnik] *adj* (eruption) 火山の kazàn no; (rock etc) 火山性の kazànsei no

volcano [vɑːlkéinou] (*pl* **volcanoes**) *n* 火山 kazàn

volition [voulíʃən] *n*: *of one's own volition* 自発的に jihátsuteki ni, 自由意志で jiyúishì de

volley [vɑːliː] *n* (of stones etc) 一斉に投げられる ... issèi ni nagérareru ...; (of questions etc) 連発 reṅpatsu; (TENNIS etc) ボレー borè
a volley of gunfire 一斉射撃 isséishagèki

volleyball [vɑːliːbɔːl] *n* バレーボール barḗbōrù

volt [voult] *n* ボルト borúto

voltage [voul'tidʒ] *n* 電圧 deñ-atsu

voluble [vɑːlʲəbəl] *adj* (person) 口達者な kuchídasshà na; (speech etc) 流ちょうな ryūchṓ na

volume [vɑːlʲuːm] *n* (space) 容積 yōsèki; (amount) 容量 yōryò; (book) 本 hoǹ; (sound level) 音量 oǹryō, ボリューム boryū́mu
Volume 2 第2巻 daínikan

voluminous [vəlúːminəs] *adj* (clothes) だぶだぶの dabúdabu no; (correspondence, notes) 大量の taíryō no, 多数の tasū̀ no

voluntarily [vɑːləntərʲiliː] *adv* (willingly) 自発的に jihátsuteki ni, 自由意志で jiyúishi de

voluntary [vɑːləntèriː] *adj* (willing, done willingly: exile, redundancy) 自発的な jihátsuteki na, 自由意志による jiyúishi ni yoru; (unpaid: work, worker) 奉仕

の hōshí no

volunteer [vɑːləntiːr] *n* (unpaid helper) 奉仕者 hōshísha, ボランティア borántìa; (to army etc) 志願者 shigánshà
♦*vt* (information) 自発的に言う jihátsuteki ni iú, 提供する teíkyō suru
♦*vi* (for army etc) ...への入隊を志願する ...e no nyū́tai wo shigàn suru
to volunteer to do ...しようと申出る ...shiyṓto mōshíderu

voluptuous [vəlʌp'tʃuəs] *adj* (movement, body, feeling) 官能的な kañnōteki na, 色っぽい iróppoi

vomit [vɑːmit] *n* 吐いた物 haìta monó, 反吐 hedò
♦*vt* 吐く hakù
♦*vi* 吐く haku

vote [vout] *n* (method of choosing) 票決 hyṓketsu; (indication of choice, opinion) 投票 tṓhyō; (votes cast) 投票数 tṓhyōsū; (*also*: *right to vote*) 投票権 tṓhyōkèn
♦*vt* (elect): *to be voted chairman etc* 座長に選出される zachṓ ni señshutsu saréru; (propose): *to vote that* ...という事を提案する ...to iú koto wo teían suru
♦*vi* (in election etc) 投票する tṓhyō suru
vote of thanks 感謝決議 kañshaketsugì

voter [vou'təɾ] *n* (person voting) 投票者 tṓhyōshà; (person with right to vote) 有権者 yū́keñshà

voting [vou'tiŋ] *n* 投票 tṓhyō

vouch for [vautʃ-] *vt fus* (person, quality etc) 保証する hoshṓ suru

voucher [vau'tʃəɾ] *n* (for meal: *also*: **luncheon voucher**) 食券 shokkèn; (with petrol, cigarettes etc) クーポン kū́pon; (*also*: *gift voucher*) ギフト券 gifútokeǹ

vow [vau] *n* 誓い chikái
♦*vt*: *to vow to do/that* ...する事[...だという事]を誓う ...surú koto [...da to iú koto] wo chikáu

vowel [vau'əl] *n* 母音 boín

voyage [vɔi'idʒ] *n* (journey: by ship, spacecraft) 旅 tabí, 旅行 ryokṓ

V-sign [viː'sain] (*BRIT*) *n* V サイン buìsain ◇手の甲を相手に向けると軽べつのサイン；手のひらを向けると勝利のサイ

ン te no kō wo aíte ni mukéru to keíbetsu no saín; te nó hirá wo mukéru to shórì no saín

vulgar [vʌl'gə:r] *adj* (rude: remarks, gestures, graffiti) 下品な gehín na; (in bad taste: decor, ostentation) 野暮な yabó na

vulgarity [vʌlgær'iti:] *n* (rudeness) 下品な言葉 gehín na kotóba; (ostentation) 野暮ったい事 yabóttai kotó

vulnerable [vʌl'nə:rəbəl] *adj* (person, position) やられやすい yaráreyasuì, 無防備な mubôbì na

vulture [vʌl'tʃə:r] *n* ハゲタカ hagétaka

W

wad [wɑːd] *n* (of cotton wool, paper) 塊 katámari; (of banknotes etc) 束 tabà

waddle [wɑːd'əl] *vi* (duck, baby) よちよち歩く yochìyochi arúkù; (fat person) よたよた歩く yotáyota arúkù

wade [weid] *vi*: **to wade through** (water) …の中を歩いて通る …no nakà wo arúite tōrù; (*fig*: a book) 苦労して読む kurô shité yomù

wafer [wei'fə:r] *n* (biscuit) ウエハース uéhāsu

waffle [wɑːf'əl] *n* (CULIN) ワッフル waffùru; (empty talk) 下らない話 kudáranai hanáshi
♦*vi* (in speech, writing) 下らない話をする kudáranai hanáshi wo suru

waft [wæft] *vt* (sound, scent) 漂わせる tadayowaseru
♦*vi* (sound, scent) 漂う tadáyou

wag [wæg] *vt* (tail, finger) 振る furù
♦*vi*: **the dog's tail was wagging** イヌはしっぽを振っていた inú wà shippó wo futté ità

wage [weidʒ] *n* (*also*: **wages**) 賃金 chíṅgin, 給料 kyúryò
♦*vt*: **to wage war** 戦争をする señsō wo suru

wage earner [-ə:r'nə:r] *n* 賃金労働者 chíṅginrōdōsha

wage packet *n* 給料袋 kyúryōbukùro

wager [wei'dʒə:r] *n* かけ kakè

waggle [wæg'əl] *vt* (hips) 振る furu; (eyebrows etc) ぴくぴくさせる pikùpiku saséru

wag(g)on [wæg'ən] *n* (*also*: **horse-drawn wag(g)on**) 荷馬車 nibásha; (BRIT: RAIL) 貨車 kashà

wail [weil] *n* (of person) 泣き声 nakígoè; (of siren etc) うなり unári
♦*vi* (person) 泣き声をあげる nakígoè wo agéru; (siren) うなる unarù

waist [weist] *n* (ANAT, *also* of clothing) ウエスト uésùto

waistcoat [weist'kout] (BRIT) *n* チョッキ chókki, ベスト besùto

waistline [weist'lain] *n* (of body) 胴回り dōmawàri, ウエスト uésùto; (of garment) ウエストライン uésùtorain

wait [weit] *n* (interval) 待ち時間 machí jikan
♦*vi* 待つ matsù
to lie in wait for …を待伏せする …wo machíbuse suru
I can't wait to (*fig*) 早く…したい hayàku …shitái
to wait for someone/something …を待つ …wo matsu

wait behind *vi* 居残って待つ inokotte matsù

waiter [wei'tə:r] *n* (in restaurant etc) 給仕 kyújì, ウエーター uéta, ボーイ bôi

waiting [wei'tiŋ] *n*: **"no waiting"** (BRIT: AUT) 停車禁止 teísha kiñshi

waiting list *n* 順番待ちの名簿 juñbanmachi no meíbo

waiting room *n* (in surgery, railway station) 待合室 machíaìshitsu

wait on *vt fus* (people in restaurant) …に給仕する …ni kyújì suru

waitress [wei'tris] *n* ウエートレス uétòresu

waive [weiv] *vt* (rule) 適用するのをやめる tekíyō suru no wò yaméru; (rights etc) 放棄する hōkì suru

wake [weik] (*pt* **woke** *or* **waked**, *pp* **woken** *or* **waked**) *vt* (*also*: **wake up**) 起す okósù
♦*vi* (*also*: **wake up**) 目が覚める me gá samérù

♦*n* (for dead person) 通夜 tsuyà, tsūya; (NAUT) 航跡 kôseki

waken [wei'kən] *vt, vi* = **wake**

Wales [weilz] *n* ウェールズ uêrùzu

the Prince of Wales プリンスオブウェールズ purînsu obu uêrùzu

walk [wɔːk] *n* (hike) ハイキング haîkingu; (shorter) 散歩 sańpo; (gait) 歩調 hochô; (in park, along coast etc) 散歩道 sańpomichi, 遊歩道 yūhodô

♦*vi* (go on foot) 歩く arúkù; (for pleasure, exercise) 散歩する sańpo suru

♦*vt* (distance) 歩く arúkù; (dog) 散歩に連れて行く tsurétè ikú

10 minutes' walk from here ここから徒歩で10分の所に kokô karà tohô do juppùn no tokôro ni

people from all walks of life あらゆる身分の人々 aráyurù mibùn no hitôbìto

walker [wɔːk'əːr] *n* (person) ハイカー haîkā

walkie-talkie [wɔː'kiːtɔː'kiː] *n* トランシーバー toránshībà

walking [wɔː'kiŋ] *n* ハイキング haîkingu

walking shoes *npl* 散歩靴 sańpogutsu

walking stick *n* ステッキ sutékkì

walk out *vi* (audience) 出て行く detè ikú; (workers) ストライキをする sutôraìki wo suru

walkout [wɔːk'aut] *n* (of workers) ストライキ sutôraìki

walk out on (*inf*) *vt fus* (family etc) 見捨てる misúterù

walkover [wɔːk'ouvəːr] (*inf*) *n* (competition, exam etc) 朝飯前 asámeshimaè

walkway [wɔːk'wei] *n* 連絡通路 reńrakutsūrò

wall [wɔːl] *n* (gen) 壁 kabé; (city wall etc) 城壁 jôheki

walled [wɔːld] *adj* (city) 城壁に囲まれた jôheki ni kakômareta; (garden) 塀をめぐらした heî wo megúrashita

wallet [wɑːl'it] *n* 札入れ satsúire, 財布 saîfu

wallflower [wɔːl'flauəːr] *n* ニオイアラセイトウ nióiaraseitô

to be a wallflower (*fig*) だれもダンスの相手になってくれない darê mo dańsu no aîte ni nattè kurénai, 壁の花である kabé no hana de arù

wallop [wɑːl'əp] (*inf*) *vt* ぶん殴る buńnaguru

wallow [wɑːl'ou] *vi* (animal: in mud, water) 転げ回る korôgemawarù; (person: in sentiment, guilt) ふける fukérù

wallpaper [wɔːl'peipəːr] *n* 壁紙 kabégami

♦*vt* (room) ...に壁紙を張る ...ni kabégami wo harú

wally [wei'liː] (*BRIT: inf*) *n* ばか bakâ

walnut [wɔːl'nʌt] *n* (nut) クルミ kurúmi; (also: **walnut tree**) クルミの木 kurúmi no kì; (wood) クルミ材 kurúmizaì

walrus [wɔːl'rəs] (*pl* **walrus** *or* **walruses**) *n* セイウチ seîuchi

waltz [wɔːlts] *n* (dance, MUS) 円舞曲 eńbukyòku, ワルツ warûtsu

♦*vi* (dancers) ワルツを踊る warûtsu wo odôru

wan [wɑːn] *adj* (person, complexion) 青白い aôjiroi; (smile) 悲しげな kanáshige nà

wand [wɑːnd] *n* (*also*: **magic wand**) 魔法の棒 mahô no bô

wander [wɑːn'dəːr] *vi* (person) ぶらぶら歩く buràbura arúkù; (attention) 散漫になる sańman ni narù; (mind, thoughts: here and there) さまよう samáyoù; (: to specific topic) 漂う tadáyoù

♦*vt* (the streets, the hills etc) ...をぶらぶら歩く ...wo burùbura arúkù

wane [wein] *vi* (moon) 欠ける kakérù; (enthusiasm, influence etc) 減る herú

wangle [wæŋ'gəl] (*inf*) *vt* うまい具合に獲得する umái guái ni kakútoku suru

want [wɑːnt] *vt* (wish for) 望む nozômu, ...が欲しい ...ga hoshiî; (need, require) ...が必要である ...ga hitsúyô de arù

♦*n*: *for want of* ...がないので ...ga naî no de

to want to do ...したい ...shitái

to want someone to do something ...に...してもらいたい ...ni ...shité moraitaî

wanted [wɑːnt'id] *adj* (criminal etc) 指名手配中の shiméitehàichū no 「**wanted**」 (in advertisements) 求む motómù

wanting [wɑːn'tiŋ] *adj*: **to be found wanting** 期待を裏切る kitái wo urágirù

wanton [wɑːn'tən] *adj* (gratuitous) 理由のない riyū no naî; (promiscuous) 浮気な uwáki na

wants [wɑːnts] *npl* (needs) 必要とする物 hitsúyō to suru monô, ニーズ nízù

war [wɔːr] *n* 戦争 sensō
to make war (on) (*also fig*) ...と戦う ...to tatákau

ward [wɔːrd] *n* (in hospital) 病棟 byótō; (POL) 区 ku; (LAW: child: *also*: **ward of court**) 被後見人 hikôkennin

warden [wɔːr'dən] *n* (of park, game reserve, youth hostel) 管理人 kañrinîn; (of prison etc) 所長 shochô; (*BRIT*: *also*: **traffic warden**) 交通監視官 kōtsúkanshikañ

warder [wɔːr'dəːr] *n* (*BRIT*) 看守 kañshu

ward off *vt* (attack, enemy) 食止める kuftomeru; (danger, illness) 防ぐ fuségù

wardrobe [wɔːrd'roub] *n* (for clothes) 洋服だんす yốfukudañsu; (collection of clothes) 衣装 ishô; (CINEMA, THEATER) 衣装部屋 ishôbeya

warehouse [we:r'haus] *n* 倉庫 sōkò

wares [we:rz] *npl* 商品 shôhin, 売り物 urímono

warfare [wɔːr'fe:r] *n* 戦争 sensō

warhead [wɔːr'hed] *n* 弾頭 dañtō

warily [we:r'ili:] *adv* 用心深く yójinbukakù

warlike [wɔːr'laik] *adj* (nation) 好戦的な kôsenteki na; (appearance) 武装した busôshita

warm [wɔːrm] *adj* (meal, soup, day, clothes etc) 暖かい atátakaî; (thanks) 心からの kokôro kara no; (applause, welcome) 熱烈な netsúretsu na; (person, heart) 優しい yasáshii, 温情のある oñjō no arù
it's warm (just right) 暖かい atátakaî; (too warm) 暑い atsúî
I'm warm 暑い atsúî
warm water ぬるま湯 murúmayù

warm-hearted [wɔːrm'hɑːr'tid] *adj* 心の優しい kokôro no yasáshii

warmly [wɔːrm'li:] *adv* (applaud, welcome) 熱烈に netsúretsu ni
to dress warmly 厚着する atsúgi suru

warmth [wɔːrmθ] *n* (heat) 暖かさ atátakasa; (friendliness) 温かみ atátakami

warm up *vi* (person, room, soup, etc) 暖まる atátamarù; (weather) 暖かくなる atátakaku narù; (athlete) 準備運動をする juñbiundō wo suru, ウォーミングアップする uốminguappù suru
♦*vt* (hands etc) 暖める atátamerù; (engine) 暖気運転する dañkiuñten suru

warn [wɔːrn] *vt* (advise): **to warn someone of/that** ...に...があると/...だと)警告する ...ni ...ga arù to 〔...da to〕keîkoku suru
to warn someone not to do ...に...しないよう警告する ...ni ...shinái yō keîkoku suru

warning [wɔːr'niŋ] *n* 警告 keîkoku

warning light *n* 警告灯 keîkokutō

warning triangle *n* (AUT) 停止表示板 teîshihyōjibañ

warp [wɔːrp] *vi* (wood etc) ゆがむ yugámu
♦*vt* (*fig*: character) ゆがめる yugámeru

warrant [wɔːr'ənt] *n* (voucher) 証明書 shômeîsho; (LAW: for arrest) 逮捕状 taîhojō; (: search warrant) 捜索令状 sôsakureijō

warranty [wɔːr'ənti:] *n* (guarantee) 保証 hoshô

warren [wɔːr'ən] *n* (*also*: **rabbit warren**) ウサギ小屋 uságigoya; (*fig*: of passages, streets) 迷路 meîro

warrior [wɔːr'iːəːr] *n* 戦士 senshi

Warsaw [wɔːr'sɔː] *n* ワルシャワ warúshawa

warship [wɔːr'ʃip] *n* 軍艦 guñkan

wart [wɔːrt] *n* いぼ ibô

wartime [wɔːr'taim] *n*: **in wartime** 戦時中 señjichū

wary [we:r'iː] *adj* 用心深い yójinbukaî

was [wʌz] *pt of* **be**

wash [wɔʃ] *vt* (gen) 洗う aráù; (clothes etc) 洗濯する señtaku suru

♦*vi* (person) 手を洗う te wò aráu; (sea etc): *to wash over/against something* ...に打寄せる ...ni uchíyoseru, ...を洗う ...wo aráu

♦*n* (clothes etc) 洗濯物 señtakumono; (washing program) 洗い arái; (of ship) 航跡の波 kóseki no namí

to have a wash 手を洗う te wò aráu

to give something a wash ...を洗う ...wo aráu

washable [wɔ:ʃˈəbəl] *adj* 洗濯できる señtaku dekirù

wash away *vt* (stain) 洗い落す araiotosu; (subj: flood, river etc) 流す nagasu

washbasin [wɔ:ʃˈbeisin] (*US also*: **washbowl**) *n* 洗面器 señmeñki

washcloth [wɔ:ʃˈklɔ:θ] (*US*) *n* (face cloth) フェースタオル fésutaorù

washer [wɔ:ʃˈə:r] *n* (TECH: metal) 座金 zagáne, ワッシャー wasshá; (machine) 洗濯機 señtakuki

washing [wɔ:ʃˈiŋ] *n* (dirty, clean) 洗濯物 señtakumono

washing machine *n* 洗濯機 señtakuki

washing powder (*BRIT*) *n* 洗剤 señzai

washing-up [wɔ:ʃˈiŋʌp] (*BRIT*) *n* (action) 皿洗い saráaraì; (dirty dishes) 汚れた皿 yogóretà sará

washing-up liquid (*BRIT*) *n* 台所用洗剤 daídokoroyō senzai

wash off *vi* 洗い落される aráiotosàreru

wash-out [wɔ:ʃˈaut] (*inf*) *n* (failed event) 失敗 shippái

washroom [wɔ:ʃˈru:m] (*US*) *n* お手洗い o-téarài

wash up *vi* (*US*) 手を洗う te wò aráu; (*BRIT*) 皿洗いをする saráaraì wo suru

wasn't [wʌzˈənt] = **was not**

wasp [wɑ:sp] *n* アシナガバチ ashínagabàchi ◊スズメバチなど肉食性のハチの総称 suzúmebàchi nado nikúshokuseì no hachi no sóshō

wastage [weisˈtidʒ] *n* (amount wasted, loss) 浪費 róhi

natural wastage 自然消耗 shizénshōmō

waste [weist] *n* (act of wasting: life, money, energy, time) 浪費 róhi; (rubbish)

廃棄物 haíkibutsu; (*also*: **household waste**) ごみ gomí

♦*adj* (material) 廃棄の haíki no; (left over) 残り物の nokórimono no; (land) 荒れた aréta

♦*vt* (time, life, money, energy) 浪費する róhi suru; (opportunity) 失う ushínau, 逃す nogásù

to lay waste (destroy: area, town) 破壊する hakái suru

waste away *vi* 衰弱する suíjaku suru

waste disposal unit (*BRIT*) *n* ディスポーザー disúpōzā

wasteful [weistˈfəl] *adj* (person) 無駄使いの多い mudázukai no ōì; (process) 不経済な fukéizai na

waste ground (*BRIT*) *n* 空き地 akíchi

wastepaper basket [weistˈpeipəːr-] *n* くずかご kuzúkàgo

waste pipe *n* 排水管 haísuìkan

wastes [weists] *npl* (area of land) 荒れ野 aréno

watch [wɑ:tʃ] *n* (*also*: **wristwatch**) 腕時計 udédokèi; (act of watching) 見張り mihári; (vigilance) 警戒 keíkai; (group of guards: MIL, NAUT) 番兵 bañpei; (NAUT: spell of duty) 当直 tóchoku, ワッチ watchī

♦*vt* (look at: people, objects, TV etc) 見る míru; (spy on, guard) 見張る miháru; (be careful of) ...に気を付ける ...ni ki wó tsukerù

♦*vi* (look) 見る míru; (keep guard) 見張る miháru

watchdog [wɑ:tʃˈdɔ:g] *n* (dog) 番犬 bañken; (*fig*) 監視者 kañshisha, お目付け役 o-métsukeyaku

watchful [wɑ:tʃˈfəl] *adj* 注意深い chúibukaì

watchmaker [wɑ:tʃˈmeikəːr] *n* 時計屋 tokéiya

watchman [wɑ:tʃˈmən] (*pl* **watchmen**) *n* see **night**

watch out *vi* 気を付ける ki wó tsukerù, 注意する chū suru

watch out! 危ない！ abúnai!

watch strap *n* 腕時計のバンド udédokèi no bañdo

water [wɔ'tər] n (cold) 水 mizú; (hot)
(お) 湯 (o)yú

♦vt (plant) ...に 水 を やる ...ni mizú wo
yarú

♦vi (eyes) 涙 が 出る namída ga derù;
(mouth) よだれが出る yodáre ga derù

in British waters 英国領海に〔で〕eíko-
kuryōkai ni(de)

water cannon n 放水砲 hốsuihō

water closet (*BRIT*) n トイレ toíre

watercolor [wɔ'tərkʌlər] n (picture)
水彩画 suísaiga

watercress [wɔ'tərkres] n クレソン ku-
réson

water down vt (milk etc) 水 で 薄 め る
mizú de usúmeru; (*fig*: story) 和らげる
yawárageru

waterfall [wɔ'tərfɔːl] n 滝 takí

water heater n 湯沸器 yuwákashikì

watering can [wɔ'tərɪŋ-] n じょうろ
jōrð

water level n 水位 suíi

water lily n スイレン suíren

waterline [wɔ'tərlain] n (*NAUT*) 喫水
線 kissúiseǹ

waterlogged [wɔ'tərlɔːgd] adj (ground)
水浸しの mizúbitashi no

water main n 水道本管 suídōhonkaǹ

watermelon [wɔ'tərmelən] n スイカ
suíka

waterproof [wɔ'tərpruːf] adj (trousers,
jacket etc) 防水の bốsui no

watershed [wɔ'tərʃed] n (*GEO*: natural
boundary) 分水界 buńsuikaì; (: high
ridge) 分水嶺 buńsuīrei; (*fig*) 分岐点 buń-
kitèn

water-skiing [wɔ'tərskiːiŋ] n 水上スキ
ー suíjōsukī

watertight [wɔ'tərtait] adj (seal) 水密
の suímitsu no

waterway [wɔ'tərwei] n 水路 suíro

waterworks [wɔ'tərwərks] n (building) 浄水場 jōsuijō

watery [wɔ'təriː] adj (coffee) 水っぽい
mizúppoì; (eyes) 涙ぐんだ namídagundà

watt [wɑt] n ワット wattð

wave [weiv] n (of hand) 一振り hitófuri;
(on water) 波 namí; (*RADIO*) 電波 deñ-
pa; (in hair) ウェーブ uébù; (*fig*: surge) 高
まり takámarì, 急増 kyūzō

♦vi (signal) 手 を 振 る te wð furù;
(branches, grass) 揺れる yuréru; (flag) な
びく nabíkù

♦vt (hand, flag, handkerchief) 振る furù;
(gun, stick) 振り回す furímawasù

wavelength [weiv'leŋkθ] n (*RADIO*) 波
長 hachō

on the same wavelength (*fig*) 気が合っ
て ki gà attè

waver [wei'vər] vi (voice) 震 え る furúeru; (love) 揺らぐ yurágu; (person) 動揺す
る dốyō suru

his gaze did not waver 彼は目を反ら
さなかった kárè wa mé wð sorásanakat-
tà

wavy [wei'viː] adj (line) くねくねした ku-
nèkune shita; (hair) ウェーブのある uébù
no aru

wax [wæks] n (polish, for skis) ワックス
wakkùsu; (*also*: **earwax**) 耳あか mimífa-
kà

♦vt (floor, car, skis) ...にワックスを掛け
る ...ni wakkùsu wo kakérù

♦vi (moon) 満ちる michírù

waxworks [wæks'wərks] npl (models)
ろう人形 rốniñgyō

♦n (place) ろう人形館 rốniñgyōkan

way [wei] n (route) ...へ行く道 ...e ikú
michî; (path) 道 michî; (access) 出入口
defríguchi (distance) 距離 kyórì; (direction) 方向 hốkō; (manner, method) 方法
hốhō; (habit) 習慣 shūkan

which way? - this way どちらへ?-こ
ちらへ dochíra é? -kochíra e

on the way (en route) 途中で tochū de

to be on one's way 今向かっている imá
mukátte irù, 今途中である imá tochū de
arù

to be in the way (*also fig*) 邪魔である
jamá de arù

*to go out of one's way to do some-
thing* わざわざ...する wazáwaza ...suru

under way (project etc) 進行中で shiń-
kōchū de

to lose one's way 道に迷う michî ni
mayóù

in a way ある意味では arù imì de wa

in some ways ある面では arù men de wa

no way! (inf) 絶対に駄目だ zettái ni damé dà

by the way ... ところで tokóro dè

「**way in**」(BRIT) 入口 iríguchi

「**way out**」(BRIT) 出口 degúchi

the way back 帰路 kirò

「**give way**」(BRIT: AUT) 進路譲れ shìnro yuzúre

waylay [weilei'] (pt, pp **waylaid**) vt 待伏せする machíbuse suru

wayward [wei'wə:rd] adj (behavior, child) わがままな wagamáma na

W.C. [dʌb'əlju:si:'] (BRIT) n トイレ toìre

we [wi:] pl pron 私たちが〔が〕watákushitàchi wa〔ga〕

weak [wi:k] adj (gen) 弱い yowáì; (dollar, pound) 安い yasúì; (excuse) 下手な hetá nà; (argument) 説得力のない settókuryoku no naì; (tea) 薄い usúi

weaken [wi:'kən] vi (person, resolve) 弱る yowárù; (health) 衰える otóroerù; (influence, power) 劣る otóru

♦vt (person, government) 弱くする yowákù suru

weakling [wi:k'liŋ] n (physically) 虚弱児 kyojákujì; (morally) 骨無し honénashi

weakness [wi:k'nis] n (frailty) 弱さ yowàsa; (fault) 弱点 jakúteñ

**to have a weakness for ...に目がない ...ni me ga naì

wealth [welθ] n (money, resources) 富 tomì, 財産 zaísan; (of details, knowledge etc) 豊富な hốfu na

wealthy [wel'θi:] adj (person, family, country) 裕福な yūfùku na

wean [wi:n] vt (baby) 離乳させる rinyū́ saséru

weapon [wep'ən] n 武器 bukì

wear [we:r] n (use) 使用 shiyó; (damage through use) 消耗 shố̄mō; (clothing): **sportswear** スポーツウェア supốtsùuea

♦vb (pt **wore**, pp **worn**)

♦vt (shirt, blouse, dress etc) 着る kirú; (hat etc) かぶる kabúrù; (shoes, pants, skirt etc) はく hakù; (gloves etc) はめる

haméru; (make-up) つける tsukérù; (damage: through use) 使い古す tsukáifurusù

♦vi (last) 使用に耐える shiyṍ ni taérù; (rub through etc: carpet, shoes, jeans) すり減る surḯheru

babywear 幼児ウェア yṍjìuea

evening wear イブニングウェア ibúningu ueà

wear and tear n 消耗 shố̄mō

wear away vt すり減らす surḯherasu

♦vi (inscription etc) すり減って消える surḯhette kíeru

wear down vt (heels) すり減らす surḯherasu; (person, strength) 弱くする yowákù suru, 弱らせる yowáraserù

wear off vi (pain etc) なくなる nakúnaru

wear out vt (shoes, clothing) 使い古す tsukáifurusù; (person) すっかり疲れさせる sukkárī tsukáresaseru; (strength) なくす nakúsu

weary [wi:r'i:] adj (tired) 疲れ果てた tsukárehatetà; (dispirited) がっかりした gakkárī shita

♦vi: **to weary of** ...に飽きる ...ni akírù

weasel [wi:'zəl] n イタチ itáchi

weather [weð'ə:r] n 天気 teñki, 天候 teñkō

♦vt (storm, crisis) 乗切る noríkirù

under the weather (fig: ill) 気分が悪い kibún ga warúì

weather-beaten [weð'ə:rbi:tən] adj (face, skin, building, stone) 風雪に鍛えられた fū́setsu ni kitáeraretà

weathercock [weð'ə:rkɑ:k] n 風見鶏 kazámidòri

weather forecast n 天気予報 teñkiyohṓ

weatherman [weð'ə:rmæn] (pl **weathermen**) n 天気予報係 teñkiyohōgakarī

weather vane [-vein] n = **weathercock**

weave [wi:v] (pt **wove**, pp **woven**) vt (cloth) 織る orù; (basket) 編む amù

weaver [wi:'və:r] n 機織職人 hatáorishokunin

weaving [wi:'viŋ] n (craft) 機織 hatáori

web [web] *n* (*also*: **spiderweb**) クモの巣 kumó no su; (on duck's foot) 水かき mizúkaki; (network, *also fig*) 網 amí

we'd [wi:d] = **we had; we would**

wed [wed] (*pt, pp* **wedded**) *vt* (marry) ...と結婚する ...to kekkón suru

♦*vi* 結婚する kekkón suru

wedding [wed'iŋ] *n* 結婚式 kekkónshiki

silver/golden wedding (anniversary) 銀〔金〕婚式 giń(kiń)kónshiki

wedding day *n* (day of the wedding) 結婚の日 kekkón no hi; (*US*: anniversary) 結婚記念日 kekkón kinénbi

wedding dress *n* 花嫁衣裳 hanáyome ishṓ, ウエディングドレス uédingudorèsu

wedding present *n* 結婚祝い kekkón iwaì

wedding ring *n* 結婚指輪 kekkón yubíwa

wedge [wedʒ] *n* (of wood etc) くさび kusábi; (of cake) 一切れ hitókirè

♦*vt* (jam with a wedge) くさびで留める kusábi dè toméru; (pack tightly: of people, animals) 押込む oshíkomù

Wednesday [wenz'dei] *n* 水曜日 suíyōbì

wee [wi:] (*SCOTTISH*) *adj* (little) 小さい chíisaì

weed [wi:d] *n* 雑草 zassṓ

♦*vt* (garden) ...の草むしりをする ...no kusámushìri wo suru

weedkiller [wi:d'kilər] *n* 除草剤 josṓzai

weedy [wi:'di:] *adj* (man) 柔そうな yawásō na

week [wi:k] *n* 週間 shūkan

a week today/on Friday 来週の今日〔金曜日〕raíshū no kyṓ(kiń-yōbì)

weekday [wi:k'dei] *n* (*gen, COMM*) 平日 heíjitsu, ウイークデー uíkùdē

weekend [wi:k'end] *n* 週末 shūmátsu, ウイークエンド uíkuèndo

weekly [wi:k'li:] *adv* (deliver etc) 毎週 maíshū

♦*adj* (newspaper) 週刊の shūkan no; (payment) 週払いの shūbarai no; (visit etc) 毎週の maíshū no

♦*n* (magazine) 週刊誌 shūkanshi; (newspaper) 週刊新聞 shūkanshínbun

weep [wi:p] (*pt, pp* **wept**) *vi* (person) 泣く naku

weeping willow [wi:'piŋ-] *n* シダレヤナギ shidáreyanàgi

weigh [wei] *vt* ...の重さを計る ...no omósa wo hakáru

♦*vi* ...の重さは...である ...no omósa wa ...de arù

to weigh anchor いかりを揚げる ikári wo agéru

weigh down *vt* (person, pack animal etc) ...の重さで動きが遅くなる ...no omósa de ugóki ga osóku narù; (*fig*: with worry): *to be weighed down* ...で沈み込む ...de shizúmikomu

weight [weit] *n* (metal object) 重り omóri; (heaviness) 重さ omósa

to lose/put on weight 体重が減る〔増える〕taíjū ga herú(fuéru)

weighting [wei'tiŋ] *n* (*BRIT*) (allowance) 地域手当 chiíkiteatè

weightlifter [weit'liftər] *n* 重量挙げ選手 jūryṓage senshu

weighty [wei'ti:] *adj* (heavy) 重い omói; (important: matters) 重大な jūdai na

weigh up *vt* (person, offer, risk) 評価する hyṓka suru

weir [wi:r] *n* せき sekí

weird [wi:rd] *adj* 奇妙な kimyṓ na

welcome [wel'kəm] *adj* (visitor, suggestion, change) 歓迎すべき kangeisubeki; (news) うれしい ureshii

♦*n* 歓迎 kańgei

♦*vt* (visitor, delegation, suggestion, change) 歓迎する kańgei suru; (be glad of: news) うれしく思う uréshiku omóù

thank you - you're welcome! どうも有難う-どういたしまして dōmò arígàtō - dō itáshimashitè

weld [weld] *n* 溶接 yṓsetsu

♦*vt* 溶接する yṓsetsu suru

welfare [wel'fe:r] *n* (well-being) 幸福 kṓfuku, 福祉 fukúshì; (social aid) 生活保護 seíkatsuhogò

welfare state *n* 福祉国家 fukúshikokkà

welfare work *n* 福祉事業 fukúshijigyṓ

well [wel] *n* (for water) 井戸 idò; (*also*: **oil well**) 油井 yuséi

♦*adv* (to a high standard, thoroughly: *also* for emphasis with adv, adj or prep phrase) よく yokú

♦*adj*: **to be well** (person: in good health) 元気である geñkì de árù

♦*excl* そう、ねぇ sō, nē

as well (in addition) も mo

as well as (in addition to) ...の外に ...no hoká ni

well done! よくやった yokú yattá

get well soon! 早く治ります様に hayákù naórimasu yō nì, お大事に o-dáiji ni

to do well (person) 順調である juñchō de árù; (business) 繁盛する hañjō suru

we'll [wi:l] = **we will; we shall**

well-behaved [welbiheivd'] *adj* (child, dog) 行儀の良い gyṓgi no yoí

well-being [wel'bi:'iŋ] *n* 幸福 kṓfuku, 福祉 fukúshi

well-built [wel'bilt'] *adj* (person) 体格の良い taíkaku no yoí

well-deserved [wel'dizə:rvd'] *adj* (success, prize) 努力相応の doryòkusōō no

well-dressed [wel'drest'] *adj* 身なりの良い mínàri no yoí

well-heeled [wel'hi:ld'] (*inf*) *adj* (wealthy) 金持の kanémochì no

wellingtons [wel'iŋtənz] *npl* (*also:* **wellington boots**) ゴム長靴 gomúnagagutsu

well-known [wel'noun'] *adj* (famous: person, place) 有名な yūmei na

well-mannered [wel'mæn'ə:rd] *adj* 礼儀正しい reígitádashiì

well-meaning [wel'mi:'niŋ] *adj* (person) 善意の zeñ-i no; (offer etc) 善意に基づく zeñ-i ni motózukù

well-off [wel'ɔ:f'] *adj* (rich) 金持の kanémochì no

well-read [wel'red'] *adj* 博学の hakúgaku no

well-to-do [wel'tədu:'] *adj* 金持の kanémochì no

well up *vi* (tears) こみ上げる komíageru

well-wisher [wel'wiʃə:r] *n* (friends, admirers) 支持者 shijìsha, ファン fañ

Welsh [welʃ] *adj* ウェールズの uéruzu no; (LING) ウェールズ語の uéruzugo no

♦*n* (LING) ウェールズ語 uéruzugo

Welsh *npl*: **the Welsh** ウェールズ人 uéruzujin

Welshman/woman [welʃ'mən/wumən] (*pl* **Welshmen/women**) *n* ウェールズ人の男性〔女性〕uéruzujin no dañsei〔josếi〕

Welsh rarebit [-re:r'bit] *n* チーズトースト chīzùtōsùto

went [went] *pt of* **go**

wept [wept] *pt, pp of* **weep**

we're [wi:r] = **we are**

were [wə:r] *pt of* **be**

weren't [wə:r'ənt] = **were not**

west [west] *n* (direction) 西 nishí; (part of country) 西部 seíbu

♦*adj* (wing, coast, side) 西の nishí no, 西側の nishígawa no

♦*adv* (to/towards the west) 西へ nishí e

west wind 西風 nishíkaze

West *n*: **the West** (POL: US plus western Europe) 西洋 seíyō

West Country: **the West Country** (BRIT) *n* 西部地方 seíbuchihō

westerly [wes'tə:rli:] *adj* (point) 西寄りの nishíyori no; (wind) 西からの nishí kara no

western [wes'tə:rn] *adj* (of the west) 西の nishí no; (POL: of the West) 西洋の seíyō no

♦*n* (CINEMA) 西部劇 seíbugeki

West Germany *n* 西ドイツ nishídoitsu

West Indian *adj* 西インド諸島の nishíindoshotō nò

♦*n* 西インド諸島の人 nishíindoshotō no hitó

West Indies [-in'di:z] *npl* 西インド諸島 nishíindoshotō

westward(s) [west'wə:rd(z)] *adv* 西へ nishí e

wet [wet] *adj* (damp) 湿った shiméttà; (wet through) ぬれた nuréta; (rainy: weather, day) 雨模様の amémòyō no

♦*n* (BRIT: POL) 穏健派の人 oñkénha no hitó

to get wet (person, hair, clothes) ぬれる nuréru

「**wet paint**」ペンキ塗立て peñki nurítate

to be a wet blanket (fig) 座を白けさせ

る za wò shirákesaseru

wet suit n ウェットスーツ uéttòsūtsu

we've [wiːv] = **we have**

whack [wæk] vt たたく tatákù

whale [weil] n (ZOOL) クジラ kujíra

wharf [wɔːrf] (pl **wharves**) n 岸壁 gañpeki

wharves [wɔːrvz] npl of **wharf**

KEYWORD

what [wʌt] adj 1 (in direct/indirect questions) 何の náñ no, 何... náñì...

what size is it? サイズは幾つですか sáizu wa íkùtsu desu ká

what color is it? 何色ですか nánì iro desu ká

what shape is it? 形はどうなっていますか katáchi wà dő nattè imásù ká

what books do you need? どんな本がいりますか dóñna hőñ ga irímasù ká

he asked me what books I needed 私にはどんな本がいるかと彼は聞いていました watákushi ni wà dóñna hőñ ga irú kà to kárè wa kiftè imáshīta

2 (in exclamations) 何て... náñte...

what a mess! 何て有様だ náñte arísama dà

what a fool I am! 私は何てばかだ watákushi wà náñte bákà da

◆pron **1** (interrogative) 何 náñ, 何 náñ

what are you doing? 何をしていますか náñì wo shité imasù ká

what is happening? どうなっていますか nattè imásù ká

what's in there? その中に何が入っていますか sonő nakà ni náñì ga hátte imasu ká

what is it? - it's a tool 何ですか−道具です náñ desu ká - dőgu desu

what are you talking about? 何の話ですか náñ no hanáshî desu ká

what is it called? これは何と言いますか kőrè wa náñ to iímasù ká

what about me? 私はどうすればいいんですか watákushi wà dő surèba iíñ desu ká

what about doing ...? ...しませんか ...shimáseñ ká

2 (relative): **is that what happened?** 事件は今話した通りですか jíkèn wa ímà hanáshita tőri desu ká

I saw what you did/was on the table あなたのした事〔テーブルにあった物〕を見ました anátà no shitá kotð〔tèburu ni attá monð〕wo mimáshīta

he asked me what she had said 彼は彼女の言った事を私に尋ねた kárè wa kánòjo no ittá kotð wo watákushi nì tazúnetà

tell me what you're thinking about 今何を考えているか教えて下さい ímà náñì wo kañgaete irù ká oshíete kudasai

what you say is wrong あなたの言っている事は間違っています anátà no itté iru kotð wà machígattè imásù

◆excl (disbelieving) 何 náñì

what, no coffee! 何, コーヒーがないんだって？ náñì, kőhì gà naíñ datté?

I've crashed the car - what! 車をぶつけてしまった−何？ kurúma wò butsúkete shimattà - naní?

---

whatever [wʌtevˈəːr] adj: **whatever book** どんな本でも dóñna hoñ de mo

◆pron: **do whatever is necessary/you want** 何でも必要(好き)な事をしなさい nañ de mo hitsúyō(sukí)na koto wò shinásai

whatever happens 何が起っても naní ga okótte mo

no reason whatever/whatsoever 全く理由がない mattáku riyū ga nai

nothing whatever 全く何もない mattáku nañí mo nai

whatsoever [wʌtsouevˈəːr] adj = **whatever**

wheat [wiːt] n 小麦 komúgi

wheedle [wiːdˈəl] vt: **to wheedle someone into doing something** ...を口車に乗せて...させる ...wo kuchíguruma ni noséte ...sasèru

to wheedle something out of someone 口車に乗せて...を...からだまし取る kuchíguruma ni noséte ...wo ...karà damáshitorù

wheel [wiːl] n (of vehicle etc) 車 kurúma,

車輪 sharín, ホイール hoĭru; (also: **steering wheel**) ハンドル handoru; (NAUT) だ輪 darin

◆*vt* (pram etc) 押す osú

◆*vi* (birds) 旋回する senkai suru; (also: **wheel round**: person) 急に向き直る kyū ni mukináoru

wheelbarrow [wi:l'bærou] *n* 一輪車 ichírìnsha, ネコ車 nekóguruma

wheelchair [wi:l'tʃe:r] *n* 車いす kurúmaisù

wheel clamp *n* (AUT) ◇違反駐車の自動車車輪に付けて走れなくする金具 ihánchūsha no jidôshàsharin ni tsukéte hashírenaku surù kanágu

wheeze [wi:z] *vi* (person) ぜいぜいいう zeízei iú

KEYWORD

when [wen] *adv* いつ ítsù
when did it happen? いつ起ったんですか ítsù okóttaň desu ká
I know when it happened いつ起ったかはちゃんと分かっています ítsù okótta kà wa cháňto wakátté imasù
when are you going to Italy? イタリアにはいつ行きますか itárìa ni wa ítsù ikímasù ká
when will you be back? いつ帰って来ますか ítsù kaétte kimasù ká

◆*conj* 1 (at, during, after the time that) ...する時 ...surú tokî, ...すると ...surú tò, ...したら ...shitárà, ...してから ...shité karà
she was reading when I came in 私が部屋に入った時彼女は本を読んでいました watákushi gà heyá nì háìtta toki kánòjo wa hóň wo yóňde imáshìta
when you've read it, tell me what you think これを読んだらご意見を聞かせて下さい kórè wo yóňdara go-íkèn wo kikásete kudasaì
be careful when you cross the road 道路を横断する時には気を付けてね dôrò wo ôdàn suru tokî ni wa kí wò tsukétè né
that was when I needed you あなたにいて欲しかったのはその時ですよ aná-

tà ni ité hoshikàttà no wa sonô tokî desu yó

2: *(on, at which)*: *on the day when I met him* 彼に会った日は kárè ni áttà hí wà
one day when it was raining 雨が降っていたある日 áme̍ ga futté ità árù hí
3 (whereas): *you said I was wrong when in fact I was right* あなたは私が間違っていると言いましたが,事実は間違っていませんでした anáta wa watákushi gà machígatte irù to iímashita gà, jíjìtsu wa machígattè imásen deshìta
why did you buy that when you can't afford it? 金の余裕がないのになぜあれを買ったんですか kané nò yoyû gà náì no ni názè arè wò kattáň desu ká

---

whenever [wenev'ə:r] *adv* いつか ítsù
◆*conj* (any time) ...するといつも ......surù to itsùmo...; (every time that) ...する度に ...surù tabî ni

where [we:r] *adv* (place, direction) どこ (に, で) dokð (ni, de)
◆*conj* ...の所で〔で〕 ...no tokóro ni〔de〕
this is where ... これは...する所です korè wa ... surù tokoro desu

whereabouts [we:r'əbauts] *adv* どの辺にど donð hen ni
◆*n*: *nobody knows his whereabouts* 彼の居場所は不明だ karè no ibásho wa fuméi da

whereas [we:ræz'] *conj* ...であるのに対して ...de arù no ni taîshite

whereby [we:rbai'] *pron* それによって sorè ni yotté

whereupon [we:rəpɑ:n'] *conj* すると surú to

wherever [we:rev'ə:r] *conj* (no matter where) どこに〔で〕...しても dokð ni〔de〕 ...shite mo; (not knowing where) どこに ...か知らないが dokð ni ...ká shiranai ga
◆*adv* (interrogative: surprise) 一体全体どこに〔で〕 ittái zentai dokð ni〔de〕

wherewithal [we:r'wiθɔ:l] *n* 金 kané

whet [wet] *vt* (appetite) そそる sosóru

whether [weð'ə:r] *conj* ...かどうか ...ka dô kà

I don't know whether to accept or not 引受けるべきかどうかは分からない hikfukerubeki kà dô kà wa wakáranài
whether you go or not 行くにしても行かないにしても ikú nì shité mò ikánai nì shité mò
it's doubtful whether he will come 彼はたぶん来ないだろう karè wa tabùn konâi darō

KEYWORD

which [witʃ] *adj* **1** (interrogative: direct, indirect) どの dóndo, どちらの dóchìra no
which picture do you want? どちらの絵がいいんですか dóchìra no é gà iíñ desu ká
which books are yours? あなたの本はどれとどれですか anátà no hóñ wa dôre to dôre desu ká
tell me which picture/books you want どの絵〔本〕が欲しいか言って下さい dóndo é〔hóñ〕gà hoshíì kà itté kudasaì
which one? どれ dôre
which one do you want? どれが欲しいんですか dôre ga hoshíìñ desu ká
which one of you did it? あなたたちのだれがやったんですか anátà tachi no dárè ga yattáñ desu ká
2: *in which case* その場合 sonó baài
the train may be late, in which case don't wait up 列車が遅れるかもしれないが，その場合先に寝て下さい rèsshà ga okúreru ka mò shirénaì ga, sonó baài sakí ni netê kudasaì
by which time その時 sonó tokì
we got there at 8 pm, by which time the cinema was full 映画館に着いたのは夜の8時でしたが，もう満席になっていました eígakàn ni tsúìta no wa yórùno hachíjí deshita ga, mô mañseki ni nattê imashìta

♦*pron* **1** (interrogative) どれ dôre
which (of these) are yours? どれとどれがあなたの物ですか dôre to dôre ga anátà no monó desù ká
which of you are coming? あなたたちのだれとだれが一緒に来てくれますか a-nátàtachi no dárè to dárè ga ísshò ni

kité kuremasù ká
here are the books/files - tell me which you want 本〔ファイル〕はこれだけありますが，どれとどれが欲しいんですか hóñ〔fáìru〕wa korê dakè arímasù ga, dôre to dôre ga hoshíìñ desu ká
I don't mind which どれでもいいんですよ dôre de mo iíñ desu yô
2 (relative): *the apple which you ate/which is on the table* あなたの食べた〔テーブルにある〕りんご anátà no tábèta〔tèburu ni árù〕ríñgo
the meeting (which) we attended 私たちが出席した会議 watákushitàchi ga shussèki shitâ kâìgi
the chair on which you are sitting あなたが座っているいす anátà ga suwátte irù ísu
the book of which you spoke あなたが話していた本 anátà ga hanáshite itâ hóñ
he said he knew, which is true/I feared 彼は知っていると言ったが，その通りでした〔私の心配していた通りでした〕kárè wa shitté irù to ittá gà, sonó tòri deshita〔watákushi nò shiñpai shite ita tòri deshita〕
after which その後 sonó atò

---

whichever [witʃev'əːr] *adj*: *take whichever book you prefer* どれでもいいから好きな本を取って下さい dôre de mo iî kara sukí nà hon wo tottê kudasaì
whichever book you take あなたがどの本を取っても anátà ga donò hon wo tottê mo

whiff [wif] *n* (of perfume, gasoline, smoke) ちょっと...のにおいがすること chottô ...no nióì ga suru koto

while [wail] *n* (period of time) 間 aída
♦*conj* (at the same time as) ...する間 ...surú aida; (as long as) ...する限りは ...surú kagìri wa; (although) ...するにもかかわらず ...surú nì mo kakáwaràzu
for a while しばらくの間 shibáràku no aída

while away *vt* (time) つぶす tsubúsu

whim [wim] *n* 気まぐれ kimágure

whimper [wim'pə:r] *n* (cry, moan) 哀れっぽい泣き声 awáreppoî nakígoè
♦*vi* (child, animal) 哀れっぽい泣き声を出す awáreppoî nakígoè wo dasù

whimsical [wim'zikəl] *adj* (person) 気まぐれな kimágure na; (poem) 奇抜な kibátsu na; (look, smile) 変な heñ na

whine [wain] *n* (of pain) 哀れっぽい泣き声 awáreppoî nakígoè; (of engine, siren) うなり unári
♦*vi* (person, animal) 哀れっぽい泣き声を出す awáreppoî nakígoè wo dasù; (engine, siren) うなる unárù; (*fig*: complain) 愚痴をこぼす guchí wo kobósù

whip [wip] *n* (lash, riding whip) むち muchî; (POL) 院内幹事 iñnaikàñji
♦*vt* (person, animal) むち打つ muchíutsù; (cream, eggs) 泡立てる awádaterù, ホイップする hoîppù suru; (move quickly): *to whip something out/off* さっと取出す〔はずす，脱ぐ〕sattó torídasu〔hazúsu, nugù〕

whipped cream [wipt-] *n* ホイップクリーム hoîppukurîmù

whip-round [wip'raund] (*BRIT*) *n* 募金 bokíñ

whirl [wə:rl] *vt* (arms, sword etc) 振回す furímawasù
♦*vi* (dancers) ぐるぐる回る gurùguru mawárù; (leaves, water etc) 渦巻く uzúmakù

whirlpool [wə:rl'pu:l] *n* 渦巻 uzúmàki

whirlwind [wə:rl'wind] *n* 竜巻 tatsúmaki

whir(r) [wə:r] *vi* (motor etc) うなり unári

whisk [wisk] *n* (CULIN) 泡立て器 awádatekî
♦*vt* (cream, eggs) 泡立てる awádaterù
to whisk someone away/off ...を素早く連去る ...wo subáyakù tsuresarù

whiskers [wis'kə:rz] *npl* (of animal, man) ひげ higé

whiskey [wis'ki:] (*BRIT* **whisky**) *n* ウイスキー uîsukî

whisper [wis'pə:r] *n* (low voice) ささやき sasáyaki
♦*vi* ささやく sasáyakù

♦*vt* ささやく sasáyakù

whist [wist] (*BRIT*) *n* ホイスト hoísuto

whistle [wis'əl] *n* (sound) 口笛 kuchíbue; (object) 笛 fué
♦*vi* (person) 口笛を吹く kuchíbue wo fukù; (bird) ぴーぴーさえずる pîpî saézurù; (bullet) ぴゅーと unárù; (kettle) ぴゅーと鳴る pyû to narú

white [wait] *adj* (color) 白い shiróî; (pale: person, face) 青白い aójiroî; (with fear) 青ざめた aózamèta
♦*n* (color) 白 shirò; (person) 白人 hakújin; (of egg) 白身 shirómî

white coffee (*BRIT*) *n* ミルク入りコーヒー mirúkuirikōhī

white-collar worker [wait'kɑ:l'ə:r-] *n* サラリーマン sarárīmàn, ホワイトカラー howáitokarà

white elephant *n* (*fig*) 無用の長物 muyô no chōbutsu

white lie *n* 方便のうそ hōbèn no usò

white paper *n* (POL) 白書 hakùsho

whitewash [wait'wɑːʃ] *n* (paint) のろ norò ◇石灰, 白亜, のりを水に混ぜた塗料 sekkài, hakùa, norí wo mizú ni mazèta toryò
♦*vt* (building) ...にのろを塗る ...ni norò wo nurù; (*fig*: happening, career, reputation) ...の表面を繕う ...no hyômeñ wo tsukúroù

whiting [wai'tiŋ] *n inv* (fish) タラ tarà

Whitsun [wit'sən] *n* 聖霊降臨節 seírei-kōriñsetsu

whittle [wit'əl] *vt*: *to whittle away, whittle down* (costs: reduce) 減らす herásu

whiz(z) [wiz] *vi*: *to whizz past/by* (person, vehicle etc) ぴゅーんと通り過ぎる byûn to tōrisugirù

whiz(z) kid (*inf*) *n* 天才 teñsai

KEYWORD
---

who [hu:] *pron* **1** (interrogative) だれ dárè, どなた dónàta
who is it?, who's there? だれですか dárè desu ká
who are you looking for? だれを捜しているんですか dárè wo sagáshite irùñ

desu ká
I told her who I was 彼女に名乗りました kánojo ni nanórimashìta
I told her who was coming to the party パーティの出席予定者を彼女に知らせました pāti no shussékiyoteìsha wo kánòjo ni shirásemashìta
who did you see? だれを見ましたか dárè wo mimáshìta ká

2 (relative): *my cousin who lives in New York* ニューヨークに住んでいるいとこ nyúỹoku ni súñde iru itókò
the man/woman who spoke to me 私に話しかけた男性（女性）watákushi nì hanáshikaketà dañsei(josèi)
those who can swim 泳げる人たち oyógerù hitótàchi

whodunit [hu:dʌn'it] (inf) n 探偵小説 tañteishōsètsu

whole [houl] adj (entire) 全体の zeñtai no; (not broken) 無傷の mukīzu no
♦n (entire unit) 全体 zeñtai no; (all): *the whole of* 全体の zeñtai no
the whole of the town 町全体 machízeñtai
on the whole, as a whole 全体として zeñtai toshite

whole food(s) [houl'fu:d(z)] n(pl) 無加工の食べ物 mukákò no tabémonò

wholehearted [houl'hɑːr'tid] adj (agreement etc) 心からの kokóro kàra no

wholemeal [houl'mi:l] adj (bread, flour) 全粒の zeñryū no, 全麦の zeñbaku no

wholesale [houl'seil] n (business) 卸 oróshi, 卸売 oróshiuri
♦adj (price) 卸の oróshi nò; (destruction) 大規模の daíkibò no
♦adv (buy, sell) 卸で oróshi dè

wholesaler [houl'seilə:r] n 問屋 toñ-ya

wholesome [houl'səm] adj (food, climate) 健康に良い keñkō ni yoì; (person) 健全な keñzen na

wholewheat [houl'wi:t] adj = wholemeal

wholly [hou'li:] adv (completely) 完全に kañzen ni

whom [hu:m] pron 1 (interrogative) だれを dárè wo, どなたを dónata wo
whom did you see? だれを見ましたか dárè wo mimáshìta ká
to whom did you give it? だれに渡しましたか dárè ni watáshimashìta ká
tell me from whom you received it だれに〔から〕それをもらったかを教えて下さい dárè ni〔kárà〕soré wò morátta kà wo oshíete kudasaì

2 (relative): *the man whom I saw/to whom I spoke* 私が見た〔話し掛けた〕男性 watákushi gà mítà〔hanáshikaketà〕dañsei
the lady with whom I was talking 私と話していた女性 watákushi tò hanáshite itá josèi

whooping cough [wu:'piŋ-] n 百日ぜき hyakúnichizèki

whore [hɔ:r] (inf: pej) n 売女 baíta

whose [hu:z] adj 1 (possessive: interrogative) だれの dárè no, どなたの dónata no
whose book is this?, whose is this book? これはだれの本ですか koré wà dárè no hóñ desu ká
whose pencil have you taken? だれの鉛筆を持って来たんですか dárè no eñpitsu wò motté kitañ desu ká
whose daughter are you? あなたはどなたの娘さんですか anátà wa dónata no musúme-sañ desu ká
I don't know whose it is だれの物か私には分かりません dárè no monó kà watákushi ni wà wakárimaseñ

2 (possessive: relative): *the man whose son you rescued* あなたが助けた子供の父親 anátà ga tasúketa kodomò no chíchioya
the girl whose sister you were speaking to あなたと話していた女性の妹 anátà to hanáshite itá josèi no imótò
the woman whose car was stolen 車を盗まれた女性 kurúma wò nusúmareta

joséi

♦*pron* だれの物 dárè no monó, どなたの物 dónàta no monó

whose is this? これはだれのですか kó-rè wa dárè no desu ká

I know whose it is だれの物か知っています dárè no monó kà shitté imasù

whose are these? これらはだれの物ですか korérà wa dárè no monó desù ká

KEYWORD

why [wai] *adv* なぜ názè, どうして dóshìte

why is he always late? どうして彼はいつも遅刻するのですか dóshìte kárè wa ítsùmo chikóku suru nò desu ká

why don't you come too? あなたも来ませんか anátà mo kimásèn ká

I'm not coming - why not? 私は行きません-どうしてですか watákushi wà i-kímasèn - dóshìte desu ká

fancy a drink? - why not? 一杯やろうか-いいね íppài yárò ká - íi né

why not do it now? 今すぐやりません か ímà súgù yarímasèn ká

♦*conj* なぜ názè, どうして dóshìte

I wonder why he said that どうしてそんな事を言ったのかしら dóshìte sofina kotó wo ittá nò kashira

the reason why 理由 riyú

that's not (the reason) why I'm here 私が来たのはそのためじゃありません watákushi gà kitá no wà sonó tamè ja arímasèn

♦*excl* (expressing surprise, shock, annoyance etc)◇日本語では表現しない場合が多い nihóngo de wà hyógen shinaí baái gà ói

why, it's you! おや、あなたでしたか oyà, anátà deshita ka

why, that's impossible/quite unacceptable! そんな事はできません〔認められません〕sofina kotó wà dekímasèn〔mítōmeraremasèn〕

I don't understand - why, it's obvious! 訳が分かりません-ばかでも分る事だよ wákè ga wakárimasèn - bákà de

mo wakárù kotó dà yó

whyever [waiev'ə:r] *adv* 一体なぜ ittai názè

wicked [wik'id] *adj* (crime, man, witch) 極悪の gokúaku no; (smile) 意地悪そうな ijíwarusō na

wickerwork [wik'ə:rwə:rk] *adj* (basket, chair etc) 籐編みの tõami no, 枝編みの edáami no

♦*n* (objects) 籐編み細工品 tõamizaikuhin, 枝編み細工品 edáamizaikuhin

wicket [wik'it] *n* (CRICKET: stumps) 三柱門 sañchūmòn, ウイケット uíkètto; (: grass area) ピッチ pitchì

◇2つのウイケット間のグランド futátsu nò uíkettokàn no guráñdo

wide [waid] *adj* (gen) 広い hiróì; (grin) 楽しげな tanóshìge na

♦*adv*: *to open wide* (window etc) 広く開ける hiróku akéru

to shoot wide ねらいを外す nerái wo hazúsu

wide-angle lens [waid'æŋ'gəl-] *n* 広角レンズ kõkaku reñzu

wide-awake [waid'əweik'] *adj* すっかり目が覚めた sukkárì me gà saméta

widely [waid'li:] *adv* (gen) 広く hiróku; (differing) 甚だしく hanáhadashikù

widen [wai'dən] *vt* (road, river, experience) 広くする hiróku suru, 広げる hiró-geru

♦*vi* (road, river, gap) 広くなる hiróku narù, 広がる hirógaru

wide open *adj* (window, eyes, mouth) 大きく開けた ōkìku akéta

widespread [waidspred'] *adj* (belief etc) はびこった habíkottà

widow [wid'ou] *n* 未亡人 mibójìn, 後家 goké

widowed [wid'oud] *adj* (mother, father) やもめになった yamóme ni nattà

widower [wid'ouə:r] *n* 男やもめ otóko-yamòme

width [widθ] *n* (distance) 広さ hirósa; (of cloth) 幅 habá

wield [wi:ld] *vt* (sword, power) 振るう fu-rúu

wife [waif] (pl **wives**) n (gen) 妻 tsumá; (one's own) 家内 kanái; (someone else's) 奥さん okùsan

wig [wig] n かつら katsúra

wiggle [wig'əl] vt (hips) くねらす kunérasù; (ears etc) ぴくぴく動かす pikúpiku ugókasù

wild [waild] adj (animal, plant) 野生の yaséi no; (rough: land) 荒れ果てた aréhatèta; (: weather, sea) 荒れ狂う arékuruú; (person, behavior, applause) 興奮 した kōfun shita; (idea) 突飛な toppí na; (guess) 当てずっぽうの atézuppō no

wilderness [wil'də:rnis] n 荒野 kōyá, 原野 geñ-ya, 未開地 mikáichì

wild-goose chase [waild'gus'-] n (fig) 無駄な捜索 mudá na sōsaku

wildlife [waild'laif] n (animals) 野生動物 yaséidōbùtsu

wildly [waild'li:] adv (behave) 狂った様 に kurúttà yō ni; (applaud) 熱狂的に nekkyōteki ni; (hit) めくら滅法に mekúrameppō ni; (guess) 当てずっぽうに atézuppō ni; (happy) 最高に saíkō ni

wilds [waildz] npl 荒野 kōyá, 原野 geñ-ya, 未開地 mikáichì

wilful [wil'fəl] (US also: **willful**) adj (obstinate: child, character) わがままな wagámamà na; (deliberate: action, disregard etc) 故意の koí no

---

KEYWORD

---

will [wil] (vt: pt, pp **willed**) aux vb 1 (forming future tense): *I will finish it tomorrow* 明日終ります ashíta owárimasù

I will have finished it by tomorrow 明日にでもなれば終るでしょう asú ni dè mo nárèba owárù deshō

will you do it? - yes I will/no I won't やりますか−はい，やります〔いいえ，やりません〕 yarímasù ká - háì, yarímasù〔iíè, yarímaseñ〕

when will you finish it? いつ終りますか itsú owárimasù ká

2 (in conjectures, predictions): *he will/he'll be there by now* 彼はもう着いているでしょう kárè wa mō tsúite irú de-

shō

that will be the postman 郵便屋さんでしょう yūbinya-san deshō

this medicine will help you この薬なら効くでしょう konó kusuri narà kikú deshō

this medicine won't help you この薬は何の役にも立ちません konó kusuri wà nañ no yakú ni mò tachímaseñ

3 (in commands, requests, offers): *will you be quiet!* 黙りなさい damárinasaì

will you come? 来てくれますか kitè kuremasù ká

will you help me? 手伝ってくれますか tetsúdattè kurémasù ká

will you have a cup of tea? お茶をいかがですか o-chá wò ikága desù ká

I won't put up with it! 我慢できません gámàn dekímaseñ

♦vt: *to will someone to do something* 意志の力で...に...をさせようとする íshì no chikára dè ...ni ...wò saséyō to suru

he willed himself to go on 彼は精神力だけで続けようとした kárè wa seíshinryòku dakè dè tsuzúkeyō to shita

♦n (volition) 意志 íshì; (testament) 遺言 yuígon

---

willful [wil'fəl] (US) adj = **wilful**

willing [wil'iŋ] adj (with goodwill) 進んで...する susúnde ...surù; (enthusiastic) 熱心な nesshíñ na

he's willing to do it 彼はそれを引き受けてくれるそうです kárè wa soré wo hikíukète kureru sō dèsu

willingly [wil'iŋli:] adv 進んで susúnde

willingness [wil'iŋnis] n 好意 kōí

willow [wil'ou] n ヤナギ yanági

willpower [wil'pauə:r] n 精神力 seíshiñryoku

willy-nilly [wil'i:nil'i:] adv 否応なしに iyáō nashì ni

wilt [wilt] vi (flower, plant) 枯れる karéru

wily [wai'li:] adj (fox, move, person) ずる賢い zurúgashikoì

win [win] n (in sports etc) 勝利 shōrí, 勝ち kachí

♦vb (pt, pp **won**)

♦vt (game, competition) ...で 勝 つ ...de katsù; (election) ...で当選する ...de tōsen suru; (obtain: prize, medal) もらう moráu, 受ける ukérù; (money) 当てる atérù; (support, popularity) 獲得する kakútoku suru

♦vi 勝つ katsù

wince [wins] vi 顔がこわばる kaó ga kowábaru

winch [wintʃ] n ウインチ uínchi

wind[1] [wind] n (air) 風 kazé; (MED) 呼吸 kokyū́; (breath) 息 ikí

♦vt (take breath away from) ...の息を切らせる ...no ikí wo kiráserù

wind[2] [waind] (pt, pp **wound**) vt (roll: thread, rope) 巻く makú; (wrap: bandage) 巻付ける makítsukerù; (clock, toy) ...のぜんまいを巻く ...no zeñmai wo makú

♦vi (road, river) 曲りくねる magárikunerù

windfall [wind'fɔːl] n (money) 棚ぼた tanábota

winding [wain'diŋ] adj (road) 曲りくねった magárikunettà; (staircase) らせん状の raséñjō no

wind instrument n (MUS) 管楽器 kañgakki

windmill [wind'mil] n 風車 kazágurùma

window [win'dou] n 窓 madò

window box n ウインドーボックス uíndōbokkùsu

window cleaner n (person) 窓ふき職人 madófukishokùnin

window envelope n 窓付き封筒 madótsukifutð

window ledge n 窓下枠 madóshitawàku

window pane n 窓ガラス madógarasu

window-shopping [win'douʃa:piŋ] n ウインドーショッピング uíndōshoppìngu

windowsill [win'dousil] n 窓下枠 madóshitawàku

windpipe [wind'paip] n 気管 kikán

windscreen [wind'skri:n] (BRIT) n = **windshield**

windshield [wind'ʃi:ld] (US) n フロント

ガラス furóntogaràsu, ウインドシールド uíndoshīrùdo

windshield washer n ウインドシールドワシャー uíndoshīrudowashā̀

windshield wiper [-waip'ə:r] n ワイパー waìpā

windswept [wind'swept] adj (place) 吹きさらしの fukísarashi no; (person) 風で髪が乱れた kazé de kamí gà midárèta

wind up vt (clock, toy) ...のぜんまいを巻く ...no zeñmai wo makú; (debate) 終りにする owári ni suru

windy [win'di:] adj (weather, day) 風の強い kazé no tsuyoì

it's windy 風が強い kazé ga tsuyoì

wine [wain] n ブドウ酒 budōshu, ワイン waìn

wine bar n ワインバー waínbā

wine cellar n ワインの地下貯蔵庫 waìn no chikáchozōkð

wine glass n ワイングラス waínguràsu

wine list n ワインリスト waínrisùto

wine merchant n ワイン商 waíñshð

wine waiter n ソムリエ somúrie

wing [wiŋ] n (of bird, insect, plane) 羽根 hané, 翼 tsubása; (of building) 翼 yokú; (BRIT: AUT) フェンダー feñdá

winger [wiŋ'ə:r] n (SPORT) ウイング uíñgu

wings [wiŋz] npl (THEATER) そで sodé

wink [wiŋk] n (of eye) ウインク uíñku

♦vi (with eye) ウインクする uíñku suru; (light etc) 瞬く matátakù

winner [win'ə:r] n (of prize, race, competition) 勝者 shōshà

winning [win'iŋ] adj (team, competitor, entry) 勝った kattà; (shot, goal) 決勝の kesshṓ no; (smile) 愛敬たっぷりの aíkyō tappúrì no

winnings [win'iŋz] npl 賞金 shōkin

win over vt (person: persuade) 味方にする mikáta ni suru

win round (BRIT) vt = **win over**

winter [win'tə:r] n (season) 冬 fuyú

in winter 冬には fuyú nì wa

winter sports npl ウインタースポーツ uíñtāsupòtsù

wintry [win'tri:] adj (weather, day) 冬々

しい fuyúrashiì

wipe [waip] n: *to give something a wipe* ...をふく ...wo fukú

♦vt (rub) ふく fukú; (erase: tape) 消す kesú

wipe off vt (remove) ふき取る fukítorù

wipe out vt (debt) 完済する kańsai suru; (memory) 忘れる wasúreru; (destroy: city, population) 滅ぼす horóbosù

wipe up vt (mess) ふき取る fukítorù

wire [waiˈəːr] n (metal etc) 針金 harígane; (ELEC) 電線 deñsen; (telegram) 電報 deñpō

♦vt (house) ...の配線工事をする ...no haísenkōjì wo suru; (also: **wire up**: electrical fitting) 取付ける torítsukerù; (person: telegram) ...に電報を打つ ...ni deñpō wo utsù

wireless [waiˈəːrlis] (BRIT) n ラジオ rajìo

wiring [waiəˈrːiŋ] n (ELEC) 配線 haísen

wiry [waiəˈrːiˈ] adj (person) やせて強じんな yasè de kyójin na; (hair) こわい kowáì

wisdom [wizˈdəm] n (of person) 知恵 chié; (of action, remark) 適切さ tekísetsusa

wisdom tooth n 親知らず óyashiràzu

wise [waiz] adj (person, action, remark) 賢い kashíkoì, 賢明な keñmei na

...wise suffix: *timewise/moneywise etc* 時間〔金銭〕的に jikán(kíñsen)teki ni

wisecrack [waizˈkræk] n 皮肉な冗談 hiñku na jōdañ

wish [wiʃ] n (desire) 望み nozómi, 希望 kibō; (specific) 望みの物 nozómi no mono

♦vt (want) 望む nozómù, 希望する kibō suru

best wishes (for birthday, etc) おめでとう omédetō

with best wishes (in letter) お体をお大事に o-kárada wo o-dáiji ni

to wish someone goodbye ...に別れのあいさつを言う ...ni wakáre no aísatsu wo iu, ...にさよならを言う ...ni sayónarà wo iu

he wished me well 彼は「成功を祈る」と言いました karè wa 「seíkō wo inorù」to iímashìta

to wish to do ...したいと思う ...shitáì to omóù

to wish someone to do something ...に...してもらいたいと思う ...ni ...shité moraitaì to omóù

to wish for ...が欲しいと思う ...ga hoshíì to omóù

wishful [wiʃˈfəl] adj: *it's wishful thinking* その考えは甘い sonó kangaè wa amáì, それは有り得ない事だ soré wa aríenaì kotó dà

wishy-washy [wiʃˈiːwɑːʃiː] (inf) adj (color) 薄い usúì; (ideas, person) 迫力のない hakúryoku no naì

wisp [wisp] n (of grass, hair) 小さな束 chíìsana tabà; (of smoke) 一筋 hitósùji

wistful [wistˈfəl] adj (look, smile) 残念そうな zañnensō na

wit [wit] n (wittiness) ユーモア yūmòa, ウイット uíttò; (intelligence: also: **wits**) 知恵 chié; (person) ウイットのある人 uíttò no aru hito

witch [witʃ] n 魔女 majò

witchcraft [witʃˈkræft] n 魔術 majùtsu

witch-hunt [witʃˈhʌnt] n (fig) 魔女狩り majógari

KEYWORD

---

with [wiθ] prep 1 (accompanying, in the company of) ...と...に, ...と一緒に ...to íssho ni

I was with him 私は彼と一緒にいました watákushi wà kárè to íssho ni imáshìta

we stayed with friends 私たちは友達の家に泊りました watákushitàchi wa tomódachi nò ié nì tomárimashìta

we'll take the children with us 子供たちを一緒に連れて行きます kodómotàchi wo ísshò ni tsurête ikimasù

mix the sugar with the eggs 砂糖を卵に混ぜて下さい satō wò tamágo nì mázète kudásaì

I'll be with you in a minute 直ぐ行きますからお待ち下さい súgu ikímasu karà o-máchi kudásaì

I'm with you (I understand) 分かります wakárimasù

to be with it (*inf*: up-to-date) 現代的である geñdaiteki de árù; (: alert) 抜け目がない nukéme gà náì

2 (descriptive): *a room with a view* 見晴らしのいい部屋 mihárashi nò fi heyá

the man with the grey hat/blue eyes 灰色の帽子をかぶった〔青い目をした〕男 hafíiro nò bôshi wò kabútta〔aóì mé nò〕otôko

3 (indicating manner, means, cause): *with tears in her eyes* 目に涙を浮かべながら mé nì námìda wo ukábènagara

to walk with a stick つえをついて歩く tsúè wo tsuíte arúkù

red with anger 怒りで顔を真っ赤にして ikári dè kaó wò makká ni shitè

to shake with fear 恐怖で震える kyôfu dè furúerù

to fill something with water ...を水で一杯にする ...wò mizú dè ippái nì suru

you can open the door with this key このかぎでドアを開けられます konó kagí dè dôa wo akéraremasù

withdraw [wiðdrɔː'] (*pt* **withdrew** *pp* **withdrawn**) *vt* (object) 取出す torídasu; (offer, remark) 取消す toríkesu, 撤回する tekkái suru

♦*vi* (troops) 撤退する tettái suru; (person) 下がる sagárù

to withdraw money (from the bank) 金を引出す kané wo hikidasù

withdrawal [wiðdrɔː'əl] *n* (of offer, remark) 撤回 tekkái; (of troops) 撤退 tettái; (of services) 停止 teíshi; (of participation) 取りやめる事 toríyameru koto; (of money) 引出し hikídashi

withdrawal symptoms *n* (MED) 禁断症状 kiñdanshòjō

withdrawn [wiðdrɔː'n] *adj* (person) 引っ込みがちな hikkómigachi na

wither [wið'əːr] *vi* (plant) 枯れる karéru

withhold [wiθhould'] (*pt*, *pp* **withheld**) *vt* (tax etc) 源泉徴収する geñsenchōshū suru; (permission) 拒む kobámù; (information) 隠す kakúsù

within [wiðin'] *prep* (inside: referring to place, time, distance) ...以内に〔で〕...ínài ni〔de〕

♦*adv* (inside) 中の nakà no

within reach (of) (...に) 手が届く所に〔で〕(...ni) té gà todókù tokoro ni〔de〕

within sight (of) (...が) 見える所に〔で〕(...ga) miérù tokoro ni〔de〕

within the week 今週中に koñshūchū ni

within a mile of ...の1マイル以内に ...no ichímairu ìnài ni

without [wiðaut'] *prep* ...なしで ...nashì de

without a coat コートなしで kōtò nashì de

without speaking 何も言わないで naní mo iwanáìde

to go without something ...なしで済ます ...nashì de sumásù

withstand [wiθstænd'] (*pt*, *pp* **withstood**) *vt* (winds, attack, pressure) ...に耐える ...ni taérù

witness [wit'nis] *n* (person who sees) 目撃者 mokúgekishà; (person who countersigns document: *also* LAW) 証人 shônin

♦*vt* (event) 見る mirù, 目撃する mokúgeki suru; (document) 保証人として...にサインする hoshônin toshite ...ni saîn suru

to bear witness to (*fig*: offer proof of) ...を証明する ...wo shômei suru

witness stand (*BRIT* **witness box**) *n* 証人席 shônìnseki

witticism [wit'əsizəm] *n* (remark) 冗談 jôdañ

witty [wit'i:] *adj* (person) ウイットのある uíttò no arù; (remark etc) おどけた odôketa

wives [waivz] *npl of* **wife**

wizard [wiz'əːrd] *n* 魔法使い mahôtsukài

wk *abbr* = **week**

wobble [wɑːb'əl] *vi* (legs) よろめく yorómekù; (chair) ぐらぐらする gurágura suru; (jelly) ぷるぷるする purúpuru suru

woe [wou] *n* 悲しみ kanáshimi

woke [wouk] *pt of* **wake**

woken [wou'kən] *pp of* **wake**

wolf [wulf] (*pl* **wolves**) *n* オオカミ ôkami

wolves [wulvz] *npl of* **wolf**

woman [wum'ən] (*pl* **women**) *n* 女 ofína, 女性 joséi

woman doctor *n* 女医 joí

womanly [wum'ənli:] *adj* (virtues etc) 女性らしい joséirashii

womb [wu:m] *n* (ANAT) 子宮 shikyǔ

women [wim'in] *pl of* **woman**

women's lib [wim'ənzlib'] (*inf*) *n* ウーマンリブ ǔmanribù

won [wʌn] *pt, pp of* **win**

wonder [wʌn'dəːr] *n* (miracle) 不思議 fushígi; (feeling) 驚異 kyōí

♦*vi*: **to wonder whether/why** ...かしら〔なぜ...かしら〕と思う ...ka shira〔nazè ...ka shira〕to omóù

to wonder at (marvel at) ...に驚く ...ni odórokù

to wonder about ...の事を考える ...no kotō wò kangaèru

it's no wonder (that) ... (という事) は不思議ではない ... (to iú koto) wà fushígi de wà naí

wonderful [wʌn'dəːrfəl] *adj* (excellent) 素晴しい subárashiì; (miraculous) 不思議な fushígi na

wonderfully [wʌn'dəːrfəli:] *adv* (excellently) 素晴しく subárashikù; (miraculously) 不思議に fushígi ni

won't [wount] = **will not**

woo [wu:] *vt* (woman) ...に言い寄る ...ni iíyorù; (audience etc) ...にこびる ...ni kobírù

wood [wud] *n* (timber) 木材 mokúzài, 木 ki; (forest) 森 morí, 林 hayáshi, 木立 kodáchi

wood carving *n* (act, object) 木彫 kibóri

wooded [wud'id] *adj* (slopes, area) 木の茂った kí nò shigéttà

wooden [wud'ən] *adj* (object) 木でできた kí dè dekita, 木製の mokúsei no; (house) 木造の mokúzò no; (fig: performance, actor) でくの坊の様な dekúnobō no yō nà

woodpecker [wud'pekəːr] *n* キツツキ kitsútsukì

woodwind [wud'wind] *npl* (MUS) 木管楽器 mokkángakkì

woodwork [wud'wəːrk] *n* (skill) 木材工芸 mokúzaikōgèi

woodworm [wud'wəːrm] *n* キクイムシ kikúimùshi

wool [wul] *n* (material, yarn) 毛糸 keíto, ウール ǔrù

to pull the wool over someone's eyes (*fig*) ...をだます ...wo damásù

woolen [wul'ən] (*BRIT* **woollen**) *adj* (socks, hat etc) 毛糸の keíto no, ウールの ǔrù no

the woolen industry 羊毛加工業界 yōmōkakōgyōkài

woolens [wul'ənz] *npl* 毛糸衣類 keítoirùi

wooly [wul'i:] (*BRIT* **woolly**) *adj* (socks, hat etc) 毛糸の keíto no, ウールの ǔrù no; (*fig*: ideas) 取留めのない torítome no naì; (person) 考え方のはっきりしない kañgaekatà no hakkírì shinái

word [wəːrd] *n* (unit of language: written, spoken) 語 go, 単語 tañgo, 言葉 kotóba; (promise) 約束 yakúsoku; (news) 知らせ shiráse, ニュース nyūsù

♦*vt* (letter, message) ...の言回しを選ぶ ...no iímawashi wo erábù

in other words 言替えると iíkaerù to

to break/keep one's word 約束を破る〔守る〕yakúsoku wo yabúrù(mamórù)

to have words with someone ...と口げんかをする ...to kuchígeñka wo suru

wording [wəːr'diŋ] *n* (of message, contract etc) 言回し iímawashi

word processing *n* ワードプロセシング wǎdopuroseshìngu

word processor [-praˈsesəːr] *n* ワープロ wǎpuro

wore [wɔːr] *pt of* **wear**

work [wəːrk] *n* (*gen*) 仕事 shigóto; (job) 職 shokú; (ART, LITERATURE) 作品 sakúhin

♦*vi* (person: labor) 働く határaku; (mechanism) 動く ugókù; (be successful: medicine etc) 効く kikú

♦*vt* (clay, wood etc) 加工する kakô suru; (land) 耕す tagáyasù; (mine) 採掘する saíkutsu suru; (machine) 動かす ugókasù; (cause: effect) もたらす motárasù; (: miracle) 行う okónau

to be out of work 失業中である shitsúgyōchū de arù

to work loose (part) 緩む yurúmù; (knot) 解ける tokérù

workable [wəːr'kəbəl] *adj* (solution) 実行可能な jikkṓkanō na

workaholic [wəːrkəhɔːl'ik] *n* 仕事中毒の人 shigótochūdòku no hito, ワーカホリック wākahorìkku

worker [wəːr'kəːr] *n* 労働者 rṓdōsha

workforce [wəːrk'fɔːrs] *n* 労働人口 rṓdōjinkṓ

working class [wəːr'kiŋ-] *n* 労働者階級 rṓdōshakaìkyū

working-class [wəːr'kiŋklæs] *adj* 労働者階級の rṓdōshakaìkyū no

working order *n*: **in working order** ちゃんと動く状態で chańto ugokù jṓtai de

workman [wəːrk'mən] (*pl* **workmen**) *n* 作業員 sagyṓìn

workmanship [wəːrk'mənʃip] *n* (skill) 腕前 udémae

work on *vt fus* (task) ...に取組む ...ni toríkumu; (person: influence) 説得する settóku suru; (principle) ...に基づく ...ni motṓzukù

work out *vi* (plans etc) うまくいく umáku iku

♦*vt* (problem) 解決する kaíketsu suru; (plan) 作る tsukúrù

it works out at $100 100ドルになる hyakúdòru ni narù

works [wəːrks] *n* (*BRIT*: factory) 工場 kṓjō

♦*npl* (of clock, machine) 機構 kikṓ

worksheet [wəːrk'ʃiːt] *n* ワークシート wākushītò

workshop [wəːrk'ʃɑːp] *n* (at home, in factory) 作業場 sagyṓjō; (practical session) ワークショップ wākushoppù

work station *n* ワークステーション wākusutḕshòn

work-to-rule [wəːrk'təruːl'] (*BRIT*) *n* 順法闘争 juńpōtōsṓ

work up *vt*: **to get worked up** 怒る okórù

world [wəːrld] *n* 世界 sekài

♦*cpd* (champion) 世界 ... sekài...; (power, war) 国際的 ... kokúsaiteki..., 国際 ... kokúsai...

to think the world of someone (*fig*: admire) ...を高く評価する ...wo takàku hyōkā suru; (: love) ...が大好きである ...ga daísuki de arù

worldly [wəːrld'liː] *adj* (not spiritual) 世俗的な sezókuteki na; (knowledgeable) 世才にたけた sesái ni takèta

worldwide [wəːrld'waid'] *adj* 世界的な sekáiteki na

worm [wəːrm] *n* (*also*: **earthworm**) ミミズ mimízu

worn [wɔːrn] *pp of* **wear**

♦*adj* (carpet) 使い古した tsukáifurushità; (shoe) 履き古した hakífurushità

worn-out [wɔːrn'aut'] *adj* (object) 使い古した tsukáifurushità; (person) へとへとに疲れた hetóheto ni tsukáretà

worried [wəːr'iːd] *adj* (anxious) 心配している shiñpai shite irù

worry [wəːr'iː] *n* (anxiety) 心配 shíñpai

♦*vt* (person) 心配させる shiñpai saserù

♦*vi* (person) 心配する shiñpai surù

worrying [wəːr'iːiŋ] *adj* 心配な shíñpai na

worse [wəːrs] *adj* 更に悪い sarà ni wáruì

♦*adv* 更に悪く sarà ni warùku

♦*n* 更に悪い事 sarà ni warùi koto

a change for the worse 悪化 akká

worsen [wəːr'sən] *vt* 悪くする warùku suru

♦*vi* 悪くなる warùku naru

worse off *adj* (financially) 収入が減った shúñyū ga hettá; (*fig*): **you'll be worse off this way** そんな事は得策ではない sofina koto wa tokúsaku de wa naì

worship [wəːr'ʃip] *n* (act) 礼拝 reíhai

♦*vt* (god) 礼拝する reíhai suru; (person, thing) 崇拝する sūhái suru

Your Worship (*BRIT*: to mayor, judge) 閣下 kakkà

worst [wəːrst] *adj* 最悪の saíaku no

♦*adv* 最もひどく mottómo hidóku

♦*n* 最悪 saíaku

at worst 最悪の場合 saíaku no baái

worth [wəːrθ] *n* (value) 価値 kachì

♦*adj*: *to be worth $100* 価格は100ドル
である kakáku wa hyakúdoru de arù

it's worth it やる価値がある yarú kachì ga aru

to be worth one's while (to do) (...する事は) ...のためになる (...surú koto wa) ...no tamé ni naru

worthless [wəːrθ'lis] *adj* (person, thing)
価値のない kachì no nai

worthwhile [wəːrθ'wail'] *adj* (activity, cause) 良い yoî

worthy [wəːr'ðiː] *adj* (person) 尊敬すべき sońkeisubekì; (motive) 良い yoî

worthy of ...にふさわしい ...ni fusáwashiî

KEYWORD

would [wud] *aux vb* **1** (conditional tense): *if you asked him he would do it* 彼にお願いすればやってくれるでしょう kárè ni o-négai surèba yatté kureru deshô

if you had asked him he would have done it 彼に頼めばやってくれた事でしょう kárè ni tanómebà yatté kuretá kotó deshô

2 (in offers, invitations, requests): *would you like a biscuit?* ビスケットはいかがですか bisúkettò wa ikágà desu ká

would you ask him to come in? 彼に入ってもらって下さい kárè ni hâitte morátte kudasaî

would you open the window please? 窓を開けてくれますか mádò wo akéte kuremasù ká

3 (in indirect speech): *I said I would do it* 私はやってあげると約束しましたwatákushi wà yatté agerù to yakúsoku shimashìta

he asked me if I would go with him 一緒に行ってくれと彼に頼まれましたisshô nî itté kurè to kárè ni tanómaremashìta

4 (emphatic): *it WOULD have to snow today!* 今日に限って雪が降るなんてなあ kyô nî kagíttè yukí gà fúrù nánte nâ

you WOULD say that, wouldn't you! あんたの言いそうな事を言うね ánta no iísô na kotó dà

5 (insistence): *she wouldn't behave* あの子はどうしても言う事を聞いてくれないanô kò wa dô shite mò iú kotô wo kiîte kurenaî

6 (conjecture): *it would have been midnight* だとすれば夜中の12時という事になります dà tò surébà yonáka nò jûnijì to iú kotô ni narímasù

it would seem so そうらしいね sô rashiî nê

7 (indicating habit): *he would go there on Mondays* 彼は毎週月曜日にそこへ行く事にしていました kárè wa maíshū getsúyòbi ni sokó è ikú kotò ni shité imashìta

he would spend every day on the beach 彼は毎日浜でごろごろしていました kárè wa mâinichi hamá dè górògoro shite imáshìta

---

would-be [wud'biː'] (*pej*) *adj* ...志望の...shibô no

wouldn't [wud'ənt] = **would not**

wound[1] [waund] *pt, pp of* **wind**

wound[2] [wuːnd] *n* 傷 kizú

♦*vt* ...に傷を負わせる ...ni kizú wo owáseru, 負傷させる fushô saséru

wove [wouv] *pt of* **weave**

woven [wou'vən] *pp of* **weave**

wrangle [ræŋ'gəl] *n* 口論 kôron

wrap [ræp] *n* (stole) 肩掛 katakake, ストール sutôrù; (cape) マント mañto, ケープ kêpù

♦*vt* (cover) 包む tsutsúmù; (pack: *also*: **wrap up**) こん包する kofipô suru; (wind: tape etc) 巻付ける makítsukerù

wrapper [ræp'əːr] *n* (on chocolate) 包み tsutsúmi; (*BRIT*: of book) カバー kabâ

wrapping paper [ræp'iŋ-] *n* (brown) クラフト紙 kuráfùtoshi; (fancy) 包み紙 tsutsúmigàmi

wrath [ræθ] *n* 怒り ikári

wreak [riːk] *vt* (havoc) もたらす motárasù

to wreak vengeance on ...に復しゅうする

る ...ni fukúshū suru

wreath [ri:θ] n (funeral wreath) 花輪 hanáwa

wreck [rek] n (vehicle) 残がい zañgai; (ship) 難破船 nañpasen; (pej: person) 変り果てた人 kawárihatetà hitő
♦vt (car etc) めちゃめちゃに壊す mechámecha ni kowásù; (fig: chances) 台無しにする daínashi ni surù

wreckage [rek'idʒ] n (of car, plane, ship, building) 残がい zañgai

wren [ren] n (ZOOL) ミソサザイ misósazài

wrench [rentʃ] n (TECH: adjustable) スパナ supánà; (: fixed size) レンチ reñchi; (tug) ひねり hinéri; (fig) 心痛 shíntsū
♦vt (twist) ひねる hinérù
to wrench something from someone ...から...をねじり取る ...kara ...wo nejíritorù

wrestle [res'əl] vi: *to wrestle (with someone)* (fight) (...と) 格闘する (...to) kakútō suru; (for sport) (...と) レスリングする (...to) resùringu suru
to wrestle with (fig) ...と取組む ...to toríkumu, ...と戦う ...to tatákau

wrestler [res'lə:r] n レスラー resùrā

wrestling [res'liŋ] n レスリング resùringu

wretched [retʃ'id] adj (poor, unhappy) 不幸な fukő na; (inf: very bad) どうしようもない dő shiyő mo nai

wriggle [rig'əl] vi (also: **wriggle about**: person, fish, snake etc) うねうねする unèune suru

wring [riŋ] (pt, pp **wrung**) vt (wet clothes) 絞る shibórù; (hands) もむ momú; (bird's neck) ひねる hinérù; (fig): *to wring something out of someone* ...に...を吐かせる ...ni ...wo hákaserù

wrinkle [riŋ'kəl] n (on skin, paper etc) しわ shiwá
♦vt (nose, forehead etc) ...にしわを寄せる ...ni shiwá wo yoséru
♦vi (skin, paint etc) しわになる shiwá ni naru

wrist [rist] n 手首 tekùbi

wristwatch [rist'wɑ:tʃ] n 腕時計 udédokèi

writ [rit] n 令状 reíjō

write [rait] n (pt **wrote**, pp **written**) vt 書く kakù
♦vi 書く kakù
to write to someone ...に手紙を書く ...ni tegámi wo kakù

write down vt 書く kakù, 書留める kakítomeru

write off vt (debt) 帳消しにする chőkeshi ni suru; (plan, project) 取りやめる toríyameru

write-off [rait'ɔ:f] n 修理不可能な物 shūrìfukánő na mono

writer [rai'tə:r] n (author) 著者 choshà; (professional) 作家 sakká; (person who writes) 書手 kakìte

write up vt (report, minutes etc) 詳しく書く kuwáshiku kakù

writhe [raið] vi 身もだえする mimódàe suru

writing [rai'tiŋ] n (words written) 文字 mojì, 文章 buñshō; (handwriting) 筆跡 hissékì; (of author) 作品 sakúhin, 作風 sakúfū; (activity) 書物 kakìmono
in writing 書面で shomén de

writing paper n 便せん biñsen

written [rit'ən] pp of **write**

wrong [rɔ:ŋ] adj (bad) 良くない yokúnai; (incorrect: number, address etc) 間違った machígatta; (not suitable) 不適当な futékìtō na; (reverse: side of material) 裏側の urágawa no; (unfair) 不正な fuséi na
♦adv 間違って machígatte, 誤って ayámattè
♦n (injustice) 不正 fuséi
♦vt (treat unfairly) ...に悪い事をする ...ni warúi koto wo surù
you are wrong to do it それは不正な事です sore wa fuséi na koto desù
you are wrong about that, you've got it wrong それは違います soré wa chigáimasù
to be in the wrong 間違っている machígatte iru
what's wrong? どうしましたか dő shimáshita ká

to go wrong (person) 間違う machígaù; (plan) 失敗する shippái suru; (machine) 狂う kurúù

wrongful [rɔːŋ'fəl] *adj* (imprisonment, dismissal) 不当な futô na

wrongly [rɔːŋ'liː] *adv* 間違って machígattè

wrote [rout] *pt of* **write**

wrought [rɔːt] *adj*: ***wrought iron*** 練鉄 reñtetsu

wrung [rʌŋ] *pt, pp of* **wring**

wry [rai] *adj* (smile, humor, expression) 皮肉っぽい hiníkuppoì

wt. *abbr* = **weight**

X

Xmas [eks'mis] *n abbr* = **Christmas**

X-ray [eks'rei] *n* (ray) エックス線 ekkúsusen; (photo) レントゲン写真 reñtogeñshashin

♦*vt* ...のレントゲンを撮る ...no reñtogeñ wo torù

xylophone [zai'ləfoun] *n* 木琴 mokkín

Y

yacht [jɑːt] *n* ヨット yottò

yachting [jɑːt'iŋ] *n* ヨット遊び yottôasobi

yachtsman [jɑːts'mən] (*pl* **yachtsmen**) *n* ヨット乗り yottônori

Yank [jæŋk] (*pej*) *n* ヤンキー yañkī

Yankee [jæŋk'iː] (*pej*) *n* = **Yank**

yap [jæp] *vi* (dog) きゃんきゃんほえる kyañkyan hoérù

yard [jɑːrd] *n* (of house etc) 庭 niwà; (measure) ヤード yādò

yardstick [jɑːrd'stik] *n* (*fig*) 尺度 shakúdò

yarn [jɑːrn] *n* (thread) 毛糸 keíto; (tale) ほら話 horábanashi

yawn [jɔːn] *n* あくび akúbi

♦*vi* あくびする akúbi suru

yawning [jɔːn'iŋ] *adj* (gap) 大きな ōkína

yd. *abbr* = **yard(s)**

yeah [je] (*inf*) *adv* はい haì

year [jiːr] *n* 年 neñ, toshí, 1年 ichínen

to be 8 years old 8才である hassâi de aru

an eight-year-old child 8才の子供 hassâi no kodómo

yearly [jiːr'liː] *adj* 毎年の maínen no, maítoshi no

♦*adv* 毎年 maínen, maítoshi

yearn [jəːrn] *vi*: ***to yearn for something*** ...を切に望む ...wo setsù ni nozómu

to yearn to do ...をしたいと切に望む ...wo shitái to setsù ni nozómu

yeast [jiːst] *n* 酵母 kōbò, イースト īsùto

yell [jel] *n* 叫び sakébi

♦*vi* 叫ぶ sakébù

yellow [jel'ou] *adj* 黄色い kiíroi

yelp [jelp] *n* (of animal) キャンと鳴く事 kyañ to nakú koto; (of person) 悲鳴 himéi

♦*vi* (animal) きゃんと鳴く kyañ to nakú; (person) 悲鳴を上げる himéi wò agérù

yeoman [jou'mən] (*pl* **yeomen**) *n*: ***yeoman of the guard*** 国王の親衛隊員 kokúō no shiñ-eitaiiñ

yes [jes] *adv* はい haì

♦*n* はいという返事 haì to iú heñji

to say/answer yes 承諾する shódaku suru

yesterday [jes'təːrdei] *adv* 昨日 kinô, sakújītsu

♦*n* 昨日 kinô, sakújītsu

yesterday morning/evening 昨日の朝〔夕方〕 kinô no asà (yūgata)

all day yesterday 昨日一日 kinô ichínichi

yet [jet] *adv* まだ madà; (already) もう mô

♦*conj* がしかし ga shikáshì

it is not finished yet まだできていない madà dekíte inái

the best yet これまでの物で最も良い物 koré madè no mono dè mottômo yoì mono

as yet まだ madà

yew [juː] *n* (tree) イチイ ichíi

Yiddish [jid'iʃ] *n* イディッシュ語 idísshugo

yield [ji:ld] *n* (AGR) 収穫 shúkaku; (COMM) 収益 shūéki
♦*vt* (surrender: control, responsibility) 譲る yuzúru; (produce: results, profit) もたらす motárasù
♦*vi* (surrender) 譲る yuzúru; (*US*: AUT) 道を譲る michí wo yuzúru

YMCA [waiemsi:ei'] *n abbr* (= *Young Men's Christian Association*) キリスト教青年会 kirísutokyōseínenkai, ワイエムシーエー waîemushiè

yog(h)ourt [jou'gə:rt] *n* ヨーグルト yōgurùtu

yog(h)urt [jou'gə:rt] *n* = **yog(h)ourt**

yoke [jouk] *n* (of oxen) くびき kubíki; (*fig*) 重荷 omóni

yolk [jouk] *n* 卵黄 rañ-ō, 黄身 kimí

KEYWORD

you [ju:] *pron* 1 (subj: *sing*) あなたは〔が〕 anátà wa〔ga〕; (: *pl*) あなたたちは〔が〕 anátàtàchi wa 〔ga〕
you are very kind あなたはとても親切ですね anátà wa totémo shíñsetsu desu ne, ご親切に有難うございます go-shíñsetsu ni arígàtō gozáimasù
you Japanese enjoy your food あなたたち日本人は食べるのが好きですね anátatàchi nihóñjìn wa tabérù no ga sukí desù né
you and I will go あなたと私が行く事になっています anátà to watákushi gà ikú kotò ni natté imasù
2 (obj: direct, indirect: *sing*) あなたを〔に〕 anátà wo〔ni〕; (: *pl*) あなたたちを〔に〕 anátàtàchi wo〔ni〕
I know you 私はあなたを知っています watákushi wà anátà wo shitté imasù
I gave it to you 私はそれをあなたに渡しました watákushi wà soré wò anátà ni watáshimashìta
3 (stressed): *I told YOU to do it* やれというのはあなたに言ったんですよ yaré tò iú no wà anátà ni ittáñ desu yó
4 (after prep, in comparisons)
it's for you あなたのためです anátà no tamé desù

can I come with you? 一緒に行っていいですか isshó nì itté ìì desu ké
she's younger than you 彼女はあなたより若いです kánòjo wa anátà yori wakáì desu
5 (impersonal: one)
fresh air does you good 新鮮な空気は健康にいい shíñsen nà kúkì wa keñkō ni íì
you never know どうなるか分かりませんね dō narù ka wakárimaseñ né
you can't do that! それはいけません soré wà ikémaseñ

you'd [ju:d] = **you had**; **you would**

you'll [ju:l] = **you will**; **you shall**

young [jʌŋ] *adj* (person, animal, plant) 若い wakáì
♦*npl* (of animal) 子 ko; (people): *the young* 若者 wakámono

younger [jʌŋ'gə:r] *adj* (brother etc) 年下の toshíshita no

youngster [jʌŋ'stə:r] *n* 子供 kodómo

your [ju:r] *adj* (singular) あなたの anátà no; (plural) あなたたちの anátàtàchi no
¶ *see also* **my**

you're [ju:r] = **you are**

yours [ju:rz] *pron* (singular) あなたの物 anátà no mono; (plural) あなたたちの物 anátàtàchi no mono ¶ *see also* **mine**; **faithfully**; **sincerely**

yourself [ju:rself'] *pron* あなた自身 anátà jishín ¶ *see also* **oneself**

yourselves [ju:rselvz'] *pl pron* あなたたち自身 anátàtàchi jishín ¶ *see also* **oneself**

youth [ju:θ] *n* (young days) 若い時分 wakáì jibun; (young man: *pl* **youths**) 少年 shóneñ

youth club *n* 青少年クラブ seíshōnèn kuràbu

youthful [ju:θ'fəl] *adj* (person) 若い wakáì; (looks) 若々しい wakáwakashìì; (air, enthusiasm) 若者独特の wakámono-dokútoku no

youth hostel *n* ユースホステル yūsúhosùteru

Youth Training (*BRIT*) 職業訓練 shokúgyōkunreñ ◇失業青少年のためのもの shitsúgyōseishōnen no tamé no monð

you've [juːv] = **you have**

Yugoslav [juːˈɡouslɑːv] *adj* ユーゴスラビアの yúgosurabìa no
♦*n* ユーゴスラビア人 yúgosurabiajin

Yugoslavia [juːˈɡouslɑːˈviːə] *n* ユーゴスラビア yúgosurabìa

yuppie [jʌpˈiː] (*inf*) *n* ヤッピー yappì
♦*adj* ヤッピーの yappì no

YWCA [waidʌbəljuːsieiˈ] *n abbr* (= *Young Women's Christian Association*) キリスト教女子青年会 kirísutokyōjoshìseínenkai, ワイダブリューシーエー waídaburyūshìē

Z

Zambia [zæmˈbiːə] *n* ザンビア zañbia

zany [zeiˈniː] *adj* (ideas, sense of humor) ばかげた bakágeta

zap [zæp] *vt* (COMPUT: delete) 削除する sakújo suru

zeal [ziːl] *n* (enthusiasm) 熱情 netsújō; (*also*: **religious zeal**) 狂信 kyōshín

zealous [zelˈəs] *adj* 熱狂的な nekkyóteki na

zebra [ziːˈbrə] *n* シマウマ shimáuma

zebra crossing (*BRIT*) *n* 横断歩道 ōdánhodò

zenith [ziːˈniθ] *n* 頂点 chōteñ

zero [ziːˈrou] *n* 零点 reíteñ, ゼロ zerð

zest [zest] *n* (for life) 熱意 netsùi; (of orange) 皮 kawá

zigzag [zigˈzæg] *n* ジグザグ jigùzagu
♦*vi* ジグザグに動く jigùzagu ni ugóku

Zimbabwe [zimbɑːˈbwei] *n* ジンバブウエ jíñbabùue

zinc [ziŋk] *n* 亜鉛 aèn

zip [zip] *n* (*also*: **zip fastener**) = **zipper**
♦*vt* (*also*: **zip up**) = **zipper**

zip code (*US*) *n* 郵便番号 yūbinbañgō

zipper [zipˈəːr] (*US*) *n* チャック chakkù, ジッパー jippā, ファスナー fasùnā
♦*vt* (*also*: **zipper up**) ...のチャックを締める ...no chakkù wo shimérù

zodiac [zouˈdiːæk] *n* 十二宮図 jūníkyūzu

zombie [zɑːmˈbiː] *n* (*fig*): *like a zombie* ロボットの様に〔な〕robóttð no yð ni 〔na〕

zone [zoun] *n* (area, *also* MIL) 地帯 chitái

zoo [zuː] *n* 動物園 dóbutsùen

zoologist [zouəˈlɑːdʒist] *n* 動物学者 dóbutsugakùsha

zoology [zouəˈlɑːdʒiː] *n* 動物学 dóbutsugàku

zoom [zuːm] *vi*: *to zoom past* 猛スピードで通り過ぎる mōsupído de tōrísugimu

zoom lens *n* ズームレンズ zúmureñzu

zucchini [zuːkiːˈniː] (*US*) *n inv* ズッキーニ zukkínì

SUPPLEMENT

NUMBERS

Cardinal numbers:

1	一	ichi	11	十一	jūichi	21	二十一	nijūichi
2	二	ni	12	十二	jūni	22	二十二	nijūni
3	三	san	13	十三	jūsan		etc	
4	四	yon/shi	14	十四	jūyon/jūshi	30	三十	sanjū
5	五	go	15	十五	jūgo -	40	四十	yonjū
6	六	roku	16	十六	jūroku	50	五十	gojū
7	七	nana/shichi	17	十七	jūnana/jūshichi	60	六十	rokujū
8	八	hachi	18	十八	jūhachi	70	七十	nanajū/shichijū
9	九	ku/kyū	19	十九	jūku/jūkyū	80	八十	hachijū
10	十	jū	20	二十	nijū	90	九十	kyūjū

Note: the alternative forms given for 4, 7, 9 etc are not necessarily interchangeable. The choice is determined by usage.

100	百	hyaku	1,000	千 sen, 一千 issen	10,000	一万	ichiman
200	二百	nihyaku	2,000	二千 nisen	20,000	二万	niman
300	三百	sanbyaku	3,000	三千 sanzen		etc	
400	四百	yonhyaku	4,000	四千 yonsen			
500	五百	gohyaku	5,000	五千 gosen			
600	六百	roppyaku	6,000	六千 rokusen			
700	七百	nanahyaku	7,000	七千 nanasen			
800	八百	happyaku	8,000	八千 hassen			
900	九百	kyūhyaku	9,000	九千 kyūsen			

Alternate set of numbers:

These are used often for counting, particularly for counting things without "counters" (see below), and for expressing the age of children.

1	一つ	hitotsu		6	六つ	muttsu
2	二つ	futatsu		7	七つ	nanatsu
3	三つ	mittsu		8	八つ	yattsu
4	四つ	yottsu		9	九つ	kokonotsu
5	五つ	itsutsu		10	十	tō

Ordinal numbers:

"The first," "the second" etc are expressed by the formula 第 x 番目 *dai x banme*, where x is the cardinal number and *dai*, *banme* or *me* can be variously omitted. Thus "the third" can be expressed by any of the following:

第三番目　daisanbanme

三番目　sanbanme

三番　sanban

第三　daisan

The alternate cardinal numbers from 1 to 9 can also be made into ordinal numbers by the addition of 目 *me* alone: "the third" = 三つ目 *mittsume*.

Days of the month:

The days of the month are written straightforwardly by a cardinal number plus the character for day 日. But the reading is not straightforward and needs to be learned.

一日	tsuitachi	七日	nanoka
二日	futsuka	八日	yōka
三日	mikka	九日	kokonoka
四日	yokka	十日	tōka
五日	itsuka	二十日	hatsuka
六日	muika		

Days 11 to 19 and 21 to 31 are expressed straightforwardly by a cardinal number + *nichi*. Thus the 18th day of the month is *jūhachinichi*.

Fractions:

In Japanese you express fractions by the formula y分のx *y bun no x*, where *y* is the DENOMINATOR, not the numerator. In other words, in Japanese you say the denominator first, then the numerator, thus:

1/2　二分の一　nibun no ichi

2/3　三分の二　sanbun no ni

3/4　四分の三　yonbun no san

Counters:

As in English we often say "2 *head* of cattle", "a *bunch* of grapes", "a *flock* of geese", Japanese uses counters for almost all everyday things, including people. There are many counters, some common, some exotic (like using the same counter for "rabbit" as you would for "bird"). Here is a list of counters you will need for your daily life.

counter:		used for:
人	nin	people
名	mei	people (interchangeable with *nin* except in set phrases)
匹	hiki	animals in general, except birds
頭	tō	relatively large animals
羽	wa	birds
個	ko	3-dimensional, relatively rounded objects: balls, stones, apples, cups
枚	mai	thin, flat things: pieces of paper, computer disks, handkerchiefs, blankets, dishes
本	hon	long things: pencils, ropes, sticks
冊	satsu	books and things bound like books: notebooks, diaries
台	dai	cars, trucks, bicycles, large machines
足	soku	shoes, socks etc that come in matched pairs
歳	sai	age of living things in years
杯	hai	containers full of something: cupful, glassful, spoonful

Like the use in English of "an" instead of "a" before words that begin with a vowel, Japanese makes pronunciation changes depending on the last syllable of the cardinal number and the first letter of a counter. Here are the most important.

1. Counters beginning with "h"

   一本, 一匹 ippon, ippiki
   二本, 二匹 nihon, nihiki
   三本, 三匹 sanbon, sanbiki
   四本, 四匹 yonhon, yonhiki
   五本, 五匹 gohon, gohiki
   六本, 六匹 roppon, roppiki
   七本, 七匹 nanahon, nanahiki
   八本, 八匹 happon, happiki
   九本, 九匹 kyūhon, kyūhiki
   十本, 十匹 juppon, juppiki

2. Counters beginning with unvoiced consonants (k, s, t, ch) double the consonant after the numbers 1 and 10.

   一個, 一歳 ikko, issai
   十個, 十歳 jukko, jussai

3. "k" also doubles after 6.

   六個 rokko

4. The voiced consonants g, z, d, m, n, r, w generally do not change.

5. The counter 人 *nin* for persons has an atypical pronunciation for 1 and 2.

一人 hitori
二人 futari

6. The counter 歳 *sai* for age has an atypical pronunciation for 20 years of age.

二十歳 hatachi

DEMONSTRATIVES

Japanese demonstratives begin with 4 prefixes: *ko-*, *so-*, *a-*, and *do-*. *Ko-* expresses nearness to the speaker; *so-* expresses distance from the speaker but nearness to the listener; *a-* expresses distance from both speaker and listener; and *do-* forms interrogatives.

kō	like this	sō	like that	aa	like that	dō	how?
kono	this	sono	that	ano	that	dono	which?
kore	this (one)	sore	that (one)	are	that (one)	dore	which (one)?
koko		soko		asoko		doko	
kotchi	here	sotchi	there	atchi	there	dotchi	where?
kochira		sochira		achira		dochira	
konna	such a	sonna	such a	anna	such a	donna	what kind of?

UNDERSTANDING JAPANESE

Japanese has certain characteristics not always found in the European family of languages. This shows up in particular in the way the subject of the sentence is expressed (or unexpressed, as we shall see), and in the numerous particles which take the place of declensions, prepositions, auxiliaries etc in Western languages. Although it may take years to learn to use these characteristics like a native, being aware of their existance can serve as a shortcut to a fuller understanding of Japanese.

1. The hidden subject

Consider the following sentence. It is the opening line to Yasunari Kawabata's Nobel Prize-winning "Snow Country".

国境の長いトンネルを抜けると雪国であった。kokkyō no nagai tonneru wo nukeru to yukiguni de atta.

My translation would be:

"When your train emerged from the long tunnel beneath the border, you suddenly found yourself in the snow-bound countryside."

Notice that there is no "train" or "your" or "you" expressed in the original.

Japanese prefers not to express words that are apparent from the context or the choice of expression. This happens most frequently with the grammatical subject of the sentence, not only in literature, but especially in daily conversation.

A: どちらへお出かけですか dochira e o-dekake desu ka

B: 郵便局へ手紙を出しに行きます yūbinkyoku e tegami wo dashi ni ikimasu

Here there is no need for an *anata wa* in A or a *watashi wa* in B. The choice of words (the polite *dochira* with *o-...*) contains the "you" in A, and makes an "I" in B's answer superfluous.

In Japanese the verbal part of the sentence is the most important, and normally comes at the end. In a long sentence the listener has to wait till the end of the sentence in order to grasp the meaning. In English, the grammatical subject is the most important part, and is expressed at the beginning of the sentence, and auxiliary information about the subject is imparted gradually. This makes for great clarity of meaning, whereas Japanese sentences can often produce ambiguities. But this is a product of the Japanese culture, where reticence is considered virtue and outspokenness vice.

2. Particles

Japanese uses particles to make clear the relationship among words in a sentence. English frequently relies on position of words in the sentence for this. In a simple example, the meaning of A below is reversed if you reverse the position of the words, as in B.

A. John hit Sue.

B. Sue hit John.

On the other hand, consider the following example and its literal Japanese translation.

She gave me a book.

彼女は私に1冊の本をくれました.

kanojo *wa* watashi *ni* issatsu *no* hon *wo* kuremashita.

This is a standard translation. But the following are also possible, in context, without changing the meaning.

watashi *ni* kanojo *wa* issatsu *no* hon *wo* kuremashita.

issatsu *no* hon *wo* kanojo *wa* watashi *ni* kuremashita.

kuremashita, kanojo *wa* watashi *ni* issatsu *no* hon *wo*.

In other words, the particles make the meaning clear without regard to the position of the various sentence elements, even when the position is somewhat unnatural. On the other hand, if you confuse the particles, your speech becomes unintelligible. To say that someone's train of thought is illogical or contradictory, the Japanese have an old metaphor.

てにをはが合わない. te-ni-wo-ha ga awanai.

Literally, "his particles are all mixed up." This underscores the correct use of particles, even for a native speaker of Japanese.

The Japanese classify their particles as follows.

Case particles: Added to nouns and pronouns, they indicate relation to other words in the sentence: no, ga, wo, ni, e, to, yori, kara, de.

Adverbial particles: They are added to nouns, pronouns, and adverbs and restrict the meaning of the verbal parts of the sentence: sae, made, bakari, dake, hodo, kurai, nado, nanka, nante, yara, zo, ka, zutsu.

Modifying particles: They add their own meaning to the word they follow and also modify the verbal parts of the sentence: wa, mo, koso, demo (also written "de mo"), shika, datte.

Sentence particles: They conclude a sentence and indicate interrogation, exclamation, emotion, prohibition etc: ka, kai, kashira, na, zo, ze, tomo (to mo), tte, no, ne, sa, ya, yo.

Parenthetical particles: They are placed at the end of phrases and clauses and are used to adjust sentence rhythm or to express emotion, emphasis etc: na, ne, sa.

Connecting particles: They are appended to various verbal phrases and clauses to indicate their connection with what follows: ba, to, te mo (de mo), keredo (keredomo), ga, no ni, no de, kara, shi, te (de), nagara.

The following illustrate typical Japanese usage of the more important particles. The translations given show one way, but not necessarily the only way, of expressing the concept in English.

a. Case particles

§ の no: indicates possession, location etc

父の本　chichi no hon "my father's book" —possession

海の風　umi no kaze "a sea breeze" —location

大学の教授　daigaku no kyōju "a university professor" —affiliation

紫の花　murasaki no hana "a purple flower" —attribute

小説家の川端氏　shōsetsuka no kawabatashi "Mr. Kawabata the novelist" —apposition

§ が ga: follows nouns or pronouns

私が行きます　watashi ga ikimasu "I will go." —indicates subject

メロンが好きだ　meron ga suki da "I like melons." —indicates object of desire, ability, likes and dislikes etc

それがね、本当なんだよ　sore ga ne, hontō nan da yo "The thing is, the story is true." —attached to a demonstrative like a connecting particle

§ を wo: follows nouns or pronouns

本を読む hon wo yomu "to read a book" —indicates object of an action verb

歩道を歩く hodō wo aruku "to walk on the sidewalk" —indicates location with a verb of movement

この半年を堪え忍んだ kono hantoshi wo taeshinonda "I have suffered in silence for the past 6 months." —indicates duration of an action

朝9時に家を出る asa kuji ni ie wo deru "to leave the house at 9 o'clock" —indicates the place where an action commences

§ に ni: indicates the person or thing to which an action extends

朝5時に起床する asa goji ni kishō suru "to get up at 5 a.m." —indicates time

空に虹が出る sora ni niji ga deru "A rainbow appears in the sky." —indicates place

仕事に熱中する shigoto ni netchū suru "to concentrate on one's work" —indicates the object of an action

会社にたどりつく kaisha ni tadoritsuku "to reach one's office" —indicates destination or direction

悪夢にうなされる akumu ni unasareru "to be tormented by a nightmare" —indicates cause

1週間に2日はお休み isshūkan ni futsuka wa o-yasumi "We have 2 days a week off." —indicates ratio, proportion etc

犬に吠えられる inu ni hoerareru "to be barked at by a dog" —indicates the agent of an action

大人になる otona ni naru "to become an adult" —indicates the result of change

ぴかぴかに光る pikapika ni hikaru "to shine brightly" —indicates manner

§ へ e:

西へ進む nishi e susumu "to advance toward the west" —indicates the direction of an action

君への思い kimi e no omoi "my longing for you" —indicates the object of an action

学校へ着く gakkō e tsuku "to arrive at school" —indicates destination

兄がすぐそこへ来ています ani ga sugu soko e kite imasu "My brother is right near here." —indicates location of an action

§ と to:

友人と話す yūjin to hanasu "to talk with friends" —expresses the idea of "with"

以前と同じやり方 izen to onaji yarikata "the same manner as before" —indicates a term of comparison

政治家となる　seijika to naru "to become a politician" —indicates the result of change

開催地は山梨と決定した　kaisaichi wa Yamanashi to kettei shita "We decided to hold the meeting in Yamanashi." —indicates the content of an action or state

延々と続く　en-en to tsuzuku "to go on endlessly" —indicates the manner of an action or state

§ より yori:

父より背が高い　chichi yori se ga takai "I am taller than my father." —indicates a term of comparison

5時より前に帰る　goji yori mae ni kaeru "to be back before 5" —indicates a limit

§ から kara: used after nouns and pronouns, and indicates point of departure, or cause

明日から夏休み　myōnichi kara natsuyasumi "Summer vacation starts tomorrow." —indicates a spatial or temporal point of departure

窓から西日が差す　mado kara nishibi ga sasu "The western sun shines in through the window." —expresses the idea of "passing through"

何から何までお世話になりました　nani kara nani made o-sewa ni narimashita "You took wonderful care of me." —indicates extent

母から聞いた話　haha kara kiita hanashi "something I heard from my mother" —indicates a source

ビールは麦から作る　bīru wa mugi kara tsukuru "Beer is made from grain." —indicates constituent materials etc

§ で de:

プールで泳ぐ　pūru de oyogu "to swim in the pool" —indicates the location of an action.

ペンで書く　pen de kaku "to write with a pen" —indicates instrument, means, material etc

病気で死ぬ　byōki de shinu "to die from a sickness" —indicates cause, reason, motive

b. Adverbial particles

§ まで made: used after nouns and pronouns, and connects them with verbal parts or other particles

東京から北海道まで旅する　tōkyō kara hokkaidō made tabi suru "to travel from Tōkyō to Hokkaidō" —indicates the outer limits of an action in space or time

あくまで計画を実行する　aku made keikaku wo jikkō suru "to push a plan through to the finish" —expresses final extent of an action

§ だけ dake: expresses the limits of something

2人だけで話したい　futari dake de hanashitai "I want to talk to you alone." —indicates a limit

あれだけ食べたら満腹です　are dake tabetara manpuku desu "I'm full after eating all that." —expresses the idea of "that much"

§ ほど hodo: used after various noun and verb forms

後5枚ほど必要です　ato gomai hodo hitsuyō desu "I need about 5 more sheets of paper." —expresses an approximation of number or quantity

かわいそうなほどしょんぼりしている　kawaisō na hodo shonbori shite iru "He's looking so depressed I can't help feeling sorry for him." —expresses an action or state resulting from some characteristic

悪い奴ほど手が白い　warui yatsu hodo te ga shiroi "The evilest men have the whitest hands." —indicates 2 items, the second of which changes in direct proportion to change in the first

c. Modifying particles

§ は wa: used after many kinds of words. The original use was to single out one item of a group.

勉強はもう済んだ　benkyō wa mō sunda "I have finished my homework." —here singles out one item from a group of things to do

象は鼻が長い　zō wa hana ga nagai "The elephant has a long trunk." —singles out an item of subject matter about which some information is given

行きはよいよい，帰りは恐い　iki wa yoi yoi, kaeri wa kowai "Going is easy, but getting back is the problem." —expresses 2 or more contrasting judgments

君とは絶交だ　kimi to wa zekkō da "I want nothing more to do with you." —indicates emphasis

◇**Note:** in modern Japanese, wa is frequently used to express a word that corresponds to the grammatical subject of a sentence in English.

§ も mo: used after many kinds of words

花も実もある男　hana mo mi mo aru otoko "a man in both looks and deeds" —coordinates 2 or more concepts

料理もろくにできない　ryōri mo roku ni dekinai "She can't even cook properly." —singles out one among many other implied concepts

兄も病気になった　ani mo byōki ni natta "My older brother got sick too." —expresses the concept of "also"

そして誰もいなくなった　soshite dare mo inakunatta "And then there was no one." —used with a negative to express the idea of "nothing, no one"

§ しか shika:

生き残ったのは1人しかいない　ikinokotta no wa hitori shika inai "Only one person was left alive." —used with a negative to express the idea of "only"

d. Sentence particles

§ か ka: expresses a variety of questions

君はだれですか　kimi wa dare desu ka "Who are you?"

本当に行くのか　hontō ni iku no ka "Are you really going?"

散歩に行きませんか　sanpo ni ikimasen ka "How about going for a walk?"

こんなことができないのか　konna koto ga dekinai no ka "Can't you even do something as simple as this?"

そうか，失敗だったのか　sō ka, shippai datta no ka "Oh, so it ended in failure, eh?"

§ ね ne: used at the end of a sentence

まあ，きれいな花ね　maa, kirei na hana ne "Oh, look at the pretty flower!" —expresses an exclamation

この本は君のですね　kono hon wa kimi no desu ne "This is your book, right?" —expresses a tag question

遅れてごめんなさいね　okurete gomen nasai ne "Do forgive me for being late." —expresses a request for the listener's understanding, sympathy, agreement etc

e. Parenthetical particles

§ ね ne: appended to words or phrases as a transition word, or to adjust sentence rhythm etc

そうですね，考えておきましょう　sō desu ne, kangaete okimashō "Well, let me think about it."

私ね，その秘密知っているの　watashi ne, sono himitsu shitte iru no "Listen, I know the secret behind that."

f. Connecting particles

§ ば ba:

雨が降れば，旅行は中止　ame ga fureba, ryokō wa chūshi "If it rains, the trip is off." —expresses a possible condition

消息筋によれば，また株価が下がるらしい　shōsokusuji ni yoreba, mata kabuka ga sagaru rashii "According to a knowledgeable source, stock prices are going to fall again." —indicates the basis for a statement

日が沈めば夜になる　hi ga shizumeba yoru ni naru "Night comes when the sun sets." —expresses an invariable cause and effect relationship

5年前を思えば，随分楽になった　gonen mae wo omoeba, zuibun raku ni natta "Compared with 5 years ago, I am quite well off now." —indicates a past time for comparison with the present

§ **と to:** used after the present tense form of verbs

庭へ出ると，桜が咲いていた　niwa e deru to, sakura ga saite ita "When you went into the garden, you could see the cherry trees in bloom." —joins two contemporaneous actions

本を置くと，すぐ出て行った　hon wo oku to, sugu dete itta "He put down the book and left the room." —joins two successive actions

話が始まると，静かになった　hanashi ga hajimaru to, shizuka ni natta "When the lecture began, the audience became silent and listened." —expresses the beginning or cause etc of an action

はっきり言うと，それは失敗です　hakkiri iu to, sore wa shippai desu "Frankly, it's a failure." —expresses a preamble to what follows

§ **ても te mo** (with certain verbal forms it becomes でも *de mo*): used to express permission etc

果物なら食べてもいいですよ　kudamono nara tabete mo ii desu yo "Fruit is all right for you to eat."

§ **けれども keredomo:** used after verbs and -ii adjectives

貧しいけれども，心は豊かだった　mazushii keredomo, kokoro wa yutaka datta "He was poor materially, but rich in spirit." —expresses some sort of contrast

勝手な言い分ですけれども，帰らせて下さい　katte na iibun desu keredomo, kaerasete kudasai "I'm sorry to do so at this point, but I really must leave." —joins a preamble to the main point of the sentence

レコード持ってきたけれども，聞いてみる？　rekōdo motte kita keredomo, kiite miru? "I brought a record along. Do you want to hear it?" —simply joins two clauses

§ **が ga:** used after verbs and -ii adjectives

ご存知のことと思いますが，一応説明します　go-zonji no koto to omoimasu ga, ichiō setsumei shimasu "I'm sure you are already familiar with the problem, but I'll run through it briefly for you anyway." —joins a preamble to the main part of the sentence

驚いて振り向いたが，もはやだれの姿もなかった　odoroite furimuita ga, mohaya dare no sugata mo nakatta "In surprise I wheeled around to look back, but whoever it was had already disappeared." —expresses a temporal relationship between two clauses

見かけは悪いが，たいへん親切な男　mikake wa warui ga, taihen shinsetsu na otoko "He doesn't look it, but he's really a very kind man." —expresses contrast

§ のに **no ni**: expresses dissatisfaction, unexpectedness etc

待っていたのに，来なかった　matte ita no ni, konakatta "I waited and waited, but he didn't come."

§ ので **no de**: expresses cause, reason, basis etc

分からないので，質問しましたwakaranai no de, shitsumon shimashita "I didn't understand, so I asked."

§ から **kara**

暑いから，のどが渇いた　atsui kara, nodo ga kawaita "It was hot, and I became very thirsty." —expresses cause, reason, basis etc

決心したからには，やり通そう　kesshin shita kara ni wa, yaritōsō "We have made the decision, so let's see it through to the end." —expresses the notion of "having done such and such, it follows that..."

DAILY JAPANESE

Here we present a selection of very typical and idiomatic Japanese words and phrases. These examples occur with a high frequency in daily life in Japan. The English translations given in boldface provide an idea of the meaning, but are not absolute. A number of translations are possible, depending on the context, tone of voice, person speaking or spoken to, etc.

Some words occur in the examples which have no English equivalent, or are unintelligible to a person unfamiliar with Japan. Foreigners living in Japan often prefer to use these as loan words in conversation, rather than resorting to some clumsy translation. Such words are marked with an asterisk (∗) in the translation, and are explained in a short glossary at the end of the section.

1. Indispensable words

私　watashi **I**

(Note: slightly formal: 私 watakushi; familiar: male: 僕 boku; female: あたし atashi; very familiar/rough/vulgar, usually male: おれ ore)

あなた anata **you**

(Note: familiar/affectionate: 君 kimi; very familiar/rough/vulgar: お前 omae; rough/vulgar: てめえ temē; insulting: きさま kisama)

彼　kare **he**

彼女　kanojo **she**

はい　hai **yes**

いいえ　iie **no**

どうぞ　dōzo **please**

ありがとう（ございます）　arigatō (gozaimasu) **Thank you.**

どういたしまして　dō itashimashite **You're welcome./Don't mention it.**

いいえ，結構です　iie, kekkō desu **No, thank you.**

すみません　sumimasen **excuse me/pardon me/I'm sorry**

2. Greetings

General

お早うございます　o-hayō gozaimasu **Good morning.**

今日は　konnichi wa **Good morning./Good afternoon./Hello.** (said from about 10 a. m. to early evening)

今晩は　konban wa **Good evening.**

お休みなさい　o-yasumi nasai **Good night.**

ご機嫌いかがですか　go-kigen ikaga desu ka **How are you?** (very formal)

お元気ですか　o-genki desu ka **How are you?** (less formal)

ありがとう．とても元気です　arigatō. totemo genki desu **I'm fine, thank you.**

よいお天気ですね　yoi o-tenki desu ne **Nice weather, isn't it?**

今日は寒いですね　kyō wa samui desu ne **It's cold today, isn't it?**

さようなら　sayōnara **Goodbye.**

行って参ります　itte mairimasu (no English equivalent; said when leaving for a destination with the intention of returning)

行っていらっしゃい　itte irasshai (no English equivalent; said in response to the above)

ただ今　tadaima **I'm home./I'm back.**

お帰りなさい　o-kaeri nasai **Welcome home./Welcome back.** (said in response to the above, but the order may also be reversed)

Visiting

ごめん下さい　gomen kudasai **Hello./Anybody home?**

いらっしゃいませ　irasshaimase **Welcome.**

おじゃまします　o-jama shimasu (no English equivalent; said when entering a place)

どうぞこちらへ　dōzo kochira e **This way, please.**

ちょっとお待ち下さい　chotto o-machi kudasai **One moment, please.**

お掛け下さい　o-kake kudasai **Have a seat.**

お目にかかれてうれしいです　o-me ni kakarete ureshii desu **Pleased to meet you.**

長いことおじゃまいたしました　nagai koto o-jama itashimashita **Thank you for your time.**

この辺で失礼いたします　kono hen de shitsurei itashimasu **I'll be going now.**

明日またお会いしましょう　myōnichi mata o-ai shimashō **See you again tomorrow.**

Meals

お上がり下さい　o-agari kudasai **Help yourself** (literally, "please eat")

いただきます　itadakimasu (no English equivalent; said when beginning to eat or drink)

ごちそうさまでした　gochisōsama deshita **I enjoyed the meal./Thanks for the meal.**

3. Introducing oneself

私は日本人（オーストラリア人）です　watashi wa nihonjin (ōsutorariajin) desu **I am Japanese/Australian.**

名前は鈴木花子です　namae wa suzuki hanako desu **My name is Hanako Suzuki.**

私は学生です　watashi wa gakusei desu **I am a university student.**

京都からきました　kyōto kara kimashita **I come from Kyoto.**

22才です　nijūnissai desu **I am 22 years old.**

兄が2人妹が1人います　ani ga futari imōto ga hitori imasu **I have 2 older brothers and a younger sister.**

父は建築家です　chichi wa kenchikuka desu **My father is an architect.**

私は外国に行ったことがありません　watashi wa gaikoku ni itta koto ga arimasen **I have never been to a foreign country.**

私は少ししか英語を話せません　watashi wa sukoshi shika eigo wo hanasemasen **I can only speak a little English.**

趣味は音楽鑑賞です　shumi wa ongaku kanshō desu **My favorite pastime is listening to music.**

．．．が好きではありません　...ga suki de wa arimasen **I don't like ....**

私は水泳が得意です　watashi wa suiei ga tokui desu **I am a good swimmer.**

．．．が苦手です　...ga nigate desu **I am not very good at....**

4. Questions and requests

これは何ですか　kore wa nan desu ka **What is this?**

あの人はだれですか　ano hito wa dare desu ka **Who is that ?**

いつですか　itsu desu ka **When (is it etc) ?**

どこから来ましたか　doko kara kimashita ka **Where did you come from/where are you from ?**

どうなりましたか　dō narimashita ka **What happened/what is the matter ?**

どのぐらい遠いですか　donogurai tōi desu ka **How far (away) is it ?**

いくらですか　ikura desu ka **How much is it ?**

何をしているのですか　nani wo shite iru no desu ka **What are you doing ?**

何がほしいのですか　nani ga hoshii no desu ka **What do you want ?**

... がありますか　...ga arimasu ka **Is there a .../do you have ... ?**

... を持っていますか　...wo motte imasu ka **Do you have a ... ?**

これをいただいてもよろしいですか　kore wo itadaite mo yoroshii desu ka **May I have this ?**

... がほしい　...ga hoshii **I want a ....**

... がほしくない　...ga hoshikunai **I don't want ....**

... を取って下さい　...wo totte kudasai **Take ....**

5. Manners

ごめんなさい　gomen nasai **I'm sorry./Pardon me./Forgive me.**

失礼します　shitsurei shimasu **Excuse me./pardon me.**

すみません　sumimasen **Excuse me.** (used to get attention when seeking information, calling a waiter etc)

お手数掛けてすみません　o-tesū kakete sumimasen **I'm sorry to trouble you like this.**

よろしくお願いします　yoroshiku o-negai shimasu (no English equivalent; rather like a very formal "please")

ご迷惑でしょうか　go-meiwaku deshō ka **Is it too much trouble ?**

心配いりません　shinpai irimasen **Don't worry.**

かまいません　kamaimasen **It doesn't matter.**

よろしいんですよ　yoroshiin desu yo **That's all right.**

何とおっしゃいましたか　nan to osshaimashita ka **What did you say ?**

もう一度言って下さい　mō ichido itte kudasai **Please say that again.**

ゆっくり話して下さい　yukkuri hanashite kudasai **Please speak slowly.**

急いでいます　isoide imasu **I'm in a hurry.**

用意ができています　yōi ga dekite imasu **I'm ready.**

ちょっとお待ち下さい　chotto o-machi kudasai **Just a moment, please.**

6. Conveying information

私はあの少年を知っています　watashi wa ano shōnen wo shitte imasu **I know that boy.**

その人を知りません　sono hito wo shirimasen **I never heard of him/her.**

はっきりとは分かりません　hakkiri to wa wakarimasen **I really don't know for certain.**

覚えています　oboete imasu **(Yes,) I remember.**

忘れました　wasuremashita **I forgot.**

私はとても怒っています　watashi wa totemo okotte imasu **I am very angry.**

私はたいへん不愉快です　watashi wa taihen fuyukai desu **I am very upset.**

気分は最高です　kibun wa saikō desu **I feel great.**

とても幸せです　totemo shiawase desu **I feel very happy.**

残念です　zannen desu **That's too bad.**

家族と／が離ればなれで寂しい　kazoku to／ga hanarebanare de sabishii **I miss my family.**

それは正しいと思います　sore wa tadashii to omoimasu **That's correct.**

あなたは間違っています　anata wa machigatte imasu **You're mistaken.**

あなたの言う通りです　anata no iu tōri desu **It's as you say.**

一生懸命に働きます　isshōkenmei ni hatarakimasu **I'm going to work hard.**

7. Eating out

a. getting seats

私はとても空腹です　watashi wa totemo kūfuku desu **I'm very hungry.**

私はのどが渇きました　watashi wa nodo ga kawakimashita **I'm thirsty.**

食事に行きましょう　shokuji ni ikimashō **Let's go someplace to eat.**

安い店を紹介してくれませんか　yasui mise wo shōkai shite kuremasen ka **Do you know some inexpensive place？**

角のてんぷら屋がおいしいと評判です　kado no tenpuraya ga oishii to hyōban desu **They say the tempura* place on the corner is pretty good.**

1時にテーブルを予約して下さい　ichiji ni tēburu wo yoyaku shite kudasai **Reserve a table for one o'clock, will you please？**

3人連れですが、空いているテーブルありますか　sanninzure desu ga, aite iru tēburu arimasu ka **Do you have a table for 3？**

満席です　manseki desu **Sorry, we're all filled up.**

昼時はどこも混んでいます　hirudoki wa doko mo konde imasu **At noontime everywhere you go it's crowded.**

禁煙席にお願いします　kin-enseki ni o-negai shimasu **We want a non-smoking** table, please.

b. ordering

メニューを見せていただけますか　menyū wo misete itadakemasu ka **Can we see a menu, please ?**

定食はありますか　teishoku wa arimasu ka **Do you have set meals ?**

本日のおすすめ料理は何ですか　honjitsu no o-susume ryōri wa nan desu ka **What's today's specialty ?**

この地方の名物は何ですか　kono chihō no meibutsu wa nan desu ka **What's the local specialty ?**

何を食べたいですか　nani wo tabetai desu ka **What do you feel like eating ?**

これは何の料理ですか　kore wa nan no ryōri desu ka **What is this ?**

... を食べて見ませんか　...wo tabete mimasen ka **How about trying the ... ?**

私は... にしたい　watashi wa ...ni shitai **I want the ....**

私は魚が大好きです　watashi wa sakana ga daisuki desu **I just love fish.**

私は肉は嫌いです　watashi wa niku wa kirai desu **I hate meat.**

私はピーマンは食べられません　watashi wa pīman wa taberaremasen **I can't eat green peppers.**

おいしいです　oishii desu **It's delicious.**

これはまずい　kore wa mazui **It tastes awful.**

もう少しパンを下さい　mō sukoshi pan wo kudasai **Can we have some more bread, please?**

ご飯のおかわりを下さい　gohan no o-kawari wo kudasai **Another bowl of rice, please.**

塩を取って下さい　shio wo totte kudasai **Please pass the salt.**

スープがまだきていません　sūpu ga mada kite imasen **We didn't get our soup yet.**

味が薄い　aji ga usui **This needs more seasoning.**

辛すぎます　karasugimasu **It's too salty.**

おなかがいっぱいになりました　onaka ga ippai ni narimashita **I'm full.**

c. drinks

飲物は何になさいますか　nomimono wa nani ni nasaimasu ka **What will you have to drink ?**

生ビールを下さい　namabīru wo kudasai **We'll have draft beer.**

ブランディーはありますか　burandī wa arimasu ka **Do you have any brandy ?**

ミルクティーを2つ下さい　mirukutī wo futatsu kudasai **Two teas with milk,** please.

ダイエットをしているので砂糖はいりません　daietto wo shite iru no de satō wa irimasen **I'm on a diet, so no sugar, please.**

コーヒーのおかわりを下さい　kōhī no o-kawari wo kudasai **More coffee, please.**

水をもういっぱい下さい　mizu wo mō ippai kudasai **More water, please.**

このお茶は少し熱い　kono o-cha wa sukoshi atsui **This tea is too hot.**

d. paying

勘定をお願いします　kanjō wo o-negai shimasu **Can I have the bill, please?**

伝票を調べて下さい．間違っていると思います　denpyō wo shirabete kudasai. machigatte iru to omoimasu **Check this bill, will you? I think there's a mistake on it.**

サラダは取っていません　sarada wa totte imasen **I didn't order any salad.**

伝票を別々にしてくれませんか　denpyō wo betsubetsu ni shite kuremasen ka **Will you give us separate bills, please?**

e. restaurant words

レストラン　resutoran **restaurant**

軽食　keishoku **light lunches**

メニュー　menyū **menu**

勘定(書)　kanjō(gaki) **bill/check**

化粧室　keshōshitsu **restroom(s)**

ウエイトレス　ueitoresu **waitress**

ウエイター　ueitā **waiter**

板前　itamae **cook**

茶碗(ゎん)　chawan **rice bowl/teacup (for Japanese tea)**

湯呑み　yunomi **teacup (for Japanese tea)**

カップ　kappu **cup/teacup/coffee cup (with handle)**

箸(はし)　hashi **chopsticks**

つまようじ　tsumayōji **toothpick**

灰皿　haizara **ashtray**

たばこ　tabako **cigarette**

日本酒　nihonshu **sake***

銚子(ちょうし)／とっくり　chōshi*/tokkuri* **(no English equivalent; see glossary)**

熱燗(かん)　atsukan **hot sake**

水　mizu **water**

ミルク　miruku **milk**

砂糖　satō **sugar**
紅茶　kōcha **tea**
日本茶　nihoncha **Japanese tea**
塩　shio **salt**
こしょう　koshō **pepper**
芥子(からし)　karashi **mustard**
油　abura **oil**
酢　su **vinegar**
正油(しょうゆ)　shōyu **soy sauce**
どんぶり　donburi **bowl**
味噌(みそ)　miso **miso***
わさび　wasabi **wasabi***

f. some Japanese dishes

すき焼き　sukiyaki　　beef cooked at table with green onions, tofu, and leafy vegetables

寿司(すし)　sushi　　cooked rice seasoned with vinegar and served in various forms with a topping of fish, shellfish, and vegetables

てんぷら　tenpura　　fish, shellfish, and vegetables coated with batter and fried in deep fat

天丼(どん)　tendon　　a bowl of rice topped with tempura* dipped in broth

豆腐　tōfu　　white soya-bean curd with a soft, cheeselike consistency

梅干　umeboshi　　ume* pickled with salt and a pungent seasoning

刺身　sashimi　　fish and shellfish sliced and eaten raw with soy sauce and wasabi*

納豆　nattō　　fermented soy beans

うどん　udon　　wheat-flour noodles

そば　soba　　buckwheat noodles

味噌(みそ)汁　misoshiru　　soup flavored with miso

お握(にぎ)り　o-nigiri　　rice compacted into a ball or other shape for carrying on outings, to work etc

餅(もち)　mochi　　glutinous rice steamed, pounded into a paste, shaped into patties, and allowed to harden

赤飯　sekihan　　glutinous rice steamed with red beans

たくあん　takuan　　radish pickled in salt and rice bran

お好み焼き　okonomiyaki　　a sort of hotcake made from wheat flour batter to which have been added various vegetables and other ingredients and fried on a hot plate

ところてん　tokoroten　a jelly made from a species of seaweed and eaten as a refreshing dish in summer

おでん　oden　various fish and vegetable preparations stewed in a light broth

ようかん　yōkan　a jellied confection made from highly sweetened beans

雑煮　zōni　a soup with vegetables, fish, and meat to which mochi are added: a traditional New Year's dish

おせち　o-sechi　an assortment of New Year's dishes prepared several days beforehand from ingredients that will not spoil; the idea is to give the womenfolk a degree of respite from the drudgery of kitchen work on the greatest feast of the year

煎餅(せんべい)　senbei　fried crackers made from rice flour

Shopping

a. going out

私は帽子が買いたい　watashi wa bōshi ga kaitai **I need a new hat.**

どのお店が一番よいですか　dono o-mise ga ichiban yoi desu ka **Do you know a good store ?**

駅のそばの果物屋は安いので有名です　eki no soba no kudamonoya wa yasui no de yūmei desu **The fruit store near the station is known for its low prices.**

デパートで今セールをやっています　depāto de ima sēru wo yatte imasu **They're having a sale at the department store today.**

一緒に買い物に行きましょう　issho ni kaimono ni ikimashō **How about coming shopping with me ?**

... はどこで買えますか　...wa doko de kaemasu ka **Where can you buy a ... ?**

一番近い本屋はどこですか　ichiban chikai hon-ya wa doko desu ka **Where's the closest bookstore ?**

靴売場はどこですか　kutsu uriba wa doko desu ka **Where is the shoe department ?**

b. picking things out

店員さん，これを見せて下さい　ten-insan, kore wo misete kudasai **Excuse me, Miss, could you let me examine this item ?**

... を売っていますか　...wo utte imasu ka **Do you sell ... here ?**

... を買いたいのです　...wo kaitai no desu **I'm looking for ....**

こちらはいかがでしょう　kochira wa ikaga deshou **How about this one ?**

何色がよろしいのですか　nani-iro ga yoroshii no desu ka **What color would you like ?**

きれいな色ですね　kirei na iro desu ne **That's a pretty color, isn't it ?**

これが気に入りました　kore ga ki ni irimashita **I like this one.**

あちらの方が好きです　achira no hō ga suki desu **I like that one.**

この色はあまり好きではありません　kono iro wa amari suki de wa arimasen **I don't like this color.**

別な色のものがありますか　betsu na iro no mono ga arimasu ka **Do you have this in a different color ?**

別の品物を見せて下さい　betsu no shinamono wo misete kudasai **Show me something else.**

もっと安いものはありませんか　motto yasui mono wa arimasen ka **Do you have something cheaper ?**

予算は1万円です　yosan wa ichiman en desu **My spending limit is 10,000 yen.**

予算の枠内で買いたいのです　yosan no wakunai de kaitai no desu **I don't want to go over my limit.**

サイズはいくらですか　saizu wa ikura desu ka **What size do you take ?**

これはどのサイズですか　kore wa dono saizu desu ka **What size is this ?**

サイズ... を下さい　saizu... wo kudasai **Give me a size ....**

もっと大きいものがありますか　motto ōkii mono ga arimasu ka **Do you have something bigger ?**

大きすぎる　ōkisugiru **It's too big.**

高すぎる　takasugiru **It's too expensive.**

c. in various stores
clothing and shoes

セーターを見せて下さい　sētā wo misete kudasai **Show me some sweaters.**

ウインドーにあるのが好きです　uindō ni aru no ga suki desu **I like the one in the window.**

その着物は実に豪華ですね　sono kimono wa jitsu ni gōka desu ne **That kimono is really gorgeous.**

残念ながら着物は1人で着られません　zannennagara kimono wa hitori de kira-remasen **It's unfortunate, but a kimono is hard to put on by oneself.**

黒い絹の手袋がほしい　kuroi kinu no tebukuro ga hoshii **I want a pair of black silk gloves.**

試着していいですか　shichaku shite ii desu ka **Can I try it on ?**

胸まわりは... です　munemawari wa ...desu **My bust/chest measures ....**

ウエストは... です　uesuto wa ...desu **My waist measures ....**

襟(衿)のサイズは... です　eri no saizu wa ...desu **My collar size is....**

この色は今年の流行です　kono iro wa kotoshi no ryūkō desu **This color is in fashion this year.**

このスタイルは好きではありません　kono sutairu wa suki de wa arimasen **I don't like this style.**

コート売り場はどこですか　kōto uriba wa doko desu ka **Where do you sell coats?**

このネクタイは実におしゃれです　kono nekutai wa jitsu ni o-share desu **This necktie is really stylish.**

靴下を2足ほしい　kutsushita wo nisoko hoshii **I want 2 pairs of socks.**

ビーチサンダルがほしい　bīchisandaru ga hoshii **I want a pair of beach sandals.**

このかかとは高すぎる　kono kakato wa takasugiru **The heels are too high.**

food and drink

パンを1個下さい　pan wo ikko kudasai **One loaf of bread, please.**

冷凍食品コーナーはどこですか　reitōshokuhin kōnā wa doko desu ka **Where are the frozen foods?**

... を1キロ下さい　...wo ichikiro kudasai **Give me one kilo of ....**

牛乳を1瓶下さい　gyūnyū wo hitobin kudasai **Give me a bottle of milk.**

それは新鮮ですか　sore wa shinsen desu ka **Is that fresh?**

これは古くなっている　kore wa furuku natte iru **This isn't fresh any more.**

賞味期間を過ぎている　shōmikikan wo sugite iru **The date on this has expired.**

これは悪くなっている　kore wa waruku natte iru **This has gone bad.**

medicines

ばんそうこうを下さい　bansōkō wo kudasai **I'd like a roll of adhesive tape.**

バンドエイドを下さい　bandoeido wo kudasai **Give me a box of Band-Aids®.**

日焼け止めの薬ありますか　hiyakedome no kusuri arimasu ka **Have you got something to prevent sunburn?**

消化不良にきく薬を下さい　shōkafuryō ni kiku kusuri wo kudasai **Give me something for indigestion, please.**

のどが痛みます．トローチを下さい　nodo ga itamimasu. torōchi wo kudasai **I have a sore throat; give me a box of cough drops.**

虫刺されにきく薬をくれませんか　mushisasare ni kiku kusuri wo kuremasen ka **Can you give me something for insect bites?**

総合ビタミン剤を下さい　sōgōbitaminzai wo kudasai **I want a bottle of vitamin tablets.**

この処方箋（ﾝ）を調合していただけますか　kono shohōsen wo chōgō shite itadakemasu ka **Can I have this prescription filled, please ?**

小さな救急箱はありますか chiisana kyūkyūbako wa arimasu ka **Do you have a small first-aid kit ?**

アスピリンを1瓶下さい asupirin wo hitobin kudasai **Give me a bottle of aspirin, please.**

newspapers, books, stationery

英字新聞は売っていますか eijishinbun wa utte imasu ka **Do you carry English-language newspapers ?**

市街地図はありますか shigaichizu wa arimasu ka **Do you have a city map ?**

... 著の本がありますか ...cho no hon ga arimasu ka **Do you have any books by ... ?**

ノートを2冊とボールペンを1本下さい nōto wo nisatsu to bōrupen wo ippon kudasai **Two notebooks and a ballpoint, please.**

横書きの便せんはありますか yokogaki no binsen wa arimasu ka **Have you got letter paper for writing left to right ?**

d. paying for things

これはいくらですか kore wa ikura desu ka **How much is this ?**

全部でいくらになりますか zenbu de ikura ni narimasu ka **How much all together ?**

勘定をお願いします kanjō wo o-negai shimasu **Can I have the bill, please ?**

アメリカの通貨で売ってくれますか amerika no tsūka de utte kuremasu ka **Can I pay in American money ?**

トラベラーズチェックで受けてくれますか toraberāzuchekku de ukete kuremasu ka **Will you take traveler's checks ?**

少し高いですね sukoshi takai desu ne **That's rather expensive, isn't it ?**

割引きしてくれますか waribiki shite kuremasu ka **Can you give me a discount ?**

ここのレジは混んでいます koko no reji wa konde imasu **The line at this checkout counter is too long.**

レシートをいただけますか reshīto wo itadakemasu ka **Can I have a receipt ?**

おつりが間違っています o-tsuri ga machigatte imasu **You gave me the wrong change.**

e. complaints

責任者に会いたい sekininsha ni aitai **I want to speak to your superior.**

昨日これを買いました　sakujitsu kore wo kaimashita **I bought this yesterday.**

これは汚れている（破れている，壊れている，ひびが入っている，不良品だ）　kore wa yogorete iru (yaburete iru, kowarete iru, hibi ga haitte iru, furyōhin da) **This is stained (torn, broken, cracked, defective).**

この本には落丁があります　kono hon ni wa rakuchō ga arimasu **This book has pages missing.**

この薬は全く効果がありません　kono kusuri wa mattaku kōka ga arimasen **This medicine doesn't have any effect at all.**

店員の態度が悪い　ten-in no taido ga warui **I don't like your clerk's manners.**

これを取り替えて下さいませんか　kore wo torikaete kudasaimasen ka **Can I exchange this, please?**

お金を払い戻して下さいませんか　o-kane wo haraimodoshite kudasaimasen ka **Can I have my money back, please?**

f. repairing and mending

時計が壊れてしまいました　tokei ga kowarete shimaimashita **My watch is broken.**

修理できますか　shūri dekimasu ka **Can it be fixed?**

これを直して下さい　kore wo naoshite kudasai **Can you fix this?**

残念ながらそれはもはや修理できません　zannennagara sore wa mohaya shūri dekimasen **I'm sorry, but it's beyond repair.**

靴のかかとを新しいのとつけ替えていただけますか　kutsu no kakato wo atarashii no to tsukekaete itadakemasu ka **Can you put new heels on these shoes?**

待っている間にやってくれますか　matte iru aida ni yatte kuremasu ka **Can you do it while I wait?**

いつできますか　itsu dekimasu ka **How soon can you have it done?**

どのぐらい時間がかかりますか　dono gurai jikan ga kakarimasu ka **How long will it take?**

このジャケットのシミは抜けないでしょうか　kono jaketto no shimi wa nukenai deshō ka **Can you remove the stain on this jacket?**

このズボンのすそがほつれているので繕っていただけますか　kono zubon no suso ga hotsurete iru no de tsukurotte itadakemasu ka **The cuffs on these pants are worn. Can you mend them?**

…の具合が悪いのでみていただけますか　...no guai ga warui no de mite itadakemasu ka **The ... is out of order. Could you have a look at it, please?**

できるだけ早く直していただきたい　dekiru dake hayaku naoshite itadakitai **I want** this fixed as soon as possible.

費用はいくらですか　hiyō wa ikura desu ka **How much will it cost ?**

9. Postal and Telephone Service

a. the post office

一番近い郵便局はどこですか　ichiban chikai yūbinkyoku wa doko desu ka **Where is the nearest post office ?**

郵便局は何時まで開いていますか　yūbinkyoku wa nanji made aite imasu ka **What time does the post office close ?**

ポストはどこにありますか　posuto wa doko ni arimasu ka **Do you know where there's a mailbox ?**

ちょうど記念切手を売り出しているところです　chōdo kinenkitte wo uridashite iru tokoro desu **They have just issued a new commemorative stamp.**

カナダまで葉書はいくらですか　kanada made hagaki wa ikura desu ka **How much is a postcard to Canada ?**

アメリカまで航空便はいくらですか　amerika made kōkūbin wa ikura desu ka **How much is an air mail letter to America ?**

イギリスまで船便ではいくらですか　igirisu made funabin de wa ikura desu ka **How much is surface mail to Britain ?**

この小包をお願いします　kono kozutsumi wo o-negai shimasu **I want to mail this package.**

この手紙を速達で送りたい　kono tegami wo sokutatsu de okuritai **I want to send this letter by express mail.**

この手紙を書留にしたい　kono tegami wo kakitome ni shitai **I want to send this letter by registered mail.**

官製葉書を10枚下さい　kanseihagaki wo jūmai kudasai **Ten government postcards*, please.**

大体何日頃届きますか　daitai nannichi goro todokimasu ka **Do you know how many days it will take to get there ?**

b. telephones and telegrams

一番近い電話ボックスはどこですか　ichiban chikai denwabokkusu wa doko desu ka **Where is the nearest telephone booth ?**

電話を掛けたい　denwa wo kaketai **I want to make a phone call.**

オーストラリアに電話したい　ōsutoraria ni denwa shitai **I want to make a phone call to Australia.**

小銭が不足しています．テレフォンカードをお持ちですか　kozeni ga fusoku shite

imasu. terefonkādo wo o-mochi desu ka **I don't have enough small change.
Do you have a telephone card?**

コレクトコールにしたい korekutokōru ni shitai **I want to make a collect call.**

もしもし… さんですか moshimoshi …san desu ka **Hello. Is this Mr. …?**

どちら様ですか dochirasama desu ka **Who is this calling, please?**

内線… 番をお願いします naisen …ban wo o-negai shimasu **Give me extension
…, please.**

そのままお待ち下さい sono mama o-machi kudasai **Please hold the line a
moment.**

… はただ今外出中です …wa tadaima gaishutsuchū desu **… is out at the
moment.**

… はいつお戻りですか …wa itsu o-modori desu ka **When will … be back?**

伝言をお願いできますか dengon wo o-negai dekimasu ka **Will you take a
message, please?**

… より電話があったと彼に伝えて下さい …yori denwa ga atta to kare ni tsutaete
kudasai **Please tell him that … called.**

後ほどお電話します nochihodo o-denwa shimasu **I'll call again later.**

私に電話するように伝えて下さい watashi ni denwa suru yō ni tsutaete kudasai
Please tell him to call me.

話し中です hanashichū desu **The line is busy.**

電話番号が間違っています denwabangō ga machigatte imasu **You have the
wrong number.**

留守番電話にメッセージが入っています rusubandenwa ni messēji ga haitte imasu
There's a message on the answering machine.

電報を打ちたい denpō wo uchitai **I want to send a telegram.**

1語あたりいくらですか ichigo atari ikura desu ka **How much is it for each
word?**

祝電(弔電)を打ちたい shukuden (chōden) wo uchitai **I want to send a telegram
of congratulation 〔condolence〕.**

10. Transport

a. trains

駅はどこにありますか eki wa doko ni arimasu ka **Where is the train station?**

新幹線のホームはどこですか shinkansen no hōmu wa doko desu ka **Where are
the shinkansen* tracks?**

切符は自動発券機で買えます kippu wa jidōhakkenki de kaemasu **You can buy
your ticket at the automatic ticket machine.**

新幹線の座席指定はこの用紙に必要事項を記入します　shinkansen no zaseki shitei wa kono yōshi ni hitsuyōjikō wo kinyū shimasu **You have to fill out this form to get a reserved seat on the shinkansen*.**

９：３０分発京都行きの特急に乗りたいのですが　kujisanjippunhatsu kyōtoyuki no tokkyū ni noritai no desu ga **I want a ticket on the 9:30 special express to Kyōto, please.**

禁煙席を希望します　kin-enseki wo kibō shimasu **If possible I want a non-smoking seat.**

往復の切符を買いたい　ōfuku no kippu wo kaitai **I want a round-trip ticket.**

寝台車を予約したい　shindaisha wo yoyaku shitai **I want to reserve a berth on a sleeping car.**

寝台車はいくらですか　shindaisha wa ikura desu ka **How much does a sleeping car ticket cost?**

急行列車ですか，それとも普通列車ですか　kyūkōressha desu ka, soretomo futsūressha desu ka **Do you want the express train or the local train?**

この電車は...へ行きますか　kono densha wa ..e ikimasu ka **Does this train go to ...?**

もっと早くでる列車はありますか　motto hayaku deru ressha wa arimasu ka **Isn't there an earlier train?**

この列車には食堂車がありますか　kono ressha ni wa shokudōsha ga arimasu ka **Is there a dining car on this train?**

...まで片道３枚下さい　...made katamichi sanmai kudasai **Three one-way tickets to ..., please.**

この切符は何日間有効ですか　kono kippu wa nannichikan yūkō desu ka **How long is this ticket valid?**

この列車は何時に発車しますか　kono ressha wa nanji ni hassha shimasu ka **What time does this train leave?**

... 行きの列車は何番ホームから発車しますか　...yuki no ressha wa nanban hōmu kara hassha shimasu ka **Where do I get the train for ...?**

... には何時に到着しますか　...ni wa nanji ni tōchaku shimasu ka **What time does the train get to ...?**

... からの列車は何時に到着しますか　...kara no ressha wa nanji ni tōchaku shimasu ka **What time does the train from ... get in?**

この列車は...に停まりますか　kono ressha wa .. ni tomarimasu ka **Does this train stop at ...?**

この列車は遅れていますか　kono ressha wa okurete imasu ka **Is this train running late?**

指定券を持っています　shiteiken wo motte imasu **I have a reservation.**

車掌が検札に来ました　shashō ga kensatsu ni kimashita **The conductor is here to check the tickets.**

この席は空いていますか　kono seki wa aite imasu ka **Is this seat taken ?** (literally, "Is this seat open ?")

どこで乗換えですか　doko de norikae desu ka **Where do I transfer ?**

時刻表はどこにありますか　jikokuhyō wa doko ni arimasu ka **Where is the time-table ?**

近ごろは自動改札が増えました　chikagoro wa jidōkaisatsu ga fuemashita **Nowa-days you see more and more automatic wickets.**

b. buses

バス停はどこですか　basutei wa doko desu ka **Where is the bus stop ?**

... 行きのバスの発着所はどこですか　...yuki no basu no hatchakujo wa doko desu ka **Where do I get the bus for ... ?**

このバスは... に停まりますか　kono basu wa ...ni tomarimasu ka **Does this bus stop at ... ?**

... までどのぐらい時間がかかりますか　...made dono gurai jikan ga kakarimasu ka **How long does it take to get to ... ?**

定期観光バスに乗りたい　teiki kankōbasu ni noritai **I want to ride a scheduled sightseeing bus.**

そのバスは何時に... に着きますか　sono basu wa nanji ni ...ni tsukimasu ka **What time does the bus reach ... ?**

そのバスは何時に発車しますか　sono basu wa nanji ni hassha shimasu ka **What time does the bus leave ?**

このバスはどのぐらいの間隔で出ていますか　kono basu wa donogurai no kankaku de dete imasu ka **How often does this bus leave ?**

次のバスは何時ですか　tsugi no basu wa nanji desu ka **What time is the next bus ?**

... の近くを通りますか　...no chikaku wo tōrimasu ka **Does the bus pass near ... ?**

... 行きのバスはどれですか　...yuki no basu wa dore desu ka **Which is the bus for ... ?**

... まで行きたい　...made ikitai **I want to go to ....**

どこで降りたらいいでしょうか　doko de oritara ii deshō ka **Where should I get off ?**

最終バスは出てしまいましたか　saishūbasu wa dete shimaimashita ka **Has the last** bus already left ?

c. taxis

タクシー乗り場はどこですか　takushīnoriba wa doko desu ka **Where is the taxi stand ?**

空車が来ました　kūsha ga kimashita **Here comes an empty taxi.**

… ホテルまで行って下さい　...hoteru made itte kudasai **Take me to the … Hotel.**

遅れているので少し急いでくれませんか　okurete iru no de sukoshi isoide kuremasen ka **I'm late, so could you go a little faster ?**

ここで止って下さい　koko de tomatte kudasai **Stop here, please.**

待っていて下さい　matte ite kudasai **Wait for me, please.**

名所旧跡がみたい　meishokyūseki ga mitai **I want to go sightseeing.**

そこは遠いですか　soko wa tōi desu ka **Is it very far from here ?**

… までどのぐらいの時間ですか　...made dono gurai no jikan desu ka **How long does it take to get there ?**

いくらですか　ikura desu ka **How much is it ?**

d. airplanes

航空会社の営業所はどこにありますか　kōkūgaisha no eigyōsho wa doko ni arimasu ka **Where is the airline office ?**

日曜日の午後の便で... まで3席予約したい　nichiyōbi no gogo no bin de ...made sanseki yoyaku shitai **I want 3 tickets to … on the Sunday afternoon flight.**

金曜日に... までの便がありますか　kinyōbi ni ...made no bin ga arimasu ka **Is there a flight to … on Friday ?**

その便は何時に発ちますか　sono bin wa nanji ni tachimasu ka **What time does that flight leave ?**

その便は何時に到着しますか　sono bin wa nanji ni tōchaku shimasu ka **What time does that flight arrive ?**

… の予約をキャンセルして下さい　...no yoyaku wo kyanseru shite kudasai **Please cancel my reservation for …**

予約を変更したい　yoyaku wo henkō shitai **I want to change my reservation.**

次の便は何時ですか　tsugi no bin wa nanji desu ka **When is the next flight ?**

市内から空港までのバスがありますか　shinai kara kūkō made no basu ga arimasu ka **Is there a bus from the city center to the airport ?**

e. boats

その船は何時に出航ですか　sono fune wa nanji ni shukkō desu ka **What time does the boat leave ?**

次の出航は何時ですか　tsugi no shukkō wa nanji desu ka **When does the next boat leave ?**

その船はどこに入港ですか　sono fune wa doko ni nyūkō desu ka **What stops does the boat make ?**

その船は… に寄港しますか　sono fune wa …ni kikō shimasu ka **Does the boat stop at … ?**

… まで船便がありますか　…made funabin ga arimasu ka **Is there a boat to … ?**

この船でどのぐらい時間がかかりますか　kono fune de dono gurai jikan ga kakarimasu ka **How much time does this boat take to get there ?**

一人用船室を予約できますか　hitoriyō senshitsu wo yoyaku dekimasu ka **Can I reserve a single stateroom ?**

部屋にはいくつ寝台がありますか　heya ni wa ikutsu shindai ga arimasu ka **How many beds are there in the stateroom ?**

いつ入港しますか　itsu nyūkō shimasu ka **When will we reach port ?**

何時に乗船しなければなりませんか　nanji ni jōsen shinakereba narimasen ka **By what time do we have to be on board ?**

港にどのぐらい停泊しますか　minato ni dono gurai teihaku shimasu ka **How long will the boat stay in port ?**

f. cars

運転免許証を持っています　unten menkyoshō wo motte imasu **I have a driver's license.**

友人とドライブに出かけましょう　yūjin to doraibu ni dekakemashō **Let's go for a drive with some friends.**

いい車ですね. 自家用車ですか　ii kuruma desu ne. jikayōsha desu ka **Nice car. Is it yours ?**

いいえ. レンタカーです　iie. rentakā desu **No, it's rented.**

どこで車を借りられますか　doko de kuruma wo kariraremasu ka **Where can I rent a car ?**

レンタカーは1時間いくらですか　rentakā wa ichijikan ikura desu ka **What's the fee per hour to rent this car ?**

一番近いガソリンスタンドはどこですか　ichiban chikai gasorinsutando wa doko desu ka **Where is the nearest gas station ?**

満タンにして下さい　mantan ni shite kudasai **Fill it up, please.**

ガソリン，リッターあたりいくらですか　gasorin, rittā atari ikura desu ka **How much is gasoline per liter ?**

洗車して下さい　sensha shite kudasai **Wash the car, please.**

道路地図はありますか　dōrochizu wa arimasu ka **Do you have a road map ?**

駐車場はどこですか　chūshajō wa doko desu ka **Where is the parking lot ?**

ここは駐車禁止ですか　koko wa chūsha kinshi desu ka **Is this a no parking zone ?**

今どこでしょうか　ima doko deshō ka **Where are we now ?**

地図で示して下さい　chizu de shimeshite kudasai **Show me on the map.**

次のドライブインで昼食にしましょう　tsugi no doraibuin de chūshoku ni shimashō **Let's have lunch at the next drive-in.**

... にはどう行けばいいですか　...ni wa dō ikeba ii desu ka **How do you get to ... ?**

... はどこにありますか　...wa doko ni arimasu ka **Where is ... ?**

... への自動車道にはどう行けばいいですか　...e no jidōshadō ni wa dō ikeba ii desu ka **How do you get to the expressway for ... ?**

... へはどの道を行けば一番いいですか　...e wa dono michi wo ikeba ichiban ii desu ka **What's the best road to ... ?**

... までどのぐらいの距離がありますか　...made dono gurai no kyori ga arimasu ka **How far is it to ... ?**

... に夕刻までには着くのでしょうか　...ni yūkoku made ni wa tsuku no deshō ka **Will we reach ... by evening ?**

高速道路は混んでいます　kōsokudōro wa konde imasu **The expressway is clogged with heavy traffic.**

渋滞に巻き込まれました　jūtai ni makikomaremashita **I got caught in heavy traffic.**

抜け道がありますか　nukemichi ga arimasu ka **Is there a back road to get around the traffic ?**

このまま5キロほどまっすぐ行って下さい　kono mama 5 kiro hodo massugu itte kudasai **Go straight along this road for 5 kilometers.**

次の信号を右に曲って下さい　tsugi no shingō wo migi ni magatte kudasai **Turn right at the next signal.**

車の鍵(⚿)をなくさないように　kuruma no kagi wo nakusanai yō ni **Don't lose your car keys.**

　　some road signs

右側通行　migigawa tsūkō **keep right**

一方通行道路　ippōtsūkōdōro **one way**

迂回　ukai **detour**

駐車禁止　chūsha kinshi **no parking**

追い越し禁止　oikoshi kinshi **no passing**

進入禁止　shinnyū kinshi **no entry**

前方道路工事中　zenpō dōro kōjichū **construction ahead**

11. Hotels

安くてよいホテルを紹介して下さい　yasukute yoi hoteru wo shōkai shite kudasai **Can you tell me the name of a hotel that is good and also cheap ?**

今夜部屋はありますか　kon-ya heya wa arimasu ka **Do you have a vacancy for tonight ?**

2人で泊まれる部屋がありますか　futari de tomareru heya ga arimasu ka **Do you have a room for two ?**

シングルの部屋を3室予約します　shinguru no heya wo sanshitsu yoyaku shimasu **I would like to reserve 3 single rooms.**

その部屋は何階にありますか　sono heya wa nangai ni arimasu ka **What floor is that room on ?**

2階の部屋は空いていますか　nikai no heya wa aite imasu ka **Do you have a room on the second floor ?**

この部屋にします　kono heya ni shimasu **I'll take this room.**

別の部屋がありませんか　betsu no heya ga arimasen ka **Don't you have some other room ?**

ツインしかありません　tsuin shika arimasen **We only have a twin room.**

空き室はこれだけです　akishitsu wa kore dake desu **This is the only vacancy we have.**

和室の部屋はありますか　washitsu no heya wa arimasu ka **Do you have a Japanese-style room ?**

この部屋は1泊いくらですか　kono heya wa ippaku ikura desu ka **What's the rate for this room ?**

もっと安い部屋はありませんか　motto yasui heya wa arimasen ka **Don't you have something cheaper ?**

明朝7：30分に起して下さい　myōchō shichiji sanjuppun ni okoshite kudasai **Please wake me up at 7:30 tomorrow morning.**

私の部屋にはタオルがありません　watashi no heya ni wa taoru ga arimasen **There are no towels in my room.**

シーツが汚れています　shītsu ga yogorete imasu **The sheets are dirty.**

トイレの水が流れません　toire no mizu ga nagaremasen **The toilet won't flush.**

シャワーの出がよくありません　shawā no de ga yoku arimasen **There's no pressure in the shower.**

窓が空きません. 開けて下さい　mado ga akimasen. akete kudasai **I can't get the window open. Please open it.**

暑すぎます　atsusugimasu **It's too hot in here.**

暖房を強くできますか　danbō wo tsuyoku dekimasu ka **Can you turn up the heat?**

冷房がきいていません　reibō ga kiite imasen **The air conditioning isn't working.**

鍵(ぎ)を下さい　kagi wo kudasai **Give me my key, please.**

私宛のメッセージがありますか　watashi ate no messēji ga arimasu ka **Are there any messages for me?**

この洋服を洗濯してほしい　kono yōfuku wo sentaku shite hoshii **I want to get this dress cleaned.**

このスーツにアイロンを掛けてほしい　kono sūtsu ni airon wo kakete hoshii **I want to get this suit pressed.**

明日の午前中までにできますか　myōnichi no gozenchū made ni dekimasu ka **Can you have it done by tomorrow morning?**

食堂はどこですか　shokudō wa doko desu ka **Where is the dining room?**

明後日の朝立ちます　asatte no asa tachimasu **I'll be leaving the day after tomorrow in the morning.**

勘定書きを用意してくれますか　kanjōgaki wo yōi shite kuremasu ka **Will you get my bill ready, please?**

荷物を下におろしていただけますか　nimotsu wo shita ni oroshite itadakemasu ka **Can you have my luggage taken downstairs, please?**

10時にタクシーを1台呼んでいただけますか　jūji ni takushī wo ichidai yonde itadakemasu ka **Will you call me a taxi for 10 o'clock, please?**

お世話になりました　o-sewa ni narimashita **I enjoyed my stay.**

12. Leisure time

a. sightseeing

名所旧跡を見物しましょう　meishokyūseki wo kenbutsu shimashō **Let's go sightseeing.**

ガイドブックを持ってきましたか　gaidobukku wo motte kimashita ka **Did you bring the guidebook?**

当地の見所は何ですか　tōchi no midokoro wa nan desu ka **What is there to see** around here ?

この建物は何ですか　kono tatemono wa nan desu ka **What is this building ?**

いつ建てられましたか　itsu tateraremashita ka **When was it built ?**

誰(だれ)が建てましたか　dare ga tatemashita ka **Who built it ?**

このお寺は何と言いますか　kono o-tera wa nan to iimasu ka **What's the name of this temple ?**

これは美術館ですか　kore wa bijutsukan desu ka **Is this an art museum ?**

... は何時に開きますか　...wa nanji ni akimasu ka **What time does ... open ?**

何曜日が休館ですか　nanyōbi ga kyūkan desu ka **What days is it closed on ?**

入場料はいくらですか　nyūjōryō wa ikura desu ka **How much is the entrance fee ?**

切符はどこで買えますか　kippu wa doko de kaemasu ka **Where do they sell the tickets ?**

カメラを持ってきましたか　kamera wo motte kimashita ka **Did you bring your camera ?**

写真をとって下さい　shashin wo totte kudasai **Take a picture of that.**

写真をとってもいいですか　shashin wo totte mo ii desu ka **Is it all right to take pictures ?**

撮影は禁止です　satsuei wa kinshi desu **Picture-taking is forbidden.**

ガイドさんについて行って下さい　gaidosan ni tsuite itte kudasai **Follow the guide.**

ガイドは英語を話せますか　gaido wa eigo wo hanasemasu ka **Can the guide speak English ?**

ガイドはいりません　gaido wa irimasen **I don't need a guide.**

少し足をのばしてみましょう　sukoshi ashi wo nobashite mimashō **Let's walk on a little further.**

城に行くのはどのバスですか　shiro ni iku no wa dono basu desu ka **Which is the bus that goes to the castle ?**

... に行く道はこれですか　...ni iku michi wa kore desu ka **Is this the road that goes to ... ?**

... に行くにはどう行ったらよいですか　...ni iku ni wa dō ittara yoi desu ka **How can I get to ... ?**

歩いて行けますか　aruite ikemasu ka **Is it close enough to walk ?**

当地の名物料理は何ですか　tōchi no meibutsuryōri wa nan desu ka **What kind of cooking is this place known for ?**

有名なお店を教えて下さい　yūmei na o-mise wo oshiete kudasai **Can you tell me the names of important stores in this area ?**

土産には何を買ったらいいですか　miyage ni wa nani wo kattara ii desu ka **What kind of souvenirs should I buy to take home with me ?**

民芸品のお店を紹介して下さい　mingeihin no o-mise wo shōkai shite kudasai **Can you direct me to a place that sells folk art ?**

b. sports

プロ野球の観戦に行きたい　puroyakyū no kansen ni ikitai **I want to go to a professional baseball game.**

一番安い席はいくらですか　ichiban yasui seki wa ikura desu ka **How much is the cheapest ticket ?**

何時に始まりますか　nanji ni hajimarimasu ka **What time does the game start ?**

テニスをやりたい　tenisu wo yaritai **I want to play tennis.**

この海岸で泳げますか　kono kaigan de oyogemasu ka **Can you swim at this beach ?**

水泳禁止です　suiei kinshi desu **It's a no swimming zone.**

私は美容のためにヨガとエアロビクスをやっています　watashi wa biyō no tame ni yoga to earobikusu wo yatte imasu **I do yoga and aerobics for beauty care.**

相撲は日本の国技です　sumō wa nippon no kokugi desu **Sumo is the Japanese national sport.**

兄は柔道5段剣道2段です　ani wa jūdō godan kendō nidan desu **My older brother holds a fifth dan in judo and a second dan in kendo.**

釣りに行きませんか　tsuri ni ikimasen ka **Would you like to go fishing with me ?**

ボートを借りられますか　bōto wo kariraremasu ka **Can we rent a boat ?**

なかなかゴルフの腕前が上がりません　nakanaka gorufu no udemae ga agarimasen **I don't seem to make any progress at golf.**

私はマリンスポーツが得意です　watashi wa marin supōtsu ga tokui desu **I specialize in marine sports.**

運動し過ぎて体じゅうの筋肉が痛い　undō shisugite karadajū no kinniku ga itai **I exercised too hard, and all my muscles are sore.**

子供とキャッチボールをします　kodomo to kyatchibōru wo shimasu **I play catch with my son.**

家族と一緒にアウトドアスポーツを楽しみました　kazoku to issho ni autodoa spōtsu wo tanoshimimashita **I had fun playing outdoors with my family.**

c. events

映画館で何かおもしろいものをやっていますか　eigakan de nanika omoshiroi mono

... wo yatte imasu ka **Is there some good movie playing at the theater now ?**

コンサートがありますか　konsāto ga arimasu ka **Are there any concerts scheduled ?**

... デパートで生け花展があります　...depāto de ikebanaten ga arimasu **There is an ikebana* exhibition at the ... Department Store.**

... ホールで明晩オペラがあります　...hōru de myōban opera ga arimasu **There is an opera tomorrow night at the ... Hall.**

S席のチケットを2枚ほしい　esu-seki no chiketto wo nimai hoshii **I want 2 S tickets*, please.**

来週の火曜日の席を予約したい　raishū no kayōbi no seki wo yoyaku shitai **I want a reserved seat for next Tuesday.**

前売り券は明日から売り出します　maeuriken wa myōnichi kara uridashimasu **Advance tickets go on sale tomorrow.**

開演は何時ですか　kaien wa nanji desu ka **What time does the play start ?**

演目は何ですか　enmoku wa nan desu ka **What's the title of the play ?**

指揮者は誰ですか　shikisha wa dare desu ka **Who is the conductor ?**

配役を教えて下さい　haiyaku wo oshiete kudasai **Tell me the names of the actors.**

プログラムを2部下さい　puroguramu wo nibu kudasai **Two programs, please.**

日本の古典芸能に関心がありますか　nippon no kotengeinō ni kanshin ga arimasu ka **Do you have any interest in classical Japanese theater ?**

歌舞伎は見たことがありますか　kabuki wa mita koto ga arimasu ka **Have you ever been to see Kabuki* ?**

能はまだ一度も見たことがありません　nō wa mada ichido mo mita koto ga arimasen **I have never seen a Noh* play.**

13. Sickness and Accidents

a. sickness

病院へ行きたいのですが，どこがいいでしょうか　byōin e ikitai no desu ga, doko ga ii deshō ka **I want to get medical attention. Can you recommend a good hospital ?**

お医者さんを呼んで下さい　o-ishasan wo yonde kudasai **Please call a doctor.**

救急車を呼んで下さい　kyūkyūsha wo yonde kudasai **Please call an ambulance.**

私は病気です　watashi wa byōki desu **I am sick.**

とても気分が悪い　totemo kibun ga warui **I feel terrible.**

吐き気がする　hakike ga suru **I feel nauseated.**

頭ががんがん痛い　atama ga gangan itai **I have a splitting headache.**

視力が急に落ちた　shiryoku ga kyū ni ochita **My eyesight has gotten bad all of a sudden.**

耳なりがひどいのです　miminari ga hidoi no desu **I have a terrible ringing in my ears.**

虫歯が痛くてたまりません　mushiba ga itakute tamarimasen **I have a terrible toothache.**

歯医者さんへ行かなければなりませんか　haishasan e ikanakereba narimasen ka **Do you need to see a dentist?**

食あたりをしたようです　shokuatari wo shita yō desu **I must've eaten something that didn't agree with me.**

胃をこわしました　i wo kowashimashita **I've got an upset stomach.**

消化不良を起こしました　shōkafuryō wo okoshimashita **I've got indigestion.**

風邪をひきました　kaze wo hikimashita **I have a cold.**

息苦しい　ikigurushii **I have trouble breathing.**

目まいがする　memai ga suru **I feel dizzy.**

私はずっと糖尿病を煩っています　watashi wa zutto tōnyōbyō wo wazuratte imasu **I have had diabetes for a long time.**

全く食欲がありません　mattaku shokuyoku ga arimasen **I have no appetite.**

熟睡できません　jukusui dekimasen **I have trouble sleeping.**

寒気がします　samuke ga shimasu **I'm getting chills.**

咳(￥)が止まりません　seki ga tomarimasen **I can't stop coughing.**

持病の...が悪化したようです　jibyō no ...ga akka shita yō desu **His chronic ... has gotten worse.**

足首を捻挫(￥)した　ashikubi wo nenza shita **I sprained my ankle.**

右腕を骨折した　migiude wo kossetsu shita **I broke my right arm.**

やけどをした　yakedo wo shita **I burnt myself.**

切り傷をした　kirikizu wo shita **I cut myself.**

いつからそんな状態ですか　itsu kara sonna jōtai desu ka **How long have you been like this?**

昨日からこんな状態です　sakujitsu kara konna jōtai desu **I've been like this since yesterday.**

どこが痛いですか　doko ga itai desu ka **Where do you hurt?**

寝ていないといけませんか　nete inai to ikemasen ka **Do I absolutely have to stay in bed?**

絶対安静が必要です　zettai ansei ga hitsuyō desu **You need absolute rest.**

口を開けなさい　kuchi wo akenasai **Open your mouth.**

舌を出しなさい　shita wo dashinasai **Stick out your tongue.**

横になりなさい　yoko ni narinasai **Lie down.**

息を吸いなさい〔吐きなさい〕iki wo suinasai 〔hakinasai〕 **Breathe in 〔out〕.**

薬局にこの処方箋(せん)を持って行きなさい　yakkyoku ni kono shohōsen wo motte ikinasai **Take this prescription to a pharmacy.**

1日に3回これを飲んで下さい　ichinichi ni sankai kore wo nonde kudasai **Take this 3 times a day.**

注射しましょう　chūsha shimashō **I'll give you an injection.**

袖(そで)をまくりなさい　sode wo makuri nasai **Roll up your sleeve.**

少し気分がよくなりました　sukoshi kibun ga yoku narimashita **I feel a little better now.**

おかげさまですっかり元気になりました　o-kagesama de sukkari genki ni narimashita **Thanks to you, I am completely cured.**

b. accidents and disasters

交番はどこですか　kōban wa doko desu ka **Is there a police box* around here ?**

警察を呼んで下さい　keisatsu wo yonde kudasai **Call the police.**

大至急110番して下さい　daishikyū hyakutōban shite kudasai **Quick, dial 110.**

領事館に知らせて下さい　ryōjikan ni shirasete kudasai **Please inform my consulate.**

私のカバンが盗まれました　watashi no kaban ga nusumaremashita **My briefcase has been stolen.**

財布をすられました　saifu wo suraremashita **A pickpocket stole my wallet.**

パスポートがなくなりました　pasupōto ga nakunarimashita **My passport is missing.**

交通事故にあいました　kōtsūjiko ni aimashita **I have had a traffic accident.**

... に車をぶつけました　...ni kuruma wo butsukemashita **I crashed my car into a ....**

駅の階段から落ちました　eki no kaidan kara ochimashita **I fell down the stairs in the station.**

雪道で滑りました　yukimichi de suberimashita **I slipped on the snowy street.**

大けがをしました。救急車を呼んで下さい　ōkega wo shimashita. kyūkyūsha wo yonde kudasai **I am badly hurt. Please call an ambulance.**

重傷です。そっと担架に乗せて下さい　jūshō desu. sotto tanka ni nosete kudasai **He is badly hurt. Go easy when you put him on the stretcher.**

意識を失っています。大丈夫でしょうか　ishiki wo ushinatte imasu. daijōbu deshō ka **She's unconscious. Will she be okay ?**

火事だ！火事だ！　kaji da! kaji da! **Fire! Fire!**

消火器はどこですか　shōkaki wa doko desu ka **Where's the fire extinguisher ?**

今朝の地震にはびっくりしました　kesa no jishin ni wa bikkuri shimashita **The earthquake this morning was frightening.**

台風の大雨で床下浸水になりました　taifū no ōame de yukashita shinsui ni narimashita **The heavy rains of the typhoon flooded my house almost up to floor level.**

家の前の川が反乱しました　ie no mae no kawa ga hanran shimashita **The river in front of my house overflowed its banks.**

... が行方不明です　...ga yukuefumei desu **...is missing.**

山で遭難しました．救助隊を呼んで下さい　yama de sōnan shimashita. kyūjotai wo yonde kudasai **We've had a bad accident on the mountain. Please call out the rescue squad.**

仕事の現場で事故にあいました　shigoto no genba de jiko ni aimashita **He had an accident at the construction site.**

補償はどうなるのでしょうか　hoshō wa dō naru no deshō ka **What does he have to do to get compensation ?**

14. At the office

新入社員の... です．よろしく　shinnyūshain no ...desu. yoroshiku **I have just joined the company and my name is .... I am happy to meet you.**

今日からアルバイトをする事になった... です　kyō kara arubaito wo suru koto ni natta ...desu **My name is ... and I have started today as a part-timer here.**

会社の中を案内しましょうか　kaisha no naka wo annai shimashō ka **Shall I show you around the place ?**

名刺をいただけませんか　meishi wo itadakemasen ka **Could I have your card, please ?**

私のデスクはどこですか　watashi no desuku wa doko desu ka **Which is my desk ?**

初めに何をしたらいいですか　hajime ni nani wo shitara ii desu ka **What's the first thing I need to do ?**

この小包を出してきて下さい　kono kozutsumi wo dashite kite kudasai **Go mail this package, will you ?**

会議室はどこですか　kaigishitsu wa doko desu ka **Where is the conference room ?**

会議を始めます　kaigi wo hajimemasu **The meeting will now come to order.**

食事に行きます　shokuji ni ikimasu **I'm going out to lunch.**

毎日忙しい　mainichi isogashii **Every day is a busy one for me.**

残業をしなければなりません　zangyō wo shinakereba narimasen **I have to work overtime today.**

お先に失礼します　o-saki ni shitsurei shimasu (no English equivalent; said when going home ahead of one's colleagues)

お疲れさまでした　o-tsukaresama deshita (no English equivalent; said as a polite goodbye in response to the above)

忙しくていやになります　isogashikute iya ni narimasu **I'm so busy it isn't funny.**

昨日も終電で帰ったのです　kinō mo shūden de kaetta no desu **Yesterday also I worked till it was time for the last train.**

ストレスがたまっています　sutoresu ga tamatte imasu **I'm all stressed out.**

ファックスは今使っています　fakkusu wa ima tsukatte imasu **The fax machine is busy now.**

コンピュータ通信ができる人はだれですか　konpyūtatsūshin ga dekiru hito wa dare desu ka **Is there someone here who knows how to send electronic mail?**

コピーをして下さい　kopī wo shite kudasai **Make me a copy of this, please.**

ワープロを打って下さい　wāpuro wo utte kudasai **Type this out on the word processor, will you?**

ファックスを送って下さい　fakkusu wo okutte kudasai **Fax this out, will you please?**

これ，すぐお願いできますか　kore, sugu o-negai dekimasu ka **Can you handle this right away, please?**

今，ちょっと忙しいんだけど　ima, chotto isogashiin da kedo **Sorry, I'm terribly busy right now.**

この件，すぐに調べて下さい　kono ken, sugu ni shirabete kudasai **Will you look into this right away, please?**

これから課長と打ち合わせです　kore kara kachō to uchiawase desu **I've got a meeting with the manager now.**

出張で大阪へ行ってきました　shutchō de ōsaka e itte kimashita **I just got back from Osaka on a business trip.**

もうじき人事異動があります　mō jiki jinjiidō ga arimasu **There's going to be some personnel changes soon.**

根回しがうまくいっていません　nemawashi ga umaku itte imasen **The prearrangements* aren't going well.**

忘年会はだれが幹事ですか　bōnenkai wa dare ga kanji desu ka **Who's in charge of the bonenkai*?**

二次会はどこに決まりましたか　nijikai wa doko ni kimarimashita ka **Where are** you going for the nijikai* ?

彼は企画部のベテランです　kare wa kikakubu no beteran desu **He's a veteran employee of the planning department.**

この資料に目を通して下さい　kono shiryō ni me wo tōshite kudasai **I want you to read through this material, would you ?**

このパソコンの操作を教えて下さい　kono pasokon no sōsa wo oshiete kudasai **Can you show me how to run this computer ?**

... さんを応接室へお通し下さい　...san wo ōsetsushitsu e o-tōshi kudasai **Show ... to the reception room, please.**

帰りにいっぱい飲みませんか　kaeri ni ippai nomimasen ka **How about a drink on the way home ?**

もういっぱいいかがですか　mō ippai ikaga desu ka **Have another drink ?**

ちょっと酔ったからタクシーで帰ります　chotto yotta kara takushī de kaerimasu **I'm drunk, so I'll take a taxi home.**

仕事にやっと慣れました　shigoto ni yatto naremashita **I've finally gotten used to my work.**

昇進おめでとうございます　shōshin omedetō gozaimasu **Congratulations on your promotion.**

... についてご意見を聞かせて下さい　...ni tsuite go-iken wo kikasete kudasai **We'd like to hear your opinion on this matter.**

会社を辞めることにしました　kaisha wo yameru koto ni shimashita **I have decided to leave the company.**

転職することに決めました　tenshoku suru koto ni kimemashita **I have decided to look for a new job.**

15. Calendar events

a. January

日本のお正月は初めてです　nihon no o-shōgatsu wa hajimete desu **This is my first experience of the New Year's celebration in Japan.**

明けましておめでとうございます　akemashite omdetō gozaimasu **Happy New Year !**

初詣(⁀)では人がいっぱいでした　hatsumōde wa hito ga ippai deshita **The temples and shrines were crowded with people out for the first prayers of the year.**

みんなで百人一首をやりませんか　minna de hyakuninisshu wo yarimasen ka **How about all of us playing hyakunin-isshu* ?**

雑煮とお節料理を召し上がれ　zōni to o-sechiryōri wo meshiagare **Help yourself to** the zoni* and New Year's dishes.

年賀状がたくさん来ました　nengajō ga takusan kimashita **I received a whole lot of New Year's cards.**

b. February

2月3日は節分です　nigatsu mikka wa setsubun desu **February 3 is the setsubun* festivity.**

冬が終わって新春を迎える日です　fuyu ga owatte shinshun wo mukaeru hi desu **It is the day for celebrating the end of winter and the advent of spring.**

豆まきをして家の中に福を呼び込みます　mamemaki wo shite ie no naka ni fuku wo yobikomimasu **People throw beans and invoke happiness on their households.**

バレンタインデーは憂鬱(う)です　barentaindē wa yūutsu desu **I hate Valentine's Day.**

どうしてチョコレート売り場に女性が殺到するのか不思議です　dōshite chokorēto uriba ni josei ga sattō suru no ka fushigi desu **I never cease to wonder at all those women and girls crowding the chocolate candy counters.**

c. March

3月3日は桃の節句です　sangatsu mikka wa momo no sekku desu **March 3 is the peach blossom festival.**

女の子のいる家ではお雛(な)様を飾ります　onna no ko no iru ie de wa o-hinasama wo kazarimasu **In households with female children they set up a display of dolls.**

そろそろお花見のシーズンですね　sorosoro o-hanami no shīzun desu ne **It's about time for the cherry blossom season.**

桜の花が満開になりました　sakura no hana ga mankai ni narimashita **The cherry trees are in full blossom.**

卒業式帰りの女子大生をよく見かけます　sotsugyōshikigaeri no joshigakusei wo yoku mikakemasu **A conspicuous sight is women university students returning from their graduation ceremony.**

d. April

エープリルフールで以前ひどいいたずらをされました　ēpurirufūru de izen hidoi itazura wo saremashita **I once had a terrible prank played on me on April Fools' Day.**

新入生がお母さんの手に引かれて学校へ行きます　shinnyūsei ga o-kaasan no te ni

hikarete gakkō e ikimasu **Little children walk hand in hand with their mothers to their first day of school.**

会社も新しい社員が入って活気に満ちています　kaisha mo atarashii shain ga haitte kakki ni michite imasu **Companies are busy welcoming their new employees.**

e. May

5月5日は端午の節句です　gogatsu itsuka wa tango no sekku desu **May 5 is the Boys' Festival.**

男の子のいる家では鯉(こ)のぼりを飾ります　otoko no ko no iru ie de wa koinobori wo kazarimasu **Households with male children fly big cloth carps on a pole.**

まちにまったゴールデンウイークの到来　machi ni matta gōruden-uīku no tōrai **Now comes the long-awaited Golden Week*.**

今年は何連休ですか　kotoshi wa nanrenkyū desu ka **How many days off will we have this year ?**

どこへ行っても混んでいるから家でゴロゴロします　doko e itte mo konde iru kara ie de gorogoro shimasu **Everywhere you go it will be crowded, so I'm just going to lie around at home.**

f. June

梅雨に入りました　tsuyu ni hairimashita **The rainy season has started.**

毎日雨ばかりでうっとうしいですね　mainichi ame bakari de uttōshii desu ne **Isn't it dreary, all this rain day in and day out ?**

g. July

7月7日は七夕です　shichigatsu nanoka wa tanabata desu **July 7 is the Star Festival.**

何か星に願いをかけましょうか　nanika hoshi ni negai wo kakemashō ka **Shall we pray to the stars for something ?**

ようやく梅雨が上がり暑さがきびしくなりました　yōyaku tsuyu ga agari atsusa ga kibishikunarimashita **The rainy season has ended and the heat has become oppressive.**

土用の丑(?)の日には夏ばて防止にウナギを食べる習慣です　doyō no ushi no hi ni wa natsubate bōshi ni unagi wo taberu shūkan desu **On the day of the Ox in the dog days of summer, people customarily eat eel so as not to succumb to the heat.**

夏休みの計画は立てましたか　natsuyasumi no keikaku wa tatemashita ka **Have you made your plans for the summer vacation ?**

h. August

海水浴に行きませんか　kaisuiyoku ni ikimasen ka **Do you care to go to the beach with me ?**

お盆の帰省ラッシュのピークはいつですか　o-bon no kisei rasshu no pīku wa itsu desu ka **When is the back-to-the-country rush going to reach its peak during this o-bon* ?**

盆踊りを見に行きましょう　bon-odori wo mi ni ikimashō **Let's go watch the bon-odori*.**

花火大会があります　hanabi taikai ga arimasu **There is going to be a fireworks display.**

金魚すくいはなかなか難かしい　kingyōsukui wa nakanaka muzukashii **It's hard to catch goldfish with these paper nets.**

i. September

新学期が始まります　shingakki ga hajimarimasu **The new school term starts.**

今夜は仲秋の名月です　kon-ya wa chūshū no meigetsu desu **This is the night of the harvest moon.**

今年は台風が多いです　kotoshi wa taifū ga ōi desu **There are a lot of typhoons this year.**

j. October

あちこちで運動会があります　achikochi de undōkai ga arimasu **Many schools are having Field Day.**

芸術の秋です。美術館を散策します　geijutsu no aki desu. bijutsukan wo sansaku shimasu **Autumn is the season for art. I like to visit art museums at this time.**

食欲の秋です。また焼き芋(￥)を買ってしまった　shokuyoku no aki desu. mata yaki-imo wo katte shimatta **The autumn air stimulates the appetite. I bought some roasted sweet potatoes again.**

公園の樹々が見事に紅葉しています　kōen no kigi ga migoto ni kōyō shite imasu **The trees in the park are beautiful in their autumn colors.**

k. November

だんだん寒くなってきました　dandan samuku natte kimashita **It is gradually**

getting colder.

あちこちの大学で学園祭が催されます　achikochi no daigaku de gakuensai ga moyōsaremasu **Many universities are holding their school festival.**

l. December

師走は何となく気ぜわしい月です　shiwasu wa nan to naku kizewashii tsuki desu **Somehow December always makes me feel restless.**

クリスマスのプレゼントはもう買いましたか　kurisumasu no purezento wa mō kaimashita ka **Have you finished your Christmas shopping ?**

クリスマスイブは誰(淮)と過ごしますか　kurisumasuibu wa dare to sugoshimasu ka **Who are you going to spend Christmas Eve with ?**

年賀状はもう書きましたか　nengajō wa mō kakimashita ka **Have you written your New Year's cards yet ?**

忘年会が続いて少し胃がもたれました　bōnenkai ga tsuzuite sukoshi i ga motaremashita **I have been to so many year-end parties that my stomach feels queasy.**

m. Japanese public holidays

Jan. 1 元旦 gantan **New Year's Day**

Jan. 15 成人の日 seijin no hi **Coming-of-Age Day**

Feb. 11 建国記念日 kenkoku kinenbi **National Foundation Day**

March 20 春分の日 shunbun no hi **Spring Equinox**

April 29 緑の日 midori no hi **Nature Day**

May 3 憲法記念日 kenpō kinenbi **Constitution Day**

May 4 国民の休日 kokumin to kyūjitsu **Citizens' Day**

May 5 子供の日 kodomo no hi **Children's Day**

Sept. 15 敬老の日 keirō no hi **Senior Citizens' Day**

Sept 23 秋分の日 shunbun no hi **Autumn Equinox**

Oct. 10 体育の日 taiiku no hi **Sports Day**

Nov. 3 文化の日 bunka no hi **Culture Day**

Nov. 23 勤労感謝の日 kinrō kansha no hi **Labor Day**

Dec. 23 天皇誕生日 tennō tanjōbi **The Emperor's Birthday**

振替休日 furikae kyūjitsu **substitute holiday***

16. Dates and Times

日 hi/nichi **day**

朝 asa **morning**

昼 hiru **noon/daytime**
夕方 yūgata **evening**
夜 yoru **night**
午前 gozen **morning** (from daybreak to noon)
正午 shōgo **12 noon**
午後 gogo **afternoon**
真夜中 mayonaka **midnight**
今朝 kesa **this morning**
午前中 gozenchū **during the morning**
深夜 shin-ya **late at night**
今日 kyō **today**
昨日 kinō/sakujitsu **yesterday**
明日 ashita/asu/myōnichi **tomorrow**
明後日 asatte/myōgonichi **the day after tomorrow**
一昨日 ototoi/issakujitsu **the day before yesterday**
週 shū **week**
今週 konshū **this week**
先週 senshū **last week**
来週 raishū **next week**
日曜日 nichiyōbi **Sunday**
月曜日 getsuyōbi **Monday**
火曜日 kayōbi **Tuesday**
水曜日 suiyōbi **Wednesday**
木曜日 mokuyōbi **Thursday**
金曜日 kin-yōbi **Friday**
土曜日 doyōbi **Saturday**
月 tsuki/getsu **month**
今月 kongetsu **this month**
先月 sengetsu **last month**
来月 raigetsu **next month**
1月 ichigatsu **January**
2月 nigatsu **February**
3月 sangatsu **March**
4月 shigatsu **April**
5月 gogatsu **May**
6月 rokugatsu **June**
7月 shichigatsu **July**

8月 hachigatsu **August**

9月 kugatsu **September**

10月 jūgatsu **October**

11月 jūichigatsu **November**

12月 jūnigatsu **December**

年 nen/toshi **year**

今年 kotoshi/konnen **this year**

去年 kyonen **last year**

昨年 sakunen **last year**

来年 rainen **next year**

西暦 seireki **Western calendar year**

1993年 senkyūhyakukyūjūsannen **nineteen ninety-three**

年号 nengō **Japanese calendar year name**

平成5年 heisei gonen **the fifth year of Heisei (= 1993)**

季節 kisetsu **season**

四季 shiki **the four seasons**

春 haru **spring**

夏 natsu **summer**

秋 aki **autumn/fall**

冬 fuyu **winter**

閏年 uruudoshi **leap year**

今日は何日ですか kyō wa nannichi desu ka **What's today's date?**

3月3日です sangatsu mikka desu **It's March (the) third.**

今日は何曜日ですか kyō wa nan-yōbi desu ka **What day of the week is it today?**

水曜日です suiyōbi desu **It's Wednesday.**

今年は何年ですか kotoshi wa nannen desu ka **What year is it?**

1993年です senkyūhyakukyūjūsannen desu **It's nineteen ninety-three.**

今何時ですか ima nanji desu ka **What time is it?**

8時15分です hachiji jūgofun desu **It's eight fifteen.**

10時15分前です jūji jūgofun mae desu **It's fifteen to ten.**

いつ来ましたか itsu kimashita ka **When did you get here?**

お昼過ぎです o-hirusugi desu **A little after noon.**

GLOSSARY

bon-odori: A community dance held on certain evenings around the time of the o-bon festival.

bonenkai: A traditional party held at the end of the year by various work and social groups to bring the year to a happy end.

choshi: A tokkuri (see below) full of sake (see below).

Golden Week: Seven or more days, usually beginning April 29, during which 4 national holidays and 1 or 2 weekends occur.

government postcards: Postcards issued by the government on which the postage has been prepaid, so that no further postage is necessary; said in contrast to picture postcards etc which require a postage stamp.

hyakunin-isshu: A card game played at New Year's.

ikebana: The Japanese art of flower arranging.

Kabuki: A form of classical Japanese drama based on popular legends, with male actors in both male and female roles.

miso: Fermented bean paste.

nijikai: An informal drinking party taking place after a more formal party or banquet.

Noh: A form of classical Japanese drama based on religious or mythical themes and featuring very stylized dancing.

o-bon: The festival of the dead, held to commemorate one's ancestors. It is marked in modern times by a great exodus from the cities as people return to their ancestral homes in the country for the celebration. In most regions it is held on August 13, 14, and 15.

police box: A small local police station manned by 2 or more policemen 24 hours a day. It usually consists of a small office with toilet and sleeping facilities. In the cities there may be one every several hundred meters, depending on the population density.

prearrangements: Also called by their Japanese name, *nemawashi*, such arrangements usually consist of informal, often secret meetings with individual members of some decision-making committee etc to argue one's case before the full committee meets.

S tickets: Tickets to the S seats, i.e., the best reserved seats in the house in a theater or concert hall.

sake: A kind of wine made from fermented rice and often drunk hot.

setsubun: A festivity where people throw beans toward the outside of their houses to ward off devils.

shinkansen: The Japanese name for the so-called "bullet trains" that run at great speeds on wide, elevated tracks.

substitute holiday: The name given to a Monday observed as a holiday following a national holiday that fell on a Sunday.

tempura: Fish, shellfish, and vegetables dipped in batter and fried in deep fat. Spelled with an *n* in romaji, but with an *m* as an English loan word.

tokkuri: A small bottle for heating sake (see above).

ume: A green, very sour relative of the plum, used for various kinds of pickles and flavorings. Its tree, also called ume, is also cultivated for its beautiful white, pink, or red blossoms, which open in very early spring.

wasabi: A kind of horseradish, cultivated in cold mountain streams, and used as a pungent spice.

zoni: A broth containing vegetables and mochi (see page 605) and eaten at New Year's.